Kayaks of Greenland

The History and Development of the
Greenlandic Hunting Kayak, 1600-2000

By Harvey Golden
2006

Cover: A hunter from Arsuk (between Paamiut and Qaqortoq) with a seal in tow and a light dusting of snow. 1937, Photographer: Jette Bang /Arktisk Institut (gjb02548).

Copyright © 2006 by Harvey Golden. All rights reserved.
No part of this book may be reproduced in any manner
without written permission from White House Grocery Press.
No liability is assumed with respect to use of the information
herein.

Printed in China

Publisher's Cataloging-in-Publication
(Provided by Quality Books, Inc.)

Golden, Harvey.
Kayaks of Greenland : the history and development of
the Greenlandic hunting kayak, 1600-2000 / by Harvey
Golden. — 1st ed.
       p. cm.
       Includes bibliographical references and index.
       Preassigned LCCN: 2006930555
       ISBN 0-9787221-0-8

       1. Kayaks—Greenland—History. 2. KayaksGreenland
—Design and construction. 3. Inuit—Greenland—
Boats.
       I. Title.

VM353.G65 2006   623.82´9
                             QBI06-600301

Book Design by Susan Bard; Portland, Oregon

Questions or comments regarding the content of this book
should be addressed to:
White House Grocery Press
2000 SE 47th
Portland, OR 97215
USA

for Kathy and Max

Contents

Preface vii

Introduction ix

Acknowledgements xii

Maps 1-5 xv

History of Greenland Kayaks 23

Notes Pertaining to Terminology and Illustration 41

Greenland Kayak Construction 47

Polar Greenland Kayak Construction 96

Repairs and Modifications on Greenland Kayaks 101

Types of Greenland Kayaks: A New Typology 106

104 Greenland Kayaks 118

    Type I
        Plates 1-7 119

    Type II
        Plates 8-14 144

    Type III
        Plates 15-25 169

    Type IV
        Plates 26-38 204

    Type V
        Plates 39-55 244

    Type VI
        Plates 56-73 296

    Type VII
        Plates 74-81 358

    Type VIII
        Plates 82-83 388

Type IX
    Plates 84-91 .... *399*

Type X
    Plates 92-93 .... *435*

Type XI
    Plates 94-98 .... *441*

Type XII
    Plates 99-101 .... *460*

Type XIII
    Plate 102 .... *470*

Mixed Types
    Plates 103-104 .... *474*

Greenland Kayak Paddles
    Paddle Plates 1-79 .... *481*

Analysis and Speculation on the Origins, Development,
and Variations of Greenland Kayaks *530*

APPENDICES: *546*
    A. Ratios and Proportions
    B. Two Medieval Kayaks: Conjectural Drawings.
        Plates 105-106
    C. Greenlanders Paddling to Europe
    D. Lifting Offsets

Glossary *558*

Bibliography *563*

Index *576*

Preface

For many kayakers this weighty volume titled *Kayaks of Greenland: The History and Development of the Greenlandic Hunting Kayak, 1600-2000* is immediately meaningful as being about a kind of arctic kayak design. But for most readers it may be helpful to first set the work in a wider context of watercraft studies about that very varied category called "canoes" without restriction to the North American Indian designs based on bark covering or carving a log. A kayak is skin-covered, of course, with "skin-on-frame" construction, and together with its open sister-craft, the umiak ("oo-mee-ak"), makes up that far-flung family of northern "skin boats" which has existed for ages in northeastern Asia and northern North America. They likely developed from the very ancient skin-covered boat known as the coracle whose varied occurrences around the world are well described in *Water Transport: Origins and Evolution* by James Hornell (1946). The coracle in basic form is roundish with a basket-like framework of bent branches. Such a blunt vessel won't do well in the sea with its large waves although a large elongated form in western Ireland called "curragh," which is "coracle" pronounced differently, is sea-going. The kayak and umiak are also much elongated forms with the important additional feature of a main central longitudinal or "keel" piece which turns up into bow and stern members to give sharp rather than blunt ends. Thus they can better cut through the waves. As to when and where this happy design transformation occurred, arctic archaeologist William S. Laughlin in conversation thought it happened on the Asia side of the North Pacific north of the trees some 13,000 or more years ago. The swift Arctic kayak is such a unique and captivating craft, especially in action, that it has long caught the eye of Europeans. It is a highlight in many early descriptions of native arctic life, and the focus of numerous scholarly studies. Perhaps the best of the latter is *Skinboats of Greenland* by the Greenlander H. C. Petersen (1986) who covers both kayak and umiak in the context of Inuit life.

In first hand study Harvey Golden has concentrated on Greenland kayaks as artifacts and did not himself really get into hunting with them or their socioeconomic and overall cultural frameworks; however, he is aware of these aspects and cites other sources. He has had first hand contact with the Inuit in North Baffinland after kayaks disappeared there and in Central West Greenland where kayaks have revived, mainly for sports and recreation. Harvey is very accomplished at rolling, excelling in the now annual Greenland national competition in 2000. In the U.S.A. and Canada he occasionally gives demonstrations, and if so inclined, could write a rolling manual. In short, he is not just an armchair kayak scholar. It is mostly the lack of language, of Inuit and Danish, which has hindered him from getting into the ethnography of Greenland kayaking. The present study stops short of describing the hunting gear since that entails the activity, but no matter since kayak gear is well presented by the inimitable H. C. Petersen and a few others like P. Scavenius Jensen (1975). As for kayak hunting techniques, we have the remarkable 18th century descriptions of Otto Fabricius (in Holtved, 1962). Also for kayaking as Greenland life experiences there are a number of native accounts available such as the eye-opening ones from the 19th century which have just appeared in English in the new journal *Qajaq* (S. Rink, [1897] 2005).

In the 21st century Arctic skin boats have pretty well disappeared except around the Bering Straits where umiaks survive and in Greenland where kayaks continue. To study the latter comparatively for their variations by locale and over four centuries of historically known time, Harvey Golden has energetically tracked down over a hundred examples preserved in museums and private collections to make "surveys," i.e., measuring and, usually, producing "lines drawings." Such scale representations on paper are fundamental in comparative study providing four views: profile or "elevation," top and bottom or "plan," and "cross-sections," in halves from bow and stern. The heart of the present study is a set of 104 lines drawings, done, or in some cases redone, by Harvey. They are presented under thirteen types identified by Roman numerals which Harvey has distinguished for Greenland kayaks. Types I to IX encompass forms from West, South, and East Greenland over four centuries of development. Type X is a new specialized form designed for the recently formalized sport of rolling rather than hunting. Types XI to XIII cover the rapidly changing forms of the isolated northwest extreme where kayaks had disappeared until reintroduced from Baffinland in the 1860s. In addition are shown two kayaks of mixed features which fall outside of Harvey's typology. Each drawn example is accompanied by detailed description. Another set of 78 drawings are of paddles which, unlike hunting gear, can hold interest for non-native recreational kayakers as useable alternatives to the wide-bladed commercial products. Since paddle specimens often lack certain association with particular kayaks, they are presented separately.

Harvey has built replicas of eighteen different Greenland kayaks thereby deepening his understanding of the family. Incidentally, in comparative study the total number of design types we can distinguish seems at present to be on the order of around eighty, grouped into a dozen regional families. Harvey's large sample of Greenland designs is a treasure trove for replica builders. His descriptions of construction which precedes the lines drawings explains the framework parts and their assembly in detail. It follows a comprehensive opening review of historical records on Greenland kayaks which covers a number of established study topics such as the capture of kayakers by Europeans, whether Greenlanders ever kayaked to Europe, kayaking deaths, and recent hunting decline due to economic change. At the other end of the main text is Harvey's developmental analysis of his types giving a picture of Greenland kayak design history. To read this museum study with its dense artifactual detail from cover to cover is rather heavy going, but in whole or in part it does contribute substantially to our knowledge and appreciation of the seemingly simple but finely tuned *Kayaks of Greenland*, the only Arctic ones to really live on in the 21st century. Congratulations to the author!

E. Arima. Ottawa, May 2006.

INTRODUCTION

This project began in 1998, when I surveyed a Greenland kayak for the first time at the Hull Maritime Museum, Humberside, England. That year I traveled to twelve museums in England, Scotland, and The Netherlands specifically to see and study kayaks from the Arctic. The form and construction of kayaks from the Arctic tradition greatly appealed to me—they are not only beautiful works of art and brilliant designs, they are relatively easy to build and use. I had already built about twenty full-size replicas of them from a variety of published sources before my 1998 travels.

Having worked from scale drawings to build kayak replicas, I was interested in working from a kayak (in a museum) to make a scale drawing—reversing the process, thereby documenting a kayak. In doing so, I was certain I, as an experienced builder, could glean many details and nuances of the kayak that don't usually find their way onto a scale drawing. During the 1998 trip I surveyed twenty-four kayaks, and decided to write an article about what I had seen. But first, I had to see more . . .

Eight years and eighty Greenland kayaks later, the 'article' is finished. It is the very book I had wanted to find on a library shelf years ago. The book is done, but the learning is not. The more I have seen, the more questions I'm left with; this book is just another stepping stone along the narrow and windy path of Arctic kayak studies. The point of this study is to not find answers, but to look for them.

The period that this study covers— the last 400 years— is not arbitrarily picked: Very few full-sized intact kayaks from Greenland (or anywhere) pre-date the 1600s, but since then there has been a fairly constant movement of Greenland kayaks to European museums. A developmental study of the kayaks spanning 400 years is attainable despite the fact that several of the types of Greenland kayaks described in this study have been extinct for over a hundred years.

Telling the history of a particular type of object is no easy task. The 'who, what, when, where, and how' are mere starting points—and not always answerable. While every kayak presented in this study has its own story of building and use, this has been recorded all too rarely. If museums have any documentation, it is often only the collector's name, the place it was collected (sometimes as general as "Greenland"), and when it was collected (or accessioned by the museum). Even this information is usually lacking. For those kayaks whose acquisition has been recorded, the stories reveal a broad range of ways in which kayaks ended up in museum or private collections. The stories also reveal a broad range of European attitudes towards a completely different culture.

In studying the kayaks of the Greenlanders, I've heeded (as best I was able) the Ethnologist Morten Porsild's very obvious but often overlooked solution to achieving a higher level of understanding:

In order to carry out an investigation ... one should preferably be able to use the implement which is to be investigated, and preferably be able to make it oneself from the materials, and tools used by the aborigines. Because, not until we ourselves have made use of a complicated implement do we fully understand all its small details, which, at first sight, we either do not notice at all, or regard as unimportant for the purpose of the implement ... (1915:119-120)

To accomplish this, I have built replicas of eighteen kayaks presented in this study.[1] This has helped me understand the variations in Greenland kayak construction, as well as how to achieve some of their more complex forms. Building replicas of a variety of kayaks has also given me a sense of their development over time. Each kayak replica had its own construction challenges— techniques, tricks, and methods to figure out. This has allowed me to better interpret what I had not only been looking at, but also to notice what I had been overlooking.

Of course, a replica kayak also provides information through its use. Sea-trials— casually known as the fun part— are serious research nonetheless. The feel and characteristics of a kayak on the water are the manifestation of its form and the desires of the original builder/user. I cannot overstate the importance of this experiential aspect of my research. But at the same time, it is highly subjective and difficult to articulate. For example, no two people will necessarily feel the same characteristics (such as stability, maneuverability, and comfort) in the same way in a particular kayak. This can be due to different body sizes, different backgrounds in paddling, different skill levels, and different expectations. Not everyone will like or even be able to paddle a kayak that I find to be superb. My experiences from building and using the replicas are presented at the end of each replicated kayak's section.

With all of my replicas, my experiences have been skewed by the absence of sealskin coverings— a significant aspect of the Arctic kayak tradition. Instead I have used either canvas or nylon 'skins' sewn over the frame and sealed with paint or varnish. Other substitutions have had to be made as well, for instance: nylon or hemp cord in lieu of seal-skin or baleen for lashings, hardwood, antler, or metal for ivory, and locally grown species of timber instead of what would have either been found as driftwood on Greenland shores or imported lumber from Europe.

Even more significant than my not using skin coverings is the fact that I have not used the replicas as the originals were intended: for hunting. These kayaks were made to be seaworthy and capable vessels in their own right, and I have learned much from paddling them, but I have not truly used them.

My research has been entirely within museums and private collections, and hardly at all with actual functioning kayaks in Greenland. I do not have interviews with kayakers from various vicinities of Greenland to support my observations, and nor do I always know the provenance of a particular museum kayak. But the value of having conducted the bulk of my research among museum collections is that I was able to study a broad temporal range as well as a broad geographical range of kayaks from Greenland.

---

[1] The kayaks selected for replication were the Lübeck kayak (plate 1), the DHNS 2 (plate 4), the KNK 1161 (plate 9), the RvV 349-1 (plate 15), the HMG E.102 (plate 26), the KNK 2050 (plate 49), the PQN (plate 50), the KNK 2237 (plate 66), the EK 1959 (plate 72), the RvV 1076 (plate 75), the DNM L.9726 (plate 77), the DNM Lc.148 (plate 82), the DNM L.19.157 (plate 86), the MUS 48057 (plate 87), and the KNK 1007 (plate 97). I have also built but not spent significant time in replicas of the WFM 232 (plate 2), the DR 42 (plate 3), and the CMC IV-A-432 (plate 103). The experiences with the latter three replicas, while helpful to my understandings of form and construction, are not discussed in this text.

I also saw, studied and/or surveyed all of the kayaks featured in this book, except for two examples surveyed by Vernon Doucette and Richard Nonas (Kunuunnguaq Davidsen's rolling kayak, and the KNK 1906, plates 93 and 104), and a Polar Greenland kayak surveyed by Dr. Eugene Arima (ROM 950-219, plate 102). Another two kayaks were surveyed by others, but I also studied them first-hand and with additional data re-drew them: The Medico-Chirurgical Society's kayak, surveyed by Dr. William Fortescue (plate 27), and the Greenland National Museum's kayak KNK 1215 (plate 61), surveyed by John Heath.

With an interest in making as complete of a study of Greenland kayak development as possible, I excluded no Greenland kayaks that I surveyed, thus leaving in examples that could be considered degenerate, redundant, acculturated, or not particularly fine. The same can be said for the Greenland paddles I have surveyed. I also wish to avoid a romanticized portrayal of what is simply a hand-made tool: some kayaks are prettier and better-made than others, but the less-aesthetic kayaks often reflect significant changes in their cultural/ecological context and are thus every bit as valuable.

I hope this book will appeal to a wide audience— museum curators seeking to identify a kayak model in their collection; kayak builders looking for inspiration; engineers admiring ancient genius; students and scholars of Arctic studies; and Greenlanders interested in what a kayak from their vicinity looked like 300 years ago— perhaps built by a relative.

Acknowledgements

The research for this work directly involved some forty museums and private collections in ten countries; this is a sincere attempt to recall the names of those who went out of their way to facilitate or assist me in my research:

In the U.K.: Dr. Alexander Adam & the Medico-Chirugical Society in Aberdeen, Mr. Neil Curtis & the Marischal College Museum of Anthropology also in Aberdeen. Dr. Dale Idiens, Ms. Chantal Knowles, Ms. Briony Crozier, and Ms. Allison Petterson & the National Museum of Scotland, Edinburgh. Mr. S. Pinder, Mr. Woodward, Captain Ledger, Captain Holmes, and all the gracious and hospitable Captains at the Trinity House, Hull. Mr. Arthur Credland of the Hull Maritime Museum, who facilitated my very first museum kayak survey in 1998, and welcomed me back for three more in 2002. Elder Brother and House Archivist Captain Stephen Healy of Trinity House, Newcastle. Mr. Graham Pickles and Mr. Roger Pickles, brothers, both of the Whitby Museum. Dr. Keith Headland of the Scott Polar Research Institute, Cambridge. Dr. Euan MacKie, Dr. Lawrence Keppie, and Ms. Aileen Nisbit & the Hunterian Museum, Glasgow. Mr. John Old & Mr. Robert Elsey of Tyne and Wear Museums, Newcastle, and Mr. Les Jessop & the Hancock Museum also in Newcastle. Mr. Adrian Zealand of the McManus Galleries in Dundee.

In the Netherlands: Dr. Corine Bliek and Ms. Giselle Van Eyck of the Museon, Den Haag, facilitating visits in 1998, and 2002. In Rotterdam, Dr. Kees Van Den Meiracker, Dr. Sietske Kentie, and the staff at the Wereldmuseum storage depot. Many thanks to Dr. Cunera Buijs of the Rijksmuseum voor Volkenkunde in Leiden for studies conducted in both 1998 and 2002— Mr. Dorus Kop Jansen and Mr. Conn Barret graciously assisting during those two visits, as well as Ms. Karin Booij and Ms. Ester De Bruin during the latter visit. Dr. Peter Priester of the Gemeentelijke Musea Zierikzee in Zierikzee. Dr. Cees Bakker of the Westfries Museum in Hoorn. In Hindeloopen, Ms. C. Hack of de Hidde Nijland Stichting, and in De Rijp: Ms. Jenny Lind of T'Houten Huis.

From the Oslo University Museum, Norway, Ethnology Department, Dr. Tom Svensson, Mr. Eivind Bratlie and Ms. Farideh Faramarzi. In Finland, Dr. Heli Lahdentausta and Ms. Marja Puhakainen of the National Museum of Finland, Helsinki. In Germany, Capt. Rudiger Pfaff of the Schiffergesellschaft in Lübeck, and Dr. Mona Suhrbier and Mr. Uhl of the Weltmuseum, Frankfurt. In France, Dr. Héléne Tromparent and Mr. Laville of the Musée De La Marine in Paris. In Greenland, the staff and members of the Nuuk Kayak Club—Peqatigiiffik Qajaq Nuuk, and the National Organization: Qaannat Kattuffiat.

Ms. Kelly Cameron and Ms. Nadja Roby of the Canadian Museum of Civilization, Hull. In the United States, Mr. Val Berryman of Michigan Sate University, Mr. Mark Starr of Mystic Seaport Museum, Mr. Lyles Forbes of the Mariners' Museum, and Dr. Laila Williamson of the American Museum of Natural History. At the Smithsonian Institution's Museum of the American Indian: Dr. Mary Jane Lenz and Dr. Patricia Nietfeld. At the Smithsonian Institution's Museum of Natural History: Dr. Deborah Hull-Walski and Ms. Felicia Pickering.

Three museums in particular distinctly stand out as not only having gone out of their way for me, but having done so for more than a week's time each: Dr. Claus Andreassen, Dr. Emil Rosing, and Dr. Joel Berglund of the Greenland National Museum. In Denmark, Dr. Anne Bahnson, Ms. Anne-Marie Legaard, Dr. Hans-Christian Gulløv, and Dr. Martin Appelt of the Danish National Museum. And in Canada, Ms. Dawn McColl and Mr. John Stevenson of the Canadian Canoe Museum, Peterborough.

The support, hospitality, and contributions from many individuals have also made this book possible: Sincerest appreciation to my parents Steve and Nancy Golden, Dr. Eugene Arima, Susan Bard, John and Stella Brand, Vernon Doucette, George Dyson and the Baidarka Historical Society, Anders Gedionsen and Kirsten Madsen, Dr. Keld Hansen, John and Jessie Heath, Kimberly Kinchen, Hans Kleist-Thomassen, Martin Nissen, Richard Nonas, members of the Oregon Ocean Paddling Society, Maligiaq Padilla, Brian Schulz, Skip Snaith, Robin Snow, Greg Stamer, Ken Taylor, Dr. Jaap Tinbergen, Kathy Tucker, Uncle Dave, Duncan Winning, OBE, and Norm Wyers.

Maps

Map 1: Regions of Greenland. (Map after Bure, ed., n.d: 6).

A. Polar Greenland

B. West Greenland

C. South Greenland
   (Part of West Greenland)

D. Southeast Greenland/
   King Frederik VI's Coast

E. East Greenland/Ammassalik
   District

F. Scoresby Sound
   (Part of East Greenland)

(Northwest Greenland or the Northern West Coast generally refers to points North of Sisimiut).

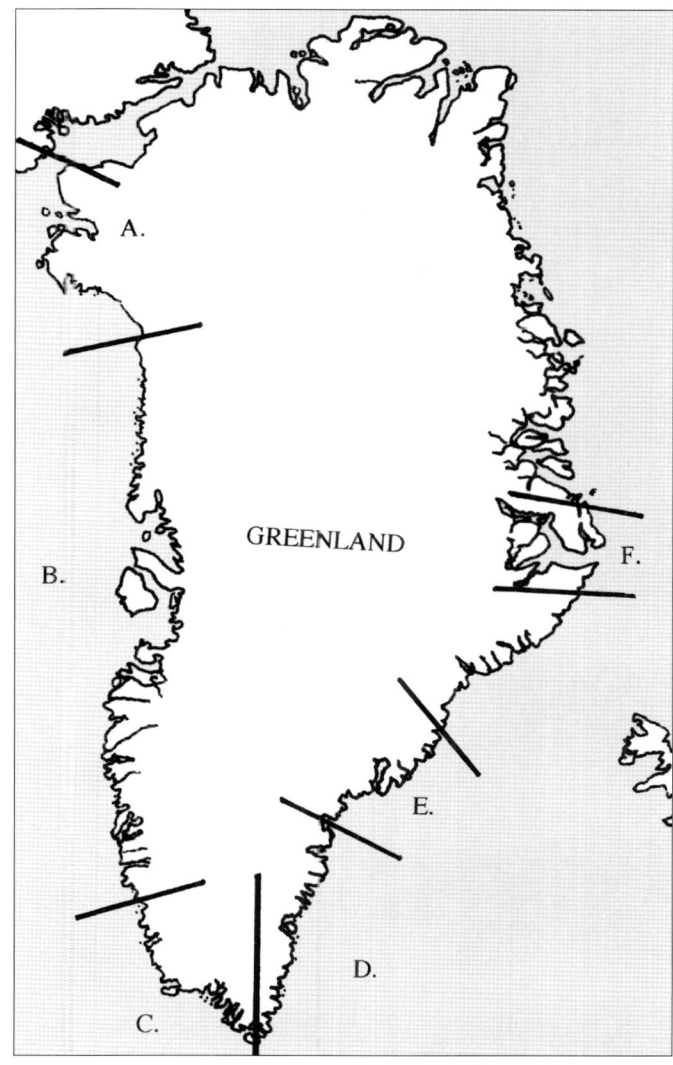

Map 2: Some key Greenlandic settlements (After Petersen, 1986, Gad, 1982, and Bure, ed., n.d.). Note that Uummannaq appears twice; in the text, no. 2 is referred to as "Uummannaq (Polar Greenland)."

1. Etah
2. Uummannaq
3. Cape York
4. Upernavik
5. Illorsuit
6. Uummannaq
7. Qeqertarsuaq
8. Ilulissat
9. Aasiaat
10. Sisimiut
11. Kangaamiut
12. Maniitsoq
13. Nuuk
14. Paamiut
15. Qaqortoq
16. Nanortalik
17. Kap Farvel
18. Ammassalik
19. Scoresby Sound

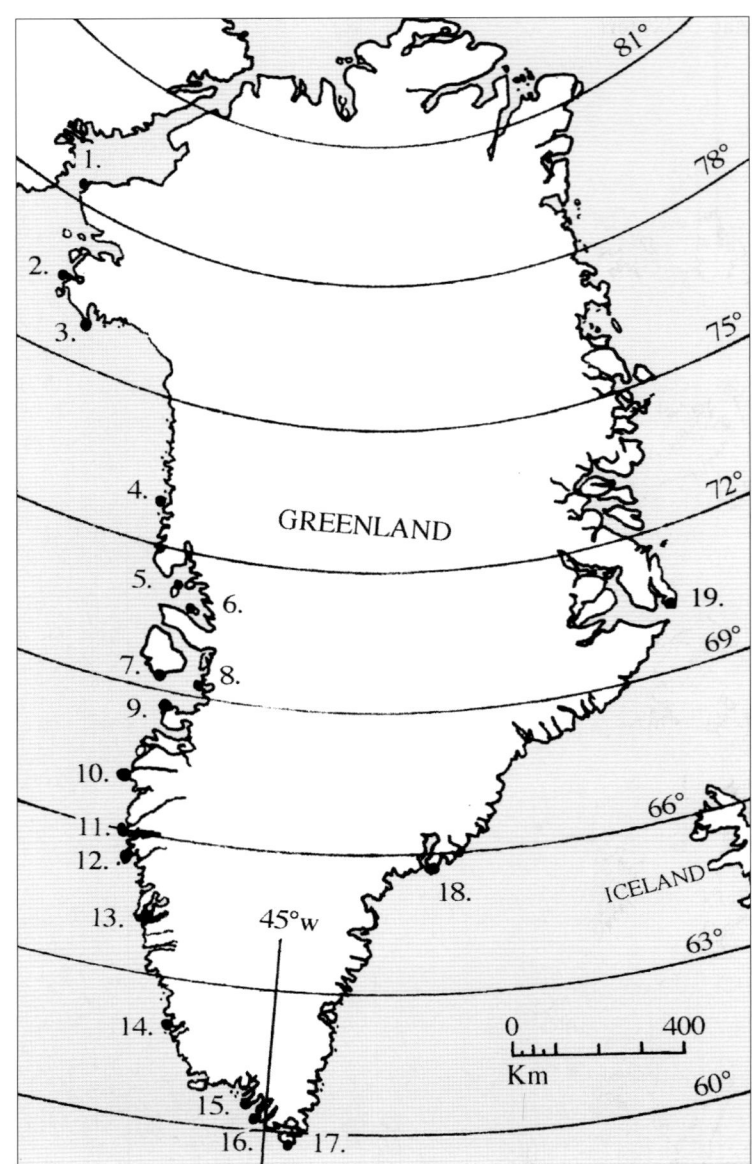

Map 3: Waters and Lands surrounding Greenland.

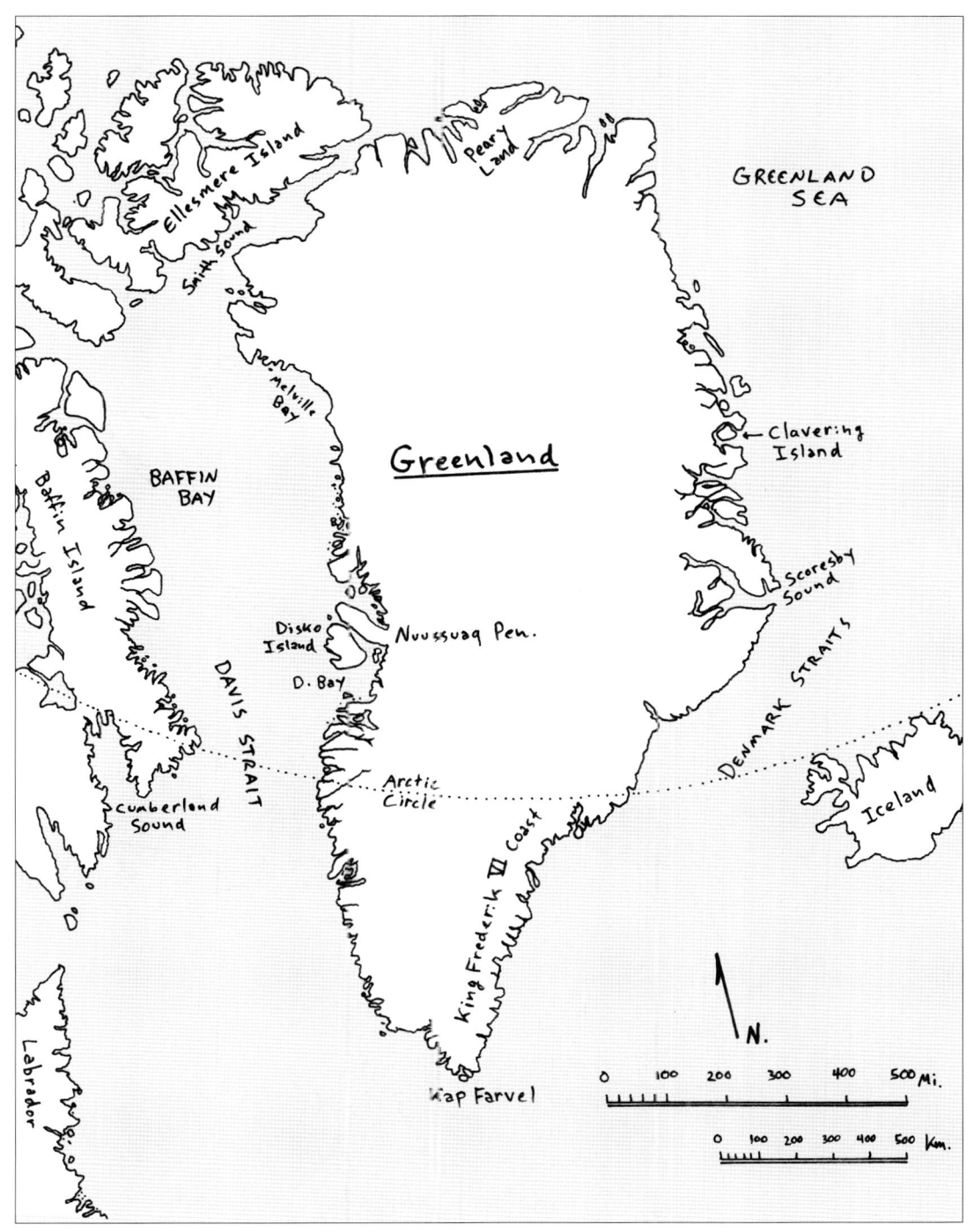

Map 4: Map of Polar Greenland.

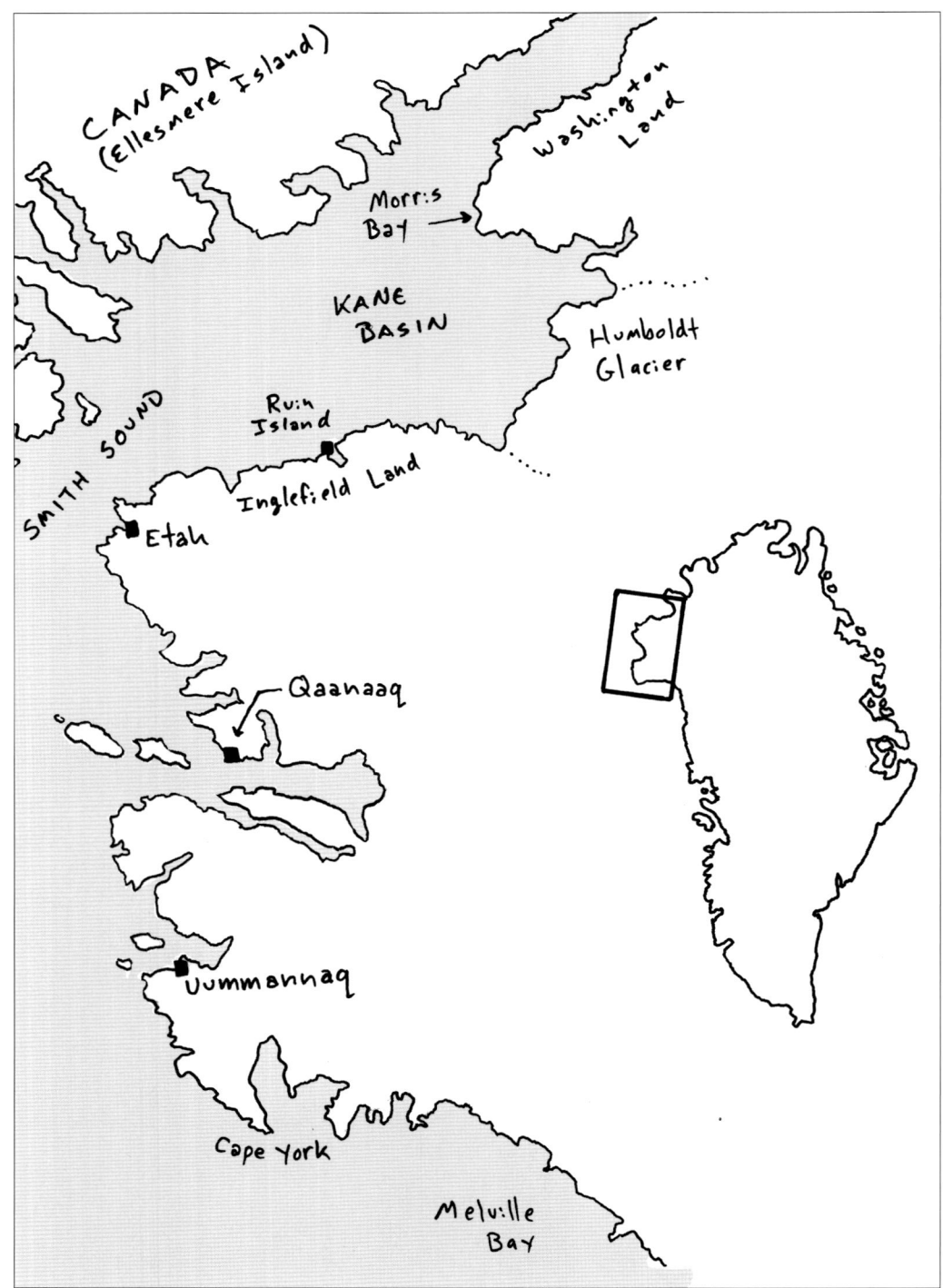

Map 5: Map of the Central and North West Coast of Greenland.

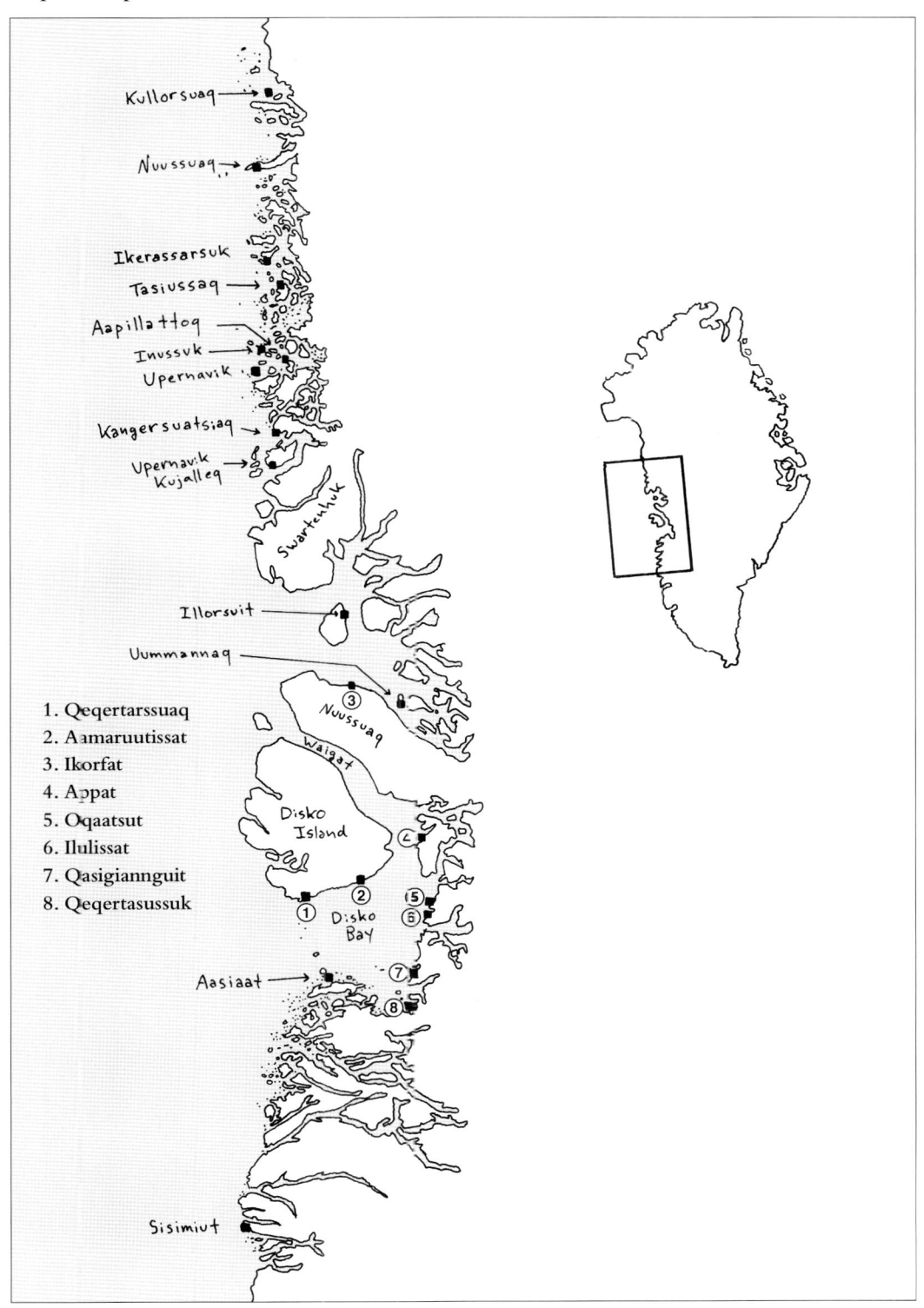

Map 6: Map of South West Greenland, left, and East Greenland, right.

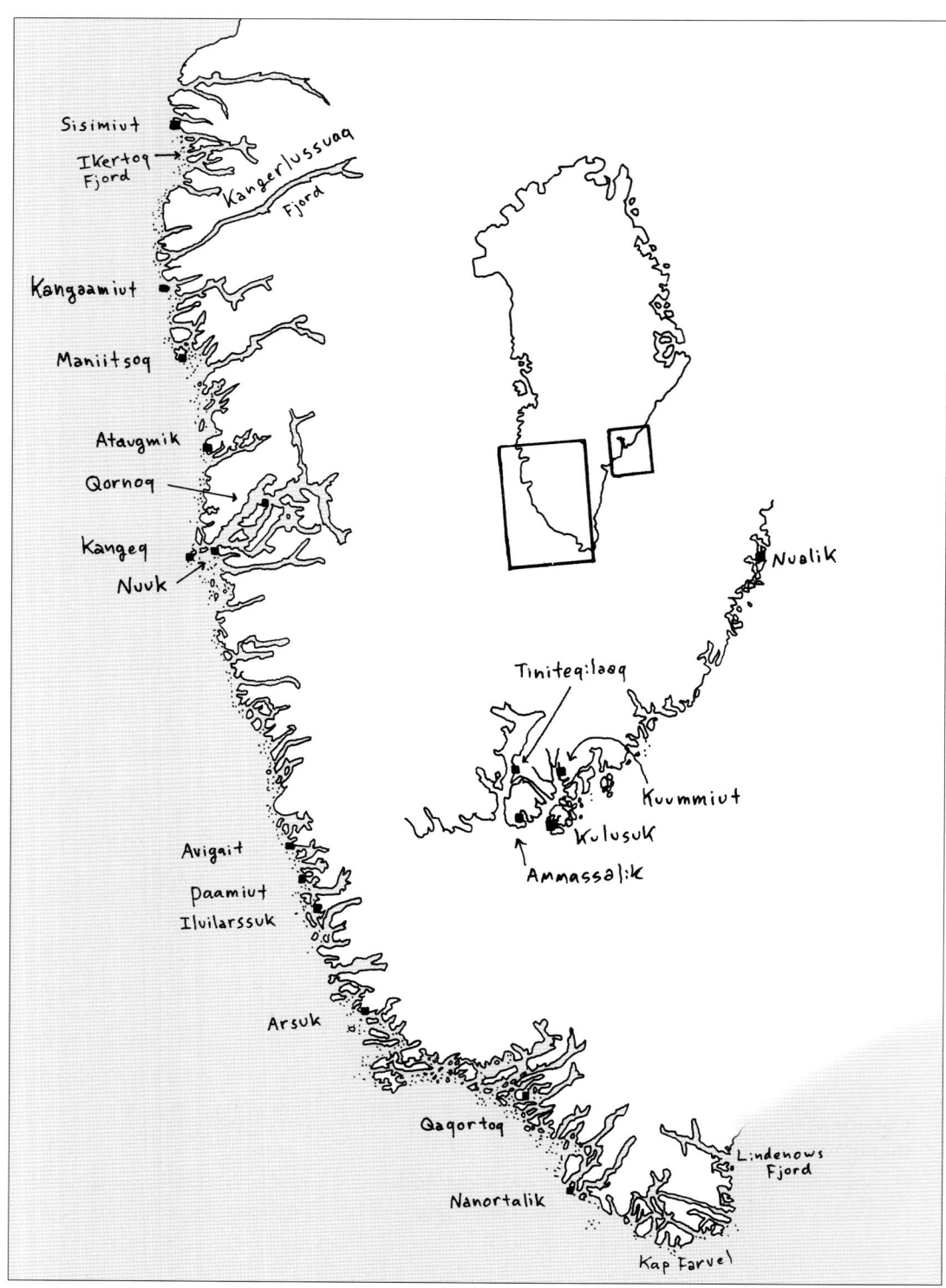

Table of Current, Danish, and Archaic Place Names

Current Spelling	Danish Names	Archaic Spellings	Map No.
Aasiaat	Egedesminde	Ausiait	5
Ammassalik		Angmagssalik	6r
Appat	Ritenbenk	Agpat	5
Aamaruutissat	Skansen	Aumarutigsat	5
Etah		Itah	4
Ikorfat		Ekorgfat	5
Illorsuit		Igdlorssuit	5
Ilulissat		Jakobshavn	5
Inussuk		Inugsuk	5
Kangaamiut	Old Sukkertoppen		6l
Kangersuatsiaq	Prøven		5
Kulusuk	Kap Dan		6r
Maniitsoq	Sukkertoppen		6l
Nuuk	Godthåb	Nûk	6l
Nuussuaq[2]	Kraulshavn		5
Oqaatsut	Rodebay	Oqaitsut	5
Paamiut	Frederikshåb		6l
Qaanaaq	Thule		4
Qaqortoq	Julianehåb		6l
Qasigiannguit	Christianshåb		5
Qeqertarsuaq	Godhavn		5
Qornoq		Karnok	6l
Sisimiut	Holsteinsborg (Hosteensborg, etc.)		6l
Upernavik		Upernivik	5
Upernavik Kujalleq	Søndre Upernavik		5
Uummannaq (North West Gl.)		Umanak, Omanaq	5
Uummannaq (Polar Greenland)	Dundas/Thule Air Base	Thule	4

[2] Nuussuaq is also the name of the large peninsula just North of Disko Island; see map 3.

Kayaks of Greenland

A kayak is a unique type of canoe with a rigid internal framework with skins stretched around it to form the hull and decks. A kayak has an opening (or openings) for the kayaker to sit in. Kayaks are propelled with paddles— with either a double- or single-blade. Greenland kayaks, as with the kayaks of all Arctic traditions, are primarily working boats— the work being hunting. In seasons where the water was navigable, i.e., not ice-packed or frozen over, hunters took to the water in kayaks to pursue seals, walrus, whales, sharks, caribou, fish polar bears, and birds.

The word 'kayak' is the common modern English spelling of an Inuktitut word; Inuit did not have a written language. Before the spelling of 'kayak' was standardized, the word appeared in many different forms, such as 'kayack,' 'kaiak,' 'caiack,' 'kyak,' etc. Very often kayaks were just referred to as canoes or boats. As Europeans struggled not only to accurately record Inuktitut words in the Roman alphabet, but also to arrive upon some consistency, certain spellings were loosely adapted as standard. The

Figure 1: Kayaks and up-turned umiaks used as shelters at Aasiaat, 1909. (Photographer: Arnold Heim/Arktisk Institut 25665)

present spelling for kayak used in modern written Greenlandic is "qajaq" (singular), "qajaat" (dual), and "qaanaat" (plural).

East Greenlanders in the vicinity of Ammassalik use an entirely different word to refer to the hunting kayak: sarqit, or sakkit, which translates into "a means of wandering" (Rink, H., [1887]1914: 210; Nooter, 1991:322). Rink notes that "It seems that the word qajaq must have been formerly used; for a person's name, *Qajāteq*, and the name of an island *Qajartilik*, was in use" [1887]1914:221). Gustav Holm clears this matter up in explaining that the custom of not naming the name of the dead was observed in Ammassalik vicinity, and that a man named Kajarpak had died there, hence the change to sarkit (as Holm spells it) from kayak (1914:79-80). Because the word and spelling "kayak" has so permanently entered the English language, this spelling will be used within the text except in citations, where the authors' original spellings are used.[3]

Figure 2: A hunter landing a Greenland shark, Ilulissat vicinity, 1939. (Photographer: Jette Bang/ Arktisk Institut. gjb03980)

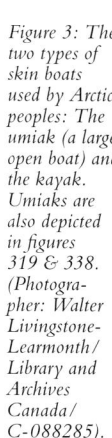

Figure 3: The two types of skin boats used by Arctic peoples: The umiak (a large open boat) and the kayak. Umiaks are also depicted in figures 319 & 338. (Photographer: Walter Livingstone-Learmonth/ Library and Archives Canada/ C-088285).

---

[3] "Kajak" is the Danish spelling of kayak, and appears in many English translations of Danish texts; the pronunciation is the same as the English kayak.

While kayaks originated and reached a high level of sophistication for ocean hunting in the Bering Straits, archaeologists found the earliest remains of an Arctic skinboat in Greenland.[4] In the 1980s, the Qasigiannguit Museum excavated remains of a kayak-like skinboat's rib at Qeqertasussuk (east of Aasiaat), West Greenland. The remains date from the early third of the Saqqaq period, some 3,900–3,100 years ago (Grønnow, 1994: 201, 216, 221, fig.23). Archaeologists also found a piece of wood that was quite likely a paddle-blade (1994:222, fig.24): it compares in form to the earlier paddle blades presented in this study (leaf-shaped, i.e., broad in the middle of the blade, narrowing towards the tips).

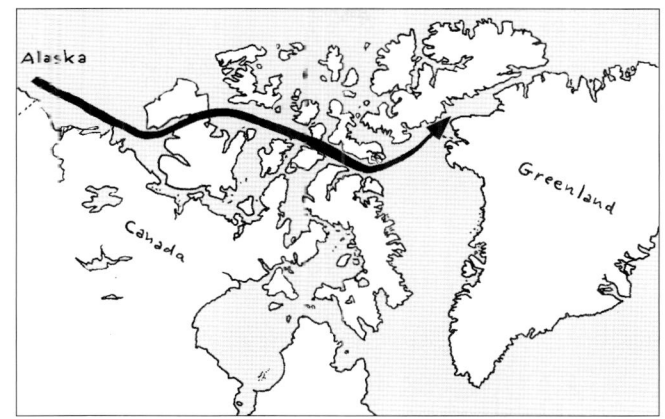

Figure 4: General path and directions of the Thule Culture migrations from Alaska to Greenland, circa 900-1100c.e. (After McGhee, 1984:370 fig.1)

The Qeqertasussuk skinboat remains do not necessarily represent the precursor of modern Greenland kayaks. Since the Saqqaq period, Greenland has had different cultural migrations as well as periods where it was likely uninhabited. It is also possible that some of the cultures that came to Greenland may not have had kayaks at all. The Greenland kayaks that we know from museum collections and present-day use are descendent from those of the Thule Culture migrants that first entered Greenland around 1050-1100 c.e., or in the case of Polar Greenland kayaks, a much smaller modern Inuit migration in the 1860s (Jordan 1984:540, Mary-Rousselière, 1991:113).

The Thule Culture originated from two distinct earlier cultures in Alaska/Siberia after about 900 c.e.: the Birnirk of North Alaska, and the Punuk from Bering Straits (McGhee, 1984:369). Archaeologists have found small carved kayak models from each of these cultures. Multi-chined (or rounded) hull, reverse sheer, and projecting end-horns characterize the Birnirk kayak models, while the Punuk models have hard-chined flat bottoms, slight sheer, and straight raked stems (Arima, 2002:12; 1985:24-25; 1975:53,238-239).

A warming climate that allowed Thule hunters to pursue whales to their summer feeding grounds in the Beaufort Sea and the Canadian High Arctic Archipelago facilitated the Thule migration to Greenland (McGhee, 1984:370). Prior to the peak of warming trends around 1000 c.e., the Thule had been relegated to hunting whales in near-shore ice-leads as the whales migrated to (in the spring) and from (in the fall) their feeding grounds (McGhee, 1984:370-371; Dumond, 1987:140-141).

Kaj Birket-Smith notes, "The kayak is the element of Eskimo culture which, almost before any other, impressed the European mind" (1929:166). Europeans' early comparative analysis of kayaks usually involved a comparison to weaving shuttles— common objects from their own material culture that closely resembled the Greenland kayak in form. Isaac De La Peyrère, writing in the 1640s, elaborates on such an otherwise dry comparison:

> To understand the shape and style of these boats, picture to yourself, sir, a weaver's shuttle.... It was not without reason that I have compared these boats to weaver's shuttles; for the shuttles from the hands of the most skilful weavers, do not run faster in the loom than the boats managed by these oars, with the skill of these savages, run on the water ([1647] 1855:223-224).

---

[4] That the oldest skin boat remains were found in Greenland is quite by chance, and in no way is it accepted to mean that the Arctic kayak originated or was invented in Greenland.

Using the same metaphor, David Crantz describes the kayak of the Greenlanders in greater detail in his 1767 *The History of Greenland*:

Figure 5: An engraving from Harper's Weekly Supplement, September 9th, 1876 after a Danish painting titled "The First Lesson." (Collection of the author).

The little Man's-boat, called in Greenlandish kaiak, *is 6 yards in length, sharp at head and stern, just like a weaver's shuttle, scarce a foot and half broad in the broadest middle part, and hardly a foot deep. It is built of a keel like a slender pipe-staff, long side-laths, with cross hoops not quite round, bound together with whale-bone, and is covered over with some fresh-dressed seal's leather as the women's boat [umiaks]; only the leather incloses it like a bag on all sides, over the top as well as beneath. Both the sharp ends at head and stern are fortified with an edge of bone, having a knob at top, that they may not receive damage so soon by rubbing against the stones. In the middle of the covering of the Kaiak there is a round hole, with a rim or hoop of wood or bone, the breadth of two fingers. The Greenlander flips into this hole with his feet, and sits down on a board covered with a soft skin; when he is in, the rim reaches only above his hips. He tucks the under-part of his water-pelt or great-coat so tight round this rim or hoop of the kajak, that the water can't penetrate any where.*[5] *The water-coat is at the same time buttoned close about his face and arms with bone buttons (i,150).*

Greenland kayaks represent a particular culture's answer to the question of survival— a compromise of thousands of possibilities, specific and random. A successful working boat is, and must be: 'just right' according to its users. In being just right, the kayak of the Greenlander— in all its variations— is a critical tool and symbol of survival, the importance of which cannot be understated. In 1767 missionary David Crantz observed "...every man must have a kajak and all the necessary implements, to the end that if he even is not capable of catching seals, he may at least be able to come at some fowls and fish for his sustenance"(Crantz, 1767:ii, 402).

Seal catching was essential to being a Greenlander; Crantz also writes:

"... (Therefore)... No man can pass for a right Greenlander, who cannot catch seals. This is the ultimate end they aspire at, in all their device

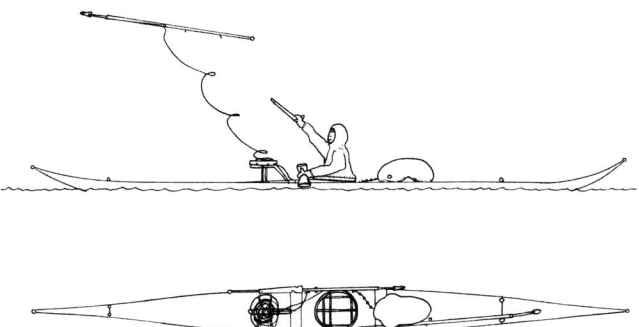

Figure 6: The throwing of a harpoon. Note the line tray ahead of the hunter, and the float on deck behind him. The lower image depicts a kayak's deck as it would be set up for hunting: The harpoon points aft with the throwing board attached to it, the line is coiled in the tray, the float is ready to be set loose, and a lance lies in readiness on the aft deck. Numerous other tools and projectiles would also typically be carried; see figures 96 and 98, and pages 76 – 78 .

[5] The "water-pelt" refers to the spray skirt (*akuilisaq*) and the "great-coat" refers to the paddling jacket (*tuilik*) of the Greenlander. Examples of these are depicted in figures 113 and 114.

and labour from their childhood up. It is the only art (and in truth a difficult and dangerous one it is) to which they are trained from their infancy, by which they maintain themselves, make themselves agreeable to others, and become beneficial members of the community"(Crantz, 1767:i, 131).

One of the most accurate and detailed descriptions of seal hunting from a kayak comes by way of Otto Fabricius, a Danish missionary who lived at Iluilarssuk (30km southeast of Paamiut) from 1770 to 1773. Fabricius was not only a very keen observer, but he was also a capable kayaker who hunted seals himself (*in* Holtved, ed., 1962:8-10, 24).

Usually several [seal hunters] start together from the shore; but arriving at the haunts of the seals, and especially when they observe one with its head above the water, they spread out in order not to get in one another's way, but usually so that they can see each other and get help if needed; all with the exception of some few dare devils and cranks who, relying upon themselves, go far away from the others. Then each one remains quietly at his post, waiting for the seal to emerge. In sunshine he keeps the sun behind him, so that the seal when looking into the sun will not readily become aware of him. If it is blowy he keeps before the wind in order to not make too much noise. He makes just as much movement as is required for wielding the paddle, and so neatly and gently that it makes scarcely a sound, at which the Greenlanders are quite masters. Then when a seal bobs up, the hunter studies its behaviour in order to decide whether he has any hope of catching it and how to attack it (Fabricius in Holtved, ed., 1962:103-104).

If the seal is unaware, the hunter will sneak up on it using "long deep strokes of the paddle" and "by urging the kayak forward with his body alone." Fabricius notes that many are "so highly trained at this that they can get the seal alongside the kayak without its noticing it" (*in* Holtved, ed., 1962:104). When a seal is more cautious, the hunter must approach only when the seal has submerged, remaining still when the seal's head is above water. In this situation, the hunter must be contented to "throw the harpoon at it from as far away as the [harpoon] line can reach"(*in* Holtved, ed., 1962:104). A harpoon's line measures about 11-14 meters (36-46 feet) long, although a strong hunter can throw a harpoon as far as 18 meters, or 60 feet (Birket-Smith, 1924:291, 319).

When finally he has come within striking distance in one way or the other he throws the harpoon at the seal, having previously attached the [harpoon] head; the line, which has lain coiled on the kayak stand, runs with it; as the harpoon head is barbed the hunter can see at once whether the seal has been hit or not, for if so the seal cannot easily get free of it but is compelled to pull more and more of the line out; then there is no time to waste; as soon as he sees that the seal is hit the hunter must at once throw the float overboard, as otherwise it would receive a hard jerk when the seal had run the line out, whereby the kayak would be liable to capsize.

If the harpooned seal gets the float in tow – it is rarely able to drag it below the surface – the hunter watches the direction it takes, follows it and with the lance tries to kill it; for the lance has no barbs but slips out of the wound and floats up every time it is thrust into the seal; in the end it has to yield to the repeated wounds, for it has also become exhausted by dragging the large, blown-up float; when at last the hunter gets close enough he gives the seal the death blow by hitting it on the snout with his fist, which stuns it immediately; and if necessary it is stabbed with the killing knife.

After that it has to be made fast for the tow home: first of all the wounds are closed with wound-plugs to prevent the blood from going to waste . . .; at the same time air is blown in between skin and flesh to make the carcase more buoyant. If the seal is only small it is laid aft in [on] the kayak, furnished at about the navel with a small bladder to keep it afloat in the event of its falling off. But if the seal is a large one it has to be towed in the water alongside the kayak and with a float so large that the carcase can be left to drift without risk in case the hunter sees another seal to catch; if several are caught they are made fast to the first ones, and thus a lucky hunter may paddle home with four or five seals in tow at one time (in Holtved, ed., 1962:104-105).

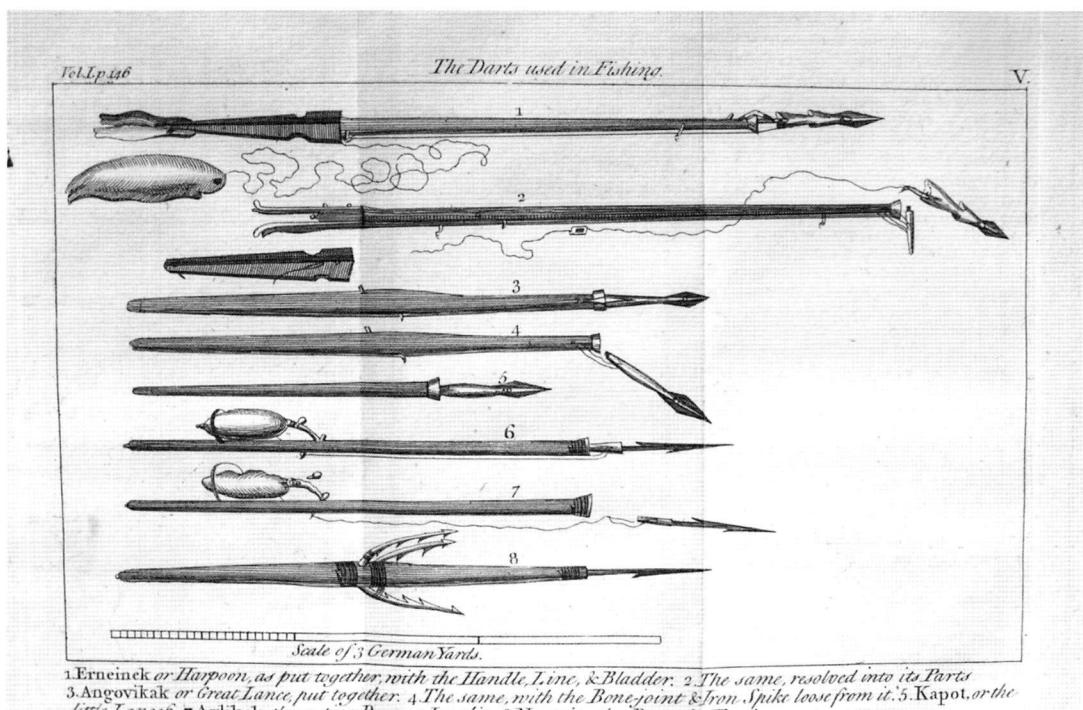

Figure 7: An early detailed depiction of common West Greenland hunting weapons (Crantz, 1767: i, pl.V.) (John Wilson Room, Special Collections, Multnomah County Library, Portland, Oregon.)

It was around 1740 that the Greenlanders were first sold firearms and related supplies (Gad, 1984:560-561), but it wasn't until the mid 1800s that firearms were effectively used for hunting from kayaks. The fact that the rifles were difficult to load apparently didn't prevent kayakers from using them, as Fridtjof Nansen writes of the kayak hunters at Kangek (Nuuk vicinity) only having muzzle-loaders in the late 1880s (1895:430). Nansen describes their loading:

The loading of these guns when the sea is breaking over the 'kayak' is not easy. The natives put the butt of the gun forward on the canoe, and hold the muzzle against the face, or rest it on the shoulder, while they take out the powder, cap, and wadding, which they always keep in their caps to keep them dry. In this way they manage to load in almost any sea without getting water down the barrel. There is a special bag to contain the gun on the canoe in front, so that it is always ready to hand (1895:431).

Rifles did not put an end to harpoon hunting, and they were often used in conjunction with one another. Generally, rifles were preferred for seal hunting in calm conditions, whereas harpoons were preferred in rougher conditions. Depending on the season (which directly relates to the amount of fat [buoyancy] on a seal), seals that were shot with the rifle would have quickly sunk if they were not also harpooned (Birket-Smith, 1924:320).

The use of rifles from kayaks is one of many weavings of European influence into Greenlandic culture. The time frame of this study— 1600 to 2000— encompasses European contact with at least some populations in Greenland, if only intermittently at first. These four centuries of contact with European peoples are a second phase of such contact, as the Norse had small, isolated settlements in Southwest Greenland from about 985 c.e. into the 1400s (Gad, 1971:29-33, 149).

The Norse began to settle in South West Greenland at about the same time the Thule culture expanded into Greenland. The two peoples likely first encountered each other in the 13th century,[6] probably in Northwest Greenland, i.e., Disko Bay or points north (Jordan, 1984:544; Gad, 1971:88). The Norse are known to have traveled as far north as Upernavik vicinity by the end of the 13th century (Mathiassen, 1930:300). The last direct contact between the Norse settlers of Greenland and Scandinavia occurred no later than 1414 (Gad, 1971:149).

The Western Norse Settlement (greater Nuuk fjord system) disappeared by 1355, while the Eastern Settlement (greater Qaqortoq/Nanortalik fjord systems) may have lasted as late as the 1480s (Gad, 1971:147,154-156). The cause of the decline of the Norse settlers is unknown, but a deteriorating climate and its effect on subsistence is a common theory. Plague, lack of trade and communication with Scandinavia, war or assimilation with the Neo-Eskimos, emigration, and destruction by pirates are also possible factors (Gad, 1971:146-147, 154-164; Kleivan, 1984a:554-555).

European explorers have likely been bringing Greenland kayaks to Europe since the 14th century, and conceivably as early as the 13th century. Danish cartographer Claudius Clavus Swart recorded seeing both small (kayaks) and large (umiaks) skin boats hanging in the Nidaros (now Trondheim) cathedral in the 1420s (Gad, 1971:174; Nansen, 1911:269).

Figure 8: An un-identified woman, Josva Mathæussen, and Tækild Egede standing in front of two kayaks, West Greenland, 1908. (Photograph: Marius Nyboe/ Arktisk Institut 47268.)

---

[6]The early Norse settlers of South West Greenland did not record seeing living inhabitants, but did record finding abandoned settlements, stone tools, and the remains of skin boats (Gad, 1971:19). These skinboats did not belong to the Thule culture ancestors of modern Greenlanders, but are probably from the Paleo-Eskimo Dorset Culture, which had come to Greenland by circa 550 b.c.e. and disappeared around 900 c.e. (Fitzhugh, 1984:537-538; Kleivan, 1984:551).

Figure 9: Museum Wormianum, ca. 1655. Note the kayak at the top of the picture as well as the paddle directly above the mannequin at the back wall. (Danish Royal Library and Archives)

In his 1555 *Descriptions of the Northern Peoples*, the Archbishop of Uppsala Olaus Magnus presents a chapter titled "On the boats of Greenland made of hide or leather." Magnus describes a kind of "pirate" found on a rock called Hvitsark "who sails about in a craft made of hide, with no set goal, and lies in wait so that he can bore into the bilges of merchant ships from below, rather than above the waterline"([1555] 1996:102). While his description is naïve, he does write of having seen

> ...Two such boats of hide in the year 1505 above the west door inside the cathedral church at Oslo, dedicated to St Hallvard and hung up in the wall as exhibits. King Håkon of that kingdom was said to have picked them up as he was sailing with a fleet of war-ships past the shores of Greenland, in case those on board might be harbouring a design to sink his vessels"([1555] 1996:102-103).[7]

The skin boats that Clavus Swart and Magnus each claimed to have seen are presently unaccounted for and it can be assumed that they no longer exist.

Traffic between Europe and Greenland ceased in the early 1400s, and it wasn't resurrected until 1577, when the English navigator Martin Frobisher landed in Southwest Greenland. English incursion to lands claimed by Denmark-Norway[8] spurred the Union's King to re-start expeditions to Greenland. The purpose was to exercise sovereignty and over Greenland undoubtedly to reap any commercial

---

[7] John Granlund's annotations of Magnus' *Descriptions* are included in the 1996 edition; Granlund writes that "Hvitsark . . . was probably a peak south of Angmagssalik" and was said to be visible halfway between Iceland and Greenland. Furthermore, Granlund writes that ("as far as we know") no King Håkon was ever known to have gone anywhere near Greenland (*in* Magnus, [1555]1996:137).

[8] An agreement between the Norse settlers and King Hakon in 1261 resulted in Greenland becoming a possession of Norway (Gad, 1971:120-121). From 1380 to 1814 Greenland belonged to the unified Denmark-Norway; the 1814 Treaty of Kiel resulted in Denmark alone possessing Greenland.

gain, to spread the gospel, and to contact the descendants of the Christian Norse settlers who had been abandoned for almost 200 years (Gad 1984:56; 1971:193-194.)

The Dutch began intermittent whaling and trading in the Davis Straits in 1614, but it wasn't until the collapse of the whale fisheries off East Greenland and Spitsbergen in the late 1600s that their commercial whaling off West Greenland (Davis Straits) picked up considerably. An average of 75 vessels a year sailed from the Netherlands to Davis Straits in the years 1719 to 1728 (Gad, 1970:229, 256, 311; 1973:9).

Dutch whaling declined abruptly after a catastrophic season in 1777 in which a number of ships were lost in pack ice. A complete collapse of Dutch whaling occurred during the French Revolution and Napoleonic wars (Ellis, 1999:66; Gad, 1973:383). The English started whaling in the Davis Straits around 1773 (Lubbock, 1978:114), and in 1776 had 32 ships whaling in the straits (Bobé, 1929:129). English commercial whaling in the Davis Straits peaked in 1823; that year whalers from Hull (some 17 ships) killed at least 469 whales, rendering 3810-1/2 tons of oil (Lubbock, 1978:251-256).

With increased visits to Greenland, Europeans brought back souvenirs of their interactions with the Greenlanders— sometimes traded for, but also stolen. Europeans did not draw the line at stealing objects alone, as there are several cases of Greenlanders being kidnapped and exhibited in Europe for money. A Danish expedition led by Godske Lindenov kidnapped six Greenlanders in the early 1600s (Hall *in* Gosch, 1897:70,71). All six were taken with their kayaks, one of which is preserved at the Schiffergesellschaft in Lübeck, Germany (see plate 1). Historian Finn Gad estimates that ships from Denmark-Norway and the Netherlands kidnapped about 30 Eskimos between 1605 and 1660 (1970:238).

Eventually kidnapping Greenlanders became illegal. A decree ordered by King Christian VII of Denmark in 1776 included this provision: "Furthermore it was forbidden, either ashore or at sea, to steal from the Greenlanders, to kidnap them or to use force against them or 'the Danish colonies and trading posts and their men' or their property" (Gad, 1973:381-82). This provision was part of a larger attempt to emphasize Danish sovereignty over Greenland and the adjacent waters as well as to stop foreigners from exploiting Greenlanders. At the time, the main rivals of the Danes were the English and Dutch whalers, who despite the latter's own Staaten Generaal's decree of 1720 barring robbery and violence against Greenlanders, continued to do so well after 1720 (Gad, 1973:194, 380).

There are several recorded instances of Greenland kayaks— with kayakers alive and paddling— being sighted from the coasts of Northeast Scotland and the Orkney Islands in the late 1600s (MacRitchie, 1912:213-241). Many scholars have mulled over how such occurrences happened. Theories range from Greenlanders washing out to sea, and ending up in Scotland (Whitaker, 1954:99-102, Heath, 2004:13,14) to Greenlanders escaping or being set adrift from ships returning to Europe (Souter, 1934:17, Nooter, 1971:10,11, and Whitaker again, who modified his 1954 thinking, 1977:42).

Another possibility is that the kayakers escaped from captors in Europe— from Denmark in particular, where several Greenlanders captured by Lindenov are known to have escaped by kayak (de La Peyrére, [1647] 1855:223-226). Some analysis on the subject determined these kayaks were of European origin, specifically the Lapps of Northern Scandinavia (MacRitchie, 1912:130,133). This analysis is based largely on the name given to these mysterious kayakers by naïve witnesses: "Finnmen." This latter possibility has been solidly refuted (Birket-Smith, 1924:266; Whitaker, 1954:101). In any case, this is one of the most perplexing mysteries concerning kayaks much less navigation in general.[9]

There is a long history of Greenlanders willingly traveling to more southerly nations aboard ships. Many of the early Greenlanders visiting Europe brought kayaks with them to demonstrate their

---

[9] Appendix C. addresses these mysteries at greater length and includes my own theories about the appearances of Greenlanders in kayaks off the British Isles.

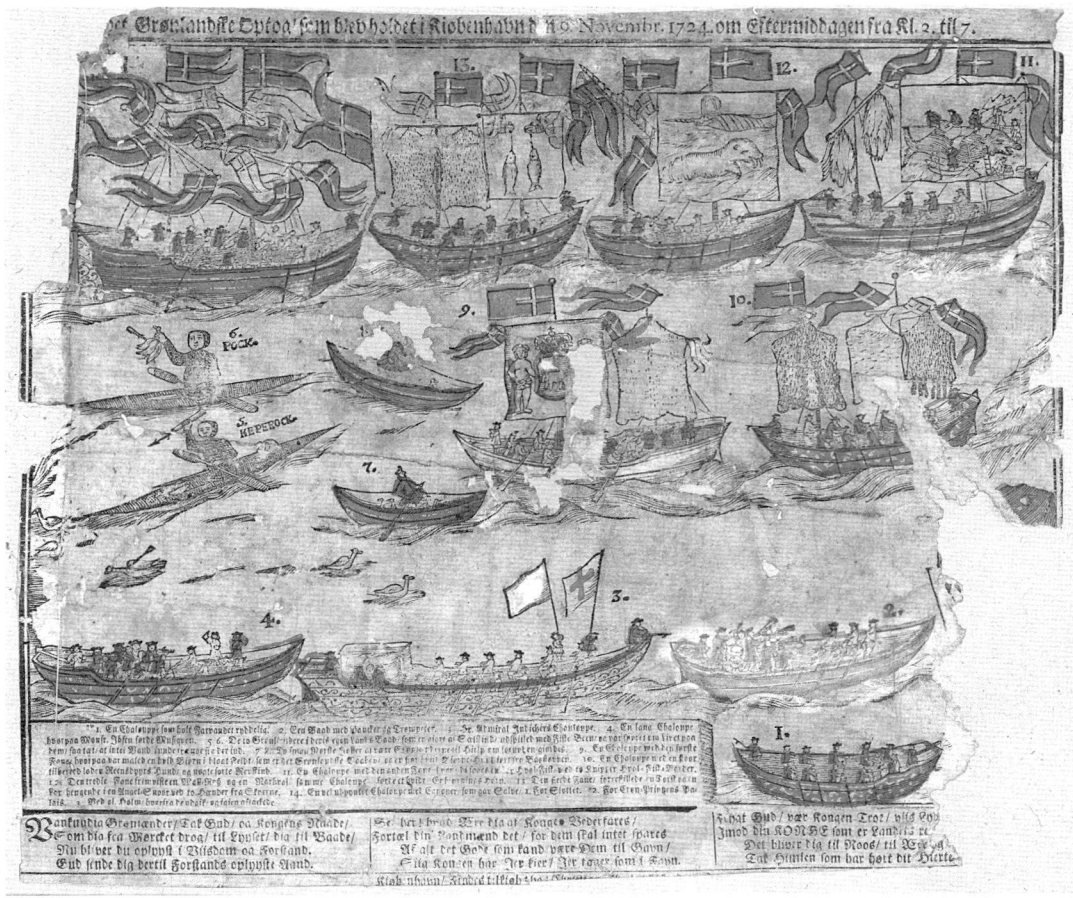

Figure 10: Pôq and Qiperoq giving a kayak demonstration (left) during a regatta through the canals of Copenhagen in 1724. (Courtesy of the Danish Royal Library and Archives.)

renowned skills and abilities. It is also the case that some of them left their kayaks in Europe, occasionally due to the visitor's untimely death after exposure to disease.

Pôk and Qiperoq from Nuuk vicinity were among the first Greenlanders to travel willingly to Europe. Both men were persuaded to travel to Denmark-Norway in 1724 only after being promised a return to Greenland. While in Denmark, Pôk and Qiperoq demonstrated kayak rolling and bird hunting for King Frederik IV and other royalty. During this same visit, the two Greenlanders in their kayaks were featured in a regatta promoting the Greenland trade through the canals of Copenhagen (see figure 10). Pôk returned to Greenland the following year, but Qiperoq died in Bergen, Norway (Gad, 1973:47-49).

A Greenlander called 'John Sakeouse' came to Scotland aboard a whaler in 1816, bringing his kayak with him. He gave paddling and kayak-rolling demonstrations in Leith harbor, and served as an interpreter on John Ross's 1818 Arctic expedition. Seven or eight Greenlanders visited Dundee Scotland between 1873 and 1924 (Idiens, 1987:166,169-170). Dale Idiens of the National Museum of Scotland writes

> It appears that many Eskimos arrived in Scotland with their own dress, kayaks, and hunting equipment. The kayaks especially excited much interest among Scots, themselves being a sea-going people, so one would expect some of the early examples to be retained in Scottish collections. However, Scots whalers and explorers also

brought back kayaks from expeditions to the Arctic and now, with only a few exceptions, it is no longer possible to distinguish between these two categories (1987:170).

One of the three Greenland Kayaks at the Hull Maritime Museum likely belonged to a Greenlander who visited Hull in the early-to-mid 1800s, and drowned in his kayak while giving a kayaking demonstration; he had apparently gotten tangled in weeds while rolling his kayak (Anonymous, 1860:9-10; Symons, 1898:14). The kayak in plate 29 is very likely the kayak he died in.

The tradition of Greenlanders willfully visiting Europe (and North America and Asia) is a continuing one. The Greenlander Manasse Mathaeussen traveled to Europe in the 1960s and 70s, giving kayak-rolling demonstrations in Paris and Monte Carlo as well as Kotzebue Alaska and Quebec. In more recent years the Greenlanders Ove Hansen, Pavia Tobiassen, John Petersen, and Maligiaq Padilla have all given kayaking demonstrations in the United States; Padilla has also visited Japan (twice), Canada, and Europe.[10]

Observers have only intermittently recorded the numbers of kayaks in specific locales or regions of Greenland. In Egedesminde District (on the central West Coast) in 1918, of a total population of 1589, there were 513 kayaks (Birket-Smith, 1924:33,260). Birket-Smith also provides kayak censuses in this district for the years 1881, 1893, and 1901— the numbers being 268, 292, and 316 respectively (1924:260).

Figure 11: A seal hunter in Northwest Greenland, circa 1889. (Photographer: Walter Livingstone-Learmonth/ Library and Archives Canada/ C-088254.)

---

[10] Manasse Matheussen's kayak is presented in this study (plate 104), as is a kayak Maligiaq Padilla built and left in the United States after giving demonstrations in 1998-99 (plate 52).

In East Greenland, (Ammassalik District), the first European visitors recorded that among a population of 413 there were 119 kayaks (Holm, 1914:202). A census published in the same work records population and kayak numbers throughout Greenland (excepting Polar Greenland) for the year 1884: (The names and spellings of locales have been changed to reflect current practice. See maps 5 and 6.)

Vicinity	Male	Female	Kayaks	Kayaks per 1000
Ammassalik district	193	220	119	288
South part of the East coast	52	83	32	237
Qaqortoq and Paamiut districts	1387	1646	715	236
The central districts	1142	1294	469	193
Colonies around Disko Bay	1259	1362	668	255
Uummannaq and Upernavik districts	803	904	336	197

Table 1: Population and kayak ownership in Greenland 1884 (after Holm, 1914:185, table II).

Kaj Birket-Smith presents a similar kayak census for the year 1923 in his 1928 *Greenlanders of the Present Day*; it is reproduced in table 2 (below) with current place name spellings in parenthesis (1928:167, table XI).

District	Total Number of Kayaks	Kayaks Owned by Hunters Fisherman	Kayaks Owned by Boys	Kayaks Owned by Employed Natives	Male-to-Kayak Ratio
Julianehaab (Qaqortoq)	609	495	73	41	2.6
Frederikshaab (Pamiut)	172	148	16	8	2.4
Godthaab (Nuuk)	207	199	5	3	3.0
Sukkertoppen (Maniitsoq)	215	205	5	5	2.7
Holsteinsborg (Sisimiut)	136	101	28	7	3.0
Egedesminde (Aasiaat)	405	324	54	27	1.9
Christianshaab (Qasigianguit)	128	96	24	8	2.1
Jacobshavn (Ilulissat)	79	67	12	0	3.4
Ritenbenk (Appat)	146	102	35	9	1.9
Godhavn (Qeqertarsuaq)	82	63	9	10	2.1
Umánaq (Uummannaq)	332	280	31	21	2.1
Upernivik (Upernavik)	270	223	31	16	1.9
WEST Greenland	2781	2303	323	155	2.4
EAST Greenland	138	128	3	7	2.5

Table 2: Number of Kayaks in West and East Greenland in 1923 (after Birket-Smith, 1928:167, table XI). Current place names have been added in parenthesis.

Subsistence hunting with kayaks is very dangerous. Birket-Smith, citing A. Bertelsen's data published in 1910, writes that hunting accidents made up 16.8% of all deaths in North Greenland, and 19.1% in South Greenland. Of these, 60% of the accidents in N. Greenland were kayak-related, a figure which reaches 80% in South Greenland. Birket-Smith adds, "In South Greenland the curve [of ac-

Figure 12: An engraving from an 1889 popular text "The Story of Man" titled 'Seal fisher in his long canoe' (Buel: 89). The paddle is naively depicted, but the kayak is rendered very accurately. (Collection of the author.)

cidental death figures] reaches its highest point during the winter with its rough sea and terrible gales" (1924:427). In the 10 months that Gustav Holm was in Ammassalik District (East Greenland) in 1884, he writes that there were 13 deaths total— three of which were kayak-related (Holm, 1914:183).

Freezing and drowning were common causes for kayak-related deaths, but such deaths were usually related to hunting accidents. If the harpoon line became entangled with the kayak or hunter on one end, and a large seal on the other, the kayaker could be quickly dragged to his death. Seals sometimes attacked the hunter and his kayak and could bite holes in the kayak's skin, thus sinking it (Fabricius, *in* Holtved, ed., 1962:104).

Weather and ice conditions could also contribute to freezing or drowning. Sea ice could quickly be blown into what was open water, leaving kayakers to either flee, or to try to climb on top of the ice. If the pack was thick, kayaks trapped in it could be crushed to splinters. Calving glaciers and unstable icebergs could create immense waves with very little notice, knocking kayaks over or washing them onto shore. New or fresh-water ice is sharper and more brittle than sea-ice, and could cut through skin kayaks like a knife.

Reckless behavior was also a factor, as related by Otto Fabricius: Some bold hunters "tie the [harpoon] line round their waist, thus making themselves and the kayak serve the purpose of a float and by hauling on the line get closer and closer to the [harpooned] seal; this however, requires no small strength and only extremely few are able to do it; the kayak is easily overturned and such venturesome hunters mostly become their own murderers" (*in* Holtved, ed., 1962:47).

The anthropologist Joëlle Robert-Lamblin has compiled mortality data in her paper *Death in traditional East Greenland: Age, causes, and rituals*. Of the 71 recorded kayak-related deaths in Ammassalik district between 1885 and 1968, Robert-Lamblin shows that 51% of these deaths involved hunters aged 15 to 24 years old, inexperience no doubt playing a large part. One of the hunters who died in a kayak was a 32-year-old woman. Surprisingly, at least seven of the 71 kayak deaths were also considered to be homicides, and one was considered a suicide (Robert-Lamblin, 1997:263-264).

Aside from hunting, kayaks were used for other important purposes, particularly during post-European contact periods. In 1929, H. Ostermann described kayakers aiding ships in navigation: "As soon as a vessel is sighted, the Greenlanders immediately paddle out to it in their kayaks. In former times it was a matter of great importance to get there at once, as the first comer was taken onboard and received pilot money. Therefore, a Greenlander did not hesitate to go far out from the shore, however heavy the seas"(210).

Piloting or guiding larger vessels from a kayak is a tradition that pre-dates European navigation: kayaks always escorted umiaks during longer voyages (Petersen, 1986:184-186). Kayaks were the hunting platform that could ensure food for large traveling parties, but they also served as messengers if an umiak was in trouble. Kayaks could also be used to increase an umiak's speed with the use of "push straps" with which a kayak or two could serve as auxiliary motors (Petersen, 1986:152, 187).

As early as the late 1700s, kayakers served as postal carriers. "Very often the post was carried between Frederikshåb and Godthåb [Paamiut and Nuuk] by kayak and this distance was covered in an incredibly short time. The kayakers considered this task a great honour, and did not stop when they came to a settlement in mid-journey"(Gad, 1973:308).

During the early 20th century, a combination of ecological factors and European contact rendered kayaks obsolete and nearly extinct in certain portions of the central South West coast of Greenland— previously a region where hunters of renowned skill and capability used kayaks year-round for subsistence. From about 1920 through 1960 milder sea conditions off South West Greenland led to a marked decrease in seal populations that coinciding with increases in the cod and shrimp fisheries. Historian Inge Kleivan writes:

The number of kayaks declined in the 1920s, especially in the central areas around Sukkertoppen [Maniitsoq] and Godthåb [Nuuk]. The decreasing use of kayaks is related to the development of fishing, which in many

Figure 13: A motorized boat transporting three kayaks in East Greenland, 1961. (Photographer Jette Bang/Arktisk Institut gjb08873.)

areas was more profitable than sealing, and to the fact that more and more Greenlanders were able to assure themselves of a steady income through paid employment (1984b:602).

The fisheries were an export industry and provided many jobs for Greenlanders, who in turn increasingly relied on imported foods. Kayaks were of course unsuitable vessels from which to sustain a viable commercial fishing industry; the first Greenlanders purchased motorized fishing boats (imported from Europe) in 1924 (Kleivan, 1984b: 603). Kayak use in South West Greenland came to a near stop in the mid-20th century, and while a renaissance of sorts occurred in the mid 1980s, kayaks today are primarily used for recreation or sport hunting.

In the more remote regions of Greenland, the adaptation of motorboats was more gradual, and did not necessarily coincide with a termination of kayak use. Motorboats could either be used for hunting seals with rifles, or for transporting kayaks to hunting grounds. Kleivan writes "Sometimes a kayak is brought along on the motorboat, partly to be used in sealing, and partly for getting help if the motorboat should develop engine trouble or become icebound"(1984:603). In Uummannaq (NW Greenland) vicinity, anthropologist Kenneth Taylor observed, "In villages where they are owned, it is common for three or four men together to make week-long hunting trips by motor boat." The hunters would bring their kayaks and camping gear, and conduct all the hunting from the kayaks (Taylor, 1961:498-500).

In the context of 1960-1970s Tiniteqilaaq, East Greenland, ethnologist Gert Nooter writes, "The ownership of . . . [outboard motorboats] . . . has increased so rapidly that almost every hunter now has one. There is still some resistance in the settlement, based on the noise and fumes generated by these boats, but not sufficient to prevent most people from buying one"(1976:34). Nooter also notes the comforts and discomforts of motorboats: "Paddling is . . . very tiring, and many hunters complain of painful limbs and

Figure 14: A Polar Greenlander in his kayak, ca. 1900. (From Peary, 1903:120)

feet after long trips. A boat with an outboard motor is of course much more comfortable, but one becomes much colder than in a kayak"(37).

The history of the kayak among the Polar Greenlanders (or "Inuhuit"— great Inuit) from the extreme Northwest coast of Greenland is an interesting and recent one warranting separate attention. During the late 1850s and early 1860s, a small migration led by the shaman Qillaq left the vicinity of Cumberland Sound, Southeast Baffin Island, Canada. This group hunted and wandered for several years up to and across Smith Sound to settle among the Polar Greenlanders who did not then have kayaks. These immigrants brought kayaks and kayak building knowledge with them (Mary-Rousselière, 1991:30-31).

In 1903-04, the Greenlandic philologist and explorer Knud Rasmussen interviewed Merqusâq, one of the few Canadian immigrants from that journey still alive in Polar Greenland at the time. Merqusâq remembered the reintroduction of kayaks to Inuhuit:

...We taught them to build kayaks, and to hunt and catch from kayaks. ... They told us that their forefathers had known the use of the kayak, but an evil disease had once ravaged their land, and carried off the old people. The young ones did not know how to build new kayaks, and the old people's kayaks they had buried with their owners. This was how it had come about that kayak hunting had been forgotten (Rasmussen, 1908:32).

The Danish ethnologist H. P. Steensby was not swayed by this explanation of the kayak's demise in Polar Greenland: "Had the Polar Eskimos been accustomed to and felt the need of building kayaks, they would certainly have found some way of continuing to do so" (1910:402). Steensby maintained that the original Polar Greenland populations (i.e., pre 19th century Baffin-immigration) were a people adapted entirely to land-based and frozen sea subsistence. Responding to the story told by Merqusâq (presented by Rasmussen), Steensby writes that it

...Does not give a rational explanation either of why they should give up the use of the kayaks, since such a cause could have no effect with a tribe accustomed to use the kayak. A probable explanation of the story is, that these kayak builders who died were immigrants— presumably from Baffin Land— who continued their customary summer mode of life, without at that time finding any imitators among the true Polar Eskimos (1910:403).

Whatever the case may be, after the migration of the 1860s kayaks have found imitators among Inuhuit of Polar Greenland — the northernmost people of the world— who use them to this day to hunt seals, walrus, and narwhal during the limited open-water season.

These Polar Greenland kayaks have inspired an unusual range of commentary by southern scholars. Naval architect and historian Howard Chapelle writes quite favorably of these kayaks: "(They) are highly developed craft— stable, fast, and seaworthy— and the construction is light yet strong enough to withstand the severe abuse sometimes given them" (1964:206). H. P. Steensby wrote in 1910 after his visit to Polar Greenland that the kayaks there were " . . . clumsy, heavy, and open . . ." (290).

Steensby's description is more accurate— especially since he is comparing them to more southerly Greenland kayaks. Chapelle's observation however, is not untrue: These kayaks were used quite ably, and certainly met the needs of those relying on them. Knud Rasmussen emphasizes this point: "What the craft lacks in seaworthiness is compensated for by the astounding skill with which the Polar Eskimo gets near to his prey, so that with ease and without the aid of a throwing-stick he harpoons his prey at quite close range" ([1921] 1976:12).

Over the years since Inuhuit regained kayak technology, their kayaks have undergone a distinct evolution away from the Baffin Island kayak type to the more seaworthy Greenland kayaks from further down the West Coast. Steensby describes this transition, writing that on account of the Polar Greenland kayaks being less than ideal for sea use, "...the Polar Eskimos ... took great interest in the West Greenland kayaks, which the [1909] Expedition had brought with it, and a West Greenland kayak which Knud

Figure 15: Angerlak Andersen of Ilulissat in her kayak at Nuuk in 2000. (Photograph by author.)

Rasmussen had taken up on an earlier occasion [1903-04] had even already produced an effect, which could be traced in some kayaks at Umanark [Uummannaq, Polar Greenland]"(1910:360).

At the end of the 20th century, the state of kayaks in Greenland is still varied: Narwhal are still hunted from kayaks with harpoons in Polar Greenland, and West Greenlanders as young as five years old and as old as 70 (men and women) compete in the annual Greenland National Kayaking Championships.

Kayaking in East Greenland has not faired so well: Gert Nooter counted 23 kayaks at Tiniteqilaaq (30k north of Ammassalik) in 1965, and only four in 1986 (1991:322). A traditional kayak renaissance in Ammassalik district is now beginning in no small measure thanks to the efforts of several Danish recreational kayakers interested in Greenland kayaks.

A couple of the kayaks in this study that were brought to Europe have now been returned to Greenland through repatriation programs and as gifts of goodwill from European museums and institutions. The Rijksmuseum voor Volkenkunde in Leiden, The Netherlands, gave a 300-400 year old kayak (plate 9) to the Greenland National Museum in 1983, after an exhibit of the kayak and two others loaned by the Rijksmuseum. This exhibit spurred a renaissance of kayak interest and use in Southwest Greenland (Heath, 1987:15), in no small part assisted by the availability of H. C. Petersen's *Qaanniornermut ilitsersuut*, or 'Instruction in Kayak Building,' published in Greenlandic, Danish, and English (1981).

The Greenland National Museum has also received several kayaks from the Danish National Museum: An 1889 child's kayak, a 1909 Polar Greenland kayak, and a 1930 Upernavik kayak (plates 35, 97, and 66, respectively). These kayaks helped build the Greenland National Museum's Greenland kayak collection into the most extensive and diverse of all.

Two of the Greenland kayaks in this study have never even been to Greenland: Greenlanders built them while traveling abroad. An elder from Nanortalik built one at the Viking Ship Museum in Denmark, where it remains (plate 81), and Maligiaq Padilla of Sisimiut built one in Texas to use for kayaking demonstrations (plate 92). In recent years many amateur kayak builders outside of the Arctic have emulated the general form and construction methods of Inuit kayaks; at least four 'how-to-build' Greenland-style kayak books are currently on the market.

It would be incorrect to assume that advances in conservation technology, cultural sensitivity, and storage in large modern facilities will necessarily preserve all museum kayaks. Kayaks are particularly difficult to store and conserve due to their size and susceptibility to insect damage, humidity changes, brittleness, and mold among other threats; it is quite remarkable that so many kayaks from the 1600s exist to this day. Because of this and other factors (e.g., a museum's mission/priority, etc.) most kayaks are not even on exhibit for public viewing.[11] In my estimation, there are at least 200 kayaks from Greenland in museum collections worldwide.

The tenuous existence of historic kayaks is emphasized by the American Museum of Natural History's disposal in the 1980s of at least 20 kayaks scarcely 100 years old, including many rare types from Canada and Polar Greenland. In 1976 a large collection of 'conservationaly-challenged' watercraft in the Heye Foundation's Museum of the American Indian was sold for $150,000.00 to the Canadian Canoe Museum (Hoyle, 2002:246). If anything, this should strongly suggest that better options than disposal may be at hand should they be sought. Regardless of a kayak's condition or appearance, there is still much to be learned from whatever pieces remain.[12]

---

[11] Of the 104 kayaks in this study, only 31 of the 97 in museum collections (i.e, non-private collections) were on display—visible to the general public—at the time of my visit, or the visit of the surveyor. That leaves 66 of the kayaks in this study in-storage.

[12] Significant cases in point would be the frame fragments of the Museon's kayak 57966—which were preserved in a small cardboard box (plate 7 and figure 195), and the Marishcal College kayak ABDUA:5736 (plate 17), which the collector had sawn in half. Some of the more remarkable examples of kayak conservation are the Museon kayak 57966 again—its skin being restored by conservationists to a convincing kayak-shape despite its original frame being mere fragments. Also, a kayak in the Netherlands whose collector had sawn it in half (plate 11) had since been rejoined by conservationists. A particularly damaged and forlorn kayak—the Newcastle Trinity House's kayak (plate 25) is presently undergoing conservation Merseyside Museums, U.K. Such conservation efforts are very expensive, and many museums struggle with merely maintaining an artifact's stability.

Notes Pertaining to Terminology and Illustration:

The kayaks in this study are referred to by their respective museums' catalogue number preceded by the museum's name or initials, e.g., the Museon's 48057 and the DNM's L.18.178. If a kayak has not been assigned a catalog number by the museum or owner, a tentative letter is used with the holders' name abbreviated, e.g., the HMM's "B" and THH's "A." The museum or organization abbreviations used in this study are given below:

AMNH:	American Museum of Natural History (New York City)	**MSM:**	Mystic Seaport Museum
CCM:	Canadian Canoe Museum (Peterborough)	**MSU:**	Michigan State University (East Lansing)
CMC:	Canadian Museum of Civilization (Ottawa)	**(N)MAI:**	(National) Museum of the American Indian (Washington, D. C.)
DHNS:	De Hidde Nijland Stichting (Hindeloopen)	**NMF:**	National Museum of Finland (Helsinki)
DNM:	Danish National Museum (Copenhagen)	**NMNH:**	National Museum of Natural History (Washington, D. C.)
FRAM:	*Fram* Museum (Oslo)	**NMS:**	National Museum of Scotland (Edinburgh)
GMZ:	Gemeentelijke Musea Zierikzee	**PQN:**	Peqatigiiffik Qajaq Nuuk
GNM:	Greenland National Museum; Also abbreviated KNK, after its Greenlandic name. (Nuuk)	**RM:**	Rijper Museum (De Rijp)
		RvV:	Rijksmuseum voor Volkenkunde (Leiden)
HMG:	Hunterian Museum (Glasgow)	**ROM:**	Royal Ontario Museum (Toronto)
HMN:	Hancock Museum (Newcastle)	**THH:**	Trinity House, Hull
HMM:	Hull Maritime Museum	**THN:**	Trinity House, Newcastle
KNK:	—*See GNM*	**UMCH:**	Univ. Museum of Cultural Heritage (Oslo)
MC:	Marishcal College (Aberdeen)		
MedChi:	Medico Chirurgical Society (Aberdeen)	**VSM:**	Viking Ship Museum (Roskilde)
		WFM:	Westfries Museum (Hoorn)
MM:	Mariners' Museum (Newport News)	**WMF:**	Weltmuseum (Frankfurt)
MdlM:	Musée de la Marine (Paris)	**WMR:**	Wereltmuseum (Rotterdam)

So as to make locating a scale drawing and/or the descriptive passage about a particular kayak, the kayaks in this text are also numbered 1-104, and the numbers are the same for the scale drawing (plate) and description.

The scale drawing of a kayak consists of the kayak's elevation (side view), and plan (top and bottom view). Trim and balance (or waterline) on the kayaks has not been accounted for in the orientation of the kayaks' elevations— this is a highly variable factor in such small boats. Instead, the orientation of the kayak in elevation-view is based on the ability to depict the cross-sections more clearly, hence the lowest part of the keelson being at the kayak's midpoint.

The plan view of a kayak is divided along its centerline, the upper half depicting the deck line arrangement, deck stringer placement, and the layout of the cockpit. Deck stringers are depicted with long-dashed lines along their respective centerlines. Occasionally a kayak will have a deck stringer placed in the middle of the kayak's deck— the text should be consulted to find out if that is the case for a particular kayak, and if so, its length.

The lower half of the plan-view depicts a kayak's bottom, showing the course of the chine and gunwale lower-edge (if present). To more accurately illustrate a particular kayak's deck lines, they are continued across the bottom view with a dashed line, fittings being depicted with a dotted line.

Cross sections of each kayak are also presented in the scale drawings, the right-half being forward stations, the left being aft stations. Adjacent to these cross sections is a structural cross-section with the scantlings. These measurements are taken inside the cockpit, and may vary in size and appearances towards the kayaks' ends.

Due to the damaged and/or deformed nature of some kayaks, several of the survey drawings present restored or 'conjectural' lines and measurements. These represent dimensions and shapes conjecturally arrived upon through evidence within the particular kayak as well as comparisons to similar kayaks. Such measurements and lines are plainly marked as conjectural, and are my own interpretations. Consult the texts (for the individual kayaks) and drawings for further notes on their respective restorations; in many cases, the artifactual lines are presented (artifactual being the representation of the damaged original).

Several kayaks in this study are frames or 'skeletons.' In rendering these in scale, two plates are used: One to depict the framework and its joinery in elevation, plan, and amidships cross-section. The second plate depicts the kayak hull-lines— essentially capturing the form and shape of the kayak as if it had a skin covering.

Scale three-view drawings cannot capture certain details and nuances of the original kayaks, so sketches are also used to show these features, as well as interior views and over-views of the kayaks. To remedy this, I have traced numerous photographs on a light-box and included them throughout the text. Another purpose of the sketches is to illustrate the organic nature of kayaks, whereas the scale-drawings are deceptively sterile and unnatural.

Kayak paddles are presented in their own section, and their scale drawings (paddle-plates) are numbered 1-79. A number of paddles are positively associated with particular kayaks in this study— others are not, and their provenance, if known, is discussed in the texts.

Offsets (measurements along x, y, and z axis) are not provided for the kayaks depicted in the survey drawings, though appendix D describes a simple technique for 'lifting' them from this book, for those that wish to loft or draw the kayaks full-size.

I have provided metric conversions for measurements; all of my measurements were made with the English system (feet and inches to fractions). The metric conversions are generally rounded to the nearest millimeter— if figures of exactitude are needed, please defer to my English measurements.

My presentation style of the scale drawings is borrowed primarily from the kayak surveys of Dr. Eugene Arima and John Heath, though certain adaptations have been made. I hand-inked the scale drawings with Stædtler Marsmagno and Copic Multiliner drafting pens, using ship's curves, an adjustable spline, and straight edges.

Some terms used throughout this text are best defined and illustrated together. A glossary is also provided, but certain terms and concepts should be given attention here due to their variable natures, especially pertaining to this study. These points consist of the pieces of a kayak, the elements of a kayak's hull (shape), and aspects of measurements and dimensions.

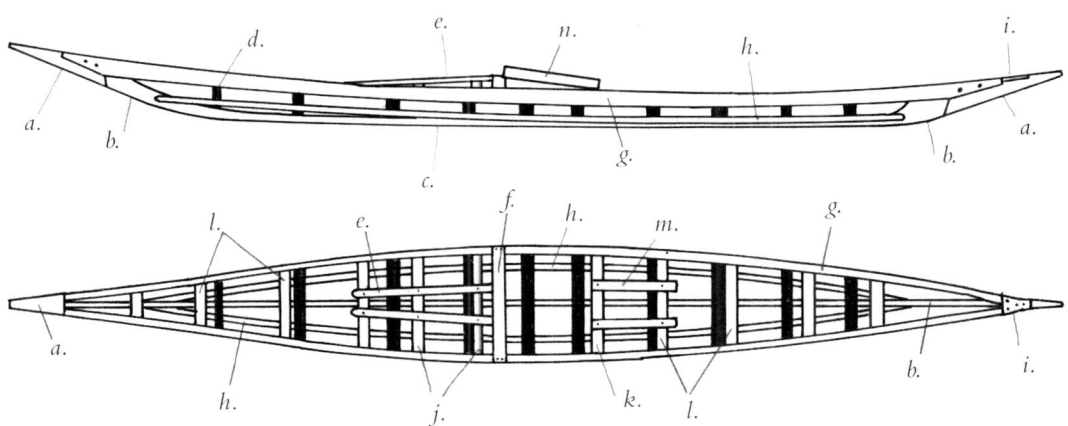

Figure 16: Structural pieces of the kayak, illustrated on a simplified West Greenland kayak frame.

The English terms for the pieces of the kayak frame, as shown in figure 16:

A. Stem board, bow/stern	D. Ribs	H. Chine	deck beam
B. Keelson ends, bow/stern	E. Forward deck stringers	I. Stem cap	L. Deck beams (straight)
C. Keelson	F. *Masik*	J. Curved deck beams	M. Aft deck stringers
	G. Gunwale	K. Aft cockpit	N. Coaming

In Greenlandic (West Greenlandic, modern spelling), the terms listed in figure 16 are:

a. *Usuusaq*	e. *Tunersuk*	i. *Qalluit*	m. *Isserfiup Tunersui*
b. *Niutaaq*	f. *Masik*	j. *Seeqqortarfik*	n. *Paaq*
c. *Kujaaq*	g. *Apummaq* (*Apummat, pl.*)	k. *Isserfik*	(after Petersen, 1981:80, and Jensen, 1975:30)
d. *Tippik*	h. *Siaaneq*	l. *Ajaat (pl.)*	

Greenlandic terms in this text are written in italics, the spellings are based on more recent texts, notably Petersen (1981 and 1986) and Heath (2004). These words are fairly up-to-date spellings of West Greenlandic vocabulary; it has proven hard to find a current terminology and/or spelling for the East Greenlandic dialect that has some of the more obscure kayak-related words. While it is a less than ideal shortcut, I have used West Greenlandic vocabulary for the sections on East Greenland kayaks. Sources for certain East Greenlandic terms and spellings can be found in Thalbitzer (1914), and Victor (1989:38-42). The use of common West Greenland spellings and vocabulary is also used in the description of Inuhuit (Polar Greenland Kayaks).

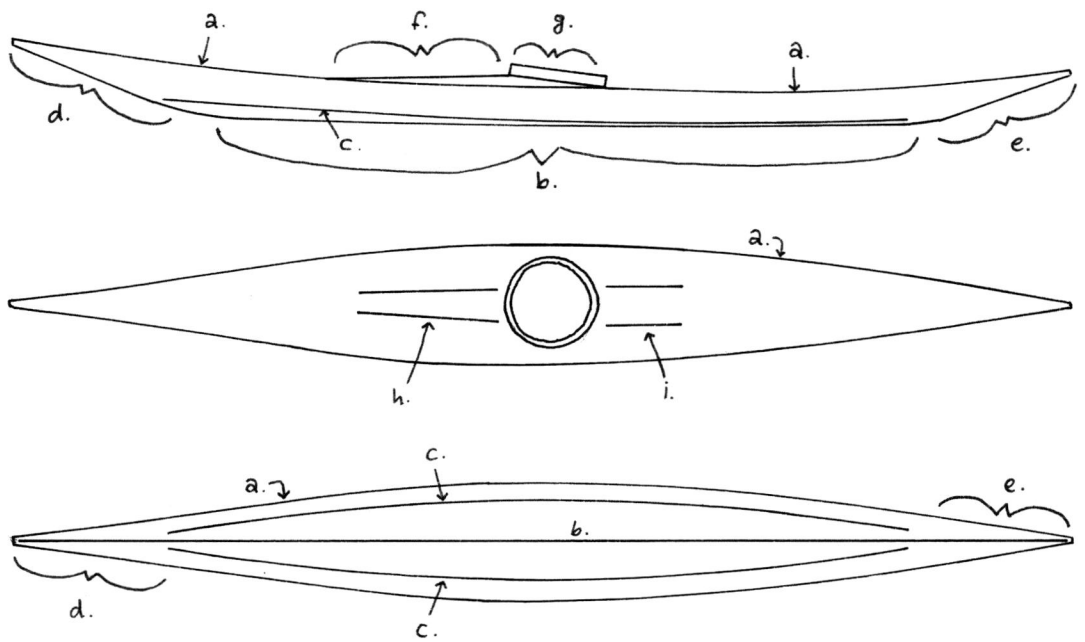

Figure 17: Elements of the kayak's hull: Lines and regions that define its shape.

a. Sheer or Sheerline
b. Keel
c. Chine
d. Stem: Bow
e. Stem: Stern
f. Fore deck, raised fore deck
g. Cockpit
h. Fore deck Stringers
i. Aft deck Stringers

Length of a kayak is just that— the length-overall, though may as well be considered a general measurement for the following reasons: Some kayaks have end-knobs, some don't, some are missing them, and in fact, some kayaks have broken and/or missing ends.

A kayak's beam or breadth is measured at the widest part of the gunwales (figure 18a), which often, though not always will be in the vicinity just ahead of the cockpit. In cases where the *masik* or coaming extends beyond the breadth of the

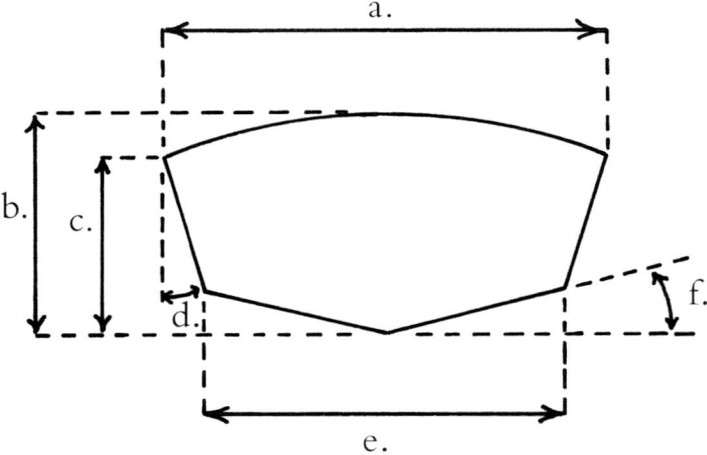

Figure 18: Some key dimensions of a kayaks' hull. Breadths are always measured at the widest point along a kayak's sheer; depths are always measured at the forward edge of the cockpit.

a. Beam (or breadth, Bmax.)
b. Depth overall (Doa.)
c. Depth to sheer (Ds.)
d. Gunwale or side flare
e. Chine Breadth
f. Deadrise

gunwales at their widest, it is still the breadth of the gunwales (at the sheer-line) that is measured, as this is more pertinent to hull-dimensions. (An example of a kayak whose *masik* is wider than its hull is the Museon's kayak 57992, plate 68.)

The depth-to-sheer of a kayak is measured from the bottom of the keel (outside the skin) to the upper-most edge of the gunwales — at the sheer-line (figure 18c). This is measured at the forward edge of the cockpit so as to correspond in position to where the depth overall is measured.

Depth overall is measured from the bottom of the keel (outside the skin) to the crown of the raised deck, just ahead of the cockpit (figure 18b). It is *not* measured to the top of the coaming. This measurement provides an idea of the deck-height above the sheer-line when the depth-to-sheer is subtracted from it. In some instances, a kayak's deck may be higher some distance forward of the cockpit (e.g., the Greenland National Museum's kayak KNK 1990 [plate 89], and the rolling-kayak "MP" [plate 92]) — the Doa. (depth overall) is still taken at the cockpit.

The above-mentioned dimensions are all provided for each kayak in the scale drawings (plates) and in Appendix A, but other dimensions not provided merit attention as well. The flare of the sides of the kayak is measured (in degrees) at 18d. In some cases gunwale flare is referred to: This is the angle of the gunwale, measured much the same way as the flare of the sides of a kayak. Figure 18f is the deadrise, also measured in degrees. It represents the incline from the keelson to the chines. Chine breadth is measured at 18e; it denotes the maximum breadth of the kayak's bottom.

Due to the pliable skin covering of a Greenland kayak, their actual cross-sectional shape when in the water is apt to look slightly different than the cross-section drawings. Water pressure around a kayak's hull presses the skin inward a bit (depending on the stiffness of the skin and the distance the skin spans between structural pieces) so as to give a concave section, as in figure 19.

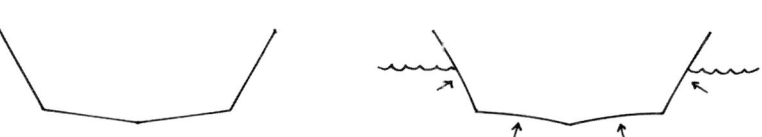

Figure 19: Water-pressure pushes the skin in between the keelson, chines, and gunwales. The extent of this depends on the pliability and tautness of the skin, the span of the skin between structural elements, and the weight of the kayak and its load.

Some other often-used descriptors should be discussed and illustrated here; these relate to the shapes of the kayaks' ends as well as the general shape of the kayak as a whole. 'Concave' and 'convex' are used to describe the curves of a kayak's end. Figure 20 left shows the profiles of two ends; the upper is concave (also known as 'clipper'), and the lower example is convex. These same terms are also used in describing kayak ends as viewed from above (plan-view): 20 right shows a concave stem (above) and a convex stem (below) — note how the convex stem carries considerable volume forward, whereas the concave stem is sharp and narrow. A kayak with concave stems in profile can have a convex stem in plan, and vice-versa.

When looking at a kayak in plan-view, one will note that the kayak's point of maximum breadth can be ahead of the kayak's midpoint, behind it, or right at it. Each of these positions has a name, respectively: fish-form, Swede-form, and symmetrical or balanced (see figure 21). These features have much to do with the distribution of a kayak's volume. These same terms can be used to describe the shape of the chines, and it should be noted that a kayak with a Swede-form sheer may not necessarily have a Swede-form chine curve. (The curve of the chine in plan view is shown in half-breadth on the scale drawings.)

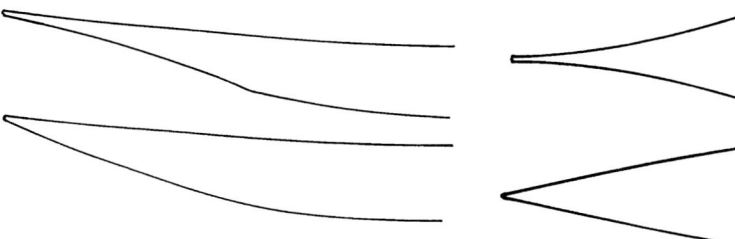

Figure 20: Kayak end-forms. Left, profile views showing concave and convex stems, and right, concave and convex stems in plan-view. A convex stem viewed 'in-plan' may have a concave form in profile, and vice-versa.

Several maps of Greenland are provided on pages xv–xx. I have tried to use the Greenlandic names in their present spellings throughout the text, but many of the sources I cite use either an older spelling or the Danish names of settlements. On page xxi I've included a table of current Greenlandic names/spellings, Danish names, and archaic names/spellings so that the reader will be able to discern accurately which locale is being discussed and where it is.

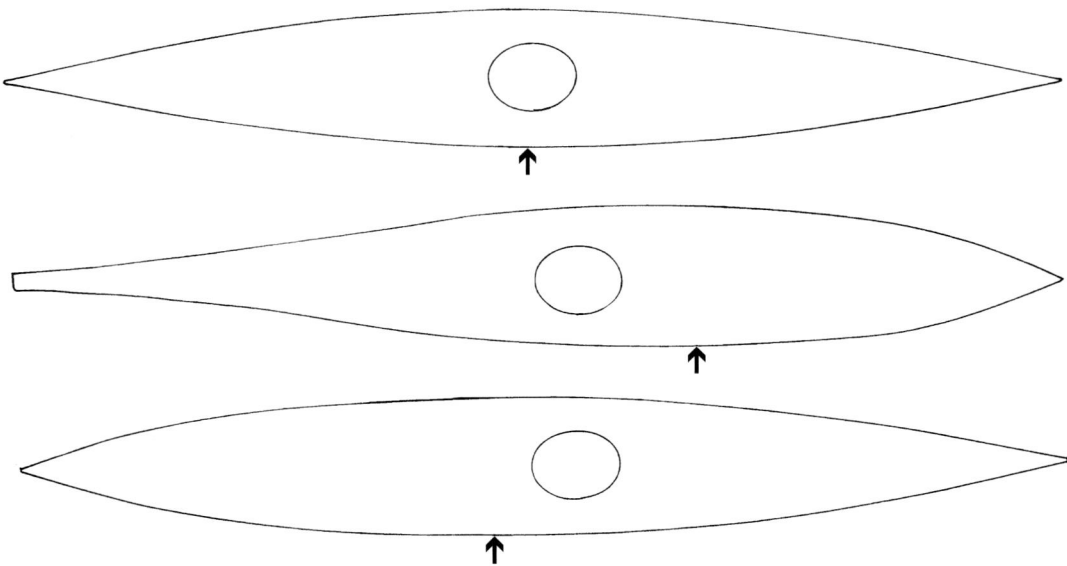

Figure 21: Top to bottom: symmetrically formed, Swede-formed, and fish-formed sheer shapes. These kayaks are viewed from above, their bows pointing left. The arrows indicate the vicinity of maximum breadth.

Greenland Kayak Construction

"We . . . see in the kayak evidences of the constructiveness, neatness, ingenuity, and resourcefulness of the Eskimo. Probably nowhere else in the World is finer naval architecture or design to be seen, even in places where materials are far more abundant."
~ William Clark Souter (1934:7)

The building of wooden boats— highly sophisticated ones— in a treeless land is nothing short of remarkable. The Arctic kayak is a skeleton of pieced-together driftwood, rendered seaworthy by its watertight seal skin covering. In regions further south in North America, bark was the common envelope to which a denser structure of wood lent rigidity. With kayaks, the frame was completed first, and then the seal skin was sewn around it; with Birch bark canoes, the bark was roughly shaped into a boat, and then the frame was built into it (Adney and Chapelle, 1964:27-57). Further south yet, where much larger trees were available, dugout canoes were more common. This latter type is the antithesis of the process of building a kayak— instead of piecing together many odd bits of wood to produce a boat, building dugouts involves the removal of large amounts of wood.

The construction method of the Inuit kayak is commonly termed a 'skin-on-frame' boat, (or 'skinboat') and this method of boatbuilding is also known among many other cultures. Indigenous forms of skin-on-frame boats exist or have existed in the United Kingdom, Northern Europe, Siberia, the Aleutian Islands, Tibet, and among certain Plains Indians of North America.

Often, a Greenland hunter would build his own kayak. Hunters would also build kayaks for their young sons, so as to prepare them to function in society as capable kayakers and hunters. William Thalbitzer, in the context of East Greenland writes, "Every adult man

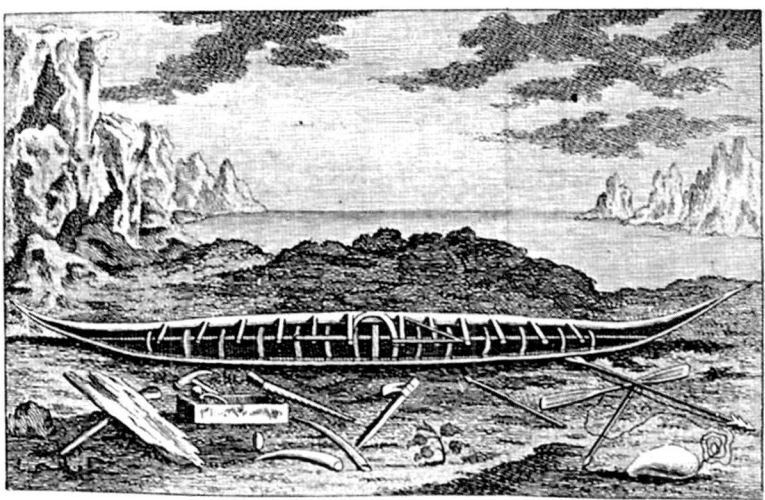

Figure 22: An engraving of a Greenland kayak frame from Crantz 1767. Oddly, the kayak is depicted as if cut in half down the middle. (John Wilson Room, Special Collections, Multnomah County Library, Portland, Oregon.)

has his kaiak, exceptionally two kayaks. Most are able to build and steer their kaiak themselves. Boys have as a rule small kayaks, built by their father and provided with miniature equipment" (1914:381-382). Gustav Holm, also in the context of East Greenland, writes "At what age the boy gets his kaiak, depends very much on how well-off the parents are; but the usual age seems to be about twelve" (1914:63).

Boys who did not have close older male relatives were typically doomed to not being kayakers or provider. Welfare funds were set up by Danish administrators in several settlements in West Greenland to provide lumber for these boys to build kayaks; hunters were encouraged and even paid to teach them the art kayaking and seal-hunting (Gad, 1982:143-146).

F. Spencer Chapman writes in 1934 of 'professional' kayak makers in East Greenland: "It interests me to hear that Kidarsi, though an excellent wood-worker, is getting his uncle to make his new kayak: so specialized is the construction that the good hunters prefer to get their kayaks made by one of half-a-dozen noted experts" (1934b: 277). Kayaks being built by professionals was not such a rare or new thing: Historian Finn Gad quotes C. Møller, a Danish trader at Christianshåb (now known as Qasigiannguit, S. E. Disko Bay) who wrote in the 1790s that "...good fangers seldom or never make their own kayaks, but pay someone else to do it..."(Gad, 1982:145).[13] But, Gad adds, "As far as kayak equipment is concerned, it has always been considered as the prevalent custom that the fanger made it himself" (1982:146).

The importance of quality work with in kayak construction and hunting equipment cannot be overstated. This basis of this pressure is of course both subsistence and safety, but what comes with successful hunting is respect. Gert Nooter describes the power of this concept in his *Leadership and Headship*:

In settlements like Tineteqilaq the language of things is extremely important, because such objects [one's tools and/or possessions] immediately convey the prestige and status of a hunter. With a little experience, a stranger

Figure 23: A successful hunter in Nuuk, ca. 1910— a photograph that exemplifies the 'language of things' discussed by Nooter in the above passage. (Photograph by John Møller/ Courtesy of Vernon Doucette.)

---

[13] The word fanger means catcher in Danish, and refers to seal-catchers. Fangst is the art and endeavor of catching sea mammals and other quarry.

can learn a good deal about the qualities of a man from his kayak and the equipment on it ... The insiders, the inhabitants of Tineteqilaq and the other settlements, do not have to learn this language; they understand it instantly. ...There can be no question that that status and prestige are highly visual matters in the East Greenland hunting communities. If a hunter sets out in a well-built kayak with a new float, a good harpoon and harpoon line, clean white camouflage screens, good rifle cases known to contain well cared for and well oiled rifles, those who watch his departure from their houses understand the language of things (1976:51-52).

This status conveyed by the quality and appearances of a hunter's possessions was undoubtedly as true for 17th century West Greenland as it was for East Greenland in the 1960s. By virtue of this concept, one would expect that the tools and kayaks of respected hunters would be emulated. Not much has been written about how hunters with poor equipment were regarded, but a passage by Nooter suggests it was at times harsh and degrading: "When a rather young hunter with poor kayak equipment took to his kayak as one of the last hunters, one of the watching women asked: 'You too?' The hunter did not answer but many of the women laughed as he set out for the narwhal hunt"(1976:51).

A kayak's frame is mostly made of wood, although other structural materials can occur, such as baleen, bone, plastic, and antler. The woods used range from various driftwoods to trade lumber and also locally grown varieties. Of the latter category, such pieces are usually so small as to be only practical for ribs. Writing in the context of East Greenland, Gustav Holm writes

The polar current which goes south along the coast carries drift-wood, wrecks etc. with it in towards the coast. The wood most frequently met with is fir. The trunks will sometimes be found to be whole trees which have been torn up by the roots, sometimes to be hewn timber; and it is no rare thing to see drift timber with a length of 20 feet and a diameter of 1 foot (1914:21).

Moravian missionary David Crantz, although theorizing at the time, correctly noted that much of the driftwood came from rivers draining into the Arctic seas above Asia.

From thence it is driven with the floating ice by the easterly current towards the pole, and then the northerly current that comes by Spitsberg meets it, and conducts it between Iceland and Greenland to the east-side, round Statenhook [Cape Farvel], into Davis's-straits, up to the 65th degree. As the stream varies there, the wood goes no farther north, and accordingly none is found at Disko nor above it, but the small remainder of this wood is driven by a contrary current westward to America (1767:I, 39).

Crantz also writes that oak was not found "except some shattered ship-planks"(1767:38). When wood from a wrecked ship was to be had, metal was apt to be found as well. Holm writes of a deserted ship drifting past Ammassalik vicinity (some 40 years before his 1884 arrival) from which "...two kaiak loads of iron were obtained. . ."(1914:21). Holm gives further mention of items found by East Greenlanders prior to his visit: Norwegian glass floats, a coconut, a bamboo cane, and brass that made its way into mountings for hunting equipment (1914:21).

The salvage of flotsam and of wrecked craft did not pass with the age of wooden ships: Gert Nooter writes of the inhabitants of Tiniteqlaaq, East Greenland visiting a wrecked helicopter in 1973 and promptly retuning home to get "saws and other tools to remove pieces of it." Pieces of the helicopter "were to be found in almost every house in the settlement." Harpoon heads among other things were fashioned from this metal (Nooter, 1980:116). Several East Greenland kayaks in this study make use of scrap metal— even scraps of plastic are known to have been used in kayak construction.

Parts of inhabited Greenland were not known to have driftwood due to unfavorable currents. Trade between Greenlanders (domestic trade) was critical in the distribution of raw materials used for subsistence technologies: Missionary David Crantz, writing in the 1760s, relates,

... As those in the south have no whales, and those in the north no wood, many boats of the Greenlanders coast every summer out of the south, ray from the east-side of the land, and proceed from two to four hundred

leagues [600-1200 miles] as far as Disko, with new kajaks and women's boats [umiaks], and the tackle and implements belonging thereto, and barter wood for the horns of the unicorn-fish, teeth, bones, whale-bone and whale's sinews, and part of this they truck on their way back (1767:I, 174).

Milled lumber became available through European trade in many areas of the West Coast during the seventeenth and eighteenth centuries. In many instances, lumber was imported from Denmark for the specific purpose of being used in kayak making (Gad, 1982:167). In describing the process of kayak construction in Egedesminde District (Aasiaat vicinity), Kaj Birket-Smith gives the first step: "At the store wood is bought..."(1924:262).

Before European tools were imported, Greenlanders made use of adzes, axes, knives, scrapers, bow-drills, and bone sewing needles for making kayaks. The edges on these tools were primarily stone, but meteoritic iron as well as metal gleaned from shipwrecks would have been used when available. Wedges of wood or stone would be helpful in splitting out boards from driftwood.

With increasing visits from Europeans, metal tools became available along with milled lumber. A list of the most requested trade items from circa 1730 includes chisels, tenon saws, laths and broad boards, rasps, and sewing needles— tools and materials well suited for kayak making (Bobé, 1952:67). Kaj Birket-Smith, in the context of early 20th century West Greenland, writes "The bow drill is to this day a favourite implement of most Greenlanders, even though European tools are now at their disposal"(1924:89). This preference may be on account of its ability to be used with one hand free, although at the expense of a socket piece being held in the mouth.

While a man (or men) did all of the carpentry, the *amiq*, or skin was prepared and sewn exclusively by women, although men often had a hand in stretching the skin over the kayak's frame. Despite such fairly clear-cut gender roles, Greenlandic women are historically known to have kayaked, and owned kayaks (Holm, 1914:46,187). In a census of inhabitants of the southeast Greenland coast, Johannes Hansen lists a twenty year-old woman, Kutsukujók, and a ten year-old girl, Kekartek, as each owning a kayak (1914:191). Today in Greenland, women build kayaks, and compete in the Greenland Kayaking Championships, and men have no qualms about sewing a cloth skin onto a kayak.

The construction of Greenland kayaks has been described in varying details in numerous sources. Kaj Birket-Smith presents the general construction process for West Greenland kayaks in his 1924 *Ethnography of the Egedesminde District* (262-265). H.C. Petersen brings a more 'how-to' approach to the process in his *Instructions in Kayak Building* (1981), and documents the building of a kayak by an elder in Kangaamiut in his *Skinboats of Greenland* (1986:17-41). Gert Nooter describes the kayak building process in East Greenland (briefly, but with numerous photographs) in his paper *The East Greenland Kayaks* (1991:325-334). Polar Greenland kayak construction is presented in Erik Holtved's 1967 *Contributions to Polar Eskimo Ethnography* (74-82).

The construction section of this study focuses on the variation of principles and solutions found in the 400 years of collected Greenland kayaks I've studied. I've presented their construction and joinery in a general chronological order of assembly, gleaned from the above-mentioned sources. Because the kayaks of the Polar Greenlanders (Inuhuit) are of very different construction, they have been excluded from the present section but are addressed separately immediately afterwards (pages 96 – 100). Following both of these sections, I have included a chapter on repairs and modifications that I have seen in the kayaks in this study.

In discussing the individual pieces of the kayak, it is important to first introduce some elements and principles that are pertinent to terminology as well as the larger picture of a kayak's structure. The numerous pieces of a kayak can be broken down into four main elements:

1. **The upper frame:** This is the rigid structure that defines the kayak's breadth; it is the strongest element of a kayak, and is rather analogous to a ladder in appearance and structure, although with tapered and joined ends. The upper frame consists of the gunwales and the deck beams.

Figure 24: Kayak building at Upernavik Kujalleq, 1939. (Photographer: Jette Bang/ Arktisk Institut gjb03712.)

2. **The lower frame:** This general element contributes the kayak's depth as well as its hull-shape and volume. It is somewhat analogous to a basket, not being so stout as the upper frame, though as a combined unit (a complete skeleton) the two are remarkably sturdy and resilient. The lower frame consists of the ribs, chines, and keelson.

3. **The skin, or** *amiq:* While the frame determines the kayak's outer shape, the skin literally becomes this shape. The nature of the skin and its attachment is such that it provides compression to the entire framework, and is therefore a structural element.

4. **Fixed accessories:** These are for the most part non-structural elements that contribute to the kayak's function, effectiveness, and durability as a hunting craft. Fixed accessories include the cockpit coaming, deck lines, deck fittings, keel edging, drain plug, and end knobs.

PRINCIPLES OF KAYAK JOINERY:

Three basic principles of joinery appear in kayak frames throughout this study, and it is often the case that two or even three of the principles are used in conjunction.

1 Lashing (Tying)
2 Pegging or Nailing
3 Mortise/Tenon

Many different materials are used for lashing kayak pieces together. Baleen, which significantly occurs most often in the oldest kayaks in this study, is indicative of a period when baleenous whales were more common and actively hunted.[14] In more recent kayaks seal skin line, sinew, cotton cord, fishing line, and even copper cable occur. The lashing of joints adds to the remarkable resiliency of a kayak, giving the kayak framework the edge of flex in lieu of fracture.

In all instances where lashings are used, a kayak builder took good care to prevent the lashing from protruding into the skin. To do this, the builder cut grooves in the frame to accommodate the lashings. This prevented both wear and hydrodynamic drag on the kayak's hull.

Pegging is the use of wood, bone/ivory, or metal nails to fasten pieces together (screws and rivets would also be in this category). In many instances, pegs or nails replace lashings, or vice-versa. In some cases they are both used together. Occasionally pegs used to fasten pieces together will also be pinned in place, so as to prevent the loosening of the pegs. Figure 25 depicts a pegged and pinned joint. Such joints are most commonly seen on coamings, and keelson, gunwale, and chine scarfs.

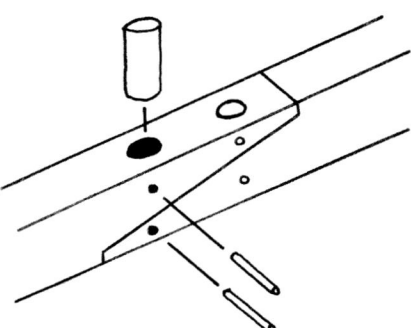

Figure 25: Pins of bone can be used to lock pegs in securely in place.

Mortise and tenon joints are nearly universal among the kayaks in this study, though the specific joints may vary somewhat, and some kayaks do not make use of them, e.g., certain Polar Greenland kayaks. It is essentially the fastening of one piece of the kayak directly into a mortise (a hole, slot, or divot) in another piece. Such pieces are secured via pegs/nails and/or lashings, though sometimes they are not fastened at all, and are held in place by compression. Figure 26 depicts the basic concept behind a mortise and tenon joint. As seen in figure 26, tenons can be thinned down tab-like extensions from a larger piece or can simply be the end of piece.

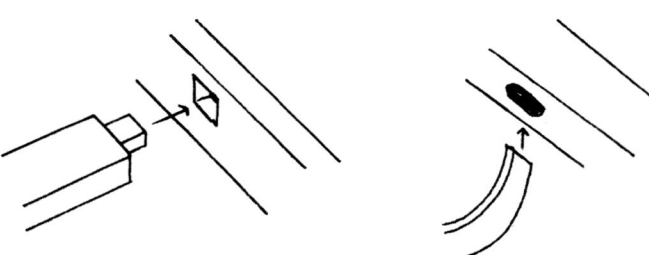

Figure 26: Mortise and tenon joints: Left, deck beam tenoned into a mortise in the gunwale; Right, rib end tenoned into a mortise in the gunwale's bottom edge.

---

[14] I've cited a passage from missionary David Crantz on page 26; in it he writes of parts of the kayak's frame being ". . . bound together with whale-bone . . ."(1767:I,150). Many early texts also mention the use of whale bone being used in kayak construction— this 'bone' is not actually hard, white bone, but instead flexible baleen from filter-feeding whales' mouths.

GUNWALES:

The main pieces of a kayak are the gunwales, or *apummat*. They are the primary load-bearing pieces, forming the deck and sheer-line of the kayak. The depth (or height) adds stiffness and strength to the kayak. The gunwales also receive other pieces such as the stem pieces, keelson ends, ribs and deck beams.

Because the gunwales of a kayak are often the longest pieces, it is common to see scarf joints. Most often, gunwale scarfs are situated right behind the cockpit. These joints can be made very simply (slant-cut and nailed together) or very complexly, such as a stepped double birds-mouth fastened with ivory pegs that are secured in place with smaller ivory pins, as shown in figure 27. Figure 28 depicts some simpler scarfs, one with peg fasteners and the other with lashings. The advantage of the birds-mouth scarf is that it will not splay when the assembled gunwale is flexed; the birds-mouths keep the wood aligned and a fair curve is ensured.

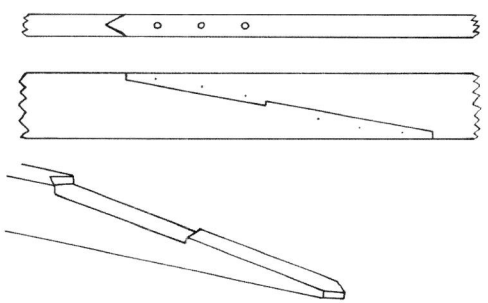

Figure 27: A stepped birds-mouth scarf joint. Note the use of locked pegs to secure the joint.

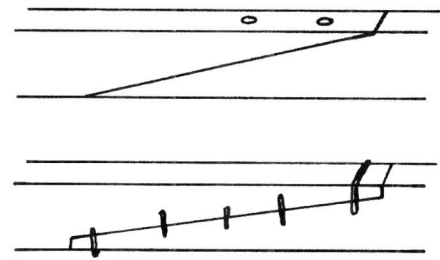

Figure 28: Scarf joints—Top, simple slant scarf with nails or pegs; bottom, stepped scarf, lashed together. These scarfs (and others) can appear on gunwales as well as chines and keelson.

A kayak's gunwales often appear as simple boards, but there is usually some complex shaping that goes into them in order to give the kayak the desired sheer. Another factor directly related to achieving the desired sheer is the flare of the gunwales. These considerations are best illustrated: Figure 29, top, shows an unshaped gunwale plank; when it is bent without any flare introduced, it will result in a flat-sheered kayak, or a kayak without sheer. The middle illustration takes another unshaped gunwale plank; only in this case flare is introduced to the plank. The result of this is a kayak with sheer. The bottom drawing in figure 29 depicts a shaped gunwale— with a humped center and raised ends. When flare is introduced and the plank is bent, the result is a kayak with little sheer amidships with raised ends.

The shaping of the gunwales can include the removal of wood, as in figure 30a, the addition of wood, and of course the combination of the two, as in figure 30b. Added pieces of wood (also referred to as 'gains') are usually nailed or pegged atop the gunwales.

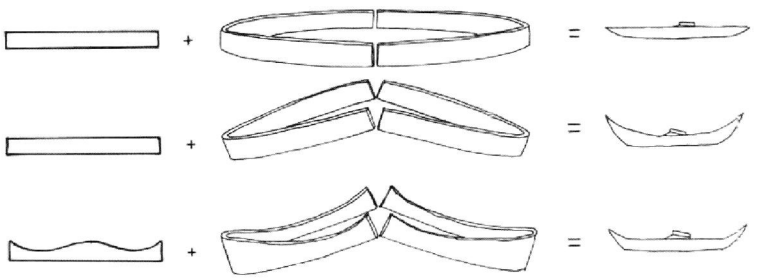

Figure 29: The shape of a gunwale plank and the flare it is given helps determine a kayak's sheer line. (after Cunningham, 2003:36). Essentially, the gunwale board's profile + a pair of such gunwales spread to a 'boat-shape' (the top example having no flare) = the resulting sheer-line in a kayak with such flare. For illustrative purposes, this presumes a fair and constant bend.

Other factors affect a kayak's actual sheer line; the examples in figure 29 presume a constant bend for illustrative purposes. Few kayaks actually have a constant fair bend of the gunwales. For example, the kayaks of East Greenland often have a subtle re-curve in their sheer. While this is generally achieved with un-shaped

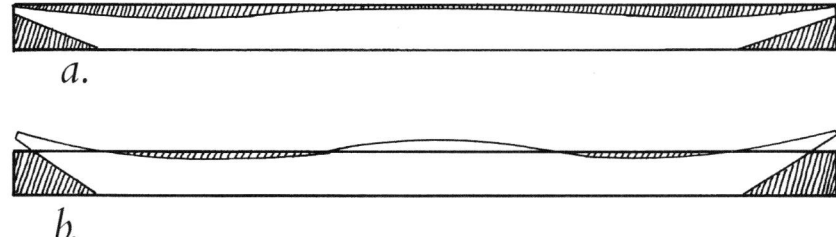

Figure 30: Gunwales can be shaped by removing wood from the boards and/or adding separate pieces (bottom).

gunwale boards with considerable flare, the re-curve results from the fact that the curve of the gunwales is not a constant fair curve. This is illustrated in figure 31; the example on the left shows a fuller-ended kayak and the resulting sheer with flared gunwales. On the right, a pinch-ended kayak's sheer typically levels out towards the tips.

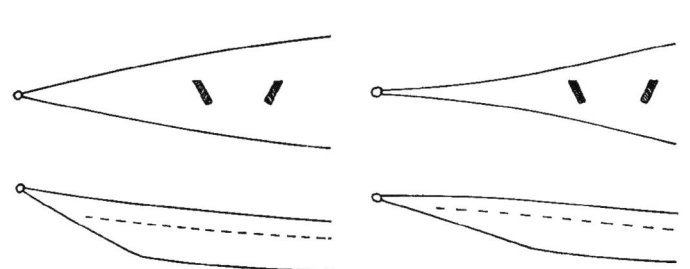

Figure 31: The fullness of a kayak's ends has an effect on the its sheer. Note how the pinched ends of the example on the right cause the sheer to level out towards the bow. (Both examples have flared gunwales; the course of the gunwales' lower edges is depicted with a dashed line.)

Again, sheer shape with pinch-ended kayaks can be adjusted through the use of shaped or built-up gunwale ends. Figure 32 shows how a pinch-ended kayak can still maintain a steep rising sheer end through gunwale shaping; the hatched area depicts the required build-up or shaping.

Most Greenland kayak gunwales have their top inside corners planed down so they do not protrude into the skin. This provides a flatter and more aesthetic deck. Figure 33 illustrates a cross-section of a planed gunwale corner, and an unplaned example for contrast.

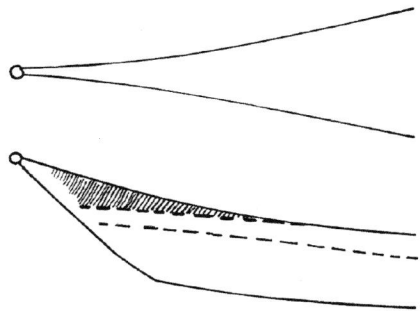

Figure 32: Kayaks with pinched ends can have raised ends if the gunwales are built-up. The dashed line shows the course of the gunwale and the hatched area depicts the required built-up area.

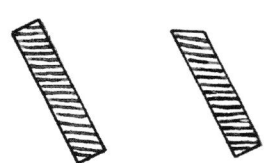

Figure 33: The inside upper corner of the gunwales is often planed down so as to not protrude into the skin-covering.

DECK BEAMS:

The kayak's deck beams run transversely from one gunwale to the other and essentially hold the gunwales apart, and in their multiplicity, add to the overall rigidity and strength of the upper-frame. Deck beams also lend considerable support to loads on deck via the deck stringers that span them.

Deck beam mortises do not always go entirely through the gunwales. It seems that in older West Greenland kayaks, noted particularly among their archaeological remains, the mortises were shallow— referred to as

Figure 34: Mortises in the gunwales to receive deck beams. Left, through mortise; right, shallow mortise.

'cavities' by Birket-Smith (Birket-Smith, 1924:79, 266-267). Later West Greenland kayaks seem to have mostly through-mortises, although shallow mortises persisted in the northern corner. East Greenlandic kayaks have as a rule only shallow deck beam mortises. Through and shallow mortises are depicted in figure 34. Unfortunately it is not always possible to tell which type of mortise a kayak has if its skin is intact.

As simple as the straight deck beams sound, their appearances are quite varied, ranging from mundanely rectangular to quite elegantly shaped. Figure 35 shows several variations of their forms. 35a depicts the form common among earlier kayak examples— rounded on all sides, with ends that taper into a tenon, while b depicts a cambered-bottom deck beam with a shouldered tenon and chamfered end. 35c depicts a plain rectangular form— occasionally this form will have the chamfered end as well.

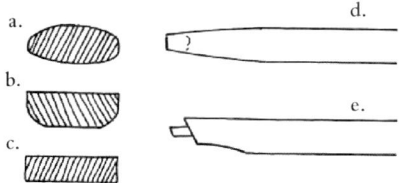

Figure 35: Cross sections of deck beams (left), and two different deck beam end-shapes.

There are several methods for securing the deck-beams in place: They are illustrated in figure 36. The most common lashing method among West Greenland kayaks is depicted in figure 36a. Method b is a slight variation of a in that the lashing passes through two holes in the gunwale instead of one. This situates the lashing higher up on the gunwale perhaps to be more effective when particularly deep gunwales are used. Figure 36b is only present in two kayaks in this study (the WMF 36841 and the Whitby kayak, plates 10 and 18 respectively).

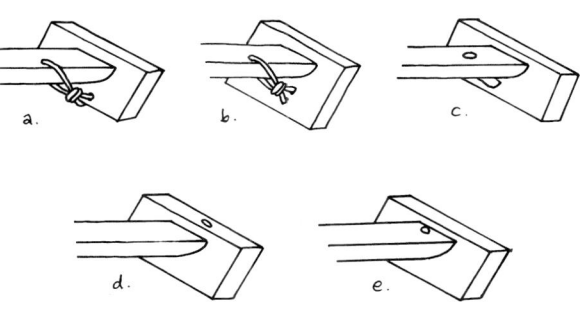

Figure 36: Fastening methods for the deck beam-to-gunwale joints.

Figure 36c is the 'oblique' peg method for fastening deck beams. Almost every East Greenland kayak exhibits the oblique peg method for securing deck beams. In these kayaks, the pegs are usually about 3/8"-1/2" (9-13mm) diameter and are used at each deck beam/gunwale joint. This same method does occurs in a number of West Greenland kayaks, although the pegs are as a rule thinner (1/4" [6mm] diameter) and are used intermittently, perhaps only on two deck beams forward and two aft of the cockpit. In a later East Greenland kayak, screws are used in-lieu of pegs for obliquely fastening some of the deck beams (as on the Museon 57602, plate 91). Several of the East Greenland kayaks have their oblique pegs locked in place with a peg or a nail set through the gunwale's lower edge.

The 'top-peg' method of deck beam fastening is depicted in figure 36d. A dowel or nail is set directly through the gunwales' upper edge, and down through the deck beam's tenon. Top-pegged deck beams apparently only occur in kayaks whose beams are through-mortised. Kayaks from the Bering Straits also utilize this method (H. Golden, field notes: 2000, 2003).

A shallow-mortise variation of the top-peg deck beam fastening method has been noticed in two of the kayaks in this study. In one example from northwest Greenland (NMS 1894.227, plate 57), the curved deck beams had fallen out of their places, and one's end exhibited an oblique hole through it— perhaps having a diameter of 1/8" (3mm). The hole passed directly through the tenon, which was only 1/4" (6mm) long, indicating the use of shallow mortises. This method of fastening, illustrated in figure 36e, makes sense when one considers that pegging through the top of the gunwale will not be effective with anything but through-mortised deck beams. The other kayak exhibiting the shallow-mortise top-peg method is a kayak skeleton from 1959 Illorsuit (EK 1959, plate 72), and instead of pegs, metal nails are used.

The presence of the two 'top-peg' methods are not always evident when one looks inside of a covered kayak, so their presence cannot always be known for certain, short of X-raying a kayak. In a few of the kayak-frames in this study (the PQN, 1Bs.8, and EK1959— plates 50, 44, and 72 respectively), there are deck beam joints in which both lashings and top-pegs are used (or oblique-pegs *and* top-pegs).

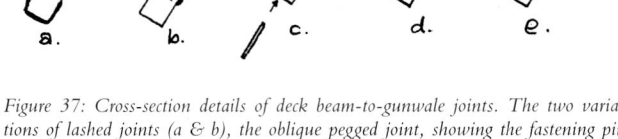

For clarity as to their exact configuration, cross-sectional views of the deck beam-to-gunwale joints are illustrated in figure 37. They are, from left to right: the two variations of lashed joints, the oblique pegged joint (showing the fastening pin occasionally used), the top-nailed joint, and the shallow-mortise variation of the top-nailed joint.

Figure 37: Cross-section details of deck beam-to-gunwale joints. The two variations of lashed joints (a & b), the oblique pegged joint, showing the fastening pin occasionally used (c), the top-nailed joint (d), and the shallow-mortise variation of the top-nailed joint (e).

It is common for lashed deck beams to have the lashings come off alternating sides of the deck beam. This is done to prevent torque on the deck beam; such a force can fracture the deck beam's tenons. There are examples however where this has not been done. A good example of both solutions is visible on the Nuuk Kayak Club's kayak "PQN," plate 50. In this example, the first two deck beams have alternating lashings, while the rest of the lashed beams are lashed on the same side.

Figure 38: Occasionally the forward edge of the isserfik will be cut away so as to make the cockpit more roomy and/or comfortable. (This is a top-view, the kayak's bow being towards the bottom.)

In Greenlandic, the deck beam placed at the aft end of the cockpit is: *Isserfik*. Often a kayak's *isserfik* will be carved back a small distance so as to effect a curved 'back-rest.' A view of such an *isserfik* is presented in figure 38, and can also be seen in plates 14, 19, 25, and 31 etc. Occasionally a kayak's *isserfik* will be of heavier dimensions than the rest of the deck beams because it needs to support the coaming, aft deck stringers (if present) and the kayaker when entering and exiting. The fastening of deck beams is often intermittent, but usually the *isserfik* is among those lashed or pegged to the gunwales.

Deck beams are usually placed towards the upper edge of the gunwales; they hold the sheer edge out, while the lower edge of the gunwale can be drawn in by lashings or clamping ties so as to give the gunwales flare. Not having deck beams placed lower on the gunwales would also of course provide more room inside of the kayak for the kayaker.

There are instances of deck beams placed lower on the gunwales— even at their bottom edges, in conjunction with higher-placed beams (as in figure 39). H. C. Petersen writes in the context of older Greenland kayaks: "To make a kayak more stable the cross beams were set at different heights, as

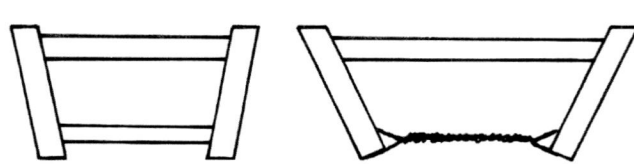

Figure 39: Lower-placed deck beams resist additional gunwale flare (left), and clamp ties are used to increase gunwale flare.

in other kayaks... In older kayaks there are also a pair of cross beams by the foot support placed one over the other" (1986:56). (By "stable," Petersen likely refers to structural stability— strength and/or stiffness, as these pieces would have nothing to due with a kayak's hydrodynamic stability on the water.)

The deck beams placed at varying heights that Petersen describes would have certainly contributed to a stouter structure, but they were likely placed at different heights for a more specific reason: Certain kayaks have a marked change in gunwale flare from the forward half of the hull to the aft-half— essentially a compound-flare, the gunwales being twisted. The paired deck beams were likely used to ensure that the forward ends of the gunwales would have little flare, while the flare towards the stern could be increased through the use of clamping ties. Such low-placed deck beams are depicted in figures 180, 200, and 318. It is rare to see low-placed deck beams aft of the cockpit in any Greenland kayak; none of the kayaks in this study have such a configuration.

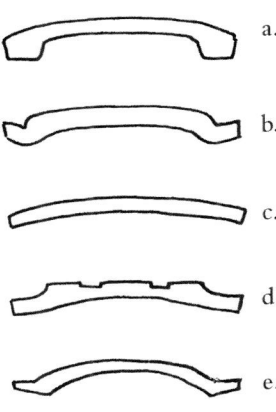

Figure 40: A variety of curved deck beam shapes.

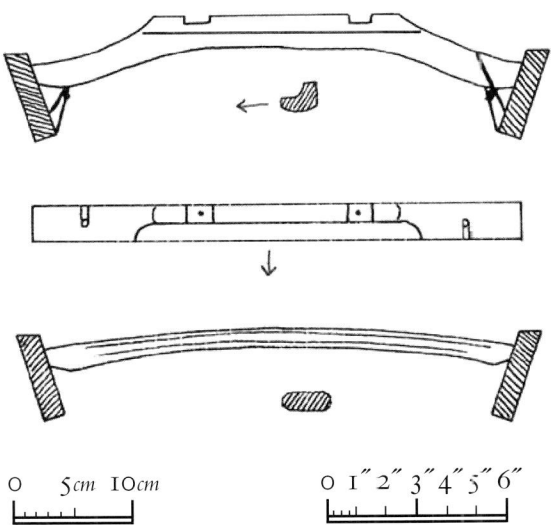

Figure 41: Curved deck beams in the Musée de la Marine': kayak 1Bs.8. The example at the top is nearest the masik. *Note the carved finger grip in the cross-section. The arrows point towards the kayak's bow.*

Curved deck beams are used in Greenland kayaks where the deck slopes up to meet the cockpit. Aside from the *masik* (the deck-beam defining the forward edge of the cockpit described later), a kayak may have one or more such pieces, though rarely more than four. These curved pieces support the forward deck stringers, and thereby the hunting equipment stored on the fore deck. Due to the shallow nature of most Greenland kayaks, the curved deck beams also make for more leg-room for the kayaker.

The shape of the curved deck beams ranges from simple arches to very curvaceous and stylized pieces with sculpted facets and chamfered corners (see figure 40). Some curved deck beams receive the deck stringers in notches, while others simply have the stringer resting atop or on shims if a gap is present. In cases where more complex formed curved beams occur, it is usually the aft-most example that is shaped such, while the forward one is usually plainer.

Figure 41 shows two curved deck beams from the same kayak: the Kangaamiut kayak of circa 1900 in the Musée de la Marine, Paris (1Bs.8, Plate 44.) A rabbet or ledge carved into the upper-front corner of the longer deck beam (fig. 41, top) serves as a hand-grip for carrying: The arm is put through the cockpit opening, and the hand grasps this deck beam between the deck stringers; this rabbet seats the fingers perfectly.

The two curved deck beams of the National Museum of Scotland's kayak 1984.277 (plate 19) are depicted in figure 42. They are less complex in form than the 1Bs.8's aft curved deck beam, but are shapelier than the 1Bs.8's forward curved deck beam. The shaping of the 1984.277's curved deck beams is very reminiscent of the curved deck beams seen in many Alaskan kayaks— wider and flatter at the ends, and taller and narrower in the middle (Golden, field notes: 2002; Zimmerly, 2000:16,29,32.)

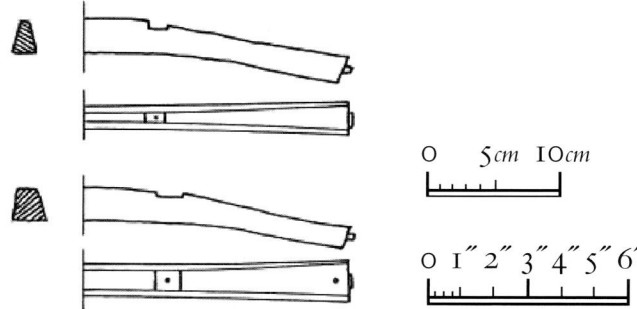

Figure 42: Curved deck beams in the National Museum of Scotland's kayak 1984.277 (shown in half-breadth). The deck beam at the bottom is nearest to the masik.

As discussed earlier, the fastening of deck beams to the gunwales is often intermittent. Typically, (and the case with figures 41 and 42), it is the aft-most curved deck beam that is usually lashed or pegged in place, while the forward curved deck beam may just have a top-peg if any fastener.

GUNWALE ENDS:

The gunwales of Greenland kayaks come together at both ends, and are fastened to each other. The most common method of joining the gunwales' ends is with pegs (figure 43). Metal nails occur in later examples (e.g., the kayak EK 1959, plate 72). It is very critical that this joint is held firmly and not allowed to shift or flex, for in doing so the entire symmetry of the kayak would be compromised.

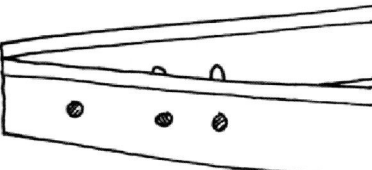

Figure 43: Pegs used to fasten the gunwale ends together.

Usually the gunwale ends are chamfered at their lower inside edges so that the pieces have a considerable 'mating' surface area (figure 44). This makes for a firmer joint and allows the upper outside edges of the gunwales (the sheer line) to be quite close, i.e., narrower and closer to the end of the kayak, thus requiring shorter stem pieces (if any). Furthermore, the chamfering helps to set the flare of the gunwales, as seen in figure 45.

Figure 44: Inner face of a gunwale's end, showing the chamfer.

Towards the ends of the gunwales (ahead of the first deck beam and/or behind the last one), there is usually a clamping-tie or dowel at the gunwales' lower edge. This not only holds the gunwales together, but it also helps maintain their flare. Examples of each of these are illustrated in figure 46. The dowel method involves the through-mortising of the dowel into the gunwales; the dowel is secured by a peg or nail set through the gunwale's lower edge, as in figure 47.

While the use of a windlass (figure 48) is generally associated with being a technique for holding pieces tightly during construction, there are several kayaks in this study in which

Figure 45: Chamfering the gunwale ends so that when they are flared and joined, they meet flush.

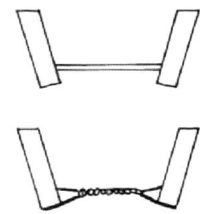

Figure 46: Top: Cross piece (a thin stick or dowel) at the lower edge of the gunwales, towards the gunwale ends. Bottom: A clamp tie in the same position.

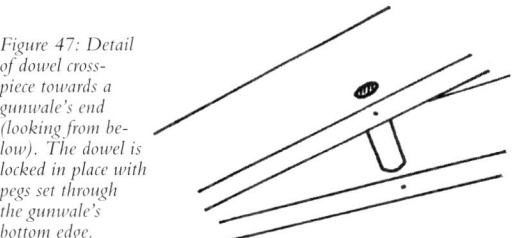

Figure 47: Detail of dowel crosspiece towards a gunwale's end (looking from below). The dowel is locked in place with pegs set through the gunwale's bottom edge.

the windlass remains in place. In this permanent application, they appear just like a normal clamping tie, except instead of wrapped and tied-off, they have a stick threaded between the lines, wound several revolutions, and then parked against a deck beam to prevent unwinding. See figure 280, a forward interior view of the National Museum of Natural History's kayak 160325 (plate 56) to see a permanent windlass.

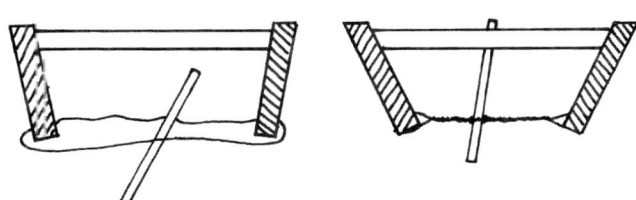

Figure 48: Windlass used to tighten gunwales and/or increase gunwale flare. Occasionally these windlasses are left inside a completed kayak.

RIBS:

The ribs of a kayak are the foundation for the kayak's ultimate hull-shape. Their shape and form contributes to kayak's depth and how its volume is distributed along the kayak's length.

Many types of wood can be used for kayak ribs, including some that grow in Greenland, such as birch, willow, hazel, rowan, and alder; these are mostly dwarf varieties that grow in fjords. H. C. Petersen mentions the use of wooden barrel hoops for ribs (1981:32, 1986:24)— these were likely widely available for trade aboard whaling ships and colonial stations, but are undoubtedly harder to come by nowadays. Kaj Birket-Smith, writing in the early part of the 20th century, writes that ribs are "now most frequently made of hoops, but on rare occasions willows are still said to be used" (1924:262). One kayak in this study (plate 104) has plastic ribs— cut from fish buckets.

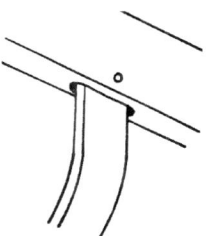

Figure 49: Pegged rib-to-gunwale joint.

Ribs are not always fastened into their mortises, but when they are, the common method seems to be via small pegs (1/8"-3/16" [3 – 5mm] diameter) set through the gunwale's face and through the tenon (figure 49). In later examples, thin metal nails can be used for this purpose, the ends being bent over inside the kayak. Figure 50 depicts an alternate method of rib fastening with metal nails.

The spacing of ribs, particularly in the vicinity of the cockpit, is highly variable and seems to be based on local tradition. H. C. Petersen writes, "In Maniitsoq— Kangaamiut there are no ribs under the cockpit, but the ribs under the kayaker's legs are closer together" (1986:25). The scale drawing of the 1.Bs.8 kayak skeleton from Kangaamiut shows this exact arrangement (Plate 44). A quick flip through the scale drawings reveals that West Greenland kayaks very

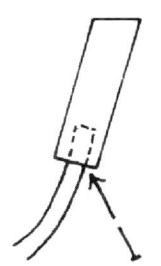

Figure 50: Oblique fastening of the rib to the gunwale.

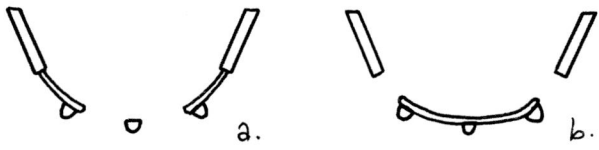

Figure 51: Two variations of the use of "Half-Ribs." The example on the left functions as a seat, while the example on the right usually appears forward in the cockpit, where the kayaker's legs would lay.

Figure 52: Two methods of forming ribs at the ends of a kayak: Left, tying two sticks together; right, kerf-bending.

rarely have a rib positioned right in the middle of the cockpit; those that do are mostly from 20th century South Greenland. East Greenland kayaks almost as a rule have ribs placed in the center of the cockpit. Many kayaks have half-ribs. These come in two forms, both illustrated in figure 51. 51a. has the center portion of the rib removed; ribs such as these are usually in the vicinity of the kayaker's legs, and may represent a modification so as to make the cockpit either more comfortable or easier to get into. This is also illustrated in the scale drawing of the South Greenland kayak VSM 810-34 (plate 81). Figure 51b is essentially the opposite of a.— where the middle part is left in place, the ends being removed, or more likely never having been present. This type of half-rib is a form of floor or seat, and is described in further detail below in the section "Seats."

One kayak in this study has a unique variation of the half-rib that spans the gunwale to the chine; it is unique in that it appears to be tenoned into the chine. This strut of sorts would hold the chine firmly in place, preventing it from slipping up the curve of the ribs. Oddly, it only appears on one side of this kayak in one place; see figure 197.

Towards the ends of a kayak, the bend in the ribs becomes more acute. There are several ways to make these extreme bends without breaking the ribs. The simplest method is to use thinner ribs that will take a tighter bend. Another method is to use kerf-bent ribs. To kerf-bend ribs, the inside of the bend is cut thinner with a knife thereby allowing a tighter bend or even an angular fold. In some cases it is more practical to just use two sticks tied together at the keelson; this and the kerf-bent method are both depicted in figure 52.

In many kayaks in this study, the ribs taper towards their ends. This allows them to be fit into small mortises and yet be sizable enough to support the keel and chines, not to mention the kayaker. In the example of the PQN (plate 50), the rib mortises are circular holes, 3/8" (9mm) diameter, while towards the keelson the ribs measure 3/8" (9mm) thick by 5/8" (16mm) wide. Some kayaks have gently tapering rib ends while others are more crudely whittled down at their ends; these extremes are depicted in figure 53. It is also sometimes the case that the rib ends are not tapered at all.

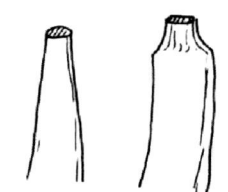

Figure 53: Two forms of tapered rib-ends. Round tapered (left) for placement in a drilled mortise. Right: square tapered or 'chamfered' rib end for chiseled mortise.

KEELSON:

A kayak's keelson is its centerline hull stringer. It is fastened to the ends of the gunwales as well as to the ribs. The shape of the keelson can vary considerably. Two forms are depicted in figure 54. The top example is a thin board, bent up at the ends to form the raked stems. This method of forming a keelson and stem ends is known throughout the Canadian Arctic (Arima, 1987:112-113 and 216, fig.27), and apparently is the structure found in the Lübeck Schiffergesellschaft kayak (plate 1, and figure 56) of circa 1607 (Neugebauer, 1993:38, Heath, 2004:12, fig.1.6a)

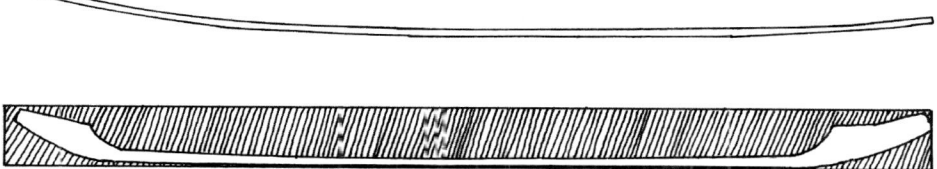

Figure 54: Keelson profiles. Top: batten keelson, sprung to desired shape. Bottom: keelson with broad ends (to form the base of the stems) sawn from a plank.

The lower example in figure 54 is a form of a typical 20th Century West Greenland kayak's keelson. As can be seen, it broadens considerably at the ends, giving the kayak a good sturdy cutwater as well as ample material to run lashings through for attaching to the gunwales. I find this latter form of keelson puzzling: it appears much sturdier than the bent-board method, but by nature of its being sawn from a long plank, there is substantial grain run-out at the turn of the stems. Consequently, several of the keelson ends I observed in kayak frames were fractured along this point and exhibited repairs.

Kaj Birket-Smith in his *Ethnography of Egedesminde District* describes a variation of the rib-to-keelson joint: "The middle part of the keelson is low, at the upper edges provided with cross grooves, into which the ribs are grooved and then fastened with treenails" (1924:262). This description is vague, and ironically this grooving, as I understand it, appears in only three *very* different kayaks in this study. One is from 1960s East Greenland (Museon's 57602, plate 91), another from Polar Greenland (Mystic Seaport's 1964.1562, plate 101), and the last is a 17th or 18th century West Greenland kayak (the RvV's 349, plate 15); the first and last of these three kayaks only exhibit keel 'grooving' intermittently.

Birket-Smith concludes that this grooving is "evidently due to European influence"(1924:269). Whether or not this is based on exposure to European technology or European solutions is unknown, and while so few kayaks in this study exhibit this 'grooving' consistently, it remains a mystery as to what Birket-Smith meant by grooving. A look at the complexity of Greenland scarf joints— even among the oldest kayaks in this study— suggests that the lack of grooving had nothing to do with the technological limitations of Greenlanders.

In some cases, a kayak's ribs may not always match up perfectly with the keelson or chines; sometimes a gap will be present, and other times a rib will stick out too far. In order to ensure a

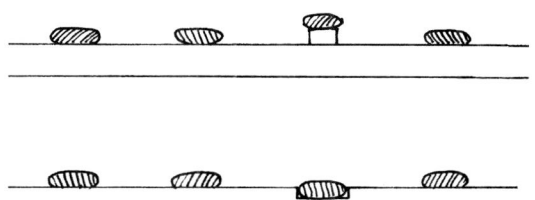

Figure 55: Occasionally a rib will not match up perfectly with a chine or the keelson. If the rib falls short of it, a shim can be added; if the rib sticks out, a notch can be made in the stringer to accommodate it.

snug fit and fair lines, kayak builders would insert shims to fill the gaps, or carve a divot in the chine or keelson where a rib protrudes. Figure 55 top shows cross sections of four ribs— one of which does not quite reach the chine, hence it is shimmed; 55 bottom shows a rib that protrudes too far, and is therefore notched into the chine. The "grooving" that Birket-Smith refers to above may be the consistent use of rib-notches as depicted in figure 55 bottom.

The methods of attachment of the keelson to the kayak's ribs are identical to those of the chine-to-rib attachments; these are all described and illustrated in the section on "Chines."

KEELSON AND GUNWALE END JOINTS:

The joint between the gunwale's ends and the keelson's ends is often very complicated — it is the convergence of the upper and lower frame, and it must be sturdy. The keel rises up to meet the gunwales, and they are usually lashed together. Often a series of steps or notches helps hold the keel firmly in place. Many different forms of these joints occur;

Figure 56: The Lübeck kayak's ends (Plate 1) (after Neugebauer et. al, 1993:38/1982:229).

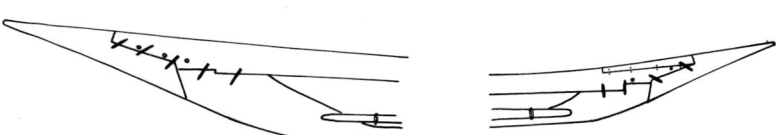

Figure 57: The 1Bs.8 from Kangaamiut, 1900 (plate 44).

the following figures show several methods that appear in kayaks in this study. (These drawings omit certain idiosyncratic details, e.g., repairs, damage, etc.; Consult the scale drawings for further aspects and actual appearances.)

The structure of the Lübeck kayak of ca. 1607 is presented in *the Greenlander— An Eskimo Kayak at the Lübeck Barge Masters Guild* (Neugebauer, 1993:38/1982:229); whether or not its structure was x-rayed or 'inferred' is not known, but in any case, it is presented in figure 56, albeit not to-scale (The survey drawing of this kayak is presented in plate 1).[15]

Figure 57 depicts the bow and stern structures of a Kangaamiut kayak from 1900 (1.Bs.8). The form of these assemblies is fairly simple and executed with few pieces. The bow and stern pieces are broader at their top faces. In the case of the 1.Bs.8, its stem pieces' sides are hollowed and carved down for a sharp keel-edge; a cross-section of this is depicted in figure 58, left.

The following two examples (figs. 59 and 60) come from very similar kayak skeletons from mid 20th century Nuuk (the KNK "C" and PQN, plates 51 and 50 respectively.) Both kayaks have separate end caps[16] attached to their stem pieces. The reason for these end caps is that the stems are made from a milled board, and not a thick chunk of wood easily hollowed out. Essentially the cap ensures a fair and smooth transition of the sheer line as it follows the gunwale ends to the stems' termini. See figure 58 for cross sections of a 'capped' stem piece and a solid stem piece (left and right, respectively).

Figure 58: Two cross sections of stem-pieces: Carved, left, and capped, or built-up.

Despite their great similarities in form and construct, a few varying elements of their end-joinery are apparent. Note how the depth of the stem was adjusted in the PQN's bow. The KNK 'C's gunwale

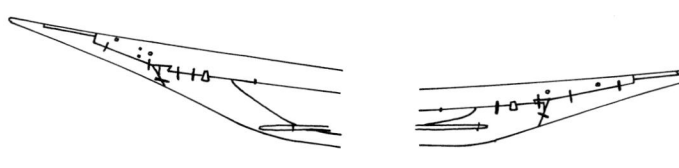

Figure 59: KNK "C" (plate 51).

---

[15] The depiction of the Lübeck kayak's end-structures in Neugebauers strikes me as being oddly devoid of ribs or any other means of support—I think the depiction is conjectural instead of based on X-raying.

[16] The West Greenlandic name for the cap-piece is given as "*qagdliut*" in P. Scavenius Jensen (1975:30); this is an older spelling, and while I have not seen the term updated, I would figure it to be *qalliut*.

ends have a step in them to further stiffen the joint. Both have small transverse pieces of wood— 'keys,' trapezoidal in cross-section— holding the keel ends firmly in place (see figure 61). These key pieces are apparently not fastened to the kayak frames in any manner; while the PQN's keys were present, the KNK C's key-pieces were both missing.

Figure 60: The PQN (plate 50).

The kayak whose stems are depicted in figure 62 is of an unknown provenance, but I think it must come from the northern West Coast of Greenland (Greenland National Museum's kayak KNK 1550x18, plate 71). Each end shows evidence of having been deepened via shim pieces inserted between the keelson ends and the gunwale ends. Despite the numerous repair and adjustment pieces, the simplicity of this kayak's end structures is plain to see when compared to those in figures 59 and 60.

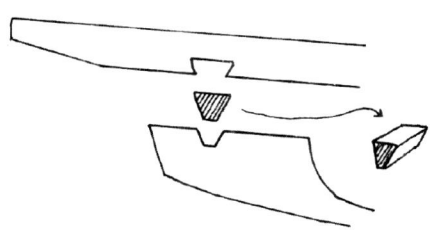

Figure 61: A trapezoid-sectioned 'key' locks the keelson end to the gunwale ends in certain kayaks. Note how this key piece appears in two different orientations in figures 59 and 60.

The ends of a Northwest Greenland kayak (from Illorsuit, 1959) are depicted in figure 63. It is very simply made— no steps, transverse pieces or fanciness. It has cap pieces both at the bow and stern, and unlike the previous kayaks in this section with cap pieces, the present examples' are set onto the stem pieces *and* gunwale ends. Also note how the cap-pieces form the kayak's tips. In lieu of pegs securing the gunwales' ends, metal nails are used— each side gets a nail, and each end is bent over on the other side.

Figure 62: KNK 1550x18 (plate 71).

Figure 63: The "EK" from Illorsuit, 1959 (Plate 72).

Figure 64: VSM 810-34: a South Greenland kayak (plate 81).

A 1990s South Greenland kayak's ends are illustrated in figure 64 (The Viking Ship Museum's kayak 810-34, plate 81). A kayak from 1935 Qaqortoq at the Greenland National Museum is nearly identical in its end-joinery pattern, save for one little triangular patch of wood where the keelson end meets the stem piece at the stern. The 1935 kayak does not appear in this study, however its lines are presented in *Skinboats of Greenland* (Petersen, 1986: 48, fig.44). Like the 1959 Illorsuit kayak, the end cap pieces of the VSM 810-34 continue over the gunwale ends, to which they are also fastened, via pegs set through its edges. A small step in the gunwale ends helps lock the keelson ends in place.

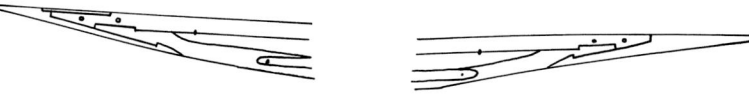

Figure 65: The East Greenland kayak 57602 (plate 91).

Appearing in stark contrast to the previously illustrated stem assemblies, the East Greenland kayak (figure 65) is not so reliant on lashings to secure its joints. The keelson end is stepped into the gunwale ends, and unlike prior examples, the stem piece is hook-scarfed to the keelson ends. These joints are secured with pegs; the pegs attaching the keel edging also add to the fastening of this joint.

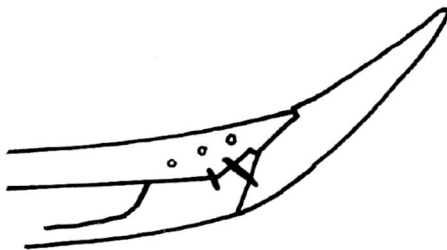

Figure 66: Stern structure of a kayak in the Canadian Canoe Museum (977.182). This is a reconstructed view; see plate 60.

A very damaged kayak in the Canadian Canoe Museum's collection (the 977.182, plate 60) was missing a bit of its skin such that its stern assembly could be seen and measured: Its form appears in figure 66. The stern structure of the 977.182 is nearly identical to a kayak collected in 1810 off Hunde Island (between Disko Island and Aasiaat); this kayak is in the Lincoln Museum, U.K. (Vernon, 1984:416, fig.1).

Each of the kayak's ends depicted in figures 57 through 66 would exhibit just one piece of wood if just their very tips were exposed. For several of the other kayaks in this study, it is the case that the skin at the tips of the bow and stern are worn away, giving a glimpse of the structure. Four of these examples are depicted in figure 67, showing further variation in how the ends are assembled. In each case, there is evidence that the gunwales extend to the very ends— at least on one end if not both.

Figure 67a is the bow and stern tip of a kayak likely from the 1600s: The Danish National Museum's Lb.101 (plate 5). The bow tip consists of just the gunwales; the keelson may have been fastened to the bottom, but is now missing. The stern tip of this kayak does have the keelson (or stem) fastened beneath the two gunwale ends. Figure 67b shows the bow and stern of the Rijksmuseum voor Volkenkunde's kayak 351-77 (plate 8)— another kayak likely from the 1600s. The tip of its bow consists of what is likely a cap piece on top of the keelson or stem piece; the stern does exhibit the ends of the gunwales.

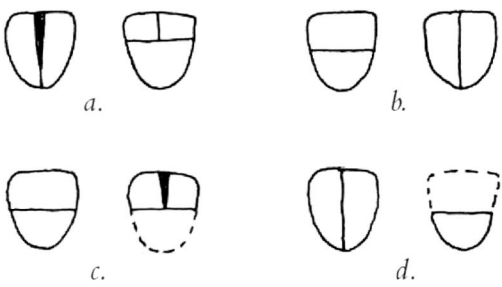

Figure 67: End structures of four kayaks as seen at their tips, where the skin has worn away. A. is the Lb.101 (plate 5). B. is the RvV 351-77 (plate 8). C. is the THN kayak (plate 25). D. is the CMC IV-A-447 (plate 48). The bow is on the left of each pair.

Figure 67c depicts the tips of the Newcastle Trinity House's kayak (plate 25), and figure 67d shows the tips of the Canadian Museum of Civilization's kayak IV-A-447 (plate 48). The dashed lines denote missing but evidenced elements, e.g., the keelson or stem of the THN kayak, and a cap-piece on the CMC kayak.

In showing this variety of stem joints, I do not wish to suggest that the depicted methods are all that are out there; other variations of gunwale end-joinery can be seen in H.C. Petersen's *Skinboats of Greenland* (1986:27) and P. Scavenius Jensen's *Den Grønlandske Kajak og dens Redskaber* (1975:28, 30, and plate IV).

CHINES:

The chines of a kayak are likely the most critical element in regards to a kayak's hull-shape. The gunwales and keelson define a kayak's sheer and breadth, and the depth and rocker respectively. The ribs are the foundation for a kayak's hull, but the positioning of the chines along the ribs sets the kayak's deadrise and bottom-breadth (chine breadth), which in turn have results affecting the kayak's hull-volume, stability, and waterline shape.

Figure 68: Flat top and channel top chines; note how the channeled chine allows for two points of contact with the ribs, and is therefore less likely to get displaced.

Chines are often triangular in cross-section, but in some later Greenland kayaks the chines are rectangular or squarish in section-view. Several West Greenland kayaks have their top surfaces channeled slightly, as in figure 68. It is definitely rare among the kayaks in the present study, but its function can be inferred, or at least naively reasoned: The channeling, while not necessarily matching the curve of the ribs, does ensure that each chine has two points of contact against each rib instead of just one. (A flat-topped chine would seat against a rib at only one point.) Kayaks in this study that exhibit channeled chines are the Hancock Museum's G.109 (plate 14), the Danish National Museum's Lc.43 (plate 31), and the Greenland National Museum's kayak KNK "C" (plate 51).

The chines (and keelson) of a Greenland kayak are lashed, pegged, or nailed to the ribs. In instances where lashings are used, the lashings are often continuous. That is to say the builder works with a considerable length of cord, and weaves it through the frame, fore-to-aft (or vice-versa) working along one longitudinal member at a time.

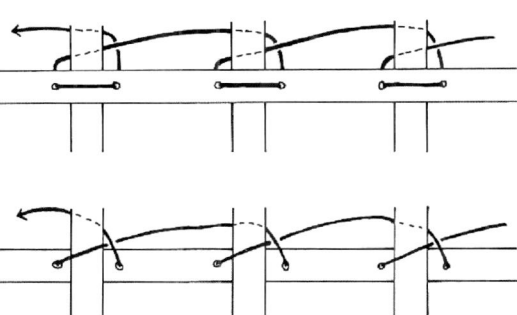

Several methods of lashing the keelson and chines to the ribs are used in Greenland. Figure 69 depicts the single-pass method common among the oldest West Greenland kayaks in this study (It is termed 'single-pass' in that it passes over the rib once.) This method is lashed through two holes drilled through the keelson or chines. When taut, this single-pass method appears in the pattern in figure 70. If the lashing is passed through a single hole in the side of the chines or keelson, it could be patterned in any of the ways depicted in figure 73, passing just once over each rib.

Figure 69: Single-pass lashing method for attaching the chines and keelson to ribs. Top, viewed from the outside of the frame; Bottom, viewed from the inside.

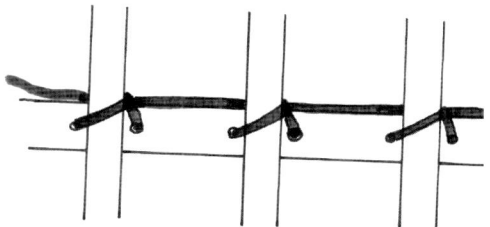

Figure 70: The single-pass lashing pattern as it appears taut.

Figure 72 shows the double-pass method as it appears both inside and outside of the hull. This technique is called double-pass because the lashing passes over the ribs twice. Note that the single-pass method typically uses two holes drilled through the top of the chine or keelson; the double-pass lashing method almost as a rule seems to use just one hole drilled through the side of the chines or keelson, directly below the rib. The Canadian Museum of Civilization's kayak IV-A-432 (plate

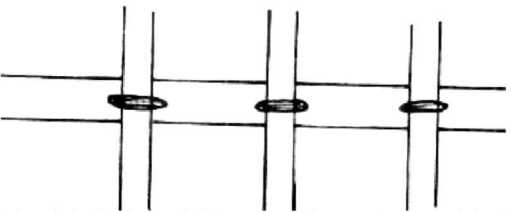

Figure 71: Single-pass lashing, non-continuous, i.e., cut and tied off at each junction.

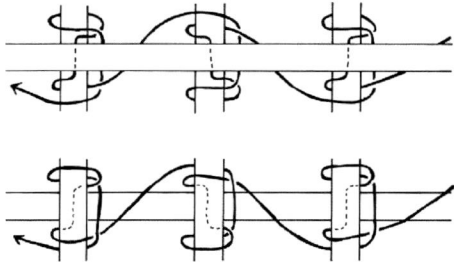

Figure 72: Double-pass lashing method for attaching the chines and keelson to ribs. Top: viewed from the outside. Bottom: viewed from the inside. The lashings are passed transversely through a single hole in the chines and keelson.

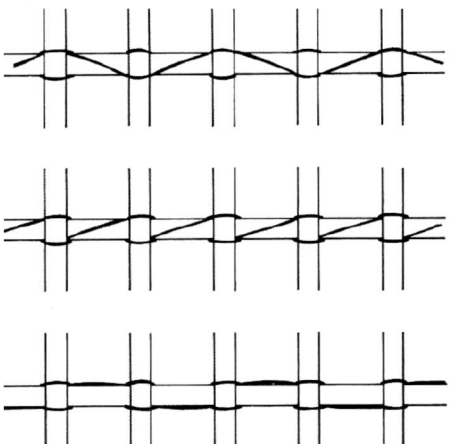

Figure 73: Some of the patterns resulting from the continual lashing of the chines and keelson. Top-to-bottom: alternating diagonal, constant diagonal, and alternating straight.

103) however has the double-pass method with two transverse holes at each junction.

Such lashing techniques, being continuous, often result in a consistent pattern. Figure 73 depicts a number of lashing patterns seen in kayaks in this study. Top-to-bottom, the patterns are alternating diagonal, constant diagonal, and alternating straight (a constant straight pattern also exists).

Lashings as a rule do not go around the outside face of the keelson or chines. Instead, the lines pass through holes drilled through the respective pieces. Where gaps occur between the ribs and chines, shims are used, much as is done with gaps between the keelson and ribs, described above and illustrated in figure 55. This allows for a solid structure and a fair-bend of the chines despite imperfectly formed ribs.

Pegging or nailing the ribs to the longitudinals is not as common as lashing in West Greenland, but it does occasionally appear, and usually in later and more southerly examples. In East Greenland it would appear that the pegging (or nailing) of the chines and keelson to the ribs is the rule, no examples in this study being lashed.

One kayak in this study exhibited pegs set through every other rib just above the chines— such that the chines were not pegged in place per-se, but rather held into position, as in figure 74. The peg is clearly placed so as to prevent the chine from slipping up and around the curve of the rib. This kayak, the Canadian Museum of Civilization's IV-A-427 (plate 62), also has each rib-to-chine joint lashed using the double-pass method.

Figure 74: Peg set through a rib in order to prevent a chine from 'slipping-up.'

The forward and aft ends of the chines can be secured by a number of methods. They need to be drawn inward somewhat so as to not poke into the skin at their ends. Figure 75a depicts a method in which the chine ends are fastened to the keelson. Either nails or a lashing are used to attach the chines to the keelson. Both fasteners are depicted in 75a, but in many cases only one method will be used. Occasionally a kayak's chines will terminate before reaching the keelson ends. In such cases the chines are usually drawn together and lashed, as in figure 75b.

While one of the popularly defining features of Greenland kayaks is their single-chine construction (a single chine on each side of the keelson), it must be pointed out that multi-chine (non-Polar) Greenland kayaks do exist— three are presented in this study (the KNK 1161 [plate 9], the MSU 4274cw [plate 45], and the KNK 2237 [plate 66]).

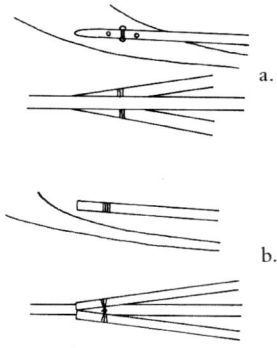

Figure 75: Methods of securing the ends of the chines. The upper pair of drawings show the side and top view of chine fastened to the keelson's end with a lashing and pegs (sometimes just one of these methods is used). The bottom pair shows chine ends fastened to each other with a lashing— essentially floating, as the ends are not attached to anything.

MASIK:

A kayak's *masik* defines the forward edge of the cockpit, holding up the front of the coaming. Writing about Eastern Canadian kayaks; Eugene Arima translates the word *masik* as 'gill'— as in a fish's gill (1987:103).

In East Greenland kayaks, the *masik* is usually attached just like the other curved deck

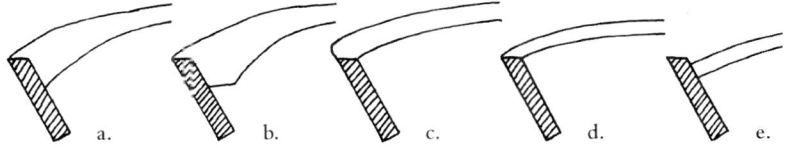

Figure 76: Profiles of different masik-to-gunwale joints.

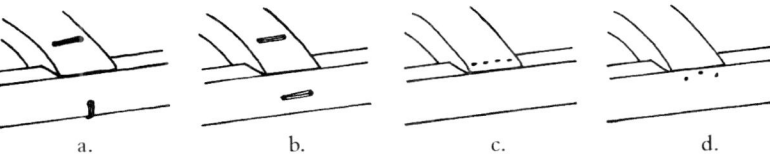

Figure 77: Several methods of attaching the masik *to gunwales. The two examples on the left utilize lashings; the two on the right utilize nails or pegs. In some instances, both nailing combinations may be used simultaneously.*

beams. In West Greenland however, the *masik* is generally set on top of the gunwales, thus it is very different from the other deck beams. H. C. Petersen writes that there is "no corresponding English word for this extra deck beam" (1981:48), and for practical purposes, i.e., distinguishing it from the straight and curved deck beams, this is essentially correct.

The variations of West Greenland *masik*-gunwale joints are depicted in figure 76a-d, as is the typical method seen in East Greenland kayaks (figure 76e). In West Greenland they are usually placed on the gunwale's top edge instead of being tenoned into the gunwale.

This is not the case in East Greenland, where a *masik* is tenoned into the gunwales much like the other deck beams, and is often fastened with oblique pegs or screws (on account of this, it would be fitted along with the rest of the deck beams as opposed to later in the construction process as in West Greenland).

Four different methods of fastening the *masik* to the gunwales are used in the West Greenland kayaks in this study (Figure 77). The two examples on the left utilize lashings; a. is lashed around the bottom edge of the gunwale, and b. is lashed through two holes in the gunwale's face. Figure 77c depicts nails or pegs being set through the end of the *masik* and into the gunwale's top edge. 77d shows nails or pegs set through the gunwale's face and into the end of the *masik*. This last example requires the *masik* be shaped as in figure 76a or b. Sometimes 77c and d will both be used simultaneously. A couple of modified *masik*-to-gunwale joints are depicted in figure 170 in the chapter on repairs and modifications.

Occasionally a *masik* will be thicker in the middle so as to accommodate a carved handhold. Petersen describes this function: "In the old days the *masik* was shaped as a handle. A thickening in the middle underneath the *masik* formed a groove which gave the fingers a good grip when the kayak had to be carried by hand" (1986:28). While kayaks are easily lifted this way, they are rarely carried this way due to balance concerns, particularly when any variety of hunting equipment could be on deck. Kayaks are instead carried either upside-down on one's head or with one's arm in the cockpit, the hand grasping a curved deck-beam specifically carved for this purpose (see figure 41 top, and figure 283).

The handhold in the *masik* is made primarily for pulling one's self into the cockpit. Greenland kayaks were and are made as small as practical, and even considering different body proportions and a smaller stature on average, many must have been snug for Greenlanders themselves. A tug on this handhold can make all the difference between fitting and not fitting into a kayak, as it fairly painlessly forces the knees to reverse slightly, allowing one to seat properly. Not every kayak has such a handhold; often the *masik* will be a smooth arch without such features. A number of different types of handholds are illustrated in figures 78-80, cross-sections and face-views being shown.

Figure 78 depicts a simple arched *masik*. Shallow grooves or holes cut through the *masik* can function as handholds, as illustrated in the cross-sections. The bottom cross-section shows a *masik* without a handhold, but with thinned aft-edge sure to make getting in and out of the kayak easier. Below the cross-sections in figure 78, a handhold consisting of three individually divoted finger-holds is depicted, as seen only on the Hull Maritime Museum's kayak "64" (plate 29).

Figure 79 depicts a *masik* with a raised handhold. These occur very intermittently in 17th-18th century west Greenland kayaks, but are very common in East Greenland kayaks— particularly the form illustrated in the upper cross-section of figure 79.

The form depicted in figure 80 only occurs in one kayak in this study (the Wereldmuseum 32848, plate 11). By appearances it is formed much like the example in figure 79, only the finger grip has been cut all the way through the *masik*.

A kayak's *masik* is generally wider than the other deck beams, perhaps 3" (76mm) wide on average, and as thin as 1/4" (6mm) at their aft edge. In several kayaks from the West Coast of Greenland, the *masik* will project outboard of the sheer by some fraction of an inch (about 1/4" to 3/8" [6 to 9mm] in many cases.) The purpose of this is a mystery; it seems to have no particular function, but this may not be the point of its existence. A theory I have is that if a *masik* is being re-used on a kayak that is narrower than the original, there are two choices to make the *masik* work. First, one could place the *masik* as-is and leave the overhang, or second, one could cut the *masik* to the proper length and then fit it. The second choice seems logical, but in doing so this could decrease the height of the arch, and/or make the end of the *masik* thinner and potentially weaker.

As with the *isserfik*, a kayak's *masik* is occasionally cut forward a bit at the cockpit so as to afford more room for the kayaker. Such a cut-away *masik* would appear just as in figure 38, only the kayak's bow would be towards the top of the figure.

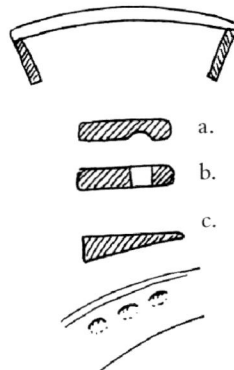
Figure 78: Common West Greenland kayak's masik appearance, also showing a variety of finger grips and cross-sections.

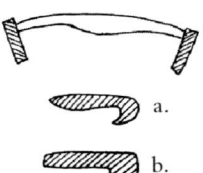
Figure 79: Common East Greenland kayak's masik appearance, showing finger grips in cross section. Some earlier West Greenland kayaks have similar masik shapes and grips.

Figure 80: A variation of figure 79, as seen on an older West Greenland kayak (WM 32848, plate 11).

DECK STRINGERS:

Where the fore deck is raised as it meets the height of the *masik*, stringers are placed so as to create a smooth slanted deck that is also stout enough to support a considerable weight of hunting equipment. In many cases, kayaks will have deck stringers on the aft deck as well, just behind the cockpit. For some areas of Greenland, aft deck stringers were not used, but in no instances were there kayaks without one or more forward deck stringers.

For the most part, West Greenland kayaks have taller narrower forward deck stringers and broad flat aft deck stringers. The forward deck stringers as a rule slant downwards, their top forward edges ending below the sheer line to ensure a smooth transition between the raised and the flat sections of the forward deck.

East Greenland kayaks generally have broad and flat forward deck-stringers and none aft. Generally, the fore deck stringers in East Greenland kayaks do not slant downwards and are instead more or less parallel to the sheer line. Their forward ends are rounded so as to not present a sharp edge into the kayak skin.

In the earliest collected kayaks in this study, baleen lashings seem to have been the common way to attach the deck stringers to the deck beams. In later examples pegs or nails seem to have replaced lashings entirely.

Figure 81a depicts a common deck stringer layout for a West Greenland Kayak, and figure 81b depicts the same for an East Greenland kayak. As elaborated on below, many other forms and methods occur. Notice on the West Greenland example how the taller deck stringer is undercut at its aft termini so as to meet flush with the thinner edge of the *masik*.

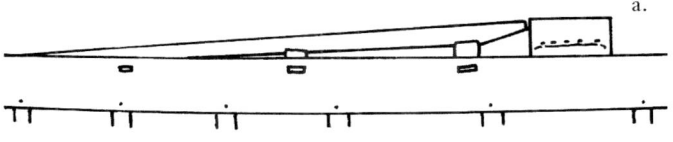
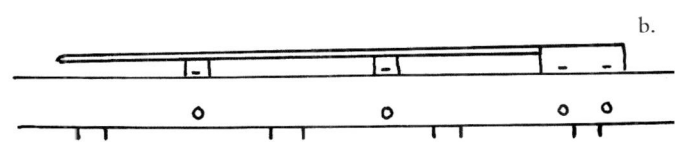

Figure 81: Deck stringer profiles. a.: Typical West Greenland arrangement; b.: Typical East Greenland method.

As described in the section on curved deck beams, the forward stringers are attached to these pieces, though at their forward extremity, stringers will often alight on a straight deck beam. In some cases, stringers will be too high to seat on straight deck beams, so shims are occasionally used. As with any piece of a Greenland kayak, these deck stringer shims can take many forms; figure 82 depicts a variety of solutions.

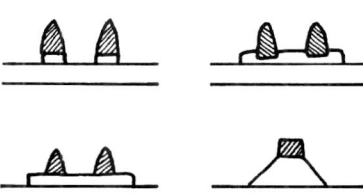

Figure 82: Shims supporting deck stringers above a straight deck beam.

Greenland kayaks have a very broad range of deck-stringer arrangements, as illustrated in figure 83. Figure 83a is the most common deck stringer arrangement among West Greenland kayaks— a 'two forward, two aft' pattern; older West Greenland kayaks often have just two stringers forward and none aft, as in figure 83b. Figure 83c appears in only one example in this study: a West Greenland kayak (ca.1770s-1830s?), the Trinity House Hull's kayak "B," plate 13.

Figures 83d and e appear on two 20th century Northwest Greenland kayaks: The KNK 2237 (plate 66) and the DNM L.18.273 (plate 73). Figure 83f appears once in this study— on a child's kayak from West Greenland (plate 47).[17] Figure 83g appears in a kayak that may have been fitted with out riggers at one time (plate 40)— much as was likely the case with the child's kayak. Figure 83h has the most deck stringers (five), and is a pattern that hails from South Greenland. East Greenland kayaks do not have aft deck stringers, and they typically

Figure 83: Deck stringer arrangement variations seen in kayaks from Greenland. (Each kayak's bow is toward the bottom.)

---

[17]Figures 83d and f are common deck stringer arrangements for the Polar Greenland kayaks in this study; consult the chapter on Polar Greenland kayak construction for further information.

have three broad deck stringers forward, as in figure 83i, though 'four forward' (figure 83j) appears on one example in this study (the DNM 19.157, plate 86).

H. C. Petersen describes the attachment of deck stringers in both his 1981 and 1986 works; in his latter work he wrote "There should be a slight gap between the deck stringers and the *masik* so they will not touch. Otherwise the kayak framework might creak, which would be easily heard by a seal" (1986:28). This is likely a localized rule, as many Greenland kayaks from the West Coast have their deck stringers set into the *masik*; it seems to be the rule in East Greenland that the stringers are set into the *masik*.

Figure 84 shows two typical methods for attaching the aft deck stringers to a kayak's *isserfik*. The 'inset' method on the left is apparently more rare, and usually appears in only kayaks from the northern West Coast; The example on the right is much more common throughout West Greenland.

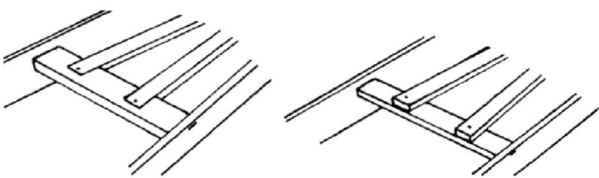

Figure 84: Aft deck stringers—left, set into the isserfik; *right, set atop the* isserfik.

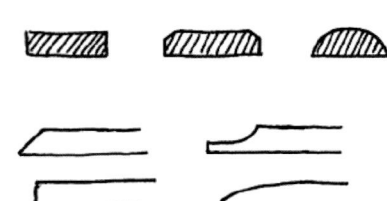

Figure 85: Aft deck stringers may take on a variety of forms, such as the examples depicted here. The hatched examples show a variety of cross-sections; below are four end profiles of aft deck stringers.

Despite being just a simple batten, aft deck stringers take on many forms, some rather elegant. Figure 85 (top row) shows three typical cross-sections of aft deck stringers; the chamfered and rounded examples cause less wear on the kayak's *amiq*. The four profiles at the bottom of figure 85 depict common end-shapes of the aft deck stringers. The cut at their forward edges can make it easier for the kayaker to get in and out of the kayak and is less likely to snag clothing.

SEATS:

Most kayaks in this study do not have anything of an integral (non-removable) seat to the kayak, save for the keel and ribs themselves. Comfort could be added in the form of an animal skin— perhaps polar-bear fur, or caribou. Several kayaks in this study had de-haired seal skin pieces set inside the cockpit. These seal skins were obviously recycled kayak skins, in that they exhibited the creases and wear formed by kayak chines and keelson. One kayak in this study (Fram Museum 176, plate 42) had small oval pieces of skin in the cockpit below the ribs between the chines and keelson— this may have been placed more in the interest of thermal insulation than actual padding.

F. Spencer Chapman, a member of the British Arctic Air Route Expedition, sings the praises of the skin seat in a kayak: "I find the getting in and out of a kayak in a rough sea, especially with a full deck of cargo, by far the hardest thing of all, but it makes a lot of difference putting a piece of an old kayak skin inside so that one's feet don't catch on the ribs of the kayak"(1934b: 267).

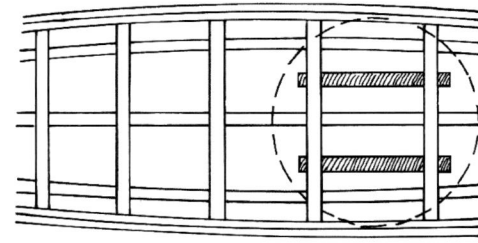

Figure 86: Typical seat-slat arrangement for West Greenland kayaks (deck beams omitted).

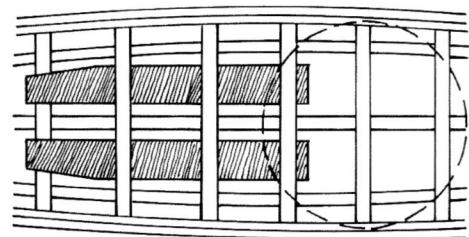

Figure 87: Typical leg-slat arrangement for East Greenland kayaks (deck beams omitted). Note how the slats are positioned above the rib at their forward termini.

Integral seats that do appear in kayaks take on many forms; for the most part they are made of wood. Among the West Greenland kayaks, short slats are occasionally found slung beneath the two ribs exposed in the cockpit. These pieces are most often lashed in place. The shaded pieces in figure 86 show the most common seat slat placement in West Greenland kayaks; deck beams have been omitted from the drawing.

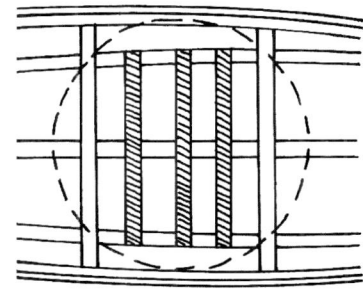

Figure 88: Transverse seat slats; these are essentially just half-ribs, as in figure 51b.

Broad slats that more support the legs instead of the seat are common in East Greenland kayaks. These slats generally start at or forward of the cockpit mid-point and extend forward to where the kayaker's feet would be. These slats are lashed or nailed beneath the ribs, so they do not take up the very limited room inside an East Greenland kayak. In these examples, the forward end of these thin and broad slats is usually brought above a rib. Figure 87 shows the typical leg slat layout for an East Greenland kayak.

John Brand refers to the leg slats as "heel guides" in his writings (1988:13, 47, etc.); the slats would certainly function as such when the kayaker enters the kayak; it would prevent the heels from getting hung up on the ribs. Writing in the context of East Greenland kayaks, Dr. Gert Nooter writes that the leg slats in a kayak ". . .also keep the legs and feet of the kayaker dry if some water gets into the kayak" (1991:330).

A kayak from South Greenland (KNK 1550x1, plate 80) has what could be called extra ribs in the cockpit— some only spanning chine-to-chine (as in figures 88 and 51b.), instead of gunwale-to-gunwale. These half-ribs function as seats. Several kayaks from East Greenland utilize half-rib seats in conjunction with the leg slats described above (e.g., the DNM Lc.19.157, and the RvV 2823, plates 86 and 88 respectively.)

The highly specialized rolling kayak (plate 93) made by Kunuunnguaq Davidsen of Sisimiut has a large piece of very thin plywood covering as much of the cockpit and leg area as possible; this kayak is so shallow (4-3/4" [12cm] to sheer) that this would take up little room and provide a smooth surface to ease entry.

One of the more elegant seating solutions I have seen appeared in the Canadian Museum of Civilization's kayak 76/13/88 (plate 64): It was a length of cotton twine laced back and forth between the two ribs in the cockpit, and can be easily placed and adjusted.

SKIN COVERING— THE *AMIQ*:

Arctic peoples have used both sea mammal and land mammal skins for covering kayak frames. Of the sea mammals, walrus, seal, and sea lion are preferred skins, varying by region, availability, and tradition. For Greenland, Petersen lists four types of seals (with variations of the names) used in covering kayaks: Greenland/saddle/harp seal, hooded/bladder-nose seal, ringed/fjord seal, and bearded seal (1986:29). Illustrating the tenuous existence of the Greenlanders, Otto Fabricius writes that people resorted to eating old boat skins in times of famine *(in* Holtved, ed., 1962:115).

Three to six skins are required to cover a kayak, depending on the kayak's length and the type and size of the seals used. Dr. Gert Nooter writes (in the context of East Greenland kayaks) that it takes two skins of a mature bearded seal or hooded seal to cover a kayak (1991:330); Birket-Smith writes of three or four saddle seals being used in Aasiaat vicinity (1924:264).

The color of seal skin kayaks varies greatly, spanning the tonal spectrum from lamp-black to bright white. Reddish-browns and yellows to deep buffs and chocolaty browns are also common. Much of this color variation has to do with how the skins are prepared: Fridtjof Nansen describes seal skins being either unscraped or scraped of their dark membranes (1893:127).

While Nansen writes that light colored skins are preferred in the summer, and dark in the winter (1893:128), Kaj Birket-Smith attributes the darker and lighter skins as being regional preferences: darker skins in Nuuk vicinity and north, and lighter skins in South Greenland (1924:271). Petersen reinforces the latter suggestion (1986:31), however many of the examples in this study known to be from South Greenland in fact do have dark skins; one of them (albeit canvas-covered) is even painted black (KNK 1550x1, plate 80).

The preparation of seal skins for the covering of a kayak involves many steps. Petersen writes that once the seal has been flayed, the blubber is removed and residual fat must be scraped off. Next, the hair on the skin must be dealt with— either pulled out or shaved with a very sharp *ulu*, or woman's knife. Pulling the hair out could be made easier by soaking the skins in a tub of urine for a few days and then rubbed with ashes, otherwise a woman might use her teeth to pull out the hairs (Petersen, 1986:30).

For kayaks whose skins are to be white, there is a different process of preparation, also presented by Petersen: The skin is scraped of its fat and then folded up after a saltwater bath. It is then covered with turf for a couple of weeks. As the meat and blubber rot they are scraped away. "When the skin is 'ripe' (mature) the hairs are rubbed off and then the grain, or dark membrane, can be removed. The result is a white skin"(Petersen, 1986:31).

To help ensure that the seal skins are waterproof, they must be closely inspected for punctures or holes. Birket-Smith writes, "all the holes must be carefully patched, both the round ones which are due to the natural apertures of the animal . . . and the oblong ones which are due to the hunting weapons..."(1924:264).

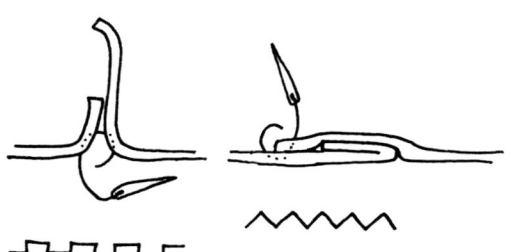

Figure 89: Transverse seams, showing the stitching pattern for each pass below; the inside of the skin (to be inside the kayak) faces up. (After Victor and Robert-Lamblin, 1989:42, figs. 39-44)

Gert Nooter writes that the sewing of the *amiq*'s seams is done with seal tendon, and later nylon. "The ivory needles of the past have been replaced by steel needles" (1991:330). Unlike with woven cloth, seal skin is a thick membrane that does not need to be fully punctured through to be sewn— again, in Nooter's words: "The needle is not allowed to pass all the way through the skin, which is thick and strong enough to permit this method"(1991:330). By sewing only part way through the skin, fewer holes are present, and therefore the covering is inherently more waterproof.

Before the skins are wrapped around the kayak frame, they must first be sewn together so as to create a single skin (*amiq*) to fit and sew around the kayak. These seams— transverse seams— are typically sewn with the method depicted in figure 89. The flatter and smoother this seam is, the less wear it will receive under use, and the less water resistance will be created; the lap in these seams always faces aft.

Once the splicing is finished, resulting in a single long skin, the skin must be stretched along the kayak's length. Gert Nooter writes that the new kayak skin begins with "the thumb"— an end of the skin is sewn around the tip of one's thumb to form a pocket, and this is then slipped over the kayak frame's tip (1991:329 fig.11, 330). This is repeated for the kayak's other end as well, thus the skin is attached to the frame by being 'hooked' over its ends.

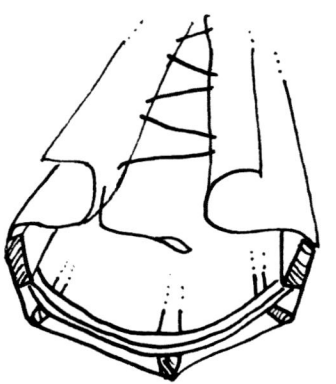

Figure 90: A zigzagging line is sewn along a kayak's deck to draw the amiq *tightly around the kayak's bottom.*

Figure 91: Karolus from Kuummiut, East Greenland, stretching the amiq *over his kayak, 1933. With regards to attaching the* amiq *to a kayak skeleton, the stretching is typically the only part a man would do; the sewing is, at least historically, women's work. (Copyright Greenland National Museum and Archive.)*

A kayak's *amiq* must also be stretched around the bottom of the hull so it can be sewn taut along the deck. The common method for this transverse stretching was to use a zigzag line sewn into the seal skin so as to tighten it much like a laced-up shoe (figure 90). Gert Nooter, writing in the context of East Greenland (1960s-1970s) writes,

> The skin cover could be stretched tight by pulling on a zigzag lacing made of seal tendon and applied before the two sides are sewn together. Starting in the 1970s, nylon fishing-line was almost invariably substituted for the tendon. The production of a line made of tendon is time-consuming, requires great precision, and can still be done only by older women, whereas a roll of nylon cord can be bought at will in the store and does not even cost much (1991:325).

The zigzag lacing is sewn into the inside of the *amiq* and it does not penetrate the skin entirely, thus there are no holes all the way through the skin where it is attached. Because the skin is stretched at these points, pucker marks are left in the *amiq*. If there are places where the *amiq* does not reach all the way around the kayak's girth, patches can be sewn in where needed.

Two distinct types of seams are found on Greenland kayaks, apparently varying by region. One is the flat seam (figure 92), which gives a smooth deck surface, but is not as waterproof as the raised seam (Birket-Smith, 1924:269). The flat seam is found along the west coast, from Sisimiut vicinity to south-

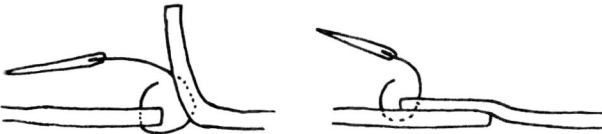

Figure 92: Flat seam (After Victor and Robert-Lamblin, 1989:42, figs. 47 & 48).

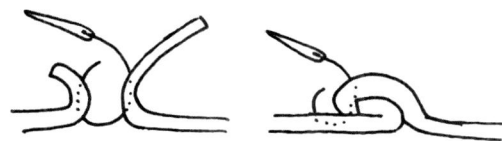

Figure 93: Raised or 'rolled' seam.

ernmost Greenland (Birket-Smith, 1924:270-271); flat seams are also typically used in East Greenland (Victor and Robert-Lamblin, 1989:42).

The second type of seam is the raised or rolled seam, which is more waterproof, but makes the kayak's deck harder to keep ice-free (Birket-Smith, 1924:264; Petersen, 1986:33). Figure 93 shows the cross-section of the raised seam; the height of the seam depends on tension of the stitching.

After the skin has been stretched and sewn around a kayak frame, it must be oiled and the seams must be sealed. Fresh seal blood is sometimes smeared over a new kayak skin; once the blood dries, the *amiq* becomes less quickly saturated with water (Fabricius, in Holtved, 1962:110). Otto Fabricius writes of the post-sewing work of finishing the *amiq*:

> *When the boats have been covered the seams especially are rubbed with old, tough blubber collected at the blubber pits, but the entire cover is also rubbed with fresh blubber or boiled oil long enough to produce a sort of glaze on the outside; the one and the other serve to keep the water out and cure the skin against it; thus, such a boat-cover will not leak or become slack unless it is used too much and the renewal of its greasing is neglected (in Holtved, ed., 1962:114)*

Gert Nooter also refers to the collection of and use of aged seal fat for sealing a kayak's seams: "The seams joining the skins require an extra treatment to make them watertight or at least almost watertight, and for this purpose use is made of old seal fat. Very old fat of this kind is found in abandoned settlements . . . on the ground in spots where the women chose to flay seals"(1991:331).

In his *Instructions In Kayak Building*, Petersen writes ". . . When the seal population of Greenland began to decline at the beginning of the present (20th) century, it became difficult for many hunters to get hold of the required number of suitable kayak-skins. More and more hunters have therefore started to cover their kayaks with canvas or duck"(1981:55). Several of the kayaks in this study have cloth skins; all of these are painted in order to render them waterproof.

Paint is also sometimes used on seal skin-covered kayaks. Morten Porsild, writing in 1915 relates that, ". . . in recent times it has become more and more common to paint the skin covering of the kayak with white oil colour, which prevents the skin from absorbing so much water and becoming so heavy and also increases its durability" (181). Porsild adds that the white-painted kayak, in conjunction with a white-clad hunter and a white shooting screen, is apt to resemble a block of ice; essentially, the kayak becomes a camouflaged shooting blind of sorts.

P. Scavenius-Jensen cites the high demand and resulting high prices of seal skins for the use of canvas as a kayak covering in Greenland: "As the skins for a kayak cost about Dkr. 200 (around 1965), it is no wonder that a hunter chooses to use canvas which can be bought for half the price" (1975:24).

The reason canvas or other cloth was not used as a kayak covering earlier may be explained by Scavenius-Jensen: "(Canvas) is more vulnerable to and inclined to split and break and more difficult to repair in an emergency. As the canvas is not elastic, it does not respond to the movement of the wooden framework, and the seams are the weakest spot requiring broad overlaps" (1975:24). John Heath, in his article "The Greenland Kayak and the Canadian Connection," relates from Ken Taylor that Taylor's canvas covered kayak was thought to be "much too noisy" by Illorsuit seal hunters (1987c:15).

Taylor himself (in the context of Northwest Greenland circa 1959) writes:

> *The number of Harp Seal caught is insufficient for all kayaks to be covered with seal skin and in many cases canvas has to be used. In Umánatsiaq, all eight kayaks were canvas covered, and in Igdlorssuit [Illorsuit] one of the eighteen. All canvas-covered kayaks observed were painted white, as were also seven of the skin-covered kayaks in Igdlorssuit. The canvas-covered and painted kayaks offer the best possible camouflage, but the canvas, being less strong than seal skin, cannot withstand the scraping of the first thin sea ice forming in early winter (1960:495)*

Figure 94: Women sewing a seal skin on a kayak frame, Kraulshavn, northern Upernavik District, 1936. Note how the skin is pulled taut across the cockpit opening prior to the fitting of the coaming. (Photographer Jette Bang/ Arktisk Institut gjb00908).

Decorative painting does not exist within the Greenland kayak tradition, but today some Greenlanders will paint faux seams on their cloth-covered kayaks to make them look more like seal skin kayaks. Europeans have painted several of the kayaks in this study, most likely for display purposes (the Lübeck kayak, the Rijper Museum's 42, the DHNS' 2, and the Museon's 57966, plates 1, 3, 4, and 7 respectively).

The longevity of a kayak-skin is determined by many factors such as the type of skin used, whether it is scraped or not, how often the kayak is used, how well it is maintained, etc. Nansen (writing in the context of central West Greenland) writes that "a well-appointed hunter . . . ought to recover his kaiak twice a year: nowadays, however, he can generally do so only once, and sometimes only once in two years"(1893:128).

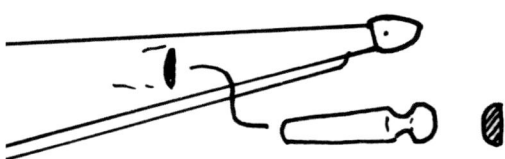

Figure 95: Typical drain plug detail common on East Greenland kayaks.

For East Greenland in the 1960s, Gert Nooter writes that "Kayaks require a great deal of maintenance; depending on the luck or skill of the hunter who uses it, once every two or at most five years he will need two bearded or hooded seals to recover the frame" (1976:35-37).

In East Greenland, a phenomenally practical accessory is often seen on kayaks: a drain plug. East Greenland kayaks are the only kayaks from Greenland known to have these accessories, although drain holes of various forms occur in kayaks from the central Canadian Arctic (Arima, 1987:209, fig.20), Baffin Island (Arima, 1987:219,fig.30), and the Aleutian Islands (Laughlin et al, 1991:171). The form of the plug itself is reminiscent of wound plugs— carried on a kayak and used to stop up a wound on a seal for example, to prevent blood and/or buoyancy loss. The function is more or less the same— to firmly seal a hole in a skin. The drain plug however has one face flattened, as it is wedged against the gunwale. Figure 95 depicts a drain plug's general appearance; note the cross-section.

DECK LINES and DECK FITTINGS:

It is the deck lines and fittings that make a Greenland kayak a *hunting* kayak. These hold the sophisticated array of tools, accessories, and projectiles used in the Greenlander's pursuit of food. To give an idea of the gear that a kayak may carry, the following list would not be uncommon for a well-equipped West Greenland kayak of the late 1800s:[18]

1. Camouflage screen
2. Harpoon
3. Harpoon head and line
4. Harpoon line-stand
5. Harpoon throwing board
6. Lance
7. Long knife
8. Knife
9. Kayak scraper (for removing ice)
10. Wound plugs
11. Bird spear
12. Throwing board for bird spear
13. Hunting float (avataq)
14. A variety of towing gear
15. Pieces of blubber

A West Greenland kayak of the early 20th century could well expect the same equipment as well as:

1. Small-bore rifle
2. Rifle bag
3. Deck-mounted rifle-stand
4. Ammunition

(Lists compiled from Fabricius [*in* Holtved, ed., 1962], Gad [1971:269-270], Scavenius-Jensen [1975], and Petersen [1986].)

---

[18] For detailed illustrations and descriptions of Greenlandic hunting equipment, the author would refer the reader to Fabricius (*in* Holtved, ed., 1962), Birket-Smith (1924), Jensen (1975), and Petersen (1986) for West Greenland, Thalbitzer (1914) and Victor/Robert-Lamblin (1989) for East Greenland, and Holtved (1967) and VanStone (1972) for Polar Greenland. Greenlandic fishing tackle is given special treatment by Hansen (1997). Several figures in the present text do show scale drawings of certain pieces of hunting equipment, e.g., figures 183, 218, 244, 310, & 349.

Figure 96: Hunter's-eye-view of an equipped kayak's foredeck, in this case an East Greenland kayak. From left to right: Killing knife, bird-dart (laying over a paddle holder), bladder dart (laying over several wound-plugs), the harpoon line stand, rifle and its holster and stand, kayak knife, and a harpoon with throwing board attached. The camouflage-shooting screen is deployed ahead of the line-stand. Omitted are the harpoon line and head, and a throwing board for the bird-dart and bladder dart.

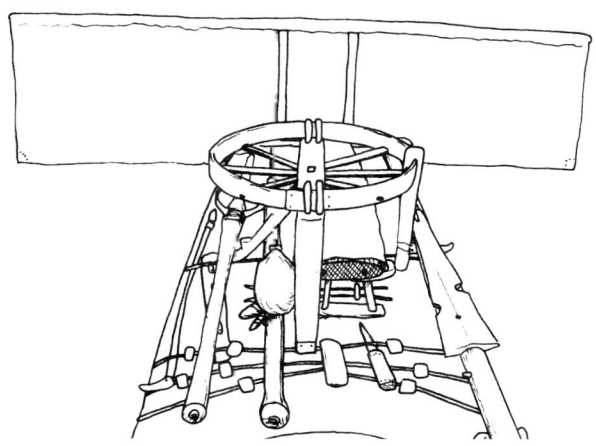

Gert Nooter describes both rifles and shotguns being carried on-deck in East Greenland in the 1960s and 70s (1991:334). In Nuuk, 2000, I saw hunters with very limited gear seeking seals with a small caliber rifle, rifle bag and stand, extra paddle (likely to aid in

Figure 97: A kayak from Godhavn (Qeqertarsuaq) being brought aboard a steamer in 1965. The rifle holster and harpoon line tray are visible as is the stand used to support a camouflage screen. (Photographer Jette Bang/Arktisk Institut cjb08065.)

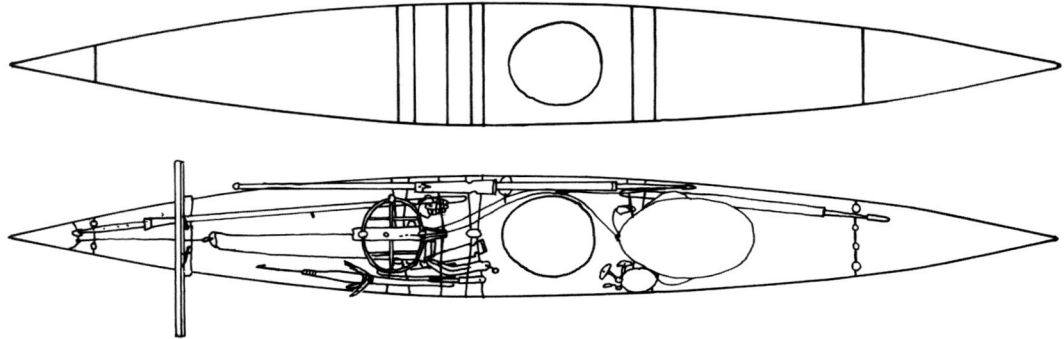

Figure 98: Top: Common deck line arrangement seen in West Greenland kayaks (fittings omitted) as described by Kaj Birket-Smith (1924:263). Bottom: Kayak equipped for hunting.

balancing while waiting for seals), knife, and a towing hook of steel on a polypropylene rope. A snack consisting of a Snickers bar and 'Faxe Kondi' ginger ale were also aboard. One kayaker also carried a *nuiq*, or bird-hunting spear, though presumably for use in dispatching seals rather than bird hunting.

F. Spencer Chapman, writing in the context of East Greenland kayaks in the 1930s writes of carrying a rifle, and a kayak jacket (*tuilik*) "— in case of stormy weather," and a sleeping bag inside of the kayak (1934b: 263).

Historian Finn Gad, writing in the context of 1750-1774, relates, "Very often the post was carried between Frederikshåb (Paamiut) and Godthåb (Nuuk) by kayak and this distance was covered in an incredibly short time. The kayakers considered this task a great honour..." (1973:308).

Kaj Birket-Smith gives a good description of the deck lines and their fittings in his 1924 *Ethnography of the Egedesminde District*: (brackets are mine.)

> *The thongs across the deck are passed through the holes in the gunwales and corresponding holes in the covering, and fastened with knots. Immediately in front of the manhole there are three thongs and slightly in front of these two more; they are all called tarqaq (sing.) except the one in the middle, asatdlerfik. Behind the manhole there are two thongs close to one another, avatserfik. Right fore and aft there is a single thong, tarqausaq. Below these thongs the hunting weapons and the remaining outfit of the kayak are attached. In order...[to better]...keep this in place various buttons and buckles of ivory are placed on them, sing. Tarqausarmio and qôrut. (1924:264)*

The general placement of deck lines described by Birket-Smith is very consistent with many of the West Greenland kayaks in this study, although exceptions do exist. (Figure 98, top, illustrates this general layout, without deck fittings). Exceptions to this pattern are found among older kayaks (circa 1600-1800), as well as those from the more northerly regions of the West Coast.

Figure 99 depicts the deck-line placement of an East Greenland kayak as described by William Thalbitzer (1914:392). Significantly, not a single East Greenland kayak in this study has identical rigging to this example, and also significantly: No two East Greenland kayaks in this study have deck line arrangements identical to each other.

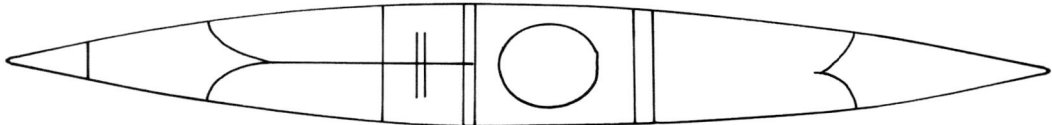

Figure 99: Deck line positions for an East Greenland kayak, as described by William Thalbitzer (1912:393); the bow points left.

Most of the examples in this study have deck lines that enter/exit the gunwales at the upper-outside corner, i.e., the sheer-line, as depicted in figure 100a. On the inside of the kayak, the deck-lines come out of the gunwale at about 1/3–1/4 the way down from the upper edge.

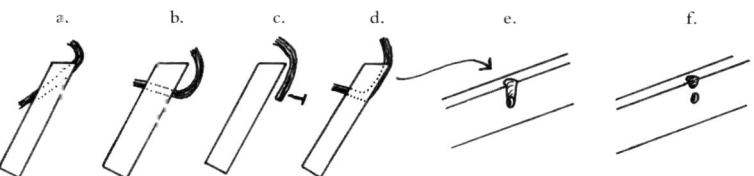

Figure 100: Methods of anchoring deck lines through/to gunwales. (A) Through an oblique hole in the gunwale (through the gunwale's sheer), (B) straight through the gunwale's face, (C) nailed to the gunwale face (through the amiq), (D) through the gunwale face again, but set in a groove to the gunwale's sheer. E shows a face-view of D, and F shows a variation of this where the sheer has a divot cut into it.

Exceptions to the deck-line's passing through the sheer-edge of the gunwale occur in Polar Greenland kayaks, some North Greenland kayaks, and many modern West Greenland kayaks. In these cases the deck line is often passed perpendicularly through the face of the gunwales, a half-inch or so below the sheer-line, as in figure 100b. This method, while appearing stronger, leaves the lines more susceptible to wear during transportation, storage, or paddling in icy seas. Figure 100d depicts a method that utilizes a perpendicular set deck line with a channel cut so as to prevent the line from protruding below the sheer line. In this latter example, the deck line exits through a hole in the *amiq* (kayak skin) above the sheer line.

As Birket-Smith writes, the deck lines are fastened with knots, however there is much more to be said about their fastening. While the deck lines are indeed tied off (in a manner) at the ends, the lines themselves are often continuous, which is to say that the lines just ahead of the cockpit are usually all one long piece threaded through. This same line will often continue through the cockpit to become the deck-lines just behind the cockpit. The continuous deck lines can be seen in many of the figures depicting the inside of the kayaks, notably figures 232 and 248.

Figure 101: Deck line "knots" made from seal skin line. A start-knot, left, and an end-knot, right.

The knots that the lines are given at their termini are not always 'knots' as we know them. Being that the deck-lines are typically made of a non-woven/braided material (i.e., seal skin), the line can be slit and divided without fraying or un-raveling. Figure 101 shows what appears to be the most common method of 'knotting' the ends. Rarely will both termini of a deck line be completed in this fashion: Usually one end will be wrapped around a rib several times and then hitched-off in the cockpit. This provides enough extra slack for repair if the line breaks or needs adjusting. (Hitched-off continuous deck lines in kayaks can be seen in figures 227, 267, and 288 among others.)

For the ease of explaining the regions of a kayak's deck, with regards to the positioning of deck lines and fittings, I have divided the deck into the four areas depicted in figure 102. These areas are somewhat vague for certain kayak types, as will be seen later. Generally, the fore deck and aft deck lines are within reach of the kayaker.

Figure 102: Areas of the deck. A. bow; B. fore deck; C. aft deck; and D. stern. These areas refer to positions of deck lines and fittings.

DECK FITTINGS:

Birket-Smith gives a reason as to why certain kayaks may have fewer deck fittings than others: "In cold weather there is . . . the following drawback about these buttons: They make it difficult to remove the ice from the kayak, and consequently there are many who only have a few or none at all" (1924:264). This statement seems supported by the number of kayaks known to be from the northern West Greenland coast having sparse deck fittings compared to more southerly examples that have numerous fittings, at least among 20th century examples. Other factors behind the sophistication of deck fittings would be access to raw materials and the tools and time to work them, as well as the complexity of the hunting implements a hunter needed to carry on his kayak.

The deck fittings on hunting kayaks come in many different forms, and they serve many different specific purposes. The common denominator of purposes is to aid in holding hunting implements so that they are not lost in heavy seas, and so that they can be retrieved quickly and easily when needed. The means by which the fittings serve this purpose is varied: Some stick up above the deck to prevent harpoons from slipping off, and some slide left and right to tighten down deck lines over implements. Some fittings merely hold the deck lines slightly above the deck so implements can be slid beneath them easier. For the purposes of the present study, I've noted what could consist of four types of deck fittings:

1. **Buttons/tabs/beads/cones** – all with a single deck line passing through them.

2. **Links** – pieces with two or more deck lines passing through them.

3. **Harpoon holders** – distinct from category 1 based on their proximity and specific function. They are placed adjacent the coaming on either the right or left side.

4. **Miscellaneous** – comprising of hooks, deadeyes, clasps, points, plates, leashes, and other specialized pieces.

The general forms of the first type of deck fittings are illustrated in figure 103. These pieces serve to keep the deck lines slightly elevated off the kayak's deck, thereby making it easier to put implements underneath the lines. Taller pieces— such as cones or tabs also serve to keep implements from rolling off the kayak's decks.

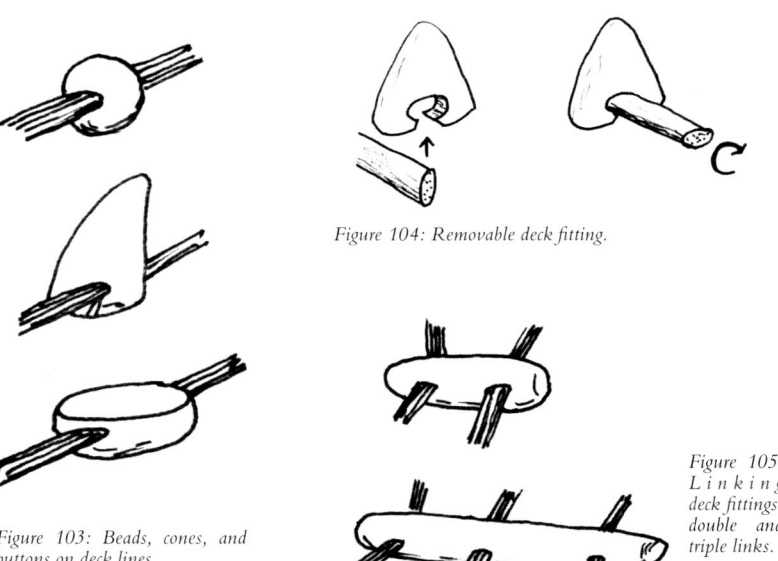

Figure 104: Removable deck fitting.

Figure 103: Beads, cones, and buttons on deck lines.

Figure 105: Linking deck fittings; double and triple links.

Removable deck fittings occur on some East Greenland kayaks. They typically are only present at the bow-most deck line, although I have seen removable harpoon leash bases as well. These fittings are made to be removable (or retro-fitted, as the case may be) by a cut made in their base, as in figure 104. On account of their being easily removed, some of the East Greenland kayaks in this study are missing a bow deck line fitting or two.

Linking pieces are the second type of Greenland kayak deck fittings. These pieces let two or three lines through them, and by sliding these pieces from side-to-side, the tension of the deck lines can be adjusted. These link pieces come in many forms, but their general appearance is depicted in figure 105. None of the kayaks in this study have such pieces linking four or more deck lines together, though they may have existed.

The harpoon holder (third type of deck fitting) is a piece of equipment that is present or evidenced on most every kayak in this study, and there are many different styles of fashioning these important fittings. They are generally situated adjacent to the cockpit coaming, at its front quarter along the sheerline. Most often, a short deck line set through the gunwale and/or the *masik* holds the harpoon holder in place.

Harpoon holders are usually made of bone, ivory, or antler, and there are several basic shapes it may take. Figure 106a depicts a simple tab-shaped harpoon holder, while figure 106b is a saddle-shaped holder. A stump-shaped holder is depicted in figure 106c. Figure 106d is a raised variation of the saddle type occasionally seen on East Greenland kayaks. Numerous other forms appear, but are generally less common than the above types, or are variations of them. Other deck fittings on a kayak may take the form of the tab-shaped harpoon holder, but only those positioned adjacent the cockpit are considered to be the kayak's harpoon holder. Three of the above harpoon holders are illustrated as they appear on a kayak's deck in figure 107.

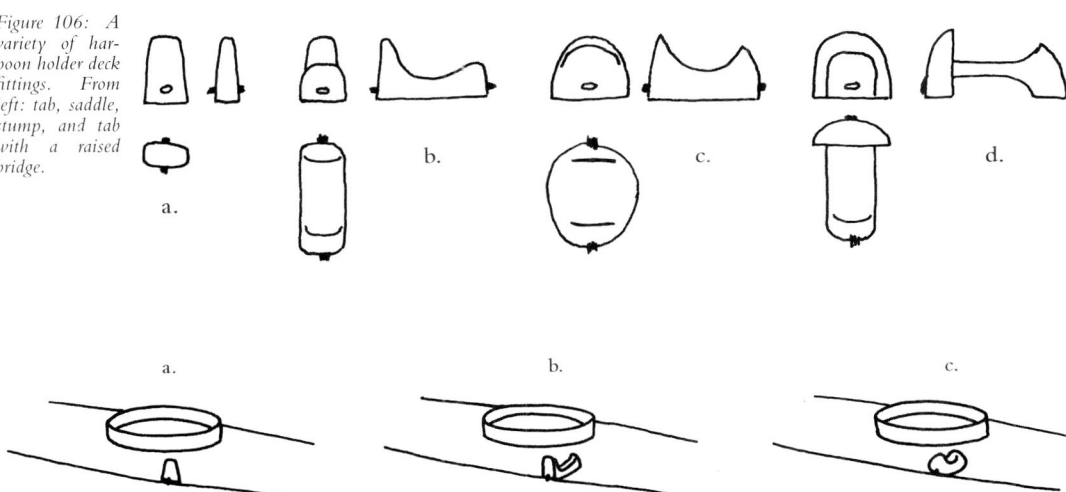

Figure 106: A variety of harpoon holder deck fittings. From left: tab, saddle, stump, and tab with a raised bridge.

Figure 107: Oblique views of a variety of harpoon holders as they would be positioned on a kayak's deck. From left, tab, saddle, and stump forms. (The kayaks' bows are towards the right).

While a few kayaks have no evidence of having had harpoon holders, or they may have a simple taut strap incapable of holding a harpoon, there were other ways to hold harpoons at the ready on deck. Figure 108 shows a removable harpoon holder made from wood as seen on the deck of the KNK 1215 (plate 61). In this kayak's case, it supplemented a permanent tab-shaped harpoon holder; the wooden piece was slipped under one of the fore deck deck lines, the deck line passing through the deep notch, leaving the two upright prongs to function as a holder.

Figure 108: A detachable wooden harpoon or implement holder, supplementing the permanent tab-form on the KNK 1215 (plate 61).

A unique harpoon holder seen only on some East Greenland kayaks is depicted in figure 109. The upright plate is lashed to the kayak's sheer adjacent the cockpit, and the line runs up and through an ivory tube joined to the face of the kayak's coaming. This forms an elevated bridge to support the harpoon, and the vertical plate prevents the harpoon from tumbling overboard. This only appears on one full size kayak in this study (the Danish National Museum's kayak Lc.148 [plate 82]), but is evidenced in two kayak models described in the text (the UMCH 6488 and the DNM's Lb.387).

Figure 109: The Lc.148's harpoon holder.

The fourth type— or 'miscellaneous' deck fittings generally consist of loops, leashes, hooks, deadeyes, and adjustable deck lines. Most examples seen in this study hail from the South or East Coast, though in the case of rifle-bag anchor points, from the Northwest coast.

The adaptation of the rifle for sea hunting led to the need for special equipment to support the rifle and keep it dry. Rifle bags could be anchored to the bow of the kayak via a looped lanyard, or tied to the foremost deck line. In one case among the kayaks in this study a second deck line adjacent to the forward line is placed to hold the rifle bag, so as to not lose the

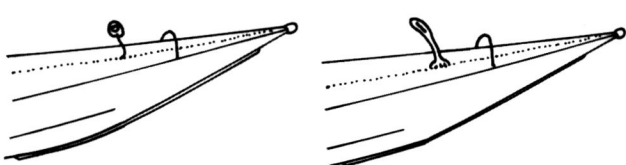

Figure 110: Anchor points for rifle holsters. Right, a seal skin cord with a slit in the end sewn to the kayak's fore deck; left, an ivory deadeye attached to a short cord sewn into the seam of the amiq.

usefulness of the other forward deck line (e.g., the Greenland National Museum's kayak KNK 1550x1, plate 80). Several kayaks in this study have special anchors sewn into the *amiq* so as to receive the rifle bag clasp. Two examples of these are depicted in figure 110.

Some of the more distinctive features of East Greenland kayaks are their elaborate deck fittings— in particular their hooks, deadeyes, and clasps used to attach game and equipment to the kayak's deck. Figure 111 depicts these fittings; the upper shows the deadeye (left) and hook (right) as often found on the fore deck of East Greenland kayaks. The hook is typically set such that it attaches to one of the two or three deck lines just ahead of the kayak's cockpit. Tension of this line can be adjusted by threading more or less line through the hook-piece.

Figure 111 (lower) depicts a typical adjustable deck line found at the stern of East Greenland kayaks. The deadeye piece is often much the same as found on the fore deck, but instead of a hook attachment, the stern lines use a series of clasps for adjusting tension. The stern adjustable deck lines are not made to attach to other deck lines.

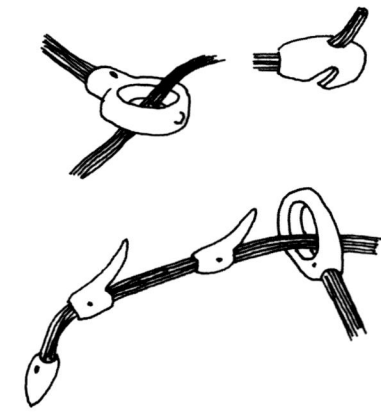

Figure 111: Deadeye, hook, and deadeye with clasps and a point. The former generally appears on an East Greenland kayak's foredeck, while the latter is on the aft deck.

At the terminus of deck lines with clasps or hooks, a point is occasionally affixed (in other cases, the point may have been omitted or lost). This point likely eased in the threading of the line through the deadeye. Such clasps and deadeyes do appear in West Greenland, although usually not on their kayaks: The suspenders and tighteners of a *tuitsoq* or *tuiliq* make use of them.

East Greenland kayaks sometimes have leashes for the harpoon. This leash is a string of bone or ivory beads that terminates in a long thin spike set 90° to the line. The spike acts as an anchor, being easily slipped beneath a deck line. Figure 112 shows its arrangement. East Greenland kayaks have very little free-board and even in light seas, the harpoon could easily float off the deck if it were not leashed.

The deck fittings of most of the kayaks in this study are drawn in scale and are presented at the end of each kayak's description.

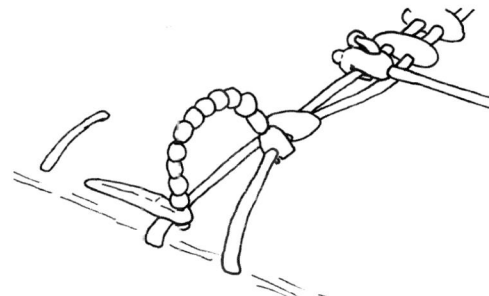

Figure 112: A harpoon leash (center), as seen on the Danish National Museum's kayak L.19.157 (plate 86).

COAMING:

Despite its being made of wood or baleen,[19] a kayak's coaming is actually not part of the kayak frame, but instead it is an element of the *amiq*, in that the *amiq* is the only thing the coaming is actually fastened to. Aside from keel edging and end-knobs, the coaming (*paa*) is usually one of the last parts of the kayak to be attached.

The coaming is a rigid rim attached to the *amiq* that defines the cockpit. The Greenlanders attach their paddling jackets (*tuiliq*, sing.) and spray skirts (*akuilisaq* or *tuitsoq*, both sing.) to kayak coamings in order to keep water out of the kayak. A paddling jacket is depicted in figure 113, and spray skirts are depicted in figures 114 and 136.

Several kayaks in this study use mast-hoops from sailing ships as coamings— these are generally perfectly round, though are often somewhat modified for their new function. Ash seems to have been the most common material for mast-hoop coamings, though many mast-hoop coamings used today in Greenland are made of European beech. Two of the wooden coamings in this study are actually made of thin plywood.

The shape of kayak coamings is variegated, particularly before the advent and widespread availability of round mast-hoops. Figure 115 depicts some of the more common coaming shapes among Greenland kayaks: from left to right, triangular (whose 'angles' are of course very rounded), oval, and round.

The scarf joints on coamings range from a simple over-lap with nails, to an intricate hook-scarf with large pegs securing the joint, and tiny pins used to lock the pegs in place. Generally, the scarf is placed at the back of the coaming, but they can also be found at the front, side, or even at the back 'quarters' if a two-piece coaming is used.

Scarfs can be cut along two different facets of a coaming: the face or the edge. The first seven examples are all face-joint scarfs. 116a depicts a simple lap joint, with the inside end thinned down. Figure 116b shows a joint with the mating faces thinned so as to meet flush without a thicker over-lap. Figure 116c shows a scarf similar to 116b., only the ends are thicker and inset so as to remain flush; this form of terminating a joint is called a stop. This essentially is a stronger version of b. in that it doesn't have the thin and delicate scarf-ends.

Figures 116d and e are each hook-scarfed joints; d. has un-stopped ends, and e. has stops at its scarf's ends. These scarfs are fairly common among older West Greenland kayaks, as well as in later coamings made of mast-hoops from sailing ships. Figure 116f is a variation of the hook-scarf seen on the Whitby kayak (plate 18).

---

[19] Baleen coamings are often referred to as "whale bone" coamings, particularly in older texts (pre 1850s), e.g., the 1767 passage by David Crantz cited on page 26.

Figure 113: A tuilik— *the full paddling jacket. The hem at the waist fits snugly around the kayak's coaming keeping water out. The* tuilik *seals around the paddler's face and wrists as well. (Photographer: Jette Bang/Copyright: Greenland National Museum and Archive.)*

The last face-scarfed coaming joint is depicted in figure 116g. It is essentially a variation of 116a, with the overlapping piece faired flush at the bottom, but not at the top edge, thus leaving a 'strap' or lip at the coaming's upper edge. This serves to hold the *tuitsoq* or *tuilik* in place more effectively, and is also markedly stronger than the scarfs in figures 116b and c. This method appears exclusively in East Greenland kayaks.

Figure 114: Qarqutsiaq and Maigssánguaq, two Inuhuit (Polar Greenlanders) photographed in 1930s. Each is a wearing sprayskirt [20] (akuilisaq or tuitsoq, both sing.), and Qarqutsiaq is also wearing kayak sleeves (aaqqat) to keep his arms dry. (Photographer: Erik Holtved/Arktisk Institut 42156.)

Figures 116h, i, and j are edge-scarfed coaming joints. 116h is a fairly simple joint with a stop in the upper terminus. 116i is about as complex as a coaming joint can get: It is hook-scarfed with stopped ends— and these ends have birds-mouth joints carved into them to prevent splaying. Figure 116j shows a simple edge scarf with stopped and birds-mouthed ends. Another method to prevent scarf ends on edge-fastened coamings from splaying is depicted in figure 117. It essentially uses an ivory 'key' piece to lock the joint in place. As elegant as this solution is, it only appears on one kayak in this study— the CMC IV-A-447 (plate 48).

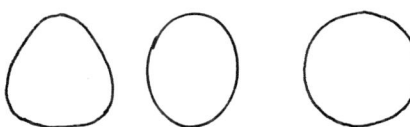

Figure 115: Coaming shapes, L-R: Triangular (much rounded at its 'points'), oval, and round. Egg-shaped coaming also occur, and are sort of middle-of-the-road between triangular and oval shapes.

Typically, coaming scarfs are fastened with pegs (wooden or bone/ivory) or metal fasteners. Figure 118 depicts fastenings of both a face-scarf and an edge-scarf coaming; these are just two examples of a broad variety and pattern of fastenings. Note how the pegs in the edge-scarfed coaming are pinned in place to prevent their loosening. Coamings that are made from sailing ship mast-hoops will occasionally retain their factory-fastened bronze or copper rivets, although often the kayak builder has refastened the scarfs with pegs. Lashings are also used to fasten coaming scarfs, but this is very rare among the non-Polar Greenland kayaks in this study.

---

[20] Polar Greenlanders only used sprayskirts after they adapted the round coamings of more southerly Greenland in the 1930s; See plate 102 for a Polar Greenland kayak whose coaming would facilitate a sprayskirt.

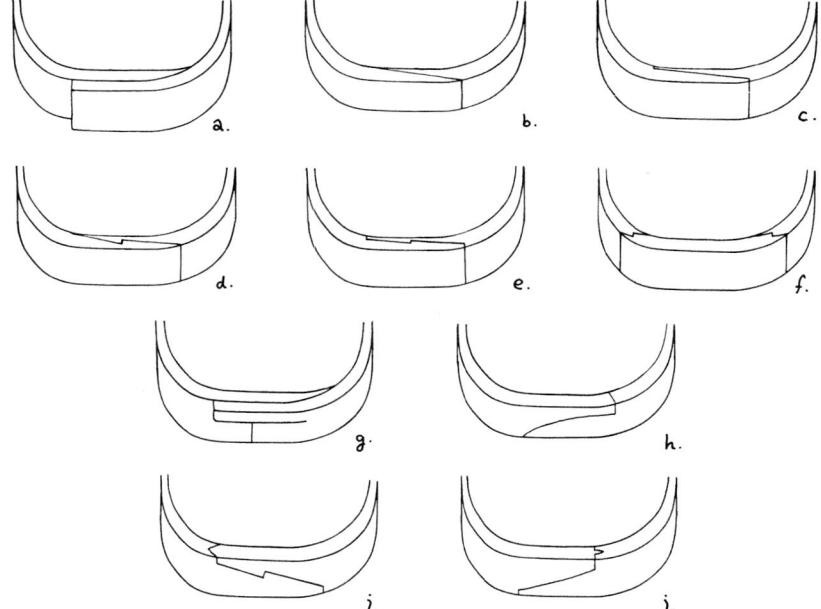

Figure 116: Types of kayak coaming scarfs. Examples a. through g. are scarfed on the coaming's face; h., i., and j. are scarfed along the coaming's edge.

It is often the case that the scarfs on coamings will be re-enforced with small ivory or bone strips. This adds strength to the joint via the numerous pegs holding these strips in place, and it also prevents the fine edges of the scarf from wearing or snagging on the *tuitsoq* or *tuilik*. In one example in this study, baleen is used for this purpose (UMCH 95, plate 74). Coaming scarf protection strips are depicted in figure 119. The ends of these strips are usually square, but occasionally they will have more elegant forms, as in figure 120.

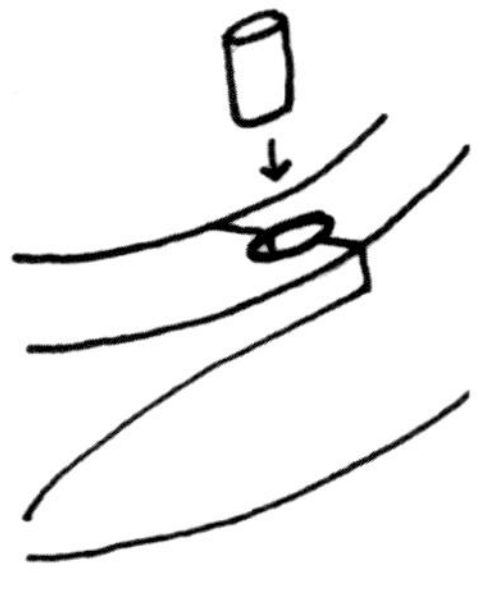

Coaming edging is pegged or nailed to the coaming with bone or ivory pegs— with metal nails in certain kayaks. The pegs used to fasten the edging to the coaming are often lock-pinned in place, thus ensuring the edging will not spring loose; this is depicted in figure 121. The pegs used to secure the edging are not always round in cross-section, but are often flat and broad.

Figure 117: Ivory 'key' piece used to prevent splaying of a coaming scarf.

Coamings are attached to the kayak's skin (*amiq*) alone, and not to the frame. As a rule, in Greenland the *amiq* is pulled up inside the coaming and is fastened to it with pegs, tacks, or lacing. Figure 122 shows the peg placement, as well as some typical cross-sections of coamings.

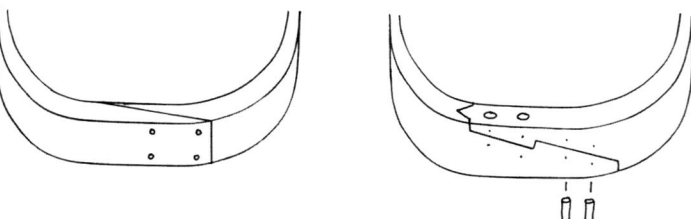

Figure 118: Two examples of how coaming scarfs may be fastened: on the left, a face-scarf, and on the right, an edge-scarf. The pegs are often ivory, but bone, wood, nails, and rivets also occur; pegging and nailing patterns vary considerably.

The pegging or lashing of the *amiq* to the kayak's coaming can be done in a number of different ways resulting in different appearances. Figure 123a is a fairly common method in much of Greenland for attaching a coaming to the *amiq*. The skin is pulled up inside the hoop, and slits cut into the skin's edge are hung on ivory or bone pegs set into the inner-face of the coaming. 123b depicts a method seen on some of the oldest kayaks: the *amiq* is attached to the coaming via the same means as in figure 123a, only at the back of the hoop, the skin is pulled up and over the hoop, and is anchored to pegs set in its back face. This method also appears in relatively modern kayaks from Northwest Greenland, such as the KNK 1215 (plate 61), and the CMC IV-A-375 (plate 67), among others (see also figure 298). In cases where canvas or cloth is used in lieu of a seal skin *amiq*, metal tacks are used instead of pegs.

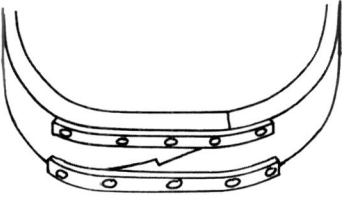

Figure 119: Bone scarf protection on the back of a coaming.

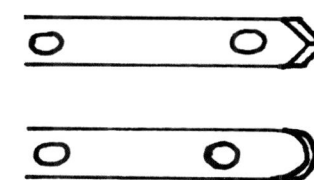

Figure 120: End shapes of coaming edging. The upper-example is apparently quite rare.

The lacing methods of attaching a coaming are depicted in figure 123c, d, e, and f. 123c shows the 'over-the-top' lacing method that occasionally is used on kayaks from North West Greenland. An older variation of this is shown in figure 123d; this method appears only on the Lübeck kayak of circa 1607 in this study (plate 1), and is a combination of methods 123b and 123c. Figure 123e shows an even more common method of lacing the *amiq* to the coaming. This lacing pattern can be either continuous or intermittent (as depicted). A variation of this last example is depicted in 123f: The skin is pulled up through the coaming, and folded down over the outer face, whereupon it is laced using the continuous method. I have only seen one such Greenland kayak using this method: A child's kayak at the Ethnographic Museum in Stockholm (not in this study).

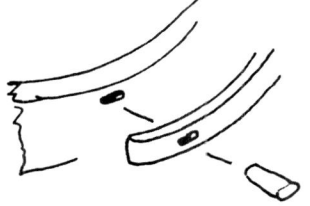

Figure 121: Details of how coaming edging is fastened with a peg that is then pinned in place.

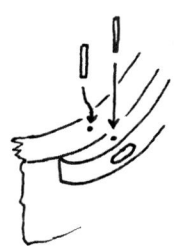

Figure 122: Cross-sections of three different kayak coamings. Note the bone pegs for hanging the *amiq*.

Occasionally, bone or ivory tabs will be placed on the forward quarters of a coaming (figure 124): This is described by H. C. Petersen as being done in Qaqortoq (1986:36), though this tab also occurs on more Northerly kayaks (e.g., MM BF-47, plate

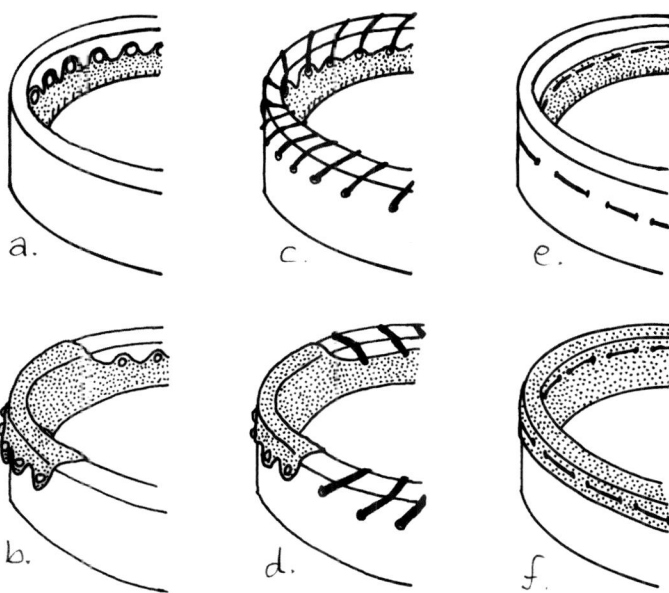

Figure 123: Six methods of mounting the coaming to the kayak's amiq, or skin.

58). A couple of kayaks in this study (the RvV 1076, and the WMF 36481, plates 75 and 10 respectively) have a bone lip nearly all the way around the upper-face of the coaming, which would've certainly prevented any *tuitsoq* or *tuilik* from slipping off.

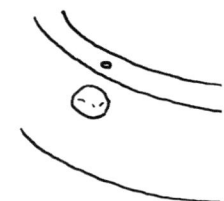

Figure 124: Ivory tab set through a coaming's upper face. The tab is secured with a pin set through the coaming's upper edge.

It is also the case on a few kayaks in this study that the coamings are entirely capped with bone or ivory (the WMF 36481, the RvV 351-77, and the Whitby kayak, plates 10, 8, and 18 respectively). Such an arrangement must have guarded against wear and splintering as well as providing further re-enforcement for the scarfs. Both coaming lips and caps are illustrated in figure 125.

Coamings are not always centered on Greenland kayaks: H. C. Petersen writes that this is "...Because that is a poor working position for the hunter... If (the hunter) is right handed, for example, the coaming is moved to the right so that he can come nearer to the seal when he is using the towing gear"(1986:36). This is the case for many of the kayaks in this study, though the opposite arrangement seems to be common with older kayaks— kayaks often narrower than more recent ones. (One can tell a left-handed kayak from a right-handed one by noting which side the harpoon holder is on.) The reason for the contrary arrangement on older kayaks is likely to afford more room on deck for the harpoon itself, which lays adjacent the cockpit. In a particularly narrow kayak, one is of course very close to both sides simultaneously. Such arrangements are depicted in figure 127.

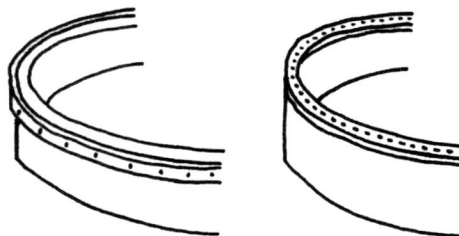

Figure 125: Left, ivory or baleen coaming lip; Right, ivory coaming cap.

Figure 126: Hunters securing a white whale for towing, Aasiaat vicinity, circa 1935. (Photographer: Sylvester Saxtorph/ Arktisk Institut 50852.)

(Right) Figure 127: Offset coamings—the two principles: top, narrow kayak with coaming set away from harpoon holder so as to make room for the harpoon; bottom, wide kayak with coaming set towards harpoon holder so as to afford the paddler better access to the side of the kayak where a captured seal would be secured. (The bows of the kayaks are pointed left.)

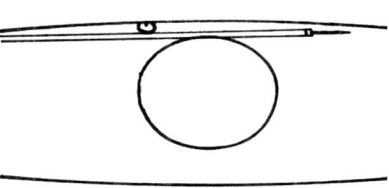

SEAM AND EDGE PROTECTION:

Certain parts of a kayak are prone to considerable wear and damage. A seal skin *amiq* is susceptible to abrasion during encounters with sea-ice as well as when landing, and being portaged. The keel, particularly at the bow and stern where it curves upwards, is quite vulnerable, and is therefore often shod in strips of bone or ivory. Older Greenland kayaks tend to just have such edging at the bow, while later West Greenland kayaks have keel protection at the bow as well as the stern.

At points where the transverse seams of the *amiq* pass across the keel, smaller pieces of bone or ivory can often be found— the resulting lump of a seam is a particularly susceptible wear-point. These seam-protection pieces are often only one to two inches long, and their inside faces are occasionally hollowed so as to straddle a seam more effectively (see figures 128 and 129).

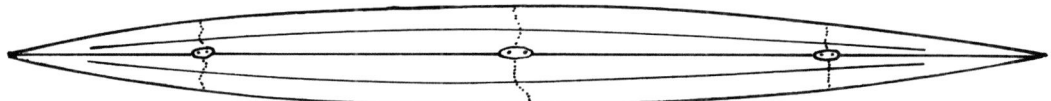

Figure 128: Bone or ivory protection pieces along the keelson at transverse seams. East Greenland kayaks will often have such pieces along the chines as well.

East Greenland kayaks often have more extensive keel and stem edging, often occurring at the bow and stern as well as a large portion of the amidships keel section. It is also common for East Greenland kayaks to have bone or ivory pieces— some quite long— along the chines in certain places, usually straddling seams.

Bone or ivory nails are typically used to attach such protection strips, though in later kayaks, metal nails or screws are used. Wood and even metal strips have replaced bone and ivory in some later examples. Some 20th century kayaks utilize aluminum weather stripping or other metal channeling as edge protection (e.g., the Museon 59876, and the KNK 1990 [Plates 90 and 89 respectively]). Plastic is often used for edge protection in Greenland today.

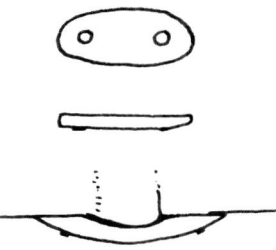

Figure 129: Detail of seam protection pieces. Note the two profiles, one for flat seams (middle), and one for raised seams (bottom).

Figure 130 shows the common form of bone or ivory stem edging. It is usually quite thin towards the kayak's tips, being fairly thick below the stem-to-keelson joint area. Birds-mouth joints are occasionally used to join several strips together, although most kayaks have simpler butt-scarfed edging.

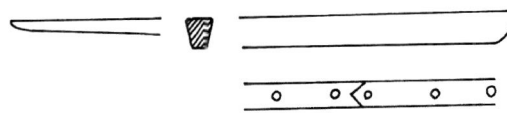

Figure 130: Stem edging Typical tapered end (left) towards bow or stern, thicker termination inboard of bow or stern (right). A birds-mouth scarf joint is depicted below, right.

END PROTECTION:

The very ends— or tips— of a kayak are very susceptible to getting banged-up. Because the kayak's *amiq* is stretched longitudinally, being anchored on the tips, if the skin wears down at these points, the *amiq* is prone to tearing back a distance, loosening the entire *amiq* and letting water in. The tips of the kayak are therefore often protected with bone, antler, ivory, or wood knobs that in essence function as bumpers on land and at sea.

H. C. Petersen writes that kayaks used only during the summer season will often not have such end knobs (1986:38). This is very consistent with what I have found among the kayaks in this study: Kayaks from regions with year-round open water (South, Southwest, and East Greenland) are seldom without end-knobs. Kayaks from Northwest Greenland are more likely to not have end-knobs.

The end knobs are hollow and are slipped over the kayak's tip as if a thimble on a finger. They are generally secured in place by use of a single thin bone peg or nail set through their side or top all the way through the kayak's tip. Generally, the knob will cover the first 3/4″ to 1″ (19-25mm) of the kayak's tips and will usually be anywhere from 1″ (25mm) long to 1-1/2″ (38mm) long. Their diameter varies as well, being 5/8″ to 1-1/4″ (16-32mm) generally. Figure 131 depicts several variations of end knobs as well as their fastening method.

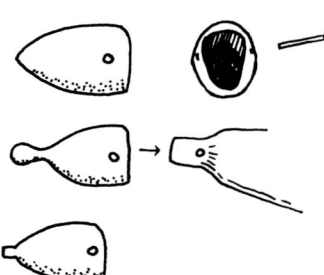

Figure 131: End knob shapes, and their method of attachment. (e shows the chamfered tip of a kayak, shaped so as to receive an end-knob.)

H. C. Petersen describes some end knobs on Greenland kayaks having been fastened to the kayak via tack set through the tip of the knob itself, the tack's head acting as decoration (1986:38). This is not the case in any of the kayaks in this study except for one, and therefore may be an isolated preference. The kayak with an end-fastened knob is the RvV 1076— from South Greenland, ca. 1892 (plate 75); this kayak's bow knob is end fastened with a metal screw, but its stern knob is conventionally fastened. Several end knobs in this study are carved as if they had a nub at their tips, but they are either side- or top-pegged.

As these end-knobs do take the brunt of impact— particularly when being carried by the kayaker, collector, or museum workers— they are often missing. It is usually apparent if a kayak had end-knobs at one time by the fastening holes left in the kayak's tips. As mentioned in the introduction, missing knobs may throw a kayak's overall length off by a couple of inches; when knobs are missing but evidenced, this will be noted in the text.

SKEGS:

Morten Porsild describes the purpose of a skeg (*aquut*) on a kayak: (Porsild uses the term 'rudder' in the following quote, but 'skeg' is a more accurate description as they are fixed, immovable, i.e., not controllable by the kayaker.)

> *When one steals upon a seal the rudder has to counteract the effect of the wind catching the shooting screen[21] which may force the kayak out of the desired direction, or it has to counteract the effect of the last stroke of the paddle which would otherwise cause the kayak to veer and render concealment illusory (1915:182).*

Skegs are usually thought of as an object affixed to the outside of a kayak's hull, but they may in certain cases be integral to the kayak's frame, i.e., fitted before the *amiq* is attached. Figure 132a depicts

---

[21] The "shooting screen" mentioned above is a broad piece of white cloth suspended transversely above and across the kayak's fore-deck, and is essentially a piece of camouflage that conceals the kayak, harpoon line stand, and the kayaker's torso. See figures 283 and 341 for photographs of kayaks with such screens.

a kayak without any skeg; 132b depicts a kayak with an integral skeg, which is essentially a re-curving or built-up keelson-end. Figure 132c shows a kayak with an externally attached skeg, and figure 132d shows a combination of the two skeg-forms— the KNK 2050 is an example of a kayak having both external and integral skegs (plate 49).

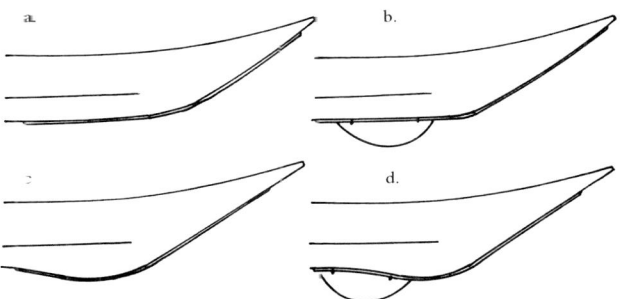

Figure 132: Kayak without skeg (a), kayak with external skeg (b), kayak with integral skeg (c), and kayak with external and integral skeg (d).

External skegs are usually lashed to the kayak, and there are several ways in which this may be done. Figure 133a depicts the method of attaching the skeg to the kayak by means of two transverse lashings. Figure 133b depicts the 'stick' method; the stick lies across the gunwales, and the skeg is lashed to the stick. Both of these methods allow for easy removal if desired— even while afloat if another kayaker is nearby to assist.

Morten Porsild describes a later improvement in the mounting of kayak:

> Originally [the skeg] was simply tied round the stern of the kayak, but the . . . family Geisler here [Disko Bay] made a small improvement by cutting a couple of incisions in the keel timber of the kayak, before the skin was drawn on. When, during the process of drying, the skin shrinks, a hole for the lashing appears between the skin and that strip of bone which at this point strengthens the kayak, and which acts as the runner when the kayak is pushed across the ice (1915:182, "Disko Bay" reference on pg. 142).

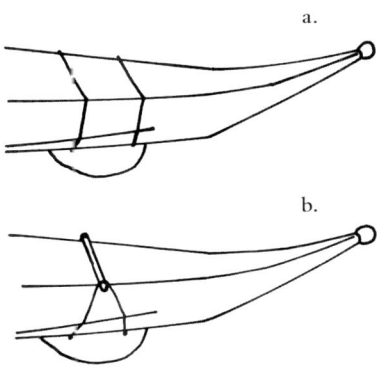

Figure 133: Two methods of attaching a skeg to a kayak. The lower example is suspended by a cross-stick.

Another method of attaching the skeg to the kayak without tying it all the way around the hull are evidenced in the stern keel edging of the MSU 4274cw (plate 45) and the CCM 977.180 (plate 38): Both of these kayak's stern keel edging has transverse holes drilled through, suggesting that skegs had been lashed to them, as in figure 134a.

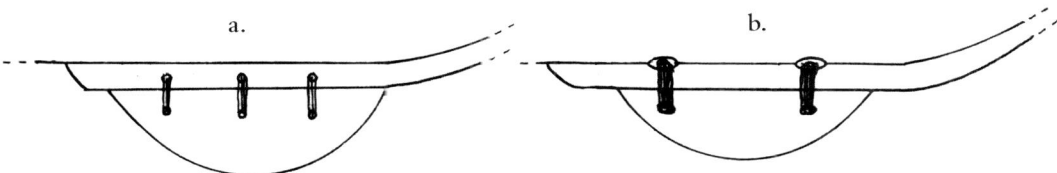

Figure 134: Two methods of attaching a skeg to a kayak's stern keel edging. The figure on the right shows the method described above by Morten Porsild.

Skegs do not seem to be used on East Greenland kayaks, but F. Spencer Chapman does mention an East Greenlander who did have one:

One of the Eskimos here has a small wooden fin attached to the bottom of his kayak about a yard from the stern: it is ten inches long and four inches deep at the most ... It is unsuitable for conditions here, as it would be more difficult to dodge about in thick ice and would prevent the hunters sliding in their kayaks from an ice-floe down into the water (1934b: 281).

Morten Porsild writes that the skeg attachment method in West Greenland was specially made to endure some hard use: "The lashing is just sufficiently tight to keep the rudder in a vertical position, but not too tight to permit its folding up without breaking when, on landing, the kayak takes the ground" (Porsild, 1915: 182).

BALANCE AIDS:

Several methods are used in conjunction with training children how to use and balance a kayak; each method functions as an outrigger of sorts, giving both buoyancy and resistance to heeling. Technically, none of these are 'parts' of a kayak, but, as with skegs, they directly affect the hydrodynamic properties of a kayak, they are discussed here.

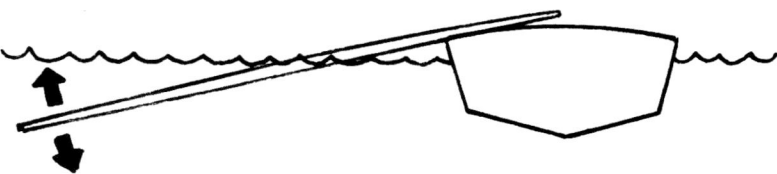

Figure 135: A paddle deployed as a balance-aid. The paddle is slipped firmly underneath deck lines just ahead of the cockpit; with one blade in the water a few inches below the surface, the kayak has tremendous resistance to leaning and tipping.

The simplest method of stabilizing a kayak is to run the kayak paddle beneath the fore deck lines of the kayak (see figures 135). For most purposes, the paddle is angled perpendicular to the kayak. If however it is used in teaching a child to balance and paddle a kayak, an extra paddle can drag somewhat behind the child where it won't affect their paddling or steering significantly.

In East Greenland a special made paddle-holder (*nootaaki-taa*)— dubbed a 'paddle-pinch' by Thalbitzer — is used in lieu of

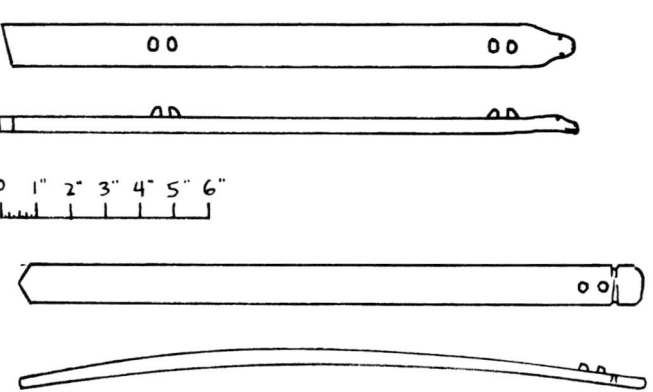

Figure 137: Two paddle holders from East Greenland, of the type seen in figure 136. The upper example from the Rijksmuseum voor Volkenkunde[22] measures 16-11/16" (42.3cm) long, 1-1/4" (32mm) wide, and the wooden portion measures 7/16" (11mm) thick. The buttons are ivory, and the forward end of this holder is shaped like a seal's head. The lower example is in the Danish National Museum—lying on the deck of their kayak L.19.157 (plate 86). It measures 18-1/2" (47.0cm) long and 1-1/8" (28mm) wide, and is bent to better hold the paddle.

---

[22] This paddle holder was measured at the Rijksmuseum voor Volkenkunde in Leiden; it was found on the deck of kayak 351-77 (plate 8)—a West Greenland kayak likely dating from the 1600s or 1700s. It undoubtedly did not belong to that kayak, and it is the author's opinion that it instead belongs to the East Greenland kayak 2823 (plate 88). The button placement on this paddle holder further re-enforces this, as their distances correspond perfectly to the 2823's deck-line spacing.

Figure 136: A boy getting into a kayak in Ammassalik district, 1961. Note how the paddle is used as an outrigger for balance—it is tucked below a paddle holder specially made for this purpose. (Photographer: Jette Bang/ Arktisk Institut gjb02198.)

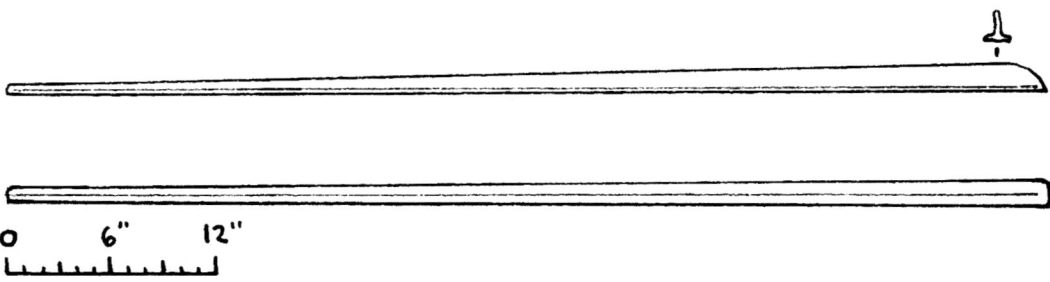

Figure 138: A balance stick from East Greenland at the Museon, The Hague (no. 57531). The stick measures 60" long (152.4cm).

deck lines to hold the paddle in an outrigger position (Thalbitzer, 1914:386-387). This holder consists of a thin flat board that is placed underneath the deck lines just ahead of the cockpit, as in figure 136. Some examples of these paddle holders have raised ivory buttons placed such that they abut the kayak's deck lines to prevent the holder from shifting or sliding out. Two such paddle-holders are illustrated in scale in figure 137.

In East Greenland, Gert Nooter collected a specially made substitute for the 'extra-paddle' technique described above; this balance stick is depicted in figure 138. This balance stick has a raised ridge along its length in order to stiffen and strengthen it; the narrow end would be tucked under a deck line on the fore deck, and the wide end would drag in the water behind and off to the side of the kayaker. Such a stick can also be seen stowed on the aft deck of the kayak in the foreground of figure 341.[23]

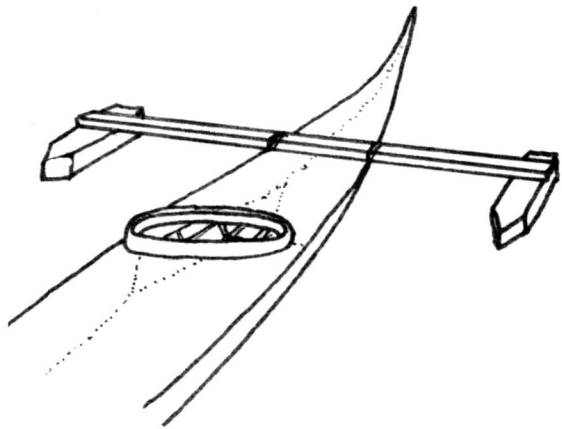

Figure 139: General appearance of wooden outriggers, lashed to a kayak's aft deck. In more recent years, the wooden floats have been replaced with plastic detergent bottles, having better buoyancy, an ideal shape and size, and even a handle to lash to.

Another outrigger-method used in kayak training is a pair of wooden floats attached to a long stick laid across the aft deck of a kayak and lashed in place— essentially converting the kayak into a tri-maran (figure 139). Fridtjof Nansen made use of such a balance-aid when getting accustomed to his kayak: "I got on better still when I had a pair of outriggers or supports made to help me. These are miniature 'kayaks,' about two feet long, and are fastened one on each side of the canoe, just behind the seat. They make things considerably easier for the uninitiated of course, but the Eskimo themselves rarely use them, and I myself abandoned them after a while"(1895:403).

---

[23] Another use of this balance stick could have been to keep smaller game (fish, birds, etc.) from tumbling off a kayak's deck. Note how harpoons and lances are used for this purpose in figure 328.

AMULETS:

Kaj Birket-Smith writes, "There is naturally much superstition in connection with a pursuit so full of dangers as kayaking" (1924:277). Most mentions of amulets or other magico–spiritual objects associated with kayaks are specifically within the context of hunting, although amulets were also used in keeping mythological beings at bay. Birket-Smith writes of kayak hunters placing tufts of heather at the stems of kayaks to ward off the mythological beings *"atdliarútit"*— beings known to hunt humans (1924:224, 277.).

Other documented instances of spiritual beliefs relating to the kayak-object are, for example: Boys not allowed to use hare skins as kayak seats for the concern it will make them timid hunters, and the placement of a small wooden kayak model, or a page of a hymn book inside a kayak (Birket-Smith, 1924:277, 413). The Moravian missionary David Crantz describes kayak amulets used to prevent turning over:

They like to fasten to their kajak a model of it with a little man holding a sword in his hand; or only a dead sparrow or snipe, or a bit of wood, stone, some feathers, or hair, that they may not overset; although those chiefly are lost, that had armed themselves most in this manner against it, but only were unskilled or timorous, or relied so much on their superstitious preservatives, that they ventured beyond their power (1767:i 216-271).

H. C. Petersen writes of special deck fittings on kayaks' bow deck lines: "... In the old days there was also a middle figure of tooth, carved in the shape of a man or seal... This figure was a kind of amulet. It ceased to be used after the introduction of the rifle holster on the West Coast, but can still be seen on several kayaks on the East Coast"(1985:40). The suggestion that the rifle holster had anything to do with the man or seal figures no longer being used is likely circumstantial.

Greenlanders have historically observed many other taboos and methods not directly related to the kayak itself in order to ensure successful kayak hunting. These traditions will not be addressed here, but I refer you to Birket-Smith, 1924:277, 282-283 446-447, and Porsild, 1915:149-150.

Polar Greenland Kayak Construction

As mentioned before, the structure and construction of Polar Greenland kayaks is very different than that of West and East Greenland kayaks, hence its separate attention here. I've also mentioned that the kayaks of the Polar Greenlanders have changed dramatically since their re-introduction in the 1860s. By about the middle of the 20th century, Polar Greenland kayaks had assimilated nearly fully with the West Greenland types. This section will deal with the pre-assimilated forms (early and transitional forms), i.e., those with pieced-frame construction.[24]

Several Polar Greenland kayaks in this study have gunwales that have been shaped such that the outside corners were removed and replaced with facets, such as in figure 140. This is exposed in a section of a kayak where the skin has separated; the gunwale side is oxidized dark brown and gray, while the planed facets expose bright new wood. This form of gunwale shaping is occasionally seen in East Canadian kayaks, which is not surprising given the roots of Polar Greenland kayaks (Golden, field notes: 2002, 2003).

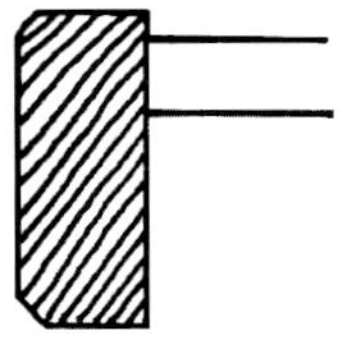

Figure 140: Polar Greenland gunwale cross-section showing rounded outside edges.

The deck beams in most examples are simply butted against the gunwales and lashed firmly in place, as illustrated in figure 141, left. As can be seen, the lashings are oriented quite snugly against the top and bottom faces of the deck beam to prevent their shifting out of place. In the case of later examples, such deck beams are not lashed, but nailed in place, (with one to three nails) as in figure 141, right.

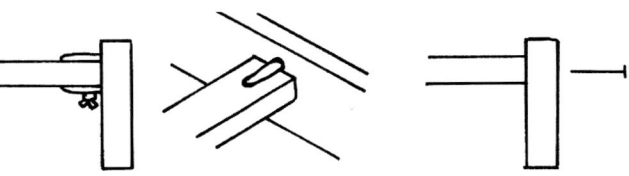

Figure 141: Lashed deck beam joint (left and middle). Right: Nailed deck beam.

One Polar Greenland kayak (NMAI 165227, plate 95) exhibits a unique method of tightening lashings: This is done by inserting wedge-shaped chips of wood between the lashing and the deck beam as depicted in figure 142. This same method is also used at the rib-to-gunwale lashing joints as well as on the coaming joints of this same kayak.

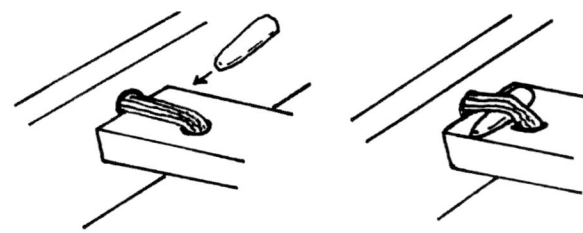

Figure 142: Wooden wedges can be slipped beneath lashings in order to tighten them.

---

[24]Only one assimilated-form Polar Greenland kayak is presented in this study: The Royal Ontario Museum's 950-219, surveyed by Eugene Arima (plate 102). There is one early-form Polar Greenland kayak in this study with bent ribs (the CCM 977.181, plate 98)—apparently a very unusual example.

In comparing the kayak building technology of Baffin Islanders with the Polar Greenlanders, anthropologist Franz Boas writes, "The art of steaming wood does not seem to be known to the latter tribe. For this reason the ribs of their kayaks are made of three pieces,— one for the bottom, and one for each side"(1901:12). The joints between the rib pieces are usually lashed or nailed together. The middle piece appears as a 'floor' of sorts, and will be referred to as such throughout the text. Figure 143 depicts the cross section typically found in Polar Greenland kayaks. Only one example of a pre-assimilation Polar Greenland kayak in this study has bent ribs— the CCM 977.181 (plate 98).

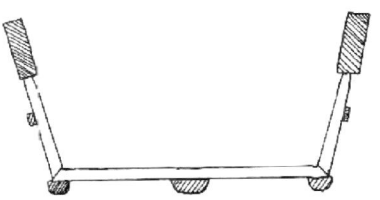

Figure 143: Typical framing cross-section of a Polar Greenland kayak. Note the pieced ribs and the smaller 'secondary' chines.

Mortise and tenon joints are used in a number of Polar Greenland kayaks, but this is usually just at the rib-to-gunwale joints in later examples. Ribs in the examples not using mortises are simply butted against the bottom edge of the gunwale— sometimes in a transverse notch, and lashed in place through a hole in the rib and one in the gunwale. This is depicted in figure 144, left. In instances where the ribs are mortised into the gunwales, lashings or pegs are often used to secure them in place, as in figures 144, middle and 144, right. One Polar Greenland kayak, the CCM 977.181 (plate 98), has bent-over metal nails in lieu of pegs.

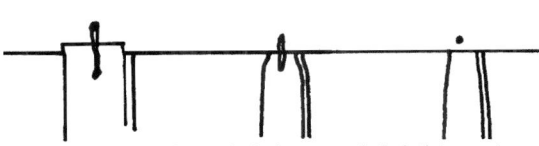

Figure 144: left to right: Lashed rib in grove, lashed rib in mortise, and pegged/nailed rib in mortise.

One Polar Greenland kayak in this study exhibited a variation of the mortise-less rib attachment method (the NMNH 160388, plate 94). A birds-mouth notch was cut into the rib's top end so as to lock it against the bottom inside edge of the gunwale. This method is depicted in figure 145. This joint is lashed in place the same as is depicted in figure 144, left.

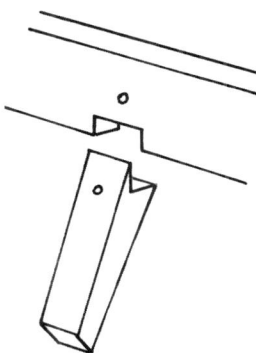

Figure 145: Birds-mouth-joint rib set into groove.

Figure 146a and b show details of Polar Greenland kayak rib, floor, and chine joints. 146a depicts the rib juncture at the bilge prior to the fitting of the chine. The joint is mitered and lashed through both rib pieces; this joint is fastened first, and then the chines are attached. The chine lashing goes over the rib juncture lashing, thereby cinching it tighter, as shown in figure 146b.

One Polar Greenland kayak in this study, the CCM 977.179 (plate 96), has a notched step cut into the ends of the floor-pieces, as shown in figure 147. The rib is butted into the floor's notch; compared

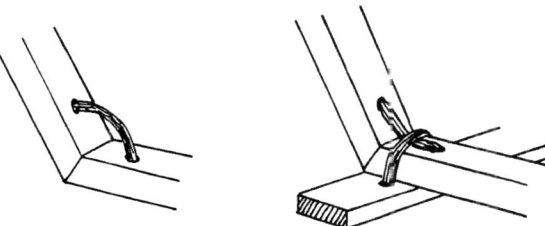

Figure 146: Lashed rib-to-floor joint (left); lashed chine to rib joint (right).

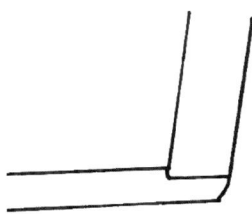

Figure 147: Notched floor piece.

Figure 148: Qarqutsiaq framing his kayak at Inglefield Land, Northeast of Etah, 1936. (Photographer: Erik Holtved / Arktisk Institut 52133.)

to the miter joint shown in figure 146, this method may be less likely to shift.

Nails or pegs have replaced the rib-floor-chine lashings in later kayaks from this region, e.g., the KNK 528, DNM L17.125, and the Mystic 1964.1562 (plates 100, 101, and 102 respectively). The nailed rib-to-floor and chine joint is depicted in figure 149.

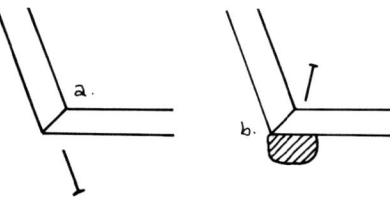

Figure 149: Nailed floor-to-rib joint (left). Chine fastened to rib with nails (right).

Several Polar Greenland kayaks in this study have secondary chines that run along the forward half of the hull between the gunwales and the primary chines. These secondary chines are usually very thin battens— not so much a structural element as a means to keep the *amiq* off the ribs in the vicinity where there would otherwise be a large gap between the gunwale and primary chine. Figure 143 shows the general positioning of the second-

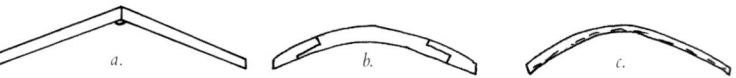

Figure 150: Three masik *forms seen in Polar Greenland kayaks. Left, straight pieces mitered and lashed; middle, curved piece with extensions scarfed on the ends; right, a natural crook of caribou antler.*

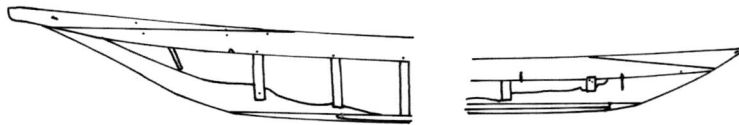

Figure 151: End structures of a Polar Greenland kayak (the Mystic Seaport Museum 1964.1562, plate 101).

ary chine; see plates 94 and 96 for examples of Polar Greenland kayaks with such chines. Secondary chines are very common among East Canadian kayaks as well (Arima, 1987; Golden, field notes: 2002, 2003).

The *masiit* (*masik*, plural) of Polar Greenland kayaks appear in three different forms and materials among the examples in this study. One is a pieced-together *masik* made of straight pieces of wood, as in figure 150a. Another form is the pieced-together example shown in figure 150b, made from a short natural crook that has been lengthened with straight pieces. The third form is made from a natural crook— not of wood, but of caribou antler (figure 150c). The antler *masik* is present in three of the eight Polar Greenland kayaks in this study: The NMNH 160388, CCM 977.179, and the NMAI 165527 (plates 94, 96, and 95 respectively.) Figures 366 and 368 show how the antler *masik* is attached to the gunwales.

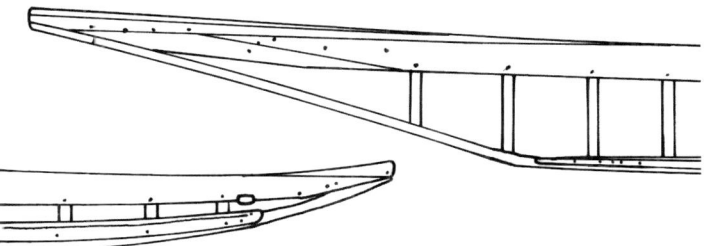

Figure 152: Bow (top) and stern structures of a Labrador kayak in the Canadian Canoe Museum (CCM no. 980.20).

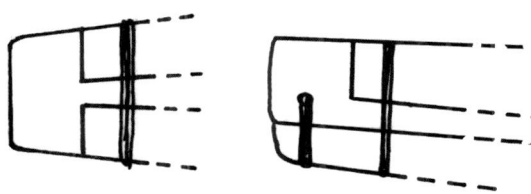

Figure 153: Bow joinery as it appears on the National Museum of the American Indian's kayak 165227 (plate 95). Top view, left, and side view, right.

Only one Polar Greenland kayak frame is present in this study (MSM 1964.1562, plate 101), and it is a transitional form, being a mix of older techniques and forms combined with influences introduced from more southerly Greenlanders. Its end joinery is depicted in figure 151, (as well as on the survey drawing).

A full view of the bow structure of an older Polar Greenland kayak was not possible among the examples I saw. However being that they are not-too-distant cousins of East Canadian kayaks, it is worth presenting the bow and stern structure of an East Canadian kayak (figure 152), Labrador, kayak from ca. 1920s. It illustrates many similar principles depicted in figure 151. Most notable are the chines affixed to the keelson ends, and the gunwales that course the full length of the kayak. Also note how each kayak's gunwales have built-up ends.

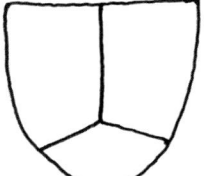

Figure 154: The bow structure evidenced on the L.17.125 (plate 99).

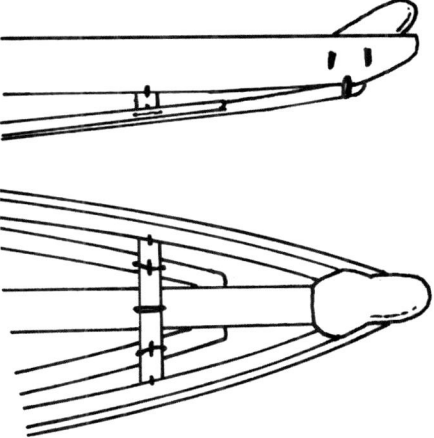

Figure 155: Stern assembly (not to scale) of the Canadian Canoe Museum's Polar Greenland kayak 977.179 (plate 96).

An older Polar Greenland kayak that I observed (the NMAI 165227, plate 95) had a couple inches of skin missing at its bow, and it revealed some interesting features. The gunwales did not quite reach the tip; instead they were set into a small block carved to receive them. The keelson (or at least the stem-piece) did reach to the tip. This joint, as much as could be seen, was entirely lashed (figure 153).

Missing skin at the bow of a Polar Greenland kayak at the Danish National Museum (L.17.125, plate 99) exposed two gunwales and the keelson, as depicted in figure 154. The keelson is shaped such that it firmly seats against the gunwales' lower edges.

Another Polar Greenland kayak in this study had a generous section of its stern assembly exposed: The CCM 977.179 (plate 96). A side and top view of the visible structure is depicted in figure 155. The up-turned stern is not part of the gunwales as in the East Canadian example (figure 152), but instead it is a separate piece of wood especially carved to receive the gunwale ends, being fastened by lashings. The keelson is lashed to the gunwales where their lower edges meet.

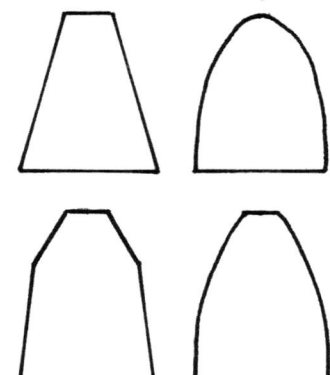

Figure 156: Shapes of Polar Greenland kayak coamings.

The pre-assimilation Polar Greenland kayaks in this study just have single deck stringers ahead of the cockpit. Of the eight of these kayaks, five have single stringers on the aft deck while the other three have no aft deck stringers.

Most Polar Greenland coamings are quite distinct in their form— they are usually not round like other Greenland kayaks' coamings, but are instead more trapezoidal, with angular corners, such as depicted in figure 156. The several pieces used in making such a coaming are lashed together at their junctures. Later Polar Greenland kayaks do make use of round or oval coamings, for example, the ROM 950-219 (plate 102).

The narrower front-piece often found on Polar kayaks is usually thicker than the sides and serves not only as a solid receiving block for the coaming sides, but also as a mounting for the paddle rest. This type of paddle rest is quite exclusive to Polar Greenland: The paddle can rest on this mounting while being used. This technique is described for East Canadian kayaks, but in these cases, the paddle is just rested on the coaming's front (Arima, 1987:120-121). Whalebone is used for the Polar Greenland kayak's paddle rest, though several examples in museums have mahogany pieces instead. A paddle rest's attachment is illustrated in figure 157 and also in figures 368 and 369.

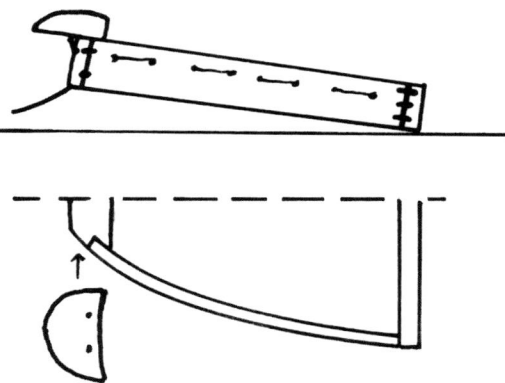

Figure 157: Joinery details of a Polar Greenland kayak coaming. Note the paddle rest mounted on the front of the coaming.

Three Polar Greenland kayaks in this study have bent cockpits: One is the kayak with the bent ribs mentioned above (the CCM 977.181, plate 98). In this example, the coaming is only bent at the front and has a straight back piece, as in figure 156, top right. The forward face of this kayak's coaming is re-enforced with a strip of bone or antler. The other Polar Greenland kayaks with bent coamings are the MSM 1964.1562 (plate 101), and the ROM 950-219 (plate 102) — the former example's coaming is mostly missing; the only intact section is the front quarter with its paddle-rest intact. That this length is made from one piece of wood suggests it at least had a curved front. Like the CCM 977.181, the Mystic Seaport kayak likely had a straight back-piece as well.

Polar Greenland kayak coamings are typically lashed to the kayak's *amiq*, most examples in this study use an intermittent lineal pattern (as in figure 123e), but the CCM 977.179 (plate 96) uses an over-the-top pattern, as depicted in figure 123c.

Repairs and Modifications

It is of no surprise that hunting tools depended on so critically for subsistence in a broad range of conditions would exhibit both damage and repair. Wood being the commodity it is and was in Greenland, the recycling, repair, and modification of wooden pieces is commonly present. Such changes and improvisations evidenced in kayaks are every bit as interesting as their general construction.

Historian Finn Gad writes of the importance of maintaining good hunting equipment: "Before the Eskimos took to the water, their frail little boats were always checked, and the work of maintenance was carried out with the most meticulous care and solicitude. It was a matter of life and death, and even the smallest defect had to be mended in time" (1971:269).

By virtue of kayak skins rarely lasting more than a year, each time a skin is removed, the builder/hunter has access to the kayak's frame in order to repair it or make changes to the design. I have seen the following repairs and adjustments in the kayaks presented in this study.

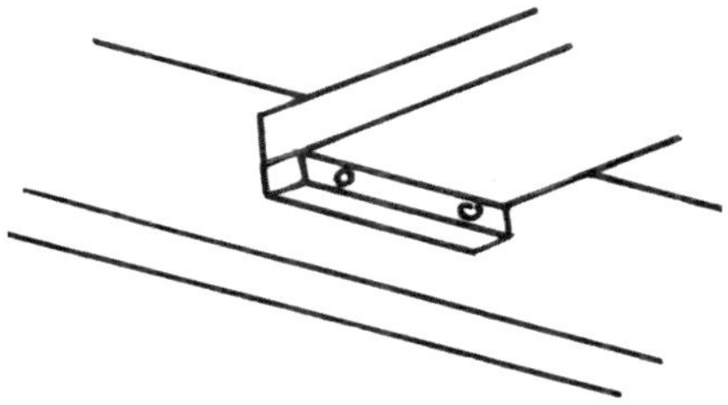

Adjustments and the recycling of pieces in kayaks are usually apparent by the presence of unused deck beam or rib mortises. The question arises however whether these represents modifications per-se, or just the re-use of older kayak parts. In the case of the PQN's 'old frame' (plate 50), one can see that the *isserfik* has effectively been moved forward by the placement of a new *isserfik* ahead of the old one. The new one is not through tenoned (i.e., tenoned all the way through) to the gunwales like the other deck beams, thus indicating it may have been placed without disassembling the frame.

Figure 158: A deck beam 'hanger'—a strip of wood fastened to the gunwales supporting a deck beam. A hanger enables a deck beam to be inserted into a covered kayak without having to mortise and tenon the joints.

The NMF 5023 (plate 63) exhibits a similar *isserfik* modification. In this example, the presumed newer deck beam is resting on top of two 'hangers' nailed to the gunwale's faces (figure 158). It is not certain how the deck beam was fastened here; it may not be fastened at all, or is perhaps side-nailed through the gunwales' outside face.

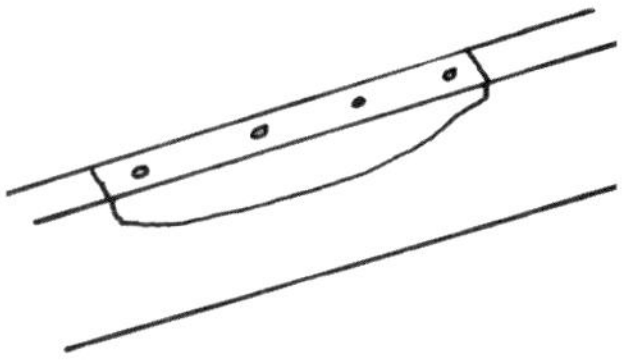

Patches of wood can be used to replace rotted or broken sections of larger planks. A kayak frame from East Greenland (the Museon 57602, plate 91) exhibits such a patch atop the forward end of one of the gunwales. The patch is nailed in place, and appears as in figure 159. On this same kayak the joint between the gunwale ends and the stem piece is wrapped with a piece of tin, and tacked along its edges. This metal cladding would not only strengthen this joint considerably, but would also ensure a fair-lines transition between the gunwale ends and the stem piece.

Figure 159: Patch of wood used to mend a damaged gunwale.

In the cases of two East Greenland kayaks (the DNM L.19.157 and the KNK 1990, plates 86 and 89 respectively), trusses have been inserted between the deck beams and the bottom edge of the gunwales, as in figure 160. The purpose of these must be guessed at: I think they were used to hold and lock these kayaks' considerable gunwale flare in place. They would also by virtue of their attachment hold the deck beams firmly in their mortises. These trusses can also be seen in figures 343 and 352.

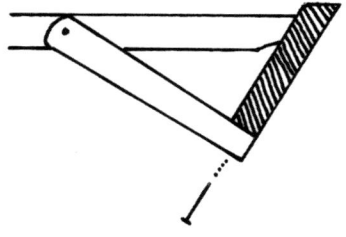

Figure 160: Truss, as seen in two East Greenland kayaks in this study.

The recycling of deck beams— particularly noted with curved deck beams— is often evidenced when a kayak's breadth is widened. In some cases, the deck beams might be too short to reach the gunwales where they are needed. This is remedied by the attachment of short boards or blocks to the inside face of the gunwales. This essentially 'narrows' the kayak on the inside so the deck beams will fit (figure 161). The deck beams are then mortised and tenoned into these pieces, just as if they were the gunwales proper. Being that these blocks are often in the forward cockpit area, their corners are as a rule rounded so as to not chafe the kayaker's legs. This solution appears in East Greenland kayaks (MUS 59876 and KNK 1990, plates 89 and 90 respectively) as well as in a West Greenland kayak (NMS 1866, plate 32)— see figure 358 in particular.

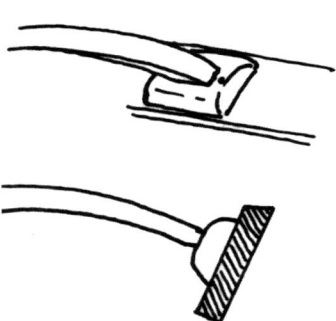

Figure 161: Block used to 'narrow' gunwales so as to accommodate a shorter deck beam.

A similar block attached to the inboard face of gunwales also appears in the West Greenland kayak MSU 4274cw (plate 45), only its function is not to provide a footing for deck beams, but instead to re-enforce a weak segment of the gunwale (figure 267). Its placement is from about 4" (10.2cm) behind the *masik*, extending about 10" (25.4cm) forward; it measures 1-1/2" high by 1" (38 x 25mm) thick, and is nailed in place with metal nails. Like the above-mentioned blocks, the corners of the MSU's block are rounded over— to the point where the entire block looks like a piece of half-round molding. The KNK 2237 (plate 66) has a gunwale re-enforcement block behind the cockpit; it is not rounded over at all.

Another way to effectively increase the reach of a deck beam occurs in several West Greenland kayaks in this study. This is accomplished by setting a peg or thin shim through the base of the deck beams' tenons, essentially making the deck beams reach further, i.e., the thickness of

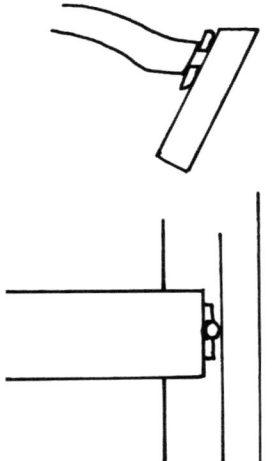

Figure 162: Peg shims used to 'lengthen' or tighten a deck beam.

Figure 163: Repairs to broken ribs. Splint repair to a fracture (b.), and replaced rib tenon (c.).

the peg or shim. This is illustrated in figure 162, and can also be seen in figures 256 and 257. By virtue of this method decreasing the distance that the tenon reaches into the mortise, it can only be used for fine-tuning; it would not be a viable option in kayaks with shallow mortises and short tenoned deck beams.

In an instance where a kayak's deck beam has broken, the fracture can often be wrapped with numerous passes of twine; this repair is present on an East Greenland kayak's curved deck beam, and is visible in figure 342.

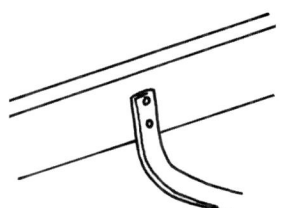

Figure 164: Rib nailed to the inside face of a gunwale.

Where kayak's ribs have fractured, or they need re-enforcing, splints of wood are often bound to them with lashings (figure 163b). Another method of repairing a broken rib is depicted in figure 163c: A new tenon end is placed in the mortise and is lashed to the existing rib remnant.

Another way to repair a rib— particularly if the mortise in the gunwale has split out— is to fasten a new rib to the gunwale sides with nails or pegs, as in figure 164. If the repair is to be made in the cockpit, it can be done without removing the *amiq*. This solution was noted in the cockpit of the CMC IV-A-427 (plate 62).

Figure 165: Splint lashed to a rib to prevent hogging of the keel.

Greenland kayaks with broad flat bottoms are particularly prone to hull-collapse— especially shallower kayaks. Deeper V-bottomed kayaks have more arch-shaped ribs, a shape with much better resistance to deformation. One method used in arresting and/or preventing such hull-collapse appears in the KNK 1215 (plate 61). This is done by lashing a straight piece of wood (a splint) to the rib to help hold its shape, as in figure 165. Several ribs inside this kayak have this treatment; interestingly, the splint pieces are made from crown molding.

Figure 166 shows a modified/recycled/repaired end structure of a kayak in the Greenland National Museum (catalog no. 2057; not in this study). Other kayaks exhibiting such repairs and shims are the PQN and the KNK 1550x18 (plates 50 and 71; these are also illustrated in figures 60 and 62.)

Two different solutions to repairing a broken keelson have been observed in the kayaks in this study. In the case of the MSU 4274cw (plate 45), its keelson had been shaved down a bit to make the cockpit more comfortable, and at this location, it had fractured. A bone or antler splint has been lashed across the top of the keelson to prevent its shifting. This sort of repair is depicted in figure 167, although in this case the splint is nailed in place.

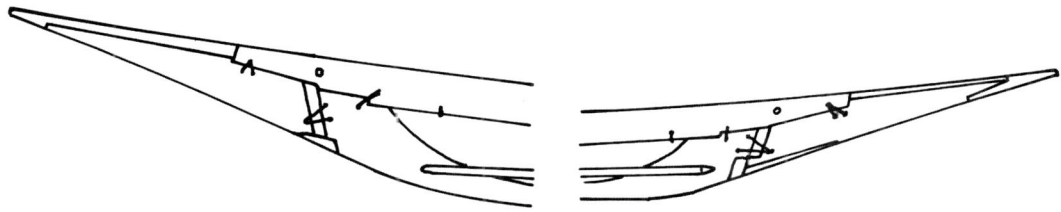

Figure 166: End structures of the Greenland National Museum's kayak KNK 2057. Many repairs and modifications are evident in this illustration. (A scale drawing of this kayak does not appear in this study.)

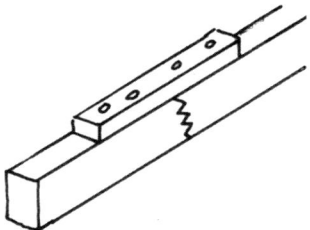

Figure 167: Repair of fractured keelson or chine. Occasionally the splint-portion is situated on the side of the member.

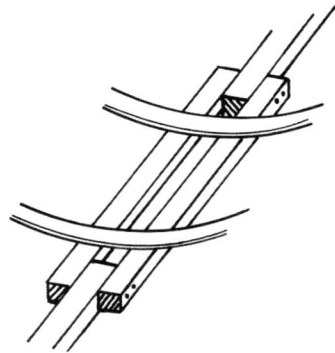

Figure 168: Broken keelson partnered with two pieces of wood. Note the removed portion of the keelson.

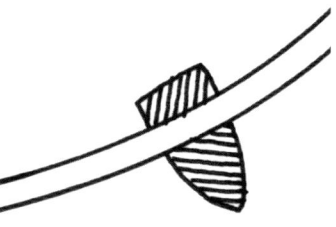

Figure 169: Chine partnered on the inside of the ribs with a batten of wood.

The other example of keelson repair is inside the Museon 57992 (plate 68). A section of the keelson about the length of the cockpit hoop was entirely missing, and the gap is spanned by two lengths of wood partnered aside the gap, being fastened to the fractured keelson's ends with nails, as in figure 168.

A few West Greenland kayaks have battens that are partnered to chines above the ribs, a cross section of which is depicted in figure 169. The exact function of these battens is not known, but they may help in adjusting the amount of curve in a chine, or are perhaps reinforcing a damaged section of chine. Such a reinforcing batten can be seen in figure 285 (right chine, towards the bow), a forward interior view of the KNK 1215, plate 61.

Two kayaks in the Canadian Museum of Civilization (plates 64 and 67) have had *masik* modifications. In both cases the aim seems to have been to make it easier to get inside the kayak— by either raising the *masik* height, or by tilting it forward, thus raising the back edge of the *masik*. Both examples are depicted in figure 170. Each method is achieved by inserting a shim between the *masik* and the gunwale— the former uses a 3-5/8″ (92mm) long, 1/2″ (13mm) square shim, the latter uses a wedge shaped shim; each is top-nailed to the gunwales.

Bone or ivory strips are commonly seen over coaming scarfs, but occasionally they appear to be placed randomly and asymmetrically along the face of a coaming. Upon closer inspection, one will often find that these pieces usually cover fractures or splinters, thus it is used as a repair strip (figure 171, left). Metal is used for such repairs on two East Greenland kayaks in this study from the 1930s (the DNM L.19.157, plate 86, and the AMNH 60.1/6003, plate 85). If a grain splinter occurs along the edge of a coaming, a nail or peg can be set through the edge to arrest it, as in figure 171, right.

A kayak's deck lines are somewhat prone to being broken or cut— they are exposed to abrasion, ice, and implements with sharp blades, and stresses from towing seals. Several methods of repairing the deck lines are present in the kayaks in this study. These repairs range from meticulously executed to rather crude but functional field repairs. The seal skin straps used to make the deck lines can be scarfed and/or sewn together via several methods; figure 172 depicts several of these. Figure 173 shows how the leather line is spliced without sewing.

In the case of the KNK 2237 (plate 66), the bow deck line seems to have been broken, and may have been cut back to small stubs at each side. Holes have been cut in these stubs, and a cord has been fed through them making up the new deck line; it is passed back and forth several times.

A more crude but simple method for fixing broken deck lines is present in the DNM's L.18.273 (plate 73). This kayak's broken deck lines have been cut off flush at the sheer line, and replacement lines have been nailed to the gunwales adjacent to the original lines' posi-

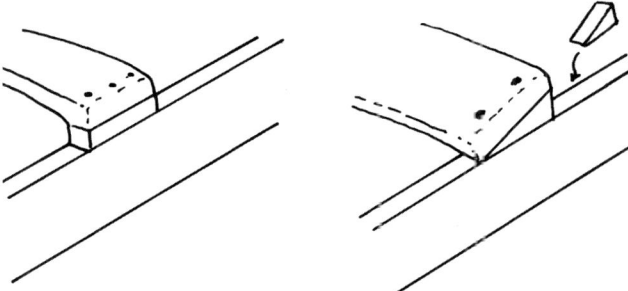

Figure 170: Shims used to raise the masik. *The example on the right is a wedge-shaped shim that tilts the masik forward, thereby raising its aft-edge.*

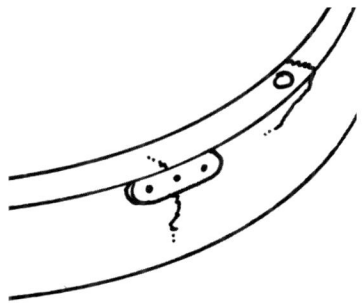

Figure 171: Two forms of coaming repairs: Left, a plate of bone/ivory/metal used to arrest and reinforce a fracture. Right, a peg or nail used to arrest a splinter.

tion. In some instances several of the nailed replacement lines have also broken, whereupon the initial solution is repeated, leaving a row of nailed-on seal skin stubs.

Repairs to deck lines seem more common among later kayaks, such as those from the mid to late 20th century onward. This was perplexing at first until I noticed that these same kayaks were usually painted. Essentially kayaks with painted skins would not need re-covering as often, so the *amiq* was liable to outlast the deck lines; removing and replacing the *amiq* gave easy access to replacing broken deck lines.

A kayak's *amiq* is susceptible to wear and puncture. While the seal skins used to cover a kayak have considerable strength, they often must endure scuffs and bumps with ice, abrasion from storage and transportation, and a close working proximity to sharp hunting implements. Historian Finn Gad writes that holes in kayaks could be quickly plugged with pieces of blubber that were always carried for that purpose (1971:269). Holes from abrasion along the keel and chines cannot be plugged, due to the kayak's structure being in the way; in many Greenland kayaks such areas of high-wear are protected with thin strips of bone or ivory, as in figures 129 and 130.

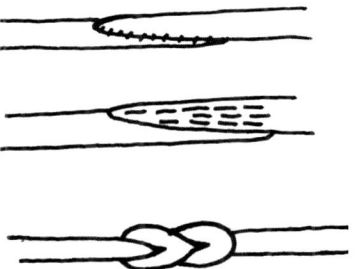

Figure 172: Splices/repairs to broken deck lines. Top two examples are sewn; the lower is threaded through slits cut in the line.

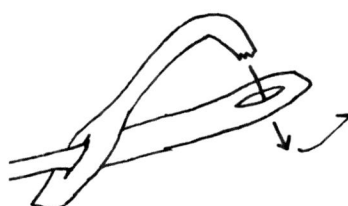

Figure 173: Detail of how the splice in figure 172 (bottom) is made.

Types of Greenland Kayaks

*"Until the comparative morphology of the kayak genus
be studied intensively, we cannot be certain how many
genuinely distinct types should be recognized."*
~ James Hornell, 1946:165

*"What should the typological criteria be? How long must the
kayak have been in use? And along how great a stretch
of coast must it have been built? Which year or
period should be the demarcation line?"*
~ H. C. Petersen, 1986:48

Hornell's 1946 statement is no less true today, and Petersen's questions, while not in response specifically to Hornell, hints at the difficulties of creating a typology of kayaks. Despite the difficulties involved, scholars have been presenting increasingly detailed comparative morphologies (or typologies) for at least the last 100 years.

Explorers have been noting the different types of kayaks around the Arctic coasts for centuries, but in the late 1800s ethnologists and anthropologists described these variations in detail and began to relate them to their cultural context as well as to analyze their development and origins. Their research comes from having traveled in Greenland and having seen a variety of kayaks first-hand as well as through building upon previous writings about kayaks.

Anthropologist Morten Porsild provides a brief and limited typology of Greenland kayaks consisting of six kayak-types named for their respective regions (1915:121-122). Porsild's typology lacks a visual reference (i.e., comparative illustrations, etc.), and some of the types receive no description at all. Porsild does however recognize that there is much more to kayak differences than is liable to meet the outsider's eyes:

> *On a trip last year [to Upernavik]...[a kayak].... struck me as extraordinary from the fact that the stern almost formed a right angle with the deck, but my companion, a hunter and kayak builder from Disco Bay, told me that there were many other and far more decisive differences in the construction of the frame-work than the one mentioned above (1915:121).*

In the *Ethnography of Egedesminde District* (1924), Danish ethnologist Kaj Birket-Smith offers one of the more complete and effective typologies of Greenlandic kayaks (268-271). It encompasses kayaks from all inhabited coasts of Greenland and is thorough in description and attribution to geographic areas, although it lacks drawings or photographs. Birket-Smith's summary list of his typology is quoted in full below: (While Danish place/vicinity names are used, the Greenlandic place-names, concurrent with modern practice, have been added in brackets.)

By their appearances we may thus comprise the kayaks on the west coast of Greenland under the following types, with which are further associated the types from Angmagssalik, Frederik VI's Kyst and the Thule District:

1. *Julianehaab— Frederikshaab [Qaqortoq— Paamiut]. Hardly any sheer. Long Stems. Almost only light skin. Flat seams. — Introduced by the immigrated Eskimos from Frederik VI's Kyst: similar type, though with a nearly flat bottom and vertical sides.*

2. *Godthaab [Nuuk]. Distinct sheer. Shorter stems. Dark skin with flat seams.*

3. *Sukkertoppen— Holsteinborg [Maniitsoq— Sisimiut]. Sheer. Very short stems, the stern formerly curving upwards, as is still done in Kengâmiut [Kangaamiut]. Dark Skins. Flat seams.*

4. *Egedesminde— Disko Bay [Aasiaat— Ilulissat vicinity]. Sheer; in out-of-the-way places still the shape of a tall, sharply built stem with a deck inclining strongly backwards. Long stem, shorter stern which until a short time ago was curved upwards. Dark skin. Raised seams.*

5. *Ûmánaq— Søndre Upernavik [Upernavik Kujalleq]. Like the preceding type, but with a somewhat shorter stem and stern. The latter still curved upwards.*

6. *Upernavik District, north of Søndre Upernavik. No sheer. Short stem and quite a short stern, the former slightly, the latter very strongly curved. Dark skin. Raised seams. The two straps immediately in front of the manhole as a rule oblique.*

*Within these principal types there are **sub-types**, according to local conditions. Thus the kayaks from the inner dwelling places of the Godthaab Fjord [Nuuk vicinity] are longer and narrower than the kayaks at the outer coast. The flat stern, however, is gradually spreading from the south. At Angmagssalik [Ammassalik] it also has penetrated everywhere in the years after the stay of Holm 1883–'84. Thus there can be no doubt that it originally belongs on the southern West Coast (1924:270-71).*

Birket-Smith briefly alludes above to the forms of Thule (Polar Greenland) and "Angmagssalik" (Ammassalik vicinity, East Greenland) kayak types, both very distinct forms, although the former has assimilated with the West Greenland types in later years, while the latter has remained distinct. The kayaks of King Frederik VI's Coast remain a bit of a mystery as to their precise form and construct; detailed descriptions are lacking, and I've not come across any full-size kayaks known to be from this region (extreme South-East Greenland). A map showing the general vicinities cited by Birket-Smith is presented in figure 174.

It is important not to overlook Birket-Smith's brief reference to "sub-types." His example of kayaks of varying proportions along a single fjord is significant because it shows a fine-tuning of form within types based on local conditions. Birket-Smith also records some changes and evolutions as related to him by Greenlandic hunters, as well as the rather sudden shape transformation with East Greenland kayaks. Several examples of sub-types will be pointed out throughout the presentation of kayaks.

As complete and exacting as Birket-Smith's Greenland kayak typology seems, it cannot be relied upon too heavily when applied to kayaks before circa 1900, or post circa 1950. Gert Nooter, in his *Old Kayaks of the Netherlands* (1971), applies Birket-Smith's typology in identifying places of origin for some

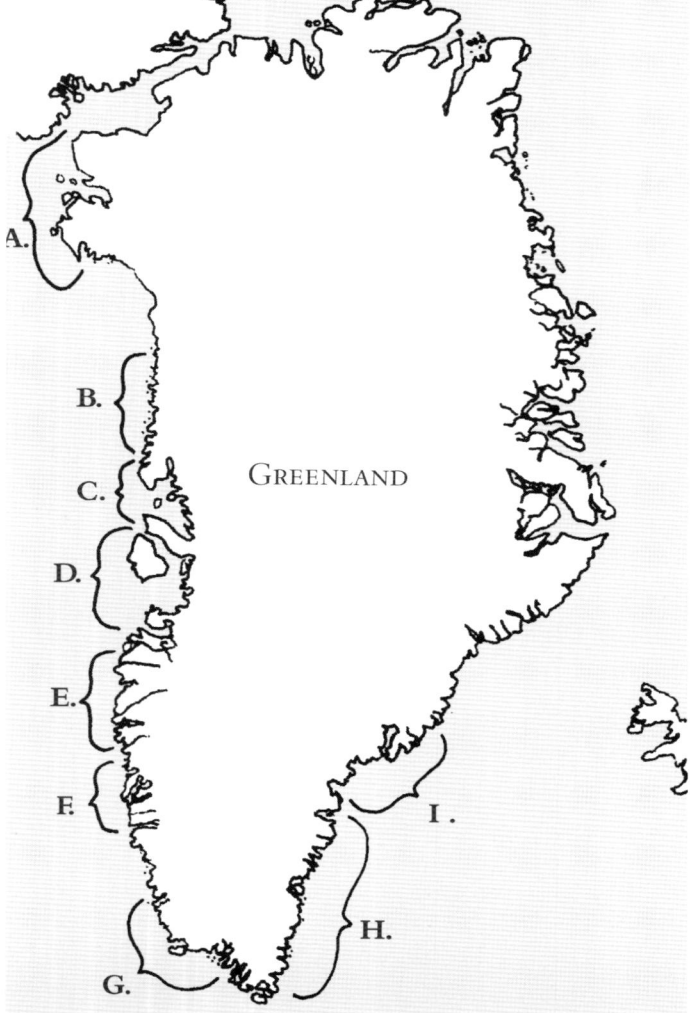

Figure 174: Regions mentioned by Birket-Smith in summarizing his typology of Greenlandic kayaks. Current place names are added in parenthesis.

A Thule District (or Polar Greenland)

B Upernavik District, north of Søndre Upernavik (Upernavik Kujalleq)

C Ûmánaq (Uummannaq) to Søndre Upernavik (Upernavik Kujalleq)

D Egedesminde (Aasiaat) to Disko Bay

E Sukkertoppen (Maniitsoq) to Holsteinsborg (Sisimiut)

F Godthaab (Nuuk)

G Julianehaab (Qaqortoq) to Frederikshaab (Paamiut)

H King Frederik VI's Coast

I Angmagssalik (Ammassalik)

of the more ancient intact Greenland kayaks. This application is inherently flawed because it ignores centuries of distinct changes and adaptations, not the least of which was the tremendous influence of rifle-use in kayak hunting in the mid-1800s.

H. C. Petersen, writing in the 1980s, discusses and presents a typology of Greenland kayaks in his landmark *Skinboats of Greenland*. Significantly, he discusses the difficulties in this undertaking:

> *There are many problems inherent in trying to categorise Greenland kayaks. The kayak has undergone considerable alteration in the past 100 years. East Greenlanders have adopted the Kap Farvel type in place of their own traditional type. The avisissartoq[25] type disappeared and another type or types appeared. These and a score of other reasons have made it difficult to group kayaks in Greenland (1986:48).*

---

[25] *Avasissartoq* is defined in a passage by Petersen cited on page 204 of the present text.

108

To overcome these issues, Petersen presents the variety of Greenland kayak types using different criteria for the selection and attribution. They fall into four main types. The comments in brackets are mine:

1. **Present kayak types** [based on sheer form primarily]:
   - The flat type
   - The curved type
   - *Avasisaartoq* type
   - The North Greenland type

2. **Specialised kayak types** [based on purpose of use/function]:
   - The portable kayak
   - The storm kayak
   - The cult kayak

3. **Local kayak types** [based on region]:
   - Ikerassarsuk kayak
   - Ammassalik kayak
   - Thule kayak

4. **Old Greenland kayaks**
   (1986:48-60).

This breakdown provides an effective typology, although there are overlaps, for example: The flat type also encompasses the Ammassalik type. Several of the types noted by Petersen (e.g., the storm and cult kayaks) apparently do not exist in museums, either full-size, or in model form, and therefore are not included in my proposed typology below.[26]

Although it is tucked away at the end of his chapter "Change and Development," H.C. Petersen succinctly divides all Greenland kayaks into four simple categories. These four categories are all encompassing and without overlap. They are:

1. Kayaks of the latest migration period— different types

2. A Greenland kayak from 1600-1700 adapted to the Greenland environment. It was developed during a period of growing cold and its use in the winter was very restricted. The main type was very long, narrow and shallow.

3. *Avasisaartoq* type with exaggerated sheer, developed in the 18th and 19th century.

4. 20th century type of kayak with distinctive local adaptations. (1986:63)

Petersen's first category here is the kayaks of Polar Greenland— those of Inuhuit from Northwest Greenland above Melville Bay. The second category is much more general, and by acknowledging a "main type" Petersen recognizes further variations of form. The third type is self-explanatory, and one will see that these forms represent a considerable number of kayaks in the present study. Petersen's fourth category is very important— specifically the "distinctive local adaptations," for these adaptations have resulted in a very large and diverse spectrum of kayak form and construction in Greenland during the 20th century. Petersen's four categories serve extremely well as the genus for my typology's species.

---

[26] The omission of these types from my typology is not to question their existence or Petersen's accuracy. My typology is based primarily on the collected material culture that I have studied that is also supported by historical texts.

I am seeking to replace Kaj Birket-Smith's typology with a model that is not so temporally or geographically constrained. Birket-Smith's is essentially a snapshot of the Greenland kayak 'situation' in the early 20th century— a useful and accurate one though. (Furthermore, two distinct forms of Greenland kayaks have made appearances since the publication of Birket-Smith's typology.) I also hope to build upon both the types and categories outlined by Petersen, specifically by omitting certain overlaps in his types and by adding more criteria and divisions to his categories.

The key bases of the new typology I am presenting are details of form, construction, deck line arrangements and fittings (when known). These elements can be very consistent among a particular kayak type, though they can also be variable or transitory as a type persists through time. Because of this, some of the kayaks in this study, being transitional, extreme, mixed, or anomalous, will fall between or even straddle types. Geographical and temporal origins also play a crucial factor in my typology, although the specific origins of many kayaks in this study have not always been recorded.

I have divided the Greenland kayaks in this study into thirteen distinct types. Salient features of each type are illustrated below their descriptions. This is a summarized presentation of the typology; the types are explained in greater detail in their respective introductions later in this study. Due to the fact that this new typology encompasses varying periods and regions, it mostly defies the naming of individual types: As a result I have chosen to use roman numerals to distinguish them. In certain instances kayak types could well be given a name in lieu of a number, but in the interest of consistency, I will use only numbers.

Greenland Kayak Types:

I. Circa 17th and 18th centuries, and likely earlier; West Greenland. Little sheer, often multi-chined in cross-section due to the gunwales' lower edges protruding into the *amiq*. The bows are moderately long, and the keel-to-stern transition is gradual. Cockpit slightly aft of center; maximum breadth adjacent cockpit. Baleen lashings, oval cockpits, simple deck lines and fittings. Bottom structure usually lashed.

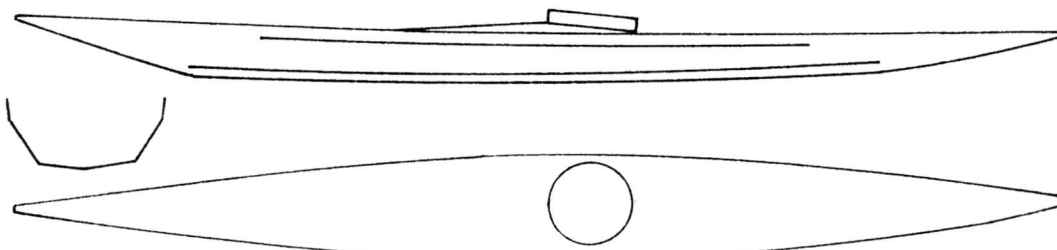

II. Circa 17th and early 18th centuries, and likely earlier; West Greenland. Reverse sheer amidships, very short and low bow, and gradual stern transition. Cockpit at or slightly aft of center; maximum breadth adjacent cockpit. The cross-sections of many of these kayaks changes from a boxy flat-bottom shape forward to a V-bottomed dish-shape aft. Baleen lashings, oval cockpit, simple deck lines and fittings. Bottom structure usually lashed.

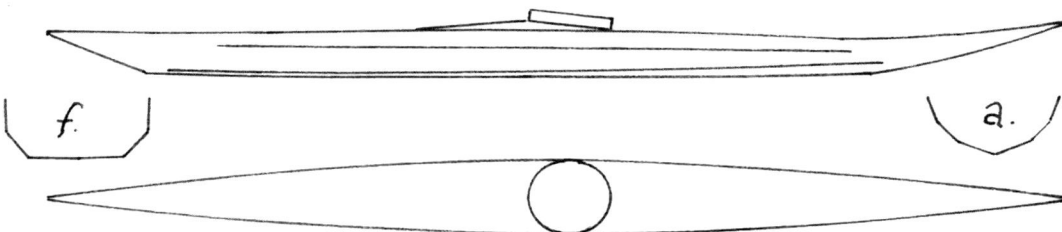

III. Circa 17th century into 1800s; West Greenland. Moderate/low or reverse sheer amidships with distinctly high and fine ends, boxy cross-section though occasionally with considerable deadrise. Ends of moderate length and rake. Cockpit at center; maximum breadth adjacent cockpit. Bottom structure usually lashed. There is often a distinct symmetry of ends when viewed from the side.

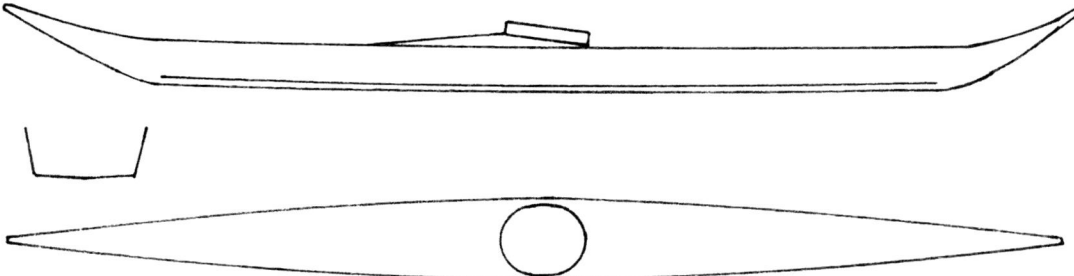

IV. Circa late 1700s into 20th century. Occurring along the whole of West Greenland at varying times. Moderate to high sheer, high stern, moderate bow, short but fuller ends than type III kayaks, moderate deadrise. Cockpit slightly aft of center; maximum breadth at or ahead of cockpit. Keel rocker highly variable. Bow stem convex or straight, only rarely concave; stern stem always convex. Bottom structure usually lashed. This type could well be called "*avasisaartoq*," as-per H. C. Petersen's definition and description (see page 204).

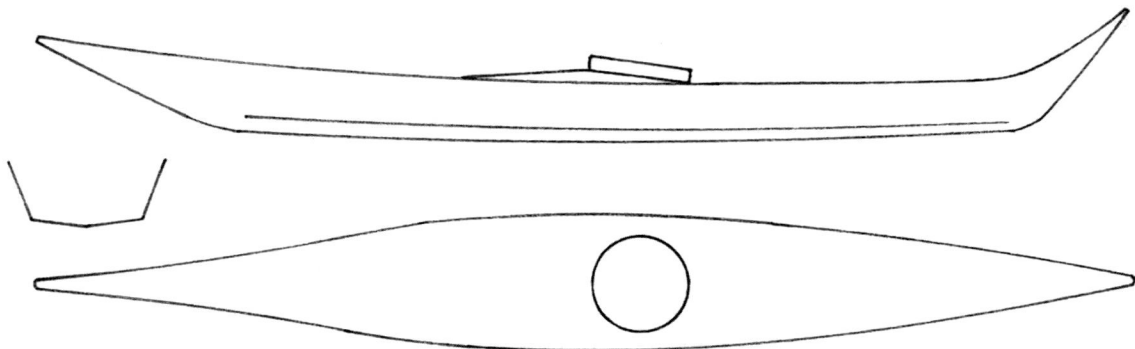

V. Circa late 1800s through present; Central West Greenland. Moderate sheer, moderately high and moderately short ends. Occasional sinuous keel line. The bow stem is usually straight or slightly concave, stern stem usually concave. Cockpit aft of center; maximum breadth ahead of cockpit. Fairly deep amidships. Bottom structure usually lashed. Some of the type V kayaks in this study are likely what H. C. Petersen calls "curved-types," or *pequngasoq*; his description is cited at length on page 276-277.

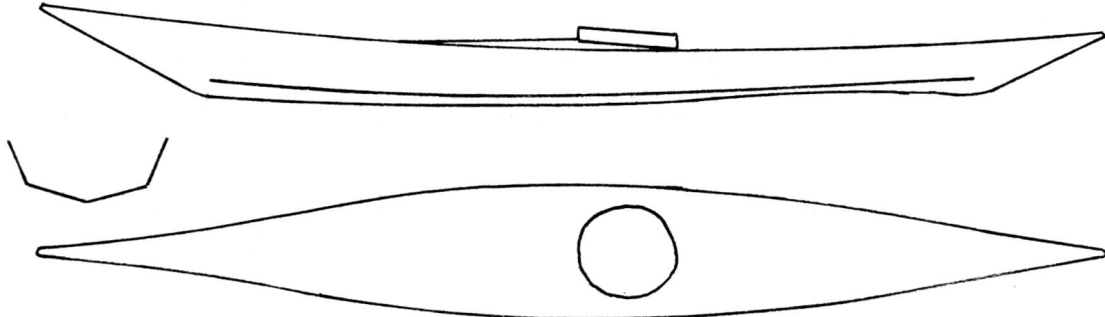

VI. Circa late 19th through 20th century; generally from Northwest Greenland (Disko Bay and North). Later type VI kayaks— particularly those with more southern origin— increasingly resemble type V kayaks. Low sheer, short moderately high bow, with even shorter stern of varying height—usually low (Note the variation of stern shapes). Gradual keelson-to-stem transition. Both stems usually convex. Usually little or no gunwale flare, thus the gunwale's lower edge adds a chine edge. The chine stringer usually terminates rather high forward. Type VI kayak's cockpits are often distinctly aft-of-center, with their maximum breadths being ahead of the cockpit. The cross-sections are highly variable; typically they are multi-chined and flat-bottomed, with later and/or more southerly examples having sections that approximate those from type V kayaks, i.e., V-bottomed.

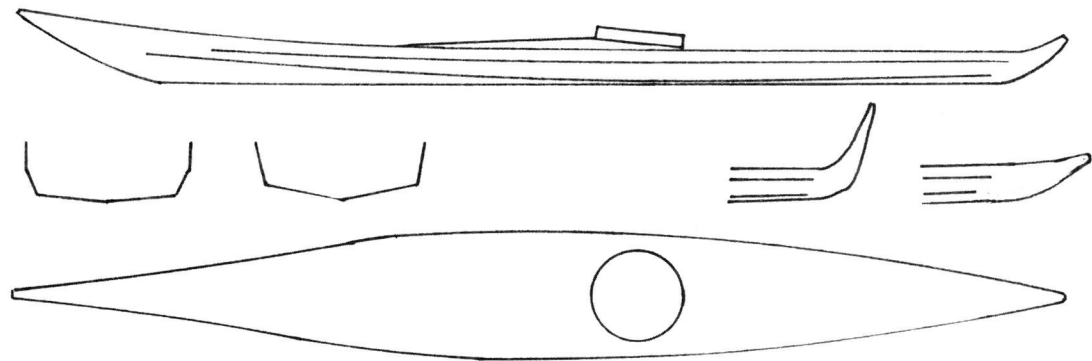

VII. Circa 1850s through 20th century; South Greenland early, spreading northward on the west coast in 20th century. Very long ends— often clipper cut, distinct sheer and rocker with considerable deadrise. The bow and stern profiles are often very identical to each other; they are also nearly identical in plan-view, both being pinched or concave. Cockpit at center or slightly aft; maximum breadth slightly ahead of cockpit. Bottom structure usually pegged or nailed.

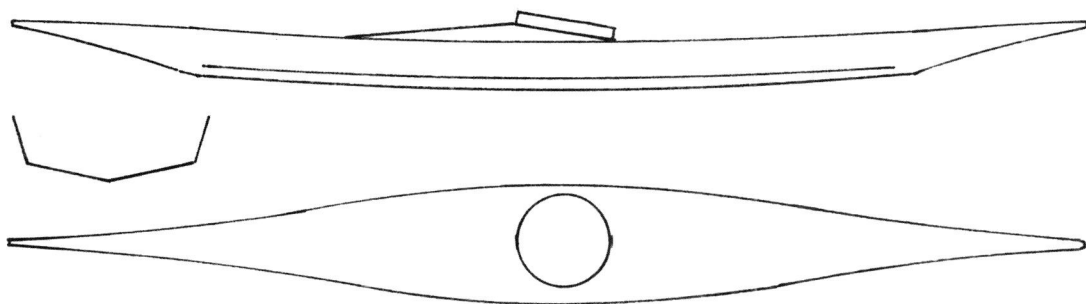

VIII. Pre 1884, becoming wholly extinct shortly thereafter; East Greenland. Short and flat bow, with high, fine stern, boxy cross-section. Slight reverse sheer, and considerable rocker. Convex stems. Cockpit slightly aft of center; maximum breadth ahead of cockpit.

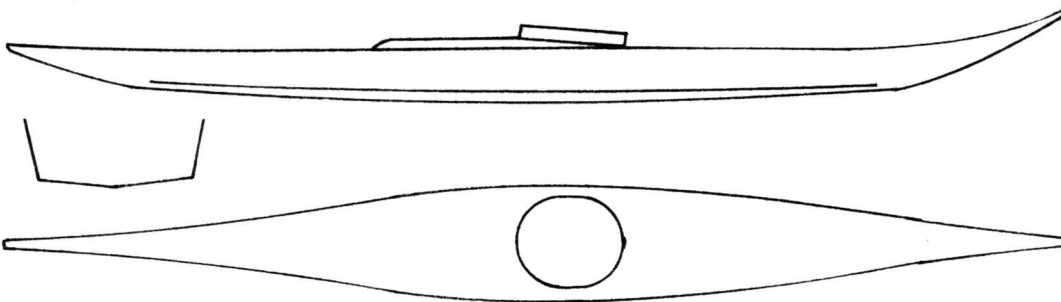

IX. Post circa 1884 through 20th century; East Greenland. Low sheer— nearing flat, very long ends. Minimal deadrise, highly flared sides. The chine breadth is quite narrow, and the hull is shallow. The construction is fairly distinct. Bottom structure always pegged or nailed. Concave stems in both elevation and plan. Cockpit slightly aft of center; maximum breadth ahead of cockpit.

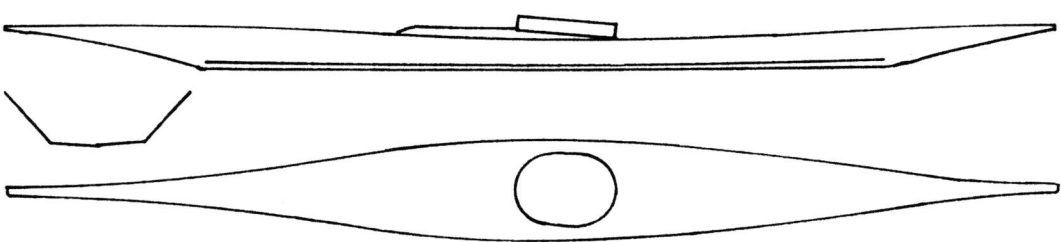

X. Circa 1990s to present; West Greenland. Shorter lengths (< 15′) and extremely shallow depths. Usually very low short ends. These are built to train kayakers for rolling and also to be used in kayak rolling competitions; they are especially designed to make rolling easier.

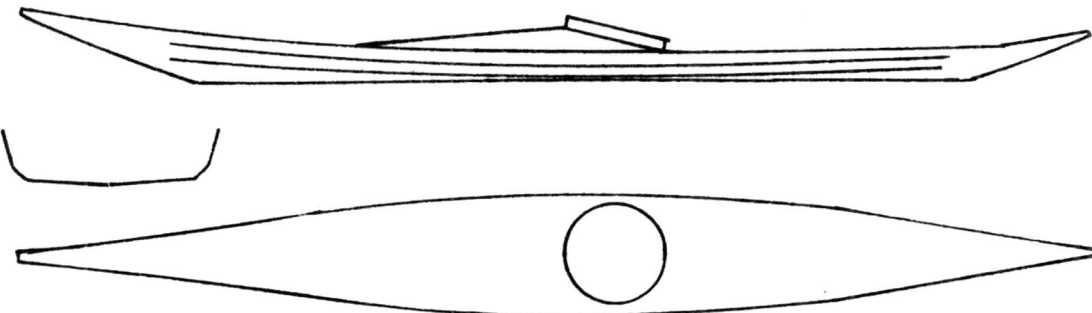

— And including the kayaks of Polar Greenland (three types):

XI. Pre circa 1890s to circa 1910s; Polar Greenland. Short, deep bow. Flat bottom, shallow aft-hull, and an indefinite stem transition astern. Distinct Swede-form, with the maximum breadth occasionally being behind the cockpit. Cockpit itself usually well behind the kayak's mid-point. Distinct pieced construction including coaming.

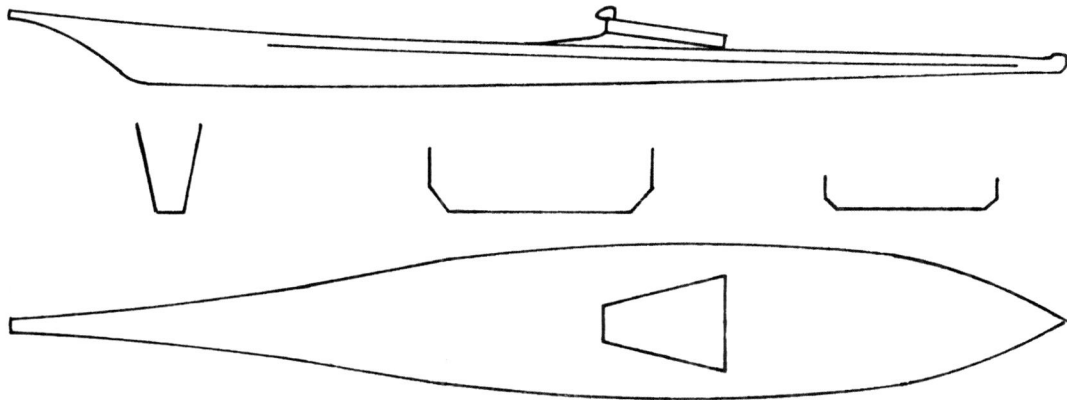

XII. Circa 1910s— mid 20th century; Polar Greenland. Longer bow, more distinct stern form, and more constant depth along hull. The bow and stern both curve up above the flat sheer-line. Slight rocker, less distinct Swede-form. Cockpit behind center. Distinct pieced construction. (This kayak type could be called a transitional Polar Greenland kayak, having been influenced by West Greenland kayaks.)

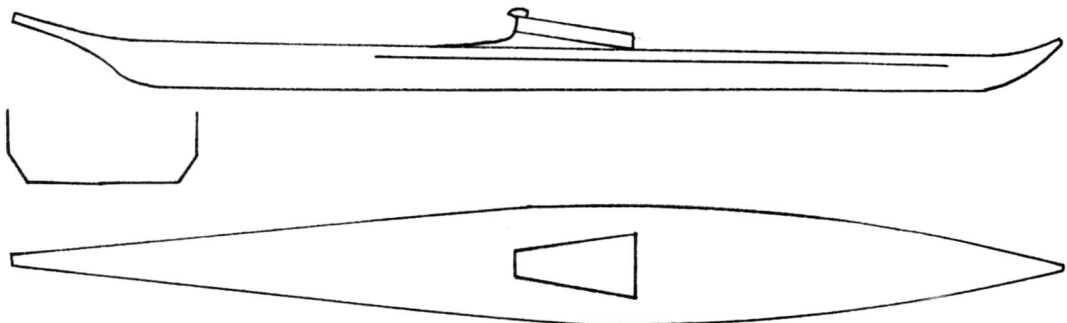

XIII. Circa mid 20th century to the present; Polar Greenland. Appearing very much like certain type VI kayaks, specifically those with low sterns. Only one such kayak is present in this study— one surveyed by Eugene Arima (plate 102). While I presume it to be somewhat representative of the type based on comparisons with photographs of other modern Polar Greenland kayaks, such assumptions are potentially flawed when based on just a single example.

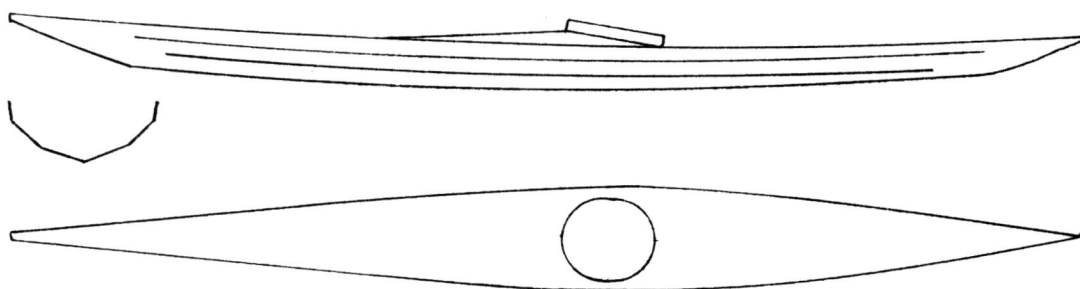

Co-existence of forms within the same vicinities has of course occurred and is mentioned in Petersen (1986:81) as well as in Thalbitzer (1912:384) and Birket-Smith (1924:269). This co-existence is often transitory, as one form supplants others (see figure 175). It is likely that forms evolved both subtly and gradually, and yet also suddenly on account of new tools and materials or even by emulating a design used by a particularly successful hunter.

What follows is the presentation of 102 Greenland kayaks in description and scale illustration — each grouped into the thirteen types described above. Two additional Greenland kayaks are presented as well; these examples transcend my typological basis in that they are 'melting-pot' kayaks of a sort, as will be demonstrated.

Figure 175: Co-existence of varying kayak forms, Nuussuaq vicinity, Northern Upernavik district, 1936. Both are type VI kayaks despite the phasing out of the form in the foreground in favor of the flatter-sterned kayak behind it. (Photographer: Jette Bang/ Arktisk Institut gjb01166.)

One Hundred and Four Greenland Kayaks

This section presents the thirteen types of Greenland kayaks as proposed in the typology. (Within each type, the kayaks are presented chronologically where possible.)

TYPE I.

Simple lines define this type of Greenland kayak: a gentle sheer, little rocker, a moderately long bow and a subtle keel-to-stern transition. The deck line's arrangements are quite simple, having few deck lines and scarcely more than one fitting per kayak. Occasionally a pair of deck lines on a type I kayak will be crossed.

Typically, type I kayaks are lashed with baleen and often have clamp ties in several places along the gunwales— not just at their ends. Deck beam tenons seem to be as a rule shallow. Several examples have the *amiq* secured up and over the aft edge of the coaming.

Type I kayaks are usually very long— on average, this type is longer than any other type in this study, their average being 18′9-7/8″ (573.7cm) long; the shortest is 17′5-3/4″ (532.7cm) (see appendix A). Generally, type I kayaks are moderately deep, and have (in proportion to the beam at the sheer) narrow chine breadths. The breadths of the type I kayaks in this study range widely from 21-3/16″ (53.8cm) to 15-5/8″ (39.7cm) wide, but average 17-7/8″ (45.5cm) wide.

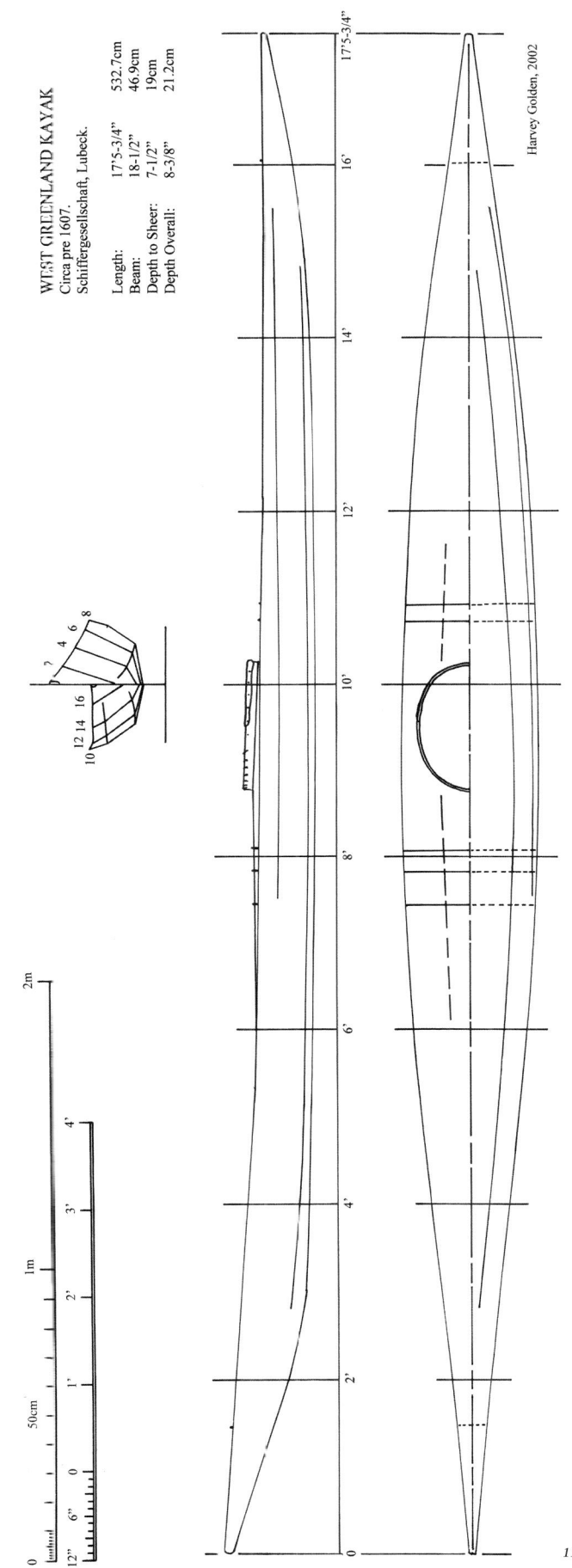

1. Schiffergesellschaft, Lübeck (N/N)

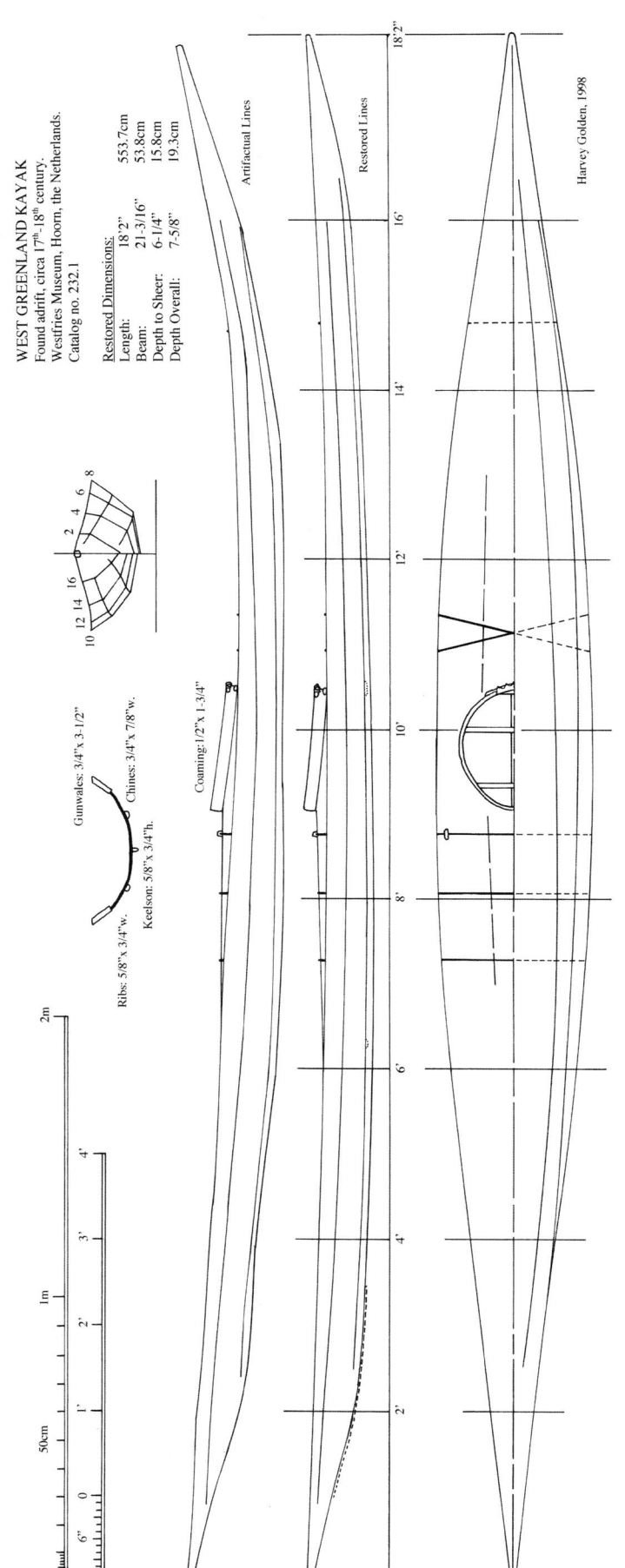

2. Westfries Museum catalog no. 232

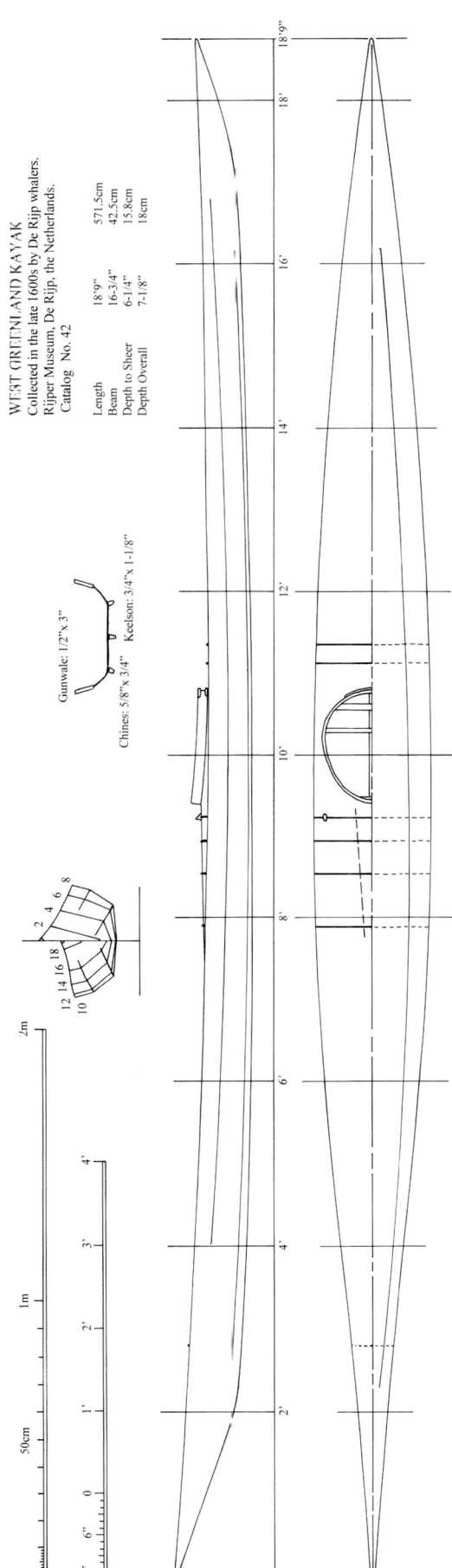

3. Rijper Museum catalog no. 42

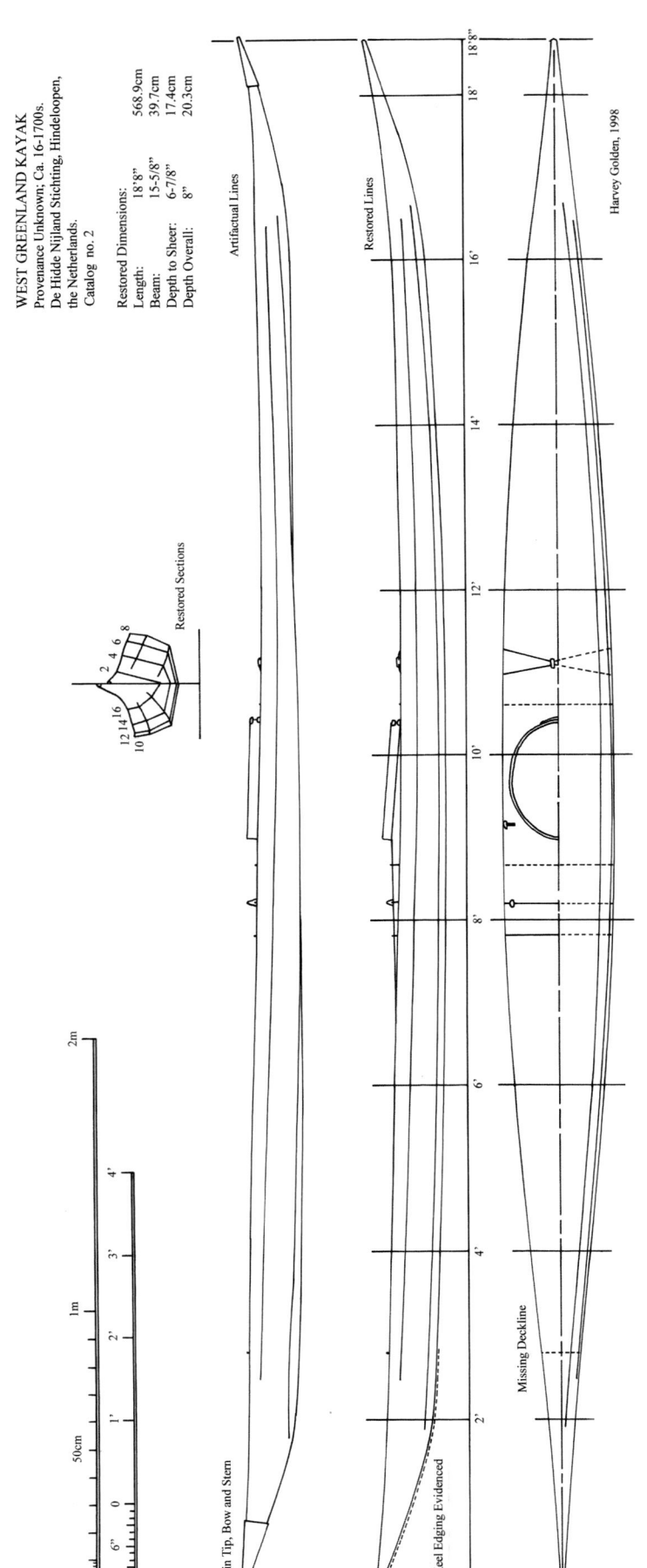

4. De Hidde Nijland Stichting catalog no. 2

5a. Danish National Museum catalog no. Lb.101

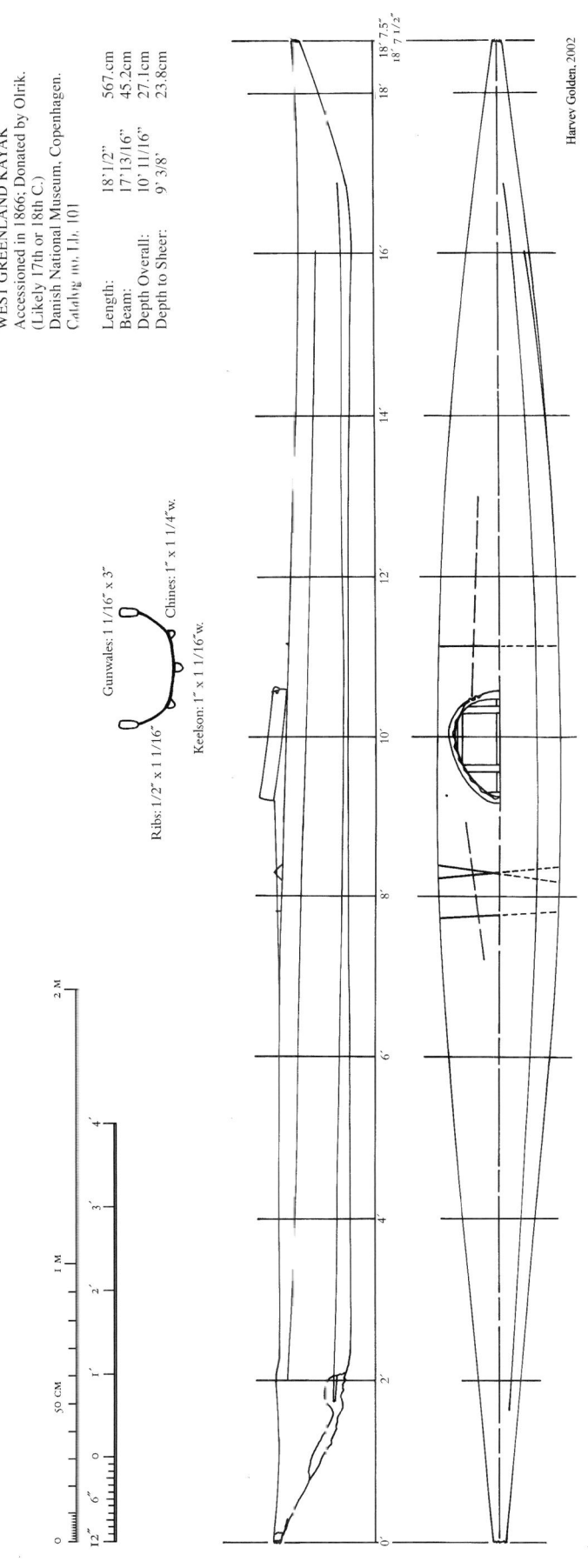

WEST GREENLAND KAYAK
Accessioned in 1866; Donated by Olrik.
(Likely 17th or 18th C.)
Danish National Museum, Copenhagen.
Catalog no. Lb. 101

Length:	18' 1/2"	567.cm
Beam:	17' 13/16"	45.2cm
Depth Overall:	10' 11/16"	27.1cm
Depth to Sheer:	9' 3/8"	23.8cm

Gunwales: 1 1/16" x 3"
Chines: 1" x 1 1/4" w.
Ribs: 1/2" x 1 1/16"
Keelson: 1" x 1 11/16" w.

Harvey Golden, 2002

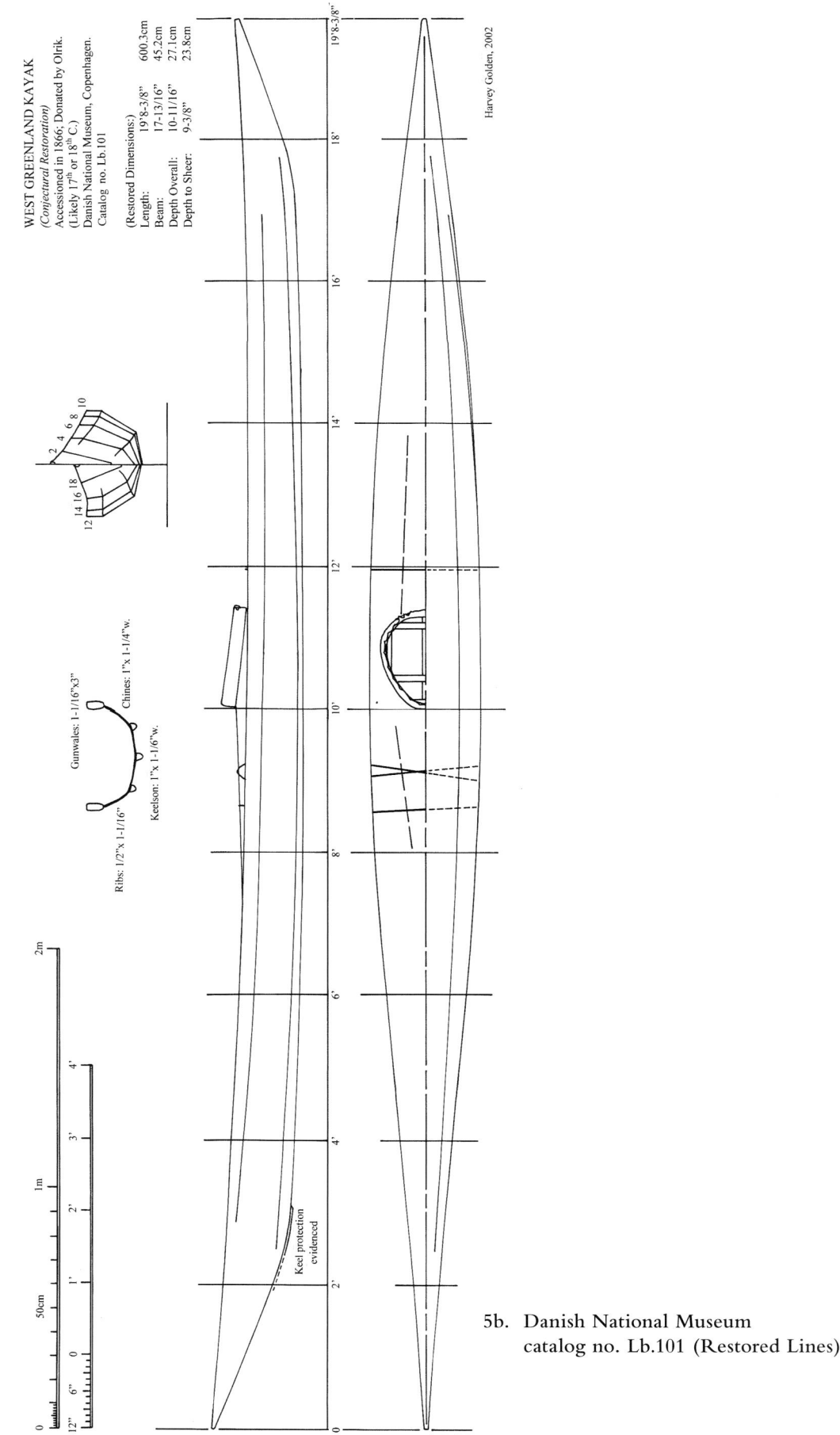

5b. Danish National Museum catalog no. Lb.101 (Restored Lines)

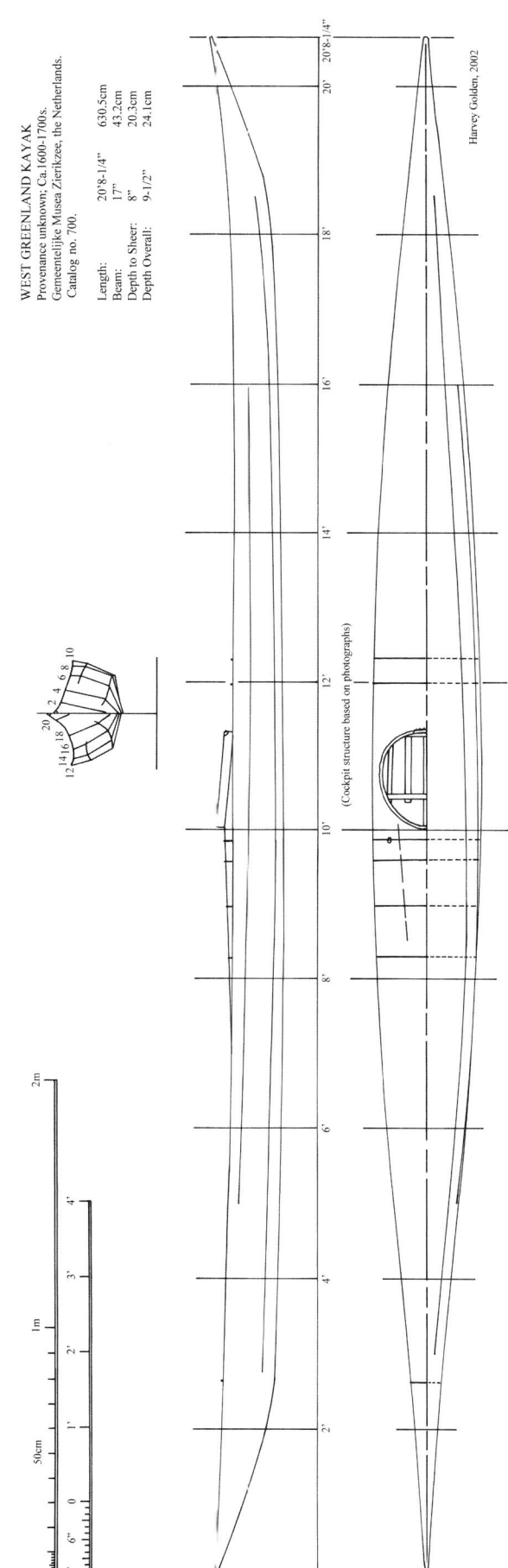

6. Gemeentelijke Musea Zierikzee catalog no. 700)

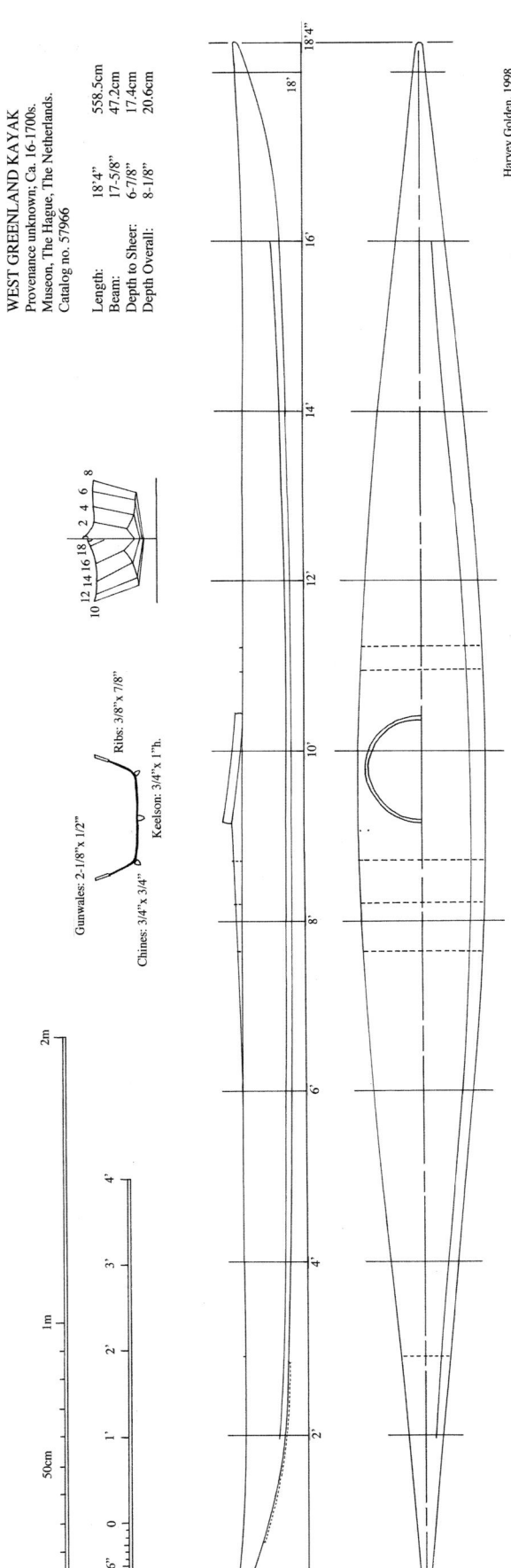

7. Museon catalog no. 57966

1. West Greenland Kayak of ca. 1607: Schiffergesellschaft, Lübeck, Germany. (N/N).

"1607" is twice painted on the hull of the Lübeck Schiffergesellschaft (Barge Master's Guild Hall) kayak. The names of numerous guild members over the years as well as four dates of conservation (1668, 1821, 1911, and 1979) are also painted on the kayak. A poem further graces the kayak's hull: "The yacht from Greenland is my name, from there to the skippers company I came. I wish no longer to go to sea, would God save all good seafairing people like me" (as translated from the German original in Steffan-Schrade, 1997:14).

Werner Neugebauer cites a passage from *Lübische Geschichten und Sagen* (edited by Ernst Deecke, 1890: entry no.214):

Figure 176: Mannequin in the Lübeck kayak of ca. 1606. The paddle is a naïve European-made accessory.

In 1607, the Lübeck barge masters brought with them from the North Sea a Greenland vessel, which had perhaps been carried away by a storm, and a man was sitting in it who died shortly after. So it was kept in the building of the Barge Masters Guild... (in Neugebauer, et al., 1982:2).

Neugebauer writes in his 1982 text's postscript: "Only after the paper went to press did it become known that, in the *Danske Bibliografisk Leksikon XVI* (pp. 384f), H. Ostermann refers to the Lübeck kayak as loot taken by the Danish seafarer Godske Lindenov[27] during his 1606 Greenland expedition" (1982:39). (As it is, there is a possibility that Lindenov collected this kayak the year before [Gosch, 1897:xc-xcii]).

James Hall, an English pilot with the Lindenov expedition of 1606, writes of some Greenlanders visiting the ship *Trost*: " . . . after Dinner, some of the people came vnto vs, of whom we caught fiue, with their Boates, and stowed them in our ships, to bring them into Denmarke, to enforme our selues better, by their meenes, of the state of their Countrie of *Groineland* . . ." (in Gosch, 1897:70,71). In a footnote, Gosch adds that the kayak in the Schiffergesellschaft is "probably one of those here alluded to"(1897:71, footnote 5).

The 1606 kidnapping of Greenlanders and the stealing of their kayaks occurred at Ikertok (Foss Bay) on August 6th (Gosch, 1897:xc). It is certain that the Greenlanders were not willing travelers, a sixth having jumped overboard at sea (de La Peyrère, [1647] 1855:221-222). Ikertok, or Ikertoq as it is presently spelled, is a fjord 20km southeast of Sisimiut.

Lindenov's having 'collected' the kayak in 1606 at Ikertoq does not necessarily preclude its having been found adrift in the North Sea by Lübeck barge masters in 1607. Scholar Isaac De La Peyrére writes of several attempts made by the Greenlanders to escape Denmark:

[The kidnapped Greenlanders] often looked towards the north, and sighed with so much regret after their own country that their guards, being lenient, those who could seized their little boats and oars and put to sea to try the passage. But a storm which surprised them at ten or twelve leagues from the Sound, cast them on the coasts of Schonen [Skåne, Sweden], where the country people took them and sent them back again to Copenhagen. ...Two of those who had put out to sea and whom the storm had cast on Schonen, and who were less suspected than the others, because it seemed unlikely that they would expose themselves a second time to the perils they had encountered, seized their boats and succeeded in regaining the north. They were pursued and overtaken near the mouth of the sea, but only one was taken, the other escaped, or, rather was lost; for it does not seem probable that he ever could have arrived in Greenland ([1647] 1855:223,225).

---

[27]This name appears in some texts as "Gotske Lindenow."

It is entirely possible that Lübeck masters could have found the lost kayak in the North Sea, and in fact several kayaks in the present study also are alleged to have been found in European waters, in one case (the Westfries Museum's kayak [plate 2]), with a body inside. The Lindenov expeditions are but two definite instances of Greenlanders being unwillingly brought to Europe with their kayaks— it is certain that many more were brought on other ships from other countries.

Lindenov's pilot James Hall, who had by 1612 sailed to Greenland three times, provides a vivid but somewhat naive description of Greenland kayaks and their use:

> ...*The other sorts of their Boats are such as Captaine* Frobisher *and Master* Iohn Dauis *brought into England, which is but for one man, being cleene couered over with Seale skins artificially dressed, except one place to sit in, being within set out with certaine little ribs of Timber, wherein they vse to row with one Oare more swiftly than our men can doe with ten; in which Boates they fish, being disguised in their Coates of Seale skinnes, whereby they deceiue the Seales, who take them rather for seales then men; which Seales or other fish they kill in this manner: — They shoot at the Seales or other great fish with their Darts vnto which they vse to tye a bladder, which doth boy vp the fish in such manner that, by the said means, they catch them (in Gosch: 1897:36-37)*[28].

A carved mannequin is sitting in the cockpit of the Lübeck kayak (figure 176). The figure is naively made, although an attempt to capture the essence of a hooded paddling jacket of seal skin (a *tuilik*) has been made. The paddle that the mannequin carries was obviously made by one not familiar with Greenland kayak paddles; the carver was likely simply told to 'make a paddle' and was then left to his own wits. An oversize cloth spray skirt is wrapped around the mannequin's waist, and is draped loosely around the cockpit.

The Lübeck kayak may be the oldest intact kayak in the world— 'intact' distinguishing it from archaeological remains. It has fairly good documentation, though one cannot rule out that other examples may be older, particularly those lacking documentation. A child's kayak in Munich is purported to date from the 1580s or 1590s (Sturtevant and Quinn, 1989:117-118, note 12).

For a kayak nearing 400 years of age at the time of this writing, it is in remarkable condition: It does exhibit age — not damage, per-se, but just slight deformation— mainly sag. The scale drawing of the Lübeck kayak depicts my conjectural restoration, being based on similar kayaks as well as artifactual evidence.

Although the Lübeck kayak's coaming has been described as being fashioned of wood (Steffan-Schrade, 1997:15), it is actually a light colored piece of baleen; it measures 3/8″ (9mm) thick by 1-3/8″(35mm) high. The coaming is laced on in front, using the over-the-top method, but at the back and rear quarters, the skin is pulled over the top of the coaming, and is secured to the coaming's upper face with bone or ivory pegs. This combination of pegs and lacings for securing the coaming (as in figure 123d) is not to be seen in any other kayaks in this study. (The scale drawing of this kayak depicts the *amiq* as having slipped off one of the pegs.) A second pass of pale thin leather strapping is wrapped around the entire coaming's face at the front; it is by appearances a later repair, and was likely done in Europe.

The amidships deck lines on the Lübeck kayak are present and intact. No harpoon holder is evidenced, and the three deck lines just ahead of the cockpit and the two just aft do not have any fittings on them. It cannot be ruled out that some deck lines may have broken and have since been re-attached— perhaps after the loss of a bone/ivory fitting.

There are slight divots in the sheer-line 18″ (45.7cm) behind the bow and 17-1/2″ (44.4cm) ahead of the stern that may suggest the one-time presence of deck lines, though holes were not noted in the skin

---

[28] A Greenlander in a kayak killed Hall on July 23, 1612 with one such dart; Hall was apparently trying to trade a piece of iron for the man's dart.

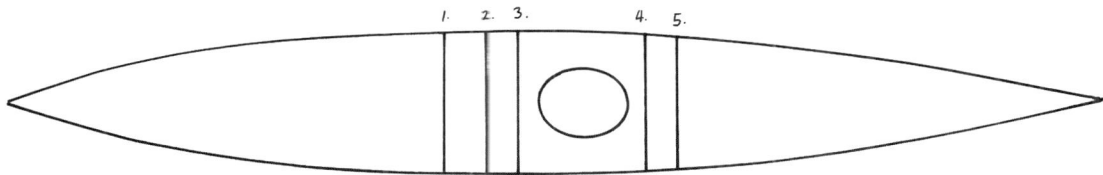

Shiffergesellschaft Zu Lübeck (n/n)

at these positions. The kayak has been painted and varnished, so there is a chance that any holes were filled. I would think that these were *not* deck line positions due to their considerable distance from the other lines. In any case, the positions of these divots are indicated on the scale drawing.

I built a replica of the Lübeck kayak in order to feel how such a craft would paddle in varying conditions. It is an agile craft— it turns very quickly on account of the deep bow and rather shallow and gradual stern. Because of this, however, the kayak is somewhat more prone to weather cocking than most West Greenland kayaks, so one has to stay one step ahead of it in a sense. Fortunately it corrects very easily, so it couldn't be considered a problem. The bow, elevated as it is, is very buoyant and maintains a fairly dry deck in all but especially rough seas or surf.

The Lübeck kayak is very comfortable— for me at least; I weigh 130 pounds and am 5′8″ tall. It has plenty of volume, such that it would maintain a reasonable freeboard with a kayaker as heavy as

Figure 177: The replica of the Lübeck kayak in 2005. (Photograph by Kathy Tucker.)

180 pounds or so. The narrow chine breadth allows it to heel easily and yet its overall beam lends a distinct firmness once the sheer nears the water— essentially what would be called 'good secondary stability.' I didn't need to make any adjustments to the coaming's size or the distance between the *masik* and *isserfik* in order to fit in this kayak.

Figure 178: Front quarter view of the Lübeck replica. The paddle being used is a replica of the Danish National Museum's Elc.9, depicted in paddle-plate 1. (Photograph by Kathy Tucker.)

2. West Greenland Kayak of ca. 1600s: Westfries Museum, Hoorn, the Netherlands. Catalog no. 232 ("Hoorn")

This kayak is alleged to have been found adrift with a body inside. It is not too clear when it was found, nor by whom. Dr. Gert Nooter describes this kayak at length in his book *Old Kayaks in the Netherlands*, 1971. Unfortunately, the earliest written source of information about this kayak is an entry in a museum catalog from 1890 (Nooter, 1971: 24). Nooter suggests that the Hoorn kayak is from the Sukkertoppen/Holsteinborg (Maniitsoq/Sisimiut) vicinity of West Greenland (1971:24). This is based on Birket-Smith's typology (1924:271), and should be held as suspect considering the 232's age and damaged state.

It is conceivable that this kayak may be one of those used by Greenlanders fleeing from Denmark, or perhaps fleeing from a ship bringing them from Greenland to Europe. Isaac De La Peyrère described several successful as well as failed escapes from Denmark in the early 1600s ([1647] 1855:221-227). Success is relative of course, for surely none made it even

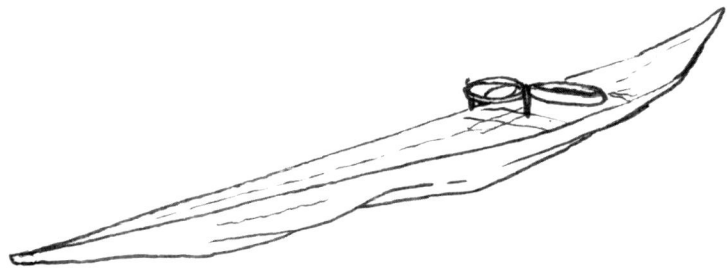

Figure 179: The Westfries Museum Kayak (232). A harpoon line stand (asaloq) is on the fore deck. The hull damage to this kayak is readily apparent.

close to Greenland, and they certainly met death on the seas or shores of northern Europe. Another possibility is that Dutch whalers or explorers in Greenland may have acquired it in Greenland during the 17th or 18th centuries.

For many years, there were human remains associated with this kayak, and they were at the museum when I visited in 1998. The remains are just a hollowed out shell of skin. It is really only obviously human by the ear on the right side of what could otherwise be mistaken as the hood of a seal skin tuilik (paddling jacket); the face is missing. It is a horrifying thing to see and hold, and the irony of it is plain to see: the kayaker preserved in much the same way as the seals he has covered his kayak with.

At the time of my visit, museum tradition was that the mummified remains were those of the Greenlander found in the kayak, but it was soon after that the remains were found to be of a European. The mystery was scientifically solved after Greenlanders tried to have the remains repatriated for a proper burial (Anonymous, 2001).

The average width of the nine full-size "old kayaks" in Nooter's book is 16-1/2" (42.1cm). The Hoorn kayak (WFM 232) is one of these nine kayaks, and is almost 4-3/4" (12.0cm) wider than this average, and almost 4" (10.1cm) wider than the next widest kayaks.[29] Such an anomaly suggests certain possibilities about the intended use and/or user of this kayak. The likelihood of the Hoorn kayak having been made for a larger person is nil: Its cockpit opening is quite small, even by Greenlandic standards, (15-3/4" long, by 14" wide [40.0x35.5cm]) and the kayak is very shallow: 6-1/4" (15.8cm) depth-to-sheer, with a depth overall of 7-5/8" (19.3cm).

The builder has paid great attention to ensuring that an unusually wide kayak would paddle very much like its narrower counterparts in certain rougher conditions. A proportionally wider kayak will inherently result in a larger volume, but the builder of the Hoorn kayak countered this result by

---

[29] The average width of the type I kayaks in this study—excluding the Hoorn kayak—is 44.1cm (17-3/8"); see appendix A.

decreasing the depth and making the sides greatly flared via a narrow chine breadth. Petersen describes the importance of properly balanced volume:

> *[A kayak] must have a certain volume so that it will not sink too quickly in the water. But it must not ride too high in the water, either. With too little air it would be difficult to rise above storm waves. Too much air makes it ride high in the water and increases the wind pressure and drift of the kayak. (1986:42).*

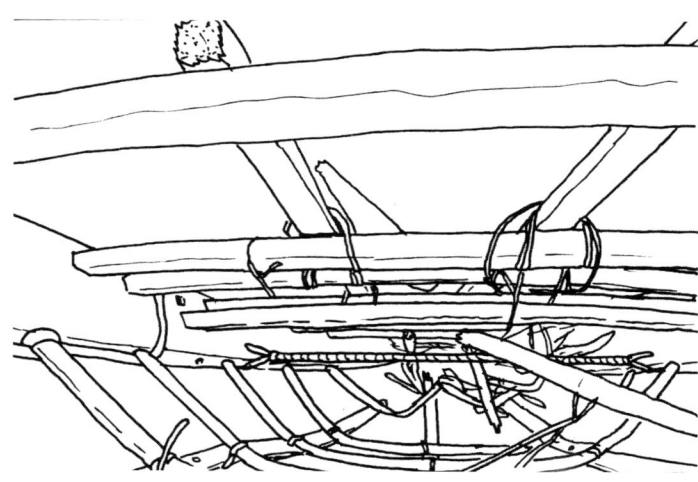

Figure 180: Forward interior of the WFM 232.

Form-wise, the WFM 232 compares favorably to the Lübeck kayak of circa 1606: both have long, low bows and sterns that are much less defined in their transition from the keelson, although also low. Despite their considerable difference in beam, their hull shapes are very similar, both having a narrow chine breadth with moderate deadrise.

The survey drawing of the WFM 232 depicts both artifactual and restored elevations. Over the centuries it has endured poor storage practices— likely being suspended by the ends, hence the exaggerated sheer. There are also several areas of hull-collapse, though the gunwales themselves have held their shape very well, at least in plan-view.

Two sketches made from photographs illustrate interior views of the "Hoorn" kayak. Figure 180 shows the forward interior: There is a fairly dense clustering of deck beams— one of them is loose and dangling by a lashing. Just forward of this is a clamping tie pulling the lower gunwale edges in. Note the lashings along the chines and the deck stringers; all of the lashings are baleen, as in the Lübeck kayak.

Looking at the aft interior view (figure 181), one can see how the deck stringers have slipped out of place. Another heavy clamping tie helps hold the flare in the gunwales. Cluttered debris and loose deck beams obscured the view further towards the stern.

Bone or ivory edging is evidenced along the keelson at the bow; a dashed line on the survey drawing shows where it had been. The only other evidence of bottom protection are two sets of holes along the left chine: The first two holes are at 6′4″ (193.0cm) and 6′4-7/8″ (195.2cm) from the bow, the third and fourth are at 10′6″ (320.0cm) and 10′8″ (325.1cm). The pieces were each situated over transverse seams (high-wear areas), but strangely they only appear along the left chine. A

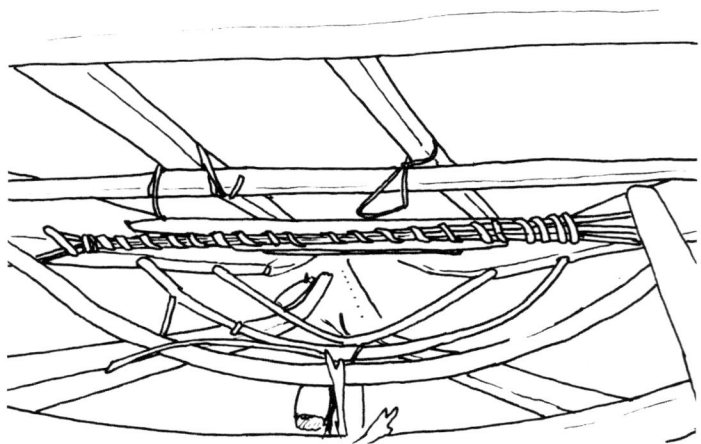

Figure 181: Aft interior view of the WFM 232.

deck line is missing but evidenced at 14′9″ (449.5cm) from the bow. There is no evidence of end-knobs, although part of the stern seems to be missing.

A harpoon line stand is associated with the kayak and is depicted in figures 182 and 183. The presence of a harpoon line stand suggests that whoever was 'found' in the kayak was intending to hunt sea-mammals. The stand is symmetrically constructed unlike later types that have one leg protruding diagonally from the center of the rack, and one descending vertically from the rim's edge. The rack is missing the transverse crosspieces that support the line, but their positions are indicated. A paddle is also associated with the Hoorn kayak, and is depicted in paddle-plate 4.

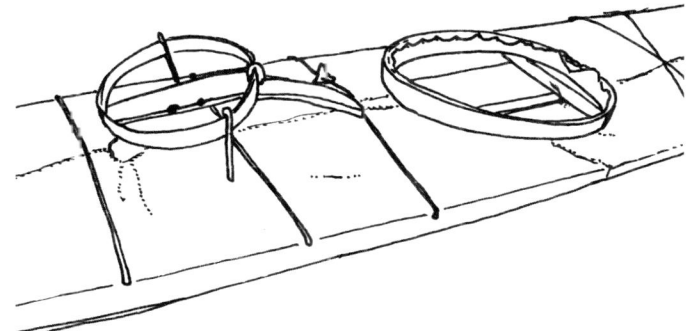

Figure 182: Close-up of the 232: harpoon-line stand (asaloq) at left.

The coaming of the 232 is attached to the *amiq* with bone or ivory pegs, and the *amiq* is pulled up and over the back edge of the coaming. Two ivory or bone bands cover the coaming's scarf at the back, the *amiq* being anchored to the upper one. The 232's coaming measures 1/2″ (13mm) thick by 1-3/4″ (44mm) high.

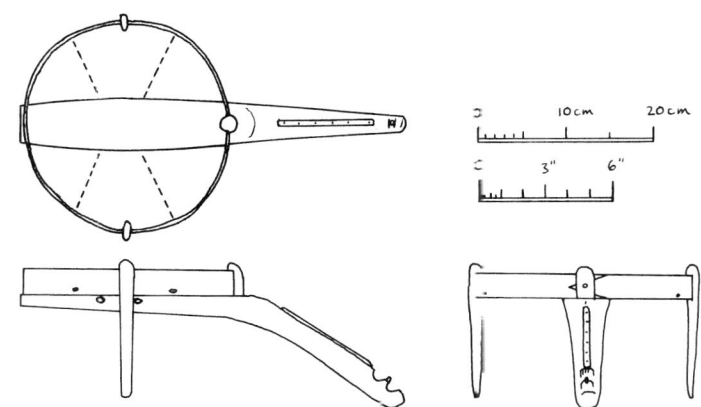

Figure 183: Scale drawing of the WFM 232's asaloq or harpoon line stand. The dashed lines indicate the positions of missing pieces, as evidenced by holes.

The Westfries Museum kayak lacks any evidence of having had a bow deck line. It does however exhibit evidence of having had a stern deck line at one time. Only one fitting is present (3a), and it is an implement holder attached to the deck line immediately in front of the cockpit. A *masik*-mounted harpoon holder is not present or evidenced. The deck lines behind the cockpit (4-5) cross each other, though are not linked or fastened together.

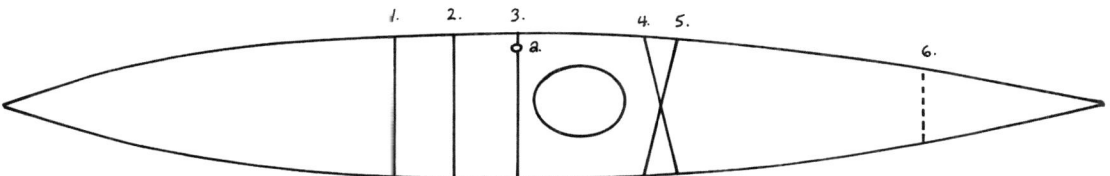

Westfries Museum, Hoorn: Cat. no. 232

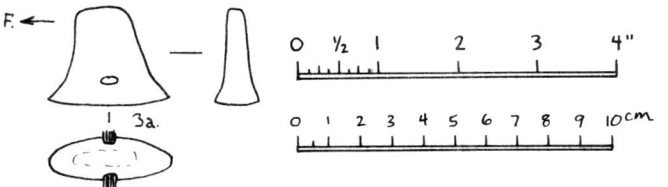

3. West Greenland Kayak from ca. 1600s: Rijper Museum, De Rijp, the Netherlands. Catalog no. 42. ("De Rijp")

While the town of De Rijp is now in the middle of sprawling farmlands, in the 1600s it was a seaport that was active in the Greenland whale fisheries. At the Rijper Museum, I was told that their kayak is the oldest in Holland, and the accession file for the kayak lists its period as being "1500-1600."

This is another kayak featured in Gert Nooter's *Old Kayaks in the Netherlands*; Nooter writes "Until a few years ago a card on the kayak in de Rijp stated that the boat had been brought home in 1675 on a ship from de Rijp . . ." (1971:6). Apparently this is not to be held as entirely conclusive, as Nooter writes that the earliest reliable report regarding the kayak dates from 1845 (1971:6). The suggestion by the present file that it may well pre-date 1600 is doubtful; the year 1675 is plausible given the occasional Dutch visit to the Davis Straits at that time.

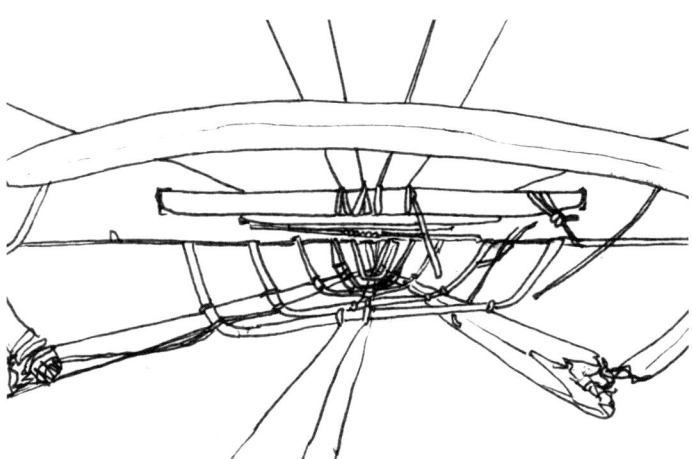

Figure 184: Forward interior of the Rijper Museum kayak.

The De Rijp kayak is very damaged and distorted, and its method of display made surveying it a physical and mental challenge: It is stored about 9′ up, hanging from the ceiling, and is heeling about 40 degrees. I had to take elevations (hull heights/depths) using the kayak's sheer (instead of the floor) as a baseline, so the curve of the sheer and the rocker were restored through comparisons with similar kayaks as well as photographs.

The damage to the kayak consists of the hull having shifted to one side— essentially wracked, instead of the more common hull-collapse. Through a combination of averaging angles, 'virtually' straightening ribs, and comparison to similar kayaks, the conjectural restoration of the kayak was completed, and is presented in the lines drawing.

The De Rijp kayak's *masik* is missing, but the deck-height is drawn restored, based on the run of the fore deck stringers. The condition as well as general structural features can be seen in figure 184. There are no aft deck-stringers in the De Rijp kayak; its *isserfik* measures 3/4″ (19mm) thick by 1-3/8″ (35mm) wide and is oval in cross-section.

The framing in the cockpit warrants a bit of explanation: The scale drawing depicts two crosspieces in the cockpit— the one on the left is a rib, and the one on the right is the *isserfik*. I checked for empty rib mortises beneath the gunwales elsewhere in the cockpit, but there weren't any; the next rib forward is at 9′ (274.3cm) from the bow.

Figure 185: Paint scheme of the Rijper Museum kayak (also seen on the De Hidde Nijland Stichting kayak [plate2]).

The De Rijp kayak is painted in a very striking manner: entirely black (or perhaps an extremely dark blue), with a white wave-pattern at the waterline. The keel and a narrow area around it were left black. The coaming was also painted black, as well as the deck lines and even the ivory fitting. This white wave-pattern is also seen on Dutch sailing ships from the 17th century— a pinnace, dating from circa 1650, in the National Maritime Museum (Amsterdam) bears this pattern in white, although the rest of its hull was not painted black. Figure 185 depicts the pattern painted on the De Rijp kayak.

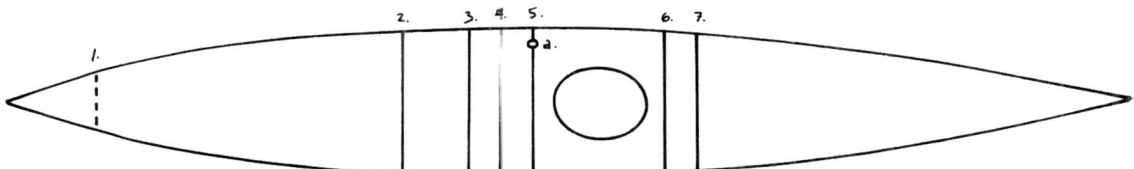

Rijper Museum, DeRijp: Cat. no. 42

Only one deck fitting (5a) is on Rijper museum's kayak: a harpoon holder attached to the first deck line ahead of the cockpit. This implement holder is nearly identical to the example on the WFM 232 kayak only it comes to a point at the top. A *masik*-mounted harpoon holder is not present or evidenced. The foremost deck strap is missing, and may or may not have had fittings on it. A stern deck line was not evidenced.

Two Greenland paddles are present at the Rijper Museum. I surveyed one of them, and it is depicted in paddle-plate 6.

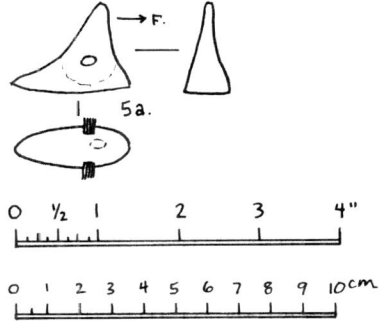

4. West Greenland Kayak from ca. 1600s: De Hidde Nijland Stichting, Hindeloopen, the Netherlands. Catalog no. 2. ("Hindeloopen")

Gert Nooter cites two sources, both from 1919, that offer conflicting information on the history of the Hindeloopen kayak: One reports that the kayak was collected by Hindeloopen whalers at "Iseland," and the other states that it had washed ashore at Hindeloopen " . . . at the beginning of this century . . ." (Museum catalog, 1919, entry 2, and Boeles 1919:236 respectively, in Nooter, 1971:18,21). I think the latter history provided by Boeles may be discounted (unless he is in actuality citing an earlier quotation without compensating for elapsed centuries) as the kayak certainly long pre-dates circa 1900.

This kayak has extensive hull collapse, though it is mainly concentrated behind the cockpit. Planking had been inserted in the cockpit area to maintain rigidity— likely an early attempt at conservation. Tin tips cover the bow and stern of this kayak; their purpose is mysterious and Europeans likely made and attached them. It is on display in a case at De Hidde Nijland Stichting under extremely heavy plate-glass; when Nooter had visited, the Hindeloopen kayak was suspended from the ceiling (1971:18-21).

The Hindeloopen kayak's fore deck is completely collapsed, so the restored depth-overall of 8˝ (20.3cm) is conjectural, having been based on similar kayaks. The chine breadths are also conjecture and based primarily on the De Rijp kayak (plate 3), which also needed much reconstruction, but had more 'evidence' to work with, e.g., a hull that I could see into.

Like the De Rijp kayak, the Hindeloopen kayak has a wavy waterline painted on it. The wave pattern is white and it descends to just below the chines. The upper part of the kayak is painted in a very dark green— nearing black. The coaming is painted red, and the paddle associated with the kayak is painted the dark green color. (See figure 185 for the paint scheme on the kayak.)

A series of 1/8″ diameter holes spaced every inch or so are present along the bow's keel edge. These indicate the onetime placement of keel edging that extended three feet behind the bow of the kayak. Keel edging at the stern was not present or evidenced. The Hindeloopen kayak has a paddle associated with it, and it is depicted in paddle-plate 7.

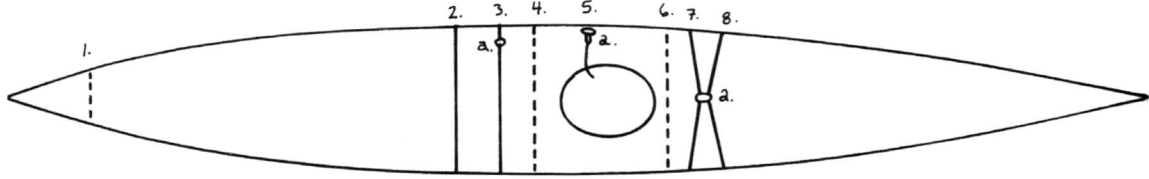

De Hidde Nijland Stichting, Hindeloopen: Cat. no. 2

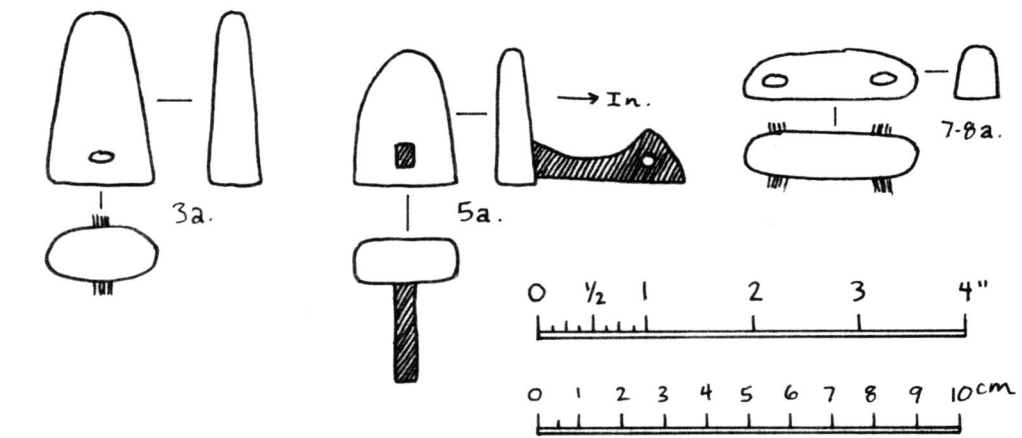

Two deck lines are missing from the Hindeloopen kayak— the bow deck line, and one immediately behind the cockpit. Behind this latter missing deck line is a pair of lines linked together with a single ivory piece. It is an anomaly for an older West Greenland kayak to have three such lines behind the cockpit, however this typical is typical among 20th century South and East Greenland kayaks (type VII and IX).

Two equipment holders are present on the Hindeloopen kayak. The forward piece is a simple tab-shaped piece (3a) threaded onto deck line 3. The other piece is a composite piece, with an upright tab of ivory, and a saddle-rest carved from baleen; the baleen is tenoned into the ivory tab. This harpoon holder is dangling loosely from the cockpit, being attached with a baleen cord.

Despite its seemingly impossible beam of only 15-5/8″, I built a replica of the Hindeloopen kayak. While all of the replica's hull dimensions are exactly as the survey drawing depicts, I did have to enlarge the cockpit coaming to 19″ (48.2cm) long and 15-1/2″ (39.3cm) wide (from the original's dimensions of 16-7/8″ by 14″ [42.8 x 35.5cm]) so I could manage to fit inside of it. It is still a snug fit, but very comfortable to sit in.

Perhaps the most surprising aspect of paddling such a narrow kayak was how stable it was— not at all expected. Helpful, undoubtedly was the fact that the waterline beam was nearly the kayak's overall beam on account of the nearly plum gunwales and the freeboard being up alongside of the gunwales.

Figure 186: The author in the replica of the 'Hindeloopen' kayak. (Photograph by Kathy Tucker.)

(It is not unusual for certain kayaks being 18″ wide or so to have waterline breadths nearing or even less than 15-5/8″, depending on the shape and depth of their hulls. These wider kayaks may even feel tippier on account of having higher freeboard and the resultant higher center of gravity.)

The Hindeloopen kayak maneuvered very well— almost as well as the Lübeck kayak replica, on account of the former having a shallower bow. The speed of the Hindeloopen was exhilarating: Kayaks with such narrow breadths move through the water so easily, and whether or not they actually measure faster than other kayaks is perhaps besides the point— they feel fast, being very easily driven.

In waves, the Hindeloopen replica is a wet ride, but not so sloppy. It maintains its course well, and does not get too thrown about, likely on account of its low volume and small surface area. Wind hardly

Figure 187: The 'Hindeloopen' replica underway, Whidbey Island, 2006. The replica is painted the same as the original—in a seventeenth-century Dutch Naval scheme. (Photograph by Kathy Tucker.)

nudges it around, but again, it is a very wet ride, the deck being under a good deal in one-foot waves. Surf on the other hand did not treat this kayak so well: I had taken it out in 6′ winter surf on the Washington coast, and its great length paired with its low volume lead to a fairly violent pitch-pole— the kayak flipped end-over-end, breaking off the bow knob in the process. Remarkably, that was the only damage.

In 1999, the multiple Greenland Kayaking Championship winner Maligiaq Padilla of Sisimiut visited and used this kayak on the Columbia River and for rolling demonstrations in Washington State. Padilla remarked that it was the fastest kayak he'd ever been in; the racing kayaks he'd been used to were typically a foot shorter and at least 3″ wider.

5. West Greenland Kayak of ca. 1600-1800: Danish National Museum, Copenhagen. Catalog no. Lb.101.

Only one hint as to this kayak's history is present in museum accession data: An "Olrik" is listed as the donor. It was received or at least accessioned by the Danish National Museum in 1866.

It is quite clear through comparisons to other kayaks— both in form and construct, that this kayak could easily predate 1866 by a century or two. For example, the Lb.101 has baleen lashings used in 'old' patterns (i.e., single-pass), an *amiq* that is pulled up and over the coaming back, and it has very simple deck lines, a pair of which cross each other. These are all features commonly found in type I and type II kayaks. The Lb.101 is in fair condition considering its probable age, although it has had some rough treatment at the stern and especially the bow.

Both artifactual and restored lines are presented of the Lb.101. The artifactual lines depict its sagging bow, which is in fact missing the stem-piece and a bit of the gunwales' length. The stern is not quite so damaged, but is still missing a few inches of length. Through fairing and comparison to similar kayaks, a conjectural restoration was made (Plate 5b), which includes a replaced bow and stern, adding some 12-7/8″ (32.7cm) to the length. (Note: the stations in the conjectural restoration do not correspond to those in the artifactual lines drawing [Plate 5a].)

The scantlings of the Lb.101 are remarkably heavy. The gunwales are 1-1/16″ (27mm) thick whereas most gunwales in 17th-18th century kayaks are only 1/2″-5/8″ (13-16mm) thick. The chines and keelson are also substantial, being 1-1/4″ wide by 1″ thick (32 x 25mm) and 1-1/16″ wide by 1″ thick (27 x 25mm) respectively.

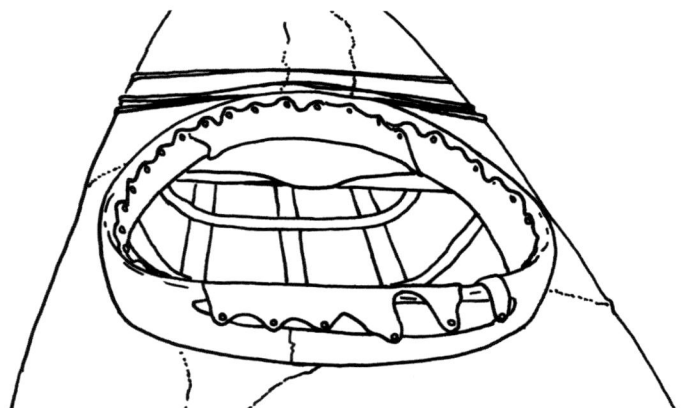

Figure 188: The cockpit of the Lb.101. Note the amiq *having been pulled up and over the coaming at the back; the pegs securing it are tacked into a strip of bone. Also note the hand-grip carved into the* masik, *and the deck beam immediately ahead of it.*

As can be seen in the scale drawing, the gunwales are taller aft of the cockpit, and become much shorter towards the bow: This is the case with the Gemeentelijke Musea Zierikzee's kayak no. 700 (plate 6) as well. At the bow, the gunwale ends are exposed and measure 1-9/16″ (40mm) high (see figure 67a). The gunwales are very rounded in cross-section— they have no sharp corners.

The Lb.101's *masik* has a handle carved into it— not so

much a pocket as seen on the kayak KNK 1161 (plate 9), nor a through-slot as seen in the Hull Trinity House kayaks 'A' and 'B,' (plates 16 and 13) but instead just an inverted step with a cross-section as depicted in figure 79 bottom. The *masik* measures 5/8" (16mm) thick at the ends, and 1-3/4" (44mm) thick at the handle; it is 3-1/4" (8.2cm) wide. The Lb.101's *isserfik* is 1" (25mm) thick by 1-1/2" (38mm) wide and is oval in cross-section.

The forward interior view of the Lb.101 is presented in figure 189. All of the lashings are baleen, and those attaching the stringers to the ribs were largely sprung or missing adjacent the cockpit. The deck stringers are also lashed in place with baleen as well as being pegged further forward. A long shim-piece is used to support the deck stringers over a straight deck beam. A gunwale scarf is also visible in figure 189. It is on the left gunwale towards the bow; its exact form was indeterminable due to its proximity, but baleen lashings and a 'step' were noted.

Figure 190 shows the aft interior view of the Lb.101. Note the heavy baleen clamping tie at the gunwales' lower edges; it has slackened a bit on the right end. Interestingly, the aft deck stringers are

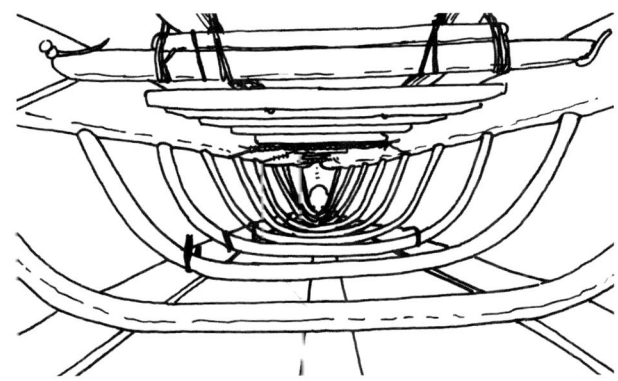

Figure 189: Forward interior of the Lb.101. Note the shim supporting the deck stringers.

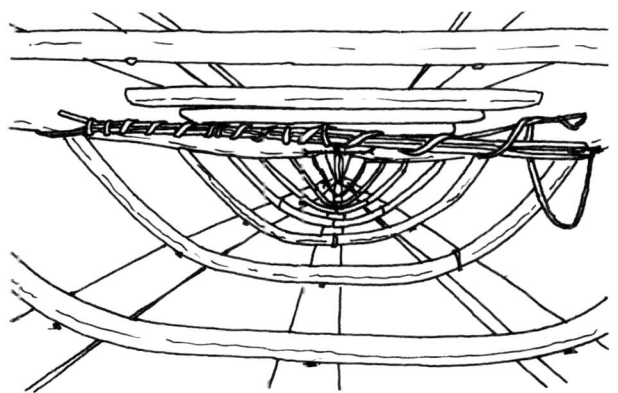

Figure 190: Aft interior view of the Danish National Museum's Lb.101. Note the baleen clamp tie, one end of which has unwound a bit.

pegged to the deck beams, whereas the forward stringers are lashed.

The Lb.101's *amiq* is drawn over the top of the cockpit coaming's backside, and is set with six pegs into an 8-1/2" (21.6cm) long antler strip mounted on the coaming's face. The antler strip measures 1/4" (6mm) thick and is 1/4" high on the left side and 7/8" (22mm) high on the right. The pegs are set into it 7/8" (22mm) below the coaming's top edge. The coaming measures 3/4" (19mm) thick by 2-1/8" (54mm) high, and has a rounded top.

Bow and stern deck lines are not present or evidenced on the Lb.101. Only four deck lines are present: one behind the cockpit, and three ahead of the cockpit. The two deck lines on the fore deck closest to the cockpit cross each other. A *masik*-mounted harpoon holder is evidenced but missing.

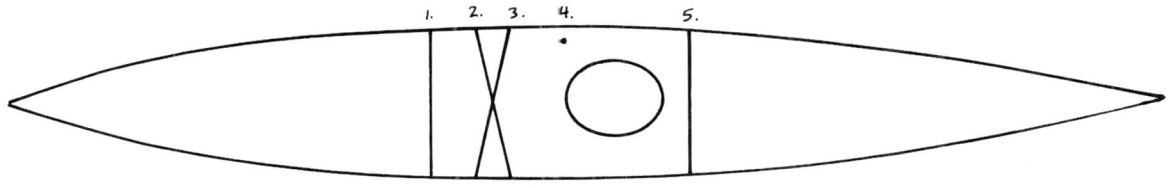

Danish National Museum: Cat. no. Lb. 101

6. West Greenland Kayak of ca. 1600-1800: Gemeentelijke Musea Zierikzee, Zierikzee, the Netherlands.
Catalog no. 700. ("Zierikzee")

The history of the 700 is mysterious, and its 'popular' history can certainly be discarded, though of course repeated as it is interesting and mythological: The city of Zierikzee was founded by Zierik who in 849 A.D. arrived there in the kayak (Nooter, 1971:64-69). Figure 191 depicts the effigy of Zierik in his kayak; he is wearing a seal skin *tuilik*, or paddling jacket. The presence of the *tuilik* may suggest that this kayak was brought to Europe with a Greenlander. A paddle associated with the GMZ 700 is depicted in paddle-plate 11.

The GMZ 700 distinctly resembles the Lb.101 described previous. Both are large in all dimensions except breadth when compared to other early Greenlandic kayaks, and their cross-sections are nearly identical, being deep with narrow chine breadths.

Unfortunately, due to the placement of the effigy of Zierik, I was unable to gain a view

Figure 191: 'Zierik' – The effigy inside the GMZ's kayak 700.

of the interior of the 700, so construction details and scantlings remain unavailable, although Nooter has fortunately published photographs of the interior (1971:65,66). His photos depict short, narrow seat-slats and the *amiq* being pulled up and over the back of the cockpit coaming. Figure 192 is a cockpit sketch after Nooter's photograph; my scale drawing illustrates the cockpit arrangement based this photograph.

The dimensions of the structure (scantlings) are not given in Nooter, nor can they be accurately inferred from the photographs. The only scantlings I was able to acquire were a coaming height of about 1-1/4" (32mm), and a gunwale height of about 2-3/8" (60mm) at the cockpit front. Based on marks in the *amiq*, I think the GMZ 700's *masik* must be about 2" (50mm) wide.

Evident in the scale drawing are gunwales whose height changes considerably along their visible length: They maintain a fairly constant height aft of the cockpit, but become significantly shallower ahead of the cockpit, as evidenced by the gunwale's lower edge protruding into the *amiq*.

The kayak GMZ 700 is of striking dimensions, and at 20'8-1/4" (630.5cm) long and only 17" (43.2cm) wide, it has a very high length-to-width ratio (14.60); this is the second highest in this study, exceeded

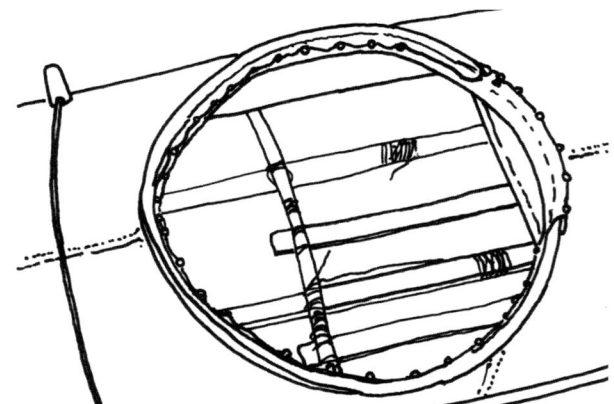

Figure 192: Cockpit view of the 700; after a photograph by Gert Nooter (1971:65, fig.33).

Figure 193: A Greenland kayak in an engraving from 1658. The kayak appears to have similar proportions to the GMZ 700, i.e., very long. (Courtesy of the Netherlands Maritime Museum, Amsterdam.)

only by the Weltmuseum kayak 36481 (plate 10) at 15.22.

A *masik*-mounted harpoon holder is not present or evidenced, but an ivory implement holder is present on the deck line just ahead of the cockpit. All of the GMZ 700's deck lines are present and intact; no other fittings are present and a stern deck line was not evidenced.

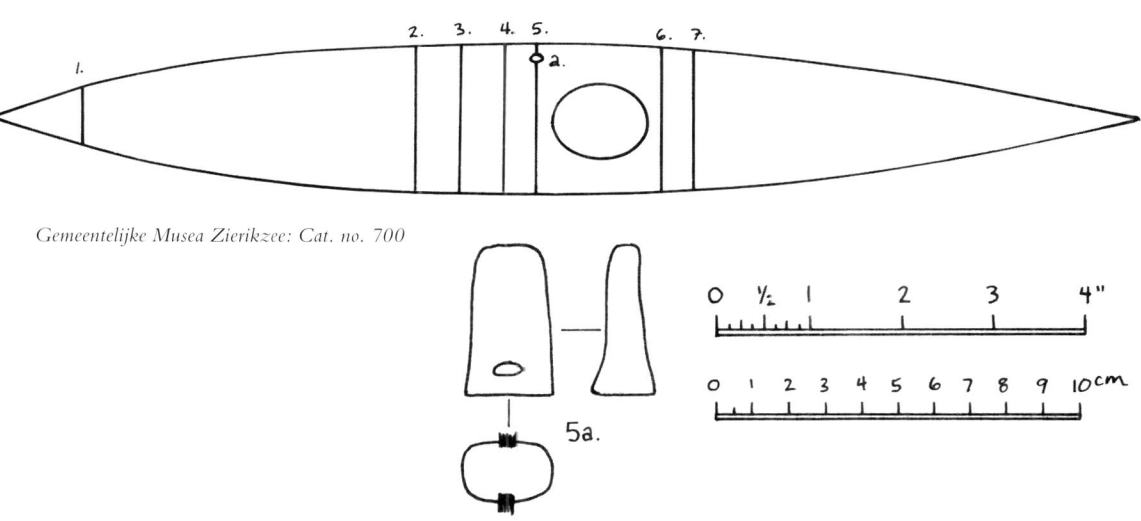

Gemeentelijke Musea Zierikzee: Cat. no. 700

7. West Greenland kayak of ca. 1600 – 1800: Museon, Den Haag, the Netherlands. Catalog no. 57966. ("Enkhuizen")

This kayak is described by Nooter in his *Old Kayaks in the Netherlands* (1971:22-23) and is referred to therein as the "Enkhuizen"— after the town it had been in for centuries before its 1966 transfer to the Museon in The Hague. Photographs of the "Enkhuizen" kayak in Nooter's book show it in a very neglected state: The coaming is missing, much of the frame is gone, and the skin is very damaged. Interestingly, the kayak had been painted with traditional Dutch floral embellishments and a yellow dragon along the sides.

Visiting 27 years after Nooter, I expected to see this kayak in the same if not worse condition. To my surprise, it had been restored— and very well restored at that. A new coaming had been fitted— one that took close examination to affirm that it was not original. New framework had been inserted in the cockpit area and plywood bulkheads further in helped hold the kayak's shape; all the original woodwork was gone. The kayak has been restored with end-knobs, but they are omitted from the scale drawing.

The "Enkhuizen's" skin was held in such a shape that it did not require much correcting in the scale drawing. Various rumples exist along the bottom of the kayak, but the creases where the chines and keelson had been were very obvious. While the scale drawing presents a slightly faired version of a museum conservationist's restoration, it should be considered that certain elements and characteristics of the original kayak's form are lost. My placement of this kayak in the type I category is a tenuous one, as the kayak could have very well been of the type II form originally. My scale restoration of the "Enkhuizen" kayak (Museon 57966) is deliberately simplified, as I did not want to introduce stylistic elements when none were evidenced.

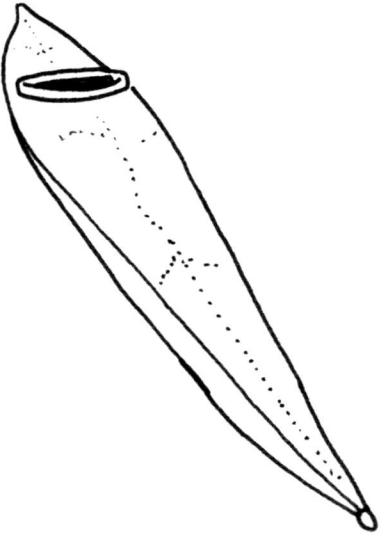

Nooter gives the length of the "Enkhuizen" as 554cm long, 45cm wide, and 20cm deep; he adds, "...these measurements are highly unreliable due to the poor condition of this kayak" (1971:22). They are however very close to my measurements taken of the restored kayak (558.5cm, 47.2cm, and 20.6cm respectively), though these too must be held as unreliable due to the kayak's condition.

Upon finishing the survey, I inquired about the original framework, which I had assumed had been long since discarded. What was left of it was brought to me in a 20" long box. Inside were twenty-five or so little pieces of wood— each meticulously cataloged. I was very thrilled to see these pieces as the original scantlings and certain details of joinery are preserved. The scantlings given on the scale drawing are not those of the frame inserted by conservationists, but are those gleaned from the fragments of the original frame.

Figure 194: The "Enkhuizen" kayak—restored.

Several key pieces of the "Enkhuizen's" salvaged frame are illustrated in figure 195. Piece a is a deck beam (viewed from either above or below) with the tenon intact. The end of the tenon is 1/2" (13mm) wide and 1/4" (6mm) high. The center of the deck beam measures 1-1/8" (28mm) wide and 15/16" (24mm) thick, rounded as shown in the shaded cross-section. Piece b is also a deck beam (viewed from the side), with holes drilled through it. The hole on the left likely anchored the piece to the gunwales, while the two holes to the right may have held the pegs or lashings attaching the deck stringers. (If I'm correct about what these holes are for, the length of this piece was probably 15" [38.1cm] originally, and therefore was probably situated just behind the cockpit.) Piece c, shown in two views, is likely the furthest forward rib. It is made of two separate pieces lashed together at the base. These pieces are each only 5/16″ (8mm) thick, while fragments of other ribs measure 3/8″ (9mm) thick.

Piece d is the largest fragment and it tells much of the "Enkhuizen's" construction and joinery. One end has been fractured, but the other end consists of a nicely preserved scarf joint— half of one. This scarf joint is stepped and had been pegged as well as lashed. The deck beam mortise is 5/8″ x 1/4″ (16 x 6mm) and is 3/8″ (9mm) deep. The angle at which it is cut into the gunwale reveals a possible gunwale flare of about 26 degrees. Two rib mortises are cut into the gunwale piece: one at about the middle, and the other at the far right, just before the fracture, spaced 10″ (25.4cm) on-center.

A paddle is not associated with the "Enkhuizen," though in Nooter, there is a photograph of the kayak with a paddle (1971:25). Nooter writes in the caption: "The paddle did not originally belong to the kayak." Nothing else about this paddle is mentioned, and one might wonder the paddle's history or current whereabouts, as I did not see it at the Museon.

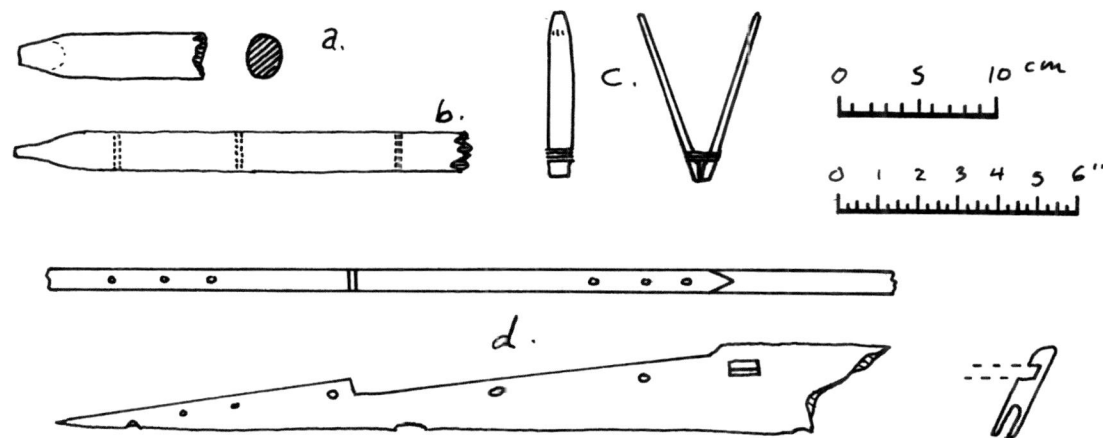

Figure 195: Several key remnants of the Museon kayak 57966's framework.

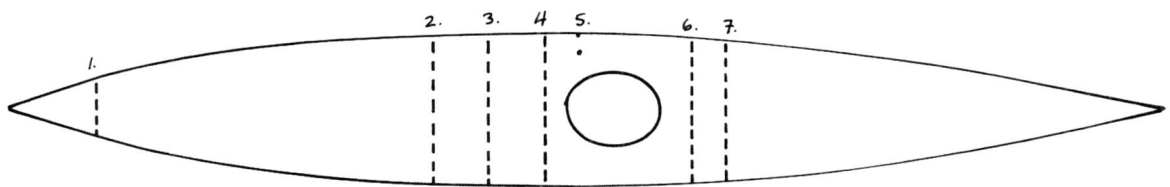

Museon, the Hague: Cat. no. 57966

This kayak— rather the intact skin of this kayak— is missing all of its original fittings and deck-lines. Their positions are of course evidenced by holes along the sheer-line creases, and their positions are indicated in the scale drawing with dashed lines. The two holes where a harpoon holder had been attached are also depicted. The actual orientation of the deck lines is unknown; some of them may well have been crossed, as seen on the Westfries Museum's kayak 232 and the Danish National Museum's kayak Lb.101. Nooter described having seen deck lines on this kayak, but no deck fittings (1971:22).

TYPE II.

In stark contrast to type I kayaks, type II kayaks are characterized by very complex lines. Typically, these kayaks have a slight reverse sheer amidships with low or gently raised ends, and their deep gunwales often exhibit considerable shaping. Like type I kayaks, the keelson-to-stern transitions are not particularly distinct. The bows of type II kayaks are usually very short, the one exception in this study being a later example of the type (plate 14). Two type II kayaks exhibit dramatic gunwale twisting— a feature not seen in any other Greenland kayaks in this study. Baleen lashings, simple deck line arrangements, and shallow deck beam mortises are common characteristics of these kayaks.

Type II kayaks are generally very narrow— the average beam of the seven examples in this study is only 40.4cm (15.9"). The cross sections of type II kayaks are fairly boxy, having a proportionally wide chine breadth. The two examples with distinctly twisted gunwales have boxy sections forward, and more rounded sections aft. Five of these seven kayaks have bow keel edging— only one has stern edging.

None of these kayaks have had their provenance recorded in any detail, so it remains a mystery as to where in West Greenland these kayaks come from. Most type II kayaks are (or were) in Dutch museums: In 1656, the Dutch trader Nicholas Tunes is said to have brought a large number of kayaks back from a voyage to Greenland, landing them in Vlissengen (Gad, 1971:256). The kayaks that Tunes brought to The Netherlands may account for some of the older preserved kayaks (both types I and II) in that country's museums.

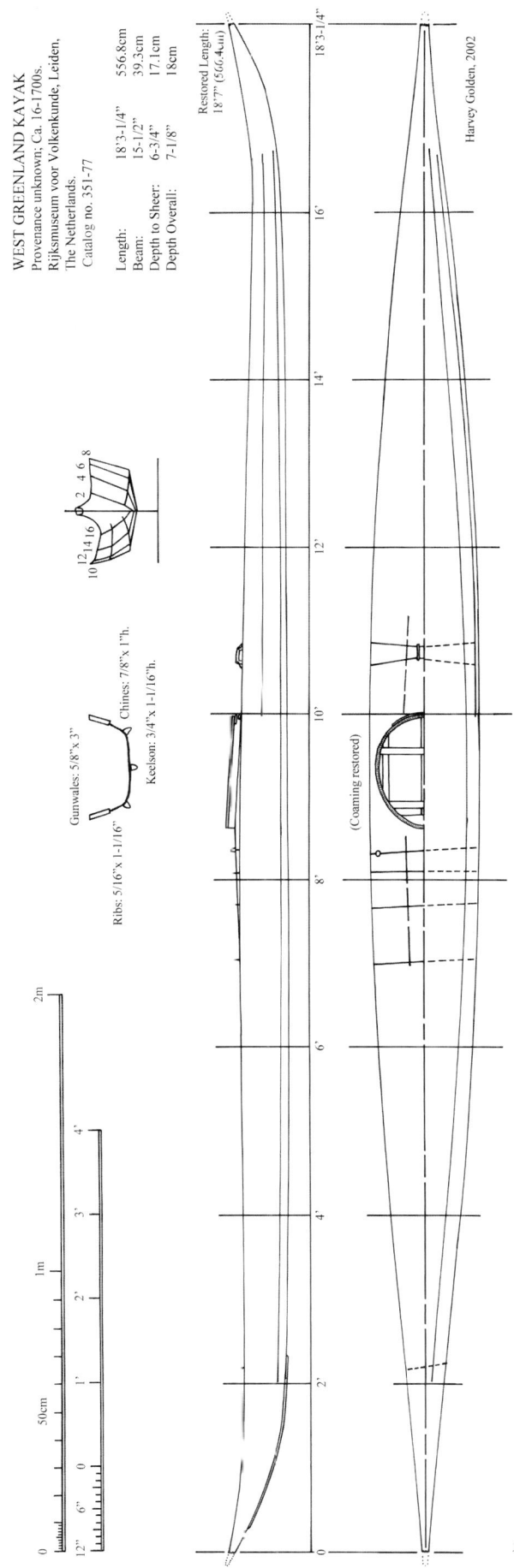

8. Rijksmuseum voor Volkenkunde catalog no. 351-77

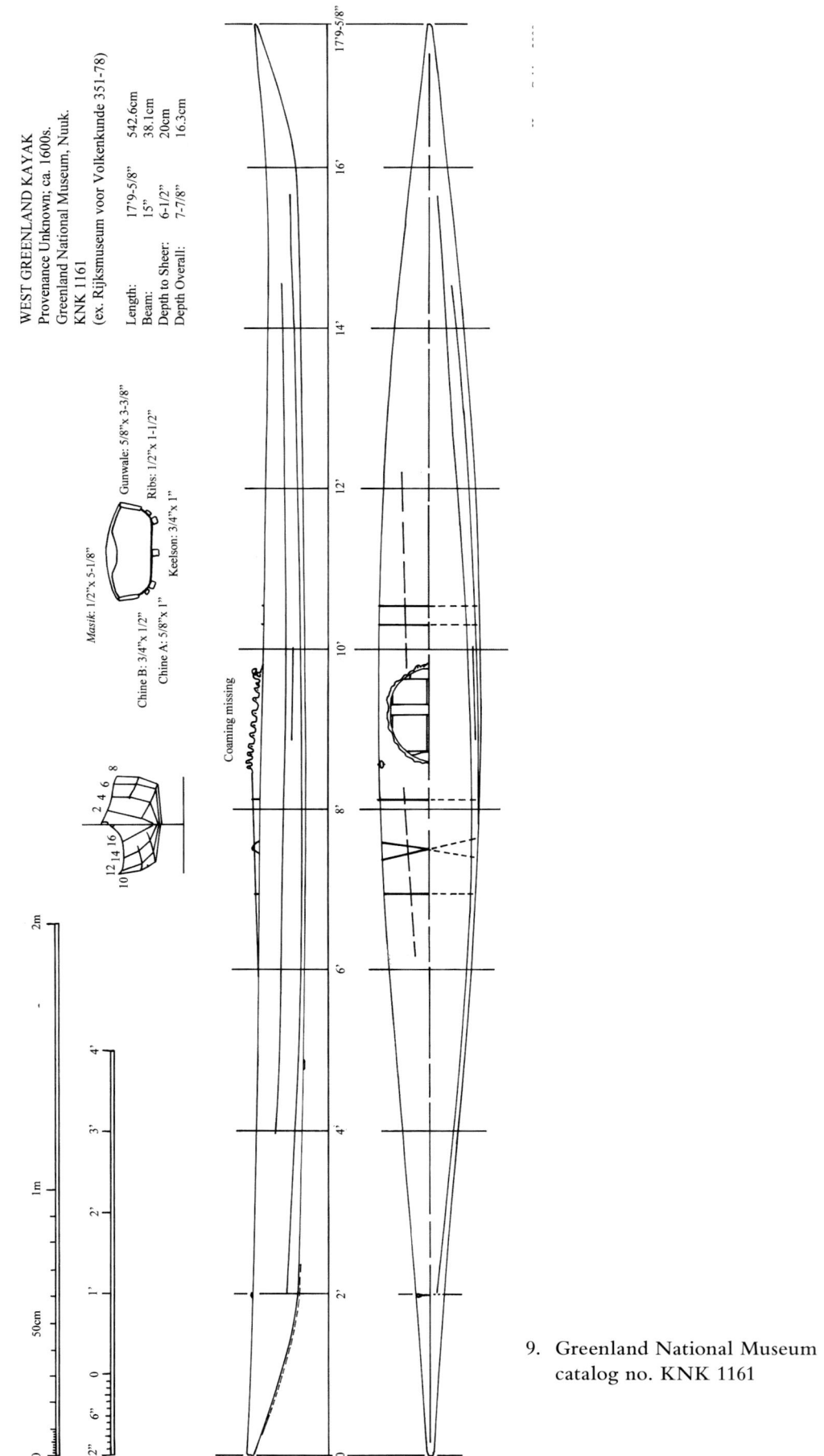

9. Greenland National Museum catalog no. KNK 1161

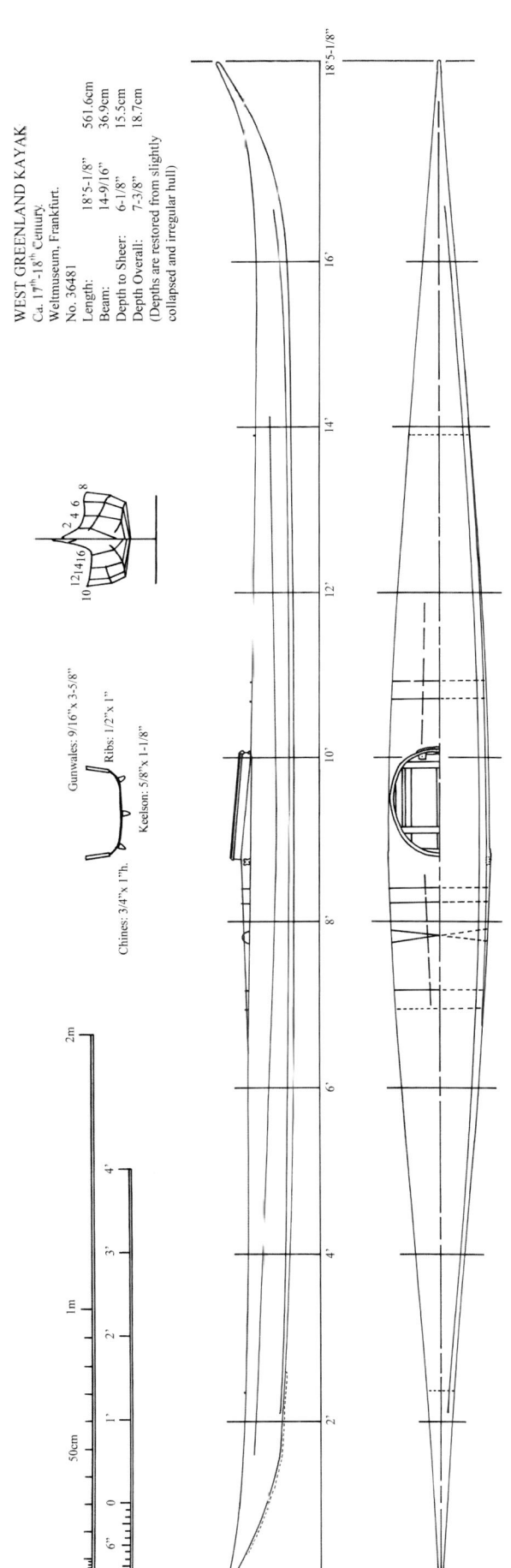

10. Weltmuseum catalog no. 36481

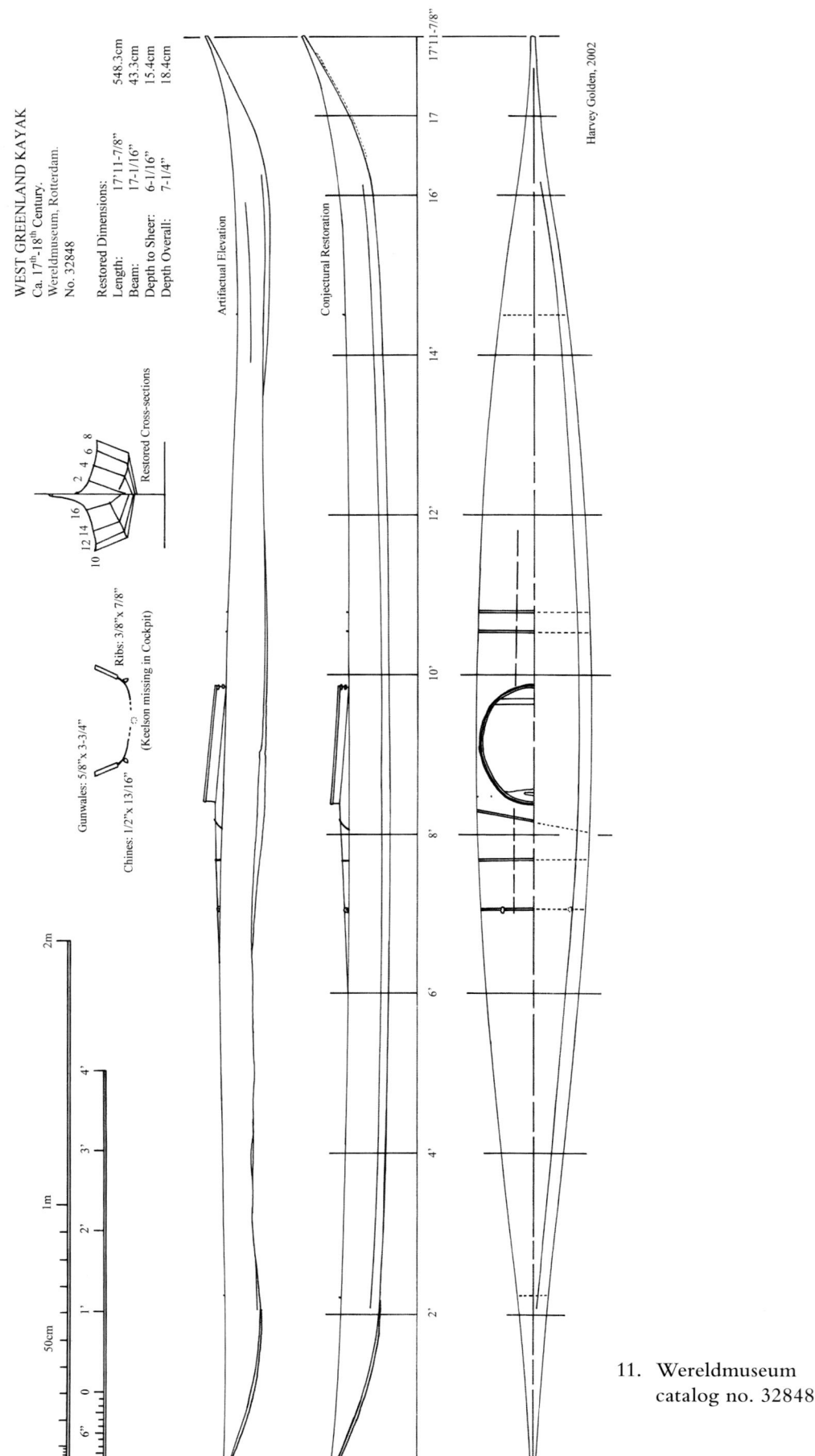

11. Wereldmuseum catalog no. 32848

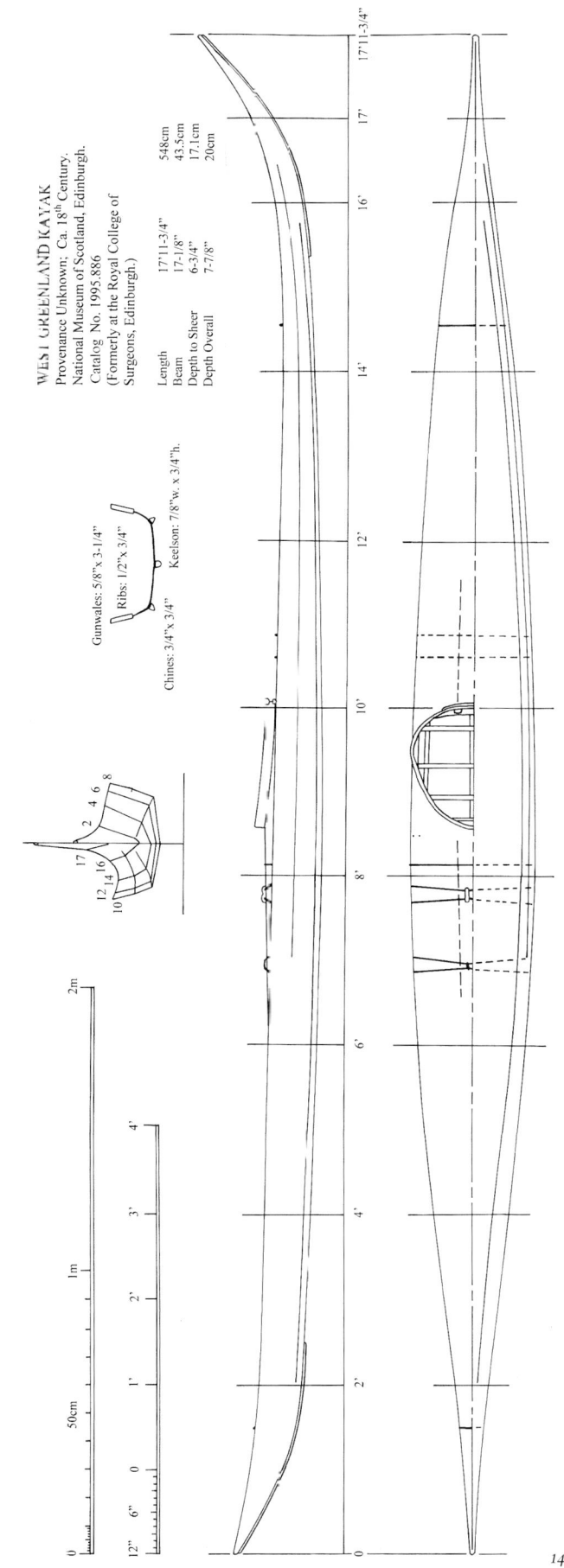

12. National Museum of Scotland catalog no. 1995.886

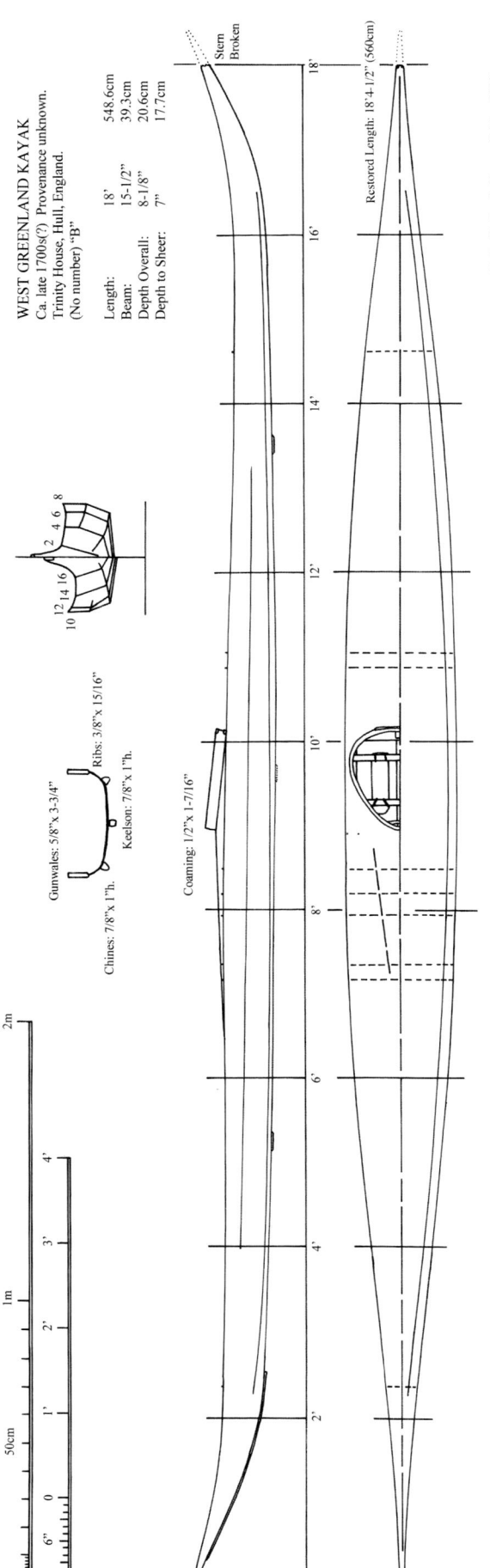

13. Trinity House Hull (N/N 'B')

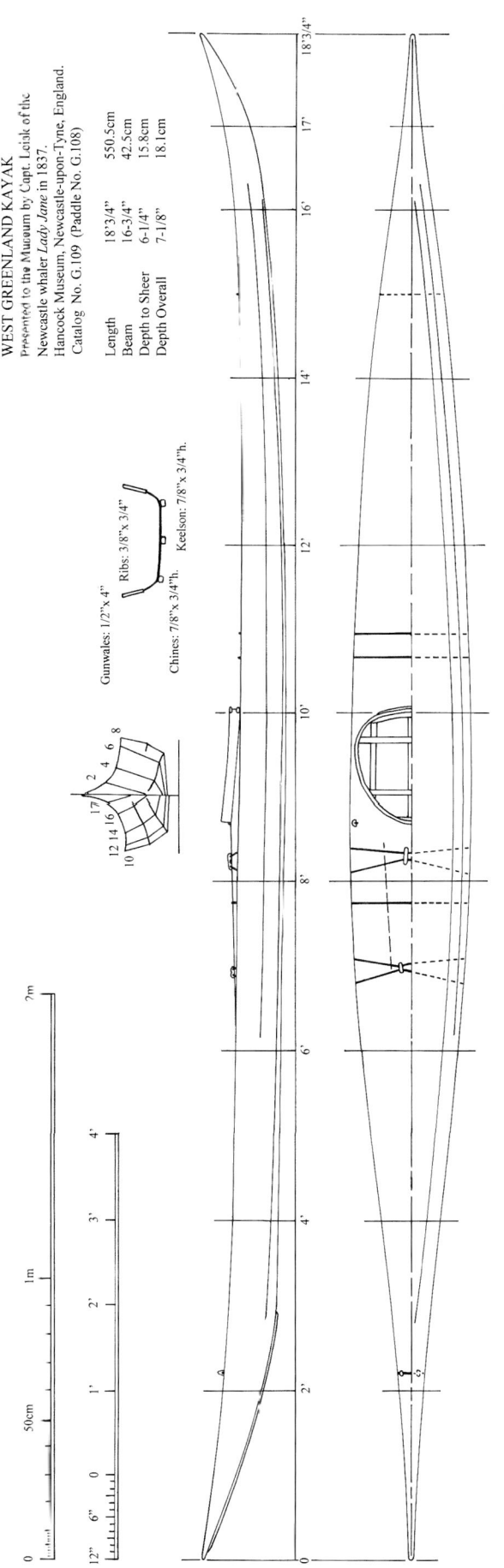

14. Hancock Museum catalog no. G.109

8. West Greenland Kayak of ca. 1600-1800: Rijksmuseum voor Volkenkunde, Leiden, the Netherlands.
Catalog no. 351-77 ("the Hague")

Formerly at the Ministerie van Marine (the Hague), this kayak was transferred to the Rijksmuseum in Leiden in 1883. It appears in Nooter's 1971 work as "The Hague"— specifically (Nooter's) number 15, as there are two kayaks referred to as "The Hague" in his work.[30]

Measuring 556.8cm (18′3-1/4″), the RvV 351-77 has broken ends that suggest an original length of about 566.4cm (18′7″)— a figure arrived upon conjecturally via fairing the lines out (Nooter's length for this kayak is 555cm [1971:74]).

The 351-77 has boxy hull cross-sections forward, but a round-ish multi-chine section aft. This form is due to the gunwales being flared very little ahead of the cockpit, and flared considerably aft of the cockpit. The compound gunwale flare in this kayak is achieved through the placement of a deck beam towards the gunwales' lower edges ahead of the cockpit in order to hold the lower edges of the gunwales out— i.e., less flared (see figure 197). Behind the cockpit, clamping ties have been placed to pull in the gunwales' lower edges. This hull form, including the reverse sheer, is somewhat typical of type II Greenland kayaks.

Some of the 351-77's scantlings not shown on the scale drawing are as follows: The *masik* is a simple arch measuring 1/2″ (13mm) by 3-1/2″ (8.9cm) wide; the *isserfik* measures 5/8″ (16mm) thick by 1-1/2″ (38mm) wide. At their mid-points, the deck beams measure 3/4″ (19mm) thick by 1″ (25mm) wide, with an oval cross-section (i.e., rounded edges). At their ends, these deck beams are chamfered to 3/16″ (5mm) thick and 3/4″ (19mm) wide; these ends are the tenons. The forward deck stringers measure 5/8″ (16mm) square at their aft edge; the aft deck stringers are both missing, but their original positioning is evidenced by creases in the kayak's *amiq*.

Figure 196: The Rijksmuseum voor Volkenkunde's 351-77—"The Hague"

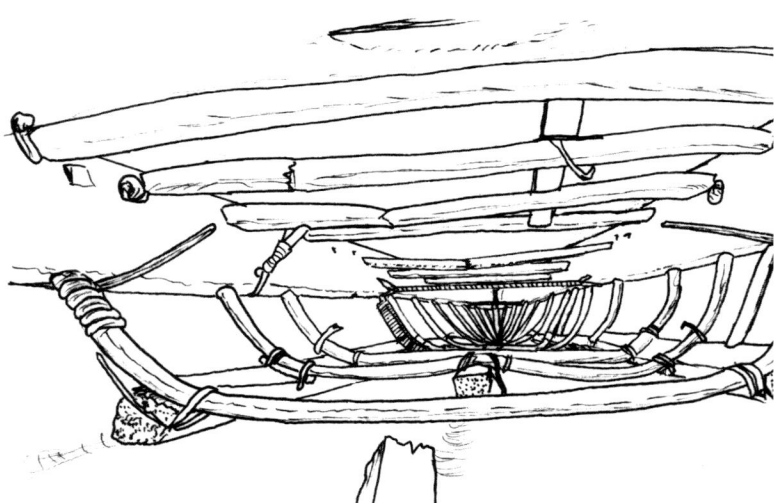

Figure 197: Forward interior view of the Rijksmuseum's 351-77. Note the broken curved deck beams; one of the deck stringers is missing. On the right, there is a partial rib that appears to be tenoned into the chine.

---

[30] It must be pointed out that some of the photographs of kayaks in Nooter's *Old Kayaks in the Netherlands* (1971) are erroneously labeled: Figure 21 is the Brielle, *not* the Hague (no.15), and figure 28 is the Hague (no.16), *not* the Brielle. There are two "Hague" kayaks mentioned in Nooter, no.15 being the present (351-77), and the other, no.16, is now the Greenland National Museum's kayak 1161 (plate 9).

Much of the RvV 351-77's coaming is missing, though it is drawn restored in the scale drawing. Two bone pieces cover the coaming's scarfs: The upper piece is 8-1/2" (21.6cm) long, and the lower piece is 6-1/4" (15.9cm) long. Both pieces are 1/8" (3mm) thick by 3/8" (9mm) high, and are pegged in place with oval bone or ivory pegs— seven on the upper, and six on the lower piece. The top surface of the 351-77's coaming is ivory-shod, the strip being 1/8" (3mm) high and 5/16" (8mm) wide, pegged about 1/8" (3mm) on center with many tiny ivory pegs— well over 100 pegs must have been present. The coaming's cap is pieced together from many short pieces of ivory, each junction being a birdsmouth joint. The coaming, sans ivory cap, measures 3/8" (9mm) thick by 1-3/8" (35mm) high.

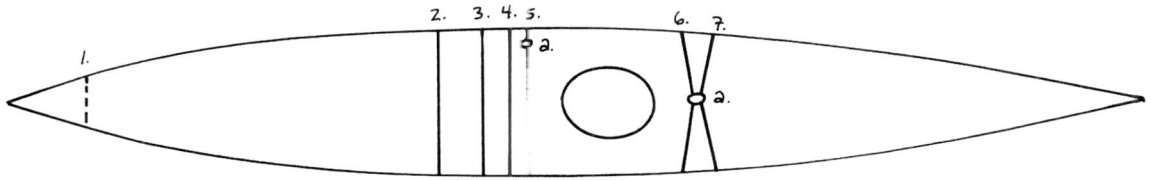

Rijksmuseum voor Volkenkunde, Leiden: Cat. no. 351-77

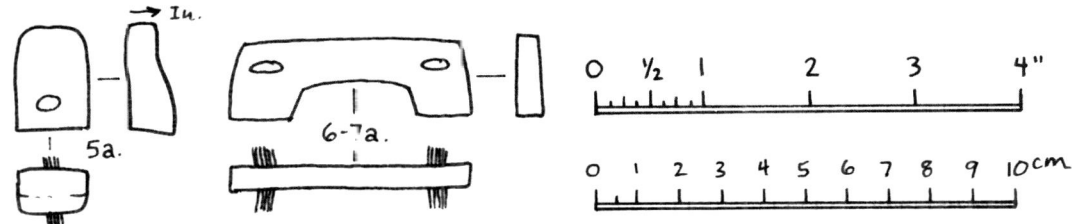

The deck lines of the 351-77 are largely intact — only the bow deck line is missing. A *masik*-mounted harpoon holder is not present or evidenced, but an ivory implement holder is present on the deck line just ahead of the cockpit. A link-piece is present between the two deck lines just behind the cockpit; its form is that of a 'suitcase handle'— a form that recurs in this same position among many West Greenland kayaks in this study. A stern deck line was not present or evidenced.

9. West Greenland Kayak of ca. 1600–1800: Greenland National Museum, Nuuk, Greenland.
Catalog no. KNK 1161 ("the Hague")

This kayak formerly belonged to the Rijksmuseum voor Volkenkunde in Leiden (catalog no. 351-78), and before 1883, it belonged to the Ministerie van Marine, in The Hague. Dr. Gert Nooter described this kayak in his book *Old Kayaks in the Netherlands* (1971:53-54), and is therein referred to as "The Hague." (There are two such named kayaks in Nooter; he distinguishes them with the no. 15 [plate 8 in this study] and no. 16; The KNK 1161 is the no. 16.)

One hundred years after its transfer to Leiden, it was sent to the Greenland Museum (now the Greenland National Museum) in Nuuk, along with two other old kayaks for an exhibit. The exhibition of these kayaks had a significant impact on kayaking in Greenland, as historian John Heath relates:

Some young Greenlanders, seeing these old kayaks, were instilled with pride in their heritage.... the kayak had fallen into disuse in most of Greenland by the middle of the twentieth century, and a whole generation of Greenlanders had virtually no knowledge of them. The young men decided to form a club that would preserve Greenland's kayaking heritage (1987:15).

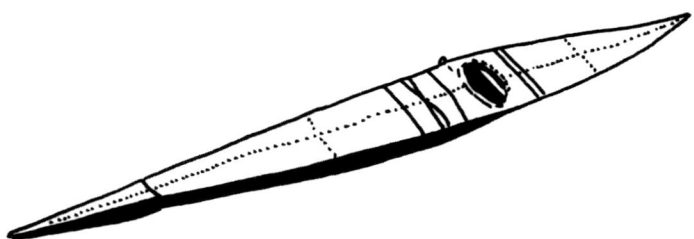

Figure 198: The Greenland National Museum's KNK 1161.

Rijksmuseum voor Volkenkunde curator Gert Nooter himself arranged for this kayak to be permanently transferred to the Greenland Museum— a very profound gesture, considering the Greenland Museum's second-oldest kayak is only from circa 1889 (the KNK 1849, plate 35). (The KNK abbreviation refers to the Greenland National Museum via its Greenlandic name: Kalaallit Nunaata Katersugaasiviata.)

The KNK 1161, depicted in figures 198 and 199, is in very good condition, though it is entirely missing its coaming. The scale drawing of the 1161 shows the broad ribs and the very unusual addition of a shorter second pair of chines. These are distinguishable from seat slats in that they are placed between the main chines and the gunwales and they present an edge into the kayak's *amiq*.

Figure 199: The Greenland National Museum's KNK 1161.

Figure 200 shows the inside-view of the 1161, looking forward. The substantially deep gunwales are immediately obvious; the continuous deck lines are also apparent on both gunwales. Adjacent to these continuous lines is a pair of empty deck beam mortises (the mortise on the left being mostly obscured by the continuous deck lines). As can be seen in this view, there are deck beams placed at three different heights along the gunwales: Most at the upper edge, but one at the bottom edge, and one in the middle.

Also evident in figure 200 are the sharp angles the ribs are bent at so as to achieve the boxy forward cross-sections. A scarf joint can be seen in the second rib forward from the bottom of the drawing: It is essentially a simple lap joint, given extra turns of baleen to better secure it. The rib-to-chine lashings are extant on the right side, but are broken or

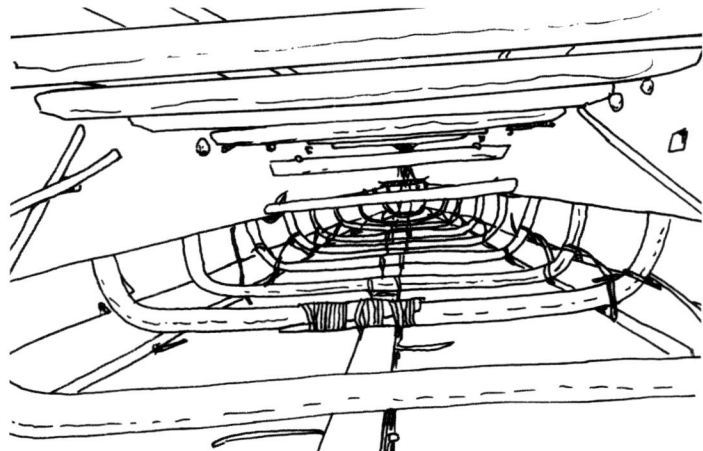

Figure 200: Forward interior view of the KNK 1161. Note the deck beam placed at the gunwale's lower edge.

missing on much of the left side. All of the lashings are baleen.

Figure 201 shows the aft-view inside, with less angular ribs, so as to achieve the more dish-shaped cross-section. The ribs in fact are not so much set into the bottom edge of the gunwales as they are into the inside lower corner. A fractured deck beam can also be seen further back in the hull.

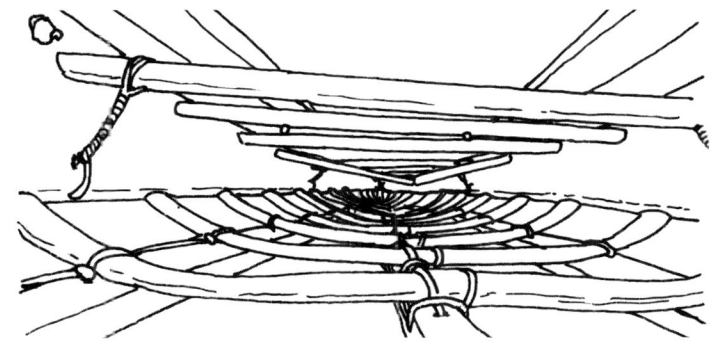

Figure 201: Aft interior view of the KNK 1161.

As can be seen in both interior views of the KNK 1161, two different lashing methods are used for the longitudinals. The keelson-to-ribs lashing is the same throughout, using the double-pass lashing method seen in many modern West Greenland kayaks (figure 72), but the chine-to-ribs lashings uses the single-pass lashing method, but only inside of and aft of the cockpit. The single-pass lashing method is depicted in figure 69, and can also be seen in other early kayaks, such as the DNM Lb.101 (plate 5). (Unlike the double-pass method seen in later kayaks, the pattern in the KNK 1161 does not meander, and instead it repeatedly angles inward [towards the keelson] as it continues from the bow towards the stern, as in figure 73, middle.)

To the extent that I could see and reach with a tape measure, I documented the positions of the framing in and around the cockpit of the KNK 1161; the results are depicted in figure 202. Note the

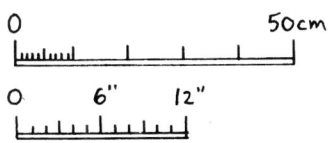

Figure 202: Amidships framing pattern of the Greenland National Museum's kayak 1161.

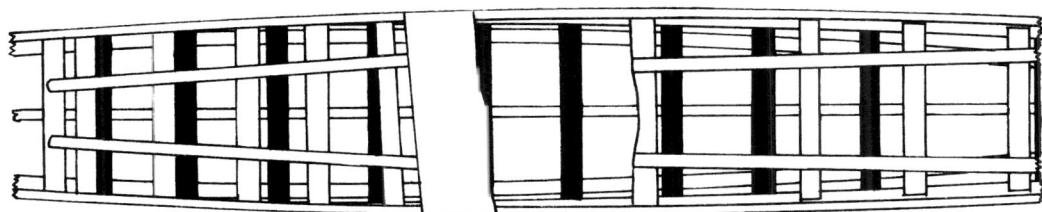

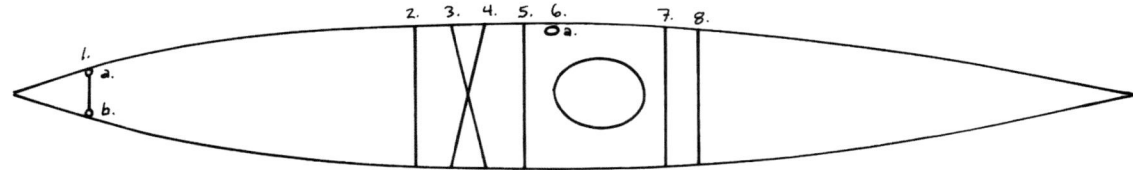

Greenland National Museum: Cat. no. 1161

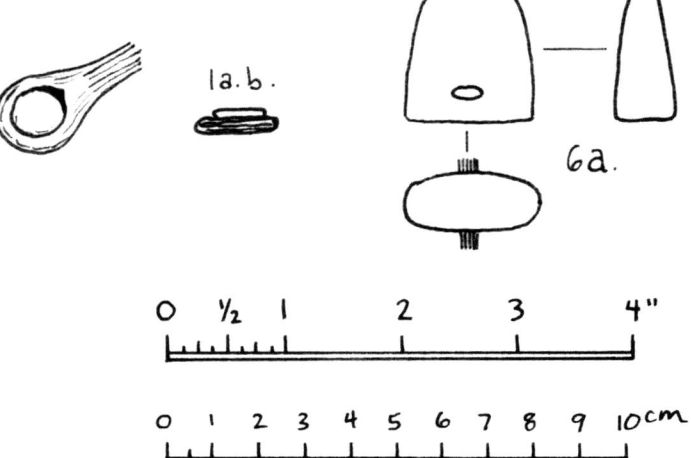

secondary chines and extremely wide *masik*, which had either shifted or was placed slightly crooked.

While the coaming of the 1161 is missing, the skin that had been attached to it is longer in back and folded backwards, indicating it had been pulled up and over the coaming's back edge, much as is the case with several of its contemporaries, e.g., the DNM Lb.101, WFM 232, and the Lübeck kayak.

The foremost deck line on this kayak is attached with two bone or ivory pegs. The pegs are set into the top-edge of the gunwale; the line is fairly snug, and is attached to the pegs via slits cut into the seal skin line's ends. The *masik* mounted harpoon holder is of a simple tab-form. Deck lines 3 and 4 cross each other. No stern deck line is evidenced.

The KNK 1161 is the narrowest kayak I have replicated. Building this kayak was especially challenging on account of the gunwale flare changing from plumb forward to considerable flare aft of the cockpit. The gunwales had to essentially be

Figure 203: The completed frame of the KNK 1161 replica. (Photograph by author.)

Figure 204: Replica of the KNK 1161. (Photograph by author).

tortured into place with straps and levers. As in the original, I used lower-placed deck beams to push out the lower edges of the gunwales in the front of the kayak, and I used many lashings to pull them in aft of the cockpit; there is a phenomenal amount of tension and compression in this otherwise dainty structure.

At the same time I was trying to manage the gunwale's compound flare, I had to ensure that the sheer-line was correct in all its subtleties. I had known this would be particularly challenging so I used over-height gunwales and shaped them down to the proper appearance once the flare had been set. Essentially the experience building this kayak was a crash-course in learning what wood wants to do and how to change its mind. The result is a phenomenal kayak, and a much better understanding about the how and why of this unique form— discussed at length in this study's analysis.

In order to fit inside this kayak, I had to adjust the span between the *masik* and *isserfik*: The original's span— measured along the kayak's centerline— is 10-7/8″ (27.6cm); my replica's measures 16-3/4″ (42.5cm), and is still painfully tight. The original's coaming is missing, but I estimate that it measured 14-3/8″ (36.5cm) long by 13-1/8″ (33.3cm) wide; my replica's coaming is 18″ (45.7cm) long by 14-3/8″ (36.5cm) wide.

The launching of this replica was very challenging— the cockpit, although lengthened to accommodate me, was still very tight. This kayak was also much tippier than expected given my positive experiences with the Hindeloopen replica. I had to brace constantly when not paddling, although after 30 minutes I could calmly just rest the paddle in the water to hold myself up. The tippiness is likely on account of half the hull being fairly rounded in section; while the forward half is squarish, it seems to contribute more volume than stability.

The handling of this replica was much the same as my experience with the Hindeloopen kayak replica. Brian Schulz took it offshore in the Pacific during a low swell at Depoe Bay, Oregon. At the bar he ran into some larger waves and noted that the kayak had absolutely no inclination to rise up the wave faces, instead it just needled through them, leaving him to take their entire wave force on his chest. With the kayak submerged well over 50%, the kayak's stability was next to nothing; it's also especially difficult to turn a kayak that is underwater.

Figure 205: Another view of the replica of the KNK 1161. (Photograph by author).

As expected, the KNK 1161 replica is hardly affected by winds at all— on all quarters and beam, but if the winds stir the water up considerably, it can be a very wet and sloppy ride.

10. West Greenland Kayak of ca. 1600-1800: Weltmuseum, Frankfurt, Germany. Catalog no. N.S. 36481 ("Amsterdam")

Referred to as the "Amsterdam" kayak in Nooter's *Old kayaks of the Netherlands*, this kayak had been transferred from the Koninklijk Insitut voor de Tropen to the Museum für Völkerkunde in Frankfurt, Germany in 1954 (Nooter, 1971:43). (The Museum für Völkerkunde has been renamed Weltmuseum). Its one time presence in the Royal Institute of the Tropics is curious. Prior to this kayak's 1914 transfer to the Royal Institute of the Tropics it had been in the ethnological collections of the Zoological Gardens (Nooter, 1971:44). How the kayak got to the Netherlands remains a mystery, but presumably Dutch whalers returned with it as a souvenir.

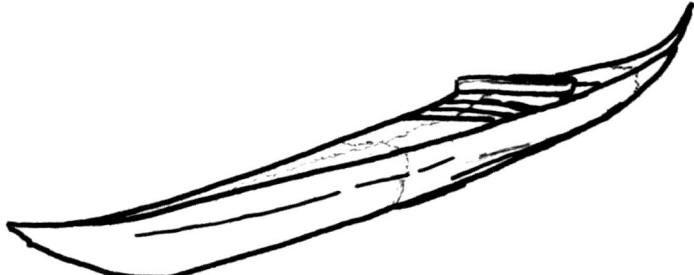

Figure 206: The Weltmuseum's kayak 36481.

While this kayak is among the longest examples in this study (18′ 5-1/8″; 561.6cm), it is also the narrowest adult-size kayak, being 14-9/16″ (36.9cm) wide. Its extreme narrowness and formidable length give this kayak the highest length-to-width ratio of any in this study: 15.22; see appendix A.

Some slight hull collapse is present in the 36481: At the *masik* the depth to sheer measured 5-3/8″ (13.6cm) I conjecturally restored the depth to sheer in the survey drawing to 6-1/8″ (15.5cm). The hull collapse is evident in figure 207.

The 36481's lower gunwale face inside the cockpit area have been shaved down about 1/4″ (6mm) thinner than the upper face— likely to accommodate, albeit snugly, the kayaker. The notion of a half-inch gain being that critical to one's ability to use this vessel speaks much of the original builder/hunter's desire for a narrow-as-possible kayak

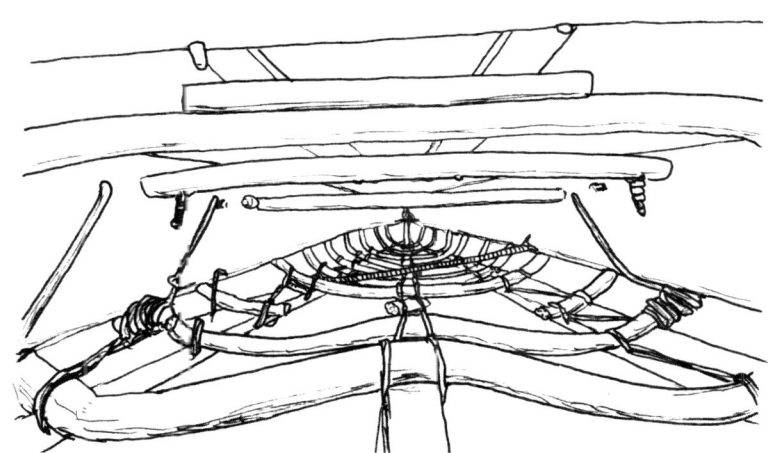

Figure 207: Forward interior view of the Weltmuseum's kayak 36481. The slight hull-collapse is evident; remarkably the ribs have not broken. Note the shim beneath the deck stringers and the broken baleen clamping tie.

All of the 36481's lashings are baleen. Continuous lashings are present securing the chines and keelson to the ribs. The lashing pattern used is the double-pass method depicted in figures 72 and 73 middle. The deck beams are lashed to the gunwales using the method depicted in figure 37b. As narrow as this kayak is, it still bears the common pattern of two deck stringers forward, and two aft of the cockpit. The forward deck stringers on the 36481 measure 3/8″ (9mm) thick and 7/8″ (22mm) wide; the aft deck stringers are 9/16″ (14mm) thick and 1-1/16″ (27mm) wide.

The *masik* in the 36481 is 3-13/16″ (9.7cm) wide and 1/2″ (13mm) thick at the ends. In the middle of the *masik* there is a bulge 3-3/8″ (8.5cm) long that thickens to 1-3/16″ (30mm) (see figure 208); this bulge is a hand grip carved into the *masik*'s lower face, and it has a cross-section as in figure 79 middle. The 36481's *isserfik* measures 3/4″ (19mm) thick by 1-1/16″ (27mm) wide and is oval in cross-section.

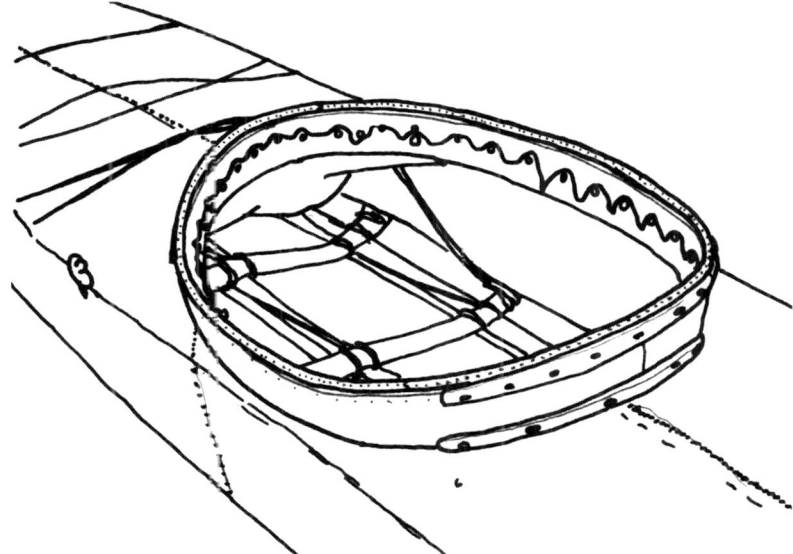

Figure 208: A cockpit view of the Weltmuseum's 36481. Note the handhold carved into the masik.

The 36481's coaming is fitted with the usual ivory or bone back-bands, but also has a circumfrencial band of bone/ivory that continues from the upper back-piece. Further, the coaming has a cap-piece all the way around as well. The circumfrencial band is 1/16″ (1.5mm) thick by 3/16″ (5mm) wide; the cap-piece is 3/16″ (5mm) high and 1/4″ (6mm) thick. The former is pegged every 15/16″ (24mm) to 1-1/8″ (29mm), and is positioned 1/4″ (6mm) below the coaming's top edge. The cap piece is pegged every 1/4″ (6mm) or so with 1/16″ (1.5mm) diameter pegs— "More than one hundred," Nooter writes (1971:43).

The coaming's back-band pieces are 8-1/4″ (21cm) long, 1/4″ (6mm) thick, and 1/2″ (13mm) wide, and the upper one is placed 1/4″ (6mm) below the top of the cap-piece. The coaming itself measures 1/2″ (13mm) thick by 1-5/8″ (41mm) high, sans cap-piece. A view of the cockpit and coaming back is depicted in figure 208.

Keel edging is missing but evidenced between 4-3/4″ and 2′7-1/8″ (12.1cm to 79.1cm) from the bow; edging is not present or evidenced astern. The 36481 originally had a stern knob, as evidenced by a side-peg hole 1/4″ (6mm) from the tip; the tip at the bow is damaged such that I couldn't tell if a knob had been present, but I think it would be unusual to have a stern knob and not a bow knob as well.

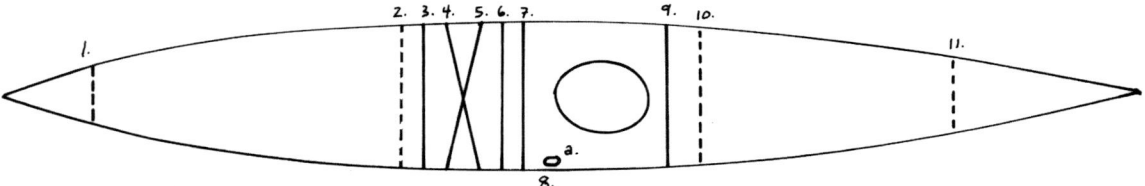

Weltmuseum, Frankfurt: Cat. no. 36481

Not so significant, but nonetheless of interest is the fact that this kayak belonged to a left-handed hunter. This is based on the placement of the harpoon-holder on the left side of the coaming, being adjacent to the hunter's throwing hand. The harpoon holder itself is of a unique motif— unique at least as a fitting on kayaks, but actually fairly common as a motif on the bone or ivory wings of winged-harpoons. This motif, while somewhat 'heart-shaped' in European culture, represents the tail of a seal in Greenlandic culture (Petersen, 1986:95), as well as among Inuit of Eastern Canada (Boas, 1901-07:19-18). This seal-tail shape appears on two other kayaks in this study: the National Museum of Natural History's kayak 160325 (plate 56), and the Danish National Museum's kayak Lc.148 (plate 82).

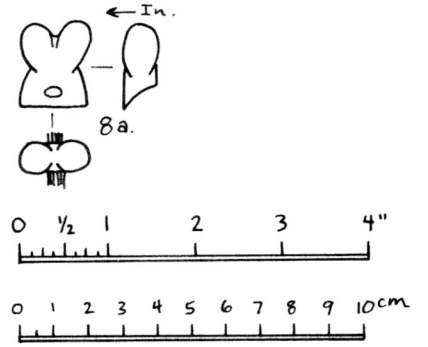

11. West Greenland Kayak of ca. 1600–1800: Wereldmuseum, Rotterdam, the Netherlands. Catalog no. 32848.

Apparently 'discovered' among the Rotterdam Rijksmuseum voor Volkenkunde's collections in 1952, this mysterious kayak's history is entirely unknown prior to 1952 (The Rotterdam Rijksmuseum is presently known as the Wereldmusem). I found out about this kayak during an appointment in 2002 to see the Wereldmuseum's Caribou Inuit kayak; fortunately I was able to study both.

Based on its form, construction, proportions, and rigging, it would stand to reason that this kayak could easily date from the 1600s or 1700s. Despite its damage, its profile is very similar to that of the 36481, having a very short and low bow, and a graceful up-turned stern.

This kayak had been sawn in half— a fairly sure indicator it was collected by a ship with limited storage space; this is one of two kayaks in this study that have been sawn in half— the other is the Marischal College Museum kayak ABDUA:5736 (plate 17). While time does not usually treat museum kayaks well, this one has greatly improved since having been sawn up. Conservators have re-assembled the kayak, and in such a manner that it was difficult to see that it had ever been halved.

The 32848 still exhibits considerable damage, particularly hull-collapse, and sagging of the sheer. The upper profile (or elevation) in plate 11 is an artifactual presentation; the lower profile is a conjectural interpretation of the original form. The plan-view shows only one rib in the cockpit— there was likely another originally, but the gunwales in this vicinity are new pieces added by conservators, and they lack the mortises to indicate any ribs' original placement.

Figure 209: The Wereldmuseum's 32848.

Being that the conjectural restoration is just one possible answer to this kayak's original form, one may consider that it had cross-sections more like those of the previous kayak: The 36481. They bear distinct similarities in their elevations, and if the 32848's gunwales were originally more vertical (such that their lower edges produced a 'chine'), their sections would be nearly identical.

Figure 210 shows an aft interior view of the 32848. As can be seen, much of the keelson and many of the ribs are missing; the aft hull was in much better condition than the forward hull. Note the rib mortises carved into the gunwales— they are

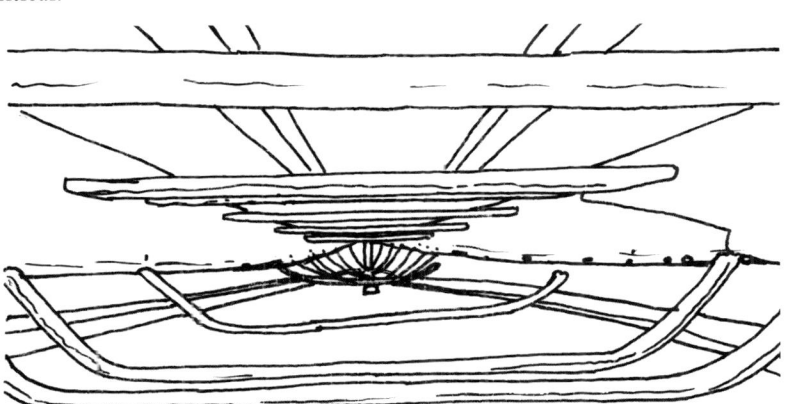

Figure 210: Aft interior of the Wereldmuseum's kayak 32848. Note the scarf on the right.

161

carved into the lower corner of the gunwale instead of into the lower edge. Also note the scarf joint on the gunwale at right.

The 32848's *masik* measures 2-1/2" (63mm) wide and 1/2" (13mm) thick at its forward edge and ends. At its center aft edge, the *masik* bulges downward to 1-1/4" (32mm) thick; this bulge is a handhold cut through as in figure 80. The 32848's *isserfik* was missing, as were the forward deck stringers; their positions are noted on the scale drawing but their precise length remains uncertain.

The 32848's coaming measures 3/8" (9mm) by 1-3/4" (44mm) high, and a 1/8" (3mm) thick by 1/4" (6mm) high ivory rim is fastened to the coaming's upper face (not edge) all around except for 6" (15.2cm) adjacent the coaming's scarf in back. The coaming also has two bone strips spanning its scarf joint: both measure 1/4" (6mm) square, and the upper piece is 9-3/4" long (24.7cm) (covering part of the ivory rim), and the lower is 8-1/4" (20.9cm) long, placed 1/4" (6mm) above the bottom edge of the coaming.

Keel edging on the 32848 is present at the bow and evidenced at the stern. The bow is shod from the very tip to 2'1" (63.5cm) aft. It tapers gradually, and reaches its maximum height of 1/2" (13mm) between 6" to 1'6" (15.2 to 45.7cm) from the bow. The edging at the stern is evidenced from 16'5-3/4" to 17'9-1/2" (502.2 to 542.2cm). It is worth noting that most of the 'early-period' examples of collected Greenland kayaks (circa 1600-1800) exhibit no keel edging at the stern.

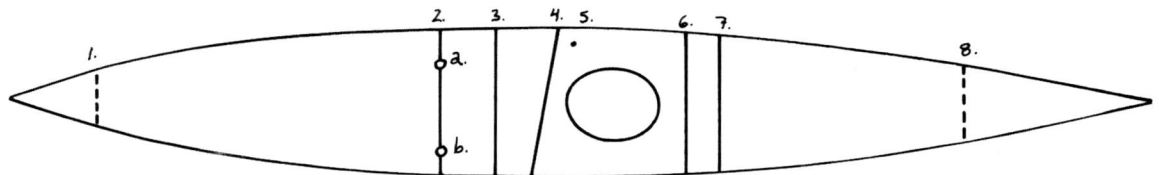

Wereldmuseum, Rotterdam: Cat. no. 32848

More than half of the 32848's deck lines are missing, but those that are intact are of a unique arrangement. Deck line 2 has two fittings— not cones, but low elongated buttons; these are the only fittings present. Deck line 4 is an oblique line, spanning the entire deck. A *masik*-mounted harpoon holder is missing but evidenced.

It appears that the 32848 had at one time been painted black, although the stern on the right side appears to have been painted gray. A paddle at the Wereldmuseum is associated with the 32848 and is depicted in paddle-plate 12.

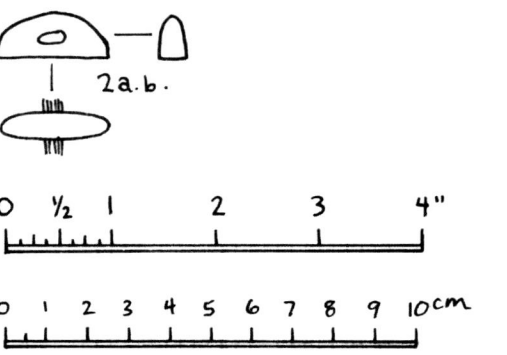

12. West Greenland Kayak of pre-1865: National Museum of Scotland, Edinburgh. Catalog no. 1995.886.

The provenance of the 1995.886 is unknown, but I would estimate that it dates from the mid-to-late 1700s. It was accessioned by the National Museum of Scotland in 1995, having been received from the Royal College of Surgeons, Edinburgh. This kayak's onetime presence at the college suggests it may have been a gift from an alumni, perhaps a ship's surgeon; the college's history does little to narrow down a possible date of origin, as it was founded as a guild in 1505. Figure 211 depicts the 1995.886.

The shallow sweeping tail of the 1995.886 is a stunning marvel of carpentry. The lower edge of the gunwale gradually presents a chine just ahead of the cockpit, and reaches quite far aft, following the raised stern before fading.

This kayak exhibits typical type II features: a short bow, reverse sheer, and rounded sections behind the cockpit and boxier sections forward. The 1995.886 does have slightly more deadrise than most other type II kayaks and the forward section's sides have considerable flare. While the hull's sections do change shape forward-to-aft, the gunwale flare stays relatively constant.

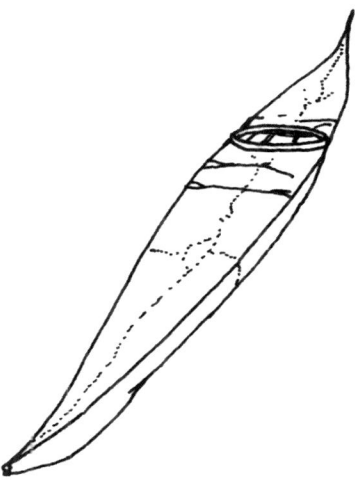

Figure 211: The NMS 1995.886.

Figure 212 shows the forward interior view of the 1995.886. The ribs are double-pass lashed to the keelson and chines with seal skin line. The deck beams are lashed to the gunwales with baleen.

The seal skin *amiq* is a rich dark brown, but it appears as if the entire deck and the coaming have been painted black. It is uncertain whether Greenlanders or Europeans painted the deck, and it is also a mystery as to why the deck was painted at all. Paint has been used on seal skin as both camouflage and as a sealant, but in neither case would it be of particular advantageous to paint just the deck.

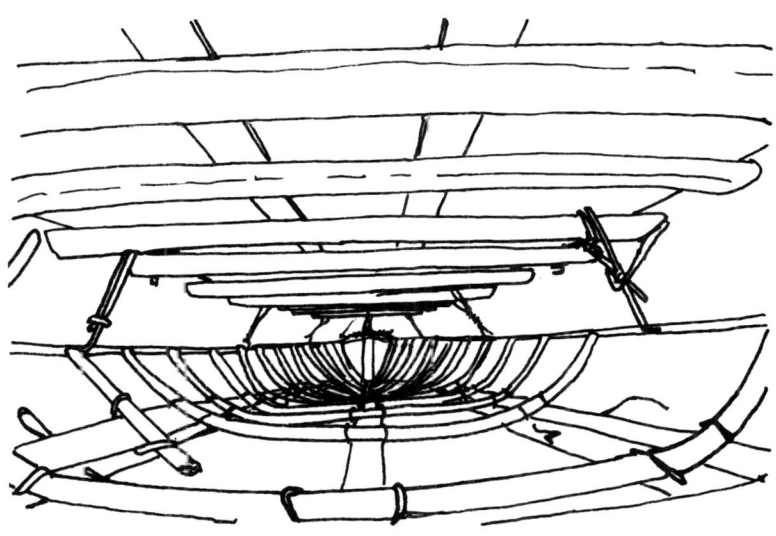

Figure 212: Forward interior view of the NMS 1995.886.

Both deck-lines immediately behind the cockpit are broken, so it is impossible to determine whether or not they were linked together or had any fittings. The other lines are unbroken, and the furthest lines fore and aft have no fittings. Just ahead of the cockpit is a single line; this line is most commonly linked to the line just ahead of it, but this is not the case in this example; such an exception may simply reflect the personal preference of the hunter.

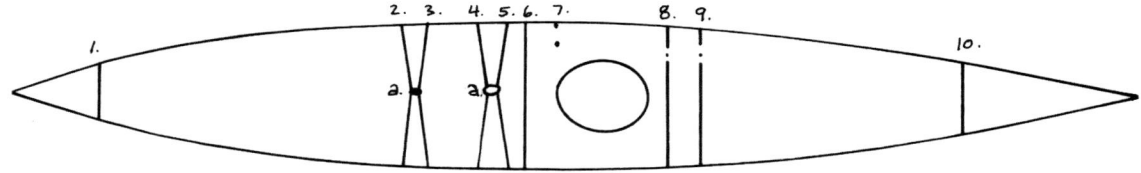

National Museum of Scotland: Cat. no. 1995.886

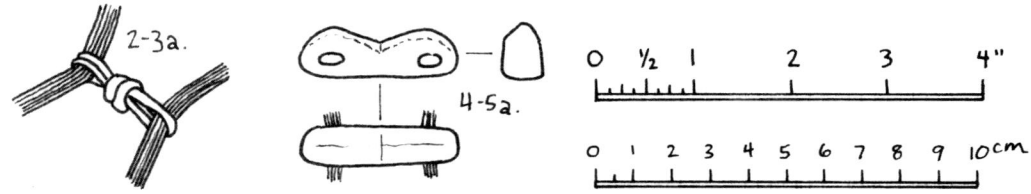

The forward linked pair of deck lines doesn't have a link-fitting per-se, but are instead tied together with a few turns of seal skin line. This may have been an afterthought on the part of the builder/kayaker, or a quick replacement for a missing deck fitting. The harpoon holder is missing, but is evidenced on the right side of the cockpit, having been set through the *masik*.

13. West Greenland Kayak of ca. Late 1700s – early 1800s: Trinity House, Hull, England. (N/N) 'B'

The most famous kayak at the Hull Trinity House is the kayak collected during James Hall's Greenland voyage of 1612. Hall turned over his command of the ship to Andrew Barker after being mortally wounded by a harpoon thrown by a Greenlander in a kayak (Gosch, 1897:cix; Baffin, in Gosch, 1897:124). Barker's name has been painted on the kayak, the full inscription reading: "ANDREW BARKER ONE OF THE MASTERS OF THIS HOUSE ON HIS VOYAGE FROM GREENLAND ANNO DOMINI 1613 TOOK UP THIS BOAT AND A MAN IN IT OF WHICH THIS IS THE EFFIGY"(Brand, 1984: 2).

The 1612 kayak has been studied and documented by John Brand and is presented in *The Little Kayak Book, Vol.I* (Brand, 1984:1-10), and in Heath, et al. (2004:84). While it is widely known and is the pride of the Trinity House, it is the other two kayaks at the House that are presented in this study, as they are in fact finer examples in much better condition, although not as old and less historically interesting.

Commander Arthur Storey, in his book *Trinity House of Kingston upon Hull, Vol. II*, writes that in 1753 there was only one "canoe" in the Canoe Room, and that today there are three (1969:161). It is obvious that the example of circa 1613 was at the Trinity House from early on, as the collector himself (Andrew Barker) gifted it to the house.

Of the other two kayaks, Commander Storey writes:

The other two canoes, twenty feet and seventeen and a half feet in length, are of similar design and make to that given by Captain Barker. One of them, it is not known which one, was given to the Guild by Captain W. Clark at the time of his election as a Younger Brother in 1776. The order in the Vote book, dated August 9th, 1776, reads, "That W. Clark be presented with his Brotherhood of this House free of all expenses in consideration of his having given this Corporation a boat which belonged to a Native of Davis Straits with all the Fishing Apparatus" (1969:162)

A ship's master "Wm. Clark" of the *Unicorn* appears in the Lloyds Register for the 1775-1776 seasons (Jones, 1996:4). The *Unicorn* apparently sailed from Liverpool to Greenland, assuming I have interpreted the voyage abbreviations "Liv-Gld" correctly (Jones, 1996:4). Whether or not it is the same Captain Clark is unknown.

Only meager evidence suggests that the Trinity House kayak 'A'—the larger of the two mentioned above— is the kayak dating from 1776. W. C. Souter's table of "33 Kayaks in Great Britain" lists the shorter (non-1613) kayak as having been acquired "about 1830." The longest one at Trinity House (237" by his measurements) is not provided a date of acquisition in his table (1934:13). Unfortunately, Souter provides no source with regards to the date of circa 1830. It is the present kayak—the 'B'—that would be the 1830 kayak, assuming the above information is correct. (The Trinity House 'A,' a type III kayak, is presented in plate 16).

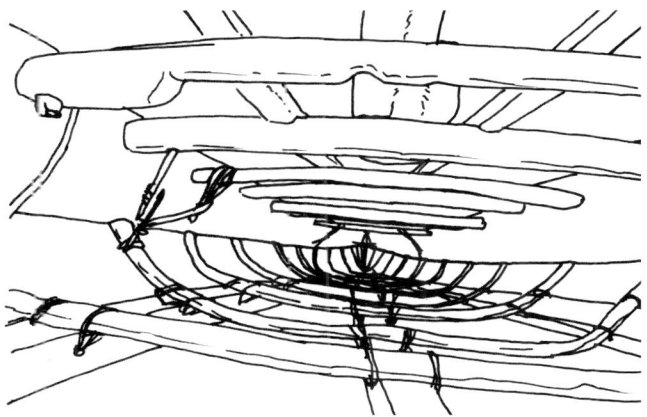

Figure 213: Forward interior of the Hull Trinity House's kayak 'B.' Note the shaping of the curved deck beam and the three forward deck stringers.

For all their time on this earth, the kayaks of the Trinity House nearly met their demise in the 1920s when a fire in an adjacent kitchen came quite close to their hulls. They all three survived, and perhaps are conserved for eternity as their shellac-finishes seem to have 'caramelized' into an armored layer from the heat.

The Trinity House kayak 'B' exhibits several distinct type II features: The gunwales are fairly plumb forward, but gradually twist as they pass the kayak's midpoint. Also, there is a slight reverse sheer, and the gunwale's lower edges protrude distinctly into the *amiq* for much of the kayak's length.

Four deck stringers are present in the 'B': Three forward and one aft, along the centerline. The forward deck stringers converge at their forward end; the middle stringer is 2" (50mm) wide, and the outer stringers are 1/2" (13mm) wide. The aft deck stringer is 1/4" (5mm) thick and 1-1/2" (38mm) wide, and extends aft of the *isserfik* to about 11' 9" (358.1cm) from the bow. The *masik* measures 5/8" (16mm) thick by 3-1/2" (89mm) wide in the middle, and has a rectangular hole cut through it that serves as a handhold. The *isserfik* measures 5/8" (16mm) thick by 1-1/4" (32mm) wide.

Several inches of the stern are missing from the 'B,' but by continuing the existent lines, I've arrived at a conjectural original length of about 18' 4-1/2" [560cm]). Other than this damage, the 'B' is in exceptional condition.

Shims appear regularly in Greenland kayaks—chips of wood lashed-in to fill any gaps between the ribs and the chines or keelson. The 'B' has a very unusual form of shim that is long—spanning two rib/chine junctions. It would seem unlikely that these two ribs were just bent too short on accident, so the shims may have served as a way of elevating the seat, seeing as how they are in the cockpit area. This type of shim appears on both sides, abreast of each other, and at 7/16" (11mm) high, is fairly tall as well. The shims are further held in place by small splints tenoned into the shim's sides and into the gunwale's lower edge, as if a rib. Further aft in the 'B,' there are normal-size shims, some even in a row, and not made of single long strips.

The Trinity House kayak 'B's' ribs are lashed with the double-pass method to the chines and keelson with baleen in the alternating-straight pattern as depicted in figure 73 bottom. The deck-beam-to-gunwale joints are also baleen-tied. Baleen clamping-ties appear inside both ends of the kayak. A seat slat is present in this kayak: It is 8-7/8" (22.6cm) long, 2-1/4" (5.7cm) wide, and is tied with baleen beneath two ribs in the cockpit; the opposite slat is missing, but is depicted in the scale drawing. Figure 214 is a cockpit-view of the 'B,' and it shows the seat slat as well the forward end of a long rib-shim and the splint used to hold it in place. Also note the handhold cut into the *masik*.

The coaming on the THH 'B' is of a much-rounded triangular shape, and it is scarfed in the back with a stepped edge scarf, as in figure 116i. The coaming is 1/2" (13mm) thick by 1-7/16" (36mm) high, and has two bone strips fastened to its back face: The upper strip is 7-1/4" (18.4cm) long, and the lower is 6-5/8" (16.8cm) long. Both strips are 3/16" (5mm) thick and 3/8" (9mm) wide.

Keel edging is present at the bow, from 3-7/8" to 2'6-1/2" (98mm to 77.4cm), and measures 5/16" (8mm) square, tapering to 3/16"

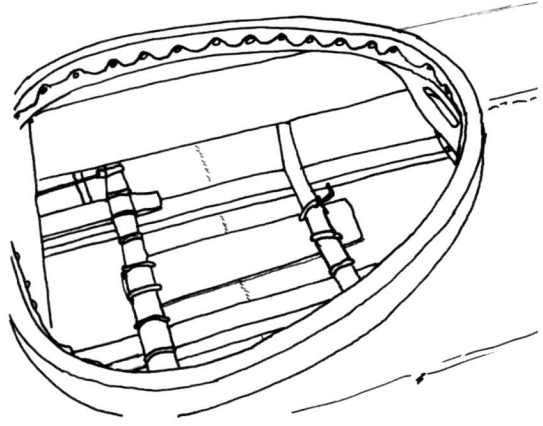

Figure 214: The cockpit of the Trinity House kayak 'B.' Note the seat-slat, masik *handhold, chine/rib shim and the unique splint holding it in place.*

(5mm) thick at the aft end. Stern edging was not present or evidenced. A bow knob was present at one time, evidenced by a hole 1/4" (6mm) aft of the kayak's tip; a fair amount of the stern is missing, and it may have had a knob as well.

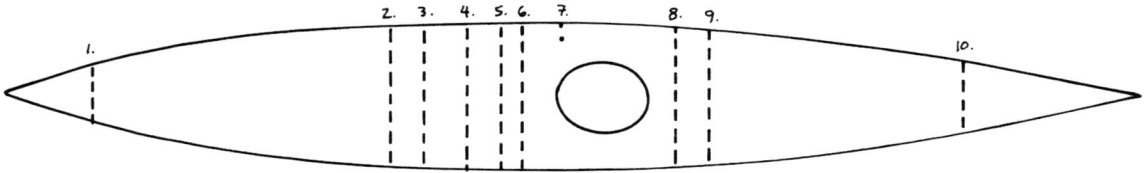

Trinity House, Hull: (n/n) "B"

Unfortunately, not a single deck line is present on the 'B,' though their placement is indicated on the scale drawing with dashed lines; their positions are evidenced by holes in the *amiq*. A paddle was laying on the THH "B's" deck; it cannot be certain that the paddle belonged to this kayak. This paddle is depicted in paddle-plate 13.

14. West Greenland Kayak: Hancock Museum, Newcastle upon Tyne, England. Catalog no. G.109.

Early mention of the Hancock Museum's kayak appears in *Transactions of the Natural History Society of Northumberland, Durham, and Newcastle upon Tyne, Volume II,* published in 1838 (Anonymous). Page 432 contains a continuation of a "List of Presents" arranged by year. Under the year 1837, among such mundane items as "A curious Walking Stick," and "Nuts found when cutting the Foundation for Sunderland Docks," appears "An Esquemaux Canoe"— donated by Captain Leisk, of the *Lady Jane*. A "J. Leask" is listed as one of the *Lady Jane*'s masters in the Lloyd's Register for 1838 (Jones, 1996:136); Leask

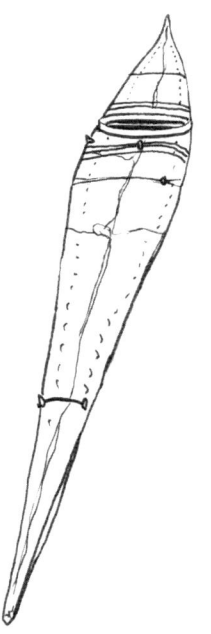

Figure 215: The Hancock Museum's kayak G.109.

may have collected the kayak while acting in a lower capacity prior to 1838. For 1838, the *Lady Jane* is listed as having sailed "Sh-NWF:" presumably from Shields to the Northern Whale Fishery (Jones, 1996:136).

The G.109 is in exceptional condition, appearing quite newly made. It has a remarkably flat bottom, and it is perhaps the flattest of the non-Polar Greenland kayaks in this study. No aft deck stringers are present or evidenced. Figure 215 shows a frontal view of the G.109: The dash-marks paralleling the sheer are anchor points for the internal lacing-line used to stretch the skin over the kayak's frame.

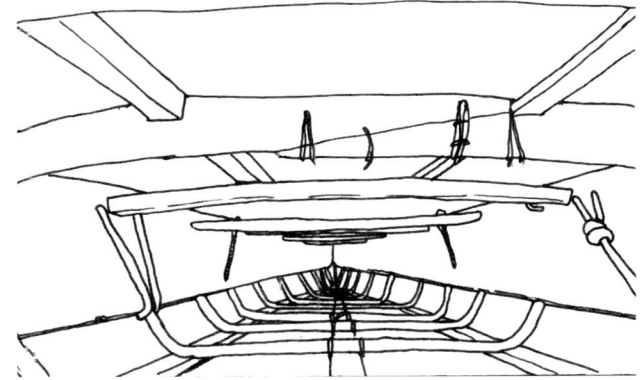

Figure 216: Forward interior view of the Hancock Museum's kayak G.109. Note the deep gunwales and abrupt bend in the ribs. The ribs are lashed to the keelson, but are pegged to the chines. The curved deck beam is made from two pieces of wood lashed together.

Figure 216 shows an inside view of the G.109, looking forward. Note the scarfed curved deck beam and the continuous deck lines threaded through the gunwales and around a rib. Also note the abrupt bend of the ribs at the bilge to achieve the very flat-bottomed hull shape.

The G.109's keelson is lashed to the ribs while the chines are pegged to the ribs. Such a combination of fastening methods is very rare among the kayaks in this study, although it is plain to see why it was done in this example:

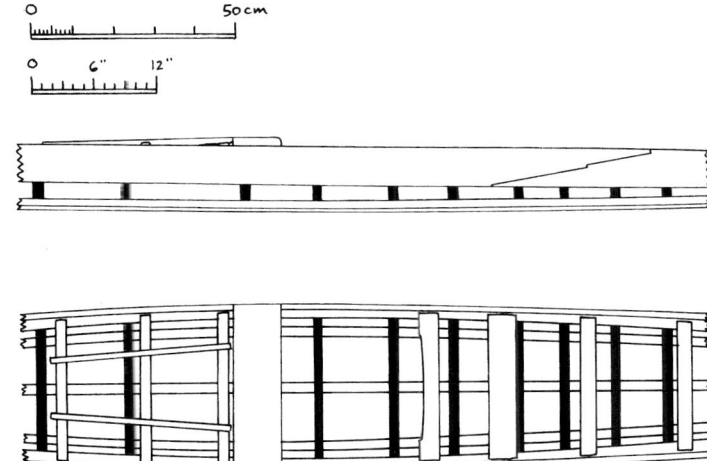

Figure 217: Framing details of the kayak G.109.

The chines could easily have slipped up and around the abrupt bend in the ribs had they not been pegged. The chines' upper facets are slightly channeled, as in figure 68, likely to achieve a firmer contact with the ribs.

To the extent that I could see and reach with a tape measure, I documented the positions of the framing in and around the cockpit of the G.109; the results are depicted in figure 217.

Some of the scantlings not depicted in the scale drawing are as follows: The *masik* measures 1/2" (13mm) thick and 4-1/2" (11.4cm) wide in the middle, and 1" (25mm) thick and 4-3/4" (12.0cm) wide at the ends. The *isserfik* is 1/2" (13mm) thick and 1-1/2" (38mm) wide in the middle, and 2" (51mm) wide at the ends. The coaming is 7/16" (11mm) thick and 1-3/8" (35mm) high.

One of the forward deck stringers is much thinner than the other; this can be seen in figure 216. The thicker stringer measures 1/2" (13mm) wide and 5/8" (16mm) high at its aft end. The G.109 has three curved deck beams (excluding the *masik*); they are positioned 5", 12-5/8", and 20-3/4" (12.7, 32.0, and 52.7cm) ahead of the *masik*'s aft edge, and they all are 1" square in cross-section.

The form of the G.109 is a bit anomalous—it hails from a period where most Greenland kayaks being brought south were of high-sterned forms (e.g., types III and IV). It isn't known what region the G.109 comes from, but it is perhaps a link to the forms brought to Europe over 100 years earlier by Dutch whalers. The G.109's cross-section is boxy and its stern is gradually elevated. It compares favorably to the likes of the KNK 1161 and RvV 351-77 (plates 9 and 8), albeit with a bow some 12″ (30.4cm) longer. They may all come from the same vicinity, the G.109 being a later example of the type.

Much of the G.109's hunting equipment is preserved: A lance, a harpoon shaft, throwing board, seal skin float (with the line and harpoon point attached) a bird spear, and a harpoon-line stand (damaged) are all kept with the kayak at the Hancock Museum. The projectiles and the throwing board are depicted in figure 218. The paddle associated with the kayak G.109 is depicted in paddle-plate 23.

Two conical implement holders are present on the G.109's bow deck line—this line is very slack, such that the holders are not especially prone to staying upright. These two pieces lean in towards each other. The deck fitting 2-3a is of an interesting form—perhaps an exaggerated version of the type seen on the NMS 1995.886 (piece 4-5a). Every deck line was present and intact on this kayak, which is often not the case, even with much newer kayaks.

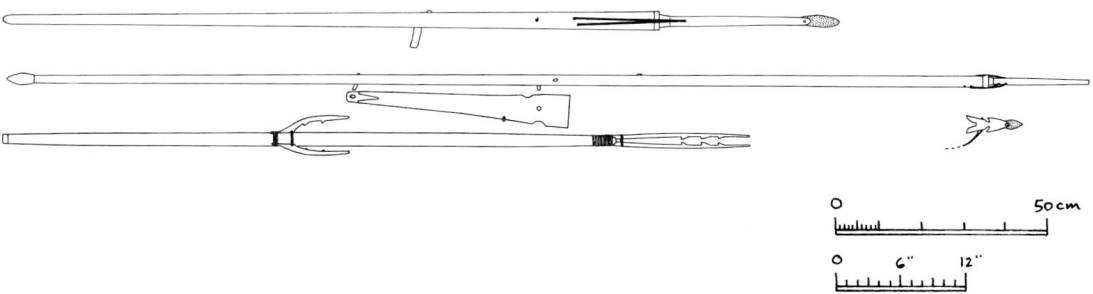

Figure 218: From top to bottom, the G.109's lance, harpoon and throwing board, and bird spear.

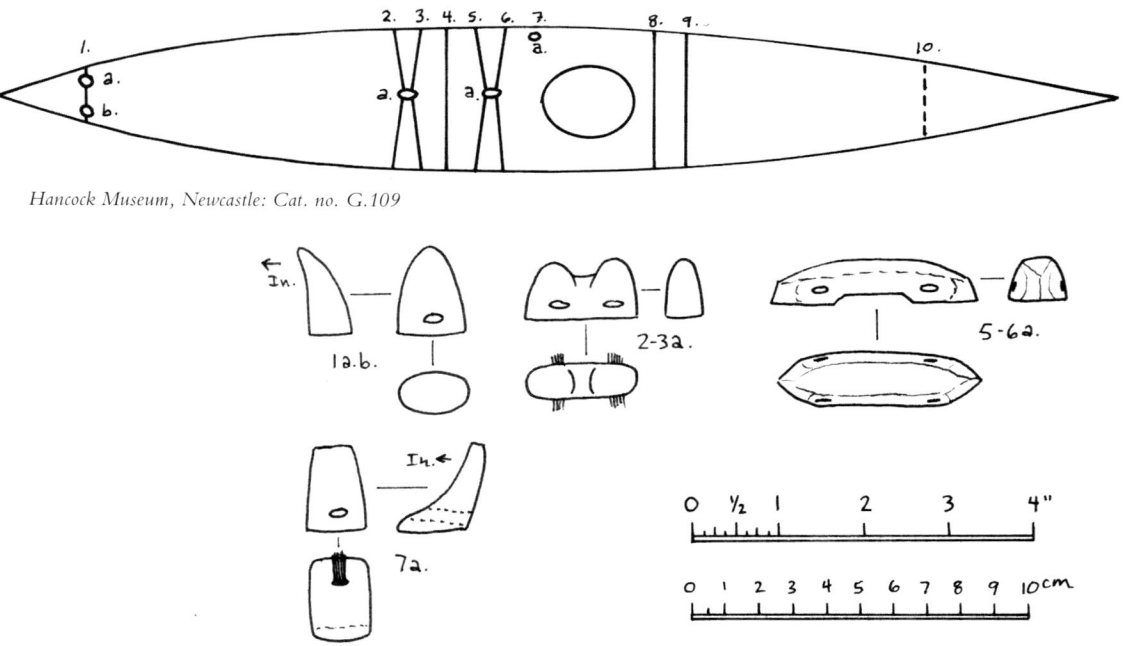

Hancock Museum, Newcastle: Cat. no. G.109

TYPE III.

Abruptly raised ends (bow and stern) with very fine profiles—spike-like—are the most characteristic features of this kayak type. In the earlier examples the profile of the bow is almost identical to the profile of the stern. In later examples, the stern tends to be raked much steeper, and the bow becomes more understated. The sheer amidships is generally very slight if not even reversed a bit. The shape of the cross-sections is fairly inconsistent, having steep deadrise in certain examples, and flat and boxy sections in others.

The vicinities where the type III kayaks in this study were collected were unfortunately not recorded; their form may have been fairly widespread on the West Coast at one time. Collection dates are mostly vague, but most seem to be from the late 1700s to the early 1800s; one example may be from the 1600s (plate 15). Of the 11 examples in this study, nine are in English or Scottish museums; the remaining two are in The Netherlands and France.

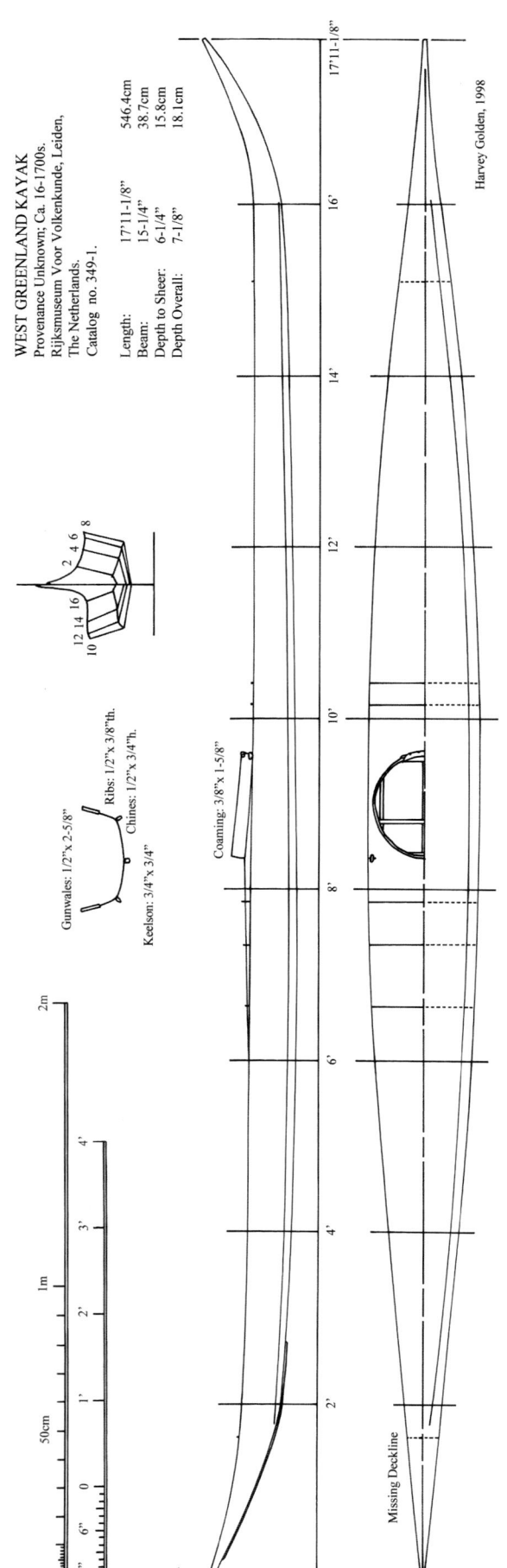

15. Rijksmuseum voor Volkenkunde catalog no. 349-1

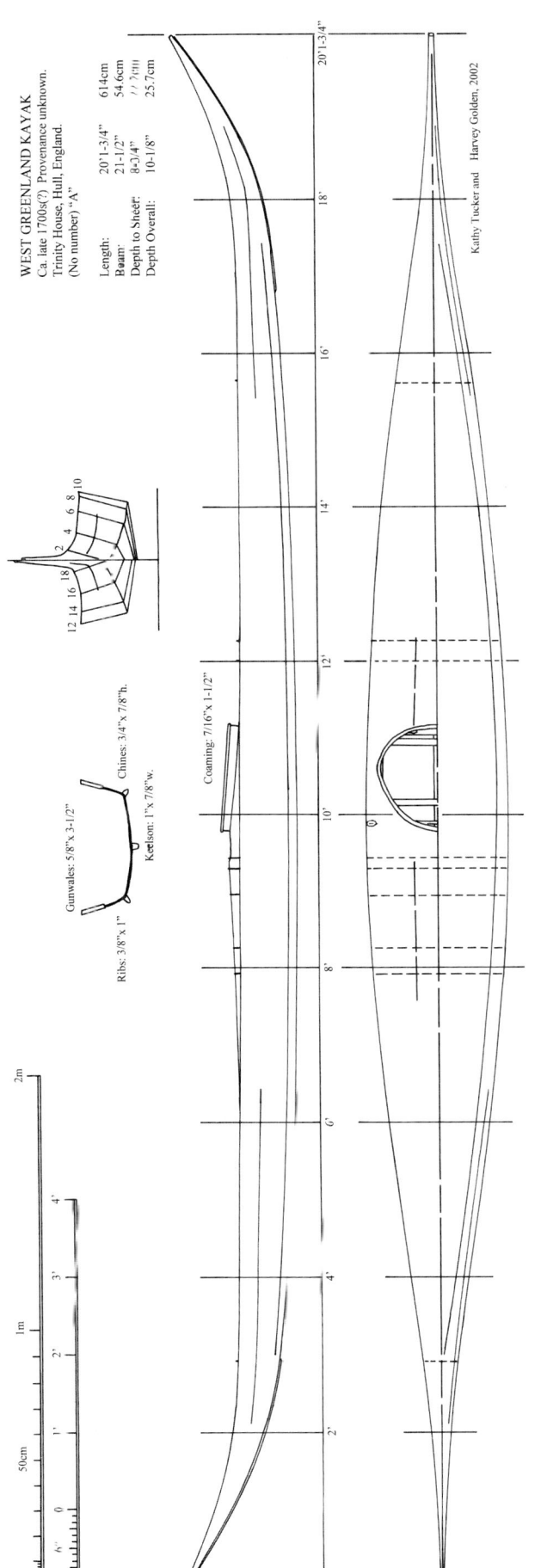

16. Trinity House Hull (N/N) "A"

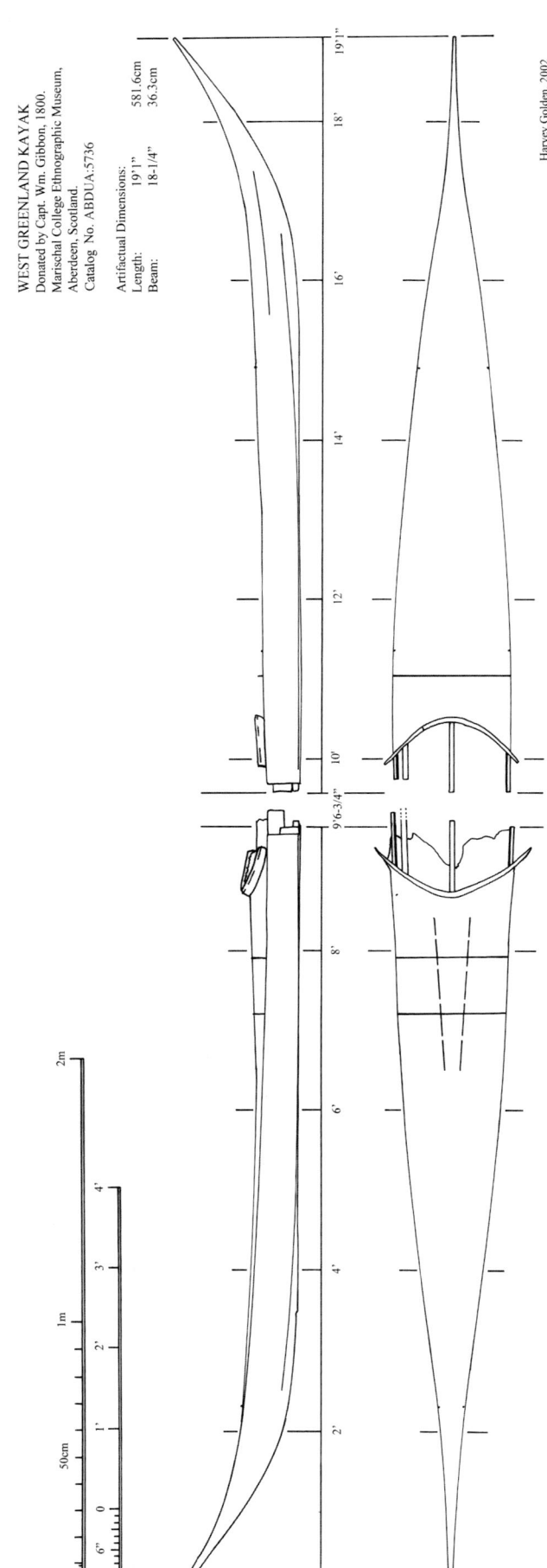

17a. Marischal College Museum catalog no. ABDUA:5736

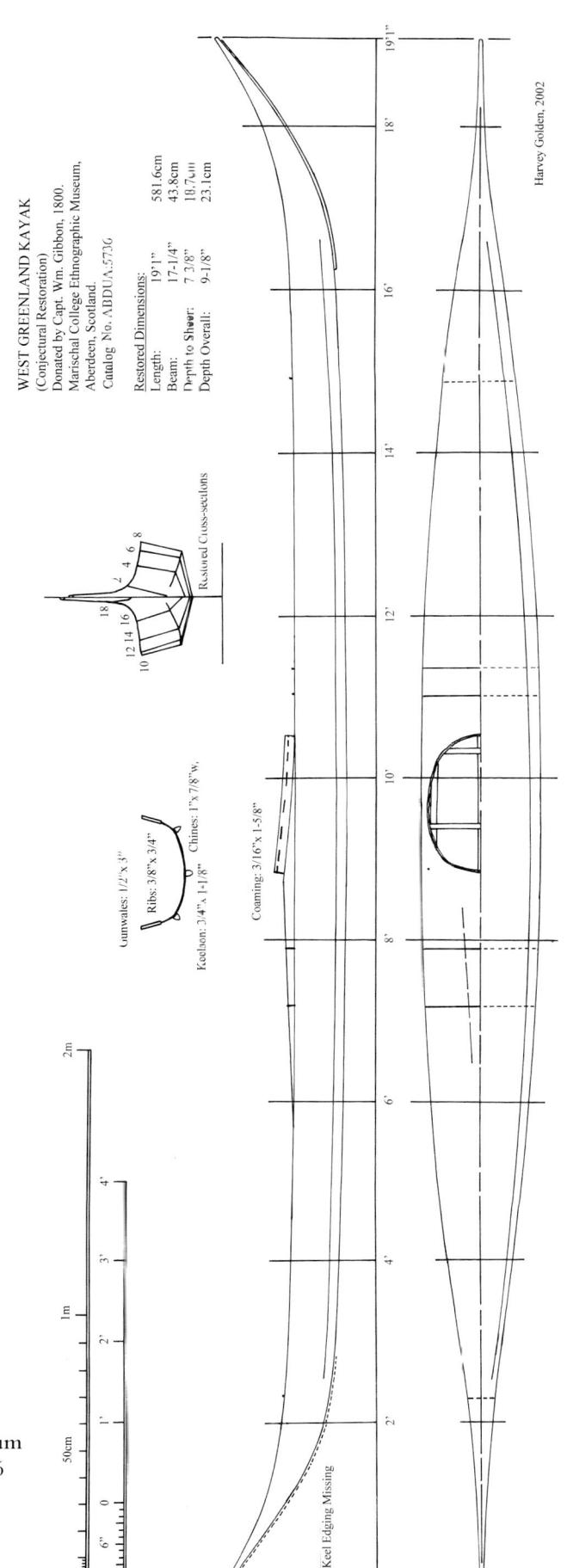

17b. Marischal College Museum catalog no. ABDUA:5736 (Restored Lines)

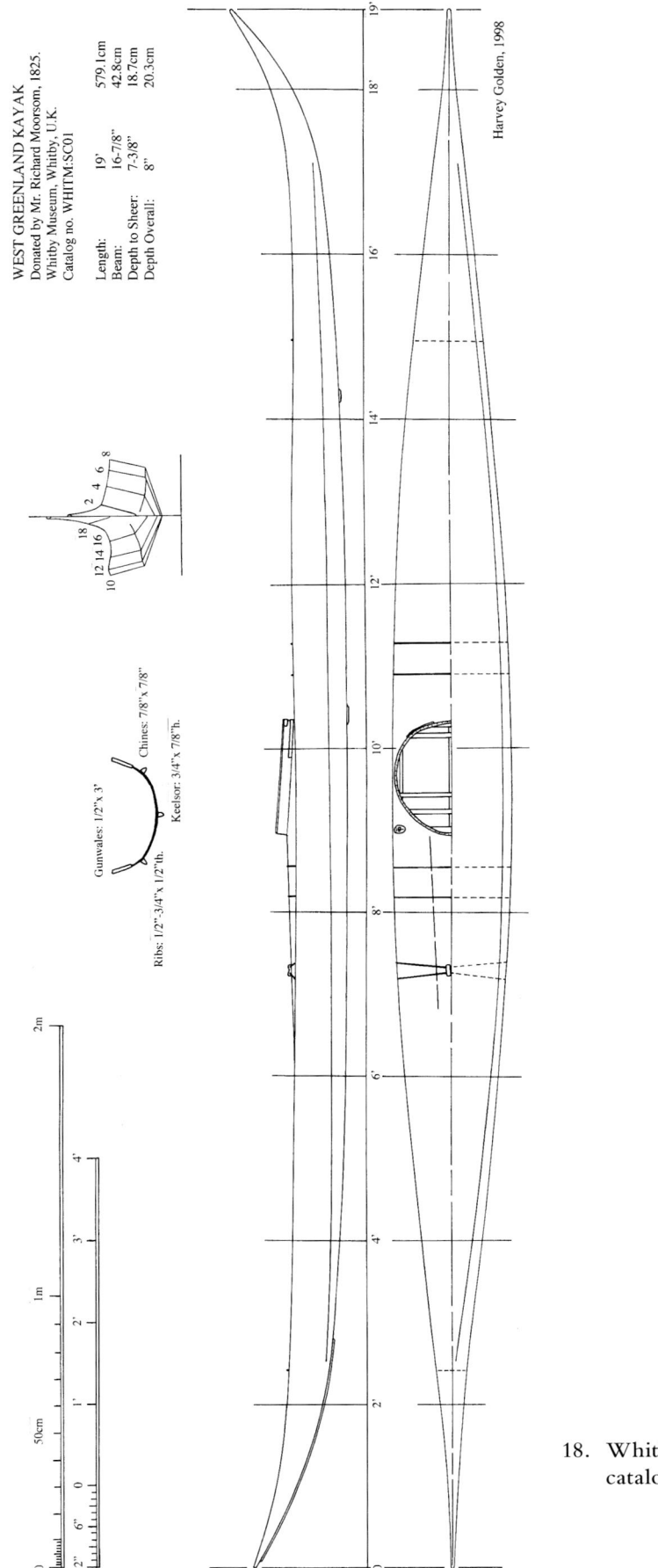

WEST GREENLAND KAYAK
Donated by Mr. Richard Moorsom, 1825.
Whitby Museum, Whitby, U.K.
Catalog no. WHITM:SC01

Length: 19'	579.1cm
Beam: 16-7/8"	42.8cm
Depth to Sheer: 7-3/8"	18.7cm
Depth Overall: 8"	20.3cm

Gunwales: 1/2" x 3"
Chines: 7/8" x 7/8"
Ribs: 1/2"–3/4" x 1/2" th.
Keelsons: 3/4" x 7/8" th.

Harvey Golden, 1998

18. Whitby Museum
catalog no. WHITM:SC01

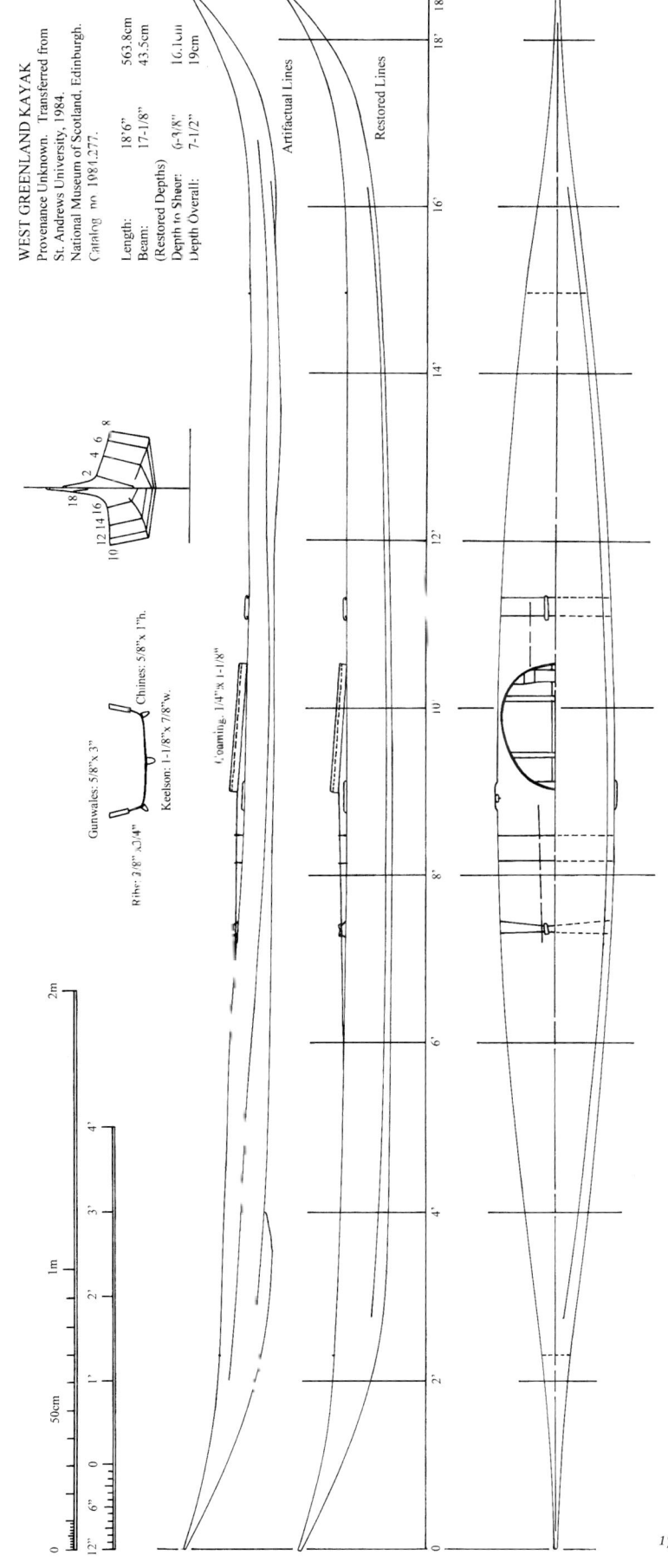

19. National Museum of Scotland catalog no. 1984.277

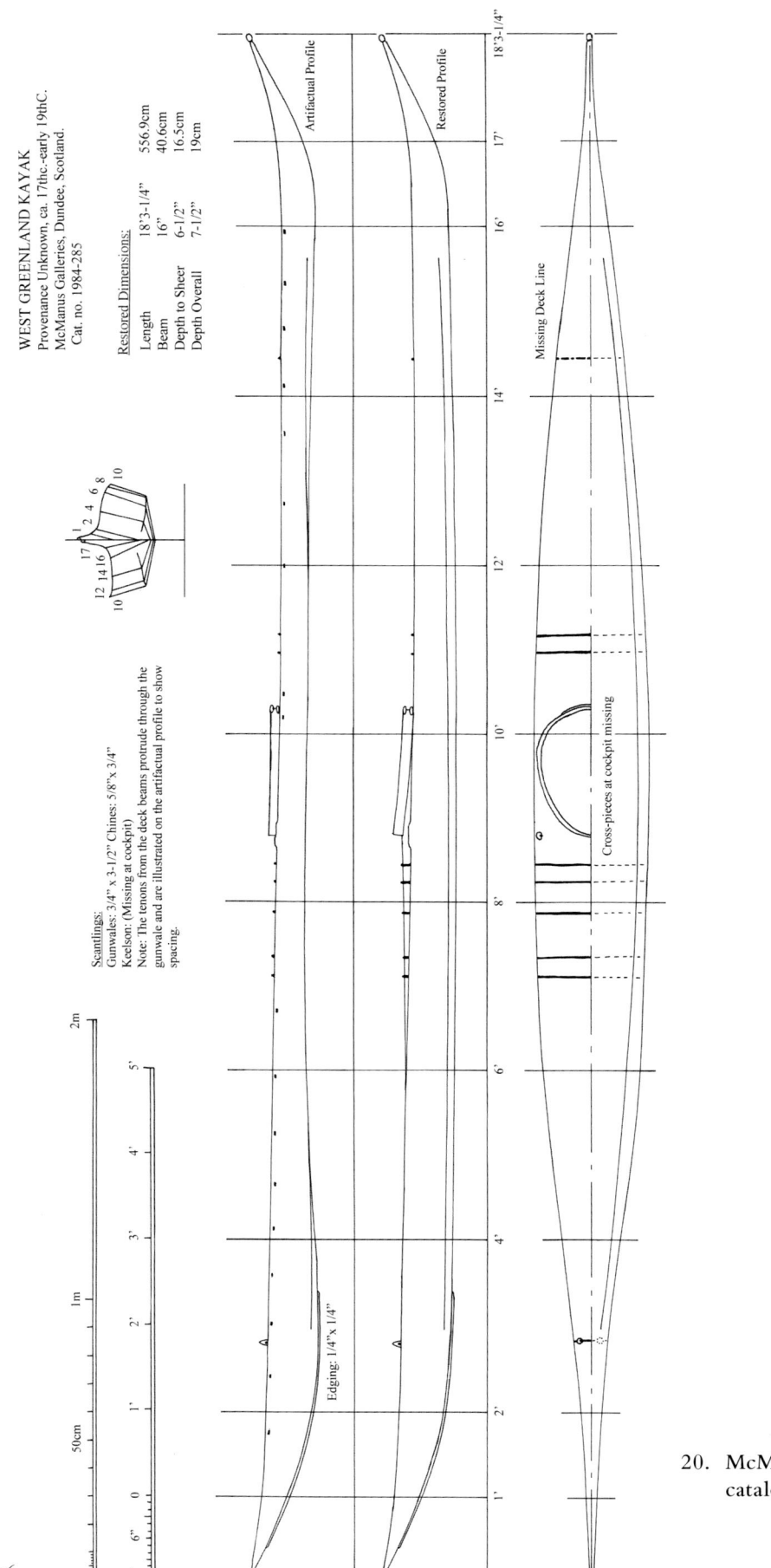

20. McManus Galleries catalog no. 1984.285

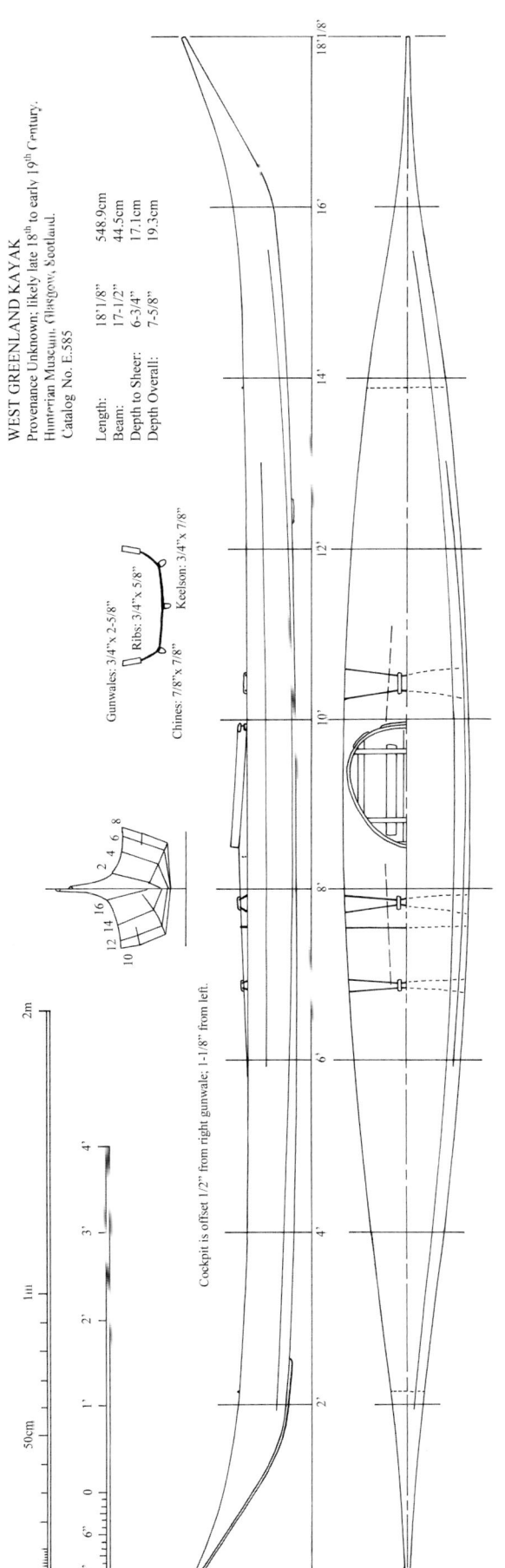

21. Hunterian Museum catalog no. E.585

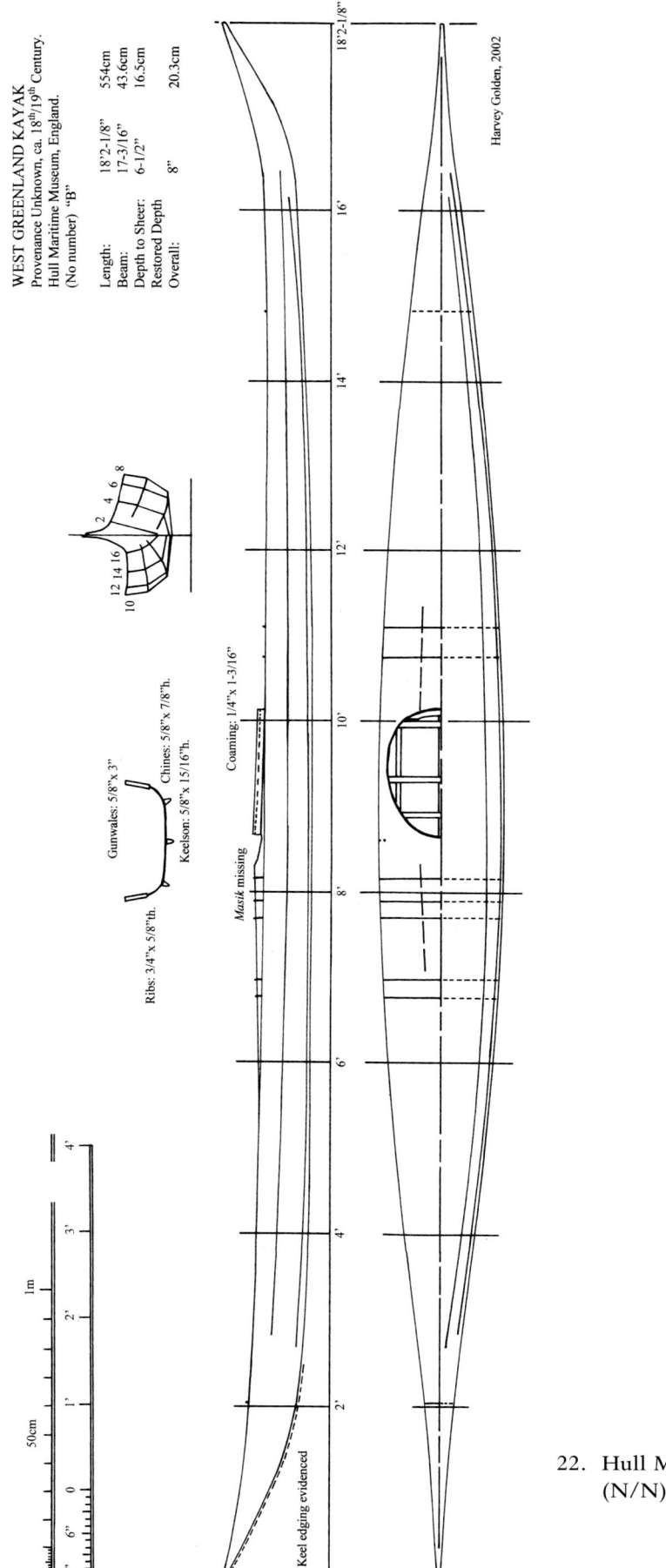

22. Hull Maritime Museum (N/N) "B"

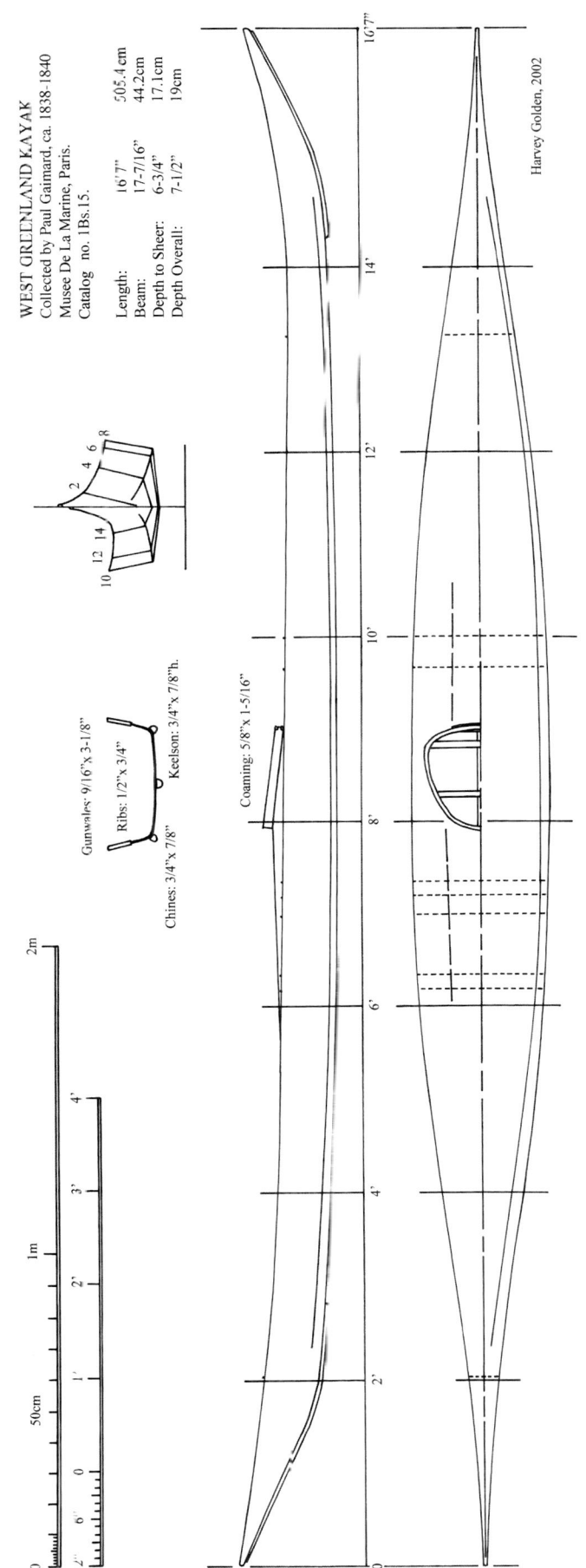

23. Musée de la Marine catalog no. 1Bs.15

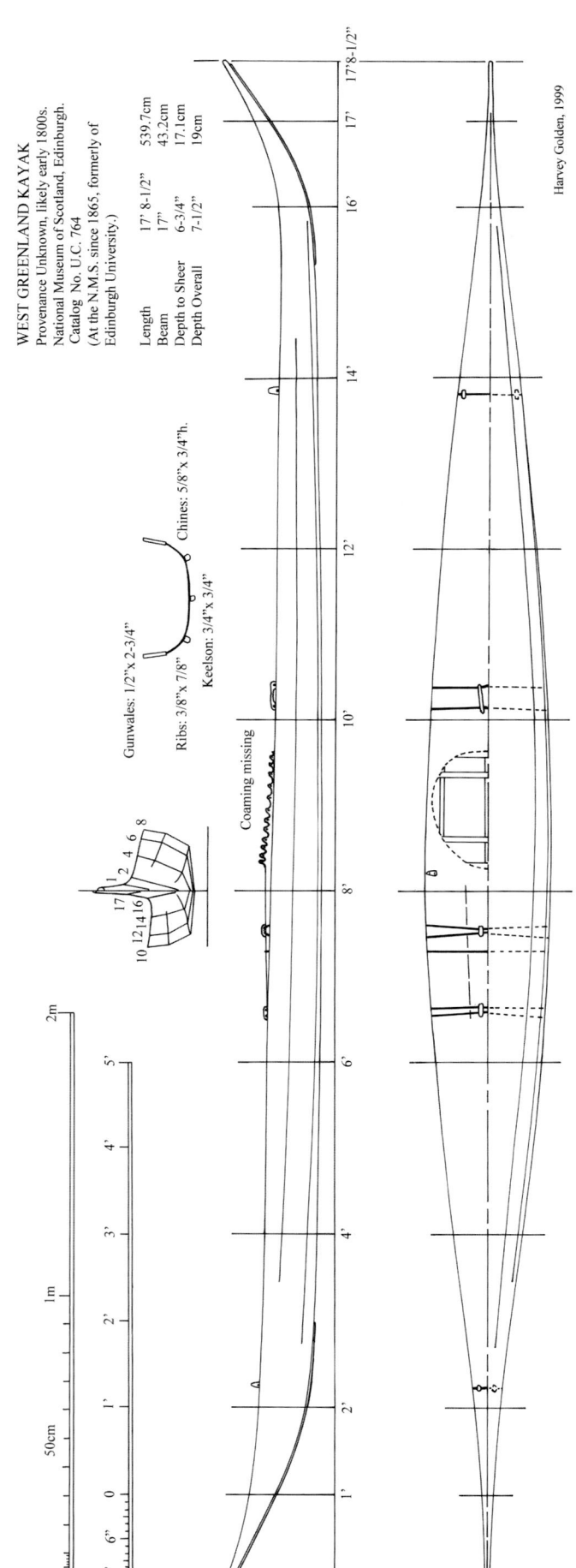

24. National Museum of Scotland catalog no. U.C. 764

WEST GREENLAND KAYAK
Provenance Unknown, likely early 1800s.
National Museum of Scotland, Edinburgh.
Catalog No. U.C. 764
(At the N.M.S. since 1865, formerly of Edinburgh University.)

Length	17' 8-1/2"	539.7cm
Beam	17"	43.2cm
Depth to Sheer	6-3/4"	17.1cm
Depth Overall	7-1/2"	19cm

Gunwales: 1/2"x 2-3/4"
Ribs: 3/8"x 7/8"
Chines: 5/8"x 3/4"h.
Keelson: 3/4"x 3/4"

Coaming missing

Harvey Golden, 1999

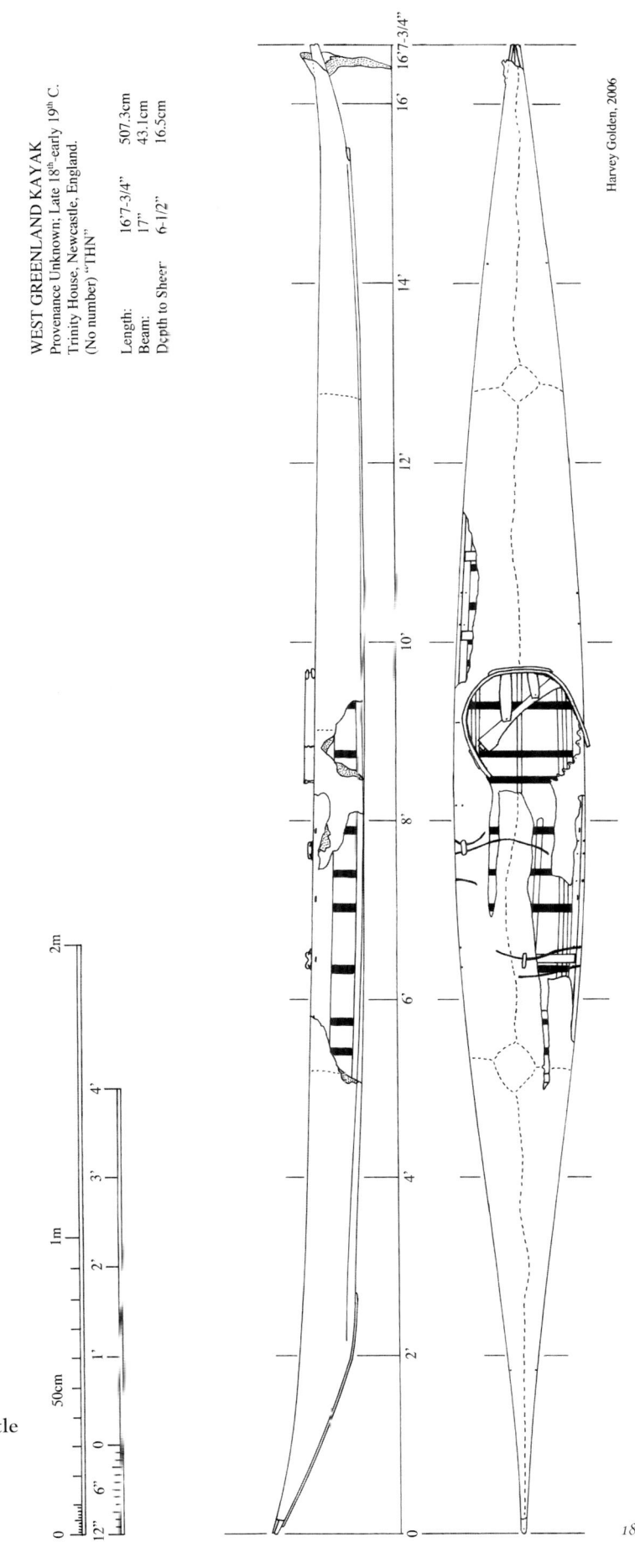

25a. Trinity House Newcastle (N/N) "THN"

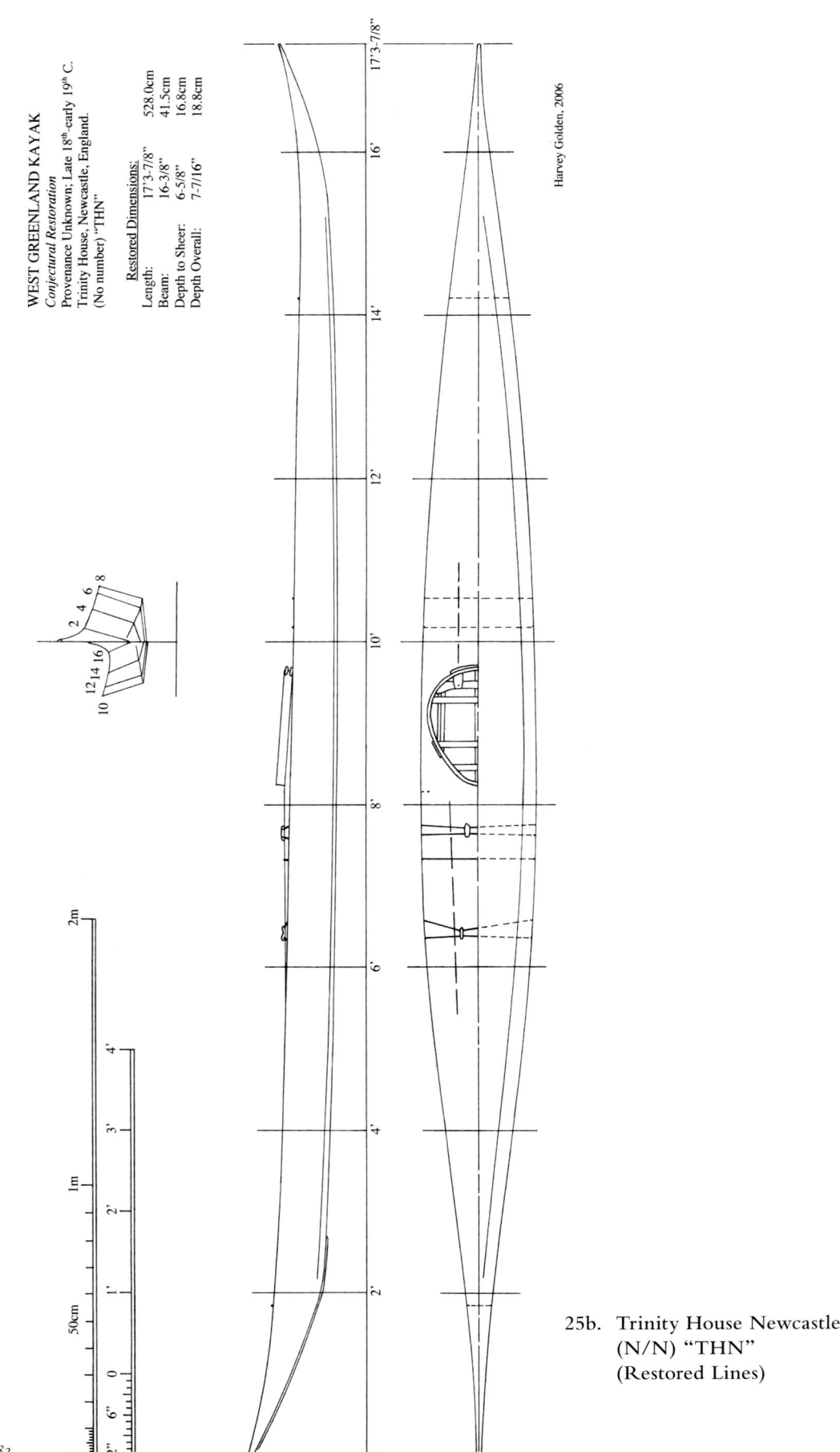

25b. Trinity House Newcastle (N/N) "THN" (Restored Lines)

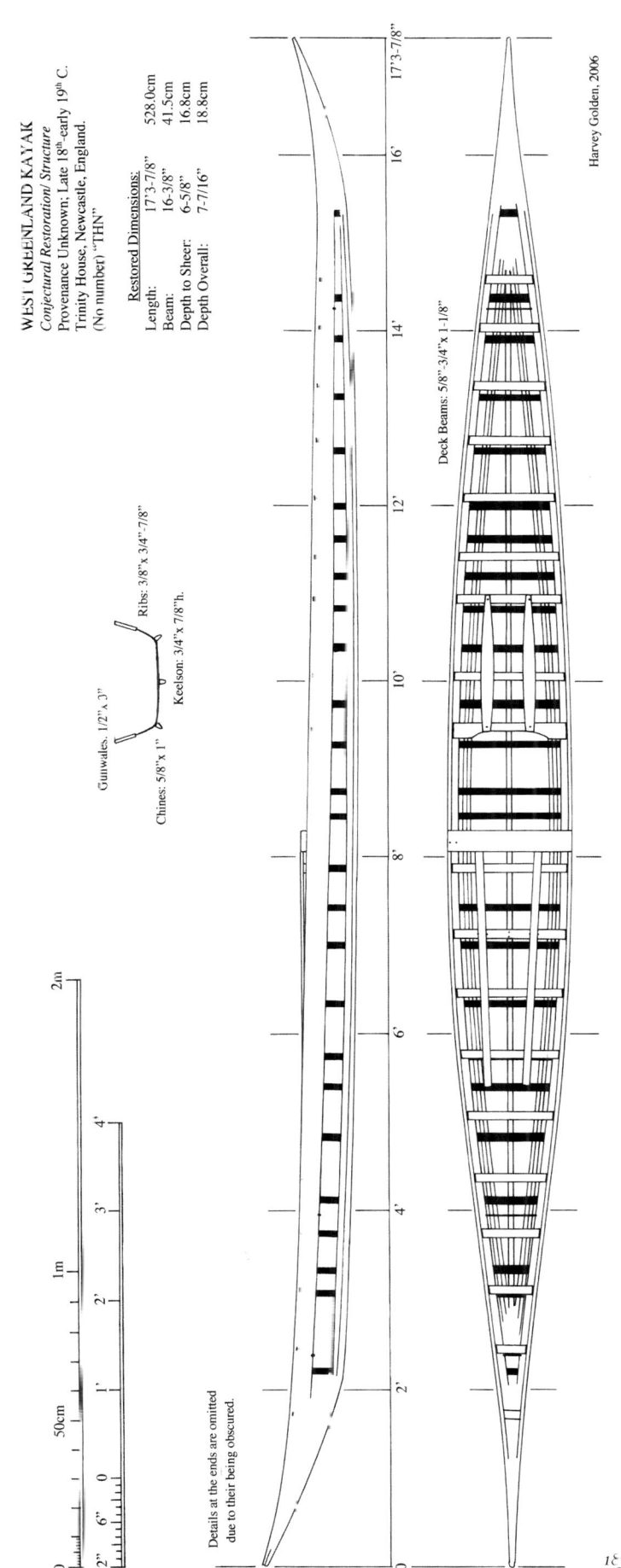

25c. Trinity House Newcastle
(N/N) "THN"
(Restored Lines: Frame)

15. West Greenland Kayak of ca. 1600-1800: Rijksmuseum voor Volkenkunde, Leiden, the Netherlands. Catalog no. 349-1. ("Brielle")

This is yet another kayak that Gert Nooter includes in his 1971 *Old Kayaks in the Netherlands*. He refers to the 349-1 as the "Brielle", after the Dutch town whose museum it had been in prior to transfer to the Rijksmuseum in 1883 (1971:61-62).

Nooter suggests that it originates from Disko Bay vicinity (1971:61) based on Birket-Smith's kayak typology (1924:271). Birket-Smith's typology again must be held suspect: It is a 'snapshot' of the situation in Greenland in the early 1900s. Nooter conservatively offers, "that a dating between 1600 and 1800 may be accepted" (1971:62). I would agree, but lean towards the mid- or late- 1600s, based on its tiny breadth, simple deck rigging, and *amiq*-to-coaming attachment method. Most of the type III kayaks in this study (whose dating is known) seem to span from late 1700s to the 1830s.

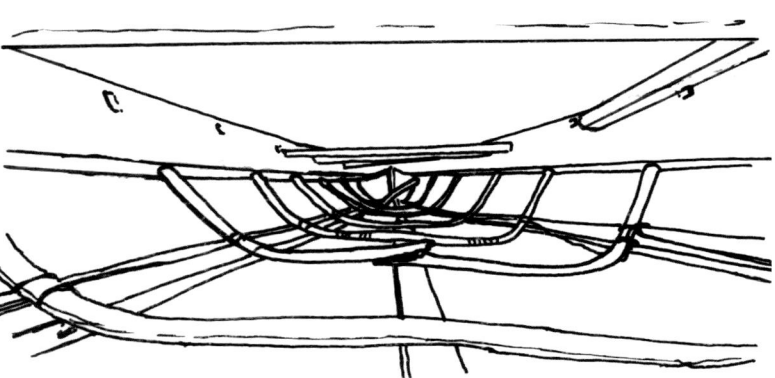

Figure 219: Aft interior view of the Rijksmuseum voor Volkenkunde's kayak 349. Two deck beams are missing.

The 349 is in a very damaged state: viewed from above, it winds like a snake. Extensive hull collapse exists, primarily in the stern. The interior is cluttered with broken deck beams, chines, and ribs. The *amiq* is in fair shape and is a dark rusty-brown color. The drawing presents a reconstructed kayak—drawn with a straight centerline, as it was certainly built.

Unlike the Lübeck, De Rijp, Hindeloopen, and Hoorn kayaks (all type I), this kayak has very boxy cross-sections—i.e., a hard chine with rather plumb-sides, and slight dead rise, as well as a lack of the gunwale's lower edge protruding into the skin. The 349's cross-sections are very similar to the KNK 1161's (plate 9) forward sections.

All of the lashings in the 349 are baleen. Several of the deck beams are lashed to the gunwales. The chines and keelson are double-pass lashed to the ribs. Forward of the coaming, the ribs are let into the keelson (as in figure 55 bottom), perhaps to make for more room inside the cockpit as well as to make getting in and out easier. (The keelson was missing below the coaming, and was unreachable with my tape measure; by appearances it was about 3/4" (19mm) square.) None of the deck stringers remained in place, so their positions were undeterminable; there were two deck stringers aft and two forward.

The cockpit placement of the 349 is worth noting here as it is proportionally placed quite far forward, even compared to other Type III kayaks. (See Appendix A, column 7 for length-to-cockpit mid-point ratios). The cockpit coaming measures 3/8" (9mm) thick by 1-5/8" (41mm) high. Like several type I and II Greenland kayaks, the *amiq* is drawn up and over the back of the 349's coaming, as in figure 123b.

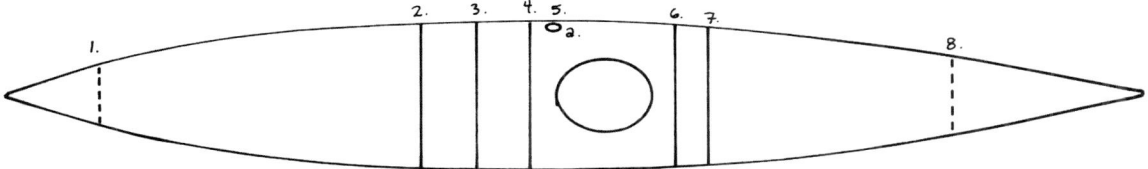

Rijksmuseum voor Volkenkunde, Leiden: Cat. no. 349

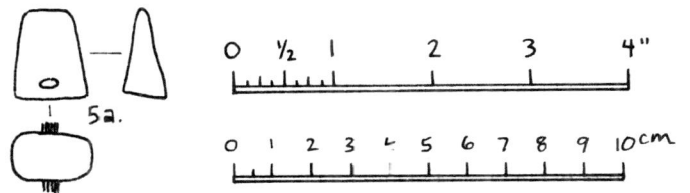

Just a single deck fitting is present on the RvV 349— a *masik* mounted harpoon holder. The deck lines at the bow and stern were each missing but evidenced. Like several type I kayaks, there are only three deck lines on the 349's fore deck. These lines are all intact on the 349. A paddle associated with the 349 is depicted in paddle-plate 14.

I built a replica of the RvV 349 in 1998, not long after I had surveyed it. Forming the highly raked ends of the gunwales was particularly challenging, but ultimately solved by scarfing inclined and oversized boards to the gunwales' ends, after which they were shaved down to the original form. The shallowness of this kayak necessitated a much longer coaming/opening than on the other very narrow replicas I'd built. My replica's cockpit opening measures 19″ (48.3cm) long, and 14-7/8″ (37.8cm) wide, and is still a painful fit.

The boxy hull-shape of the 349 is inherently a stable one, however when it is only 15-1/4″ (38.7cm) wide, 'inherently stable' means little. The kayak did sit firmer upright than the Hindeloopen and

Figure 220: The replica of the RvV 349 in 2005. (Photograph by Kathy Tucker.)

Figure 221: A forward-quarter view of the 349 replica. (Photograph by Kathy Tucker.)

KNK 1161 replicas, but the 349 replica was still very easily heeled over. The lack of stability or ease of heeling in so many Greenland kayaks strikes me as being a good advantage in that when the seas are rough, the kayak will resist getting thrown around so much giving the kayaker much better control over the kayak. Volume is also a critical factor in rough conditions— this narrow kayak, on account of its boxy cross-sections, seems to be an optimization of higher volume but lower stability.

16. West Greenland Kayak of ca. 1770s: Trinity House, Hull, England. (N/N) 'A'

No specific provenance has been recorded for this kayak, identified here as the THH 'A.' Souter's 1934 table of kayaks in Great Britain shows three kayaks present at the Trinity House: The shortest is given a date of 1613, and is well documented (see pg. 164). The second longest kayak is given a date of 1830— the second longest kayak there is the THH 'B' (plate 13) of this study. Souter provides no acquisition date for the longest kayak at the Trinity House, but historian Commander Storey writes that one of the House kayaks ("...it is not known which one...") was acquired in 1776, having been gifted by Captain W. Clark (Souter, 1934:13; Storey, 1969:162). Thus it is reasoned that the THH 'A' is the kayak from 1776.

Quite massive for a Greenland kayak of its time, the Trinity House kayak 'A's' length is exceeded in this study by the GM 700 alone (plate 6). The breadth of the 'A' is however 4-1/2″ (11.4cm) greater than that of the 700. For such a large kayak, no grace was spared, and the ends appear very fine and elegant.

Four of the Trinity House 'A's' deck beams are fastened to the gunwales via the oblique peg method (as in figure 36c); two of these are forward of the cockpit. The chines and keelson are lashed to the ribs with a seal skin cord using the double-pass method (as in figure 72).

A handhold is carved into the 'A's' *masik*, and it is cut all the way through, thus appearing identical to the handle in the other Trinity House's kayak (plate 13). The handhold is a rectangular hole 3/4" by 3-1/8" (19 x 79mm), 5/8" (16mm) ahead of the *masik*'s aft edge. The *masik* itself measures 9/16" (14mm) thick by 4-7/16" (11.3cm) wide. The 'A's' *isserfik* is 1" (25mm) thick by 1-5/8' (41mm) wide, and oval in cross-section.

The coaming of the 'A' is shaped like a much rounded triangle, and it has a bone lip all the way around its upper edge;

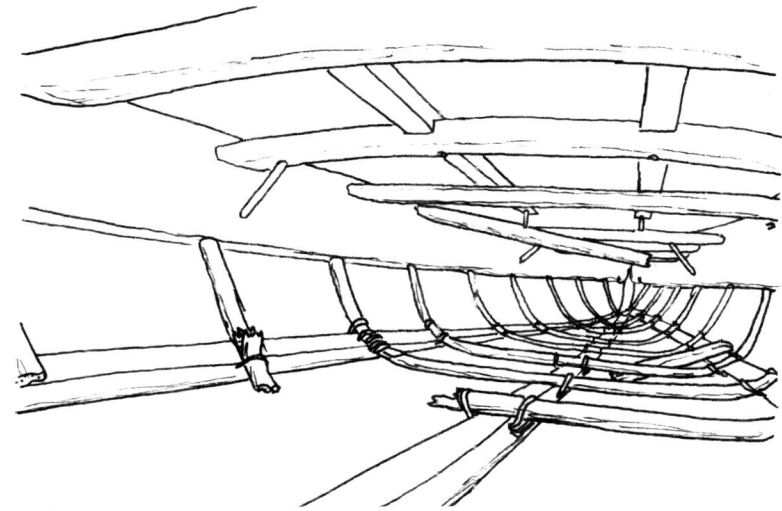

Figure 222: Forward interior of the Hull Trinity House's kayak 'A'.

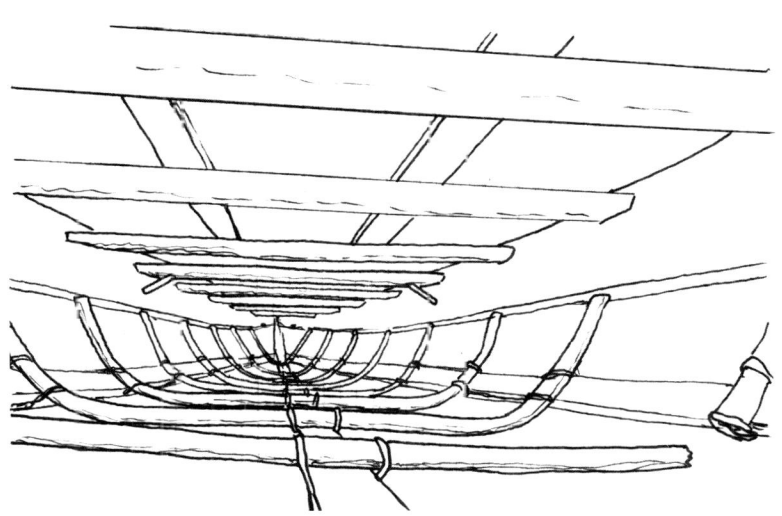

Figure 223: Aft interior view of the THH 'A'.

this lip measures 1/4" high by 3/16" (6 x 5mm) thick. On the coaming's lower-aft face, there is an 8-1/2" (21.6cm) long bone strip 3/16" (5mm) thick and 3/8" (9mm) high. The coaming is 7/16" (11mm) thick by 1-1/2" (38mm) high.

Keel protection is present both fore and aft. This edging covers from the bow-knob to 2' 11-1/4" (89.5cm) aft of zero, and at the stern from 16' 9-1/2" (511.8cm) to the end.

None of the deck lines of the Trinity House 'A' were present except for the harpoon holder (7a). This harpoon holder was not actually in place, but instead was dangling from a cord holding other miscellaneous chunks of ivory that were from hunting equipment. The positions of the missing deck lines are indicated above and on the scale drawing.

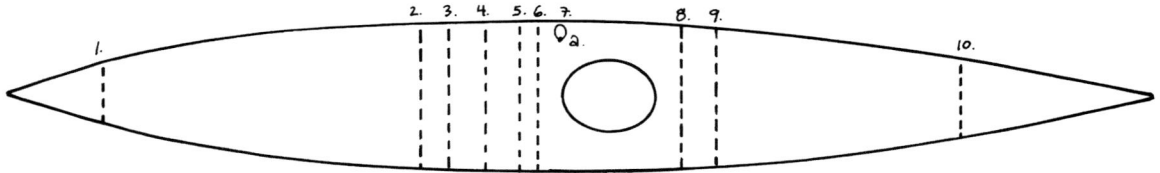

Trinity House, Hull: (n/n) "A"

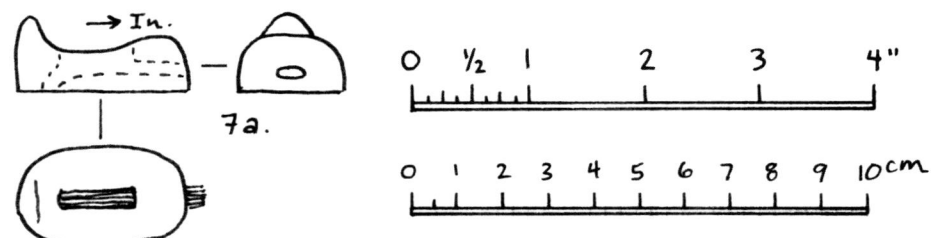

I surveyed the paddle laying on the THH 'A's' deck; it isn't certain that the paddle belongs to this kayak. The paddle is depicted in paddle-plate 16.

17. West Greenland Kayak of ca. 1800: Marischal College, Aberdeen, Scotland. Catalog no. ABDUA:5736.

Captain William Gibbon donated this kayak to the Marischal College museum in 1800. Gibbon commanded the whaler *Latona*, which sailed from London to the Greenland fisheries in 1784, 1785 and/or 1786, and 1787 (Jones, 1996:13, 16, 23, 186). It is not known for certain if the Marishcal College kayak was collected on any of these voyages, and nor is it known whether or not Gibbon was the collector. At the time of my visit in 2002, the catalog number for this kayak was V-87, but it has since been changed to ABDUA:5736.

This kayak had been sawn in half—really the only reason this would've been done was for easier transportation aboard a ship. Figure 224 shows the 5736's present state. The plasticity of the baleen coaming is plainly seen, as it has tried to spring-free of the kayak's *amiq*. For some reason, this kayak is omitted from W. C. Souter's table of kayaks in Great Britain; Souter lived and worked in Aberdeen, and was familiar with the College Museum's other kayak, the ABDUA:6.013, published in *Eastern Arctic Kayaks* (Heath, 2004:10, fig.1.5).

The damage inflicted on the 5736 is substantial, though its grace and beauty are still plain to see. Drastic as sawing a boat in half is, the remains left enough information that the kayak could be re-constructed on paper. This conjectural restoration is presented in plate 17b.

The 5736's ends are very distinct, and are matched quite evenly in form and height, whereas it is more common for the stern to be at least slightly higher than the bow. Its lines are extreme but they call to mind the RvV 349-1 (plate 15), and the Whitby kayak described next.

The deck height of the 5736 has been conjecturally restored to 1-3/4″ (45mm) above the sheer, based on similar kayak types as its *masik* was entirely missing. Despite its being lost, the gunwales show evidence

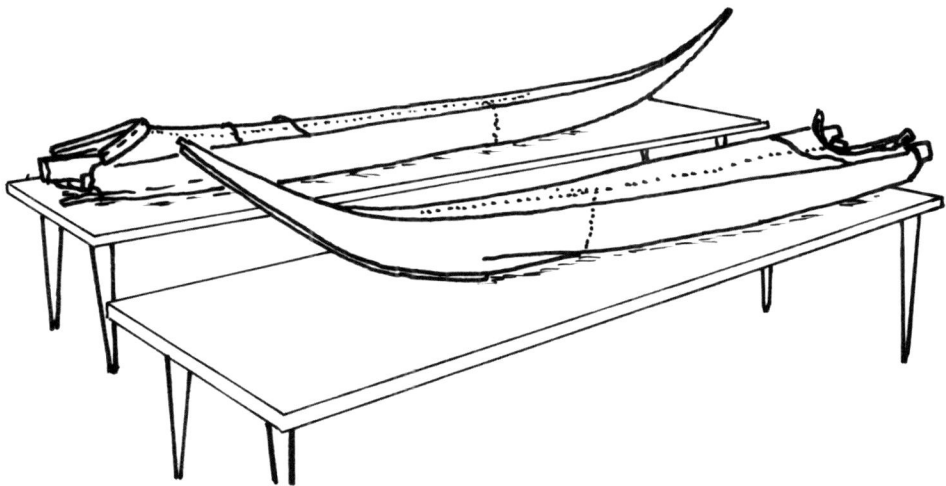

Figure 224: The Marischal College kayak ABDUA:5736—sawn in half.

of the *masik* having been 4" (10.1cm) wide at its ends; it had been top-pegged to the top of the gunwales with four pegs, such as is depicted in figure 77c. The 5736 is also missing its *isserfik*; it had been set into shallow mortises in the gunwales.

Oblique pegs are intermittently used to secure deck beams to the gunwales—a method seen in the THH 'A' kayak (plate 16). The chines and keelson are pegged to the ribs. It was not possible to determine whether or not the 5736 ever had aft deck stringers, though they might be expected.

The 5736's keel edging is missing but evidenced at the bow from 1-1/4" (32mm) aft of the tip to 2' 9-3/4" (85.7cm) aft. The stern edging is present from 16'3" (495.3cm) to 19'1/2" (580.3cm), and measures 7/16" (13mm) square towards the front end and 1/4" (6mm) square towards the stern. (The existent stern edging has accidentally been omitted from the artifactual scale drawing.) The only end-knob placement evidenced was at the bow, as inferred from top-peg holes 1/2" (13mm) behind the kayak's tip.

The deck lines on the 5736 are very sparse, there only being two lines on the fore deck. Most kayaks of this type have at least three, and usually five. No fittings were present on this kayak, though the deck lines at each end were missing, as was the harpoon holder. The paddle associated with this kayak is depicted in paddle-plate 17.

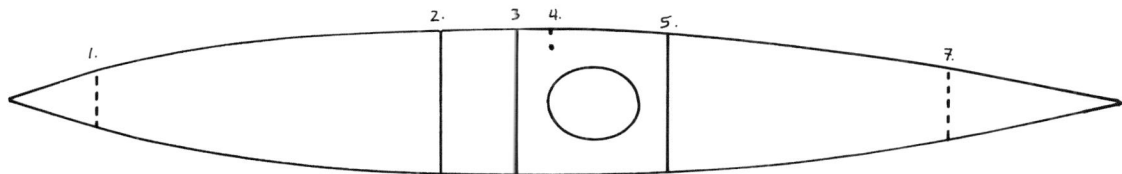

Marischal College Museum, Aberdeen: Cat. no. ABDUA.5736

18. West Greenland kayak: The Whitby Museum, Whitby, England. Catalog no. WHITM:SCO1.

A Mr. Richard Moorsom donated this kayak to the Whitby Literary and Philosophical Society in 1825. The Whitby Museum, operated by the Whitby Literary and Philosophical Society, was founded in 1823.

Deductive reasoning, albeit non-conclusive, may suggest that the kayak was collected by or through Moorsom's father, Richard Moorsom III. The elder was involved in Greenland whaling after circa 1774, (co-owning eight whaling ships), and died in 1809 (Ventress, 1998:2,3). If acquired by the elder Moorsom (either personally or through his captains), the kayak likely dates between 1774 and 1809.

Figure 225: An engraving from Crantz, 1767. Note the high ends, and their relative symmetry—typical of type III kayaks such as the ABDUA:5736, and the WHITM:SC01. (Courtesy of the John Wilson Room, Special Collections, Multnomah County Library, Portland, Oregon.)

Ventress writes that Richard Moorsom III's interest in Arctic whaling "explains Cape Moorsom on the east coast of Greenland and several large Narwhal tusks . . . which used to be part of the decorations in Airy Hill" – Airy Hill being the family home in Whitby (1998:3).

The cross-section of the Whitby kayak is remarkable in that it has a very steep angle of dead rise and that the chines are placed quite high. Such a deep V-bottom is not common in West Greenland kayaks from this period and earlier, though it gradually became more common later in the 19th century, particularly among type IV and V kayaks. H. C. Petersen, in *Skinboats of Greenland*, writes of the advantage of V-bottom kayaks: ". . . It is of course more difficult to maintain one's balance but the shape does give the kayaker more control over his craft" (1986:46).

Petersen describes a specialized kayak used exclusively in rough water: the storm kayak— *kujaannalik*[31] ("one with only a keel"). They are described as having had very high gunwales, a high keelson, and no chines. "It was first necessary to accustom oneself to the extremely delicate balance and therefore it could not be used by just anyone. But once one had got used to it, it was far and away the best kayak to use in a strong wind" (Petersen, 1986:50-51).

While the Whitby kayak is not structurally a *kujaannalik*, it may be an intermediate type suited for a particular region or an evolution towards or from the *kujaannalik* form. The shape of the Whitby kayak's hull suggests this possible relation. If the gunwales were two inches (51mm) deeper, the Whitby kayak wouldn't need its chines, and it would by definition become a *kujaannalik*. With such a prominent keel, the Whitby kayak would presumably track well, though its considerable rocker and shallow ends ought

---

[31] Examples of the historic *kujaannalik* are not known to exist; H. C. Petersen presents the only drawing of a "storm kayak"—a conjectural cross-section (1986:51, fig.48).

to still allow for considerable maneuverability.

The structure of this kayak is light, yet well made: The gunwales are 1/2″ (13mm) thick, but amply supported by numerous ribs and a stout keel and chines. There are 26 ribs in all: three in the cockpit, 11 forward of these, and 12 aft. There is a gap of 26″ (66.0cm) between the forward cockpit rib and the next one towards the bow. Teeth marks are evident on the ribs from bending.

Several of the deck beams in the kayak are lashed in place. The lashing pattern is as depicted in figure 36b, in which the lashing passes through two holes in the gunwale

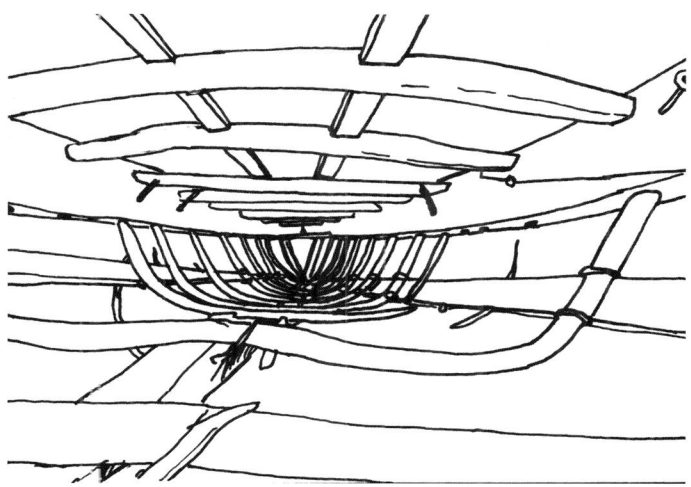

Figure 226   Forward interior view of the Whitby Museum kayak.

instead of just one. This method is very rare and only occurs in one other kayak in this study: the WMF 36841 (plate 10). No aft deck stringers are present in the Whitby kayak. The Whitby kayak's deck beams measure 1/2″ (13mm) thick by 1-1/2″ (38mm) wide, although the *isserfik* is only 1-1/4″ (32mm) wide; the *masik* is 2-1/4″ (57mm) wide.

The Whitby kayak's coaming is made from two pieces of wood, step-scarfed (on the face) in the aft quarters, and appears as in figure 116f. The coaming measures 3/8″ (9mm) thick by 1-1/4″ (32mm) high. Three 3/8″ (9mm) wide bone or ivory strips are attached to the coaming's face. The middle piece is 3″ (76mm) long, and is pegged to the rear of the coaming at the upper edge. The other pieces span the coaming's two scarfs—the starboard piece being at the upper

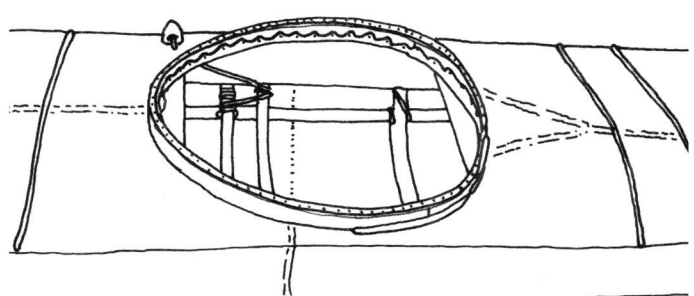

Figure 227   Cockpit of the Whitby Museum kayak.

edge of the coaming, and the port-side piece being at the lower edge. The middle piece was likely just used to help fasten the *tuitsoq* or *tuiliq*, as it does not span either of the coaming scarfs. An ivory cap is present on the coaming's upper rim. It measures 3/16″ (5mm) high and is attached with pegs. The cap's purpose is not specifically known, though it must have afforded good wear-resistance; similar coaming caps appear on the kayaks RvV 351-77 and WMF 36481 (plates 8 and 10, both type II kayaks).

Keel edging is present at the bow, but there is no evidence of edging at the stern. A 1-1/2″ (38mm) long protective piece of ivory covers the keel where the transverse seam crosses beneath the cockpit. Another piece 1-1/8″ (29mm) long protects the aft transverse seam. End protection knobs are evidenced both at the bow and stern, but neither was present.

The rigging on this kayak is simple in having only one deck fitting aside from the harpoon holder. Two deck lines are missing but evidenced: the furthest forward and the furthest aft. These deck lines

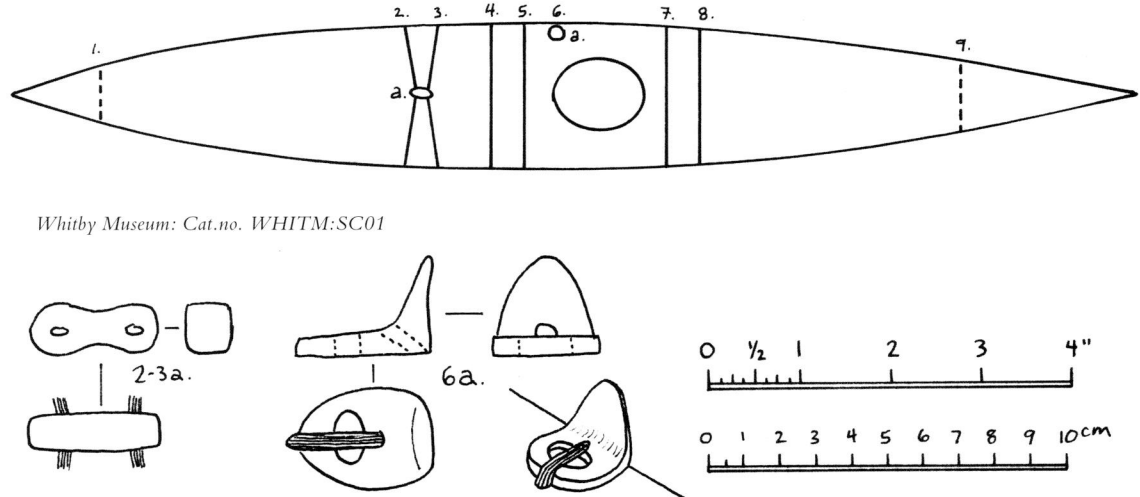

Whitby Museum: Cat.no. WHITM:SC01

may or may not have had deck fittings. The harpoon holder on the Whitby kayak is of an unusual form— it is quite elegant, and there are no others like it among the 100-plus Greenland kayaks in this study.

19. West Greenland Kayak of ca. 1800s: National Museum of Scotland, Edinburgh. Catalog no. 1984.277 (Ex. St. Andrews University).

This kayak has no accession information aside from its having been transferred to the National Museum from St. Andrews College circa 1980s. How it got to the College is a mystery; the kayak does not receive mention in Souter's 1934 paper. Of the kayaks listed in Souter's table of kayaks in Great Britain, several are presently missing or destroyed; the ex-St. Andrews kayak could possibly be one of these, or simply one entirely unknown to him. The National Museum of Scotland's accession files list this kayak as being from the "late 19th century," but I tend to think it may be from the early part of that century based on comparisons to similar kayaks.

The 1984.277 has several distinctive features: A baleen coaming, high ends, and simple deck-lines and fittings. It is highly damaged, the hull being collapsed nearly to the gunwales for much of the length. One can't help but compare the 1984.277 to the Marischal College 5736 (plate 17) and the Hull Maritime Museum's "B" (plate 22) on account of their high ends, baleen coamings, and sparse deck rigging ahead of the cockpit.

All of the lashings inside the 1984.277 are of baleen; the chines and keelson are fastened to the ribs via the double-pass method, the pattern of which was not visible due to broken lashings and the collapsed hull. Two of the curved deck beams were lying loosely inside the kayak—their profiles are depicted in scale in figure 42. These deck beams (and presumably the rest of them in this kayak) have short tenons, suggesting shallow mortises in the gunwales.

The 1984.277's *masik* measures 5/8″ (16mm) thick by 3-7/8″ (9.8cm) wide; the *isserfik* measures 3/4″ (19mm) thick and 1-11/16″ (43mm) wide in the middle, and 1-15/16″ (49mm) wide at the ends.

The forward deck stringers are 3/4″ (19mm) thick by 5/8″ (16mm) wide; the aft deck stringers are 1/2″ (13mm) thick by 1-5/8″ (41mm) wide.

The baleen coaming is lashed to the kayak's *amiq*, using an intermittent lineal pattern as in figure 123e. The scarf of the coaming is a simple lap and is fastened with three ivory pegs— two near the top edge, and one at the bottom edge. These pegs are 5/16″ (8mm) diameter, and protrude 3/16″ (5mm). The bottom of the scarf is further re-enforced with two turns of baleen lashings Keel edging and end knobs were not present or evidenced on the 1984.277.

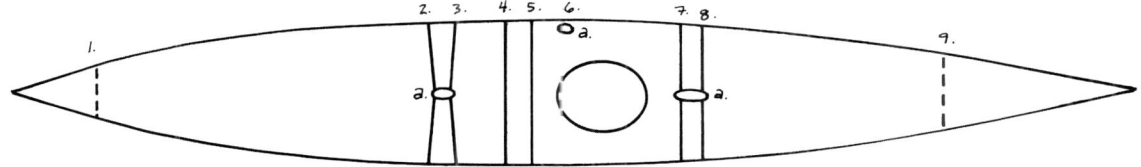

National Museum of Scotland: Cat. no. 1984.277

Only the bow and stern deck lines are missing from the 1984.277. Four deck lines are present on the fore deck— the forward pair is linked. The pair of deck lines behind the cockpit is also linked. The harpoon holder is of a simple tab-shape.

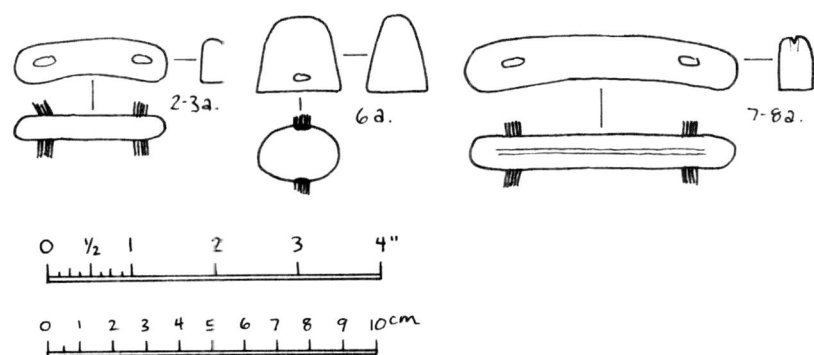

20. West Greenland Kayak from ca. 18th or 19th Century: McManus Galleries, Dundee, Scotland. Catalog no. 1984-285.

William Clark Souter, in his 1934 paper lists a kayak at the Montrose Museum in Montrose, Scotland. According to Dale Idiens of the National Museum of Scotland, the kayak was transferred from the Montrose Museum to Dundee in 1958 (Idiens in Feest, et.al, 1987:171). I found this out the hard way, by inquiring to perplexed museum staff at the front desk of the Montrose Museum, asking if I could see their kayak. Such is the problem with relying too heavily on sixty-four-year-old information. Off to Dundee . . .

Souter gives the dimensions and scant provenance information: "Greenland . . . before 1844" (1934:13). (Souter offers no reference source for these dates). The McManus Galleries' catalog information is more specific geographically, but more vague temporally: "West Greenland . . . 19th century?" James Low writes in *Industry in Montrose* that "The passing of an Act by Parliament in 1771 for the better prosecution of the whale fishing in the Arctic regions, with bounties paid by the government, tempted Montrose to form a company in 1785, under the name of 'The Montrose Greenland Fishing Company'" (1943:39). If collected by ships of the Montrose Company, it is likely that the kayak dates from between 1785 and the 1844 date cited in Souter.

Upon seeing the 1984-285, I was struck by its great similarity to the RvV 349-1 (plate 15), which I had studied only weeks before: The 1984-285 is also very narrow (16"; 40.6cm), very long (18' 3-1/4"; 556.9cm), has fine ends, simple deck lines with few fittings, and it lacks stern keel protection. The sheer-line viewed from above is convex or full-ended, i.e., not pinching inward towards the ends as in later West Greenland kayaks.

The 1984-285 has extensive hull collapse, as shown in the artifactual elevation in the scale drawing. The ribs, keelson, and chines are missing in the cockpit area, and in fact the hull is flattened right up to the bottom of the gunwales. While their exact placement is impossible to determine, I have included a conjectural lines restoration based on evidence as well as on comparisons to similar kayak types. Due to the extensive hull-collapse and general disarray inside, not too much of the 1984-285's construction could be seen. Deck beams, at least those still intact seem to have alternating methods of attachment: Lashings and the oblique peg method are both present. A view forward into the kayak was obscured by what appeared to be a turtle shell of all things.

Apparently the tenons of the deck beams of the 285 were either slightly longer than their respective mortises, or else the gunwales have shrunk in thickness slightly over the years: The tenons are poking into the *amiq*, showing their placement. Their positions are illustrated in the artifactual lines. These tenons measure 1/4" (6mm) high by 5/8" (16mm) wide. Notably, the curved deck beams in the cockpit do not have projecting tenons; it is not known whether they had through mortises or not. Both the *masik* and *isserfik* were missing; the *masik* appears to have been about 3" (76mm) wide.

The 1984.285's coaming measures 5/8" (16mm) thick by 1-1/2" (38mm) high, and has two 8-3/4" (22.2cm) long bone strips on its back face. These strips are 1/4" (6mm) thick and 1/2" (13mm) wide.

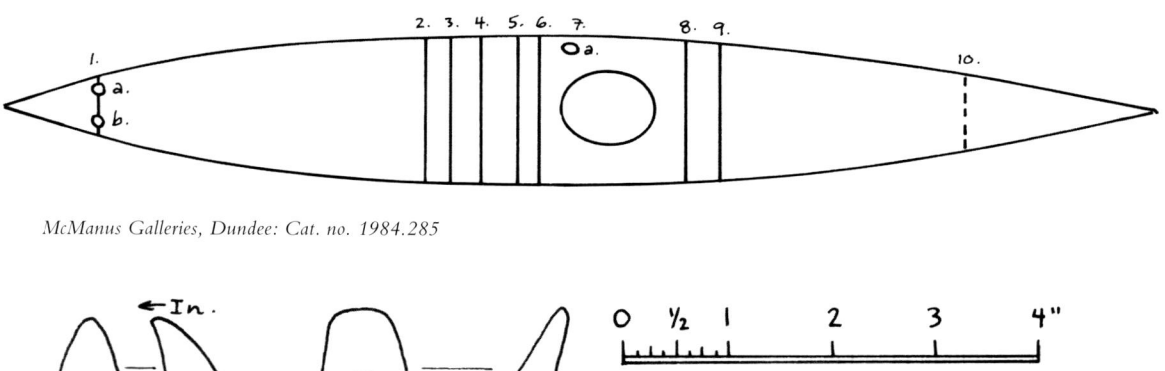

McManus Galleries, Dundee: Cat. no. 1984.285

Three fittings are present on this kayak's decks: Two 'cones' (a and b) are on deck line 1, and piece c is a harpoon holder. All of the deck lines on this kayak are intact except for the stern line, which may or may not have had fittings.

21. West Greenland kayak from ca. Late 1700s to early 1800s: Hunterian Museum, Glasgow, Scotland. Catalog no. E.585.

The history of the University of Glasgow Hunterian Museum's E.585 is not known beyond the listing "Davis Straits -Greenland" on the identification card. It is sequentially cataloged with the E.584 (plate 28), for which only the same data appears, although the two kayaks are very different (the E.584 is a type IV kayak). Both kayaks are listed in the museum catalogs as having been donated by a J. Dalrymple of Glasgow in 1819, although the donations book cites a canoe instead of two. Souter lists three Hunterian Museum kayaks in his table, but none are provided with any origin information or dates of acquisition (1934:13).[32]

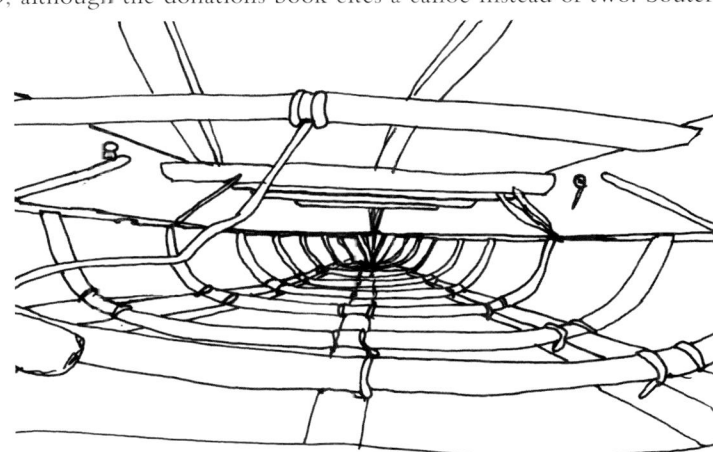

Figure 228: The forward interior of the Hunterian Museum's E.585. Note the carrying toggle anchored to the curved deck beam.

The E.585 is in very good condition, with only slight and intermittent hull collapse. Like the two other kayaks at the Hunterian Museum, the 585 has no stern keel protection. Incidentally, this kayak was made for a left-handed hunter as the harpoon rest is on the port side. The 585's coaming is shifted away from the left side (1/2" [13mm] from right sheer, 1-1/8" [29mm] from left) despite the original owner being left-handed, though still likely for a good reason: This would in fact make more room for the harpoon, as the E.585 is quite narrow to begin with.

A carrying toggle is anchored to one of the deck-beams ahead of the *masik*, and is evident in figure 228, at the extreme left. The toggle is a piece of bone or antler 3/4" (19mm) by 7/8" (22mm), and 3-1/2" (8.9cm) long, and is attached to a 9" (22.8cm) long

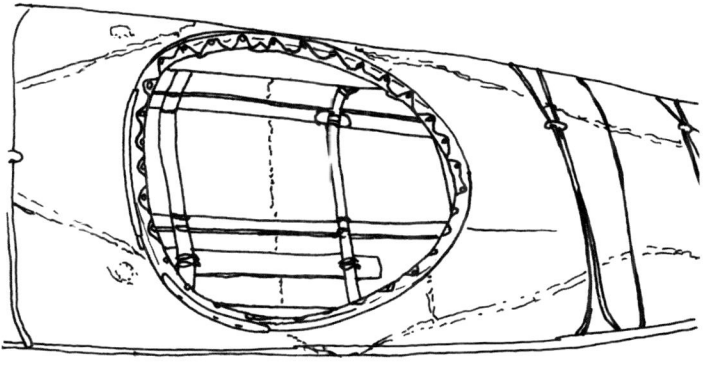

Figure 229: Cockpit of the Hunterian Museum's E.585. One of the seat-slats is missing.

---

[32] The third Hunterian Museum kayak is the E.102, plate 26 in this study.

piece of seal skin line anchored to a deck beam 14-1/2" (36.8cm) ahead of the cockpit front. Carrying toggles such as this are not too common among West Greenland kayaks, but seem to be fairly common in East Greenland kayaks; several in this study have them. Continuous deck lines are also present and can be seen in figure 228. The forward deck stringers have shifted considerably, but are drawn 'restored' (based on comparisons to similar kayaks and evidence seen inside the E.585's hull) in the scale drawing.

Figure 229 shows a cockpit view of the E.585. The adjacent deck lines are depicted as well as the one remaining seat-slat, anchored below the ribs in the cockpit. The seat slat measures 3/16" (5mm) thick by 1-1/2" (38mm) wide and is 12-3/4" (32.4cm) long. A shim can be seen between the left chine and a rib. Also note the two patches behind the rear quarters of the coaming—based on their symmetrical appearance, the holes were likely naturally occurring in the seal skin.

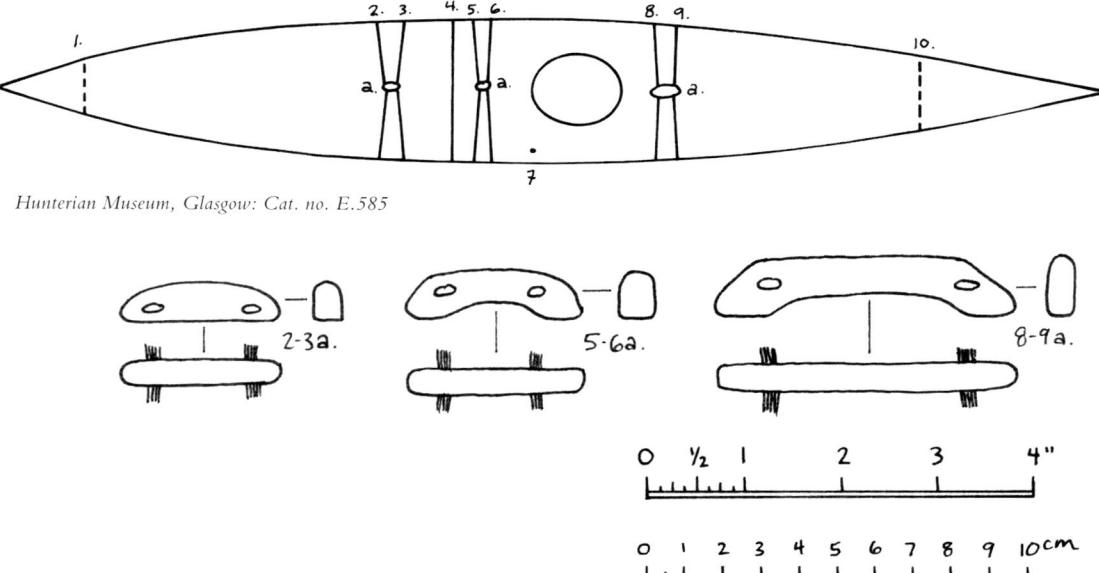

Hunterian Museum, Glasgow: Cat. no. E.585

Only three deck fittings remain on the E.585's deck lines; all three are link pieces. The piece behind the cockpit has the re-curring 'suitcase handle' form, and interestingly so does the link piece just ahead of the cockpit. As mentioned, the harpoon holder had been situated to the left of the cockpit, but is missing. The bow and stern deck lines are both missing, and they may or may not have had fittings.

22. West Greenland Kayak of ca. Early 1800s: Hull Maritime Museum, Hull, England. (N/N) HMM 'B'

Four kayaks are listed in William Souter's table of 'Kayaks in Great Britain' for "Hull Museum" (1934:13). This example is one of two listed without any provenance information. The four kayaks are currently in the collection of the Hull Maritime Museum, and of the three from Greenland, the 'B' is in the best condition. Souter provides only basic dimensions that are in instances very different from mine, such that the "B" may in fact be either his Hull Museum no. 2 or no.3 (1934:13).

While The Hull Literary and Philosophical Society's records were likely lost in the bombing of Hull in 1939-41. Despite the loss, information does exist, albeit not so detailed: For example, In the 1914 *Illustrated Catalogue to the Museum of Fisheries and Shipping, Pickering Park, Hull* there is in the list of 'Esquimaux Objects' "Three Esquimaux Kayaks (canoes)" followed by another item: "Esquimaux Kayak with model of man in native costume, provided with harpoon, etc" (Anonymous, 1914:20).

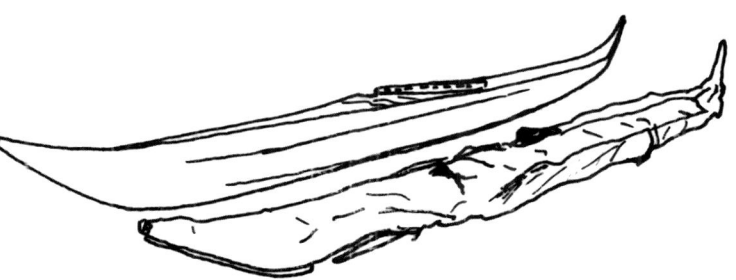

Figure 230: Hull Maritime Museum kayaks 'B' (rear), and 'C' (foreground).

In *A Guide to The Museum of the Literary and Philosophical Society of Hull* (Anon., 1860) mention is made of two 'Esquimaux canoes;' these are said to have been "presented to this Museum by Captain, afterwards Sir John Ross" (9-10). Two of the kayaks in Souter's table under "Hull Museum" are attributed to Ross (1934:13). According to museum tradition, the present kayak is not one of them, its history being unknown[33] (Arthur Credland, 2002: personal communication).

The HMM 'B' has a moderately fine bow and stern, each with a gentle rise to it—very balanced in appearance. The *masik* is missing, but the original depth overall can be inferred, as the forward deck stringers are intact. (The scale drawing depicts the artifactual condition of the kayak, i.e., with its *masik* missing, and thus the fore-deck collapsed adjacent the coaming.) The original depth overall is estimated to have been 8″ (20.3cm).

The position and length of the missing aft deck stringers is conjectural, however there was evidence of their placement by pegs set through deck beams as well as creases in the *amiq*. The fore deck stringers are present and measure 5/8″ (16mm) wide by 3/4″ (19mm) high at their aft end. The *isserfik* measures 5/8″ (16mm) thick by 1-7/8″ (48mm) wide at the ends, but is cut to 1-9/16″ (40mm) wide at the middle.

The rib-to-chine and keelson lashings are all of baleen, though much of it has broken and sprung loose over the years. Only one deck beam forward and one deck beam aft are lashed to the gunwales (with baleen), the others being unfastened or perhaps top-pegged. Clamping-ties are evidenced at both ends of the gunwales. The aft-ends of the forward deck stringers have steps cut into them that suggest that they were once set into notches in the *masik*.

The cockpit of the 'B' is very egg-shaped, although with a slightly flattened backside. It is made from baleen and is lashed in place with seal skin cord: The lacing is intermittent with the cord running an

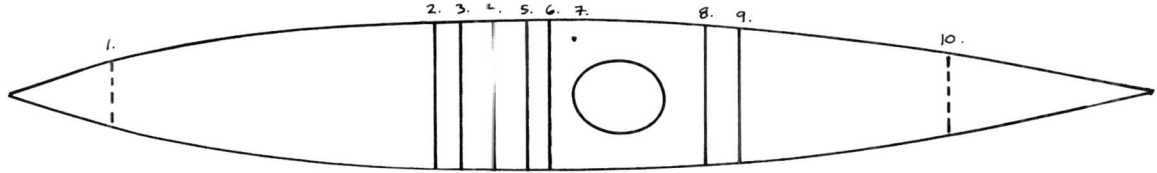

Hull Maritime Museum (n/n) "B"

---

[33] The two kayaks attributed to Ross are the HMM "C" (plate 30), and a kayak from Baffin Island, not in this study.

inch (25mm) on average with a gap of 1-1/4" (32mm) in between. The lacing runs 1/4" (6mm) below the top of the coaming. The coaming is distinctly offset on this kayak, being 13/16" (21mm) from the left sheer, and 1-1/8" (28mm) from the right sheer.

Bow edging was missing on the 'B' but was evidenced, its position being from 7/8" (22mm) aft of the bow to 2'6" (76.2cm). No stern edging was evidenced, nor were bow and stern knobs. One seam protection piece is present on the keel at 9'5-1/4" (287.6cm) reaching 2-1/8" (54mm) forward. This piece is 5/8" (16mm) wide and 1/8" (3mm) thick.

Deck fittings were not present on the 'B,' though most of the deck lines were intact. The stern deck line was broken and may have had fittings. The harpoon holder was missing, but evidenced on the right of the cockpit, having been mounted through the now-missing *masik*.

23. West Greenland Kayak of ca. 1830s: Musée de la Marine, Paris, France. Catalog no. 1.BS.15.

Musée de La Marine inventory lists the history of the 1Bs.15 as having been collected by Naval Surgeon Paul Gaimard during the 1838-1840 expedition to Iceland, Greenland, and Northern Europe, aboard the French corvette *Recherche*. The 1.Bs.15 is one of the shorter adult-size kayaks in this study. It is about a foot-and-a-half shorter than the two previous kayaks, which it otherwise resembles in form, breadth, and depth.

Appearing much like the Hull Maritime Museum's 'B,' this kayak is rather different in construction. For example, the rib lashings are of seal skin cord instead of baleen, pegs are used in lieu of lashings for deck beam-to-gunwale joints, and dowels have replaced the clamping-ties at the ends. Also, the coaming is made of wood instead of baleen.

The 1.Bs.15 has three forward deck-stringers, the middle one being almost twice as wide as the outer two, calling to mind the arrangement in the THH 'B' (plate 13). These two kayaks also have similarly shaped coamings— rather egg-shaped with a flattish back. These kayaks differ in that the 1.Bs.15 has two aft deck stringers instead of the one stringer in the THH 'B'. The *masik* is broken in the 1.Bs.15, although it is 'restored' to its original height in the scale drawing. The 1Bs.15's *masik* measures 2-9/16" wide and the *isserfik* is 11/16" thick by 1-3/16" wide. The outer fore deck stringers are 7/8" (22mm) wide, while the middle one is 1-7/8" (48mm) wide. The two aft deck stringers are 1/2" (13mm) thick by 1-1/16" (27mm) wide.

Two bone strips are present on the coaming's aft face (see figure 231); both strips are 8-5/8" (21.9cm) long, and are 1/4" thick by 3/8" wide (6 x 9mm). The coaming measures 5/8" (16mm) thick by 1-5/16"

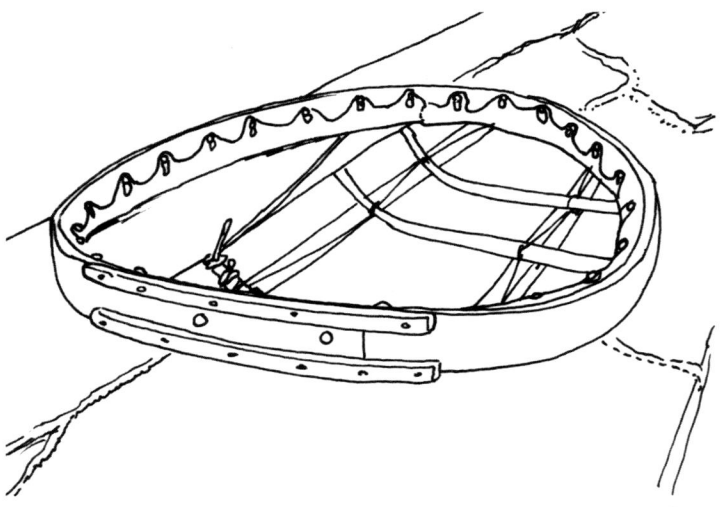

Figure 231: Cockpit-view of the Musée de la Marine's 1Bs.15, looking forward.

(33mm) high. Keel edging is present on the 1.Bs.15: It spans from 1/2″ (13mm) to 2′10″ (86.3cm) along the keelson from 'zero,' and from 14′4-1/4″ (437.5cm) to 16′6-3/4″ (504.8cm) at the stern. This edging is 1/2″ (13mm) tall by 1/4″ (6mm) wide on average, and is fastened with bone or ivory pegs.

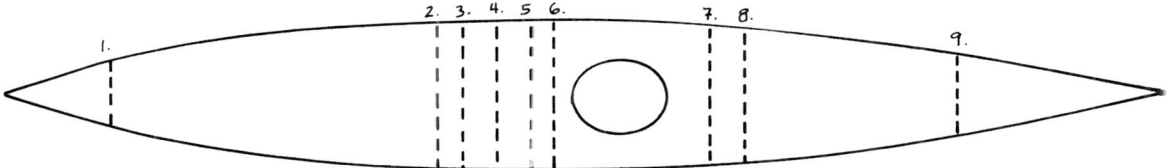

Musée de la Marine, Paris: Cat. no. 1Bs.15

No deck lines remain on the 1Bs.15, although their placement is evidenced. A harpoon holder is not evidenced, which is rather unusual for a Greenland kayak.

24. West Greenland Kayak of pre-1865; likely late 18th-early 19thC.:
National Museum of Scotland, Edinburgh.
Catalog no. U.C.764.

The U.C. 764 is known to pre-date 1865, the year of its transfer from Edinburgh University to the National Museum of Scotland (Souter, 1934:13). Dale Idiens writes that this kayak . . . "Must have come into the University collection after 1780..." (Feest, et.al. 1987:173). Beyond this, no history is known at all.

The U.C. 764 is in superb condition except for its missing coaming. Continuously threaded double-pass lashings are used to assemble the U.C. 764's lower frame—instead of the lashings continuing on the upper faces of the chines and keelson, they are passed alongside these members, alternating from side to side, as in figure 73 bottom. Several deck beams are lashed in place, and clamping ties are present at the gunwales' ends both fore and aft. The ribs are not fastened into their mortises.

Several of the deck beams behind the cockpit exhibit what may be shims set through their tenons to prevent them from seating fully into their mortises. This would have been done as a modification—to effectively widen the kayak without having to replace all of the deck beams. Other kayaks in this study, notably the MSU 4274cw (plate 45), and the NMNH 35667 (plate 33), exhibit this same feature. Forward of the cockpit, the 764 has several empty mortises, which suggests that the gunwales had been used in previous incarnations. The 764's *masik* is 3″ wide (76mm).

The U.C. 764 has all of its deck lines and fittings intact. Three linking

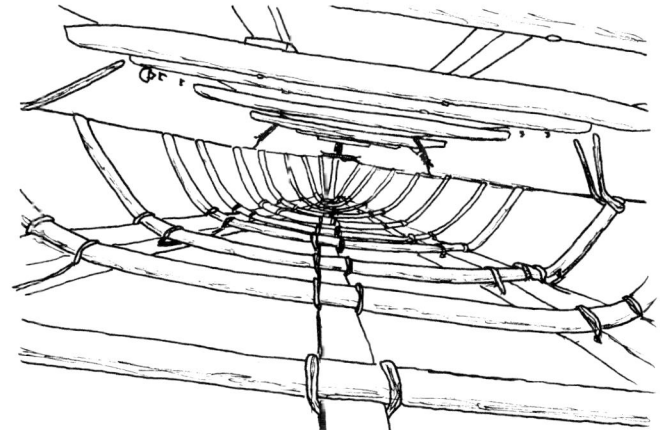

Figure 232: Forward interior view of the U.C. 764.

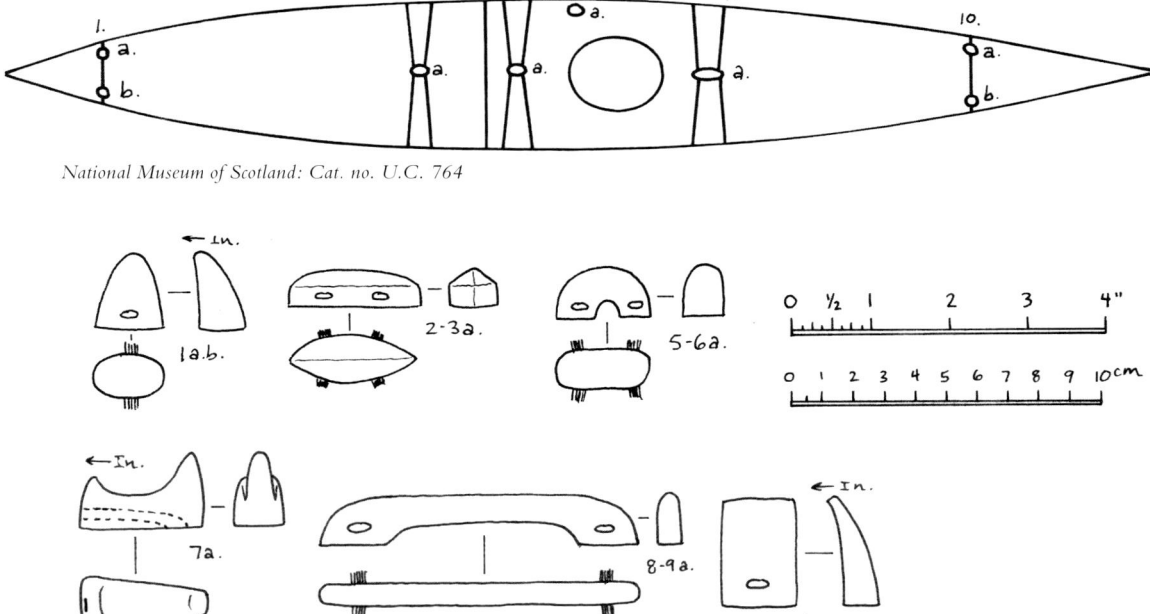

National Museum of Scotland: Cat. no. U.C. 764

pieces are present on three pairs of deck lines: The pair on the aft deck, the pair just forward of the cockpit, and the pair aft of the bow deck line. The link piece between the lines just ahead of the cockpit is of an unusual arch form. It may have functioned as an anchor point for the harpoon-line stand (*asaloq*).

The bow and stern deck lines each have a pair of tab-shaped fittings. Each of these two lines has been severed but re-connected via large knots on deck. Consequently, the tabs are flopped over as these lines are quite slack. A saddle-form harpoon holder is present to the right of the cockpit. Keel edging is present at both the bow and stern.

25. West Greenland Kayak: Trinity House, Newcastle, England.
(Surveyed at the Laing Gallery, Newcastle).
(N/N) "THN"

I surveyed this kayak in a storage room of the Laing Gallery in Newcastle in 1998. The only thing I was told about the kayak at the time of my visit was that it *didn't* belong to the Laing Gallery—it was just being stored there. This kayak does not appear in Souter's "Table of Data of 33 kayaks in Great Britain" (1934:13).

Tyne and Wear Museum's conservation officer R. Elsey answered my inquiry about this kayak's history and present ownership: The kayak belongs to the Corporation of the Trinity House, Newcastle-upon-Tyne. "It is the kayak that was formerly displayed in the James Mather Memorial Center in South Shields as part of an exhibition put together by the late Cap't A. Johnson in 1968" (personal communication, 1999).

Elsey recalled seeing the kayak in 1976 at the Memorial center, but between then and 1979 the unthinkable happened:

> *How exactly the kayak found its way into the hands of the Marsden Bay life guards in South Shields we do not know, however once it was brought to our attention steps were quickly taken to recover it. A brief conservation report prior to its recovery indicated considerable deterioration in the vessels covering, sewn seams, etc., and there was encrustation with what appeared to be salt; these evidences suggested that the Kayak had actually been used in the sea (R. Elsey, 1999: Personal communication).*

The paddle associated with the Newcastle Trinity House kayak is unusual in that it is feathered. It appears in *The Complete Book of Sea Kayaking* (first published in 1976 as *Sea Canoeing*) by Derek Hutchinson, a British Canoe Union Coach (1995:162), but is properly documented and described by John Brand in his *Little Kayak Book*, vol. II (1987:47-50). In researching the paddle's origins, Brand also uncovered the kayak's sad history, referring to it as the "South Shields Kayak:"

> *On 13th Jan. 1987 Mr. A. Osler, Senior Museum Officer, Maritime History, at Newcastle upon Tyne Museum of Science and Engineering sent some good news: 'Thank you for your inquiry re: the South Shields kayak, an intriguing craft which the Museum Service rescued from near oblivion—it having been lent by a former South Shields curator to a 'club' which, by all appearances, had attempted to use it. It is therefore in very poor condition, stabilized, but beyond our current means to restore... despite its condition a lines and constructional plan should be achievable' (1987:50).*

Indeed the Trinity House ("THN") kayak does appear to have been used recently with complete disregard to its value. The *masik* is missing, the coaming front is broken off and missing, and the deck skin has been slit open so as to make the kayak roomier, and easier to enter— essentially it had been converted into a 'sit-on-top' kayak. The inside of the kayak had a fair amount of coarse sand in it as well—something any Greenlander would not let happen, knowing full well that it would quickly wear holes through the skin. Figure 233 shows the general condition of the kayak in 1998. In my estimation, this kayak probably dates from between the late 1700s and the mid 1800s.

As can be seen in the artifactual drawing (plate 25a), the kayak's stern is missing, and a remnant of skin about 8″ (20.3cm) long dangles off the stump of the stern. The artifactual drawing also depicts the general disarray of the THN kayak: Several deck beams are missing or displaced. The breadth of the kayak measured at 17-1/4″ (43.8cm), although based on evidence of the remains, it was originally about 16-3/8″ (41.5cm). The fractured coaming, slashed deck, broken or missing deck lines, and the seams are also depicted. A peg is present at the bow of this kayak, and it likely was the fastener for a now-missing end knob.

Plate 25b shows my conjectural restoration of the Trinity House Newcastle kayak. The dimensions are restored based on evidence and comparisons with similar kayaks; the breadth and depth have been re-drawn, and the sheer-line has been restored.

My conjectural restoration of this kayak's lines has been an unusual ordeal for somewhat interesting

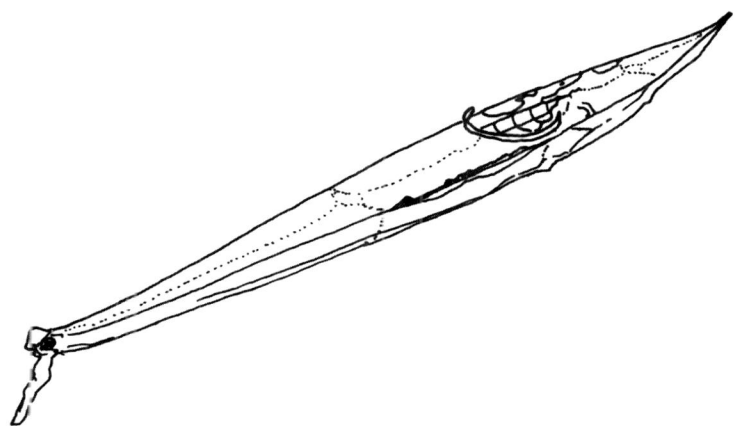

Figure 233: The Newcastle Trinity House kayak. The stern is broken and missing; the cockpit and fore deck are trashed.

reasons: I had originally based it on Hutchinson's description, illustration, and measurements of the "South Shields" kayak in his *Complete Book of Sea Kayaking*. In his chapter on kayak origins, Hutchinson describes the South Shields kayak as having an extremely high stern, and the accompanying drawing shows it as being considerably more raked than the stern of the Whitby Kayak; he gives the length of the 'South Shields' kayak as being 17'6" (533.4cm) (1995:155-157). This was the only information available to me as to what the kayak had looked like and measured prior to its abuse.

Long story short, it has turned out that the South Shields kayak in Hutchinson is an entirely different kayak than the kayak I surveyed; I based much of my conjectural reconstruction on the *wrong* kayak. The good news is that I did not like my initial results anyways—I felt that the high stern shape paired with the existing fractured stern within the constraints of the 17'6" length given by Hutchinson simply looked odd. While the restoration in plate 25b is updated, it is still conjectural: The true shape of the original stern may be lost to history unless old photographs of the kayak exist.

So where is the kayak depicted in Hutchinson? Elder Brother and Trinity House archivist Captain Stephen Healy related to me that it is still unaccounted for, but a photo from circa 1948 depicts it at the Trinity House and in good condition—and with a stern identical to that depicted by Hutchinson. So, does the kayak in plate 25 belong to the Trinity House in Newcastle? According to Captain Healy, it does, and this kayak is presently undergoing much needed conservation at Merseyside Museums prior to its return to Newcastle.

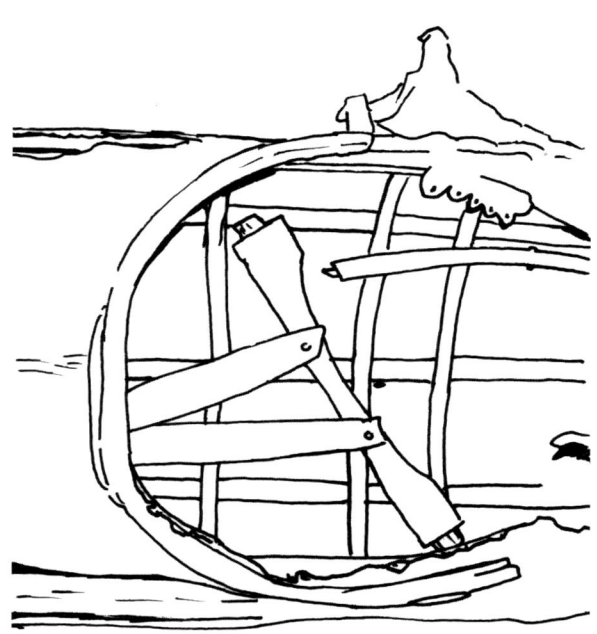

Figure 234: The cockpit of the Newcastle Trinity House kayak. Note the displaced isserfik, *with the aft deck ridges still attached. A loose curved deck beam can also be seen.*

Because the Newcastle Trinity House kayak's *amiq* is broken and missing in places, a somewhat clear view into the framework was possible. From what I could see and/or reach with a tape measure, I took structural survey measurements. The structural survey (plate 25c) shows the results of these measurements overlaying my conjecturally restored lines; the ends are left blank, as a clear view of their joinery was not possible.

A concave cut is present along the forward edge of the *isserfik*: This was done to make more room or provide better comfort for the kayaker. The *isserfik* measures 5/8" (16mm) thick by 2-1/8" (54mm) wide at the ends, narrowing to 7/8" (22mm) in the middle. The structural reconstruction also shows the pair of aft deck-stringers with their curved edges. These stringers are cambered in cross-section, and measure 1/2" (13mm) thick and 1-5/8" (41mm) wide at the widest.

The curved deck beam ahead of the *masik* has two small holes drilled through it at its mid-point. It likely was the attachment point for a carrying handle, as seen in the Hunterian Museum's E.585 (plate 21, figure 228). Another possible explanation is that it was an attachment point for a middle deck stringer, though aside from these holes, no further evidence of such a stringer was noted.

Twenty-six ribs are present inside of the THN kayak, and I didn't see any empty rib-mortises. I also counted nineteen deck beams and/or deck beam mortises, though one or two may have been obscured in the stern. The deck beams have chamfered ends and rounded bottoms and typically measure 5/8"

(16mm) thick by 1-1/8" (28mm) wide. The deck beam mortises are through mortises and they measure 3/16" (5mm) high by 11/16" (17mm), and their upper edges are situated about 1/2" (13mm) below the sheer line.

The THN kayak has two seat slats slung beneath ribs, only instead of being placed in the usual position, they are situated ahead of the *masik* and they function more as 'leg-slats.' The use of leg-slats is common in East Greenland, but is rare among West Greenland kayaks; One other West Greenland kayak has leg-slats: the Hunterian Museum's kayak E.584 (plate 28).

The coaming and its shape have also been restored in the conjectural drawing; the coaming measures 1/2" (13mm) thick and 1-1/4" (32mm) high. A short bone strip is situated on the right side of the coaming just aft of the fracture. It is not clear whether or not one was on the opposite side of the coaming as well. Occasionally such pieces would come in pairs in order to better hold the *tuitsoq* or *tuilik* in place, or it could have been a repair piece, perhaps arresting a splinter in the coaming.

Every deck line on this kayak was either broken or missing. Among those broken but present are lines 2-3, and 5-6—each pair linked by ivory pieces that were miraculously not pilfered during its years of abuse. The bow edging has also survived intact. It measures 5/16" (8mm) square.

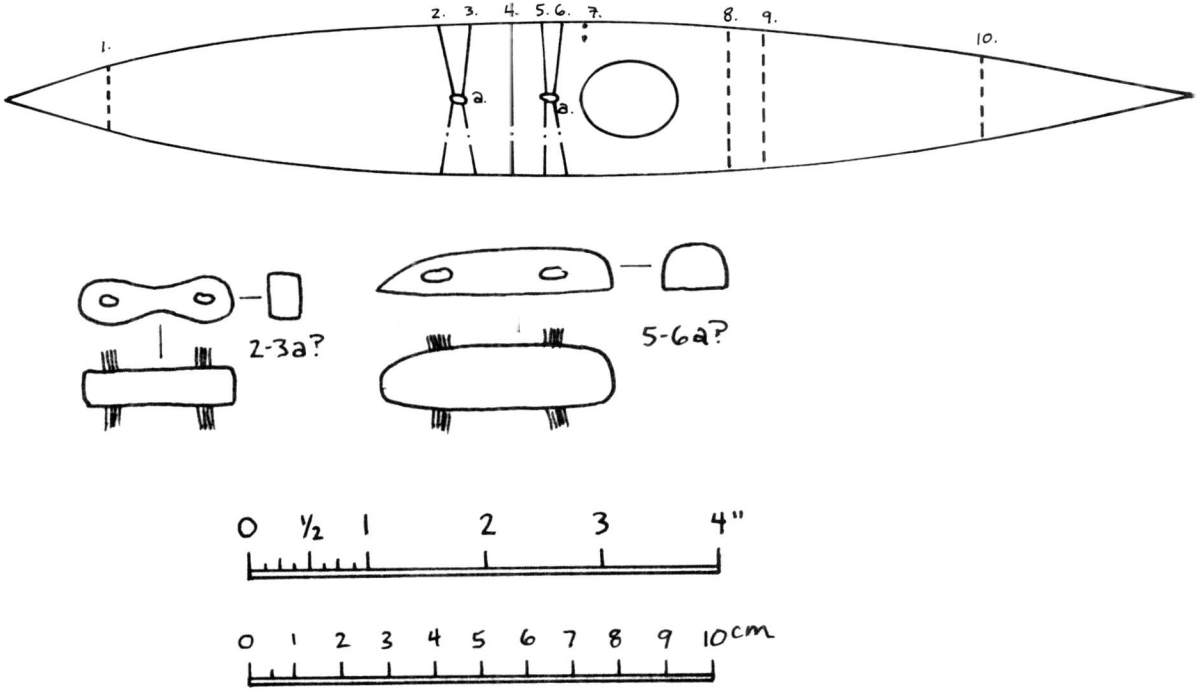

TYPE IV.

Type IV kayaks are characterized by their very high sterns. In contrast to the kayaks of type III, the sterns of type IV kayaks are fuller—more voluminous. There is moderate sheer forward, but the bow is generally much lower than the stern, and again deeper and fuller than type III kayak bows. Type IV kayak hull-sections are typically moderate-to-deep V with slab sides and a generous chine breadth. A considerable range of keel-rocker can be seen among type IV kayaks; these are likely local preferences.

Most every type IV kayak in this study is a form of kayak known as the *avasisaartoq*, described by H.C. Petersen. The *avasisaartoq* is "...concave...and its ends turn up sharply." According to Petersen, the *avasisaartoq* was "widespread until the end of the 19th century. After the introduction of the rifle it became necessary to straighten out the sharply rising ends and after that the type quickly disappeared from the areas where it had formerly been in use" (1986:49).

While Petersen's description is very brief, he illustrates the *avasisaartoq* form with a photograph of the Danish National Museum's kayak Lc.157. The Lc.157 has a moderately high bow, with a distinctly higher and steeper stern. This distinguishes the form from my type III, which Petersen's description could've well described. (A scale drawing of the Lc.157 appears in Brand, 1984:13).

Many theories abound for the reason behind the high sterns of the *avasisaartoq*. P. Scavenius-Jensen writes that it may have been used as a handle with which to drag the kayak over ice floes, or that it served as a 'vane' to further effect weather-cocking (1975:23). Birket-Smith, writing 50 years earlier, describes another practical function: "The up-curved stern was said to have the advantage that the boat was not heard, when bumping in the seas, but all the same it was abandoned, because it caught the wind and was apt to turn the kayak"(1924:269).

Type IV kayaks are for the most part classic *avasisaartoq* forms, but the form gradually becomes more subtle throughout time—the ends become lower and more subdued despite the continuity of considerable sheer. This follows Petersen's statement about the ends being straightened (i.e., lowered) as the rifle became widely used in the mid-to-late 1800s.

The *avasisaartoq* in particular, and my type IV in general parallel Kaj Birket-Smith's type 4 which he describes as having "sheer; in out-of-the-way places still the shape of a tall, sharply built stem with a deck inclining strongly backwards. Long stem, shorter stern which until a short time ago was curved upwards" (1924:271). The passage "until a short time ago" effectively refers to the bulk of the kayaks in my type IV. Those kayaks that do not have the upward curved sterns (referring to the sheer; i.e., and *avasisaartoq*) retain the inclining fore decks and the bow longer than the stern. In fact, the strongly inclining fore decks seem to have become more distinct among the later type IV kayaks in this study, as will be seen.

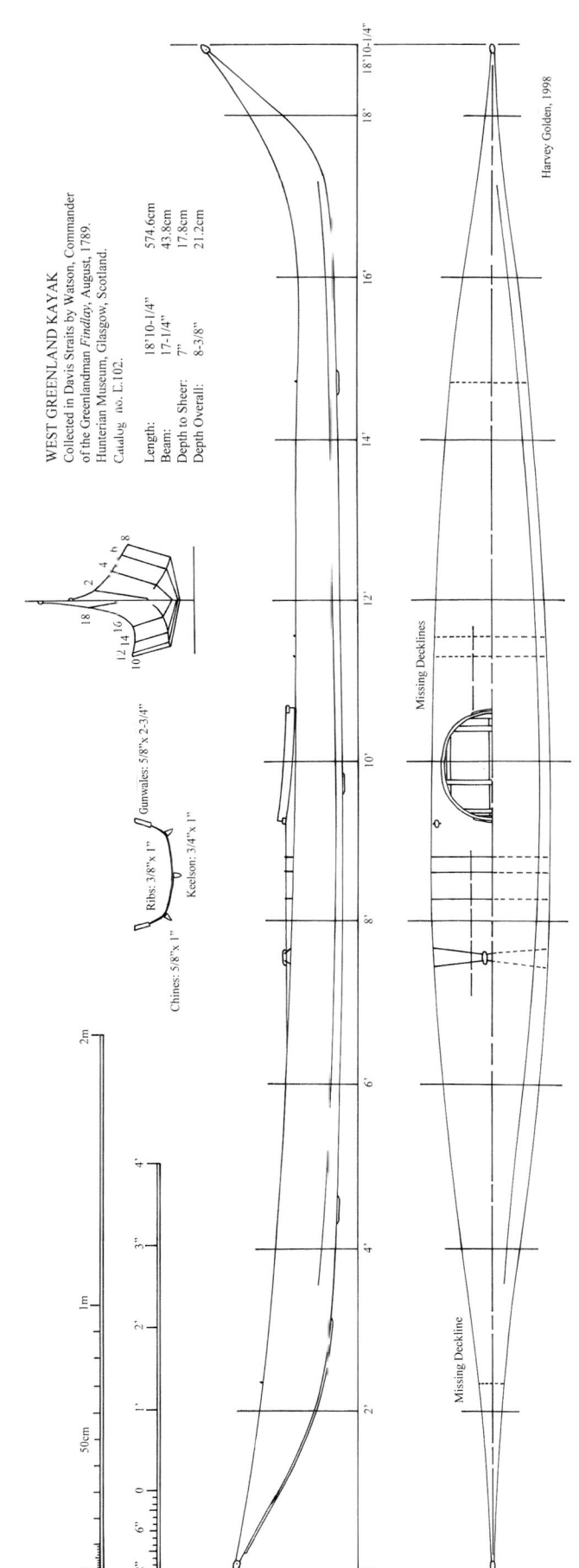

26. Hunterian Museum catalog no. E.102

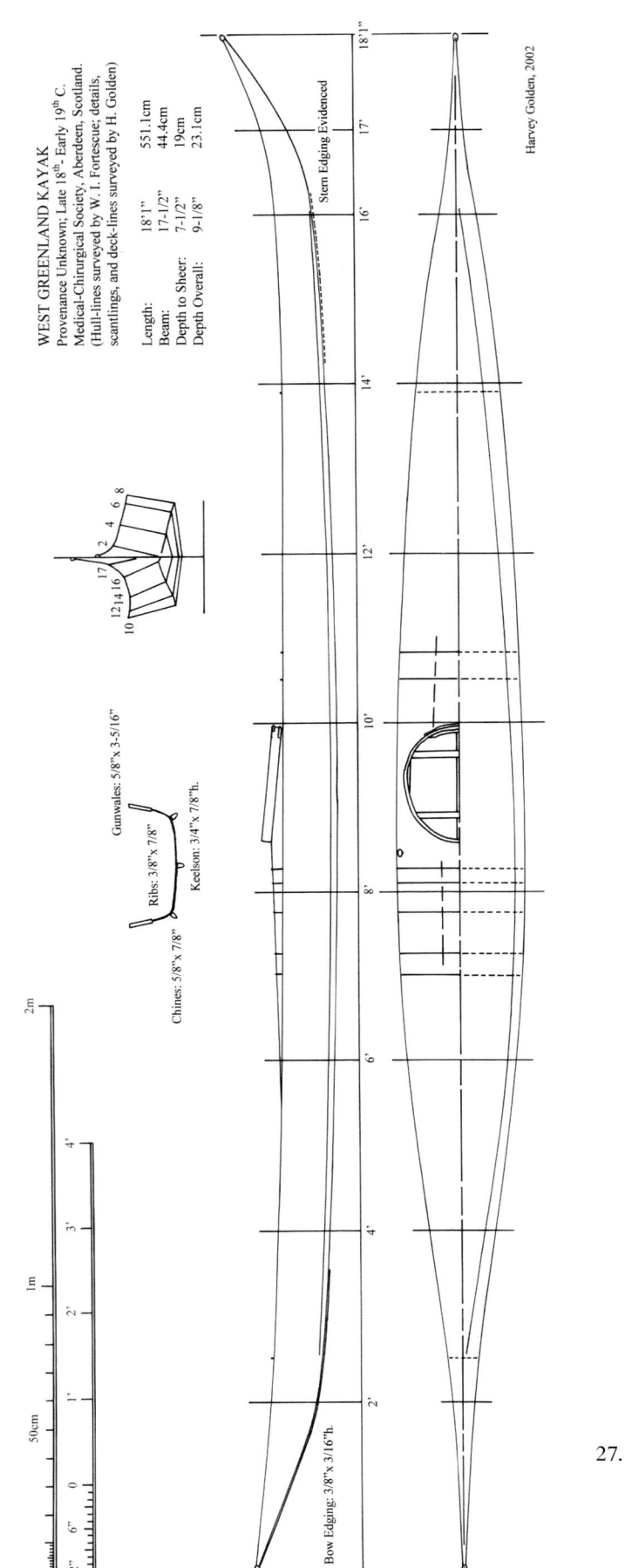

27. Medico Chirurgical Society (N/N) "Med-Chi"

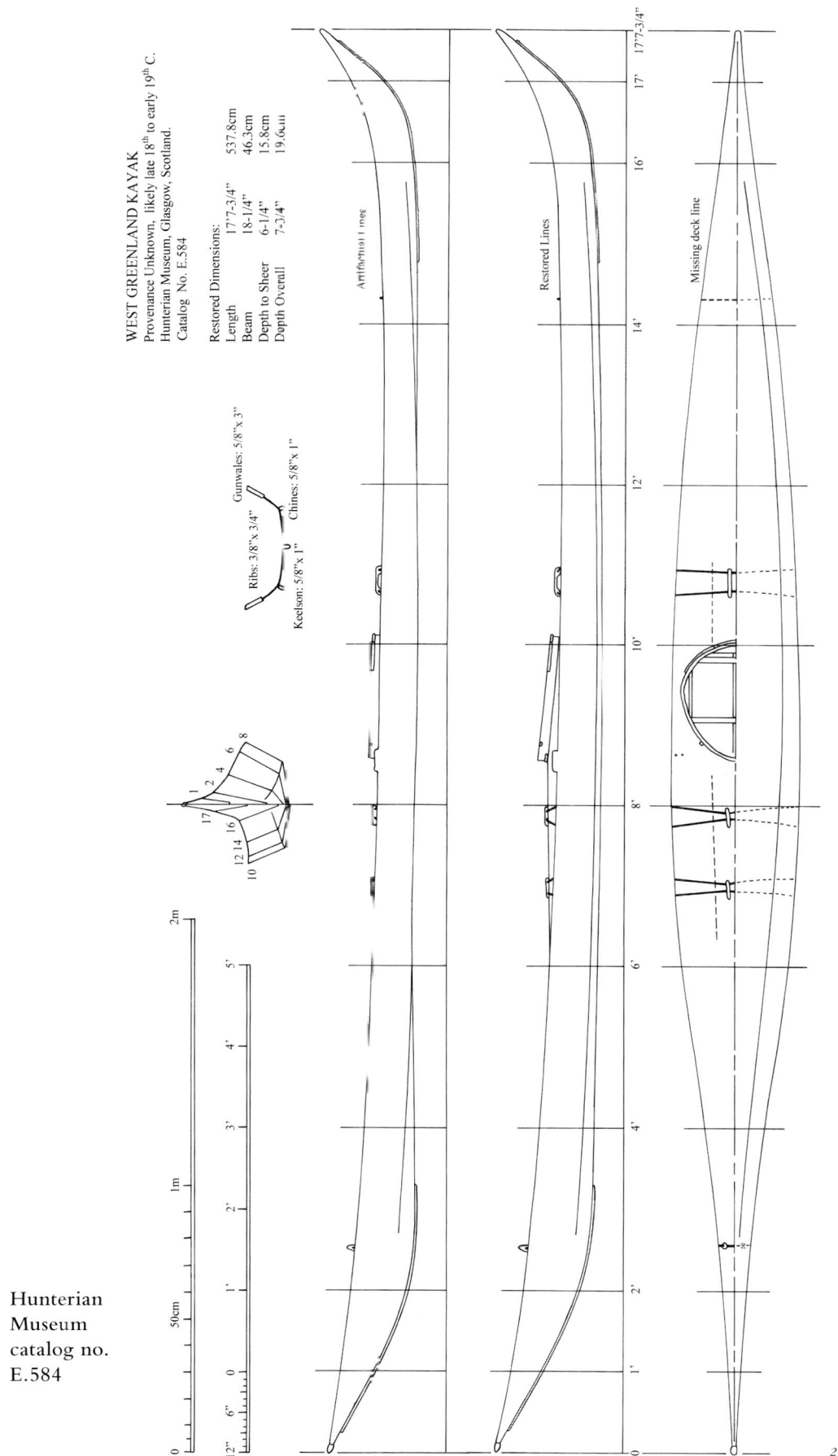

28. Hunterian Museum catalog no. E.584

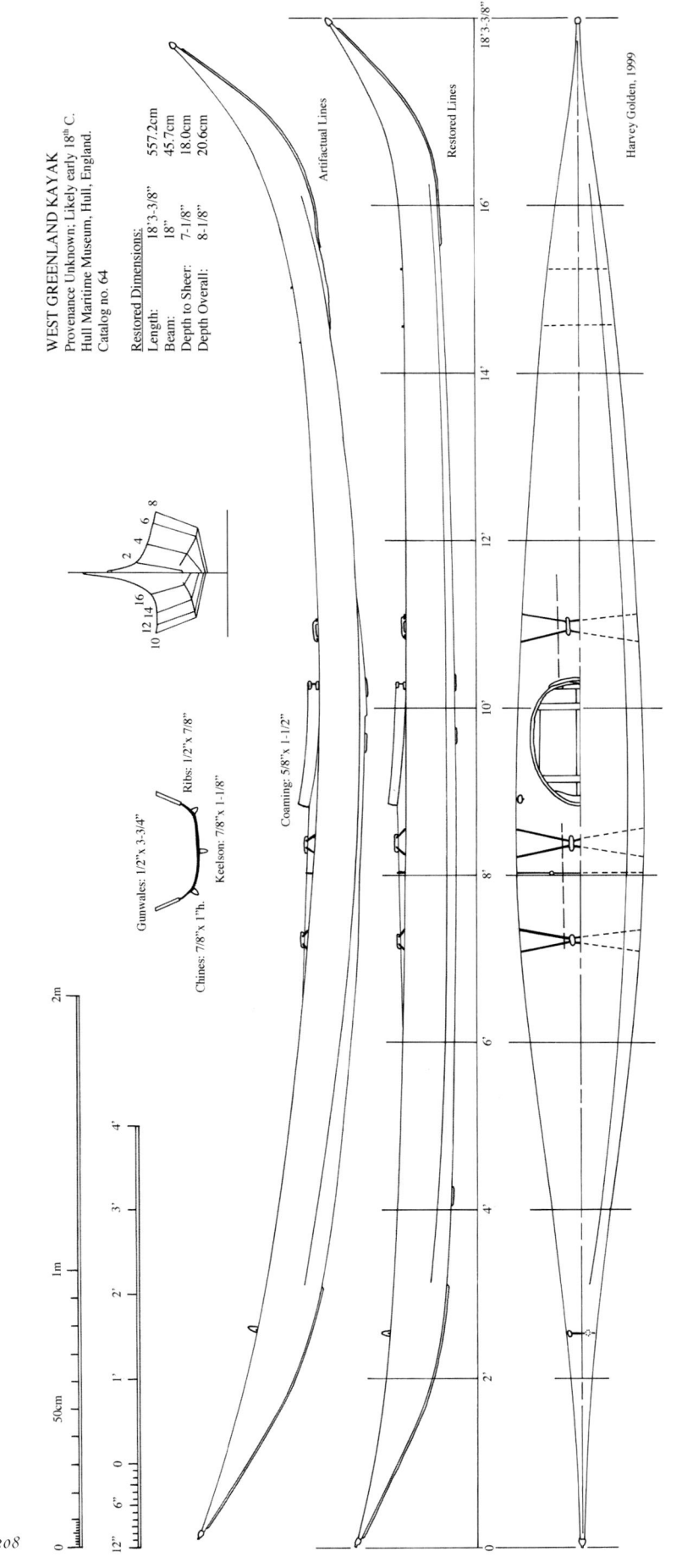

29. Hull Maritime Museum catalog no. 64

30. Hull Maritime Museum (N/N) "C"

WEST GREENLAND KAYAK
Stern elevations from highly damaged kayak.
Collected by Sir John Ross, ca.1830s
Hull Maritime Museum, Hull, England.
No catalog no. ("C")

Length: 17'1-1/2"   521.9cm
Beam: 19-1/2"   49.5cm

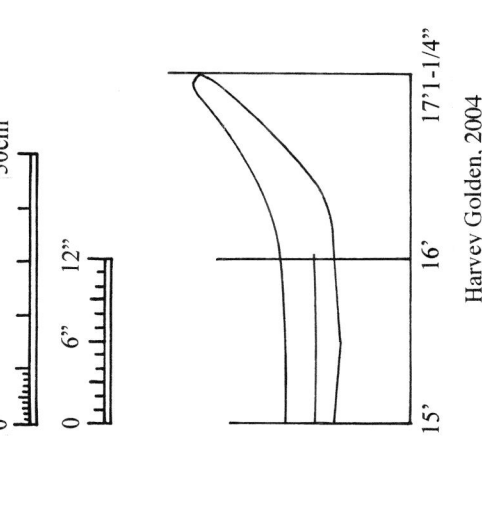

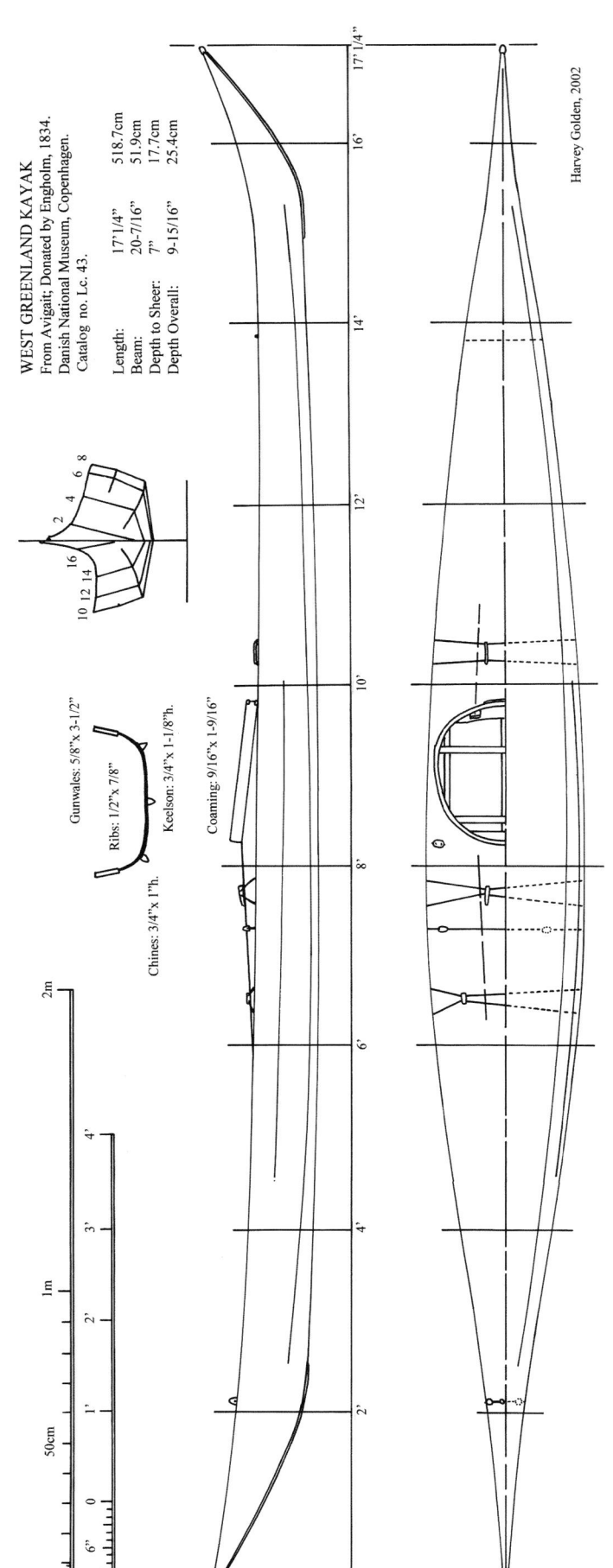

31. Danish National Museum catalog no. Lc.43

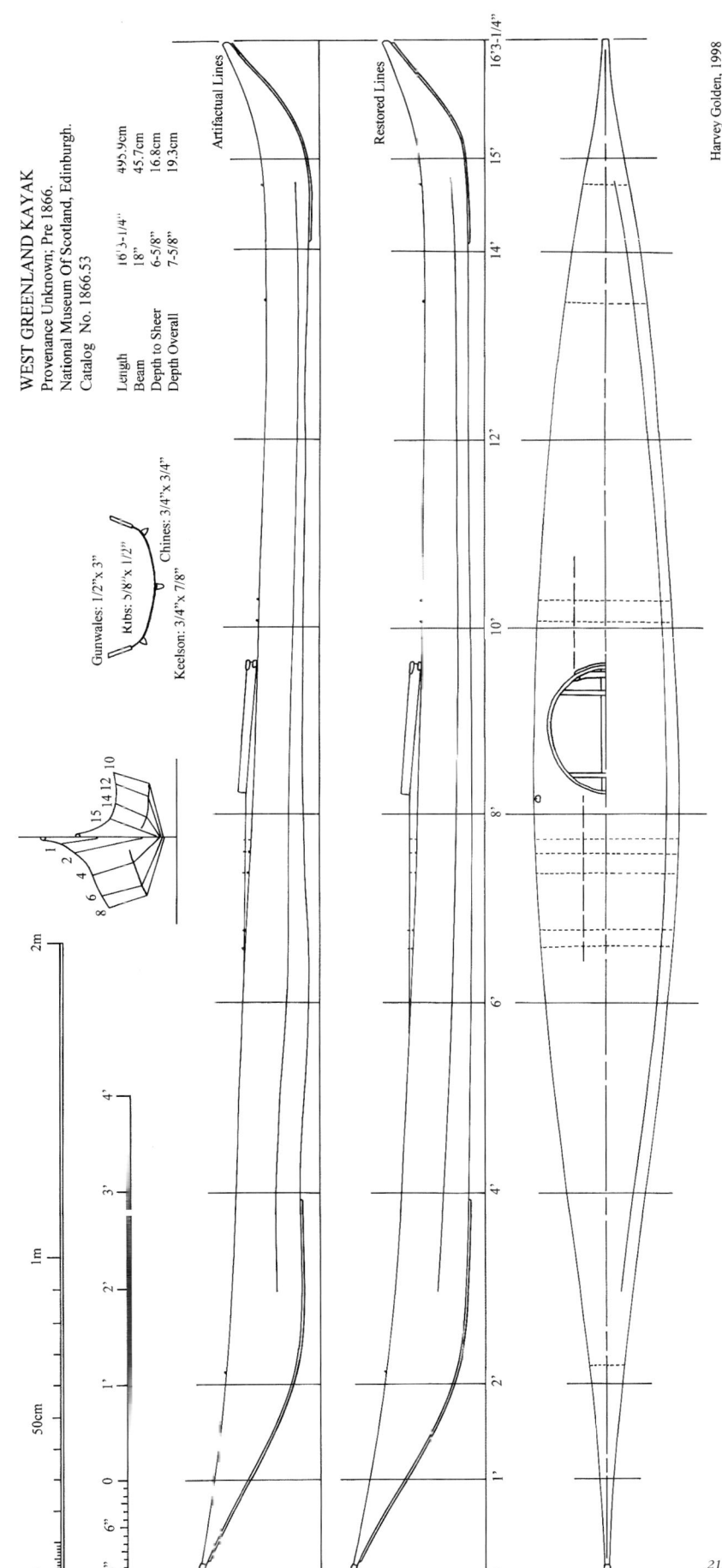

32. National Museum of Scotland catalog no. 1866.53

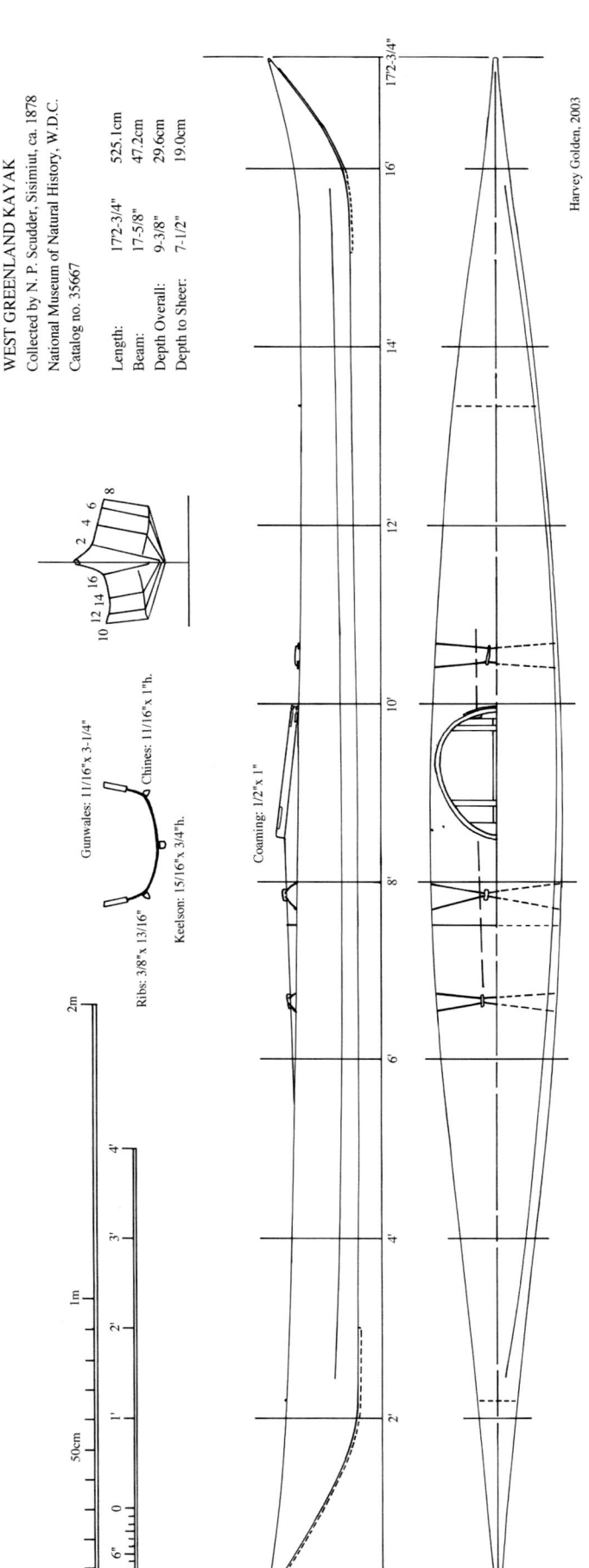

33. National Museum of Natural History catalog no. 35667

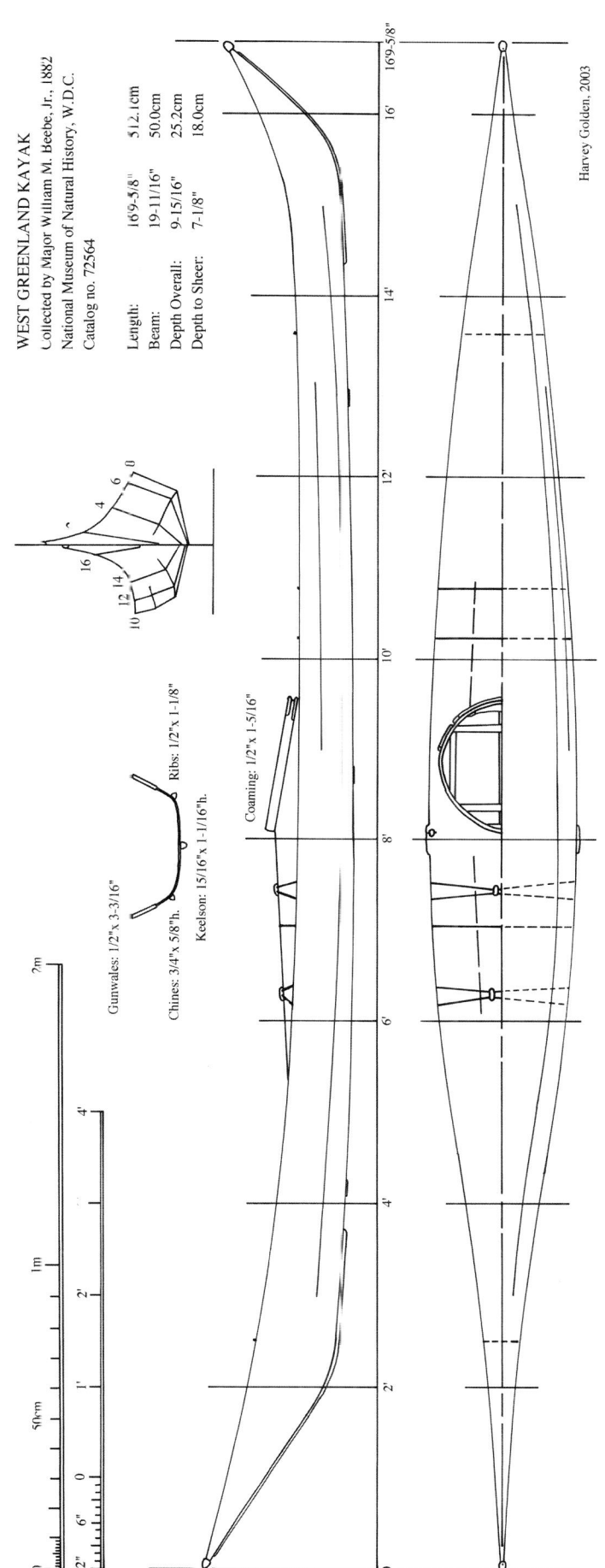

34. National Museum of Natural History catalog no. 72564

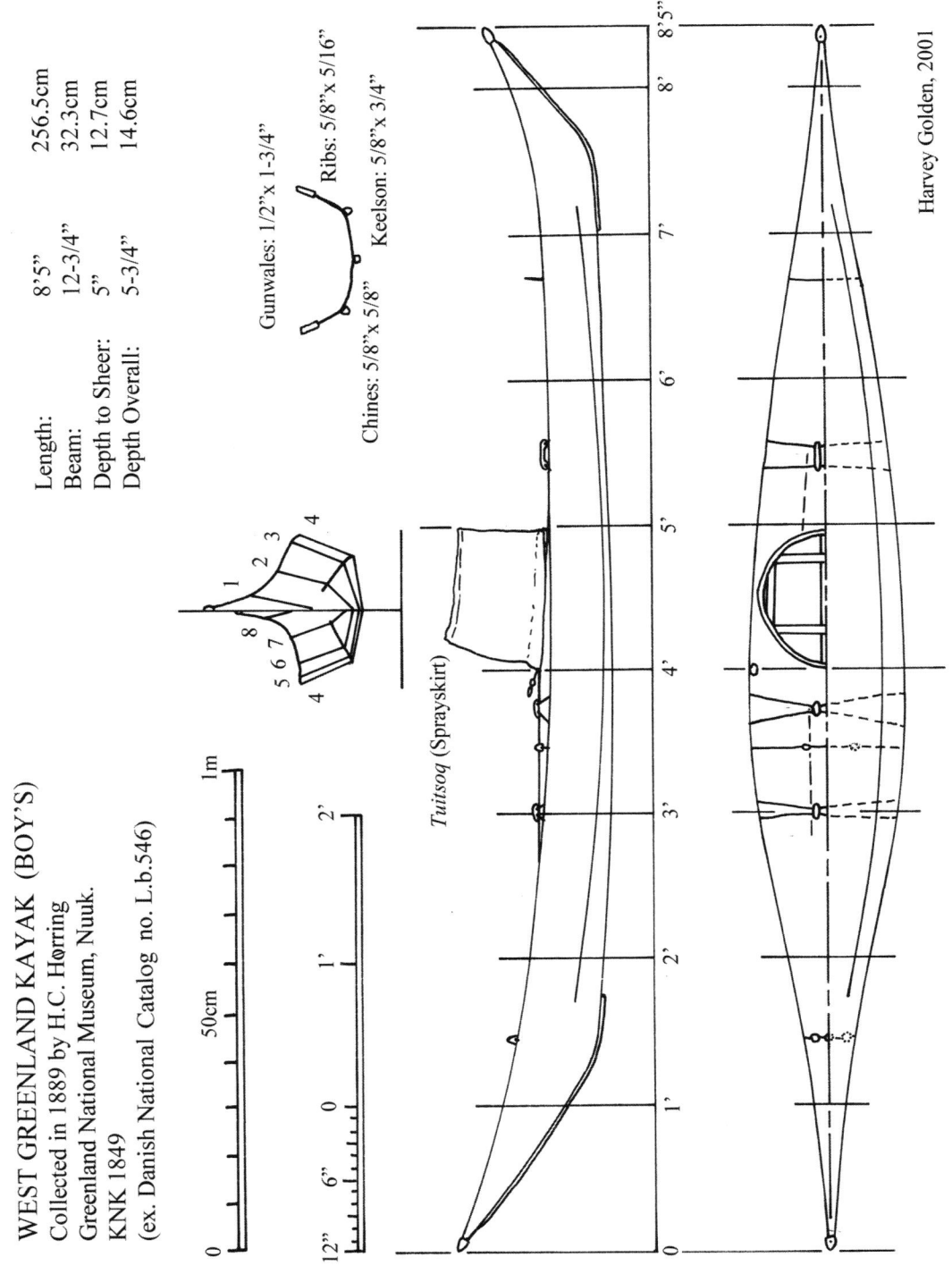

35. Greenland National Museum catalog no. KNK 1849

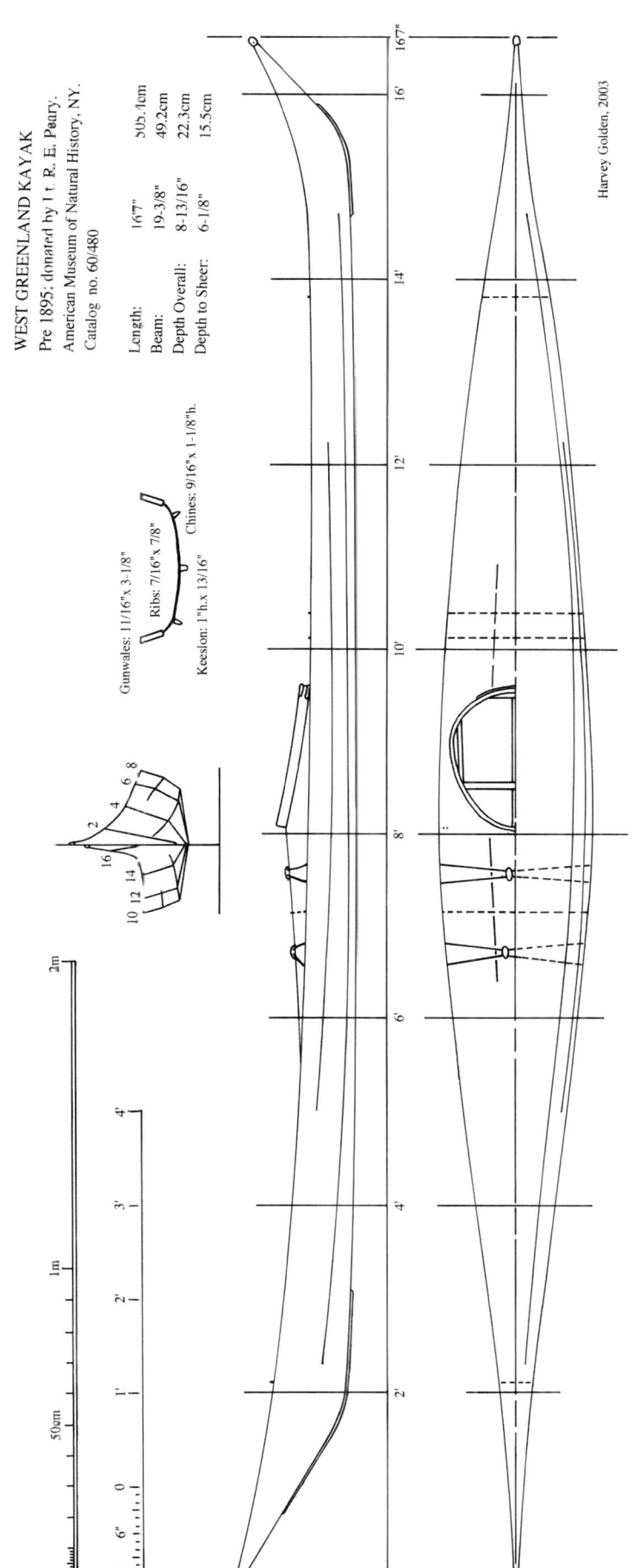

36. American Museum of Natural History catalog no. 60/480

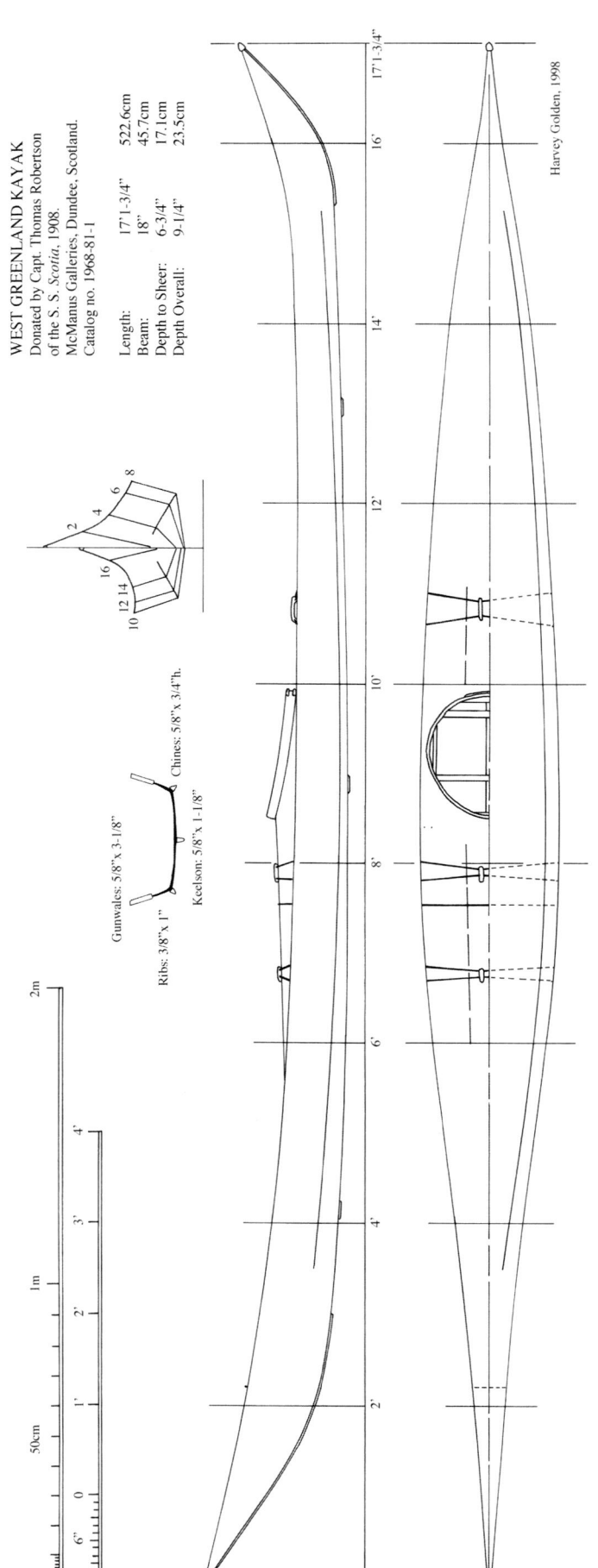

WEST GREENLAND KAYAK
Donated by Capt. Thomas Robertson
of the S. S. *Scotia*, 1908.
McManus Galleries, Dundee, Scotland.
Catalog no. 1968-81-1

Length:	17'1-3/4"	522.6cm
Beam:	18"	45.7cm
Depth to Sheer:	6-3/4"	17.1cm
Depth Overall:	9-1/4"	23.5cm

Gunwales: 5/8"x 3-1/8"
Chines: 5/8"x 3/4"Th.
Ribs: 3/8"x 1"
Keelson: 5/8"x 1-1/8"

Harvey Golden, 1998

37. McManus Galleries catalog no. 1968.81

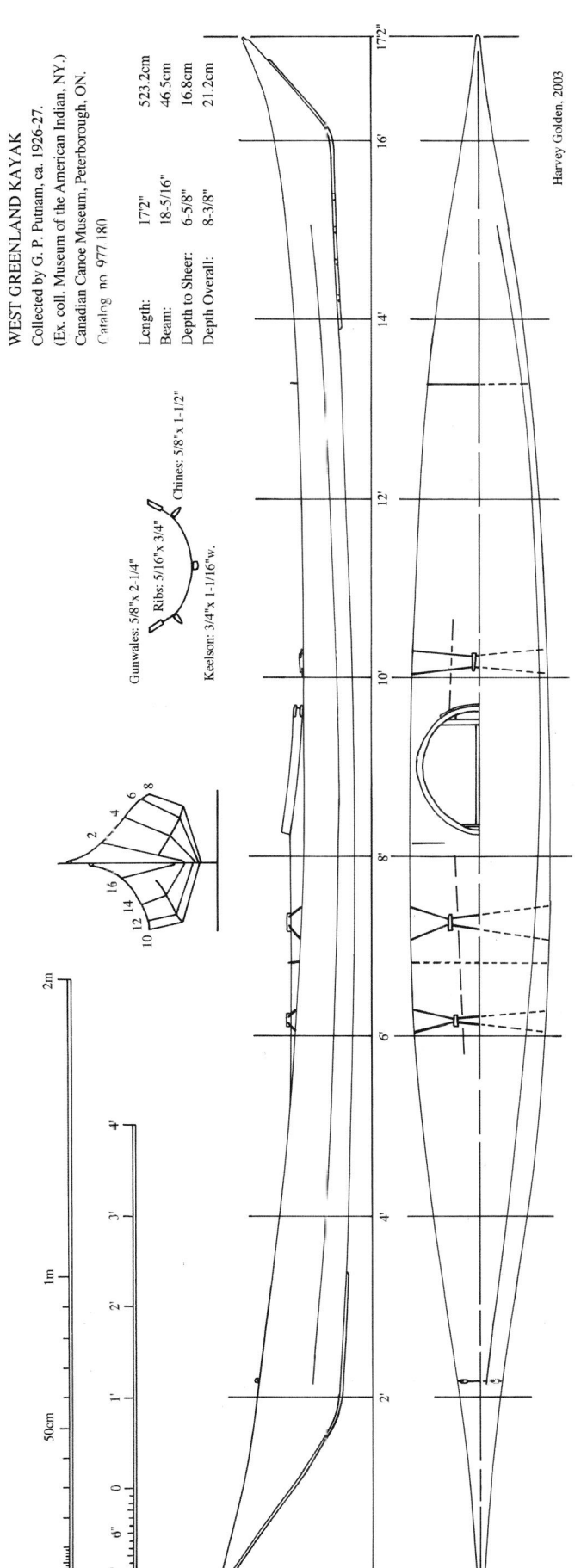

38. Canadian Canoe Museum catalog no. 977.180

26. West Greenland Kayak from ca.1789: The Hunterian Museum, Glasgow, Scotland. Catalog no. E.102.

Museum catalog information shows that a Mr. Watson, commander of the Greenlandman *Findlay*, collected this kayak during the summer of 1789 in the Davis Straits. The Glasgow Whale Fishing Company presented it to Glasgow University the following year. The E.102's data card lists "Davis Straits" as the place of origin; not a very specific one as the Straits entail the coast of Southeast Baffin Island and the entire shore of central and South West Greenland.

Dale Idiens of the National Museum of Scotland writes in *Eskimos in Scotland: c.1682-1924* that "a kayak in the Hunterian Museum, Glasgow . . . was brought back on a whaling ship in 1787 . . ." (in C. Feest, et al, 1987:173). It is not known whether the kayak of 1787 is the E.584, E.585, or even the E.102.[34] The year of 1819 is attributed to one of the two former kayaks—it is not known which one; see entries for kayaks E.584 (plate 28) and E.585 (plate 21).

This kayak is in excellent condition for its age. Its *amiq* is a very clean creamy yellow color and the coaming is of a bright reddish-colored wood. One hasty looking repair to a cut or tear in the *amiq* is present just forward of the cockpit: It is stitched closed with a non-waterproof seam.

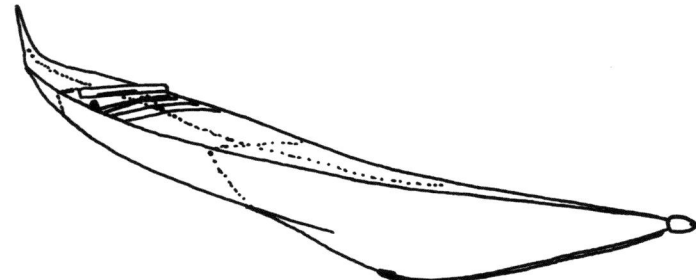

Figure 235: View of the Hunterian Museum's kayak E.102.

An interior view looking forward into the E.102 is presented in figure 236: A dowel cross piece at the lower edge of the gunwales towards the bow holds the gunwales together and helps set the gunwale flare. The deck stringers are shimmed to the correct height with small wooden blocks. Chines and the keelson are lashed to the ribs using the double-lash method.

The E.102's two curved deck beams are 1-1/4″ (32mm) tall and wide, and are trapezoidal in cross-section, their top facet being about 3/4″ (19mm) wide. The E.102's *masik* measured 1/2″ (13mm) thick by 3-5/8″ (9.2cm) wide; the *isserfik* is 3/4″ (19mm) thick by 1-1/2″ (38mm) wide with rounded corners and a cambered upper-face. The fore deck

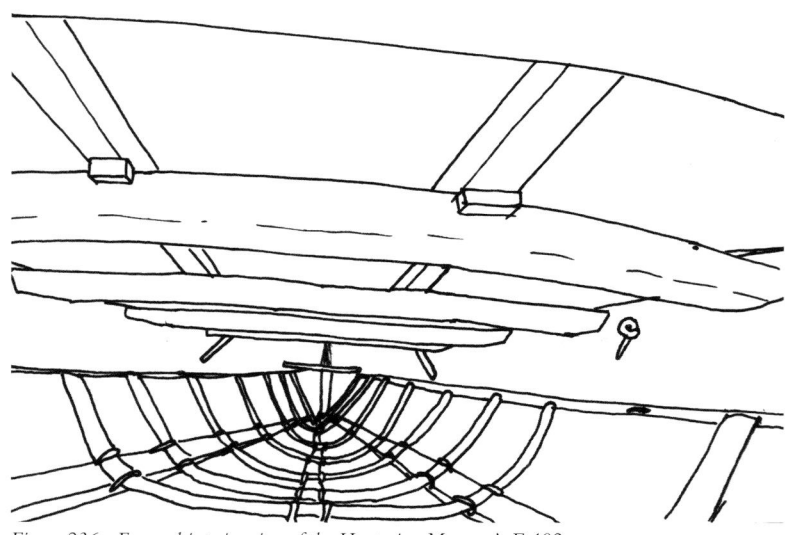

Figure 236: Forward interior view of the Hunterian Museum's E.102.

---

[34] The *Findlay*, with Mr. Watson commanding, did sail to Davis Straits in 1787 as well as 1789 (Jones, 1996:22,27).

stringers are 3/4" (19mm) wide and 7/8" (22mm) high at their aft end; the aft deck stringers are 1/4" (6mm) thick and 2" (51mm) wide.

Only four of the E.102's deck beams are visibly fastened to the gunwales; they are fastened by the oblique peg method. It is very likely that the E.102's deck beams are also top-pegged in place.

To the extent that I could see and reach with a tape measure, I documented the positions of the framing in and around the cockpit of the E.102; the results are depicted in figure 238.

The bow deck line of the E.102 is missing, as are all three deck lines aft of the cockpit. The pair behind the cockpit may have had a link, much like the pair of lines just forward of the cockpit. A tab-shaped harpoon holder is present to the right front quarter of the coaming. The E.102's coaming is placed slightly off the kayak's centerline: It is 1" (25mm) from the right sheer, and 1-3/8" (35mm) from the left sheer. The coaming measures 5/8" (16mm) thick by 1-5/16" (33mm) high. Both end-knobs are present on this kayak as is keel edging at the bow. The transverse seams in the *amiq* are spanned along the keelson by several small pieces of bone or ivory.

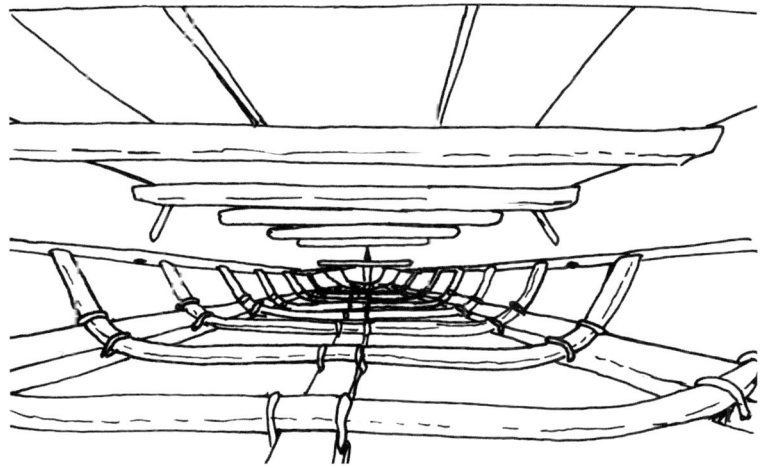

Figure 237: Aft interior view of the Hunterian Museum's E.102.

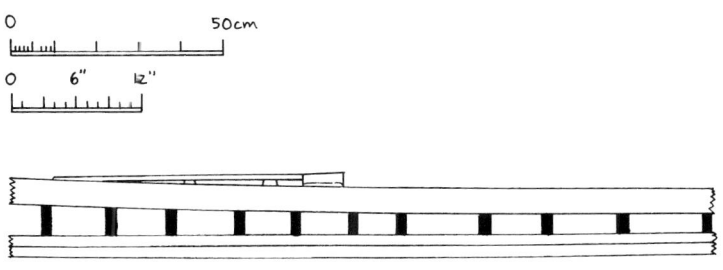

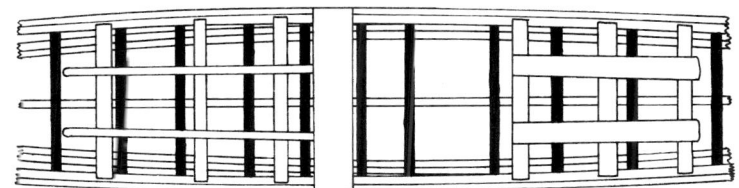

Figure 238: A midships framing pattern of the Hunterian Museum's E.102.

The Hunterian Museum's kayak E.102 is an extremely appealing kayak, and there was no doubt at first glance that I was going to build a replica of it. It did take me two years after surveying it (in 1998) to feel confident about doing the extreme sheer justice. It was quite a challenge and involved extensive shaping and scarfing—and even re-scarfing when things came out wrong. The E.102 and the KNX 1161 (plate 9), share the distinction of being the two most difficult kayaks I've ever replicated.

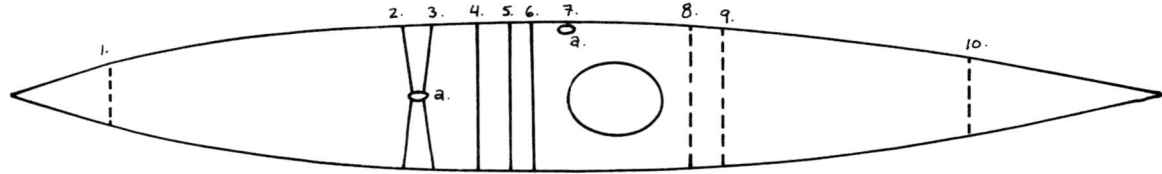

Hunterian Museum, Glasgow: Cat. no. E.102

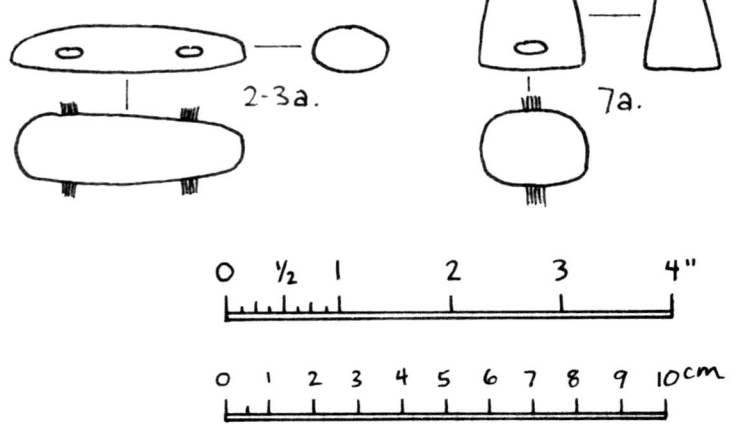

The E.102 replica was a dream to paddle. It struck me then, and I still maintain this notion, that it is the finest kayak I've ever paddled. Its balance of volume, stability, tracking, agility, rough water and wind handling, comfort, and ultimate seaworthiness is as perfect as I could imagine. This high praise must of course be taken for what it is: extremely subjective. Any other person's experience is likely to vary based on any number of factors including prior experiences, preferred characteristics, sense of balance, their size and weight, their expectations, etc., etc. Kayaks are by their nature very individual experiences, unlike freighters and tankers perhaps. In order to be able to fit in the E.102 replica's cockpit, I had to lengthen the coaming from 17-1/4" (43.8cm) long to 18-3/4" (47.6cm).

That the E.102 replica is manageable (if not plain comfortable) in high winds (beam, quartering, etc.) tends to surprise many people. By its very appearance the stern seems to be a weather vane, but in actuality it has a considerably neutral helm. The high stern is compensated for by the kayak's low rocker and slight deadrise—these aspects lend considerable resistance to weather cocking.

As Birket-Smith described (see type IV introduction, page 204), the high stern makes an immense different with regards to noise: The upsweep of the stern mimics the curve of following waves and dampens or

Figure 239: Stern view of the E.102 replica's frame. Note how the gunwales curve upwards at their ends—this was conjecturally interpreted, but is fairly consistent with other kayaks, e.g., the KNK 1550x18 (plate 71). Photograph by the author.

Figure 240: The E.102 replica being paddled by Brian Schulz, Portland, Oregon, 2006. (Photo by author.)

Figure 241: The E.102 replica in Portland, 2006. (Photo by author.)

even prevents the loud *THWOMP* one tends to hear in flatter kayak types. Likewise, the bow, though less elevated, greatly aids in preventing submarining in all but the larger waves.

It may not be productive to offer up a sweeping opinion on kayak aesthetics, but I think that the E.102 is by far the most beautiful kayak in this study. I also think its aesthetics are in perfect harmony with its on-the-water performance and handling.

27. West Greenland Kayak: Medico-Chirurgical Society, Aberdeen, Scotland. (N/N) 'Med-Chi'

Dr. William I. Fortescue surveyed this kayak early in the 20th century, and his drawing has been published in William Clark Souter's paper *The Story of Our Kayak and Some Others* in 1934 (1934: facing title page). 'Our Kayak' refers to the present kayak; the paper was Souter's address to the Medico-Chirurgical Society (of which he was president) given in 1933. It isn't known for certain when the kayak was surveyed or drawn-up by Fortescue, but Honorary Librarian Alexander Adam of the Medico-Chirurgical Society writes "From 1897 until 1910 he [Fortescue] was Assistant Surgeon at the Children's Hospital. During those years he was a member of our Society and regularly attended meetings... It seems almost certain, though I cannot prove it, that the drawing was made before 1910" (2002, personal correspondence).

Fortescue's drawing is very well executed, but is limited to elements of form instead of construct and detail—essentially omitting details of deck-line placement, scantlings, etc. The drawing presented here is re-drawn from Fortescue's hull-lines; I have added the above-mentioned details.

Souter does not come up with solid conclusions as to the Med-Chi kayak's history, but he does arrive at the theory that it may have been used by a patient at the hospital—specifically an Eskimo brought to Aberdeen by Captain Penny of the *Neptune* in 1839: "I (further) venture to suggest that our kayak was the one used by Eenoolooapik in 1839. . . The other obvious alternative, though perhaps less of a flattering unction to our medical souls than a present from a grateful patient, is that the kayak was brought to Aberdeen on a whaler by some unrecorded medical student or recent graduate on completion of his trip to the Arctic as a ship's surgeon" (1934:19-20).

The first possibility may be rejected on account that Eenoolooapik was a Baffin-Land Inuk (specifically, from Exeter Sound, Cumberland Peninsula [Ross, 1985:112-113]), and the kayak is unquestionably Greenlandic in origin. Souter's second theory is much more likely. As learned from the mummy in

Figure 242: From David Crantz's 1767 The History of Greenland *(Vol. I, plate III). The kayak, while naively portrayed, is of the classic type IV form—an abruptly up-turned stern and a gradually sheered bow. (Courtesy of Vernon Doucette.)*

Hoorn (page 133), and Zierik's 9th century civic planning (page 142), the most interesting and unusual story is not always the true one.

Form-wise, the Med-Chi kayak bears great resemblance to the E.102, though its curves and ends are slightly more subdued; their construction methods also vary slightly. The joinery in the Med-Chi kayak is all pegged—deck-beams use the 'oblique' pegged method intermittently to fasten to the gunwales; the chines and keelson are pegged to the ribs. In lieu of a clamping tie at the gunwales' ends, a dowel is used, as illustrated in figure 46 top. The ribs are not pegged the gunwales.

The Med-Chi kayak's *masik* is 2-1/2" (63mm) wide, but is cut back along its middle 4-3/4" (12cm) to 2" (50mm) wide. The *isserfik* is 3/4" (19mm) thick and 1-5/8" (41mm) wide at its ends, and is also cut back 1/2" (13mm) at its mid-point. The coaming measures 1/2" (13mm) thick by 1-1/4" (32mm) high. The fore deck stringers are 1/2" (13mm) wide, and the aft deck stringers measure 1/2" (13mm) thick by 3/4" (19mm) wide.

Bow edging is present and indicated on the drawing and stern edging is missing but evidenced and is depicted in the scale drawing as a dashed line. It is unusual that the stern edging does not continue well up the stem, instead ending 22-1/2" (57.1cm) from the tip of the stern, with no evidence of having extended further.

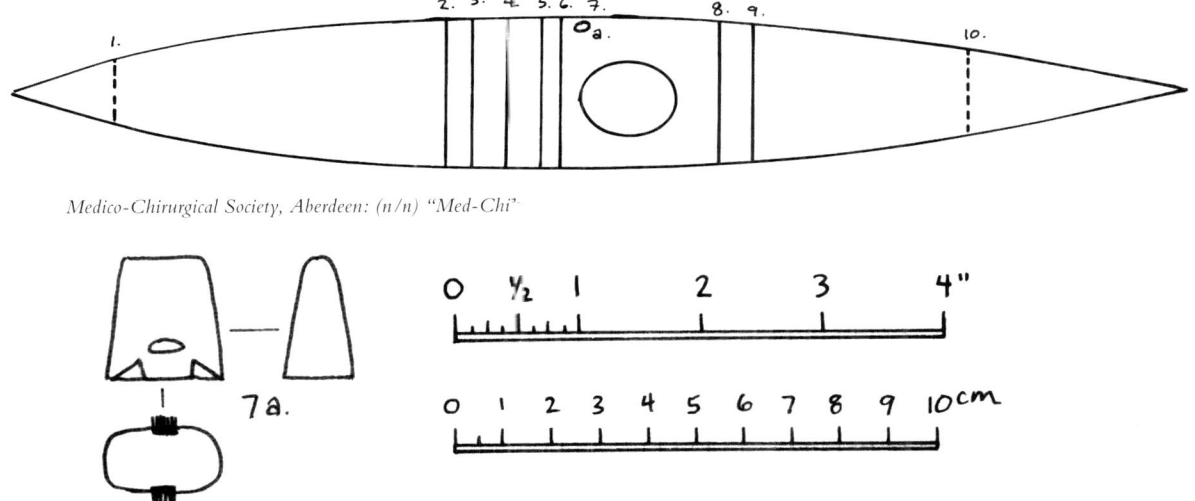

Medico-Chirurgical Society, Aberdeen: (n/n) "Med-Chi"

The deck lines on the Med-Chi kayak are very simple; the only fitting present is the harpoon holder. The two end-most deck lines are entirely missing and may or may not have had fittings.

28. West Greenland kayak from ca. Late 1700s to early 1800s:
   Hunterian Museum, Glasgow, Scotland.
   Catalog no. E.584.

The history of the E.584 is unknown beyond its possibly of having been donated in 1819 by a J. Dalrymple of Glasgow (museum catalog.) Another kayak in the Hunterian's collection (the E.585) shares this possible provenance—it is not known which of these is the 1819 kayak. Historian John

Heath writes that both the E.584 and the E.585 (plate 21) date from 1819, which could be the case, but does run contrary to Hunterian Museum records (Heath, 2004:11). The three kayaks presently in the Hunterian's collections are recorded in Souter's table of kayaks in Great Britain, but origins and acquisition dates are left blank (1934:13).

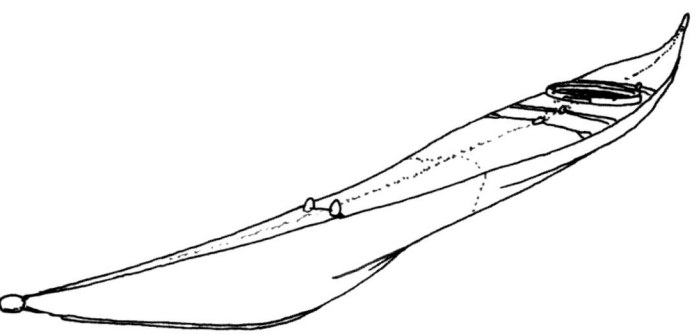

Figure 243: The Hunterian Museum's kayak E.584.

This kayak appears to be of the same general form as the Medico-Chirurgical Society's kayak, although the ends are slightly fuller in volume when viewed in profile. This increase of bow and stern volume seems to be a consistent trend from older to more recent type IV kayaks.

The E.584 has extensive amidships hull collapse, and the framing is broken up a bit in the cockpit. The ends however are in good condition, especially the bow. The scale drawing shows an artifactual elevation as well as a conjecturally restored elevation.

Two deck beams aft, and two deck beams forward of the cockpit are lashed to the gunwales. Gunwale clamp ties are present both fore and aft at the gunwales' ends. The chines and keelson are double-pass lashed to the ribs with a non-continuous line—curiously, many turns of the lashing are present over the ribs—as many as eight passes in places. The lashing material is twine, and either little regard was given to wasting the material, or the builder had little faith in its durability. The ribs are not fastened to the gunwales.

The E.584 has a pair of seat-slats, or more appropriately, leg-slats. This particular arrangement is rare among the West Greenland kayaks in this study, but is very typical of East Greenland kayaks (see the DNM's kayak L.19.157 [plate 86] and especially the Museon's kayak 57602 [plate 91]). The E.584's slats are 1-1/4″ (32mm) wide, and they begin 14-1/4″ (36.2cm) forward of the coaming's front edge, and extend forward for 24″ (61.0cm). The slats are slung beneath the ribs, and are lashed in place.

Another interesting feature of the 584 is the pair of bone buttons at the forward quarters of the coaming (appearing as in figure 124). The buttons are positioned 7/8″ (22mm) up from the coaming's bottom edge, and they are 3/16″ (5mm) high by 7/16″ (11mm) wide, and they project out 3/16″ (5mm). These buttons would have served to better hold the *tuitsoq* or *tuilik* in place. One other kayak in this study has the same form of coaming button: The Mariners' Museum kayak BF-47 (plate 58). The E.584's coaming measures 1/2″ (13mm) thick by 1-1/4″ (32mm) high.

Most of the 584's deck lines are present and intact; only the stern deck line and the harpoon holder are missing. Two large cones are present on the bow deck line; these two pieces are slightly hollowed

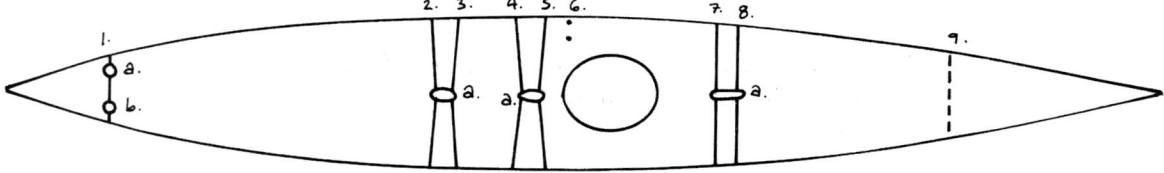

Hunterian Museum, Glasgow: Cat. no. E.584

at their crowns. Two of the four deck lines ahead of the cockpit are linked together; usually a single unlinked line would be present between these pairs, but such a line was not evidenced on this kayak. The pair of deck lines behind the cockpit is also linked together. A bow end knob is present, but there is none aft. Bow and stern keel edging is present.

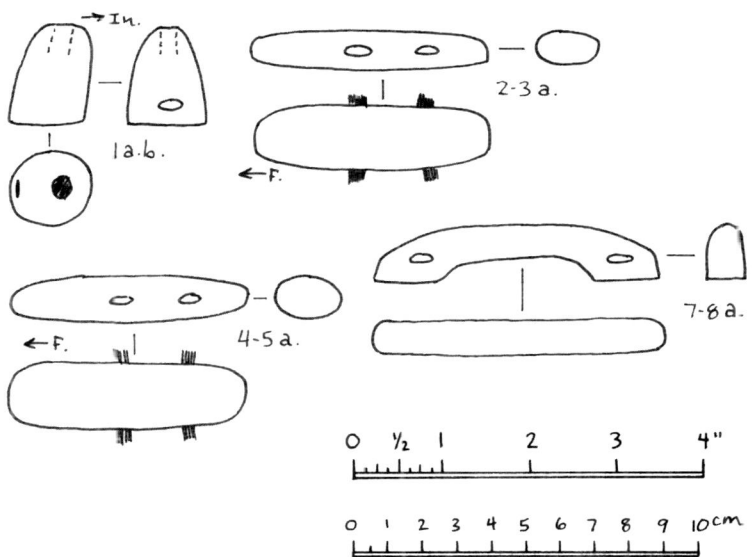

29. West Greenland kayak from ca. Late 1700s to mid 1800s: Hull Maritime Museum, Kingston Upon Hull, England. Catalog no. 64(?)

The history of the '64' is lost, likely having been destroyed during the Battle of Britain, 1939-40. Responding to my inquiry, Arthur Credland (Keeper of Maritime History, Hull Maritime Museum), writes that, "64 may have been the old Literary and Philosophical Society daybook number, but the old books are all gone" (1998: personal correspondence).

Souter, in his 1934 table of kayaks in Great Britain, lists four kayaks in Hull. Measurements are given for each, though none match up precisely enough with my measurements of the '64' to tell which one it may be. One of the kayaks in Souter's table can be ruled out on account of its 258″ (21′6″; 655.3cm) length (1934:13). This long kayak—by all appearances from Baffin Island—is given (by Souter) a tentative provenance of "Sir John Ross ? Davis St. 1833" (1934:13). This same attribution (with question-mark) is given to another kayak in Souter's list (1934:13). While the measurements I made of the three Greenland kayaks there don't match precisely with those of Souter's, it is the Hull Maritime Museum tradition that Ross collected the kayak in plate 30 (A. Credland, personal communication, 2002).

If one takes both what is known from Souter's table and the Hull Maritime Museum tradition, we see that the present kayak—the '64'—was not collected by Sir John Ross, although even this is questionable, sure as Souter has placed question-marks with his attributions.

An effigy of a Greenlander is present in the kayak—wearing a seal skin *tuilik*, or paddling jacket. This simple fact may hint towards the origin of this kayak as an effigy associated with a kayak is mentioned in the Hull News Supplement of February 12th, 1898 (Symons, 14), kindly provided by Mr. Credland:

Above the window in the right wing may be seen suspended the effigy of an Esquimaux in his canoe. It was presented by the valiant Arctic explorer, Captain Sir John Ross. It appears that one of the Hull whaling ships, owned by the late Mr. Wm. Collinson brought to Hull on a visit an Esquimaux and his boat. The latter would betake himself and the canoe to the Garrison Cut, so called, but it was really a moat . . . The

Esquimaux used to amuse the people by an exhibition of how his people jumped in and out of their Kyaks, as Dr. Nansen terms them. However, during one of his exhibitions, the poor fellow dived under the canoe and got entangled in the weeds at the bottom of the moat, and was drowned. The effigy and canoe are mementos of him. It is the identical boat and the effigy is clad in the same garments that he wore.

The article above, while vividly describing the demise of the Greenlander, tends to confuse the reader with mention of Sir John *and* a Mr. Collinson. A passage in *A Guide to the Museum of the Literary and Philosophical Society of Hull* from 1860 somewhat clears this up (or further confuses, as the case may be) by stating that there were two kayaks with effigies at the museum (**emphasis mine**):

> ... Under the skeleton of the whale, in the right wing of the museum, are **two** Esquimaux canoes, with models of the natives in their own dresses, which were presented to this Museum by Captain, afterwards Sir John, Ross. The Esquimaux, who was the owner of one of these canoes, having come to Hull in a whale ship, belonging, we believe, to Mr. Collinson, used to amuse the people of this town, by shewing [sic.] the way in which he could jump in and out of his canoe, and even dive under it, to escape the attack of any sea-monster which might attack it ... His canoe remains here a memento of him and his people (Anonymous, 1860:9-10).

The '64' is presently the only kayak at the Hull Maritime Museum with an effigy in-place. Still, nothing is known for certain of its history, as enticing as it is to suppose that Ross had collected it and/or it was the kayak used by the 'Esquimaux' who amused people in the moats of Hull.

The '64' is quite damaged, though intact and very presentable. The extent of the damage was not immediately clear due its being stored in a confined space, though its damaged state became quite apparent as I drew up its lines. While the '64' does have a very high stern, the sagging of the kayak accentuates this greatly. The hull aft of the cockpit is collapsed up to the chines and beyond. Slight hull collapse exists in the forward half.

The *masik* is quite wide: 4-1/4" (10.8cm) at its ends, but has a concave curve cut into its aft edge making it 3-1/4" (8.2cm) wide in the middle. At this narrowest point, there are three shallow divots carved at the lower surface: Likely finger-grips for pulling one's self into the kayak.

An unusual combination of joinery techniques is present in the '64:' Behind the cockpit, several of the deck beam-to-gunwale joints are fastened via the oblique-peg method (figure 36c), but ahead of the cockpit, lashings are used instead (as in figure 36a). A dowel is used to join the gunwales at their forward end; the stern end inside is obscured by debris. The longitudinals are double-lashed to the ribs, resulting in the lashing pattern depicted in figure 73, top.

The '64's' coaming measures 5/8" (16mm) thick by 1-1/2" (38mm) high, and is scarfed on the face as in figure 116c. There are two

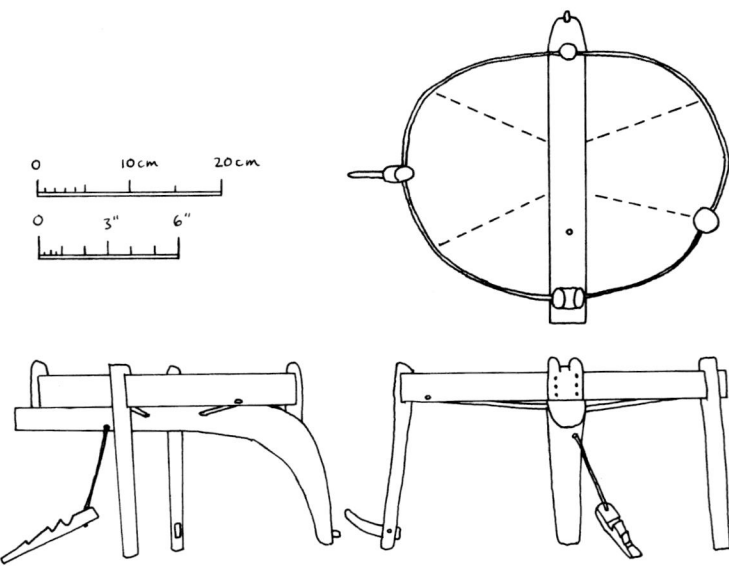

Figure 244: The asaloq, or harpoon line stand displayed with the Hull Maritime Museum's kayak no. 64.

parallel bone strips 9-1/2″ (24.1cm) long covering the scarf at its upper and lower edges; these strips measure 1/4″ (6mm) thick by 3/8″ (9mm) high.

Bow and stern keel edging is present, the stern's rising up very close to the highest reach of the keel. Both end knobs are also present. The '64' has three seam protection pieces, though one is not actually covering a seam, and is situated just aft of the piece that protects the seam at the cockpit.

An *asaloq*, or harpoon-line stand was on the deck of the '64'— It is depicted in scale in figure 244. The *asaloq* is missing the thin splints between the rim and the backbone (a natural crook of wood, actually), but their original positions are indicated with dashed lines. Note the toggle used to secure the stand to the kayak's deck lines. A paddle is on display with the kayak, though it cannot be 100% positively associated with the kayak. see paddle-plate 21.

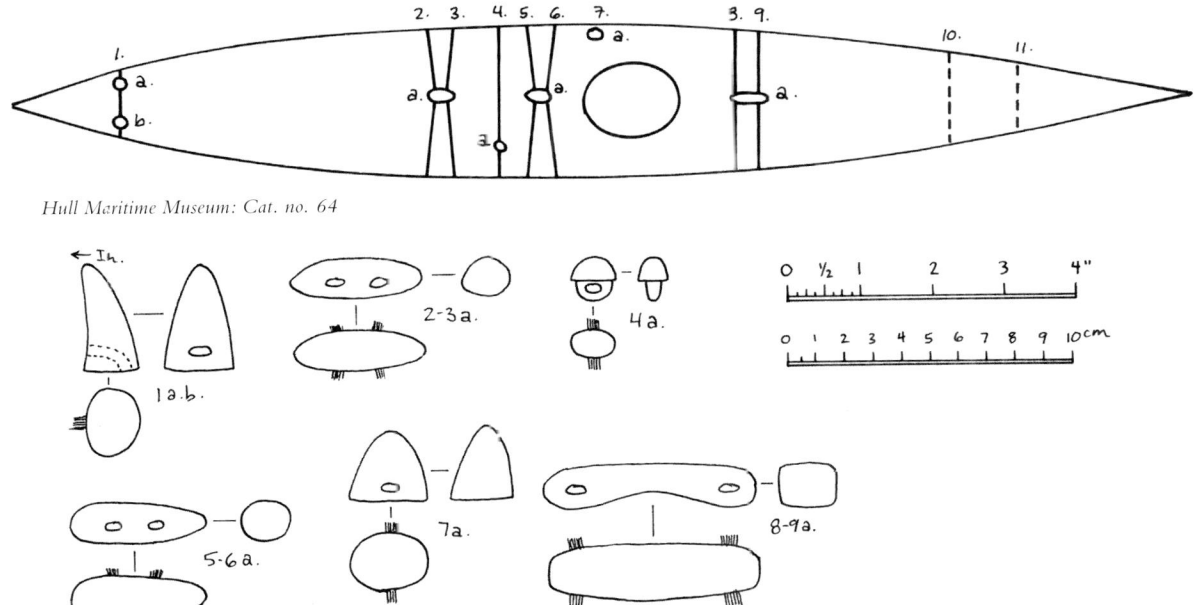

Hull Maritime Museum: Cat. no. 64

All existing deck lines on this kayak have fittings on them. Three link-pieces are present, as is a harpoon holder. This kayak had two deck lines close to the stern— both are missing, but evidenced. One deck line (no. 4) often left without fittings on older kayaks has a small bead with an oblong mushroom top.

30. West Greenland Kayak from ca. 1833: Hull Maritime Museum, Kingston Upon Hull, England. (N/N) 'C'

While no detailed records exist of the Hull Maritime Museum's kayaks, it is the museum's tradition that Sir John Ross collected this kayak (A. Credland, personal communication). No catalog number has been assigned to this kayak, hence its being labeled 'C' in the present work.

Souter's table of kayaks in Great Britain offers the acquisition date of 1833 for two of the Hull Maritime Museum kayaks; these same two kayaks also have the name "Sir John Ross ? Davis St." provided in the table (1934:13). Taking the museum tradition as truth, one can assume that this is the shorter of the two kayaks associated with Ross in Souter's table, as one is over twenty feet in length and clearly from Eastern Canada.

Souter's dimensions for this kayak are 213″ long (17′ 9″) and 19-1/2″ wide (1934:13). The results of my measurements are somewhat different: 205-1/2″ (17′ 1-1/2″; 521.9cm) long, but the width is identical. It had not struck me that some seven inches (17.8cm) were missing off the damaged kayak—perhaps as much as three or four inches (7.6-10.2cm) however.

The 'C' is in an extreme state of damage, resembling little more than a loose floppy bag containing a small amount of sawdust. Figure 245 depicts the kayak's condition in 2002: flattened, fore deck collapsed, the coaming is missing, gunwales splayed outward at their bottom edge, and a stringer protruding through the skin. This kayak is not at all beyond saving via conservation, much as was the case with the "Enkhuizen" kayak and the Weltmuseum's kayak 32848 (plates 7 and 11, respectively).

It is with some regret that I did not survey the 'C', but its condition was such that any rendering would've been over 90% conjectural interpretation and thus of little comparative value. Merely adapting the 'C's' overall dimensions to any other type IV kayak's form would be just as reasonable. A profile of the stern was taken, and it is depicted in scale in plate 30. The stern's actual shape is still questionable as it was wrapped tightly with cloth tape— perhaps to hold loose pieces together. The tip of the stern seems awfully blunt— there is a good chance it had been longer, terminating in a finer point.

Figure 245: The very damaged kayak 'C' At the Hull Maritime Museum.

Only four deck fittings are preserved with the HMM 'C,' and of these, only the harpoon holder is still attached to the kayak. I am assuming the link piece was on deck lines 2 and 3, as the other fore deck lines are intact and the only other possible location would be on lines 8 and 9, which usually would

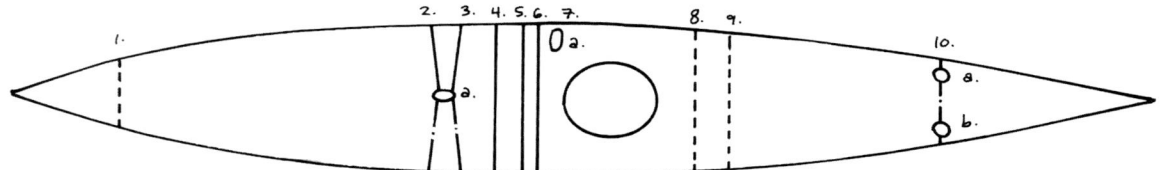

Hull Maritime Museum: (n/n) "C"

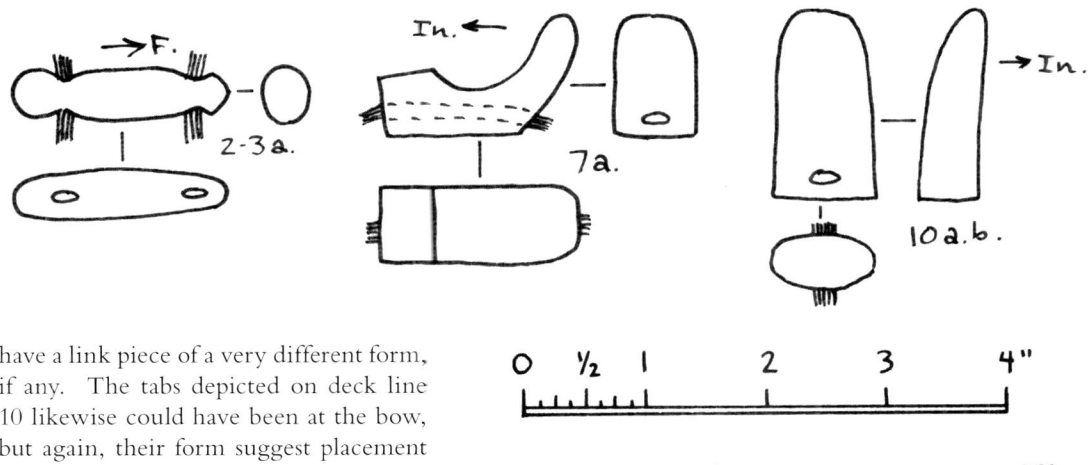

have a link piece of a very different form, if any. The tabs depicted on deck line 10 likewise could have been at the bow, but again, their form suggest placement at the stern when compared to other kayaks from this period, e.g., the U.C.764 (plate 24).

31. West Greenland Kayak of ca. 1834: Danish National Museum, Copenhagen. Catalog no. Lc.43.

This finely formed kayak is fairly well documented for a kayak of its age. It is from Avagait, just north of Paamiut vicinity. It was received by the Danish National Museum in 1834. Earlier kayaks' origins are rarely recorded in detail beyond "Greenland" if even that. The donor's name is given as "Engholm" (Museum Catalog).

This kayak is a very southerly example of the *avasisaartoq* form of kayaks. While the kayak typology of Kaj Birket-Smith should be held as suspect when considering earlier kayak examples (i.e., pre 1900), it is interesting to compare his early 20th century observations to a kayak from 1834. He describes the kayak-type from Julianehaab to Frederikshaab (Qaqortoq to Paamiut vicinities): "Hardly any sheer. Long stems. Almost only light skins. Flat seams. — Introduced by the immigrated Eskimos from Frederik VI's Kyst: Similar type, though with a nearly flat bottom and vertical sides" (1924:271). The Lc.43 is entirely the opposite—even down to the color of

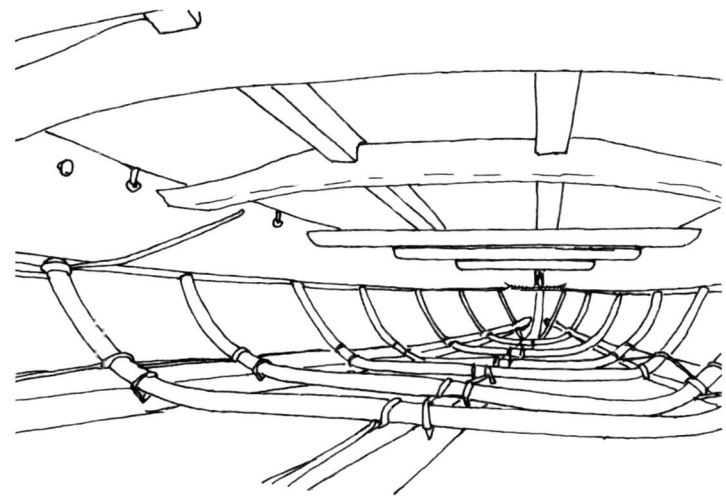

Figure 246. Forward interior of the Danish National Museum's kayak Lc.43.

its *amiq* (dark brown). This suggests a change in Southwest Greenland kayak form occurred between the 1830s and the early 1900s.

It is also valuable to compare and contrast this example with earlier *avasisaartoq* examples, notably the E. 102 and the Hull Maritime Museum '64.' The Lc.43 has much the same lines, though in a much shorter and wider package. Later type IV kayaks maintain these stubbier proportions but are often deeper in the ends and more abrupt in the rake of the stems (notably 60/480, and 977.180—plates 36 and 38).

None of the deck beams in the Lc.43 exhibit any fastening technique; this suggests the exclusive use of the top-peg method as illustrated in figure 37d. The keelson and chines are lashed continuously to the ribs, but the lashing pattern varies randomly such that no attention to following a certain pattern was given by the builder. The upper surfaces of the chines exhibit a slight channeling, as seen in figure 68. This channeling is occasionally seen in kayaks, but is more the exception than the rule. The purpose of channeling may simply aid in getting better chine-to-rib contact at the bend of the ribs.

The Lc.43's *masik* is 3-5/16″ (8.4cm) wide, and the *isserfik* is 5/8″ (16mm) thick and 2-5/16″ (5.9cm) wide at its ends, but 2-3/16″ (5.5cm) wide at the middle, being cut-away as in figure 38. The aft deck stringers measure 5/8″ (16mm) thick by 1-3/16″ (30mm) wide; the fore deck stringers are 13/16″ (21mm) wide. Keel edging at the bow begins at the base of the bow knob, and is 1/4″ (6mm) high, becoming 3/8″ (9mm) high at 1′6″ (45.7cm) from the tip (zero); the edging is 3/8″ (9mm) wide. Edging at the stern starts at 15′2″ (462.2cm) from zero and reaches to 16′10″ (513.0cm).

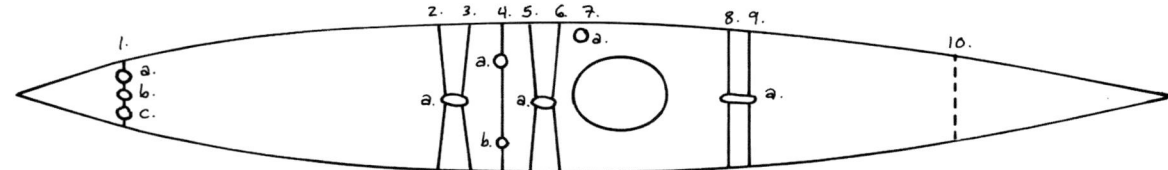

Danish National Museum: Cat. no. Lc.43

Only the stern deck line is missing from the Lc.43. Three deck fittings are present on the bow deck line; this line has a meticulously cut and sewn scarf joint, appearing as in figure 172 top. The fore deck has two pairs of linked deck lines, and the two aft deck lines are also linked. Deck line 4 has two conical fittings, each leaning towards the other. The Lc.43's harpoon holder is saddle-shaped.

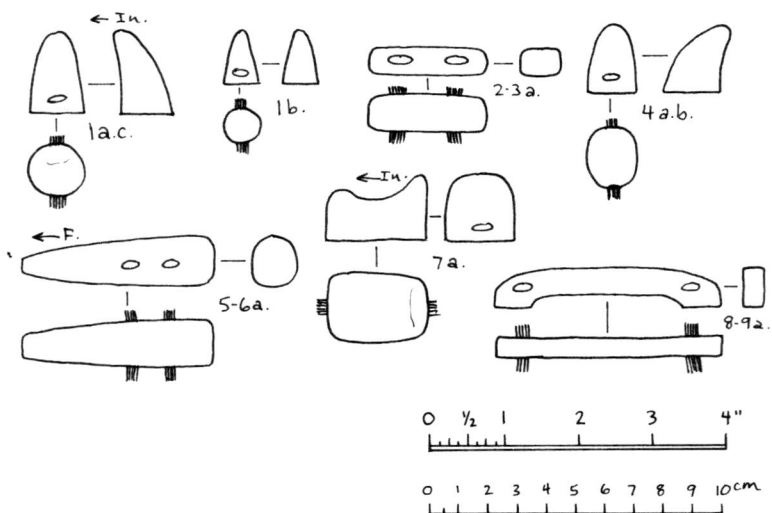

32. West Greenland Kayak: National Museum of Scotland, Edinburgh. Catalog no. 1866.53.

William Clark Souter, in his table of 33 kayaks in Great Britain presents an acquisition date of 1866, reflecting the catalog number of '1866' (1934:13). The National Museum of Scotland's accession files provide no further information. The 1866.53 is in fair condition, though the hull exhibits intermittent collapse; this collapse is depicted in the upper elevations drawing.

The 1866.53 is a very elegant kayak despite its short length. The cockpit is situated well aft of the kayak's mid-point, its center being at 57% of the kayak's length;[35] the type IV average cockpit-center placement is 52.9% (see Appendix A, column 7).

The forward deck stringers are missing from the 1866.53, but their placement and length was inferred from wear and creases in the skin. The aft deck stringers measure 3/8" (9mm) thick by 1-3/8" (35mm) wide. Longitudinals in the 1866.53's lower frame are double-lashed in place with seal skin cord, and are tied off at each junction. Deck beams are intermittently lashed in place, also with seal skin cord. A clamping tie is visible at the aft gunwale ends, but there aren't any clamping ties in the forward half of the hull.

All of the deck lines are missing except for the harpoon rest. Fortunately, the detached deck lines and fittings were saved in a plastic bag stuffed inside the kayak. Their precise placement cannot be known for certain, but the rigging must have looked much like that of the Hunterian's E.584 (plate 28), although

Figure 247: Photograph of a hunter about to set out in his kayak, 1869. Note the classic type IV kayak form. (Photographer: William Bradford/ Library and Archives Canada/ C-082024.)

---

[35] This figure is exceeded by only one other kayak in this study: A Polar Greenland kayak from the early 20th century (plate 98), whose cockpit center is at 57.5% of overall length.

no remains of the bow and stern deck lines were found. With regards to the aft deck lines, the 1866.53 had two such lines just over a foot apart, the furthest aft being 1′ 7″ (48.3cm) ahead of the stern. A similar arrangement is present on the stern of the HMM 64 (plate 29). A bow end knob is present, but there is no evidence of a stern knob having been placed.

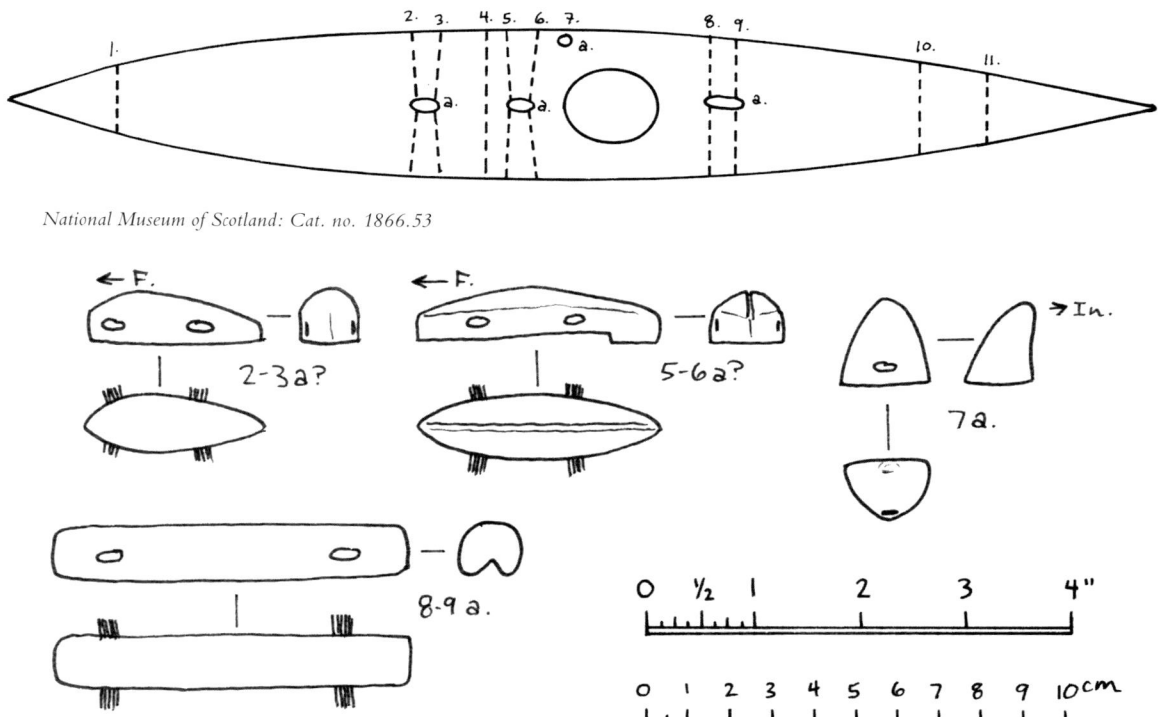

National Museum of Scotland: Cat. no. 1866.53

33. West Greenland Kayak: National Museum of Natural History, Smithsonian, Washington, D.C. Catalog no. 35667.

Inked in cursive directly on the kayak's *amiq* are the words "Holsteenburg, Greenland, N.P. Scudder," and a tag affixed to the kayak gives the date of 1878, and names Scudder as the collector. This is one of several kayaks in this study known to originate from "Holsteenburg," presently known as Sisimiut. While not at all old by European museum standards, this kayak may be one of the oldest kayaks presently in North American museum collections.

The 35667 somewhat resembles the National Museum of Scotland's kayak 1866.53 (plate 32), but is subtler in the rise of its ends. Also, the 35667 has a much straighter sheer and keel line as well as much less side flare. Structurally, the 35667 is fully intact and exhibits no sign of deformation or hull-collapse.

It is interesting to compare the 35667 to other kayaks listed as having come from Sisimiut only some 40-50 years later: The Canadian Museum of Civilization's kayak IV-A-483 from circa 1935 (plate 46), and the Michigan State University's cw4274 from the 1920s (plate 45). Essentially, the 35667 could hardly be more different than these others: The 35667 is very straight—rigidly so, and the others are very long ended and curvy. This fact brings attention to the likelihood of different forms coexisting or the sudden change in kayak-form in Sisimiut vicinity. The Lübeck kayak from circa 1606 (plate 1) also comes from Sisimiut vicinity, and it is significantly different from the 19th and 20th century Sisimiut vicinity kayaks.

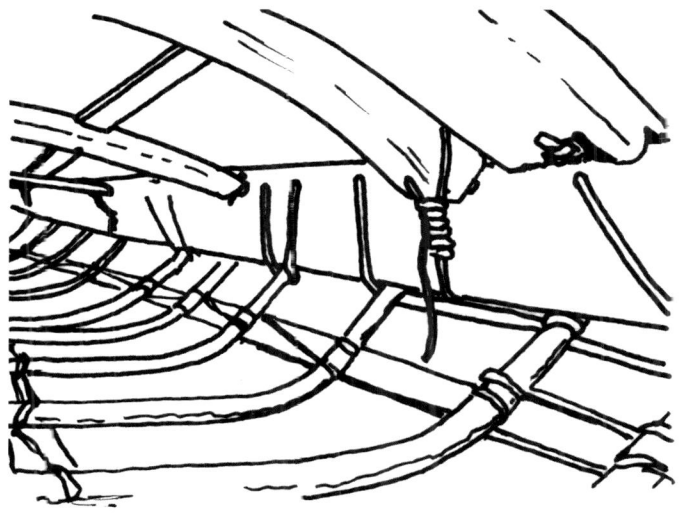

Figure 248: Forward interior view of the National Museum of Natural History's kayak 35667. The cord knotted at the masik joint and exiting the gunwale just below the joint is the deck line holding the harpoon holder in place.

The bottom structure of the 35667 is all lashed, using seal skin line in the double-pass method. Its lashing pattern is very random, varying from that of figure 73a to figure 73b, among others. The *masik* is attached to the gunwales with a birds-mouth joint as in figure 76a, and is probably top-pegged in place; the *masik* is 2-3/4" (70mm) wide. Figure 248 shows these features and the general appearance of the forward interior of the 35567.

The second curved deck beam forward of the *masik* exhibits an interesting modification: The piece was not wide enough for its position (having likely been re-used), and the builder fixed this by setting a wooden pin through each tenon's base effectively lengthening the deck beam. Figure 162 depicts this adjustment as clearly as I could infer it had been done. The 35667's *isserfik* is 5/8" (16mm) thick and 1-1/2" (38mm) wide.

At only 1" (25mm) high, this kayak has a very short coaming. A repair strip of bone is pegged to the coaming's left forward quarter; this strip measures 5-3/8" (13.6cm) long, 1/8" (3mm) thick and 1/2" (13mm) wide. Two scarf protection pieces are on the coaming's back face: The upper piece is 9-1/2"(24.1cm) long and the lower is 10-1/4" (26.0cm) long. The coaming's scarf joint is made as in figure 116d.

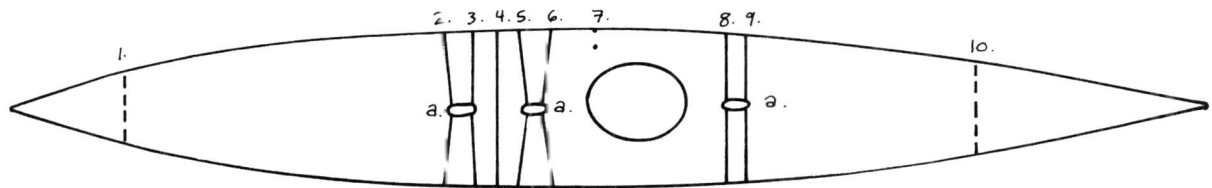

U.S. National Museum of Natural History: Cat. no 35667

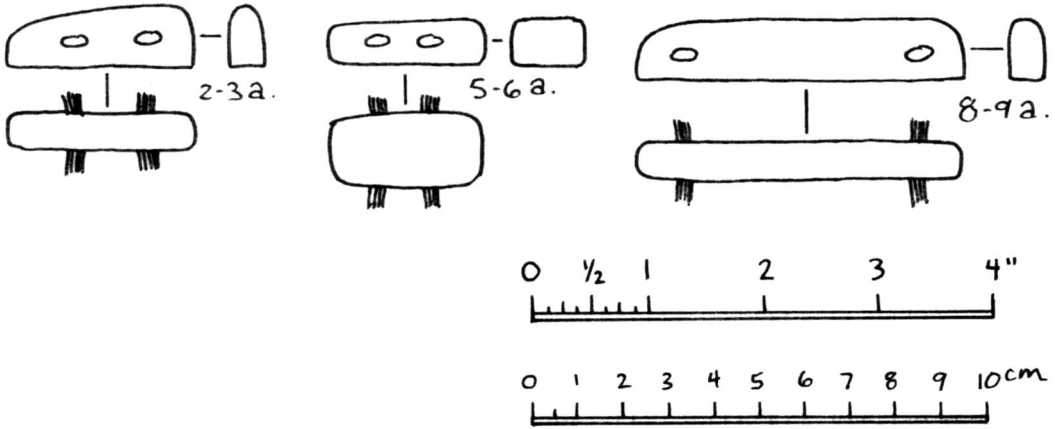

Most of this kayak's edge protection is missing; just a short segment 3/8″ (9mm) wide and 5/16″ (8mm) high remains astern. Evidence of placement exists, and these vicinities are shown as dashed lines in the scale drawing's elevation view. A side-pegged bow knob is present, and a stern knob is evidenced but missing. The bow knob is 1-3/16″ (30mm) long and 13/16″ (21mm) diameter.

34. West Greenland Kayak from ca. 1882:
   National Museum of Natural History, Smithsonian, Washington, D.C.
   Catalog no. 72564.

Major William M. Beebe Jr. collected this kayak in or before 1882, and the NMNH catalog card indicates the "Chief Signal Officer, War Dept" had deposited it at the museum. (I've not been able to determine if the Major and Chief Signal Officer are the same man.) A provenance of "Disko Bay, W. Coast of Greenland" is also listed on the card.

The 72564 is in astonishingly superb condition, and does not seem to show any age, save for a small crack in the skin here or there. The *amiq* is a bright creamy yellow, such as chamois. This kayak's form is equally astonishing: Its extreme sheer and deep ends are marvels of carpentry and design.

An inside forward view of the 72564 is depicted in figure 250. Note the half-rib in the vicinity of where the kayaker's

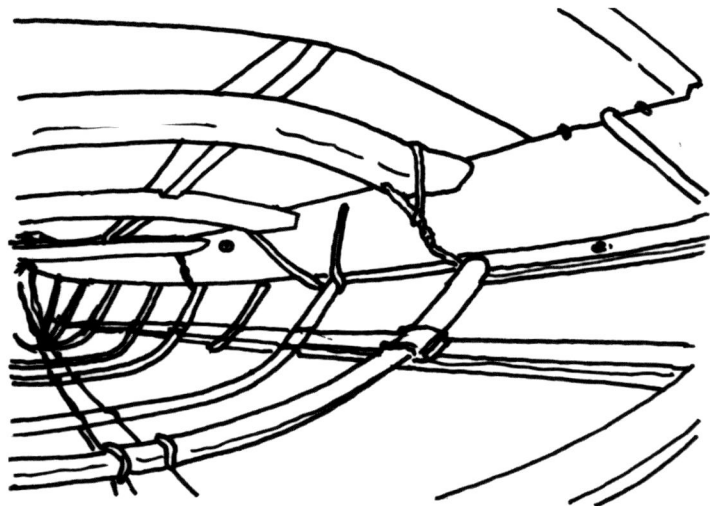

Figure 250: Forward interior view of the National Museum of Natural History's kayak 72564.

Figure 249: A boy from the Geisler family at Aaruaruutissat on S.E. Disko Island, 1906. (Photographer: Arnold Heim/ Arktisk Institut 25716.)

feet would be. The *masik* sits atop the gunwale, as in figure 76a. Also note the continuous deck lines, particularly the line going through the *masik* to attach the harpoon holder.

Both seal skin line and twine are used as lashings in this kayak, the bottom joinery having a mix of the two, while the deck beams and the clamping ties are lashed with twine. The chine and keelson lashings are continuous, and their pattern is that seen in figure 73 top. Only one of the 72564's ribs are pegged to the gunwales: The rib at the cockpit back.

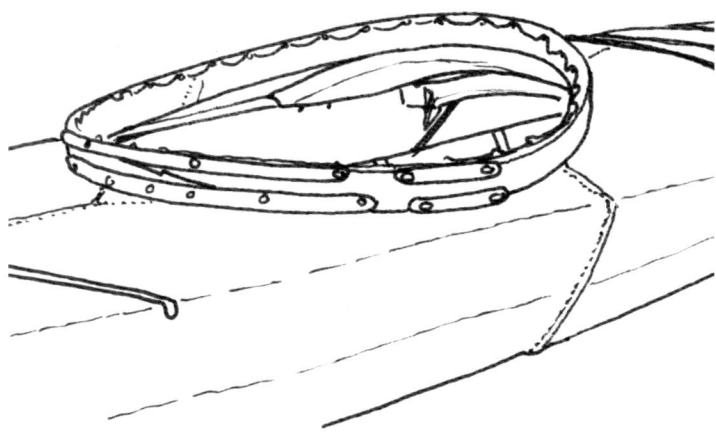

Figure 251: Cockpit view of the 72564.

The *isserfik* has been carved back 13/16" (21mm) at the midpoint so as to make the cockpit slightly roomier; at its widest it measures 2" (51mm), and is 1" (25mm) thick. The *masik* projects beyond the sheer by 3/8" (9mm) on each side, and is 3-3/4" wide (9.5cm). It is fastened to the gunwales with two top-pegs per-side.

The 72564's coaming is scarfed via the method depicted in figure 116i. Keel edging is present both fore and aft, being 3/16" (5mm) wide and 5/16" (8mm) high. Three seam protection pieces are also present, these being 5/8" (16mm) wide and 3/16" (5mm) high. Both end knobs are present and each is top-pegged into place.

Photographs of the 72564 have been published in *The Bark Canoes and Skinboats of North America* (Adney and Chapelle, 1964:208,209). The top-view photograph on the bottom of page 208 clearly shows two deck fittings on the bow deck line. When I surveyed the kayak in 2003, this deck line and its two fittings were missing. They were most likely conical, and about the size of the kayak's harpoon holder. The stern deck line was missing in 2003, and it doesn't seem to appear in the above-mentioned photographs either.

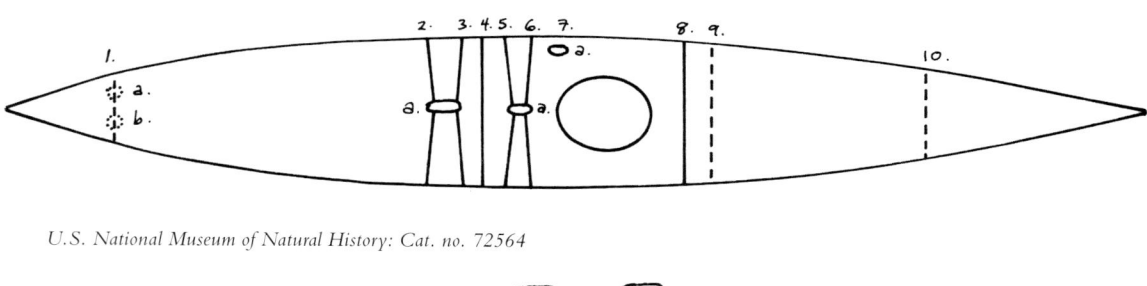

U.S. National Museum of Natural History: Cat. no. 72564

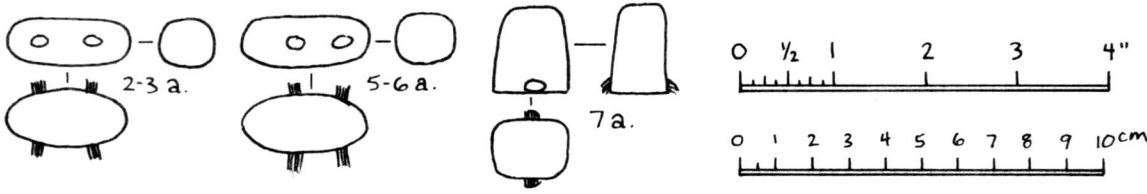

35. West Greenland Kayak from 1889: Greenland National Museum, Nuuk. Catalog no. KNK 1849.

H. C. Hørring collected this boy's kayak in 1889; this is the only provenance information present in the Greenland National Museum's catalogs. The kayak is in exceptional condition and is extremely well made. The museum data card describes it as being made for a six or seven year old. Two general views of the KNK 1849 are presented in figures 252 and 253.

Some of the scantlings not given on the scale drawing are as follows: The coaming measures 7/16" (11mm) thick by 7/8" (22mm) high; the *masik* is 2" (51mm). The aft deck stringers measure 1/4" (6mm) thick by 7/8" (22mm) wide; the spray skirt impeded an accurate measuring of the forward deck stringers, but I estimate them as being about 1/2" (13mm) square.

A spray skirt (*akuilisaq* or *tuitseq*) is fastened to the KNK 1849's coaming. It is dried and rigid, but it holds the shape as if being worn by the kayaker. When I saw it in 2000, it was missing its suspender straps; a color photograph by Werner Forman in Ernest Burch, jr.'s *The Eskimos* (1988:84-85) shows this kayak with the straps still intact.

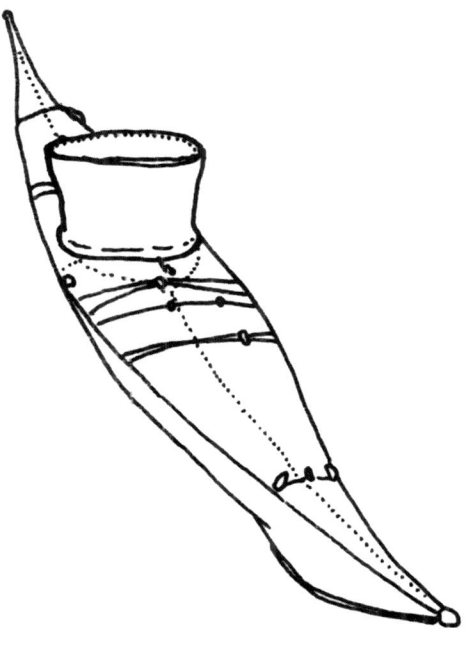

Figure 252: View of the GNM's KNK 1849. The 'tube' extending up from the coaming is a spray skirt.

Every deck line on the KNK 1849 is intact. Three pieces are present on the bow deck line. The outer two are cones, leaning inward, and the middle piece (1b), is of an unusual shape—perhaps representative of a person. A pair of conical upright pieces, such as are those on the bow-most deck line, are placed on deck line 4, leaning towards each other. The aft-most deck line is very slack and has no fittings.

Figure 253: Aft view of the KNK 1849.

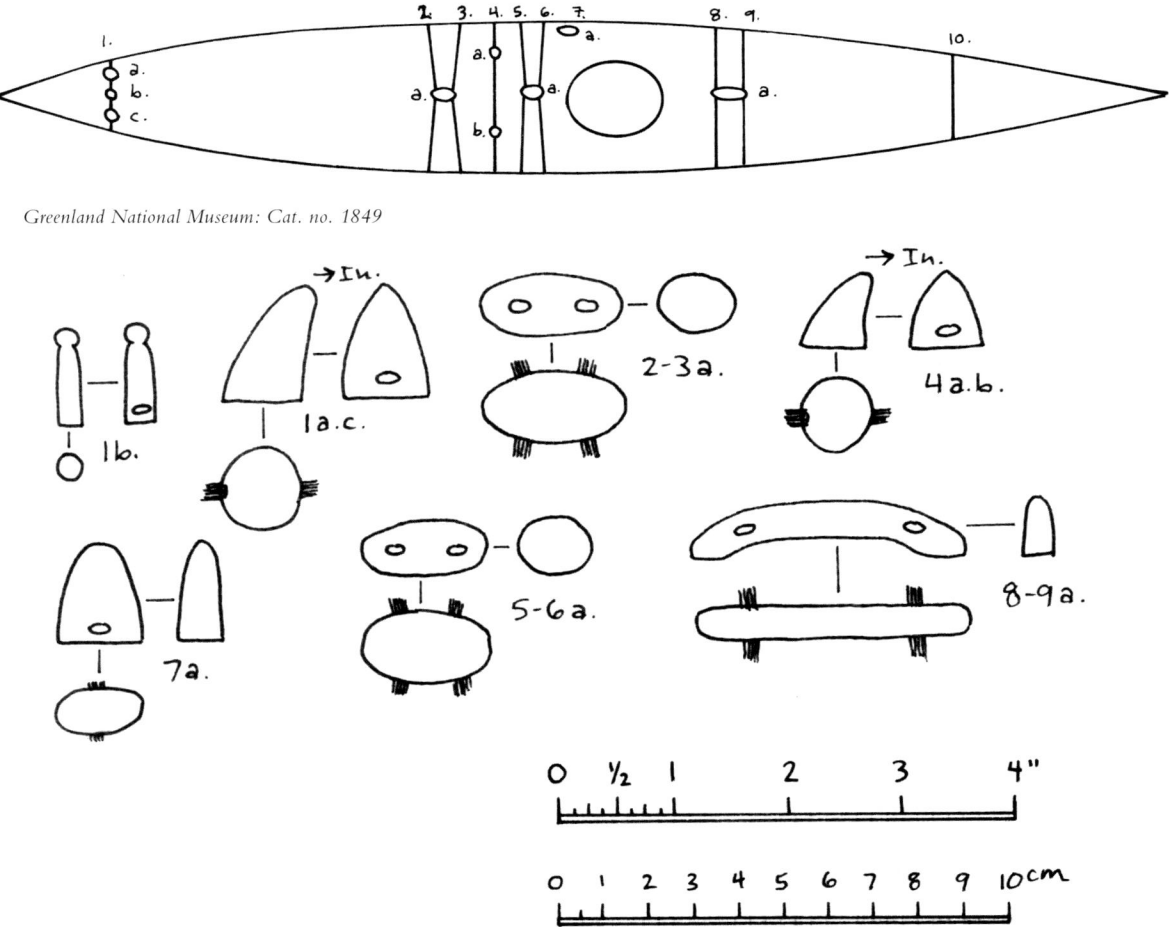

Greenland National Museum: Cat. no. 1849

36. West Greenland Kayak from ca. 1895:
   American Museum of Natural History, New York, New York.
   Catalog no. 60/480.

The American Museum of Natural History's kayak 60/480 is catalogued as being from "South Greenland." Lt. Robert E. Peary collected it in or before 1895; the kayak was accessioned by the AMNH in 1895. The 480's attribution of South Greenland may be a reflection of Peary's possible Polar-centric view of Greenland; i.e., anything south of Melville Bay being 'southern.' The likelihood of such an *avasisaartoq* persisting to the late years of the 19th century in what is generally accepted to be "South Greenland" (Paamiut to Kap Farvel) is slim. This kayak could be presumed to be from well north of Sisimiut if not north of Disko Bay during this period.

The AMNH 60/480 is a very elegant example of the *avasisaartoq* form. It is a fairly late example being from the 1890s, though a similar kayak from the mid-teens (20th century) exists at the Sisimiuni Katersugaasivik in Sisimiut (Blæsild, 1988:33; V. Doucette, personal communication). The 60/480

Figure 254: A seal hunter in a particularly fine example of a type IV avasisartoq, West Greenland, 1869. (Photographer: William Bradford/Library and Archives Canada/C-081978.)

compares nicely to the NMNH's kayak 72564 (plate 34). Both have very similar stem rakes and heights, and are roughly the same size, although the 480 is an inch shallower.

Some structural damage is present in the 480: The *isserfik* is missing, though the aft deck stringers are still in place, dangling free at their forward ends (the spread at their forward end in the scale drawing is conjectural). A slight hull collapse is present from about 5' to 13'6" (152.4 to 411.5cm). This was restored in the drawing, but the artifactual depths-to-sheer are 6-1/4" (15.9cm) at 6', 5-3/16" (13.2cm) at 8', 4-13/16" (12.2cm) at 10', and 4-5/8" (11.7cm) at 12'. My conjectural restoration may still fall short of the 60/480's original depths: as much as 1" (2.5cm) could be added to the depth-to-sheer at the cockpit.

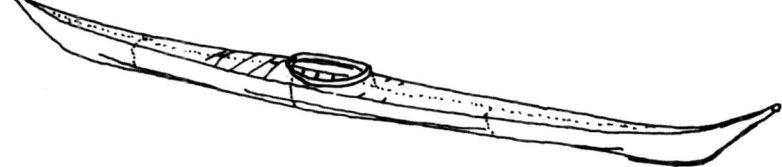

Figure 255: The American Museum of Natural History's kayak 60/480.

The 60/480's chines and the keelson are all lashed to the ribs, and in the cockpit they are also pegged. The ribs did not appear to be pegged into their mortises. The deck beams are intermittently lashed to the gunwales, and the *masik* is fastened to the gunwales via the method in figure 76c. The deck lines are not threaded continuously through the hull; instead, each end is knotted or hitched off on adjacent ribs.

The cockpit coaming is distinctly egg-shaped, and not likely made from a mast-hoop. It is fashioned from oak, and is joined by a stepped scarf with birds-mouth joints. Two parallel bone strips are present on the coaming's backside: These are both 9-3/4" (24.7cm) long and 3/16 (5mm) thick by 3/8" (9mm) wide.

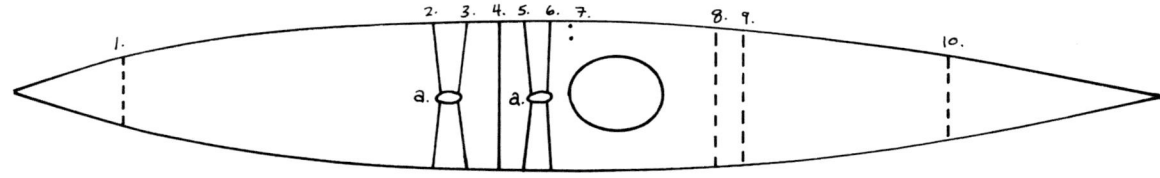

American Museum of Natural History, New York: Cat. no. 60/480

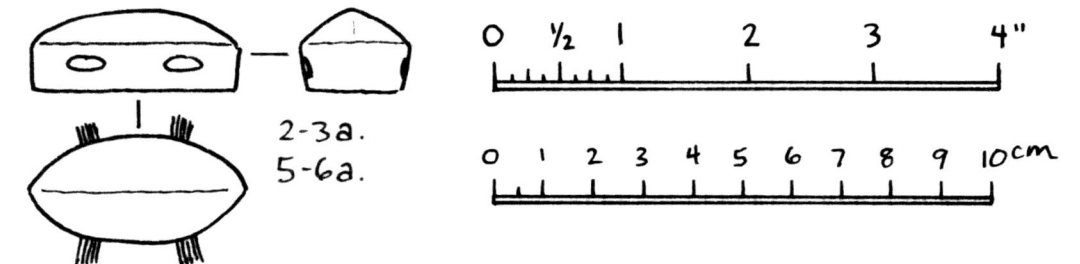

A stern knob is present on the 480 and is side-pegged in place. The bow knob is missing, but is evidenced as having been fastened by a top-peg. Bow and stern edging are both present, but unlike on the NMNH 72564, the edging on the 480 does not extend to the tips. The edging is 3/8″ (9mm) square.

Only two deck fittings remain on the 60/480's deck lines: two identical link pieces on the fore deck. The only deck lines present are the five on the fore deck. The harpoon holder's placement is evidenced on the right side of the *masik*.

37. West Greenland kayak from ca. 1908: McManus Galleries, Dundee, Scotland. Catalog no. 1968-81-1.

The 1968-81's accession card offers only meager information as to the kayak's history: "Brought back from Arctic by Dundee Whaler." A brief paragraph in the McManus Galleries' catalog is more specific: "A kayak was donated in 1908 by Captain Thomas Robertson of the S. S. *Scotia*. It was said to come from the 'Great Northern River.'" Historian Basil Lubbock describes the *Scotia* as having been active in the Greenland fisheries in the summers of 1905 through 1908 (1978:447-49). On which voyage the kayak was collected is not known. The location or meaning of the 'Great Northern River' leaves me at a loss— it could refer to a specific locale or fjord in Greenland or perhaps may just be 'whaler-lingo' for Davis Straits.

Birket-Smith's kayak typology could be held in a high degree of accuracy for a kayak of this period. His typology would suggest this kayak might be from Uummannaq Fjord: "Sheer; in out-of-the-way places still of the shape of a tall, sharply built stem with a deck inclining strongly backwards. Long stem, shorter stern which until a short time ago was curved upwards" (1924:271). The 1968-81 distinctly exhibits the 'curved-up' stern, and in fact fits Birket-Smith's description quite well, save for the bow not being remarkably long. 1908 would likely fit into Birket-Smith's notion of "...a short time ago."

The 1968-81 is in excellent condition: It has no hull-collapse or any distortion. The bow is distinctly curved upwards, and the keelson is significantly rockered from 6′ (182.9cm) forward. The stern is turned upwards as well, though the keel runs fairly straight up to the curve of the stem.

Several of the deck beams of the 1968-81 are pegged in place, using the oblique-method. Clamping ties are found at the fore and aft ends. The forward deck stringers are square in cross-section, while the aft stringers are broad and thin, very typical of west Greenland kayaks. The 1968-81 is one of several kayaks in this study to have shims used to effectively lengthen deck beams, a method depicted in figure 162. Three of these shims can be seen in figure 256: two on the first straight deck beam, and one on the right side of the curved deck beam.

An aft view into the hull of the kayak 1968-81 is presented in figure 257. Note the difference in hull-shape between this view and the view forward (figure 256). Stepped scarfs are present in both gunwales, behind the second deck beam aft of the cockpit; more deck beam shims can also be seen.

The 1968-81's coaming measures 1/2" (13mm) thick by 1-1/4" (32mm) high, and has two parallel bone strips attached to its aft face. The upper strip

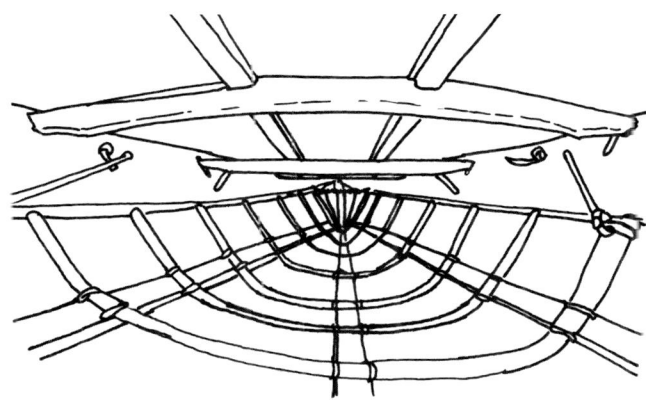

Figure 256: Forward interior view of the McManus Galleries' kayak 1968-81.

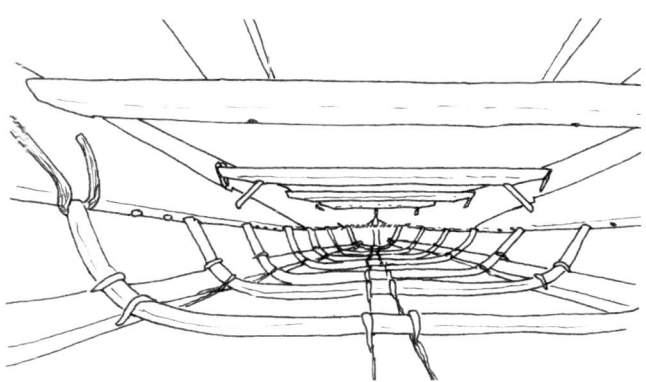

Figure 257: Looking aft in to the hull of the 1968-81. Note the scarf joints in the gunwales.

is 10" (25.4cm) long, and the lower is 8-1/2" (21.6cm) long; both are 1/4" (6mm) thick and 1/2" (13mm) wide. Ice protection along the keelson is present at the bow as well as the stern—in both cases extending all the way up to the end-knobs. The harpoon holder is missing but is evidenced on the front right quarter of the cockpit. A paddle (MMG 1968-81-3) is associated with the kayak, and is depicted in paddle-plate 24.

A stern deck line is not present on this kayak, nor evidenced on the outside. A view inside the hull did reveal the knotted ends of a deck line towards the stern, so in at least one previous incarnation of this

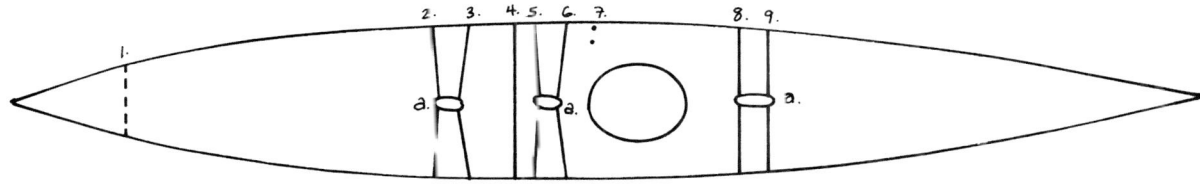

McManus Galleries, Dundee: Cat. no. 1968-81

kayak's skeleton, it had been rigged with a stern deck line. A link piece on the fore deck has a broken end, and it has been repaired with a cord of sinew threaded through the piece and around deck line 2.

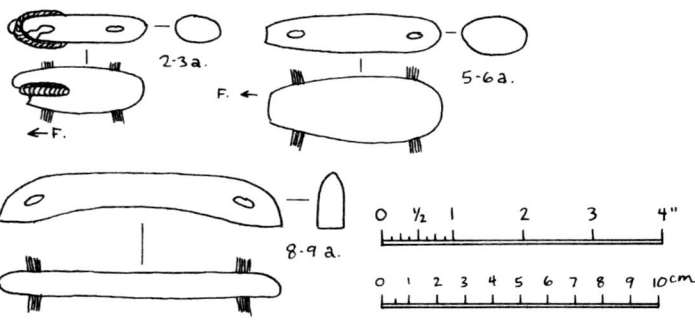

38. West Greenland Kayak: Canadian Canoe Museum, Peterborough, Ontario. Catalog no. 977.180

This is the first of several kayaks in this study that were transferred in 1976 from the (U.S.) Museum of the American Indian to the Kanawa International Museum in Ontario, Canada. "Through the noted anthropologist, Dr. Edmund Carpenter, it became known that the Museum of the North American Indian in New York City was having difficulty housing and maintaining the Heye Foundation's collection of rare canoes and kayaks." The canoe and kayak collection—numbering forty-four boats—was sold to the Kanawa International Museum at Camp Kandalore, Ontario, for $150,000 U.S. (Hoyle, 2002:246). The Kanawa Museum relocated to Peterborough, Ontario, and changed its name to the Canadian Canoe Museum. (The Museum of the American Indian is now the *National* Museum of the American Indian, Smithsonian, and has since moved to Washington, D.C.)

The Museum of the American Indian's records list this kayak as having been collected by publishing heir George Palmer Putnam, and gives an accession date of 1927 (Its MAI catalog number was 15/6264). Putnam went to Cape York Greenland in 1926 aboard the *Morrisey* to assist in the gathering of bird and animal specimens for the American Museum of Natural History.

Perplexingly, this kayak's provenance is listed as being from "Cape York"— in both CCM and MAI records. While Putnam may have collected this kayak during his trip to Cape York, the likelihood of the kayak being from there is nil. Other stops in Greenland during the *Morrisey's* 1926 voyage included Sisimiut, Qeqertarsuaq (Godhavn), and Kangersuatsiaq (Prøven), and Upernavik (Putnam, 1926).

This kayak is a good example of what the *avasisaartoq* form has evolved into: The sharply rising stern has been lowered considerably, although there is still substantial sheer, and the bow is in fact still rather elevated. Both ends are very raked, and the transition from keel-to-stem is very abrupt or angular. The 977.180 still remains distinct from type V kayaks (to which its sheer line otherwise resembles) in that its ends are quite short—the stern being distinctly shorter than the bow.

A distinct gap between ribs is present in the 977.180's cockpit. A missing rib was checked for, but no empty mor-

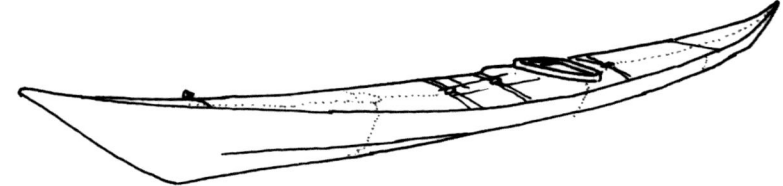

Figure 258: The Canadian Canoe Museum's kayak 977.180.

tises were present. H. C. Petersen writes that "In Maniitsoq—Kangaamiut there are no ribs under the cockpit, but the ribs under the kayaker's legs are closer together" citing comfort and ease of entry as reasons (1986:25). I doubt the kayak is from this vicinity, based mainly on comparisons to two Kangaamiut kayaks in this study (1Bs.16 and 1Bs.8, plates 43 and 44). Of the places visited by the *Morrissey* in 1926, I think Qeqertarsuaq is the likeliest point of the 977.180's origin.

Oblique pegs are used intermittently to fasten deck beams to the gunwales aft of the cockpit, and lashings are used for the same purpose intermittently ahead of the cockpit; this makes for a rare combination of joinery methods.

The 977.180's *masik* measures 3″ (76mm) wide, and the *isserfik* is 3/4″ (13mm) thick by 1-1/4″(32mm) wide, but is partnered up against another beam measuring 2″ (51mm) wide. The fore deck stringers are 15/16″ (24mm) wide, and the aft deck stringers are 2″ (51mm) wide.

The keelson and chines are continuously lashed to the ribs, however they do not continue across the rib-gap in the cockpit. While the chine height is given as 1-1/2″ (38mm) in the scantlings of the scale drawing, the chines are actually built-up from two pieces of wood to that height: The lower/outer piece is 1″ (25mm) high. The pieces are fastened with metal nails spaced approximately every 7″ (17.8cm).

The 977.180's coaming is 5/8″ (16mm) thick and 1-3/8″ (35mm) high. Two 11″ (27.9cm) long bone strips are fastened to the back face of the coaming— one at the upper edge, and the other at the lower edge. Each strip measures 1/4″ (6mm) thick by 5/16″ (8mm) wide. End knobs were evidenced at both the bow and stern, but neither knob was in place. One knob was found inside the kayak: It measured 1-5/8″ (41mm) long by 1″ (25mm) diameter.

All deck lines are present on this kayak, except for one: the line between the linked pairs of deck lines on the fore deck. While the foremost deck line has two fittings on it, one is atypical and out of place: It is a suspender hook as seen on spray skirts (*tuitsoq*, sing.) or paddling jackets (*tuiliq*, sing.). The other piece is of a form expected to be here— a cone shaped piece leaning inboard.

A long harpoon holder strap is present on the CCM's 977.180, adjacent the cockpit coaming on the right, but the holder itself is not present. The aft-most deck line on this kayak is nailed to the gunwale's sides, about 3/4″ (19mm) below the sheer. The keel edging at the stern of the 977.180 has transverse holes drilled through it. These were likely used to fasten a skeg to the kayak.

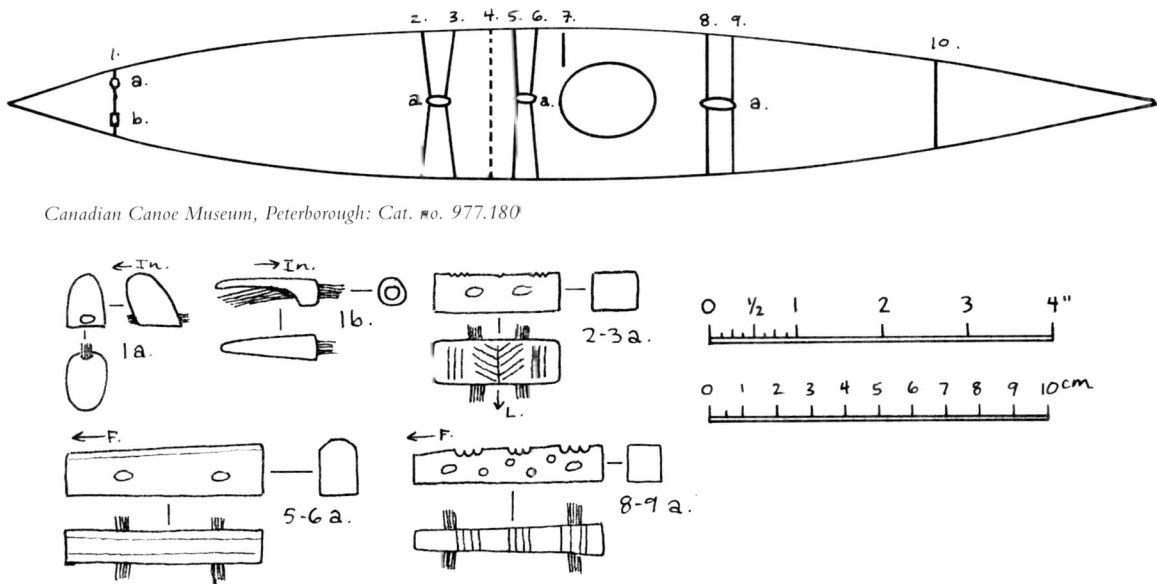

Canadian Canoe Museum, Peterborough: Cat. no. 977.180

TYPE V.

Type V kayaks seem to be an out-growth of Type IV kayaks— resulting from changing fashions, influenced no doubt by the advent of the rifle for kayak-hunting, as discussed at length in this study's analysis. The emergence of this type (among collected museum examples) seems to correspond with the later years of type IV kayaks. That the type IV kayak 977.180 described above could just as easily be considered a type V emphasizes this point. Constructionally, type IV and V kayaks are quite similar.

The defining characteristics of type V kayaks are moderate-to-low sheer, stems of moderate lengths, and bottoms with slight to considerable deadrise. The sheer at the ends does not abruptly angle upwards, the curve being rather constant. The bow and stern profiles are usually straight or slightly concave. The maximum breadth of type V kayaks is almost always just ahead of the cockpit. A number of type V kayaks have integral skegs, as in figure 132c.

Type V is the first kayak type in this study to largely hail from a known vicinity, albeit a large one: Southwest Greenland— roughly from Paamiut to Sisimiut—most being from Nuuk. This is known on account of better museum documentation for most of these kayaks. The type V kayaks in this study span from circa 1888 to the 1990s. Being that H.C. Petersen's *Instructions in Kayak Building* (1981)— published in English, Danish, and Greenlandic— is based on a typical type V kayak, the form's continuity has likely been assured for many years to come; such kayaks continue to be built and used in Southwest Greenland today.

Two examples of type V kayaks could be considered to represent a sub-type of the form, having a strong sheer and very sinuous keel line. Between the stems, the keel is very concave for the first half, and then markedly convex for the second half, terminating with an integral skeg—a very unique combination. Furthermore, one of them (CMC IV-A-483, plate 46) has a total of four chines; the other example (MSU 4274cw, plate 45) essentially has a similar configuration only the 'extra' chines are nailed to the lower sides of the gunwales.

The selection of kayaks in this type is a fortunate one. For example, the first four kayaks are all from Nuuk, 1888, thus giving a unique glimpse of variation of form and rigging within a sampling from the same time and place. Also, two especially fine examples from Kangaamiut, 1900 are represented— one in *amiq*, and the other a frame.

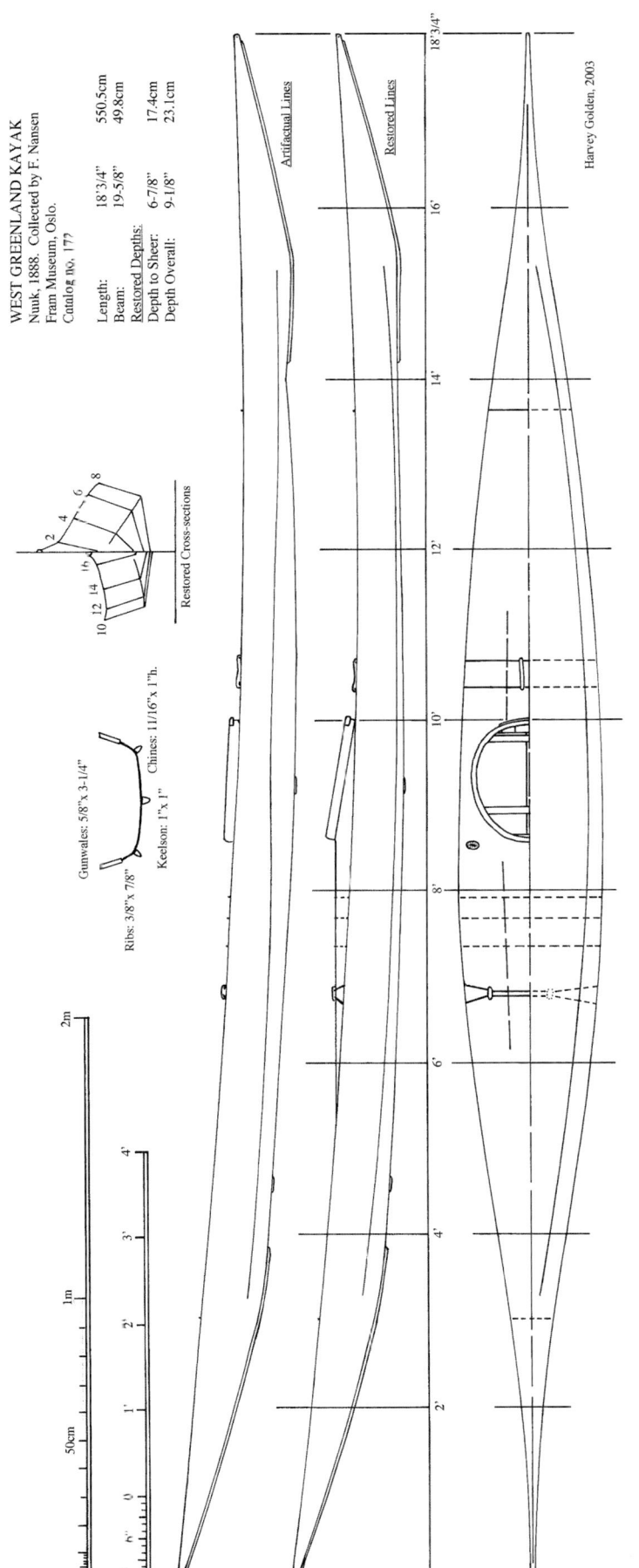

39. Fram Museum catalog no. 172

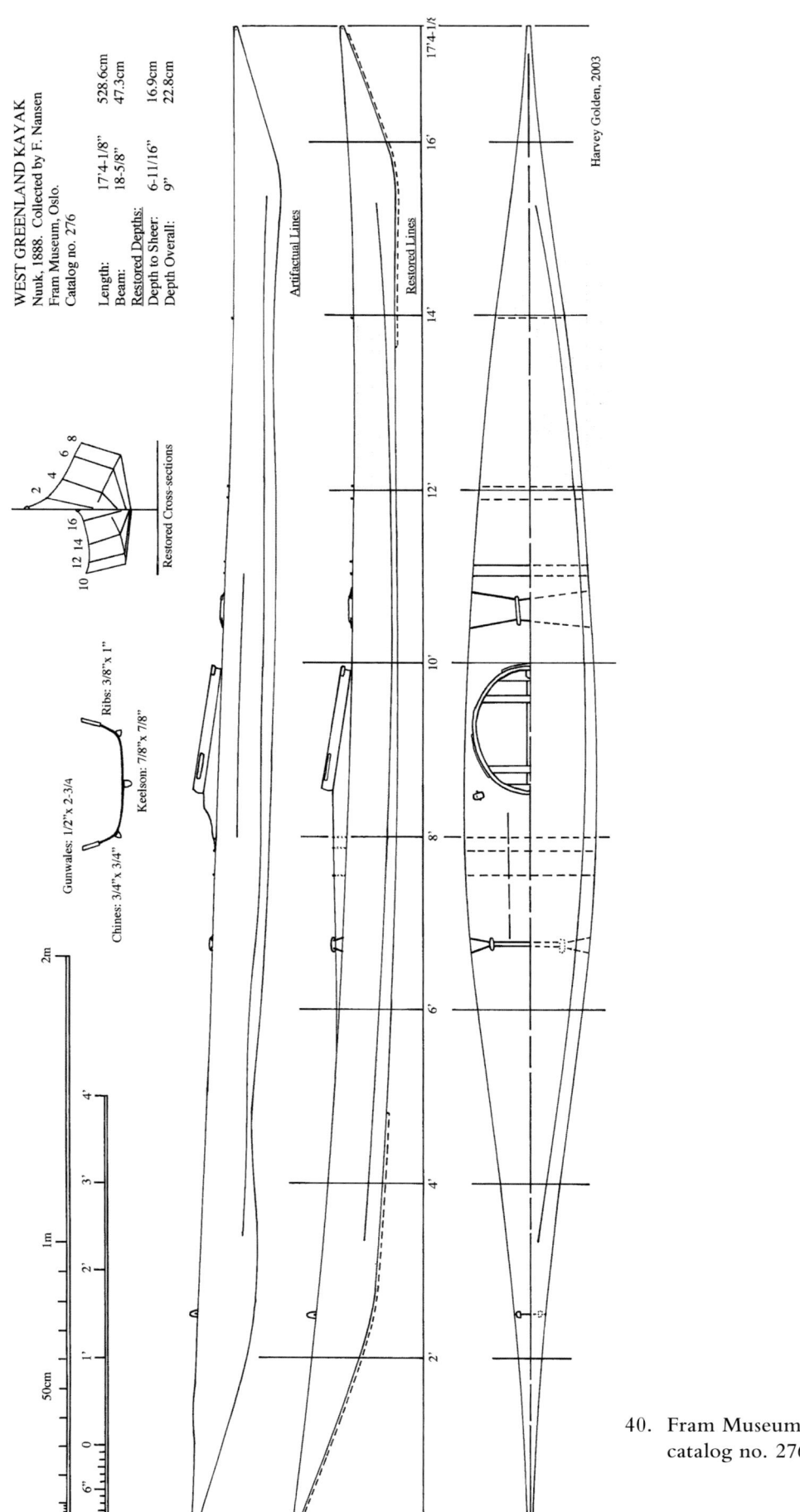

40. Fram Museum catalog no. 276

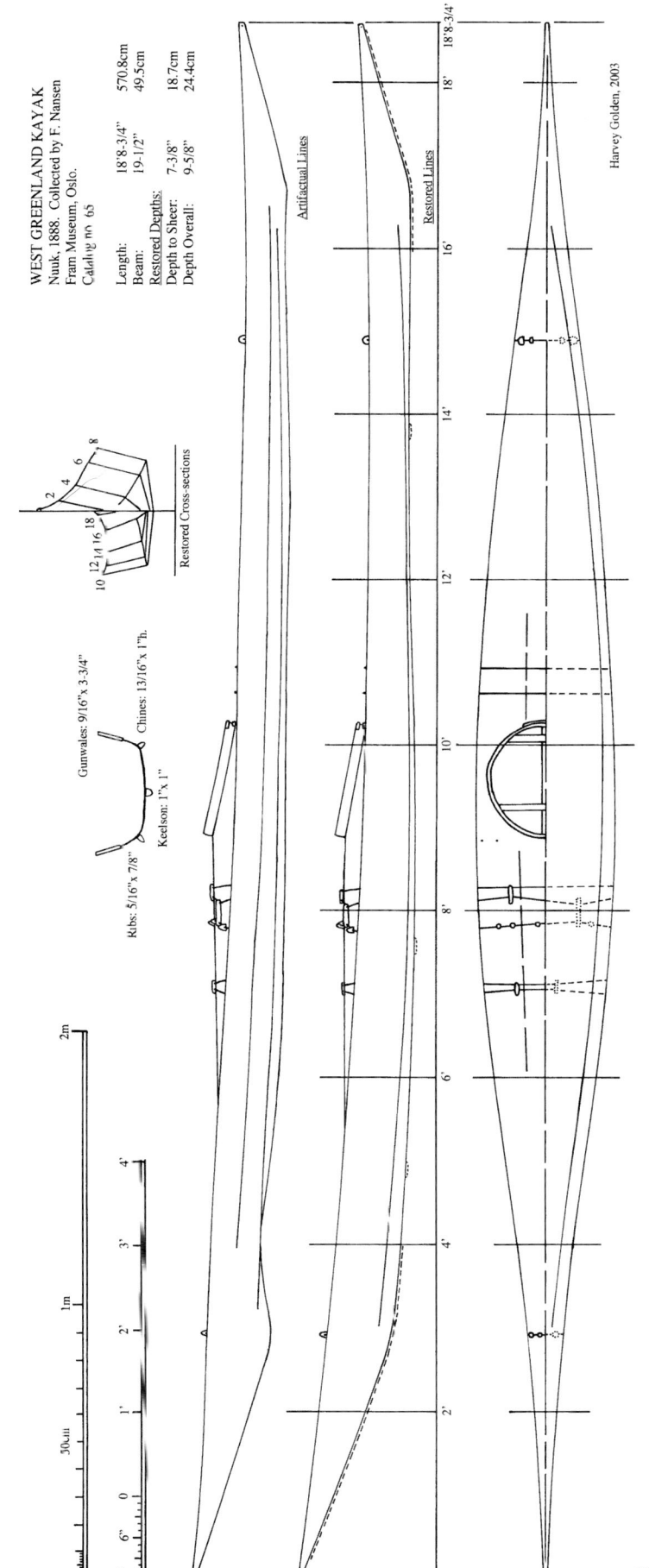

41. Fram Museum catalog no. 65

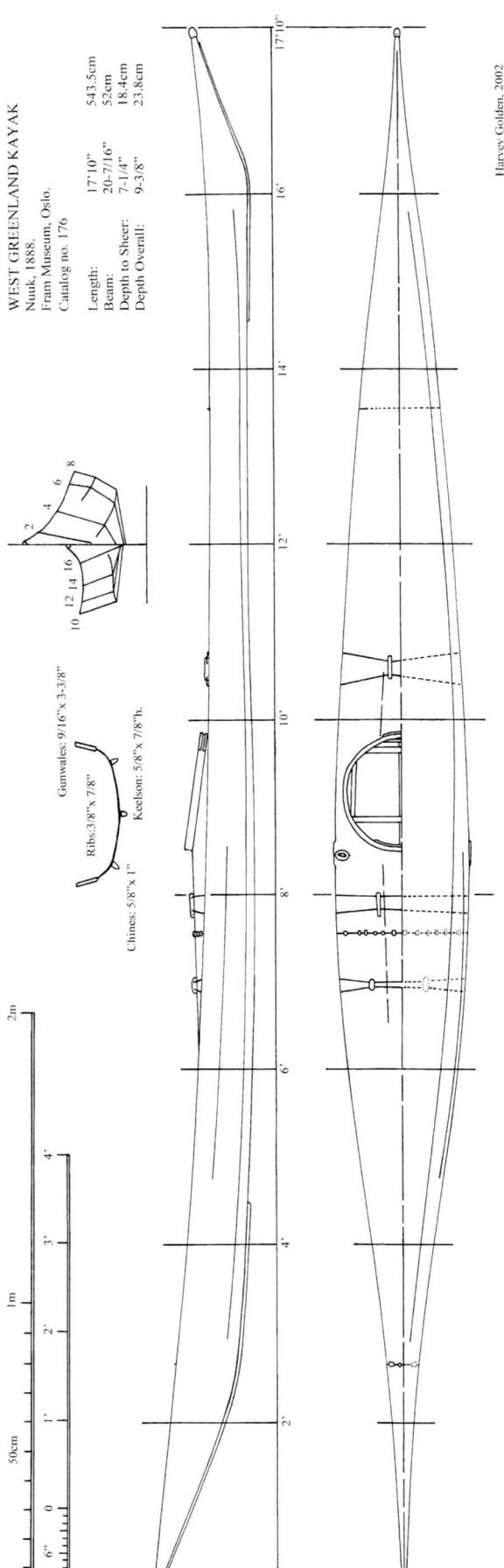

42. Fram Museum catalog no. 176

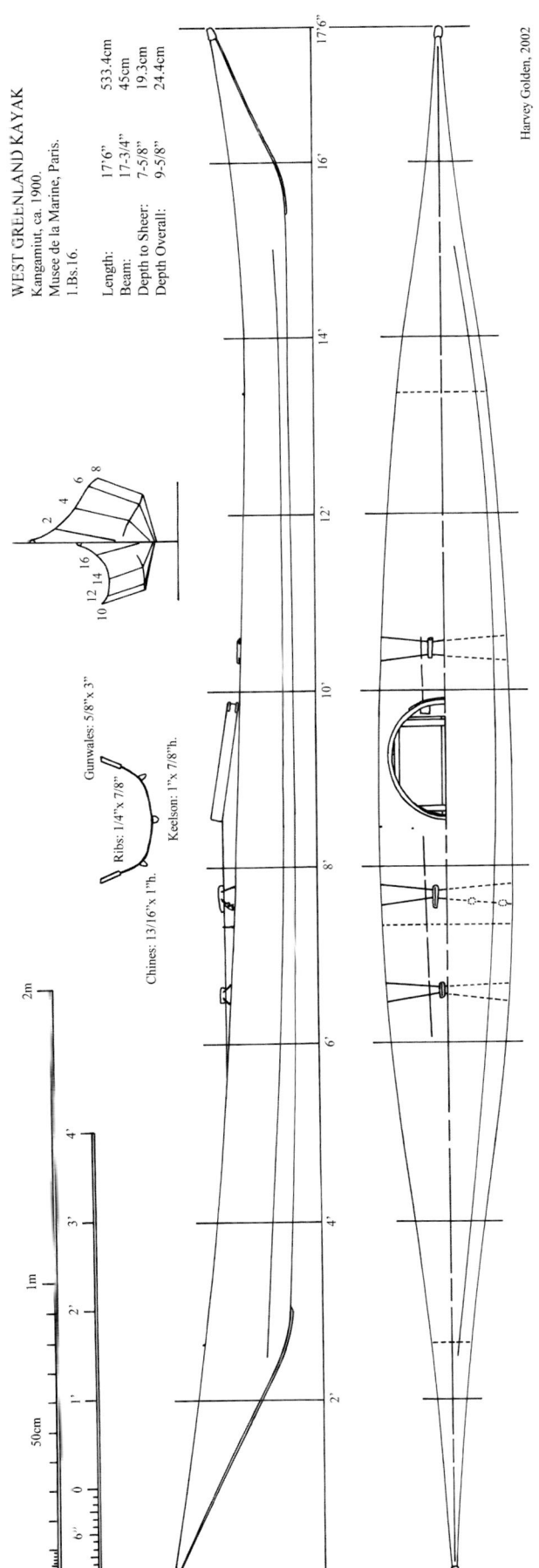

43. Musée de la Marine catalog no. 1Bs.16

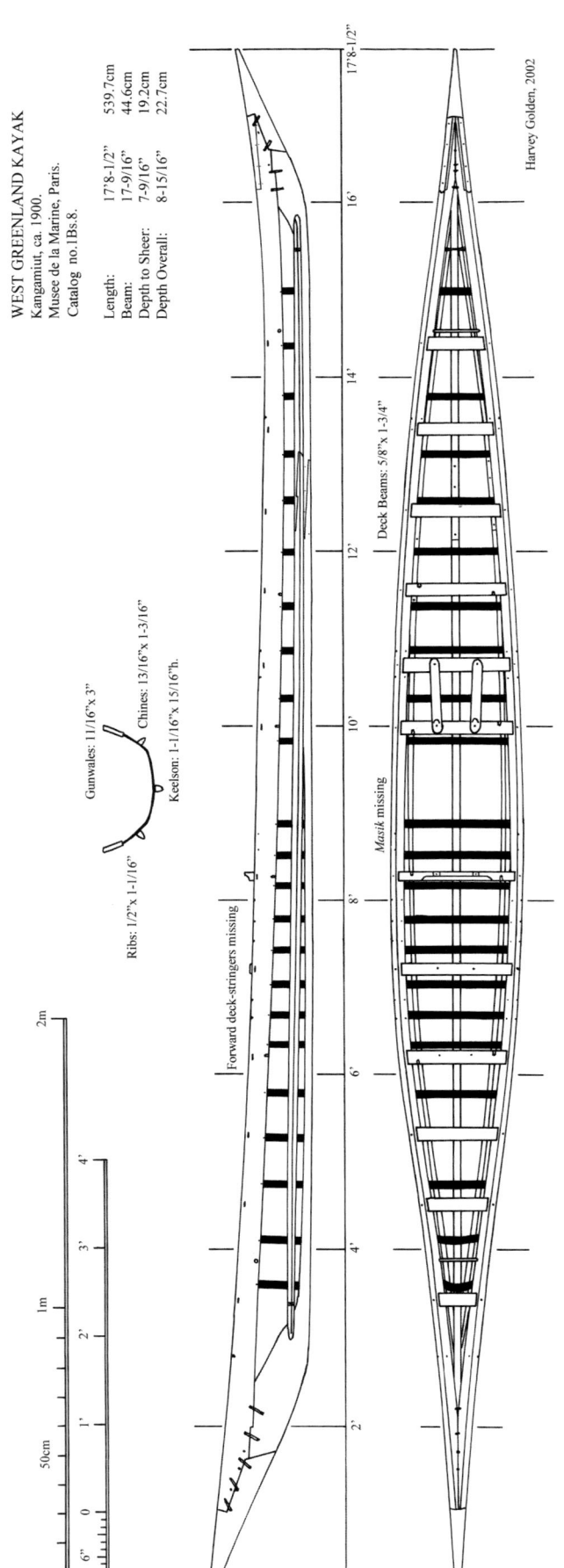

WEST GREENLAND KAYAK
Kangamiut, ca. 1900.
Musée de la Marine, Paris.
Catalog no.1Bs.8.

Length:	17'8-1/2"	539.7cm
Beam:	17-9/16"	44.6cm
Depth to Sheer:	7-9/16"	19.2cm
Depth Overall:	8-15/16"	22.7cm

Gunwales: 11/16"x 3"
Chines: 13/16"x 1-3/16"
Ribs: 1/2"x 1-1/16"
Keelson: 1-1/16"x 15/16"h.

Deck Beams: 5/8"x 1-3/4"

Masik missing

Forward deck-stringers missing

Harvey Golden, 2002

44a. Musée de la Marine catalog no. 1Bs.8

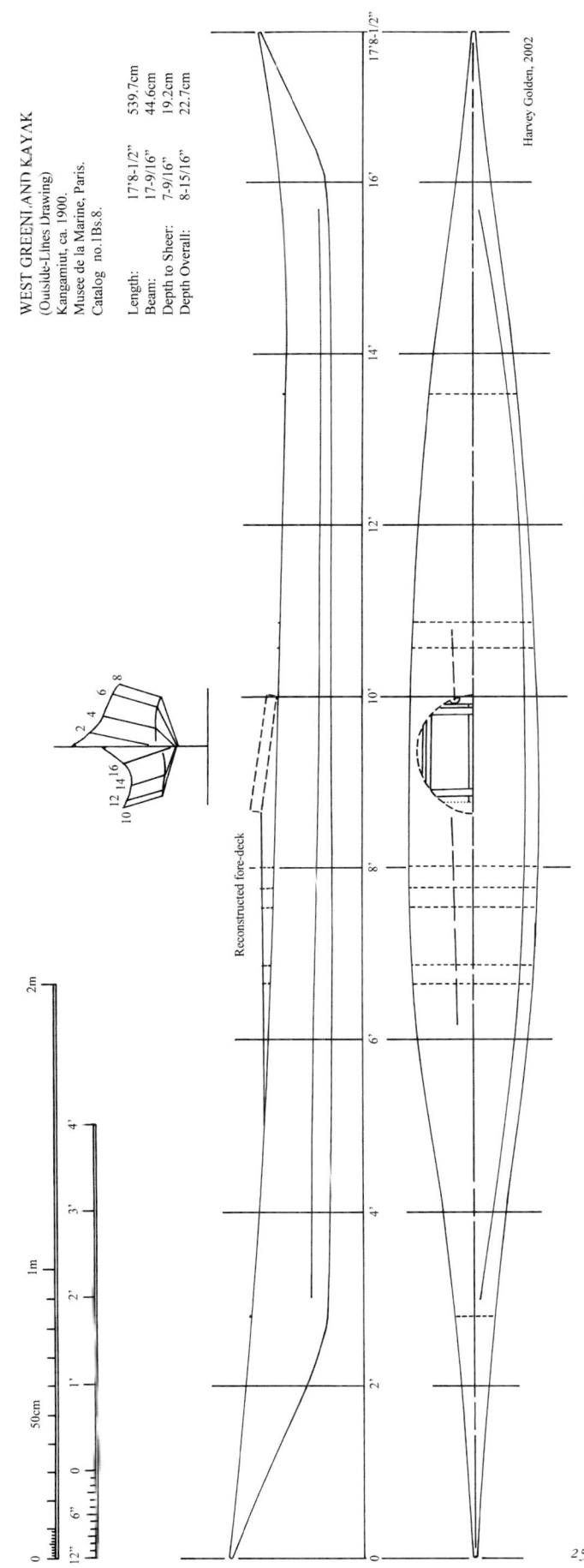

44b. Musée de la Marine catalog no. 1Bs.8 (Hull Lines)

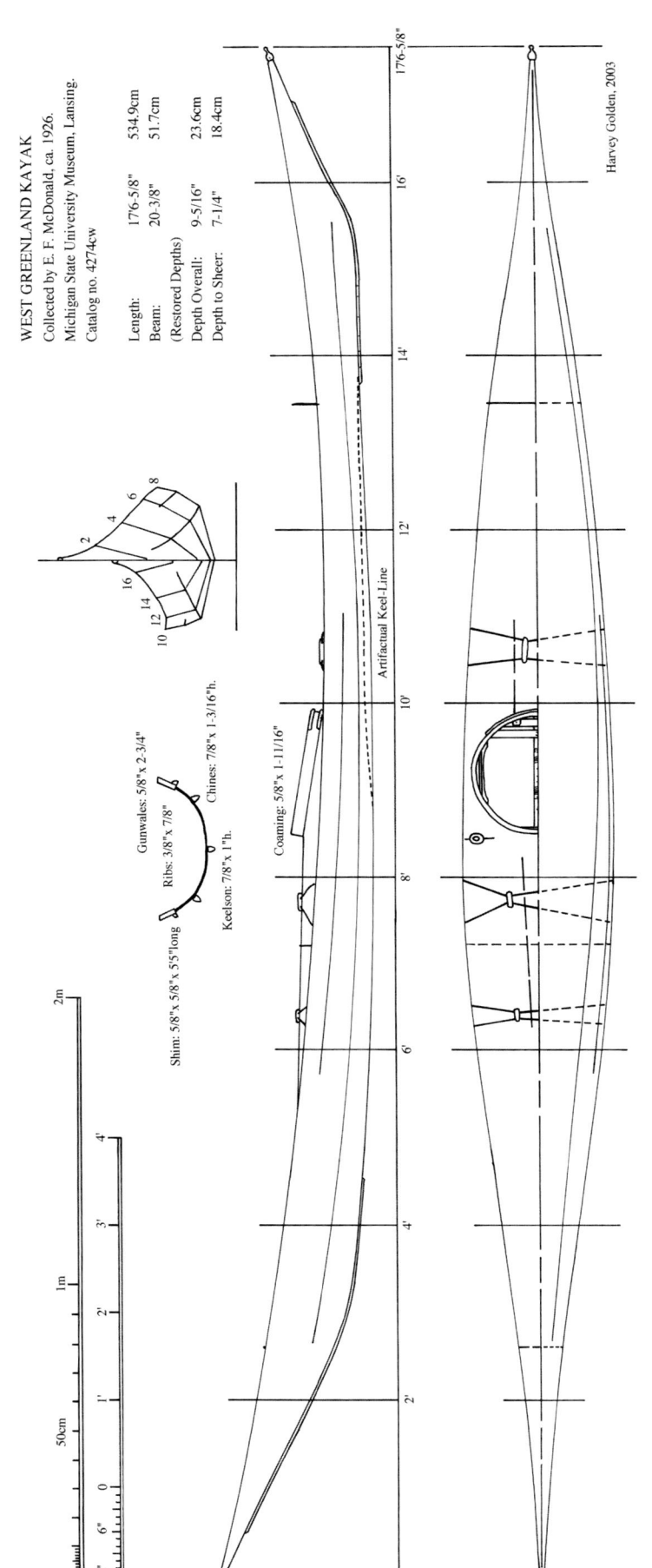

45. Michigan State University catalog no. 4274cw

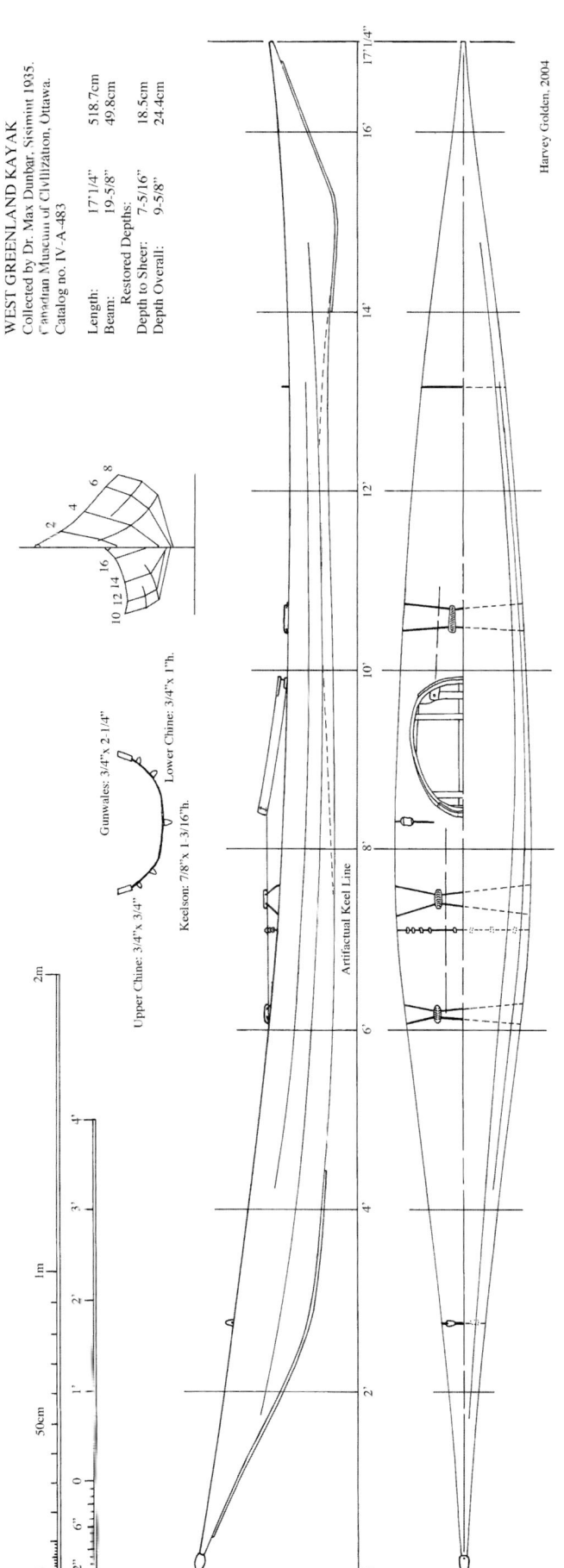

46. Canadian Museum of Civilization catalog no. IV-A-483

WEST GREENLAND KAYAK

Commissioned by Knud Rasmussen, early 1930s
Museon, the Hague, the Netherlands.
Catalog no. 117798

Length: 6'10-3/4"   210.1cm
Beam: 16"   40.6cm
Depth Overall: 6-1/8"   15.5cm
Depth to Sheer: 5-13/16"   14.7cm

Gunwales: 7/16" x 1-7/8"
Chines: 3/8" x 7/16" w.
Ribs: 1/8" x 7/8"
Keelson: 3/4" x 3/4"

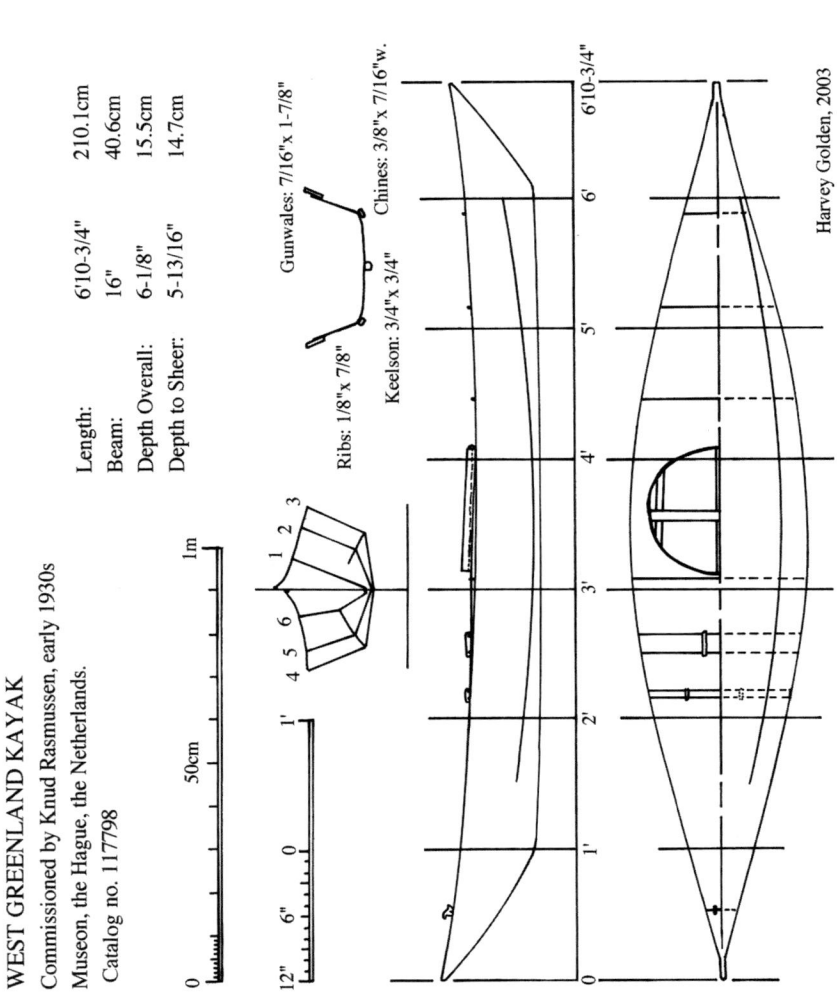

Harvey Golden, 2003

47. Museon catalog no. 117798

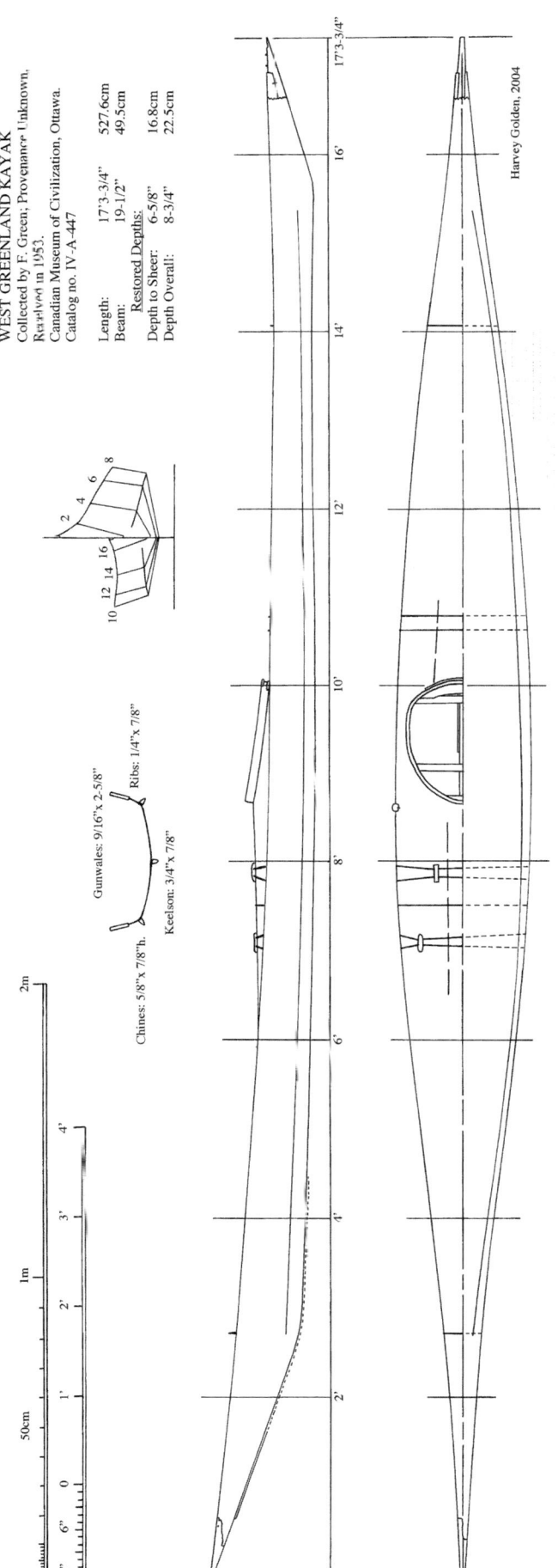

48. Canadian Museum of Civilization catalog no. IV-A-447

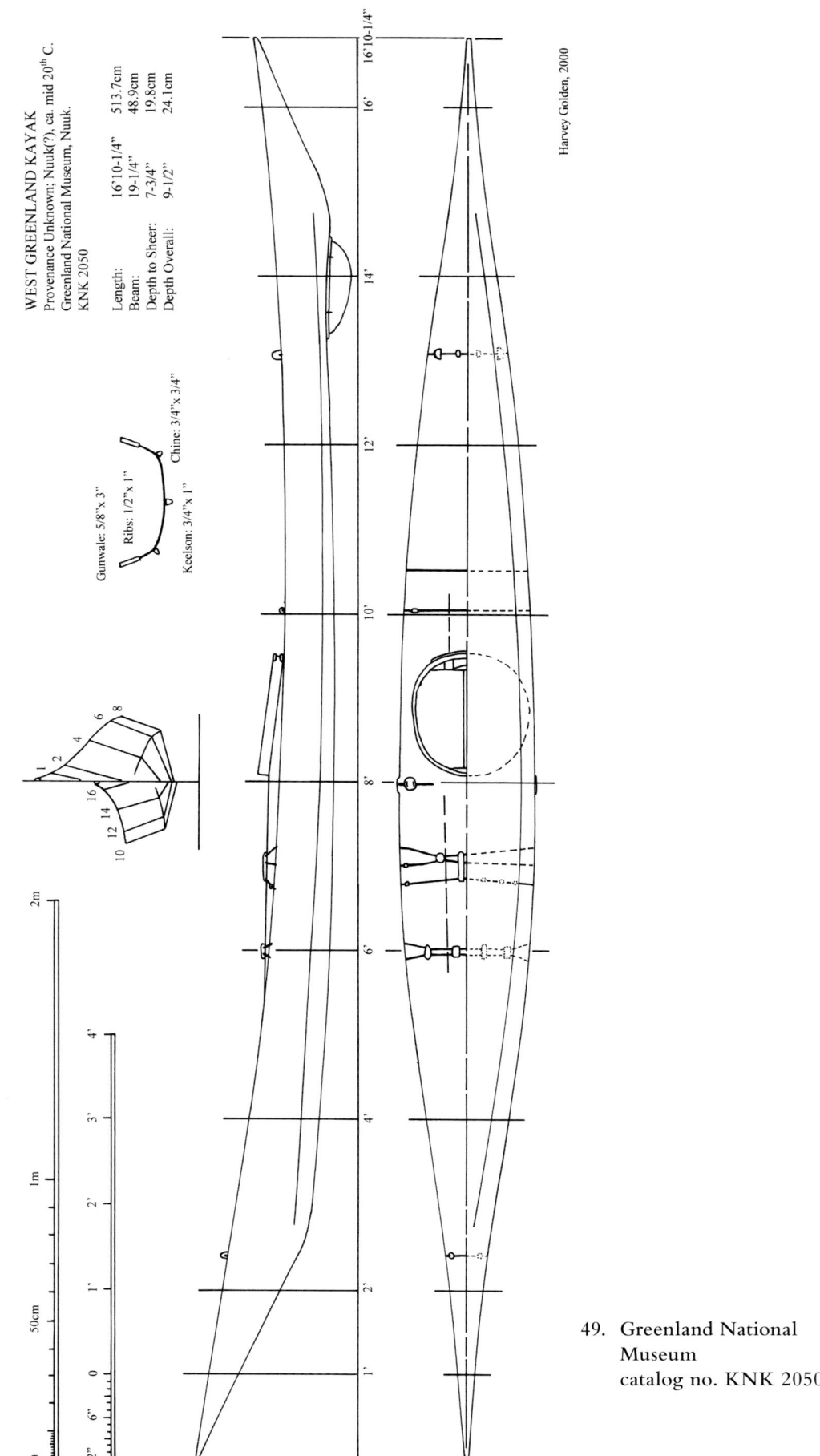

49. Greenland National Museum catalog no. KNK 2050

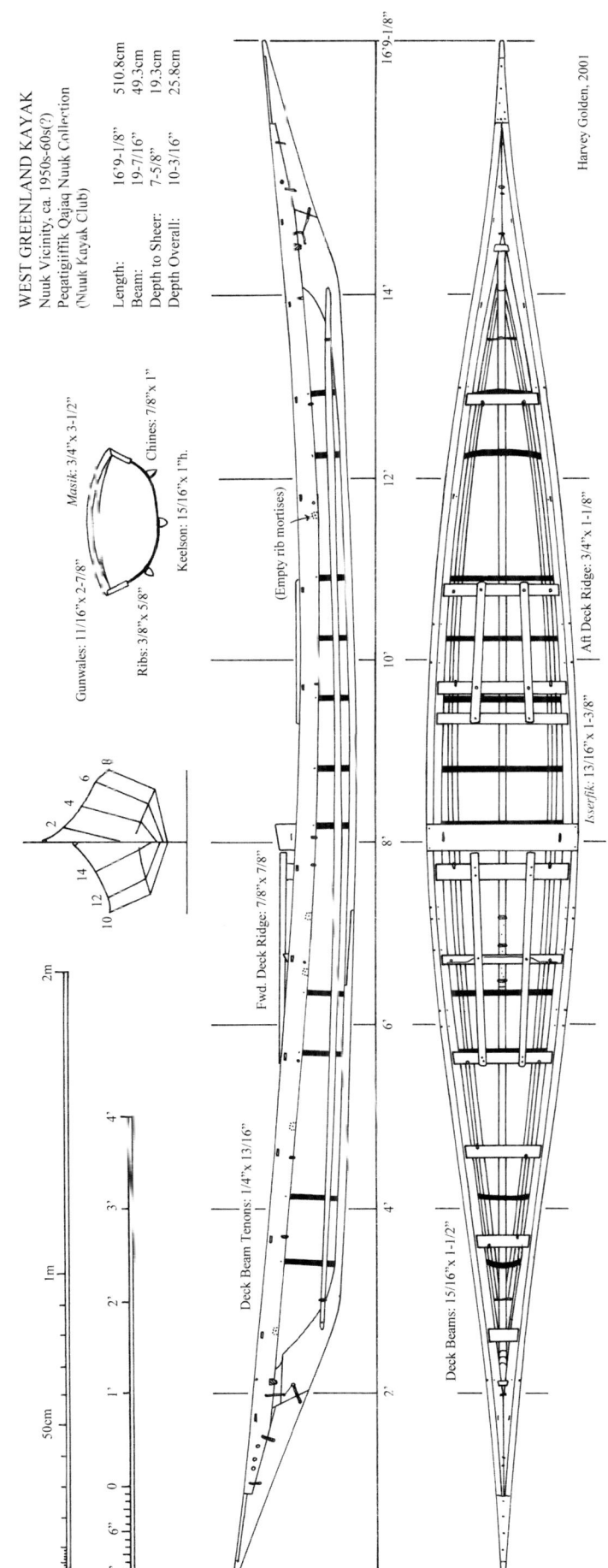

50a. Peqatigiiffik Qajaq Nuuk (N/N) "PQN"

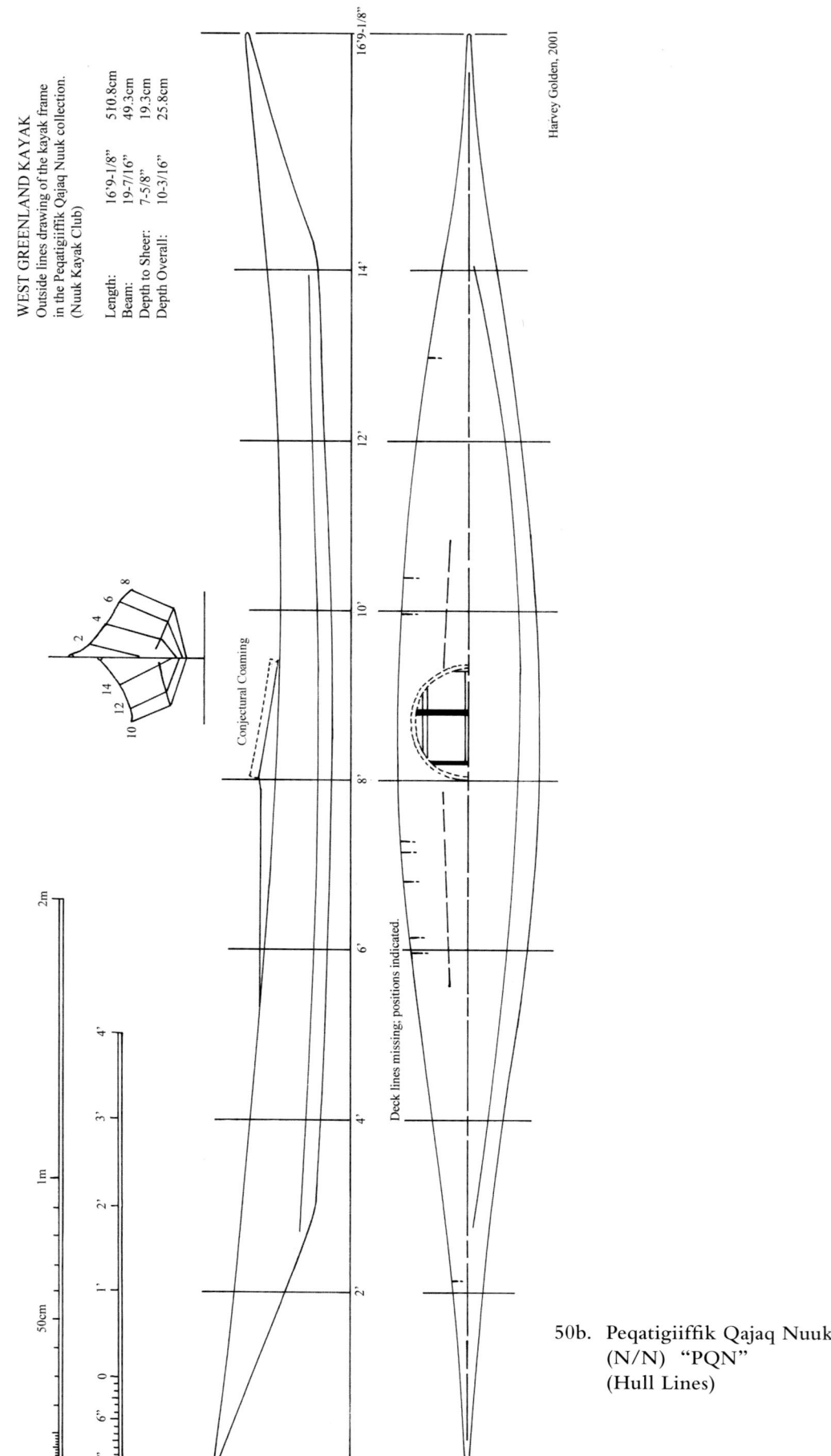

50b. Peqatigiiffik Qajaq Nuuk
(N/N) "PQN"
(Hull Lines)

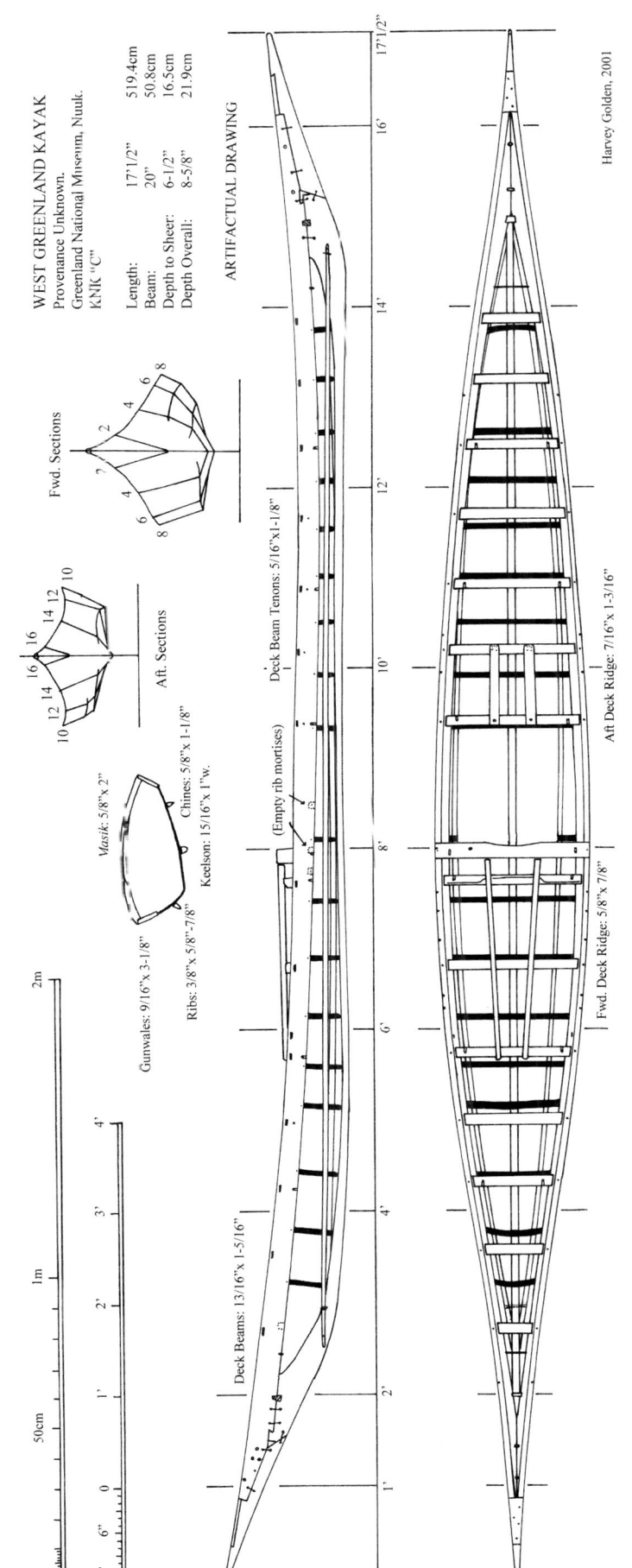

51a. Greenland National Museum (N/N) "C"

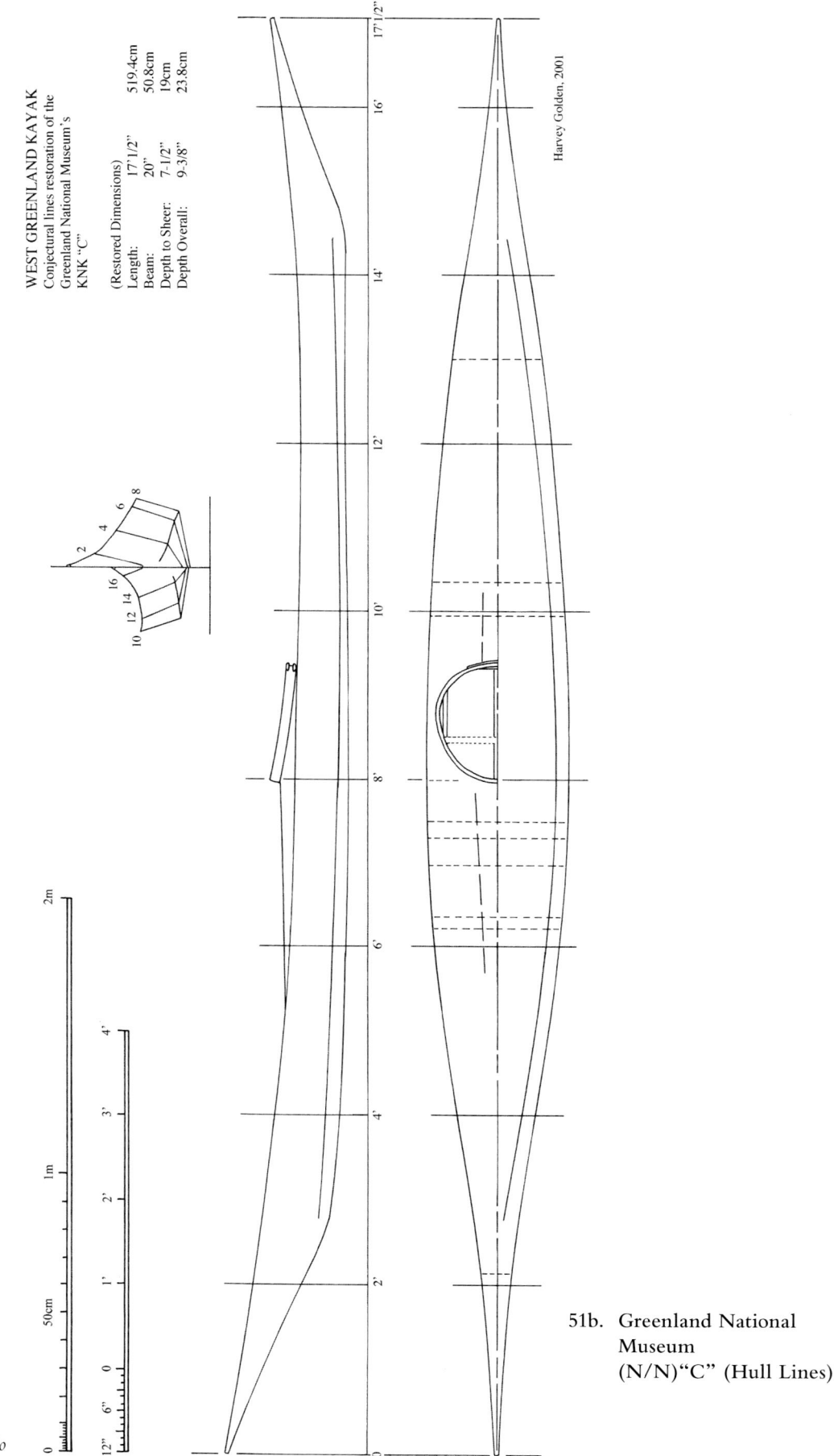

51b. Greenland National Museum (N/N) "C" (Hull Lines)

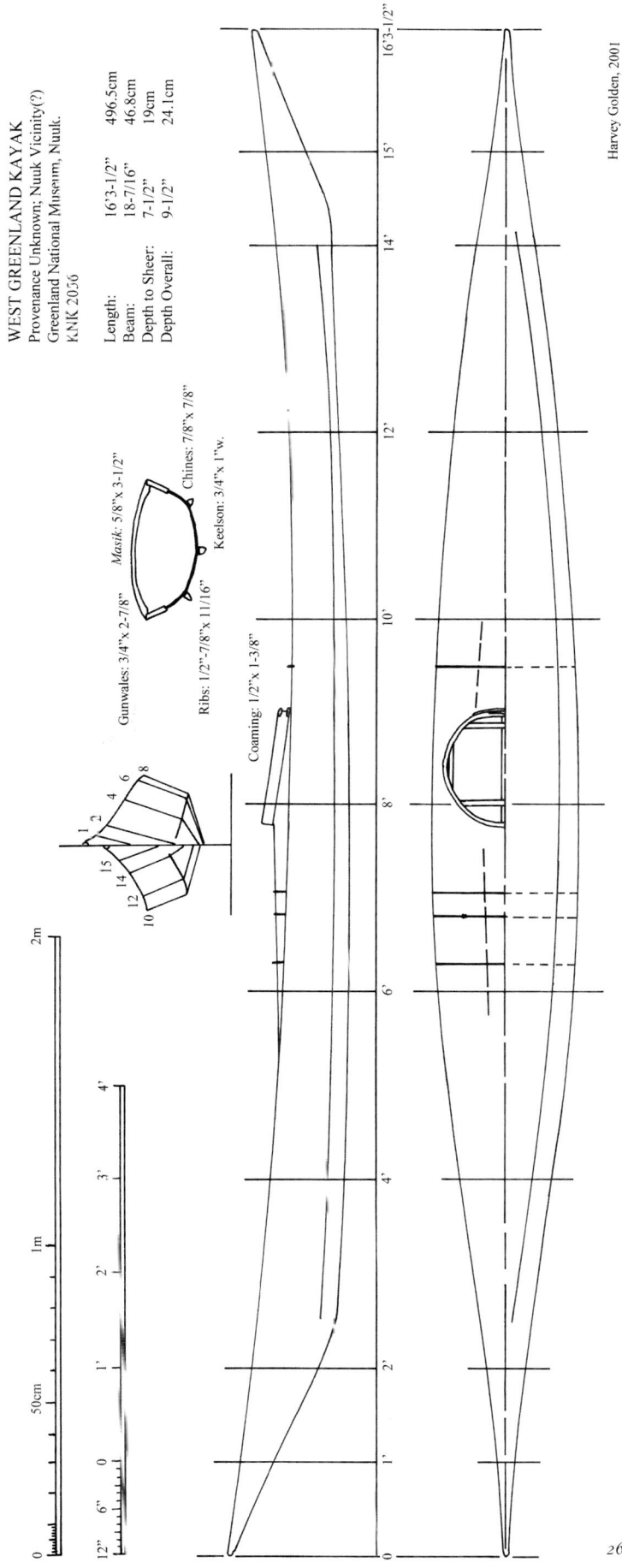

52. Greenland National Museum catalog no. KNK 2056

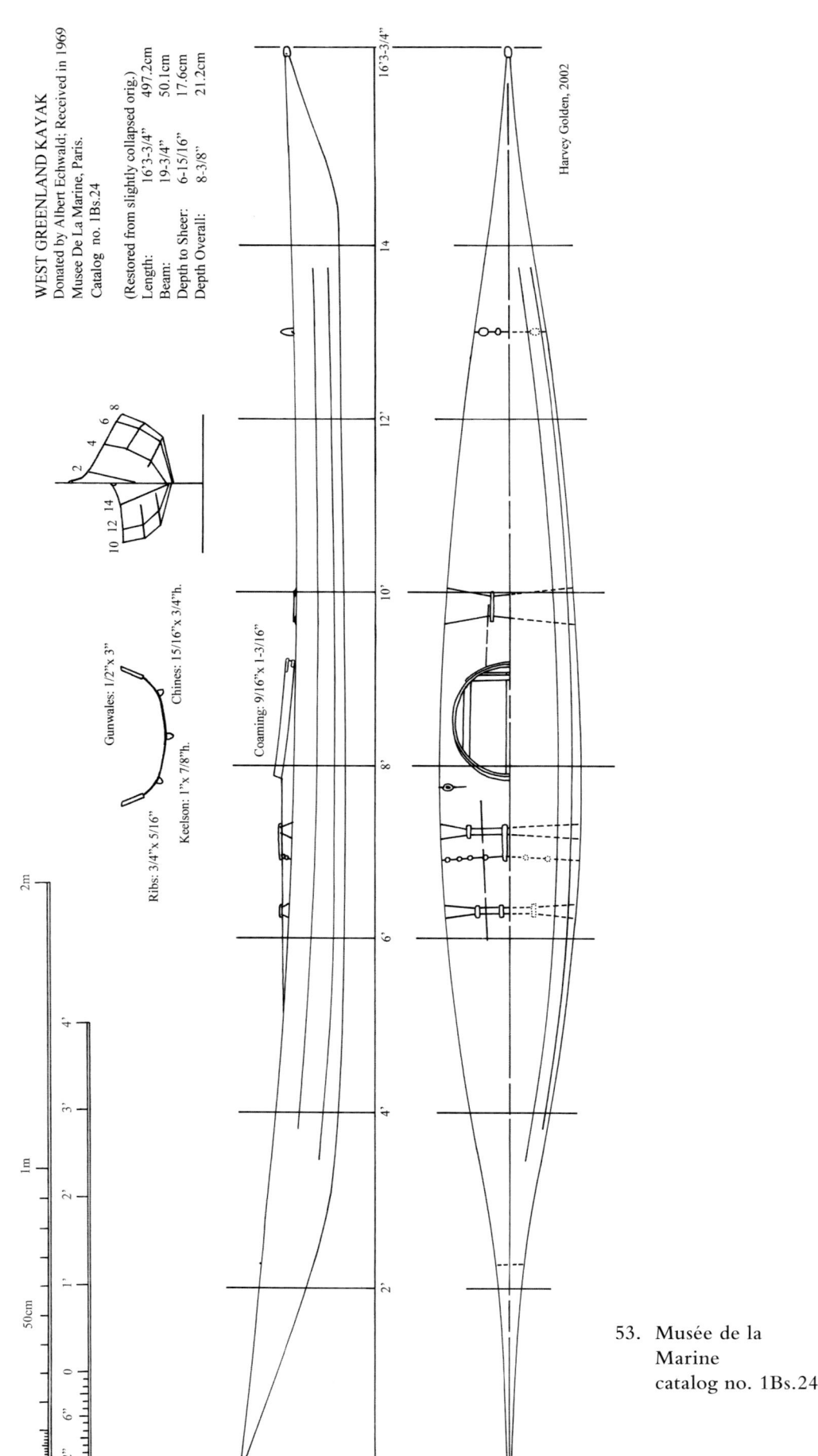

53. Musée de la Marine catalog no. 1Bs.24

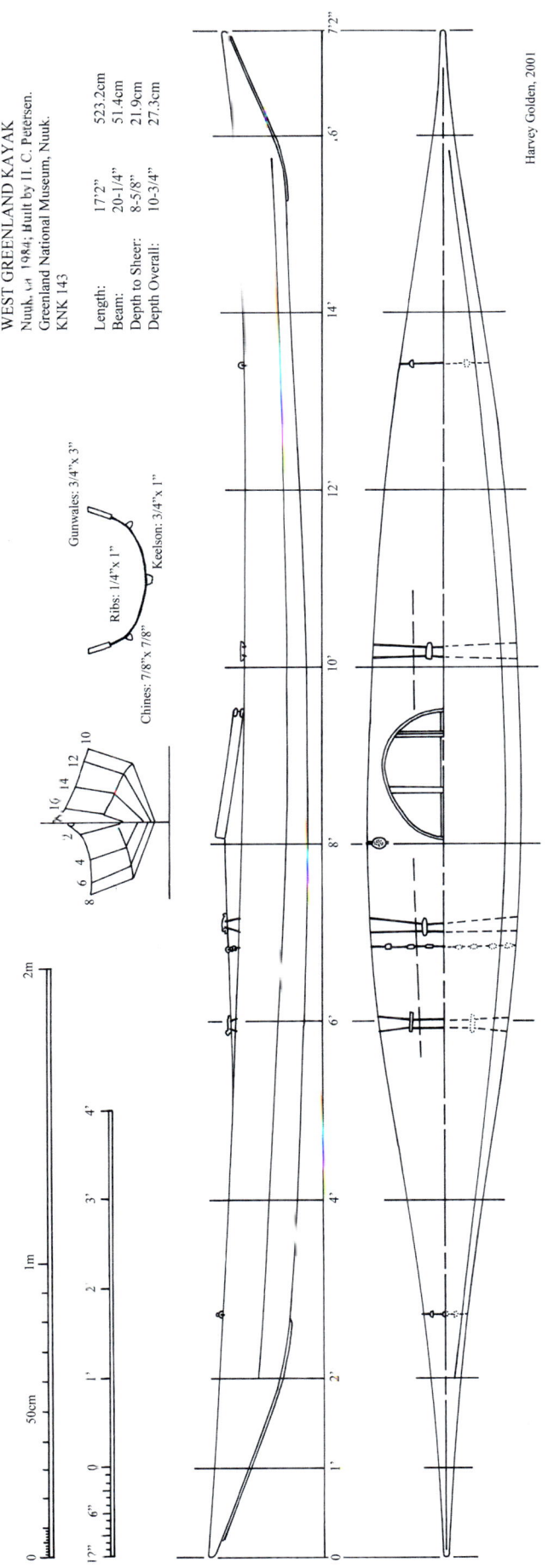

54. Greenland National Museum catalog no. KNK 143

WEST GREENLAND KAYAK (BOY'S)
Paamiut, ca. 1991.
Built by Karl Samuelsen.
Greenland National Museum, Nuuk.
KNK 1966x1

Length:	8'11"	271.7cm
Beam:	12-5/8"	32.0cm
Depth to Sheer:	4-7/16"	11.2cm
Depth Overall:	5-3/8"	13.6cm

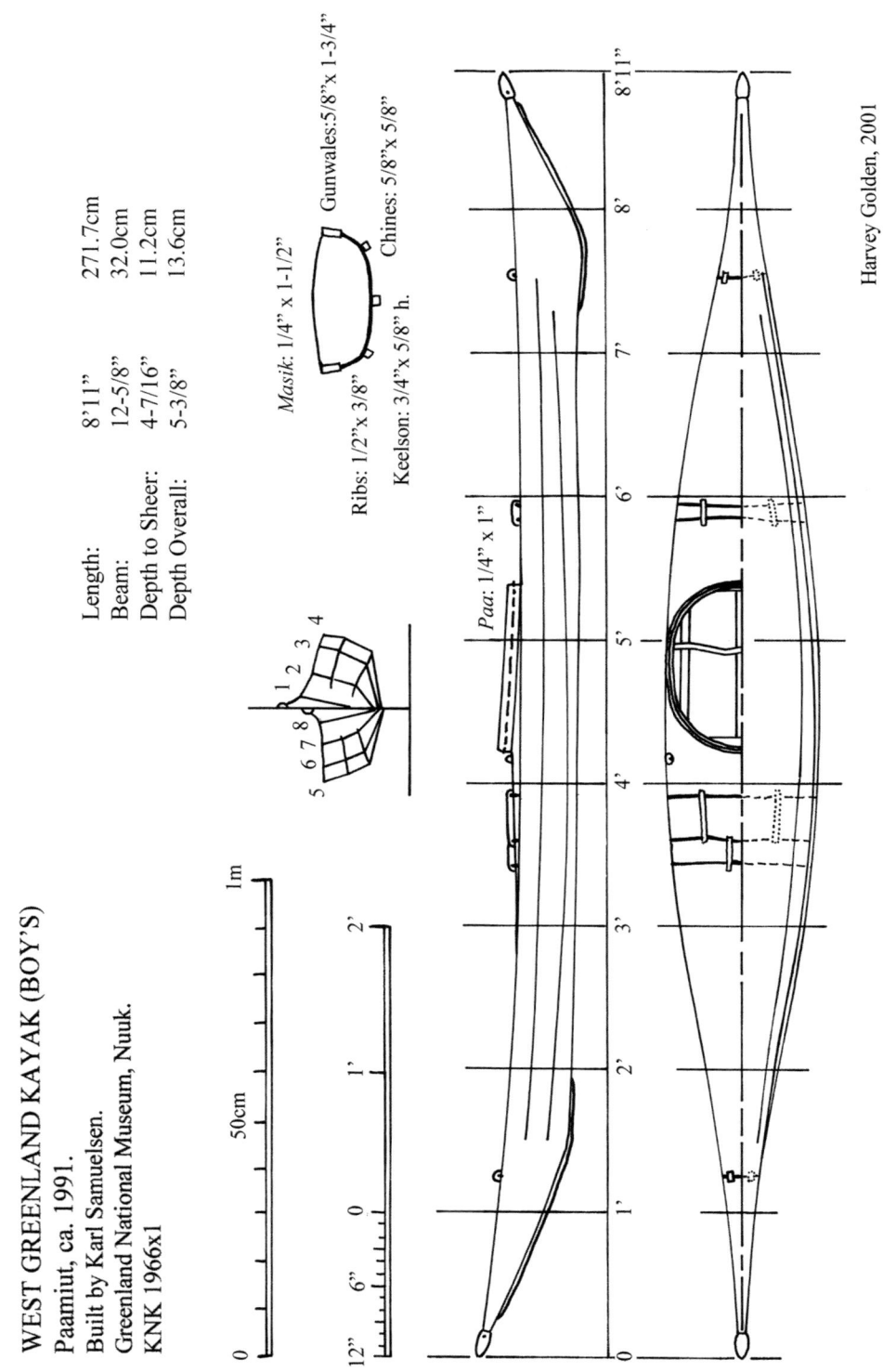

Harvey Golden, 2001

54. Greenland National Museum catalog no. KNK 166

39. West Greenland Kayak: Fram Museum, Oslo, Norway. Catalog no. 172

This kayak and the three that follow are all kayaks used by members of Fridtjof Nansen's 1888 cross-Greenland expedition. The Fram Museum's 172 is in the most damaged condition of them all, although its artifactual form still shows a kayak of considerable grace and quality; the Fram Museum's kayak 176 (plate 42) was the basis for my conjecturally restored rendering of the Fram 172.

As can be seen in the artifactual elevation, the 172's fore deck is collapsed. The *masik* is fractured, but present, and by all appearances the original deck height would have been about 2-1/4" (5.2cm) above sheer. The 172's *masik* measures 1/2" (13mm) by 3-7/8" (9.8cm) at its midpoint; the *isserfik* is 5/8" (16mm) thick by 1-1/2" (38mm) wide. The *masik* is lashed in place and its forward edge reveals notches and peg-holes that firmly received the aft ends of the forward deck stringers.

The gunwales are joined forward and aft via the dowel method, as depicted in figure 46 top. Only two deck beams forward and two aft exhibit fasteners: Pegs set obliquely. This is not to say the other deck-beams are unfastened, likely some or all use the top-peg method, which is not visible in a covered kayak. Lashing materials on the lower-frame all seem to be cotton twine. The lashing pattern is a

Figure 259: Fridtjof Nansen's Cross-Greenland Expedition members on a beach in West Greenland with their kayaks: Nansen stands third from left; to his left are Otto Sverdrup, Oluf Dietrichson, and Kristian Kristiansen, 1888-89. (National Library of Norway, Picture Collection.)

zig-zagging single-pass instead of the much more common double-pass pattern. Three of the Fram Museum's Greenland kayaks have this same lashing pattern with the same material.

The Fram 172 has just a single bone strip on its coaming's aft face; this is positioned at the upper edge and is 8-1/8" (20.6cm) long, and 3/16" (3mm) thick by 7/16" (11mm) high. The coaming itself is made of ash and measures 5/8" (16mm) thick by 1-1/4" (32mm) high. The keel edging on the Fram 172 is 7/16" (11mm) high by 7/16" wide overall, with the edge's face being 1/4" (6mm) wide. It is missing in places, but is drawn intact. Two seam protection pieces are along the keelson as well: These pieces are 1/4" thick and 1/2" wide (6 x 13mm). A third piece is evidenced as having been placed 13' 8-1/2" (417.8cm) aft of the bow.

Many of the 172's deck lines are missing, but their positions are evidenced by holes in the *amiq* along the sheer; their placement is indicated on the scale drawing. Those intact are the aft-most deck

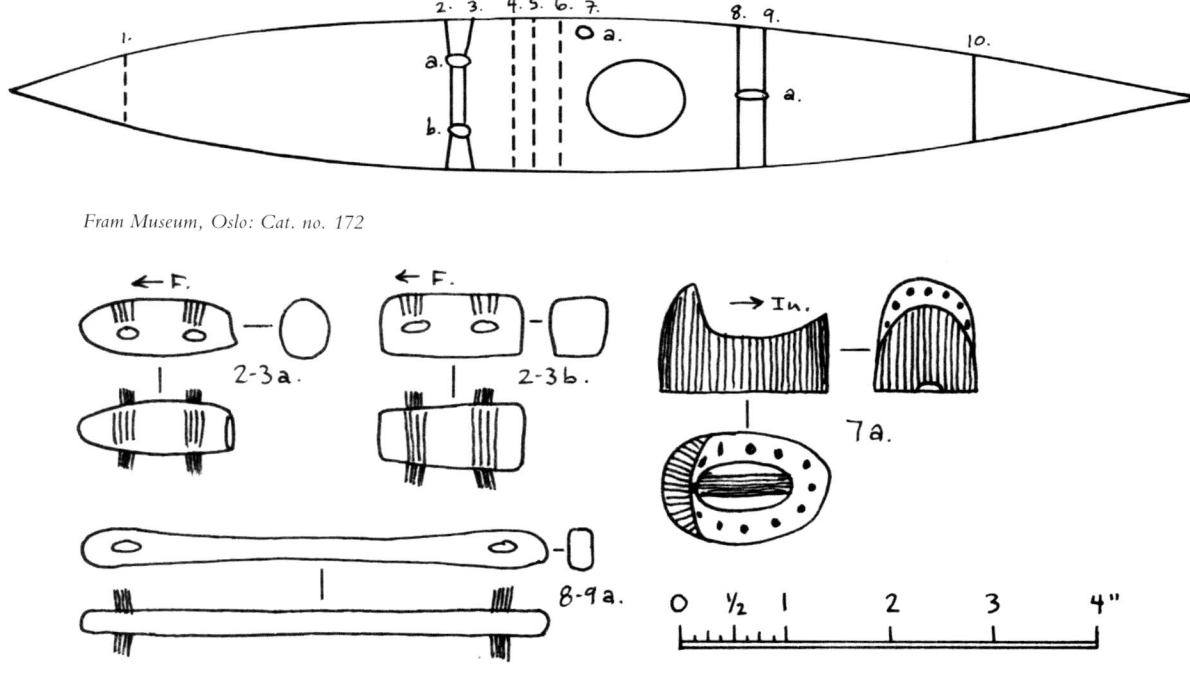

Fram Museum, Oslo: Cat. no. 172

line, a linked pair behind the cockpit, and a double-linked pair at the forward end of the fore deck. A very elegant harpoon holder is also present: it has fluted sides, a hollow core, and a rim around the top decorated with a ring of black dots.

40. West Greenland Kayak: Fram Museum, Oslo, Norway.
   Catalog no. 276

The Fram Museum's kayak no. 276 is the kayak that belonged to Fridtjof Nansen himself. Nansen writes extensively in his 1895 *The First Crossing of Greenland* about his experiences with his kayak: "The Eskimo 'kayaks' were, of course, a great attraction to us strangers, and as soon as possible I possessed myself of one." He describes their stability as if swinging on a knife-edge; "...It is very necessary, so to speak, to keep your hair parted well in the middle" (402).

Of the Fram Museum kayaks, the 276 is most unique: It has only one deck stringer behind the cockpit, and an excess of deck-lines (present and evidenced) on the aft deck. Nothing else would suggest it is in anyway different from the others— it is about the same size as the other Fram Museum kayaks, and also has a harpoon holder. The aft deck stringer measures 3/8" (9mm) thick by 7/8" (22mm) wide.

The extra lines on the aft deck were perhaps used to fasten outriggers— with a choice of two different positions. Two children's kayaks presented later in this study (the Museon's 117798 and the GNM's KNK 1966, plates 47 and 55) also have such extra deck lines, and even the single aft deck stringer—these children's kayaks were undoubtedly used with outriggers because of their tiny size and inexperienced users. Nansen writes that he had used outriggers to get accustomed to the kayak's stability (1895:403 –see also page 96 present volume). It should also be considered that some of the 'extra' deck lines on the aft deck might have been placed to hold Nansen's skis and poles.

Figure 260: Fridtjof Nansen, foreground, and four fellow members of his cross-Greenland expedition in local-made Greenland kayaks, Nuuk vicinity, 1888-89. National Library of Norway, Picture Collection.

The coaming on the 276 has three bone pieces fastened to its outer face. The piece at the upper back covers the scarf joint and is 3" long by 5/16" square (20.3cm x 8mm). The two pieces at the front quarters are situated 1/8" (3mm) below the coaming's top edge, and are 3/16" (5mm) thick by 5/16" (8mm) high the piece on the left is 3-1/2" (8.9cm) long, and the piece on the right is 6" (15.2cm) long. These latter pieces likely were placed to provide a better grip on the kayaker's *tuilik*, or paddling jacket.

The construction of the 276 is much the same as in the Fram Museum's kayak 172. The bow interior of the 276 is obscured by what appears to be a hornet's nest, thankfully inactive. As can be seen in the artifactual elevation, the fore deck ahead of the *masik* has completely collapsed, and the keel line indicates areas of hull collapse. The restored lines are based on comparisons to similar kayaks, notably the Fram Museum's kayak 176.

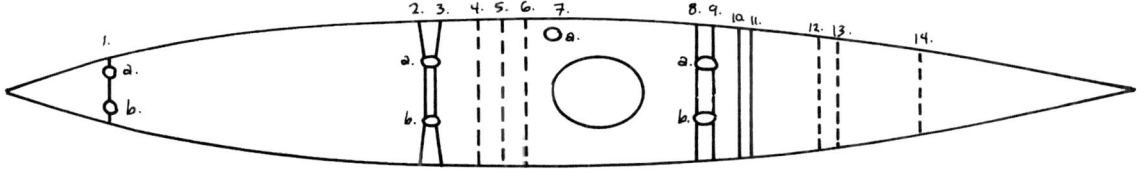

Fram Museum, Oslo: Cat no. 276

The harpoon holder on the 276 is not ornately fashioned in the least, but the two fittings on the bow deck line have very elegant and unique shapes. The pair of deck lines immediately behind the cockpit is double-linked. The pairs of deck lines 10-11 and 12-13 are as mentioned above, likely attachment points for outriggers. It isn't known why there would be two such pairs— perhaps so that the outriggers can be placed in either position.

If Nansen is in this same kayak in the photo in figure 260, this kayak had fittings on the stern deck line, much like those on the Fram Museum kayak no. 65 (plate 41). Bow and stern knobs are missing but evidenced, as is bow and stern keel edging.

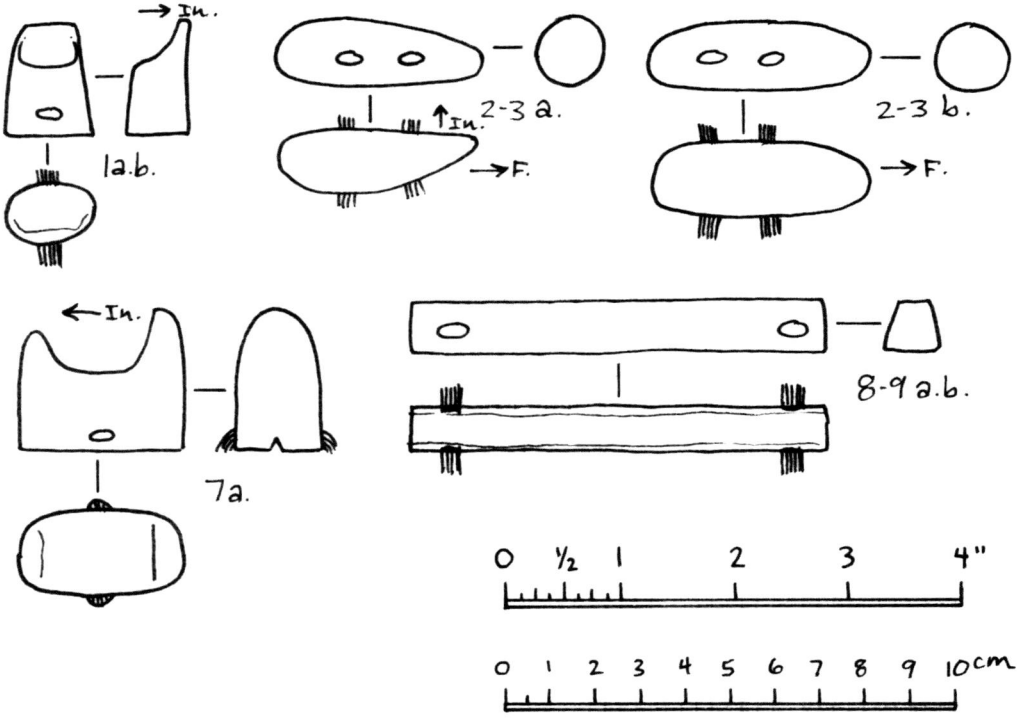

41. West Greenland Kayak: Fram Museum, Oslo, Norway.
   Catalog no. 65

Another kayak from Nuuk, 1888, the Fram Museum's kayak 65 exhibits hull damage but mainly at the bow, with the stern being in moderately good condition. The scale drawing depicts the damaged artifact and the conjectural reconstruction, based on the Fram Museum kayak 176 (plate 42).

The 65's *masik* is very wide at 4-1/16" (10.3cm), but it is cut back in the middle such that its narrowest point is only 2-13/16" (7.1cm) wide; at its mid-point, the *masik* is 1/2" (13mm) thick. The *isserfik* measures 3/4" (19mm) thick by 1-1/2" (38mm) wide.

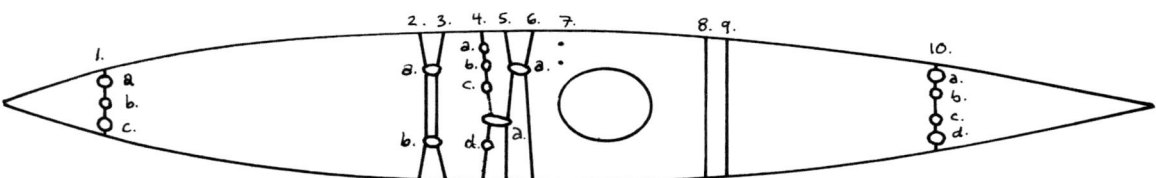

Fram Museum, Oslo: Cat. no. 65

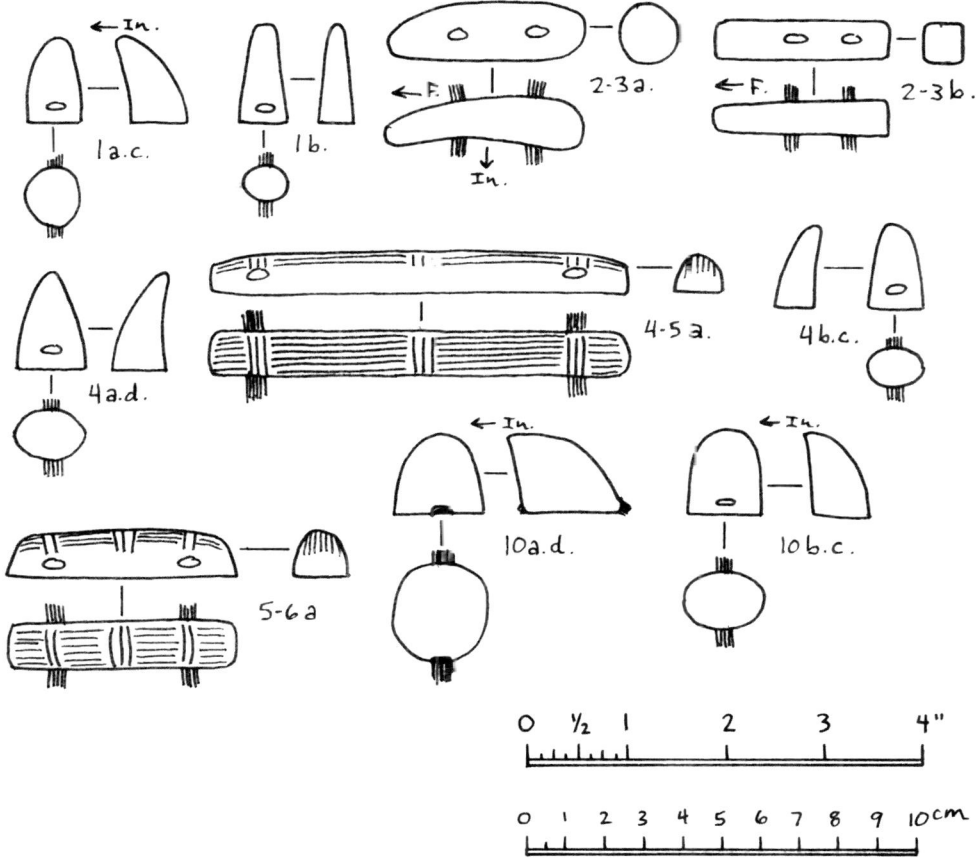

Of all the Fram Museum kayaks, the 65's deck lines are most intact: The only missing element of the lines and fittings is the harpoon holder, whose position was evidenced, and is noted on the scale drawing.

The fittings on the Fram 65 are very elaborately carved; many pieces have intricately carved ridges, and all of them are finely polished. As ornate and decorative as these pieces appear, it must be considered that they would at times need to be moved about in possibly icy conditions, so these ridges would have afforded a better grip for the kayaker. Bow and stern keel edging is evidenced but missing, and is presented in the drawing with a dashed line. The construction is much the same as in the Fram Museum kayak 172 (plate 39). A paddle associated with the kayak no. 65 is depicted in paddle-plate 25.

42. West Greenland Kayak from 1888: Fram Museum, Oslo, Norway.
Catalog no. 176

Of the four Greenland kayaks from Nuuk, 1888, at the Fram Museum, the 176 is in the best condition. The conjectural restorations of the three previous Fram Museum kayaks are largely based on this kayak. The 176 sits in a cradle astern of the *Fram* herself (figure 261). Form-wise, the 176 is very attractive, with a stern much shorter than on the Fram Museum kayaks 172 and 65 (plates 39 and 41); it bears more resemblance to the Fram 276 (plate 40). A paddle associated with the kayak 176 is depicted in paddle-plate 38.

The continuous lashings in the Fram 176 are cotton twine, and are secured via the double-pass method depicted in figure 73 top. Deck beams are secured to the gunwales with pegs, set obliquely, and the gunwale ends are secured with a peg, both fore and aft. The 176's *masik* measures 5/8" (16mm) thick in the middle and 3-5/16" (84mm) wide; the *isserfik* is 13/16" (21mm) thick by 1-3/4" (44mm) wide.

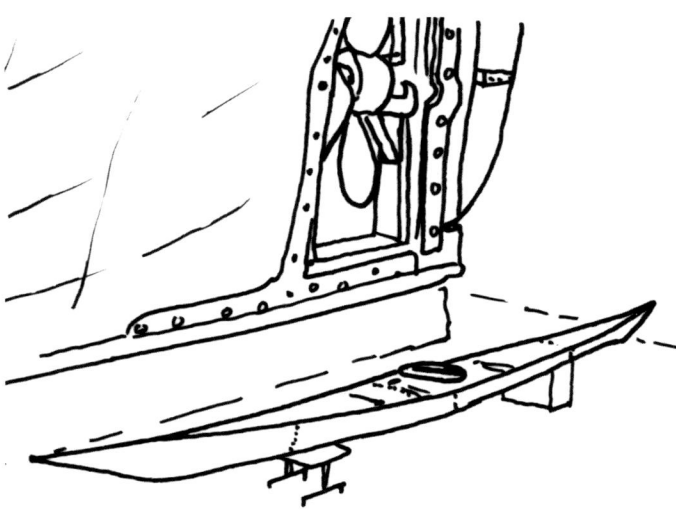

Figure 261: The Fram Museum's kayak 176, beneath the Fram *herself.*

Four small oval pieces of skin have been set beneath the ribs in the cockpit— these are likely just extra padding or insulation. Since they do not cover the ribs, it could be presumed that other padding would also be used, such as an old remnant of a kayak *amiq*. No other kayaks I've studied had such pads in them, although one kayak had wool socks or sweater remnants stuffed beneath its ribs (plate 61).

While the other three Fram Museum kayaks are in very poor condition, the integrity of the 176 allows a surety regarding the presence of an integral skeg at the stern. As the keelson slowly rises up behind the cockpit towards the raked stern, it makes a subtle dip back down before transitioning into the stern. This subtle yet significant feature is known as an integral skeg, being just like a skeg or 'fin' but instead of one that is attached to the outside of the kayak, the integral example is permanent and is inside the *amiq*. See figures 132, 133, and 134 for examples of skegs and their attachments.

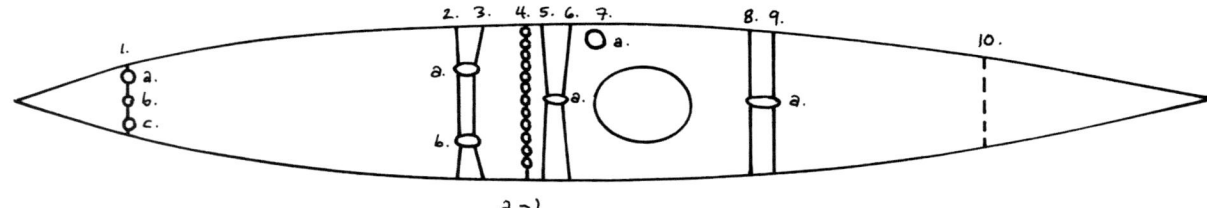

Fram Museum, Oslo: Cat. no. 176

All of the deck lines on the Fram 176 are intact except for the stern line. Three fittings are present on the bow-most deck line. The next pair aft is double linked, and behind this is a single unlinked line bearing twelve beads. Just ahead of the cockpit is a single linked pair of deck lines. The harpoon holder is a hollowed section of walrus tusk, incised with a series of rings and dots. A single linked pair of deck lines is on the aft deck.

The four Fram Museum kayaks offer an intriguing glimpse into elements of variation among kayaks built in the same region at the same time. There are the obvious considerations made for accommodat-

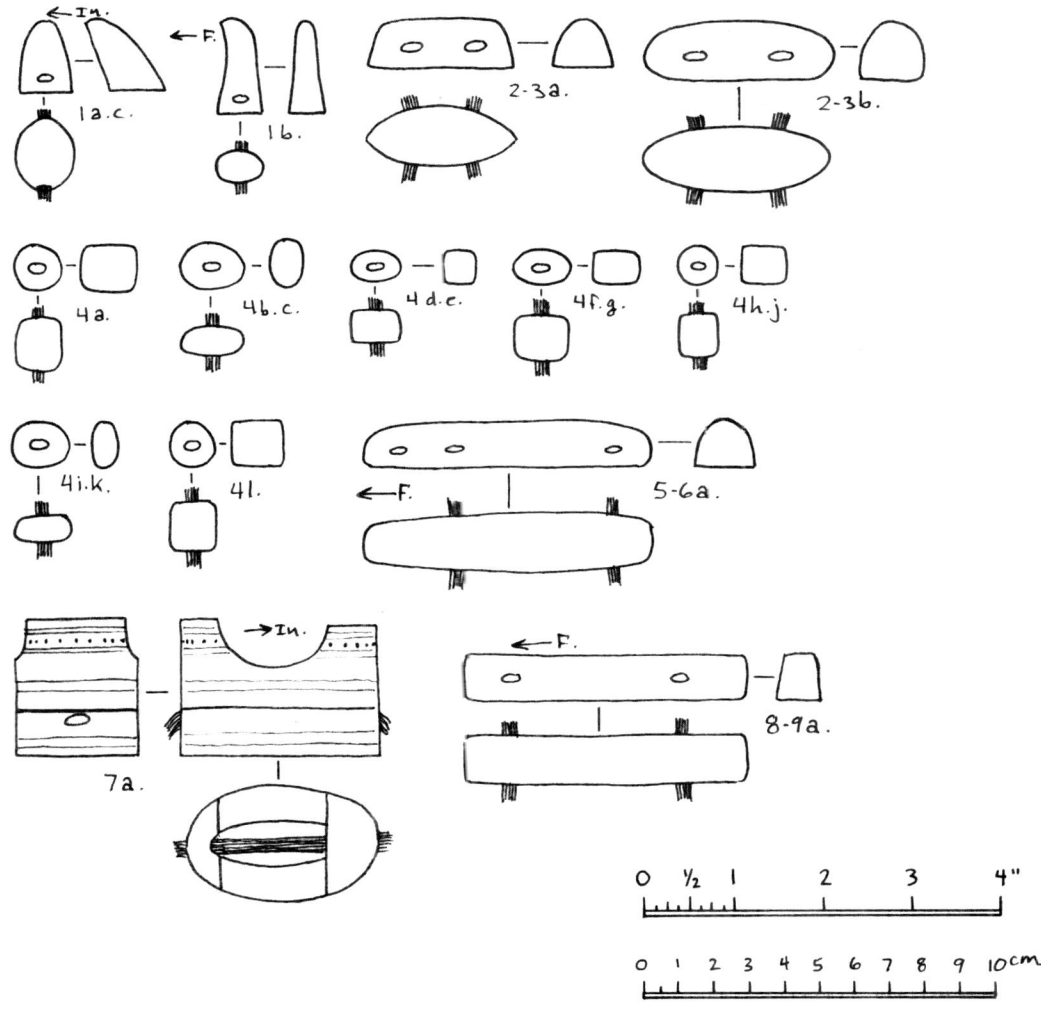

ing varying-sized kayakers, but other variations are more mysterious. Why is each kayak's deck rigging so different? Why the differences in stem lengths?

Fridtjof Nansen describes in his *Eskimo Life* the reasons behind certain proportional variations of kayaks in the fjords adjacent Nuuk: "...the kayaks in Godthaab fiords— as, for example, at Sardlok [Sardloq] and Karnok [Qornoq]— were longer and narrower than kayaks on the sea-coast, for example at Kangek, obviously for the reason that on the open coast they are exposed to heavier seas, and must therefore be stiffer and easier to handle. The shorter and broader kayaks are better sea-boats, and ship less water"(1893:47).

Nansen's reasoning makes sense, and there is no reason to doubt what he claims to have observed. However, H.C. Petersen shows that Nansen's statement about shorter and wider kayaks being preferred on the outer coasts isn't always the case. Using measurements gathered by Ole Bendixen, Petersen shows that the opposite is the case for Godthaab fjord (1986:43). The different results between Nansen's observations and Bendixen's measurements may be due to limited sample sizes and/or population movements. The differences in proportions and rigging could simply reflect the personal preferences of the builders.

43. West Greenland Kayak: Musée de la Marine, Paris, France. Catalog no. 1Bs.16.

The 1Bs.16 is an especially fine looking kayak from Kangaamiut— a locale whose inhabitants were renowned kayak hunters. This kayak's provenance is by deduction: The 1Bs.8 (next in this study) is nearly identical in shape, size, construction, and even in materials used— particularly the jute-like cord used for the lashings; the two kayaks also have the same donor. While the museum did not have data as to where either of these kayaks are from, the 1Bs.8 had a faint pencil inscription on the gunwale, some of it readable: "(??)... af Ulrik Rosing ... Kangâmiut ... (? ?) ... 1900." Musée de la Marine inventory cards list this kayak as having been donated by Laurits Hans Christian Bistrup in 1901.

Kaj Birket-Smith, in his *Ethnography of the Egedesminde District*, offers a kayak typology for the districts of Sukkertoppen-to-Holsteinborg (Maniitsoq/ Sisimiut): "Sheer. Very short stems, the stern formerly curving upwards, as is still done in Kangaamiut. Dark skin. Flat seams" (1924:271). Distinct sheer and short stems are accurate descriptions of the 1Bs.16. The stern of this example is not curved particularly high, especially when compared to other kayaks in this study, though "curving upwards" is a very relative description.

Birket-Smith sheds light on the changes of stern-shape in this vicinity: "During my stay at Sukkertoppen [Maniitsoq] in 1918 a number of men from Kangaamiut came to visit the settlement, and among them several with kayaks, the sterns of which were curved upwards just as on the type from Disko Bay.... At Kangaamiut the up-turned stern was beginning to disappear, but as yet it was not entirely abandoned" (1924:269).

The stern of the 1.Bs.16 is considerably higher than the Kangaamiut kayak presented in P. Scavenius-Jensen's *Den Grønlandske Kajak og den Redskaber* (1975:22, Plate I.). This example has a very low

Figure 262: Kayakers at Ataugmik, between Nuuk and Maniitsoq, 1918. (Photographer: Ole Bendixen/Arktisk Institut 45572.)

and short stern, and being from circa 1959, it illustrates the continuation of trends described by Birket-Smith in 1918 above.

A view into the 1Bs.16 is presented in figure 263, looking towards the bow. The curved deck beam ahead of the *masik* is shown quite well in this image, as is the dense rib spacing and continuous deck lines. An interesting feature is also to be seen in this figure: a piece of flat wood spanning the two forward deck-stringers. Considering its placement, it must have served as a firm footing for the aft-leg of the harpoon-line stand (*asaloq*).

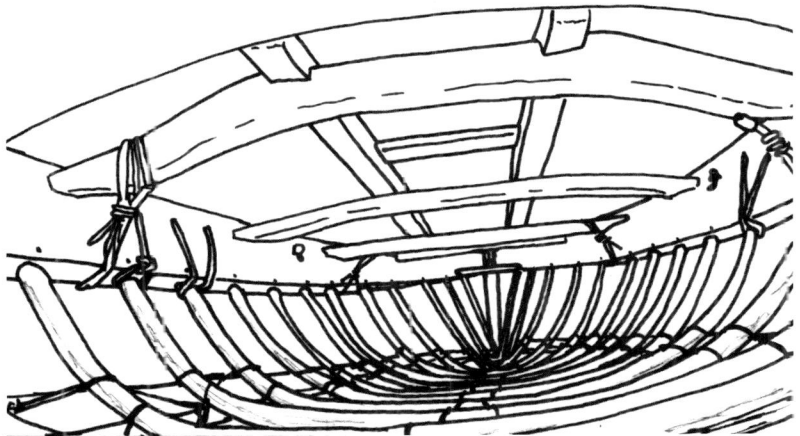

Figure 263: A forward interior view of the Musée de la Marine's kayak 1Bs.16. Note the short cross piece spanning the two forward deck stringers and the continuous deck lines passed below the gunwales and around the ribs.

Some scantlings not depicted on the scale drawing are as follows The *masik* measures 3-1/4″ (6mm) wide and 3/4″ (19mm) thick, but its aft-edge comes to a sharp tapered point, as in figure 78c. The *isserfik* is 5/8″ (16mm) thick and 1-11/16″ (43mm) wide. The forward deck stringers are 3/4″ (19mm) wide, and the aft deck stringers are 5/8″ (16mm) thick by 1-3/16″ (30mm) wide.

Bone bands are present on the back of the 1Bs.16's coaming: The upper band is 9-3/4″ (24.7cm) long, and the lower is 9-3/16″ (23.3cm) long; both strips are 1/8″ (3mm) thick by 5/16″ (8mm) wide. The coaming itself measures 5/8″ (16mm) thick by 1-1/2″ (38mm) high, and is made of ash.

Another feature of the 1Bs.16 worth noticing is the lack of an integral skeg astern on this kayak presumably from Kangaamiut, 1900, whereas the Fram Museum kayaks from circa 1888 Nuuk (e.g., plate 42) do have such skegs.

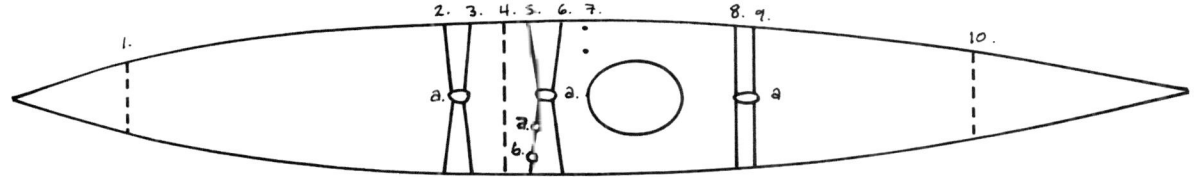

Musée de la Marine, Paris: Cat. no. 1Bs.16

Three deck lines and the harpoon holder are missing from the 1Bs.16, but the remaining deck lines have very elegantly carved fittings on them. The two link pieces just fore and aft of the cockpit have very finely polished raised piping— aesthetically brilliant, but also functional in that they afford a good grip when the hunter needs to adjust them. The two cones on deck line 5 are leaned such they point towards each other; the bow deck line likely had a similar pair of fittings on it as well.

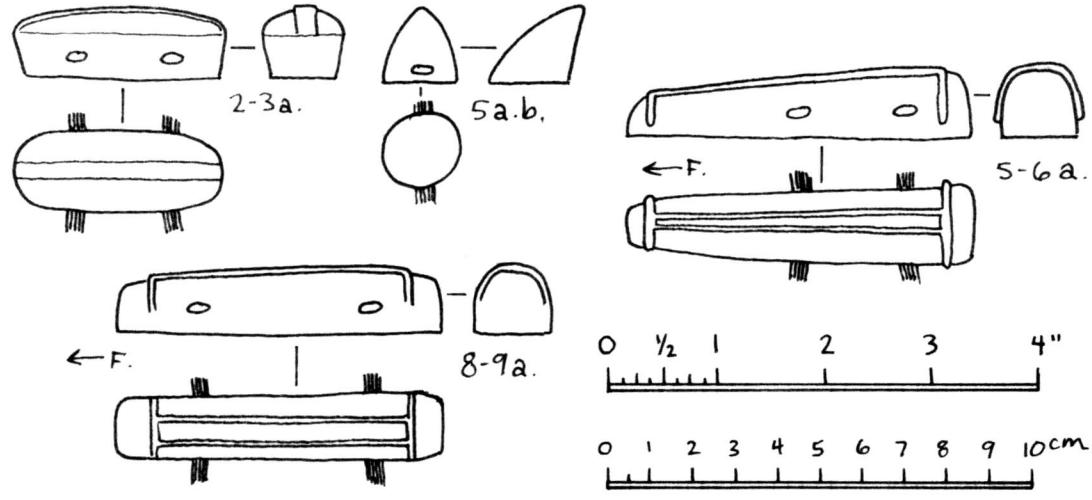

44. West Greenland Kayak from 1900: Musée de la Marine, Paris, France. Catalog no. 1Bs.8.

It is very fortunate to have an uncovered frame of what is more or less the same kayak as the 1Bs.16 (plate 43). It is usually the case that a covered kayak retains its construction details hidden from sight, and a bare frame usually has no hints as to how its deck-fittings were arranged. Same as the Musée's 1Bs.16, the 1Bs.8's inventory card lists this kayak as having been donated by Laurits Hans Christian Bistrup in 1901. This kayak bears the penciled inscription "... af Ulrik Rosing ... Kangâmiut ... 1900."

Further adding to the value of this framework's presentation is H. C. Petersen's descriptions of kayaks and their construction in his *Skinboats of Greenland* and his *Instructions in Kayak Building*. His works, while combining research gleaned from builders in a variety of regions, draws heavily on his observations of a kayak builder in Kangaamiut: David Rosing— likely a relative of Ulrik Rosing (1986:17-41).[36]

The 1Bs.8's chines and keel are lashed to the ribs using a continuous run of twisted cord. The continuity of the lashings is interrupted between the two cockpit ribs. This is also the case in the 1Bs.16, and it was likely done to prevent the seated kayaker from causing the lashings to wear.

As can be seen in the scale drawing of the 1Bs8, several of the deck beams are lashed to the gunwales. Another fastening method is also used: Every deck beam except one is top-peg fastened. Figure 264 depicts a joint with both methods used. With so many kayaks in this study being 'with-*amiq*,' it is impossible— short of X-raying the kayaks— to know to what extent top pegging was used. It can be inferred that it is used in kayaks that exhibit few (if any) lashed or oblique-pegged joints inside. The deck beam mortises in the 1Bs.8 measure 3/16" (5mm) high by 1" (25mm) wide, and have squared corners; they are positioned about 1/2" (13mm) below the gunwales' top edge.

---

[36] Of further interest is the harrowing story by Kangaamiut-born Johannes Rosing (Ataralaa) about his having been blown out to sea in his kayak during a storm over New Year's Eve 1899-1900. This vivid testament to the renowned skill of the kayakers of Kangaamiut has been published in Danish (Rosing, 1991:29-33) and English (Rosing, 2004:103-105).

The 1Bs.8 has a dowel joining each end of the gunwales, as illustrated in figure 265. These dowels are 3/8″ (9mm) diameter, and are locked in place with 1/16″ (1.5mm) diameter pegs set through the gunwale's lower edge. Kaj Birket-Smith mentions such a feature in describing kayaks from Egedesminde District (Aasiaat vicinity), writing that beyond the furthest fore and aft deck beams " . . .the gunwales are tied together, but nowadays there are some who instead of that use a wooden stick" (1924:262). This seems to suggest that the dowels, or "sticks" are new methods: This may be the case for that particular vicinity, but such dowels do appear in considerably earlier kayak examples, notably the E.102 (plate 26) from circa 1789.

Three— maybe four— pieces are missing from this kayak frame: the *masik*, the two forward deck stringers, and likely a piece that spanned the latter two, as seen in the 1Bs.16 (figure 263). The scale lines drawing of the frame depicts the kayak as seen in 2002, while the hull-lines drawing shows a conjecturally restored fore deck, based on the depth overall of the kayak 1Bs.16.

Figure 266 shows the complexly shaped and faceted second curved deck beam with the cockpit beyond. Note the two peg-holes for attaching the missing *masik* behind the starboard end of the curved deck beam. Also note the notches cut to receive the deck stringers, the deck line holes along the sheer, and the lashings for ribs and deck beams. Scale drawings of the 1Bs.8's curved deck beams are presented in figure 41.

H. C. Petersen writes that "In Maniitsoq— Kangaamiut there are no ribs under the cockpit, but the ribs under the kayaker's legs are closer together" citing comfort and ease of entry as reasons (1986:25). This is very much the case with the 1Bs.8 as well as with the 1Bs.16. Numerous other kayaks in this

Figure 264: Construction detail of the Musée de la Marine's 1BS.8 showing a deck beam-to-gunwale joint and a chine-to-rib joint. Note the top-peg securing the deck beam's tenon in the gunwale.

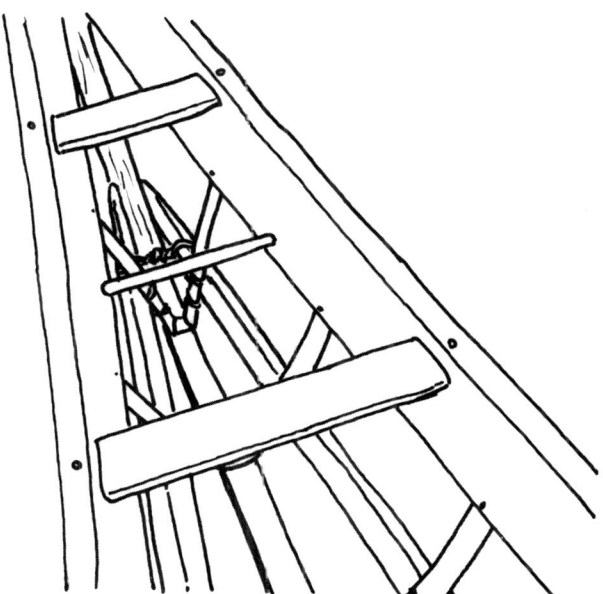

Figure 265: Chine ends at the bow of the 1Bs.8. Also note the dowel crosspiece between the gunwales and the kerf-bent rib.

study exhibit this characteristic as well: the Canadian Canoe Museum's 977.180 (plate 38), the Musée de la Marine's 1.Bs.24 (plate 53), and the Greenland National Museum's KNK 2050 (plate 49), among others.

The deck line positions of the 1Bs.8 are indicated on the hull-lines drawing (plate 44b). Evidence of a harpoon holder was not noted on account of the missing *masik*, to which it would have been anchored. The 1Bs.8's rigging can be presumed to have been identical to that of the 1Bs.16 (plate 43).

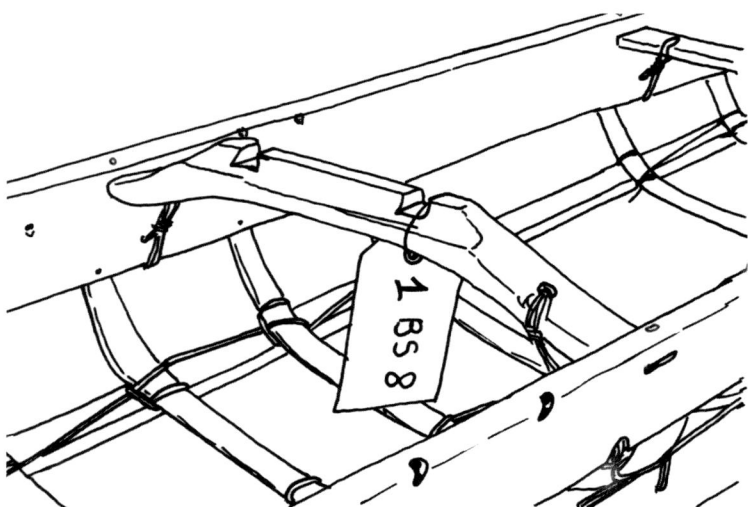

Figure 266: Curved deck beam in the 1Bs.8. The deck stringers are missing; two peg holes on the far gunwale indicate the position of the missing masik.

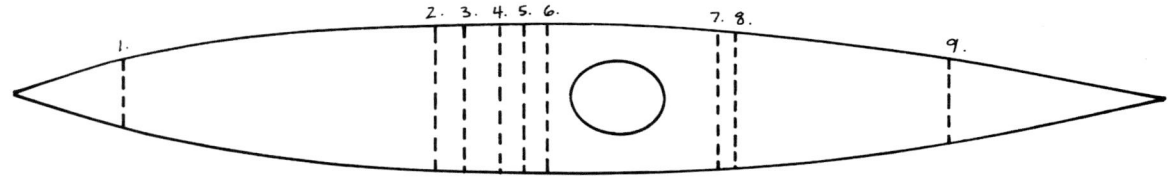

Musée de la Marine, Paris: Cat. no. 1Bs.8

45. West Greenland Kayak: Michigan State University Museum, East Lansing. Catalog no. 4274cw.

While presently at the Michigan State University Museum, this kayak was originally donated to the Chamberlain Memorial Museum in Three Oaks, Michigan. It arrived there in 1928, having been donated by Commander Eugene F. McDonald, president of the Zenith Radio Corporation. In a letter dated Nov. 27, 1928, McDonald writes: "This model that I am sending to you is one of the best models I have ever seen in Greenland... (It) is the model used in the middle Greenland Coast" (letter, MSU Archives). Eugene McDonald was second in command of the MacMillan Arctic Expedition of 1925, and commanded the steamship *Peary*, carrying the Navy Arctic Unit (commanded by Lt.Cmdr. Byrd) and its three airplanes (MacMillan, 1925:482).

For some reason, this kayak acquired a provenance of "North Greenland" that persists from the Chamberlain Memorial Museum's Receipt Blank right up to its transfer to the MSU in 1952. McDonald's letter runs contrary to the "North" suggestion, as does the appearance and construction of the kayak itself.

This kayak is a classic example of the 'curved kayak,' or *pequngasoq* described by H.C. Petersen in his *Skinboats of Greenland*:

> Following the lines in this type along the top of the sheer boards the kayak is almost straight at the middle. Only fore of the foot support do the lines begin to go up, rising a bit more farther forward. The straight line continues aft of the cockpit and only rises a bit at the end. The line of the keel is sinuous, convex for its first half, and the height of the ribs increases from the cockpit to the foot support, becoming lower father forward. Aft of the cockpit the bottom of the kayak is concave. It is narrowest about one foot from the end of the keel and the beginning of the stem and stern. For the last part of the keel the ribs are higher and therefore bulge out at this point (1986:48).

("Stem and stern" would read 'bow and stern stems' by my terminology, or just 'stems.') Petersen adds, "The curved type is the deepest of all Greenland kayaks. Its overall length and the length of the stem and stern are average" (1986:49).

Petersen goes on to ascribe vicinities where its form is more extreme as well as a broader locale where this kayak could be found.

> This type is only found in the area between Sisimiut and Maniitsoq. Where this kayak has spread to other areas the profile of the keel has become less sinuous and may even be concave for the whole of its length . . . It is found between the coast from Paamiut to Sisimiut, where kayaks are used all year round (1986:49).

The attribution of this form to the first regions Petersen cites places this kayak firmly in the central West Coast— the "middle" that Commander McDonald stated in his letter. Comparisons with the CMC IV-A-483 (plate 46), a kayak unquestionably from Sisimiut, furthers my thinking that the MSU kayak also hails from there.

The MSU 4274cw exhibits hull collapse from about 8′ (243.8cm) to 13′ (396.2cm) from the bow. The artifactual keel-line is depicted in the scale elevation by a dotted line, the solid keel line being my conjectural restoration. Comparisons to the Fram Museum's 176 (plate 42), the Greenland National Museum's KNK 2050 (plate 49), and especially the CMC-IV-A-483 (plate 46) show very similar forms.

A cockpit-view of the 4274 is shown in figure 267. Note the coaming scarf protection pieces and the continuous deck lines with numerous turns of slack hitched around the ribs. The block of wood attached to the starboard gunwale's inside face is a repair piece used to re-enforce the gunwale.

Several of the 4274's deck beams are lashed to the gunwales with twine. All of the ribs are metal-nailed to the chines, gunwales, and keelson. The rib-to-gunwale joints had been nailed from the outside, the points being simply bent-over on the inside. The forward cockpit rib (centered

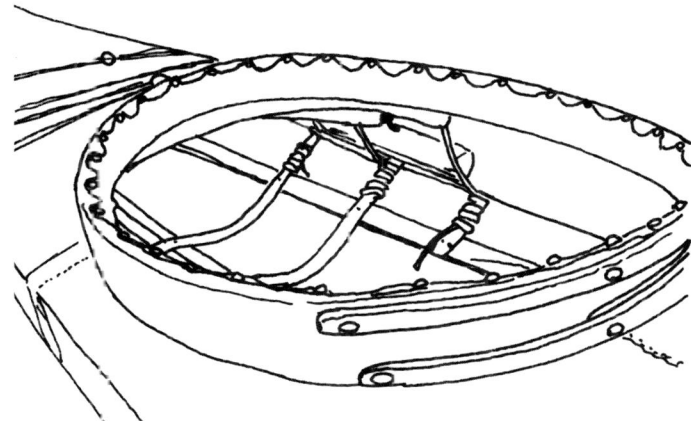

Figure 267: Cockpit view of the MSU 4274cw. Note the hitched-off deck lines on ribs below and ahead of the masik. A block has been nailed to the gunwale in this same vicinity—likely to re-enforce a weak spot.

at 8′ 9-7/16″ [267.8cm] from zero) is a partial rib, extending from the gunwales to the chines. This was likely a modification as a nail hole was present in the keelson adjacent this position. The MSU 4274's *masik* measures 5/8″ (16mm) thick by 3-1/8″ (80mm) wide; the *isserfik* is 5/8″ (16mm) thick and 2-13/16″ wide. The forward deck stringers are 5/8″ (16mm) square at their aft terminus; the aft deck stringers are 5/8″ (16mm) thick and 2″ (51mm) wide.

A fracture in the keelson has been repaired with a bone splint twine-wrapped to the keelson's top face. This fracture is due to the keelson being shaved down to 9/16" (14mm) high (from 1" [25mm]) and the coincidence of a knot being present at this position. Such shaving appears in some kayaks and was likely done for comfort, but also would result in a slightly lower center of gravity. The chines are similarly shaved down as well, the inner/upper corner being worked down a bit. These hollows are about 7" (17.8cm) long and are centered between the two cockpit ribs.

A particularly interesting modification has been done to this kayak, one that wasn't immediately apparent. I looked inside the cockpit and noted considerable gunwale flare, and while measuring the heights, noted the lower edge of the gunwale protruding. Usually one of these features would preclude the other, and upon closer examination, the thickness of each gunwale's lower edge had been doubled by means of a 5/8" (16mm) thick strip attached to the gunwales' lower face. The forward lower corners of these two strips (one on each side) had become points of wear, and holes in the *amiq* were present. The aft end could also be felt through the *amiq*; these strips run from 5' 9" (175.3cm) to 11' 2" (340.3cm). This unique feature is essentially a second pair of chines— instead of being fastened to the ribs, they are attached to the gunwales.

The purpose of this strip is assumed to be a means of adding volume and/or stability, as it effectively widens the kayak's beam in the vicinity of its waterline. This method preserves the kayak's original sheer (achieved through the considerable gunwale flare), and increases stability and volume, all without widening the kayak as a whole.

The coaming on the MSU kayak measures 5/8" (16mm) thick by 1-11/16" (43mm) high, and has two parallel bone strips on its back face. The upper strip is 14-5/8" (37.1cm) long, and the lower is 13-7/8" (35.2cm) long; both are fastened with metal nails.

The MSU 4274 has keel edging at the bow and the stern. This edging is 3/8" (9mm) high and 1/2" (13mm) wide, and is fastened with bone or ivory nails. The forward portion of the stern edging has six holes drilled transversely through it; these are likely for lashing a skeg to the kayak. The holes are positioned 2-1/4", 4-1/2", 6-5/8", 9-1/4", 12-1/4", and 13-3/4" (5.7, 11.4, 16.8, 23.5, 31.1, and 34.9cm) behind the stern edging's forward end.

The bow knob of the 4274 is missing, but the stern knob is intact and in place. Its form is very unusual in that its tip does not come to a point but instead narrows greatly and then widens into a ball-shaped terminus, as in figure 131b. The form of this knob calls to mind Petersen's quote about knobs being end-fastened with buttons (see page 90), but this example is a single solid piece, being attached with a top-peg.

The fittings on the kayak 4274 are elegantly made, though simple. The two link pieces on the fore deck have 'pitched roofs' as it were, and their pointed ends face aft. The top-view of piece 5-6a shows the head of a nail, set flush with the top of the piece— its purpose is unknown, and it does not appear to be a repair. The harpoon holder is fashioned from a hollow section of walrus tusk, and while it is only 1-7/8" (48mm) long, it is attached to a 4-1/8" (10.5cm) long deck line. The MSU kayak's paddle is depicted in paddle-plate 31.

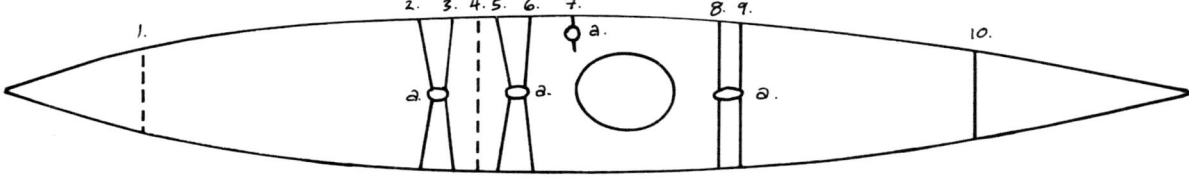

Michigan State University Museum, Lansing: Cat. no. 4272cw

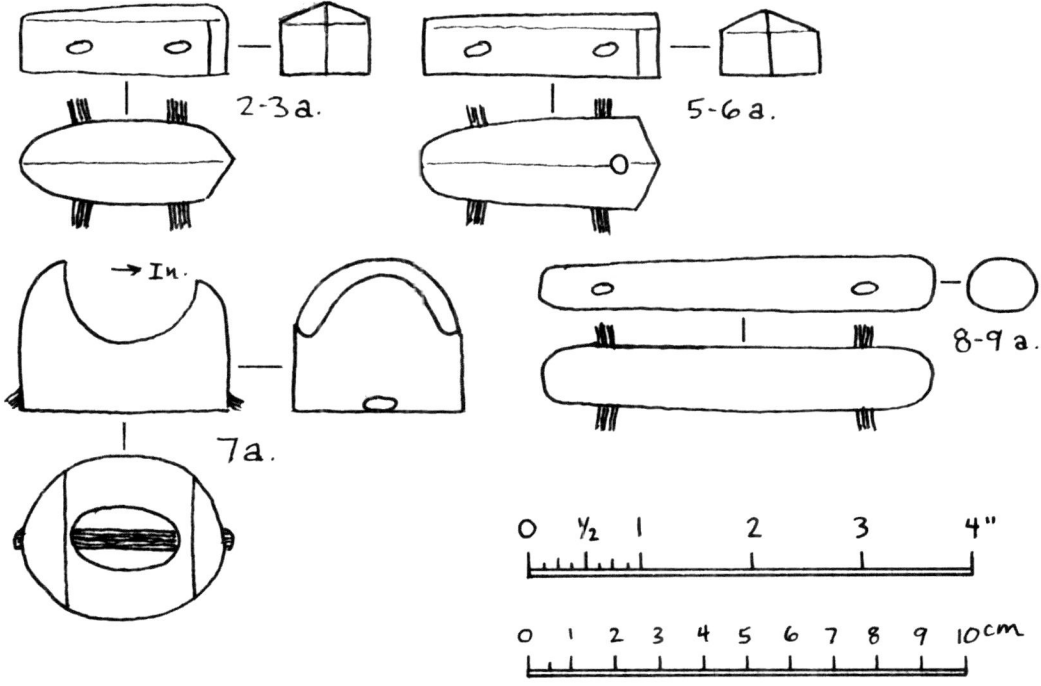

46. West Greenland Kayak: Canadian Museum of Civilization, Ottawa. Catalog no. IV-A-483

The Canadian Museum of Civilization accession card lists this kayak as having been collected by Dr. Max Dunbar in the Holsteinsberg (Sisimiut) District in 1935. Further, the kayak was "probably made at least twenty years before that." This is a curious statement— did the kayak sit completed and covered for twenty years before being collected? Or was the skeleton in use during the twenty years, being re-covered as needed? This brings up the question of 'how old is a kayak, anyways?' considering that pieces are replaced and recycled over the years. The CMC received the kayak in 1975.

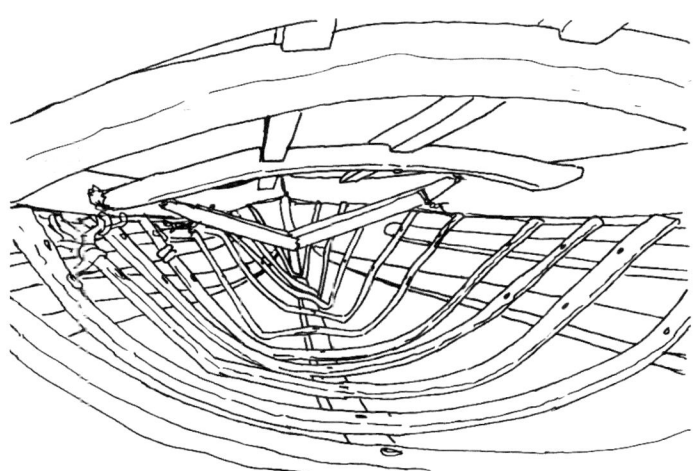

Figure 263: Forward interior view of the IV-A-483. One deck beam has buckled due to the shrinking skin. The bottom has held its shape surprisingly well forward of the cockpit. Note the fact that there are four chines in this kayak, as opposed to the usual two.

The most interesting element regarding this kayak is that it is multi-chined. Unlike other multi-chined kayaks in this study (i.e., KNK 1161 [plate 9], and the KNK 2237 [plate 66]), the 'second' chines in the 483 are very long, spanning 8′3″ (251.5cm) of the kayak's length.

Kayak historian John Heath documented a kayak similar to the 483 in an un-published survey drawing; the kayak is at the Missouri State Historical Society (catalog no. 1934.24.47). This kayak is known to be from Sisimiut, having been purchased there by Charles A. Lindbergh in 1933 during his Atlantic air-route survey flight in the *Sirius* with Anne Morrow Lindbergh (Lindbergh, 1974:70).

That the IV-A-483 is attributed to Sisimiut strongly suggests that the MSU 4274cw (plate 45) is from the same vicinity, on account of their very similar forms. This is further suggested by the 'Lindbergh' kayak's origin from the same vicinity. While all three of these kayaks do figure in my "type V" category, they form a fairly distinct sub-type with their multi-chine construction, deep ends, and sinuous keel lines. (The MSU 4274cw might not be considered a multi-chine kayak, but in a sense it is, simply having the extra chine between the gunwales' lower edge and the skin instead of it being between the ribs and the skin.)

Figure 268 shows the forward interior of the IV-A-483. The deck beams are intermittently lashed with twine. All four chines are nailed to the ribs with what appear to be roofing nails with 3/8″ (9mm) diameter heads. The ribs are nailed through their tenons to the gunwales.

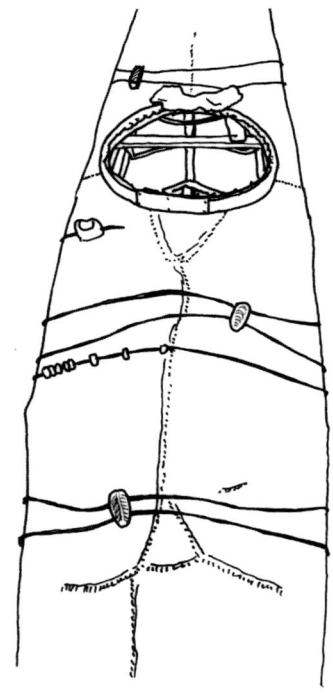

Figure 269: The fore deck of the CMC's kayak IV-A-483. Note the bone plate set into the coaming's forward face and the cloth padding on the coaming's back.

The IV-A-483's coaming measures 9/16″ (14mm) thick by 1-3/8″ (35mm) high, and it has two bone strips fastened to its backside. The upper strip is 13-1/2″ (34.3cm) long, and the lower is 11″ (28.0cm) long; both strips are 3/16″ (5mm) thick by 3/8″ (9mm) wide. A bone plate is set into the coaming's front face. This plate measures 5-7/8″ (14.9cm) long, 1-3/8″ (35mm) high and 1/8″ (3mm) thick, and is fastened to the coaming with six nails. At the back of the coaming, a square patch of cloth has been nailed to the inside face. Its purpose may be padding, but it is just a thin piece of cloth; perhaps it used to have stuffing sewn into it.

Some of the deck fittings on the 483 are incredible works of art— one appears as if it were a fossilized trilobite cast in ivory. Deck line four, however, has eight crudely shaped chunks of ivory— their only curves merely being from the shape of the walrus tusks they were cut from.

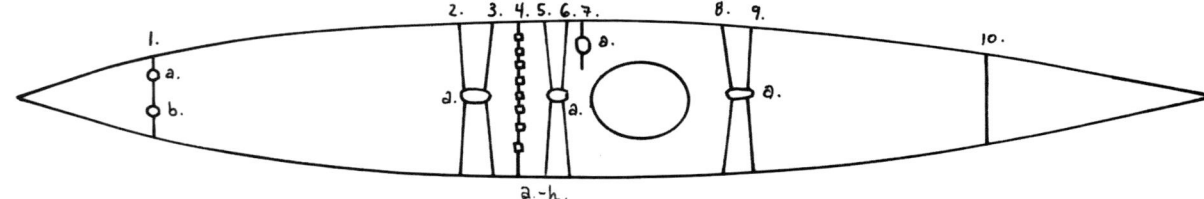

Canadian Museum of Civilization: Cat. no. IV-A-483

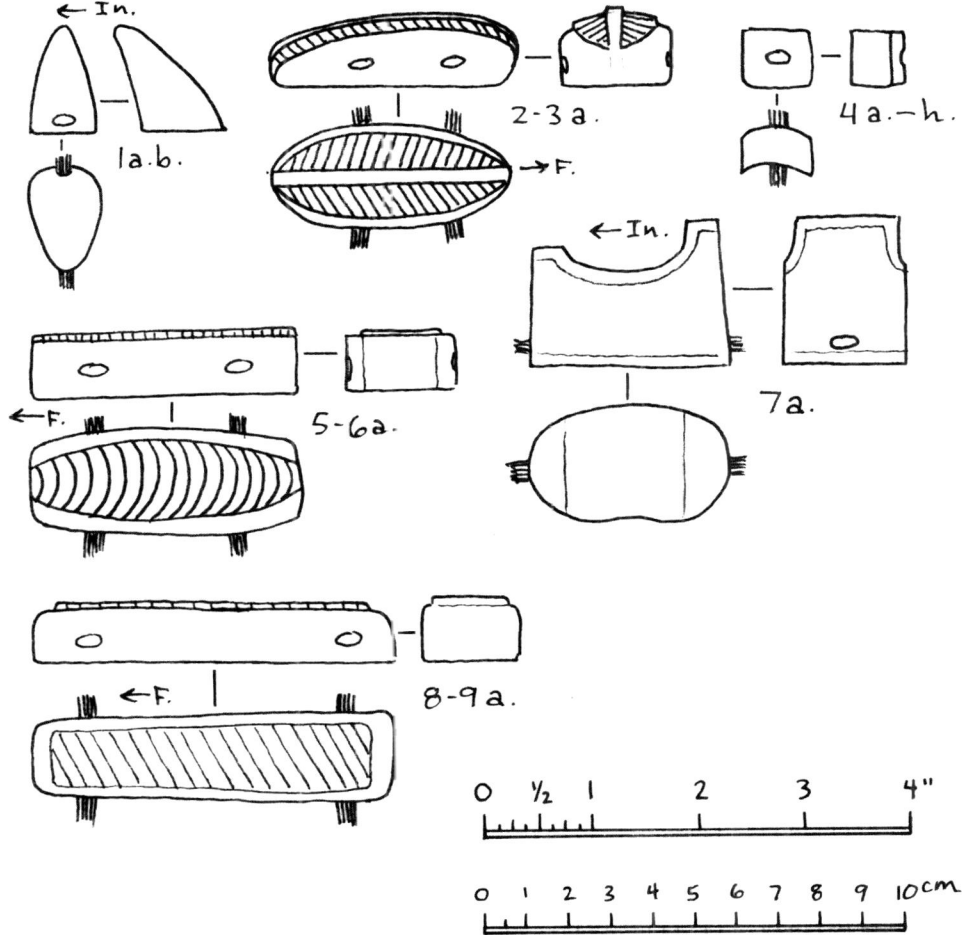

As with the kayak 4274cw described previously, the harpoon holder is fashioned from a section of walrus tusk, although the appearance is quite different, being solid and less sharp at the crests. The length of the harpoon holder is 1-7/8″ (48mm) long, but the strap it is attached to is 5-5/8″ (14.3cm) long. The IV-A-483's paddle is depicted in paddle-plate 39.

47. West Greenland Kayak: Museon, Den Haag, the Netherlands. Catalog no. 117798.

The Museon purchased this child's kayak in 1998 from an Inuit art gallery in Denmark. Dr. Corine Bliek of the Museon responded to my inquiry regarding the kayak's history:

According to the gallery owner where this kayak was bought, the kayak was made around 1930 [by] order of Knud Rasmussen. He had this kayak made as a present for the 6 year old son of one of his crew members... For a long time the kayak was in the possession of the family until a distant relative of the boy brought it to an auction (2002, personal correspondence)

The kayak is of a very simple form and construct, and seemingly wide (at 16"; 40.6mm) for a child's kayak; perhaps it was made wider on account of it going to a non-Greenlander. It has a single deck stringer ahead of and behind the cockpit. The coaming itself is made of 1/8" (3mm) thick plywood, 13/16" (21mm) high, and is sewn on; the coaming may have been added later or may be a replacement.

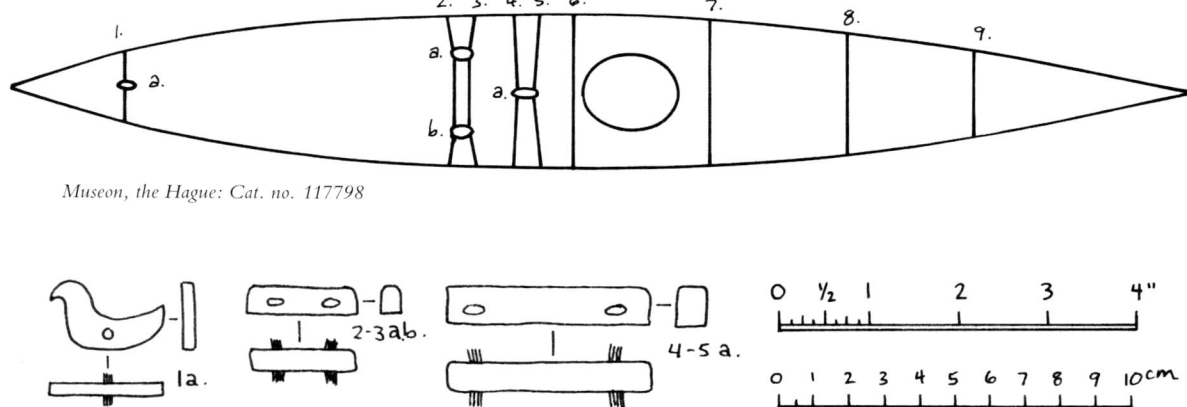

Museon, the Hague: Cat. no. 117798

The ribs of the 117798 are not mortised into the gunwales, and are instead double-nailed to the inboard faces of the gunwales. This method is more commonly used in repairs than actual construction— see figure 164. No keel edging or end-knobs are evidenced. The covering of the 117798 is a black-painted muslin— it appears rather baggy, and probably is not original.

An ivory bird-figure is placed on the foremost deck line, the usual cones being absent. The deck lines just ahead of the cockpit are also of a unique arrangement: a single unlinked strap being placed right at the coaming's forward edge. Three bare deck lines span the 117798's aft deck, the middle one likely used as an anchor-point for outriggers. A paddle is associated with this kayak, and is phenomenally well made, leaving me to think the kayak had been re-skinned with less care than the original builder would have allowed; the paddle is depicted in paddle-plate 48.

48. West Greenland Kayak: Canadian Museum of Civilization, Ottawa. Catalog no. IV-A-447

The only useful information on the accession card with regards to this kayak's history is its date received of 1953, and the note that it was "found under a verandah." F. Green is listed as the collector, although if the extent of the kayak's recorded history is having been found beneath a porch, Green was perhaps just the donor.

The 447 is not in very good condition: Its hull has collapsed considerably between the cockpit and the bow. The artifactual depth-to-sheer at the 447's *masik* is 5-3/8" (13.6cm), but I have conjecturally restored this to 6-5/8" (16.8cm).

The ends are damaged a little, exposing a bit of their structure. Interestingly, the gunwales at the bow do not meet up to a stem piece and terminate. Instead, the gunwales carry on right up to the kayak's tip, as is the case with several old (17th-18th century) kayaks. The stern exhibits more damage, but does in fact end with a stem piece, the gunwales terminating 4-3/4″ (12.0cm) behind the end. A cap piece is evidenced as having been fitted at the stern, but is now missing; I would estimate that about an inch of the stern is missing.

A repair to the keelson is present inside the cockpit: The keelson is splinted on the sides and the top (between the two ribs in the cockpit); splinting is a common method of repairing keel or chine fractures. All of the ribs are nailed through their tenons to the gunwales. The chines and keelson are both nailed and lashed with twine to the ribs. The deck beams are lashed intermittently to the gunwales, and at the gunwales' ends, clamping ties are present— also of twine.

The keel edging astern has two divots carved in its upper face (adjacent to the kayak's keel) at 14′ and 14′6″ (426.7 and 441.9cm) from the bow. These are lashing points for an external skeg, as in figure 134b; the skeg is missing. The keel edging measures 5/16″ (8mm) thick by 3/8″ (9mm) wide.

The 447's coaming measures 7/16″ (11mm) thick by 1-3/16″ (30mm) high. The two bone strips attached to the coaming's aft face are secured with square-cut bone nails whose heads measure 1/8″ by 1/4″ (3 x 6mm). The edging measures 1/8″ (3mm) thick by 3/8″ (9mm). The coaming's scarf is a stepped edge-scarf (as in figure 116i), but instead of having birds-mouth ends, it has a unique 'key' set into its upper edge to prevent splaying, as in figure 117.

For such a damaged kayak, it is very remarkable that all of the deck lines and fittings were intact— such elements seem to be the first to go missing. The bow and stern deck lines are slack and without fittings, and the harpoon holder is of a simple tab-shape. Aside from the harpoon holder, there are only two other deck fittings— both link pieces on the fore deck.

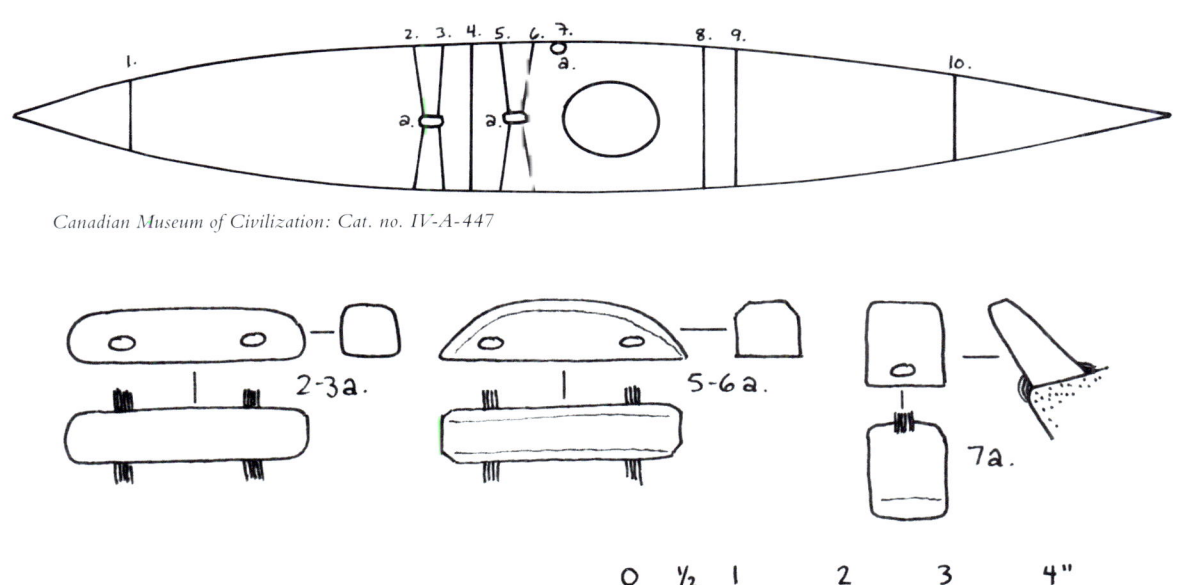

Canadian Museum of Civilization: Cat. no. IV-A-447

49. West Greenland Kayak: Greenland National Museum, Nuuk. Catalog no. KNK 2050.

Nothing of the KNK 2050's history has been recorded in the Greenland National Museum catalogs; in fact the accession file for 2050 says it is an umiak from Upernavik— clearly a mix up with the umiak KNK 2005. The 2050 was likely a local kayak— hailing from the greater Nuuk vicinity.

The KNK 2050's bow is very high and deep. The stern is more subdued in form, but has a very distinct integral skeg. Both stems are slightly more 'clipper-cut' than those of the MSU 4274cw and the CMC IV-A-483 (plates 45 and 46). Unlike these two kayaks, the KNK 2050 does not have a second chine, nor does its lower gunwale edge protrude into the *amiq*.

A beam of 19-1/4″ (48.9cm) is given on the scale drawing for the KNK 2050, but the widest part of the kayak is 19-3/4″ (50.2cm) — where the *masik* extends beyond the sheer line. Having a *masik* longer than a kayak is wide is an occasional occurrence with West Greenland kayaks; other examples can be found among the type V and VI kayaks in this study.

Petersen's description of the *pequngasoq* kayak, or 'curved' kayak, does describe the KNK 2050's form, though Petersen suggests the form is somewhat diluted outside of Sisimiut-Maniitsoq vicinities: "Where this kayak has spread to other areas the profile of the keel has become less sinuous and may even be concave for the whole of its length" (1986:49).

The KNK 2050 has an external skeg affixed to the stern keel edging. This method of attachment is depicted in figure 132d. What is particularly unusual is that this kayak also has an integral skeg— one that is inside the *amiq* (as in figure 134b).

An interesting feature of the seal skin-covered 2050 is the fact that it had been painted. The entire hull is painted a pale gray, as are the ends of the decks and the seams. While in Nuuk, Greenland, I saw

Figure 270: Frederik Balle in a kayak off Nuuk, ca. 1910. (Photograph by John Møller/Copyright: Greenland National Museum and Archive.)

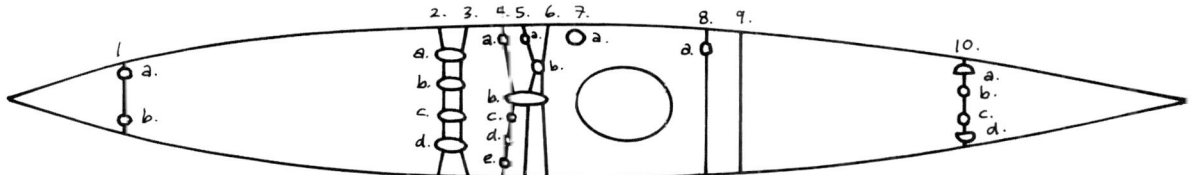

Greenland National Museum: Cat. no. 2050

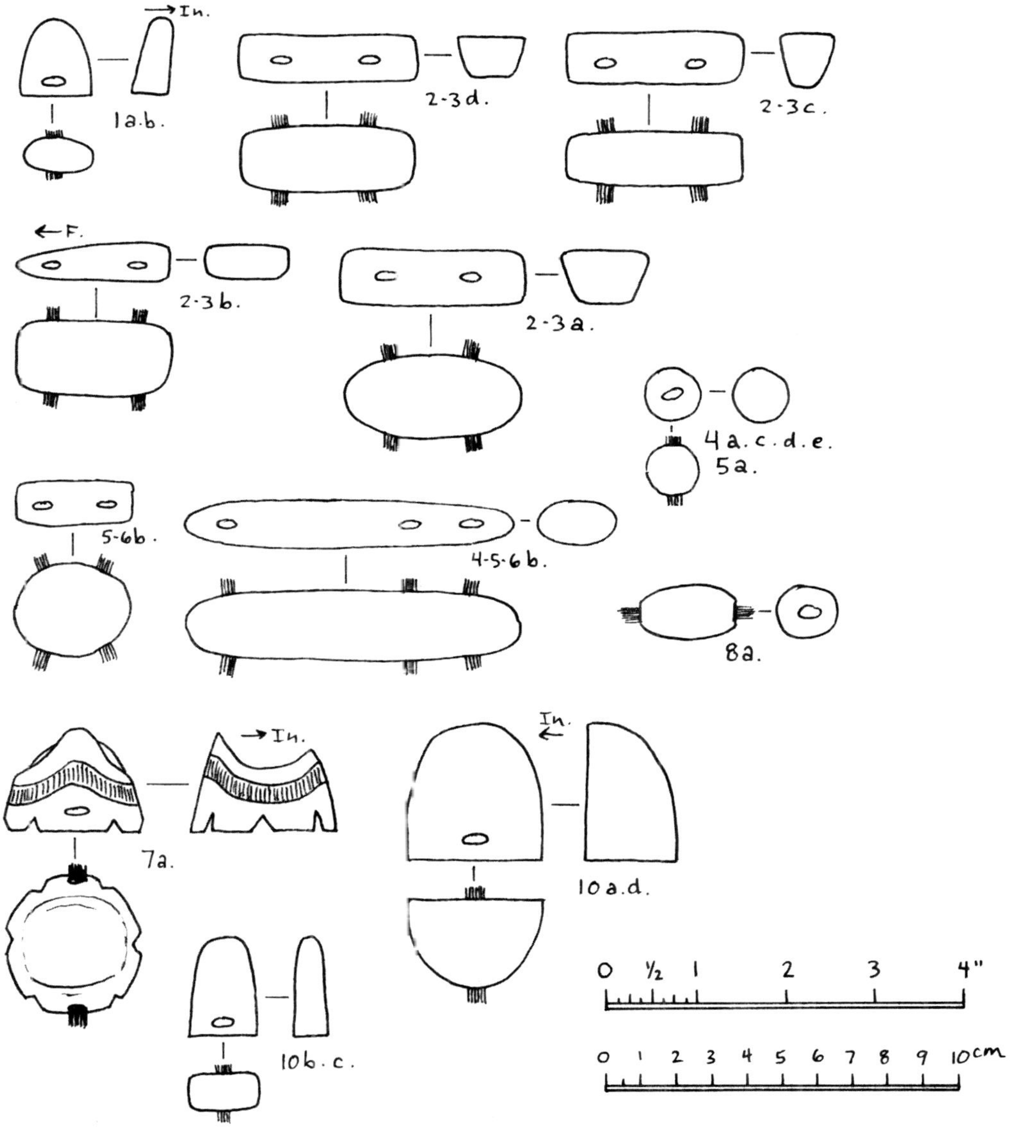

many painted kayaks— most of them entirely painted on account of being covered with canvas or nylon. I was struck with the tonal-range of neutral colors— from black to white, and many shades of gray in between. I was surprised to see that black kayaks were every bit as camouflaged as the white ones when the wind was producing whitecaps. The gray kayaks were nearly invisible as well.

The deck lines and fittings on the KNK 2050 are fairly sophisticated and ornate. Their layout bears close resemblance to the existing deck lines on the Fram Museum's kayak 65 from Nuuk. One of the deck fittings on the fore deck is a large flat disc made from a cross-section of ivory tusk. The harpoon holder on this kayak is unique and well made: It is a large and moderately high, truncated cylinder— appearing much as a stump. It is ornately carved with a band of grooves circumscribing the rim, and 'pinks' circumscribing the base. The harpoon holder is attached to a 5-1/8" (13.0cm) long deck line.

I built a replica of the KNK 2050 in 2005, five years after surveying the original. While it had always appealed to me, I did not see it as unique, old, extreme, or immediately compelling, hence the delay in building a replica. It is of course a beautiful kayak with interesting lines and a comfortable and manageable size.

My first time in this replica was on a small lake, and my initial reaction was very positive although it felt much tippier than I had expected. I got used to this fairly quickly and was in short time able to let go of the paddle without fear of a dunking. It likely felt tippy on account of my light weight and the kayak's deep hull and narrow bottom; the high ends and deep hull set a fair amount of weight up high. I estimate the waterline breadth to have been about 16-1/2" (39.6cm) wide or so with my 130 pounds in it.

The integral skeg is one of more unique features of this kayak— as is its external skeg in addition (I omitted the external skeg, although I plan to install it later for comparisons). I distinctly felt the extra grip aft afforded by this feature; the replica turned well enough, but simply felt a bit stiffer than most other Greenland kayak replicas. Likewise, the 2050 replica was less inclined to swerve to a gliding stop— undoubtedly the reason behind it (i.e., good directional stability when one has set down the paddle and picked up a rifle).

Figure 271: The KNK 2050 replica in the Pacific Ocean off Cape Falcon, Oregon, 2005. (Photograph by Brian Schulz.)

For a second voyage, I took the replica to the coast to feel it out in surf and swells. As anticipated, the bow's great height and volume provides good resistance to submerging, especially when I landed the kayak through 5' surf. In the case of surf paddling, this resistance to submerging translates into safer, more controlled landings as it lessens the chance of broaching or pitch-poling (flipping end-over-end).

50. West Greenland Kayak: Peqatigiiffik Qajaq Nuuk (P.Q.N.)
Property of Nuuk Kayak Club
(N/N) "PQN"

The history of this kayak was not specifically known by anyone whom I asked, though Peqatigiiffik Qajaq Nuuk (PQN) secretary Hans Kleist-Thomassen suggested it might date from the 1950s. It is likely a type from Nuuk vicinity, and is clearly a *pequngasoq*, ("curved kayak") based on its sinuous keel and moderate sheer. The PQN frame hangs inside of the clubhouse in the historic colonial harbor of Nuuk.

The PQN kayak is nearly identical to the KNK 2050 above, and they are practically the same size, though the PQN has a longer and more elegant stern. The PQN, being just a skeleton, serves to not only show how the KNK 2050's joinery might appear, but is also a fine looking craft in itself.

Heavy-gauged fishing line lashings are used throughout the PQN, although some of the joints are a bit loose. The PQN kayak exhibits a variety of ways that the deck beams are joined to the gunwales: Most of the beams are lashed to the gunwales, but two deck beams exhibit the oblique pegging method. One of these beams is missing, but the other is intact; the pegs do not go all the way through the gunwales, and therefore must have been fitted from above, i.e., through the deck beam and then into the gunwale. One other deck beam and four ribs are missing although the fore and aft-most deck-beam mortises

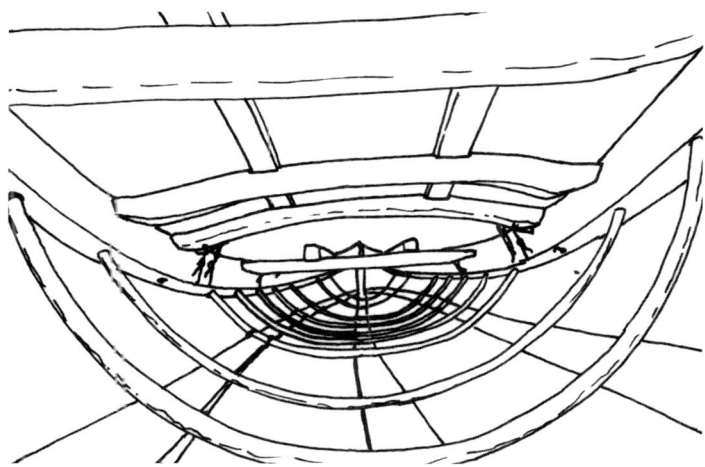

Figure 272: An interior view of the 'PQN,' looking aft towards the cockpit from the bow. In this view, the masik is entirely obscured by the second curved deck beam, although its lashings are visible.

and the fore-most rib mortise were likely never used. The deck beam mortises measure 1/4" (6mm) high by 13/16" (20mm) long, and have rounded sides.

The ribs in the PQN are pegged through their tenons to the gunwales, though several have recently been glued in place with polyurethane glue. The keelson of the PQN is made from two pieces, the scarf being of a simple stepped form. Where the wide keelson end's top-edge meets the gunwales, there is a 'key' block, as in figure 61. The keelson does not hook onto the gunwales at either end, as is the case with the KNK "C" (plate 51). At the forward keelson-to-gunwale joint, a shim is set atop the keel-end to build up extra height. The chine ends (both bow and stern) are tied to each other; the bow chine ends are nailed to the keelson end as well.

An interesting thing to note about the PQN is its *isserfik* and its placement: It is mortised and tenoned in place, but the mortises do not go all the way through. The *isserfik* is also about 3/8″ (9mm) lower than the deck-beam behind it. It is likely that it was added as a modification; the beam presently behind the *isserfik* was likely the *isserfik* at one time. The obvious result of this is a much shorter cockpit opening— only 13-1/4″ (33.6cm) long.

A hull-lines scale drawing accompanies the scale drawing of the PQN frame; the coaming is rendered conjecturally, based on the size of the cockpit, as a coaming was not with the PQN. This drawing exposes a fine looking kayak with long slender ends, and a concave stern. Deck line positions are indicated in the drawing, but their original appearance is unknown but may have resembled the KNK 2050's somewhat.

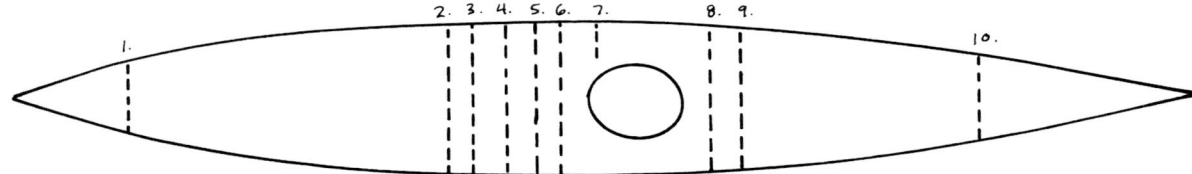

Peqatigiffik Qajaq Nuuk: (n/n) "PQN"

I made a replica of the PQN in 2001. The gunwales required a considerable amount of shaping so as to achieve the sheer shape; risers had to added to the upper ends of the gunwales to achieve the proper height.

The PQN replica felt very buoyant compared to most of the other replicas I had made. In retrospect this could have been expected as I was paddling it without any hunting equipment on-deck. The original PQN was undoubtedly made to carry one or two rifles among the typical assortment of hand-cast projectiles and associated equipment; such a fore deck load could weigh at least 30 pounds or so.

Figure 273: Greg Stamer in the PQN replica, Hood Canal, Washington, 2001. (Photograph by the author).

51. West Greenland Kayak: Greenland National Museum, Nuuk. Catalog no. KNK 'C'

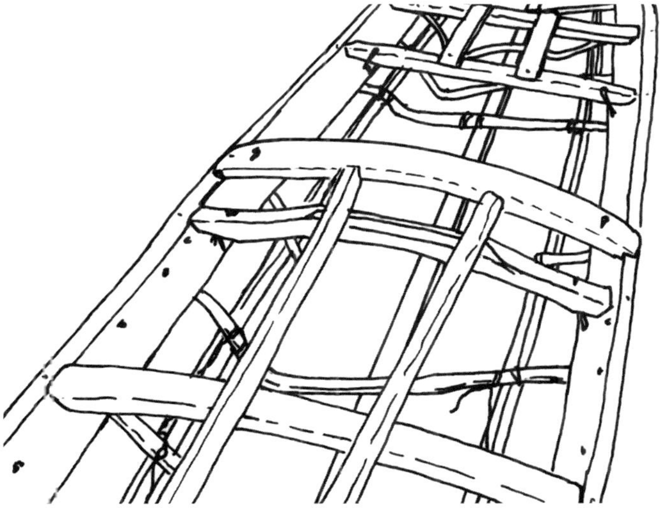

The Greenland National Museum's kayak 'C' is fairly intact, though very damaged. The profile and plan both look quite nice, but upon closer observation, severe hull collapse and shifting is evident— The hull cross-sections show this most plainly (full forward and full aft section-views are depicted). No provenance data is linked to this kayak, and in fact 'C,' as a catalog number, may simply represent an artifact separated from its accession information.

Figure 274 shows the deck of the 'C.' Note the curved deck beam shapes: The forward beam is a simple form, while the aft curved deck beam has a facet on the upper forward face that functions as a hand-grip for lifting and carrying. The deformation of the ribs is also plain to see.

Figure 274: The foredeck of the Greenland National Museum's kayak 'C,' also showing the deformed ribs.

Four pairs of rib mortises are empty, though the foremost pair was likely never used. All ribs are pinned to the gunwales with 1/8" to 3/16" (3-5mm) diameter pegs. The chines and keelson are lashed to the ribs, though three ribs (one of which is missing) also show evidence of having been double-nailed to the chines and keelson. These ribs are the three nearest the *masik*; the rib just behind the *masik* is a half-rib.

All of the 'C's' deck beams are top-pegged to the gunwales (as in figure 37d) except for the last two. The deck beam mortises measure 5/16" (8mm) high by 1-1/8" (28mm) long, and their upper edge is generally 3/8" (9mm) below the gunwale's top edge. The scale drawing shows the positions of oblique pegs that are also used to secure the deck beams to the gunwales: All of these pegs have been sawn-off flush with the gunwales, and there is no evidence of their having been set through the deck beams. This is of course evidence of the gunwales having been used before, as the deck beams in the present incarnation are lashed and/or top-pegged.

The keelson of the 'C' is made of one piece of wood, no scarfs being present. Small trapezoidal blocks 'key' the keelson's ends to the gunwales ends. Further, the keelson's ends are also hooked onto the gunwales as well as lashed in place. The chines are slightly hollowed out on their top surface— a somewhat rare feature in Greenland kayaks. Figure 275 shows the bottom of the KNK 'C.' The chine ends, both bow and stern, are nailed to the keelson end boards and are tied to each other, the lashing passing through the keelson ends.

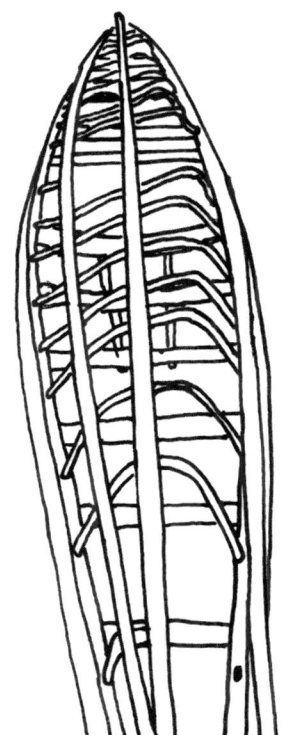

Figure 275: The bottom of the Greenland National Museum's kayak 'C.'

No deck lines were present on this frame, but their placement holes were evident and it could be accurate to presume they were rigged similarly to those of the KNK 2050 (plate 49), as these two kayaks greatly resemble each other and are likely contemporaries from the same vicinity.

The hull-lines drawing depicts the 'C' as it may have looked with its *amiq* and *paa* in place. It is not only a presentation of outside-lines, but is also a conjectural restoration based on the artifact, and comparisons with similar kayaks, e.g., the KNK 2050 and the PQN's kayak (plate 49 and 50).

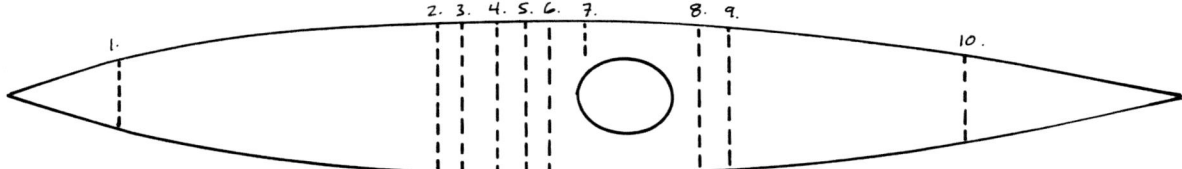

Greenland National Museum: (n/n) "C"

52. West Greenland Kayak: Greenland National Museum, Nuuk.
Catalog no. KNK 2056

This kayak greatly resembles the KNK 2050 and the PQN kayak in form, though this example is canvas covered and has just a few bare straps as deck-lines. The canvas is painted khaki, and the original color of the canvas was olive drab. The canvas has been tacked along the gunwales, as well as sewn down the center of the deck; the canvas is full-length so there are no transverse seams. This kayak is very well made and quite shapely. No accession data was present for the 2056 in the Greenland National Museum's card catalog.

The chines are lashed to the 2056's ribs, using the double-pass method with an alternating straight pattern. The keelson is nailed to the ribs. This kayak's *masik* is lashed to the gunwales via the method depicted in figure 77a, the joint-shape being like that in figure 76b. Two deck beams forward and two aft of the cockpit are oblique pegged. The chines are lashed together at each end, and may or may not be nailed to the keelson ends as well. Clamp ties are present at both ends of the gunwales; all of the lashings are natural fiber— perhaps jute.

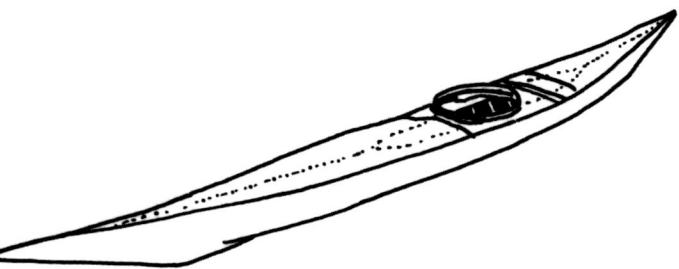

Figure 276: The Greenland National Museum's kayak 2056. The stern is at the left foreground.

Some of the scantlings not shown on the scale drawing are as follows: The coaming is 1/2" (13mm) thick by 1-3/8" (35mm) high; the *masik* is 3-1/2" (8.9cm) wide and 5/8" (16mm) thick in the middle. The forward deck stringers are 3/4" (19mm) square at their aft-end; the aft deck stringers are 1/2" (13mm) thick by 1-1/4" (32mm) wide. The *isserfik* is 1" (25mm) thick by 1-3/8" (35mm) wide.

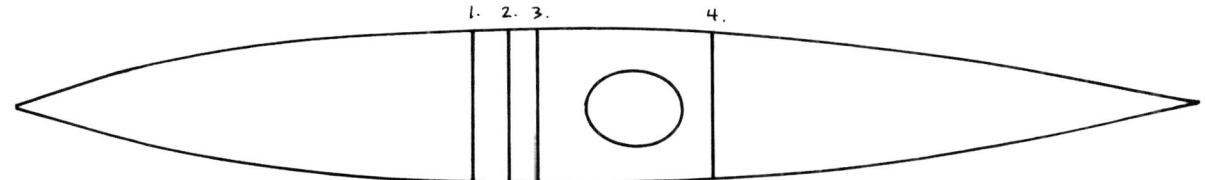

Greenland National Museum: Cat. no. 2056

The deck lines and rigging on the KNK 2056 are very austere and must have been the very least a Greenlander would've gone to sea with— perhaps it was just used for fowling with a shotgun? Deck line 2 has an interesting scarf in it, as depicted in figure 172 bottom; this is the only remarkable aspect of this kayak's deck lines. The deck lines are nailed on to the gunwales instead of being fitted through them. The 2056's coaming is made of oak, and it has two ivory strips covering the scarf at its backside.

53. West Greenland Kayak: Musée de la Marine, Paris, France. Catalog no. 1Bs.24.

This kayak was given to the Musée by Albert Echwald, president of the Naval Society of Nuuk, and was received by the museum in 1969. I've restored this kayak's depth-to-sheer in the scale drawing to 6-15/16″ (17.6cm) from the 6-3/16″ (15.7cm) of the slightly collapsed original.

The 1Bs.24 is a very graceful looking craft with a very long stem and rather short stern. It has modest sheer, the bow rising distinctly, though not nearly so dramatically as the *pequngasoq* forms (e.g., KNK 2050 [plate 49], etc.) also from Nuuk vicinity.

The longitudinals are all nailed in place, and the deck beams are intermittently lashed with cotton string. The ribs are of split branches— perhaps Arctic birch or willow as can be found in many fjords, or possibly imported barrel hoops. The ribs are half-round in section, with the bark-side turned downward. The inside chine edges in the cockpit area are shaved-down so as to afford more comfort for the kayaker.

A fore deck and cockpit view is depicted in figure 277. Note the repair piece on the coaming's lower front face, and the slightly compressed ribs inside the cockpit. No keel edging was evidenced fore or aft, though a bow knob is evidenced (via a side-peg hole); a stern knob is present. The 1Bs.24's coaming has two bone bands at its backside: Each mea-

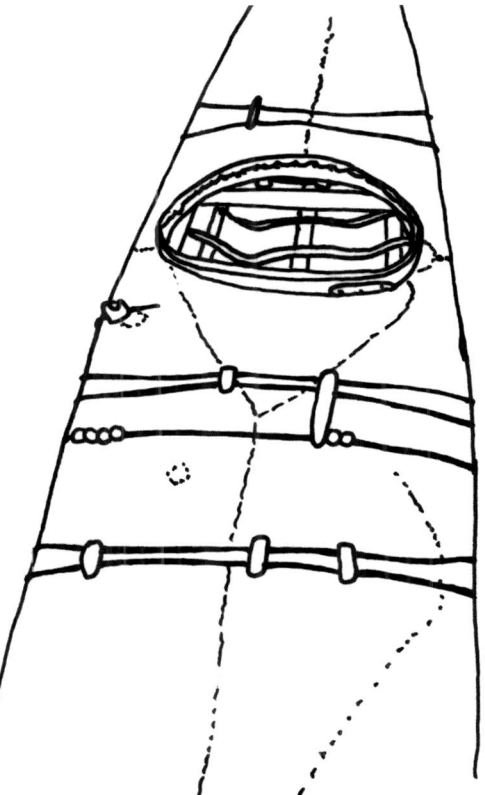

Figure 277: Fore deck of the 1Bs.24, looking aft.

sure 3/16″ thick by 5/16″ high (5 x 8mm). The upper strip is 9-5/8″ (24.4cm) long, and the lower is 11-1/8″(28.2cm) long.

The fittings on the 1Bs.24 are plain in form, though numerous and well made. Deck lines 2-3 share three fittings, an unusual number, as one, two, or four pieces seem most common in this position. Likewise, the aft-most deck line also has just three fittings, two or four being most common here. The aft three fore deck lines are all linked together with one piece (4-5-6a); deck line 4 has six identical beads on it, and deck lines 5 and 6 are linked again with piece 5-6a. The two aft deck lines are linked with a single piece. The bow deck line is missing.

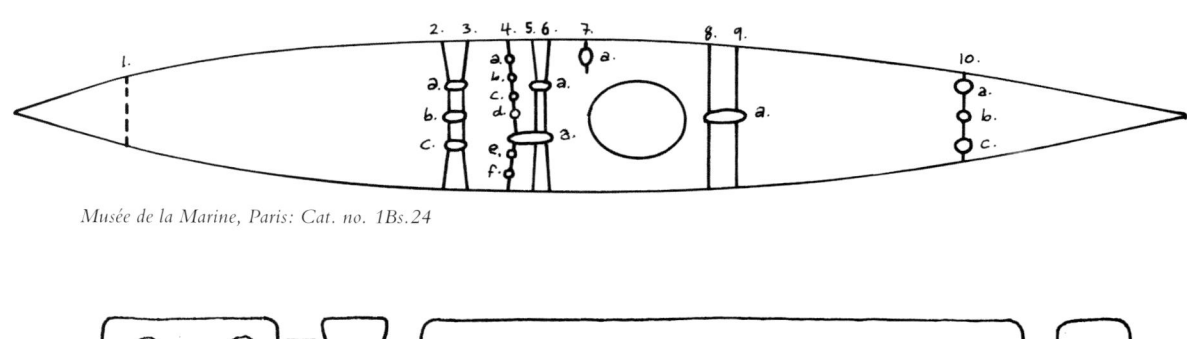

Musée de la Marine, Paris: Cat. no. 1Bs.24

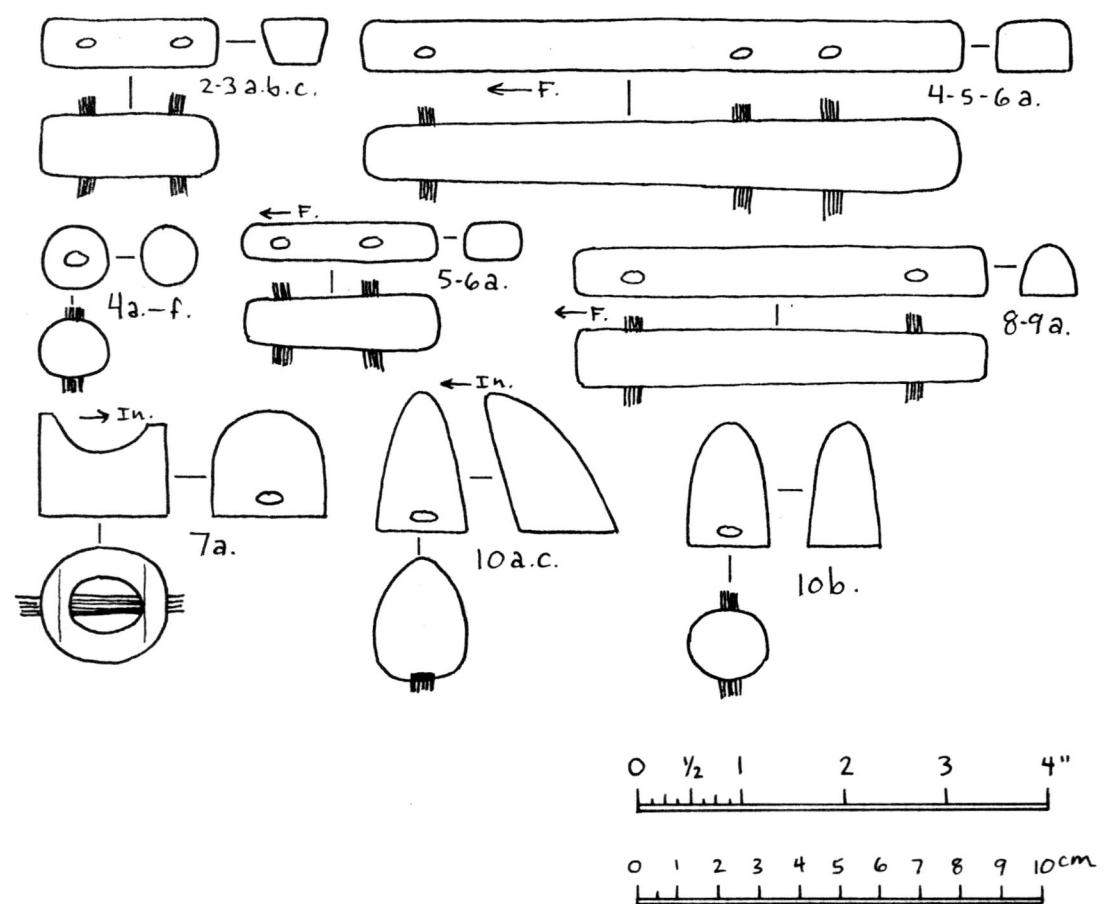

54. West Greenland Kayak from the 1980s: Greenland National Museum, Nuuk. Catalog no. KNK 143

The name H. C. Petersen comes up fairly regularly throughout this work; he is unquestionably the pre-eminent scholar of Greenlandic kayaks. His interest in kayaks coincided with the period of sharp decline in kayak use, especially so in Southwest Greenland. Being a Greenlander, he was in a unique position to interview many elders, hunters, and kayak-builders, and to travel to many regions of Greenland as well as to museums in Europe in order to study kayaks.

Petersen's first great kayak-related work is his *Instruction in Kayak Building*, in which he describes the construction process of a kayak in great detail. The kayak described is not a specific type, and Petersen emphasizes this point:

The kayak to be described here is a Greenland type— or rather it is a composite of a number of technical solutions from various parts of Greenland. For this reason it cannot be localised as a particular type and it should not, therefore, be looked upon as an ethnographical specimen. The technical solutions are all satisfactory in themselves, although many old Greenland kayak-builders will doubtless have their objections. (1981:6)

Petersen built the Greenland National Museum's kayak KNK 143 in the early 1980s. It is, like his book, a composite of technical solutions, and cannot be held as an example of a specific type.

The KNK 143's seal skin *amiq* is as black as can be— unpainted. The inside of the seal skin is manila-envelope yellow, being the inner-skin of the seal. Keel edging is present both forward and aft. The aft edging is 1/4" high and 3/8" wide (6 x 9mm), and the forward edging is the same, although it tapers to 1/16" (1.5mm) high over the foremost 6" (15.2cm) of the edging. End knobs are not evidenced at the bow or the stern. The coaming makes use of a tropical wood: mahogany— and it is edge scarfed in the back and fastened with bronze nails. Two 14" (36.8cm) long bone strips cover the scarf joint; these strips measure 1/4" x 3/8" (6 x 9mm), and are fastened with bronze nails.

The deck fittings on the KNK 143 are very well made: They are all finely polished, and several pieces are in the form of sea mammals and fish, each carved in great detail. Petersen himself writes, "Previously the tighteners were fashioned as ornaments and for decoration on the deck, but by the middle of this century they had become simpler, fashioned with no imagination and purely functional" (1986:39). Petersen clearly felt compelled to restore the ornamentation to the kayak's deck fittings. The fitting between the two cones on the bow deck line is shaped like a man and is facing aft— another feature Petersen describes as having been lost over the years (1986:40).

The harpoon holder is an oblong stump form that not only holds the harpoon, but also elevates it well above the deck, much like the harpoon holder on the KNK 2050. The KNK 143's holder is less ornate, though still elegant having a band carved into the base. It is interesting to note that the deck lines and fittings of this kayak are identical in placement and arrangement with the Fram Museum's 176 (plate 42) of 100 years prior— at least with what lines are still present on the 176.

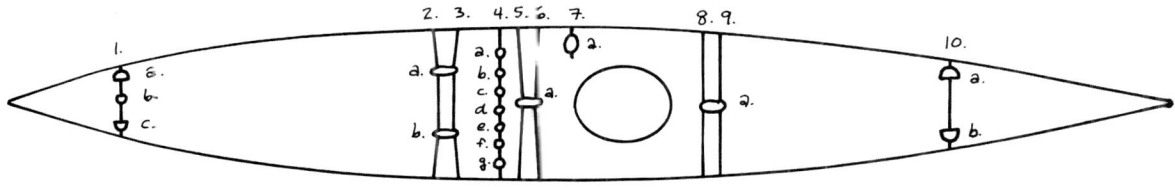

Greenland National Museum: Cat. no. 143

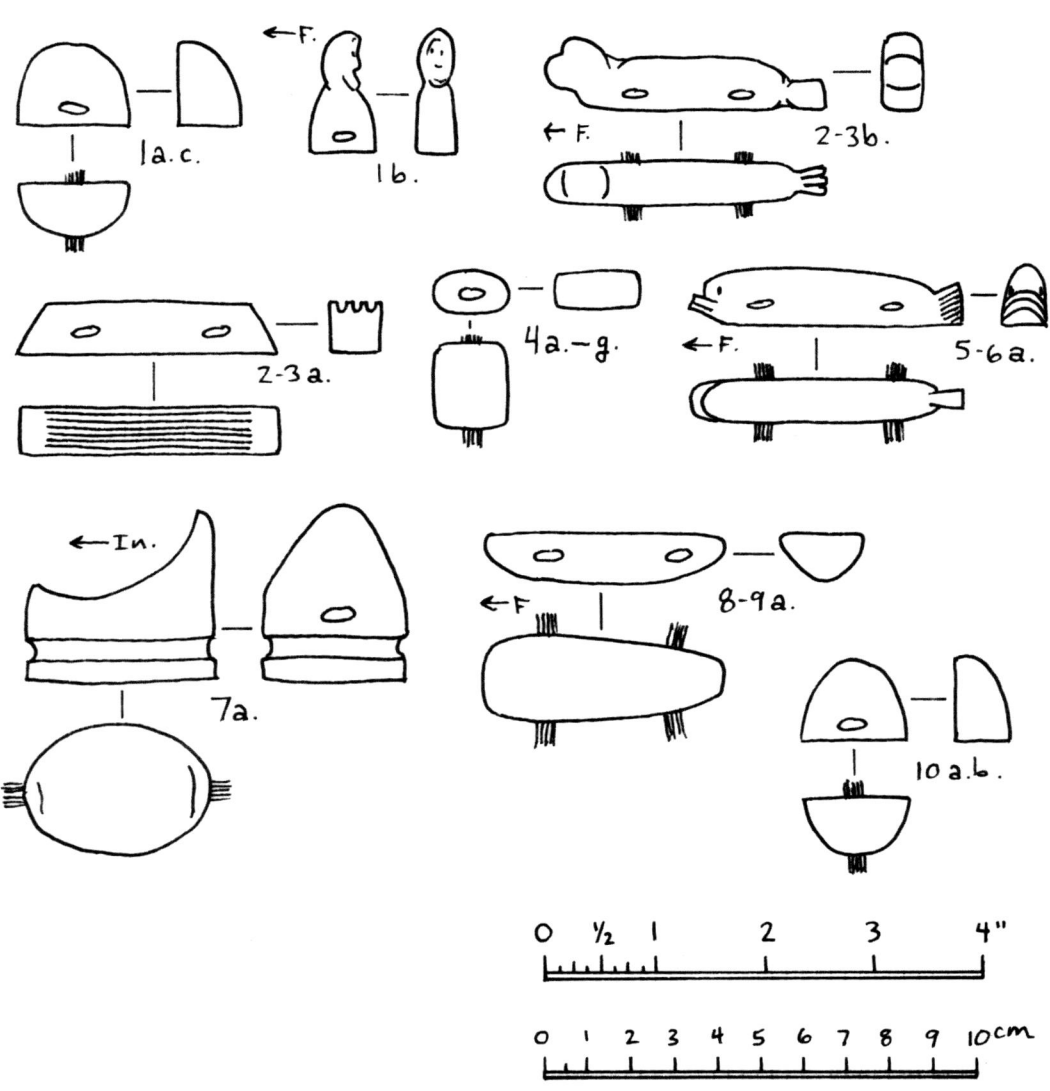

55. West Greenland Kayak from the 1990s: The Greenland National Museum, Nuuk. Catalog no. KNK 1966.

Karl Samuelsen of Paamiut built this boy's kayak in the 1990s. It is fully 'kitted' out for hunting— right down to its harpoon line tray, tiny rifle bag, and spray skirt. It is roughly proportional to the KNK 1849, but is more of the quality of smaller models made for the tourist trade.

The sheer of the 1966 is quite flat and the depth is fairly constant, though it reaches maximum depth at the internal skeg. The coaming is made of 1/8" (3mm) thick birch plywood, bent around twice to achieve a total of 1/4" (6mm) thickness. The *amiq* is jet-black in color. The KNK 1966 has end knobs, but lacks keel edging.

All of the KNK 1966's ribs are made from split branches. The lashings are made from a three-strand tarred nylon and the chines and keelson are double-pass lashed to the ribs; these lashings are non-continuous. The fore deck has just a single deck stringer, and the same configuration is present on the aft deck. The 1966's *masik* is 1/4" (6mm) thick by 1-1/2" (38mm) wide; the deck stringers are 3/8" (9mm) thick by 1-1/4" (32mm) wide. The *isserfik* is 1/2" (13mm) thick by 1-1/2" (38mm) wide.

All of the fittings on this kayak are crudely formed, but entirely functional. The fore deck only has three lines, but they are linked in interesting and symmetrical pattern. The pair of aft deck lines is double linked. A paddle is positively associated with the kayak 1966, and is depicted in paddle-plate 36.

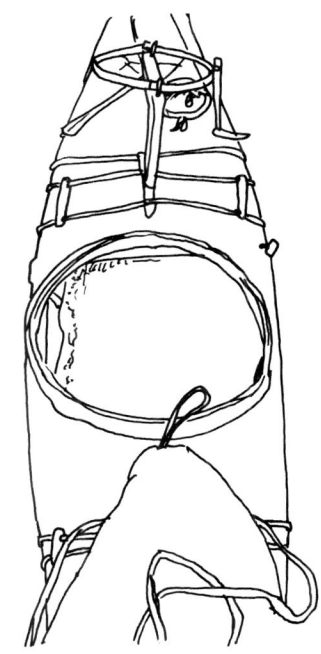

Figure 278: Cockpit view of the KNK 1966. A seal pelt seat obscures the framework.

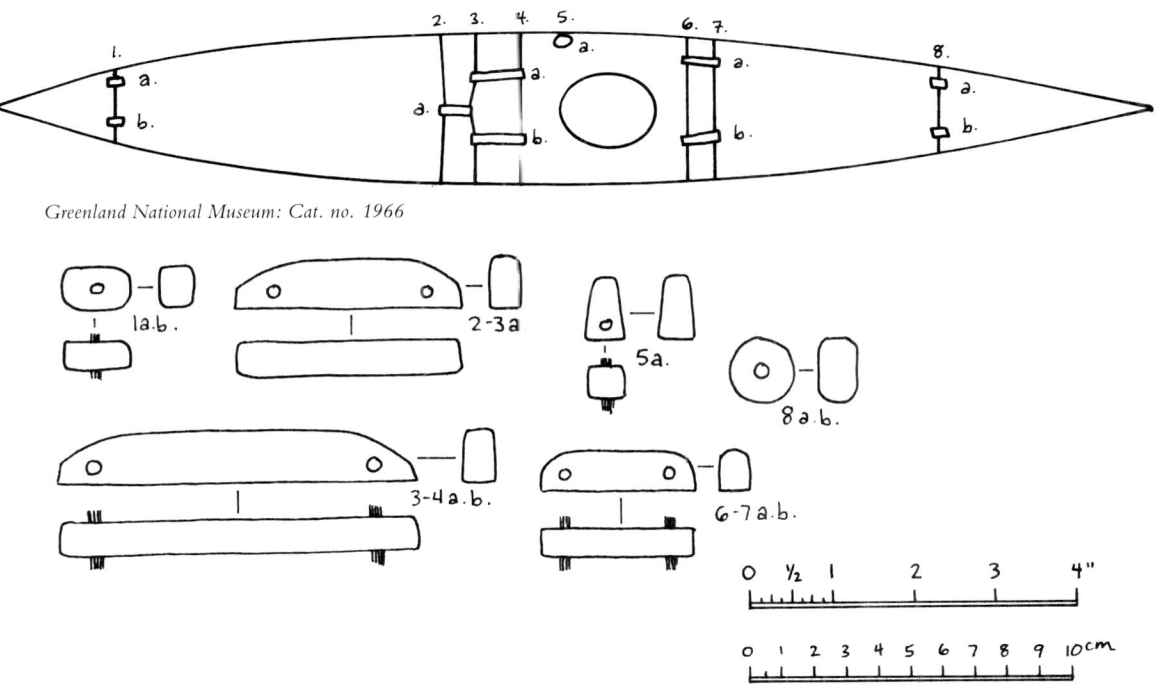

Greenland National Museum: Cat. no. 1966

TYPE VI.

While less than 100 years of type VI kayaks are presented here, they are essentially kayaks with distinct 17th and 18th century forms and features that are quickly exposed to 20th century kayak influence from further down the coast. By the mid 20th century, many of the old forms were dissolved, but many details and features consistent with the older kayaks persisted. Type VI kayaks are still being built and used in Greenland today (see figure 15). The common denominator of type VI kayaks is their coming from the Northwest Coast of Greenland— from Disko Bay to Upernavik District. The earliest example in this study is from the 1880s, and the latest is from the 1960s.

There is considerable variation in form within type VI kayaks. Forms range from bow and stern shapes reminiscent of type III kayaks to stems nearly identical to type V kayaks. Stem profiles are mostly convex, but they become straighter or even concave in later examples— notably around Disko Bay vicinity circa 1930s, and in Upernavik District by the 1960s. Type VI kayak hull-shapes can be flat-bottomed and slab sided but also deep-V bottomed with flared sides. Certain examples have considerable keel rocker, while others have a very flat keel— hogging in some instances, although this could be attributed to damage, i.e., hull-collapse. A high peaked chine terminus at the bow is fairly consistent among type VI kayaks in all but the older and most northerly examples (e.g., the NMNH 160325, plate 56, and the KNK 2237, plate 66).

Type VI kayaks are also very diverse in size, the length of adult-kayaks ranges from 14′3″ to 19′6″(434.3 to 594.4cm) long; breadths range from 18″ to 22″ (45.7 to 55.9cm). For the most part, the longest examples are among the widest; this suggests a considerable range in hull-volume among type VI kayaks.

H. C. Petersen writes, "the shortest kayaks [in Greenland] are built in the Northern part of Disko Bay, in the Ilulissat-Appat[37] area" (1986:43). Petersen himself found the average kayak length at Ilulissat in 1970 to be 497cm (16′ 3-11/16″) (1986:42). Four of the adult-size type VI kayaks in this study are shorter than 497cm, although one is from Illorsuit in Uummannaq district. The exact origin of the other three is unknown, although they are in my mind undoubtedly from Disko bay. Historic photographs suggest that shorter kayaks were also used at Qeqertarsuaq (Godhavn) on the Southwestern tip of Disko Island; e.g., figure 287.

The longer type VI kayaks (for example, plates 56, 60, 69, and 70) likely hail from Upernavik Kujalleq and points north; the average length of the four longest type VI kayaks in this study is 570.2cm (18′ 8-7/16″)— an average length only exceeded by type I kayaks of circa 17th century.

Why are type VI kayaks that exhibit type V influences not simply considered to be type V kayaks? Despite significant changes to the outside of the kayak— its very shape— certain aspects remain consistent within type VI kayaks that are not commonly found in type V kayaks. These include light scantlings (especially gunwale heights), very simple deck line patterns (e.g., four lines on the fore deck and one on the aft deck), lack of keel edging at the stern, and lashed-on coamings. Some of the type VI kayaks that do have pegged-on coamings have their *amiq* pulled up and over the back of the coaming where it is fastened with pegs to the coaming's outer face. This method is known from kayaks dating from the 1600s and 1700s (types I, II, and early type III), and is unknown in Greenland in the 20th century except for along the Northwest coast, i.e., type VI kayaks.

---

[37] Appat is 61km north of Ilulissat. It is sometimes spelled *Agpat*, and its Danish name is Ritenbenk.

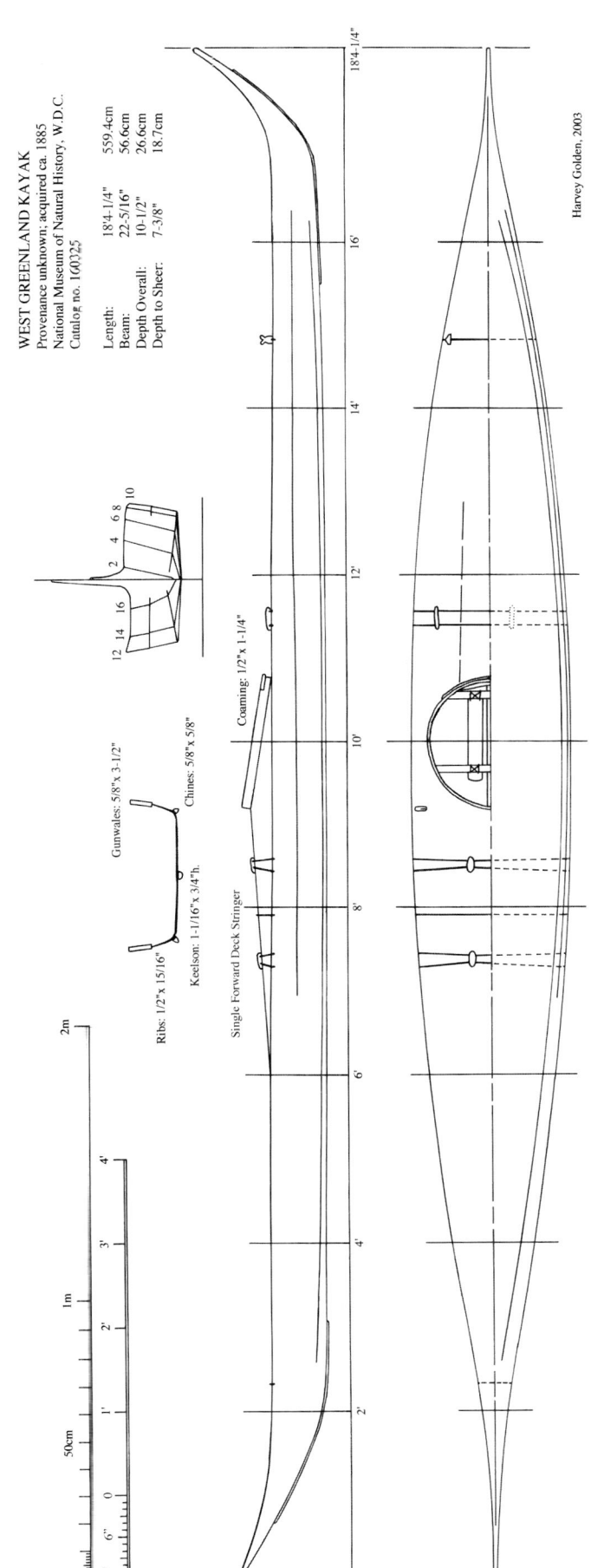

56. National Museum of Natural History catalog no. 160325

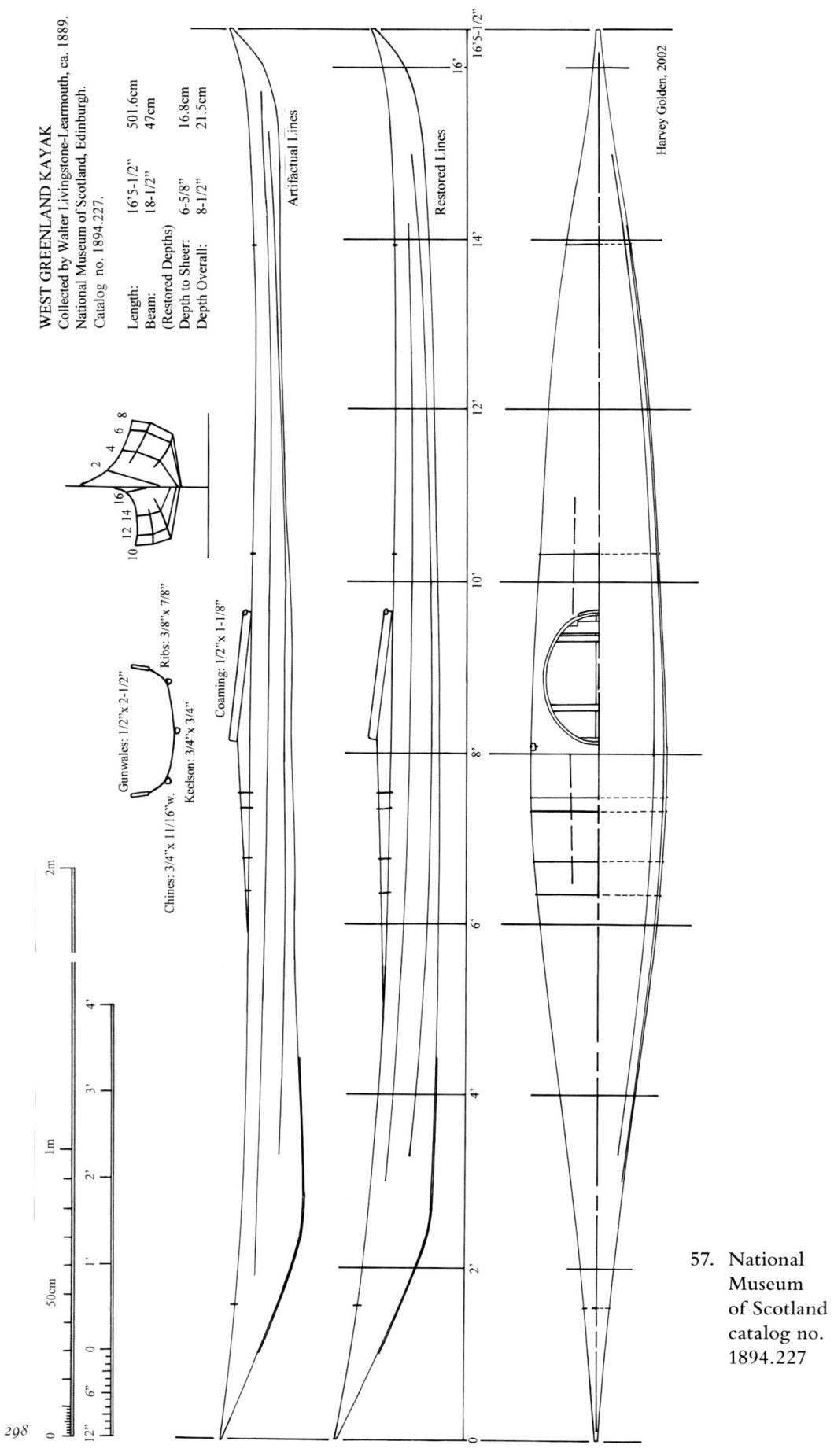

57. National Museum of Scotland catalog no. 1894.227

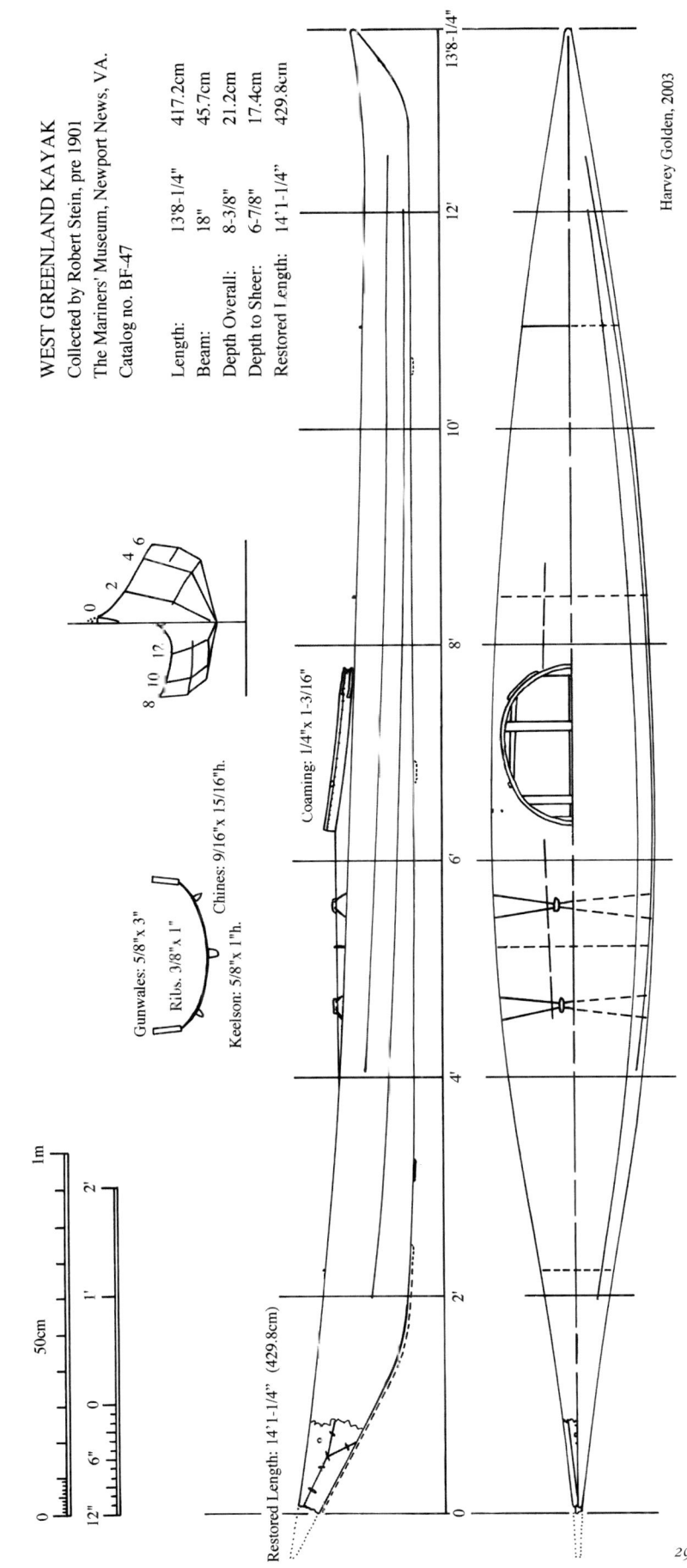

58. Mariners' Museum catalog no. BF-47

WEST GREENLAND KAYAK

Collected by Capt. Comer, 1917(?)
American Museum of Natural History, NY.
Catalog no. 60.1/5253

Length:	8'1/2"	245.1cm
Beam:	12-3/8"	31.4cm
Depth Overall:	5-11/16"	14.4cm
Depth to Sheer:	4-13/16"	12.2cm

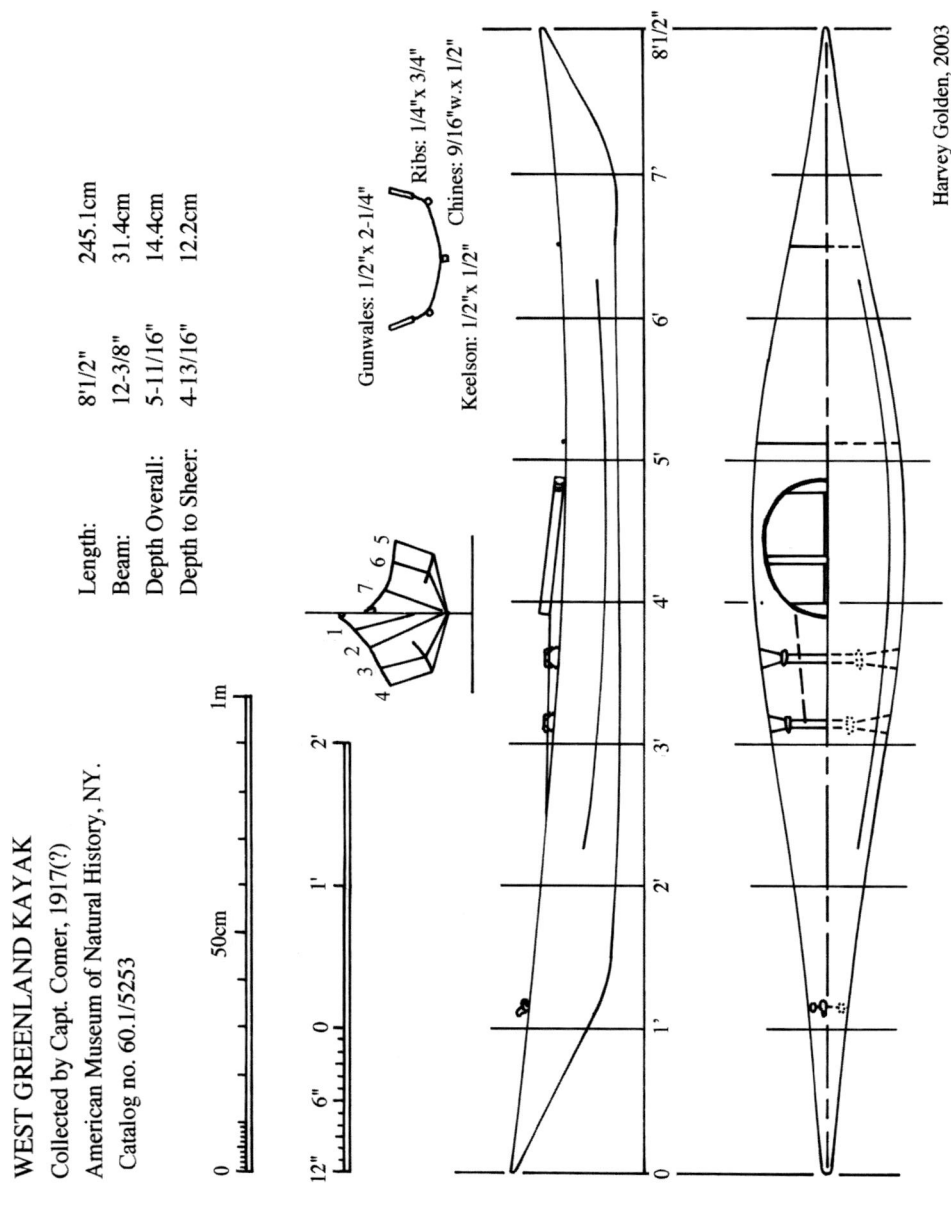

59. American Museum of Natural History catalog no. 60.1/5253

60. Canadian Canoe Museum catalog no. 977.182

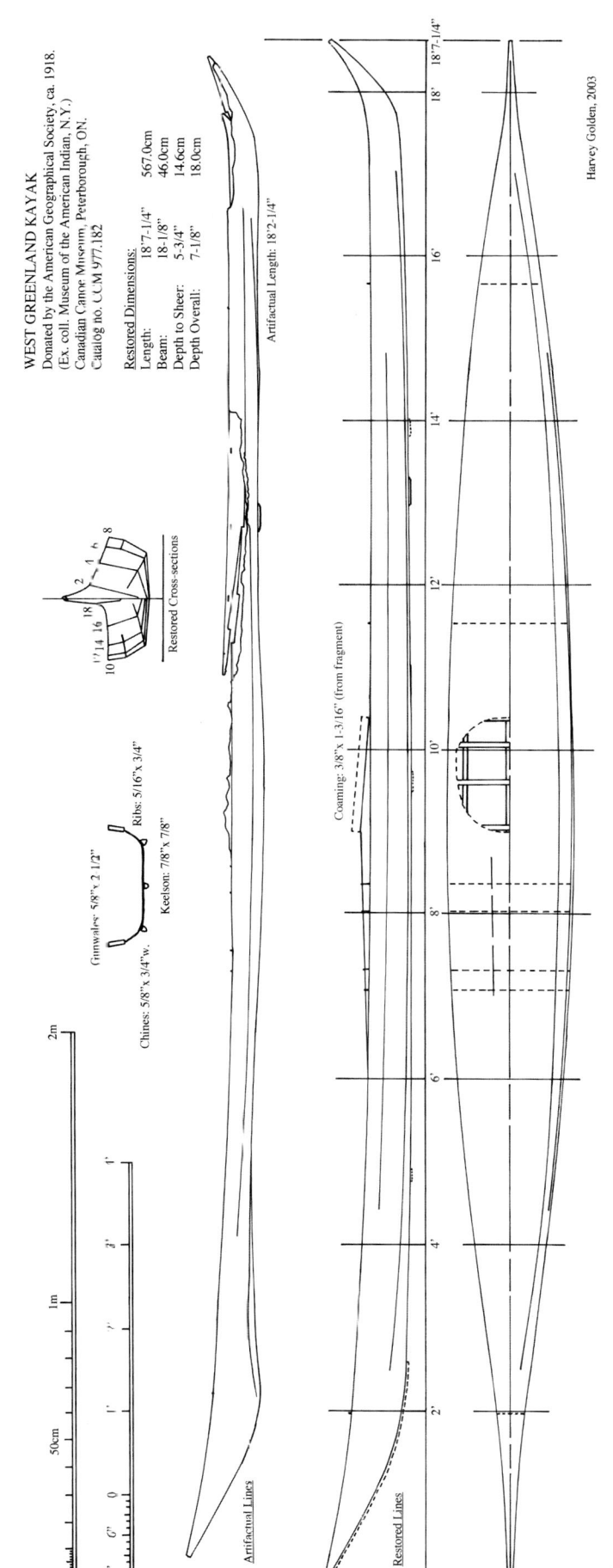

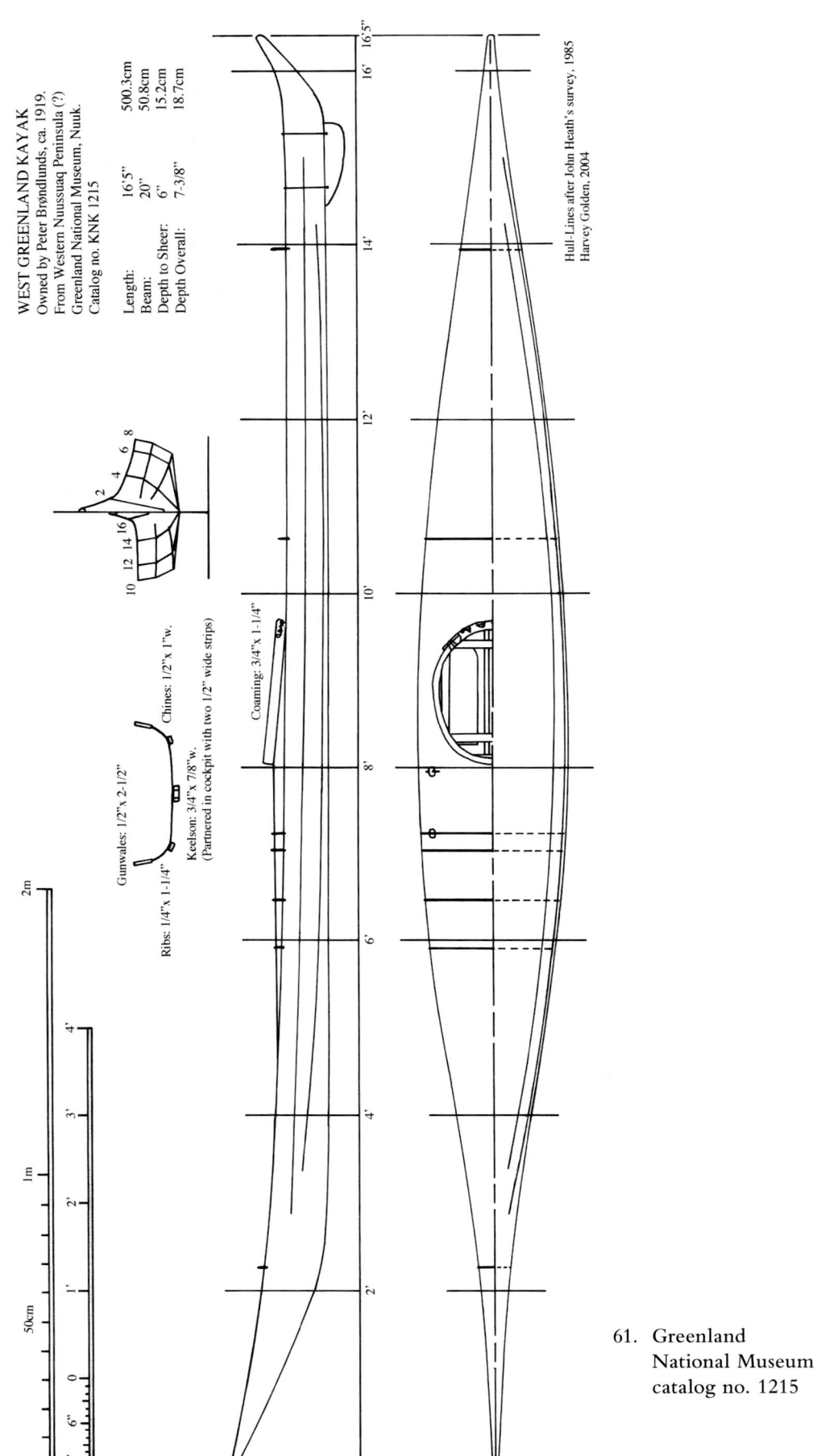

61. Greenland National Museum catalog no. 1215

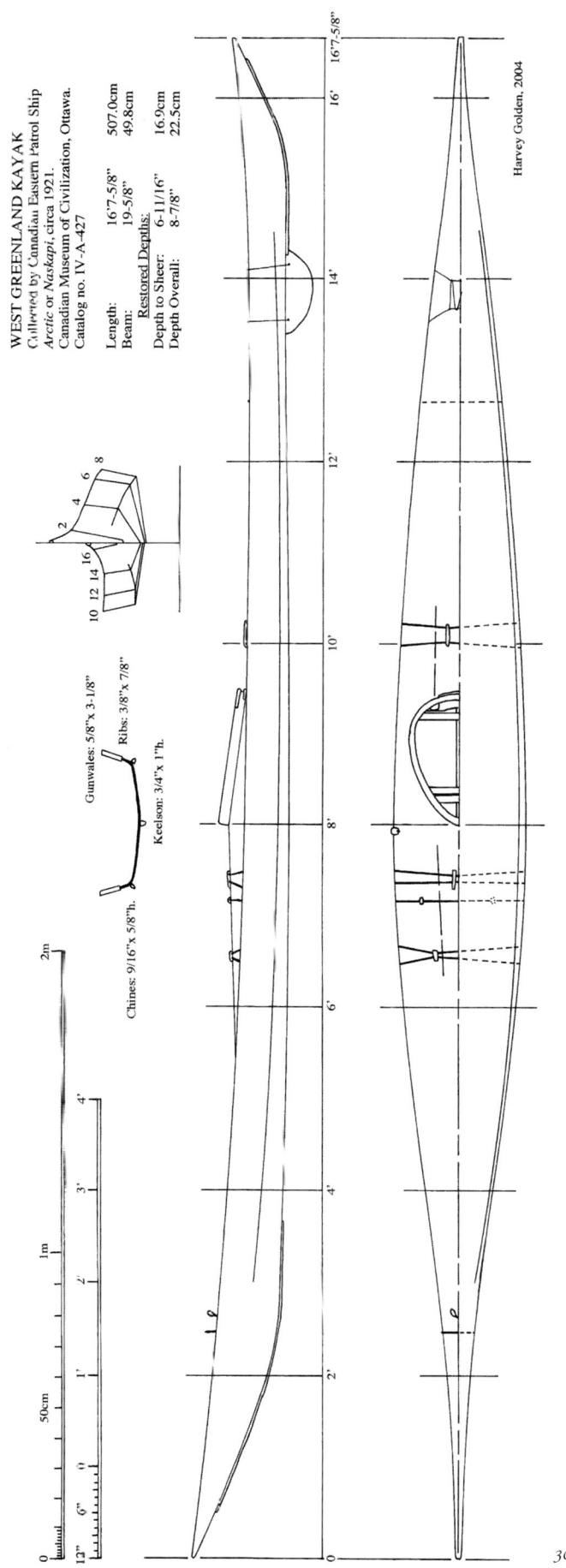

62. Canadian Museum of Civilization catalog no. IV-A-427

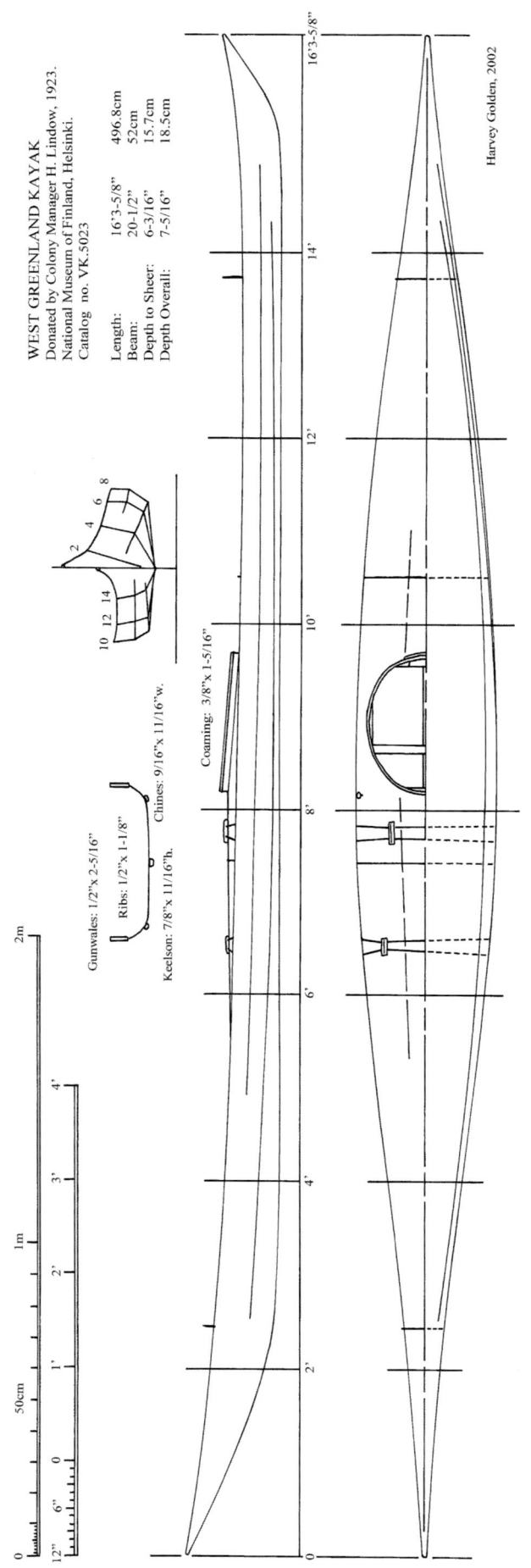

63. National Museum of Finland catalog no. 5023

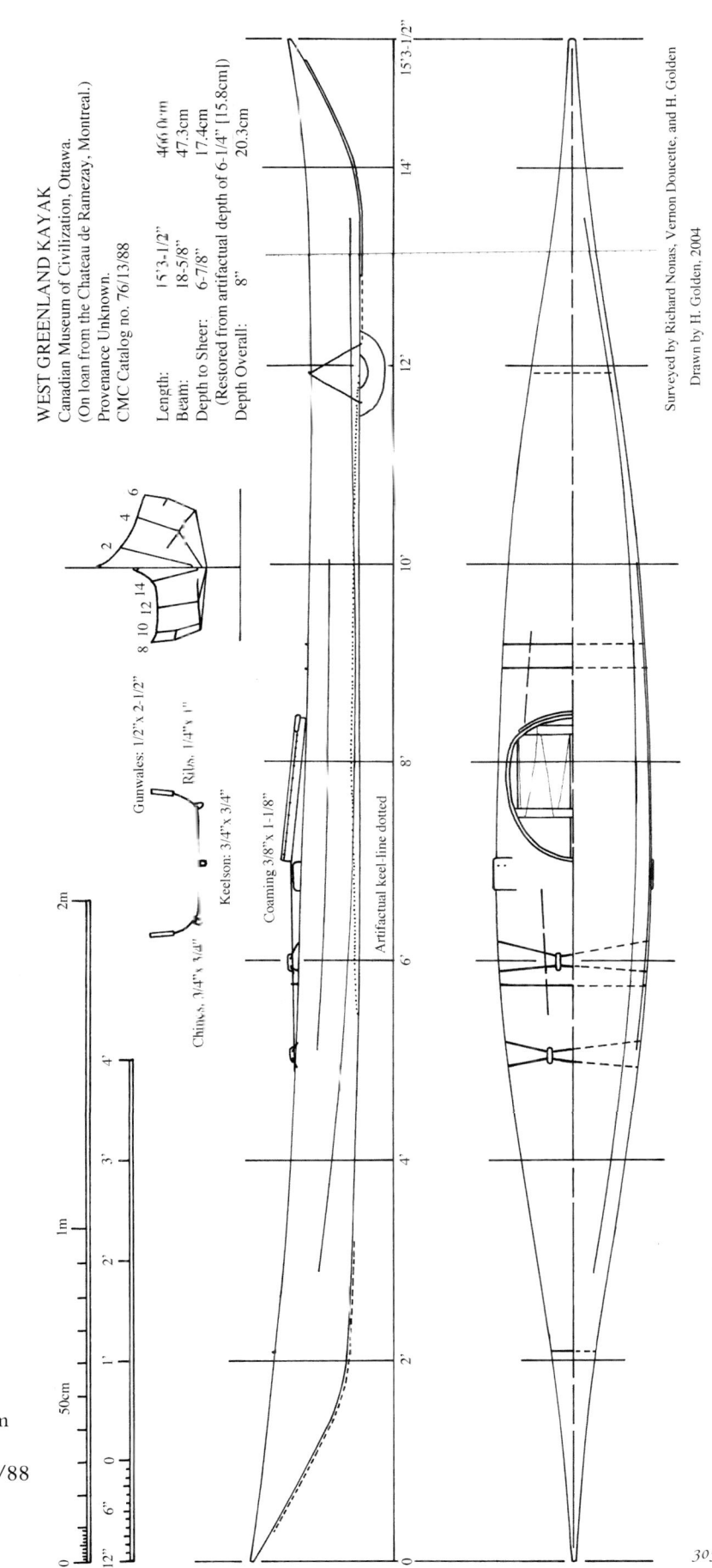

64. Canadian Museum of Civilization catalog no. 76/13/88

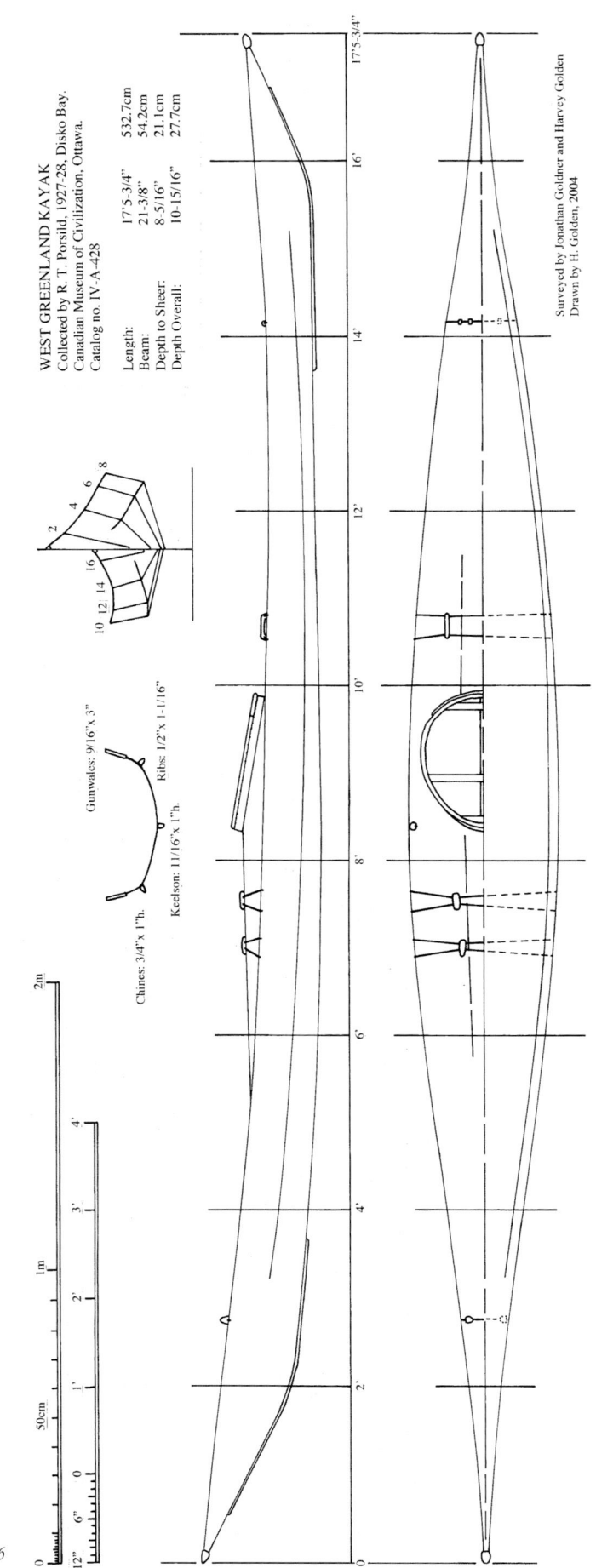

65. Canadian Museum of Civilization catalog no. IV-A-428

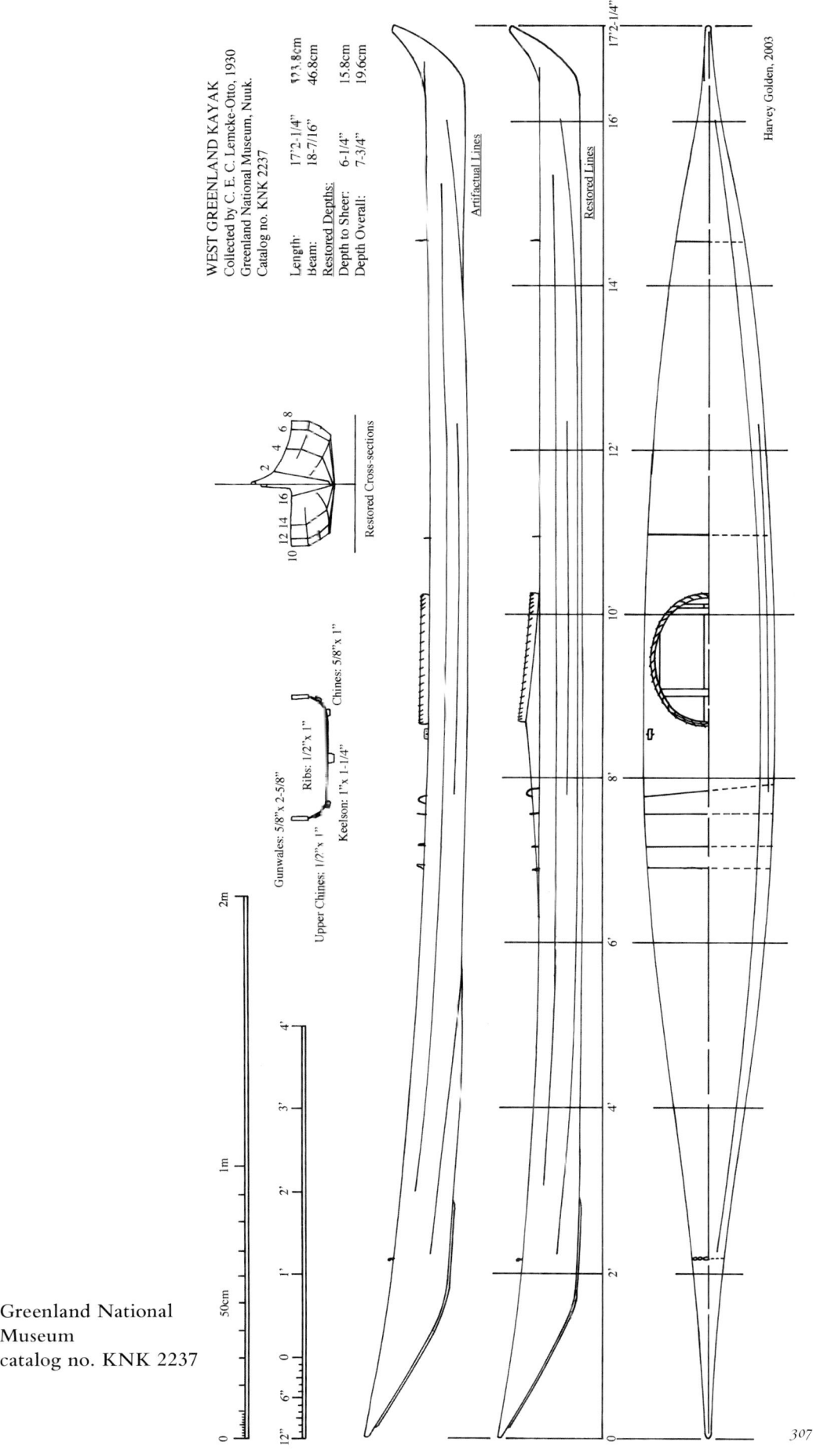

66. Greenland National Museum catalog no. KNK 2237

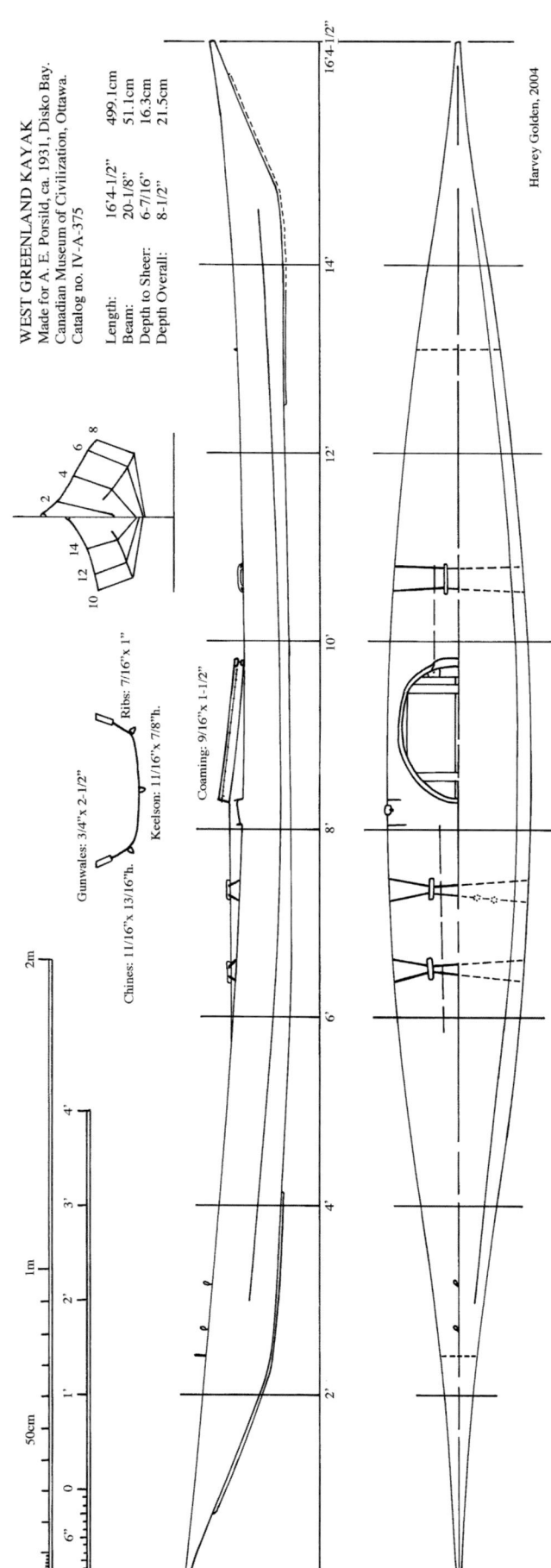

67. Canadian Museum of Civilization catalog no. IV-A-375

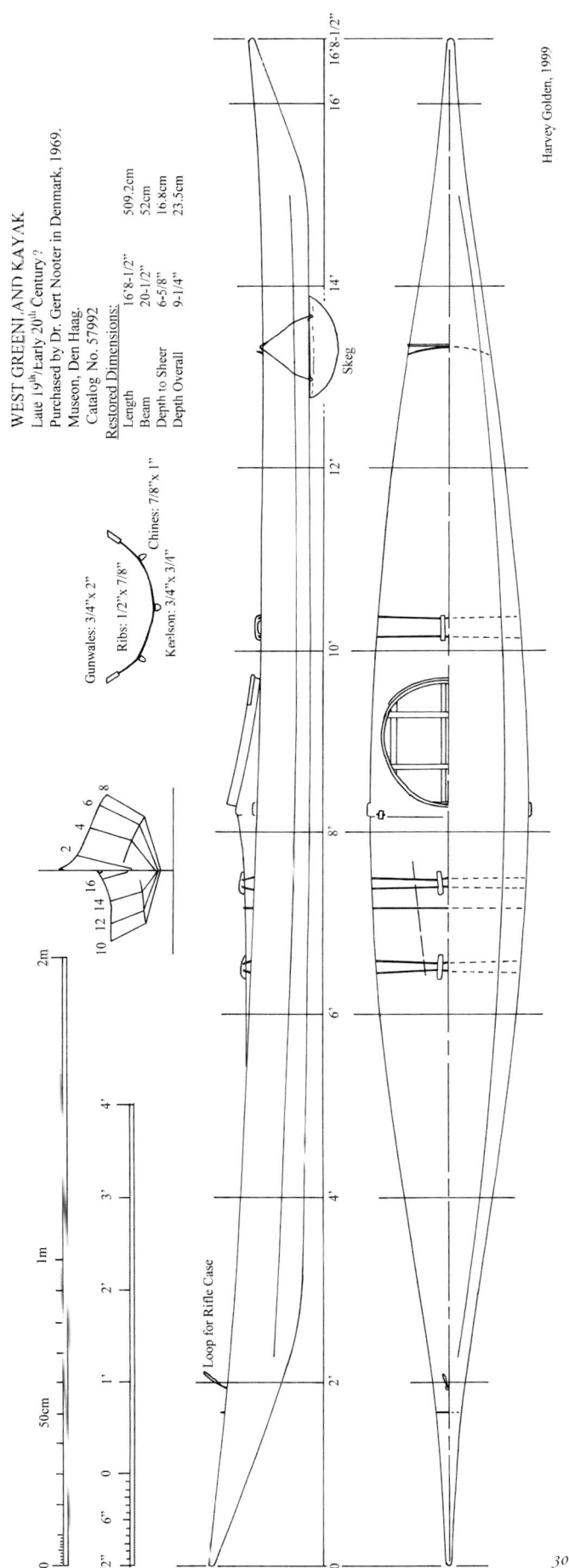

68. Museon catalog no. 57992

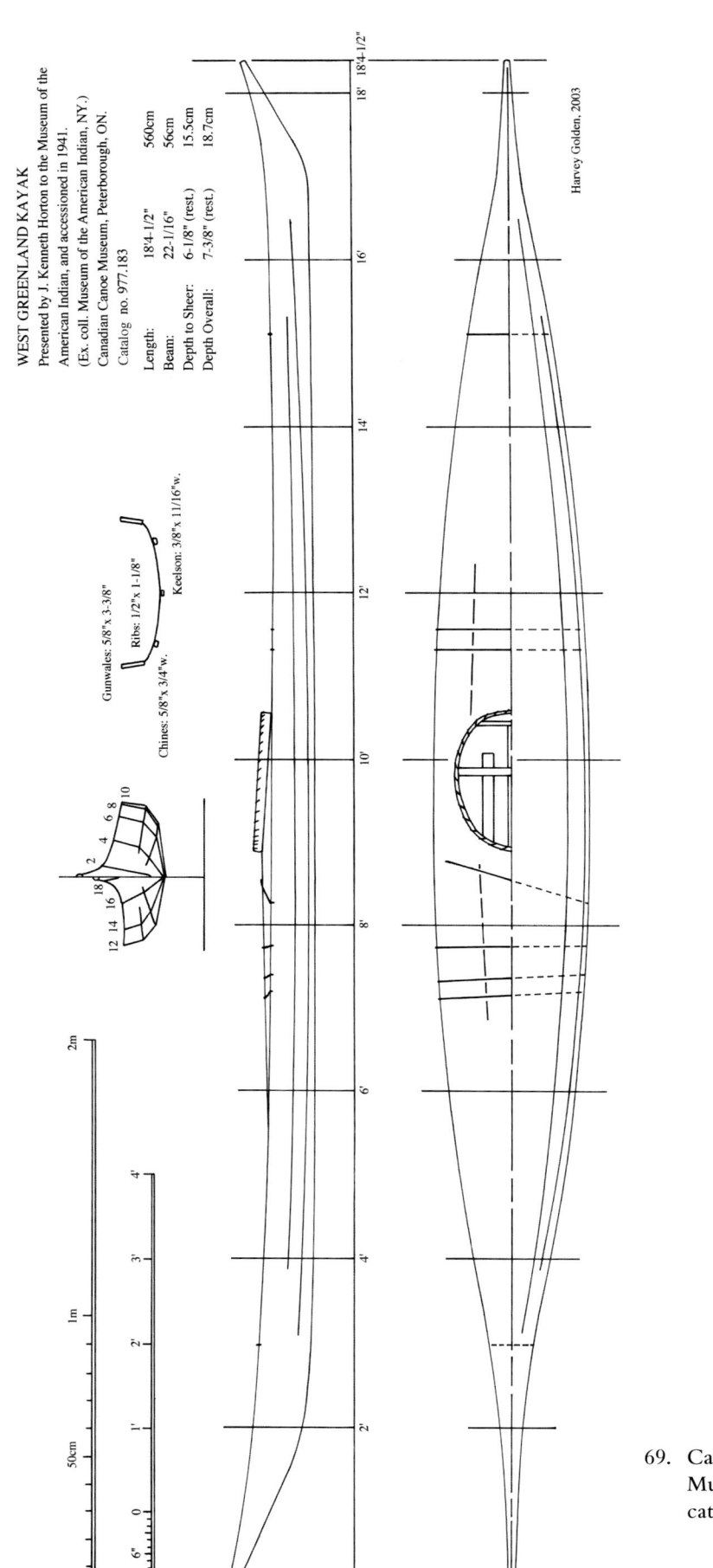

69. Canadian Canoe Museum catalog no. 977.183

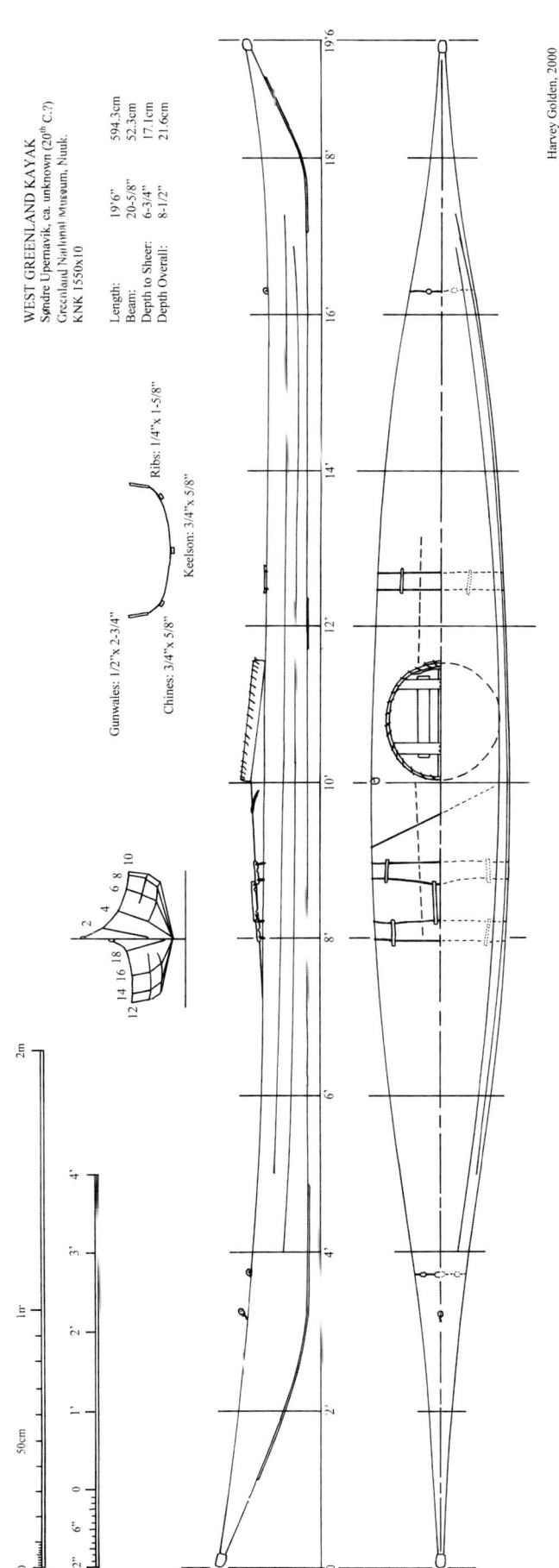

70. Greenland National Museum
    catalog no. KNK 1550x10

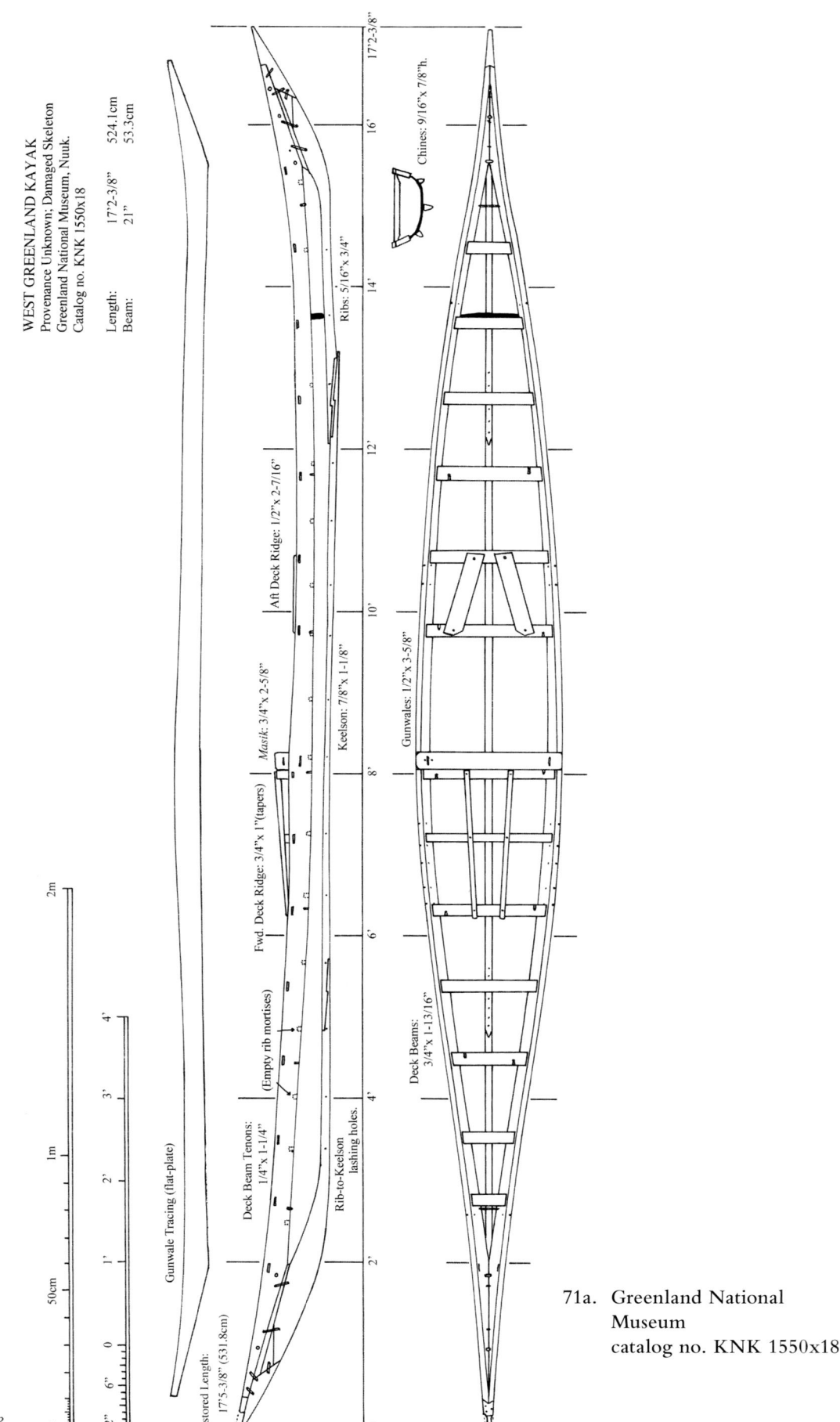

71a. Greenland National Museum catalog no. KNK 1550x18

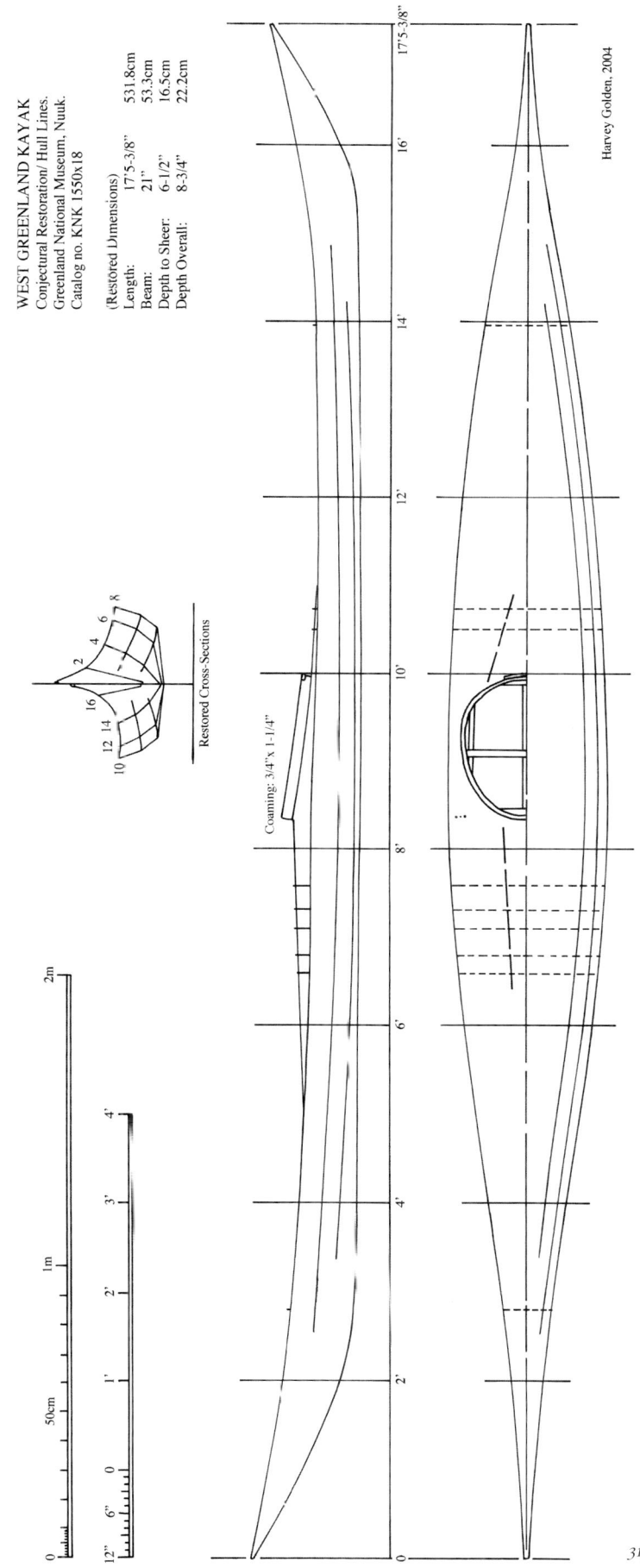

71b. Greenland National Museum catalog no. KNK 1550x18 (Hull Lines)

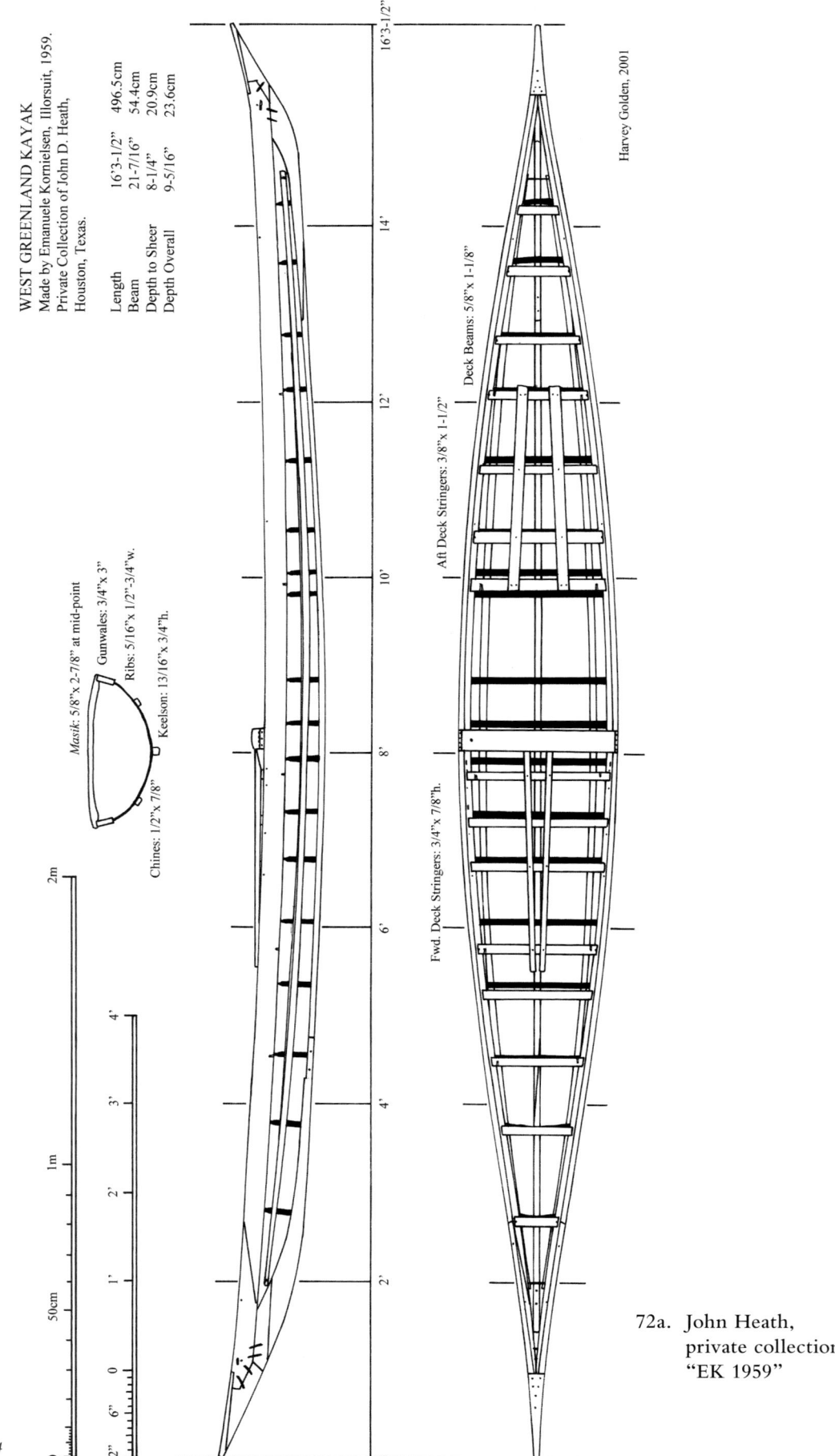

WEST GREENLAND KAYAK
Made by Emanuele Kornielsen, Illorsuit, 1959.
Private Collection of John D. Heath,
Houston, Texas.

Length	16'3-1/2"	496.5cm
Beam	21-7/16"	54.4cm
Depth to Sheer	8-1/4"	20.9cm
Depth Overall	9-5/16"	23.6cm

Masik: 5/8"x 2-7/8" at mid-point
Gunwales: 3/4"x 3"
Ribs: 5/16"x 1/2"–3/4"w.
Keelson: 13/16"x 3/4"h.
Chines: 1/2"x 7/8"
Aft Deck Stringers: 3/8"x 1-1/2"
Deck Beams: 5/8"x 1-1/8"
Fwd. Deck Stringers: 3/4"x 7/8"h.

Harvey Golden, 2001

72a. John Heath,
private collection
"EK 1959"

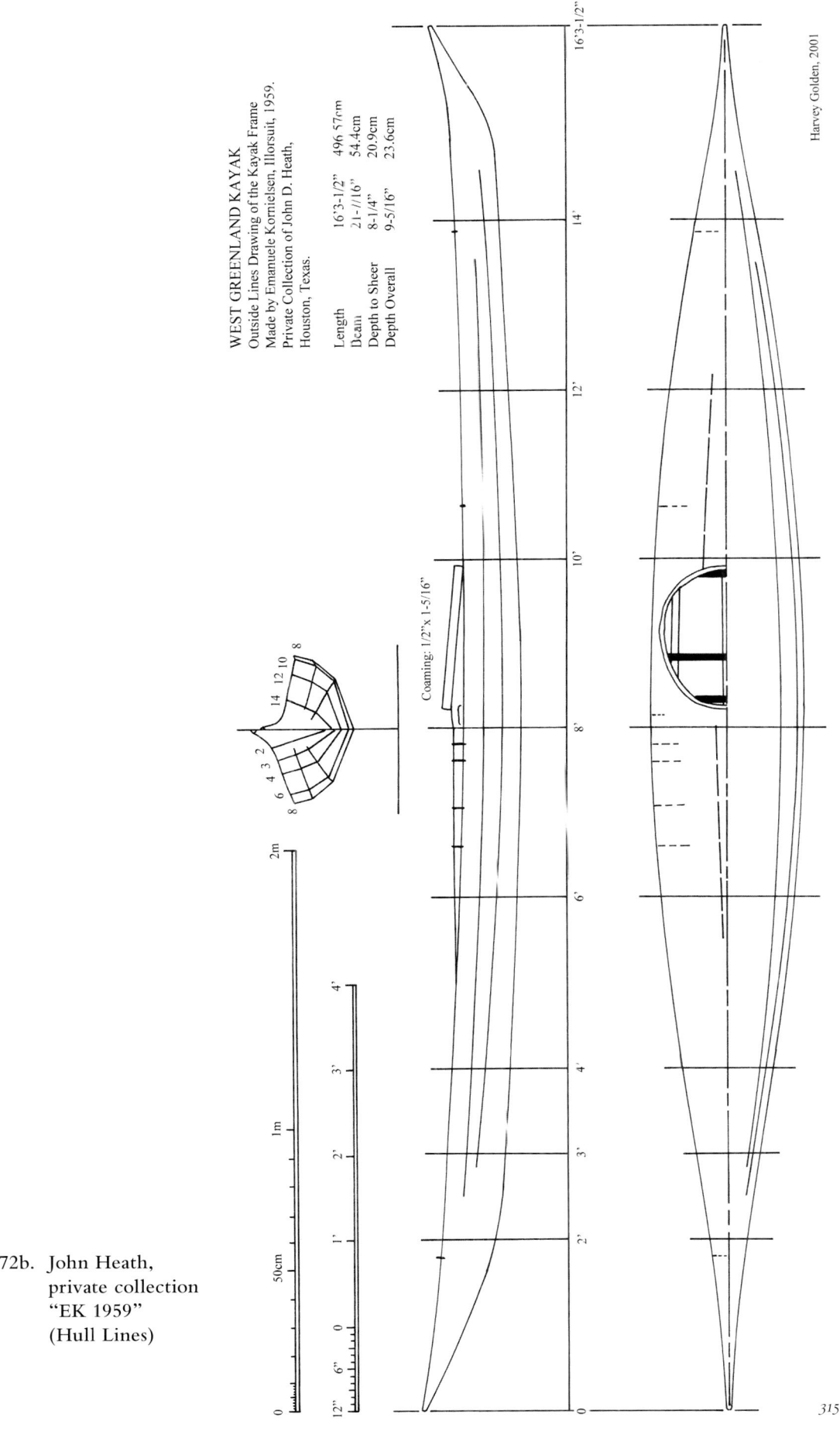

72b. John Heath, private collection "EK 1959" (Hull Lines)

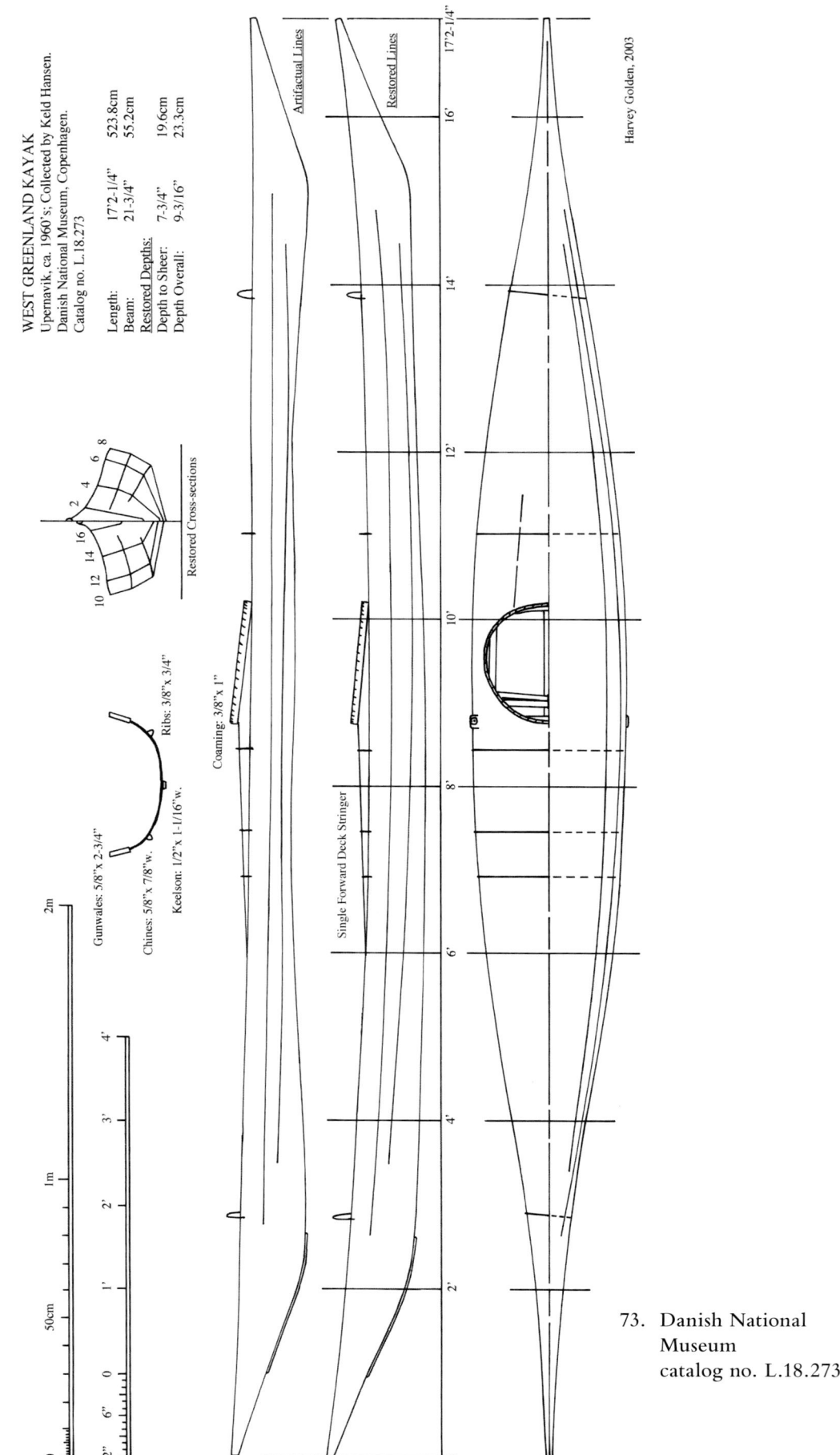

73. Danish National Museum catalog no. L.18.273

56. West Greenland Kayak from ca. 1885: National Museum of Natural History, Smithsonian, Washington, D.C.
Catalog no. 160325

Howard Chapelle surveyed and drew the lines of the NMNH's kayak 160325 in 1948. His drawing appears in the book *The Bark Canoes and Skinboats of North America* (Adney and Chapelle, 1964:203, fig. 191). I visited the 160325 in order to study its fittings, construction, and other details more thoroughly, as Chapelle's drawing more or less simply captured the lines of the kayak, as well as the scantlings. Our respective drawings are quite identical, the overall dimensions only slightly varying; my length-overall being 3/4" (19mm) less than Chapelle's and his beam being 3/16" (5mm) wider than my results.

As Chapelle notes, the kayak had been attributed to "Mackenzie River," but it was as he writes, "... apparently an eastern kayak from Upernavik, West Greenland" (1964:203). A 1963 entry on the catalog card for the 160325 acknowledges the likelihood of error "... According to studies of Howard Chapelle, Kaj Birket-Smith, Philip Heath."[38] The date of 1885 appears on Chapelle's drawing as well as on the NMNH catalog card, but no collector's name is given.

Historian H. C. Petersen gleaned the following information from a hunter originally from Upernavik Kujalleq (Jens Karlsen, born in 1902), relating a form of kayak unique to a particular community (Ikerasaarsuk, about 85 kilometers due-north of Upernavik) in Upernavik district:

> *The settlement lay between two islands by water with many strong currents which kept the sea open even when areas around were frozen. The kayaks there were used for more of the year than in the surrounding communities. The pile-up of ice on the beach made it difficult for the hunters to get in and out of their kayaks, though. They had to hold on tightly not to be swept away by the current. The solution to this problem was to lengthen the stern post upwards to give the hunter something to grip. The stern posts were thin and about half a meter long (1986:52).*

The 160325 is undoubtedly from Upernavik district, and the form described above especially fits this kayak— the practicality of the purpose described seems suspect. In any case, the 160325 may well be from Ikerasaarsuk.

The 160325 is a very large kayak, having about the same volume as the THH 'A' (plate 16), an 18th century type III kayak. Of the other type VI kayaks, the 160325's general dimensions are close to the CCM 977.183's (plate 69), but with the very square cross-sections and deeper hull, the 160325 has considerably more volume. The 160325's stern is a very steeply inclined tall spike, and the bow-shape is not unlike those of much older kayaks, such as the Hunterian Museum's E.585 and the National Museum of Scotland's U.C.764 (plates 21 and 24 respectively).

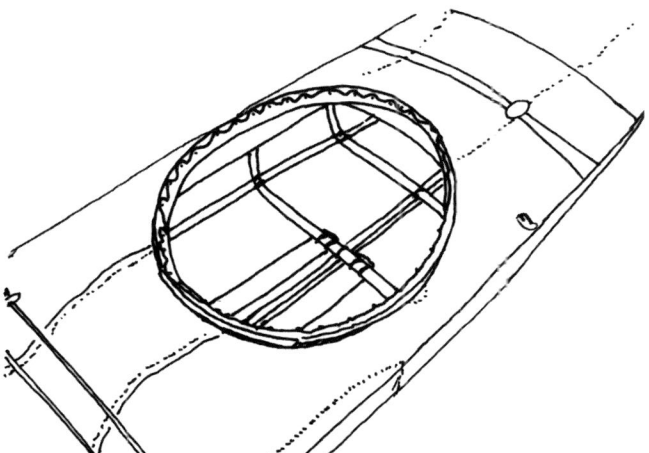

Figure 279: Cockpit-view of the NMNH 160325.

---

[38] "Philip Heath" is probably a mistake, as kayak historian John Heath likely contributed information that led to this kayak being identified as Greenlandic.

The bottom assembly of the 160325 is lashed with a non-continuous seal skin line. The keelson is lashed with a single-pass pattern such as depicted in figure 69, although towards the ends, a double-pass method is used, as in figure 72. This latter pattern is used on the chines throughout. The rib in the forward end of the cockpit is also pegged to the chines, but not the keelson. All of the ribs are fastened to the gunwales with pegs. Two seat slats are present in the 160325, each being 13-3/8″ (33.9cm) long and 2-1/8″ (5.4cm) wide. These are lashed beneath the two cockpit ribs.

The difference between a *masik* and a kayak's other curved deck beams has been discussed in the chapter on construction, but in the case of the 160325, there are a total of four *masik*-formed deck beams below the fore deck. Each one, (including the one directly below the coaming) is set onto the gunwale's top edge. The forward three *masik*-formed deck beams are at 7′ 6″ (228.6cm), 7′ 11-3/4″ (243.2cm), and 8′ 9″ (266.7cm) on-center; each measures 1-5/8″ (41mm) wide.

While the 160325 has two aft deck stringers, it has only one deck stringer forward. The forward stringer measures 5/16″ by 2-1/2″ (8 x 63mm) wide, contrary to Chapelle's results of 1/4″ by 5/8″ (6 x 16mm) (1964:203). The aft deck stringers measure 1/2″ (13mm) thick by 1-13/16″ (46mm) wide.

As with a number of type VI kayaks, the gunwale presents a chine-edge for most of its length. At least in the cockpit vicinity, each gunwale is 3-1/8″ (7.9cm) high with a gain of 3/8″ (9mm) height attached to the upper edges (the scantlings of the scale drawing reflect the total gunwale height of 3-1/2″). As discussed in the section on kayak construction, fashioning the shapes of the gunwales sometimes includes adding wood as well as removing wood.

A forward view into the 160325's hull is shown in figure 280. The single broad deck stringer is visible as are the lashing patterns along the keelson and chines; the chine of the right has fractured and become displaced. Also note the windlass left in place towards the bow.

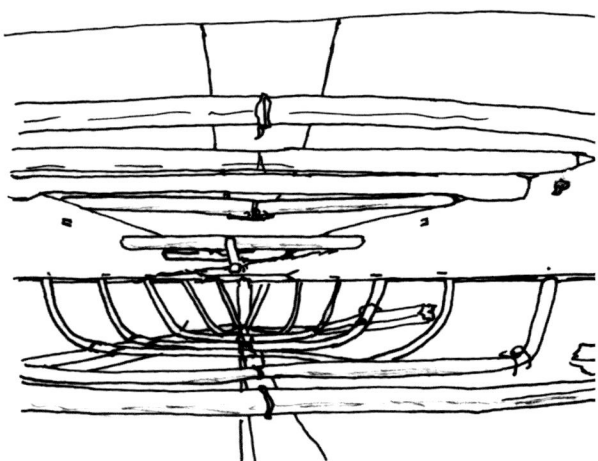

Figure 280: Forward interior view of the NMNH's kayak 160325. Note the windlass left in place towards the bow.

Figure 281 shows the *masik* joint with the gunwale. Note the other *masik*-formed deck beams as well as the built-up gunwales. Below the gunwales' upper edges, next to the continuous deck lines, two empty shallow mortises are present. This suggests not only the gunwales having been reused, but also the builder/kayaker's desire for more room in the cockpit for the present incarnation. The deck lines are set through the gunwales' faces, exiting 1/2″ (13mm) below the sheer line on the outside.

The 160325's coaming measures 1/2″ (13mm) thick by 1-1/4″ (32mm) high, and has a single bone strip fastened to the upper rear of the coaming. This strip is 9″

Figure 281: View showing the built-up gunwales of the NMNH 160325. Also note the high placed curved deck beams and the doubled masik.

(22.8cm) long, and is 3/16" (5mm) thick by 1/2" (13mm) wide. This strip is not centered on the coaming: Its right terminus is only 4-5/8" (11.7cm) from the right sheer.

Keel edging is present both at the bow and stern, and the outer ends of each edging strip exhibit a very unique but ingenious feature. Instead of ending abruptly or tapering to a thin end, the edging's tip is actually set through the *amiq*, so as to prevent anything (ice, harpoon line, etc.) from snagging it. This is the only such Greenland kayak in this study that exhibits such a method, however I have seen it on a Yukon-Kuskokwim River delta kayak from the late 1930s in a private collection (2001: Survey notes).

As will be seen among later kayaks form the northern West Coast, the 160325 has a comparatively large number of deck fittings. Whether or not the bow deck line had fittings is unknown, as it is missing. The stern deck line only has one fitting (10a), but likely had another matching piece; the line is broken and the other piece must have fallen off. The shape of fitting 10a is that of a seal's hind flippers. The harpoon holder is a simple 'reclining' tab-shape, somewhat similar to that on the MMG 1984.285 (plate 20) from circa 1785-1844.

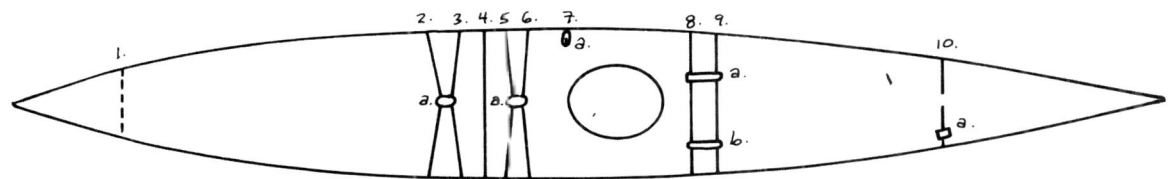

U. S. National Museum of Natural History: Cat. no. 160325

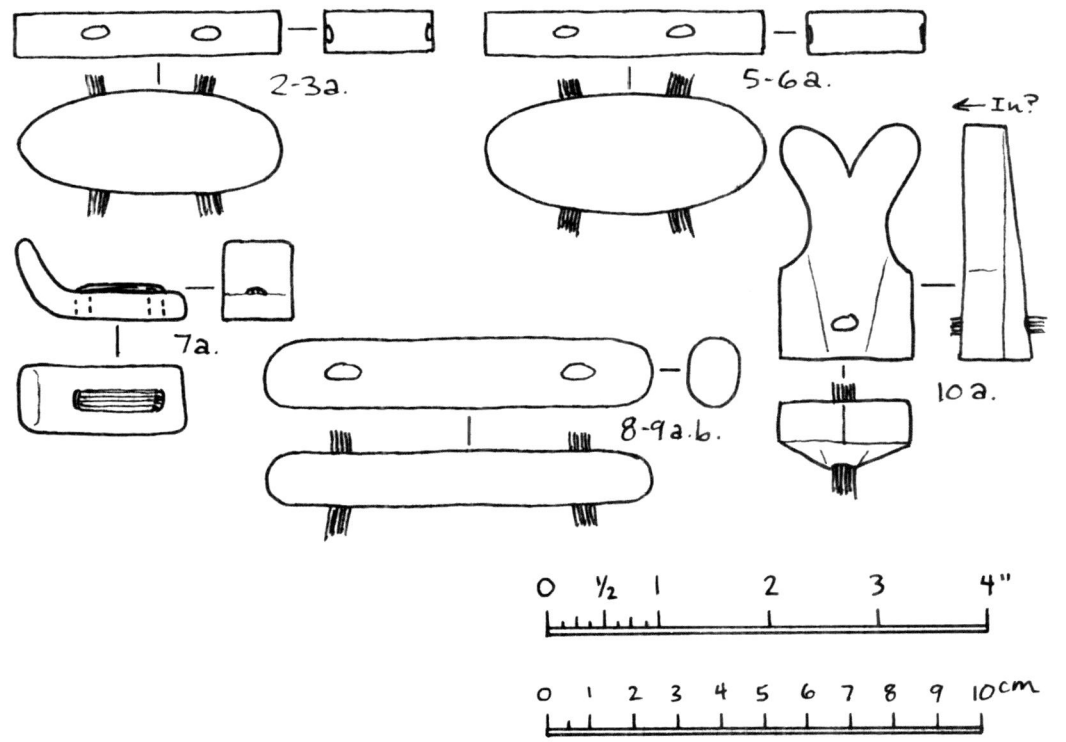

57. West Greenland Kayak: National Museum of Scotland, Edinburgh. Catalog no. 1894.227.

Museum catalog information for the 1894.227 only lists "Kayak of seal skin: Inuit, Lancaster Sound." The kayak is quite distinctly Greenlandic and could not be from Lancaster Sound (between Baffin Island and Devon Island in the Canadian Eastern High Arctic). Another kayak at the museum is undoubtedly the Lancaster Sound kayak: the U.C. 765. This confusion also surfaces in Souter's table of kayaks in Great Britain (1934:13), despite Kaj Birket-Smith having noted this error in his 1924 work (266).[39]

During my visit to the National Museum of Scotland, the paddle associated with the 1894.227 was found lying in a nearby dugout canoe, wrapped in plastic (see paddle-plate 30). A tag with the accession number and a name was attached: Livingstone-Learmonth. A Mr. Walter Livingstone-Learmonth traveled to Baffin Bay in 1889 as a passenger on the Dundee whaler *Maud* (W. Gillies Ross, 1985:213-224). It is undoubtedly this same person who collected this kayak and donated it to the National Museum of Scotland.

Livingstone-Learmonth made several photographs of Greenland kayaks during his 1889 voyage; several are presented in this book: Figures 282, 3, and 11. The kayak in figure 3 bears a very distinct resemblance to the 1894.227.

Figure 282: Seal hunters in 1889. (Photographer: Walter Livingstone-Learmonth/ Library and Archives Canada/ C-088301.)

---

[39] Birket-Smith attributes the U.C. 765 to Labrador; having seen and studied the U.C. 765 myself, I think it is more likely from North Baffin Island.

The 1894.227 is largely collapsed, though the ends— particularly the bow— are in fair condition The conjectural restoration was largely based on the National Museum of Finland's kayak no. 5023 (plate 63), to which it bears considerable resemblance.

Deck beams are intermittently lashed to the gunwales, and the ends of the gunwales have clamp-ties. The *masik* is 3/8" thick by 3-1/4" wide (9mm x 8.2cm) and it is flat for the mid-10" (25.4cm) of its length. Aside from the *masik*, there is only one curved deck beam. The *isserfik* measures 5/8" (16mm) thick by 1-5/8" (41mm) wide.

The longitudinals of the 1894.227 are both pegged and lashed to the ribs, and there doesn't appear to be any consistent pattern: In a few joints, both methods are used. The lashings are not continuous, although they do use the double-lash method. Where pegs were used in places far enough away from the cockpit, the excess was not trimmed off, so sharp spikes of 1/4" to 1" in length (6 to 25mm) are spread through the hull.

Bow and stern knobs are both missing, but are evidenced. The bow edging at the keel is intact and measures 1/4" by 1/4" (6mm square); keel edging is not evidenced at the stern. The coaming has a scarf protection strip at the upper backside, 6" long and 3/8" x 3/8" (15.2cm long x 9mm square), its outer face being rounded. A piece at the bottom edge is missing but evidenced.

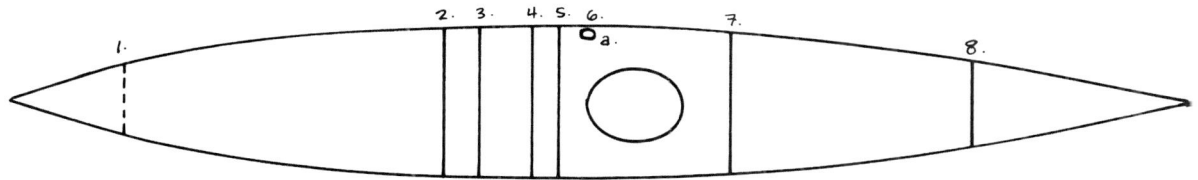

National Museum of Scotland: Cat. no. 1894.227

The only fitting present on the 1894.227 is a harpoon holder— a simple tab lashed through the *masik*. The only missing deck line is at the bow, which may or may not have had fittings. Like the 1894.227, many type VI kayaks have just four deck lines on the fore deck, although exceptions exist.

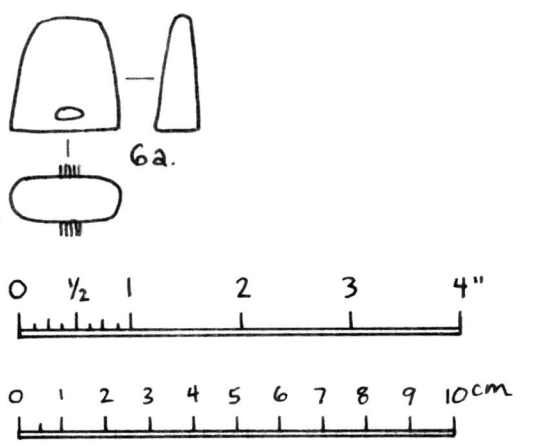

58. West Greenland Kayak: Mariner's Museum, Newport News, Virginia. Catalog no. BF-47.

This remarkably short kayak came to the Mariner's Museum after being transferred from the Smithsonian Institution in 1947. The Smithsonian's shipping invoice lists the item as "Kayak, southwest Greenland, received by the U.S. National Museum in 1901. Collector: Robert Stein."

Perplexingly, the length and width are recorded in the Mariners' Museum accession book as being 19′9″ (602.0cm) and 15-3/4″ (40.0cm) respectively. This could be a typographical error, or it could suggest that the 'Stein' kayak is not what is now the BF-47. I measured the kayak at 13′8-1/8″ (417.2cm) long, but a good chunk of the bow is missing. Projecting an original length, I came about a figure of 14′ 1-1/4″ (429.9cm). The width of this kayak is 18″ (45.7cm).

As far as the BF-47 coming from "Southwest" Greenland, I think this is unlikely. H. C. Petersen writes that the shortest kayaks in Greenland are from the Northern part of Disko Bay in the Ilulissat-Appat area (1986:43). This kayak is the shortest adult kayak in this study, and it does likely hail from Disko Bay vicinity— perhaps Godhavn/ Qeqertarsuaq as it was a common and convenient port-of-call for foreign (non-Danish) vessels traveling to North Greenland. Another short kayak is the Chateau de Ramezay kayak (76/13/88; plate 64) of unknown provenance, measuring 15′ 3-1/2″ (466.0cm) long.

All of the BF-47's ribs are pegged to the gunwales through their tenons. The double-pass lashing method is used to secure the keelson and chines to the ribs and is tied off at each joint, i.e., non-continuous. Deck beams are through-mortised and are intermittently secured to the gunwales with lashings. The BF-47's *masik* measures 7/8″ (22mm) thick and 2-3/4″ (70mm) wide; the *isserfik* is 5/8″(16mm) thick and 1-3/16″ (30mm) wide.

The coaming of the BF-47 is sewn to the *amiq* using a continuous lineal pattern, as in figure 123e. Four bone strips are present at the back of the coaming— the starboard pair spans the coaming's scarf, and the port pair may simply have been added for symmetry and/or a better grip on the spray skirt (tuitsoq) or paddling jacket (tuilik). The edging is 1/4″ (6mm) thick by 3/8″ (9mm) wide.

Two small bone buttons are present at the coaming's forward quarters— such pieces are identical to those seen on the kayak E.584 at the Hunterian Museum (plate 28). In the case of the BF-47, these buttons are set all the way through the coaming's face, and are top-pegged in place with a bone or ivory pin. The buttons measure 1/8″ (3mm) thick, 3/8″ (9mm) wide, and protrude 3/16″ (5mm) from the coaming; they are situated 1/4″ (6mm) below the top of the coaming. Keel edging is evidenced at the bow

Figure 283: Man carrying a kayak at Ikorfat, Northeast Disko Bay, 1906. (Photographer: Arnold Heim/ Arktisk Institut 25825.)

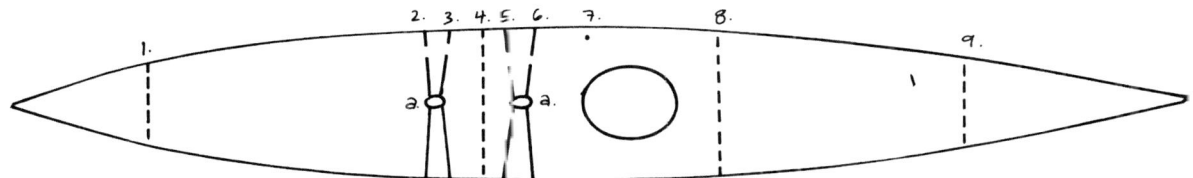

Mariners' Museum, Newport News: Cat. no. BF-47

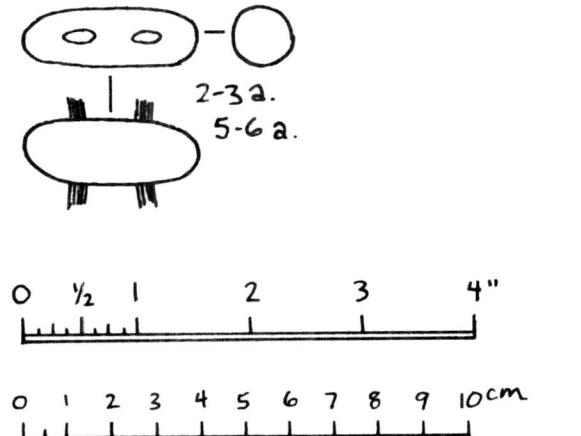

only. Two seam protection pieces are missing, but their positions are indicated on the scale drawing; one piece is present, and measures 3/16" (5mm) thick and 1/2" (13mm) wide.

None of the BF-47's deck lines were fully intact, though two link pieces were still present on the fore deck. The link pieces are identical to each other; there could have been more of them on the fore deck, such as with the following kayak, the AMNH 60.1/5253. A single aft deck line was evidenced but missing, as was the stern deck line.

59. West Greenland Kayak: American Museum of Natural History, New York, New York.
Catalog no. 60.1/5253

This child's kayak is attributed to Polar Greenland in the American Museum of Natural History's catalogs. The 60.1/5253 was accessioned in 1917. Captain George Comer, listed as the donor of this kayak, was the ice-pilot on the steam schooner *George B. Cluett*, which sailed in 1916 to relieve the Crockerland Expedition led by Donald MacMillan. The kayak clearly originates from West Greenland, and if it was collected in Polar Greenland, an earlier visitor/collector must have left it there.

Form-wise, this kayak very much appears to be a type V kayak. Its placement in the type VI section is on account of several distinct features. These are, for example, the four deck lines on the immediate fore deck, the single line just behind the cockpit, the high forward chine terminus, and the lack of aft deck stringers, which is somewhat rare for type VI, but unknown among the type V kayaks in this study.

The 60.1/5253's chines and keelson are fastened to the ribs with metal nails, and the gunwale ends are lashed together. The ribs are also nailed to the gunwales through their tenons; the nail-ends are bent over inside the kayak.

This kayak's *isserfik* is apparently a recycled section of a gunwale, as it has what appears to be a rib mortise carved into its forward edge. The *isserfik* measures 1/2" (13mm) thick by 1-5/16" (33mm) wide; the *masik* is 1/2" (13mm) thick and 1-1/4" (32mm) wide. The gunwale presents a bit of its lower edge astern, as the chine rises abruptly in this vicinity. Two deck stringers are present on the fore deck, and there are none on the aft deck.

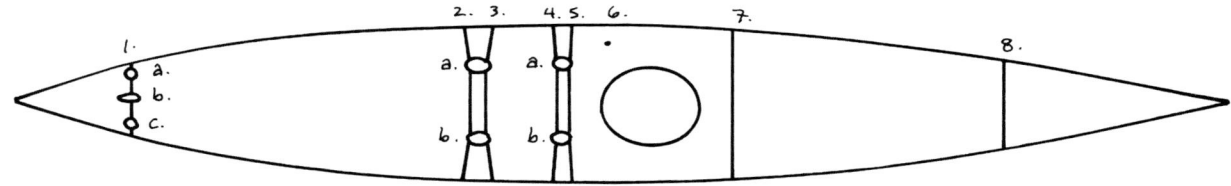

American Museum of Natural History, New York: Cat. no. 60.1.5253

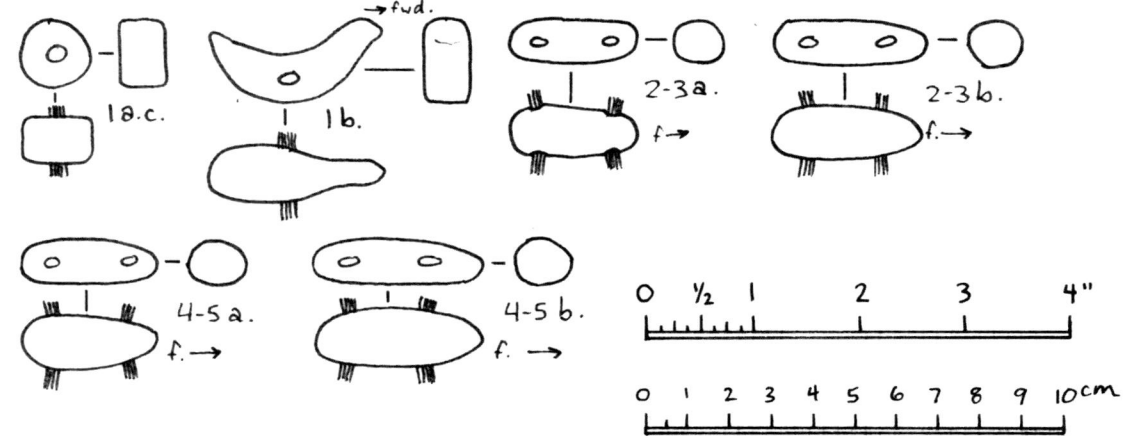

The 5253's coaming is scarfed together about as simply as can be: It is lapped and then wrapped with cord at each end. The scarf's overlap is 6″ (15.2cm) long. The *amiq* is attached to the coaming with bone or ivory pegs. The coaming is 5/16″ (8mm) thick and 7/8″ (22mm) high.

No keel-edging or end protection is evidenced on the 5253; this kayak would not have been used as extensively and as arduously as an adult's hunting kayak would be. Despite no evidence of having had end knobs, what appeared to be a kayak's end-knob was lodged inside of the kayak— well beyond my reach; it is more likely the end-knob of a harpoon.

Three deck fittings are present on the bow-most deck line. The outer two are simple beads, but the middle is a bird figure, facing forward. Between the bow deck line and the cockpit, there are only two pairs of deck lines, each pair being double-linked. There is a single deck line on the aft deck and a stern line— neither of these lines have any fittings. The harpoon holder is missing but is evidenced by a hole 5/8″ (16mm) inboard from the right sheer at the cockpit.

During the survey, museum staff asked the very good question as to whether or not this was a 'real' kayak or just a large model. The question had me wondering the same until I noticed a particular element: Inside the cockpit I was able to see a pair of deck-beam mortises that were not in present use, suggesting an alteration had been made during a re-skinning of this kayak— i.e., the lengthening of the cockpit. I believe this lends very high credibility to the notion that this was a kayak made for and indeed used by a child-kayaker in Greenland.

60. West Greenland Kayak: Canadian Canoe Museum, Peterborough, Ontario. CCM 977.182

According to both the Museum of the American Indian and the Canadian Canoe Museum's records, the 977.182 was received by the MAI via the American Geographical Society, circa 1918. No further accession information accompanied the kayak to Canada. This kayak is extremely damaged, but due to the nature of the damage, a survey was still possible; the artifactual and restored lines are both presented in the scale drawing.

The 977.182's *masik* was only 'half-there,' and entirely dislodged. The *masik* fragment measured 3″ (7.6cm) wide and showed evidence of having been pegged to the gunwales' top-edges with four pegs, appearing much like the example in figure 77c. The depth overall is conjecturally restored based on the fragment of the *masik*.

Through tenons are used in the fastening of the deck beams to the gunwales. The deck beams are intermittently top-pegged in place, such as in figure 37d. Knife marks left by the builder are present in the gunwales' top edges to indicate deck beam placement. The deck beams measure 5/8″ (16mm) thick by 1-1/4″ (32mm) wide; their tenons measure 3/16″ (5mm) high and 7/8″ (22mm) wide.

The forward deck stringers are indicated in the plan-view drawing, but their original spacing towards the bow is unknown, as they have shifted considerably. They measure 3/4″ by 3/4″ (19mm) in cross section at their aft ends. There are also two aft deck stringers; they are 19-3/4″ (50.1cm) long, 1″ (25mm) wide, and 7/16″ (11mm) thick, but their spacing and position is entirely unknown because the *isserfik* is missing.

Stern keel edging was not evidenced on the 977.182, but a series of holes indicates the one time placement of edging at the bow. Four seam protection pieces are also evidenced, one being present and measuring 1/2″ (13mm) wide and 5/16″ (8mm) thick. End knobs were not evidenced at the bow or stern.

All that remains of the 977.182's coaming are two fractured segments; the exact size of the cockpit is unknown and is therefore conjecturally suggested by a dashed-line in the scale drawing. The coaming fragments measure 3/8″ (9mm) thick and 1-3/16″ (30mm) high. The *amiq* was originally fastened to the coaming using ivory pegs as hangers, as in figure 123a.

Both artifactual and conjecturally restored lines of the 182 are presented in the scale drawing; the 5″ (12.7cm) difference of length is due to the slipped scarf joints on the gunwales just aft of the cockpit, and the displaced stern piece. Despite the scarfs being stepped birds-mouth joints, they failed in longitudinal compression due to the force of the shrinking seal skin *amiq*. The restored lines drawing of this kayak is based on similar examples as well as on the damaged remains of the 977.182 itself.

The great value of an otherwise very damaged kayak cannot be understated: The broken skin at the stern has exposed very interesting joinery. Figure 66 depicts the stern assembly— as much as could be seen.

All of the deck lines on this kayak were broken if not missing entirely. Only four lines were evidenced on the fore deck just ahead of the cockpit, and just a single line was just behind the cockpit. A harpoon holder was not evidenced. Bow and stern deck lines were also evidenced.

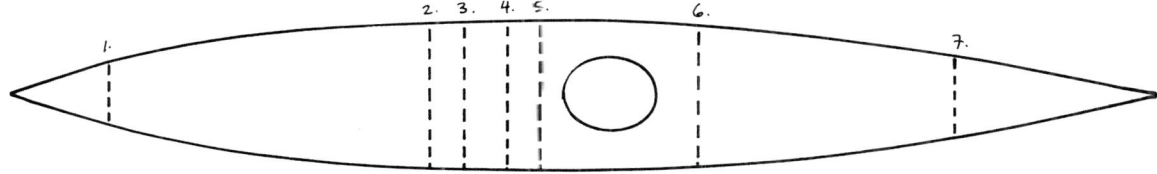

Canadian Canoe Museum, Peterborough: Cat. no. 977.182

61. West Greenland Kayak: Greenland National Museum, Nuuk. Catalog no. KNK 1215.

This kayak belonged to Peter Brøndlund of Oqaatsut, 14km north of Ilulissat (museum catalog), although another source suggests the kayak was built in 1919 on the western end of Nuussuaq Peninsula (Petersen, 1997:80, caption, fig.73). Both may in fact be true: Brønlund may have lived in or traveled to both locations. My scale drawing of this kayak is based on an unpublished survey drawing by John Heath; I have added details of the kayak's scantlings, construction, and its skeg. A paddle belongs to this kayak and is depicted in paddle-plate 26.

The KNK 1215 is in exceptional condition, although well used and repaired extensively. For example, the keelson in the cockpit has been partnered on both sides with strips of wood. The aft cockpit rib has a segment of cove molding lashed to its center in order to give it more rigidity. Other ribs forward and aft of the cockpit have splints lashed to them with many turns of fiber twine.

Three stanchions are present inside the 1215's hull. A stanchion forward of the cockpit sits between the single deck stringer and the keelson. Two stanchions behind the cockpit are positioned between deck beams and the keelson. These stanchions would prevent the hull from flattening— this kayak's numerous rib repairs and re-enforcements suggest that the rib material was not of the best quality.

Both the *masik* and the *isserfik* have one end resting in a block attached to the gunwales. This is a method for effectively lengthening a deck beam, as illustrated in figure 161. The block supporting the *masik* is on the left gunwale, and the block supporting the *isserfik* is on the right gunwale, perhaps reflecting the builder's desire to have a balanced kayak. The ribs are metal-nailed to the chines and keelson. The deck beams are intermittently lashed to the gunwales with fiber twine, and the ribs are all metal-nailed to the gunwales.

Figure 284: Group photograph taken in Ritenbenk (Appat) in 1909 by H. P. Steensby/ Arktisk Institut 45185.

Figures 285 and 286 show interior views of this kayak. (More or less the same view forward appears as a photograph in H. C. Petersen's Skinboats of Greenland [1986:54, figure 53], however it is mislabeled as a "Thule" [Polar Greenland] kayak from 1909.)

Seat slats are present in the cockpit of the 1215, but there is no evidence of permanent fastening. They are situated beneath the two cockpit ribs, but between them and the *amiq*, there is what appears to be sleeves cut from a wool sweater. A large rectangular piece of seal skin (likely a 'retired' *amiq*) was in the cockpit above the slats and the ribs. A carrying toggle is lashed to the curved deck beam nearest the *masik*, and is visible in figure 285.

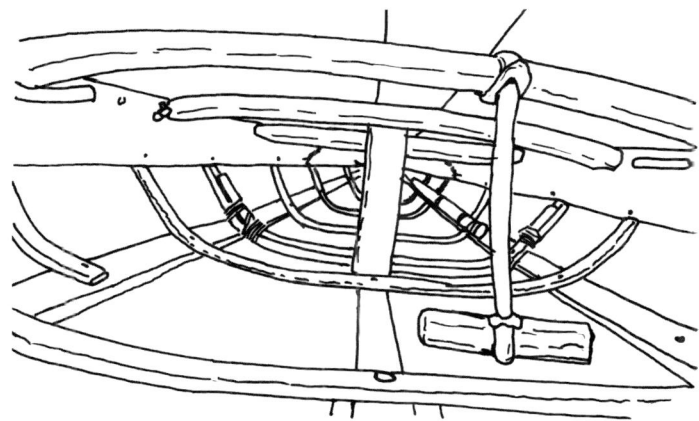

Figure 285: Forward interior view of the Greenland National Museum's kayak KNK 1215. Note the carrying toggle lashed to the curved deck beam and the stanchion.

A single forward deck stringer (2-3/4″ [7cm] wide) is present in the 1215, although two are present on the aft deck. I found an unattached skeg laying on the 1215's aft deck. Two holes drilled into its upper edge corresponded in distance with wear marks along the 1215's sides, furthering the likelihood that the skeg belonged to the kayak 1215. The skeg and

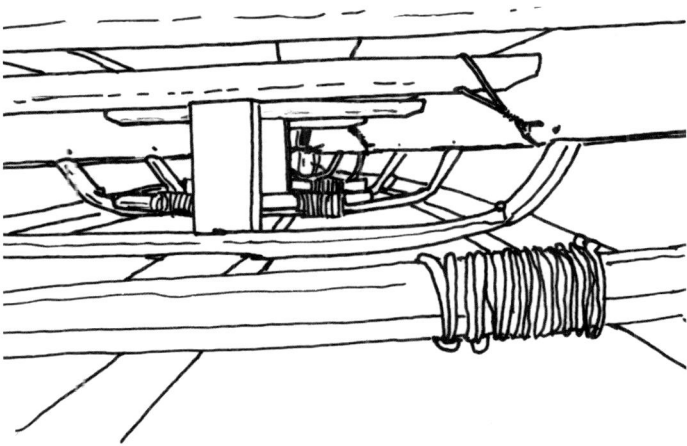

Figure 286: Aft interior view of the KNK 1215. Note the splinted ribs and the two stanchions between the keelson and two deck beams.

its position are illustrated in the scale survey drawing. The lashing marks suggest the attachment method depicted, as opposed to the method seen on the Museon's kayak 57992 (plate 68).

Another interesting feature of this kayak is that its *amiq* is pulled up and over the coaming's aft upper edge. This is a feature associated with much older kayaks (see the Lübeck kayak, the WFM 232, the DNM Lb.101, and the RvV 349 [plates 1, 2, 5, and 15] among others.) This coaming attachment is not as meticulously executed on the KNK 1215 as on the older kayaks. Instead, the pegs fastening the *amiq* to the outer face of the coaming are large stubs— not the finer buttons seen in the earlier kayaks.

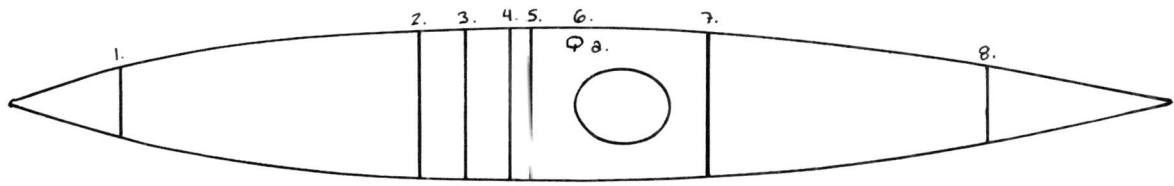

Greenland National Museum: Cat. no. KNK 1215

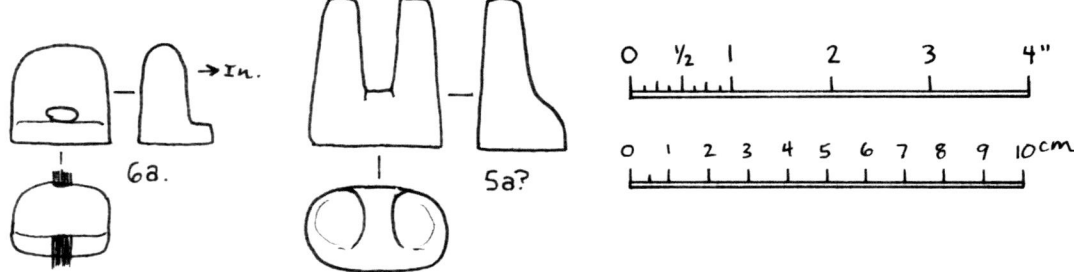

The only permanent deck fitting on the 1215 is a harpoon holder, lashed to the *masik*. This kayak does however have a removable deck fitting— made of wood. When I saw the kayak in 2000, this fitting was beneath deck line 5, though by essence of its portability, it was likely moved about as needed by the original owner. All of the other deck lines are intact. The deck line arrangement is fairly typical for type VI kayaks: four lines on the fore deck and one aft, with the bow and stern lines both quite slack.

62. West Greenland Kayak: Canadian Museum of Civilization, Ottawa. Catalog no. IV-A-427

The history of the Canadian Museum of Civilization's kayak IV-A-427 is unknown, though suggested by its accession card: "Collected possibly 1921 by Eastern patrol ships— 'Arctic' or 'Naskapi.'" Its provenance is given as "Disko Bay, Greenland." Both ships apparently called at Qeqertarsuaq (Godhavn), South Disko Island during the early years of the Eastern Patrol.

A slight flattening of the hull of the 427 is evidenced; I have restored this slightly in the scale drawing from a measured depth-to-sheer of 5-3/16" (13.2cm) to 6-11/16" (16.9cm). The 427 is otherwise in excellent condition.

Several interesting features are to be seen on the 427: The *masik* has a shallow divot— a handgrip— carved into its bottom face; the divot is rectangular. Such *masik* grips are apparently rare in West Greenland kayaks after about the mid 1800s. The *masik* measures 3/4" (19mm) thick by 3" (7.6cm) wide.

An ingenious construction solution not found in any other kayaks in this study is present on the 427: As can be seen in the cross-sections, the turn of the bilge is a very abrupt angle, increasing the likelihood of the lashed-on chines slipping up towards the gunwales. The builder prevented this by putting pegs through the ribs above the chines (as in figure 74) so as to prevent their migrating upwards. This method is present at every other rib-to-chine juncture.

Three ribs are visible in the plan-view of the scale drawing; the second and third rib back are nailed to the inside faces of the gunwales, having likely been retro-fitted. The aft rib straddles remnants of the original ribs that extend from the gunwales to the chines.

A skeg is present with the kayak 427; I had initially thought that one corner of it was chipped, and paid no further attention until Vernon Doucette pointed out that the corner had been shaped deliberately so as to fit over the forward end of the stern's keel-edging. This is a very elegant and common-sense feature that I nearly dismissed as damage. Where the skeg straps cross the kayak's sheer line, grooves have been sawn into the gunwales. The *amiq* dips into these grooves slightly allowing the skeg straps to seat

Figure 287: Kayaks tied alongside the patrol ship Arctic *at Godhavn, 1923. (Photographer: L. T. Burwash / Dept. of the Interior / Library and Archives Canada / PA-099037.)*

firmly in place. A separate cord is used to bind the skeg straps together in order to tighten them; this is depicted in the scale drawing of the IV-A-427.

Bow and stern keel edging are present; end knobs were not evidenced. The coaming is attached to the *amiq* with ivory pegs, and the coaming has two bone strips along its aft face. The coaming measures 11/16" (17mm) thick by 1-7/16" (32mm) high.

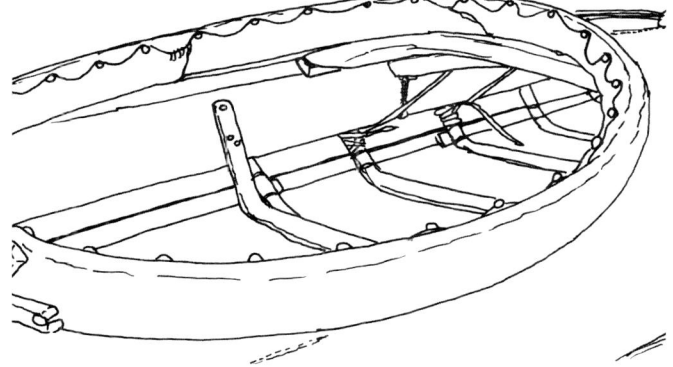

Figure 288: Cockpit view of the Canadian Museum of Civilization's kayak IV-A-427. Note the rib fastened to the face of the gunwales and the shim supporting the mask.

The bow deck line of the IV-A-427 is slack and has no fittings. At one side, the bow line had been broken and was repaired by being nailed to the kayak's sheer. Just behind it is a 1-3/8" (35mm) long loop of braided sinew sewn into the seam of the *amiq* providing an anchor point for a rifle holster. The stern deck line is missing. There are three pairs of linked deck lines on the IV-A-427: two ahead of the cockpit, and one behind it. The deck line pattern is similar to those of most type V kayaks, i.e., there are five on the fore deck and two on the aft deck, plus a bow and stern line. However, the slack bow deck line and the simple tab-shaped harpoon holder of the IV-A-427 are typical of type VI kayaks.

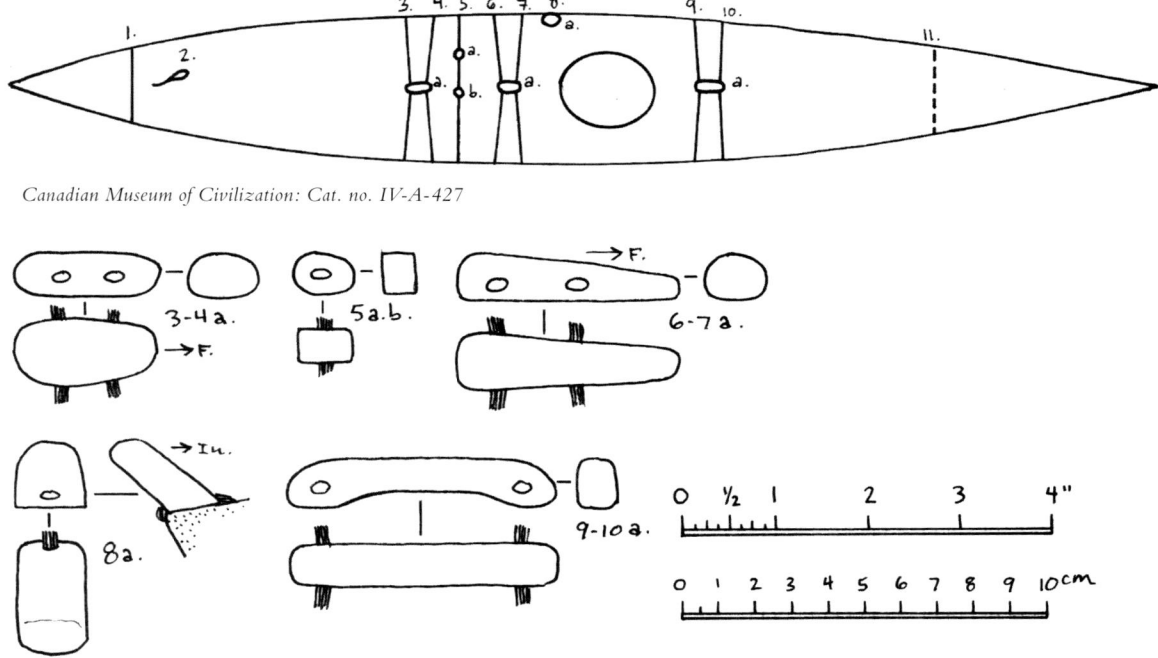

Canadian Museum of Civilization: Cat. no. IV-A-427

63. West Greenland Kayak: Finnish National Museum, Helsinki. Catalog no. 5023.

North Greenland colony official Harald Lindow donated this kayak to the Finnish National Museum in 1923. The exact geographical origin of this kayak is not known. A photograph of Harald Lindow in a kayak in Ataa Sound (Ikerasak), 40k north of Ilulissat, is presented in figure 289; this very well may be the kayak now at the Finnish National Museum

The bow of the 5023 is moderately long, while the stern is very short; both stems are gracefully convex. The sheer amidships is very slight, being rather flat, but the ends have a gentle rise to them. Viewed via the cross-sections of the hull, the 5023 appears less aesthetic, though its functionality as a low-freeboard stable hunting platform is plain to see.

Several of the deck beams in the 5023 are pegged in place using the oblique-method. The deck beams are rectangular in cross-section, not being cambered on their lower faces as is common among many Greenland kayaks. Clamping ties joining the gunwales towards their ends are present fore and aft.

The 5023's *isserfik* is 4-9/16″ (11.6cm) wide and 11/16″ (17mm) thick, but closer examination revealed it to be three deck-beams placed tightly together. The middle one is obliquely pegged in place. The aft-most one is likely just tenoned into the gunwale, but the fore-most one rests on small wooden hangers nailed to the gunwale's face (as in figure 158), and wasn't tenoned in place. An *isserfik* of this breadth would've handled considerable weight, though the fore-most piece may have been added to simply shorten the cockpit length.

Figure 289: Harald Lindow paddling a kayak in Ataa Sound (Ikerasak) north of Ilulissat. This kayak may be the Finnish National Museum's 5023. (H. Lindow/ Arktisk Institut 08108.)

The coaming of the 5023 is lashed to the *amiq*; this lashing is continuous and enters the coaming every 1-1/2″ (38mm). The face-scarfed joint in the 3/8″ (9mm) thick coaming is fastened with metal nails. Keel edging or end-knobs were not present or evidenced on the 5023.

All of the lines and fittings on the NMF 5023's were present and intact. The 5023's fittings are few however— just two link pieces on the fore deck and a thin stumpy harpoon holder. The bow and stern deck lines are without fittings and are very slacked— looping 1-1/2″ (38mm) high forward, and 3″ (76mm) high aft. Only one deck line is present on the aft deck.

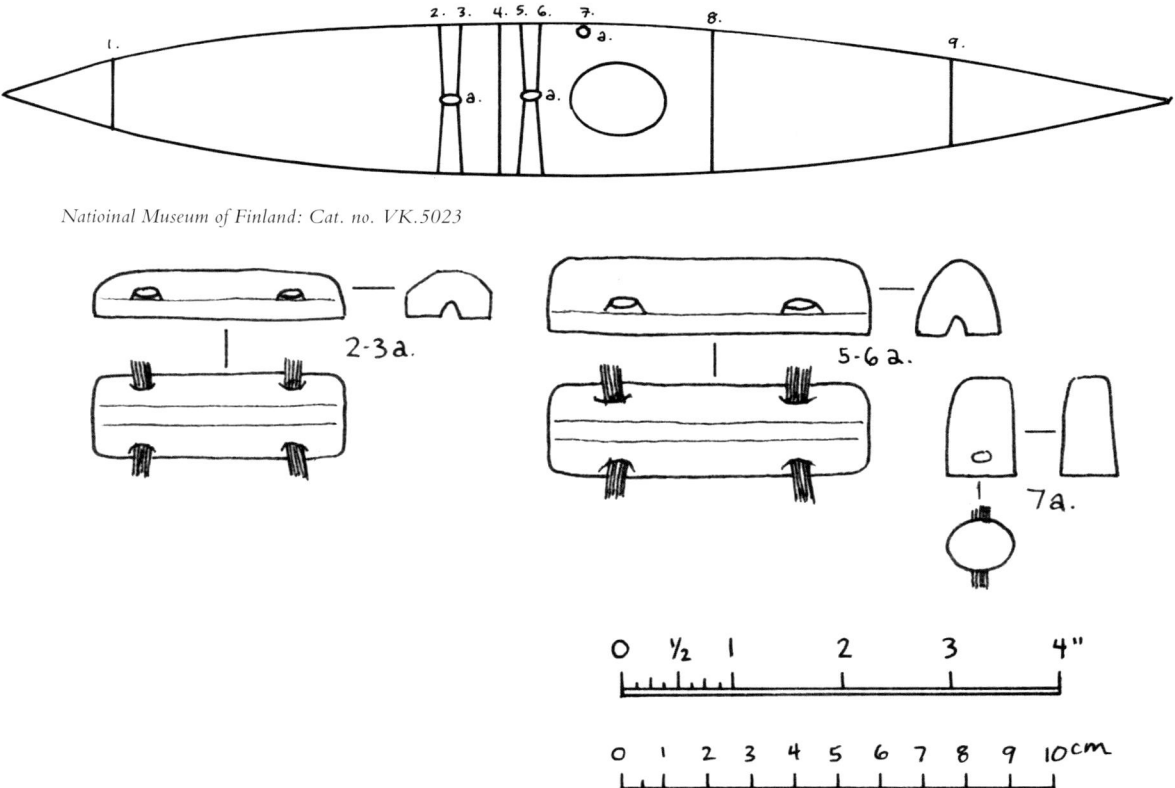

National Museum of Finland: Cat. no. VK.5023

64. West Greenland Kayak: Chateau de Ramezay, Montreal; on loan to the Canadian Museum of Civilization, Ottawa. Catalog no. 76/13/88

The kayak 76/13/88 is on a lengthy temporary loan from the Chateau de Ramezay in Montreal to the Canadian Museum of Civilization. Its history was not passed along to the CMC when transferred; the catalog number is a CMC number. Richard Nonas, Vernon Doucette, and I surveyed the 76/13/88 at the CMC in 2004.

The *masik* in the 76/13/88 is a very low shallow arch, but it has been placed atop 1/2" (13mm) high shims on top of the gunwales, the *masik* and shim being top-nailed to the gunwales. The *masik* itself measures 1/2" (13mm) thick by 3-5/8" (9.2cm) wide. Only one curved deck beam is present (or evidenced) in this kayak; it is placed 5" (12.7cm) ahead of the *masik*'s aft edge and is 1-1/4" (32mm) wide. The *isserfik* measures 3/4" (19mm) thick by 1-3/4" (44mm) wide.

Metal nails are used to fasten the ribs to the gun-

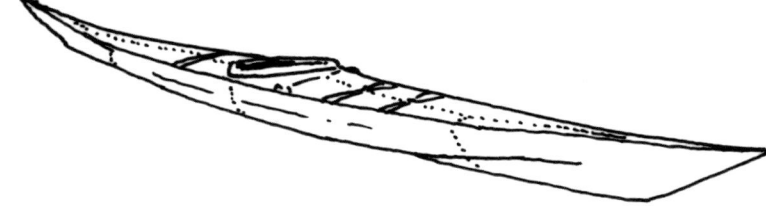

Figure 290: View of the Chateau de Ramezay's Greenland kayak, presently at the Canadian Museum of Civilization.

wales, but their exact configuration is very different from most other kayaks: The method used in this kayak is depicted in figure 50. The reason for this method is mysterious— was it used so as to weaken the gunwale less? The points of the nails do protrude into the cockpit somewhat. Both lashings and nails are used in fastening the chines and keelson to the ribs. The lashings occur at these joints towards the ends of the kayak (at the first three and last three ribs), while nails are used elsewhere.

The seat arrangement in this kayak is very unique and quite ingenious in its simplicity: A twine cord is laced back and forth around the two ribs in the cockpit— affecting a sort of hammock or cargo-net for the buttocks.

End knobs are not present, nor are they evidenced. Keel edging is present both at the bow and stern. The coaming has a single bone strip at the top of its aft-face; its length is 15″ (38.1cm) and is 1/4″ (6mm) thick and 3/8″ (9mm) high. This bone strip is fastened with square bone nails whose heads measure 3/16″ (5mm) by 9/16″ (14mm) long. These square nails are pinned in place through both the coaming's top edge and the bone strip's top edge (as in figure 121). The coaming measures 3/8″ (9mm) thick by 1-1/8″ (28mm) high.

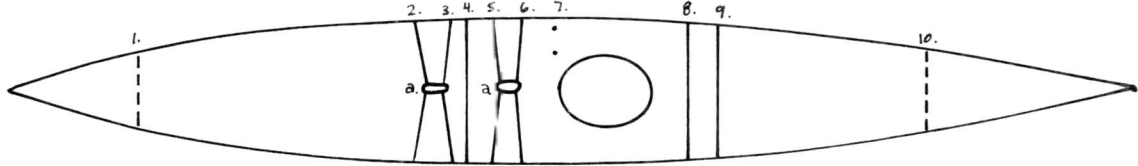

Canadian Museum of Civilization: Cat. no. 76/13/88

A skeg is present with the 76/13/88: Its profile and position is indicated in the scale drawing. There is an elegant semi-circular cutout in the skeg's upper edge; it was perhaps fashioned such to ease the skeg's grip on the water somewhat. The skeg is 9/16″ (14mm) wide at its top edge, and tapers to a sharp edge along the curve. Apparently the skeg had been lashed to the kayak's aft deck line.

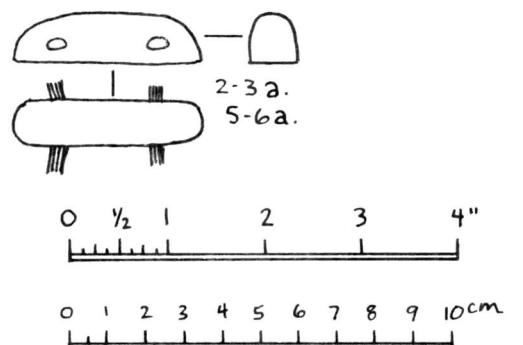

Both the bow and stern deck lines are missing from the 76/13/88, as is the harpoon holder. Only two fittings are present, both being identically sized link pieces situated on the fore deck. Aside from the missing harpoon holder, these may have been the only fittings on this kayak. There are two deck lines on the aft deck, and these have no fittings.

65. West Greenland Kayak: Canadian Museum of Civilization, Ottawa. Catalog no. IV-A-428

Museum accession cards list this kayak as having been collected circa 1927-28 by R. T. Porsild in the Disko Bay vicinity. Jonathan Goldner and I surveyed this kayak, although it was previously surveyed by John Heath and Eugene Arima, its lines having been published in *Contributions to Kayak Studies* (Arima, ed. 1991:103). The 428's paddle is depicted in paddle-plate 41.

The general form of the 428 shows distinct influence from more southerly kayaks (i.e., type V), specifically the relatively low stern, greater sheer, greater rocker, stern edging, end knobs, increased deadrise, and a longer and straighter stern. It does however retain several distinct type VI characteristics such as the laced-on coaming, the simpler deck rigging (specifically the four lines on the fore deck), and the very high positioning of the chines' forward ends.

The rib-to-gunwale joints in the 428 are fastened with thin metal nails, bent over on the inside. The ribs in the cockpit are lashed (non-continuously) to the keelson and chines, but ahead of the cockpit every other rib is nailed instead of lashed. Aft of the cockpit, the situation is random; three ribs are nailed, and four are lashed. The ribs are made from split limbs, possibly collected locally. The *masik* measures 3/4″ (19mm) thick by 2-5/8″ (66mm) wide, and is actually two pieces of wood mated together fore and aft. The *isserfik* is 3/4" (19mm) thick by 1-1/4" (32mm) wide.

The 428's seal skin *amiq* is painted silvery white— the paint is worn away around the immediate fore deck, suggesting it had gotten some use before it was shipped south. The coaming is a perfectly circular mast-hoop, and is sewn to the coaming via a continuous pattern. A single strip of bone 16-7/8″ long (42.8cm) is present at the coaming's aft upper edge, covering the scarf. This strip measures 3/16″ (5mm) thick by 1/2″ (13mm) wide.

Both end knobs are present on the 428; the bow knob is diagonally pegged, while the stern knob is side-pegged. The keel edging measures 3/8″ (9mm) thick by 5/8″ (16mm) wide, and tapers to 1/4″ (6mm) thick at its outer ends.

The deck fittings on the IV-A-428 are quite numerous for this kayak type; the taut bow and stern lines, with two and three fittings each respectively, show southerly influence. The deck lines are set into the gunwales 1/2″ (13mm) below the sheer line. Interestingly, only four deck lines are present on the fore deck— a tip-off to this kayak's more northerly heritage.

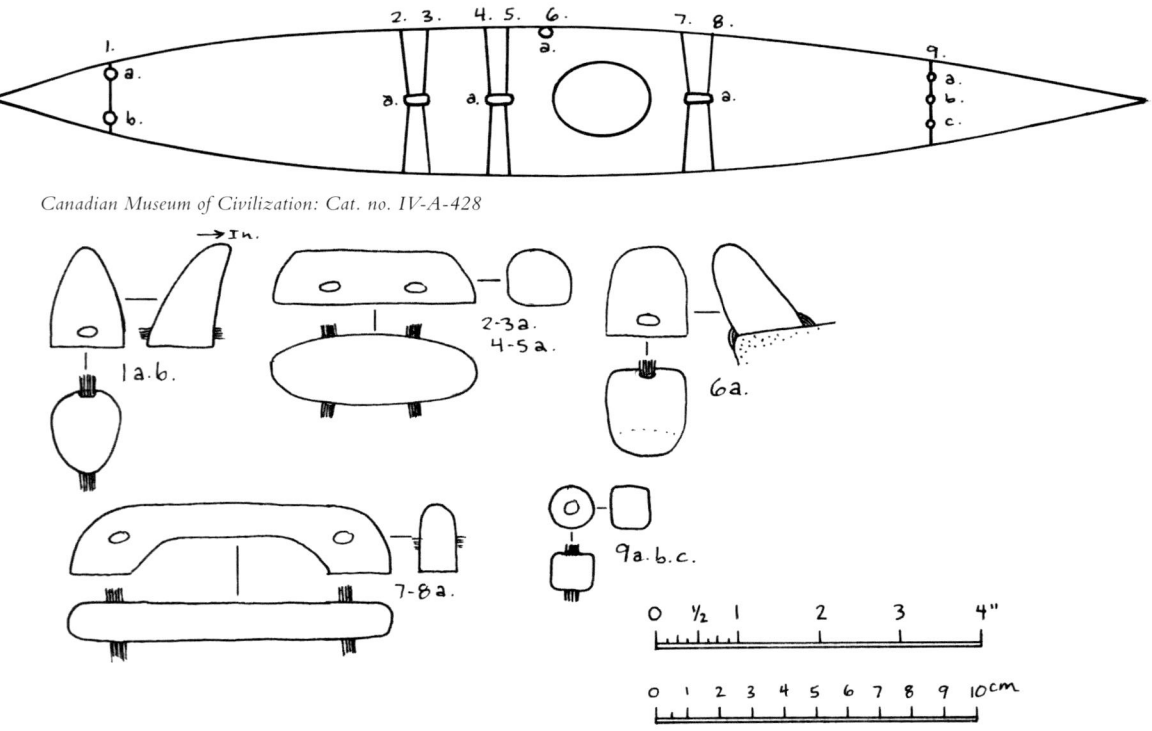

Canadian Museum of Civilization: Cat. no. IV-A-428

66. West Greenland Kayak: Greenland National Museum, Nuuk. Catalog no. KNK 2237.

The Greenland National Museum's kayak KNK 2237 was collected by Upernavik colony manager Carl Ernst Lembcke-Otto, and sent to Dr. Thomas Thomsen at the Danish National Museum in 1930. The kayak was catalogued at the Danish National Museum as the L.18.7a. In the 1990s, this kayak was given to the Greenland National Museum in Nuuk.

In the accompanying letter to Dr. Thomsen, Lembcke-Otto writes that this kayak was "probably one of the last of the original types which was being used up here before the introduction of the slender South Greenland kayaks" (letter dated August 18th, 1930; translated to me by Claus Andreassen). Lembcke-Otto's statement is a bit perplexing because the 2237 itself is quite slender; in any case it is clearly of the form and construct of the 'original type,' e.g., the NMNH's 160325 (plate 56). An example of a distinctly Southern-influenced Upernavik kayak can be seen in the DNM L.18.273 of the 1960s (plate 73).

The KNK 2237 has an abrupt, short upturned stern, and a fairly short bow as well. Kaj Birket-Smith describes Upernavik kayaks as having "No sheer. Short stem and quite a short stern, the former slightly, the latter very strongly curved" (1924:271). The abrupt and strongly curved stern of the KNK 2237 calls to mind that of the NMNH's 160325 (plate 56).

The 2237 is extremely damaged, having extensive hull-collapse from 7′ to 11′6″ (213.4 to 350.5cm) aft of the bow. Minor collapse is present from 5′ to 7′ (152.4 to 213.4cm) and from 11′6″ to 14′6″ (350.5 to 441.9cm) aft. The shrinking of the *amiq* caused the hull collapse. The scale drawing shows both artifactual and conjecturally restored elevations. Figure 291 depicts the forward inside-view of the 2237.

There is only one deck stringer on the 2237— ahead of the cockpit, measuring two feet long. This kayak has two pairs of chines, though the second pair is much shorter than the main pair; the shorter pair of chines extends from 7′10″ to 12′4″ (238.7 to 375.9cm). This rare chine configuration only appears in two other non-Polar Greenland kayaks

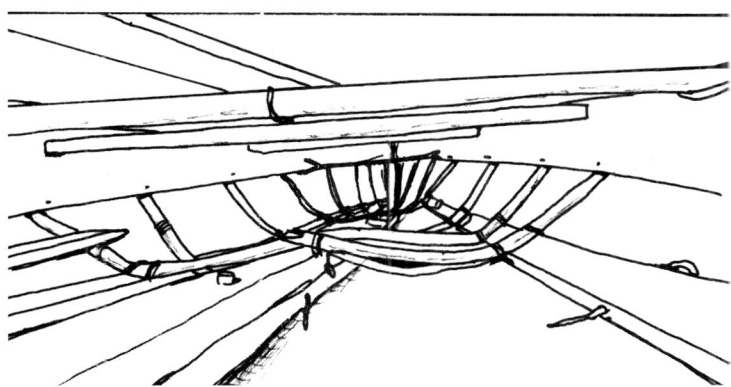

Figure 291: Forward interior view of the GNM's kayak KNK 2237. Note the secondary chine's termini at the left— its end is simply lifted above a rib.

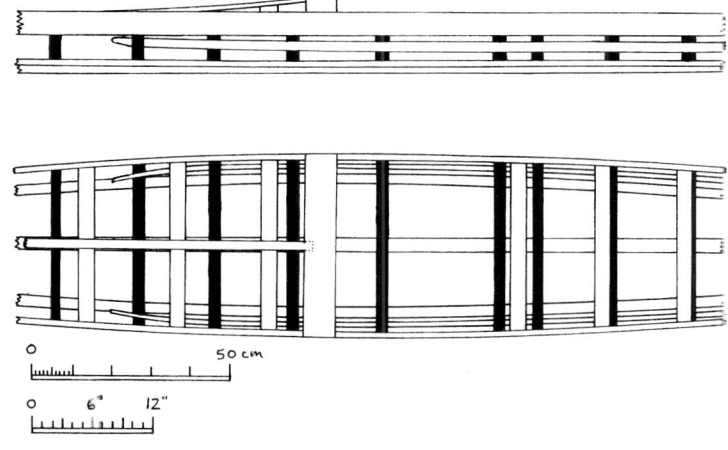

Figure 292: Amidships framing pattern of the Greenland National Museum's kayak 2237.

in this study: The Greenland National Museum's kayak 1161 (plate 9), and the Canadian Museum of Civilization's kayak IV-A-483 (plate 46).

Deck beam fasteners are not visible inside the 2237, so it could be presumed that a top-peg method is used in at least some of the deck beams. A large clamping tie is evident at the stern gunwale joint; the bow is obscured by debris and a heavily frayed jute clamping-tie with a windlass stick in its center.

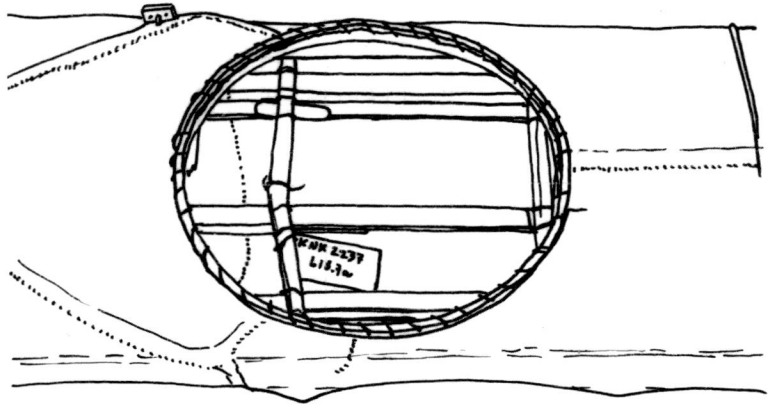

Figure 293: Cockpit view of the KNK 2237. The lumps at the bottom of the sketch are displaced or broken ribs protruding into the amiq.

The ribs of the 2237 are pinned to the gunwales through the mortise and tenon, and the ends of the pins are not sawn off, and stick as much as an inch into the kayak's interior. All four chines are lashed to the ribs via the double-lash method, though the lashings are tied off at each juncture, not being continuous. The keelson is also lashed non-continuously, and uses a single-pass lashing pattern as depicted in figure 69.

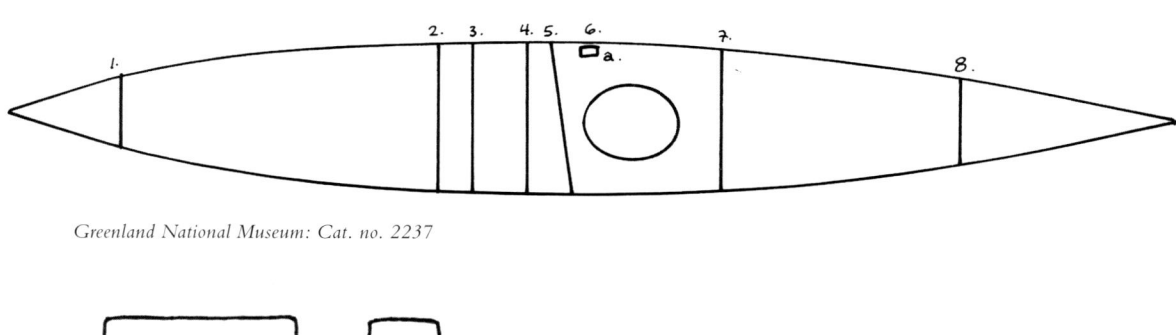

Greenland National Museum: Cat. no. 2237

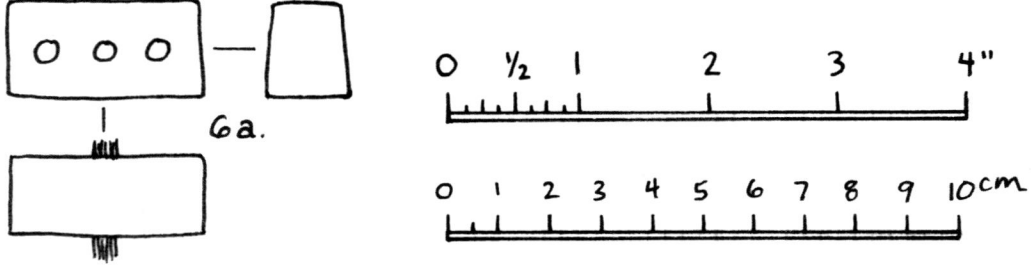

Figure 294: The replica of the Greenland National Museum's 2237, paddled by Kathy Tucker in 2005. (Photograph by the author.)

The coaming is scarfed in the front— not particularly common among Greenland kayaks. Also, the coaming is laced to the skin with a cord that is wrapped over the coaming's upper edge, as in figure 123c. The coaming measures 5/16″ thick by 1-5/16″ high (8 x 33mm). The *amiq* is entirely painted— mostly a mauvish-brown, but with a large black patch on the right-hand fore deck. Figure 293 shows the coaming, deck-seams, harpoon holder, and the cockpit layout of the 2237.

The deck-line configuration on the KNK 2237 is very simple. There are four lines on the fore deck; the two fore deck lines closest to the cockpit are oblique. The aft deck has just a single line. The harpoon holder is the only fitting on this kayak. The bow deck-line is a double-strand that winds through two small leather loops projecting from the gunwale's upper edge— perhaps stubs from a broken deck line. All of the 2237's deck lines are fairly slack. The only keel edging is at the bow, and there are no end-knobs present or evidenced. The 2237's paddle is depicted in paddle-plate 33.

The sterile lines presentation of the scale drawing does not show the KNK 2237 as a particularly pretty kayak. Even 'in-life,' the damaged original with its awful paint color was

Figure 295: The frame of the KNK 2237 replica. Note the secondary chine and how it is tucked inside of the ribs at its ends. (Photograph by the author.)

Figure 296: Kathy Tucker in the KNK 2237 replica, 2005. (Photograph by the author.)

unappealing. Still, its unique multi-chine construction and its being "...one of the last of the original types..." from Upernavik peaked my curiosity: I built a replica of this kayak in 2001.

On the water, the 2237 replica was surprisingly pleasant, comfortable, and capable— even quite pretty (see figures 294 and 296). The stability, as expected for a shallow flat-bottomed kayak, was superb. The cross-sections and shallow ends give it a relaxed grip on the water, so it is quite agile; lack of rocker, and its flat shallow decks give it very good handling, tracking, and correcting in winds from all points. The 2237 replica is a wet ride in moderate wind-chop, but its ease of handling more than makes up for this.

67. West Greenland Kayak: Canadian Museum of Civilization, Ottawa. Catalog no. IV-A-375

Canadian Museum of Civilization accession cards list the kayak IV-A-375 as having been made for the Botanist A. E. Porsild. Its origin is given as Disko Bay, 1931.

The 375, like the CMC's IV-A-428 (plate 65), exhibits distinct type V kayak influences in its general form: The stern is rather low and the stems both have a slight clipper-cut to them. Features such as the laced-on coaming, the simple deck rigging, and the shallow gunwales (being only 2-1/2" [6.3cm] high) are somewhat typical type VI features.

Figure 297: A kayak at Qeqertarsuaq ca. early-to-mid 1930s. (Photographer: Unknown/ Dept. of the Interior/ Library and Archives Canada/ PA-042116.)

The *masik* of the 375 is canted forward— similar to the *masik* of the Peqatigiiffik Qajaq Nuuk's old frame, only executed differently. In the case of the 375, the *masik* is sitting on wedges atop the gunwales; these wedges tilt the *masik* forward (as in figure 170 right), raising the depth slightly allowing for a roomier cockpit. The 375's *masik* measures 1/2″ (13mm) thick by 3-1/8″ (80mm) wide.

The first three ribs and the last two ribs are lashed to the keelson, and the first and last ribs are lashed to the chines: The rest of the rib-to-chine and keelson joints are nailed. The ribs are not fastened to the gunwales. Deck beams are intermittently lashed to the gunwales, and clamping ties

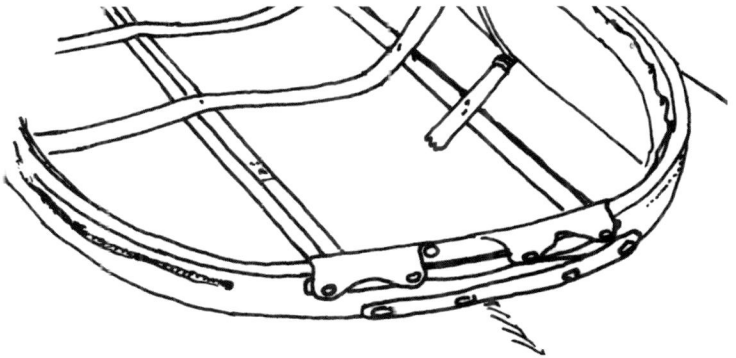

Figure 298: Detail of the IV-A-375's coaming. Note the skin pulled up and over the coaming back.

are present between the gunwales towards the bow and stern. Through mortises are used for the deck beams, as evidenced by the tenons leaving impressions in the *amiq*.

As with the Greenland National Museum's kayak 1215 (plate 61), the 375 has its *amiq* pulled up and over the back of its coaming. The *amiq* is attached to the upper coaming strip with the four ivory nails used to secure the strip. The front and sides of the coaming are sewn to the *amiq* with a continuous stitching of twine. These features are illustrated in figure 298.

An end knob is present at the bow of the 375, and while a stern knob may have been fitted, there is no evidence of one as the skin is broken and the end of the kayak's frame is chipped. Keel edging is present forward and aft, although a portion is missing aft.

Two rifle bag anchors are present along the seam towards the bow of the IV-A-375. Each of these is made of braided sinew and measure 1-1/6″ (1.5mm) long. The fact that there are two such anchor points likely suggests the use of a rifle and shotgun; it is however possible to secure two rifle bags to one anchor point. Ahead of these anchor points, a bow deck line is evidenced but missing. Four deck lines are present on the fore deck; lines 4 and 5 are linked, as are lines 6 and 7. Deck line 6 has two small beads to the left of the link piece. The two aft deck lines are linked together with a 'suitcase handle' formed piece. The stern line is missing, but evidenced.

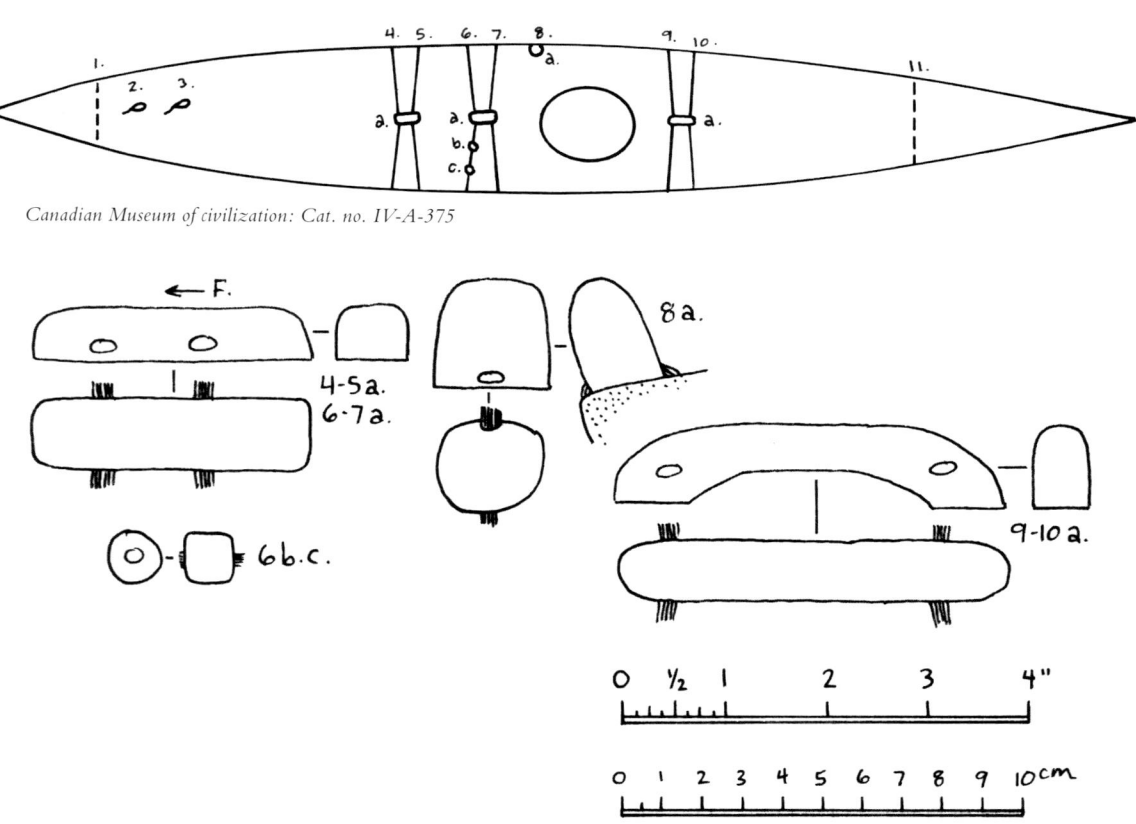

Canadian Museum of civilization: Cat. no. IV-A-375

68. West Greenland Kayak: Museon, The Hague, the Netherlands. Catalog no. 57992.

Museon accession data for the 57992 show that this kayak was purchased in Denmark by Dr. Gert Nooter in 1969. Nothing else of its history was described in the files, excepting that Nooter paid one Danish Kroner for it.

The 57992 has an elegant plainness in form, the curve of the sheer is subtle, particularly astern. While the 57992 resembles type V kayaks, numerous aspects have landed it in the type VI category. Most prominent of these are its high chine terminus forward, the slack bow and stern deck lines, the lack of keel edging and end knobs, the single bone strip on the back of the coaming, the rifle bag anchor loop, the tab-shaped harpoon holder and the relatively light scantlings— in particular the gunwale heights. It is the occurrence of all these together that lead me to think of this kayak as being type VI.

There is some hull collapse in the 57992; the artifactual depths-to-sheer are 8-1/4″ (20.9cm) at 4′, 6-1/4″ (15.9cm) at 8′, and 5-1/2″ (14.0cm) at 12′. My conjectural restoration is based on similar kayaks and by 'virtually' expanding deformed ribs.

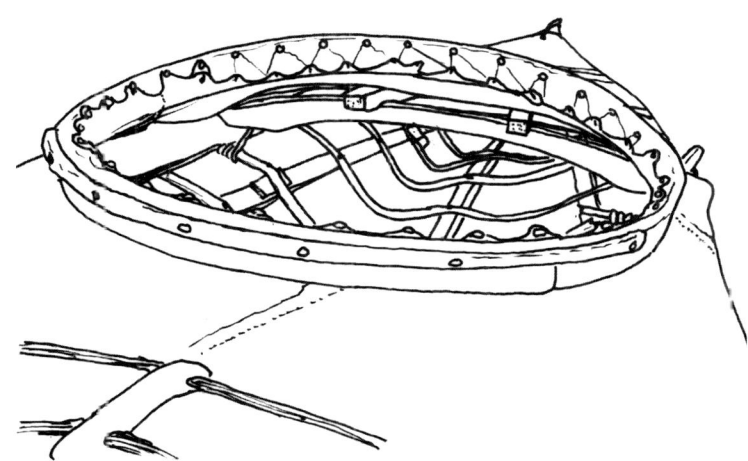

The fore deck of the 57992 is quite tall, the depth overall being 2-7/8″ (7.3cm) greater than the depth-to-sheer. The *masik* projects over the gunwale edges 5/16″ (8mm) on each side. Looking into the cockpit, (figure 299) one can see the rear-most curved deck beam and the aft ends of the deck stringers. The *masik* is considerably taller, and the deck stringers do not fair gracefully to the height of the *masik*. It appears that this kayak was hastily modified for a large or stiff-legged person. Further evidence suggests

Figure 299. Cockpit view of the Museon's kayak 57992; note the collapsed hull and raised masik.

that the modification was made after the kayak had been covered in seal skin: The *amiq* is not attached directly to the coaming's ivory pegs in the front— instead, there is a cord laced through the holes in the *amiq* and over these pegs.

One could assume the *masik* of the 57992 is top-fastened with pegs, as no fasteners are visible from inside the kayak. The longitudinals in the 57992 are all metal-nailed to the ribs, and the ribs are pegged through their tenons to the gunwales. A segment of the keelson is missing in the cockpit area, and has been partnered on both sides with equally sized pieces of wood, as in figure 168.

The 57992's coaming measures 3/4″ (19mm) thick by 1-1/4″ (32mm) high, and the bone strip attached to its upper aft face is 20″ (50.8cm) long and 1/4″ (6mm) thick by 1/2″ (13mm) wide.

A removable skeg is attached to the stern of the 57992. It is slung beneath a stick that rests transversely on the aft deck (such as depicted in figure 133 bottom). A light cord is threaded through holes in the wider upper edge of the fin. The fact that the 57992's skeg is easily removed must have been a consideration of the builder. No end knobs or keel edging are present or evidenced.

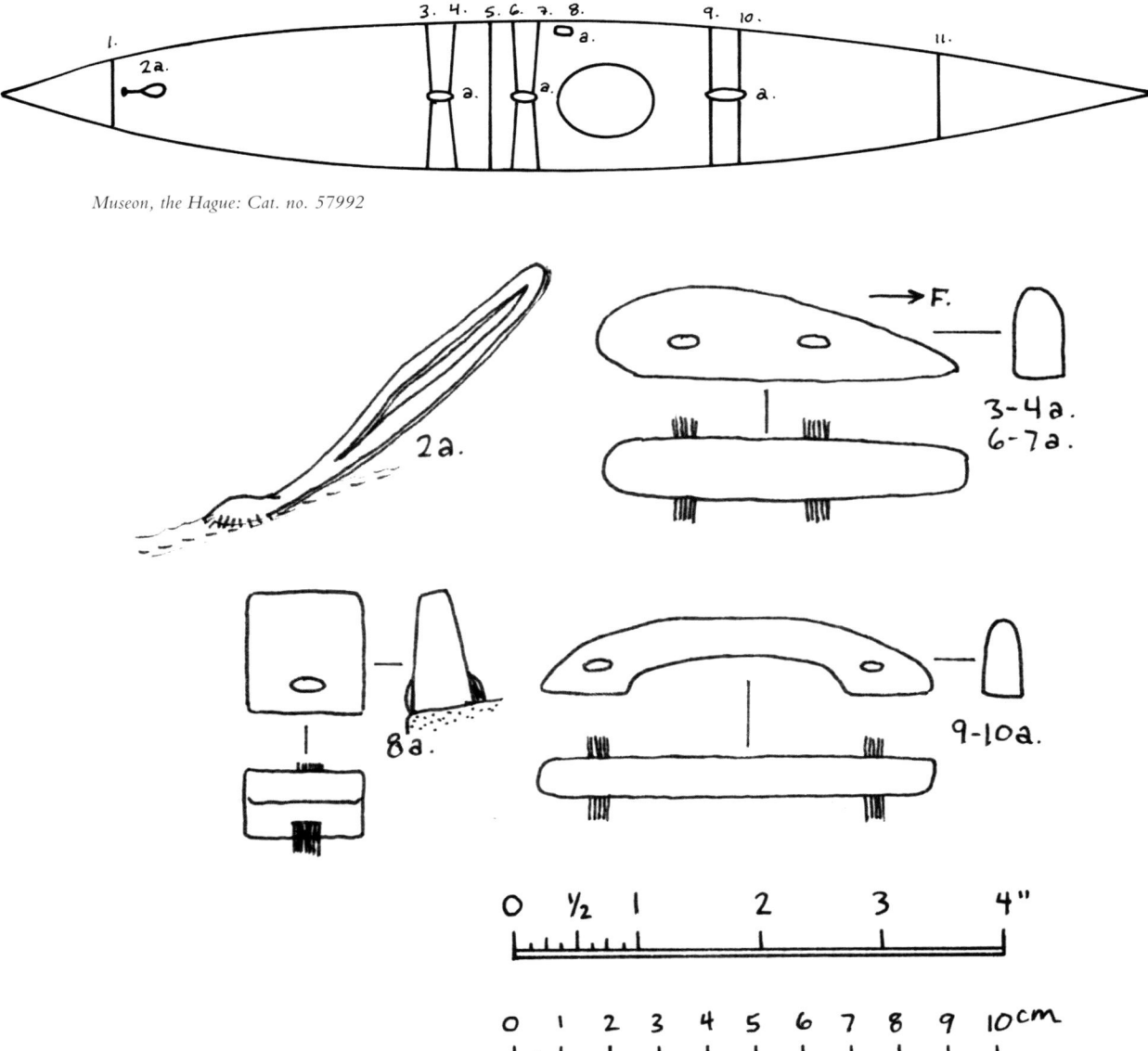

Museon, the Hague: Cat. no. 57992

Both the bow and stern deck line are present and intact; both are quite slack and without fittings. A unique attachment is present just aft of the bow deck line: It is a 3-1/2″ (8.9cm) long seal skin loop sewn into an *amiq* seam. This loop served as the anchor-point for the forward end of a rifle bag. The two link pieces on the fore deck are identical to each other, and their blunt ends face aft. A suitcase-handle shaped link is present on the aft deck. The harpoon holder is a simple tab shape.

69. West Greenland Kayak: Canadian Canoe Museum, Peterborough, Ontario. Catalog no. CCM 977.183

Catalogued as being from East Greenland, this kayak is undoubtedly from the northern part of Greenland's West Coast, likely the vicinity of Upernavik or Upernavik Kujalleq. The 977.183 came to the Canadian Canoe Museum in 1976, having been in the (US) Museum of the American Indian since 1941. Records transferred to the CCM list the same provenance of East Greenland, having been collected by J. Kenneth Horton. The 977.183's old catalog number at the MAI was H20/4863. That this kayak would be attributed to East Greenland is not too surprising: Oblique deck lines are known to have been used in East Greenland, (see DNM Lc.148, plate 82), and the size and shallowness of the 977.183 is similar to many East Greenland kayaks.

The hull of the 977.183 has flattened somewhat, though the sheer has held its form very well. (The artifactual depth-to-sheer [at the *masik*] of the 977.183 is 4-1/8″ [10.4cm]). Fortunately, a nearly identical kayak in superb condition exists (KNK 1550x10, plate 70), and was instrumental in achieving the conjecturally restored lines of the 183. Notable differences between the two exist, such as the deck-line arrangements and the slightly higher and more elegant stern of the 183.

The 977.183 has two deck stringers forward and two aft of the cockpit. The aft pair is set in flush with the upper surface of the *isserfik* (as in figure 84 left), quite unlike how it is usually done in more

Figure 300: A kayaker sharing his kayak with a young student at Kullorsuaq, northern Upernavik District in 1956. (Photograph by Jette Bang/Copyright: Greenland National Museum and Archive.)

southerly Greenland. The aft deck stringers are 2-1/2″ (63mm) wide and 22″ (55.9cm) long— fairly lengthy for a Greenland kayak, although deck stringers seem to be consistently long among Greenland kayaks from north of Disko Bay (compare to NMNH 160325, JDH 1959, and the DNM L.18.273— plates 56, 72, and 73).

The 977.183 has two 17-1/2″ (44.4cm) long seat slats in the cockpit: These slats are 3/8″ (9mm) thick by 1-1/2″ (38mm) wide. The fore deck stringers are 5/8″ (16mm) thick by 3/4″ (19mm) high and are set into the *masik* and secured with nails. The *masik* measures 1/2″ (13mm) thick by 2-3/4″ (70mm) wide. The *isserfik* is 3/4″ (19mm) thick by 2-1/4″ (57mm) wide and has a 9-1/4″ (23.5cm) long piece of wood 3/4″ (19mm) high and 5/8″ (16mm) wide nailed to its forward edge.

Figure 301: A seal hunter at Tasiusaq, Upernavik District, 1936. Note the white cloth draped over the harpoon line stand (and the piece over the hunter's head) functioning as camouflage. (Photographer: Jette Bang/ Arktisk Institut gjb01126.)

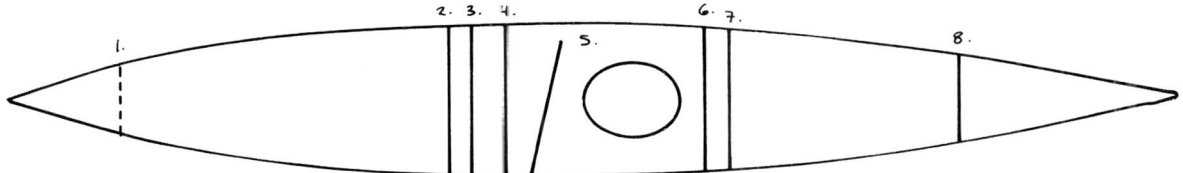

Canadian Canoe Museum, Peterborough: Cat. no. 977.183

    A distinctly offset coaming is present on the 977.183: It is 2-1/8" (5.3cm) from the left gunwale and 3" (41.1cm) from the right gunwale. The coaming measures 7/16" (11mm) thick by 1-3/8" (35mm) high. The *amiq* is laced to the coaming via the 'over-the-top' method depicted in figure 123c.

    While oblique deck lines are unusual among most West Greenland kayaks, they are typical in Upernavik District according to Kaj Birket-Smith (1924:271). Birket-Smith does however write that not one, but "the two straps immediately ahead of the manhole [are] as a rule oblique" (1924:271). None of the examples of kayaks from Northwest Greenland in this study are rigged as such, however one East Greenland kayak (the DNM's Lc.148 [plate 82]) does have a pair of oblique deck lines.

    The 977.183's oblique deck line is anchored into the top of the *masik* 1-13/16" (46mm) from the right sheer. No harpoon holder is present or evidenced on the 977.183's deck. Only the bow deck line is missing. The aft deck has two deck lines; none of the deck lines on the 977.183 have fittings.

70. West Greenland Kayak: Greenland National Museum, Nuuk. Catalog no. KNK 1550x10.

    The kayak 1550x10 is part of a large diverse collection transferred to the Greenland National Museum in 1987 from the Royal Greenland Company (Kongelige Grønlands Handel, abbr: KGH) in Denmark. The history specific to this kayak is unknown, though a tentative date of mid 20th century could be ascribed, primarily based on photographs of similar types. The 1550x10's accession card indicates that the kayak is from Uummannaq or southern Upernavik District.

    The lines and construction of the 1550x10 are nearly identical to those of the 977.183 from circa 1941— only the deck lines and fittings stand out as being very different. Both kayaks are much larger than most West Greenland kayaks, each exceeding 20" (50.8cm) wide and 18' (548.6cm) in length. Their size calls to mind the (U.S.) National Museum of Natural History's kayak 160325 from Upernavik (plate 56), as well as the Hull Trinity House's kayak "A" (plate 16.) The 1550x10 is in excellent condition, and is a very stunning kayak— immense and yet well formed and proportioned.

    Two broad but short seat slats are lashed beneath the ribs in the cockpit; these measure 1/4" (6mm) thick, 1-3/4" (44mm) wide, and 12-1/2" (31.7cm) long. Two forward and two aft deck-stringers are also present; the aft stringers are set-in flush to the top of the *isserfik*, and are double nailed in place. They are also set into their aft deck beam support, though not flush with its top. The aft deck stringers measure 1/4" (6mm) thick by 2-1/8" (54mm) wide; the forward stringers measure 1/4" (6mm) thick by 1-1/8" (28mm) wide.

    The ribs in the 1550x10 are quite thin, but wide (1/4" x 1-5/8" [6 x 41mm]), and are lashed to the chines using the double-pass lashing method, although it is not continuous instead and is tied off at each joint. The ribs are double-fastened to the keelson with flat-head screws.

    The 1550x10's end knobs are fairly large; the bow tip, made of oak, is 2-13/16" long and 1-1/2" wide (7.1 x 3.8cm), and the stern tip (ivory) is 1-1/2" long by 1-3/8" wide (38 x 35mm). The bow and

Figure 302: A hunter on glassy seas at Nuussuaq vicinity, Northern Upernavik District, 1936. (Photographer: Jette Bang/ Arktisk Institut. AI01173)

stern keel edging is 1/4″ x 1/4″ (6mm), and there is an amidship seam protection piece that is 7″ long (17.9cm) and 3/16″ thick, and 5/8″ wide (5 x 16mm). The 1550x10's coaming is laced on with the 'over-the-top' method depicted in figure 123c. The coaming measures 1/2″ (13mm) thick by 1-9/16″ (39mm) high, and apparently was a mast-hoop.

The coaming is placed off-center, being 2″ (51mm) from the right sheer and 1-3/8″ (35mm) from the left. This positioning makes more room for the harpoon, and runs counter to H.C. Petersen's reasoning for offset coamings (1986:36) (see page 88 in this volume for this passage).

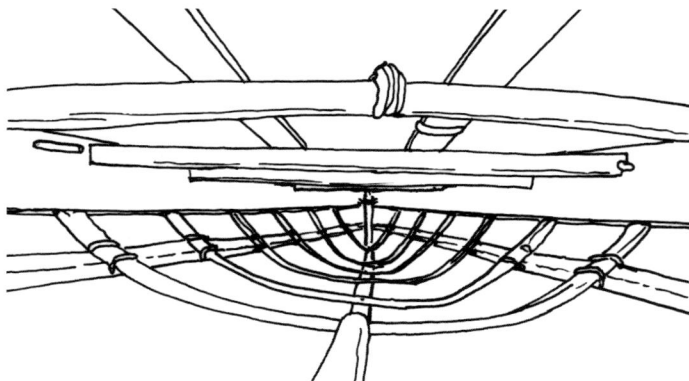

Figure 303: Forward interior view of the Greenland National Museum's kayak 1550x10.

346

An oblique deck line angles back from the 1550x10's right gunwale and is anchored to the *masik* just inboard of the left gunwale. The 977.183's oblique deck line is identical except it traverses the deck angled back from the left gunwale instead. While the x10 is a right handed kayak, the opposite angle of the 183's could suggest that that kayak is a 'lefty,' but this cannot be known for certain as a harpoon holder is not evidenced on the 183.

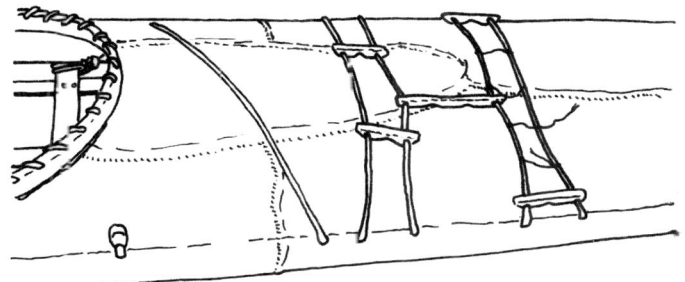

Figure 304: Fore deck of the Greenland National Museum's 1550x10. Note the oblique deck line and the lacing pattern on the coaming.

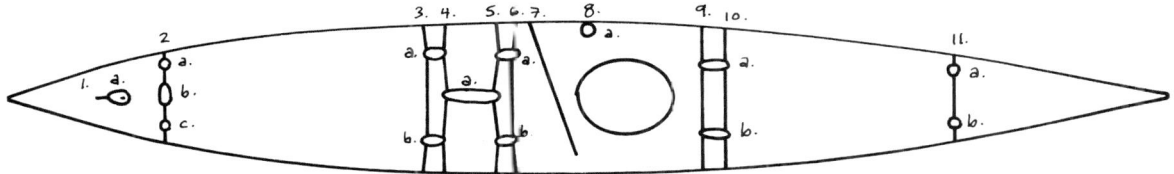

Greenland National Museum: Cat. no. 1550x10

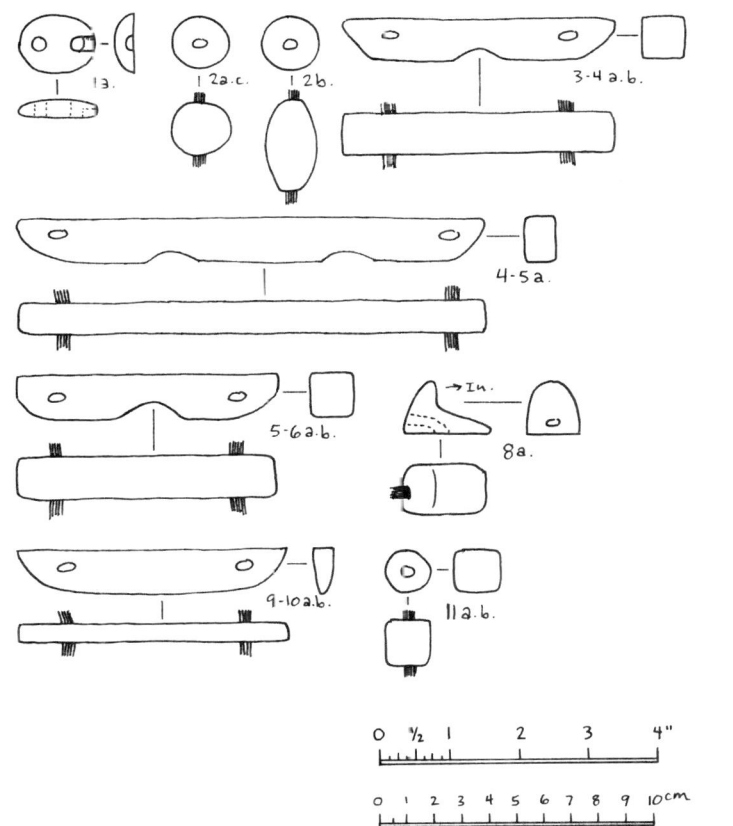

While the oblique deck line on the 1550x10 has no fittings, the other deck lines have a generous number of fittings— both beads and links. The four fore deck lines ahead of the oblique line are all linked together with symmetrically arranged ivory pieces. The deck line arrangement on the 1550x10 is worth comparing to two Illorsuit kayak's deck rigging as depicted in figure 313.

A rifle-bag anchor line appears just ahead of the usual bow deck line. It is an ivory tab with two holes in it, and it is attached to a one-inch long line of braided sinew sewn into the centerline deck seam. The bow deck line is very slack, and instead of the usual 'cones,' it has three beads— the middle one being elongated. The harpoon holder is simple yet elegant in form. A paddle is associated with this kayak and is depicted in paddle-plate 34.

71. West Greenland Kayak: Greenland National Museum, Nuuk. Catalog no. KNK 1550x18:

The kayak frame 1550x18 in the Greenland National Museum's collection is of an unknown provenance: It is part of a "diverse" collection repatriated to Greenland in 1987 from the (Danish) Royal Greenland Company. The entire "1550" series contains items from all over Greenland, and the 1550x18's object transfer list only records it as "kajakskelet," with the GNM museum records only elaborating so much to say "meget miserabel"— very bad condition.

As can be seen in the artifactual lines, this kayak is missing its chines and all of its ribs except for one. The keelson is present, and firmly lashed to the gunwale ends, although the aft scarf joint has come loose. The upper frame is in superb condition, and is only missing a bit of the bow cap-piece. Accordingly, the restoration of this kayak's lines (plate 71b) is very conjectural below the gunwales. The heights and breadths of the chines were not preserved except at the sole remaining rib, which is quite far aft. The restoration is based on comparisons to other similar kayaks, e.g., the 977.183 (plate 69) and the 1550x10 (plate 70), as well as on the meager evidence provided from the artifact itself.

I've placed the 1550x18 in type VI despite its provenance being unknown. This thinking is based mainly on the sheer line, but also on certain structural elements. The plan-view of

Figure 305: The fore deck of the kayak frame 1550x18. (The coaming is on backwards).

the kayak in the scale drawing shows a distinct pinched-narrowing of the sheer towards the stern; this is typically distinct among later Type VI kayaks such as the 1550x10 and the 977.183 (plates 70 and 69). The keelson joint with the gunwales is made without steps or locking parts, as in the Illorsuit kayak "EK" (plate 72); this simpler joint may also be a characteristic of kayaks from the northern West Coast. Other details that lead to my considering the 1550x18 as a Type VI kayak were the single scarf protection strip on the coaming and the convex stems. The generous breadth of this kayak (21″ [53.3cm]) should also be considered.

The 1550x18's keelson is formed from three pieces of wood, scarfed twice with the sophisticated stepped method using birds-mouth joints to lock it in place. Both ends of the keelson expand to form the stems of the kayak, and both are capped with shims to add extra depth. Such shims suggest a modification and/or recycling of pieces. Another unique feature of this kayak is the layout of the aft deck-stringers, seen in the scale drawing; they are dramatically angled, converging aft.

The gunwale end-to-keel joint is quite different than those on the PQN kayak (plate 50) and the KNK "C" (plate 51). As mentioned, it has no hook or 'key' piece to lock it into place, relying instead on lashings for alignment. The termination of the stern is simply constructed, while the bow has a cap-piece, parts of which are missing. Some 2-1/2" (6.3cm) or so is apparently missing from the kayak's nose. (Note: The stations in the hull restoration drawing do *not* correspond to those in the artifactual lines drawing due to the restored length.)

The gunwales of the 1550x18, with their marked rise at the cockpit, exhibit careful shaping; I made a tracing of a gunwale so that its complex form could be studied and understood better. From the tracing, a 'flat-plate' image of the gunwale was made and is depicted in the scale drawing. The years of stress have curved the gunwales' lower edges, which were likely straight during its shaping.

The through deck beam mortises in the 1550x18's gunwales measure 1/4" (6mm) high by 1-1/4" wide; the rib mortises are 1/4" (6mm) wide by 1/2" (13mm) long and about 5/8" (16mm) deep. This kayak's coaming was present with the frame: It is very round, measuring 19-1/2" (49.5cm) long and 18" (45.7cm) wide, being 3/4" (19mm) thick and 1-1/4" (32mm) high. Just a single bone strip is present at the coaming's upper aft edge, measuring 1/8" (3mm) thick, 5/8" (16mm) high, and 6-1/2" long, and is fastened with four bone nails.

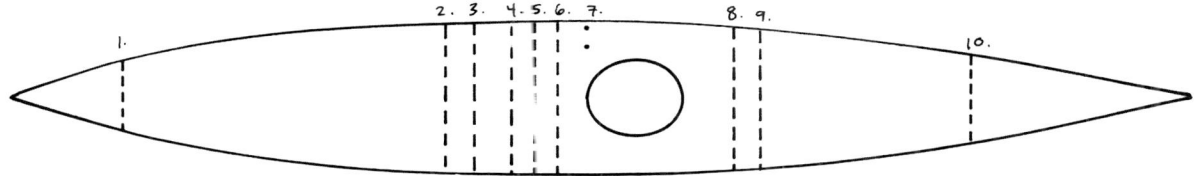

Greenland National Museum: Cat. no. 1550x18

The holes for the deck lines are present in this kayak frame, but their particular arrangement can't be known for sure. Five deck lines cross the fore deck, and two cross the aft deck. Both bow and stern deck lines are also evidenced, as is a harpoon holder line having been mounted through the *masik*.

72. West Greenland Kayak: John D. Heath, private collection, Houston, Texas. 'EK'

This kayak was commissioned by kayak historian John Heath in 1959, and was built by Emanuel Korneliussen of Illorsuit. Ken Taylor, formerly of Scotland, was visiting Illorsuit at that time and facilitated Mr. Heath's request. Taylor also had a kayak made for himself and it is nearly identical in form and shape. Taylor's kayak is 16'6-3/4" (504.8cm) long, 20-13/16" (52.8cm) wide, and 7-13/16" (19.8cm) depth-to-sheer (Winning, survey drawing: 1964). (Ken Taylor's kayak is currently in the Kelvingrove Museum, Glasgow, Scotland.) After John Heath's death in 2003, his kayak was given to Greenland kayaking technique student and scholar Greg Stamer of Florida.

Both Taylor's and Heath's kayaks have an unusual keel-line aft of the cockpit. While drawing up Heath's frame, I had initially thought I read my offsets wrong, but when I looked at Duncan Winning's

Figure 306: Emanuel Korneliussen (middle) at Illorsuit, 1959. (Photograph by Kenneth Taylor.)

1964 drawing of Taylor's kayak, I saw the same keel-line as I had just drawn. The keel rises behind the cockpit, levels out for two feet or so, and then rises abruptly up to the stern. This keel form is similar to the *pequngasoq* described by H.C. Petersen (1986:48-49), but is much subtler than more southerly examples (e.g., IV-A-483, plate 46), and may not be directly related, much less even referred to locally as a *pequngasoq*.

Ken Taylor writes about commissioning a kayak in Illorsuit, "I was able to squeeze into some of the kayaks in each village visited but some of them were too tight a squeeze for me. I'm 5 feet 8 inches and weigh 146 pounds. The way I remember it although they wanted to make it wider, I insisted that it be no wider than Ludwig Quist's, the headman of the village. But I did ask for an extra inch or so of depth at the front of the manhole" (personal communication, 2004-2006). In his article "The Construction and Use of Kayaks in North-West Greenland," Taylor writes that the frame of his kayak was built in just six days from wood imported from Denmark (1961:496).

The 'EK' is a half-inch (13mm) deeper and 5/8" (16mm) wider than Taylor's. Heath's kayak shows evidence of having been widened, perhaps during the construction: The kayak's *masik* is only 20-3/4" (52.7cm) long, and has two pieces of wood nailed to each end to make it a total length of 21-7/16" (54.4cm). Just ahead of the *masik* is a pair of empty deck beam mortises— this deck beam had likely just been bumped forward a bit so it would fit in the widened kayak. The empty mortises measure 1/2" (13mm) high by 7/8" (22mm) wide and 1/2" (13mm) deep. These features are depicted in figure 309.

Along with the kayak, a harpoon and throwing board were also sent to Heath— these are depicted in figure 310. This kayak's paddle is depicted in paddle-plate 52.

The forward deck stringers on the 'EK' kayak are spaced very close together, and are only separated by 5/8" (16mm) of space at their forward ends. Such a close spacing is unusual, though in Northwest Greenland single forward deck stringers are not at all uncommon, e.g., as on the KNK 2237, the DNM L.18.273, and the NMNH 160325 (plates 66, 73, and 56).[40]

The keelson-to-gunwale joint does not have a 'hook' or a 'key' in it, as in the PQN kayak or the KNK "C"(plates 50 and 51). Instead it relies on lashings entirely, as does the KNK 1550x18 (plate 71). Interestingly, the small cap-pieces on the 'EK' kayak do more than just fair the lines

Figure 307: The completed kayak frame built by Emanuel Korneliussen for John Heath, Illorsuit, 1959. (Photograph courtesy of Kenneth Taylor.)

---

[40] A photograph taken by Dr. Harald Drever (in Taylor's collection) at Illorsuit in the 1930s shows a kayak frame with a single forward deck stringer and two short aft deck stringers.

from gunwale-to-stem: They also form the actual termini of the stems. The gunwales are joined together with two nails at each end: A nail is set through each gunwale face, and is bent over where it exits on the opposite face.

Another interesting detail of the 'EK's joinery: The tenons of the deck beams are metal-nailed at their ends obliquely through the tenon and into the gunwale, as depicted in figures 36e and 37e. Despite each deck beam being fastened with this method, five of them are also lashed in place, as in figure 37a. All of the 'EK's deck beams are shallow-mortised.

Figure 303: Ken Taylor in the kayak he had custom made by Emanuel Korneliussen of Illorsuit in 1959. (Photograph taken at Loch Lomond, Scotland, 1960, courtesy of Duncan Winning, OBE.)

A shortage of seal skins in 1959 prevented Heath's kayak from being covered at Illorsuit. It was Heath's full intentions to canvas and use his Illorsuit kayak, but this was to never happen. Heath writes that Dick Thoms of the Seattle Kayak Club made a fiberglass copy of his frame in about 1961 (1987:14)— this may be the first Greenland kayak design adapted to fiberglass construction.

During my 2001 visit to Houston, John Heath pointed out one particularly interesting element of this kayak to me: Ribs in the vicinity of the cockpit were reversed compared to the other ribs. The ribs are semi-circular in cross-section; they have been split from thin limbs (likely imported barrel hoops), and the cambered face is the de-barked outer part of the limb. Ribs no. 6-through-13 (counting fore-to-aft) are oriented so that the cambered

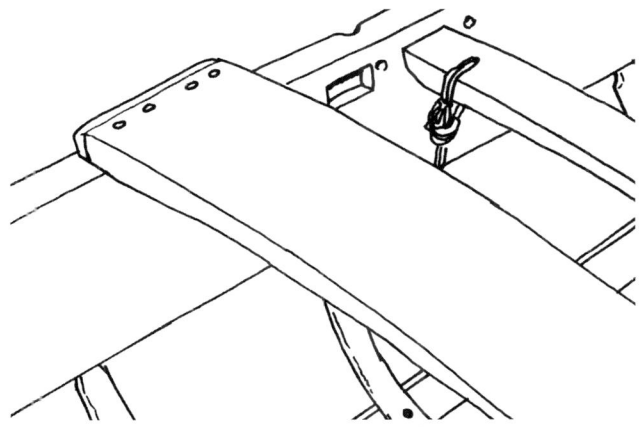

Figure 309: Construction details of the EK 1959, showing an extension piece at the end of the masik and an empty deck beam mortise.

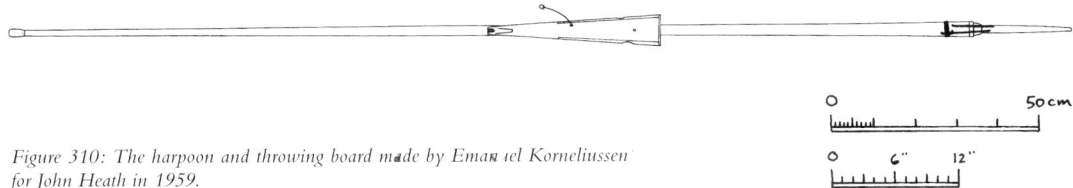

Figure 310: The harpoon and throwing board made by Emanuel Korneliussen for John Heath in 1959.

faces were turned upward— so as to prevent sharp edges from impeding the kayaker's entering or leaving the cockpit, as well as providing a more comfortable seat. The rest of the ribs are turned cambered-face down.

H. C. Petersen writes, "In North Greenland the ends of the kayak were straightened out at the end of the 19th century; the old type held out the longest in the Uummannaq Fjord." Petersen continues, explaining that such upturned sterns can still be seen: "Even today kayaks in Il-

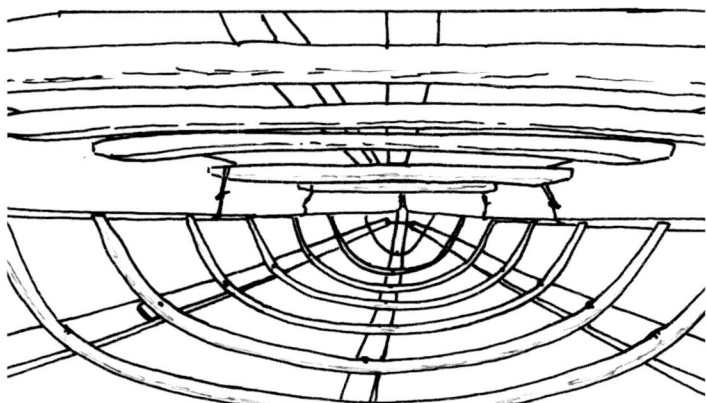

Figure 311: Forward interior of the Illorsuit kayak of 1959—the 'EK,' formerly in the collection of John D. Heath.

lorsuit are built with an exaggerated sheer and they are strongly reminiscent of the 19th century kayaks; kayaks with upturned sterns can still be seen on the northernmost part of the West Coast" (1986:63).

Being that the 'EK' is just a framework, questions arise as to how it would have been finished: How would the deck lines be outfitted, and how would the coaming be attached? Would there have been keel edging and end knobs? Such questions can't be answered for certain, but Ken Taylor sketched and described to me how his kayak had been outfitted: Figure 313 top depicts the deck line arrangements of the kayak that Korneliussen built for Taylor. Note that behind its cockpit two deck lines are present, whereas the 'EK' was drilled for just a single line. Taylor also provided the deck line and fitting layout for a kayak built in Illorsuit in 1938 for the geologist Dr. Harald Drever: This arrangement is also depicted in figure 313 (bottom).

Both Drever's and Taylor's kayaks had keel edging and bow and stern knobs. The coaming on Taylor's kayak was attached with bone pegs and the *amiq* at the cockpit's back was anchored on the coaming's aft-face— as in figure 123b (Ken Taylor, 2004: personal communication). This method of attaching the *amiq* to the coaming is apparently very old (see the Lübeck kayak [plate 1], the RvV 349 [plate 15], and the DNM Lb.101 [plate 5]), that 'held-over' in certain parts of the northwest coast (see KNK 1215 [plate 61], and the CMC IV-A-375 [plate 67] among others).

The coaming that Korneliussen provided with Heath's kayak is not fitted with bone pegs to attach to the *amiq*; instead, holes for

Figure 312: Seal Hunters at Illorsuit, 1959. (Courtesy of Kenneth Taylor.)

352

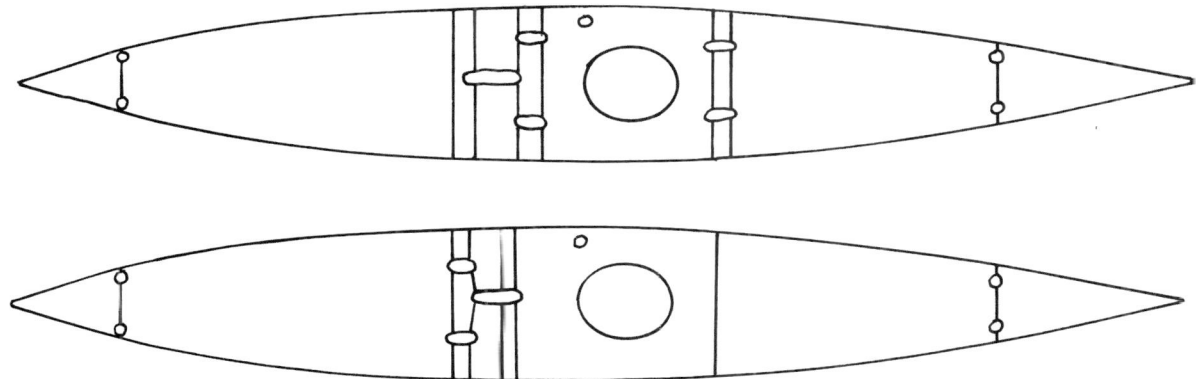

Figure 313: Deck line arrangements of two Illorsuit kayaks, as provided by Ken Taylor. The top kayak was Ken Taylor's kayak also built by E. Korneliussen in 1959. Below, a kayak built in 1938 for the geologist Dr. Drever. Both of these kayaks had end-knobs.

lacing are present, being 1/8″ (3mm) diameter, 1/2″ (13mm) on-center below the top of the coaming, spaced every 1-1/4″ (32mm). The coaming is scarfed with a simple tapered lap and secured with metal nails.

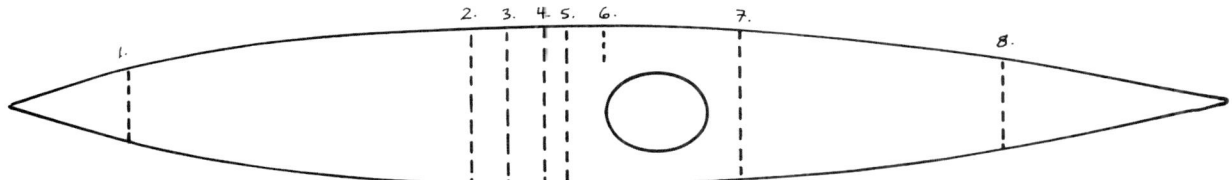

John D. Heath, Priv. coll. "EK"

Figure 314: The author paddling the replica of the 1959 Illorsuit kayak, Portland, Oregon, 2006. (Photograph by Kathy Tucker.)

Because Heath's kayak never made it to the water, I thought it would be fitting to see to it that a replica of it did. Because the original is a kayak frame, I did not need to infer the joinery methods at the ends. This was my first experience using metal nails for most of the joinery, and while it struck me as crude at first, it is actually a very elegant and effective solution.

Despite this kayak being an augmented version of the typical Illorsuit hunting kayak, it performed superbly and it didn't feel particularly big to me. It is

Figure 315: The 1959 Illorsuit kayak replica. (Photograph by Kathy Tucker.)

voluminous, but at the waterline it is not particularly wide, so feels nimble. It rides considerably higher (with more freeboard) than my other Greenland kayak replicas, but I am quite small and light (130 pounds). The freeboard doesn't seem to affect the 1959 replica's handling in wind; the considerable rocker and V-bottom must give it a handy combination of maneuverability and tracking.

73. West Greenland Kayak: Danish National Museum, Copenhagen. Catalog no. L.18.273.

Keld Hansen, now a curator at the Viking Ship Museum in Roskilde, collected the L.18.273 in Upernavik District in the late 1960s. This kayak exhibits substantial hull collapse, and the sheer has flattened as well. Hansen's photographs were crucial in my execution of the L.18.273's conjectural restoration, particularly the image in figure 316 previously published in the anthology *Kajjaker*, edited by Hansen and Birthe Clausen (1991:11). The photograph was taken at Aappilattoq, Upernavik District, and possibly depicts the same kayak— the L.18.273. Note the distinct integral skeg, (and of course the external skeg) as well as the 'chine' produced by the gunwale's lower edge.

The L.18.273 belonged to the hunter Knud Løvstrøm, although it was likely built by Wilhelm Grim, "who built most of the kayaks for others in Aappilattoq . . ." 20km northeast of Upernavik (Keld Hansen, 2005: personal communication).

Appearing in stark contrast to the Upernavik example from 1930 (the KNK 2237, plate 66), the L.18.273 does however retain a few of the 'old' features of Upernavik kayaks: a coaming lashed on via the 'over-the-top' method (as in figure 123c), and a very similar deck line arrangement to that of the KNK 2237, each having just a single fitting (a harpoon rest).

The L.18.273 definitely exhibits more Southerly Greenland kayak features: longer ends, more sheer and rocker, concave stems, considerable dead rise, and a lower stern. Unlike the 1930 example, only one chine stringer is present at each side of the keelson, and while only one deck stringer is present forward of the cockpit, two are placed behind it. An older kayak also from Upernavik district has this same deck stringer arrangement: the NMNH 160325, from circa 1885 (plate 56).

Like the KNK 2237 from Upernavik, the 18.273 is also painted, though in a more appropriate color: white. Seasons of use have also left a brown stain on the aft deck, residue from a well-oiled *avataq* (seal skin hunting float). Two gun-bags remain affixed to the deck lines, presumably one for a rifle, and the other for a shotgun.

In the cockpit, two sets of partnered ribs are present— one visible in the scale drawing, the other pair being beneath the *isserfik*. Each pair is lashed together to the keelson, but at the chines, only one rib of each pair is lashed, the other rib being nailed. The rest of the ribs in the kayak appear to be both lashed and nailed to the chines, and nailed to the keelson.

Figure 318 shows the interior of the 18.273, looking forward. Note the trapezoidal stanchion-block supporting the single deck stringer. Several of the deck beams have fallen out of their mortises. One of these was originally placed towards the lower edge of the gunwales, and one of its ends is still fitted thus, the other end being fractured, with its tenon still in the gunwale. Deck beams placed on the gunwales'

Figure 316: A 1967 photograph of kayaks at Aappilattoq in Upernavik District, taken by Keld Hansen— the collector of the DNM L.18.273 (Courtesy of Keld Hansen).

Figure 317: A hunter setting out amid icebergs in Kullorsuaq, northern Upernavik District, 1956. Note the single deck line behind the cockpit, and the single line at the stern. Also visible are three lashings holding a skeg in place. (Photograph by Jette Bang, Copyright: Greenland National Museum and Archives.)

lower edge are seen in some of the oldest preserved Greenland kayaks, for example the WFM 232 and KNK 1161 (plates 2 and 9).

The 18.273's *masik* measures 1″ (25mm) thick by 1-3/4″ (44mm) wide; the *isserfik* is 3/4″ (19mm) thick and 2-1/4″ (57mm) wide at the ends, narrowing to 2″ (50mm) wide in the middle.

All of the deck lines on the 18.273 exhibit repairs. Each has apparently been broken and/or cut off at the sheer line where they once exited the kayak. To replace the deck lines, the builder/hunter has nailed new straps to the upper edge of the gunwale's faces, using metal nails. In some instances, there are several nailed deck line stubs next to each other, indicating several replacements. For example, in the *amiq* along the sheer there is evidence of three past and present forward deck-line positions: holes with deck-line stubs at 3′ 3-5/8″ (100.6cm), a nailed-on stub at 3′ 2-5/8″ (98.1cm), and the existent nailed-on deck-line at 2′ 10-3/4″ (88.2cm).

Nailing the deck line ends to the sheer seems a hasty repair, but this was perhaps a necessary method in lieu of removing the entire skin. Sure as a painted seal skin *amiq* would last much longer than an oiled one, the access to the frame for repair and inspection would be less frequent.

The harpoon holder is a crude pyramidal chunk of bone that appears to be metal-nailed through its peak directly into the *masik*. Keel edging is present at the bow from 1´ (30.4cm) aft of zero to 2´ 7-1/2˝ (80cm), and is 1/8˝ (3mm) thick by 3/8˝ (9mm) wide. Stern edging is not evidenced.

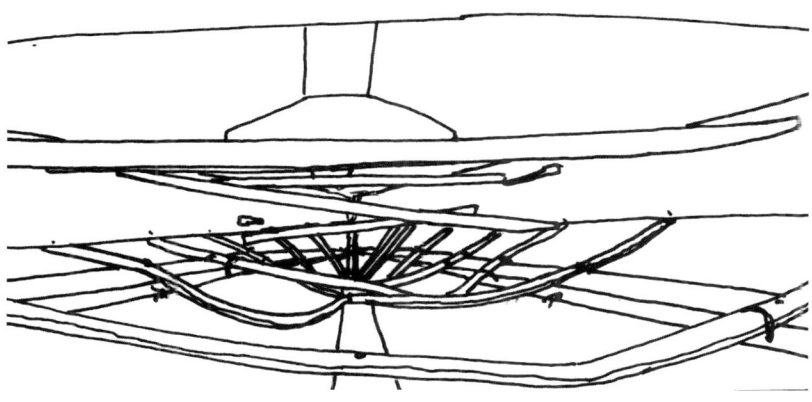

Figure 348: Forward interior of the DNM's kayak L.18.273. There is plenty of damage inside, but note the bow-placed deck beam (with the left end fractured) and the single deck stinger and the trapezoidal shim supporting it.

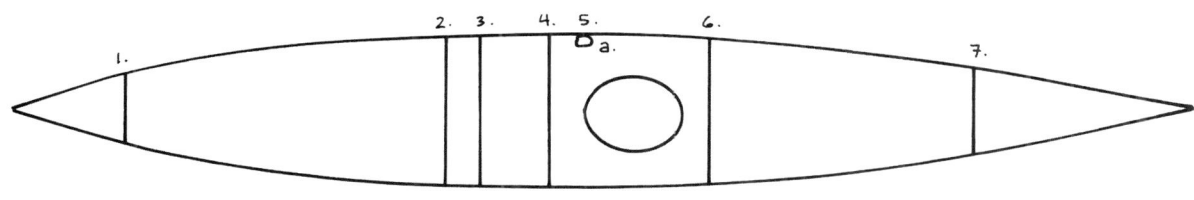

Danish National Museum: Cat. no. L.18.273

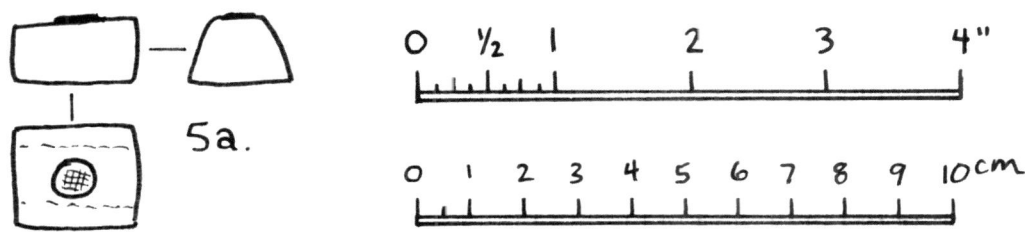

TYPE VII.

Type VII Greenland kayaks could well be called "South Greenland" kayaks, as that is where all of the examples in this study likely hail from ("South" being the greater vicinities of Qaqortoq and Nanortalik). The examples presented here span from the 1850s into the 1990s. Their form has maintained a remarkable consistency over this period— remarkable considering the fundamental changes (including extinctions) that other kayak types had gone through between those dates.

H.C. Petersen, in his discussion of present Greenland kayak types (see page 111 of the present volume), writes of a form he calls the "flat type:"

The flat kayak is built in Narsaq, Qaqortoq, Nanortalik district and in East Greenland. It is a very elongated and flat type with straight sheer boards the same width the whole of its length. The ribs are about the same height, though slightly shorter aft. The bottom of the kayak is flat and even, and the kayak is quite shallow (1986:48)

While Petersen includes the kayaks of East Greenland within his flat-type, in the present study the kayaks of East Greenland have been separated out for later attention, although his description is entirely accurate for them.

Type VII kayaks are characterized by their low sheer and a rocker that largely parallels the sheer. They also typically have long concave ends— ends that are much the same shape at the bow as they are at the stern. Viewed en-plan, the sheer at the bow and stern are both very concave, giving a distinct pinched look. Because of these features, the forward half of the kayak usually looks just like the aft half. This is also consistent with the shape of the cross-sections both fore and aft. These kayaks often have moderate deadrise, and the chines more or less follow the same curve of the sheer and keel.

The deck rigging on type VII kayaks is usually very complex and sophisticated. Link pieces, buttons, and cones are numerous on the deck lines, and occasionally adjustable hooks are present on the fore deck. Such adjustable deck lines with hooks at the end are common features of type IX (and apparently type VIII) kayaks from East Greenland. Aside from the two 19th Century examples, the type VII kayaks in this study all have their aft three fore deck lines linked together with a single piece, and the forward pair of fore deck lines is linked together with two pieces.

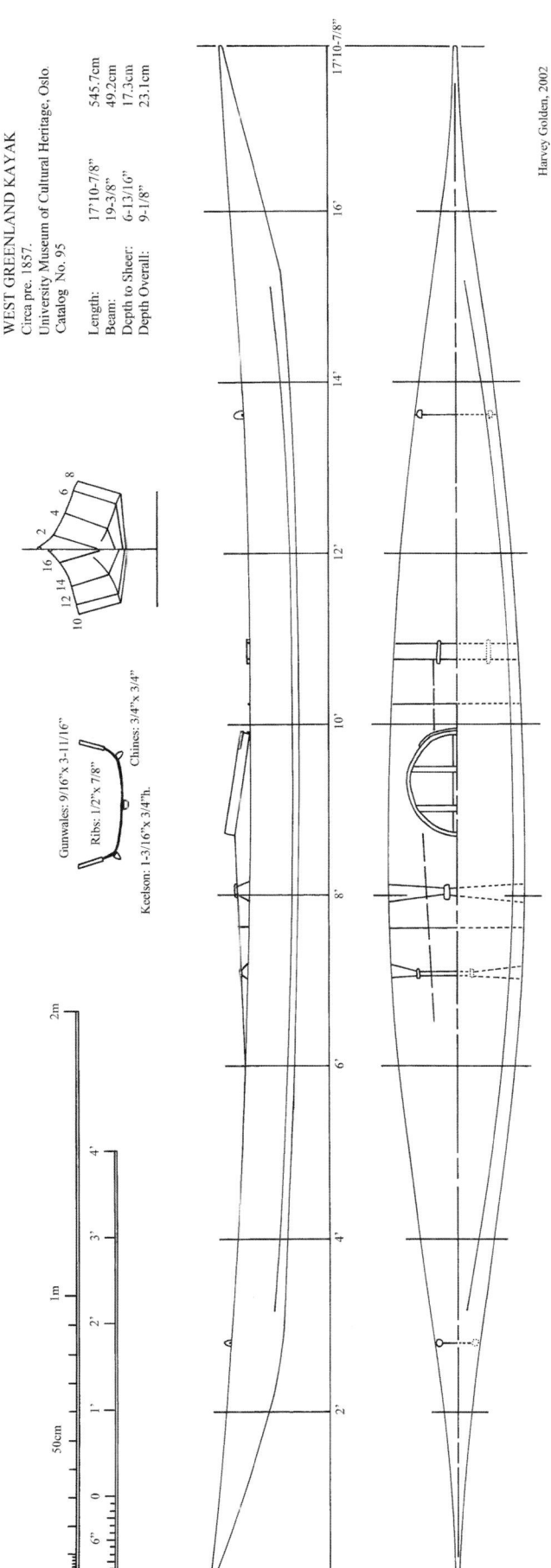

74. University Museum of Cultural Heritage catalog no. 95

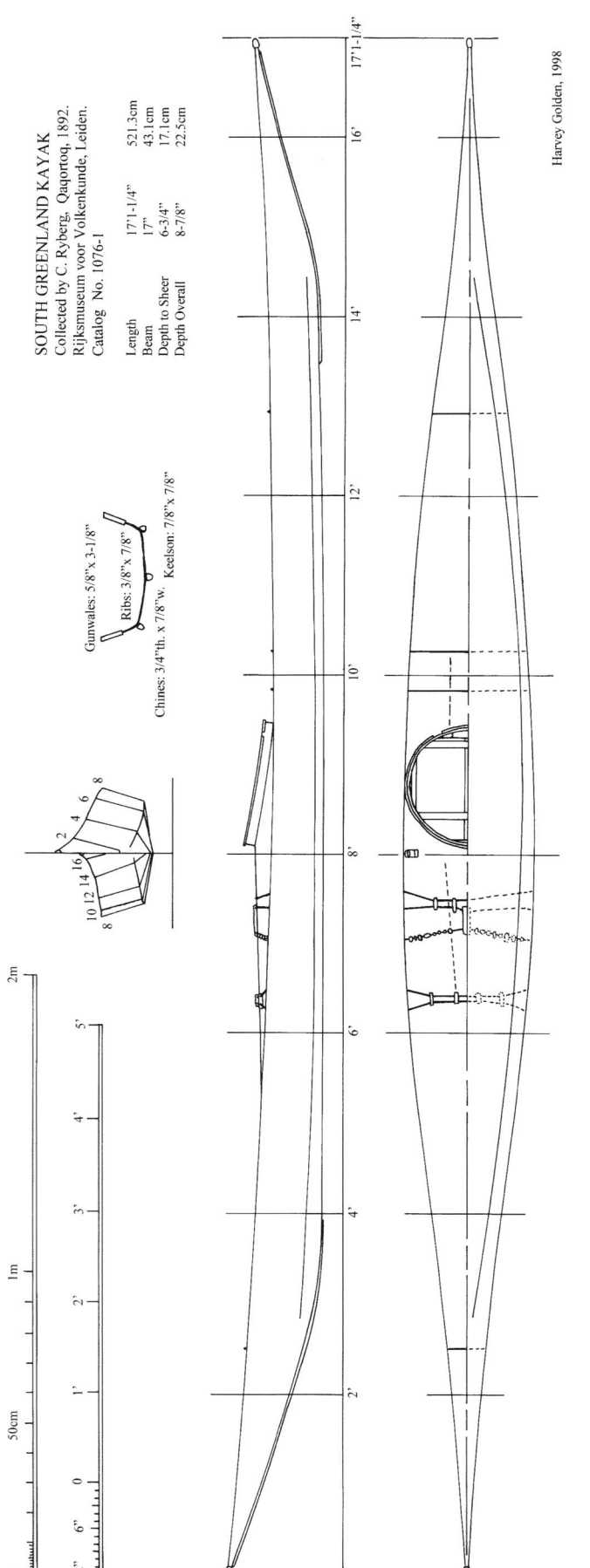

75. Rijksmuseum voor Volkenkunde catalog no. 1076-1

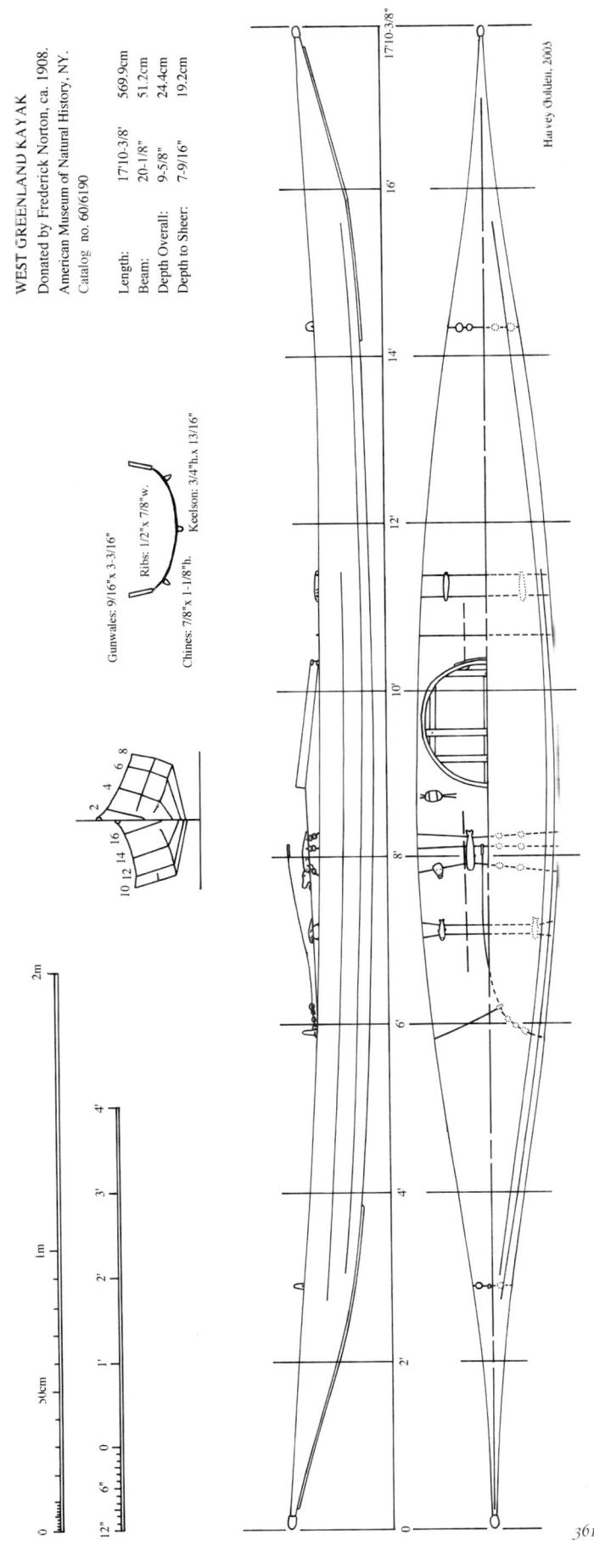

76. American Museum of National History catalog no. 60/6190

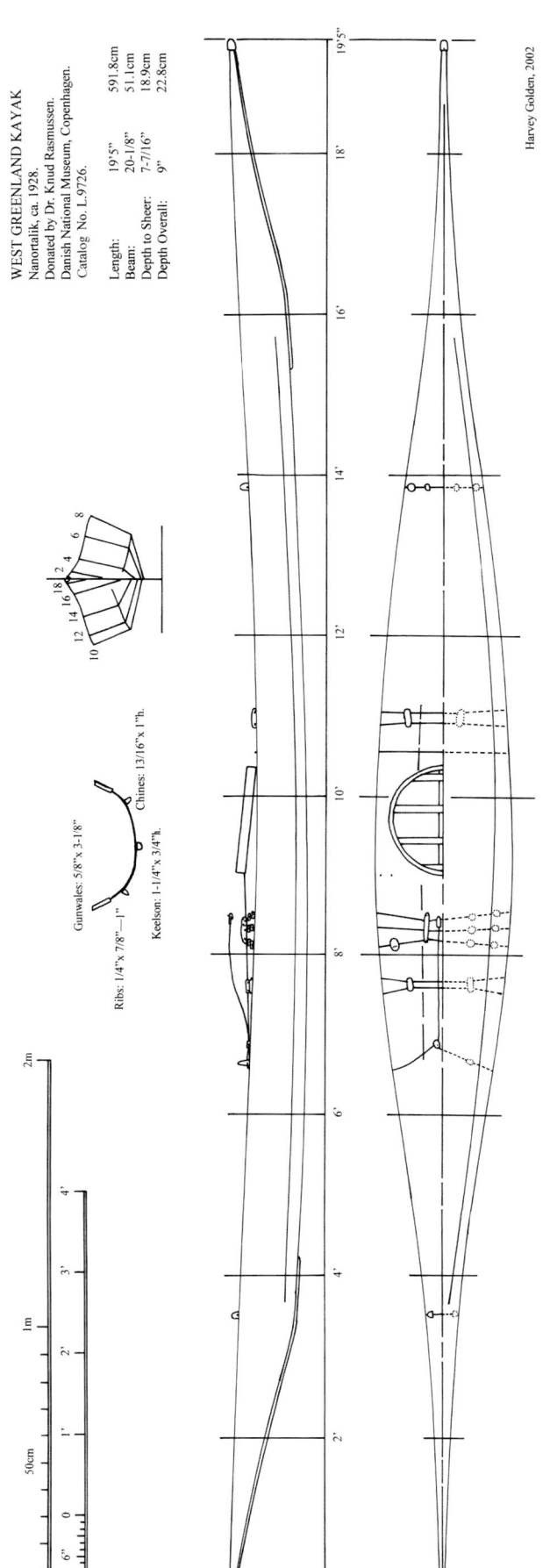

77. Danish National Museum catalog no. L.9726

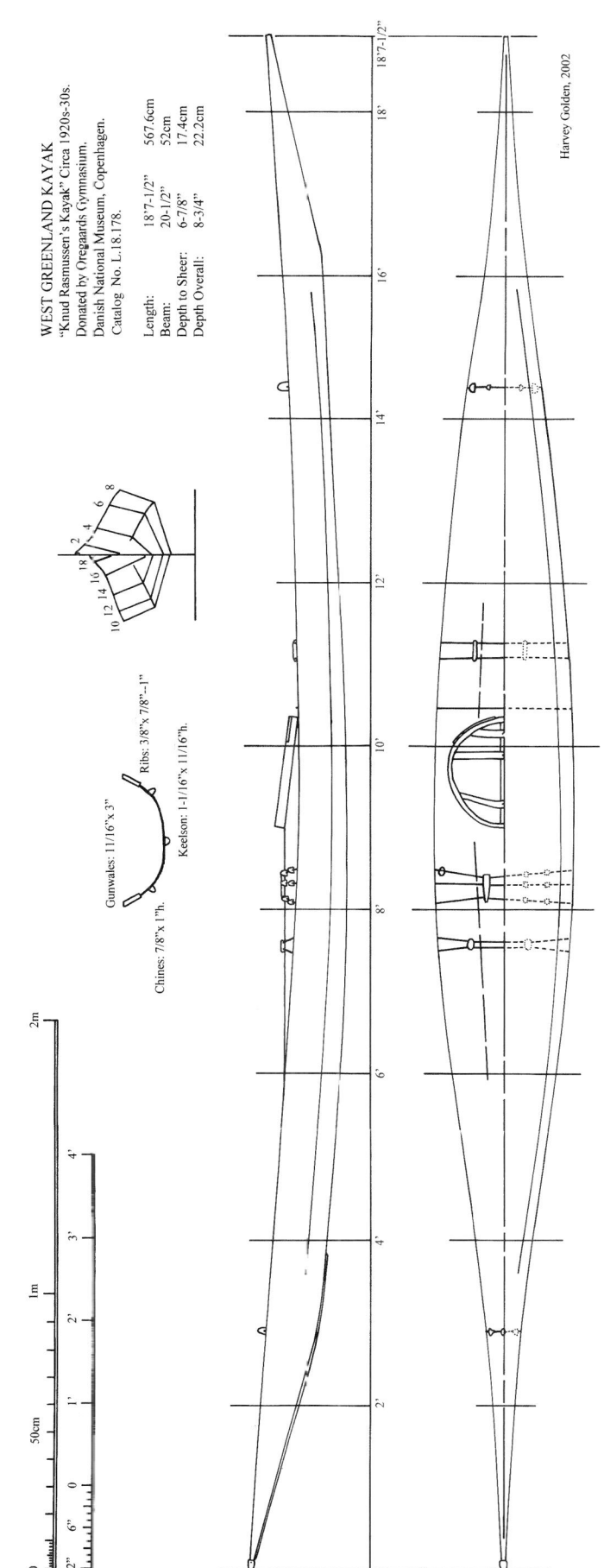

78. Danish National Museum catalog no. L.18.178

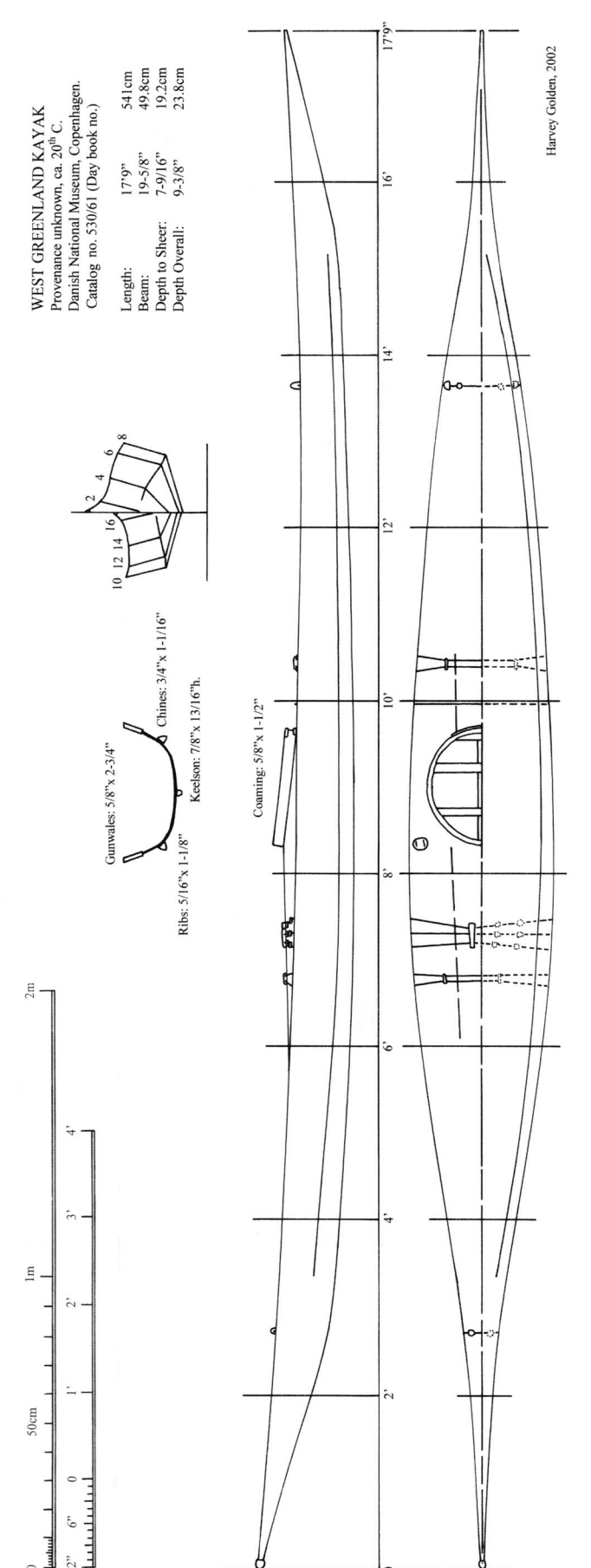

79. Danish National Museum catalog no. 530/61

80. Greenland National Museum catalog no. 1550x1

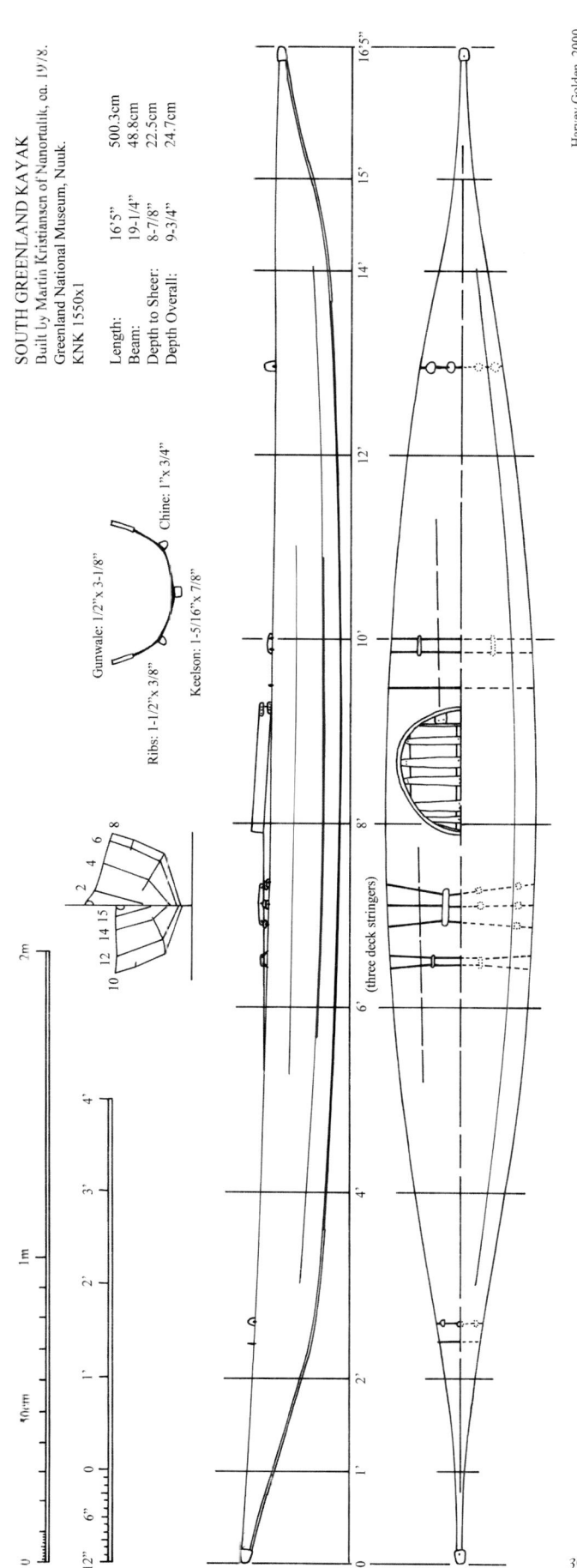

SOUTH GREENLAND KAYAK
Built by Martin Kristiansen of Nanortalik, ca. 1978.
Greenland National Museum, Nuuk.
KNK 1550x1

Length:	16'5"	500.3cm
Beam:	19-1/4"	48.8cm
Depth to Sheer:	8-7/8"	22.5cm
Depth Overall:	9-3/4"	24.7cm

Gunwale: 1/2" x 3-1/8"
Chine: 1" x 3/4"
Ribs: 1-1/2" x 3/8"
Keelson: 1-5/16" x 7/8"

Harvey Golden, 2000

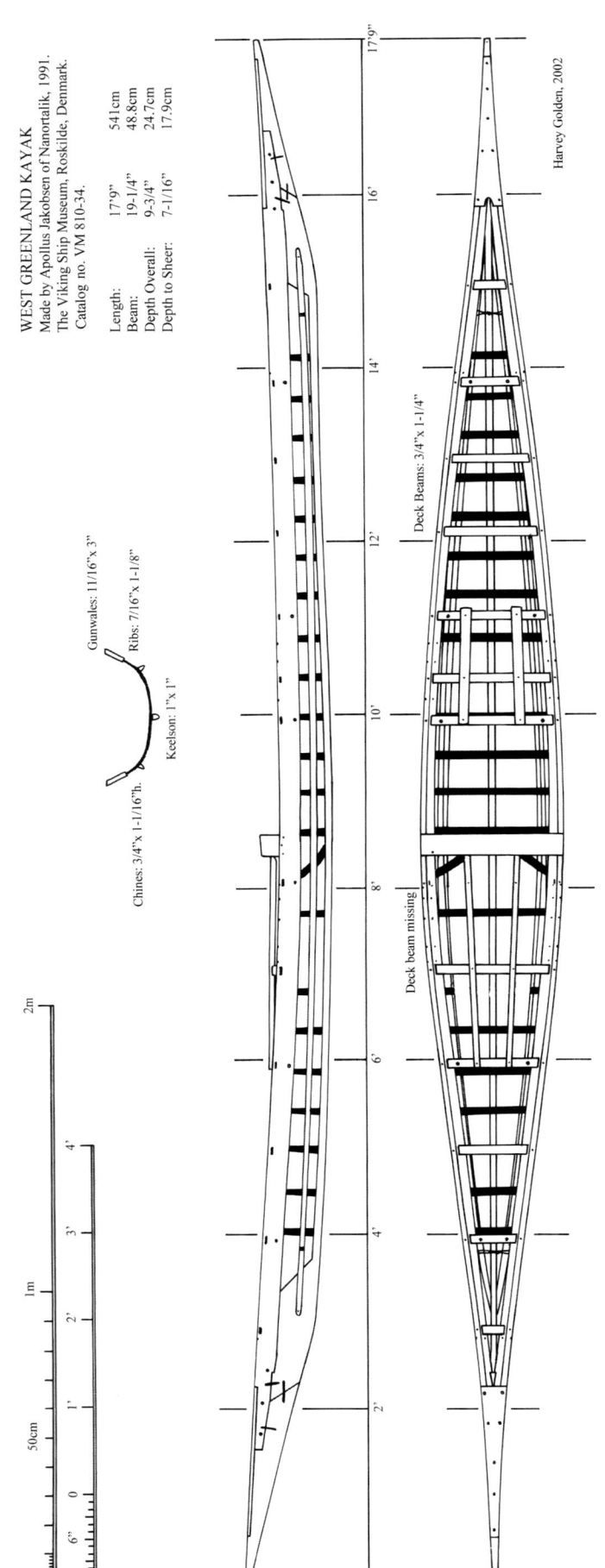

81a. Viking Ship Museum catalog no. VSM 810-34

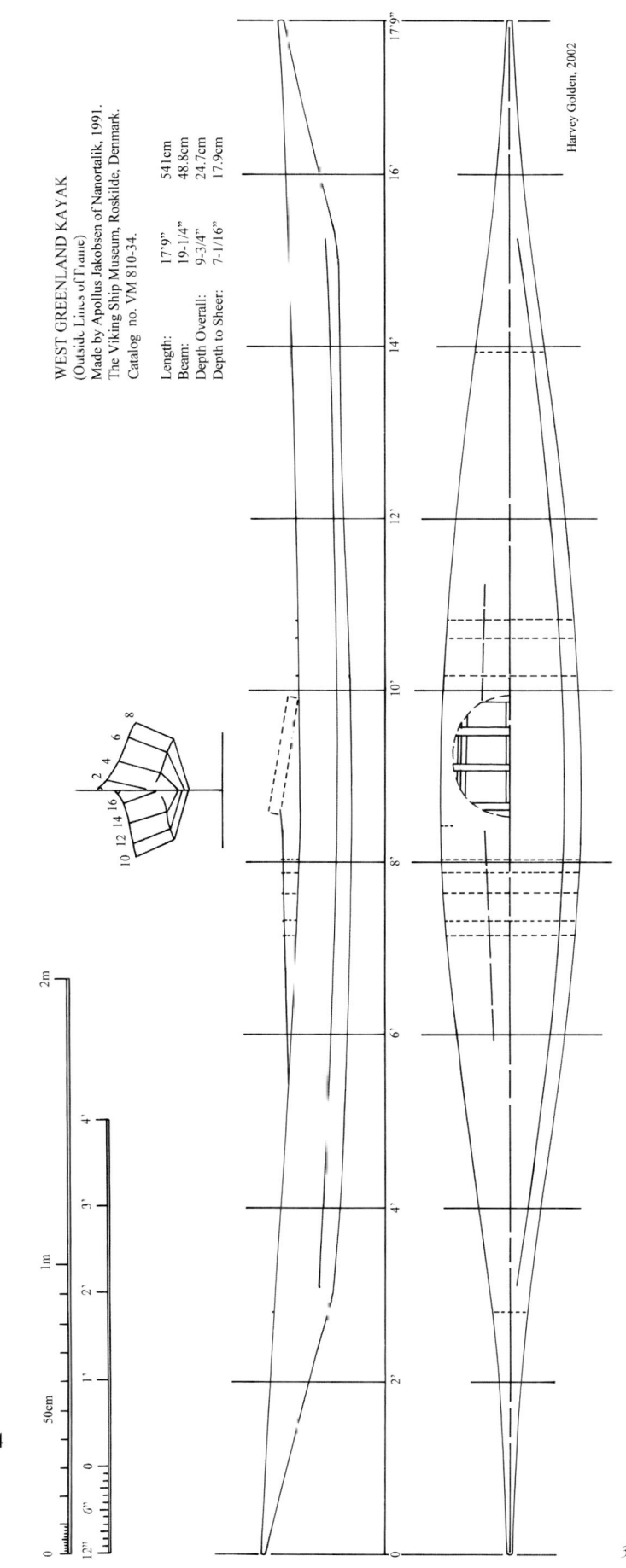

81b. Viking Ship Museum catalog no. VSM 810-34 (Hull Lines)

WEST GREENLAND KAYAK
(Outside Lines of Frame)
Made by Apollus Jakobsen of Nanortalik, 1991.
The Viking Ship Museum, Roskilde, Denmark.
Catalog no. VM 810-34.

Length:	17'9"	541cm
Beam:	19-1/4"	48.8cm
Depth Overall:	9-3/4"	24.7cm
Depth to Sheer:	7-1/16"	17.9cm

Harvey Golden, 2002

74. West Greenland Kayak: University Museum of Cultural Heritage, Oslo, Norway. Catalog no. 95.

The Oslo University Museum of Cultural Heritage conservator Eivind Bratlie translated and paraphrased this kayak's accession information for me: "Kayak from West Greenland. The year of purchase is not noted in the main protocol of the museum. It was among the first objects on display on the opening day of the Ethnographic museum in 1857" (personal communication, 2002). Nothing else is known about this kayak.

The UMCH 95 bears little resemblance to other kayaks collected during or before this period, but very much resembles the L.18.178 and the 530/61 kayaks (plates 78 and 79) in the Danish National Museum. The provenance of these latter two kayaks' has not been recorded, though its likely they are both from early-to-mid 20th century South Greenland. Significantly, the 95's deck fittings are fewer in numbers and appear much simpler— perhaps a reflection of a simpler hunting 'kit,' e.g., pre-rifle.

The 95, and the kayaks mentioned above at the DNM have distinctly long ends, considerable rocker, and a gentle sheer that, while curved, still keeps the ends quite low. One distinct difference between the 95 and its type VII successors is the lack of 'clipper' cut stems on the 95. The bow of the 95 is slightly convex while the stern is just barely concave; later type VII kayaks have stems with considerable concavity in profile. This may simply be reflective of changing fashions.

Joints between the ribs and the chines, gunwales, and keelson are all pegged. No fasteners were evidenced between the deck beams and gunwales, which may suggest exclusive use of the top-peg method of fastening depicted in figure 37d. The 95's *masik* measures 1/2" (13mm) thick by 4" (10.1cm) wide at its midpoint; the *isserfik* is 3/4" (19mm) thick by 1-5/8" (41mm) wide.

The coaming is scarfed on its edge with a step, as in figure 116i. Where the scarf reaches the coaming's upper and lower edges, pieces of baleen are tacked to the outer face so as to re-enforce the joint.

Figure 319: Kayaks and Umiaks at Paamiut, 1884. (Photograph: Fyllas *Expedition/ Arktisk Institut 45330.)*

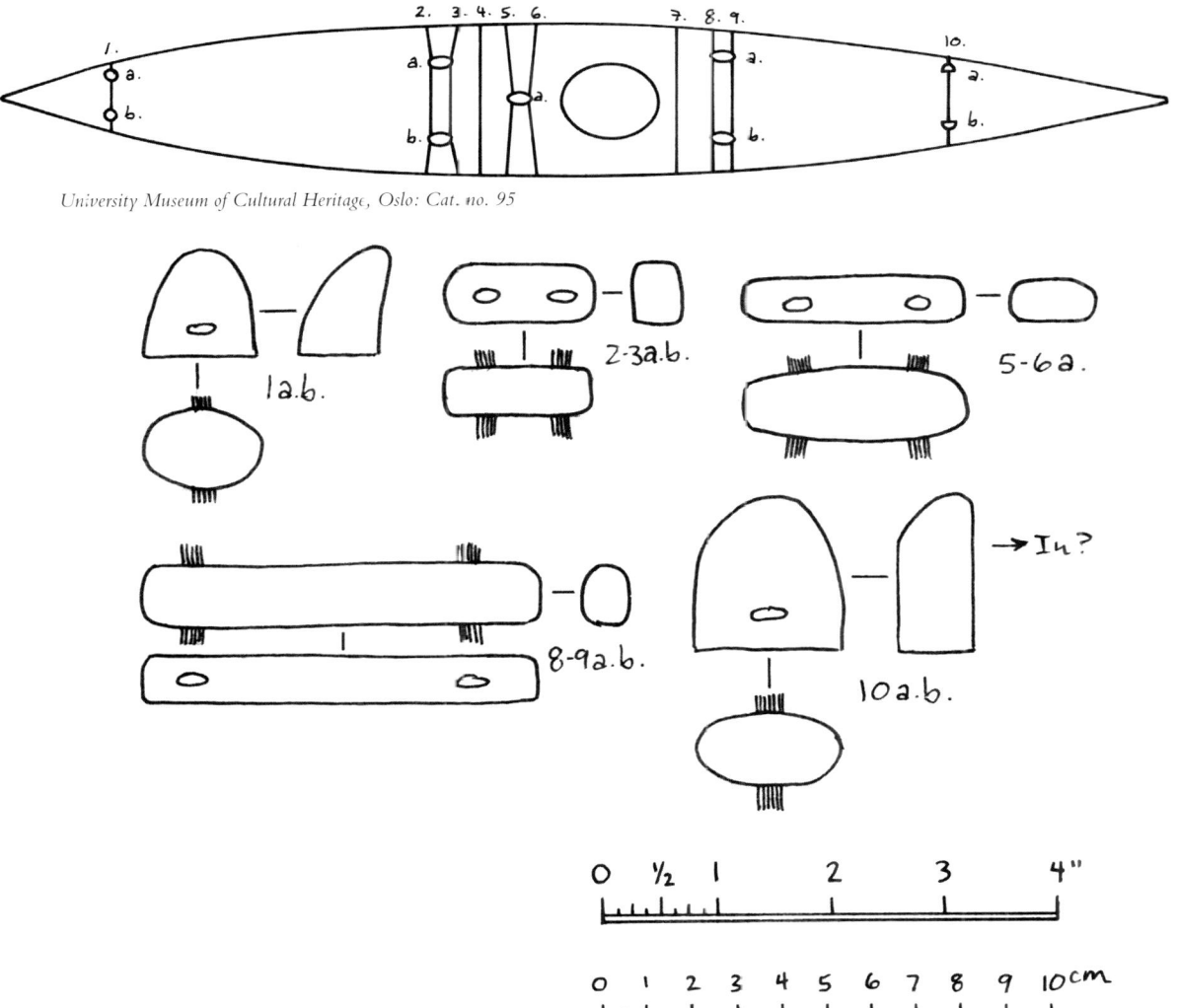

University Museum of Cultural Heritage, Oslo: Cat. no. 95

    Each baleen piece is about 1/8" (3mm) thick and 1/2" (13mm) wide, and roughly 5-3/4" (14.6cm) long, each centered over the scarf. The coaming measures 1/2" (13mm) by 1-3/8" (35mm) high. Keel edging and end-knobs are not evidenced on the 95. The 95's paddle is depicted in paddle-plate 19.

    Many of the kayaks presented so-far in this study have either one or two deck lines crossing the aft deck; on the UMCH 95 there are three, one being quite close to the coaming. This arrangement is very similar to many of the East Greenland kayaks in this study as well as in later type VII kayaks. While a harpoon holder is not present on the 95, there is a hole drilled for one through the *masik*, but not the *amiq*.

75. West Greenland Kayak: Rijksmuseum voor Volkenkunde, Leiden, the Netherlands. Catalog no. 1076-1:

Nooter briefly mentions this kayak in the introduction to his *Old Kayaks in the Netherlands*: He gives the provenance and date of acquisition as "Angmagssalik, East Greenland . . . Collected by C. Ryder, 1892." (1971:2).

Museum records retained this same information, however Dr. Cunera Buijs of the Rijksmuseum in Leiden told me that it was probably "C. Ryberg"— instead of C. Ryder— who collected this kayak (personal communication, 1998). Carl Julius Peter Ryberg was a KGH (Royal Greenland Company) district official in Qaqortoq, South Greenland circa 1891, and eventually director of the KGH in 1902 (Krabbe, 1930:59).

It is not certain how the 1076-1 got from Ryberg to the Rijksmuseum voor Volkenkunde, but a "C. A. Trolle" appears on the museum catalog sheet as the donor. A "Captain A. Trolle" receives mention in Dr. Thomas N. Krabbe's *Greenland, Its Nature, Inhabitants and History* as having captained the research ship *Danmark* in 1906-08 (1930:115, 127). The kayak may have been sent south in the care of Captain Trolle, though this is pure speculation. The 1076's paddle is depicted in paddle-plate 53.

The 1076 is a fine looking craft, and is in excellent condition. It has a very flat stern, and a fairly low bow. The kayak's keel seems to almost parallel the curve of the sheer, keeping fairly constant depths amidship and astern; the bow is a bit deeper and is inclined along the sheer. The 1076 has very long stems— the long shallow raking ends take up nearly a third of its length. It is not particularly rockered, not nearly as much so as the DNM's L.18.178 (plate 78) from Nanortalik, appearing later in this study. This lack of rocker may be a localized characteristic for Qaqortoq vicinity: A kayak skeleton from 1935 Qaqortoq at the Greenland National Museum also has a very flat keel-line.[41]

Several of the deck beams in the 1076 are obliquely pegged to the gunwales. Both gunwales have scarfs behind the cockpit. The 1076's chines and keelson are double-pass lashed to the ribs with string following the pattern depicted in figure 73 top. The ribs are not fastened to the gunwales.

The coaming has a bone or ivory rim pegged to it. It forms a 1/4" (6mm) square lip almost all the way around the coaming: There is a 1/2" (13mm) wide bone band for 10" (25.4cm) at the coamings backside.

Keel edging is present at both the bow and stern. It measures 1/4" (6mm) wide and 3/8" (9mm) high at the highest point, but tapers to just under 1/4" (6mm) high at the bow and stern. The bow end knob is fastened to the kayak through the knob's tip— with a screw. The stern knob is conventionally fastened and is made of wood.

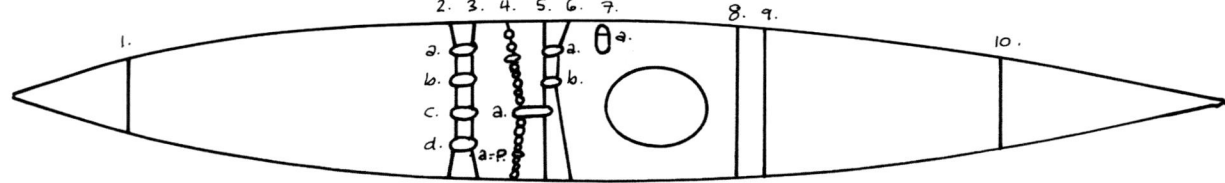

Rijksmuseum voor Volkenkunde, Leiden: Cat. no. 1076

---

[41] This kayak is illustrated in the *Skinboats of Greenland* (Petersen, 1986:48, fig.44).

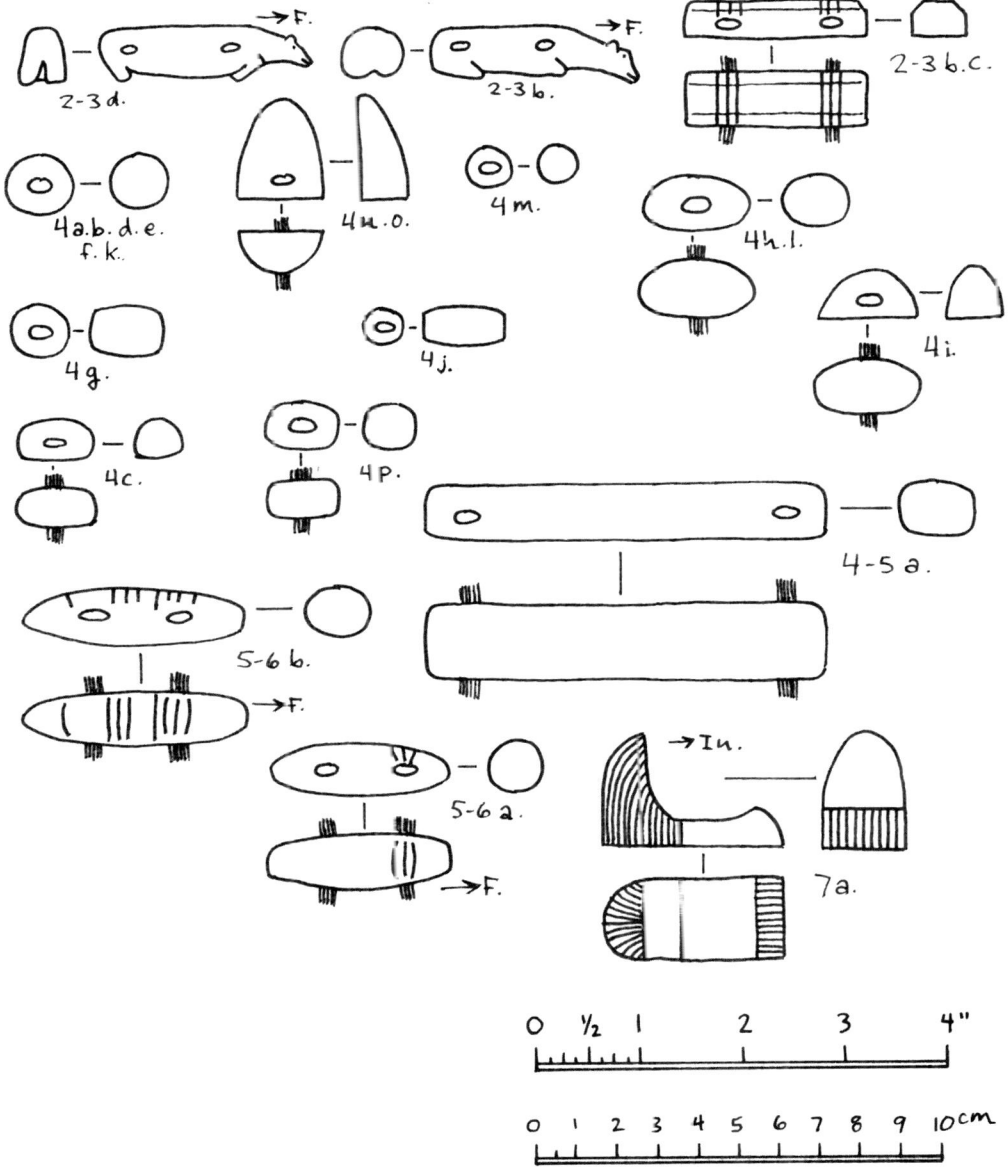

The 1076 has a very large number of fittings: 24 pieces to be precise, and remarkably, not a one behind the cockpit. A couple of the link pieces are carved into the shape of caribou. Between the caribou-shaped pieces are two rectangular pieces with chamfered corners, each with grooves cut transversely across their tops. The harpoon holder is made of two pieces, and has intricate ridging carved into it.

It is a good question as to why there are so many pieces on the third fore deck line. One familiar with the sophisticated hunting equipment and tools and their arrangement on deck can readily see the advantage of a certain number of fittings, but the 16 beads on this line are perhaps excessive in terms of

Figure 320: The author in the replica of the Rijksmuseum voor Volkenkunde's kayak 1076-1, Whidbey Island, 2006. (Photograph by Kathy Tucker.)

pure functionality; it could be simply aesthetics (we never ask what the purpose or meaning of the 16th pearl is on a lady's necklace).

I built a replica of the RvV 1076 in 1998, the same year I surveyed it. At the time, my only experiences in Greenland kayak replicas were limited to a classic-form type IV in the British Museum surveyed and published by John Brand (1988:21), and an East Greenland kayak in the Danish National Museum[42] also documented by Brand (1988:87-91). The 1076 replica handled somewhat like the type IV replica only it was noisier in waves on account of the much lower ends. It is one thing to read of and even experience the silencing effect of high-sterned kayaks, but to experience the noisiness of a low-sterned kayak in waves makes the understanding twice as valuable.

In order to be able to use this replica, I had to adjust the size of the cockpit. The original's cockpit opening (inside diameter of the coaming) was 16-1/4″ (41.2cm) long, and the distance between its *masik* and *isserfik* was only 14″ (35.5cm); my replica's coaming measures 18-3/4″ (47.6cm) long with a *masik*-to-*isserfik* distance of 16-1/2″ (41.9cm) and it is still painfully tight.

---

[42] See plate 86, as I have also surveyed this kayak.

I had the rare opportunity to paddle this replica kayak in winds that were gusting to 70 miles per hour, being at least 50 mph sustained. This was in Nuuk, Greenland in August 2000. The seas had stacked up pretty well— perhaps five or six feet, which actually created some shelter from the gale, except for when you topped the crests. Topping steep waves into such high winds puts the kayaker at risk of being blown around quite violently or even being blown over.

I was very comfortable in this kayak in those conditions— it handled marvelously; I couldn't have wanted anything different. The deep bow cut the waves very nicely and kept the deck fairly dry considering the conditions (the 1076 does have an unusually deep bow when compared to other type VII kayaks).

As expected, the stern made quite a racket in all the pitching— *THWOMP*-ing as it went under each wave. Certainly it wasn't annoying, but I could definitely see the wisdom and purpose behind the higher sterns on many kayaks (e.g., types III and IV) if one were stalking seals.

Figure 321: The author landing the 1076 replica in light waves, Whidbey Island, 2006. (Photograph by Kathy Tucker.)

76. West Greenland Kayak: American Museum of Natural History, New York, New York.
Catalog no. 60/6190

The American Museum of Natural History's kayak 60/6190 is cataloged as being from "Holstensborg," now known as Sisimiut. Frederick G. Norton donated this kayak to the AMNH in 1908. Dr. Clark Wissler's 1909 *Notes on New Collections* features among other things the museum's acquisition of this kayak, although nothing of pertinent interest is mentioned: "The kayak seems to be of the typical Greenland type..." being the most profound passage (1909:318-320). The 60/6190's paddle is depicted in paddle-plate 55.

Many elements about this kayak suggest that it is not from Sisimiut vicinity, but instead from South Greenland. The low shallow ends, the very extensive array of deck lines and fittings, and the nailed construction all suggest a provenance of Nanortalik vicinity or thereabouts— South Greenland in any case.

Figure 322: A boy receiving a kayak-lesson, Qaqortoq, 1939. (Photographer: Jette Bang/ Arktisk Institut gjb04210.)

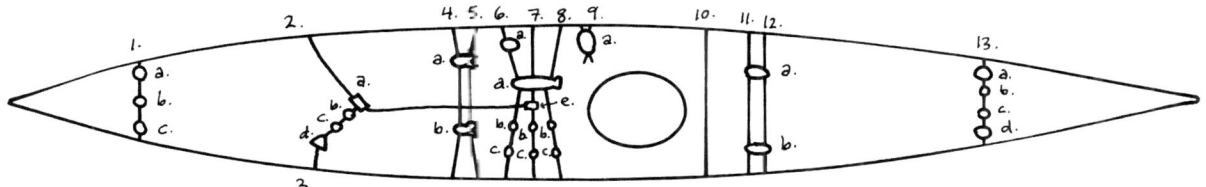

American Museum of Natural History, New York: Cat. no. 60/6190

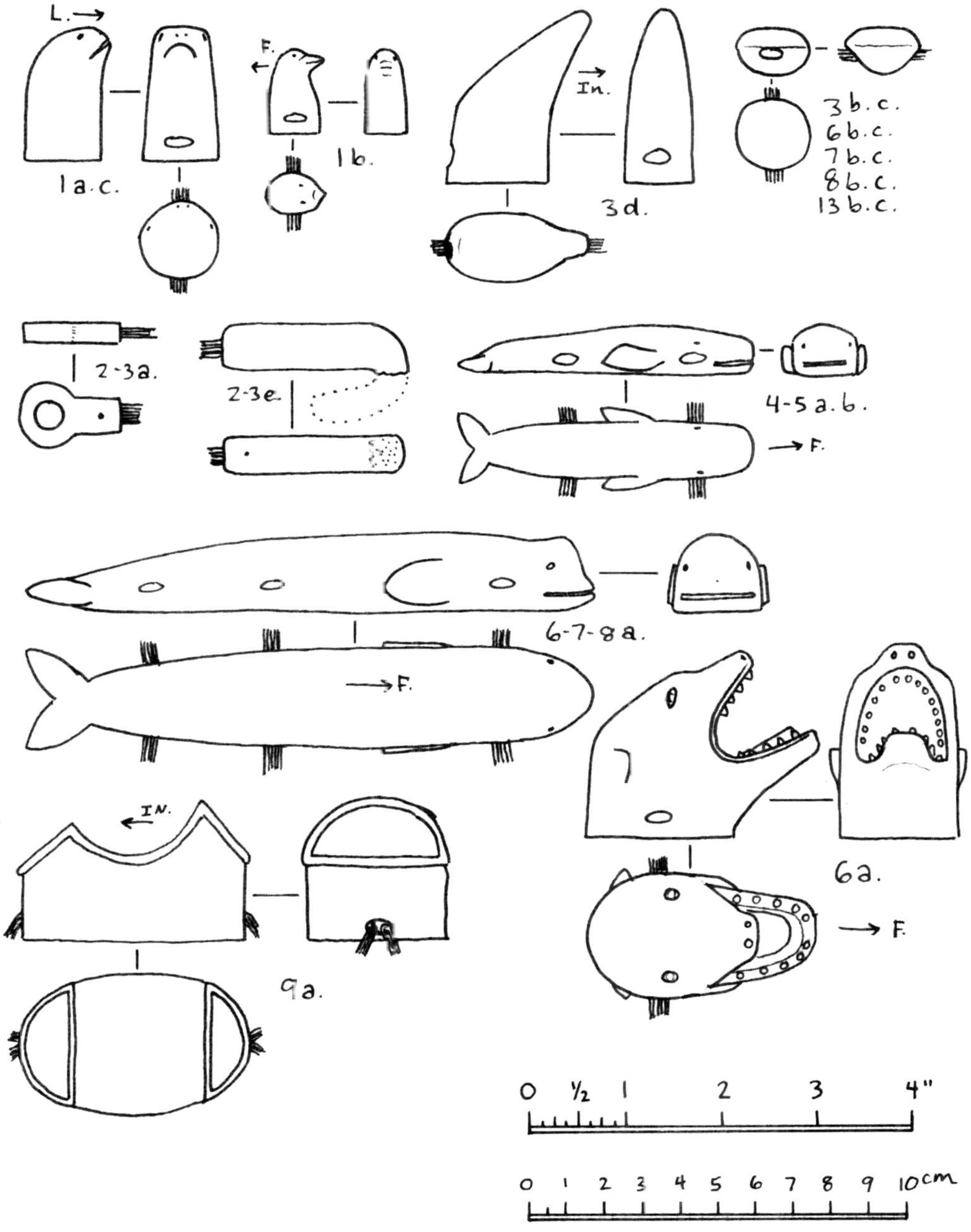

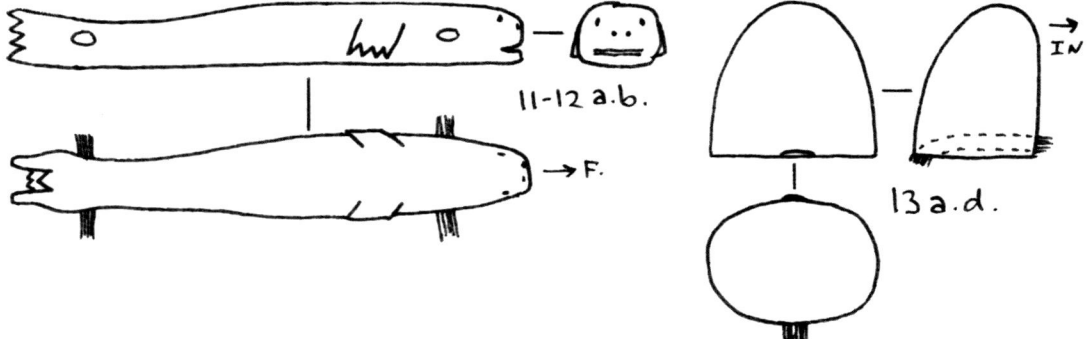

Consistent with most type VII kayaks, the 60/6190 has a very distinct fore and aft symmetry in elevation view. This is to say that the stern's profile is nearly identical to that of the bow's profile. Fore and aft hull symmetry is plain to see in the cross sections as well.

Several of the deck beams are fastened to the gunwales using the oblique peg method: two deck beams forward, and three in the aft half of the kayak. The ribs are not fastened into their mortises, but they are all metal-nailed to the chines and keelson. The chines have a channeled upper edge as in figure 68 right; in fact, both sides of each chine are also slightly channeled.

The 60/6190 has two deck stringers forward and two aft of the cockpit. The forward stringers are 3/8″ (9mm) thick by 7/8″ (22mm) wide; the aft stringers are 9/16″ (14mm) thick and 1″ (25mm) wide. The *isserfik* measures 7/8″ (22mm) thick and 1-1/4″ (32mm) wide, and the *masik* is 3-1/16″ (78mm) wide. The coaming measures 5/8″ (16mm) thick by 1-5/16″ (33mm) high.

A similarity with East Greenlandic kayaks is evident on this kayak, namely its "Y" shaped adjustable deck-line on the fore deck. The right side's line extends to the 6th line aft of the bow and terminates with an ivory hook. The left side's line ends in a deadeye through which the right line runs. A nice feature on the left-side line is a conical implement rest— a feature also seen on the DNM L.9726 (plate 77) from Nanortalik. Two disc-shaped pieces are also present on this line, inboard of the implement rest. (The 60/6190's being an East Greenland kayak can be ruled out based on its specific form, construction, deck fittings, and deck stringer arrangements.)

Most stunning about the 60/6190's rigging are the deck fittings themselves: They consist of a bird figure, four seals, two baleenous whales, a beluga, and a very large polar bear head— complete with a mouth full of teeth— twenty-two individually set ivory teeth! The high level of workmanship of these figures cannot be conveyed enough: The scale-drawings of these pieces hardly do their quality justice.

The bow-most deck line on this kayak seems to have been replaced at some time— likely by a museum conservator, as the line material is not finished to the standards of the rest, and the ivory pieces are improperly arranged. The two outboard figures (surfacing seals) are both facing the same direction (left).

77. West Greenland Kayak: Danish National Museum, Copenhagen. Catalog no. L.9726.

Accessioned in 1928, the donor of this kayak is Dr. Knud Rasmussen, the renowned explorer and philologist. In the Danish National Museum's accession catalog, the L.9726's origin is listed as Nanortalik, South Greenland.

The L.9726 is rather extreme in form, its ends being very long and narrow. About 6′ 6″ (198.1cm) of its 19′ 5″ (591.8cm) length is comprised of raked stems; six feet (182.9cm) of this kayak's length is less than 5″ (12.7cm) wide. It has a remarkable fore and aft symmetry as well, the bow being nearly identical to the stern in profile and plan.

Shape-wise, the L.9726 compares very favorably with the UMCH's kayak 95 (plate 74) of some 70 years prior. The primary difference is the much longer and concave ends of the 9726; both kayaks have very similar cross-sections. The depth to sheer is fairly constant along the hull on both kayaks. These similarities support my theories that the UMCH 95 and the AMNH 60/6190 (plate 76) are both from South Greenland.

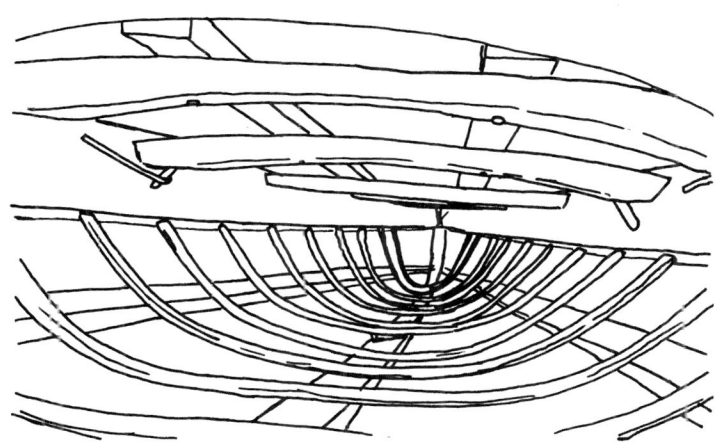
Figure 323: Forward interior view of the Danish National Museum's kayak L.9726.

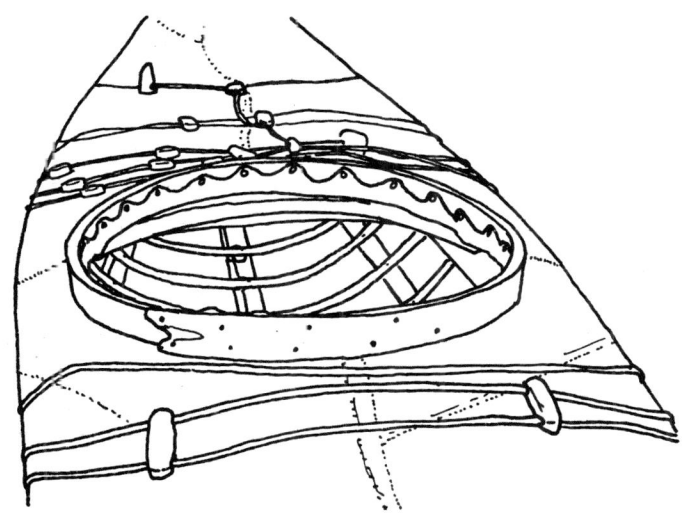
Figure 324: Cockpit view of the Danish National Museum's kayak L.9726.

Figure 323 shows the forward inside view of the L.9726. Several of the deck beams are pegged to the gunwales using the oblique method. The ribs are not pegged or nail-fastened into their mortises, but they are metal-nailed to the keelson and chines. The 9726's keelson is laid on-flat (i.e., the width being greater than its height) instead of on-edge; the chines are on-edge.

This kayak's coaming has no scarf protection pieces, which is very unusual for a kayak from the West Coast of Greenland. This is possibly on account of East Greenlandic influence, where such pieces are not used. The scarf is fastened with bronze nails. A groove in the face of the coaming's overlap scarf ensures a more waterproof seal for the *tuilik*; this feature can be seen in figure 324, a cockpit view of the L.9726. The coaming itself measures 5/8″ (16mm) thick by 1-3/8″ (35mm) high, and is made of ash.

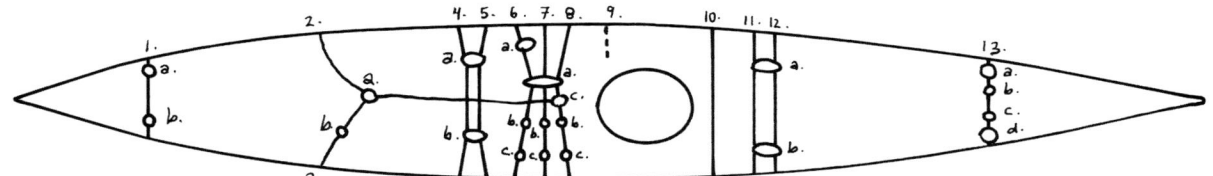

Danish National Museum: Cat. no. L.9726

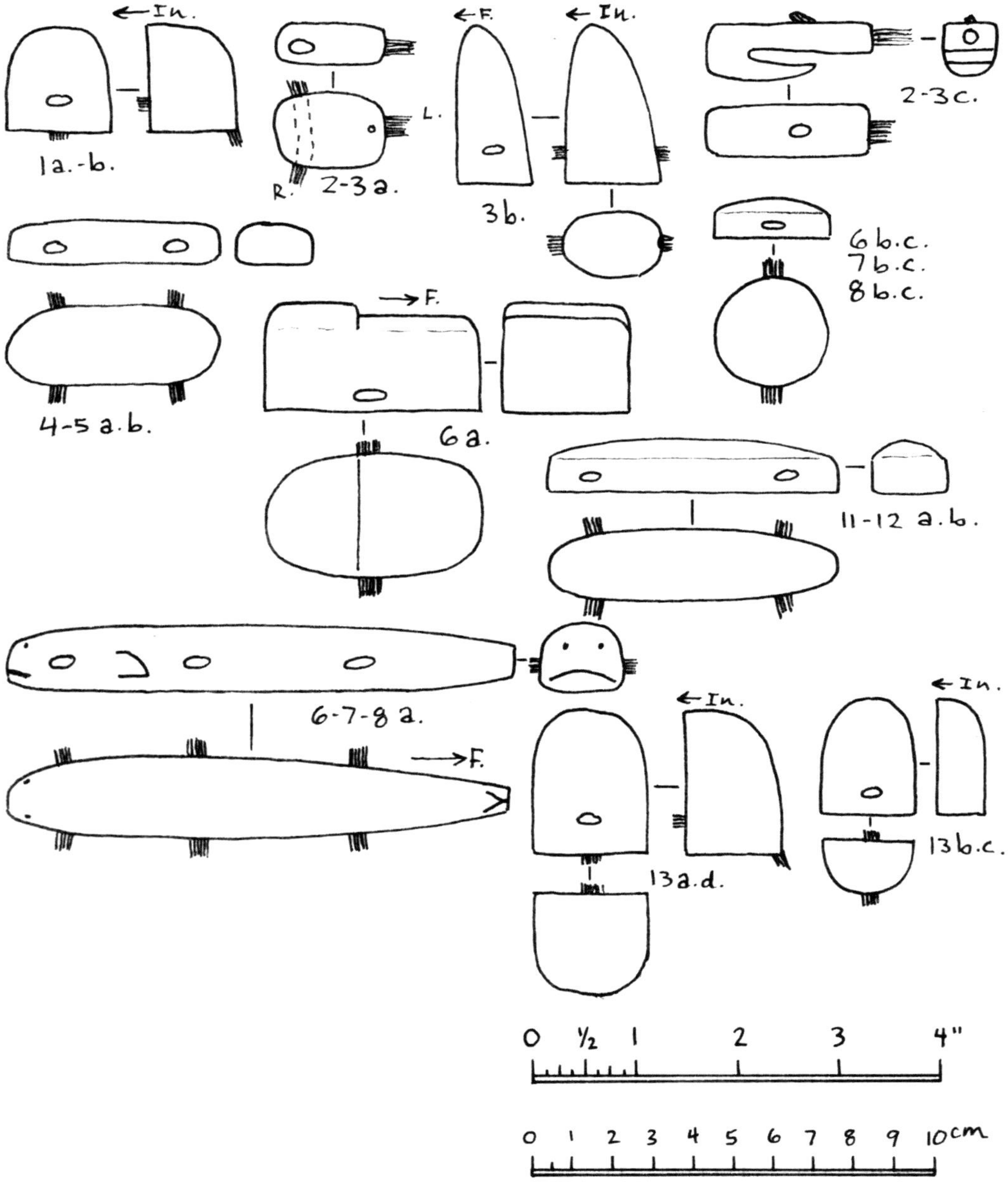

Some of the scantlings not presented on the scale drawing are as follows: The *masik* measures 1/2" (13mm) thick at the aft edge in the middle, and is 3" (7.6cm) wide. The *isserfik* is 3/4" (19mm) thick and 1-1/4" (32mm) wide. The fore deck stringers are 1/2" (13mm) thick by 1-3/8" (35mm) wide; the aft deck stringers are 1/2" (13mm) thick and 1"(25mm) wide.

Every deck line is present on the DNM's kayak 9726 except for the harpoon holder, which is evidenced to the right of the cockpit on the *masik*. Where the previous kayak had the large polar bear head fitting, the 9726 has a large split-level piece (6a), the specific function of which I don't know. The higher end of this fitting is towards the stern; a similar piece can also be seen on the following kayak, although it is placed just a bit further aft on the deck.

A Y-shaped deck line is present on the 9726, and it appears very much like that on the AMNH 60/6190 (plate 76), except for the buttons. A large seal-shaped figure links the three deck lines just ahead of the cockpit. To the left of the seal link, each of the three deck lines has two ivory discs. Deck lines 4 and 5 on the fore deck and lines 11 and 12 on the aft deck are each double linked. A single deck line (10) is situated just ahead of the linked deck lines on the aft deck.

The bow deck line has two large implement holders— too blocky to be considered conical, but of an elegant form, nonetheless. The stern deck line has four implement holders of the same form as the bow deck line; the outer two are much larger than the inner pair.

Figure 325: The replica of the L.9726 off the Oregon Coast, 2006. (Photograph by Brian Schulz.)

In 2005, I built a replica of the DNM L.9726— I had wanted to since the day I saw the original. It appears much grander than other type VII kayaks on account of its very long ends and greater length.

For what is a fairly large Greenland kayak, the L.9726 replica feels very swift and is a very solid feeling ride, the long ends dampening waves somewhat being reserve buoyancy. As expected the 9726 replica turns very easily, likely on account of its generous rocker. It lean-turns exceedingly well, such that one can nearly steer with one's hips alone. (Lean-turning involves heeling a kayak during the turn such that a curved asymmetrical hull is presented to the water— this curved immersed hull shape tends to cause the kayak to turn, some more readily than others. In the case of the 9726, this characteristic is optimized when the kayaker heels towards the outside of the turn.)

Figure 326: The replica of the DNM L.9726 being paddled by the author on the Willamette River, Portland, Oregon, 2005. (Photograph by Brian Schulz.)

78. **West Greenland Kayak: Danish National Museum, Copenhagen. Catalog no. L.18.178.**

Little is known of the L.18.178's history, though it is known informally at the Danish National Museum as "Knud Rasmussen's kayak." The vicinity it hails from is only noted as "South West Greenland" (Dr. Anne Bahnson, 2002, personal correspondence). When compared to the L.9726 (above) and others known to be from Nanortalik (e.g., the KNK 1550x1, and the VSM 810-34 [plates 80 and 81]), it is almost certain that this kayak is also from that vicinity.

The rib-to-chine and keelson joints are fastened with copper or bronze nails with 1/4″ (6mm) square heads. The keelson is laid flat, instead of on-edge, like many type VII kayaks in this study. The chines in this kayak are placed fairly high, giving a moderate dead rise and shallower sides. As can be seen in the survey drawing, the ribs are not particularly straight— squirrelly at best. They are fashioned from split limbs (de-barked), likely harvested in local fjords.

The 18.178's *masik* is 3-1/8″ (79mm) wide, and its *isserfik* measures 5/8″ (16mm) thick by 1-3/8″ (35mm) wide. The deck beams are intermittently fastened to the gunwales with oblique pegs; they may also be fastened with top-pegs, as is often the case.

Coaming protection pieces consist of two ivory strips placed along the upper backside of the hoop. There is a gap between them of about 2-1/4″ (5.7cm) between the 7-1/4″ (18.4cm) long strips. The strips are 1/2" (13mm) wide and 1/4" (6mm) thick, and are fastened to the coaming with metal nails. The coaming itself measures 5/8" (16mm) thick by 1-1/4" (32mm) high and is fashioned of ash.

The L.18.178's deck lines are rigged similarly to the 530/61 and the KNK 1550x1 (plates 79 and 80). The ivory fittings on the L.18.178 are very well made and are

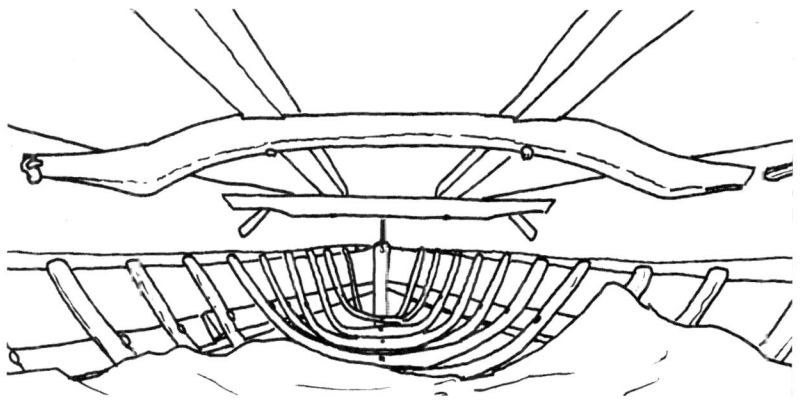

Figure 327: Forward interior view of the Danish National Museum's kayak no. L.18.178. A seal skin seat pad obscures the foreground. Note the shape of the curved deck beam and the density of the ribs.

uniquely angular and geometrically-faceted, appearing almost 'art-deco'— my drawings do not do them justice. On the fore-most deck-line between the two implement holders is a carving of a bird, facing the kayaker. Deck lines 4, 5, and 6 are all linked together, and to the left of the link piece are six implement holders— two on each of the lines. The implement holders are situated such that they face their 'opposite' on the same line.

Deck lines 2 and 3 on the fore deck and 8 and 9 on the aft deck are each double linked. A single line is situated just ahead of deck line 8. The stern deck line has four implement holders, the outer two being quite large with rounded backs, and the inner two being more angular.

A harpoon holder was not evidenced on either side of the cockpit. A bow knob and bow keel edging was present, though no stern knob or stern edging was present or evidenced.

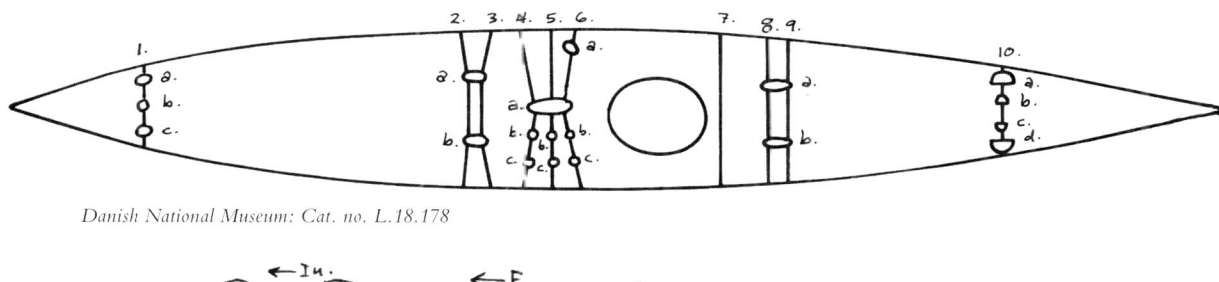

Danish National Museum: Cat. no. L.18.178

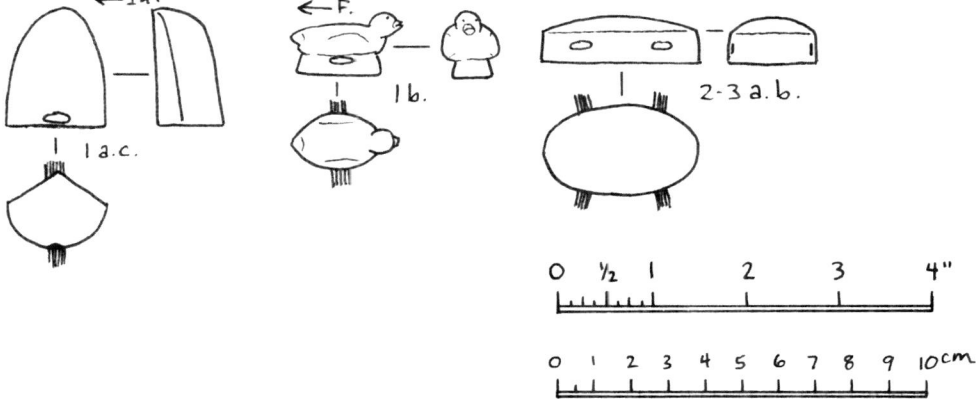

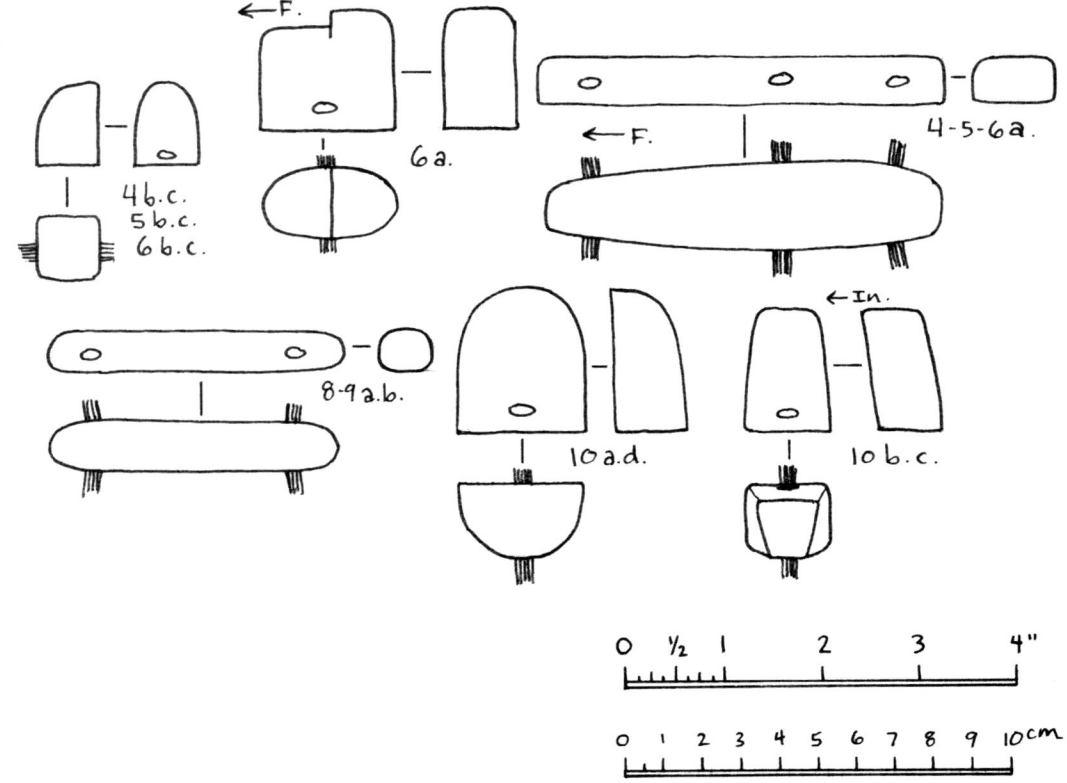

79. West Greenland Kayak: Danish National Museum, Copenhagen. Catalog no. 530/61.

The Danish National Museum's 530/61 is another kayak of unknown provenance, although it bears a close resemblance to the previous example, the DNM's L.18.178. (The designation "530/61" is the DNM's daybook heading number; a catalog number hadn't been issued.) Considering distinct resemblances to other type VII kayaks in this study, I think it is very obvious that the 530/61 is a kayak from South Greenland.

The *masik* in the 530/61 is 2-1/4" (57mm) wide at the gunwales, and is carved down to 1-3/8"(35mm) wide at its mid-point. The next deck beam forward of the *masik* is 4-1/8" (10.5cm) ahead of it. Every other deck beam is obliquely pegged to the gunwales and the lower frame is metal fastened. The 530/61's *isserfik* measures 5/8" (16mm) thick and 1-1/4" (32mm) wide. The fore deck stringers measure 3/4" (19mm) wide and the aft deck stringers are 1/2" (13mm) thick and 1-1/2" (38mm) wide.

The 530/61's seal skin *amiq* is painted entirely in a battleship-grey, and little care was taken with regard to getting paint on the ivory fittings and on the coaming, much less inside the cockpit itself. That gray paint should be slopped over ivory deck fittings should re-enforce the fact that this kayak was first and foremost a hunting tool. No keel edging was evidenced fore or aft, but a bow knob was present (1-3/16" long, 1-1/16" h., and 1" wide [30 x 27 x 25mm]). There was no evidence of a stern knob having been fitted. Two bone strips are present at the back of the coaming; the upper is 9" (22.8cm) long, and the lower is 8-1/2" (21.6cm) long. Both strips are 3/16" (5mm) thick by 3/8" (9mm) high. The coaming's scarf joint is secured with three copper rivets.

Figure 328: Hunters unloading fish from their kayaks, Nanortalik, 1937. (Photograph by Jette Bang. Copyright: Greenland National Museum and Archive.)

All the deck lines are present on the 530/61, and their fittings are very well made. The harpoon holder is a very low and rounded 'stump' type— a form very unlikely to snag a harpoon line or scrape the kayaker's knuckles.

The pattern and rigging of the 530/61's deck lines is very similar to that of the previous kayak, the L.18.178 (plate 78). The exceptions are that the 530/61 has a harpoon holder and lacks the large split-level fitting on the L.18.178's deck line 6 (piece 6a)— Perhaps the piece missing from the 530/61 functions as the harpoon holder on the L.18.178? For two such similarly rigged kayaks, it is interesting to compare the stylistic variation in the actual form of the deck fittings.

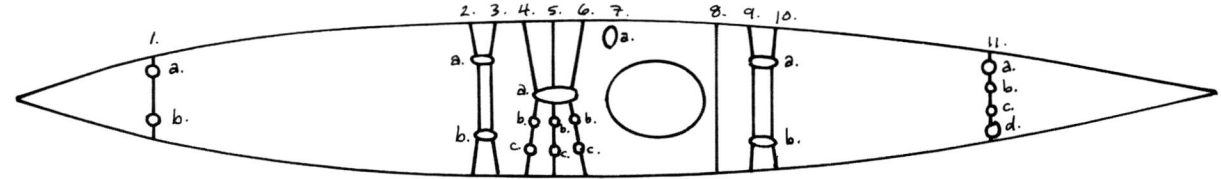

Danish National Museum: Cat. no. 530/61

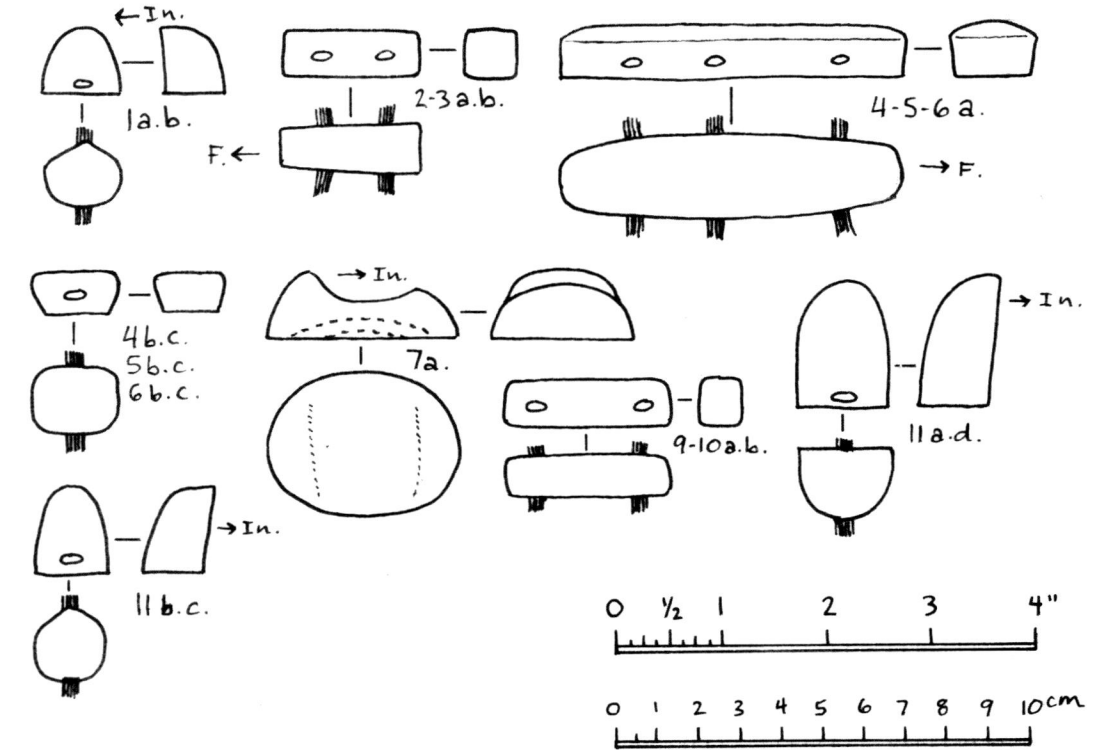

80. West Greenland Kayak: Greenland National Museum, Nuuk. Catalog no. KNK 1550x1

The 1550x1 was built in Nanortalik around 1978 by Martin Kristiansen. The 1550x1 is from the large diverse collection (the "1550" series) transferred to the Greenland National Museum from the Royal Greenland Company (KGH) in 1987.

This kayak has a very flat sheer that even dips downward at the stern. It is unusually deep for the type, especially considering its breadth. As if to compensate for its great depth-to-sheer (8-7/8"; 22.5cm), its depth overall is only 7/8" (22mm) greater, giving it a very low flat deck. The 1550x1 is rather short for the type, at only 16'5" (500.3cm); its length and depth give it a rather heavy appearance, unlike the dainty and fine appearance of the flamboyant L.9726 (plate 77), also from Nanortalik.

An interior view of the 1550x1 is presented in figure 329. The rib-to-chine and keel joints are all metal-nailed, and the deck beam-to-gunwale joints are lashed with many turns of fine fishing line.

The rib spacing in the 1550x1's cockpit is very dense; three of these ribs (as seen in the survey drawing) are actually half-ribs extending from just chine-to-chine (as in figure 88). These half-ribs are positioned at 8′ 7/8″ and 8′ 11″ (246.0 and 271.7cm) on-center. A third half-rib is well forward of the cockpit, situated at about 6′ 7″ (200.0cm) from the bow. Behind the cockpit, there is a full-length rib that is not set into mortises; instead its ends are carried up adjacent to the inside face of the gunwales to which it is metal-nailed. This was probably done due to a fractured mortise wall.

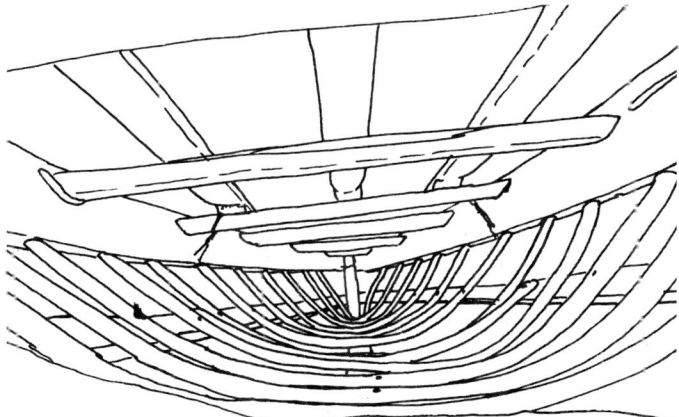

Figure 329: Forward interior view of the Greenland National Museum's kayak 1550x1. Note the three forward deck stringers.

The 1550x1 is canvas covered, nd is painted with gloss-black enamel paint. Despite its 1/2″ (13mm) thick gunwales, it is stoutly built and fairly heavy, perhaps 45 pounds. The bottom of the 1550x1 is well protected against ice and wear. Keel edging extends the entire length, the mid-section being of wood in lieu of ivory (from 3′ 7″ to 13′ 7-1/2″ [109.2 to 415.2cm], 7/16″ [11mm] thick, 9-1/16″ [14mm] wide). The chines also have wooden edging, extending from 5′ 7-3/4″ to 10′ 10-1/2″ (172.0 to 331.4cm). Protective edging along the chines is a feature more commonly associated with East Greenland kayaks.

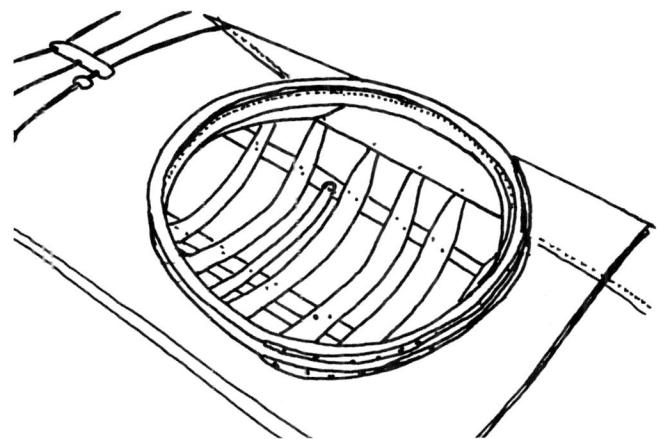

Figure 330: Cockpit view of the KNK 1550x1. Note the multitude of upholstery tacks used to attach the canvas amiq to the coaming, and the "cut-away" masik.

The bow-most deck line is unadorned and taut, though just 2″ (5 1cm) behind it is another deck line, this one with three ivory cones. The forward line may have served as an anchor point for a rifle bag. The three deck lines just ahead of the cockpit are all linked by one long piece of ivory, and several buttons are present on the deck lines to the left of the longer piece. The two deck lines ahead of these three are linked together with two small ivory pieces. No harpoon holder was evidenced on this kayak.

The 1550x1 has three lines on the aft deck, the aft two being linked with two ivory pieces. These pieces are thin and curved, such that their concave faces are faced inboard. The 1550x1's aft-most deck line has four very large fittings— presumably whale teeth. The outer two lean inwards, while the inner pair leans outboard.

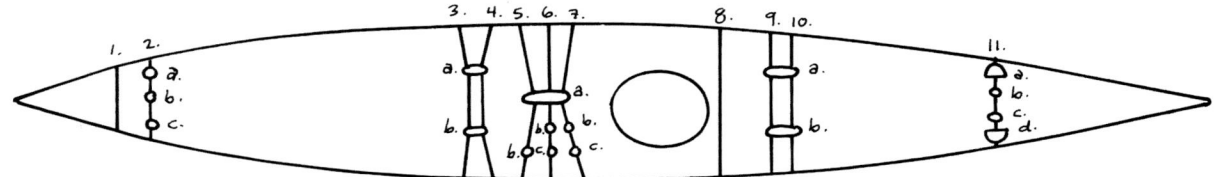

Greenland National Museum: Cat. no. 1550x1

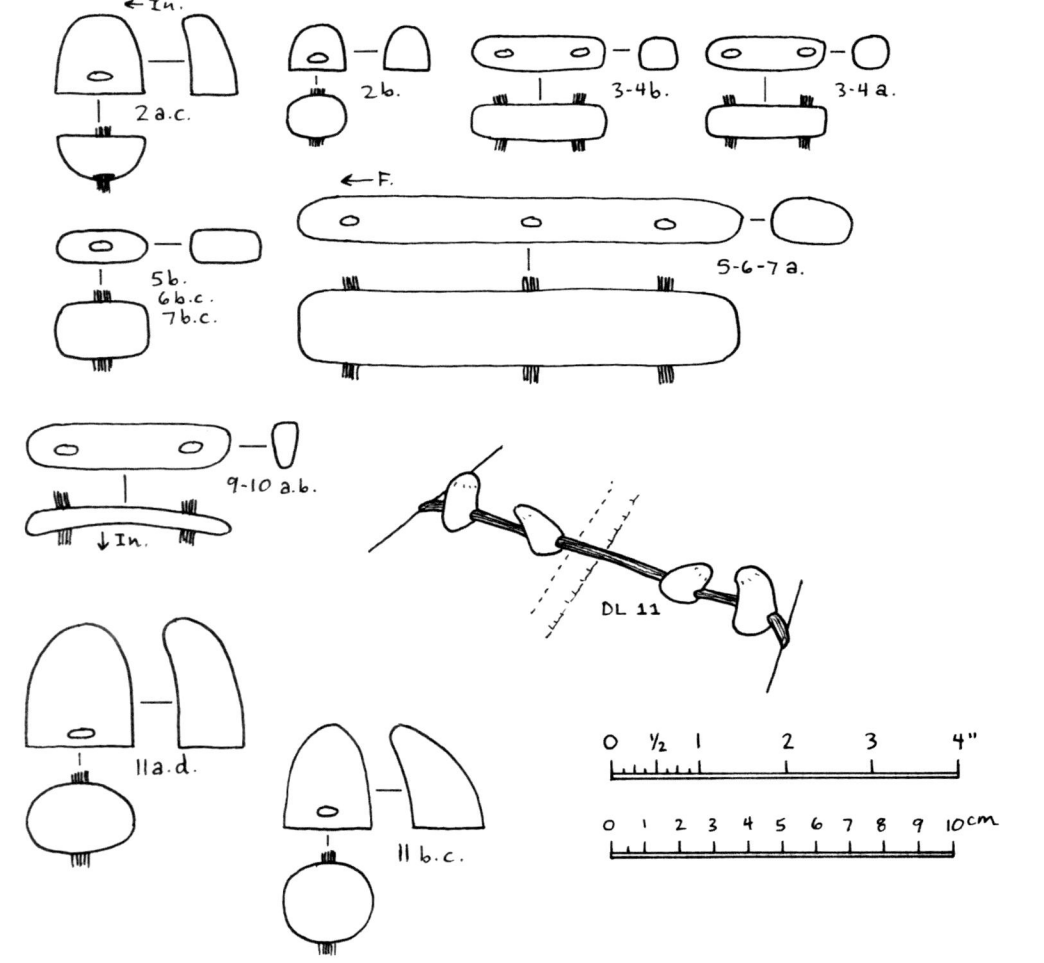

81. West Greenland Kayak: Viking Ship Museum, Roskilde, Denmark. Catalog no. VSM 810-34.

Apollus Jakobsen of Nanortalik built this kayak at the Viking Ship Museum in Roskilde, Denmark in 1991. It was, at the time of my visit, on display at the Danish National Museum, Copenhagen.

Only two pieces seem to be missing from the 810-34's frame: the curved deck beam just ahead of the *masik*, and a rib, whose mortise is evidenced at 7′ 3″ (221.0cm) aft of zero. The forward deck stringers sag to well below their original height on account of the missing deck beam. The drawing of the frame (plate 81a) depicts this omission and deformity, though the fore deck height is restored on the hull-lines drawing (plate 81b). There are two other pairs of empty rib-mortises, but the likelihood that ribs were missing is slim; most likely they were never fitted. These mortises are the fore- and aft-most, being at 3′ 7″ (109.2cm) and 14′ 6-1/2″ (443.2cm) from zero. None of the ribs exhibit any peg or nail fastening to the gunwales.

The chines and keelson are metal-nailed to the ribs. The first two ribs in the cockpit opening are each double-nailed to the chines and keelson. The *masik* is side pegged to the gunwales, as in figure 77d. The ends of the *masik* are shaped as in figure 76b. The forward edge of the *masik* is 3/4″ (19mm) thick in the middle, and the aft-edge is 3/16″ (5mm) thick. This thinning of the aft-edge allows for easier entry and exit. To further aid in this, the *masik* has been carved with a forward tilt, or cant, such that the aft upper-edge is 3/8″ (9mm) higher than the forward edge; the *masik* measures 3″ (7.6cm) wide.

The deck beam mortises in the 810-34's gunwales are 5/16″ (8mm) high and 1-1/8″ (28mm) wide, with rounded corners. The upper edges of the mortises are 5/16″ (8mm) below the top of the gunwales. Six of the deck beams are oblique-pegged; the pegs are 1/2″ (13mm) diameter, and exit the gunwales' outer faces about 7/8″ (22mm) on-center above the gunwales' lower edges. All of the deck beams are also top-pegged in place.

The only lashings on the 810-34 are at the keel ends' junction with the gunwales and the stem pieces, and at the chine-ends. At their termini, the chines are also nailed to the keelson ends. Clamping ties near the gunwale ends are not present, nor are there clamping dowels in this vicinity. This omission seems to be the exception in Greenland kayaks, most using one or the other method. Unlike many of the kayak frames in this study, the keelson piece with its tall bow and stern sections is all one piece, no scarfs being present at all.

The hull-lines of the VSM 810-34 depict a very fine looking kayak— very reminiscent of the DNM's 530/61, and nearly identical in size. A very slight integral skeg is present; the ribs in this section were intact and holding their shape well, so this re-curving of the keelson was intended by the builder.

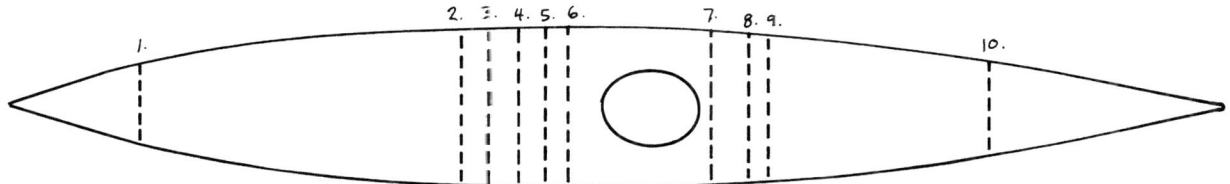

Viking Ship Museum, Roskilde: 810-34

The 810-34's deck line placement was evidenced from holes drilled in the gunwales and the *masik*, and are drawn with dashed-lines on the hull-lines plate (81b). The original fittings and arrangement of the 810-34 likely resembled those on the 530/61; both have three deck lines just behind the cockpit, as do two other kayaks from Nanortalik: the DNM L.9726 (plate 77), and the KNK 1550x1 (plate 80). Holes suggesting a presence of a Y-shaped deck line were not present.

TYPE VIII.

East Greenland is considered to consist of vicinities north of Cape Farewell (Kap Farvel) along the East Coast to well north of Scoresby Sound, the northernmost settlement along this coast. While no kayak examples in this study are known to hail from Scoresby Sound or from King Frederik VI's Coast in the South, 'East Greenland' shall primarily refer to Ammassalik District.[43]

Greenlanders were the first of the Eskimos to have contact with Europeans— they have been in contact off and on since the 1200s, and fairly consistently since the 1600s. Despite 800 years of contact with Greenlanders, Europeans had not visited the Ammassalimmiut in East Greenland until the comparatively recent date of 1884. Europeans first heard reports of the Ammassalik population in 1752, although by 1728 the missionary Hans Egede had heard that the southern regions of the East Coast were populated (Birket-Smith, 1928:14-15).

Type VIII kayaks are one of two types from East Greenland discussed in this study. Type VIII is the 'old-form' East Greenland kayak, distinguishable from the new form (type IX) by its high stern, reverse sheer, considerable rocker, greater chine breadth, and convex stems. Aside from the elevated stern, reverse sheer, and convex stems, type VIII kayaks resemble the South Greenland kayaks (type VII) rather closely in form, particularly in cross-section.

Despite resembling the South Greenland kayaks in form, the construction of the type VIII kayak is distinct and has remained that way even in the newer form East Greenland kayaks. The most significant difference is the attachment of the *masik*, which, in East Greenland is shallow mortised into the gunwale, as in figure 76e, as opposed to resting on top of the gunwale. The *masik* in East Greenland kayaks has a handle carved into its center, as depicted in figure 79. Deck beams in East Greenland kayaks are unshouldered (as in figure 35d); deck beams are always shallow mortised, and typically fastened obliquely with large wooden pegs (as in figure 37c). East Greenland kayaks seem to never have aft deck stringers, and typically have three (four, in one case) broad stringers on the fore deck.

Unfortunately, the sample size of type VIII is as limited as it could be— just one kayak, which may in fact be the only one in existence. I have supplemented this section with a survey of a particular fine model of the old type (a frame) as well as notes on the rigging of two other models. Type VIII kayaks became extinct by 1894 (Thalbitzer, 1914:284).

---

[43] Scorseby Sound, while having been inhabited in pre-historic times, was re-populated in 1924; King Frederik VI's Coast had become entirely de-populated by the early 1900s; Gustav Holm had only counted 135 inhabitants in 1884 (Birket-Smith, 1928:14).

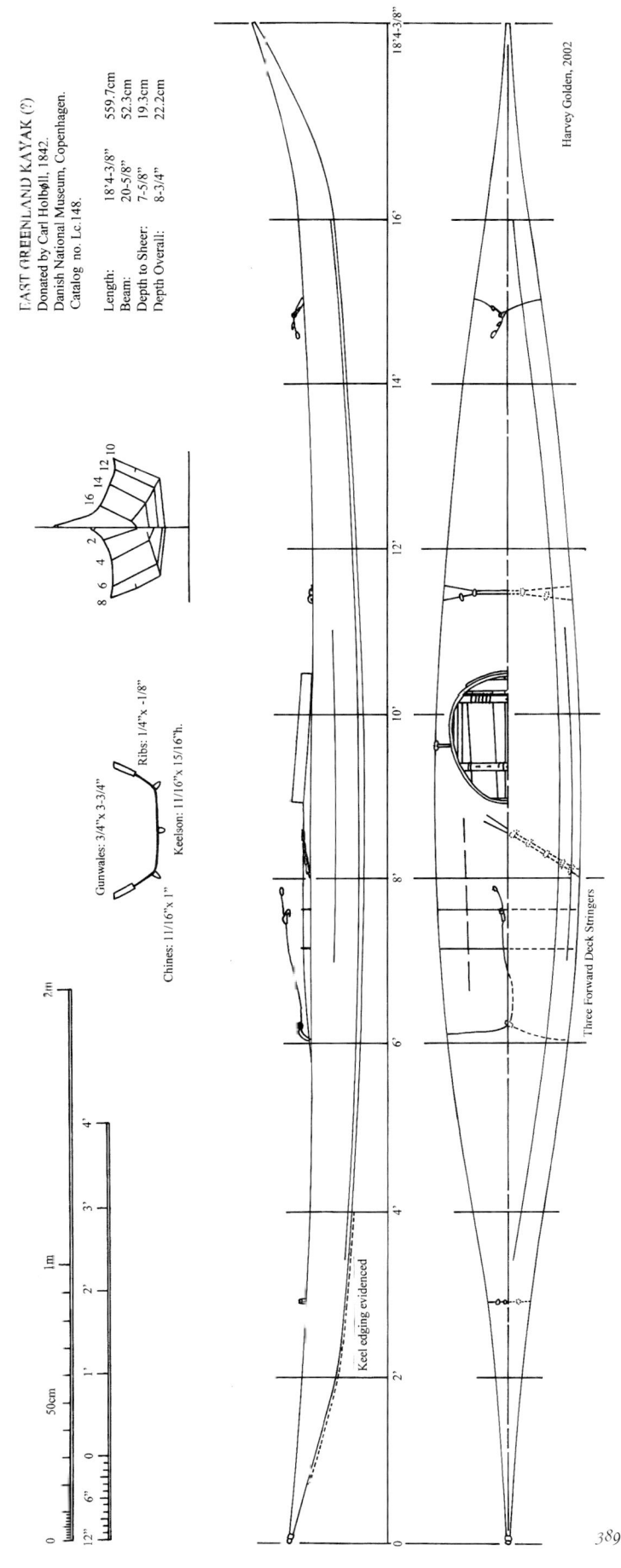

82. Danish National Museum catalog no. Lc.148

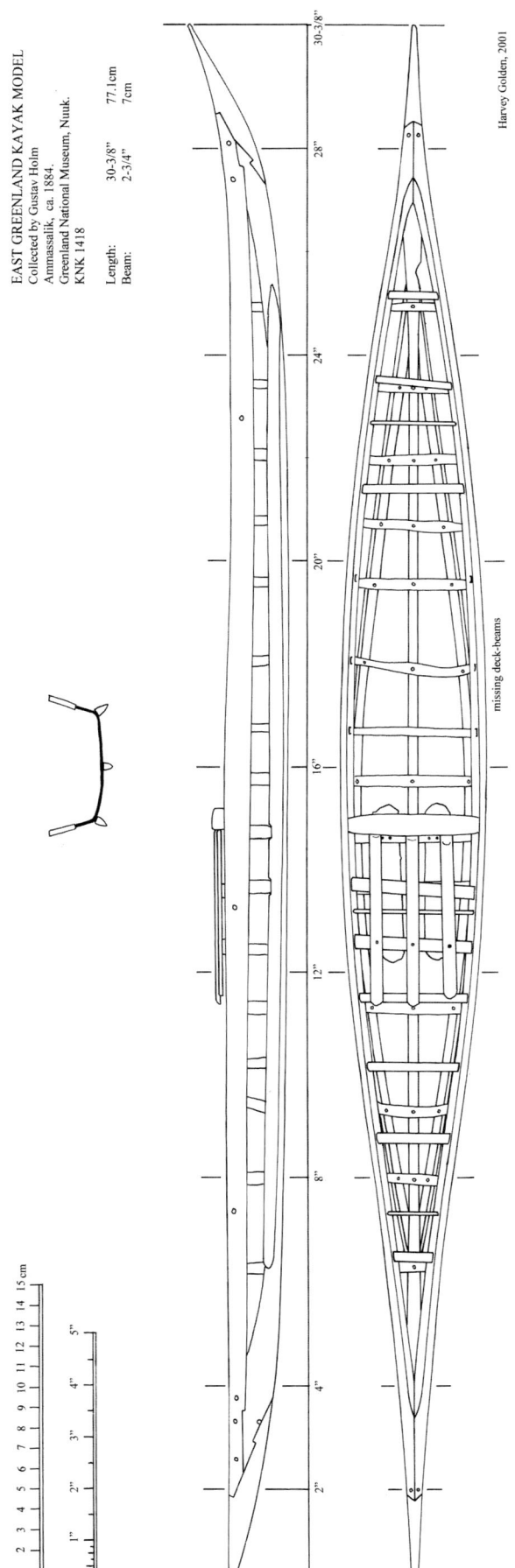

83a. Greenland National Museum catalog no. KNK 1418

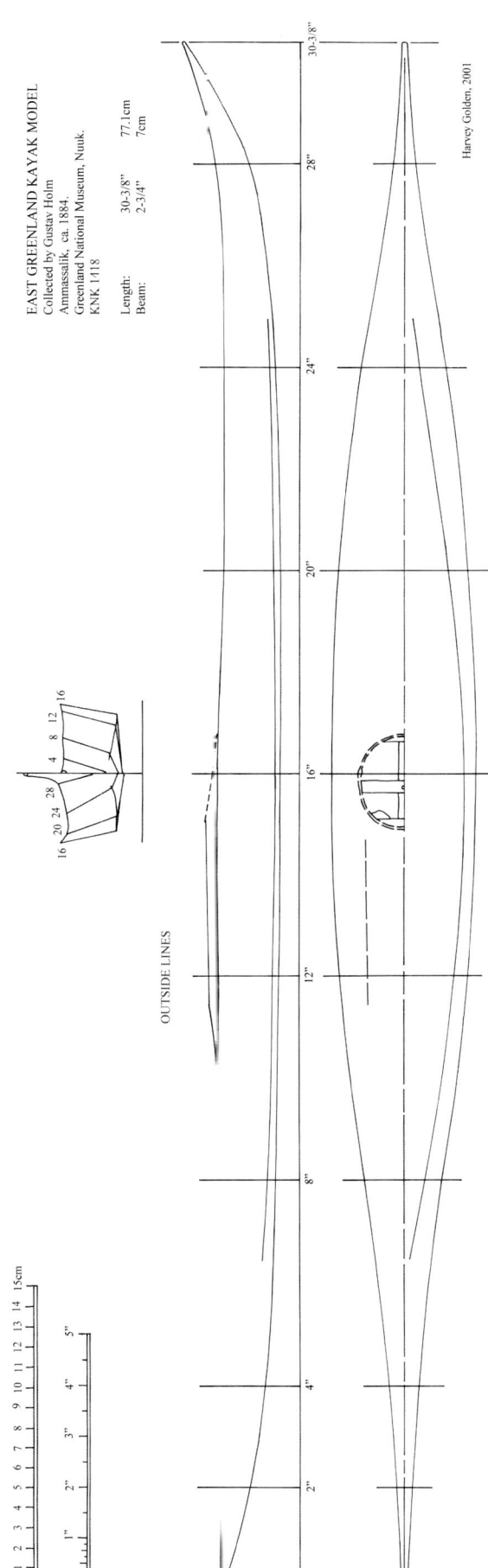

83b. Greenland National Museum catalog no. KNK 1418 (Hull Lines)

82. East Greenland Kayak: Danish National Museum, Copenhagen. Catalog no. Lc.148.

It has turned out that the Lc.148 had already been surveyed by John and Stella Brand in 1975, and published in John's *The Little Kayak Book, vol. III* (1988:82-86). John Brand writes that his contact at the DNM had little information about the kayak. The designation of "no.3" is explained by Brand as being "little help because, if I remember correctly, it is something we adopted to differentiate it from the other Greenland kayaks, from a wooden label found loose in the cockpit with 'no.3' penciled on it"(1988:82). The conflict of catalog numbers led me to conduct a survey of my own on the Lc.148 thinking it may be a different kayak. It has since turned out that Brand's "no. 3" and the Lc.148 are one and the same.

While the museum accession card presently attributes the kayak's origin to "West Greenland," Brand writes of his uncertainty as to where he thought it was from, deciding East Greenland initially, then thinking more South Greenland. "Later I thought that if it was from the Angmagssalik area it would be late C.19th. because of the elegant ends" (Brand, 1988:82). Kaj Birket-Smith makes reference to an "... older kayak of South Greenland type in the National Museum..."(1924:270) regarding its oblique deck-lines; the Lc.148 is the only kayak at the DNM with such deck lines.

I strongly think that it is an East Greenland kayak, despite its having been collected in "West" Greenland, as-per DNM records. This theory is based on the models collected by Holm (described next), Holm's expedition results (Holm, 1914), and Thalbitzer's own reports also published in the 1914 volume. Furthermore, there are no West Greenland kayaks similar to the Lc.148— perhaps an element here or a detail there, but all in all the Lc.148 has numerous unique details— many of which are to be seen in later East Greenland kayaks. John Brand, much to his credit, was quite correct to think "East Greenland" when he saw this kayak. I hope I am mistaken but I believe the Lc.148 may be the only full-size kayak of its type left in the world.

Current Danish National Museum accession information lists the Lc.148 as having been given to the museum by Carl Holbøll in 1842. From 1828 to 1856, the year of Holbøll's death in a shipwreck, he was the South Greenland Inspector (Krabbe, 1930:100). That this East Greenland kayak pre-dates European visits to the East Greenland populations at Ammassalik by forty-two years is remarkable but not surprising. Holbøll's position in South Greenland was ideal for not only collecting South Greenland 'ethnographica,' but also to see and acquire objects traded down the Southeast coast from Ammassalik vicinity.[44]

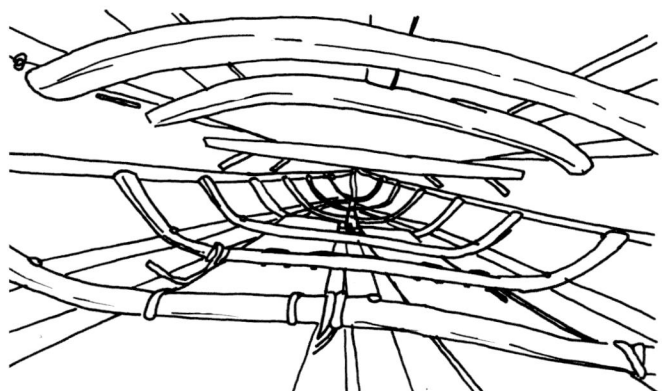

Figure 331: Forward interior view of the Lc.148: Note the three deck stringers and leg-slats. All of the straight deck beams in this kayak are oblique-pegged. Also note the built-up gunwales.

Figure 330 shows a view inside of the Lc.148, looking forward. The curved deck-beams are not too symmetrically cut, but one wouldn't know by looking at the outside form of the kayak. The slight reverse sheer of the Lc.148 is actually built-up: Pieces have been added to the gunwales' upper edges

---

[44] The kayak Lc.148 is not the only artifact from Ammassalik vicinity to reach Denmark before the first European visit to Ammassalik in 1884. For example, Kaj Birket-Smith writes of a water-pail and dipper that was acquired by the trading post manager in Qaqortoq circa 1849 from "Eastlanders;" this same manager was apparently the first to record "Angmagssalik" as a locale in stating the pail and dipper's origin (1928:15).

to increase their height. This exact method has been described before, in the case of the NMNH 160325: a type VI kayak from Upernavik (plate 56).

The chines and keelson are pegged to the ribs with a single wooden peg at each joint. The ribs are not fastened to the gunwales. All of the straight deck beams have large oblique pegs securing them to the gunwales; the curved deck beams show no evidence of having fasteners: They may be top-pegged, although I suspect their tenons are set into shallow mortises. The deck stringers of the Lc.148 are narrow compared to later East Greenland kayaks, being only 1-1/4" (32mm) wide for the outer two, and 1" (25mm) wide for the middle. No aft deck stringers are present in the Lc.148.

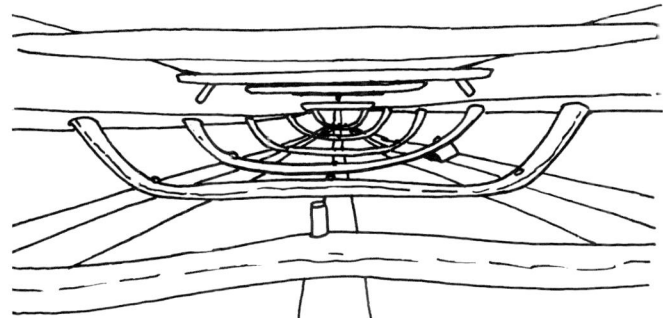

Figure 332: Aft interior view of the Lc.148. By all appearances, the cross-piece at the lower edge of the gunwales was made of bone.

The Lc.148's *masik* measures 1/2" (13mm) thick by 3-1/4" wide (8.2cm); at its mid-point, the *masik* thickens to about 1-1/4" (32mm) and has a hand grip carved into its under-side. The *isserfik* measures 1" (25mm) thick by 1-3/4" (44mm) wide; its thickness tapers to about 5/8" (16mm) at the ends. The coaming measures 1/2" (13mm) thick by 1-3/4" (44mm); its scarf is secured with two parallel rows of ivory nails with 1/2" (13mm) heads.

While West Greenland kayaks have seat-slats (if any) as in figure 85, and modern East Greenland Kayaks typically have leg-slats, as in figure 86, the Lc.148 has slats that would support the kayaker's seat and legs. The slats are about 5' (152.4cm) long, 1/4" (6mm) thick, and 3-1/2" (89mm) wide and are lashed beneath the ribs, and at the forward end, the slats are resting on top of a rib. These slats are attached with lashings— some joints are wrapped over the ribs and passed through holes in the slats, but other joints are intermittently stitched through holes in the ribs and slats. The second rib forward in figure 330 exhibits this latter method.

An aft interior view of the Lc.148 is presented in figure 331. Note the single yet large shim between the chine and rib on the right. The oblique-peg fastening system is used sparingly in the Lc.148, compared to later East Greenland kayaks (type IX). The cross-piece at the lower edge of the gunwales towards the stern is not a wooden dowel as in several West Greenland kayaks, but is instead a piece of bone. A closer observation wasn't possible, but similar configurations (also with bone) have been noted among East Canadian Kayaks (Golden, field notes: 2003). Such a crosspiece was not present in the bow of the Lc.148.

The Lc.148's deck lines are entirely different in their layout and sophistication compared to any kayak described prior in this study. Its sophistication lies in the use of adjustable-length deck lines forward *and* aft of the cockpit. As mentioned above, the 148 also has a pair of oblique deck lines just ahead of the cockpit; these deck lines do not reach all the way across the kayak's deck, and are instead anchored into the *masik* just to the right of the kayak's centerline. Birket-Smith writes that he never came across it in West Greenland except for at Upernavik (1924:270).

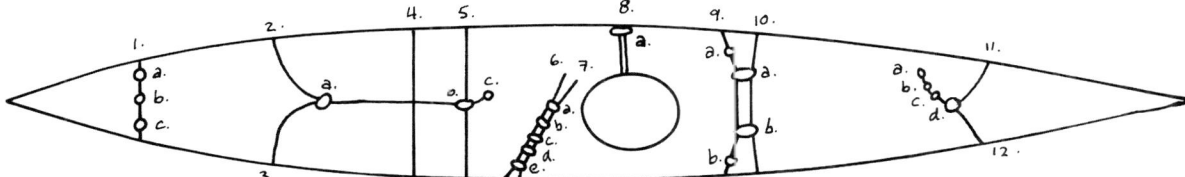

Danish National Museum: Cat. no. Lc.148

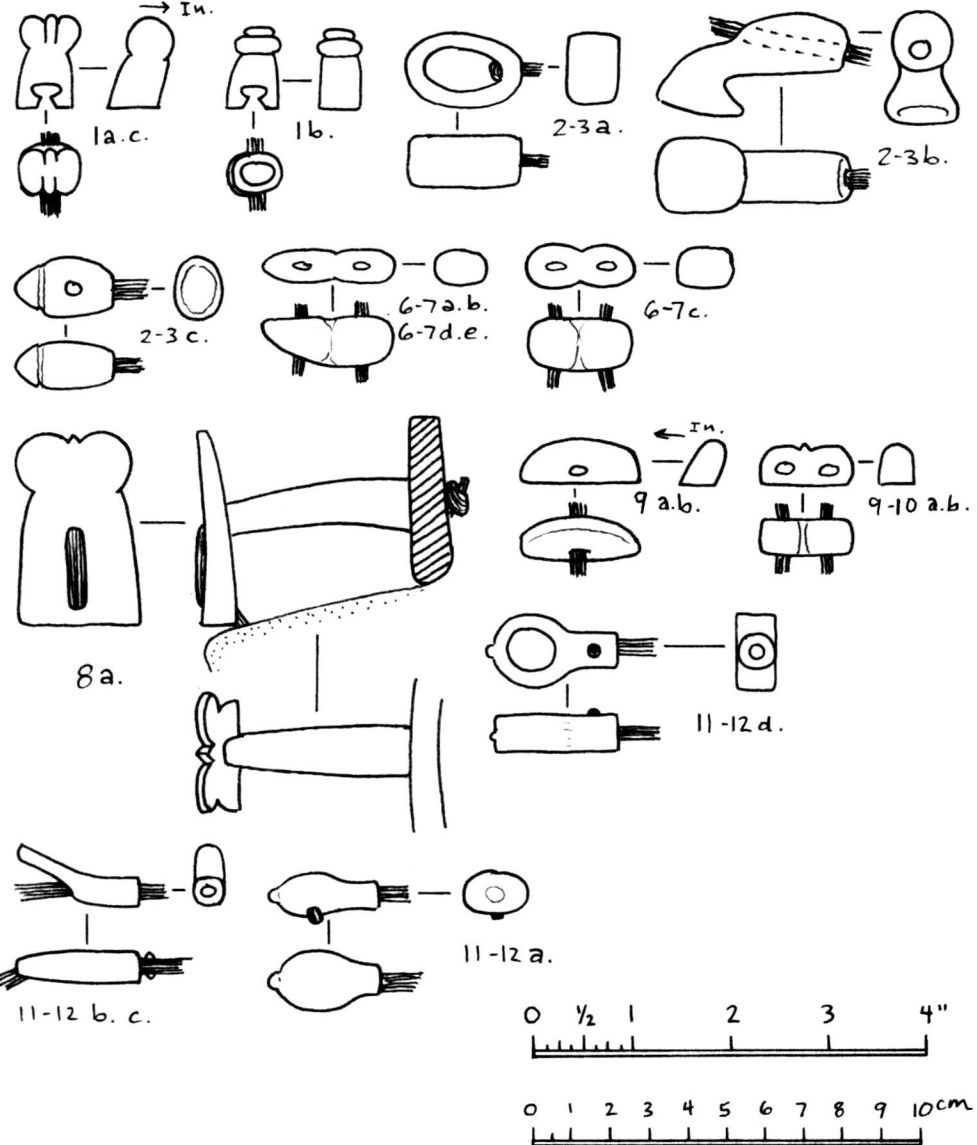

Figure 108 depicts the Lc.148's harpoon holder, and it is again illustrated in scale above (piece 8a). This form and placement is entirely different than any seen thus far in this study. It consists of two pieces of ivory— one is a flat plate, and the other is a hollowed tube, which forms a bridge from the plate to the side of the coaming. The line holding this fitting in place comes up through the kayak's sheer line and through two holes in the plate; at the upper hole, the line passes through the ivory tube and through the coaming where it is knotted.

The general motif of the Lc.148's harpoon holder can be seen in the tab-shaped harpoon holder on the Weltmuseum's kayak 36841 of ca. 1600s (plate 10), and on the aft deck line's fitting of the 1885 Upernavik kayak, the NMNH 160325 (plate 56). The two link-pieces on the Lc.148's aft deck (9-10a and b) mirror this motif in profile.

A Y-shaped deck line is not only present on the fore deck of the Lc.148, but also at the stern. This configuration is fairly typical of and unique to East Greenland kayaks of both types VIII and IX, as will be seen. The stern Y-shaped line is rigged somewhat differently than the Y-shaped line seen on East Greenland kayaks' fore decks. Piece 11-12d serves as a dead-eye through which a length of deck line runs— in this case the dead-eye is attached to line 12. Pieces 11-12b and c are shaped such that they can be threaded through the deadeye, but when put under tension they prevent slipping back through. Piece 11-12a is an ivory point attached to the tip of line 11; this point undoubtedly provided a better grip when pulling the line through the deadeye. Any adjustments to this deck line would have to be done either ashore or by another kayaker rafting up alongside the kayak needing adjustment.

No questions existed about whether or not to build a replica of the Lc.148: It may be the sole remaining kayak of its type, and it would be hard to imagine a finer example even if dozens existed. The sheer of this kayak was an intimidating prospect, much as it was with the replica of the E.102 (plate 26). Building in the reverse sheer amidships of the Lc.148 replica was simple: I used the same method as in the original of attaching a separate piece of wood atop the gunwales; figure 332 shows a flat-plate gunwale tracing of the replica's gunwale. For the end-joinery, I emulated that of the model described below (plate 83). This pattern was fairly difficult to execute— at least as cleanly as the model had been made.

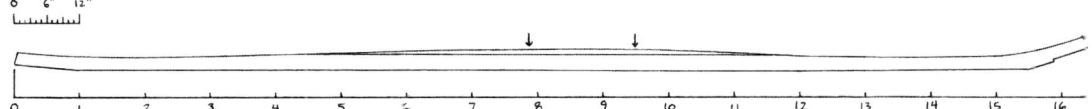

Figure 333: Flat-plate tracing of the gunwale shape used in the replica of the Lc.148; the arrows point to the position of the two cockpit deck beams. The total length of this gunwale is 16'5-1/8" (500.6cm). Also note the position and length of the gain.

The replica of the Lc.148 handled fairly predictably, being very agile and easy to correct in winds due to the very generous rocker and stems with very little grip. It rides waves very well, maintaining a dry deck fairly well and the elevated stern has a definite silencing effect in waves— this design feels quite at home in rough water. This replica is very comfortable and fairly roomy; it is a very sleek and low kayak despite its fairly large dimensions.

Figures 334a & b: Dr. Pavia Lumholt giving a harpoon throwing demonstration from the replica of the Lc.148, Rehoboth Bay, Delaware, 2004. (Photographs by the author.)

Figure 334b

Figure 335: The author in the replica of the Lc.148, Portland, Oregon. (Photograph by Brian Schulz.)

83. East Greenland Kayak Model: Greenland National Museum, Nuuk. Catalog no. KNK 1418.

The first European expedition to reach Ammassalik was lead by Captain Gustav Holm, of the Danish Royal Navy in 1884. While in Ammassalik, the Holm expedition made very extensive ethnographic collections— everything from pails, visors, clothing, to hunting equipment. A full-size kayak was unfortunately not brought back with the expedition, although two kayak paddles were, one of which is presented in paddle-plate 59.

In his *Ethnological Sketch of the Angmagsalik Eskimo*, Holm makes brief mention of Ammassalik kayaks and compares them to other kayaks: "The kaiaks here are in general longer and broader than those of the West Greenlanders, and terminate behind in an upturned point" (Holm, 1914:45). Holm presents an image of such an East Greenland kayak in this same work (facing pg.45; fig.33). The sketch, while of a kayak's framework, appears naively drawn, not to scale, and it has vague structural elements. For example, it has numerous ribs, but the deck-beams appear as very tiny spindles, and there are only four of them, along with the *masik*.

H. C. Petersen also expresses suspicion of the accuracy of the Holm engraving: "... a few of the dimensions seem different from the true hunting kayak's. The exaggerated size of the two ends together with the spindly cross beams and the extremely high keel seem a bit improbable" (1986:52). Not too surprisingly, such spindly deck beams were not present inside the full-size type VIII, the Lc.148 (plate 82).

While at the Greenland National Museum in 2000, I heard that a large portion of Holm's 1884 collection had been recently repatriated to Greenland— in fact, to the GNM itself. While checking accession and transfer data, I found a "kajakmodel," formerly cataloged as the Lb.386 of the Danish National Museum. Indeed the model was right upstairs and upon seeing it, the many questions I had about its odd representation by Holm were immediately answered.

The spindly deck-beams were indeed present— except for one depicted in Holm's image, which apparently was never there. They are not in-lieu of the 'true' deck-beams, which are also present in the model. Most likely, the spindles were used to hold the model together, as no lashings were used, and nor were any pegs at the deck beam-to-gunwale joints. The Holm drawing omits the nine 'true' deck-beams present on the model. Mortises for three more deck beams are evidenced, just aft of the *masik*. These may have simply fallen out, becoming lost. Furthermore, the model is more shapely and proportional than the sketch, and would almost appear to be a perfect kayak were it scaled up to a full-size boat with a beam of about 20˝ (50.3cm).

Deck line and fitting arrangements on the KNK 1418 are not evidenced, but fortunately Holm also collected two skin-covered and rigged kayak models: One is presently at the Danish National Museum (Lb.387) and the other is at the Oslo University Museum of Cultural Heritage (6488). I didn't survey either of these other models to the same extent as the KNK 1418, but I did note their deck line and fittings arrangements (see figure 336).

The Lb.387 has a Y-shaped deck line on the fore deck; a stern deck line was evidenced, and it may also have been a Y-shaped line like that on the Lc.148 (plate 82). A harpoon leash is also present on the Lb.387— such leashes are known from type IX East Greenland kayaks as well (e.g., the DNM L.19.157's [plate 86] deck line 10, pieces a-m). A harpoon holder was evidenced but missing; it appears to have been of the same configuration as that of the Lc.148 (plate 82).

The 6488 is much simpler in its rigging, having only four deck lines forward of the cockpit. It does have a curious skin loop off the left forward quarter of the coaming (the model's harpoon line ran through this loop). As with the Lb387, a harpoon holder was evidenced, though missing adjacent the coaming along the right sheer. The 6488's aft Y-shaped deck line was intact, though no evidence of such a forward line was present.

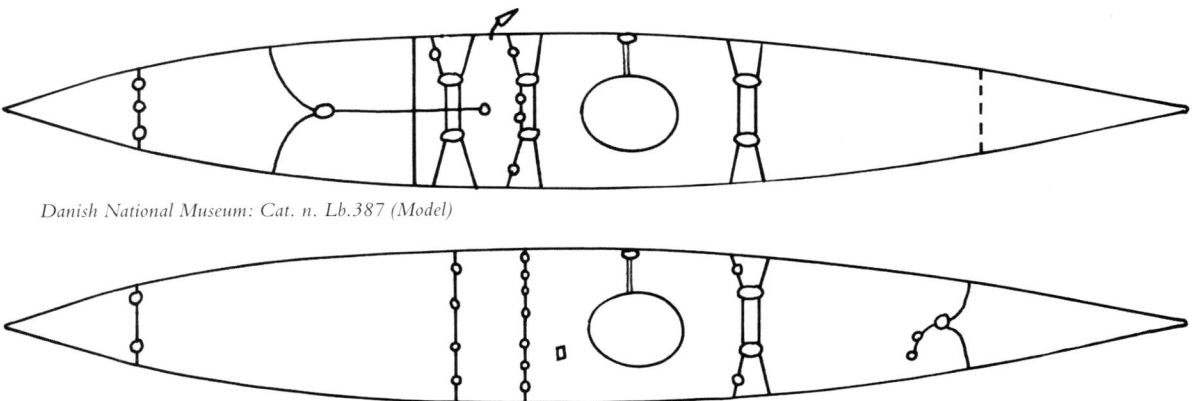

Danish National Museum: Cat. n. Lb.387 (Model)

University Museum of Cultural Heritage, Oslo: Cat. no. 6488 (Model)

Figure 336: Deck line and fittings arrangements of the two other kayak models collected by Gustav Holm in 1884: The Danish National Museum's Lb.387 (top), and the Oslo University Museum of Cultural Heritage's 6488 (bottom).

Both of these models distinctly resembled the 1418 in appearance (low bow, high stern, boxy cross-sections, etc.). Interestingly, the coamings of these models are lashed on using the over-the-top method (as in figure 123c). None of the full-size East Greenland kayaks in this study have laced-on coamings, and this may have just been done on the models due to their small size.

The hull-lines of the KNK 1418 show a very gradual keel-stem transition forward, ending in a low stiletto-like tip. The stern is curved upwards distinctly, though is fine in volume— much like those seen on type III West Greenland kayaks of the late 1700s and early 1800s (e.g., THH "B", and the Med-Chi kayak; plates 13 and 27). Cross sections of the 1418 reveal a very boxy shape, with nearly plumb sides, again being reminiscent of many type III forms.

The kayak model KNK 1418 compares phenomenally well with the full-size kayak Lc.148 (plate 82). If anything, this lends tremendous credibility to the accurate form and proportionality of the miniature kayak and to the likelihood of the Lc.148 being from Ammassalik. The only immediately obvious difference in form is the lower bow of the 1418, and the depths of its ends, as mentioned earlier by Petersen.

Aside from the three models collected by Holm and the full-size Lc.148, there may be just one other representation of the old-form East Greenland kayak: a carved model commissioned by William Thalbitzer (figure 337). Nappartuko made this model

Figure 337: Old-type East Greenland kayak and paddle models collected by William Thalbitzer ca. 1906, after figures 90 and 91 in his Ethnographic Collections from East Greenland (1914:386). The kayak's bow points to the right.

in 1906, several years after the old-form kayak had entirely disappeared. Thalbitzer quotes Nappartuko as saying the stern "was a little more bent up than the stem and the part round the man-hole reached somewhat higher up than in the present kayaks"(1914:384). The shape of this model is very true to the KNK 1418 model, only its bow is slightly fuller in depth. The elevated stern and reversed sheer are consistent with the KNK1418 and DNM Lc.148.

TYPE IX.

Type IX kayaks are the modern East Greenland kayaks— distinguished from the older East Greenland forms (type VIII) by their lower ends, concave stems, and flatter, shallower hulls. Constructionaly, they are pretty much identical. The present type seems to have appeared at Ammassalik abruptly in the very late 1800s, rendering the type VIII kayaks extinct in a matter of years. Ethnologist William Thalbitzer describes the change:

> *In earlier times the East Greenlanders at Ammassalik have only had kayaks with the stem and stern sloping upwards. According to Johan Petersen's account the old type of kciak was still in full use at Ammassalik in 1884 on the arrival of Holm's expedition. But even then, some few kayaks of the newer construction,*[45] *which had come from the south, were already noticed. On the next visit of Europeans (the founding of the Danish colony in 1894) there was not a single kaiak of the old type to be seen. all the kayaks had straight ends; the South-west mode had conquered (1914:284).*

H. C. Petersen attributes the sudden change in East Greenland kayak form to the transference of the Kap Farvel (Southern-most Greenland) kayak type to Ammassalik district. He writes "The whole kayak and stem and stern became longer. One would expect the kayak to have become deeper, but in fact it is shallower. Many technical details from the old type were retained and in some areas developed further" (1986:52).

The kayaks of South Greenland have already been presented in this study (type VII), and Petersen's statement on how East Greenland kayaks differ from them is consistent with my observations. What is distinctly consistent between type VIII and IX East Greenland kayaks is the method of attachment and form of the *masik*, and the deck stringer arrangements. The *masik* is attached to the gunwales just like the rest of the deck beams: shallow tenoned, and usually fastened with pegs. The deck stringer arrangements are 'three forward, none aft,' except for just one East Greenland kayak in this study that has four deck stringers forward (plate 36).

---

[45]Thalbitzer's mention of "newer construction" ought to be taken as 'newer form,' as the actual construction of the Lc.148 and type IX kayaks seem to be quite identical.

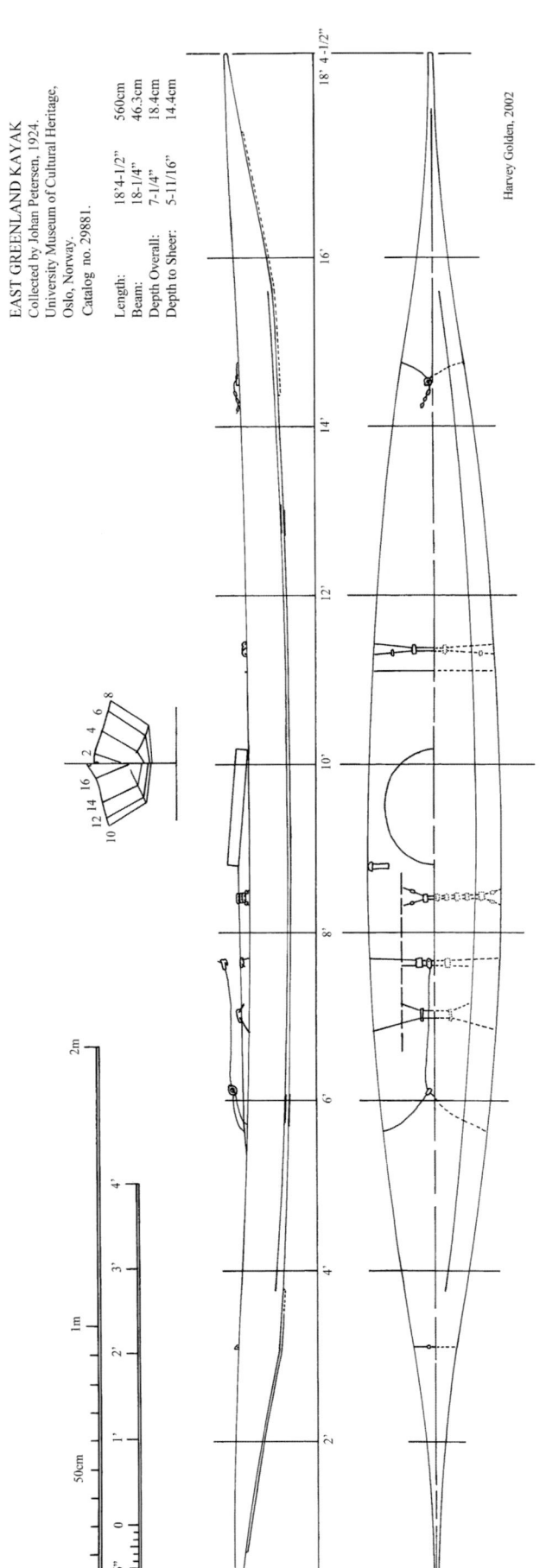

84. University Museum of Cultural Heritage catalog no. 29.881

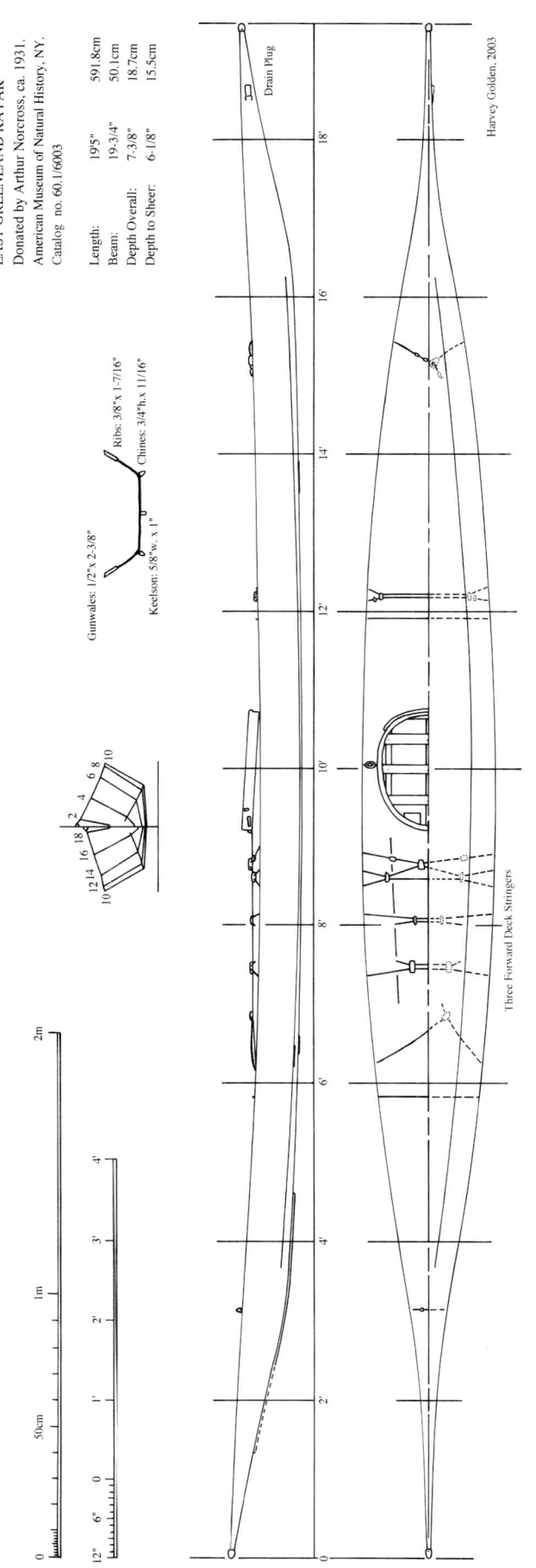

85. American Museum of National History catalog no. 60.1/6003

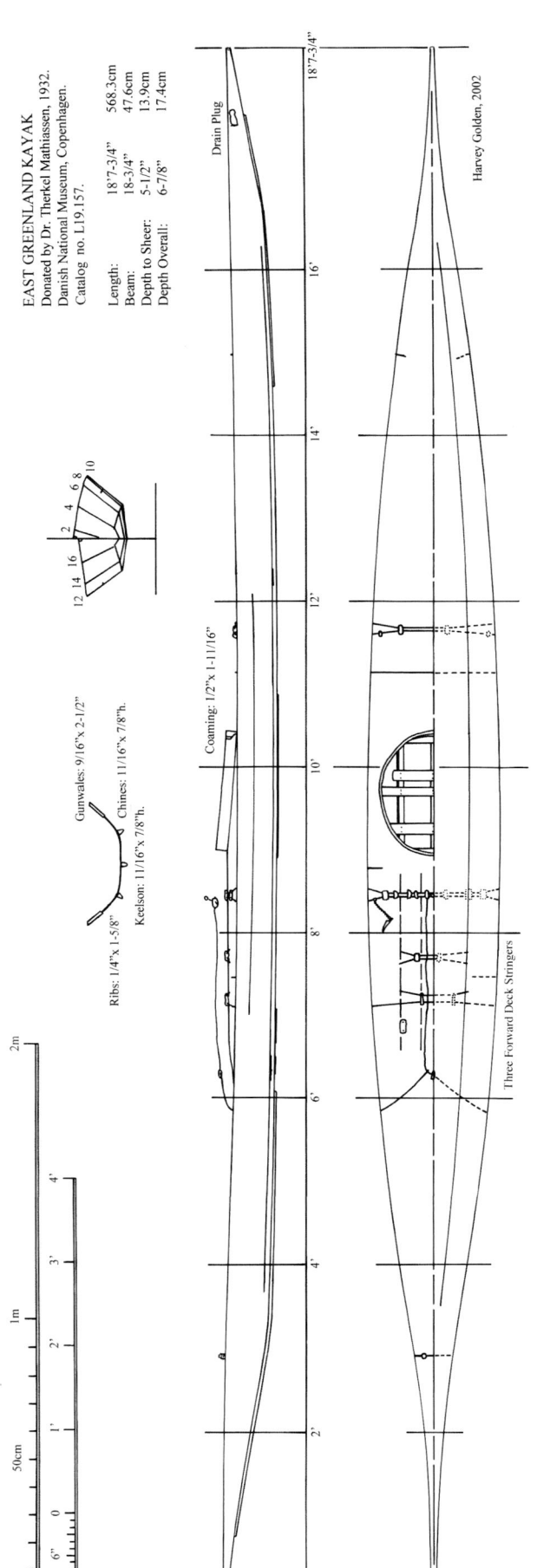

86. Danish National Museum catalog no. L.19.157

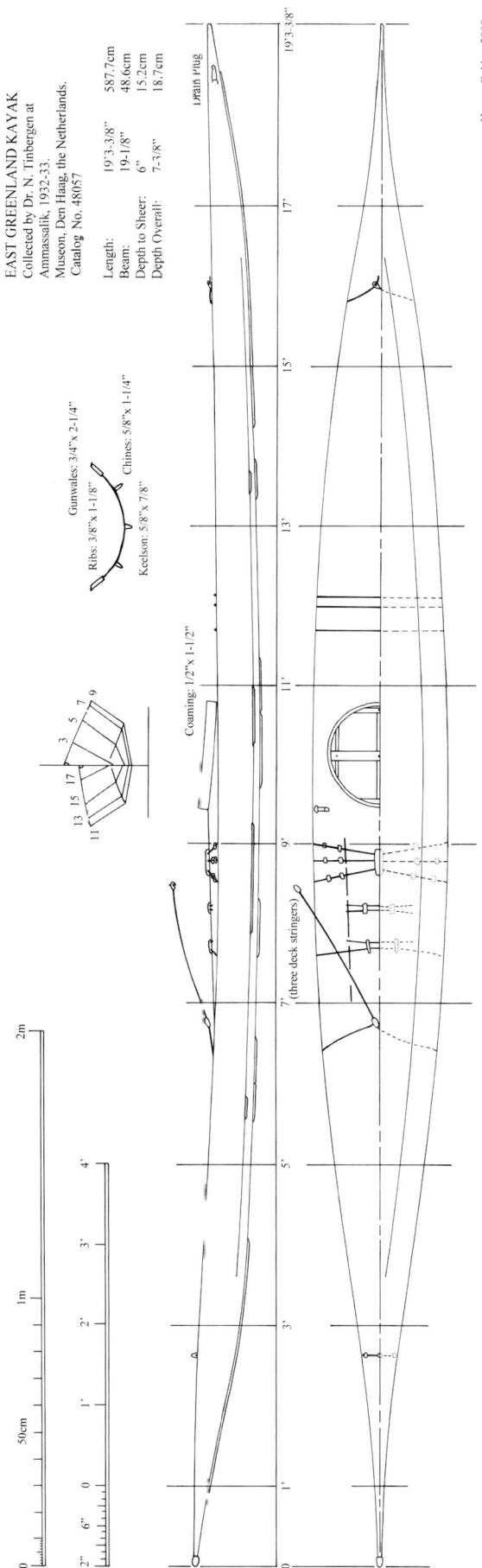

87. Museon catalog no. 48057

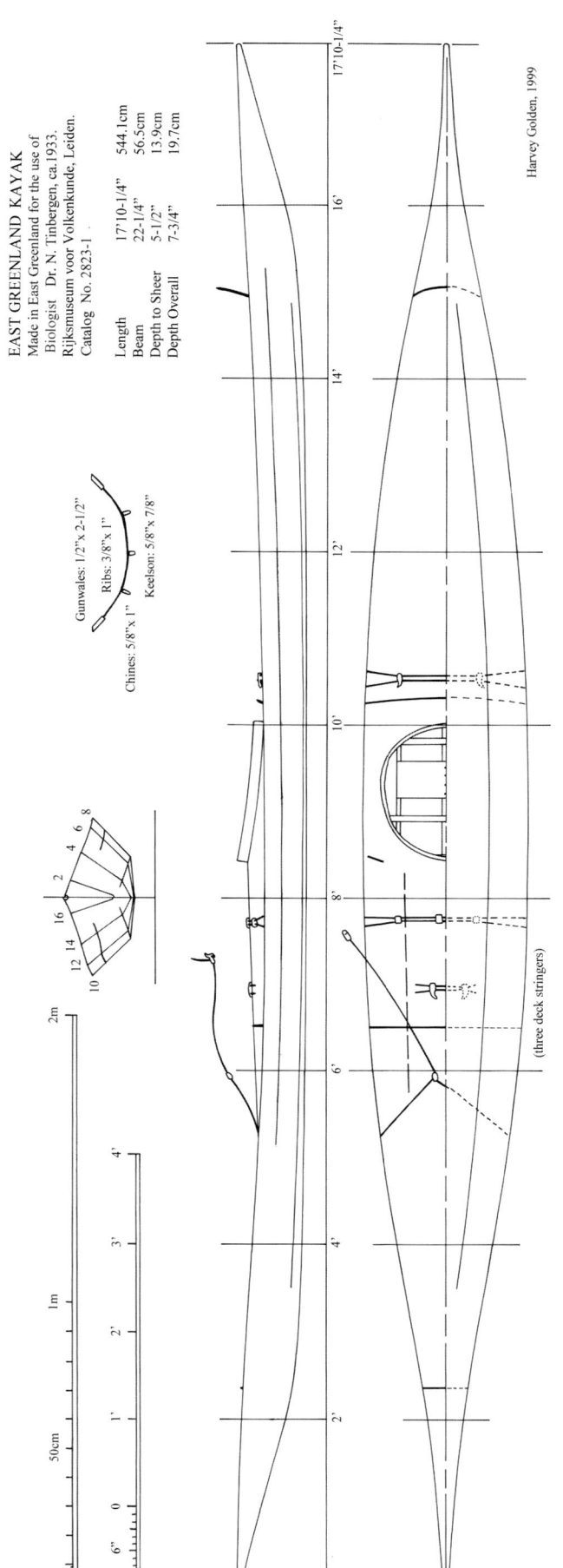

88. Rijksmuseum voor Volkenkunde catalog no. 2823-1

89. Greenland National Museum catalog no. KNK 1990x1

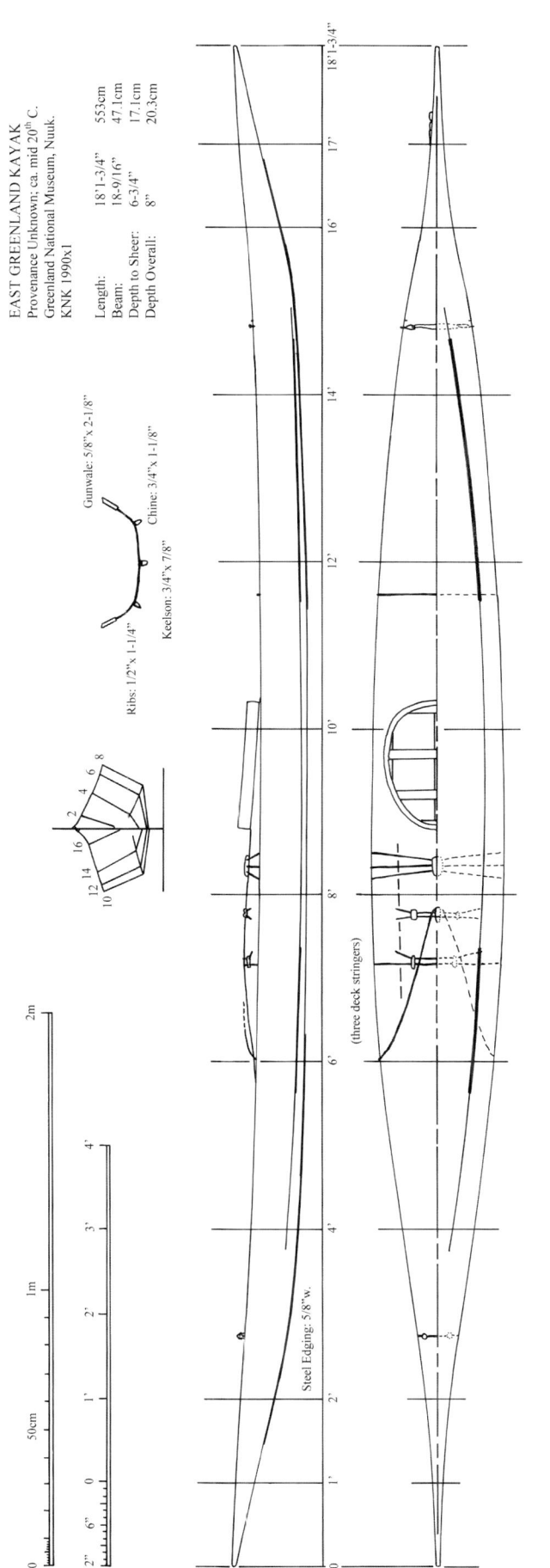

EAST GREENLAND KAYAK
Provenance Unknown; ca. mid 20th C.
Greenland National Museum, Nuuk.
KNK 1990x1

Length:	18'1-3/4"	553cm
Beam:	18-9/16"	47.1cm
Depth to Sheer:	6-3/4"	17.1cm
Depth Overall:	8"	20.3cm

Gunwale: 5/8" x 2-1/8"
Chine: 3/4" x 1-1/8"
Keelson: 3/4" x 7/8"
Ribs: 1/2" x 1-1/4"

(three deck stringers)

Steel Edging: 5/8" w.

Harvey Golden, 2000

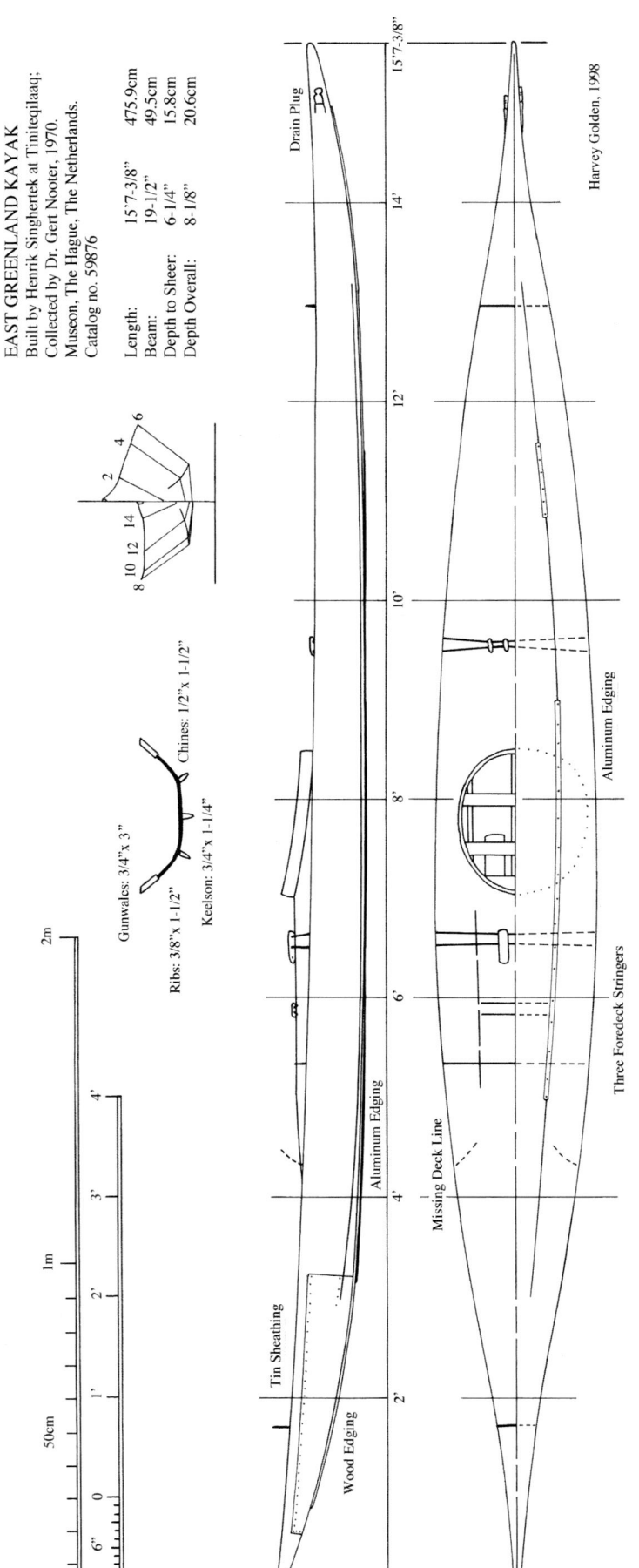

90. Museon catalog no. 59876

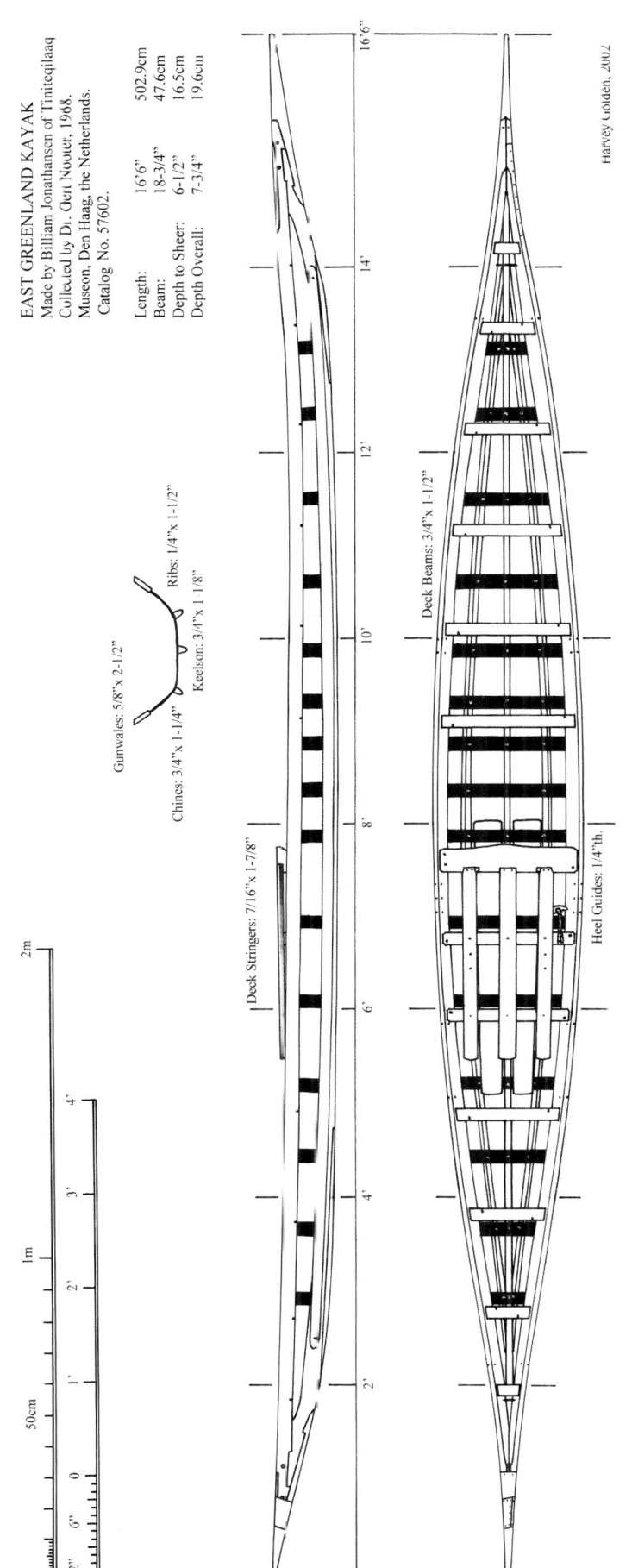

91a. Museon catalog no. 57602

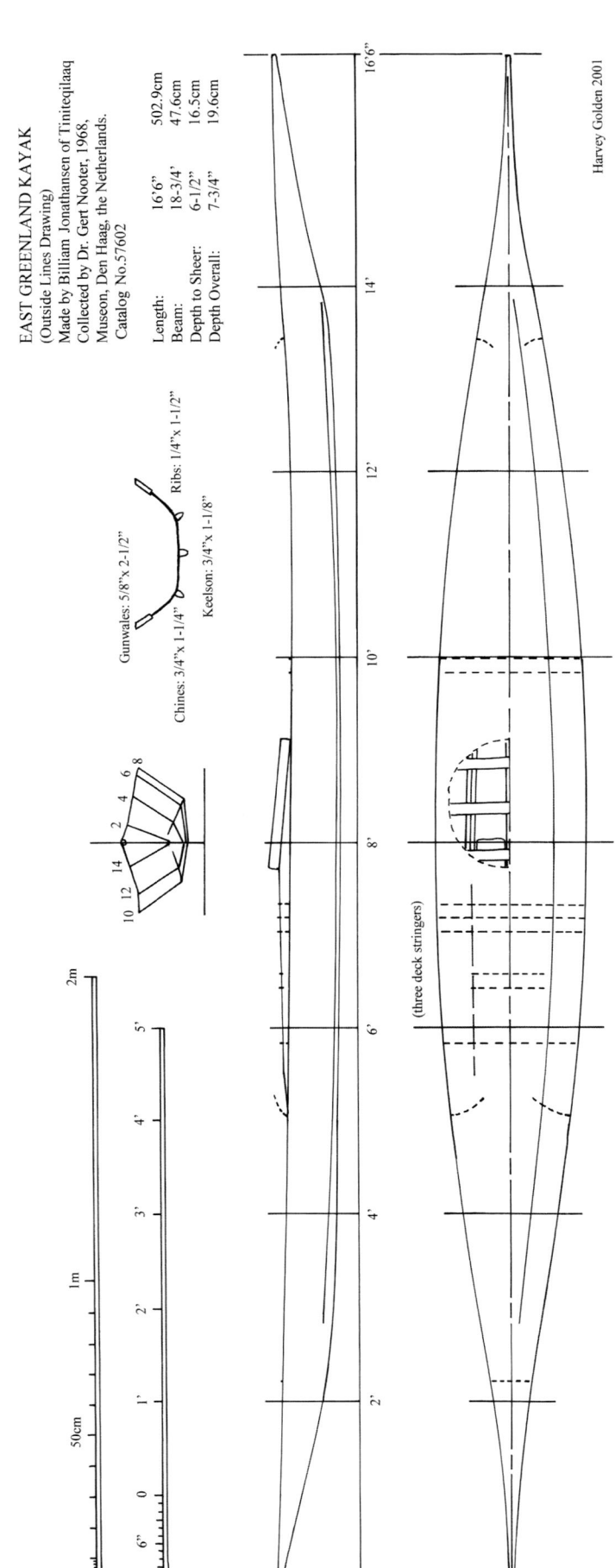

91b. Museon catalog no. 57602 (Hull Lines)

84. East Greenland Kayak from ca. 1924:
    Oslo University Museum of Cultural Heritage, Norway.
    Catalog no. 29.881.

Ammassalik Colony Manager Johan Petersen purchased this kayak for the Oslo University Museum in 1924. Johan Petersen was the first superintendent of the Scoresby Sound colony in 1925, and was the first colony manager of Ammassalik from 1894 (Krabbe 1930:112,124-125). Petersen also accompanied the Holm expedition to Ammassalik in 1884— the first European visit to the Ammassalik population.

A view inside of the 29.881 was not permitted, the cockpit being occupied by a fully dressed and equipped figure. It could be assumed that like other modern-period East Greenland kayaks, the joinery would consist of pegged or nailed longitudinals and oblique-pegged deck beams. Three forward deck stringers were present, and it would stand to reason that none were aft, as is the case with every East Greenland kayak in this study.

The 29.881 has typical modern East Greenland (type IX) kayak form— a form that is very consistent among the kayaks in this type. Its sheer is very subtle, and at the ends, its curve flattens out. The stems are quite long and they are concave and fine. The chine breadth is very narrow, and the hull being

Figure 338: East Greenland kayaks and an umiak, Ammassalik District, 1908. (Photograph by Thomas N. Krabbe/Copyright: Greenland National Museum and Archive.)

quite shallow, gives the sides of the kayak considerable flare. The bottom of the kayak has only a slight deadrise.

Keel edging is present at the bow from 8-5/8" (21.9cm) aft to 3´6-1/4" (107.3cm), but is evidenced to have run to 3´9-1/4" (114.9cm). Stern keel edging is evidenced from 14´4-1/2" to 17´5-1/2" (438.1 to 532.1cm). The edging measures 3/8" (9mm) thick by 1/2" (13mm) wide. There appeared to have been a piece of keel edging from 8´9" (266.7cm) aft, but the *amiq* was worn such that the edging's length couldn't be determined; this would not have been a seam-protection piece, as there is not a seam in the vicinity.

Seam protection pieces are present on the chines and keelson at 5´8-3/4" (174.6cm) and 12´8-1/2" (387.3cm) from zero. These pieces are 1/16" (1.5mm) thick by 11/16" (17mm) wide and are attached with metal nails; the three forward pieces are between 3-1/4" and 3-5/8" (82 and 92mm) long, and the aft three pieces are, from left-to-right, 4-1/8", 4-1/2" and 3-3/4" (10.4, 11.4, and 9.5cm) long.

The 29.881 had a slit in its *amiq* where a drain plug would normally be fitted; the plug is missing. The slit is 14" (35.5cm) forward of the stern and is 1/2" (13mm) high, 5/8" (16mm) below the sheer on the left side. A paddle is associated with the kayak 29.881, and while a complete survey was not executed, its unique tips are depicted in paddle-plate 60.

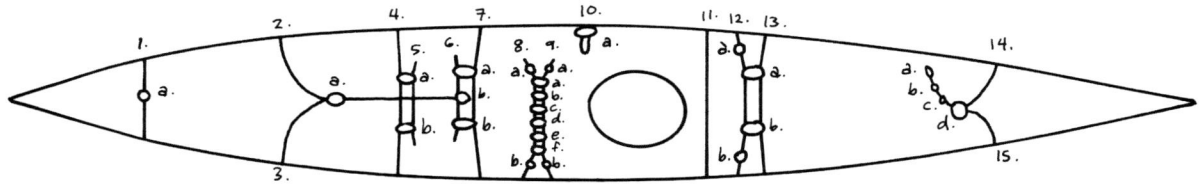

University Museum of Cultural Heritage, Oslo: Cat. no. 29.881

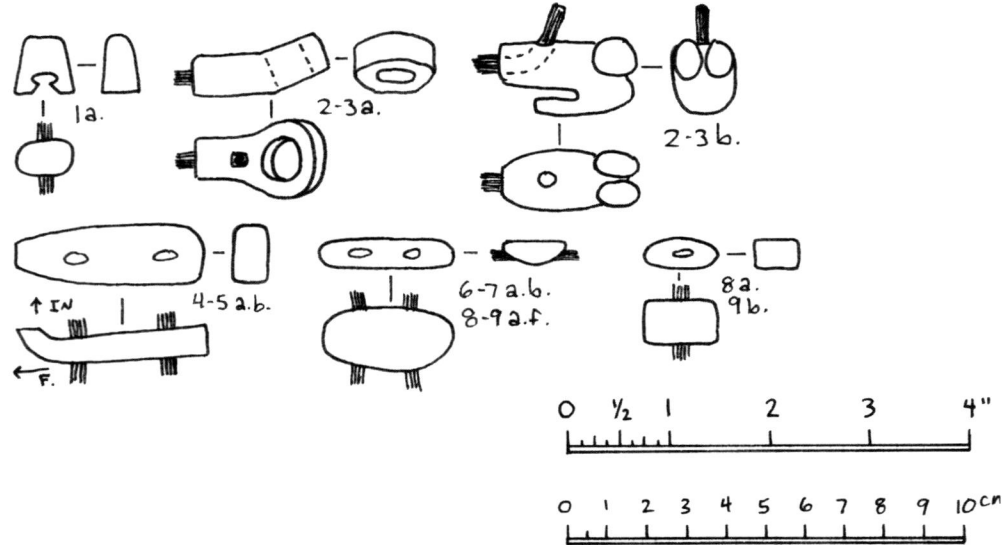

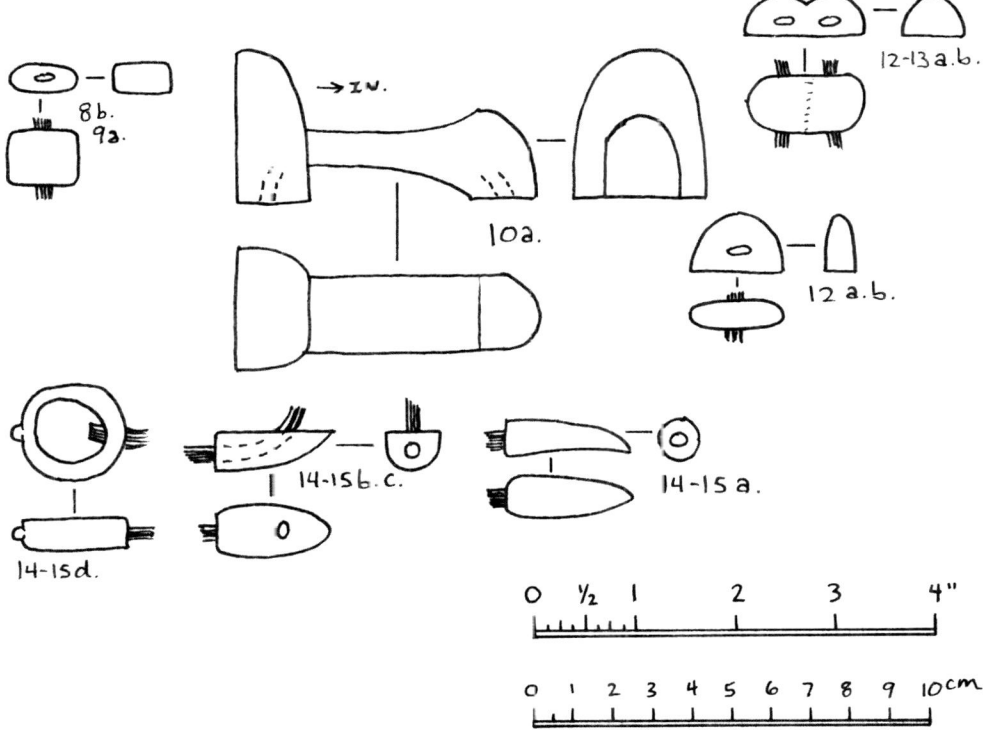

The bow deck line of the kayak 29.881 is very likely missing two cones that would normally be leaning inboard; the one piece present on this deck line (1a) is a short symmetrical tab that is made to be removable and/or retro-fitted, as in figure 104. The ability to remove the bow fittings of certain type IX kayaks has certainly lead to some of them going missing as will be seen.

Adjustable Y-shaped deck lines are present on the fore deck and on the aft deck. The Y-shaped line on the fore deck terminates with a hook-piece (2-3b) that would likely be attached to one the lines in front of the cockpit, most likely line 6. The aft Y-shaped line operates on a different principal: Instead of being hooked to another deck line, this line has two hooks or latches (pieces 14-15b/c) that catch on the deadeye piece (14-15c) providing two tension settings. Piece 14-15a acts as a needle of sorts to aid in threading the line through the deadeye. See figure 111 bottom for the general appearance of this system.

Deck lines 8 and 9 are unique in that they do not quite go all the way across the deck; their right ends terminate through the right deck stringer. The harpoon holder is made from two pieces of bone or ivory and is tab-formed with an elevated bridge to support the harpoon.

85. East Greenland Kayak: American Museum of Natural History, New York, New York. Catalog no. 60.1/6003

Arthur D. Norcross collected the AMNH 60.1/6003 in Ammassalik vicinity during the 1931 Norcross-Bartlett Expedition to Northeast Greenland. Howard Chapelle surveyed this kayak in the 1940s and his drawing was published in Adney and Chapelle's *The Bark Canoes and Skin Boats of North America* (1964:211, fig.208). Certain subtleties of form were not captured in Howard Chapelle's drawing of the 6003, e.g., the concavity of the stems and the re-curving sheer typical in East Greenlandic kayaks has either been faired-out or overlooked. Chapelle's titling of the drawing as a "S. Greenland Kayak" further complicated these points. This attribution was likely arrived upon having used Birket-Smith's kayak typology, which does not really distinguish the two forms from each other (see page 107).

The dimensions of the 6003 vary only slightly between my survey and Chapelle's: His results are a length of 19'6" (594.3cm), a beam of 20-1/4" (51.4cm), and a depth-to-sheer of 6-1/4" (15.9cm).

A forward inside-view (figure 339) of the 60.1/6003 shows the thin but numerous ribs of this kayak; this kayak has 25 ribs, each is metal-nailed to the chines and keelson. The straight deck beams are all pegged obliquely to the gunwales with heavier diameter pegs than are seen in West Greenland. The three fore deck stringers can also be seen: They are each 1-9/16" (40mm) wide.[46]

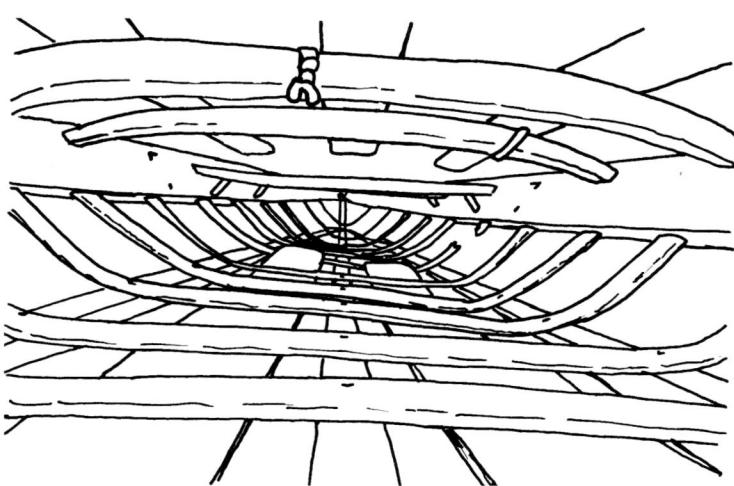

Figure 339: Forward interior view of the AMNH's kayak 60.1/6003. It is very similar to the Danish National Museum's kayak Lc.148 (figure 331).

A remnant of seal skin line appears on the aft-most curved deck beam adjacent to the central deck stringer. This was likely the anchor point for a carrying toggle, the likes of which can be seen in other East Greenland kayaks such as the DNM's L.19.157 and the Museon's 57602 (plates 86 and 91).

Figure 340 shows a cockpit view of the 6003; notice the leg slats, harpoon holder (tipped-over), and the coaming scarf. The leg slats are 1/2" (13mm) thick and 2-1/4" (57mm) wide at their aft end. The *masik* is 3-3/16" (81mm) wide and has a handhold carved into its lower face. A rib is placed right in the center of the 6003's cockpit— something rarely seen in West Greenland kayaks. This is apparently the rule in East Greenlandic kayaks, save for the early example from 1842 (plate 82), which instead has large seat slats in this same area.

Interestingly, a short mortise 1" (25mm) long and 1/2" (13mm) high is present on the gunwales' faces just behind the *masik*. Upon closer examination I was able to see that the *masik* was set into the gunwales via two tenons on each end instead of one larger one. Essentially the empty mortises I'd seen could still be used if the hunter/builder wanted to move the *masik* aft an inch or so.

---

[46] Chapelle's drawing of this kayak shows only two fore deck stringers, measuring 1" (25mm) wide (1964:211, fig.208).

The 6003's coaming measures 5/8″ (16mm) thick and 1-1/2″ (38mm) high, and is scarfed with the method common and unique to East Greenland, as in figures 340 and 116g. The scarf is fastened with nine flathead screws. Several thin plates of copper are nailed to the face of the coaming, so as to arrest fractures in the wood; their placement is depicted in the scale drawing.

A drain plug is present on the port side of the stern. Keel edging is present or evidenced from 1′4″ to 4′4-1/4″ (40.6 to 132.7cm). No keel edging is present or evidenced at the stern, though three seam-protection pieces are placed along the keel, extending aft from 6′4-1/2″, and 13′6″ (194.3 and

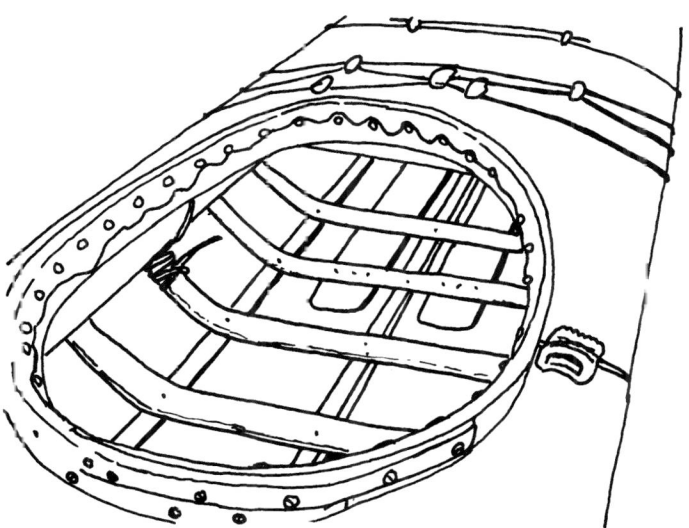

Figure 340: Cockpit view (looking forward) of the AMNH's kayak 60.1/6003. Note the unique harpoon holder—it is tipped-over in the drawing. The leg slats are also visible as is the coaming's scarf and its screw fasteners. Continuous deck lines are hitched off on the rib at left.

411.4cm), pieces being 3/16″ (5mm) thick, 3/4″ (19mm) wide, and 3″ and 4″ (7.6 to 10.1cm) long respectively. Two similar pieces were placed along the chines at 6′2-1/2″ (189.2cm), each being 3-1/8″ (7.9cm) long.

Arthur Norcross collected two paddles while at Ammassalik; it is not known if either paddle actually belonged to this kayak or not. They are depicted in paddle-plates 62 and 63.

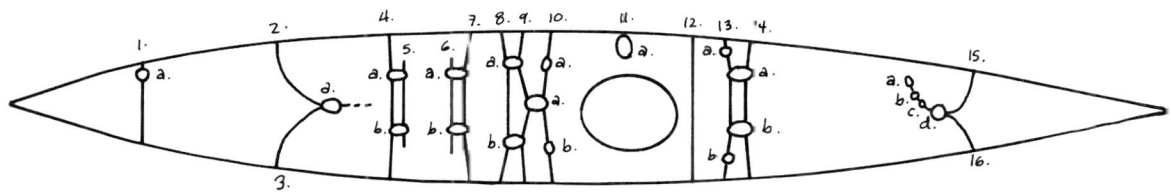

American Museum of Natural History, New York: Cat. no. 60.1/6003

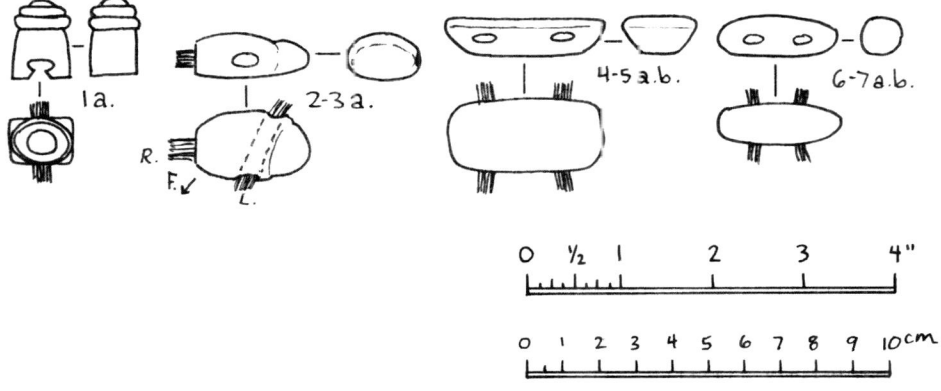

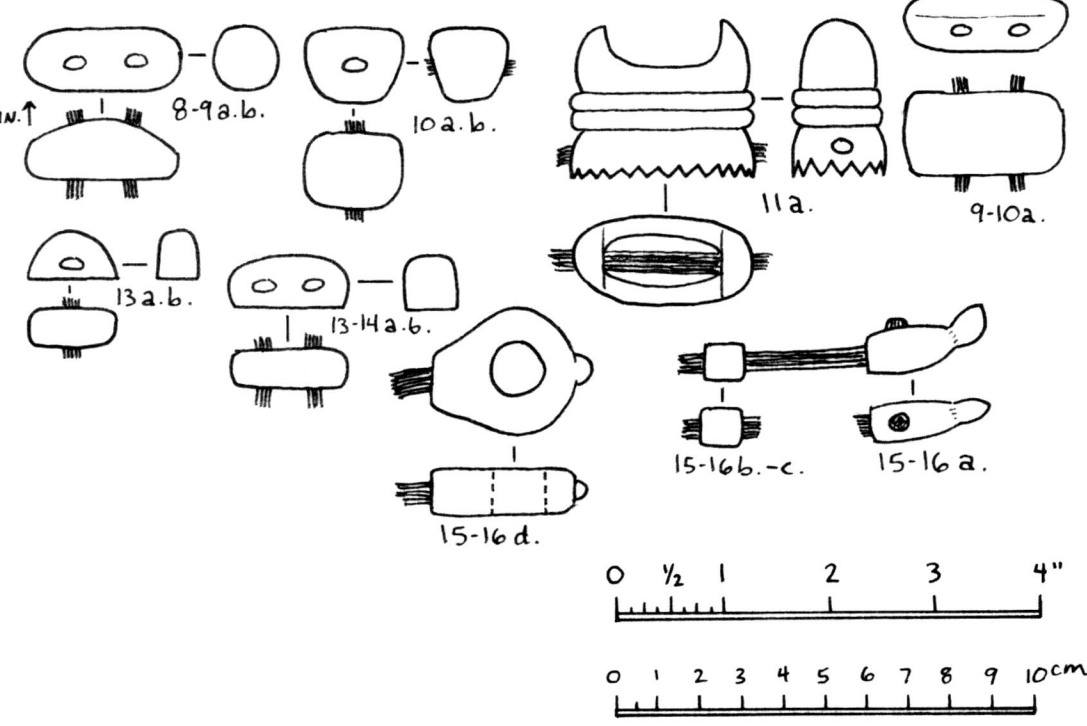

Only one deck fitting is present on the fore-most deck line, and because it is a short and symmetrical piece, it was likely the middle piece, the two outer ones being missing. Usually the Y-shaped deck line would be behind this deck line, but instead there is a simple taut strap, sans fittings. Immediately behind this line is the Y-shaped line; the long end is broken just beyond the deadeye piece. Two pairs of linked deck lines, each with a shorter segment follow; the short segments being adjacent one another.

The harpoon holder on the 6003 is placed aside the cockpit, anchored to the gunwale and through the side face of the coaming. Such placement and attachment is reminiscent of the harpoon holder on the DNM Lc.148 (plate 82), although they are each of different forms. This piece is a hollow section of walrus tusk, ornately carved with a serrated base. The Y-shaped deck line on the aft deck was broken and detached, but fortunately preserved, being in a plastic bag inside the kayak. Also inside the plastic bag was a large polar bear tooth measuring 3″ (76mm) long, 5/8″ (16mm) wide, and 9/16″ (14mm) thick, with a line anchored through the middle. This is likely the 'missing' carrying toggle described above.

Figure 341: Two East Greenland kayaks ready for hunting, Amituarsuk, 1937. (Photographer: Jette Bang/ Arktisk Institut glb02865.)

86. East Greenland Kayak: Danish National Museum, Copenhagen. Catalog no. L.19.157.

The Danish National Museum's kayak L.19.157 is another kayak surveyed and published by John Brand (1988:87-91): I re-surveyed it on account of the lack of a museum number citation in Brand as well as conflicting accession information. For example, Brand, having visited in 1975, records a note for the kayak: "Angmagsalik, no number, Knud Rasmussen's Kayak, recent acquisition, via Öregaards Gymnasium where the kayak was received as a gift from Knud Rasmussen about 1930, — no information as to origin" (1988:87).

Current DNM information records a number for the kayak (L.19.157) as well as an accession date of 1932, with the donor listed as the archaeologist Therkel Mathiassen; Rasmussen's name isn't associated with the kayak, nor is the Öregaards Gymnasium's. (See kayak L.18.178 [plate 78], associated with Rasmussen and the Ö. Gymnasium.)

The L.19.157 has several unique features not seen on any other kayaks in this study: First, it has four forward deck-stringers instead of the usual three for East Greenland kayaks. Secondly, it has a short deckline spanning from the left sheer to 3-1/2″ (8.8cm) inboard; the specific function of this line is unknown.

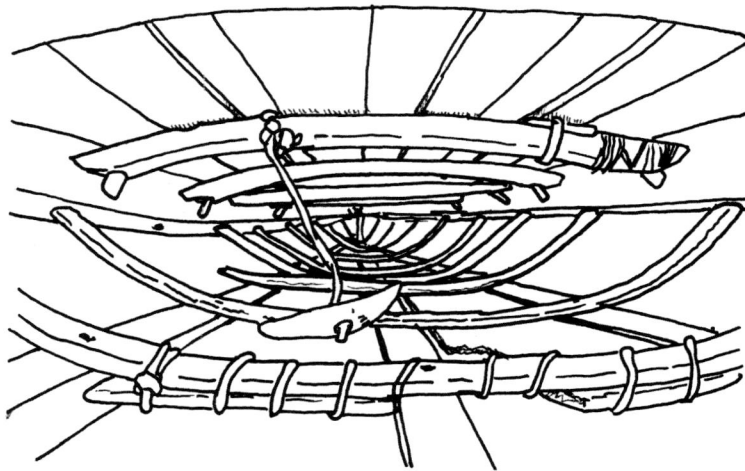

Figure 342: Forward interior of the L.19.157. The carrying handle anchored to the curved deck beam is evident as are the leg-slat end lashings and a repair to the end of a curved deck beam. This kayak has four forward deck stringers.

Thirdly, there is a low, rectangular bone plate nailed to the right-most deck stringer, 4-1/8″ (10.4cm) inboard; this may have served as a footing for the harpoon-line stand's leg. All of these features suggest the meticulous care and management of a sophisticated array of hunting equipment on-deck.

Figure 342 shows the forward interior of the L.19.157. Note the carrying toggle (made from a 3-1/4″ [8.2cm] long polar bear tooth) anchored to the curved deck beam. The L.19.157 has leg slats of the typical East Greenland form; their aft end is lashed to a rib. A curved deck beam has one of its ends wrapped extensively—likely to arrest a fracture.

Figure 343: A curious truss set between the isserfik *and the gunwale of the Danish national Museum's kayak L.19.157.*

A mysterious truss-piece is present in the L.19.157's cockpit, joining the aft cockpit deck beam to the gunwale's lower edge— only on the left side. It is inset into this deck beam's forward edge, and is depicted in figure 343. Its purpose can be imagined; possibly a repair or adjustment made to ensure the proper gunwale flare is maintained. This is the only such piece in this kayak, though another East Greenland kayak in this study has seven such pieces (the KNK 1990, plate 89).

The ribs in the 19.157 are metal-nailed to the keelson and chines, but are unfastened to the gunwales. All of the deck beams are obliquely pegged to the gunwales. The seat stringers are lashed to a single rib beneath the *masik*, and these lashing may be the only fasteners, as the seats' ends are sprung up atop the rib at their forward end, thus holding them in place.

The 19.157's *masik* is 4″ (10cm) wide, but is cut back 7/8″ (22mm) at its middle, as in figure 38. The *isserfik* measures 5/8″ (16mm) thick by 1-5/8″ (41mm) The four fore deck stringers are of different sizes:

The outer two are 1/4" (6mm) thick and 1-1/4" (32mm) wide, while the inner two are both 1/8" (3mm) thick. The right-inner stringer is 1-3/4" (44mm) wide, and the left-inner stringer is 2" (50mm) wide.

Keel and chine edging is extensively applied to this kayak: The keel has lengthy edging at the bow and stern as well as a 2-7/8" (7.3cm) long piece of bone (7/16" wide x 1/8" thick [11 x 3mm]) at 6' 3-1/2" (191.7cm) from 0. Behind this piece, there is a wooden piece, 3/4" wide x 1/8" thick (19 x 3mm), at 6' 8" (203.2cm) from 0, extending 5" (12.7cm) aft. At 8' 11" (271.7cm) from 0, there is a 7/8" (22mm) wide piece of wood, 1/4" (6mm) thick, extending to 10'10-1/2" (331.4cm) from 0.

The bow knob (1-1/8" [28mm] long by 3/4" [19mm] round) is top-pegged in place; the stern knob is missing, but its placement is evidenced by a peg-hole— side-pegged, unlike the bow. A drain plug is present in the 19.157's left stern.

Coaming scarf protection pieces are apparently not used in East Greenland, but the L.19.157 does have a small repair piece on its front right quarter: a copper plate 1/16" (1.5mm) thick, 1-1/2" long x 5/8" (38 x 16mm) with rounded corners and three nails affixing it. This piece covers up a fracture in the coaming. The coaming's scarf is fastened with six flat-head wood screws with 3/8" (9mm) heads, and the coaming itself measures 1/2" (13mm) thick by 1-11/16" (43mm) high.

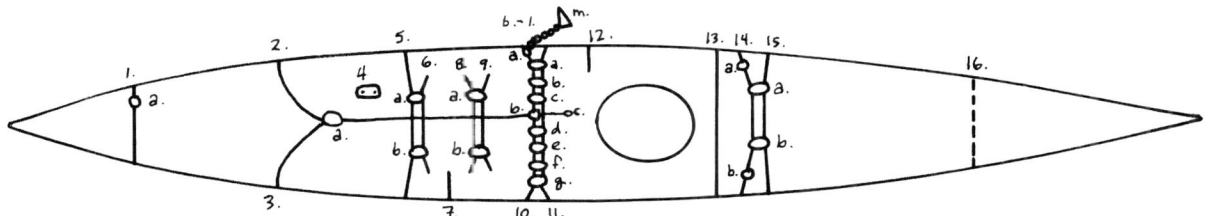

Danish National Museum: Cat. no. L.19.157

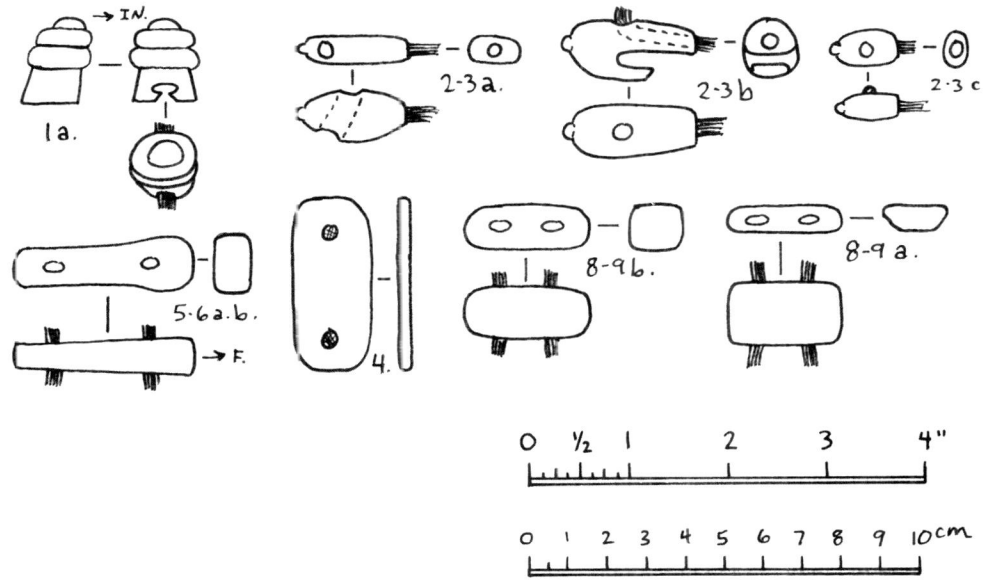

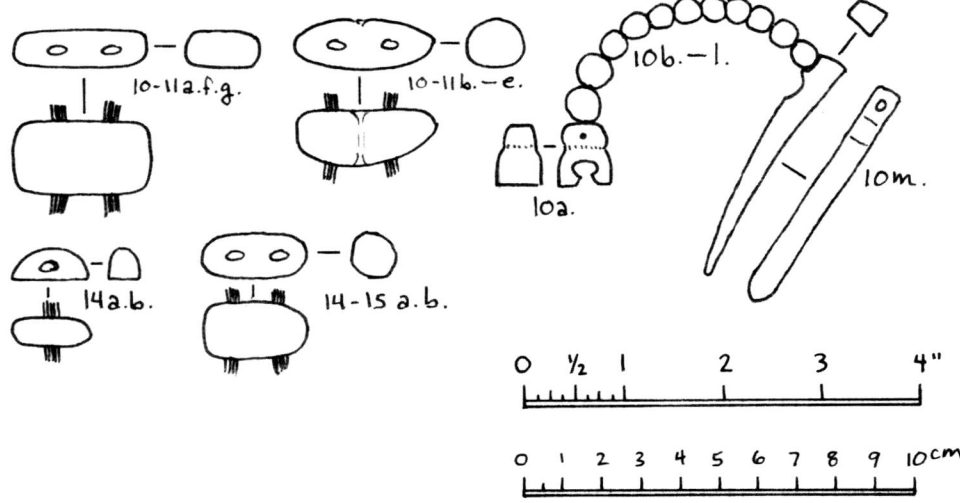

The L.19.157 has a deck fitting that seems to be unique to East Greenland: a short beaded strap that serves as a harpoon leash (figure 112, and piece 10a-m above). This leash secured the harpoon to the kayak's deck so it could not float off in waves. It simply was run over the harpoon shaft, and the long bone piece at the end was tucked under a deck line. Where a harpoon holder of the conventional form could be expected, there is instead a simple taut short strap. The leash is not long enough to be tucked under this strap, and its precise function is not known (the leash would have been secured underneath line 10, to which it is also anchored). It is not at all surprising that such harpoon leashes were used with East Greenland kayaks, as they are very shallow and prone to having lots of water sweep the decks, even in moderate conditions.

The bow-most deck fitting is cut at its base so that it can be retro-fitted to the kayak. Because this single fitting is leaning, it suggests that another piece, also leaning, had been present at one time; there may have also been a vertical piece positioned between them at one time, as is common among East Greenland kayaks. Also note how the harpoon leash's base piece is cut to be retro-fitted/removed.

The short line from the sheer to the deck-stringer (deck line 7) is of a mysterious function— no other East Greenland kayaks have such a strap in this vicinity. I think it might have been placed so as to hold the forward end of the paddle holder— a small flat board that would be placed under lines 10 or 11 and 7 that the paddle could be slipped under to function as an outrigger. The 19.157 has a paddle holder associated with it, and this is depicted in figure 137 bottom.

This was the first East Greenland kayak I replicated— I first built it in 1995 from John Brand's survey of the same kayak (1988:87). After I had surveyed this same kayak in 2002, I rebuilt my initial replica on account it had fallen into disrepair through neglect.

The most difficult part of replicating this kayak was maintaining the high degree of gunwale flare— something I had failed at the first time around. During this process, I had to have numerous straps under phenomenal tension, forcing the gunwales to flare. It helped that I over-flared them during this stage because as the straps were removed there was a slight spring-back.

I had thought that a kayak with a fairly low sheer would require considerable gunwale shaping if greatly flared gunwales were present; the sheer leveling off towards the ends further suggested this. It turned out I was incorrect: The gunwales required little shaping if any— they took the precise desired form when spread to the correct breadths and flare. The lesson learned from this is exactly as depicted

Figure 344: The author in the DNM L.19.157 replica, Whidbey Island, Washington, 2005. (Photograph by Kathy Tucker.)

Figure 345: A low front-quarter view of the 19.157 replica. This view accentuates the subtleties of this kayak's sinuous sheer line. (Photograph by Kathy Tucker.)

in figure 31 (right) in the construction chapter. In short, pinching the sheer (viewed en-plan) causes the gunwale ends to level out.

The replica of the 19.157 is a sizable craft in all dimensions *except* depth. Because of this I had to increase the distance between the *isserfik* and *masik* to 17-3/4″ (45.1cm), and the coaming's length to 18-5/8″ (47.3cm) in order to fit inside. Snug as this kayak is, it is anything but claustrophobic— more of me was outside of this kayak than with any West Greenland kayaks, and the grip it had on me was reassuring as it made balancing, control, and even rolling much easier.

With its flat sheer and shallow hull, the 19.157 replica is a very wet ride: Six-inch waves are apt to wash over the decks right to the coaming. It is however completely at home in high winds from any direction, scarcely being bothered by them at all. Where there is wind however, there are usually waves, and this design pays for its good wind handling with a very wet ride. Three-foot high waves are very likely going to hit the kayaker in the face depending on how steep and frequent they are. As waves become considerably larger with less frequency, this kayak becomes less sloppy.

Figure 346: Replica of the 19.157. (Photograph by Kathy Tucker.)

87. East Greenland Kayak: Museon, den Haag, the Netherlands. Catalog no. 48057.

The Museon's kayak 48057 was acquired by Nobel Prize-winning biologist Dr. Nico Tinbergen at Ammassalik, East Greenland in 1932-33, and is one of two Greenland kayaks he brought back with him to the Netherlands. The 48057 is an exemplar of type IX kayak form, which is to say extremely fine and graceful but not overstated. Its sheer is similar to the L.19.157's (plate 87), only the bow rises higher before leveling off; both kayaks have shorter sterns that are not so markedly concave as the 6003's (plate 85).

Figure 348 shows the forward interior-view of the 48057. Note the three wide forward deck stringers. The deck beams are all pegged obliquely into place, however one deck beam is missing. Each deck beam's oblique peg is locked in place with a thinner peg set through the gunwales' lower edges. Also apparent in figure 348 are the continuous deck lines— note where they pass through the deck stringers.

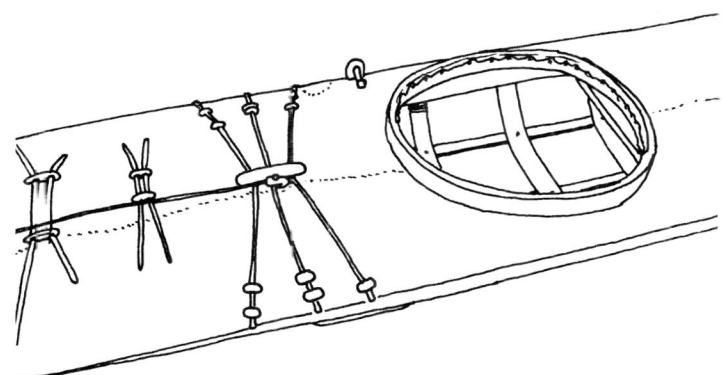
Figure 347: Fore deck and cockpit view of the Museon's 48057.

This kayak is well protected from ice: Long strips of ivory protect the stems, and intermittent pieces protect raised seams and other high-wear areas. The chines are also intermittently protected with ivory strips. The edging on the keel at the bow and stern is 1/4″ (6mm) thick and 3/8″ (9mm) wide; along the rest of the keelson and on the chines, the edging is only 1/8″ (3mm) thick, but 3/4″ (19mm) wide. The edging placement is depicted on the scale drawing.

The 48057's bow end knob is 1-1/4″ (32mm) long and 1″ (25mm) diameter at its back end; the front end is blunt and about 3/4″ (19mm) diameter. A stern knob is missing but evidenced. The 48057's *amiq* is very dark brown, almost black. There is a drain plug in the *amiq* towards the stern on the left side, 3/4″ (19mm) below the sheer. The plug is made of wood, and it protrudes 2-1/2″ (63mm) behind the slit in the *amiq*; the slit is 5/8″ (16mm) long.

An *asaloq*, or harpoon-line stand is associated with the kayak 48057: It is depicted in scale in figure 349. A paddle is also associated with this kayak and is depicted in paddle-plate 64.

The forward deck line of the 48057 has three fittings; the outer two are leaned inboard,

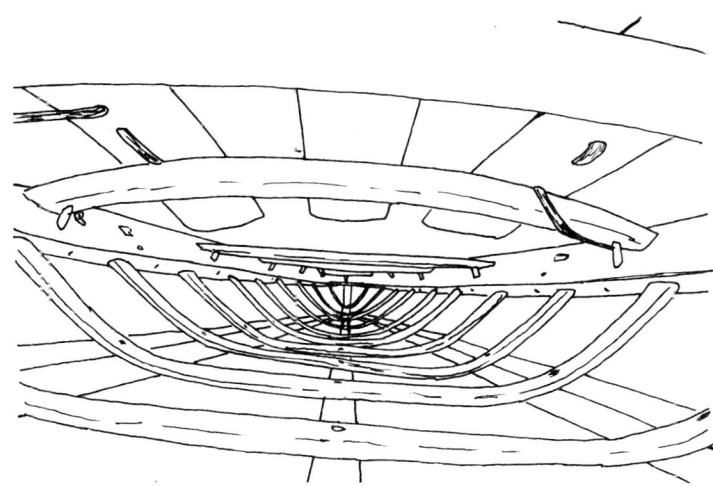
Figure 348: Forward interior view of the Museon's kayak 48057.

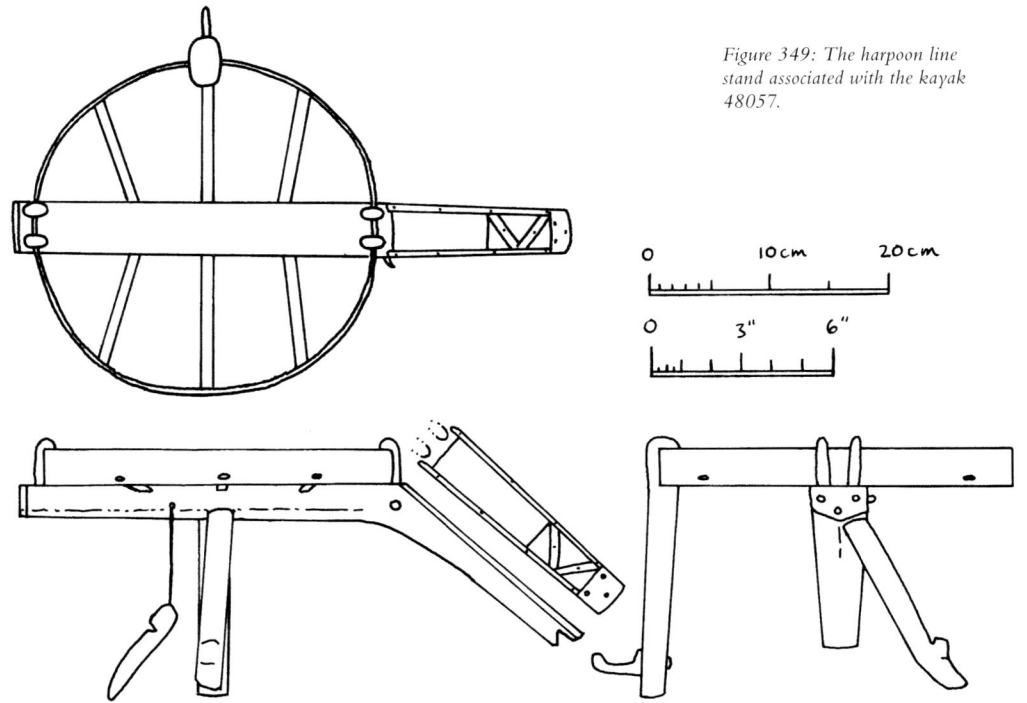

Figure 349: The harpoon line stand associated with the kayak 48057.

and the middle piece is shorter and symmetrical. All three of the bow deck line's fittings have concentric ridges around their tops. Deck lines 2 and 3 comprise the 48057's Y-shaped line: Deck line 2 carries the deadeye, and line 3 passes through it and terminates with a small hook. The aft deck's Y-shaped deck line is missing a few pieces— only the deadeye piece (15-16a) remains; the opposite side likely had clasps like those on the UMCH 29.881 or AMNH 60.1/6003 (plates 84 and 85).

Fitting 10a is missing the cord attached to its top: This was the anchor-piece for the harpoon's leash, such as that seen on the DNM L.19.157 (plate 86, and figure 112). The missing cord was perhaps four inches long or so and probably had several beads along its length and a longer clasp that, once passed over the harpoon, could be secured beneath a deck line.

I built a replica of the Museon's kayak 48057 in 1999, primarily to reaffirm understandings of East Greenland kayak construction after having seen and surveyed a few examples; my previous East Greenland kayak replica (of the DNM L.19.157, plate 86) was based on drawings by John Brand, and was built before I had seen the original. My experiences building and paddling the 48057 replica were for practical purposes identical to my experiences with the L.19.157 replica (see pages 420–422).

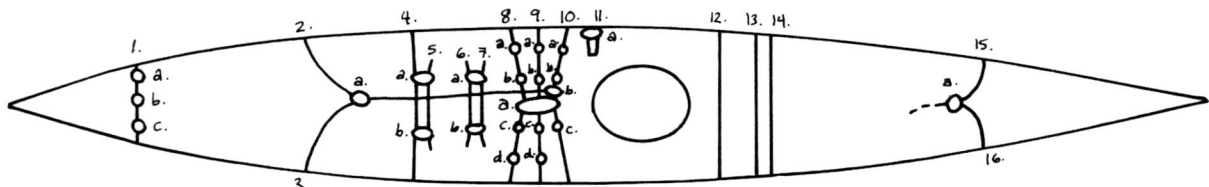

Museon, the Hague: Cat. no. 48057

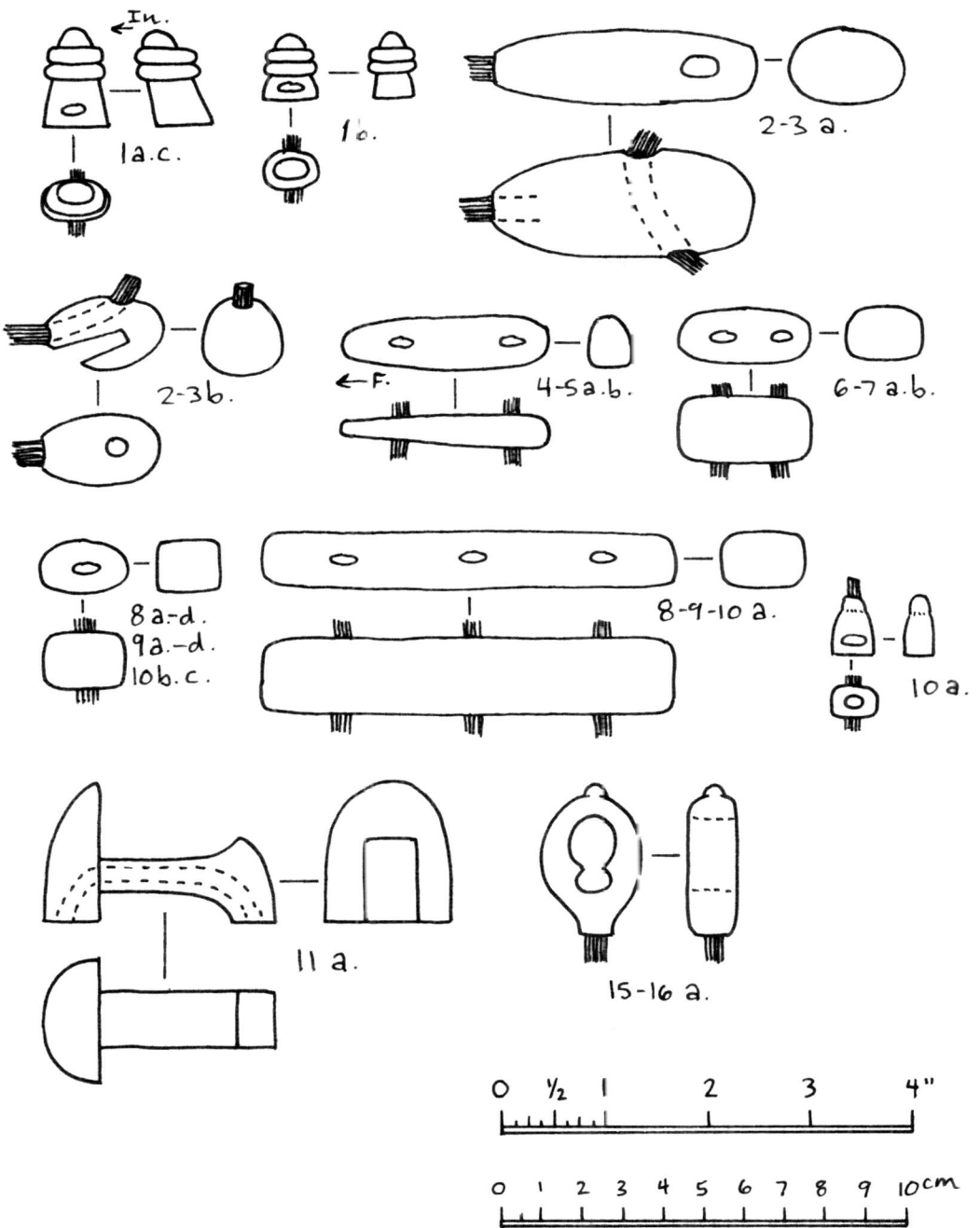

88. East Greenland Kayak: Rijksmuseum voor Volkenkunde, Leiden, the Netherlands. Catalog no. 2823-1.

The Rijksmuseum's kayak 2823-1, like the previous kayak, was collected by Dr. Nico Tinbergen: Unlike the previous kayak, the 2823 was custom-made for his own use (figure 350). It is spartanly outfitted when compared to the 48057: The 2823 does not have ivory keel and chine protection, nor does it have end knobs. Drain holes have not been cut in the *amiq*, and the deck lines and fittings are simple and spare for a modern East Greenland kayak. The paddle belonging to the 2823 is believed to be the one in paddle-plate 65.

The 2823 is wider than the average East Greenland kayak, being specially made for use by a larger and/or less practiced kayaker. As with the WFM 232 kayak [plate 2] of two hundred years before, the 2823's builder paid great attention to ensuring that a wider kayak wouldn't ride so high on the water: This was done by making the depth to sheer very shallow, and the result is the shallowest East Greenland kayak in this study. The depth overall however is greater than the average East Greenland kayak, and the coaming is large, thereby still providing enough room for the kayaker.

Figure 351 shows the forward interior view of the 2823. Note the oblique pegs fastening the deck beams to gunwales as well as the unusual position of the gunwales' scarf joints, i.e., forward of the cockpit instead of aft. The three fore deck stringers measure 1/4″ (6mm) thick by 2-1/2″ (63mm) wide.

Figure 350: Dr. Nico Tinbergen in his custom-made kayak—now the Rijksmuseum voor Volkenkunde's 2823. (Courtesy of Jaap Tinbergen/Museon.)

For added comfort, a seat board had been nailed to the keelson, and extends outwards to the chines; it measures 5-3/8″ (13.6cm) wide by 13″ (33.0cm) long. Burlap-wrapped padding is tacked to the inside coaming to function as a backrest. The coaming measures 1/2″ (13mm) thick by 1-5/8″ (41mm) high. Below the sheer line, this kayak's *amiq* is painted silvery-gray.

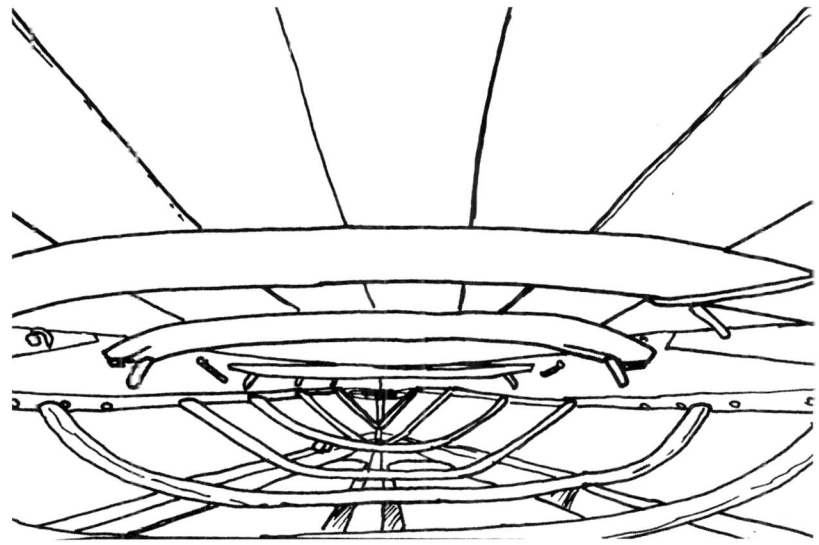

Figure 351: Forward interior view of the Rijksmuseum voor Volkenkunde's kayak 2823, built circa 1931 for the scientist Nico Tinbergen.

A forward Y-shaped line is present on the 2823, but instead of one being on the aft deck, a very slack deck line is present. The hook on the Y-shaped line is noteworthy in that it is of a very elegant and functional form: It has an extension shaped like a horse saddle's horn. This would make it quite easy to grab and unhook even while wearing thick mittens. After seeing this feature, one can suspect the hook on the 48057 must have been difficult to use by comparison.

There are few deck fittings present on this kayak (compared to other East Greenland kayaks), but those present are well made. Several fittings are made of large polar bear teeth— a very nice touch, and no doubt a source of considerable pride. The forward pair of teeth is oriented to point forward and inward; the aft pair point forward and outward.

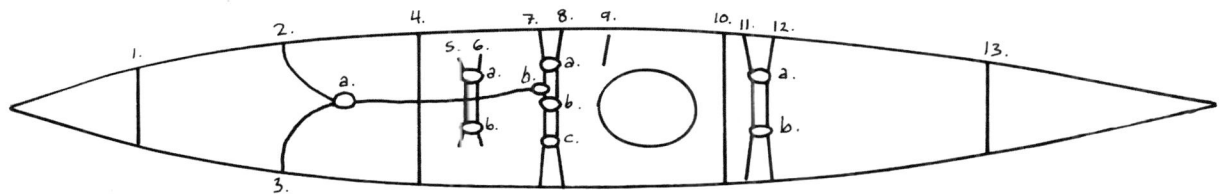

Rijksmuseum voor Volkenkunde, Leiden: Cat. no. 2823

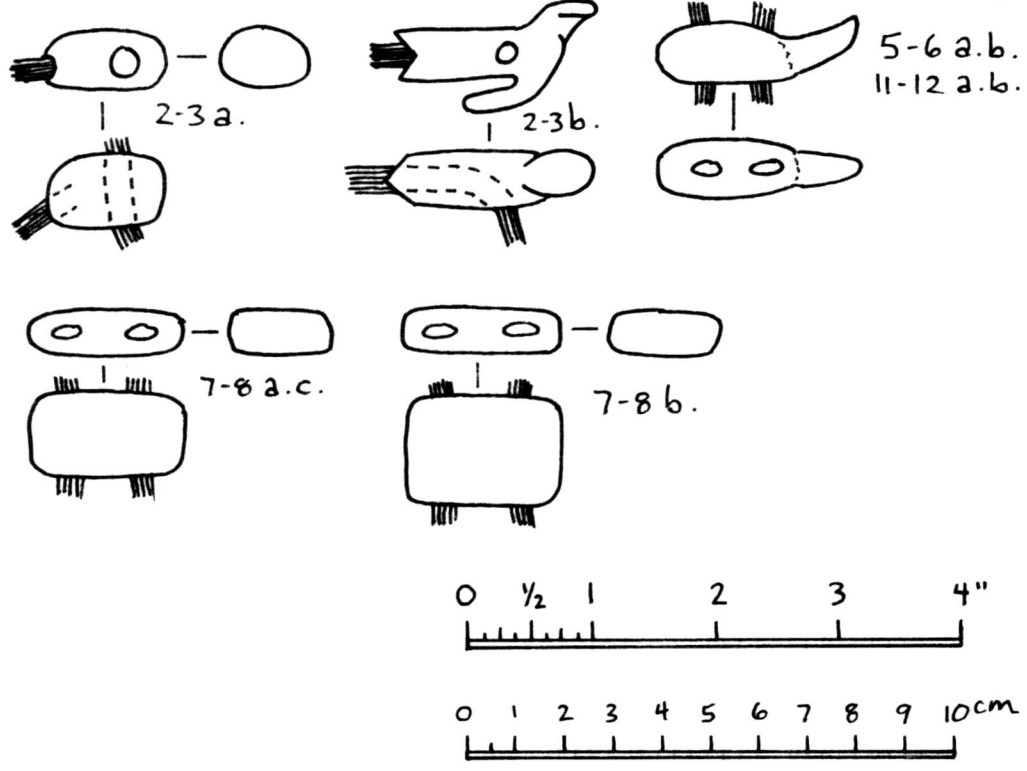

The RvV 2823 does not have a harpoon holder per-se, but instead a simple taut strap where a holder would normally be expected—this is the same case with the L.19.157 (plate 86).

89. East Greenland Kayak: Greenland National Museum, Nuuk. Catalog no. KNK 1990.

The Greenland National Museum's kayak KNK 1990 was received and/or accessioned in 1988; the donor is listed as the Arktisk Institut. A letter in the National Museum's accession files elaborates on this kayak's history somewhat: The kayak had been willed to the Arktisk Institut by Ambassador Bodil Begtrup; the A.I.'s board decided it was not an ideal recipient of such an object, and in turn they offered it to the "Grønlands Landsmuseum," as the GNM had been known. The letter, written by H. Shultz-Lorentzen, also explains that the kayak had been stored at Skagen Museum prior to Begtrup's death, and that the museum there did not know the kayak's history and presumed it had been purchased after 1962 (letter dated 8.03.88).[47]

---

[47] I owe a sincere gratitude to Martin Nissen of Denmark for providing a translation of this letter.

The KNK 1990 appears very well made, well used and in fair condition. The stern is more elevated and curvaceous than that of most type IX kayaks, but still is nothing like the high sterns of the old form East Greenland kayaks (type VIII). The KNK 1990's hull shape is boxier than many others of the type; it is moderately deep by comparison, and has less flare to the sides (i.e., a wider chine breadth).

An intriguing feature of this kayak is the reinforcements that have been nailed to the bottom edge of the gunwales that extend to the deck-beams— sort of a truss-system, perhaps to hold the gunwale flare in place. This feature alternates sides, and is only in the forward half of the kayak; seven such pieces are present (figure 352). One such truss is present in the older East Greenland kayak, the DNM L.19.157 (plate 86; figure 343).

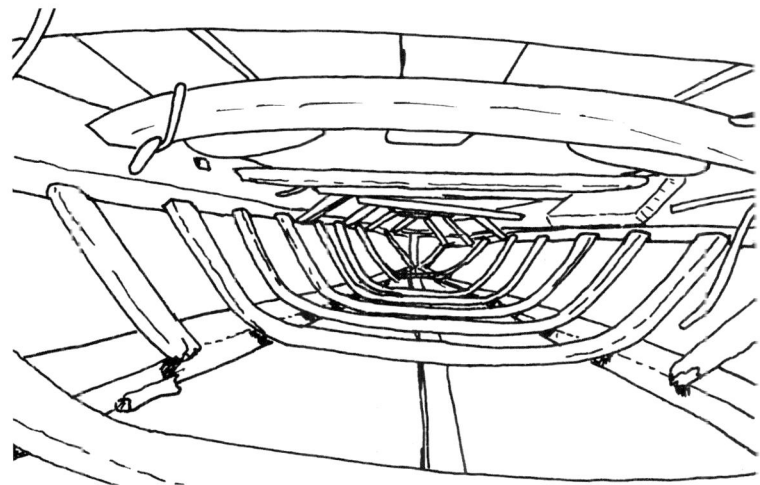

Figure 352: The forward interior of the KNK 1990. The trusses mentioned in the text are evident in this drawing. The broken rib towards the foreground may actually have been deliberately removed for the kayaker's comfort, and/or ease of entry.

The KNK 1990's fore deck is humped a bit at its forward end, perhaps for more foot room. The outer two of the three forward deck-stringers are unusual in that their tips approximate the shape of East Greenland paddle tips— being oblong; this shape is depicted in figure 353. This may have been done to prevent sharp corners from poking into the skin. At their aft ends, the deck stringers are 2″ (50mm) wide.

Figure 353: Shape of the KNK 1990's two outboard fore deck stringers. (Oblong end towards the bow.)

A cockpit view of the 1990 is depicted in figure 354. The KNK 1990's coaming is lap-scarfed in the distinctly East Greenlandic

Figure 354: Cockpit view of the Greenland National Museum's KNK 1990. Note the seal skin seat pad.

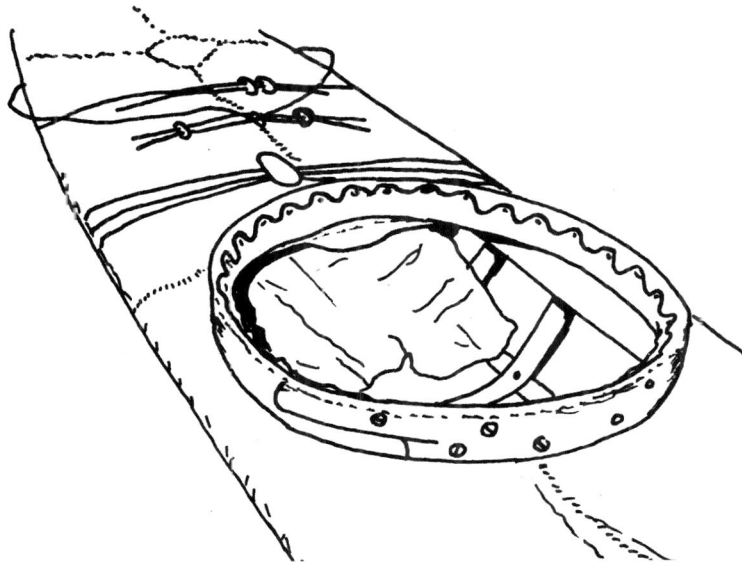

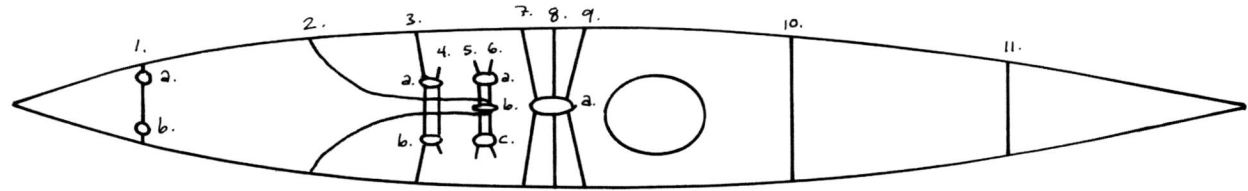

Greenland National Museum: Cat. no. 1990

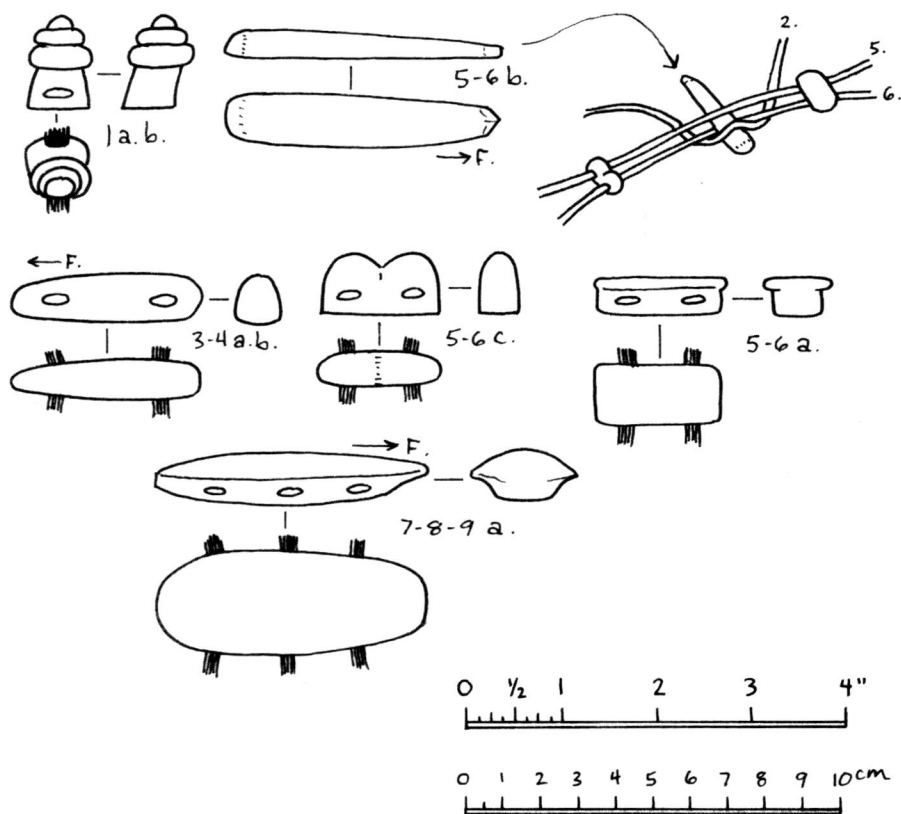

method and is secured with flathead screws. The *amiq* is attached to the coaming with pegs, as is common in most of Greenland, however in this case the pegs are oak instead of bone or ivory. The coaming measures 3/4″ thick by 1-3/4″ high (19 x 44mm).

A drain plug is present at the stern, on the port side. The KNK 1990's keel and chine edging is made from 5/8″ (16mm) wide steel channeling (i.e., slightly concave in cross-section), and is nailed to the kayak. End knobs are not present or evidenced due to wear in the *amiq* at the tips, but one could presume their one-time presence.

The two conical deck fittings on the foremost deck line are nearly identical to the corresponding pieces on the kayak 48057 (plate 97). The KNK 1990 lacks the shorter middle piece seen on the 48057, and may have had one. The KNK 1990 has a unique variation of the Y-shaped deck line: It is actually a single line (U-shaped?) and has no deadeye or hook. It is however every bit as functional— just not quite as adjustable. It runs beneath the pair of short fore deck lines, and is held in place with a loose wooden-spike, as in figure 355, and piece 5-6b.

The three deck lines just ahead of the cockpit are all linked together with a single fitting; no other fittings are on these lines. A harpoon holder was not evidenced on the KNK 1990, which is unusual. Also unusual is the lack of any fittings on the aft deck as well as there being just a single aft deck line and a single stern line. This stern line is slack, and is comprised of a thin line passed between the original deck lines' stubs; holes have been cut in the stubs to receive the thinner line

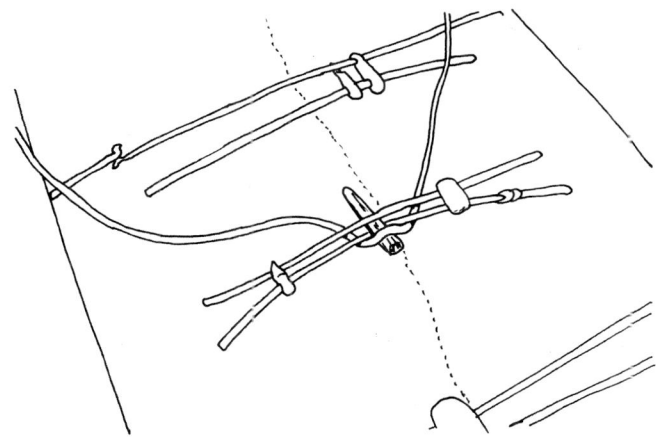

Figure 355: Fore deck details of the Greenland National Museum's kayak 1990. The cockpit is towards the bottom of the image.

90. East Greenland Kayak: Museon, den Haag, the Netherlands. Catalog no. 59876.

This kayak receives brief mention in Gert Nooter's *Old Kayaks in the Netherlands*; Nooter presents a list of the 'old' as well as newer kayaks in Dutch museums (1971:1-3). The 59876 was built by Henrik Singhertek, and was collected by Nooter himself during field work at Tiniteqilaaq, East Greenland around 1970. Nooter's paper "The East-Greenland Kayaks" published in *Contributions To Kayak Studies* (1991:319-347) has extensive descriptions and photographs of East Greenland kayaks.

This kayak stands out as being extremely short for an East Greenland kayak (15'7-3/8"; 475.9cm)— of the previously mentioned full-sized East Greenland kayaks, the average length is 566.3cm. Historian and philologist Robert Petersen, ascribes the extinction of the Ammassalimmiut "longhouse" as the factor creating particularly short East Greenland kayaks:

After the disappearance of the longhouse it was impossible to repair the kayak skin in the winter because a kayak could not be brought into a small house. Outdoor repairs were impossible at that season, because the wet skin patches quickly froze stiff. Therefore after 1930 shorter winter kayaks were built for use in addition to summer kayaks of normal length (R. Petersen, 1984:628).

The Museon 59876 is clearly a "winter kayak," and perhaps emphasizing this point, it is clad in tin armor at the bow to fend off ice. This sheet metal is tacked onto the kayak through its *amiq* along the gunwales, keelson, and chines. Figure 356 shows the treacherous ice conditions in which such kayaks were used.

Robert Petersen describes general coastal ice conditions for Ammassalik District:

Off the coast, the cold East Greenland Current flows from the north, bringing a huge mass of drift ice, the storis. . . . In the summer, however, the storis can drift so far out that one can sail even to relatively isolated

Figure 356: A hunter working his way through sea ice in a short kayak—possibly the example described here. (Photograph by Gert Nooter, Courtesy of the Rijksmuseum voor Volkenkunde, Leiden.)

places; but this travel is always undependable, and a change of wind can block the coast again in a short time (1984:623).

Gert Nooter describes how open water could persist year-round in certain areas in East Greenland—even in air temperatures of –25 degrees celsius (-13f.) due to fast water currents (1991:334-336).

Figure 357 shows the cockpit layout of the 59876. A particleboard seat is visible, as are the lines along which it has broken (this removable seat is not depicted on the survey drawing). The seat slats are visible as well, these being nailed or screwed to the ribs from beneath. The ribs are double nailed to the chines and keelson. Ivory pegs along the inner face of the coaming support the *amiq*— note how it has come loose towards the front. The coaming measures 1/2″ (13mm) thick by 1-1/2″ (38mm) high. The 59876's *masik* has a handle carved into it; this facilitated not only lifting the kayak, but also getting into it; the *masik* is 3-7/8″ (8.6cm) wide.

Figure 358 shows a forward interior view of the 59876. The curved deck beams are set into blocks on the left side— they were apparently recycled from a narrower kayak, or had damaged ends. Two of the relatively narrow deck stringers are set on shims; the stringers measure 1/4″ by 2-1/2″ (6 x 64mm) wide. The heavy line wrapped around the rib on the right of figure 358 is the tied-off end of the continuous forward deck lines. The 59876's *isserfik* measures 3/4″ (19mm) thick by 1-1/2″ (38mm) wide. Several rib shims can also be seen towards the bow. While the curved deck beams are lashed in place, all of the straight deck beams are oblique-pegged to the gunwales— these pegs are locked in place by smaller pegs set through the gunwales' lower edges.

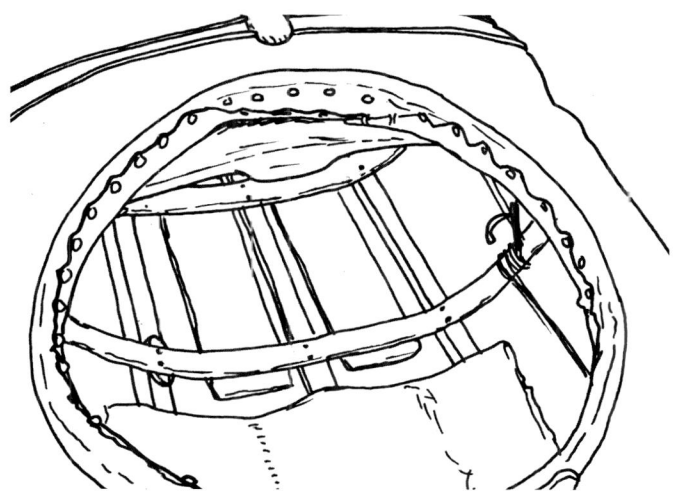

Figure 357: Cockpit view of the Museon's kayak 59876. Note the leg slats as well as the creased and fractured seat made from particleboard. The particleboard seat is omitted from the scale drawing, as it was not permanently attached to the kayak.

The 59876's coaming is offset, being 3″ (7.6cm) from the right sheer, and 1-5/8″ (4.1cm) from the left. Two drain plugs are present on the 59876, instead of the usual single plug. The plug not shown in the scale drawing's elevation is on the other side (starboard) and is an inch further forward than its counter-part.

This kayak is extensively shod with keel and chine edging. The keel has a wood strip from 10-1/2″ (26.6cm) from the bow to 6′3″ (190.5cm) aft. Astern, there is wood edging 7-1/2″

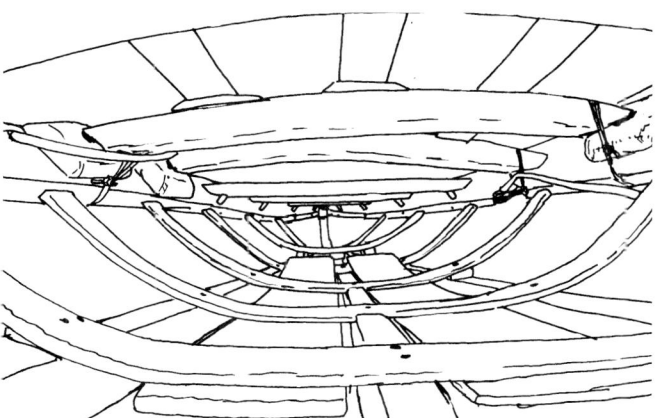

Figure 358: Forward interior view of the 59876. Note the shims beneath the deck stringers and the use of blocks attached to the gunwales to support a few deck beam ends.

(19.0cm) from the tip that reaches forward to 5′4″ (162.5cm) from the tip of the stern. This wood edging measures 3/8″ (9mm) wide and 1/4″ (6mm) high. An aluminum keel strip is also present from 4′ (122cm) to 12′5″ (378.4cm) from the bow; it overlaps the wood edging and measures 1/8″ (3mm) by 3/4″ (19mm) wide. The chines have aluminum edging from 5′ (152.4cm) to 9′ (274.3cm) from the bow, and from 4′ (122cm) to 4′9″ (144.8cm) from the stern. All of the 59876's edging is attached with metal nails. A paddle with armored blades is associated with this kayak, and is depicted in paddle-plate 71.

One unusual feature of the 59876 is its distinctly convex stems; no other type IX kayak has stems of this shape. This may have a direct relationship with how this kayak was used, i.e., in icy seas. Perhaps the convex stems are simply a means to increase the waterline length of an otherwise short "winter kayak."

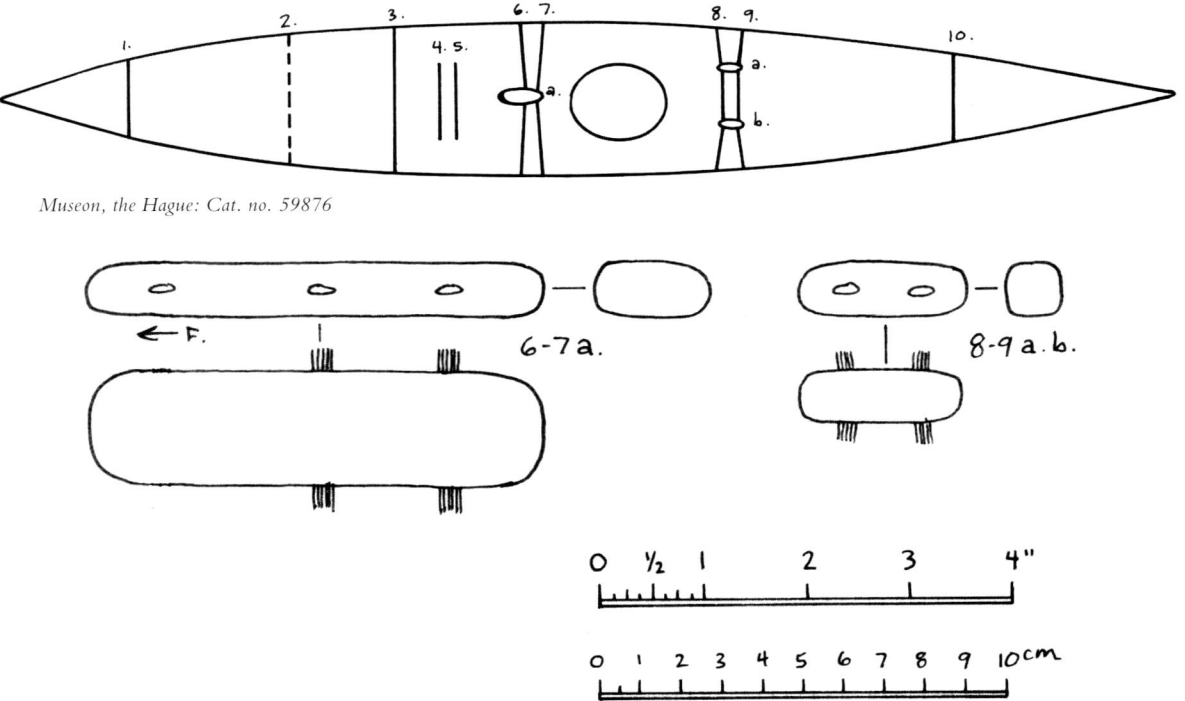

Museon, the Hague: Cat. no. 59876

A bow Y-shaped line was missing but evidenced on this kayak (deck line 2), so its exact configuration remains unknown. The first four existing deck lines have no fittings on them, and are each fairly taut. Deck lines 6 and 7 share a single link-piece. This piece has obviously been recycled from an older kayak as it has three holes drilled into it.

There isn't any evidence of a harpoon holder having been mounted on either side of the 59876's cockpit, which is unusual, but may reflect a total reliance on rifles for hunting in extremely icy seas.

91. East Greenland Kayak from late 1960s: Museon, Den Haag, the Netherlands. Catalog no. 57602.

Dr. Gert Nooter collected this kayak frame in 1968. The frame provides a detailed look at the construction of a type IX East Greenland kayak. Remarkably, the assembly compares very well with the kayak model Gustav Holm collected in 1884— the type VIII KNK 1418 (plate 82). The stem assemblies are nearly identical; the deck stringer arrangement is also the same, as are the shallow deck beam mortises and general layout of the leg slats.

The Museon's 57602 (figure 359) was made by Billiam Jonathansen of Tineteqilaaq, a locally renowned hunter and builder born in 1912. Nooter writes of him:

> *Billiam's kayak and those he built for his sons are among the best in Tineteqilâq; his fame as a kayak builder reached as far as Angmagssalik [Ammassalik] and recently even to Copenhagen. He was asked by the Kommunalbestyrelse [Settlement manager] to produce an entirely traditional set of hunting gear . . . for the King of Denmark (1976:51).*

Nooter also describes Jonathansen as being very interested in European tools and articles and quick at improvising (1976:45-51). An example of this is his emergency substitution of a rusty screwdriver with a plastic handle for an ivory harpoon foreshaft before a narwhal hunt (1976:59). Improvisation is also present in Jonathansen's kayak: The deck-beam-to-gunwale joints are not pegged as on most East Greenland kayaks, but are instead lashed— with copper cable. A piece of tin is wrapped around the bow gunwale-to-stem joint— likely a repair, or an aid in fairing the lines. The curved deck-beams and the *masik* are not lashed or pegged to the gunwales: They are fastened with screws using the oblique method usually reserved for wooden pegs.

Several repairs and/or 'gains' are evident on the 57602. The left gunwale towards the stern has a wooden patch nailed to the upper edge— perhaps to replace a rotted or damaged section. The keel has two gains fastened to it— both fore and aft at the keel-to-stem transitions. These gains are nailed in place and are depicted in the scale drawing.

The heel-guides of the 57602 are nailed onto the ribs from the bottom. At their forward end, the guides are lifted above the adjacent rib, and are not fastened to it; the slats measure 1/4″ (6mm) thick by 3-1/2″ (8.9cm) wide at their widest. The *masik* has a handle carved into it. A coaming with the 57602 measured 3/4″ (19mm) thick by 1-3/8″ (35mm) high.

The hull-lines drawing of the 57602 show a very well-formed and elegant kayak, the stern of which is lofty for a modern-period East Greenland kayak— very much like the KNK 1990's (plate 89)

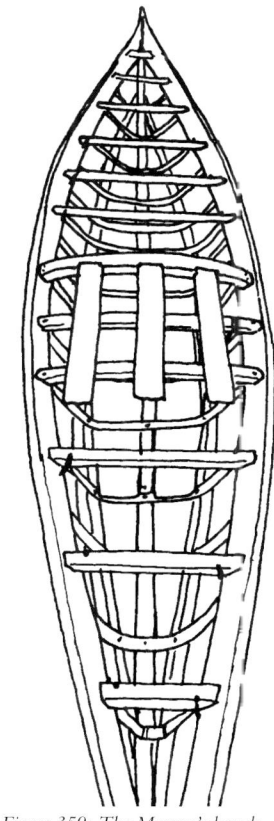

Figure 359: The Museon's kayak 57602.

Figure 360: The builder of the Museon's kayak 57602, Billiam Jonathansen, in 1973. (Photograph by Gert Nooter. Courtesy of the Rijksmuseum voor Volkenkunde, Leiden.)

At 16′6″ (502.9cm) long, this kayak is short for a type IX kayak; like the 59876 it might be considered a "winter kayak," though this is not known for certain. The average length of type IX kayaks excluding this example and the 59876 is 18′7-3/8″ (567.4cm).

The deck line placement on the Museon's 57602 is indicated on the scale drawing's hull-lines (plate 91a). Deck line 2 was likely a Y-shaped line; a harpoon holder had been fitted through the 57602's *masik*. Deck line 12 could be expected to be of the Y-shaped form as well, but the other two type IX kayaks from the 1960s (plates 89 and 90) just have a slack transverse deck line in this position. Y-shaped stern deck lines may have become obsolete by the 1960s.

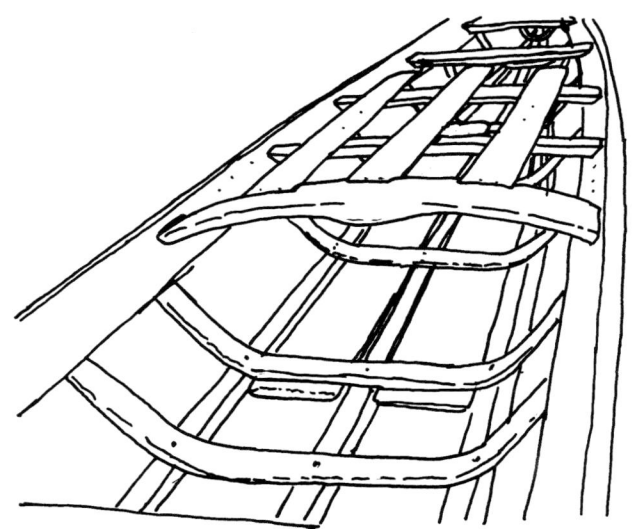

Figure 361: Cockpit view of the Museon's kayak 57602. Note the handhold carved into the masik, the leg slats, and the three forward deck stringers.

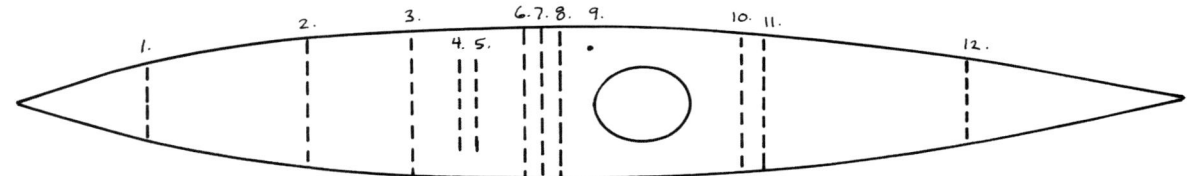

Museon, the Hague: Cat. no. 57602

TYPE X: Rolling Kayaks

Kayaking and kayak hunting remains a way of life in Greenland. Although only a small minority of Greenlanders pursue kayaking nowadays— and mainly for sport— the kayak still figures prominently as a powerful iconic symbol, certain to stir pride in any Greenlander. Importantly, the kayak of the Greenlander is still evolving. While the kayak's function has changed from subsistence seal hunting to sport (hunting, recreation, and competition) in much of Greenland, its form has continued to follow its function closely.

The competition at Greenland National Kayak Championships, presently held every year, has led to some new innovations in kayak designs. One of the more startling results is the creation of kayaks designed to have great advantages in rolling. These kayaks are extremely shallow, and generally much shorter than any hunting kayaks. Their low freeboard and narrow beam give the roller better control and less resistance from volume.

While any hunting kayak from the East and West Greenland traditions must out of necessity be plenty 'roll-able,' the rolls executed in the competitions are particularly challenging. For example, some 30 rolls or maneuvers are to be done— once on the left, and once on the right, and two tries each are allowed. By sheer numbers, this can mean a competitor may be doing as many as 120 rolls, not counting the two "as many rolls as you can do in 10 seconds" segments. What is more, the rolls progressively become more difficult; for example, these rolls, among others, are in the competition: [48]

- *Rolling the kayak with the paddle held behind the neck.*
- *Rolling with the paddle held beneath the kayak.*
- *Rolling, holding the paddle with one's arms crossed.*
- *Rolling without a paddle . . . and a 7 pound (4.4kg.) rock in one hand.*
    (Heath, 2004.33-40)

---

[48] Detailed descriptions of the traditional Greenland kayak-rolling techniques can be found in Heath (2004) and Stamer (2004).

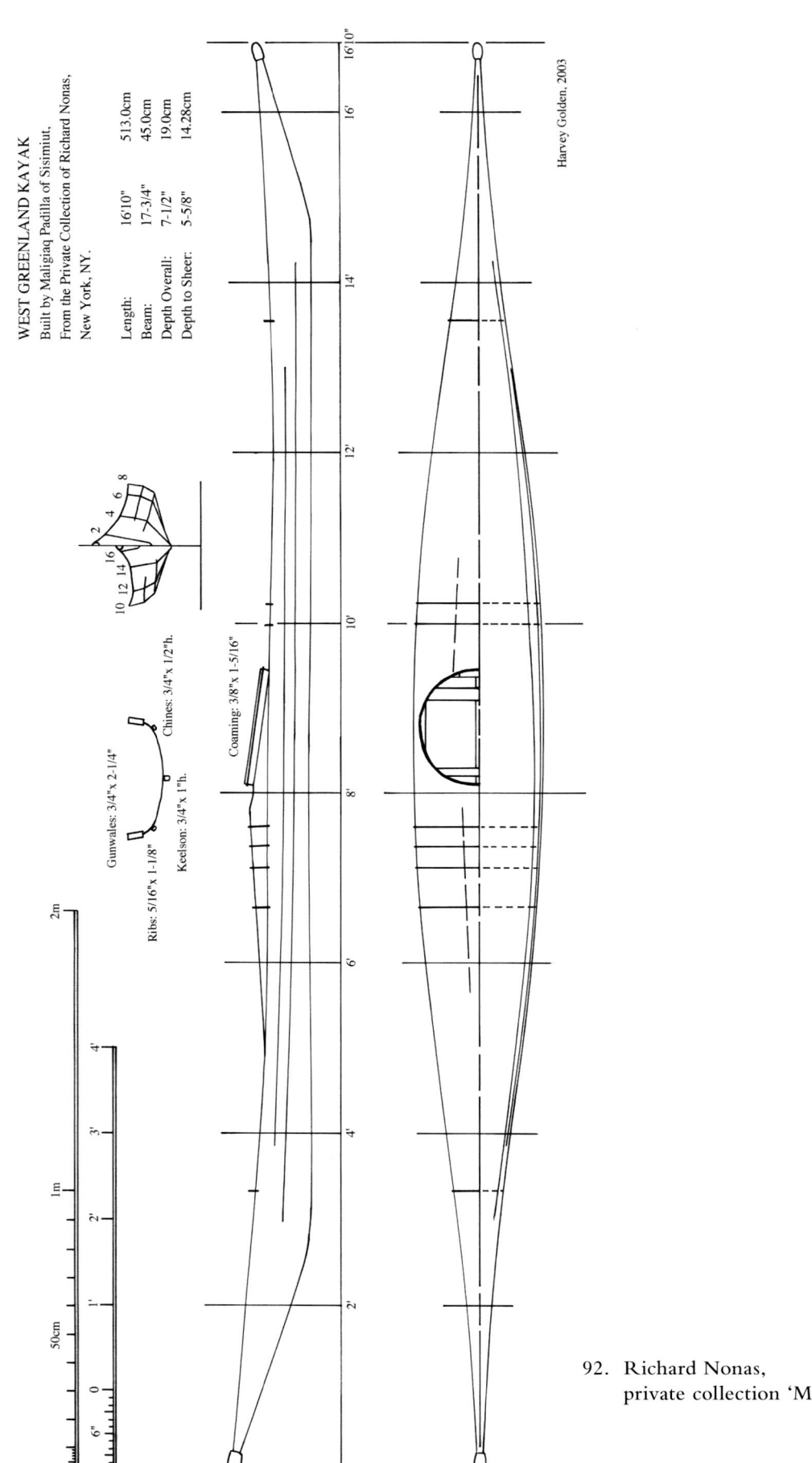

92. Richard Nonas, private collection 'MP'

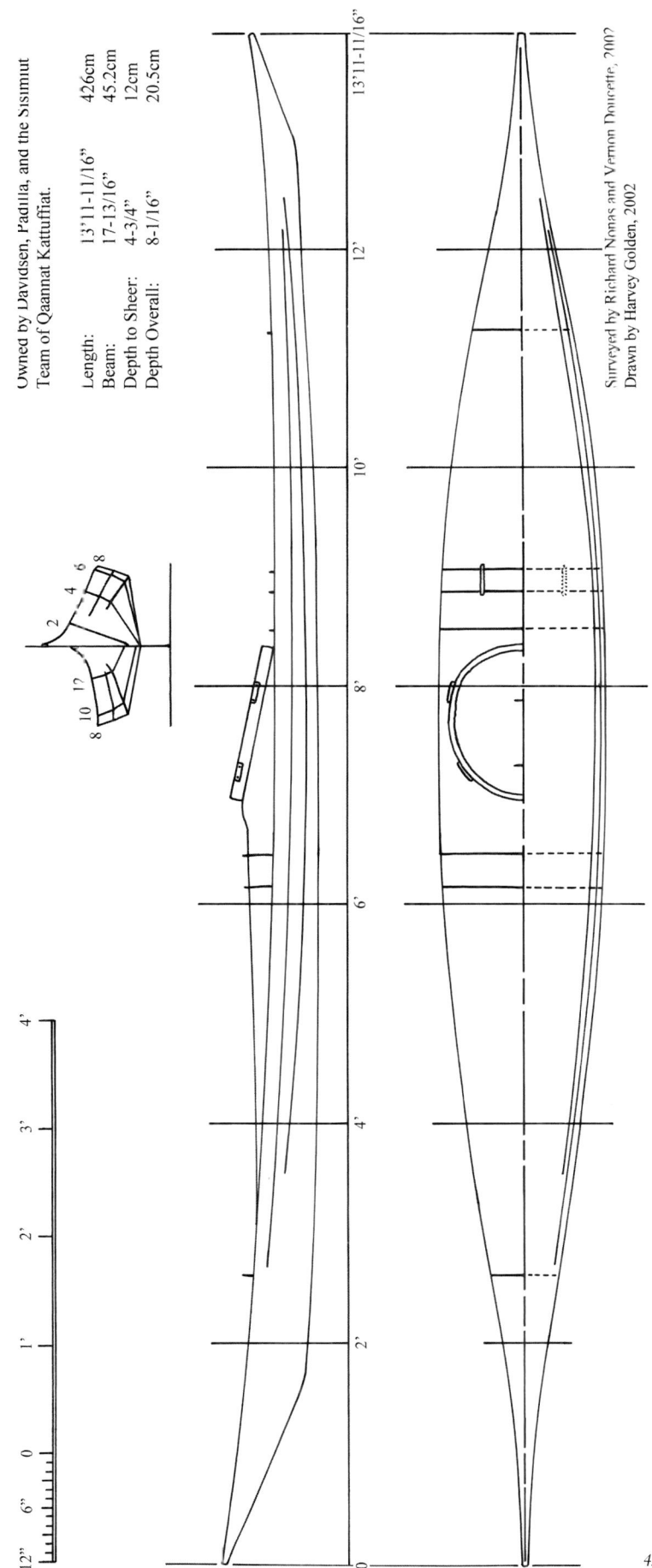

93. Kunuunnguaq Davidsen, private collection 'KD'

92. Greenland Kayak, ca. 1998:
Private collection of Richard Nonas, New York, New York.
'MP'

Maligiaq Padilla of Sisimiut built this rolling kayak in November/December of 1998. At the time it was built, Maligiaq Padilla had at age 16 become the youngest Greenlander to win top ratings at the Greenland National Kayaking Championships. This kayak wasn't used in the championships, and it was actually built in Houston, Texas for use during kayak demonstrations throughout the Southeast US Kayak historian John Heath facilitated the building of this kayak during Maligiaq's stay in Houston. The paddle Maligiaq used in the US is depicted in paddle-plate 72.

This kayak appears in the instructional videotape produced by John Heath: *Paddling with Maligiaq*, in which Maligiaq describes and demonstrates various Greenlandic paddling and rolling techniques (Heath, 2000b). I asked Maligiaq what he thought of the kayak: He replied "[at] that time I hadn't built many kayaks, so that kayak is not the best, and is not too bad" (personal communication, 2004). An oblique view of the 'MP' is

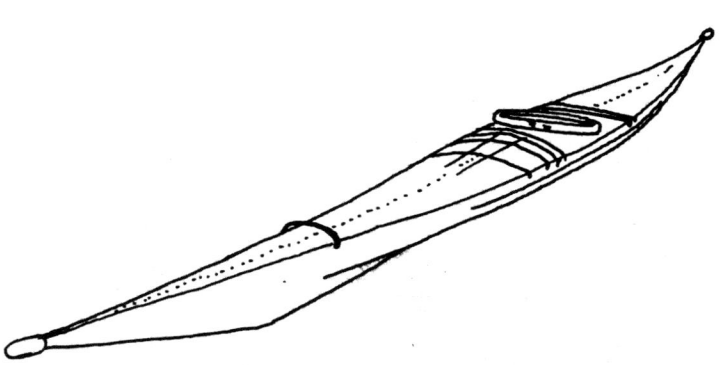

Figure 362: Maligiaq Padilla's rolling kayak. Padilla built this kayak in the U.S. by for use in demonstrations throughout North America.

shown in figure 362. The shallowness of the hull and the long fine ends are plain to see.

Figure 363 depicts the forward interior view of Maligiaq Padilla's kayak. The double-pass method of lashing the ribs to the chines and keelson is used, but instead of being continuously lashed, each juncture's lashings are tied-off. All of the ribs are fastened to the gunwales with pegs set through the mortise and tenon.

The MP's *masik* measures 13/16" (21mm) thick and 2-3/4" (70mm) wide in the middle; the *isserfik* is 3/4" (19mm) thick and 1-5/8" (41mm) wide. The fore deck stringers are 1/4" (6mm) thick by 3/4" (19mm) wide; the aft deck stringers are 1/2" (13mm) thick and 1-5/8" (41mm) wide.

The coaming measures 3/8" (9mm) thick and 1-5/16" (33mm) high. Padilla stitched a 3/16" (5mm) diameter line to the coaming 15/16" (24mm) on-center above the lower

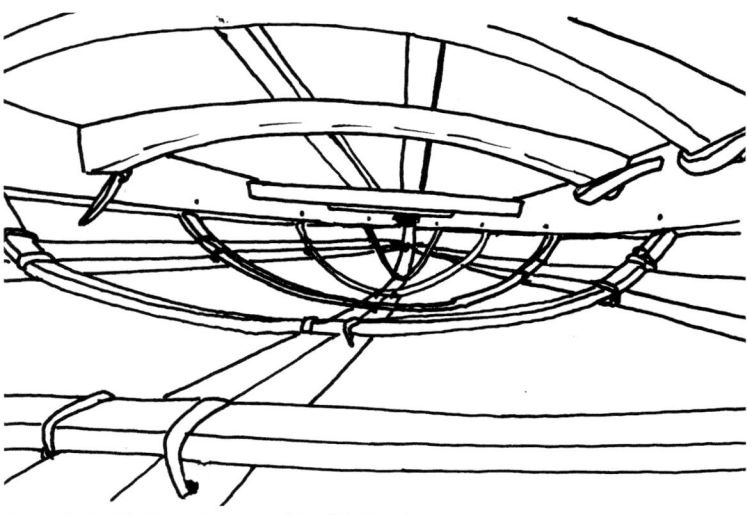

Figure 363: The forward interior of Padilla's kayak

edge. This line would function as a solid rim for the hem of a *tuilik*, particularly at the back of the coaming where the line overlaps for 12" (30.5cm). Both end knobs are carved from blocks of oak. They are unusually large, being 3-3/4" (9.5cm) long and 1-1/4" (3.2cm) diameter.

Maligiaq's kayak is covered with a synthetic cloth— likely nylon, and is coated with white marine enamel paint. The rigging is very simple, being just a few un-adorned straps crossing the fore and aft decks, as well as a single line each at the bow and stern. The deck lines are fastened through the sides of the gunwales, about 1/2" (13mm) below the sheer.

While replicas of numerous kayak types were made for this study, I was able to paddle this actual kayak at the Delmarva Kayak Rendezvous in 2003 and 2004, by courtesy of its present owner, Richard Nonas. This kayak tracks very stiffly— it is somewhat hard to turn. Its low volume is readily noticed in waves, as they easily sweep over the decks, even more than with East Greenland kayaks on account of its shorter length. It paddles nicely, and feels light, swift, and comfortable.

I personally can't claim it is significantly better in rolling than many of the hunting kayaks I have replicated. This is of course not likely to be everyone's opinion of this kayak, and indeed I think it rolls well, but I have had better luck with some of the more advanced rolling techniques in my replicas of the RvV 1076 (plate 75), and the HMG E.102 (plate 26).

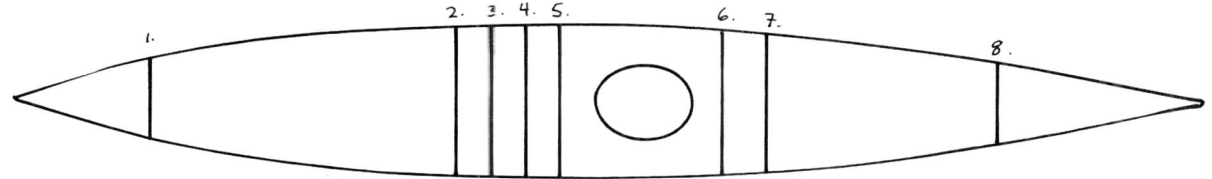

Richard Nonas, Priv. coll. "MP"

93. West Greenland Kayak, 1998: Built by Kunuunnguaq Davidsen of Sisimiut. 'KD'

Maligiaq Padilla of Sisimiut (the builder of the previous kayak) started the construction of this kayak in 1998. It was to be for his younger sister, but when Padilla was touring in the United States, Kunuunnguaq Davidsen finished it as a 'rolling kayak'— one that Davidsen hoped would allow him to do the hardest kayak rolls in competition (M. Padilla: personal communication, 2004). Vernon Doucette and Richard Nonas surveyed the 'KD' in Sisimiut in 2002; while I have not studied this kayak, I did see it in competition at Nuuk in 2000.

After the 2000 competitions, Qaannat Kattuffiat (the Greenland Kayak Association) enacted a requirement for all kayaks to maintain at least 2cm (just over 3/4") of freeboard. This rendered numerous 'rolling kayaks' to be illegal in competition— including the present example, which was actually the very kayak that provoked the ruling. Nevertheless, specialized rolling kayaks are still being used for training, and undoubtedly the minimum required freeboard is still being sought in competition-legal rolling kayaks.

H. C. Petersen writes that the shallowest kayaks he has ever measured (measured at the back of the coaming) were 10-12cm deep (3-15/16" to 4-3/4" deep) (1986:44). Being that his measurements were taken prior to the phenomenon of 'rolling' kayaks, there apparently was a precedence of kayaks this shallow within the kayak-hunting tradition. Petersen doesn't say where such shallow kayaks existed,

Figure 364: Maligiaq Padilla competing in the individual rolling category of the Greenland National Kayaking Championships at Nuuk, 2000. Padilla is using the same kayak described here – note the total lack of freeboard. (Photograph by author.)

although he does say that the deepest kayaks were from vicinities where kayaks were used year-round (1986:44). East Greenlandic kayaks, despite being used year-round, are (aside from rolling kayaks) the shallowest vessels in the present study; the average depth to sheer of type IX East Greenland kayaks is 15.2cm (5-15/16″).

Due to the shallow nature of this kayak, three stanchions are used between deck beams and the keelson to preserve the kayak's shape. The field notes of Nonas and Doucette list one stanchion below the *isserfik*, and two in the forward half of the hull, ahead of where the kayaker's feet would be.

Four plastic tabs are fastened to the front and back quarters of the coaming in order to hold the tuilik in place. A seat of sorts is present in the 'KD': A large 1/8″ (3mm) thick plywood panel, cut to cover up as much of the chines, keelson, and ribs in the seat and leg area as possible; this is undoubtedly to make getting in-and-out easier in this tiny kayak. The kayak is covered in cotton canvas and sealed with black marine-enamel paint. As required by Qaannat Kattuffiat for competitions, the deck lines of the 'KD' are made from seal skin (Nonas/Doucette, 2002: field-notes).

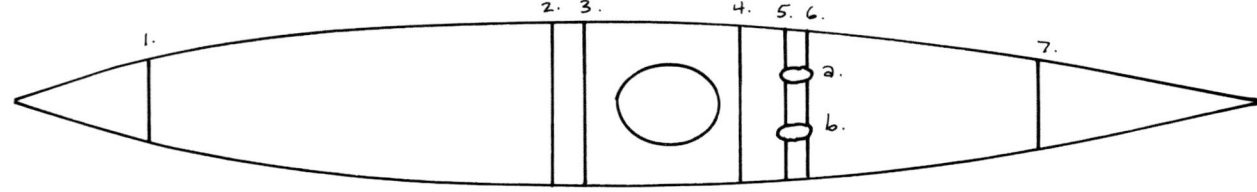

Kunuunnguaq Davidsen, Priv. coll. "KD"

TYPE XI.

The three following kayak types are all from Polar Greenland. These kayaks have received an introduction in the first chapter (pages 40–41), and their unique construction has also been presented (pages 98–102). The three types of Polar Greenland kayaks in this study are broken down into the 'older-form' (XI), the 'transitional form' (XII), and the 'assimilated' form (XIII).

Type XI— the older form— is distinguished by its maintenance of numerous features that were introduced from immigrants from Canada in the 1860s. Briefly, these are the markedly Swede-form hull, the deep raked bow and the low, shallow, and extremely short stern. The flat bottom and occasional use of secondary chines is characteristic of many East Canadian kayaks. Unlike most East Canadian kayaks, the ribs of most old-form Polar Greenland kayaks are pieced together from three separate straight pieces of wood. This technique is precedented in Eastern Canada, particularly in Northeast Baffin Island, Cumberland Sound, and East Hudson Bay (Arima, 1987: 112, 173, 222 fig.33; Golden, field notes: 1996, 2003).

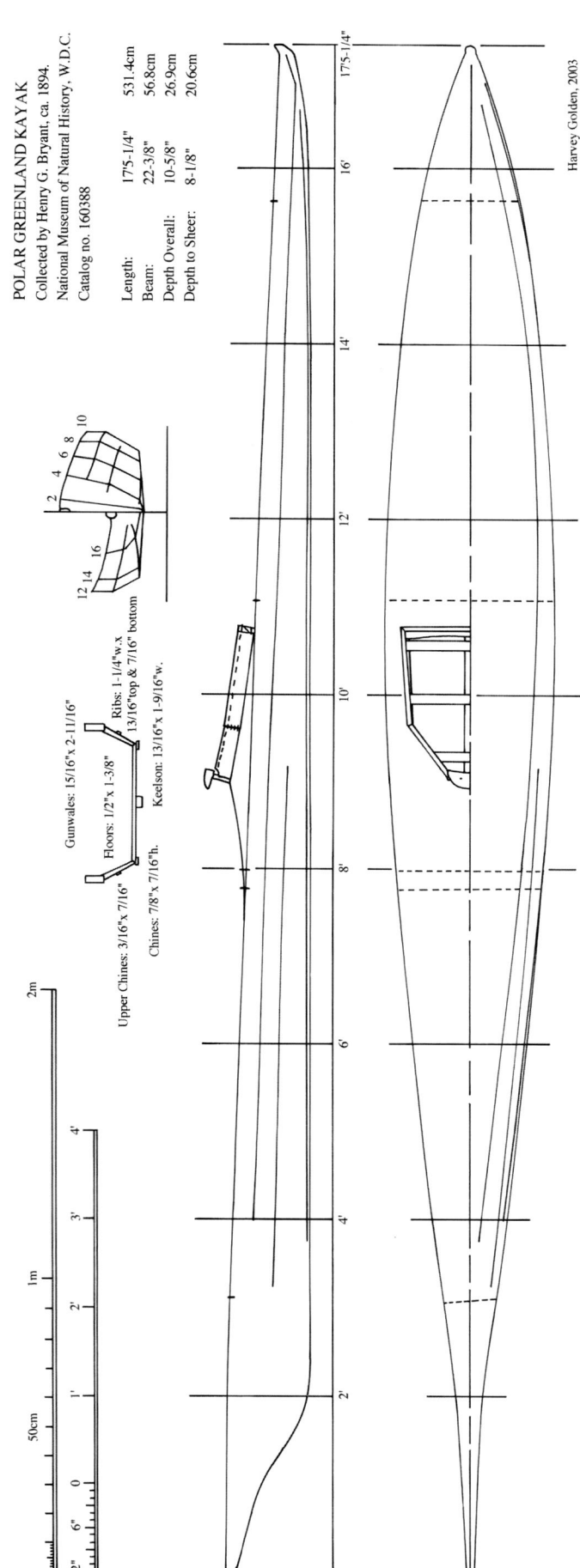

94. National Museum of Natural History catalog no. 160388

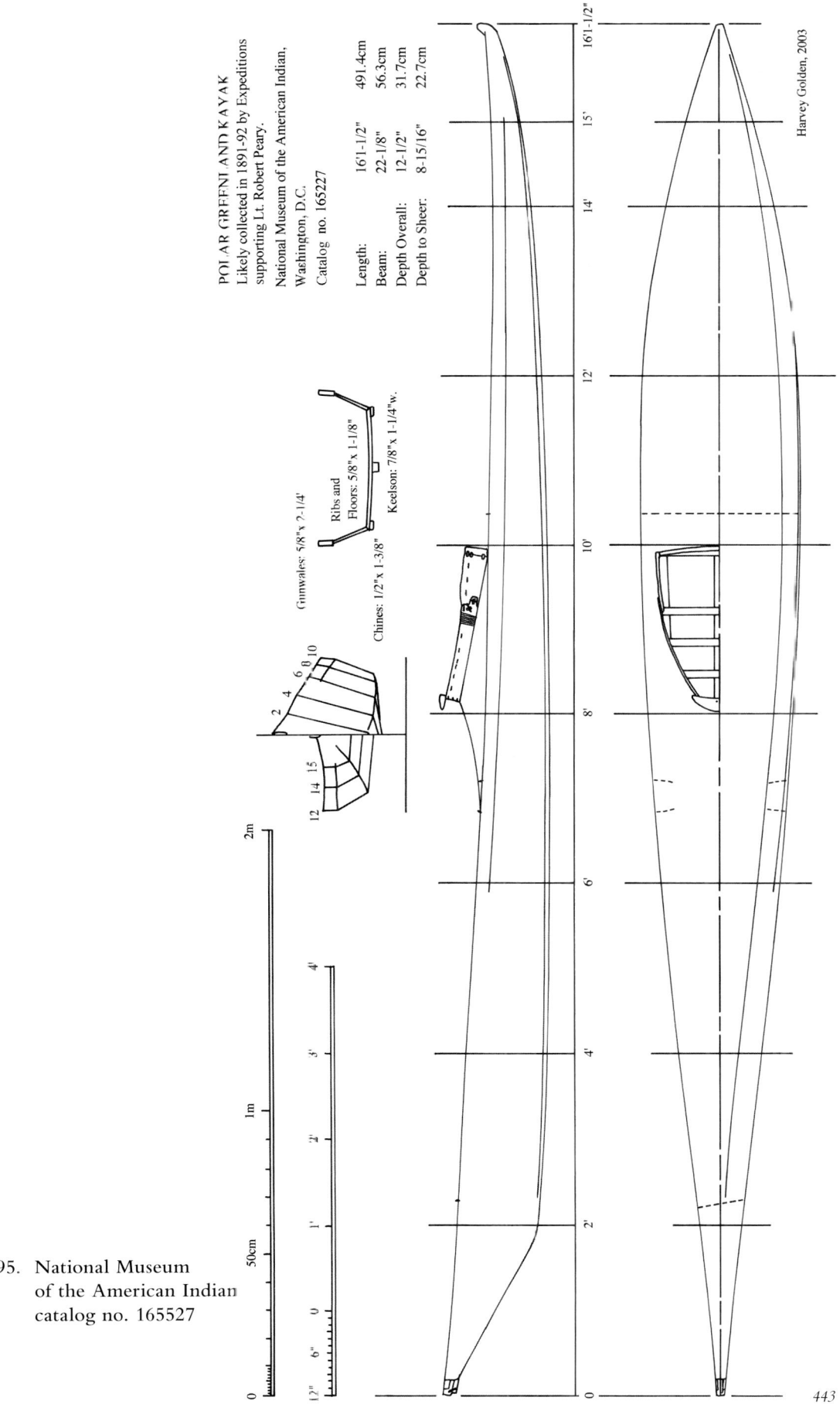

POLAR GREENLAND KAYAK
Likely collected in 1891-92 by Expeditions supporting Lt. Robert Peary.
National Museum of the American Indian, Washington, D.C.
Catalog no. 165227

Length:	16'1-1/2"	491.4cm
Beam:	22-1/8"	56.3cm
Depth Overall:	12-1/2"	31.7cm
Depth to Sheer:	8-15/16"	22.7cm

Gunwales: 5/8" x 2-1/4"
Ribs and Floors: 5/8" x 1-1/8"
Chines: 1/2" x 1-3/8"
Keelson: 7/8" x 1-1/4"w.

Harvey Golden, 2003

95. National Museum of the American Indian catalog no. 165527

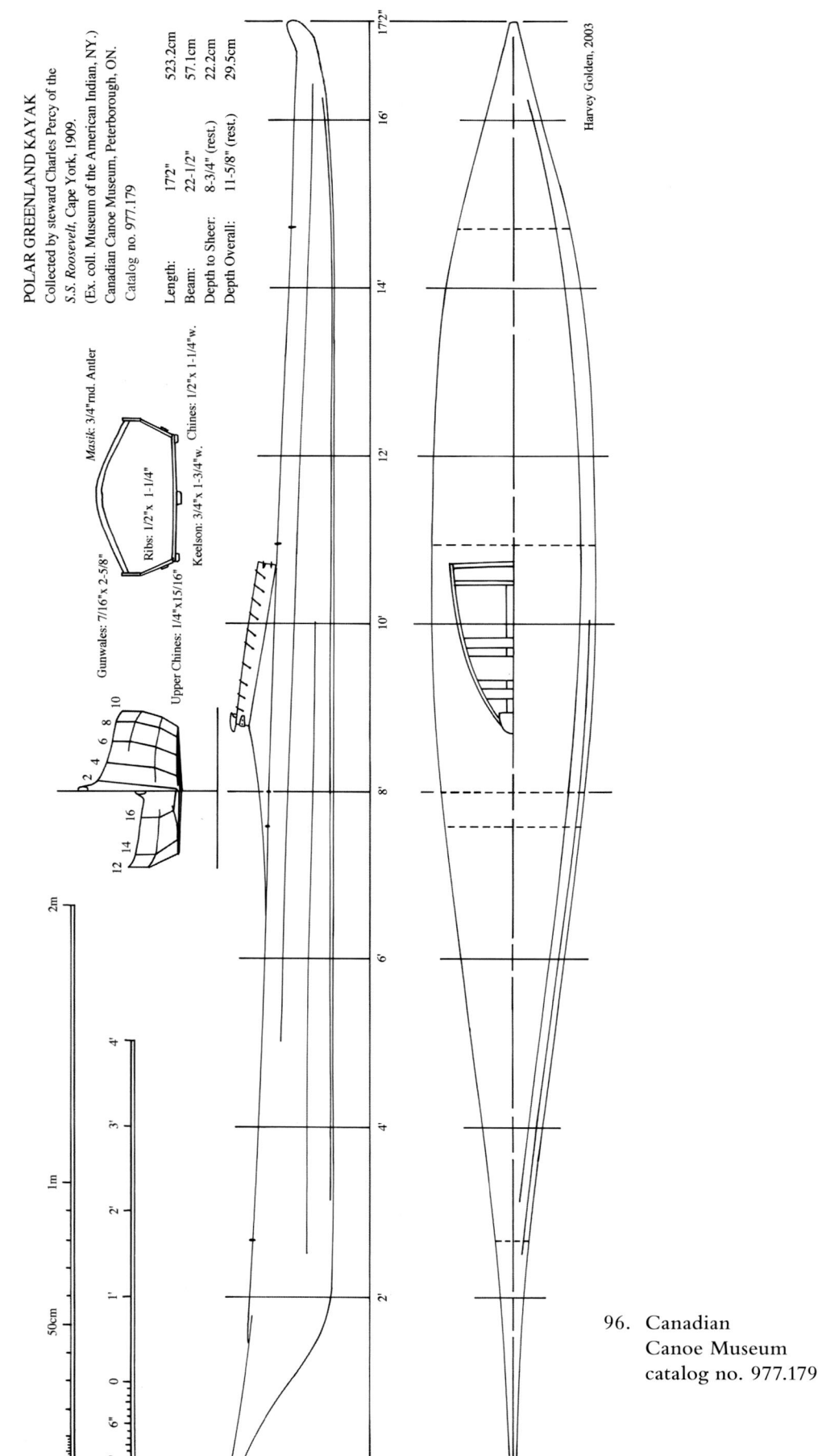

96. Canadian Canoe Museum catalog no. 977.179

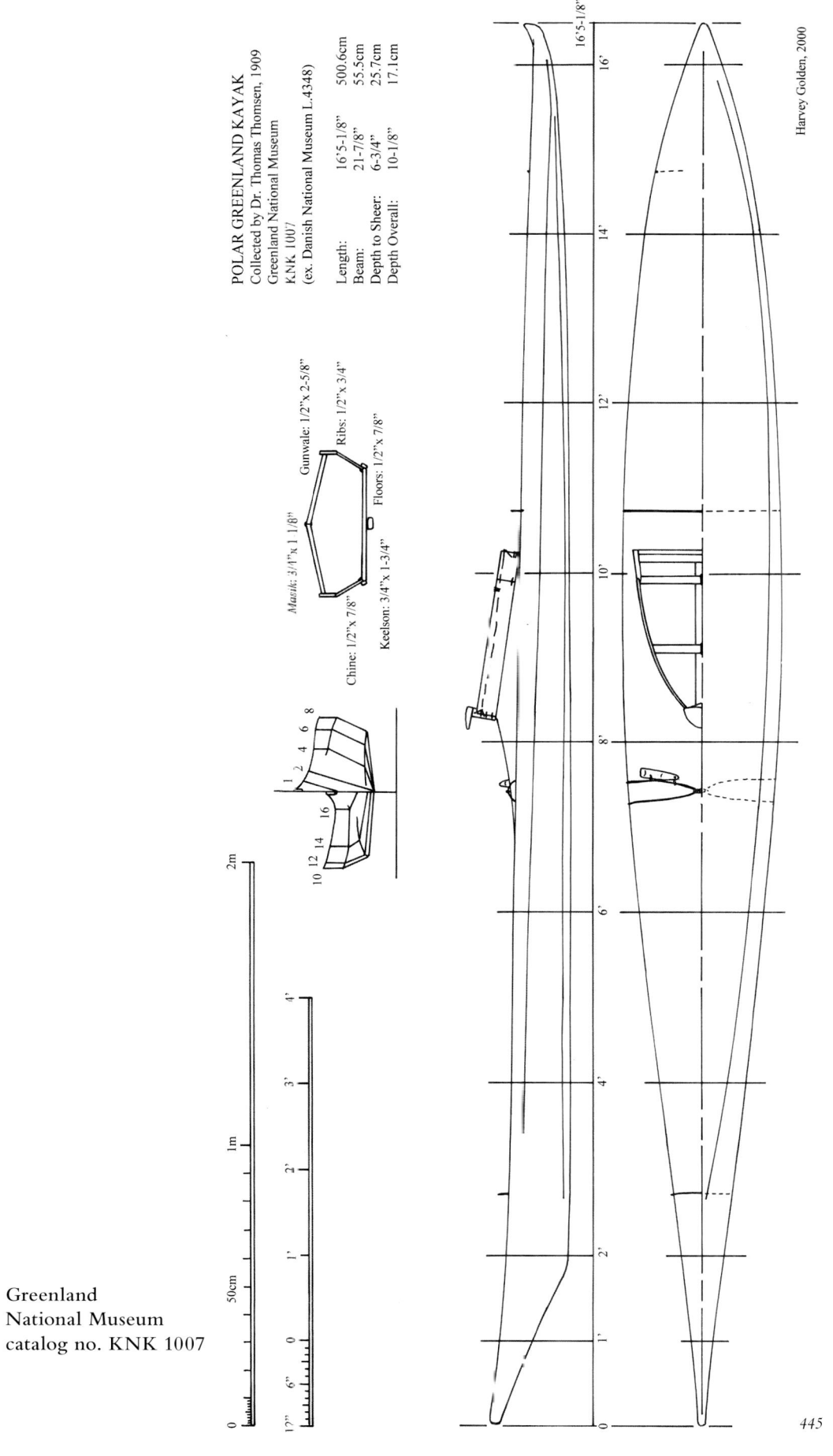

97. Greenland National Museum catalog no. KNK 1007

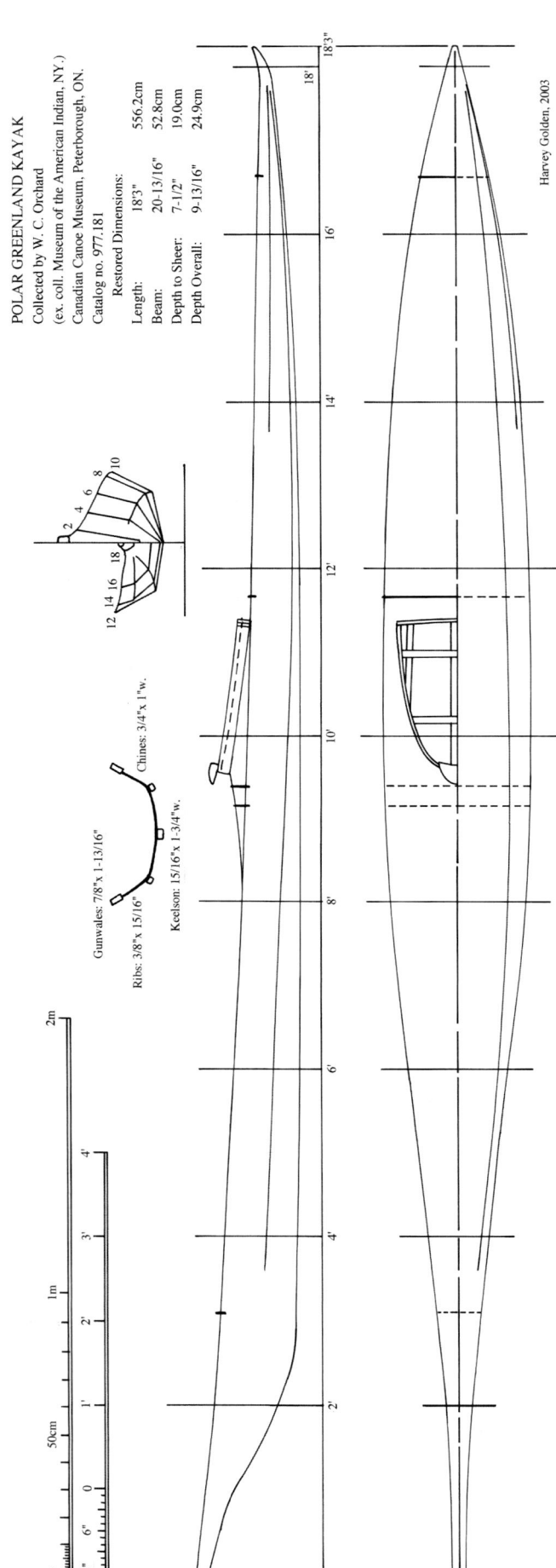

98. Canadian Canoe Museum catalog no. 977.181

94. Polar Greenland Kayak:
National Museum of Natural History, Smithsonian, Washington, DC.
Catalog no. 160388.

Henry G. Bryant donated this kayak to the Smithsonian, which accessioned it in December of 1894 (museum catalog). Bryant was second in command of the Peary Relief Expedition to West Greenland in 1892, sailing aboard the S.S. *Kite* (Keely and Davis, 1892:225). The 160388 may well have been collected on this voyage.

The Peary Relief Expedition's mission was to return Peary and his North Greenland Expedition to the United States after their over-winter stay of 1891-92. In the book *In Arctic Seas*, 1891 West Greenland Expedition[49] members Robert Keely and G. Davis write:

Until our visit to these most northern Eskimos no one had ever observed them to possess. . .boats of any description . . . but among the natives of Whale Sound we found a couple of kajaks. . . . They were similar in form and construction to some which we afterward saw lower down, at Cape York. The kajaks were of about the same size as those of the Eskimos in the neighborhood of the Danish settlements, but were neither so neatly nor so well made, being both more clumsy and heavier (1892:167).

Howard Chapelle has also surveyed the kayak 160388; the result of his survey appears in *The Bark Canoes and Skinboats of North America* (Adney and Chapelle, 1964:210, fig.205). Our respective survey results are very similar in size and form at first glance, although one chine is missing from Chapelle's drawing— a thinner and shorter chine between the main chine and the gunwale. His statement on the drawing's text "Side frames located between bottom frames" is incorrect: The side and bottom frames (ribs and floors in my terminology) are aligned and lashed firmly together.

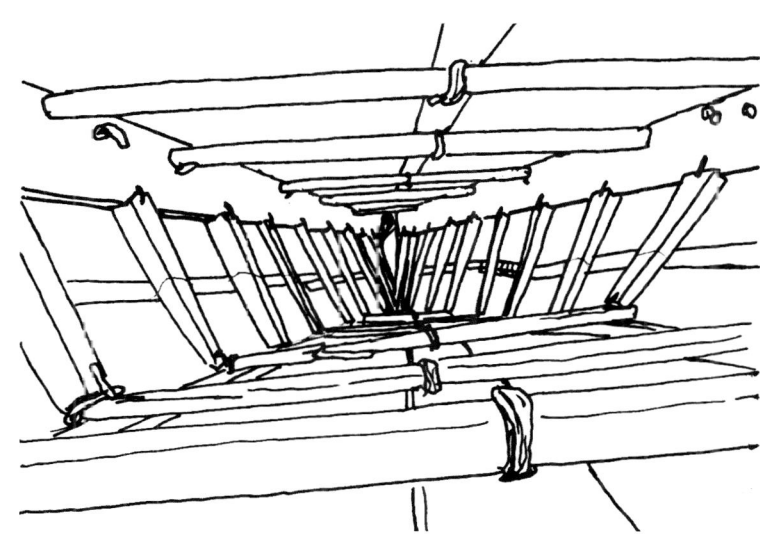

Figure 365: Forward interior of the NMNH's kayak 160388.

Figure 365 depicts the forward inside view of the 160388; note the secondary (or upper) chines. These lighter chines are lashed in place with a continuous single-passed line of cotton string. This kayak has both a single forward deck stringer, and a single aft deck stringer. The forward stringer measures 5/16" (8mm) thick by 1-3/8" (35mm) wide; the aft stringer is 1/4" (6mm) thick by 2-3/4" (70mm) wide.

Another view of the forward interior of the 160388 is depicted in figure 366. The aft terminus of the upper chines is visible as is the joint between the *masik* and the gunwales. The *masik* of the 160388

---

[49] The West Greenland Expedition of 1891 delivered the Peary North Greenland Expedition to their winter quarters in Polar Greenland.

is made of a natural crook of caribou antler, being on average 5/8″ high by 1″ wide (16 x 25mm). Several of the Polar Greenland kayaks in this study have caribou antler used for this curved deck beam (e.g., the NMNH 165527 and the CCM 977.179, plates 95 and 96).

The 160388's coaming is made up of six pieces of wood lashed together. The pieces are 5/8″ (16mm) thick by 2-3/16″ (55mm) high. The bone paddle-rest is 6-3/4″ (17.1cm) wide, 1″ (25mm) tall at the back, and 2-1/2″ (63mm) long. David Putnam, author of several titles in a popular travel series from the 1920s describes a use for the paddle rest during walrus hunts: "...The other animals in the herd often would stay close to the wounded

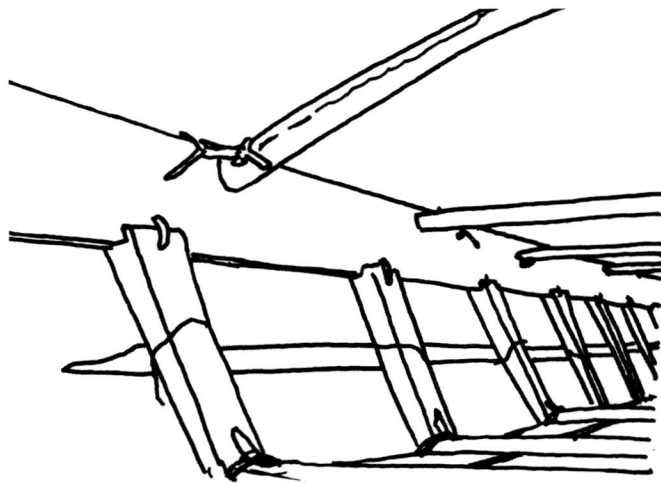

Figure 366: Depiction of the interior of the NMNH's 160388. This drawing shows the secondary chine and its aft terminus just behind the masik. *The* masik *is a natural crook of caribou antler.*

one, barking and roaring ... When the others come close, the Eskimos would bang their paddles on the paddle rest in front of them and yell, to scare off the other walrus who otherwise might attack them" (1926:118). Some years later, Erik Holtved described firing rifles to scare away walrus (1967:92). A paddle is associated with this kayak and is depicted in paddle-plate 75.

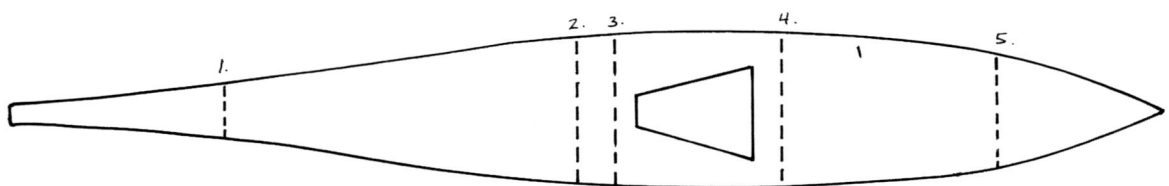

U. S. National Museum of Natural History: Cat. no. 160388

All of the 160388's deck lines were missing, however their placement was evidenced and is noted on the scale drawing.

Figure 367: Marie Peary paddling a kayak during the Peary expedition of 1900. (From Peary, 1903:106.)

95. Polar Greenland Kayak: National Museum of the American Indian, Washington, D.C. Catalog no. 165227

While this kayak had been surveyed and presented by Howard Chapelle in *The Bark Canoes and Skinboats of North America*, (Adney and Chapelle, 1964:207, fig.199), I visited and re-surveyed the kayak in the hopes of finding further details of its joinery and deck-line layout.

The 165227's history is not known beyond its provenance of "Cape York." It had been loaned to the Museum of the American Indian by the Academy of Natural Sciences of Philadelphia, and was accessioned by the MAI in 1929, no further data having been transferred with the kayak.

That this kayak was once the property of the academy in Philadelphia may suggest that it was collected during the 1891 West Greenland Expedition or the 1892 Peary Relief Expedition, the former delivering Peary's North Greenland Expedition to McCormick Bay, and the latter returning him to the US (Keely and Davis, 1892:20,225). An official of the Academy of Natural Sciences in Philadelphia, Professor Angelo Heilprin, was the leader of both of these expeditions, and most of the expedition's members were associated with Philadelphia in some manner.

One of the many purposes of Peary's North Greenland expedition was to secure a broad range of Inuhuit ethnographica for a display at the 1893 World's Columbian Exposition in Chicago (VanStone, 1972:31). Frederic W. Putnam, curator of the Peabody Museum of American Archaeology and Ethnology at Harvard University solicited Peary for this task; Putnam had been appointed Chief of the Department of Ethnology and Archaeology for the World's Columbian Exposition in Chicago (VanStone, 1972:31).

A memorandum of agreement between Peary and Putnam is reproduced in James VanStone's *The First Peary Collection of Polar Eskimo Material Culture* and lists such desired items as ". .. weapons, utensils . . . a stone house (and) all its contents . . . Several skeletons . . . and if possible, a large number of skulls of the natives." Pertinent to the present work: "If any native boats exist among the people, one or more to be secured" (1972:32).

Peary, during his many expeditions to Polar Greenland, collected a surprising number of kayaks.[50] Two kayaks ended up in the Field Columbian Museum of Chicago after the World's Columbian Exposition of 1892; both have since "disintegrated" and were discarded (VanStone, 1972:42). A list of Peary's complete 1891-92 Smith Sound collections appears in Appendix II of VanStone's *The First Peary Collection of Polar Eskimo Material Culture* (1972:78-80): The list contains four Polar Greenland kayaks. As the collection was divided between the Columbian Museum and the Academy of Natural Sciences, it can be presumed that two of these kayaks went to Philadelphia. Was the NMAI's kayak 165227 one of these? What of the other?

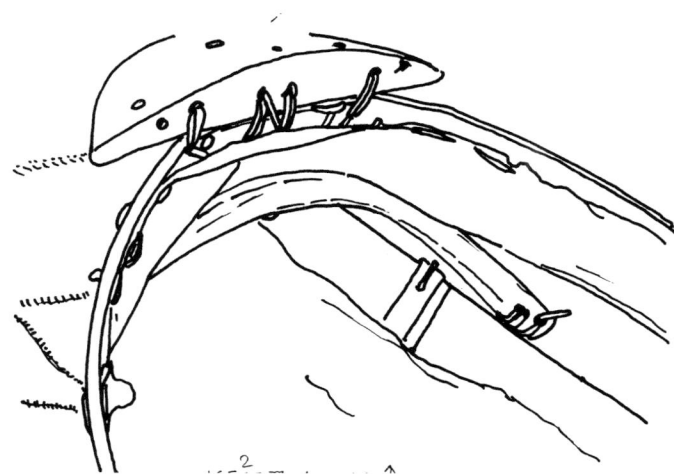

Figure 368: *Cockpit view of the National Museum of the American Indian's kayak 165227. The masik is made from a natural crook of caribou antler. A seal skin seat obscures the bottom the kayak's hull.*

The survey presented in plate 95 closely matches Chapelle's 1946 survey drawing (1964:207, fig.199). The dimensions are very close as well, and the distinct lift of the stern is captured similarly. The condition of the kayak in 2003 was fair—despite the tattered skin, the structure had has held its form well; the kayak drew up with minimal fairing/repairing required. I did arrive at a very slight dead rise to the hull, as opposed to the completely flat-bottom that Chapelle drew. In his presentation of scantlings, he suggests three deck stringers (or at least two) forward, though only one was seen in 2003. It is possible that the lap of the skin covering's seam down the fore deck may have appeared to Chapelle as if a stringer.

Figure 369: *Coaming front of the NMAI 165227. Note the center- piece and the paddle rest attached to its top edge.*

A few inches of the bow structure are exposed, due to the skin having dried, shrunk, and split back. This has revealed a few interesting elements about this kayak's bow-joinery: The actual tip of the kayak is not the gunwales' tips themselves, but is instead a block of wood extending ahead 3/4″ (19mm) into which the gunwales are set and lashed

---

[50] Five Polar kayaks ended up at the American Museum of Natural History, all being from Peary's 1895-96 expeditions. Comparison to these five kayaks is impossible, as the museum disposed of them in recent years.

(see figure 153). The keelson is lashed and pegged to the bottom of this same piece. This block extends aft between the gunwales, but how far aft is indiscernible due to the covering being in place on the rest of the kayak. The tips of the gunwales at their forward extremity are 1/2" (13mm) thick and 1" (25mm) tall, while the keelson end is 3/4" (19mm) wide and 3/8" (9mm) high.

The paddle rest assembly is detailed in figures 368 and 369, the former being viewed from inside the cockpit; the latter from ahead of the cockpit, looking aft. As can be seen, the piece is firmly lashed down to the front of the coaming and splints of wood used to tighten the lashings can be seen in the exterior-view. The paddle rest is carved from a red hardwood— possibly mahogany. A paddle is associated with this kayak, and is presented in paddle-plate 73.

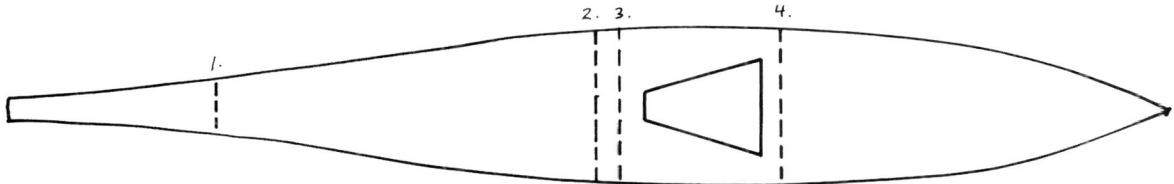

U. S. National Museum of the American Indian: Cat. no. 165227

Another interesting feature of the 165227 its *masik*: It is a natural crook of caribou antler. Its joint to the gunwales is visible in figure 368. The 165227 has a single forward deck stringer as well as a single aft deck stringer.

Chapelle makes an error in the scantlings presented with his drawing (1964:207, fig.199). He presents the ribs being spaced about 10" (25.4cm) and the floors spaced about 8" (20.3cm). In reality, the floors and ribs are aligned throughout the entire kayak, being lashed to each other at their junctions at the chines.

Howard Chapelle's drawing of the 165227 shows just a single deck line across the fore deck. While none were present when I visited, there was evidence of two lines at this vicinity as well as one at the bow and one just aft of the cockpit. It can be presumed based on other Polar Greenland kayaks that the pair of deck lines just ahead of the cockpit was fastened to each other in some manner. No evidence of a harpoon holder was present, nor was there evidence of a stern deck line.

96. Polar Greenland Kayak: Canadian Canoe Museum, Peterborough, Ontario. Catalog no. 977.179

This kayak was brought south aboard Peary's ship *Roosevelt* in 1909 from Cape York. Charles Percy is listed as the collector, and the kayak was accessioned by the Museum of the American Indian/Heye Foundation in 1934.[51] The Canadian Canoe Museum accessioned this kayak in 1977. Charles Percy served as steward aboard the *Roosevelt*, and as Peary noted, ". . . had special charge of the phonograph . . ." (1910:181).

The bow of the 977.179 is very distinctly 'clippered' or concave, and the stem itself is quite long. Like with the 160388 and 165227 above, the 977.179's *masik* is made from a natural crook of caribou

---

[51] The old MAI number was 186541; An Inuhuit paddle at the MAI retains the sequential number 186540, and while it may not be associated with this kayak, it is undoubtedly from Peary's 1909 voyage. The paddle 186540 is depicted in paddle-plate 74.

Figure 370: Three Inuhuit kayaks, ca. 1909 (Copyright: Greenland National Museum and Archive.)

antler. The deck beam ahead of the *masik* is not curved upwards to meet the descending deck stringer, but is instead lashed atop the gunwales' upper edges so as to sit higher and meet the stringer.

The lack of wood in Polar Greenland had likely only been remedied intermittently through trade or shipwreck. The Peary Relief expedition of 1892 brought many donated items for Inuhuit— Dr. Rothrock, a lecturer on botanical topics, conceived this "happy and philanthropic" idea. The expedition brought the following gifts: "... six Arctic sleds, twenty-five spears made from files ... 100 hickory spear handles ... 1000 assorted needles ... two dozen saws, many scissors

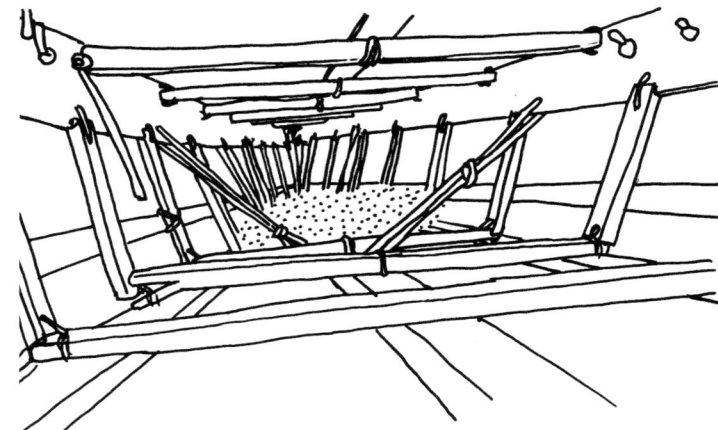

Figure 371: Unique keel-to-gunwale lashings inside the CCM 977.179 (looking forward). The 'dotted' mass in the center is the business end of a broom that somehow found its way deep into this kayak.

... hammers, braces and bits, planes, and a large quantity of cut lumber" (Keely and Davis, 1892:269-271). Not surprisingly, the 977.179 is largely made of milled lumber in lieu of driftwood: The chines and keelson all exhibit a molded bead on one face's edge, and the gunwales have a groove cut into their upper edge, as if they were once tongue-and-groove planks.

None of the deck beams or ribs appear to be mortise and tenoned into the gunwales. Instead they are firmly butted against and lashed to the gunwales. A unique tightening method is present in these joints of the 977.179: Wooden wedges have been set between the lashings and deck beams so as to tighten them. The deck beams in the 977.179 measure 1/2" (13mm) thick by 1-1/16" (27mm) wide. One of them is situated on-center at 8´1" (246.3cm) aft of the bow, and is lashed to the tops of the gunwales instead of to their upper faces. The *isserfik* measures 5/8" (16mm) thick and 3" (76mm) wide.

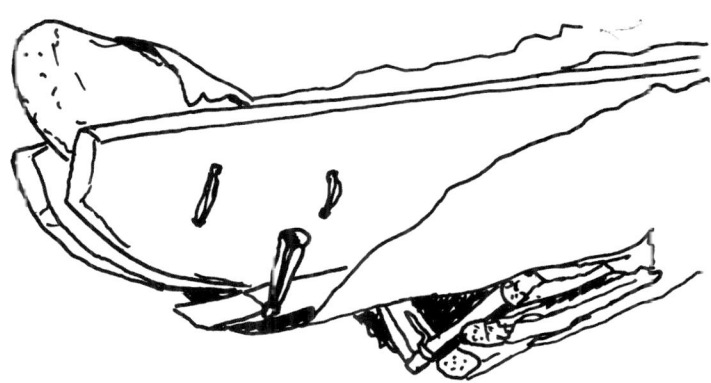

Figure 372: End joinery of the CCM 977.179, as exposed by the damaged amiq. The raised end-stub is a separate piece lashed to and between the gunwales. The keelson is also lashed to the gunwales just before their termini. The lower right depicts a collapsed rib and the fractured ends of the keelson and both chines. See figure 155 for a reconstruction of this kayak's stern assembly.

Figure 373: Two Inuhuit kayaks being used as a raft. At least five people seem to be aboard. (Photograph from Peary, 1903:41.)

A unique truss lashing is present in the hull of this kayak, both forward and aft of the cockpit: A heavy seal skin cord runs from the gunwale's lower edge directly to the keelson. The forward lashing is just ahead of where the kayaker's feet would be. Figure 371 shows the forward interior of the 977.179; the truss lashings are plain to see. Further ahead, another pair of such lashings is present, only these have pulled loose and are simply dangling from the gunwales. Aft of the cockpit, a truss lashing is situated about a foot behind the *isserfik*. The area delineated with dots turned out to be a broom of all things— perhaps stuffed inside the kayak by a surly S. S. *Roosevelt* deckhand or museum janitor.

As with many Polar Greenland kayaks, the 179 has a fairly flat stern with a short abrupt up-turned tip. The structure of this feature is exposed on the 179, due to the skin being broken open in this vicinity. The 179's stern 'bump' is a separate piece lashed in-between the thin gunwale strakes' ends. The keelson is lashed to the bottom edges of the gunwales, and the gunwales run to the very stern; this can be seen in figure 155.

Unlike most Polar Greenland kayak in this study, the 977.179 has a secondary chine. This chine becomes evident through the *amiq* at around 2′ 6″ (76.2cm) from the bow, and ends at 9′ 3″ (281.9cm) and 10' (304.8cm) on the right and left sides respectively. It runs almost in the center of the courses of the main chine and the gunwales, though is slightly favored lower towards the main chine.

The cockpit of the 179 is very damaged, the front left quarter of the coaming is missing, and the other side has straightened out considerably. The scale drawing shows the cockpit as conjecturally restored. The coaming's sides are 3/8″ (9mm) thick by 2-1/2″ (63mm) high in the middle. The back is 5/8″ (16mm) thick and 2-3/4″ (70mm) high; the front piece is 2″ (51mm) high. A 9″ (22.8cm) long antler strip is wrapped around the front of the coaming halfway up its face to re-enforce the joint; the strip is 3/4″ (19mm) wide, and is fastened with nails. The *amiq* is lashed to the coaming via the 'over-the-top' method— apparently not a common method in Polar Greenland.

A seat-board is present in the 179's cockpit: It is a single plank spanning from chine to chine and is centered between the forward pair of ribs in the cockpit. This plank is 3/8″ thick by 3-3/8″ wide (9mm x 8.5cm) and is lashed to the chines.

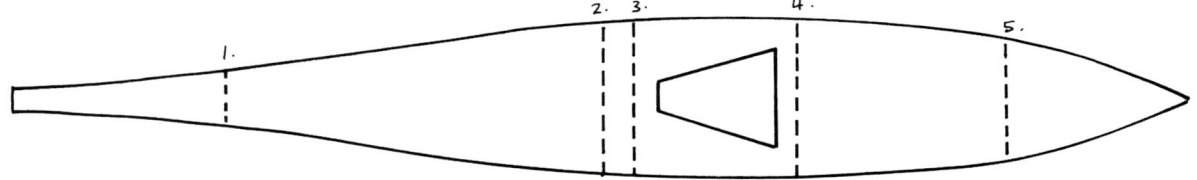

Canadian Canoe Museum, Peterborough: Cat. no. 977.179

No deck lines were present on the CCM 179, but evidence of their positions was present; the arrangement is very consistent with the other Polar Greenland kayaks in this study. The paddle-rest mounted atop the coaming's front is made of oak. It has an overhanging aft-edge, and its lashings are tightened via thin wooden wedges, much as with the rib-to-gunwale lashings.

97. Polar Greenland Kayak from 1909:
The Greenland National Museum, Nuuk, Greenland.
Catalog no. KNK 1007

Dr. Thomas Thomsen of the Danish National Museum collected this kayak in 1909. It was transferred from the DNM's collection in 1990 to the collection of the Greenland National Museum. (The DNM's original catalog number for the KNK 1007 was L.4348.) The KNK 1007's paddle is depicted in paddle-plate 76.

The KNK 1007 perhaps shows a bit of development towards the 'southernized' form of Polar Greenland kayaks: It is markedly shallower and doesn't have the dramatic depth change along its hull that other type XI kayaks exhibit. There still are classic type XI features present in the 1007, notably its Swede-form sheer, its bow and stern profiles, and numerous aspects of its construction such as the extensive use of lashings.

The ribs in the KNK 1007 are mortised into the gunwales' lower edges. Some of these joints are lashed while others are pegged— they are fastened quite randomly, and in fact some such joints are not fastened at all. The rib-to-floor joints are all lashed with several turns of seal skin line. The chines are attached at this juncture using the same lashing material.

Some of the scantlings not shown on the scale drawing are as follows: The *isserfik* is 5/8" (16mm) thick by 2-3/8" (60mm) wide; the deck stringers are 3/4" (19mm) thick by 1-1/8" (28mm) wide— this kayak has a single deck stringer on the fore and aft deck. The KNK 1007's *masik* is fashioned from two straight sticks lashed together in the middle (see figures 376 and 150 left); each stick measures 3/4" (19mm) thick by 1-1/8" (28mm) wide.

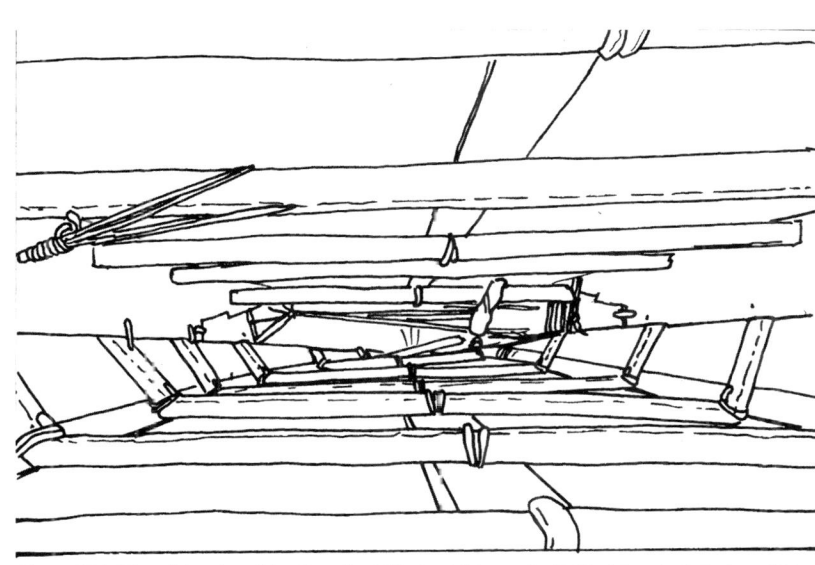

Figure 374: The aft interior of the Greenland National Museum's 1007. Note the lashed scarf joints on each gunwale. Some ribs are lashed to the gunwales while others are nailed.

All of the KNK 1007's deck lines are present except for the stern line, which was evidenced. The bow deck line is very slack; it is likely that the stern line had been slack as well. The pair of deck lines on the fore deck are not transverse— instead they are loops that enter and exit the same gunwale. These loops are connected to each other with numerous passes of 1/8" (3mm) wide seal skin line. The 1007 has just one deck fitting: a large chunk of whalebone, crudely fashioned into a wedge-shape that serves as a harpoon rest. Behind the cockpit is a single deck line, with a bit of slack in it.

The KNK 1007 was not the first Polar Greenland kayak I replicated: I had made a replica of the NMNH 160388 (plate 94) from Howard Chapelle's drawing in *The Bark Canoes and Skinboats of North America* (1964:210, figure 205). As discussed in my presentation of the kayak 160388, the framing had been mis-drawn by Chapelle, and so it has turned out that I framed that replica incorrectly.

The pieced-frames of Polar Greenland kayaks seemed to be a nice alternative to steam-bending, but in actuality it is extremely labor-intensive measuring and cutting each little piece and ensuring the miters are correct— and then there's lashing all these little pieces together. This technique is of course indispensable if one is unable to secure good bending wood.

While the chines in the KNK 1007 are positioned aside of the rib-to-floor joint (instead of below it), in retrospect it is my opinion that they may have slipped into this position. At the time I had built a replica of the 1007 (2001), I had only seen and surveyed one other Polar Greenland kayak— the KNK 528 (plate 100); this latter kayak had its chines below the rib-to-floor joint. Since then, every pieced-frame Polar kayak I've

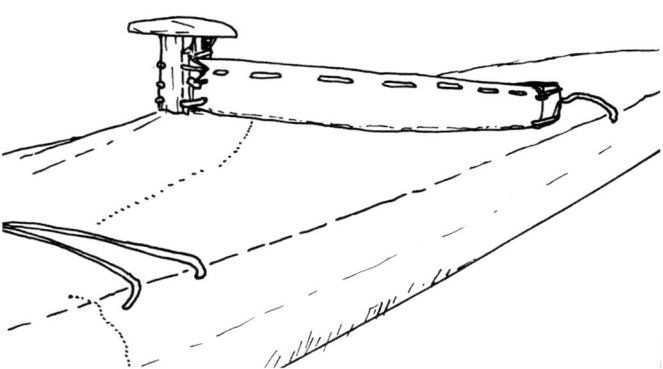

Figure 375: Cockpit of the 1007. Note how the paddle rest is elevated well above the coaming's rim.

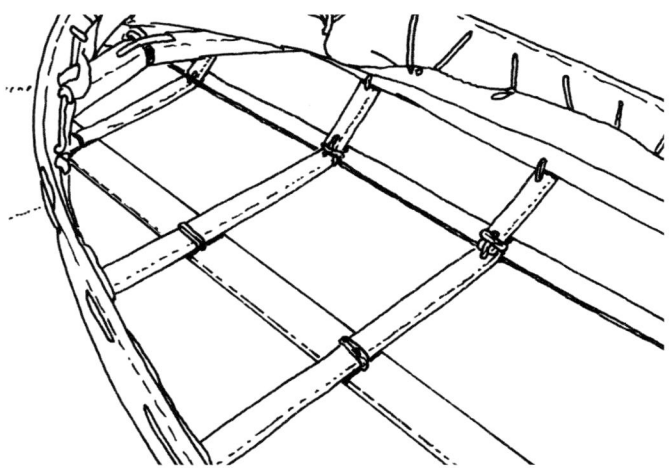

Figure 376: Cockpit view of the KNK 1007, showing the lashed joinery, including the lashing holding the two masik *pieces together.*

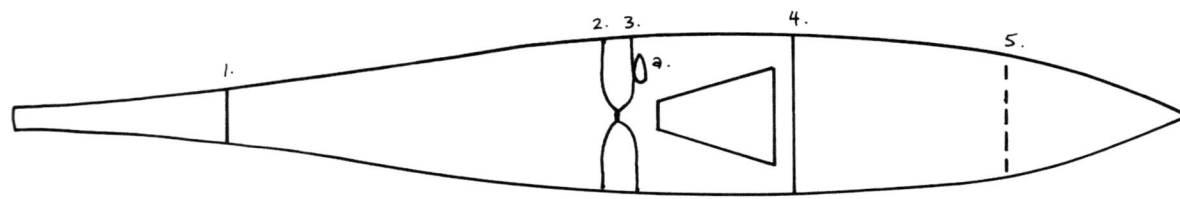

Greenland National Museum: Cat. no. 1007

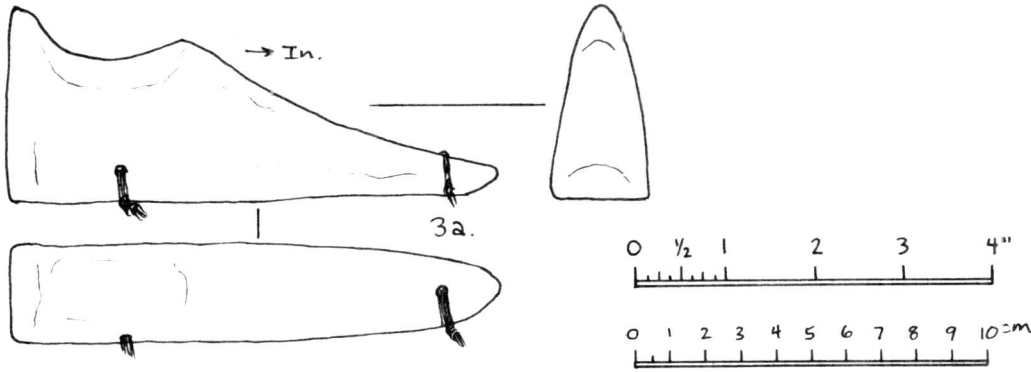

seen has had the chines below this joint. In short, the KNK 1007 may be the second Polar Greenland kayak replica I have built incorrectly.

Despite the structural glitch, the KNK 1007 replica is true to the lines in the scale drawing. As fully expected, the 1007 replica handles very similarly to the several East Canadian kayaks I've replicated—it pivots very markedly right at the forefoot of the bow, the stern skipping freely over the water on account of having little grip. Unlike the East Canadian relatives of this kayak, the 1007 is very small and light, and easier to correct when it starts to swerve.

Figure 377: Completed frame of the KNK 1007 replica. (Photograph by author.)

Figure 378: The replica of the KNK 1007 being paddled by the author, Portland, Oregon, 2006. (Photograph by Kathy Tucker.)

Figure 379: The KNK 1007 replica on the Willamette River, Portland, Oregon, 2006. (Photograph by Kathy Tucker.)

The KNK 1007 replica is very stable, giving it a very easy and comfortable ride on flat water, but a bit more jerky in rougher water. Its ultimate seaworthiness seems to be limited by its coaming's inability to accommodate a spray skirt. Otherwise I think it would be a capable vessel in seas, although less desirable than others.

98. Polar Greenland Kayak: Canadian Canoe Museum, Peterborough, Ontario. Catalog no. 977. 181

This Polar Greenland kayak was formerly in the collection of the National Museum of the American Indian, Heye Foundation. The collector is listed as W. C. Orchard, but no date is provided. The old MAI number was 8/272, as had been painted on the kayak. The Canadian Canoe Museum accessioned this kayak in 1977.

Bent frame Polar Greenland kayaks seem to be the exception in the first half of the 20th century, and therefore this example stands out as a distinct anomaly. Likewise, its coaming is bent as well— not in a hoop like more southerly Greenland kayaks, but in a horseshoe-shape with a straight back piece. Such coaming shapes are fairly common in the Eastern Canadian Arctic, but the paddle-rest— unique to Polar Greenland— is present.

Because of the presence of its bent ribs, the 977.181 could be considered a 'transitional' form Polar Greenland kayak (type XII) but its placement here is based on considerations of hull-form and other aspects of construction. For example, the deep clipper bow and shallow abrupt stern are distinctly 'old-form,' as is the extensive use of lashings. This kayak is a fascinating glimpse of what older Polar Greenland kayaks might have looked like if the Inuhuit had a consistent supply of quality bendable rib stock.

The fore deck of the 977.181 is collapsed, but the two pieces of wood forming the *masik* were intact, and their measurements suggest a deck height of about 2-1/2" (6.3cm), which is quite consistent with other Polar Greenland kayaks (the fore deck has been restored in the scale drawing). The *masik* pieces measured 1" (25mm) thick by 1-1/8" (28mm) wide.

Deck beams are not tenoned into or lashed to the gunwales. Instead they butted against the gunwale and are nailed from the gunwale's outside face into the deck beam's ends. Most of the 977.181's deck beams measure 3/4" by 1" (19 x 25mm) and are set on-edge instead of flat. The *isserfik* is 1/2" (13mm) thick and 3-3/4" (9.5cm) and is positioned flat; 3" (76mm) behind it is a deck beam on-edge that measures 1-1/4" (32mm) high by 1" (25mm) wide.

This kayak's ribs are tenoned into the gunwales, and are fastened with metal nails. The keelson and chines are all lashed to the ribs. The fore deck stringer measures 1/2" (13mm) thick and 1-1/16" (27mm) wide; an aft deck stringer is not present. The 977.181's coaming has a bent front fashioned of two pieces of wood scarfed together beneath the paddle rest. These pieces measure 1/2" (13mm) thick by 2" (51mm) high. The coaming's back piece is the same size, and has a slight curve to it. The *aniq* is lashed to the coaming with an intermittent lacing.

The length-overall of the 977.181 measured out at 18' 5-3/4" (563.2cm), but is depicted in the scale drawing as being 18' 3" (556.2cm) long. The reason for my shortening this kayak in the drawing was the fact that the broken *amiq* at the bow tip exposed the tip of the kayak's frame to be 2-3/4" (6.9cm) back. The skin migrated forward as it cycled humidity and shrunk, leaving a considerable split and gap in the *amiq* around 6' (182.8cm) from the bow. The profile of the bow is depicted as surveyed, though one could reason that the 'clipper' effect may be exaggerated somewhat due to the shrinking skin.

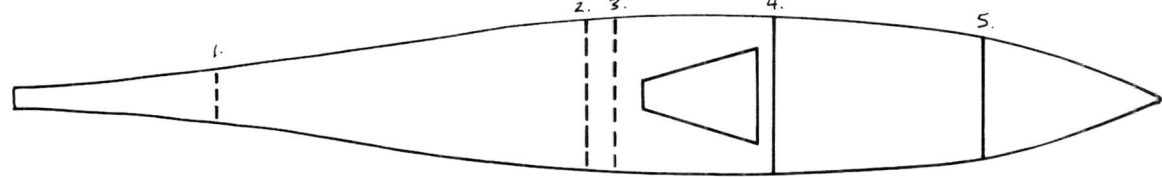

Canadian Canoe Museum, Peterborough: Cat. no. 977.181

Only the aft deck and stern line of the 977.181 were intact, but a bow deck line and a pair of fore deck lines were evidenced; their positions are indicated on the scale drawing.

TYPE XII.

Type XII kayaks are also from Polar Greenland, only these types are distinguished from the old-form Polar Greenland kayaks (type XI) in that they exhibit a distinct move away from the Canadian kayak elements typical to type XI kayaks. These changes are subtle, especially as the unique pieced-frames, flat bottom, and trapezoidal coamings are still present. The changes that are apparent are the move away from Swede-form hulls, a more constant depth-to-sheer along its length, and the adaptation of stern shapes more in fashion further south along the Greenland coast. More subtle changes include slight migration forward of these kayak's coamings and the narrower hulls when compared to type XI kayaks; see Appendix A, column 7 for types XI and XII.

As mentioned, type XII kayaks' framing is still pieced together, but in the three examples presented here, the fasteners are largely metal nails instead of lashings. Also, the ribs of these kayaks are all mortised into their gunwales' lower edges.

The instigator of the change of kayak form in Polar Greenland is fairly well documented. The Danish Ethnologist H. P. Steensby writes:

> ... *This form of kayak is only in a small degree suited for use on the sea. And the Polar Eskimos for this reason took great interest in the West Greenland kayaks, which the Expedition [the 1909 Mission Station expedition] had brought with it, and a West Greenland kayak which Knud Rasmussen had taken up on an earlier occasion [1903-04 Literary Expedition] had even produced an effect, which could be traced in some of the kayaks at Umanark [Uummannaq, Polar Greenland] (1910:360).*

Rolf Gilberg writes "After 1910, features of the West Greenlandic kayak came gradually to the Polar Eskimo so that by the 1930s the construction of the Polar Eskimo kayak generally corresponded to that of West Greenland ..."(1984:582). One lingering exception is the use of pieced-together ribs persisting through at least the mid 1930s (Holtved, 1967:75).

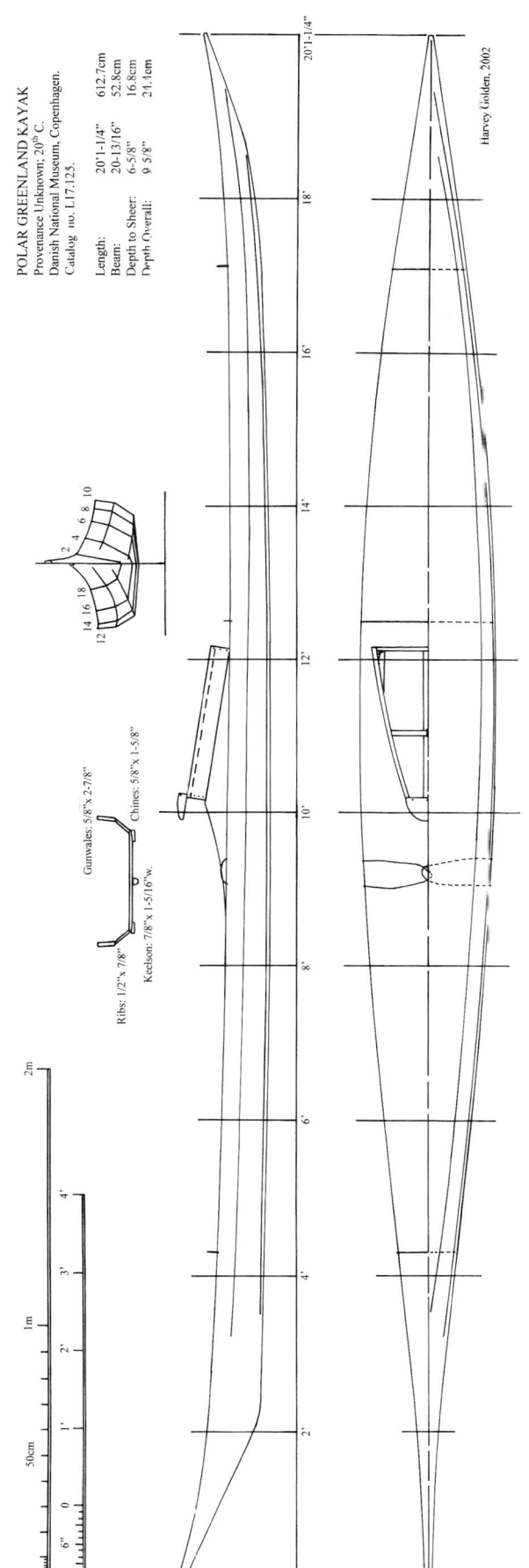

99. Danish National Museum catalog no. L.17.125

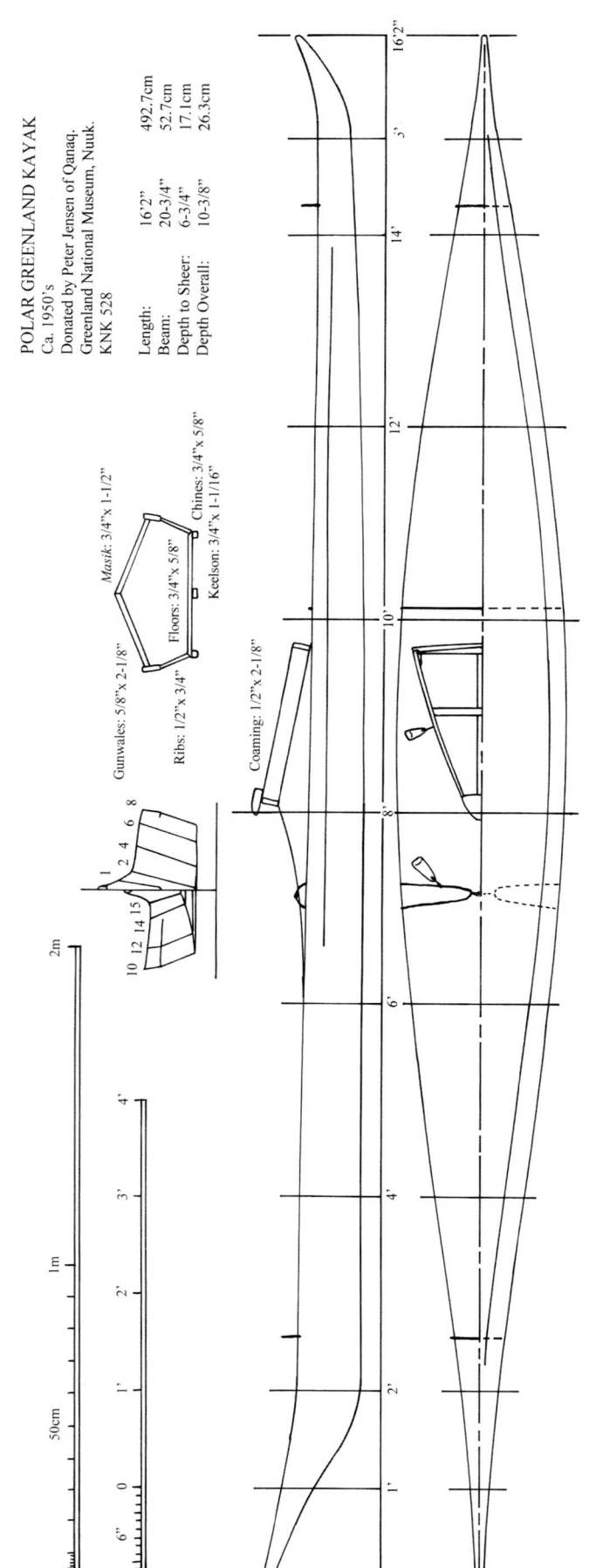

100. Greenland National Museum catalog no. KNK 528

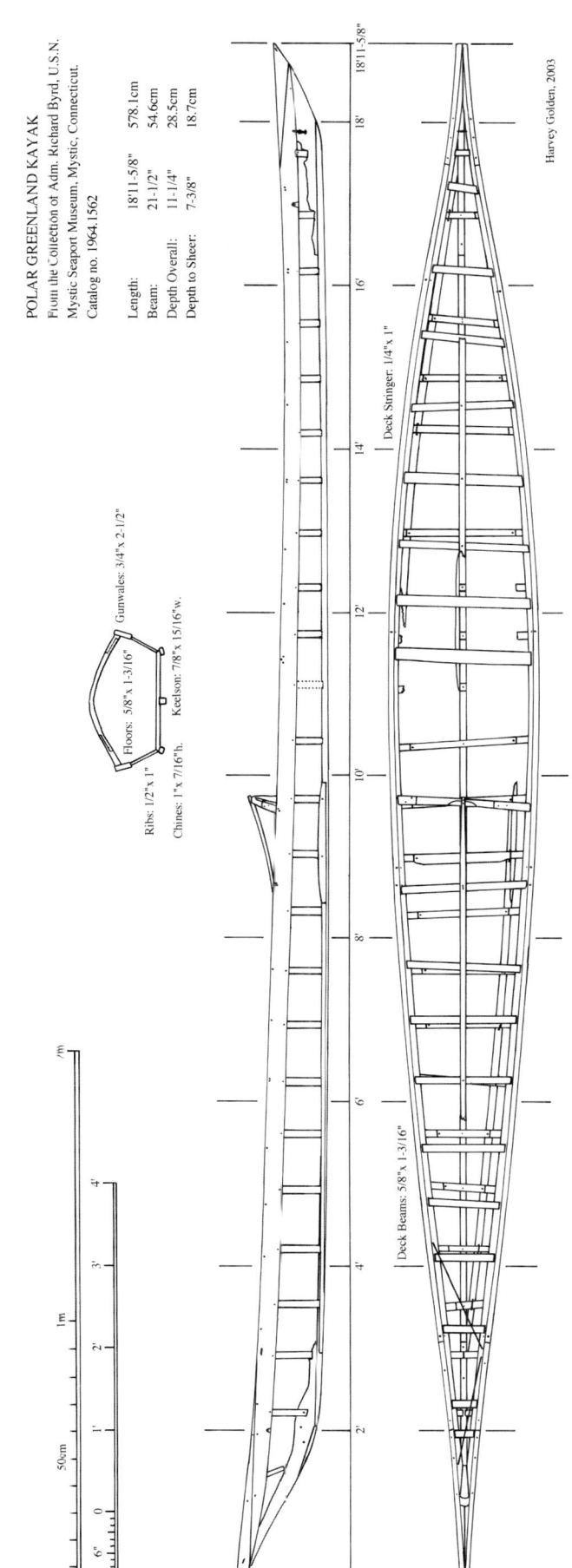

101a. Mystic Seaport Museum catalog no. 1964.1562

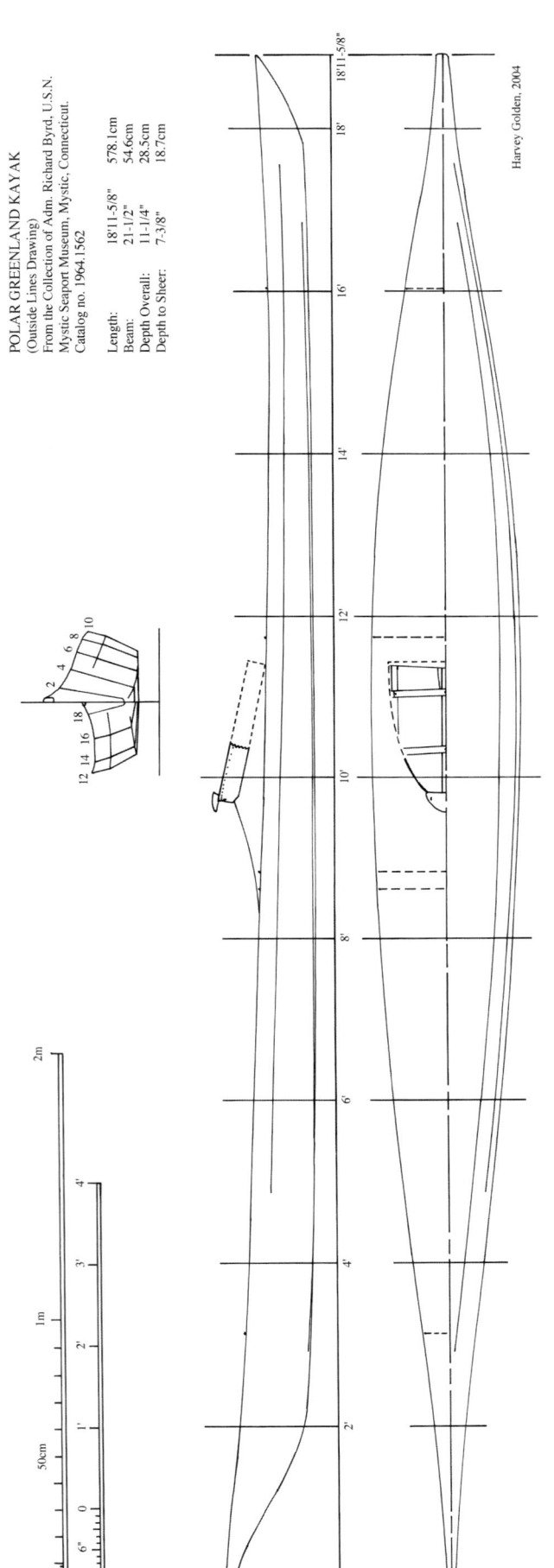

101b. Mystic Seaport Museum catalog no. 1964.1562 (Hull Lines)

99. Polar Greenland Kayak: Danish National Museum, Copenhagen. Catalog no. L.17.125.

Unfortunately, the L.17.125 has no records of collection including any dates associated with it. Based on limited descriptions of changes among the kayak types of contact-period Polar Greenlanders, one could infer that this kayak is from between 1910 and the 1930s.

The L.17.125 is by all appearances a 'super' Polar kayak— its great length, narrow hull, and fine lines are very striking. The cross-sections resemble West Greenland kayaks such as the KNK 2237 (plate 66), and the NMF 5023 (plate 63). The L.17.125's fairly constant depth between its stems and shape of the hull in plan-view reveal its transitionality— its move away from the older forms imported from Baffin Island in favor of West Greenland forms.

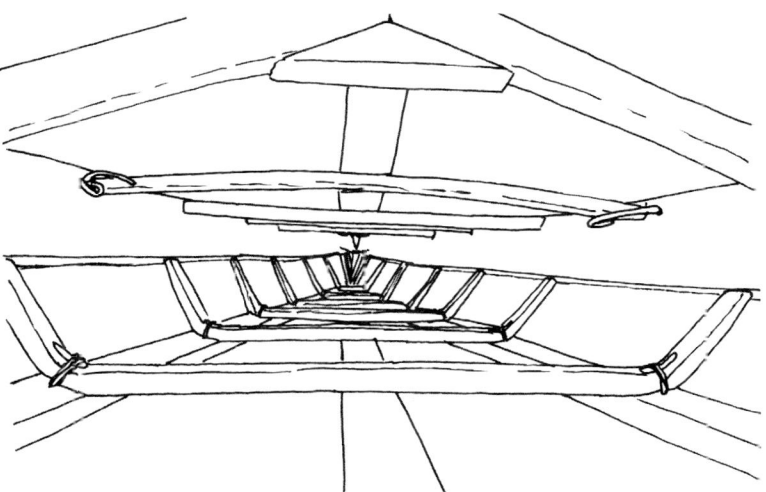

Figure 380: Forward interior view of the L.17.125. Note the triangular block at the masik joint. Its rib/floor joints are lashed together with seal skin line, and the chines are lashed to this juncture as well. The keelson is not lashed to the floors, and is instead nailed. The deck beams are butted against the gunwales and are likely nailed in place from the outside. Ribs are mortised into the gunwales, but fasteners are not evident.

While there is a single deck stringer forward, this is the only deck stringer in this kayak, and it measures 3/8" (9mm) thick by 1-1/2" (38mm) wide. The *masik* is pieced together as in figure 150 left, only with a triangular block of wood fastened beneath the joint in order to reinforce it (this reinforcement piece is visible in figure 380). The *masik* pieces measure 1" (25mm) thick by 1-1/2" (38mm) wide. The *isserfik* measures 3/4" (19mm) thick by 2" (50mm) wide. Clamping ties are present in each end of the 17.125.

The coaming of the L.17.125 is made of four pieces of wood nailed together. Each piece is 7/16" (11mm) thick by 3" (7.6cm) high. The wooden paddle rest overhangs the fore deck by 3-3/8" (8.5cm).

The L.17.125 has no deck-fittings, though its lines are similarly rigged as those on the KNK 1207. The pair of deck lines ahead of the cockpit are not transverse lines, but are instead loops that pass through each other.

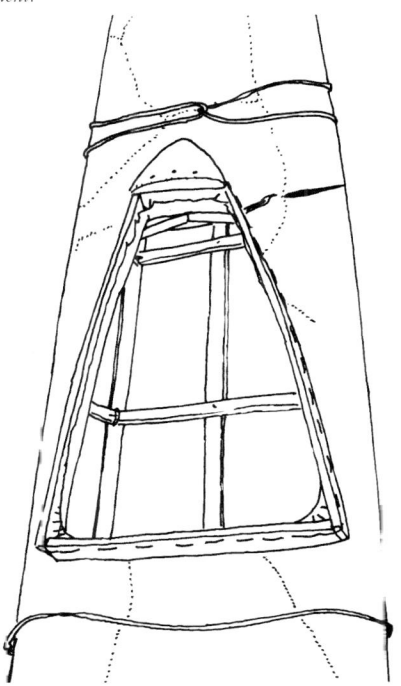

Figure 381: Cockpit view of the L.17.125.

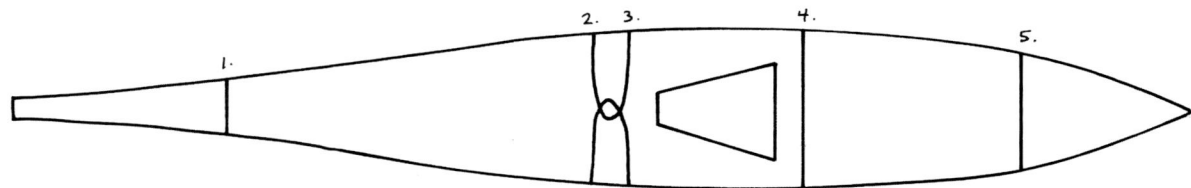

Danish National Museum, Cat. no. L.17.125

100. Polar Greenland Kayak: Greenland National Museum, Nuuk. Catalog no. KNK 528.

The name Peter Jensen of Qaanaaq is associated with this kayak— he may be the builder and/or the donor; the accession card does not specify. The card does list it as dating from the 1950s. The KNK 528's form is definitely that of a transitional Inuhuit kayak, though it must have been a bit of a hold-over as the transitional kayaks described by Holtved in the 1930s seem to have been much more West Greenlandic than this example, having round coamings (1967:74-77). The 528's appearance and condition suggests no evidence of ever having been used.

Its 'transitionality' is not clear at first due to the triangular cockpit, pieced frames, and paddle-rest, however upon seeing the drawn-up lines, the departure from distinct Swede-form is evident, and the ends are more West Greenlandic than the old-form type XI kayaks— especially the stern.

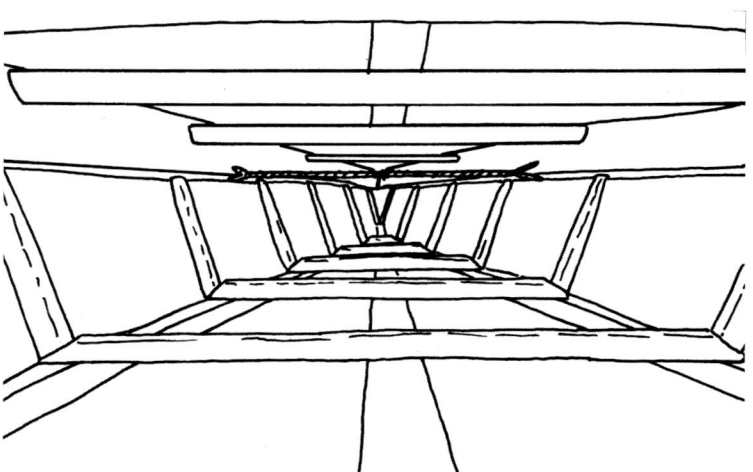

Figure 382: Forward interior of the Greenland National Museum's kayak 528. The construction is mostly secured with nails, although a clamping tie between the gunwales can be seen in this view.

The construction of the KNK 528 is almost entirely nailed. The ribs are nailed to the floors, and at this junction, the chines are also nailed in place. The keelson is apparently nailed to the floors as well, though the lack of nail heads suggests it was done from the outside of the frame. Deck beams are not tenoned into the gunwales, and are instead butted against the gunwales and nailed in place. The only gunwale lashings evident in this kayak are a clamp tie at the stern and another in the forward hull (figure 382), about half way to the bow. The 528 has a single forward deck stringer (1/4" thick by 1" wide [6 x 25mm]), but none aft; this is the same configuration as in the L.17.125 (plate 99).

Figure 383: A cockpit view of the 528. Note the pieced-together masik, *and the lashings attaching the paddle rest to the coaming's front piece.*

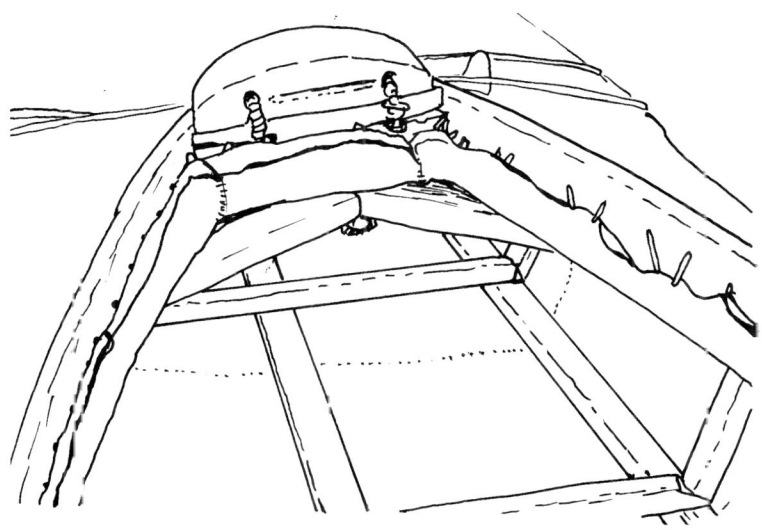

The KNK 528 is fitted with two harpoon holders: one anchored off the coaming, and the other off the deck-line just ahead of the cockpit— both on the same side. The fore and aft-most deck lines are very slack. A paddle is associated with the 528 and is depicted in paddle plate 77.

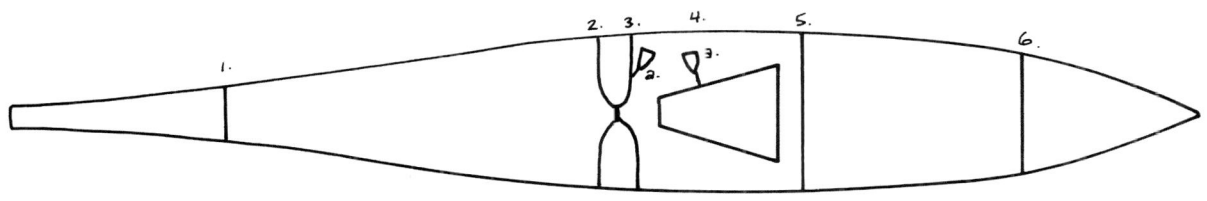

Greenland National Museum: Cat. no. 528

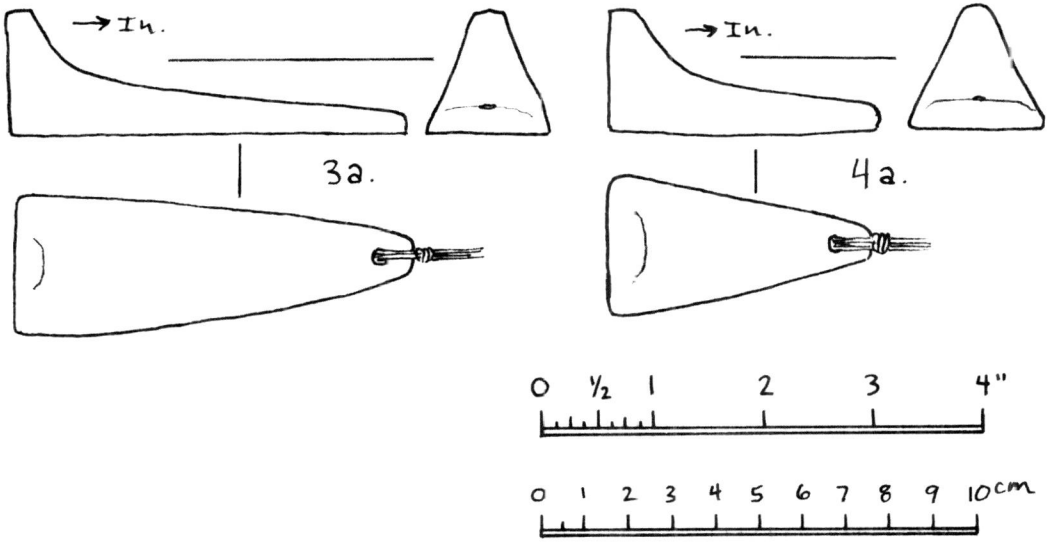

101. Polar Greenland Kayak: Mystic Seaport Museum, Mystic, Connecticut.
Catalog no. 1964.1562

Nothing is known of this kayak beyond that it once belonged to Admiral Richard Byrd (Bray, 1986:205). This was reconfirmed during my visit by Mystic Seaport Museum documentation office supervisor Mark Starr, who added that it had belonged to a sports club immediately before transfer to Mystic. (Starr has also made a survey of the 1964.1562, and it appears in his book *Building a Greenland* Kayak [2002:106-7].)

The 1964.1562 is a kayak frame, and despite its missing a few segments of chines and ribs, is in otherwise intact condition. This kayak may well be the only Polar Greenland kayak skeleton in a museum collection. The American Museum of Natural History had one that was collected by Peary in the 1890s (it is illustrated in Kroeber, 1900:273, fig.3), but this was disposed of by the museum in the 1980s.

The chines are attached to the ribs using two different methods: Some of these joints are secured with wooden pegs set through the floor-piece of the rib into the chine below, as in figure 149 right. Other chine-to-rib joints are secured with lashings set through the chines and up and around the ribs, as in figure 146. In some instances both methods appear on the same rib— one method on the left and the other on the right, for example. Most of the rib-to-gunwale joints are metal-nailed in place, the ribs being tenoned into the gunwales' lower edges. All of the rib-to-keelson joints are metal-nailed.

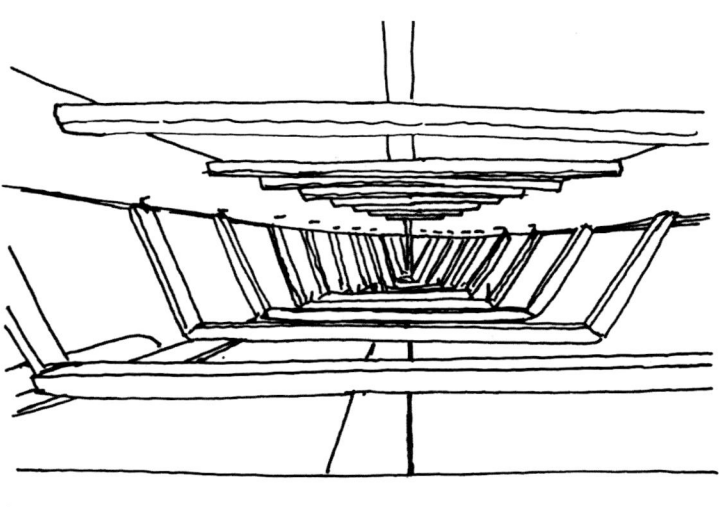

Figure 384: Forward interior view of the Mystic Seaport Museum's kayak 1964.1562. The right chine is missing.

The foremost three ribs in this kayak do not have floor pieces, and are simply just upright sticks attached to the keelson; the very first one is just one piece of wood— essentially a stanchion. It has slipped back at the keelson, never having been fastened in place at the bottom. The next rib is a pair of sticks nailed to the sides of the keelson end, set into slight grooves so as not to protrude into the *amiq*. The third rib is set into a mortise carved into the top edge of the keelson end.

This is the only type XI or XII Polar Greenland kayak in this study to have a curved wooden *masik*, the others either being pieced of straight sticks or made from natural crooks of caribou antler. The *masik* in the 1964.1562 is however made from three pieces of wood— essentially a curved middle-piece with added extensions on each end with a step-scarf, and then metal-nailed to fasten the joint. A view of this

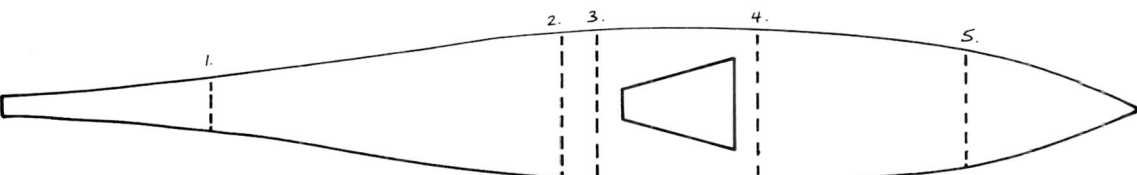

Mystic Seaport Museum: Cat. no. 1964.1562

built-up *masik* is present in the scale drawing of the kayak, particularly in the scantlings cross-section. The *masik* measures 5/8″ (16mm) thick and 1″ (25mm) wide in the middle; at the ends, it is 3/4″ (19mm) thick and 1-1/4″ (32mm) wide.

Just a fragment of 1964.1562's coaming exists: It measures 1/4″ (6mm) thick and 2-5/8″ (66mm) high. This piece is the front portion, and it has the typical Polar Greenland paddle rest fitted to its top front edge. In all likelihood, the coaming probably had a straight back piece, consistent with other Polar Greenland kayaks. The paddle associated with this kayak is depicted in paddle-plate 78.

Deck line placement is evidenced by holes drilled on the gunwales' top edges. Having the deck lines run through this edge is uncommon among Polar Greenland kayaks, most being set through the face of the gunwales.

TYPE XIII.

Type XIII kayaks are Polar Greenland kayaks from the mid-20th century to the present. They are distinguished from type XII Polar kayaks in that they have made a nearly complete assimilation into the forms seen further south along the West Coast of Greenland. Gone are the pieced frames, square-ish cockpits, flat bottoms, and the distinct coaming-mounted paddle rests.

As mentioned before, only one type XIII kayak is presented in this study. It comes by generous courtesy of Eugene Arima who surveyed the kayak in the Royal Ontario Museum, Toronto. This type of kayak is still being used today and they play the key role in the annual narwhal hunt each summer in Polar Greenland.

That there are so few of these kayaks in museums may be explained by the isolation of Polar Greenland as well as the fact that museums may see these modern kayaks as degenerate, or less than authentic on account of the kayaks being made from modern materials— particularly the *amiq*, which may be painted canvas or even plastic.

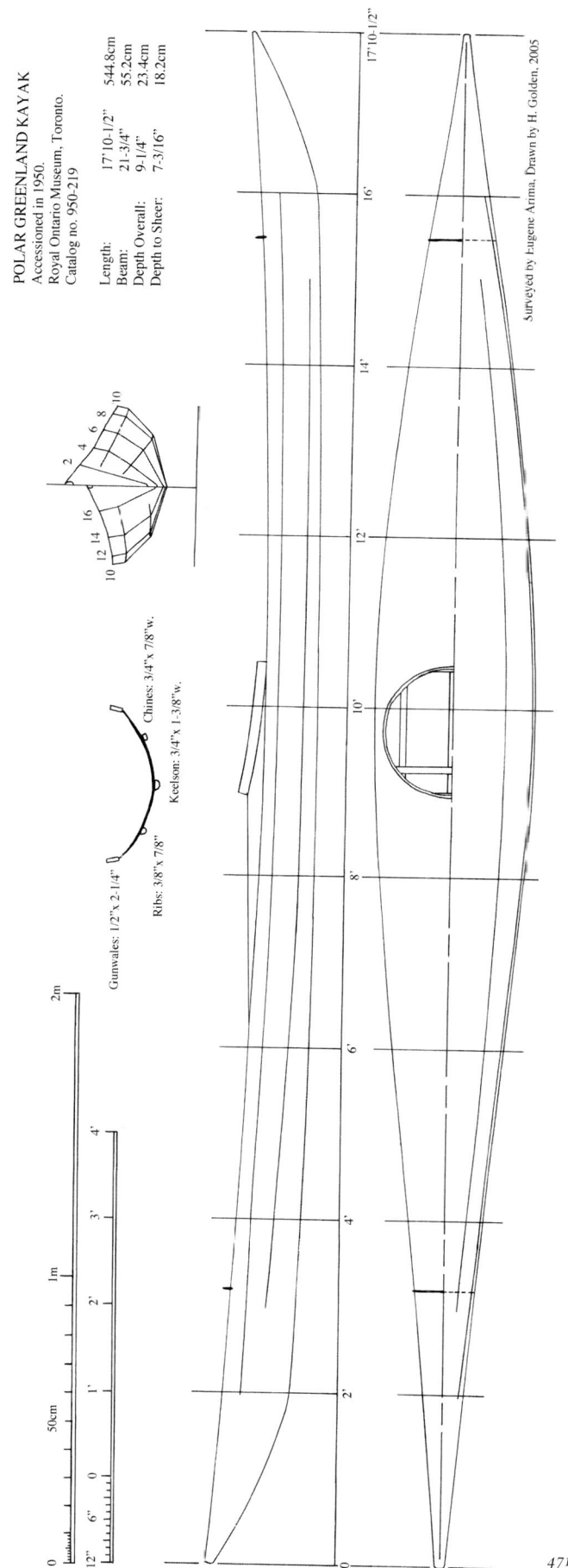

102. Royal Ontario Museum, Toronto
catalog no. 950-219

102. Polar Greenland Kayak: Royal Ontario Museum, Toronto. Catalog no. 950-219

Eugene Arima surveyed this kayak and generously allowed me to reproduce the results here; I re-inked the drawing in order to maintain a consistency among the scale drawings in this study. The Royal Ontario Museum in Toronto accessioned the kayak in 1950.

The stems on the 950-219 are fairly short and slightly concave and their transition to the keel is distinct. Neither stem is peaked very high, and they have nearly identical profiles. This kayak's sheer

Figure 385: Rowboat and kayaks at Uummannaq, Polar Greenland, 1936. Note how the kayaks have assimilated in form with more southerly Greenland kayaks. In 1936, these kayaks still may have made use of pieced-together ribs. (Photograph by Jette Bang/ Arktisk Institut gjb01217b.)

has a subtle consistent curve to it, unlike transitional Polar Greenland kayaks (type XII), whose sheer is for the most part flat, with distinct rises a the ends.

Like earlier Polar Greenland kayaks, the gunwales of the 950-219 are very plumb, despite the steep angle of the ribs. The kayak is hard-chined, but the angles between the side and bottom of the hull are very obtuse, giving the kayak a sort of broad dish-shape. The chines are peaked fairly high forward, but remain low aft, being parallel to the keelson.

Proportionally, the 950-219's cockpit is farther forward than any of the older Polar Greenland kayaks, but with its center at 54.4% of the kayak's length, it is further aft than the average of any non-Polar kayak type. Numerous type VI kayaks however do have their cockpits further aft than 54.4% of length but still, the average for type VI is only 53.5% (see Appendix A, column 7).

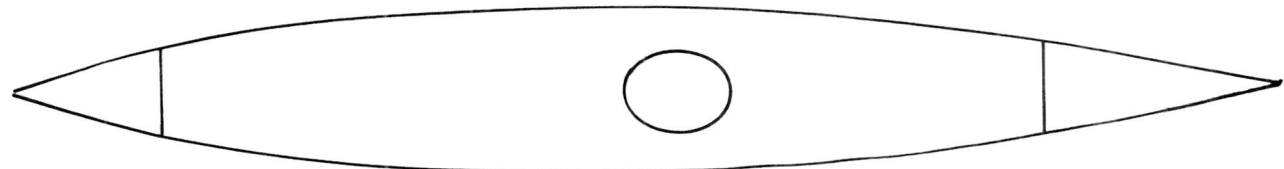

Royal Ontario Museum: Cat. no. 950-219

(Amidship deck lines were not shown on the original drawing.)

MIXED TYPES:

This category of Greenland kayak types is reserved for examples that exhibit numerous features usually not associated with one another within the same kayak; these features may be a combination of form and constructional solutions. Mixed kayaks are distinguishable from types in transition in that their features are incongruous or inconsistent with previously noted developments and changes. For both of the kayaks I've placed in this category, there are fairly clear reasons as to their being mixed in form and construct.

The first of the two kayaks classified as mixed was built in Nuuk, West Greenland in 1966-67. A number of people are known to have put this kayak together. While I do not know this for a fact, I strongly believe there was a considerable East Greenlandic influence in its form and construction. The kayak is a distinct mixture of West and East Greenland kayak building techniques as well as form— a very unique result.

One man built the second kayak in this category— one who is known to have traveled extensively, living at various times on the East coast and all over the West Coast of Greenland. As could be expected, particularly during an era where kayak use was on the decline in much of Greenland, his kayak exhibits numerous regional elements.

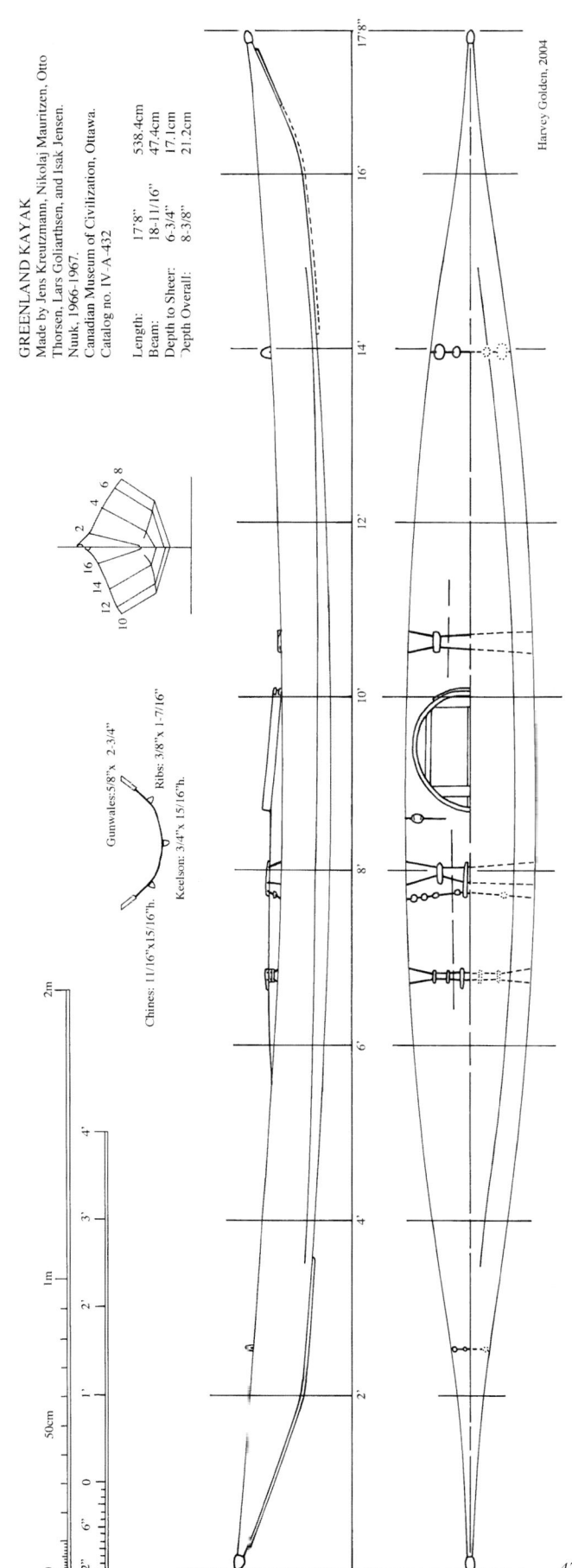

103. Canadian Museum, of Civilization catalog no. IV-A-432

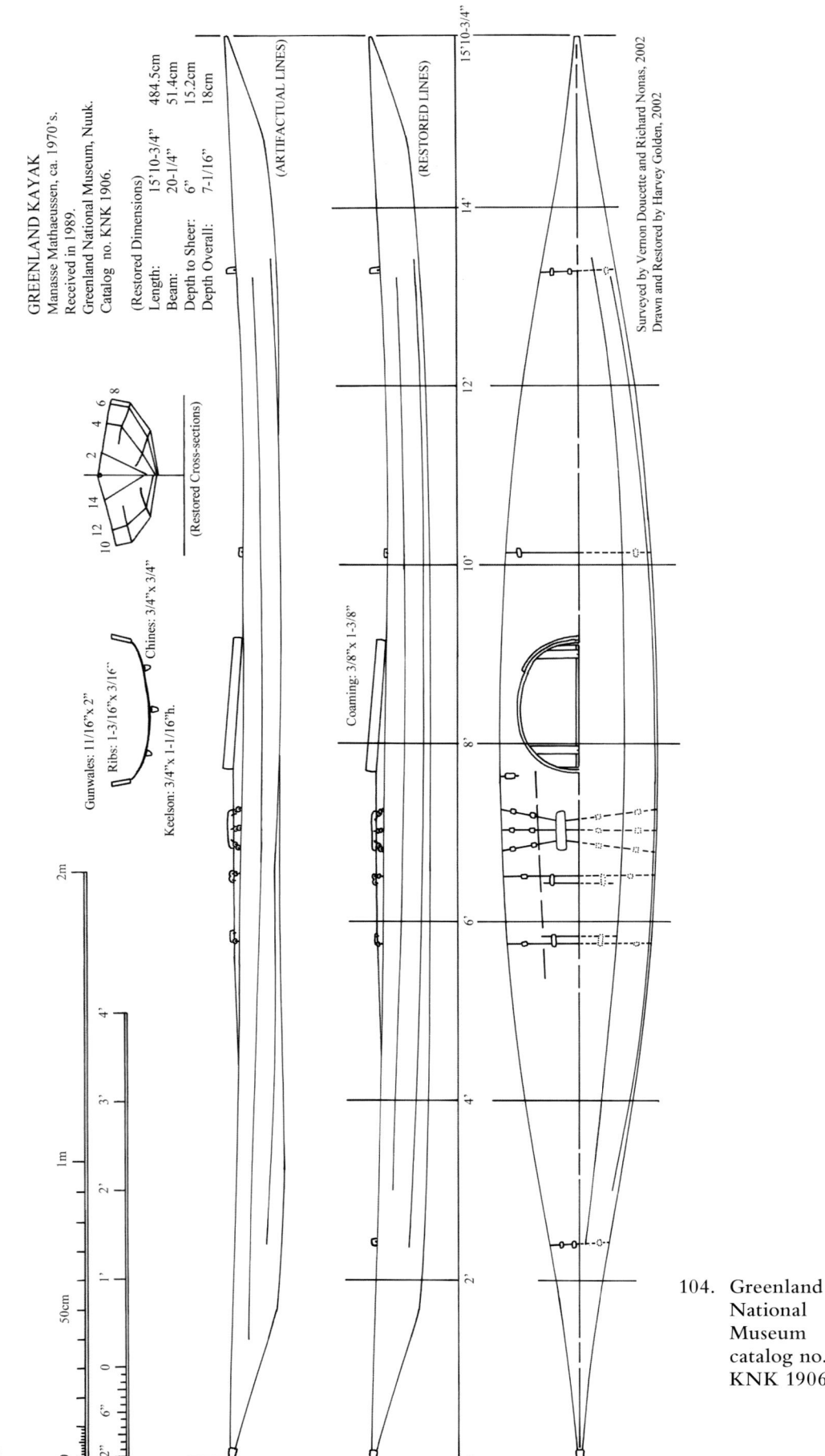

104. Greenland National Museum catalog no. KNK 1906

103. Greenland Kayak: Canadian Museum of Civilization, Ottawa. Catalog no. IV-A-432.

The IV-A-432 was made in Nuuk, West Greenland for the Montreal World Exposition of 1967. The collector is listed as the "Greenlandic Association for Folk Art and Craft;" they were more likely the donors. This kayak was received by the CMC in January 1968

The names of the builders are fortunately provided on the accession card: Jens Kreutzmann, Nikolaj Mauritzen, Otto Thorsen, Lars Goliathsen, and Isak Jessen. (Jens Kreutzmann and Lars Goliathsen [without the 'r'] appear in H. C. Petersen's name index, and both men are from Kangaamiut, West Greenland [1986:63, 129]). No women's names appear on the list, but the *amiq* was most certainly sewn by women.

Despite having been built in Nuuk by some people known to be from West Greenland, the IV-A-432 also seems to have had a strong influence rooted in the East Greenland kayak building tradition. Some of the distinct East Greenlandic elements on the 432 are its deck beams all having been fastened obliquely with larger diameter pegs, its extremely flared gunwales, and its *masik* having been set into the gunwales just as the other deck beams. Also, the *masik* has a carved handgrip of the East Greenland form, and the forward deck stringers are parallel to the sheer (when viewed from the side), thus leaving a 'bump' at their forward extremity.

Form-wise, the 432 maintains a very consistent hull depth between the stems, and has fairly symmetrical stem profiles— again fairly typical East Greenlandic features, although they lack the concave or clipper profile typical in East Greenland. The considerable deadrise is what could be expected in a kayak from Nuuk, although the chines terminate very low both fore and aft— common among East Greenland kayaks.

Unlike any East Greenland kayaks in this study, the bottom frame of the 432 is lashed. The lashing pattern seems at first glance to be of a fairly common West Greenland pattern, but upon closer examination, the lashings at each rib-longitudinal joint pass through two holes in the longitudinals instead of the usual one. No other kayak in this study is lashed like this. It appears as if someone who was familiar with the concept of lashing but not the specific 'traditional/local' method lashed the keelson and chines to the ribs.

It is somewhat ironic that this kayak, being the mixed form that it is, has become such a widely known example of a *West* Greenland kayak. Drawings of it have appeared in several publications including SeaKayaker Magazine (Heath, 1987c:17), and *Contributions to Kayak Studies* (Arima, et.al, 1991:102, fig.102). The former drawing is labeled "The Expo 67 Kayak From Nuuk, West Greenland," and the latter "West Greenland Kayak."

The coaming on the 432 appears to be considerably older than the rest of the kayak, suggesting it may have been recycled from a local kayak. It is typical for a West Greenland coaming, having bone protection strips over the scarf joint; these strips are

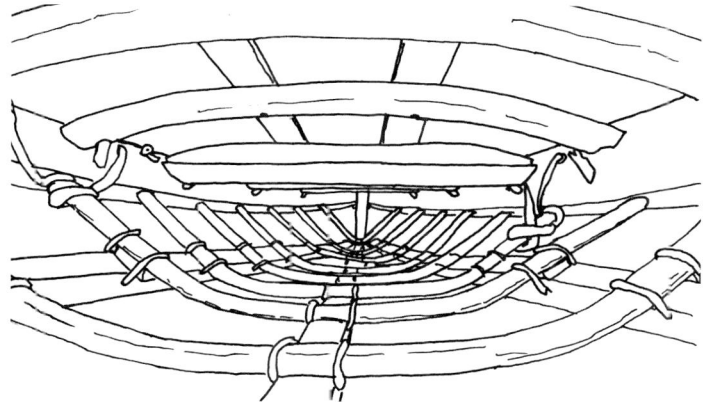

Figure 386: The forward interior view of the Canadian Museum of Civilization's kayak IV-A-432. Note the shim supporting the deck stringers: It appears as an inverted deck beam.

1/4″ (6mm) thick and 3/8″ (9mm) high and are fastened with copper nails. The coaming measures 1/2″ (13mm) thick and 1-1/4″ (32mm) high, and is positioned offset towards the right side: It is 7/8″ (22mm) from the right and 1-3/4″ (44mm) from the left side of the kayak.

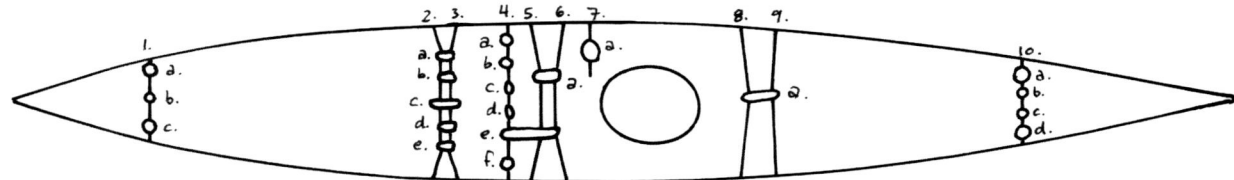

Canadian Museum of Civilization: Cat. no. IV-A-432

The deck fittings and their arrangement on this kayak are distinctly West Greenlandic, and in fact compare closely with the 1Bs.24 from Nuuk (plate 53). The IV-A-432's harpoon holder is only 1-3/4″ (44mm) long, but the strap it is attached to measures 6″ (15.2cm) long, and is fastened through the *masik*. The bow and stern deck lines have what could be considered a full complement each of fittings: three forward and four aft. The center fitting on the bow deck line is figure-shaped.

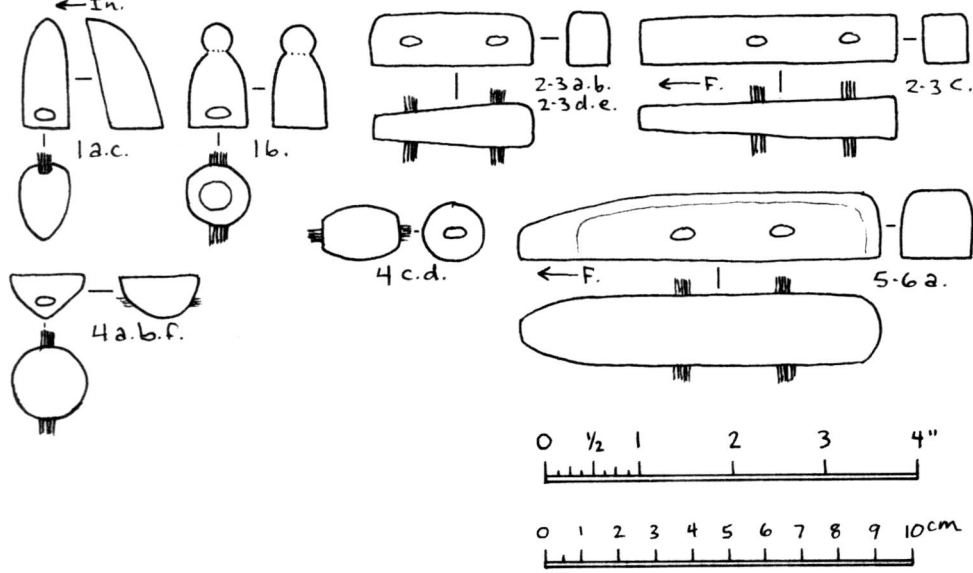

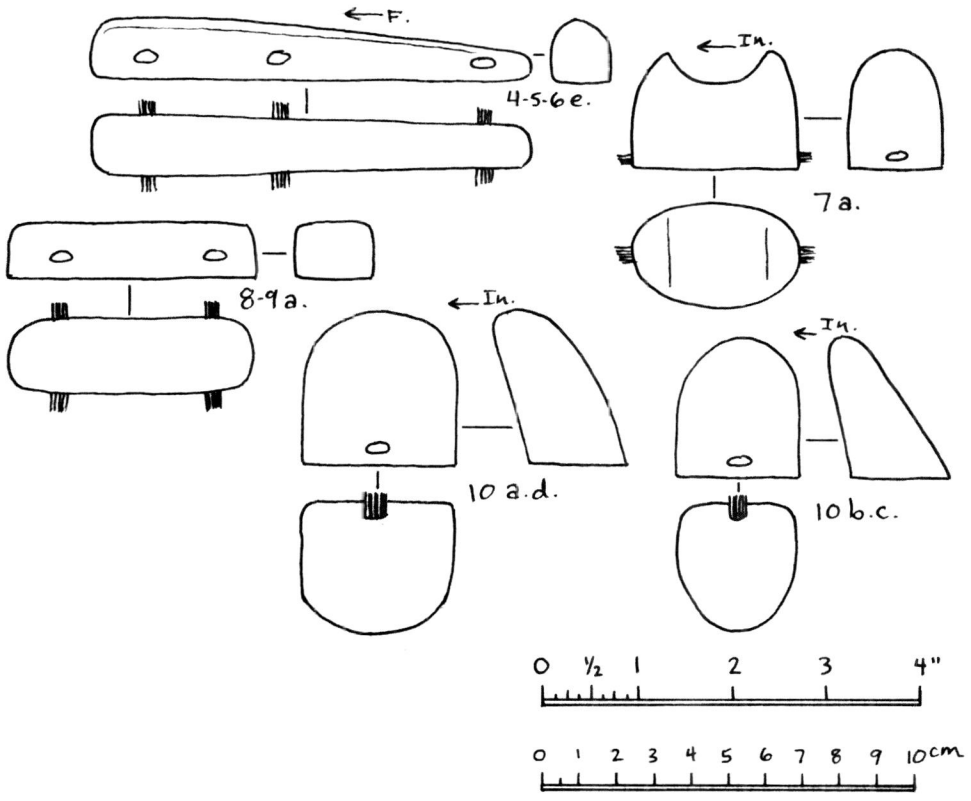

104. Greenland Kayak: Greenland National Museum, Nuuk
   (on loan to Ilulissat Katersugaasiviat [Ilulissat Museum])
   Catalog no. KNK 1906.

This kayak belonged to a very famous Greenland kayaker. His name is Manasse Mathaeussen, and he was born in Qoornoq, a settlement in a fjord north of Nuuk in 1915. Kayak historian John Heath has written what may be the only biography of Mathaeussen. Heath met Mathaeussen in 1985, and corresponded with him through the late 1980s. Mathaeussen's life included extensive kayaking paired with extensive travel throughout Greenland. Heath writes that Kulusuk (in Ammassalik District) was, at the time of Mathaeussen's living there, the home of the best seal-catchers in the world (1990:12). Mathaeussen and his kayak are depicted extensively throughout the film *Kajak Klubben* (Peqatigiiffiat Qaannat Kalaallit Nunaanni Kattuffiat, 1986). In the film, he is shown rolling this same kayak and providing instruction to students at the first Greenland kayak training camp after the foundation of Qaannat Kattuffiat— the Greenland Kayaking Association.

Photographs in John Heath's article are apparently of this same kayak, and were taken in 1976— in Kotzebue, Alaska during a kayaking demonstration. Mathaeussen writes that he was only in Kulusuk,

East Greenland for ten years (during the 1930s), and moved to Northwest Greenland afterwards (Heath 1990:12). Mathaeussen's ten years in East Greenland apparently left a deep enough impression of local kayaks that his kayak, built some 40 years later, would resemble them to the extent it does.

Mathaeussen's kayak was received by the Greenland National Museum in 1989, the year of his death. It was transferred to the Ilullissat Museum in 1991, where it remains to this day. This kayak was not surveyed nor even seen by myself, but was instead surveyed in 2002 by Vernon Doucette of Cambridge, Massachusetts, and Richard Nonas of New York City.

This kayak reflects Mathaeussen's broad travels throughout Greenland: Certain elements appear East Greenlandic, such as the shorter length deck lines on the fore deck and the deck-stringer arrangements (three forward and none aft). Its Northwest Greenland kayak elements are the lack of Y-shaped deck-lines (forward and aft), the presence of just a single aft deck line, the shorter and fuller ends, only intermittent use of oblique pegs for fastening deck beams, the lack of gunwale flare, and the lack of a drain-plug. Nonas and Doucette's field notes also mention lashings at the deck beam-to-gunwale joints.

The KNK 1906 has considerable hull-collapse, and its construction is what some would say very un-traditional, yet is, as I would argue, extremely traditional: The bent ribs are strips of plastic, likely cut from buckets or tubs. It could be emphasized here that the Arctic tradition is based entirely on making do with what resources and technology is at hand.

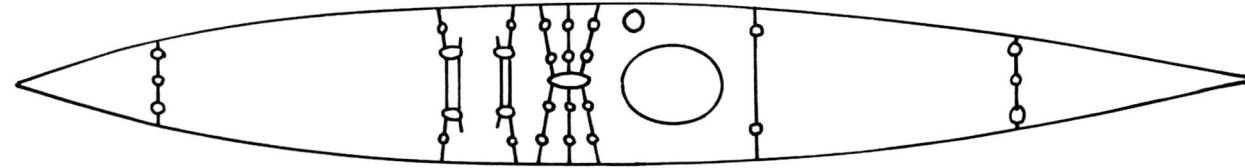

Greenland National Museum: Cat. no. 1906

Exact dimensions and forms of the 1906's deck fittings were not recorded.

Greenland Kayak Paddles

As with Greenlandic kayaks, their paddles also exhibit a wide range of shapes, sizes, proportions, and construct. Unfortunately, as with so many Greenlandic kayaks in museums, provenance records are often lacking. To further complicate things, many paddles are not positively associated with particular kayaks, the records having been lost or the paddles or kayaks were simply collected alone.

Aside from propulsion, paddles have several other functions: balancing, bracing, signaling, rolling, adjusting equipment on the deck, rafting up with other kayaks, and breaking ice. William Thalbitzer writes of paddles also being used to dispatch animals (1914:386), a practice also known from Eastern Canada (Arima, 1987:127). David Putnam describes Polar Inuit using paddles to bang on the boat in order to scare Walrus (1926 118). Morten Porsild even describes the use of kayak paddles to propel umiaks— by men— for whale hunting (1915:145). He describes the men as facing forward and rowing; it is in my mind more likely that they paddled the umiaks. In the Eastern Arctic and the whole of Greenland, rowing umiaks is the job of women.

Greenlanders are only known to have used double bladed paddles for propelling their kayaks. While single blade paddles are not used in Greenland, they do figure in West Greenlandic mythology. Hinrich Rink includes in his *Tales and Traditions of the Eskimo* the supernatural beings *kayarissat*— kayakers of extraordinary size— who control the weather. The kayarissat "use one-bladed paddles, like those of the Indians" (1875:47).

The use of Greenland-style paddles has become quite popular in more temperate regions for recreational kayaking: Some eight different commercially produced 'Greenland Paddles' were reviewed in SeaKayaker Magazine in 1999 (Andersen, 1999:39-43).

Wood is the primary material used for the shaft and blades of paddles, but other materials are often used in conjunction. Bone or ivory is commonly used for paddle tips and/or blade edging. Such attachments added longevity to the paddle; they prevented splintering and fraying during use in icy waters. It must be noted that ivory and bone were by-products of hunting— decent wood, especially prior to the European trade, was a very precious commodity. Other materials I have seen incorporated into paddles are leather strapping, nails, pot-metal, aluminum, rivets, baleen, bamboo, copper wire, and even Danish Kroner (coins).

Of the non-Polar Greenland paddles in this study, the longest paddle is (with the missing tip restored) 8′2-3/8″ (249.8cm) (likely from Sisimiut, circa 1926; paddle-plate 31), and the shortest paddle

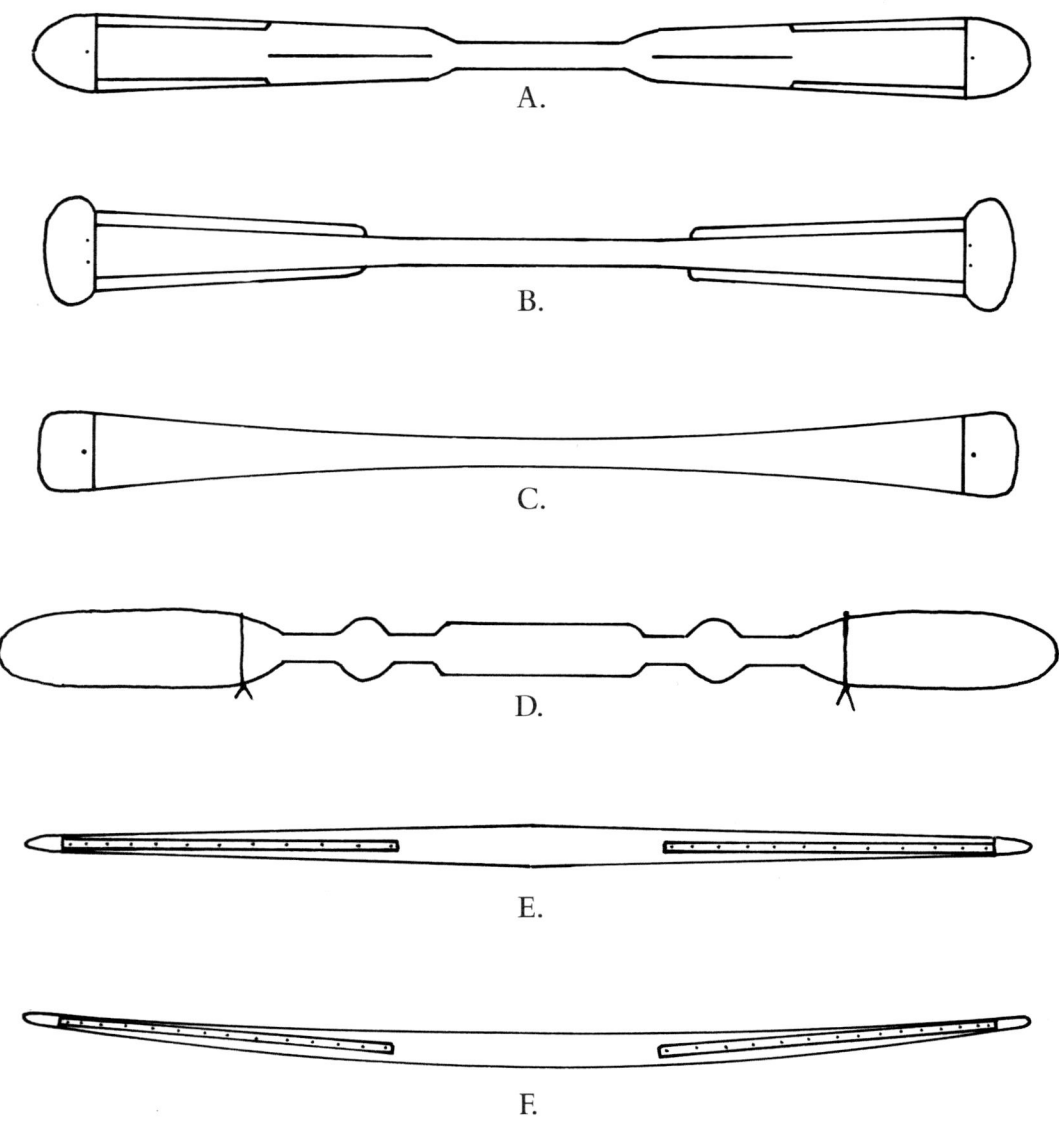

Figure 387: Features of Greenland paddles; for description and terminology, see below.

(non-child's) is 5′9-7/16″ (176.3cm) (from Nuuk, circa 1888; paddle-plate 25). H. C. Petersen writes that the longest paddles are from Uummannaq Fjord— just south of Upernavik District (Petersen, 1986:66). Short paddles were used in Disko Bay vicinities, and according to Petersen, the shortest paddles are from Qaqortoq, in South Greenland— paddles as short as 160cm (5′3″). Hunters from Disko Bay described the reason for such short paddles: " . . . There is no resistance to the wind when one is paddling against a strong wind" (*in* Petersen, 1986:65).

The width of the paddle's blades varies considerably as well: The widest in this study is 4-5/8″ (11.7cm) (DNM Elc.23, paddle-plate 2), and the narrowest blades are 2-3/8″ (6.0cm) (Numerous examples; paddle-plates 5, 8, 29, etc). These widths are of the blades proper, and not the bone tips, which are often wider than the blades.

One of the more common suggestions as to why the Greenlanders (among other Inuit peoples) had such narrow paddles is that they did not possess adequate wood to make them wider. An example of this thinking can be found in John Murdoch's *The Ethnological Results of the Point Barrow Expedition*. Murdoch describes a wide blaced (approx. 6"; 15.2cm) kayak paddle from North Alaska, and then writes: "This is a much more effective paddle than those used by Greenlanders and other Eastern Eskimos, the blades of which, probably from the scarcity of wood are very narrow, not exceeding 4 inches in width" ([1892] 1988:332).

This is a naïve interpretation based mainly on the fact that the double-bladed paddles that Europeans have been using for the last 125 years are in fact much wider, and that Europeans of course do have access to wide boards. To his credit, Murdoch includes a note that does contradict his opinion stated above: "It is a curious fact, however, that the narrowest kaiak paddles I have ever seen belonged to some Eskimo that I saw in 1876, at Rigolette, Labrador, who lived in a region sufficiently well wooded to furnish them with lumber for a small schooner, which they had built"([1892] 1988:332, note 1). It is interesting to note that some of the earliest preserved Greenland kayak paddles (1600s) are in fact much wider than examples dating from periods (e.g., today) where wide boards are plentiful and reasonably priced.

Figures 387a through c shows the general areas and parts of three forms of Greenland kayak paddles. As can be seen, the blade edging can either be raised (b) or inset (a)— as determined by the appearance of its termination towards the paddle's loom. In some cases the edging may make up the 'shoulder' of a paddle (b)— in other cases the wood of the blade's base will create the 'shoulder.' Paddle 387c has no edging and is also 'shoulder-less,' which creates an indefinite blade-to-loom transition area. Note that paddle 387a has a slight ridge on the root of the blade faces.

Paddles 387a, b, and c also show different variations of tip-shapes. Usually the tips are made of whalebone or ivory, and are fastened to the blade ends with mortises and tenons (see figure 389). Some paddles in this study have wooden tips, and several do not have separate tip-pieces. Paddle 387a has rounded tips, and b has oblong tips— tips that extend broader than the paddle's blade ends. Paddle c has squarish tips. These combinations of forms can be quite mixed— in certain cases one may find paddles with mis-matched tips, e.g., squarish on one end, and rounded on the other.

The older paddles of Inuhuit (the Polar Greenlanders) are as different from those used in the rest of Greenland as are their kayaks. The terminology crosses-over for the most part, but some additional terms are warranted. A typical older Inuhuit paddle (as would be used with type XI kayaks) is depicted in figure 387d. These paddles typically have distinct handholds cut into them, with the center of the paddle being rather wide and stout. Knobs are often present just outboard of the handgrips, and it is common to find cord attached to the base of the blades so as to leach off water before it reaches the hands. These cords are often sinew or hide, and they are set into notches in the blades' edges.

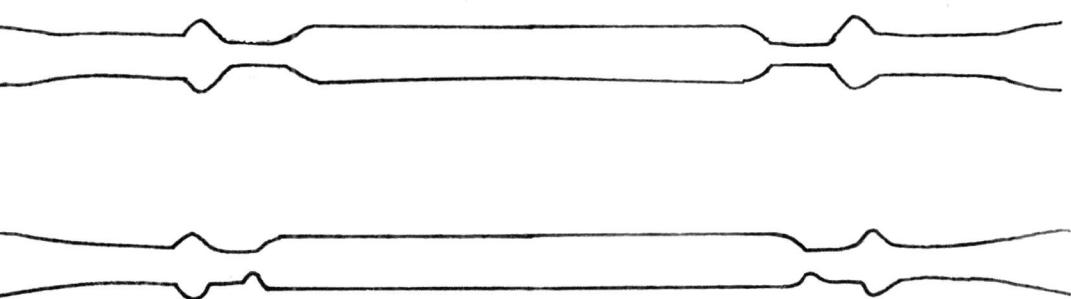

Figure 388: Two different grip/handle shapes on Polar Greenland kayak paddles. Top: regular grips with knobs outboard and a broadened center section. Bottom: grips with special thumb-divots; the knobs and broadened center section are still present.

One element apparently unique to Polar Greenland paddle is the occasional use of thumb-divots carved into the grips; rather it is the lack of carving a regular hand-grip that gives it this appearance. Figure 388 bottom depicts this form of grip; see paddle-plates 73, 74, and 78 for examples that have such grips.

Viewed on-edge (or side-view), Greenland kayak paddles are usually symmetrical, however, several paddles from East Greenland have a dihedral bend to them, as in figure 387f (The figure illustrates this principle exaggerated— consult scale drawings for actual appearances).

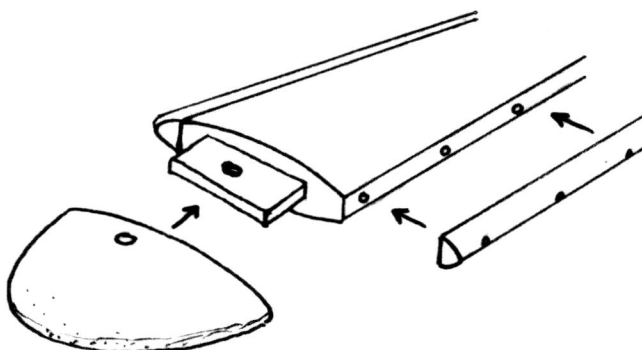

Figure 389: Detail of how tips and edging are attached to a paddle. The tip is mortised and tenoned in place, and pegged to secure it. The edging is pegged to the paddle's edge.

When used, these paddles are held with their blades angled forward— towards the bow. The intentions behind the dihedral paddle of East Greenland has not to my knowledge been recorded, but its purpose may have to do with quietness and/or a more efficient stroke, such as is the theory behind bent-shaft canoe paddles popular among canoe-racers in recent years. I have used such an East Greenland paddle replica (of the Museon 48050, paddle-plate 64) for many hours in an East Greenland kayak replica (Museon 48057, plate 87), and while I can't confidently claim it is better than any non-dihedral paddle, I can say it was a very comfortable and effective blade.

Separate tip pieces on paddles are usually attached with a mortise and tenon joint, the tenon being an extension to the blade's wooden end, and the mortise being carved into the base of the tip-piece. The tips are fastened via a peg or two— sometimes three— set through the tip's face through the tenon, as in figure 389. Paddle blade edging is usually pegged to the paddle with tiny ivory nails, also shown in

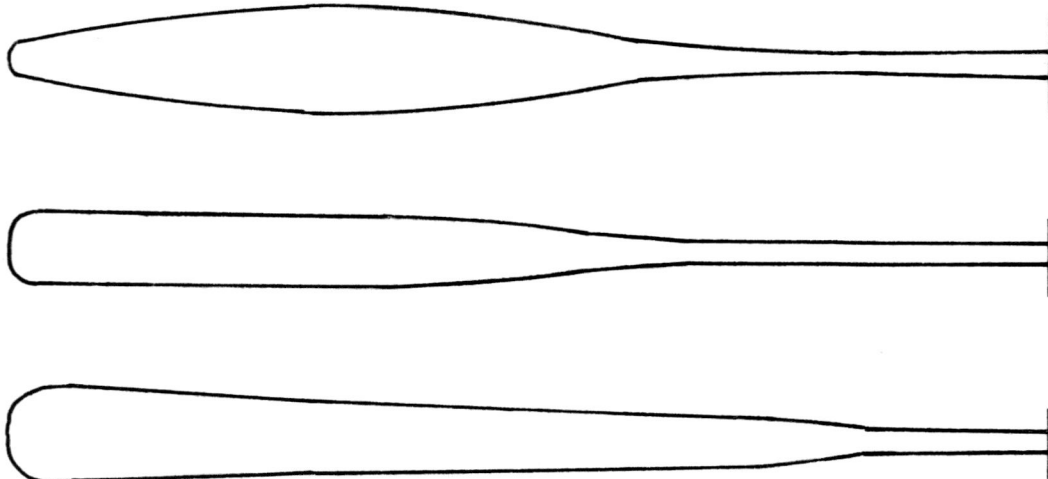

Figure 390: The general trend of paddle forms in Greenland since circa 1600— the widest point has migrated closer to the blade's ends.

figure 389. Occasionally the edging will itself be tenoned into the tip, as in figure 393; this technique is not always visible.

A little over half of the 78 paddles presented here are either positively or likely associated with a particular kayak. This association is very helpful in determining what types of paddles were used with what types of kayaks and where and when, if known for the kayak. For kayak paddles that are not associated with a particular kayak, detailed provenance information is often lacking. As with the kayaks in this study, many of the following paddles exhibit repairs or modifications. These features are described in the text for each paddle, where applicable.

Being that some 400 years of Greenland kayak paddle types are presented here, it is inevitable that certain changes in form over the years would become apparent. Several key points are:

- Some of the oldest paddles had their maximum blade width towards the middle of the blades (lasting until early [?] 1600s).

- The above type likely evolved into paddles whose blade edges were parallel (circa 1600-mid-1700s).

- In time, Greenland paddles (except Polar types) became widest at their ends (circa 1800— present).

- Paddles that would today be considered "East Greenlandic" due to their wide oblong tips once occurred in West Greenland as well, circa late 1700s to as late as early 20th century.

Unfortunately there are so many instances of dis-similarities between paddles of the same circa and vicinity that drawing specific conclusions of where certain paddles were used and when and how they evolved and exhibited influence is very difficult.

Take for example the case of the two Fram Museum paddles: Both are from Nuuk, circa 1888, but they are of entirely different forms and sizes. The FM 65 (paddle-plate 25) has semi-circular tips, raised edging and is 5′9-7/16″ (176.3cm) long; the FM 176 (paddle-plate 38) has squarish tips, inset edging, and is a foot longer than its counterpart. Such stark differences in paddles are also evident with the two paddles from Sisimiut, circa 1930s— the MSU 4274cw (paddle-plate 27), and the CMC IV-A-483 (paddle-plate 28).

The variations in paddles within a given geo-temporal frame may simply be explained by personal preferences, perhaps reflecting outside influences or results from migrations. The four points listed above are the extent of my analysis of the paddles I've studied; unlike with kayaks, detailed collection dates and places of the paddles (although mostly lacking) don't tend to expose consistent patterns of forms.

Many of the paddles presented here are drawn in 'half-length.' In cases where one side is not symmetrical with the other— either due to damage or how it was made— the opposite end is also depicted. In instances where just one half is depicted, the opposite end is identical. All lengths and breadths given are artifactual, i.e., as I found them, without restoration. With paddles, if a significant portion of one blade is missing, but the other end is fully intact, it is still possible to infer the original length with minimal error. In such cases where a conjectural length is provided, this is done so within the text describing the respective paddle.

Seventy-Eight Greenland Kayak Paddles:

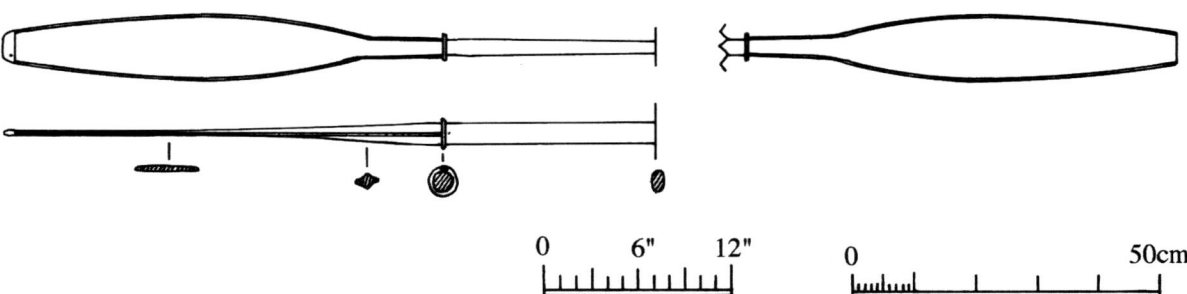

1. **Danish National Museum no. Elc.9.**
   Length: 6' 11-1/2" Width: 4-5/16" (212.0 x 10.9cm)

The Danish National Museum's paddle Elc.9 belonged to the Danish Royal Kunstkammer, founded circa 1650. How the paddle ended up at the Kunstkammer is unknown, but it appears very much like the paddle in the 1642 engraving of Ole Worm's 'Museum Wormianum' (figure 9). After Worm died, his collection was turned over to King Frederik III's Kunstkammer in 1655 (Dam-Mikkelsen, 1980:xxxiii).

A similarly formed-paddle has been published in John Brand's *The Little Kayak Book, Vol.I* (1984:7). It is historically associated with the kayak from circa 1612 at the Trinity House in Hull, England. This paddle had been sawn in half, and the ends are damaged considerably, so the actual tip-shape was unknown. Brand effected a conjectural restoration of the paddle's tips in which they come to a sharp point. While Brand's paddle-tip reconstruction varies in shape from the Elc.9 and Elc.23, the pointed tip is known from archaeological finds in Greenland (Mathiassen, 1931:88, and Plt. 2, fig. 13).

For the modern Greenland paddle enthusiast, a narrow blade— low windage, and grippable anywhere along the blade— has been the essence of a paddle; the Danish National Museum's Elc.9 appears anything but like a 'Greenland' paddle. The situation in Greenland some 400 years ago seems to have been quite different than today.

Figure 391: A Greenlander depicted in an engraving from 1683. The shape of the paddle blades is not quite as naïve and exaggerated as some may think. (From Description de L'Univers, *[pg.301] by Allain Manesson Mallet. Collection of the Author.)*

This paddle exhibits a feature that modern kayakers are very familiar with: a drip ring. This example's drip ring is a 1/8" (3mm) thick "C" shaped piece of ivory, lashed shut at its opening. The drip ring's wall-width is 5/16" (8mm). The blade edging is very thin: 1/8" x 1/8" (3 x 3mm) along the blade, and where it transitions to the loom, 1/8" x 3/16" (3 x 5mm) wide. At its mid-point, the loom measures 1-3/8" (35mm) thick and 13/16" (21mm) wide. The blade ends are 5/16" (8mm) thick, but 6" (15.2cm) inboard, they are 1/4"

(6mm) thick. One of the tips is missing, and along with it, the tenon. The other tip has just one peg securing it to the blade, and the peg is offset from center.

I have made a replica of this paddle, and it is shown being used with the Lübeck kayak replica in figures 177 and 178.

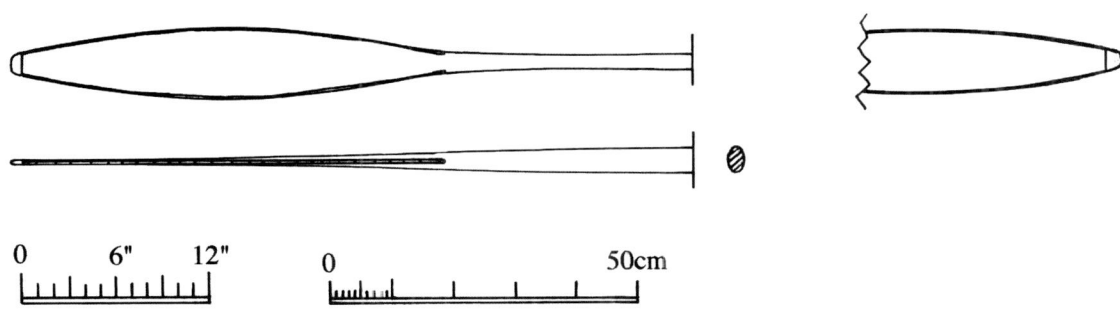

2. **Danish National Museum no. Elc.23.**
   Length: 7´3-1/4˝ Width: 4-5/8˝ (221.6 x 11.7cm)

The Elc.23 is another paddle that formerly belonged to the Royal Danish Kunstkammer. It is by 1/4˝ (6mm) the widest paddle in this study. As drawn, the left tip piece is 3/4˝ (19mm) long, and the right tip is 7/8˝ (22mm) long. Both tips are slightly thicker (5/16˝ [8mm]) than the blade ends, which measure 1/4˝ (6mm) thick. The edging is 1/8˝ thick by 1/8˝ wide (3 x 3mm), and is inset 1/32˝ (.8mm). At the paddle's mid-point, the loom measures 1-1/2˝ (38mm) thick and 15/16˝ (24mm) wide. The loom does narrow to 7/8˝ (22mm) wide 3´ (91.4cm) from the tips.

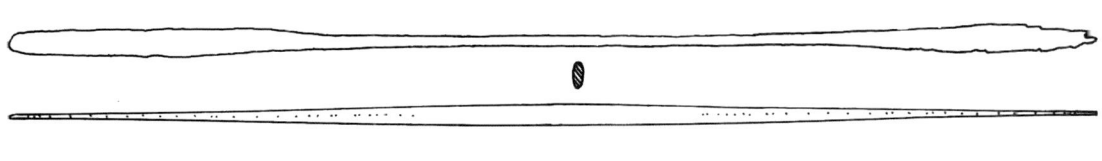

3. **Greenland National Museum no. KNK 1759x2.**
   Length: 5´9-5/8˝ Width: 1-13/16˝ (176.8 x 4.6cm)

Greenland National Museum records are vague as to where exactly this paddle was found, but it was found in a grave, and is potentially quite old. The catalog file lists Maniitsoq as the area of origin, but a tag— hand-scribbled in Danish— was paraphrased to me as being "a child's paddle from a fjord near Aasiaat."

The paddle is eroded, and is missing tips, and edging. The edging is evidenced, and the nail-positions are indicated on the drawing. It is also warped into an "S" shape, but has been drawn straight, as it likely had been made. At its mid-point, the loom measures 1-1/4″ (32mm) thick and 3/4″ (19mm) wide. The right blade (as drawn) is 1/4″ (6mm) thick 1-3/4″ (44mm) from the end. Depending on the height of the missing edging, this paddle's original width may have been about 2-1/16″ to 2-5/16″ (52 to 59mm).

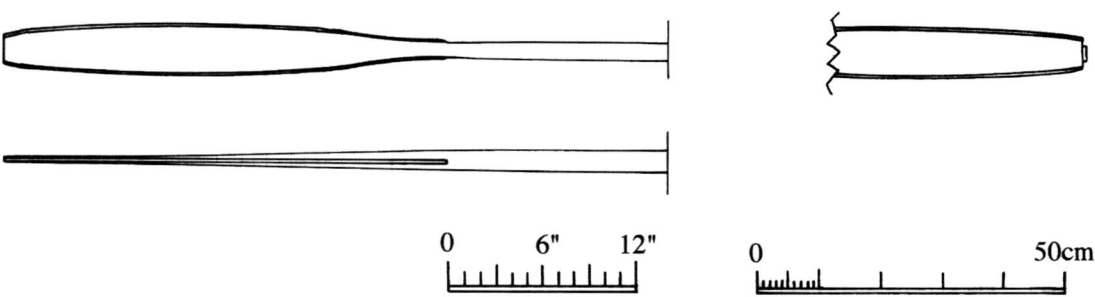

4. Westfries Museum no. 232.
   Length: 7′7/8″ Width: 3-3/8″(215.5 x 8.5cm)

The paddle belonging to the kayak in Hoorn (WFM 232, plate 2) is very well made. The blades are angled 20 degrees from each other— likely on account of twisting as the wood aged. John Brand describes a feathered Greenland paddle (1987:47) associated with the former South Shields Museum kayak (the kayak currently of Trinity House, Newcastle [in this study: plate 25]).

The example in Brand was the first feathered Greenland paddle thoroughly studied, and at the time it was likely not known if others existed. It has been suggested that such paddles are simply warped, but they may have also been carved from twisted pieces of wood, using such grain to advantage. If twisted, this paddle shows no further warps or such, and was longitudinally straight as can be. For what it is worth, I think the paddle has warped, and cannot see how a feathered paddled could've provided any advantage for a Greenlandic kayaker-hunter.

At its mid-point, the "Hoorn" paddle measures 1-1/4″ (32mm) thick and 1″ (25mm) wide. The ivory edging on the paddle is 1/8″ x 1/8″ (3 x 3mm). At the blade ends, the paddle is 3/8″ (9mm) thick. Both tips are missing, but one tenon remains in place, protruding 1/4″ (6mm) from the blade end, measuring 1″ (25mm) wide.

```
0    6"   12"         0                    50cm
```

5. Museon no. 117858.
   Length: 6′1/8″ Width: 2-3/8″ (183.1 x 6.0cm)

The origins of the Museon's paddle 117858 are not recorded, but its form and appearance suggests that it dates from the 1600s or 1700s. It is leaf-shaped like the above paddles, though this is much more subtle in the present case. The maximum blade breadth is a good 12″ (30.4cm) from its ends; both tips are missing, though stubs of the tenons are still present. The loom at the paddle's mid-point measures 1-1/4″ (32mm) thick and 15/16″ (24mm) wide. The blade ends are 5/16″ (8mm) thick.

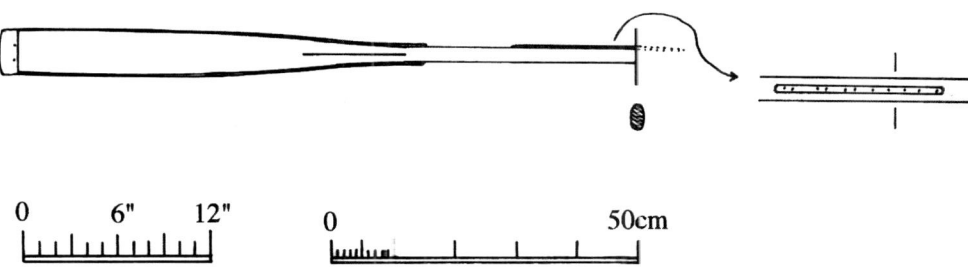

```
0    6"   12"         0                    50cm
```

6. Rijper Museum.
   Length: 6′9-3/4″ Width 3-1/8″ (207.6 x 7.9cm)

The De Rijp paddle illustrated is one of two at the Rijper Museum— the other is very damaged and eroded, and according to Gert Nooter's measurements is 196.5cm long (6′5-1/4″) with both tips missing (1971:35). While it is not known if one or both paddles are specifically tied to the De Rijp kayak (plate 3), they are likely contemporaries.

The De Rijp paddle's blades are parallel for much of their length, and it has short squarish tips. A short ridge is present on the De Rijp paddle, extending along the loom-to-blade transition area. The edging is 3/16″ x 3/16″ (5 x 5mm). The loom measures 1-1/2″ (38mm) thick and 15/16″ (24mm) wide at its mid-point. A strip of ivory 7/16″ (11mm) wide and 1/8″ (3mm) thick is pegged to one side of the paddle's loom; it measures 11-1/8″ long (28.2cm).

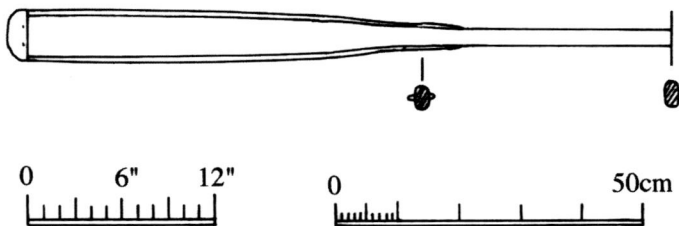

7. De Hidde Nijland Stichting.
   Length: 6′8-1/8″ Width: 3-1/8″ (203.5 x 7.9cm)

The paddle associated with the Hindeloopen kayak (plate 4) has very parallel edges on the blade. This is contrary to later paddles, with the widest section towards the ends. The paddle's end-pieces are very short, but well made.

The paddle, as with the kayak, has been painted: The paddle is very dark green, nearing black. The ivory edging and tips have also been painted this color. At its mid-point, the Hindeloopen paddle measures 1-3/4″ (44mm) thick and 15/16″ (24mm) wide. The blade ends are 5/8″ (16mm) thick.

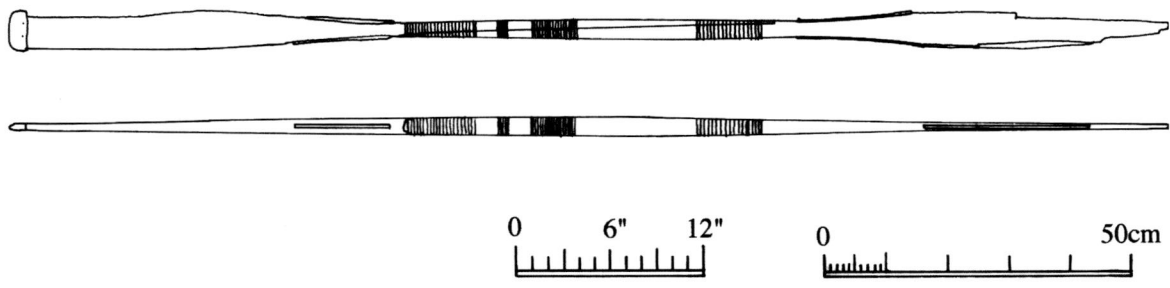

8. Marischal College Museum "A" (ABDUA:6.013?).
   Length: 6′2-5/16″ Width: 2-3/8″ (188.7 x 6.0cm)

At the Marischal College Museum in Aberdeen, there are two Greenland kayaks and two Greenland paddles: It is not documented as to which paddle goes with which kayak. Based on the kayaks' collection dates and the different forms of paddles, the present example is likely the paddle associated with the kayak of ca. 1700— the ABDUA:6.013. John Heath surveyed this kayak, and it appears in *Eastern Arctic Kayaks* (Heath, 2004:10, fig. 1.5). The kayak washed up in the Don estuary near Aberdeen with a Greenlander in it— alive. (The other Marischal College kayak is the ABDUA:5736 [plate 17], and its paddle is likely the example in paddle-plate 18.)

Numerous bits and pieces of the edging are missing as well as one of the tips. A long hook-scarf consumes the entire loom of this paddle. The scarf is wrapped in four areas— from left-to-right: with baleen, copper wire, copper wire again, and baleen again. Neither end of this paddle is in decent condition, though one end does retain its tip, though the edging is missing on one side. As can be seen in the drawing, several areas of the blade are missing, and are cut straight. The edges adjacent these portions exhibit evidence of pins, implying that patches of bone/ivory or wood were fitted, such as is the case with the lower edge of the right-hand blade (as drawn), the piece being bone/ivory.

Based on presumed symmetry, this paddle's original length would have been about 6′ 3-1/2″(191.7cm). At the midpoint, the loom measures 1-3/16″ (30mm) thick and 1-1/8″ (28mm) wide— nearly round. The blade ends are 1/4″ (6mm) thick.

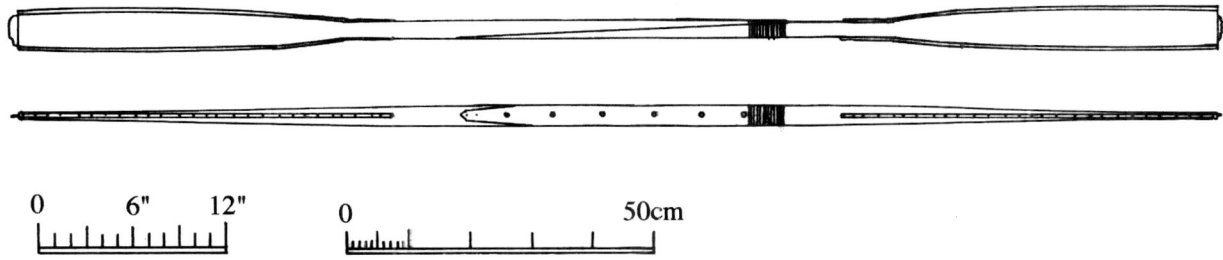

9. **Rijksmuseum voor Volkenkunde no. 360-5643.**
   Length: 6′5-3/16″ Width: 2-5/8″ (196.0 x 6.6cm)
   The RvV 360-5643 is only slightly wider in the center of the blade than at the ends of the blade. Both end pieces are missing, but the paddle is otherwise in decent condition. This paddle has a long slant scarf fastened with 1/4″ (6mm) diameter wooden pegs. At one end of the scarf, the joint is given numerous turns of string.

   At its mid-point, the 360-5643's loom measures 1-5/16″ (33mm) thick and 1-3/16″ (30mm) wide. The blade ends are 7/16″ (11mm) thick.

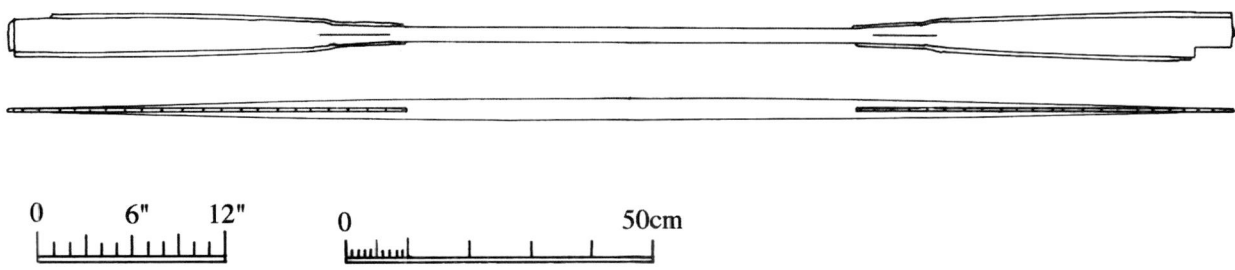

10. **Rijksmuseum voor Volkenkunde no. 351-30.**
    Length: 6′5-1/2″ Width: 2-13/16″ (196.8x 7.1cm)
    Both tips are missing from this paddle, though most of the edging is present. Its form is nearly identical to those of the Hindeloopen and De Rijp paddles— it does differ in being only slightly widest at

the ends of the blade instead of having parallel edges. Very short ridges are present at the loom-to-blade transition area.

At its mid-point, the 351-30's loom measures 1-5/16″ (33mm) thick and 15/16″ (24mm) wide, with the blade ends being 1/4″ (6mm) thick.

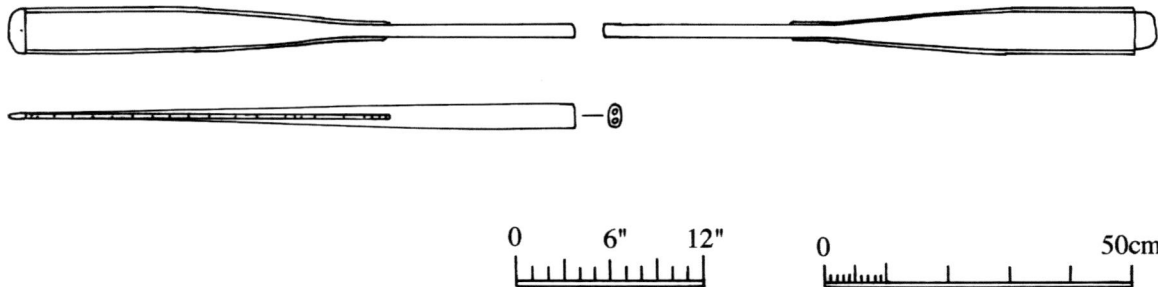

11. Gemeentelijke Musea Zierikzee no. 700.
   Total Length: 5′11-5/8″ Width: 2-15/16″ (181.9x 7.4 cm)

The GMZ kayak's paddle is sawn in two pieces, and retains peg holes to assist in re-attachment for display in the hands of "Zierik," the mannequin sitting in the kayak GMZ 700 (plate 6). The paddle's cumulative length is presently 5′11-5/8″ (181.9cm) long, which is suspiciously short for an adult Greenland paddle— especially one associated with a kayak as large as the GMZ 700.

One half's tip is intact, while the other's is missing, though a tenon is present. This tenon can be presumed to be a scarf joint in the blade instead of a tenon to receive an ivory tip: It is much too long for a tip-piece, and the blade itself is presently 1-1/2″ (38mm) shorter than the intact half (based on length of edging). Assuming symmetry, and adding the length of another tip, one could presume the original paddle to have been at least 6′1-1/4″ (186.0cm) (including saw-kerf).

At the severed loom of this paddle, the thickness is 1-1/2″ (38mm) and the width 7/8″ (22mm). The blade ends are 3/8″ (9mm) thick. Note the cross-section of the severed loom— two dowel holes are present in each half-blade's loom end.

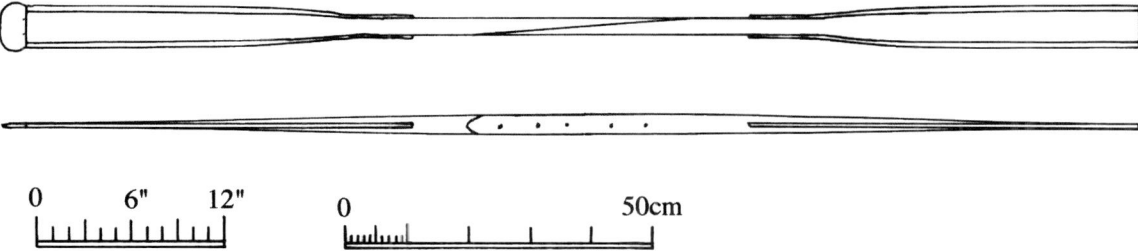

12. Wereldmuseum no. 32848.
Length: 6´2-1/2˝ Width: 2-3/4˝ (189.2x 7.0cm)

The Wereldmuseum paddle is associated with the kayak 32848 (plate 11), which was "discovered" in museum collections in the 1950s. This paddle is very similar to the previous few examples except for the longer and more oblong tip. The edging is raised and follows along the sinuous blade-to-loom transition, much as the other paddles of this type.

One of the tips is missing, and along with it, the blade's tenon. The existing tip is 1-11/16˝(4.3cm) long, so the paddle's original length would have been about 6´3-3/16˝ (191.0cm).

The 32848 is scarfed together with a simple slant-scarf, and is secured with pegs. At the mid-point of the loom, the paddle measures 1-3/8˝ (35mm) thick and 1˝(25mm) wide. The blade ends are 5/16˝ (8mm) thick.

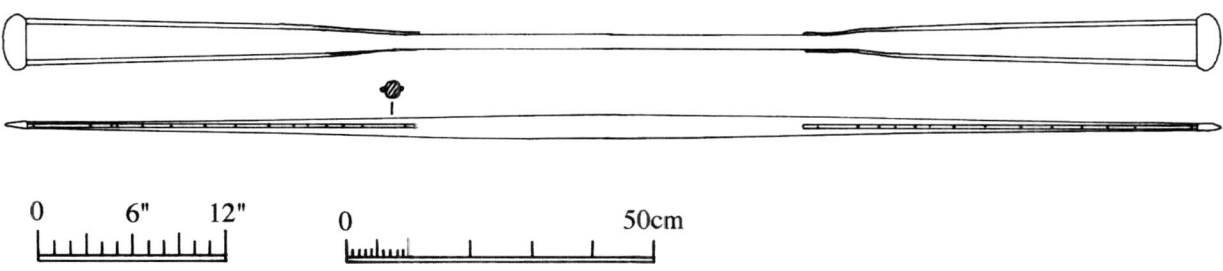

13. Trinity House, Hull "B."
Length: 6´5-13/16˝ Width: 3-1/16˝ (197.7x 7.7cm)

The Trinity House paddle "B" is associated with kayak "B" (plate 13) entirely on account of its lying on the kayak's deck. Needless to say this association is tentative.

Both Trinity House paddles weathered the heat from the same kitchen fire that 'caramelized' the varnishes on the two kayaks in the 1920s. The paddles had also been varnished, and the thick black alligatored coating obscured any fasteners used to attach the tips on the paddle "B."

The tips of the "B" are oblong, and the edging is raised. At the mid-point, the loom is 1-3/8˝(35mm) thick, and 15/16˝ (24mm) wide. The blade end is 3/8˝ (9mm) thick.

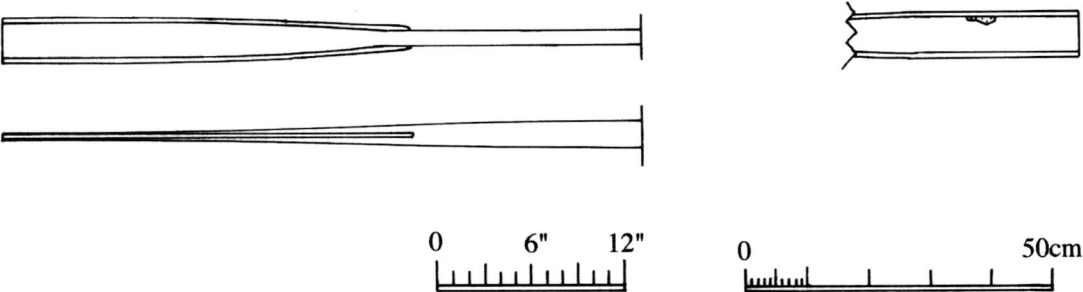

14. Rijksmuseum voor Volkenkunde no. 349.
    Length: 6´10˝ Width: 2-7/8˝ (208.3x 7.3cm)

   Both tips are missing from this paddle, but the edging is intact. By virtue of its accession number, it is associated with the kayak RvV 349, presented in this study (plate 15). While the kayak 349 is very different in form than the kayak DHNS 2 (plate 4), their respective paddles are nearly identical.

   A small ivory patch is present along one blade's edge, inboard of the edge-strip. The patch is fastened in place by five tiny pegs. At its mid-point, the loom of the 349 measures 1-5/8˝ (41mm) thick and 15/16˝ (24mm) wide. The blade ends are 7/16˝ (11mm) thick.

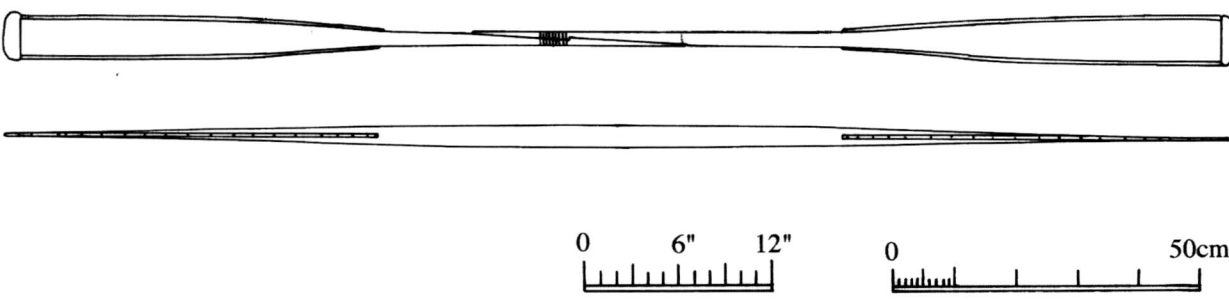

15. Rijksmuseum voor Volkenkunde no. 351-31.
    Length: 6´6-7/8˝ Width: 2-7/8˝ (200.3 x 7.3cm)

   The Rijksmuseum's paddle 351-31 has oblong tips— one more distinctly so than the other. This paddle is made from two pieces of wood, step-scarfed together and wrapped with lashings in one place; the rest of the scarf exhibits evidence of having had more lashings.

   At its mid-point, the loom is 1˝ (25mm) wide and 1-5/16˝ (33mm) thick. The edging is 1/4˝ (6mm) wide and the blade ends are 5/16˝ (8mm) thick.

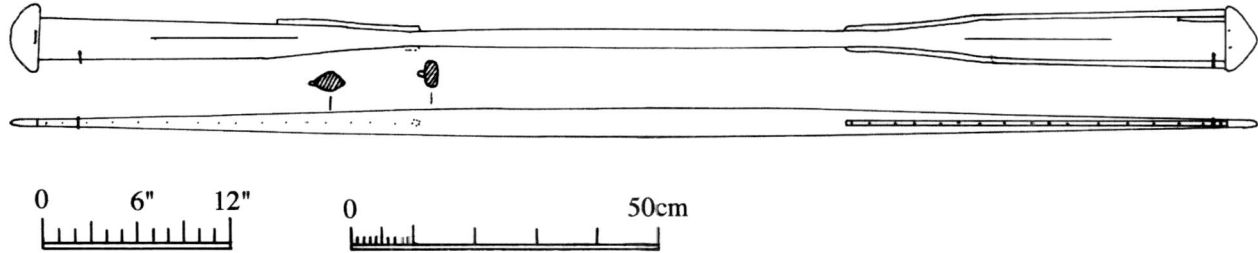

16. Trinity House, Hull "A".
Length: 6′ 7-7/8″ Width: 3-3/4″ (202.9x 9.5cm)

This damaged paddle is associated with the Trinity House kayak "A" (plate 16) merely by its having lain atop that kayak. Its tips are of a triangular form, the corners being very rounded. No other paddles in this study have such tip shapes.

One of the tips is lashed into place— possibly a field-repair or later conservation. The raised edging is also secured in one place by a lashing. Another lashing was present on the opposite blade but is presently missing along with the edging it presumably secured. Despite these lashings, the edging is also fastened with pegs.

At the "A's" midpoint, the loom is 1-11/16″ (43mm) thick and 1-1/16″ (27mm) wide. The ends of the blades are 9/16″ (14mm) thick. Short ridges are present on the inboard portions of the blades, as indicated in the drawing. A small piece of wood is pegged to one blade's end-edge— likely a repair.

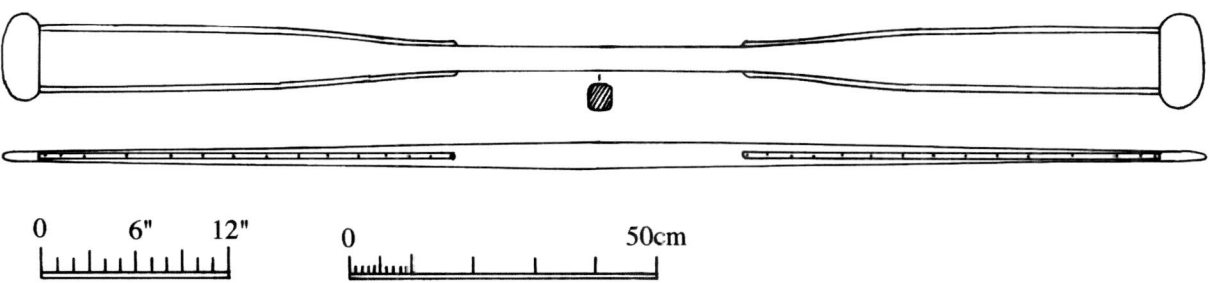

17. Marischal College Museum "B" (ABDUA:5736?).
Length: 6′ 4-1/4″ Width: 4-3/8″ (193.7x 11.1cm)

Of the two Greenland kayak paddles in the Marischal College Museum, it is my opinion that this example is the one more likely to be associated with the kayak ABDUA:5736 (plate 17). If so, the paddle would date from the 1780s, and its form would be consistent with other West Greenland paddles of the period, i.e., raised edging and oblong tips.

At this paddle's mid-point, the loom measures 1-3/4″ (44mm) thick and 1-1/2″ (38mm) wide— very substantial in size, suggesting a builder/owner with very large hands. The blade width of 4-3/8″ (11.1cm) is unusually broad. The ends of the blades are 5/8″ (16mm) thick— also substantial.

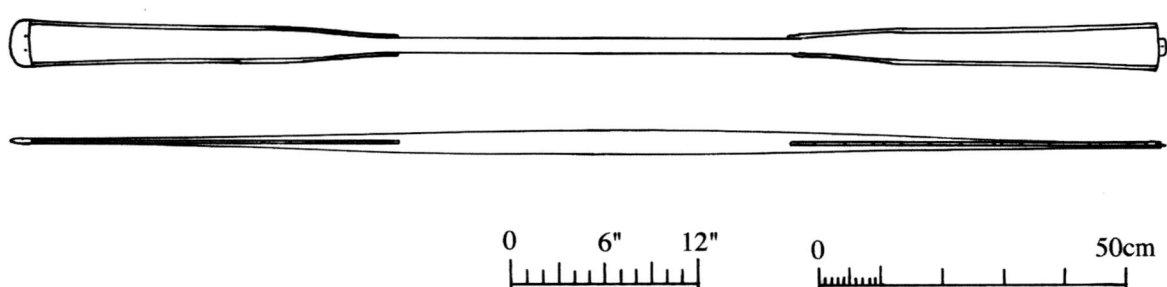

18. U. S. National Museum of Natural History no. 17520.
Length: 6´2˝ Width: 3˝ (188.0x 7.6cm)

The accession card for the US National Museum of Natural History's paddle 17520 is brief, giving only the following information: "Double Blade Paddle. Greenland. J. H. Clark. July 30, 1875." It is nearly the same size and shape as the following paddle, the UMCH 95 from South Greenland, pre-1857. Both have short tips and while the blades start off rather parallel, they flare out towards the tips somewhat. Both paddles have raised edging.

One tip is missing, having been secured by a single peg; the other tip is fastened with two pegs. The existing tip is 1-1/4˝ (32mm) long, so this paddle's original length must have been about 6´ 2-3/4˝ (189.8cm) long, subtracting of course the 1/2˝ (13mm) long tenon.

One particularly elegant touch to this paddle is its blade ends are not cut square or straight, but slightly convex when viewed en-face. The one existent tip's base has a concave cut to match the blade's end. At its mid-point, the 17520's loom measures 1-1/2˝ (38mm) thick and 15/16˝ (24mm) wide. The blade ends are 3/8˝ (9mm) thick.

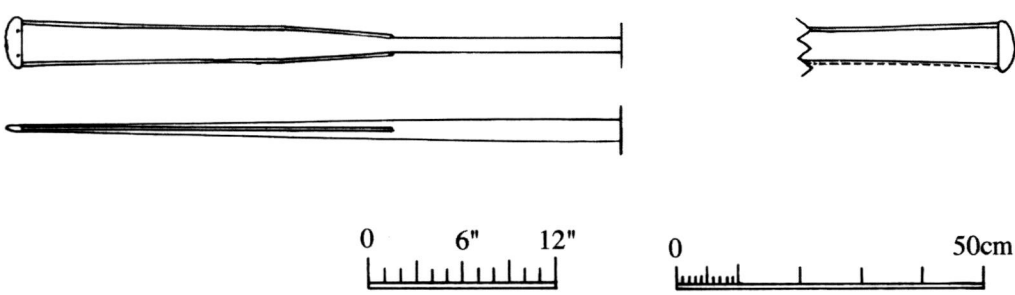

19. University Museum of Cultural Heritage no. 95.
Length: 6´ 6-7/8˝ Width: 3˝ (200.3x 7.6cm)

The paddle no. 95 pre dates 1857, having been present at the museum on opening day that year. The kayak associated with it is distinctly a South Greenland type (plate 74).

This paddle resembles several early (1600s-1700s) paddles, such as the Gemeentelijke Musea Zierikzee's 700, and the Rijksmuseum voor Volkenkunde's 351-31, although the blade widens subtly towards the tip, unlike the more parallel earlier examples. At its mid-point, the 95's loom measures 7/8˝ (22mm) wide and 1-3/8˝ (35mm) thick. The blade ends are 7/16˝ (11mm) thick. One section of edging is missing.

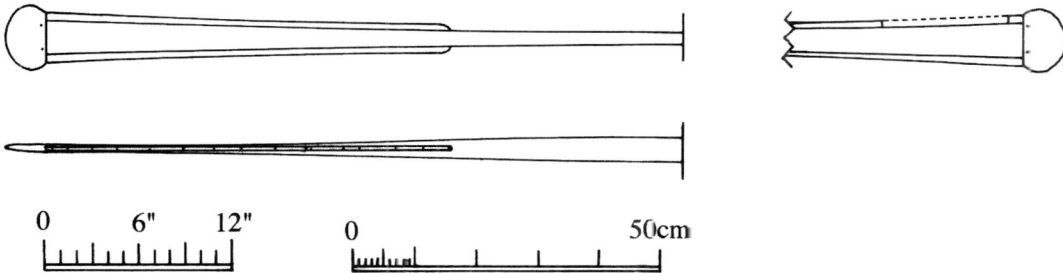

20. Hunterian Museum no. E.101.
   Length: 7′ 2-5/8″ Width: 3-5/8″ (220.0x 9.2cm)

This paddle is one of the three examples at the Hunterian Museum— each representing very different forms; the other Hunterian Museum paddles are plates 27 and 37. No history is known for this paddle, though one could infer it dates to a similar period that the three Hunterian Museum kayaks do, i.e., circa 1780s to late 1810s. This of course assumes that the paddle is associated with a kayak, which may not be the case.

The Hunterian Museum's paddle E.101 is a very nice paddle that has end-pieces that are wider than the blades. H. C. Petersen describes such paddles as being typical of East Greenland (1986:39, fig.39), but also mentions that they were once used in West Greenland as well (1986:66-67). This paddle does compare extremely well with the East Greenland paddle 48050 (paddle-plate 64).

At its mid-point, the E.101's loom is 1-1/2″ (38mm) thick and 11/16″ (17mm) wide. The blade ends are 9/16″ (14mm) thick. A considerable chunk of edging is missing along one blade. The tips are each secured to the blades with two pegs.

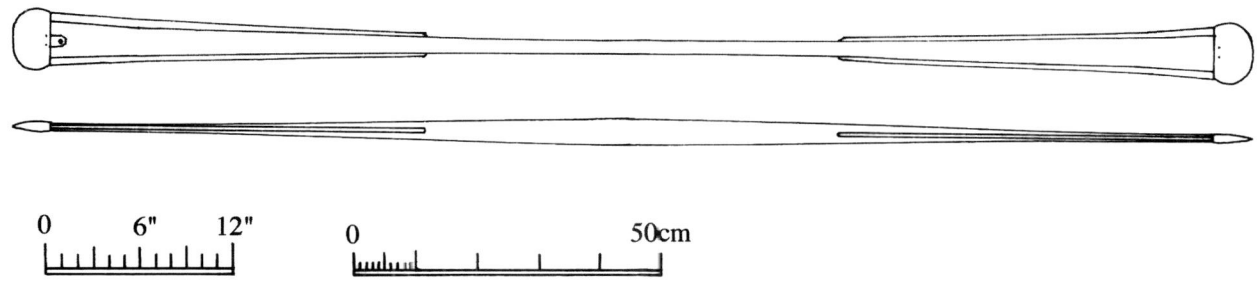

21. Hull Maritime Museum paddle '54?'
   Length: 6′ 7-5/8″ Width: 3-7/16″ (202.2x 8.7cm)

The Hull Maritime Museum's paddle is not positively associated with the kayak '64' (plate 29), but they are on display together— a tentative association. It bears great resemblance to the E.101 at the Hunterian museum: Both have tips that extend beyond the blade-width, a lack of 'shoulders' at the blade-to-shaft transition, and the edging is raised.

A patch of wood is present on one blade end, likely to replace a broken tenon. It is held in place with a copper nail. At its mid-points the paddle '64' measures 1-5/8″ (41mm) thick and 7/8″ (22mm) wide.

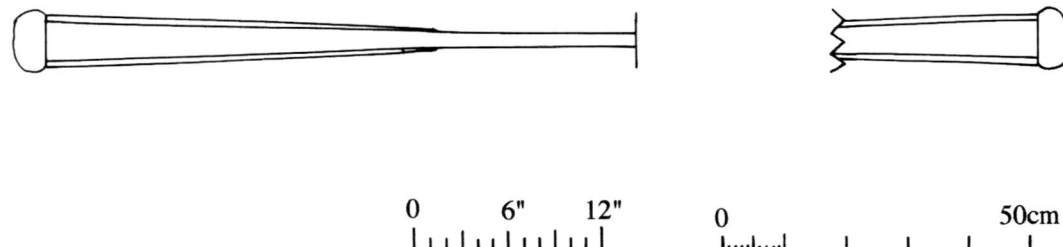

22. McManus Galleries no. 9999-430.
Length: 6' 7-1/2" Width: 3-7/16" (201.9x 8.7cm)

The MMG 9999-430 is of unknown provenance. It is very similar to the previously described paddles E.101 and HMM '64' (paddle plates 20 and 21), and like them, is probably from the early 19th century. The edging on this paddle is raised and at its inboard termination it becomes quite thin. The tips are distinctively oblong. At its mid-point, the MMG 430's loom measures 1-5/8" (41mm) thick and 7/8" (22mm) wide. The blade ends are 9/16" (14mm) thick.

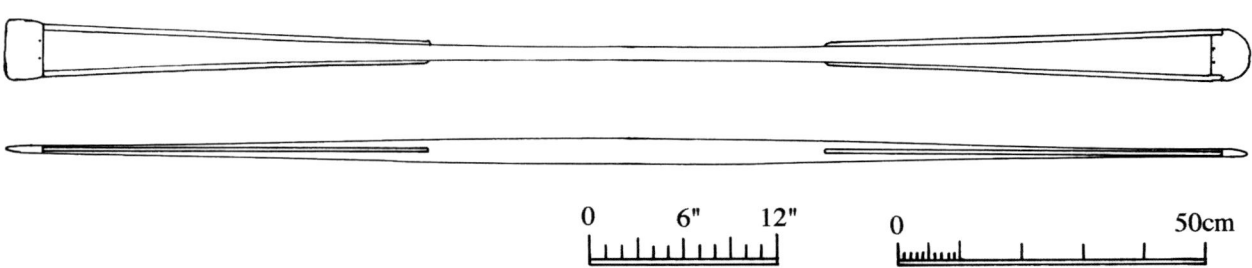

23. Hancock Museum no. G.108.
Length: 6' 7-3/8" Width: 3-1/2" (201.6x 8.9cm)

The Hancock Museum's paddle G.108 is associated with the kayak G.109 (plate 14) from pre-1837. The paddle is very well made, though it is unusual in that it has asymmetrical end-pieces. At its midpoint, the G.108's loom is 1-11/16" (43mm) thick, and 7/8" (22mm) wide. The blade ends are 5/8"(16mm) thick.

Several paddles I observed had mis-matched tips; likely from the re-using of old tips salvaged from worn-out paddles. If this is the case, one may wonder how old some of these recycled pieces may be. I don't think it is unreasonable that certain paddle tips could be at least 100 years older than the blades they are attached to.

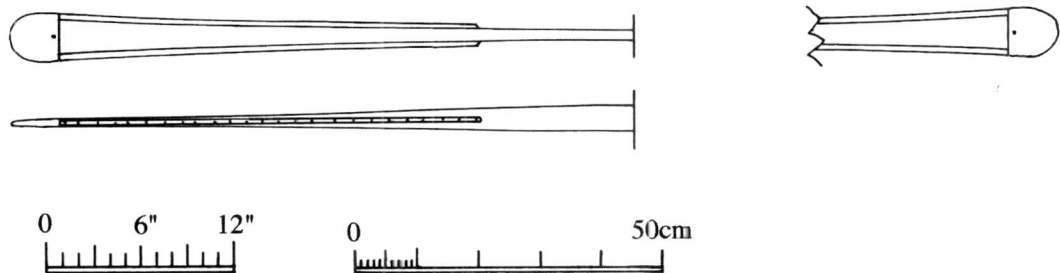

24. McManus Galleries no. 1968-81-3.
   Length: 6'7-1/2" Width: 3-1/16" (201.9x 7.7cm)

This paddle is associated with the circa 1908 kayak bearing the same accession prefix (plate 37). The edging is fairly long and wide; the loom is very narrow at 3/4" (19mm). The height of the loom at the mid-point is 1-5/8" (41mm). The thickness at the blade ends is 1/2" (13mm).

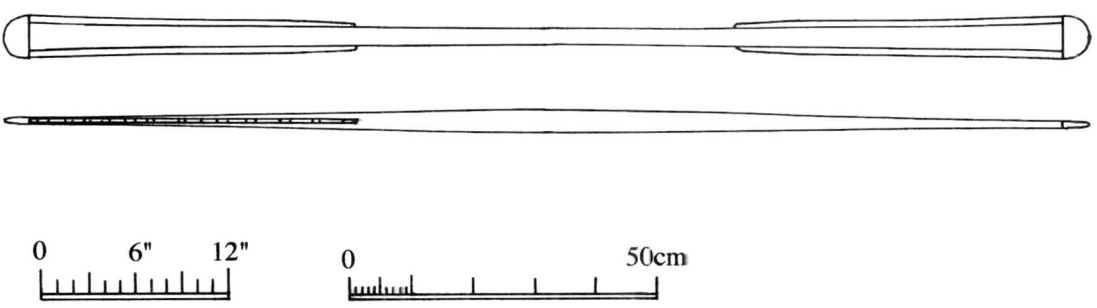

25. Fram Museum no. 65.
   Length: 5'9-7/16" Width: 2-7/8" (176.4x 7.3cm)

This paddle is associated with the Fram Museum's kayak 65 (plate 41) merely on account of its being displayed with said kayak. It has raised edging and semi-circular tips. Its blade end thickness is 9/16" (14mm). At the mid-point of the loom, this paddle is 1-7/16" (36mm) thick and 1" (25mm) wide. Presumably, this paddle was made for or purchased by members of Fridtjof Nansen's cross-Greenland expedition in Nuuk in 1888.

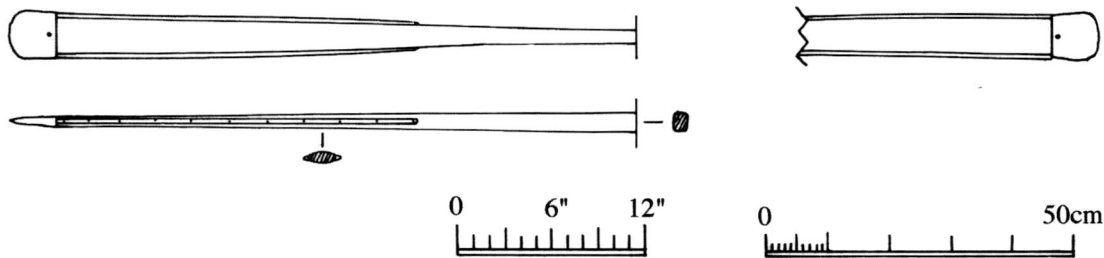

26. Greenland National Museum no. KNK 1215.
Length: 6′8″ Width: 3-1/4″ (203.2x 8.2cm)

The Greenland National Museum's paddle KNK 1215 is from circa 1919 Oqaatsut, in North Disko Bay, and belonged to Peter Brøndlund. Brøndlund's kayak is also in the National Museum, and is depicted in plate 61. The tips of this paddle are moderately long, and have very blunt ends. The edging is raised and is 3/8″ (9mm) wide and 1/4″ (6mm) thick at the ends. A very slight gradual shoulder marks the blade/loom transition area.

At the 1215's mid-point, the loom is 1-5/16″ (33mm) thick and 7/8″ (22mm) wide. The cross-section here is very squarish. The blade ends are 3/4″ (19mm) thick. The tips are each held in place by a single ivory peg.

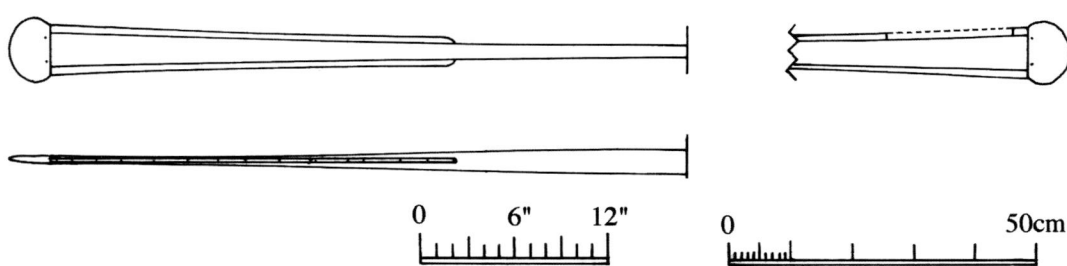

27. Hunterian Museum no. E.101/1.
Length: 6′7-7/8″ Width: 2-3/4″ (202.9x 7.0cm)

The Hunterian Museum's paddle E.101/1 is of unknown provenance but if it belongs to any of the three kayaks at the Hunterian Museum, it likely dates from circa 1780-1820. Somewhat rare among Greenland paddles, the E.101/1 has no edge protection strips. It does however have bone tips, and they are in fact oversize— they are wider than the blade itself, and are not faired into the blade width. It seems as if the tips were simply recycled from an older paddle. Also noteworthy are the blades' very smooth transition into the loom.

At the 101/1's mid-point, the loom measures 1-1/2″ (38mm) thick and 1-1/8″ (28mm) wide. The blade ends are 11/16″ (17mm) thick.

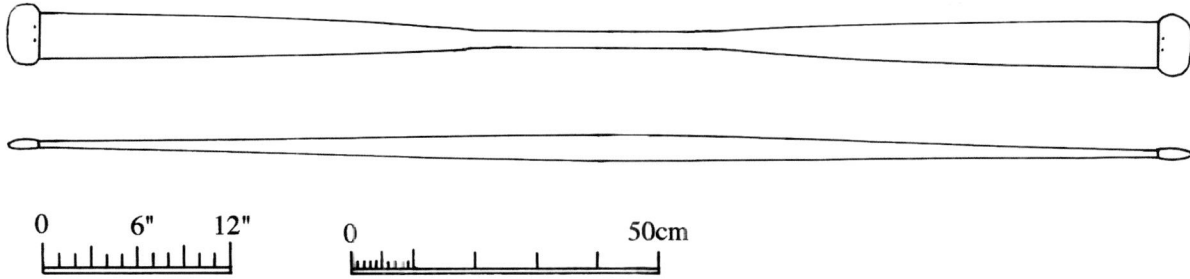

28. McManus Galleries no. 9999-428.
   Length: 6′3-7/8″ Width: 3-1/16″ (192.7x 7.7cm)

The provenance of the paddle 9999-428 is unknown, but the museum catalog lists it as being "19th century." This paddle has as no edging, but it does carry tips that extend beyond the blade-width, suggesting the tips may have been recycled. There is only a slight shoulder where the blades transition into the shaft. At this paddle's mid-point, the loom is 1-3/4″ (44mm) thick and 1″ (25mm) wide. The blade thickness is 5/8″ (16mm) at the ends.

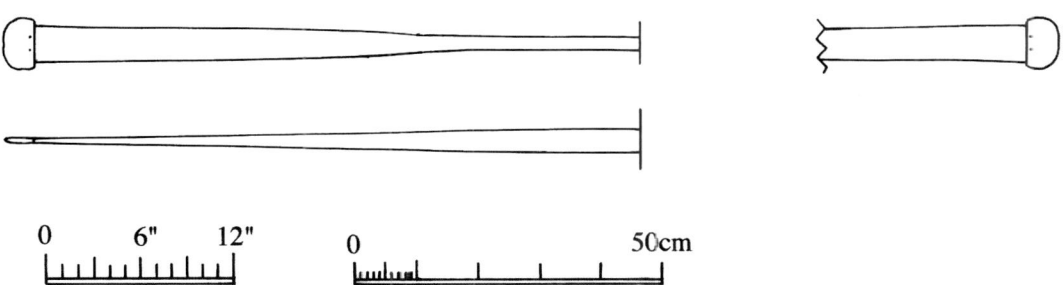

29. McManus Galleries no. 9999-429.
   Length: 6′9-3/4″ Width: 2-3/8″ (207.6x 6.0cm)

Similar in appearance to the 9999-428, this paddle is over 5″ longer, but has much narrower blades, at 2-3/8″ (6cm) wide. The tips are quite wide, and were most likely recycled from an older paddle. The MMG 429's blade edges are rounded over, and are by all appearance finished and ready for use, i.e., not awaiting edging. At its mid-point, this paddle's loom measures 1-3/4″ (44mm) thick and 7/8″ (22mm) wide. The blade ends are 3/8″ (9mm) thick. Each tip is fastened to the blade ends with two ivory nails.

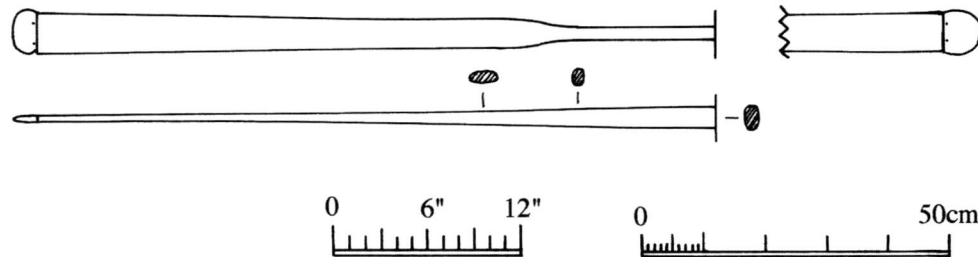

30. National Museum of Scotland no. 1894:227.
Length: 7´5-9/16˝ Width: 2-11/16˝ (227.5x 6.8cm)

This paddle was found by chance, wrapped in heavy plastic and stowed inside a dugout canoe in the National Museum of Scotland. A tag attached to the paddle read "Given by W. Livingstone-Learmonth, Parkhill, Pulmont" and gave the accession number. This paddle is associated with the kayak of the same accession number (plate 57). A photograph taken by Livingstone-Learmonth shows a kayak and paddle in the foreground (figure 3): the kayak greatly resembles the one collected by him, and the paddle on its deck resembles this one— they are likely the same.

Neither bone tip on this paddle fits the blade width precisely, the tips being distinctly undersized and not even centered. The tips were obviously recycled from a different paddle. As bone paddle tips are apt to long outlast a wooden paddle, it is natural that they would be re-used— some paddle tips may be many generations older than the paddles they are presently attached to.

At the 1894's mid-point, the loom is 1-3/8˝ (35mm) thick, and 7/8˝ (22mm) wide. The blades are quite thin as can be seen in the scale drawing. The blade ends are 9/16˝ (14mm) thick.

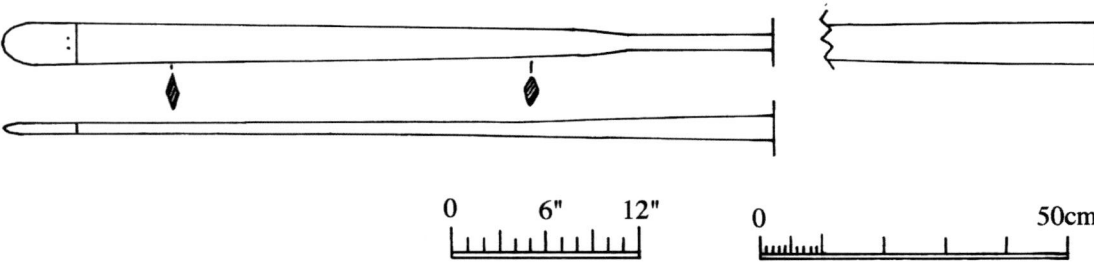

31. Michigan State University Museum no. 4274cw.
Length: 7´9-11/16˝ Width: 2-11/16˝ (237.9x 6.8cm)

This paddle was collected along with a kayak (plate 45) circa 1926 likely from the mid-West Coast of Greenland, probably Sisimiut. Even with one tip missing, this paddle is unusually long, and assuming the missing tip is the size of the existent tip, the original length of the paddle would've been 8´2-3/8˝ (249.8cm) long— the longest non-Polar Greenland paddle in this study.

Edging is not present or evidenced on the MSU's paddle. The blades have a diamond-shaped cross-section, though without a distinct ridge. At its mid-point, the loom measures 1-7/16˝ (36mm) thick and 1-1/16˝ (27mm) wide. The blade ends are 11/16˝ (17mm) thick.

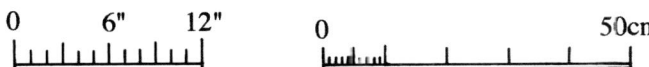

```
0    6"   12"        0              50cm
```

32. National Museum of Finland no. 5023:2.
  Length: 6′10-5/16″ Width: 3-11/16″ (209.1x 9.3cm)

This paddle is likely associated with the kayak retaining the 5023 prefix (plate 63), having been collected by Harald Lindow circa 1924. No tips or edging are present on this pine paddle: It is of considerable breadth, being 3-11/16″ (9.3cm) at the widest. It compares very favorably to the Greenland National Museum's paddle 1550x12 (paddle-plate 34), associated with the kayak 1550x10 from North Greenland (plate 70).

The blades of the 5023:2 are 9/16″ (14mm) thick at 1″ (25mm) from the ends. At the paddle's mid-point, the loom measures 1-9/16″ (40mm) thick and 13/16″ (21mm) wide.

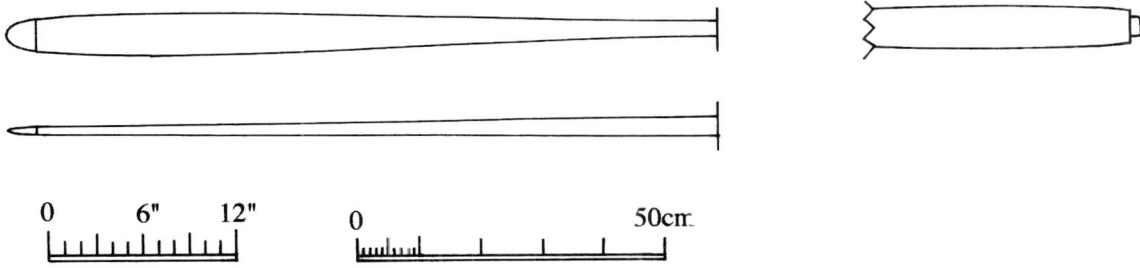

```
0    6"   12"        0              50cm
```

33. Greenland National Museum no. KNK 2237.
  Length: 7′6-3/4″ Width: 2-11/16″ (230.5x 6.8cm)

The paddle KNK 2237 is associated with the kayak bearing the same number (plate 66). The kayak and paddle are from Upernavik, 1930, having been collected by the local district administrator C. E C. Lembcke-Otto.

The 2237 has a bone tip that is fairly blunt. Interestingly, even though one tip is missing, no evidence of a fastening method could be seen, e.g., peg, glue, nail, wedge, etc. It is unusual that a 20th century non-Polar Greenland paddle would carry its maximum blade breadth inboard of the blade ends— usually the widest point is at the end of the wooden portion of the blade. This feature of the 2237 calls to mind the earliest collected paddles in this study (e.g., the DNM ELc.23, ELc.9, and the WFM 232, paddle-plates 2, 1, and 4)

At the 2237's mid-point, the loom measures 1-3/8″ (35mm) thick and 1″ (25mm) wide. The blade ends measure 1/2″ (13mm) thick. The existent tip's length is 2″ (5cm), so the paddle's original length can be estimated to have been about 7′7-7/8″ (233.3cm).

The author has made a replica of this paddle (along with the kayak), and they are both depicted in figures 294 and 296.

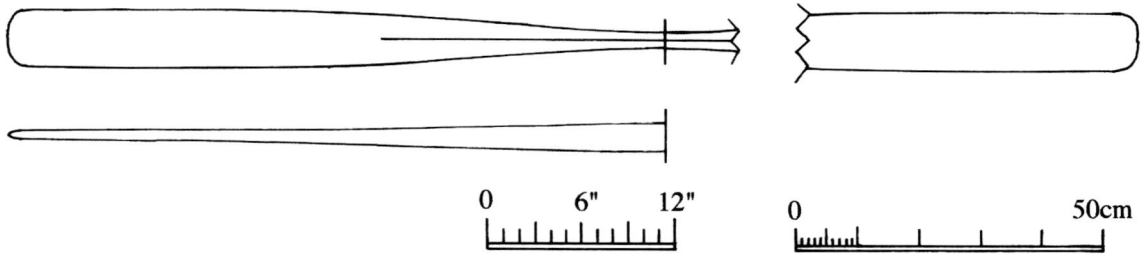

34. Greenland National Museum no. KNK 1550x12.
Length: 7' 1/8" Width: 3-7/8" (213.6x 9.8cm)

This paddle hails from Uummannaq vicinity or southern Upernavik District, and is associated with the kayak KNK 1550x10 (plate 70) that likely dates from the mid-20th century.

The 1550x12 has unusually wide blades (3-7/8"; 9.8cm) with parallel edges for a fair distance of their length. The transition from blade-to-loom is very gradual, and upon reaching the narrowest point, it immediately gets wider again: It has a very short loom— such that 'loom' is almost not the appropriate term. This paddle's tips are only slightly rounded, being very blunt— almost squared. Edging and/or end-pieces were not present or evidenced.

At this paddle's mid-point, the loom is 1-3/4" (44mm) thick and 1-1/16" (27mm) wide. A ridge is present through the entire loom of this paddle.

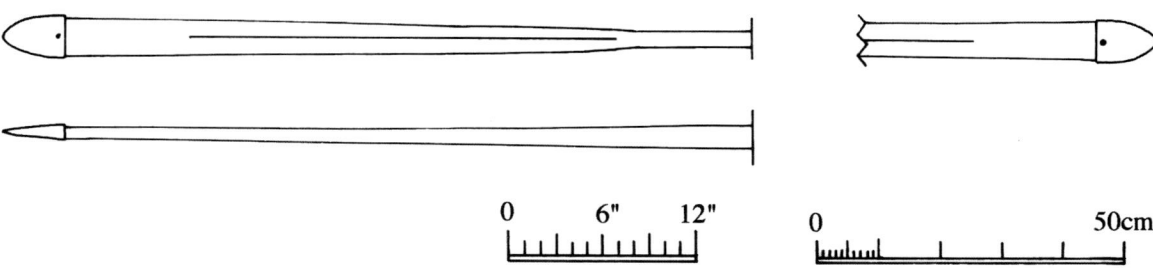

35. Greenland National Museum no. KNK 510x1.
Length: 6' 11-1/2" Width: 2-5/8" (212.1x 6.6cm)

This paddle is of unknown provenance, which is especially unfortunate as it is unlike any others in this study. Its tips are long, moderately pointed and just slightly wider than the blades. Edging is not present or evidenced. A slight shoulder marks the blade/shaft transition area. Very long ridges are present on the blades. Despite its considerable length, the loom is quite short.

The 510x1 does compare somewhat favorably with the CMC IV-A-483 (paddle-plate 39) from Sisimiut. Their tips are very similar and both paddles have ridges on the blades— the 510x1's being sharper. The CMC paddle has edging though, and with blades 3-1/2" (8.9cm) wide, is much wider than the KNK 510x1. It is also worth comparing the 510x1 with the MSU 4274 (paddle-plate 31), likely from Sisimiut.

At the 510x1's mid-point, the loom measures 1-9/16" (40mm) thick and 15/16" (24mm) wide. The blade ends are 3/4" (19mm) thick, but the inboard ends of the tips are 7/8" (22mm) thick. Each tip is secured to the blades with a single copper nail.

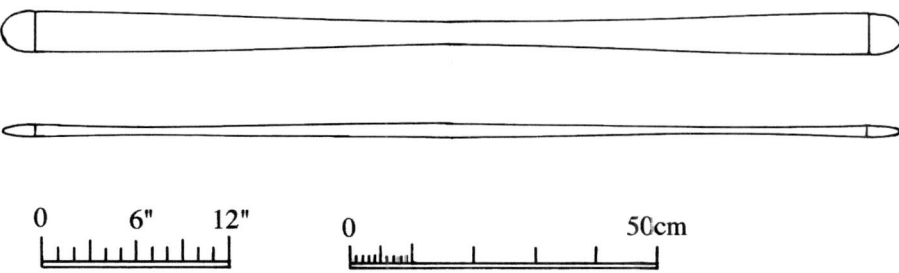

36. Greenland National Museum no. KNK 1966.
Length: 4′9-3/4″ Width: 2-9/16″ (146.7x 6.5cm)

This child's paddle, associated with the kayak KNK 1966 (plate 55), has bone tips, but no edging. The wood is apparently mahogany or sapelé. It is crudely carved, but functional by all appearances. This paddle's thickest point (at the middle of the loom) is only 7/8″ (22mm) thick. As if to make up for the thinness of the paddle, the breadth of the loom at the midpoint is a substantial 1-7/16″ (36mm) wide.

The KNK 1966's blades are 5/8″ (16mm) thick 9″ (22.9cm) from their ends. From this point towards the ends, they thicken to 13/16″ (21mm). This thickening towards a paddle's ends occurs in several paddles in this study and is a practical way to achieve a stronger mortise and tenon joint between the blade ends and the tip pieces.

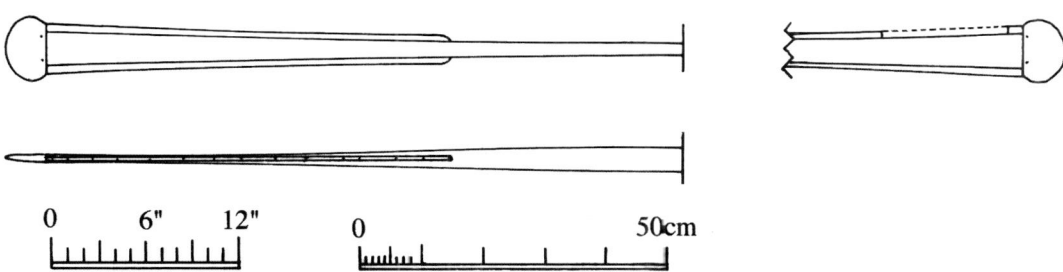

37. Hunterian Museum no. E.101/2.
Length: 7′3-3/4″ Width: 3″ (222.9x 7.6cm)

The Hunterian Museum's paddle E.101/2 is of unknown provenance, but if it belongs to any of the three kayaks at the Hunterian Museum, it likely dates from circa 1780-1820. The E.101/2 has inset edging that is only just over 12″ long— less than half of this paddle's blade length.

The tips of the E.101/2 are asymmetrical: one is long and quite squarish, whereas the other is shorter and more rounded. The edging on this paddle is fairly short at 12-5/8″ (32.0cm), and is not made of ivory or bone, but hardwood, instead. At its mid-point, the loom of the 101/2 measures 1-3/4″ (44mm) thick and 7/8″ (22mm) wide. The blade ends are 11/16″ (17mm) thick.

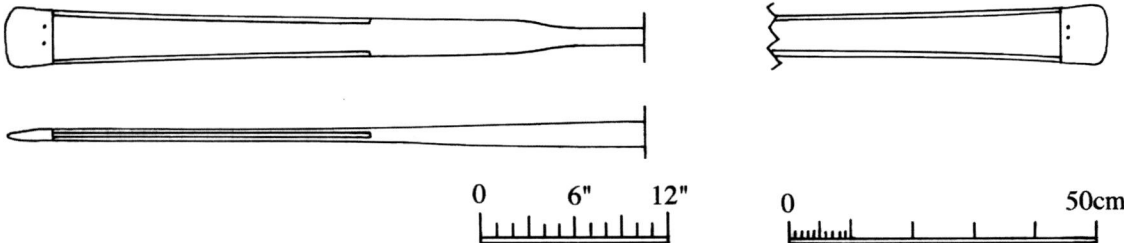

38. Fram Museum no. 176.
Length: 6′9-1/2″ Width: 3-5/8″ (207.0x 9.2cm)

The ideal of formulating a typology based on shape that can be used to identify specific geographic origin of a paddle has been confounded by the fact that the two paddles associated with the Fram Museum's kayaks are so profoundly different, though presumably made at the same time and place: Nuuk, 1888. This paddle, displayed with the Fram Museum's kayak 176 (plate 42), has very squarish tips, inset edging, and a very short loom. Its fellow Nuuk 1888 paddle— also at the Fram Museum (FM 65, paddle-plate 25)— has all the opposite features. Furthermore, the paddle 176 is a foot (30.4cm) longer and 3/4″ (19mm) wider than the no. 65.

At the blade ends, the thickness of the FM 176 is 7/8″ (22mm). At its mid-point, the loom is 1-5/8″ (41mm) thick and 1-1/8″ (28mm) wide.

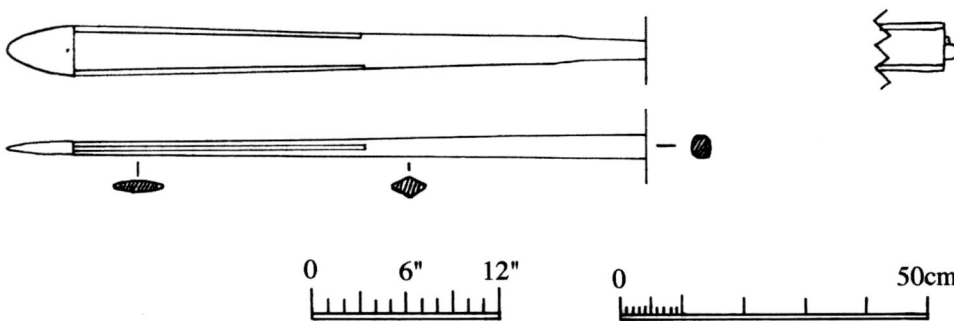

39. Canadian Museum of Civilization no. IV-A-483.
Length: 6′6-3/4″ Width: 3-1/2″ (200.0x 8.9cm)

The tip of this paddle is very long and pointed; only one other paddle's tips look like it: those of the KNK 510x1 (paddle-plate 46), of unknown provenance. The IV-A-483 is known to be from Sisimiut, irca 1935, in that it is associated with the kayak of the same catalog number (plate 46).

One of this paddle's tips is missing, leaving a chipped 3/4″ (19mm) long tenon. The existing tip is 4-3/8″ (11.1cm) long, so the paddle's original length would have been about 6′10-3/8″ (209.2cm).

The blades of this paddle are fairly thick: The terminus of the wood measures 7/8″ (22mm) thick. The paddle thickness at the shoulders is 1-1/2″ (3.8cm); at its mid-point this paddle measures 1-9/16″ thick by 1-1/4″ wide (3.9x 3.2cm).

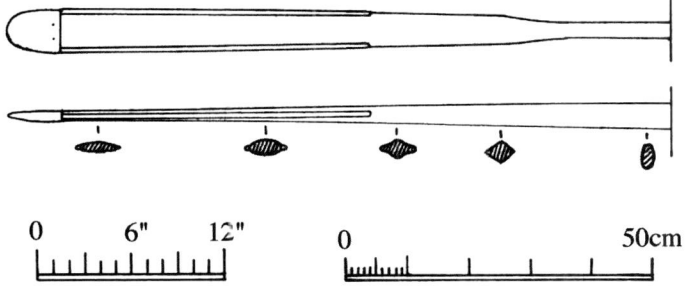

40. Canadian Museum of Civilization no. IV-A-427.
    Length: 7'1-1/4" Width: 3-7/16" (216.5x 8.7cm)

This paddle is associated with a kayak collected at Disko Bay vicinity by a Canadian Eastern Patrol ship circa 1921 (plate 62).

The ends of this blade (at the termini of the wooden portions) measure 13/16" (21mm) thick. At its mid-point, this paddle measures 1-3/4" (4.4cm) thick by 1-1/16" (2.7cm) wide. Each blade's tip is secured with two bone pegs.

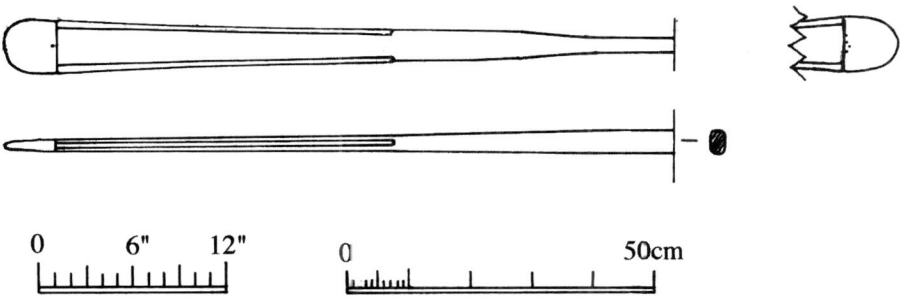

41. Canadian Museum of Civilization no. IV-A-428.
    Length: 7'1-7/8" Width: 3-7/16" (218.1x 8.7cm)

This paddle is associated with a kayak collected by R.T. Porsild at Disko Bay, circa 1927-28 (plate 65). The kayak it is associated with is a type VI kayak exhibiting distinct influences from more southerly kayak-types, i.e., type V.

Both tips measure 3-1/2" long, but they are slightly different in shape. As drawn, the tip on the left is more blunt. This same end has its edging tenoned into mortises in the tip's root (as in figure 393); the tip on the right doesn't have mortises for the edging's ends. The tip on the left has a single bone peg securing it in place while four metal nails secure the other tip.

The blade ends of this paddle are 3/4" (19mm) thick, and at the mid-point, the paddle's shaft measures 1-5/8" thick by 15/16" wide (4.1x 2.4cm).

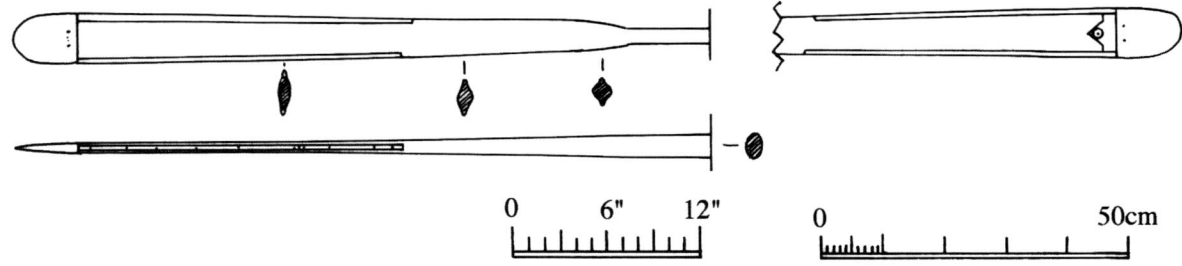

42. Greenland National Museum no. KNK 1764x1.
Length: 7´ 2-7/16˝ Width: 3-1/4˝ (219.5x 8.2cm)

The 1764x1, of unknown provenance, has long tips, inset edging, and a distinct blade-to-loom transition. It is nearly identical in shape to the KNK 1734x1 (paddle-plate 46), also of unknown provenance. This paddle exhibits a curious and complicated scarf at one blade's end. It is likely a repair, the tip having broken off, taking a bit of wood with it. What is most interesting is the use of two Danish kroners as roves, or washers (their dates unreadable, unfortunately.) A piece of metal rod or such is peened over the coins (Danish Kroners have a hole in the center). Note how short this paddle's loom is compared to similar types.

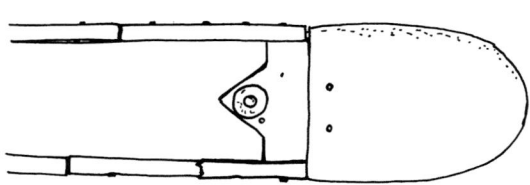

At its mid-point, the 1764x1 measures 1-5/8˝ (42mm) thick and 1-1/16˝ (27mm) wide at the loom. The blade ends are 11/16˝ (17mm) thick. The left tip exhibits four peg holes, but only the outer two holes have fasteners set through them. Cross-sections depict considerable hollowing along the base of the blades.

Figure 392: The Kroner-roved rivet and repair on the paddle 1764x1.

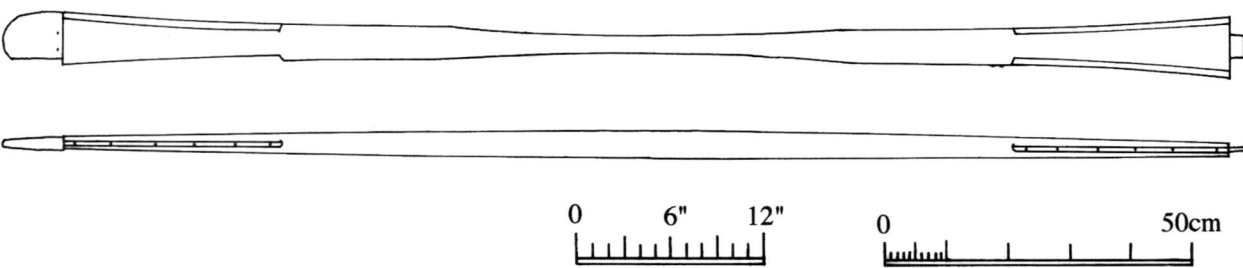

43. American Museum of Natural History no. 60.1/6004c.
Length: 6´ 7-11/16˝ Width: 3-15/16˝ (202.3x 10.2cm)

The AMNH paddle 60.1/6004c and the 6004d (paddle-plate 44) are both catalogued as having been collected by Arthur Norcross at Ammassalik, East Greenland, during the 1931 Norcross-Bartlett Expedition. The place of collection is likely incorrect because both of these paddles are distinctly West Greenlandic in form. Two other paddles at the AMNH collected by Norcross are also catalogued as being from East Greenland, and are undoubtedly from there (paddle-plates 62 and 63).

One of the 6004c's tips is missing, exposing the tenon at the end of the blade. While the other tip is present (suggesting an original overall length of 6'10-5/8" [209.8cm]), it has one edge broken off along the 'grain' of the bone.

The loom-to-blade transition is very subtle on this paddle; what could be considered to be the loom is rather short. At the mid-point, this paddle's loom is 1-3/16" (46mm) thick and 1-1/8" (28mm) wide. The blade ends measure 13/16" (21mm) thick. Richard Nonas assisted with the surveying of this paddle.

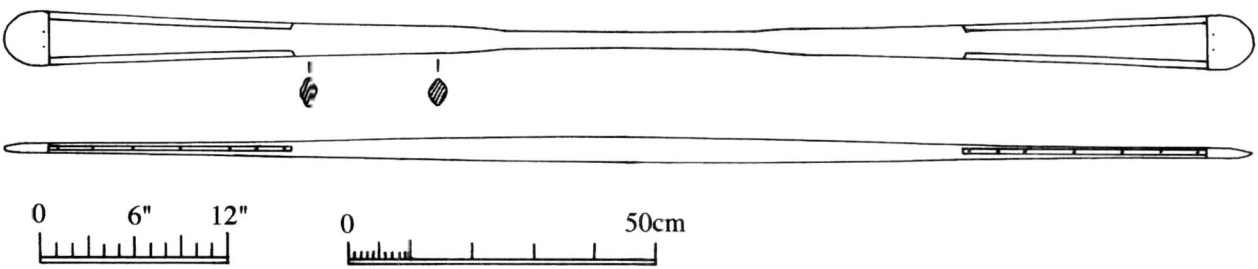

44. American Museum of Natural History no. 60.1/6004d.
   Length: 6'8-1/16" Width: 3-1/2" (203.3x 8.9cm)

The AMNH 60.1/6004d shares the same provenance information ("Angmagssalik, East Greenland") and is of the same form as the 60.1/6004c above (paddle-plate 43). Neither of these paddles are from East Greenland; they are both distinctly West Greenlandic in form. The 6004d is in perfect condition, whereas the 6004c is damaged and is missing pieces.

The blade ends of the paddle 6004d are 3/4" (19mm) thick, and at its mid-point, this paddle measures 1-3/4" thick by 1-1/16" wide (4.4x 2.7cm).

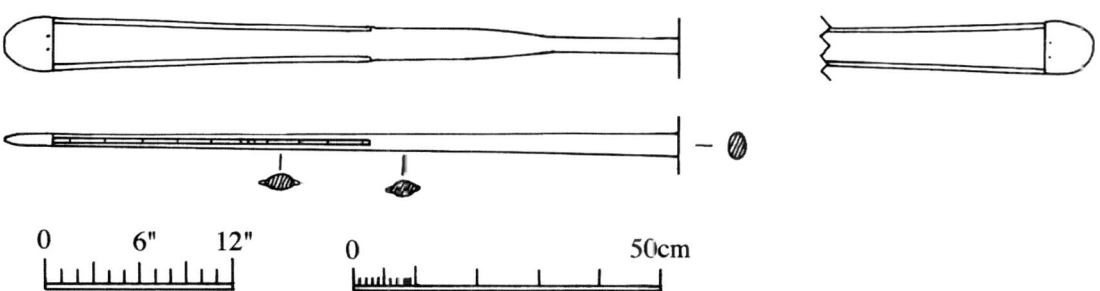

45. Greenland National Museum no. 1764x2.
   Length: 7'2" Width: 3-7/16" (218.4x 8.7cm)

This paddle has fairly wide blades— narrow at first, but they reach considerable breadth at their termini. The edging— made of beech, not ivory, is inset. There is a marked transition from loom-to-blade.

At its mid-point, the 1764-x2 measures 1-3/8" (35mm) thick and 15/16" (24mm) wide. The blade ends are 3/4" (19mm) thick. The tips are double-pegged to the blades.

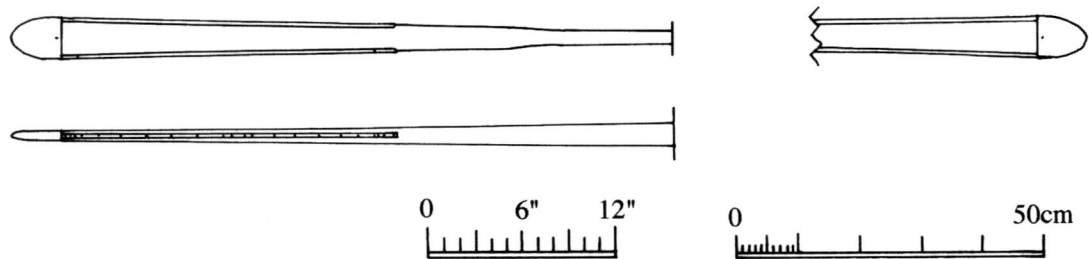

46. Greenland National Museum no. KNK 1734x1.
Length: 7′1″ Width: 2-13/16″ (215.9x 7.2cm)

This paddle has very long tips, inset edging, and a marked blade/shaft transition. The provenance of this paddle is unknown. At its mid-point, the loom measures 1-7/16″ (36mm) thick and 13/16″ (21mm) wide. The blade ends are 11/16″ (17mm) thick

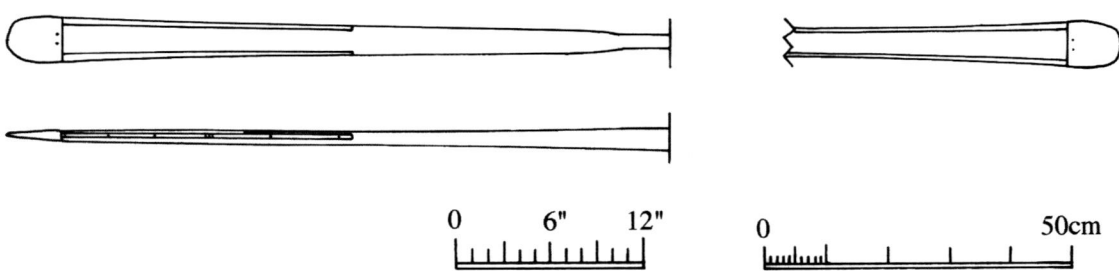

47. Greenland National Museum no. KNK 156x1.
Length: 7′7/8″ Width: 2-7/8″ (215.6x 7.3cm)

Donated to the museum by P. Scavenius Jensen (author of *Den Grønlandske Kajak og dens Redskaber*, 1975), this elegant paddle comes from Maniitsoq, 1958-60. The tips are fairly long, and blunt at the ends. The edging is inset, and the blade transitions into the shaft in a distinct 'shoulder.' At its mid-point, the 156x1 measures 1-1/2″ (38mm) thick and 7/8″ (22mm) wide. The blade ends are 3/4″ (19mm) thick.

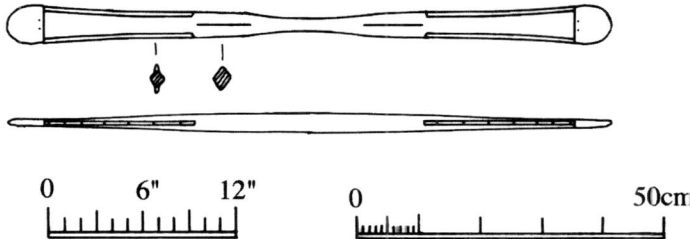

48. Museon no. 117798.
   Length: 3′2-5/8″ Width: 2-3/8″ (98.1x 6.0cm)

This paddle is associated with the kayak commissioned by Knud Rasmussen for a member of a film crew in the early 1930s (plate 47). The 117798 is extremely well made, appearing in stark contrast to the kayak it is associated with, with its baggy muslin skin.

Short ridges are present at the loom-to-blade transition; the loom is very short. At the mid-point, the loom measures 1-1/4″ (32mm) thick by 11/16″ (17mm) wide— substantial considering the associated kayak is sized for a boy of five or six year's age. The blade ends are 1/2″ (13mm) thick.

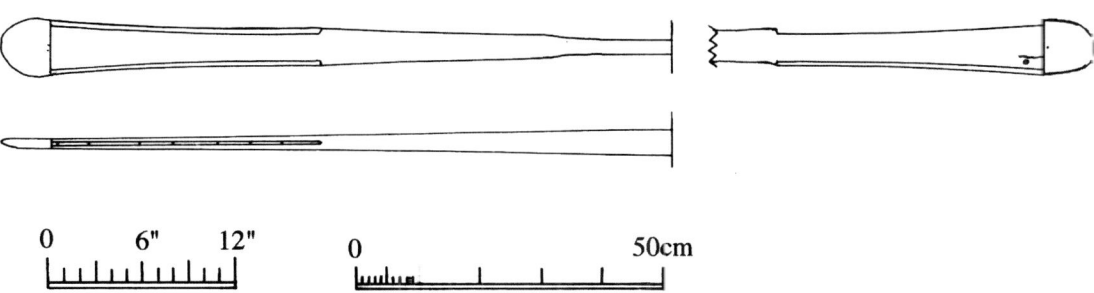

49. U. S. National Museum of Natural History no. 74126.
   Length: 7′1-7/8″ Width: 3-1/2″ (218.1x 8.9cm)

The accession card for this paddle lists an origin of "Holstenberg"— Sisimiut, West Greenland, having been collected by George Merchant, Jr. The card does not give an acquisition date.

The tips of the 74126 are slightly mismatched: As drawn, the tip on the left recurves slightly to meet the blade end, whereas the tip on the right is no wider than the blade end. Likewise, the former tip is fastened with a single peg, while the latter is attached with two pegs.

A repair is evidenced on the right blade: A peg has been set through the blade's face so as to arrest a portion of flaking grain. At the mid-point of the 74126, the loom measures 1-11/16″ (43mm) thick and 7/8″ (22mm) wide. The blade ends are 11/16″ (17mm) thick.

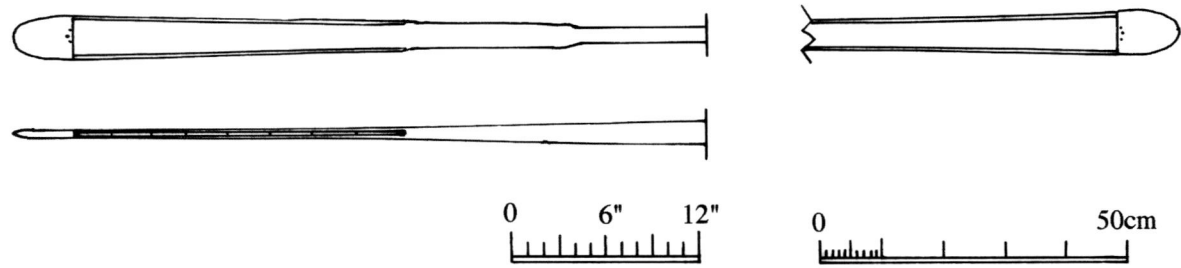

50. US National Museum of Natural History no. 398810.
Length: 7' 4-5/8" Width: 2-7/8" (225.1x 7.3cm)

The US National Museum of Natural History accessioned the paddle 398810 in 1961, having been bequest by the estate of John Oliver La Gorce. La Gorce was the Vice Chairman of the National Geographic Society's Board of Trustees when he died in 1959. The paddle's provenance is listed as Etah—the card reads "Kayak paddle used by Etah Eskimo." The form is identical to more southerly West Greenland paddles, and while the accession card does mention bone tips and edging, it gives a length of 94-3/4" (240.6cm); I measured the paddle as being 88-5/8" (225.1cm) long.

At its mid-point, this paddle measures 1-9/16" (40mm) thick and 15/16" (24mm) wide. The blade ends are 9/16" (14mm) thick. The tips are each triple-pegged to the blades. The edging measures 3/16" x 3/16" (5 x 5mm), the outer edge being rounded.

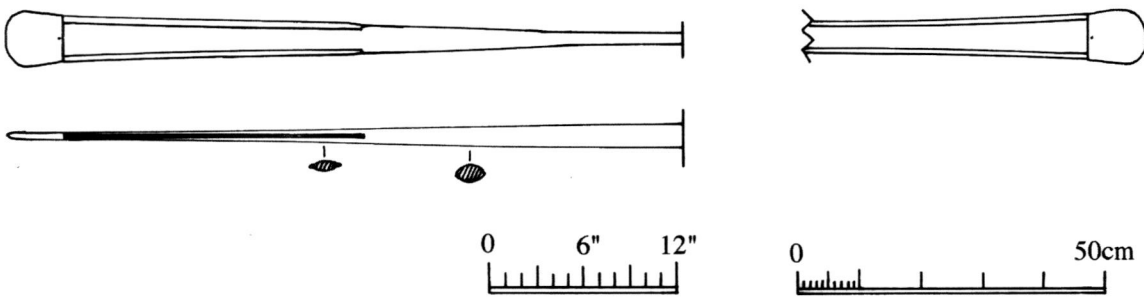

51. US. National Museum of Natural History no. 160398.
Length: 7' 2-3/4" Width: 3" (189.8 x 7.6cm)

The National Museum of Natural History's paddle 160398 has no accession data on its catalog card, but was likely entered into the inventory in the late 1800s (D. Hull-Walski: personal communication). Its form is very similar to that of the same museum's paddle 74126, from Sisimiut (paddle-plate 49), but this paddle form was apparently very widespread.

At its mid-point, the 160398 measures 1-9/16" (40mm) thick and 13/16" (21mm) wide. The blade ends are 7/16" (11mm) thick. The tips are slightly oblong, long and rather squarish.

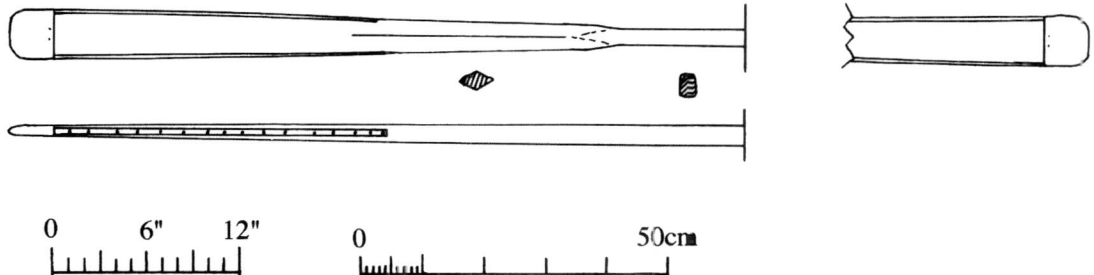

52. Emanuel Korneliussen's paddle.
   Length: 7′10-3/8″ Width: 3-5/16″ (239.7x 8.4cm)

Emanuel Korneliussen of Illorsuit made this paddle in 1959 for John Heath of Texas. Heath had also commissioned a kayak from Korneliussen— the kayak in plate 72. The paddle has bone tips and inset edging. At 7′10-3/8″ (239.7cm), this is the second longest non Polar-Greenland kayak paddle in this study, after paddle-plate 31.

A short ridge is present along the blades where they transition to the shaft; at this point the ridge changes to a flat surface, giving way to a somewhat squarish cross-section at the shaft. Midway along the ridge, the paddle's cross-section is diamond shaped. At its mid-point, this paddle's loom measures 1-1/4″ (32mm) thick and 1-1/8″ (29mm) wide. The blade ends are 11/16″ (17mm) thick.

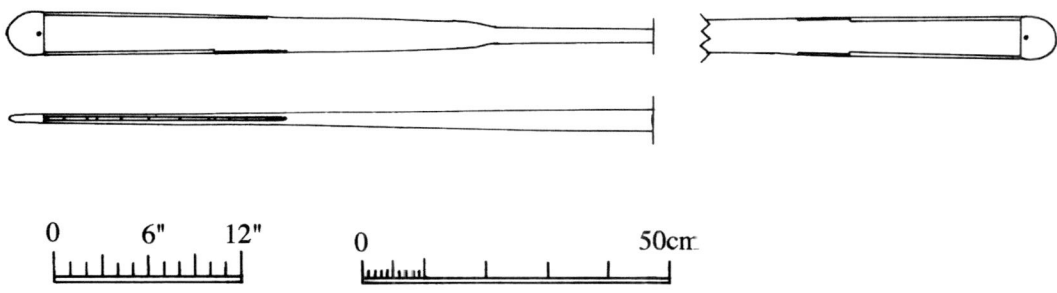

53. Rijksmuseum voor Volkenkunde no. 1076-2.
   Length: 6′10-5/16″ Width: 2-3/4″ (209.1x 7.0cm)

This paddle is positively associated with the kayak 1076-1, likely from Qaqortoq, circa 1892 (plate 75). Its edging consists of outboard strips 3/16″ (5mm) wide, with inboard pieces 1/8″ (3mm) wide. Each tip is attached with a single peg. At the 1076's mid-point, the loom is 1-3/8″ (35mm) thick, and 7/8″ (22mm) wide. The blade end is 1/2″ (13mm) thick.

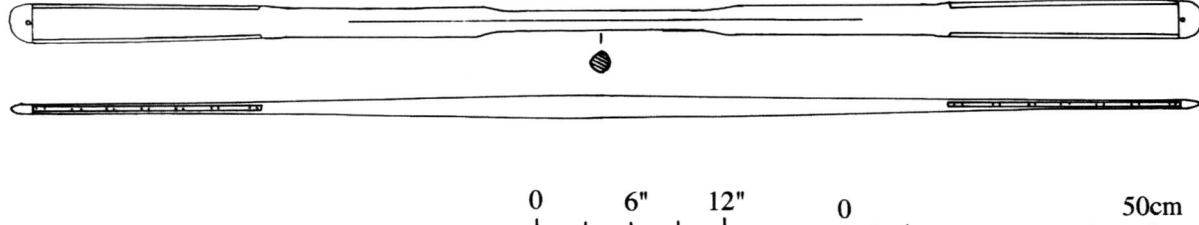

54. Greenland National Museum no. KNK 1550x20.
Length: 6´ 4-5/8" Width: 2-3/8" (194.6x 6.0cm)

The 1550x20 is not positively associated with any of the kayaks cataloged as '1550x_:' These are all items from a diverse collection sent to the Greenland National Museum from the Royal Greenland Company. This paddle has very narrow, parallel blades, with inset edging, and a marked transition from loom-to-blade. There is a slight yet distinct ridge from about 2´ (61cm) from the tips, extending inwards, through the loom. Paddles with such ridges along the entire loom are very rare.

The bone tips are fastened to the paddle with copper nails— one on each tip. The edging is secured with ivory pegs in neatly paired sets. At this paddle's mid-point, the width is 1-1/4" (32mm) and the thickness is 1-3/8" (35mm).

A replica of this paddle is depicted in figures 325 and 326, being used with the replica of the DNM L.9726 (plate 77).

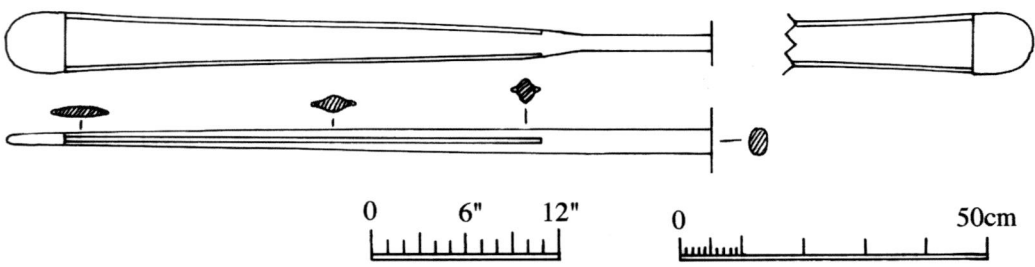

55. American Museum of Natural History no. 60/6191.
Length: 7´ 7-5/16" Width: 3-7/8" (231.9x 9.8cm)

This paddle is positively associated with the American Museum of Natural History's kayak from circa 1908 of the same number (plate 76). While the origin of the kayak is recorded as "Holstensborg" (Sisimiut) in museum catalogs, the kayak is certainly from South Greenland, most likely Nanortalik vicinity.

The 60/6191 is very heavy, being much broader and thicker than most Greenland kayak paddles. At its mid-point, the loom measures 1-9/16" (40mm) thick and 1-1/16" (27mm) wide. The blade ends are 3/4" (19mm) thick. The 60/6191's end-pieces are moderately long and broad and the paddle's inset edging extends quite close to the loom, protecting the blades entirely. The blade-to-loom transition is distinct. Despite the tips being firmly attached to this paddle, I was unable to discern any means of fastening them. Perhaps they were blind-wedged?

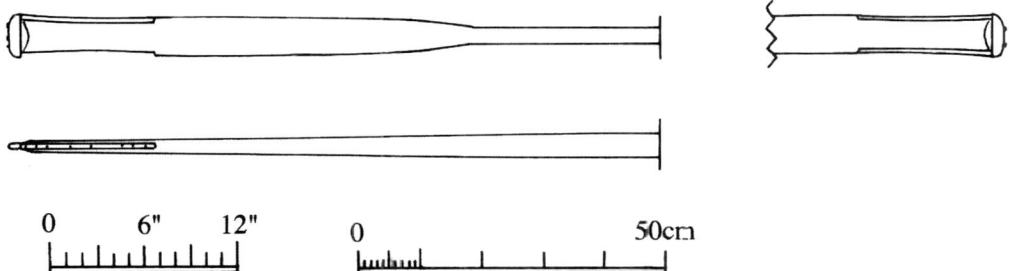

56. Greenland National Museum no. KNK 527x16.
Length: 6′ 11-1/2″ Width: 2-13/16″ (212.1x 7.2cm)

This paddle has some of the shortest edging of any in this survey, and has the shortest tips. Its blades are fairly parallel for most of the length, but actually curve inward where the edging is, and then back out to the end-tip piece. The reason for this is not known: I've not come across any references for such a paddle-shape. I could assume it may have functioned as an 'index' of sorts: It would allow the kayaker to feel where the paddle was being held— most helpful while doing the sliding-stroke.

The blade-ends of the 527x16 are beveled abruptly to receive thinner ivory tips. At their extremity, they measure 7/16″ (11mm) thick; 1/2″ (13mm) inboard of this the blade measures 11/16″ (17cm) thick. At its mid-point, the loom measures 1-9/16″ (40mm) thick and 1-1/8″ (29mm) wide. The missing edging piece has revealed that the edging is mortised into the tip.

The tips of the 527x16 are very short: 13/16″ (21mm) long— this doesn't leave much room for a mortise to receive the blade's tenon. The builder has bypassed this problem by using metal nails set through the ends of the tips and into the end-grain of the blade ends. Each tip has two metal nails securing it; the left-hand tip (as drawn) also has an ivory peg, perhaps to tighten it up a bit.

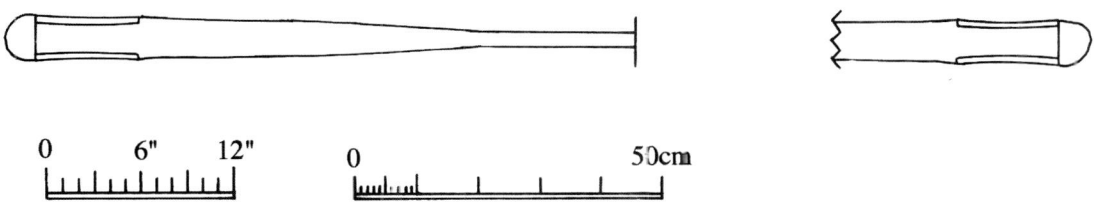

57. University Museum of Cultural Heritage no. 6463.
Length: 6′ 8-5/8″ Width: 3″ (204.8x 7.6cm)

The 6463 bears a distinct resemblance to the Greenland National Museum's paddle 527x16, in that the short edging is curved inwards, such that it has the old "Coke bottle" appearance. A detailed provenance was not available for this paddle.

I was unable to record thicknesses for this paddle due to how it was stored. I did manage to measure the thickness at the mid-point of the loom: 1-5/8″ (41mm), and the breadth at this point is 1″ (25mm). The tips are longer than those of the 527x16.

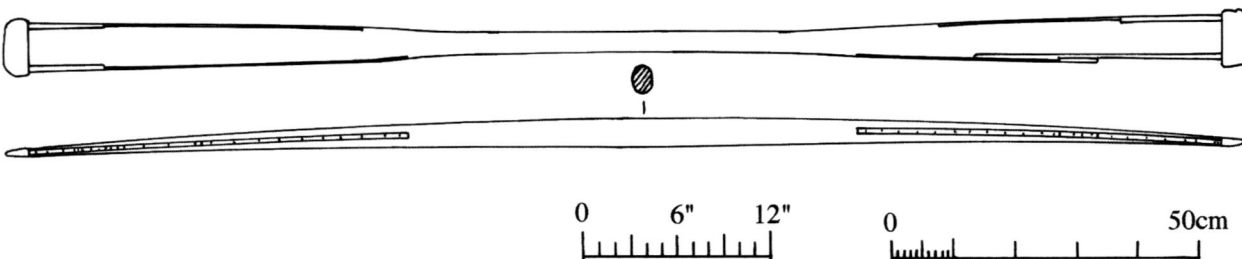

58. Greenland National Museum no. KNK 1420.
Length: 6′ 7-3/4″ Width: 3″ (202.5x 7.6cm)

This is the famous "Nualik" paddle collected by Amdrup in 1899. It was found in a "dead-house" 167 miles (269km) Northeast of Ammassalik.[52] As Amdrup passed south through Ammassalik with his Nualik collections, some items in the collection were recognized by locals as having belonged to a man who had left Ammassalik vicinity two years before Gustav Holm's visit in 1884-85 (Thalbitzer, 1914:323).

I was immediately struck by this paddle's size and weight. It seemed as if a strong giant had made it compared to most every other Greenland paddle I'd held. It is not unusually long, but the grips made me feel quite small. The wood must have been a tight-grained yew or larch, or a very resinous fir— I didn't weigh it, but estimate that it would fall into the 3-1/2— 4 pound range.

This paddle had been brought to the Danish National Museum in Copenhagen, but it has since been transferred to the Greenland National Museum in Nuuk. Its original DNM catalog number was L.6374. A photograph of this paddle appears in William Thalbitzer's *The Ammassalik Eskimo* (1914:385, fig.88).

While the 1420 is probably one of the oldest East Greenland paddles in museum collections, another form is known to have existed in East Greenland at one time. Thalbitzer commissioned a model of an old-form paddle from an East Greenlander; the paddle resembles the Danish National Museum's Elc.23 (paddle-plate 2) more than it does modern East Greenland paddles. This old-form is depicted in figure 337, after Thalbitzer (1914:386, fig. 91).

The blades of the 1420 are dihedral: The paddle is curved such that the blades reach forward at their tips. Among Greenland kayak paddles, dihedral blades seem to only occur in East Greenland, although dihedral paddles are also known from Western Alaska (Golden, field notes: 2001). While the KNK 1420 is not particularly long, it is very stoutly made. The loom thickness is 1-13/16″ (46mm), and is 1-5/16″ (33mm) wide, suggesting its owner had very large hands. The blade ends are 9/16″ (14mm) thick. The edging is generally two different widths, and one edge of one blade has extensive patching.

---

[52] The house is referred to as a "dead house" because by all appearance and investigation, it had been abandoned with all belongings in place, suggesting all the inhabitants had suddenly succumbed to death— possibly poisoning from tainted meat (Thalbitzer, 1914:323, 344-345).

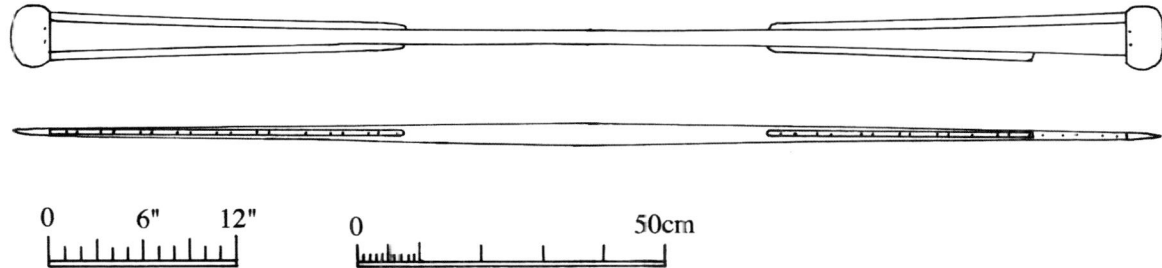

59. Greenland National Museum nc. KNK 1418.
Length: 6′7-1/8″ Width: 3-1/4″ (200.9x 8.2cm)

Collected during the Holm expedition to Ammassalik in 1884, the KNK 1418[53] is very similar to later examples from Ammassalik vicinity, notably the Museon 48050 (paddle-plate 64). The workmanship evidence on this paddle is very high— the outer ends of the ivory edging are tenoned, and the end-pieces have small mortises in the base to receive them.

At its mid-point, the 1418's loom measures 1-7/16″ (36mm) thick and 1-1/16″ (27mm) wide. The blade ends are 1/2″ (13mm) thick. The raised edging is tenoned into the base of the ivory tips, as in figure 393. The tenons measure 7/32″ (5.5mm) long, 3/16″ (5mm) square, and are positioned 3/64″ (1.1mm) above the inner face of the edging's base; the edging is 3/8″ (9mm) thick. The edging is made from narwhal ivory, and it has started to unwind, twisting and breaking the ivory pegs securing it the shaft. This paddle is symmetrical— the blades are not dihedral.

Figure 393: Detail of the KNK 1418's joinery. Note how the edging is tenoned into the ivory tip. The two pegs in the tip are fastened through a tenon projecting from the blade-end.

---

[53] This paddle and the kayak in this study— also the KNK 1418 both retain the same catalogue numbers as they are both part of the same large collection [the "Holm" collection] recently repatriated to Greenland. This paddle's catalog number at the Danish National Museum was Lb.367a.

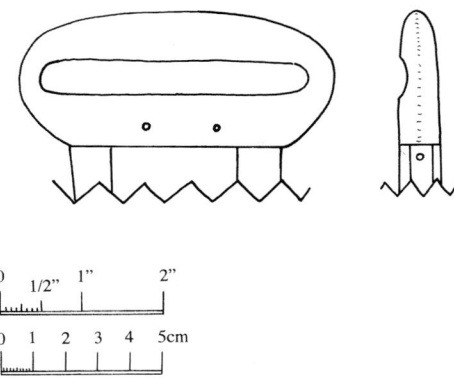

60. **University Museum of Cultural Heritage no. 29.882.**
    Length: 6′ 7-15/16″ Width: 2-5/8″ (203.0x 6.6cm)

This paddle is associated with the circa 1924 East Greenland kayak in plate 84. Only the tip of this paddle was surveyed due to access constraints. The tip was given attention on account of it's having a unique characteristic: a channel carved into one face of the tip. Likewise, the paddle's other tip had the same groove, furthering the likelihood of its being deliberate. A full-size drawing of one of the tips is depicted; the channel is open at its ends, not being a divot per-se.

The 29.882 has dihedral blades, and while it was not surveyed, I thought it important to at least record that the channels in the tips were oriented such that they face upwards when the tips are on a flat surface, the loom being arched upwards.

The purpose of these channels is a mystery, but several theories could explain them:

1. The channels could have afforded a better grip if the paddle was extended to reach something.

2. The channels might have facilitated the deployment of the shooting screen— a wooden stand attached to the kayak's bow over which a white cloth is suspended for camouflage.

3. To provide a better grip for rolling with the paddle extended.

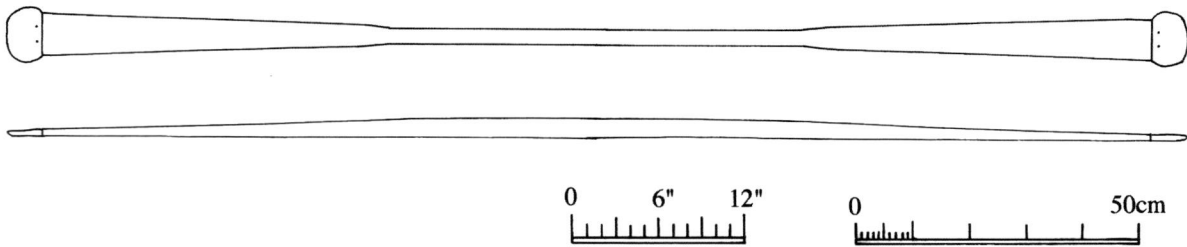

61. **National Museum of Finland no. 5023:1.**
    Length: 6′ 10-1/8″ Width: 3-1/8″ (208.6x 7.9cm)

This paddle's provenance was not specifically presented: Two paddles retain the "5023" prefix, and the kayak with that prefix is from North West Greenland (plate 63). The other paddle bearing the

'5023' prefix (5023:2, paddle plate 32) is most likely the paddle associated with the kayak; the 5023:1 appears very different, and appears to be from the opposite corner of Greenland.

The case for this paddle being of Eastern Greenlandic origin is its having dihedral blades which do not occur in Greenland outside of Ammassalik district. With its broad oblong tips, the 5023:1 does resemble some West Greenland paddles (e.g., paddle plates 27 and 28), but oblong paddle tips seem to have disappeared from the West Coast by the late 1800s.

At its mid-point, the 5023:1 measures 1-3/8" (35mm) thick and 1-3/16" (30mm) wide. The blade ends are 1/2" (13mm) thick. Both tips are held in place with two ivory pegs.

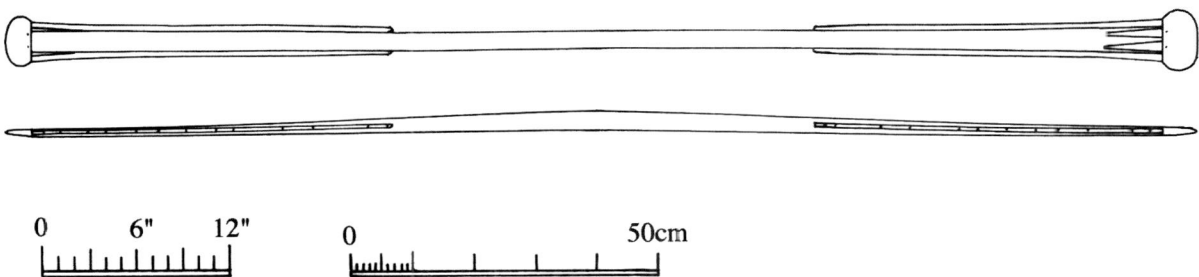

62. American Museum of Natural History no. 60.1/6004a.
Length: 6' 4-1/16" Width: 2-3/4" (193.2x 7.0cm)

This East Greenland paddle— and the following example— was collected by Arthur Norcross in 1931 during the Norcross-Bartlett Expedition to Northeast Greenland. Norcross also collected the East Greenland kayak 60.1/6003 (plate 85) during this expedition.

This paddle exhibits extensive repairs and modifications. One end has wooden triangular shims attached to the blade edge so as to achieve the desired width. The opposite end appears to have had its two tenons replaced. This was done by making two wedge-shaped cuts into the blade's face, and replacing the cutouts with wooden pieces with tenons on their outboard ends. Pegs set through the paddle's edges secure the patches.

The 60.1/6004a is a dihedral paddle. At the midpoint, the loom is 1-7/16" (36mm) thick and 13/16" (21mm) wide. At the blade ends (at the base of the tips), the thickness is 9/16" (14mm).

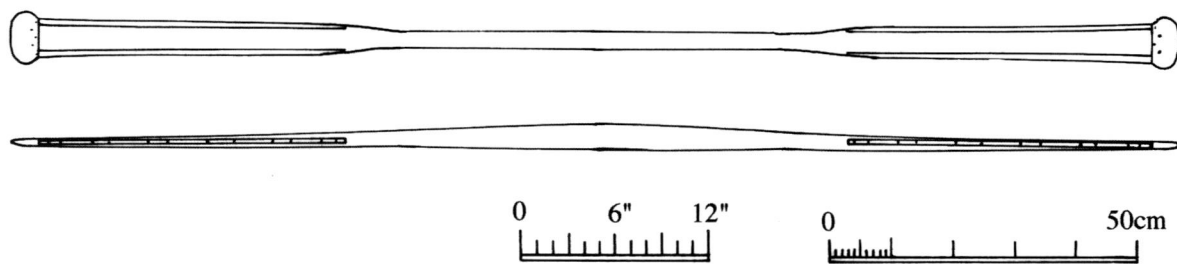

63. American Museum of Natural History no. 60.1/6004b.
  Length: 6′ 2-1/2″ Width: 2-1/2″ (189.2 x 6.3cm)

Arthur Norcross collected the American Museum of Natural History's paddle 60.1/6004b in East Greenland in 1931. The 6004b has dihedral blades, oblong tips, and what is rare for Eastern paddles: inset edging. The tips are extensively fastened: Four pegs are used on the right tip, and five are on the left tip. Two of these pegs on the latter tip are set through tenons at the end of the edging. Such tenons are depicted in figure 393.

At its mid-point, the loom of the 6004b measures 1-3/8″ (35mm) thick and 1-1/8″ (28mm) wide. At the blade ends, the thickness is 1/2″ (13mm).

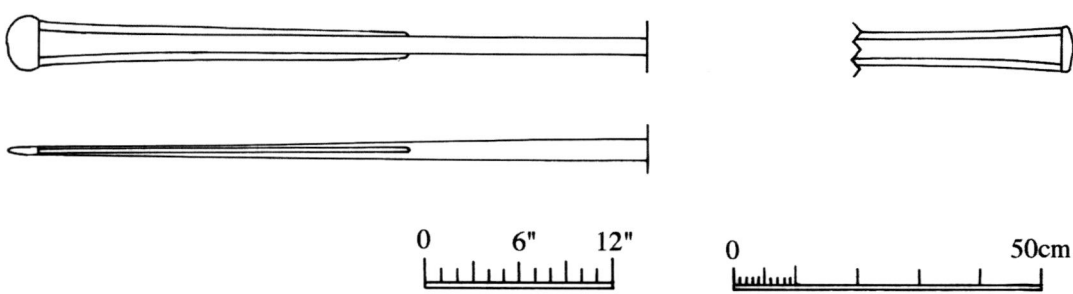

64. Museon no. 48050.
  Length: 6′ 10-3/8″ Width: 2-13/16″ (209.2 x 7.2cm)

The paddle 48050 is the paddle associated with the Museon's kayak 48057 (plate 87) collected by Dr. Nico Tinbergen in the 1930s. Like the kayak, the paddle is a marvel of workmanship, though flawed with its hastily repaired tip. It compares very well with the early-contact paddle collected by Gustav Holm in 1884: the KNK 1418 (paddle-plate 59).

At its mid-point, the loom measures 1-1/2″ (38mm) thick and 1-1/8″ (28mm) wide. The blade ends are 9/16″ (14mm) thick. The blades of this paddle are slightly dihedral.

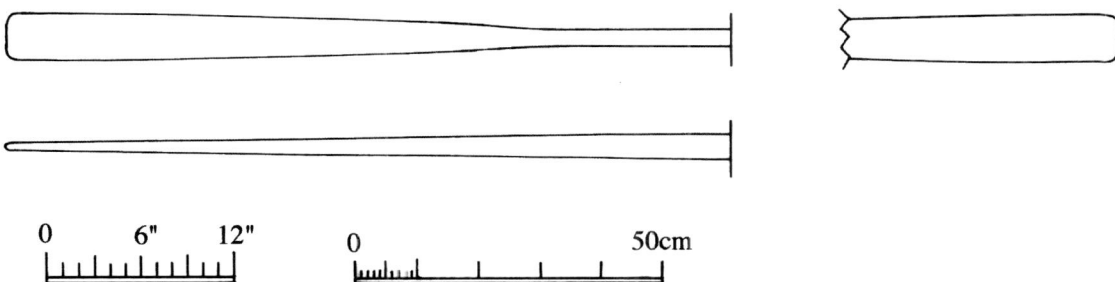

65. Rijksmuseum voor Volkenkunde no. 351-79.
   Length: 7′8-11/16″ Width: 3-1/16″ (235.4x 7.7cm)

The Rijksmuseum's catalog file lists this paddle as having come from the Dutch Ministry of Marine in 1883. The RvV's '351' series shares the same history; other items in that series include the kayaks 351-77 and 351-78 (plates 8 and 9— the latter having since been transferred to the Greenland National Museum), and the paddles 351-30 and 351-31 (paddle-plates 10 and 15). All of these items— including the present paddle, which is associated with the kayak 351-78 (now the KNK 1161), are likely from 17th or 18th century West Greenland.

So why have I placed this paddle in the middle of a batch of 20th century East Greenland paddles? This is simply a hunch, but I think that this paddle may not be what its catalog suggests, and instead I think that there is a likelihood that it actually belongs to the RvV's kayak 2823 (plate 88) from 1930s East Greenland. This is a bold speculation that warrants explanation: The 351-79 doesn't appear to me to be a particularly old paddle— especially not one as old as the kayak it is associated with. Its wood is light and not as oxidized and age-polished as the other blades in the 351 series or others known to be quite old. The form of the 351-79 also suggests that it is a later paddle: Its blade edges are not parallel (as in figure 390b), and are instead tapered (as in figure 390c)— a form that seems to have emerged after 1800.

Also, the 351-79 had never been fitted with tip pieces or edging, which is unusual for a paddle of the early historic period. It is of course also very rare for an East Greenland paddle to not have edging and tip pieces, but note the paddle in figure 350— being used by Dr. Nico Tinbergen in his kayak in East Greenland in the 1930s. My sense is that the 351-79 is the paddle in the photograph; Tinbergen's kayak (RvV 2823; plate 88) is presently in the Rijksmuseum.[54]

As simply as Tinbergen's kayak was fitted and rigged, it is not too much of a surprise his paddle would follow suit, i.e., not have edging or separate tips. At its mid-point, the 351-79 measures 1-9/16″ (40mm) thick and 1-1/8″ (28mm) wide. The blades are 1/4″ (6mm) thick at their very ends, and 1/2″ (13mm) thick 1-1/4″ (32mm) inboard.

---

[54] A similar incongruity surfaced with regards to the paddle holder shown in figure 137, top. I found this paddle holder laying inside of the kayak 351-77— a kayak likely from the 17th or 18th century; the holder itself is clearly of the East Greenland form, and the positions of its buttons aligns perfectly with the spacing of the RvV 2823's foredeck lines; see also note 22.

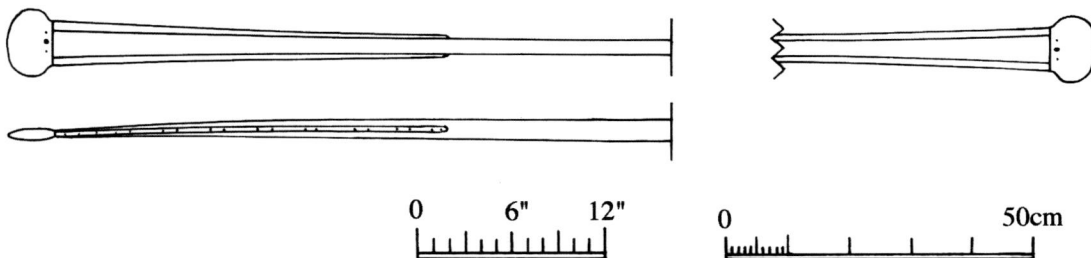

66. Greenland National Museum no. KNK 1383x3.
  Length: 7′1-1/8″ Width: 2-15/16″ (216.2x 7.4cm)

The KNK 1383x3 is a very well made East Greenland paddle with very wide tips. The ends of the blade itself become fairly thin, but the tip thickens considerably. Where the tip meets the blade, when viewed on-flat, there is an elegant re-curve in the base of the tip— a classic ogee curve. The paddle itself is slightly dihedral, as is evident in the elevation. The 1383x3 dates from circa 1938, and is from Ammassalik.

At its mid-point the loom measures 1-1/2″ (38mm) thick and 1-1/16″ (27mm) wide. The blade ends are 1/2″ (13mm) thick. The tips are not only oblong when viewed en-face, but also en-edge: The tips are 11/16″ (17mm) thick at their midpoints.

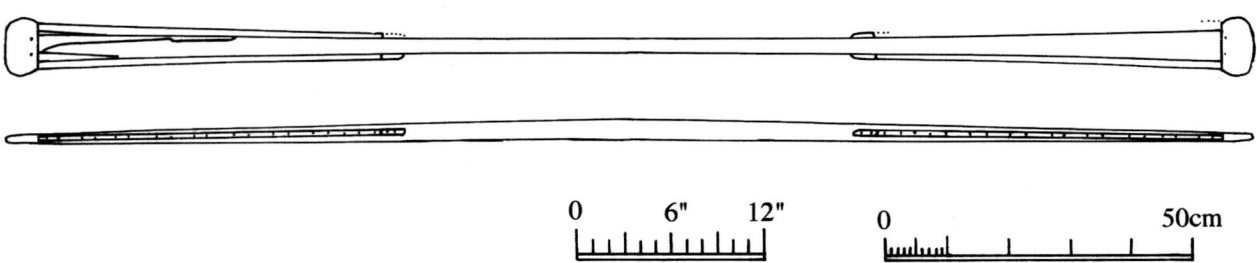

67. U. S. National Museum of Natural History no. 332423.
  Length: 6′7-3/4″ Width: 3″ (202.5x 7.6cm)

Extensive scarfing and/or repairs have been made to one end of this East Greenland paddle. By all appearances, the tenon(s) holding the end-piece on had been fractured off, and likely a good bit of the blade on that side had been damaged. The attached pieces of wood replace a fair amount of blade surface area as well as forming tenons to which an end-piece is attached.

A familiar looking code format had been inked onto this paddle— "L.5439"— and as expected it turned out that the paddle had been transferred from the Danish National Museum to the (US) National Museum of Natural History. The NMNH data cards also list an accession date of 1926, a locale of "Ammassalik Eskimo, E. Greenland," and the collectors having been "Muller Saphus et al."

At its mid-point, this paddle measures 1-7/16″ (36mm) thick and 1″ (25mm) wide. The blades are 1/2″ (13mm) thick at their ends. The 332423 has distinctly dihedral blades.

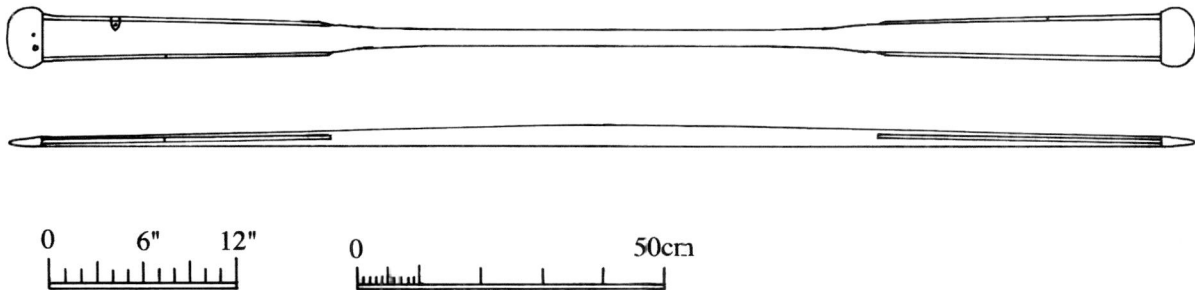

68. Museon no. 57536.
   Length: 6´4˝   Width: 3˝ (193.0x 7.6cm)

The 57536 makes use of some truly exotic (to Greenland) materials: The tips are oak, which is not too unusual, but the edging is made of bamboo— except for a short piece of fir. The story of how several pieces of bamboo made it to East Greenland would certainly be an interesting one (these pieces are too long to have been chopsticks). It is of no surprise that a Greenlander would quickly find that this 'new' material has a high crushing strength

The edging and tips are fastened to the paddle with metal nails. A small tab of tin is nailed around an edge of one blade. At its mid-point, the loom measures 1-1/4˝ (32mm) thick and 1-1/8˝ (35mm) wide. The blade ends are 11/16˝ (17mm) thick.

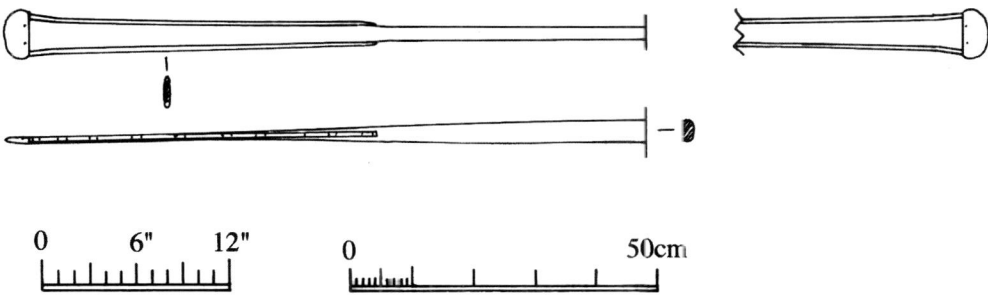

69. Greenland National Museum no. KNK 1194.
   Length: 6´10-3/8˝   Width: 2-3/4˝ (209.2x 7.0cm)

The provenance of this paddle is unfortunately entirely unknown, but I am certain it comes from East Greenland because it has dihedral blades, raised edging, and oblong tips. While all of the KNK 1194's edging was present, it was all disassembled. The outboard ends of the edging have tenons that extend into mortises in the base of the tips. At its mid-point, the 1194's loom measures 1-7/16˝ (36mm) thick and 15/16˝ (24mm) wide. The blade ends are 3/8˝ (9mm) thick.

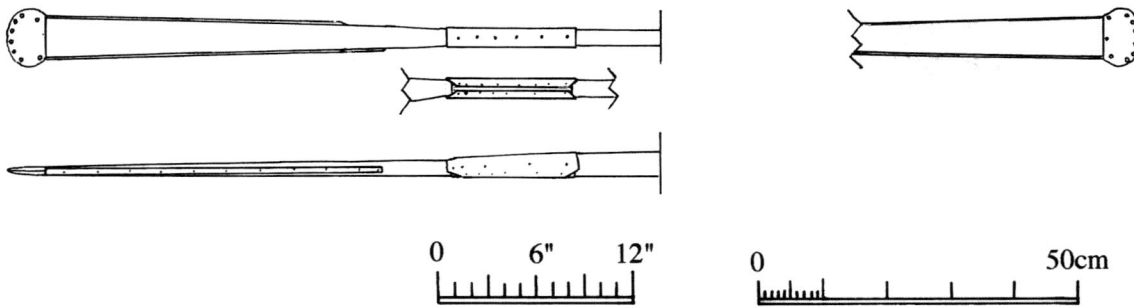

70. Greenland National Museum no. KNK 1002.
   Length: 6′8-1/2″ Width: 2-13/16″ (204.5x 7.2cm)

Catalogued as being from Maniitsoq, circa 1977, this paddle is instead distinctly East Greenlandic in origin. The tips are made from folded and riveted aluminum. A tin wrapping around the shaft may have been tacked on to mend a crack or splinter. The edging is also made from aluminum— 1/16″ (1.5mm) thick, and 1/4″ (6mm) wide. This paddle is dihedral: it is essentially straight on one face, and the other is arched. The fact that this paddle has dihedral blades and oblong tips sheds doubt on an origin of Maniitsoq. At its mid-point, the KNK 1002 measures 1-9/16″ (40mm) thick and 1″ (25mm) wide. The blade ends are 9/16″ (14mm) thick.

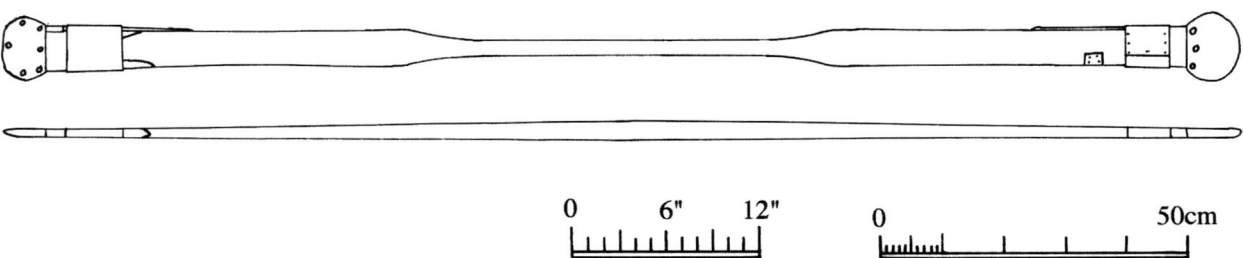

71. Museon no. 59876.
   Length: 6′7-1/4″ Width: 2-7/8″ (201.3x 7.3cm)

The paddle associated with the Museon's kayak 59876 (plate 90) is made of bone, wood, and metal. Much as the kayak is armored (with a sheet-metal clad bow), so is the paddle: Both of the tips are metal— one being of a chunk of pot-metal, the other being of folded and riveted aluminum sheet. Both blade-ends are reinforced with tin sheeting tacked to the faces. On the left blade (as drawn), the tin covers and reinforces a scarf joint. Only two small pieces of bone protect the paddle's edges, and they do so on just one side. These pieces are towards the ends, and have been further re-enforced with a tin wrapping that goes all the way around the blades.

It is hopefully obvious to the reader that I have drawn this paddle upside-down: The short strips of bone edging were certainly oriented to be closest to the water when the paddle was used around ice. Figure 356 shows the conditions in which such an armored paddle would have been prized. At the 59876's mid-point, the loom measures 1-3/8″ (35mm) thick and 15/16″ (24mm) wide. The blade ends are 9/16″ (14mm) thick.

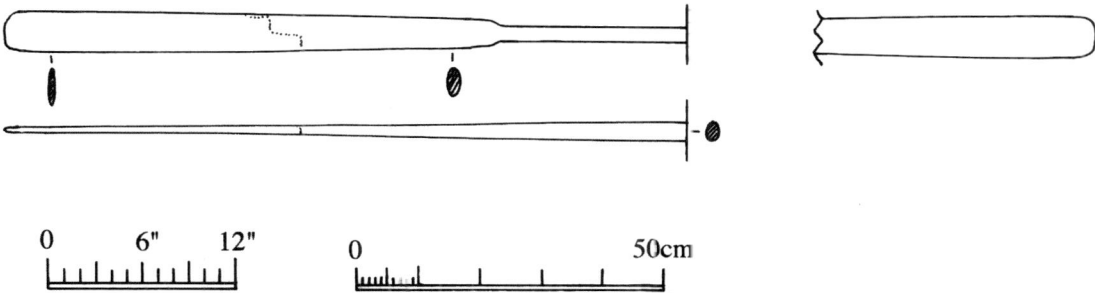

72. Maligiaq Padilla's paddle.
  Length: 7' 3-1/2" Width: 2-3/4" (222.2x 7.0cm)

This is the paddle used by Maligiaq Padilla of Sisimiut in 1998 the year he became the youngest person to win the Greenland National Kayaking Championships at age 16. Padilla is also the builder of the rolling kayak depicted in plate 92.

The dotted line that jogs across the paddle's blade in the drawing shows where it has broken. In 1999 it met its fate in of all places, the Orlando Florida Airport, where it was destroyed in Padilla's hands as it buckled against the ceiling during an otherwise uneventful escalator ride. Maligiaq writes that the paddle was his favorite at the time, and that he had to make a new one right away at Greg Stamer's house for paddling demonstrations (personal communication, 2004).

At its mid-point, Maligiaq's paddle measures 1-1/8" (28mm) thick and 1" (25mm) wide. The blades are 7/16" (11mm) thick 1-1/2" (38mm) from the end.

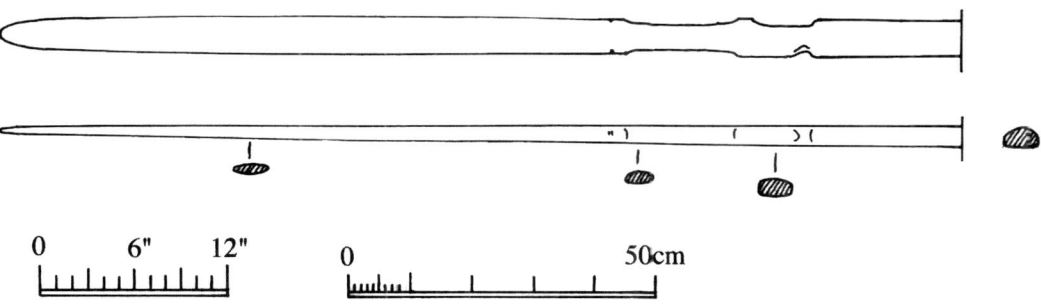

73. US National Museum of the American Indian no. 165227.
  Length: 10' 3-3/8" Width: 2-7/16" (313.4x 6.2cm)

The Museum of the American Indian's paddle 165227 marks the introduction of kayak paddles from Polar Greenland— paddles that exhibit distinct East Canadian roots. This example is associated with the kayak 165227 (plate 95) and was likely collected in the early 1890s during one of Peary's expeditions to Polar Greenland.

This paddle is asymmetrically formed in the loom— specifically the handgrips themselves. Instead of a simple symmetrical handgrip, special notches have been made to fit the kayaker's thumbs. Two other Polar Greenland kayak paddles have separate thumb notches (paddle-plates 74 and 78).

At its mid-point, the loom measures 1-1/4" (32mm) thick and 2-1/4" (57mm) wide— note the cross-section at this position. The cambered side of the loom is such that it would face upwards on the scale drawing. The blades are 1/2" (13mm) thick three inches from their ends.

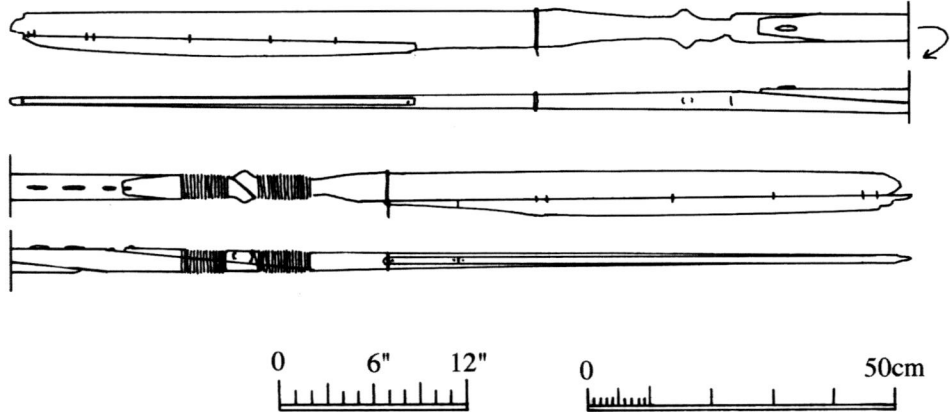

74. US National Museum of the American Indian no. 186540.
   Length: 9′ 7-3/8″ Width: 2-13/16″ (293.0x 7.2cm)

Similarly formed as the 165227 (paddle-plate 73), the NMAI's 186540 also has the asymmetrical handholds carved into it, though one of them is less distinct due to a scarf being placed in the vicinity. The 186540 was apparently associated with the kayak 977.179 (plate 96) presently in the Canadian Canoe Museum. The CCM 977.179 had belonged to the MAI, having been catalogued as no. 186541. Steward Charles Percy collected the CCM 977.179 during Robert Peary's 1909 polar expedition. Despite the kayak's transfer to Canada in 1976, the paddle was left behind in the NMAI collections.

Two scarf joints are present along this paddle's length. One is heavily bound with sealskin line; it may or may not have nails beneath this lashing. The other joint is fastened with four metal nails, each bent over.

Both of the blades of the 186540 have been widened through the addition of extra pieces of wood. These strips are lashed to the blades, although they are also pegged in several positions. Without the added strips, the blades would be symmetrical, but since the strips are just placed along a single edge, the blades have a lop-sided appearance. At the mid-point, the 186540 measures 1-1/2″ (38mm) thick and 1-11/16″ (43mm) wide. The blades are 3/8″ (9mm) thick 3″ (76mm) from their tips. The ends of the blades are slightly chipped.

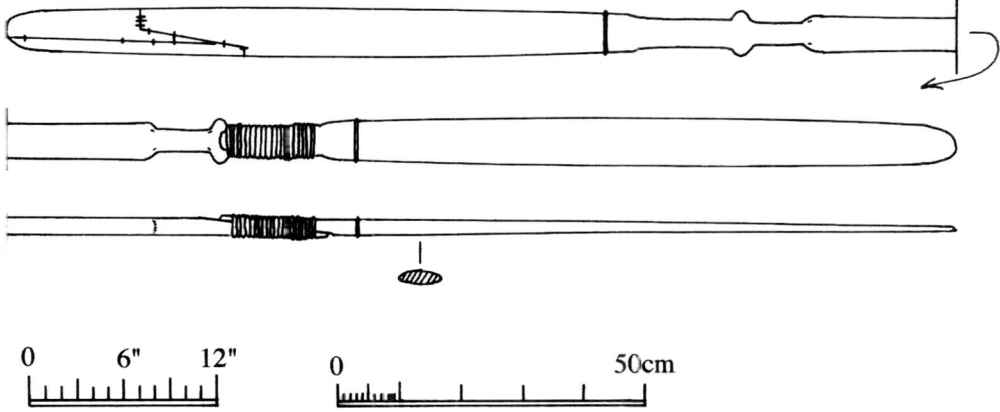

75. U. S. National Museum of Natural History no. 160383.
   Length: 10' 1-1/2" Width: 3-1/8" (308.6x 7.9cm)

Associated with the kayak of the same number (plate 94), this Polar Greenland kayak paddle has been published previously appearing in Adney and Chapelle, figure 205 (1964:210). It is reproduced here with additional details and in larger scale to further show its characteristics, particularly the scarf joint. (The original paddle is disassembled; the scale drawing shows the paddle as if re-assembled).

Chapelle's drawing of this paddle suggests that it has handgrips that are wrapped with line of some sort. A wrapping of line is present on the paddle, but it is outboard of the handgrip and binds a scarf joint. One tip of this paddle is comprised of two pieces of wood lashed together and to the blade. This may be a repair to a broken blade or simply the means by which to make an adequate paddle with limited resources. Drip rings are present on this paddle; the rings are made of thin sealskin line.

The thickness from the knobs to the paddle's mid-point is 1-1/8" (28mm) thick. The blades are 3/8" (9mm) thick 6" (15.2cm) from the ends. The width at this paddle's mid-point is 2-3/16" (55mm).

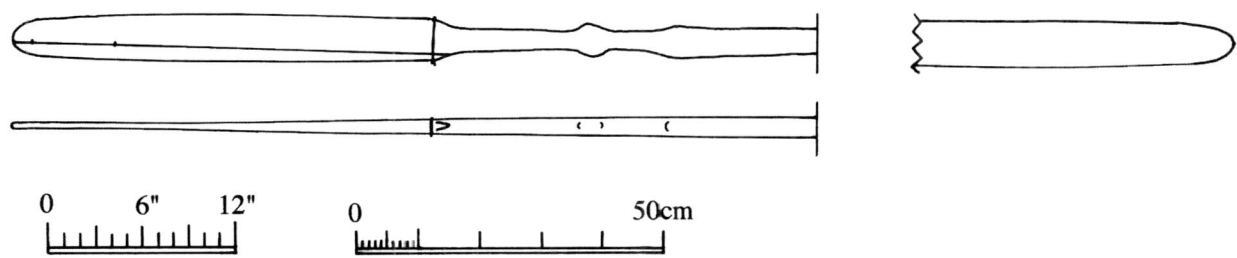

76. Greenland National Museum no. KNK 1007.
   Length: 8' 7" Width: 2-7/8" (261.6x 7.3cm)

This paddle, associated with the kayak KNK 1007 (plate 97), is smooth and very well made, though it is not entirely symmetrical: One blade is made of two pieces of wood (lashed together with sealskin line), and is a bit broader than the opposite blade. A leather cord is wrapped once around one blade set in tiny notches at the edges; this cord functioned as a drip-ring, stopping cold water from running down the blade onto the kayaker's hands. The drip ring on the other blade is missing, but the notches are evident. The knot on the existing wrap is situated right at the blade's edge, and the tails dangle a half-inch or so— these tails help lead water off the blade.

At the paddle's mid-point, the loom is 1-3/16" (30mm) thick and 1-11/16" (43mm) wide. The blades are 3/8" (9mm) thick 2" (51mm) from their ends. A replica of this paddle is shown being used with the replica of the kayak KNK 1007 in figure 379.

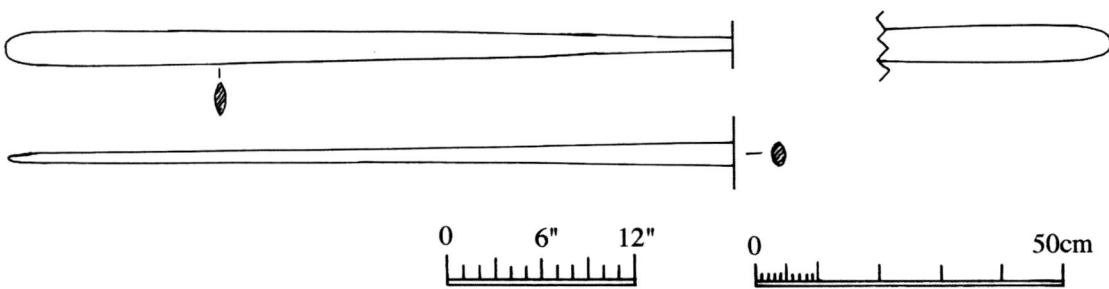

77. Greenland National Museum no. KNK 528.
Length: 7' 9-1/4" Width: 2-3/8" (236.8x 6.0cm)

The Polar Greenland paddle KNK 528 (with the kayak 528, plate 100) reflects a transition from the heavier, longer, 'knobbed' paddle-form undoubtedly brought to Polar Greenland by the Canadian immigrants of the 1860s. The 528 does not have any carved handle or drip-knob, and the blades transition smoothly into the loom. There isn't any edging or end-pieces on this paddle. It is quite simple: just one piece of wood, flat-sawn, and full of tight knots. The KNK 528's paddle bears a distinct resemblance to the Upernavik paddle from 1930 (the KNK 2237, paddle-plate 34).

This paddle maintains a considerable thickness along the blades, but the edges are actually quite sharp, as shown in the cross-sections. At the mid-point, the loom measures 1-1/2" (38mm) thick and 7/8" (22mm) wide. The blades are 11/16" (17mm) thick 2" (51mm) from the ends.

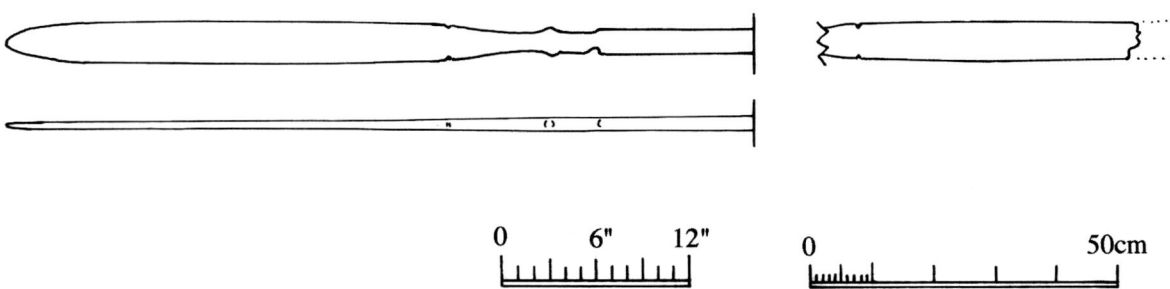

78. Mystic Seaport Museum no. 1964:1652.
Length: 7' 5-3/4" Width: 2-3/4" (227.9x 7.0cm)

This paddle is associated with the Polar Greenland kayak frame at Mystic Seaport Museum (plate 101). It is carved from a single piece of oak, and its shape is of the unique to Polar Greenland form with asymmetrical thumb-grooves. One blade-end is fractured and missing, but the original length was likely 8' 4-3/4" (255.9cm) (the mid-point in the drawing is based on this estimated length). Drip rings were not present, but notches for drip rings at the blade's edges were present. The kayak associated with this paddle is considered to be a transitional form (type XII) Polar Greenland kayak based on my typology, but the paddle is clearly of the 'older' form; compare to paddle-plate 77.

At the mid-point of the loom, the paddle is 15/16" (24mm) thick and 1-7/8" (48mm) wide. At the distinct 'knob' adjacent the handgrips, the thickness is 7/8" (22mm) thick. Five inches from the blade ends, the thickness is 3/8" (9mm).

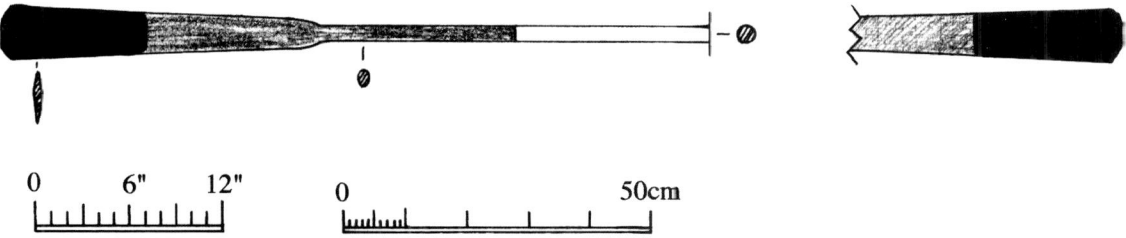

79. National Museum of Scotland no. 1884.82.
    Length: 7'6" Width: 3-9/16" (228.6x 9.0cm)

This paddle, with its unusually long loom, yet well proportioned narrow blades, is not from Greenland at all— nor even from the Arctic. It hails from the tropics: Guyana, South America, and was accessioned by the National Museum of Scotland in 1884. It is included for no other reason than that it does bear a stunning resemblance to Greenlandic Kayak paddles, and wonderfully illustrates the fact that good technical solutions are apt to occur among very diverse cultures.

This paddle is carved from a very dense hardwood— perhaps coubaril (jatoba), and is finely made and polished. The blades are stained black, the outermost portions being very dark. It was most likely used in a dugout canoe, perhaps much wider than most Greenland kayaks, which may explain its length. At its mid-point, this paddle measures 1" (25mm) diameter. The blades are 11/16" (17mm) thick 1-1/2" (38mm) from their ends. At the loom-to-blade transition, the paddle is 3/4" (19mm) thick.

Outside of the arctic, double-bladed paddles are known from Aden, on the southern coast of the Arabian Peninsula (Moser, 1918:275 [photo.]), Jolo, in the Philippines (Neyret, 1974:180), Venezuela (Neyret, 1974:287), Chile (Leshikar, 1988:27-28), Peru, Lake Titicaca, Bolivia (Madsen and Hansen, 1992:27, 31, 68-69), and among several indigenous groups in California (Cunningham, 1989:12,47,80).

Analysis and Speculation on the origins, development, and variations of Greenland Kayaks

Up to here, this study has been mainly a descriptive and illustrative exploration of Greenland kayaks. The typology I've proposed takes note of and illustrates many variations of form and structure among Greenlandic kayaks of the last four centuries, but deeper questions exist: Where did these historic forms come from? How do the many types of Greenland kayaks relate to each other? Why have they assumed the varied shapes they have?

In order to explore these questions, many factors must be considered. These factors include the distant cultural origins of the modern Greenlanders, the changing climate, migrations to more temperate regions, and domestic trade and the resultant exposure to new kayak-forms. Contact with Europeans was also a major factor in the development of Greenland kayaks. The European factor encompasses something as simple as the introduction of metal nails, as complex as the effects of commercial whaling and the introduction of rifles for kayak hunting, or as devastating as smallpox epidemics.

As mentioned in the first chapter, the kayaks of the modern Greenlanders are descendent from those of Thule culture immigrants. The Thule culture originated from two distinct cultures in Alaska/Siberia after about 900 c.e.: the Birnirk of North Alaska, and the Punuk from Bering Straits (McGhee, 1984:369). The Thule culture began their movement eastward from North Alaska circa 900 c.e.; they were drawn through the Canadian Arctic archipelago towards Greenland during a period of warming. These people first reached Greenland between 1050 and 1100c.e. (McGhee, 1984:369-370; Jordan, 1984:540).

Erik Holtved's excavations in the Thule District led him to believe that the Thule immigrants not only came to Greenland in different waves, or phases, but that certain phases had cultural elements apart from distinctly Birnirk features. Specifically, Holtved saw clear Punuk influences among artifacts from the Ruin Island site (see map 4) that were known from Punuk-Thule finds in Alaska (1944:II, 150-165). Holtved suggests that the Punuk-Thule immigrants reached Greenland by 1300c.e. (Holtved, 1944;II, 169), but subsequent carbon dating has placed other Ruin Island phase artifacts at the beginning of Thule migration to the region (McCullough, 1989:13-14).

Through analyzing the limited remains and evidence of Thule kayaks, Eugene Arima has noted their diversity as well as certain consistencies: "Thule kayaks are represented archaeologically by parts, models, and engravings on artifacts which

Figure 394: An ivory kayak model from Sevuokuk (Gambell, St. Lawrence Island, Alaska) excavated by Henry B. Collins in the early 1930s. The model is from Punuk full-phase, circa 900-1100c.e. (After Collins, 1935:plate 5, no. 9 [reversed here].)

indicate a variety in form and use, both local and temporal differentiation being involved apparently, and do not allow a simple postulation of some single Thule type. Several major features, however, such as reverse sheer, transversely flat deck, and elongated stem, are widespread" (1975:240). Arima speculates that the diversity of form within Thule kayaks is due to differing amounts of influence from Punuk- or Birnirk-kayak form— a "Birnirk vs. Punuk-derived distinction" as he refers to it (2002:12-13).

Arima characterizes Birnirk kayaks as having been multi-chined (or having round sections), with flat or reverse sheer. End horns occur, with the bow being jogged-up similar to modern period central Canadian kayak types (e.g., Caribou Eskimo and Nattilingmiut kayaks). Punuk kayaks on the other hand are characterized by their flat-bottoms, hard chines, a slight sheer, and stems of variable rake (Arima, 2002:12; 1975:237-239). Figure 394 depicts an early (circa 900-1100 c.e.) Punuk kayak model from St. Lawrence Island in the Bering Straits; the deck apparently has a slight ridge and the stems are raked very steeply.

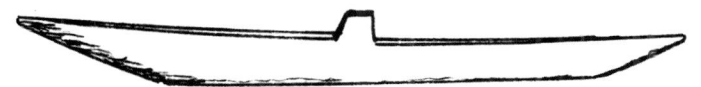

Figure 395: A kayak model excavated by T. Mathiassen in 1929 on Inugsuk (Inussuk) Island, Upernavik District. The model likely dates from the 13th or 14th century, and it exhibits strong Punuk influences. (After Mathiassen, 1930: pl.20, no.7.)

Arima originally wrote that Birnirk round sections may have changed to flat in Eastern Canada as an adaptation to ocean use (1975:88; 1994:194), but later came to see flat bottoms as a Punuk influence instead of an ecological adaptation (2002:13). Both may be the case.

Kayak models excavated in Polar and Northwest Greenland exhibit fairly distinct traits of what could be considered Birnirk-Thule and Punuk-Thule kayak elements, as described by Arima. Figure 395 shows a model excavated by Terkel Mathiassen in 1929 on Inugsuk (Inussuk) Island, Upernavik District.[55] The model exhibits Punuk traits such as a flat bottom, slight sheer, flat sides, and raked stems.

A Birnirk-derived kayak model excavated at Uummannaq (Polar Greenland) in 1935-37 by Erik Holtved is depicted in figure 396.[56] The Birnirk features, as outlined by Arima, are the reverse sheer and the raised ends; the model unfortunately offers no suggestion of its bottom shape, as it is just a silhouette carved in baleen.[57]

The Thule migration down the coasts of Greenland occurred during the Pacific Climatic Episode of circa 1200-1550 (see table 3). This period of cooling likely affected the Thule culture's reliance on open-water

Figure 396: A carved baleen silhouette of a kayak excavated by E. Holtved in 1935-37 at Uummannaq, Polar Greenland. Note the distinct Birnirk kayak-form influences. A sealskin float is represented on the model's aft deck (right), and the similar bump on the fore deck could be a second float, a seal, or even a 'humped' fore deck, similar to that of the KNK 1990 (plate 89). The dating of the model is in question (see footnote 56), but it is likely circa 1000-1300 c.e.

---

[55] This model likely dates from the 13th or 14th century and is from the early Inugsuk culture, a transitional phase between Thule culture and the modern Eskimo/Greenlander. Inugsuk culture is distinguished by the presence of Norse material and/or its influence in its material culture and archaeological sites (Mathiassen, 1931:300)

[56] Holtved attributes this model to what he calls the "Ruin Island Group," which are Thule culture house excavations in which he has found evidence of Punuk influence (namely in harpoon heads and the house designs themselves). This particular model was not excavated on Ruin Island, but in a house site at Uummannaq in which he also found what he saw as Punuk-derived items. Holtved provides a possible date of circa 14th century for the Ruin Island Group material (1944:II,57,70-71). Other Ruin Island cultural phase artifacts have since been carbon dated as being from the early part of the Thule migrations into the region (11th-12th century) and not the later part as suggested by Holtved (McCullough, 1989:13-14, 300, 301). Given the chronological reversal of Ruin Island phase, the placement of the Uummannaq model becomes less certain, as its consideration as a Ruin Island phase artifact may be in question.

[57] I have drafted a scale conjectural representation (as full-size) of this model as well as the one depicted in figure 395: These are featured in Appendix B, plates 105 and 106.

for kayak-based marine mammal hunting;[58] at the same time, the cooling period must have made their sea-ice hunting and reliance on dog sleds practical in more southerly latitudes. Meldgaard suggests that Thule immigrants had reached as far south in Greenland as Disko Bay by 1250 c.e. (*in* Bandi, 1969:169), and Jordan writes that a phase of Thule culture had reached southern-most Greenland by the late 1400s (1984:547).

We know that the descendents of the Thule culture that remained in Polar Greenland eventually abandoned kayak-based subsistence altogether, adapting instead to an entirely land/ice based subsistence pattern. Polar Greenlanders, or Inuhuit, only took kayaks up again most recently in the 1860s, when immigrants from Baffin Island re-introduced them. The warming climate in the mid-1800s no doubt made the use of kayaks for subsistence practical. This calls to mind Steensby's opinion that had the Inuhuit needed kayaks, they would have found a way to make them (see page 38).

As the Thule migrated further south in Greenland, they inevitably reached areas where the open-water period was considerably longer than they were used to at higher latitudes. This forced them to adapt to longer seasons of open water, and in a considerable portion of West Greenland, to abandon sea-ice hunting and even the use of dog sleds. Anthropologist Richard Jordan writes:

> ... *There are certain cultural ecological adjustments to Low Arctic environments and subtle changes in artifact form through time, which began to differentiate West Greenland from Thule District [Polar Greenland] cultures. For example, subsistence techniques underwent modification along the West Greenland coast. Seal ice-hunting techniques eventually disappeared south of the Holtsteinsborg [Sisimiut] region with a concomitant improvement and elaboration of kayak-hunting techniques (1984:545).*

Each Greenland kayak type in this study is linked somehow to the root forms that the Thule culture brought from Alaska and Canada. Can such links be recognized between what we know of the Punuk- and Birnirk-influenced Thule kayak-forms and the variety of kayak forms from the historic period?

To reduce the most persistent and perhaps most significant characteristics of Birnirk and Punuk kayaks to a single element, I would nominate gunwale form and shaping as the primary distinction. Gunwale form and shaping is critically linked to the appearance of a kayak's sheer and hull. Furthermore, the gunwales are the main structural elements of a kayak and therefore may be less likely to be radically changed.

As I've suggested in the chapter on construction (pages 53-54), kayaks with slight and consistent sheer lines do not require the complex gunwale shaping that kayaks with reverse or compound sheer lines need. This suggests that Birnirk kayaks, with their reverse sheer amidship and rising ends, would necessitate considerable gunwale shaping, perhaps requiring fairly wide boards to work from. Punuk kayaks, with their gentle sheer lines, would not need such shaping, and their gunwales could easily be fashioned from narrower boards.

In summary, Birnirk-Thule descendent kayaks can be identified by their taller gunwales, compound sheer lines and gunwale shaping. Punuk-Thule descendent kayaks have shorter gunwales (in height) and simple, gentle sheer lines indicative of unshaped gunwales.

The significance of these two Thule phases' distinct kayak forms with regards to modern period (after circa 1600) kayaks is that the Punuk-Thule form (as described by Arima) is essentially what I have called a type I kayak form, and the Birnirk-Thule form is a type II kayak.[59] Both types I and II Greenland kayaks in this study are some of the oldest surviving descendents of Thule culture kayaks, and they both seem to have been present in West Greenland in the 1600s.

---

[58] The evidence for this reliance is based on the remains of hunting equipment excavated in Polar Greenland by Holtved that suggests a fairly advanced develoment of kayak-based sea mammal hunting. Some of the more significant pieces of evidence are kayak pieces, models of kayaks, parts of harpoon line stands, harpoon rests, parts from bladder darts and bird darts, throwing boards, and plugs and toggles from skin floats (Holtved, 1944:I, 196-197, 207-210, 232-233).

With the presence of type I and II kayaks established in the 1600s, the question of later West Greenland kayak types emerges. There is, among the kayaks in this study, a fairly distinct period of some 100-200 years where Greenland kayaks had markedly raised ends— types III and IV. This generally covers the period starting circa late 1600s to mid 1700s through the mid-to-late 1800s. Where did the type III and type IV forms come from? Simply stated, I think that type I forms evolved into the higher and deeper stemmed type IV, and that the type II forms evolved into the higher yet finer stemmed type III. The basis of this thinking includes the complexity of sheer-form stem-length, and the distance of the cockpit's center as a percentage of the kayak's length (see Appendix A, column 7).

A distinct transition between type I and IV kayaks— at least among the collected examples in this study— is entirely lacking: There is no gradual rising of the kayak's ends, and the earliest positively dated type IV in this study could be considered an extreme example (the HMG E.102, plate 26). The basis for my speculation of type I-to-IV evolution is based on cross-sectional consistency (maintenance of slight deadrise and slab-sides) as well as the continuity of positive sheer (i.e., the opposite of reverse-sheer) adjacent the cockpit or kayak's mid-section.

Type II kayak forms evolving into type III forms is a fairly distinct transition, and there are certain type II kayaks in this study that could well be considered to be type III forms. For example, the Trinity House "B" (plate 13), and the National Museum of Scotland's 1995.886 (plate 12)— both later type II forms probably from the late 1700s— represent a move away from what are likely earlier type II forms (e.g., plates 8 and 9). Their gunwales are shallower, and the end profiles— particularly with the THH "B" are longer and more elevated. Key to this speculation is the occasional reverse-sheer present in some type III kayaks, notably the Whitby Museum's kayak (plate 18).

Type III kayaks, if indeed being descendent from type II, have entirely abandoned the compound gunwale flare (gunwale 'twist') that is apparently common in type II kayaks. The abandonment of compound gunwale flare would have left a choice of hull cross-sections to adapt: the boxier forward sections or the rounder vee-shaped aft sections of type II kayaks.[60] The boxier sections seem to have been the answer for type III kayaks, but distinct exceptions exist, for example, the Whitby kayak (plate 18).

So why did the stems of type I and II kayaks begin to rise? The function of up-turned stems is a good starting point in answering this question: According to Birket-Smith, "The up-curved stern was said to have the advantage that the boat was not heard, when bumping in the seas . . ." (1924:269)— a fact I can attest to having used both flat and curved kayaks in seas. Considering this, the question now becomes, why were quieter kayaks needed? This is probably due to declining weather conditions paired with a higher reliance on kayaks for subsistence. The period in Greenland that high-stemmed kayaks (type III and IV) are known to have existed coincides very closely with the Neo-Boreal Episode (1550-1850) or Little Ice Age.

---

[59] This conclusion is worth elaborating on: The model in figure 395 bears clear resemblance to the Lübeck kayak of circa. 1606 (plate 1), the Danish National Museum's Lb 101 (plate 5), and the Gemeentelijke Musea Zierikzee's kayak 700 (plate 6). The long, deep bow, the gentle curve of the sheer, and the shorter and more subtle straight-raked stern are common traits of each; the Inugsuk model excavated by Mathiassen is a medieval type I kayak. The 'Ruin Island Group' model in figure 396 is unmistakably of the type II kayak form. Its reverse sheer amidships with gently rising ends are nearly identical to the Rijksmuseum voor Volkenkunde's kayak 351-77 (plate 8), the Weltmuseum's 36481 (plate 10), and the National Museum of Scotland's 1995.886 (plate 12). These kayaks and the model all have shallow ends, with the stern being raked steeper than the bow. The bows of each are quite short when compared to those of type I kayaks.

[60] It is worth elaborating on the principles of the compound gunwale flare seen in several type II kayaks in this study: The gunwales of many type II kayaks are often fairly plumb (vertical) forward, and yet they become increasingly flared (literally twisting) astern. This dramatic gunwale flare change is not present in any other type of Greenland kayaks— some gunwales are greatly flared (e.g., East Greenland, type IX), and some are quite plumb (e.g., some type VI from Northwest Greenland), but none transition so dramatically from plumb to flared.

Gunwale flare that changes within a particular kayak can aid in the shaping of the kayak's hull. Ribs project more or less straight out of the gunwales so a narrow and deep hull is easier to make using un-flared gunwales, as in figure 397 left. Conversely, a wide and shallow hull is easier to make with considerably flared gunwales, as in figure 397 right. *(continues on page 536)*

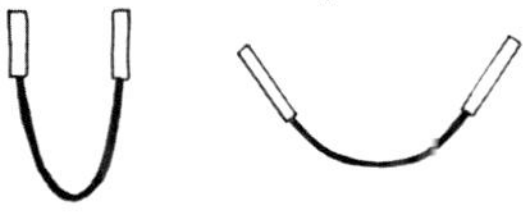

Figure 397: Gunwale flare can aid in achieving a desired hull-shape. Gunwales with little or no flare (left) are more conducive to a deep and narrow hull, and gunwales with significant flare may be more conducive to broad shallow hulls with narrow chine breadths. See also figures 200 and 201.

TABLE 3: Climatic periods and occurrences of the Greenland kayak types.

★ = present ◆ = unknown/suspected (forms may vary) ▲ = in decline

Ca.	CLIMATE/HIST.	I	II	III	IV	V	VI	VII	VIII	IX	X	XI	XII	XIII
900–1200	Little Optimum. *Peak and end of 1000 yrs, grad. Warming.* (Thule Migrations)	◆	◆											
1200–1500	Pacif. Clim. Episode *Gradual Cooling*	★	★						◆					
1550–1850	Neo Boreal Episode *Rapid Global Cooling*	★	★	Mid late ★	Mid ★				◆					
1645–1715	1st Maunder Minimum *Intense Cooling*		★	★					◆					
1790–1830	2nd Maunder Minimum *Intense Cooling*	◆		★	★				◆					
1830–	Emergence of new kayak forms; —RIFLES— *Warming trends after 1850*			★	★	★	★	★	★			From 1860		
1880–1920	Mild period				★ ▲	★	★	★	To 1894	★		★ ▲	★	
1920–1960	Decline in whales and seals. *(Mild Period)* increase in Commerce. Fisheries. Kayak decline in SW.					★ ▲	★	★		★			▲	★
1960–2000	Increase in seals.					▲ ★	▲ ★	▲ ★		▲	★			★

after Smith, 1991:100, Fossett, 2001:64–67, 115, 140, 233–234, Kleivan, 1984a: 595, and Gad, 1984:575.

For kayaks whose hulls maintain fairly constant depths from bow to stern (as is the case with most type II kayaks), the compound gunwale flare can be used to control the hull's volume. The boxier sections that result from plumb gunwales will have considerably more volume than the rounder sections resulting from gunwale flare; see figure 398.

That type II kayaks have forward sections with more volume than their stern sections is likely related to their need to support the weight of the hunting gear on the fore deck as well as the weight of the kayaker; the center of type II kayaks' cockpits are situated quite close to the kayak's mid-point, as tracked in column 7 of the table in Appendix A. The average type II's cockpit center is at 51.5% of the kayak's length; the average for type I kayaks is 53.2%. Furthermore, type II kayaks are very small kayaks to begin with— if their forward sections weren't 'bulked-out' they might not maintain adequate freeboard under normal loads.

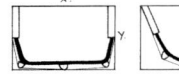

Figure 398: Gunwale flare can play a critical role in the volume of a kayak's hull: Both of these examples have the same breadth (x) and the same depth (y).

During the Neo-Boreal Episode two distinct periods of significantly reduced solar radiation (Maunder Minimums) occurred: The first, 1645-1715, is known for its intense global cooling, followed by 75 years of milder climatic conditions. The second episode, from 1790-1830, was also an intensely cold period and was followed by warming trends beginning circa 1850 that have lasted to this day (Fossett, 2001:64-66, and Smith, 1991:100). Table 3 tracks the presence of the various Greenland kayak types through periods of climatic and ecological changes (note some temporal overlapping).

Nearly all type III and IV kayaks in this study are of unknown specific geographic origin, but a pair of watercolors by Hans Willumsen reproduced in Finn Gad's *The History of Greenland, vol. III* may shed some light as to where type III and type IV kayaks could be seen around 1819. The painting of Uummannaq harbour — "*Omanak i nordre Grönland*"— depicts a very fine rendition of a type III kayak (1982: Plate VI). The other painting depicts the colony at Ritenbenk ("*Collonien Rittenben i nordre Grönland*"), and in the foreground a distinct type IV kayak (1982:Plate XII). (Ritenbenk, or Appat as it is known in Greenlandic, is 61 kilometers north of Ilulissat.) The profiles of these two kayaks are enlarged and redrawn in figure 399; the kayaks are left in 'outline' but are painted solid in the originals. (Both kayaks are equipped with harpoon line stands, sealskin floats, and perhaps harpoons on their fore decks.)

The accuracy of Willumsen's renderings can of course be questioned; many early depictions of kayaks are naïve or exaggerated. Being a carpenter, Willumsen's eye may be quite trustworthy. Taken as good representations, the painting shows type III kayaks being situated further north than type IV examples, suggesting perhaps that Nuussuaq Peninsula was

Figure 399: Two kayaks from watercolor paintings by Hans Willumsen, ca. 1819. The upper is a detail redrawn from a portrait of Uummannaq harbor (after Gad, 1982: plate VI), and the lower is a detail redrawn from a portrait of Ritenbenk Colony harbour (after Gad, 1982: plate XII).

a natural divide between the two types. This assumption is further supported by distinct type III elements persisting in Upernavik vicinity (see plates 56 and 66; specifically their stem shapes) as well as a classic type IV kayak having been collected as far south as Paamiut vicinity in the 1830s (plate 31)

From about the mid-1800s to the early 20th century, kayaks' raised ends began to disappear in favor of lower, flatter stems. The cause of these changes can be directly attributed to the advent of rifle-use from kayaks. H. C. Petersen explains that, "the upturned stem blocked the hunter's view of the animal in the water. And more than once the hunters hit the stem when they fired"(1986:61). This is undoubtedly a factor, but it does not explain why the kayak's stern was also lowered.

The lowering of kayak stems is the most overt change to West Greenland kayaks during the 19th century, but numerous other adjustments also occurred. Before elaborating on the changes to type III and IV kayaks, it is first important to summarize the dynamics of both harpoon hunting and rifle hunting. By doing so, both the overt and subtle changes in the kayaks will make more sense to the reader in that the values and necessities of such adaptations will be readily understood.

To hit a seal with a harpoon is to attach a large hunting float (*avataq*) to it, so a 'hit' to a flipper or other non-vital areas would inevitably ensure a kill, as the attached float would tire the seal and mark its position so the hunter could dispatch it with a lance. Bladder darts could also be used for this same purpose; they have a greater range than the harpoon, but have a smaller float. Birket-Smith writes "A strong man can at most throw the harpoon about 18m" (60 feet) (1924:319).

With the advent of rifles for seal hunting, the dynamics of the hunt were changed greatly. A shot to a flipper or non-vital area would most likely ensure that the seal escapes the hunter. A clean kill to the head would ensure capture. However depending on the seal's buoyancy (varying from season to season) it may start to sink if it is not also harpooned as quickly as possible.[61]

There is a direct correlation between the advent of rifle use from kayaks and the widening of kayaks. The average width of type III and IV adult kayaks in this study between 1800-1850 is 44.9cm (17-5/8"), and the average width of type IV and V adult kayaks from 1850-1900 is 48.0cm (18-7/8"). Kayaks before 1800 are narrower yet, and kayaks post-1900 are wider yet on average.

Two reasons may explain the widening of kayaks for rifle hunting— both are rather obvious: A rifle's butt measures about 4" wide, thus it takes up considerable space on an already limited fore deck. The second reason is the need for extra stability— both for aiming the rifle, and to compensate for the weight of a rifle and ammunition. Kayaks are very sensitive to the center of gravity of the load: the higher up the center of gravity is, the less-stable the kayak will be. Rifles are not just stored on-deck, but their butts rest on small wooden stands 2-4" high so the rifle holster will better resist filling with water.

Thus the lowering of the kayaks' ends could be explained by the fact that once rifles were relied upon, hunters did not need to be as close to a seal in order to kill it, so stealth (high bows and sterns) and speed (long and narrow hulls) were not as critical requirements anymore. Also, straight-ended kayaks are certainly easier to build— a fact I can personally attest to.

More subtle changes also occurred in kayaks as rifles were beginning to be used from kayaks, and some of these changes can be detected in type III and IV kayaks even before their stems were lowered. For example, the kayak's point or area of maximum breadth moved ahead of the cockpit and the cockpit position moved sternward. These adjustments relate directly to the trim (balance and distribution of weight and volume) and have been made in order to compensate for the weight of a rifle (and/or a shotgun) on a kayak's fore deck. The latter trend can be tracked in column 7 of table 4 (Appendix A), which presents the ratio of a kayak's length to the distance of the center of the cockpit from the bow. (The former trend is difficult to measure as it is an area, and not a point. The trend can be seen quite easily, however, when comparing scale drawings of the kayaks.)

The flattening or lowering-of-kayak-stems on the West Coast was not a spontaneous adaptation, but was instead the result of a trend with a fairly specific origin: Birket-Smith noted, "The flat stern... is gradually spreading from the south"(1924:271). He also notes that immigrants from Southeast Greenland (King Frederik VI's Coast) introduced kayaks of "Hardly any sheer" and "long stems" to the vicinities of the West Coast south of Paamiut (1924:271). "... I met as early as in 1912, in the Julianehaab District (Qaqortoq vicin.), several West Greenlanders who had adopted the kayak of the southern East Coast with a flat bottom and nearly perpendicular sides" (1924:269).[62]

---

[61] The use of rifles for kayak hunting did not mean the end of harpoon use. Kaj Birket-Smith describes the use of both weapons for kayak hunting: "Harpooning is chiefly practiced in rough sea, when the hunter can get close to the seals, and also when they return from their mating migrations and are so lean, that they sink when shot. In calm sea, and when the seals are fat, the rifle is preferred" (1924:320). Note the numerous 20th century kayak photographs in this book in which the kayak is outfitted with a harpoon-line holder (*asaloq*) as well as a rifle holster.

[62] This passage also provides us with one of the more detailed descriptions of the elusive southern East Coast kayaks (i.e., those from King Frederik VI's Coast).

Because, according to Birket-Smith's observations, the diffusion of kayaks with little sheer and straighter, lower ends originated in South or Southeast Greenland, certain questions arise: Did this form ebb during the Neo-Boreal Episode (circa 1550-1850)— perhaps lingering in more temperate or isolated vicinities (i.e., South or Southeast Greenland) only to flow again during warming periods (i.e., post-1850s)?[63] Did the advantages of kayaks with lower bows after the adaptation of the rifle accelerate this diffusion? It seems that both may be the case.

Figure 400: A hunter shooting a seal, Illorsuit, 1959. The photographer, Ken Taylor, writes, "This is the coup-de-grace with a .22. The absence of the avataq [sealskin float] on the afterdeck shows that he's already got the seal harpooned" (Personal Communication, 2006; Photograph Courtesy of Ken Taylor).

The fact that this stem-lowering trend was gradual and originated in the South is bourn out by many well-documented kayaks in this study as well as through comparisons of historic photographs and ethnographic record. For example, we can see that in Paamiut vicinity, kayaks went from type IV to type V or VII forms between 1834 and 1884, based on comparing the kayak from Avagait from circa 1834 (plate 31) to the kayaks in the photograph taken at Paamiut in 1884 (figure 319).

Despite their relatively recent appearance (late 1800s— based on the examples in this study), type V Greenland kayaks are mysterious in that their appearance seems to have occurred rather suddenly. Significantly, this appearance was shortly after the rifle started being used for kayak hunting. It could be presumed that type V kayaks are direct descendents of type I kayaks: their resemblance is plain to see, e.g., low gentle sheer lines with deeper bows, and a hull with flared sides and a shallow-to-moderate V-bottom. There does seem however to be a gap of at least 100 years (if not 200 years, on account of poor dating of type I kayaks) between the two forms.

Further north along the West Coast, Kaj Birket-Smith noted during his 1918 travels that, "the now common kayak in the Egedesminde District is ... not of long standing in those parts. Until 10 or 15 years ago the kayaks had a distinctly up-curved stern. ... It has long been known that the up-curved stern belonged to the northern part of the West Coast" (1924:168). This puts the demise of type IV kayaks just after the turn of the century for South Disko Bay.

Morten Porsild writes of kayaks in Upernavik and Prøven (Kangersuatsiaq) in Northwest Greenland with sterns forming "almost ... a right angle with the deck ..."(1915:121). Porsild's description of the kayaks calls to mind the NMNH 160325 (plate 56) and the KNK 2237 (plate 66)— two kayaks with extremely steep sterns.[64]

---

[63] Does the unusually late (1830s) presence of a type II kayak— the Hancock Museum's G.109 (plate 14)— suggest that it may be one of the lingering low-sheered kayaks that persisted well through the Little Ice Age?

[64] I see both of these kayaks as being close to type II kayaks— a category I had initially placed them in. The lack of continuity (some 50 years; perhaps on account of poor documentation) between these two kayaks and type III forms lead me to associate them with type VI kayaks.

By the 1930s kayaks in Upernavik District had their form and proportions influenced by "southern" forms; we know this from C. E. C. Lembcke-Otto's letter regarding his sending a particular kayak to the Danish National Museum in 1930. Lembcke-Otto wrote that the kayak (the KNK 2237, plate 66) was "probably one of the last of the original types which was being used up here before the introduction of the slender South Greenland kayaks" (Letter: Greenland National Museum catalog files, as translated by Claus Andreassen). The likes of the NMNH 160325, CCM 977.182, KNK 1215, and KNK 2237 (plates 56, 60, 61, and 66), gave way to kayak forms with less sheer at the ends such as the CMC IV-A-427, 428, 375, and the DNM 18.273 (plates 62, 65, 67, and 73).

By piecing together such information, a general timeline of the adaptation of newer kayak forms with lower ends can be traced along the West Coast of Greenland. This timeline is depicted in figure 401, along with certain trends relating to Polar and East Greenland kayaks, described in the text below.

While the kayaks in Upernavik District adapted lower sterns in the early 20th century, the kayaks from Uummannaq Fjord just south of Upernavik District retain slight but distinctly elevated sterns to the present day. This is also the case with kayaks in Ilulissat: compare figures 2 and 15, the former taken in the 1930s, and the latter in 2000. That some kayaks retain older features could be explained by any number of factors including geographical isolation, stronger traditions/rejection of outside ideas, and simply a contentment with what has worked and still works just fine.

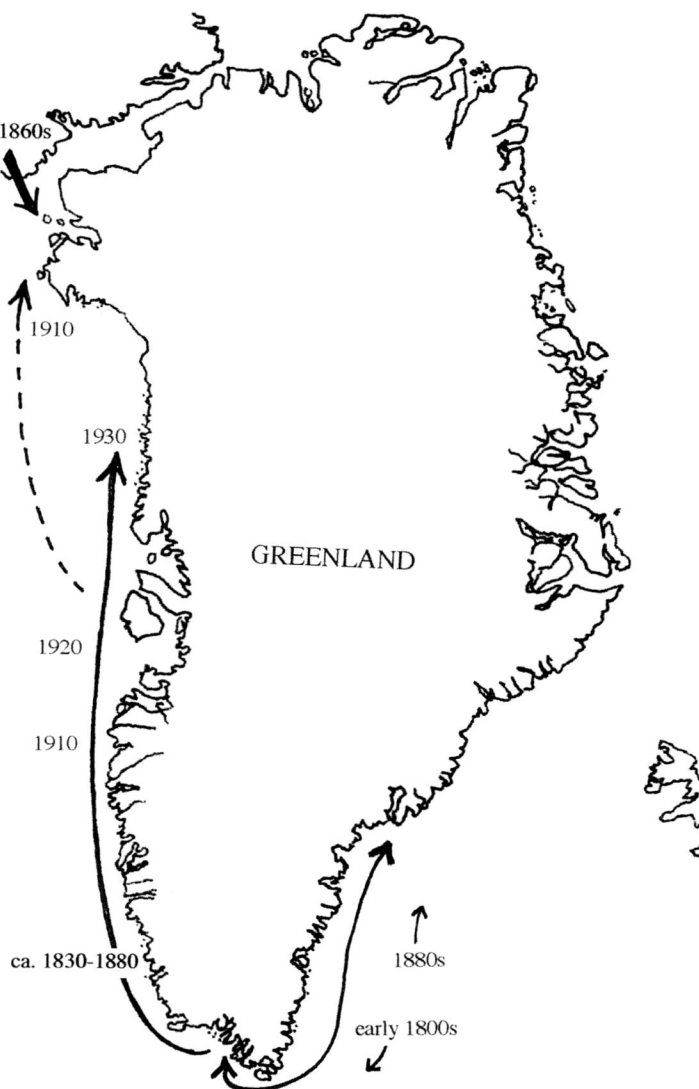

Figure 401. Map of Greenland showing possible courses of influence with regards to the trend of kayaks with lower (flatter) end shapes. The dates are conjectural, representing earliest appearances of more southerly (i.e., flatter) forms based on the collected examples featured in this study. The dashed arrow shows the leap to Polar Greenland that southerly kayak forms made during the early 1900s. The map also shows the possible two-way influences between South Greenland and East Greenland, as discussed below.

The seal hunters of the northern half of West Greenland gradually adopted more southerly forms of kayaks, but they are at the same time credited with several new innovations in kayak hunting, notably in conjunction with rifle use. A hunter from Ilulissat invented the kayak skeg in the 1860s, and the rifle holster was invented in Uummannaq district that same decade. Rifle holsters later became mandatory under penalty in several districts due to accidents related to the stowing of loaded rifles inside of kayaks. Skegs, rifle holsters, and camouflage shooting screens (also invented in northern West Greenland) were quickly adapted all along the West Coast of Greenland, and, with the exception of the skeg, in East Greenland as well (Porsild, 1915:181-183, Birket-Smith, 1928:29).

For the East Coast, William Thalbitzer writes that the Southwest Greenland "mode" of kayak had by 1894 "conquered"— indeed, entirely replaced the older forms (type VIII) seen only ten years earlier in Ammassalik district (1914:384 [cited at length in the present volume on page 399]. Thalbitzer's observation is not incorrect, but most likely the "mode" he refers to are type VII kayaks originating

Figure 402: A woman seeing a hunter off at Kullorsaaq, northern Upernavik district, 1956. (Photographer Jette Bang/ Copyright: Greenland National Museum and Archives.)

in Southernmost Greenland and/or from King Frederik VI's Coast of Southeast Greenland; Southwest Greenland kayaks were once known to have high sterns (Petersen, 1986:49).

While we are left with only one surviving full size example of the "old form" East Greenland kayaks (type VIII; plate 82), it is very consistent with descriptions of the type and the models collected by Gustav Holm in 1884-85 (see plate 83) and William Thalbitzer in 1906 (see figure 337). The reverse sheer, slightly elevated bow, and steeper, loftier stern of type VIII kayaks calls to mind the form of the kayak model excavated by Holtved at Uummannaq (figure 396), and suggests a strong Birnirk-Thule lineage.[65]

The Birnirk-Thule gunwale shapes of type VIII kayaks did not survive the East Greenlanders' adapting a new kayak form from South Greenland in the late 1800s. The kayaks from South Greenland (type VII) have shorter gunwales (in height) with simpler sheer lines and a lack of complex gunwale shaping— a form I see as being derived from Punuk-Thule influences.

The new 'flatter' East Greenland kayaks are type IX kayaks. While they were undoubtedly influenced by type VII South Greenland kayaks, they differ considerably, hence the separate type-numbers. For example, the new-form East Greenland kayaks have less sheer, less deadrise, less rocker, are shallower, and have narrower chine-breadths than type VII kayaks from South Greenland. Significant structural differences between East and South Greenland kayaks also exist, such as the use of shallow mortised deck beams in the former, and through deck beam mortises in the latter.

In 1906 William Thalbitzer spoke with several old hunters in Ammassalik district about the old form East Greenland kayaks (type VIII) as well as even earlier kayak types from the area. Thalbitzer writes that he was told that the "original kayaks" did not have bent ribs, but instead pieced ribs, as in umiaks (and incidentally, Polar Greenland kayaks). Also, instead of the kayak frames being nailed together, lashings were used (1914:384).

Further, Akernilik explained, that in his youth he himself had seen a kaiak belonging to Awkuluk's younger brother, which had the stem and stern of bone, both sloping upwards and forked (thus somewhat similar to the umiak). — Apart from the latter exaggeration, I am unable to disregard these statements, as they were confirmed by several old men and they agree, further, with the reports of the Eskimo kayaks more to the west (Thalbitzer, 1914:384).

Such fork-ended kayaks are known of from carved models (fig. 403) found by archaeologists in Siberia adjacent the Bering Straits (S. A. Arutyunov et.al. 1964:342,344 fig.7; Arima, 1985:23). Eugene Arima has already drawn a link between the fork-ended Old Bering Sea culture kayak and the modern Greenland kayak, based on archaeological evidence: The Punuk are descendent from the Old Bering Sea Culture from which the fork-ended kayak model originates (Arima, 2002:12-13; Anderson, 1984:91). That such an unusual kayak type was recounted in Ammassalik is remarkable, and perhaps less of an exaggeration than Thalbitzer thought. In any case, it isn't known for certain if such kayak types had existed in Ammassalik district; if Akernilik saw one there, it would place the form as having been present around the early-to-mid 1800s.[66]

It is easy to see how South Greenland kayaks may have influenced the new-form East Greenland kayaks but it is also important to consider how the 'old-form' East Greenland kayak (type VIII) may have influenced South Greenland types. The earliest type VII kayak in this study, the UMCH 95 from pre-1857 (plate 74), has considerable similarities with the type VIII DNM Lc.148 (plate 82)— particularly

---

[65] A flat-plate tracing of the gunwale form needed to achieve the proper sheer of a type VIII kayak replica is presented in figure 333.

[66] H.C. Petersen writes about a form of kayak that once existed in southwest Greenland that was made especially for boys who had lost older brothers in their youth (*piarkusiaq*). The kayak, known as *piaaqqisiaq*, or "cult-kayak," is of an entirely different form than the normal local types. A 19th century photograph published in Petersen (1986:51, fig.49) shows the *piaaqqisiaq* to have short convex stems that terminate in short vertical spikes. If a similar tradition existed among the East Greenlanders of Ammassalik vicinity, the unusual and ancient form described by Akernilik may indeed have existed in the 1800s.

the cross-sections, keel rocker, and bow profile and shape. The type VIII kayak is essentially a type VII with a high stern. In any case, one should consider that influence is not always a one-way street; the kayaks of South Greenland are both exhibitor and instigator of change and adaptations.

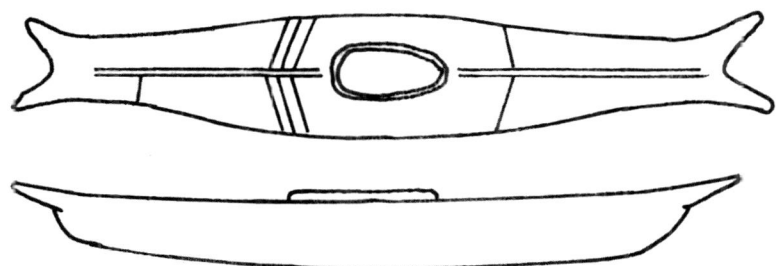

Figure 403: A fork-stemmed kayak model found in Siberia; The model is about 2000 years old and is from the Old Bering Sea culture (after Arima, 1985:23).

With the exception of gunwale shaping, this exploration of the origins and inter-relations of Greenland kayaks has largely focused on the outside of the kayak— its shape. Kayak structures and how they are assembled also sheds light on developmental trends and directions.

The early historic Greenland kayaks (types I and II) have their deck beams set into shallow mortises, and occasionally some deck beams are placed lower between the gunwales, as opposed to along the gunwales' upper-edges as with later kayaks. The joinery in these kayaks is primarily fastened with lashings— typically baleen. Several early kayaks have gunwales that apparently run the course of the kayak's entire length, as evidenced by worn areas at the bow and stern (see figures 56, and 67b).

Due to the fact that few 'early' kayaks are without their skin-coverings, it is difficult to pinpoint such trends as the adaptation of separate stem-pieces and through-mortised deck beams; in any case, such information would likely be complicated by poor provenance documentation and the likelihood of their having been adapted in various areas at different times.

One of the above-mentioned 'older' elements persisted through the 20th century: the use of shallow-mortised deck beams. Not surprisingly, the areas where shallow mortises lasted the longest are in Northwest Greenland and East Greenland— two very isolated regions. Kaj Birket-Smith noticed this in the context of the kayaks of remote Upernavik District: ". . . the Upernavik kayak is particularly interesting because of some very old features: The cross trees [deck beams] rest in cavities and are not directly pegged [tenoned] through the gunwale . . ." (1924:270).

Other old construction features that can be seen in some 20th century Northwest Greenland kayaks (type VI) are single-pass longitudinal lashings (often tied off at each joint), straight and curved deckbeams without chamfered ends or complex shaping, and the occasional fastening of the *amiq* up and over the backside of the coaming. More variegated deck-stringer arrangements, a lack of aft-keel protection, and moderately short ends are also fairly consistent features in both older Greenland kayaks (types I-III) and type VI kayaks. With the kayak DNM 18.273 (plate 73) from Upernavik vicinity, the old feature of a lower-placed deck beam can be seen (see figure 318), even though the kayak itself is of a form relatively new to the region.

The outfitting of type VI kayaks often shows continuity with kayaks from the 1600s (types I and II). Deck line patterns are more austere, typically with four on the fore deck, and one on the aft deck, and a bow and stern line. Few deck fittings are present, particularly on more northerly type VI kayaks — usually just a harpoon holder. With influence from the south, more southerly type VI kayaks (e.g., from Disko Bay) tend to exhibit more extensive deck fittings, but still often retain the simpler four lines on the foredeck pattern. Perplexingly, the oldest type VI kayak in this study (the NMNH 160325; plate 56)— one apparently from north of Upernavik— exhibits deck line patterns and rigging that could be expected on a kayak from much further south in West Greenland.

East Greenland kayaks also share some structural features seen among the older historic kayaks such as shallow deck beam mortises and simply curved deck beams. In contrast, the kayaks of East Greenland in this study— both types VIII and IX— do not have lashings at the rib-to-keelson/chine joints; these joints are all pegged or nailed. With one exception (the Museon 57602, plate 91) their deck beam-to-gunwale joints are also pegged. I do not know why East Greenland kayaks joints are pegged instead of lashed; it may suffice to say 'because it worked.'

The lashings in most of the earlier kayaks are made of baleen: Among the fourteen type I and II kayaks in this study, all but one definitely have baleen lashings.[67] The most recent kayaks in this study to feature baleen lashings are likely from the 1830s: plates 14, 19, 22, and 25. As baleen disappears, sealskin line seems to have been adapted as a lashing material, and later twine was used. Of the baleen coamings on kayaks in this study, three of the four are on type III kayaks (plate nos. 17, 19, and 22), the exception being the coaming of the Lübeck kayak, a type I from circa 1606 (plate 1).

Baleen was not widely available in East Greenland, which may explain the adaptation of pegs/nails for securing joints that were typically lashed in West Greenland (before pegs and metal nails were used in the 20th century). The disappearance of baleen in Greenland kayaks is undoubtedly explained by a combination of the market/trade value of the material with European traders and the depletion of baleenous whales in Baffin Bay and Davis Straits due to commercial whaling. The most recent utilization of baleen on a kayak in this study might be the two short coaming scarf protection strips on the UEM 95 of pre circa 1857 (plate 74).[68]

Emphasizing the idea that an increased reliance upon an object brings on inevitable changes in its form and manufacture, the kayaks of Southwest Greenland (types V and VII) exhibit construction solutions quite different from the earlier or more northerly Greenland kayaks. Types V and VII were/are used where there is open water year-round and no reliance on sea-ice hunting; this situation owes itself to both a warming climate as well as their being used in lower latitudes.

Type V and VII kayaks tend to have complexly-shaped curved deck beams (as in figure 35e), and straight deck beams with elegantly chamfered ends;(as in figure 40d and e). The deck beams in these kayaks are tenoned all the way through the gunwales. With exceptions, type V kayaks seem to have their chines and keelson lashed to the ribs, and 20th century type VII kayaks tend to use nails at these joints. Both of these types also exhibit more sophisticated outfitting than more northerly kayak types. For example, most type V and VII kayaks have keel edging at the bow and stern, end knobs, and elaborate deck line patterns with extensive deck fittings.

In the first chapter I referred to a decline of kayak use in both West and East Greenland in the mid 20th century; some direct contributors to this decline were the growing commercial fishing industry (paid employment) and the availability of motorboats. The decline of kayak usage is not just a 20th century phenomenon, and it has occurred in many areas of Greenland throughout time for many reasons.

Two of the more notable examples of this are the sophisticated kayak-hunting complex that existed at Uummannaq (Polar Greenland) during the Inugsuk phase of Thule culture in Greenland (Holtved, 1944II: 12, 73-78).[69] The early historic inhabitants of this region had been without kayaks for some time, and only took them up again after migrants from Baffin Island reintroduced them. The loss of kayaks

---

[67] The one kayak in question is the WMR 32848 (plate 11): I was unable to have a good close look at the lashings due to much of the structure being gone amidships; I would expect that its lashings would be baleen.

[68] The National Museum of Scotland's kayak 1984.277 (plate 19) has baleen lashings and a baleen coaming, and while the kayak is given a rough dating of "late 19th century" in the museum's catalog it appears to me to be older— perhaps from the early 19th century if not late 18th century.

[69] The 'sophistication' of the kayak-complex in this region is based most conclusively on the presence of throwing boards, bird spears, and parts of bladder darts (Holtved, 1944I: 156-157). Bladder darts in particular are highly developed weapons associated only with kayak hunting; harpoons and lances, while used from kayaks, could also have been used from umiaks.

in this region has been attributed to disease having killed older people who knew how to build and use kayaks (Rasmussen, 1908:32). It is also plausible that a worsening climate with the resultant decrease of open water may have been a factor.

Other examples of the ebb and flow of kayak usage are the Greenlanders of King Frederik VI's Coast having entirely abandoned the region for South Greenland by the early 1900s. Scorseby Sound, while having been inhabited in pre-historic times, was re-populated with Ammassalik Greenlanders in 1924, thus bringing kayak technology to the region. Remains of skinboats have been found by archaeologists in such remote areas as Washington Land, and Peary Land— areas which have for some time been uninhabited and impractical for open-water maritime subsistence (Mathiassen, 1929:183-212; Petersen, 1986:158-160).

As far back as the late 18th century, the employment of Greenlanders had a negative effect on kayak usage; historian Finn Gad explains, "Mostly in the whaling areas, training in kayak rowing seems to have declined during the 1780s. [Danish Colonial] Inspector Schultz noticed . . . after his arrival at Godhavn [Qeqertarsuaq] in 1790 that the Greenlanders there were not as proficient at kayak rowing as previously"(1982:144). Inspector Lund of the Southern Inspectorate, who in 1792 wrote: "Most of Holsteinsborg's [Sisimiut] and Qerortussoq's [7km East of Sisimiut] Greenlanders cannot catch a seal from a kayak because since their childhood they have considered a seal as insignificant in comparison to what they can earn with less labour as rowers on a sloop, in good whaling"(in Gad, 1982:144).

Danish employers and colonial officials understood the detrimental effect that the stifling of the fangst (traditional hunting) could have on the Greenlanders and indeed on themselves. The Royal Greenland Trade Company issued an order in 1782 that sought to encourage the fangst among the Greenlanders. Finn Gad paraphrases certain responsibilities that the trade officials would bear: The trader is to "see to it that the population does not concentrate in the settlements, but spreads out over the most favourable fangst sites." Further, Greenlanders must not be

> . . . Lured away from the fundamental occupation [the fangst] by getting dependent on the colonies for their necessities . . . The trader was to see to it that especially the boys were raised up as fangers. No competent fanger was to be employed by the Trade. Greenlanders who were bad providers were to set to work by the trader ... Otherwise, the trader, with the permission of the Inspector, would be allowed to employ a bad kayak rower in the service of the Trade or at whaling (1982:24-25).

Gad presents instances of traders trying to encourage the fangst in the late 1700s by paying hunters to build kayaks for boys, giving out free "kayak wood" and paying hunters to teach boys the fangst, but it was not always successful (1982:143-146).

Epidemics were another factor affecting kayak use. Large portions of the population in certain settlements were wiped out by smallpox in particular: Egedesminde District (Aasiaat vicinity) lost 42% of its population in the epidemic of 1800-1801; Jakobshavn (Ilulissat) lost 30% of its population between 1799-1802 (Gad, 1982: 89-91). Perhaps hardest hit by smallpox, Holsteinsborg District (Sisimiut vicinity) lost 89% of its population in 1801 (Gad, 1982:92-93).

While the factors of employment and epidemic have contributed to the decline of kayak use at various times in various regions of Greenland, these same factors also contributed to the dispersal and relocation of kayak forms. In the case of the smallpox epidemic of 1801 in Sisimiut, the settlement was re-populated with Greenlanders from communities as far away as Qaqortoq (Gad, 1982:92-93, 113), undoubtedly bringing with them differing notions of what a kayak should look like and how it should be built and used.

The domestic trade— undoubtedly pre-dating European contact— must have also contributed to a Greenlandic kayak builder/hunter's familiarity with different kayak forms. A hunter/kayak builder being exposed to new ideas and techniques during such trade voyages could result in changes in his own kayak and methods— or not.

Polar Greenland kayaks of the modern period have a brief and dynamic history. Immigrants from Baffin Island introduced these kayaks to the Polar Greenlanders in the 1860s (Mary-Rousselière, 1991:30-31), and the earliest collected examples of these kayaks (type XI) plainly exhibit their 'foreign' roots, i.e., flat-bottoms, pieced construction, extreme Swede-form hulls, and unique paddle shapes, etc. By the early 20th century, this kayak type came to be influenced by more southerly West Coast kayak forms; this transitional form of Polar Greenland kayak is the type XII of this study. Both types XI and XII became extinct in Greenland within 100 years of the kayak being re-introduced to Polar Greenland.

The transition from the early Polar kayak (type XI) to the West Greenland influenced form is distinct: The kayaks' maximum-breadth moves from behind the cockpit to ahead of the cockpit, and the cockpits themselves move forward (as can be tracked in Appendix A, column 7 for types XI, XII, and XIII). A more constant hull-depth also appears in transitional forms (i.e., type XII), as well as a stern shape distinctly 'West Greenlandic' in both plan and elevation views. Little of the old-form is left in the modern Polar Greenland kayak (type XIII). It is poignant to note the extent that the sole type XIII kayak in this study (from the 1950s; plate 102) resembles the oldest kayak in this study (circa 1606; plate 1)

I had just finished surveying the KNK 1550x10 and the KNK 1990 in an unheated warehouse in Nuuk, Greenland, and I was desperate for a hot coffee. The shock of the bright sky nearly knocked me over as I clambered down the steps out of the warehouse. As my eyes adjusted, they revealed a dismally cloudy day— summer, yes, but cold, rainy, and windy. My eyes also adjusted from staring at old kayaks,

Figure 404: A young kayaker accompanied by an adult at Nuuk, 2000. (Photograph by author.)

field notes, tables of numbers, and tape measures: I saw a harbor full of kayaks and a huge crowd lining the shore, cheering. It was August 2000, and the Greenland National Kayaking Championships had begun. I experienced a bit of an emotional dazzle from quickly moving from a museum setting to a very alive and active environment focused around the very objects I'd been studying.

The crowd was a remarkable mix of people— mostly Greenlandic of course, and there were as many old women as young men, and as many old men as young women. Kayaks are a very powerful source of pride for any Greenlander; a pride that crosses gender and age very readily. Eventually I made my way to the railing at the water's edge. Maligiaq Padilla from Sisimiut was competing in the Individual Rolling portion of the championships. The kayak was a tiny short kayak, barely afloat with the weight of the kayaker. The seas were a bit sloppy, and water readily swept over his boat with each passing wave.

This kayak— the same as in plate 93, is different than all other Greenland kayak types in so many ways, but in other ways, it is so much like them. It shares with the other types an origin rooted in purpose-driven design and adaptability. The 'rolling' kayaks (type X) are a reminder that kayaks are alive and important in Greenland. Even more significantly, it shows that kayaks are still being built and adapted to changing requirements, and that kayaks will be around— in one form or another— in Greenland for a long time to come.

Appendix A: ratios and proportions

By comparing ratios and proportions of different features of kayaks, one can usually note trends of development and change.

The kayaks in this table are arranged in the same order of presentation in the text and are grouped based on my proposed typology. I have calculated averages for each pertinent column of data excluding figures for children's kayaks. Each child's kayak is marked with (ch). The two kayak models in this study are also excluded from the averages, and are clearly marked.

Many of the kayaks in this study are damaged— some are missing several inches off one or both ends. (I have not restored lengths based on evidence of missing bone/ivory end knobs, so a minor range of error/variation can be expected.) Many kayaks are flattened, either slightly or considerably. When such damage is the case, conjecturally restored dimensions are used for the purpose of arriving at the figures in the table. When restored dimensions are used, an asterix (★) is used to denote this; Consult the text and scale drawings for details on the restoration and/or the artifactual appearance of the kayak.

1. Length overall meas.

2. Maximum breadth meas.

3. Depth to sheer meas.

4. Chine breadth (max.) meas.

5. Distance from the bow to the center of the cockpit.

6. Length to beam (width) ratio.

7. Center of cockpit position as % of length.

8. Breadth to depth-to-sheer ratio.

9. Breadth (overall) to chine breadth ratio.

TYPE I		1.	2.	3.	4.	5.	6.	7.	8.	9.
PL	KAYAK	LOA	BM	DS	CB	0-CC	L/B	CMP -0%	B-DS	BM/CB
1.	Schiffer	532.7	46.9	19.0	29.8	289.5	11.27	54.3	2.47	1.57
2.	WFM 232★	553.7	53.8	15.8	29.8	298.1	10.29	53.8	3.32	1.80
3.	De Rijp★	571.5	42.5	15.8	27.3	307.9	13.43	53.8	2.68	1.55
4.	DHNS 2★	568.9	39.7	17.4	30.4	295.2	14.33	51.8	2.27	1.30
5.	Lb.101 ★	600.3	45.2	23.8	27.3	326.0	13.28	54.3	1.90	1.65
6.	700	630.5	43.2	20.3	31.7	326.3	14.60	51.7	2.09	1.36
7.	MUS 57966★	553.5	47.2	17.4	33.6	297.4	11.83	53.2	2.71	1.40
	Average	573.7	45.5	18.5	29.9	–	12.71	53.2	2.49	1.51

TYPE II		1.	2.	3.	4.	5.	6.	7.	8.	9.
	KAYAK	LOA	BM	DS	CB	0-CC	L/B	CMP -0%	B-DS	BM/CB
8.	351-77★	556.8	39.3	17.1	29.8	285.7	14.16	51.3	2.29	1.31
9.	1161 ★	542.6	38.1	16.3	31.1	278.7	14.24	51.3	1.90	1.22
10.	36481★	561.6	36.9	15.5	27.9	287.3	15.22	51.1	2.38	1.32
11.	32848 ★	548.3	43.3	15.4	33.6	280.3	12.66	51.1	2.81	1.28
12.	1995.886	548.0	43.5	17.1	33.6	283.8	12.60	51.7	2.54	1.29
13.	THH "B" ★	548.6	39.3	17.7	33.6	289.5	13.95	52.7	1.90	1.16
14.	G.109	550.5	42.5	15.8	28.5	285.4	12.95	51.8	2.69	1.49
	Average	550.9	40.4	16.4	31.1	–	13.68	51.5	2.35	1.29

TYPE III		1.	2.	3.	4.	5.	6.	7.	8.	9.
	KAYAK	LOA	BM	DS	CB	0-CC	L/B	CMP -0%	B-DS	BM/CB
15.	349-1	546.4	38.7	15.8	31.1	273.6	14.12	50.0	2.45	1.24
16.	THH "A"	614.0	54.5	22.2	45.7	319.7	11.24	52.0	2.45	1.19
17.	AB5736★	581.6	43.3	18.7	35.5	295.2	13.28	50.7	2.34	1.23
18.	WHITM	579.1	42.3	18.7	36.8	294.9	13.53	50.9	2.29	1.16
19.	1984.277 ★	563.8	43.5	16.1	37.1	295.9	12.90	52.4	2.70	1.17
20.	1984-285 ★	556.9	40.5	16.5	33.0	291.4	13.72	52.3	2.46	1.23
21.	E.585	548.9	44.5	17.1	33.0	281.3	12.33	51.2	2.60	1.34
22.	HMM "B"	554.0	43.5	16.5	31.1	285.1	12.70	51.4	2.64	1.40
23.	1Bs.15	505.4	44.2	17.1	37.4	258.1	11.43	51.0	2.58	1.18
24.	U.C. 764	539.7	43.2	17.1	32.3	272.4	12.49	50.4	2.52	1.33
25.	THN ★	528.0	41.5	16.8	32.3	270.6	12.72	51.2	2.47	1.28
Average		556.1	43.7	17.5	35.0	–	12.76	51.2	2.50	1.25

TYPE IV		1.	2.	3.	4.	5.	6.	7.	8.	9.
	KAYAK	LOA	BM	DS	CB	0-CC	L/B	CMP -0%	B-DS	BM/ CB
26.	E.102	574.6	43.8	17.8	34.9	301.9	13.12	52.5	2.46	1.25
27.	Med-Chi	551.1	44.4	19.0	38.1	282.2	12.41	51.2	2.34	1.16
28.	E.584 ★	537.8	46.3	15.8	34.2	280.9	11.61	52.2	2.93	1.35
29.	HMM 64 ★	557.2	45.7	18.0	33.0	292.4	12.19	52.4	2.54	1.38
30.	HMM "C"★	521.9	49.5	-	-	-	10.50	-	-	-
31.	Lc.43	518.7	51.9	17.7	40.0	274.0	9.99	52.8	2.93	1.29
32.	1866.53 ★	495.9	45.7	16.8	37.8	282.8	10.85	57.0	2.72	1.20
33.	35667	525.1	47.2	19.0	39.3	280.6	11.12	53.4	2.48	1.20
34.	72564	512.1	50.0	18.0	38.1	268.6	10.24	52.4	2.77	1.31
35.	1849 (ch)	256.5	32.3	12.7	22.2	136.5	7.94	53.2	2.54	1.45
36.	60/480★	505.4	49.2	15.5	37.4	267.3	10.27	52.8	3.17	1.31
37.	1968-81-1	522.6	45.7	17.1	37.1	280.0	11.43	53.5	2.67	1.23
38.	977.180	523.2	46.5	16.8	40.0	272.4	11.25	52.0	2.76	1.16
	Adult Aver.	528.8	47.1	17.4	37.2	-	11.24	52.9	2.48	1.25

TYPE V		1.	2.	3.	4.	5.	6.	7.	8.	9.
	KAYAK	LOA	BM	DS	CB	0-CC	L/B	CMP -0%	B-DS	BM/ CB
39.	FM 172 ★	550.5	49.8	17.4	40.6	282.8	11.05	51.4	2.86	1.22
40.	FM 276 ★	528.6	47.3	16.9	39.3	281.3	11.17	53.4	2.79	1.20
41.	FM 65 ★	570.8	49.5	18.7	40.6	291.7	11.53	51.2	2.64	1.21
42.	FM 176	543.5	52.0	18.4	40.0	279.4	10.45	51.4	2.83	1.30
43.	1Bs.16	533.4	45.0	19.3	33.6	277.8	11.85	52.0	2.33	1.33
44.	1Bs.8	539.7	44.6	19.2	35.5	284.7	12.10	52.7	2.32	1.25
45.	4274cw★	534.9	51.7	18.4	40.6	280.3	10.34	52.4	2.80	1.27
46.	IV-A-483★	518.7	49.8	18.5	37.4	276.5	10.40	53.3	2.69	1.33
47.	117798(ch)	210.1	40.6	14.9	27.9	109.2	5.17	51.9	2.72	1.45
48.	IV-A-447★	527.6	49.5	16.8	42.5	283.8	10.65	53.7	2.94	1.16
49.	2050	513.7	47.6	19.8	38.1	266.7	10.79	51.9	2.40	1.24
50.	PQN	510.8	49.3	19.3	35.5	264.1	10.36	51.7	2.55	1.38
51.	KNK "C"★	519.4	50.8	19.0	40.6	265.4	10.22	51.0	2.67	1.25
52.	2056	496.5	46.8	19.0	32.3	255.5	10.61	51.4	2.46	1.44
53.	1Bs.24★	497.2	50.1	17.6	33.0	259.0	9.92	52.0	2.84	1.51
54.	143	523.2	51.4	21.9	41.2	267.6	10.18	51.1	2.34	1.24
55.	1966 (ch)	276.8	32.0	11.3	24.1	146.6	8.65	52.9	2.83	1.32
	Adult Aver.	527.2	49.1	18.6	38.0	-	10.77	52.0	2.63	1.28

TYPE VI		1.	2.	3.	4.	5.	6.	7. CMP -0%	8.	9. BM/ CB
	KAYAK	LOA	BM	DS	CB	0-CC	L/B		B-DS	
56.	160325	559.4	56.5	18.7	50.1	303.2	9.88	54.2	3.02	1.12
57.	1894.227 ★	501.6	47.0	16.8	37.4	267.6	10.60	53.3	2.79	1.25
58.	BF-47★	429.8	45.7	17.4	35.2	227.0	9.12	52.8	2.62	1.29
59.	60/5253(ch)	245.1	31.4	12.2	25.4	133.9	7.80	54.6	2.57	1.23
60.	977.182★	567.0	46.0	14.6	35.8	295.5	12.32	52.1	3.15	1.28
61.	1215	500.3	50.3	15.2	41.9	270.1	9.84	53.9	3.34	1.21
62.	IV-A-427★	507.0	49.8	14.6	44.4	266.0	10.18	52.4	3.41	1.12
63.	5023	496.8	52.0	15.7	43.8	271.1	9.55	54.5	3.31	1.18
64.	76/13/88★	466.0	47.3	17.4	37.4	235.5	9.85	50.5	2.71	1.26
65.	IV-A-428	532.7	54.2	21.1	46.5	278.7	9.82	52.3	2.56	1.16
66.	2237 ★	523.8	46.2	15.8	36.8	287.6	11.34	54.9	2.92	1.25
67.	IV-A-375	499.1	51.1	16.3	40.9	275.5	9.76	55.1	3.13	1.24
68.	57992★	509.2	52.0	16.8	36.1	273.6	9.79	53.7	3.09	1.44
69.	977.183★	560.0	56.0	15.5	40.0	295.9	10.00	52.8	3.61	1.40
70.	1550x10	594.3	52.3	17.1	44.4	328.9	11.36	55.3	3.05	1.17
71.	1550x18 ★	531.8	53.3	16.5	39.3	278.2	9.97	52.3	3.23	1.35
72.	JH 1959	496.5	54.4	20.9	37.4	276.2	9.13	55.6	2.60	1.45
73.	L.18.273 ★	523.8	55.2	19.6	40.9	288.9	9.48	55.1	2.81	1.34
	Adult Aver.	516.8	51.1	17.0	40.4	–	10.11	53.5	3.02	1.26

TYPE VII		1.	2.	3.	4.	5.	6.	7. CMP -0%	8.	9. BM/ CB
	KAYAK	LOA	BM	DS	CB	0-CC	L/B		B-DS	
74.	UMCH 95	545.7	49.2	17.3	37.4	279.0	11.09	51.1	2.84	1.31
75.	1076	521.3	43.1	17.1	35.8	266.0	12.09	51.0	2.52	1.20
76.	60/6190	569.9	51.2	19.2	41.2	291.1	11.13	51.0	2.66	1.24
77.	L.9726	591.8	51.1	18.9	38.1	297.1	11.58	50.2	2.70	1.34
78.	L.18.178	567.6	52.0	17.4	40.3	295.2	10.91	52.0	2.99	1.29
79.	530/61	541.0	49.8	19.2	40.6	274.3	10.86	50.7	2.59	1.22
80.	1550x1	500.3	48.8	22.5	34.6	251.6	10.25	52.2	2.17	1.41
81.	810-34	541.0	48.8	17.9	37.1	281.3	11.08	51.9	2.72	1.31
	Average	547.3	49.2	18.6	38.1	–	11.12	51.2	2.64	1.29

TYPE VIII		1.	2.	3.	4.	5.	6.	7. CMP -0%	8.	9. BM/ CB
	KAYAK	LOA	BM	DS	CB	0-CC	L/B		B-DS	
82.	Lc.148	559.7	52.3	19.3	37.4	294.9	10.70	52.6	2.71	1.39
83.	1418 (MODEL)	77.1	7.0	3.0	5.7	40.1	11.01	52.0	2.33	1.22
	Average	N/A	N/A	N/A	N/A	–	10.8	52.3	2.52	1.30

TYPE IX	1.	2.	3.	4.	5.	6.	7.	8.	9.
KAYAK	LOA	BM	DS	CB	0-CC	L/B	CMP -0%	B-DS	BM/CB
84. 29.881	560.0	46.3	14.4	28.2	289.2	12.09	51.6	2.52	1.64
85. 60/6003	591.8	50.1	15.5	31.9	303.5	11.81	51.2	3.23	1.57
86. L.19.157	568.3	47.6	13.9	25.0	294.9	11.94	51.8	3.42	1.90
87. 48057	587.7	48.6	15.2	31.7	308.9	12.09	52.5	3.20	1.53
88. 2823	544.1	56.5	13.9	29.2	281.6	9.63	51.7	4.06	1.93
89. 1990	553.0	47.1	17.1	33.6	291.1	11.74	52.6	2.32	1.40
90. 59876	475.9	49.5	15.8	25.4	237.4	9.61	49.8	3.13	1.94
91. 57602	502.9	47.6	16.5	27.9	255.9	10.56	50.8	2.88	1.70
Average	547.9	49.1	15.2	29.1	-	11.18	51.5	3.09	1.70

TYPE X	1.	2.	3.	4.	5.	6.	7.	8.	9.
KAYAK	LOA	BM	DS	CB	0-CC	L/B	CMP -0%	B-DS	BM/CB
92. K.D.	426.0	45.2	12	39.3	233.0	9.42	54.6	3.76	1.15
93. M.P.	513.0	45.0	14.2	38.1	266.0	11.40	51.8	3.16	1.18
Average	469.5	45.1	13.1	38.7	-	10.41	53.2	3.46	1.17

TYPE XI	1.	2.	3.	4.	5.	6.	7.	8.	9.
KAYAK	LOA	BM	DS	CB	0-CC	L/B	CMP -0%	B-DS	BM/CB
94. 160388	531.4	56.8	20.6	45.0	301.9	9.35	56.8	2.7	1.26
95. 165227	491.4	56.3	22.7	43.8	274.3	8.27	55.8	2.4	1.28
96. 977.179	523.2	57.1	22.2	47.6	294.9	9.16	56.3	2.5	1.19
97. 1007	500.6	55.5	17.1	46.9	283.2	9.02	56.5	3.2	1.18
98. 977.181★	556.2	52.8	19.0	36.8	320.3	10.53	57.5	2.7	1.43
Average	520.5	55.7	20.3	44.0	-	9.26	56.5	2.7	1.26

TYPE XII	1.	2.	3.	4.	5.	6.	7.	8.	9.
KAYAK	LOA	BM	DS	CB	0-CC	L/B	CMP -0%	B-DS	BM/CB
99. 17.125	612.7	52.8	16.8	40.9	340.6	11.60	55.5	3.1	1.29
100. 528	492.7	52.7	17.1	41.2	272.0	9.35	55.2	3.0	1.27
101. 1964.1562	578.1	54.6	18.7	38.7	327.0	10.58	56.5	2.9	1.41
Average	561.1	53.3	17.5	40.2	-	10.51	55.7	3.0	1.32

TYPE XIII	1.	2.	3.	4.	5.	6.	7.	8.	9.
KAYAK	LOA	BM	DS	CB	C-CC	L/B	CMP -0%	B-DS	BM/CB
102. 950-219	544.8	55.2	18.2	35.2	296.5	9.86	54.4	3.0	1.56

MIXED TYPES	1.	2.	3.	4.	5.	6.	7.	8.	9.
KAYAK	LOA	BM	DS	CB	C-CC	L/B	CMP -0%	B-DS	BM/CB
103. IV-A-432	538.4	47.4	17.1	32.7	286.3	11.35	53.1	2.77	1.44
104. KNK 1906*	484.5	51.4	15.2	30.4	256.5	9.42	52.9	3.38	1.69

Appendix B: Conjectural Interpretations of Two Medieval Greenland Kayaks in Scale

The two models excavated by Mathiassen and Holtved (figures 395 and 396 respectively) have inspired me to adapt their forms to interpretive renderings of full-size kayaks in scale drawing. These are highly conjectural of course, as models often suffer from having less-than-accurate proportions when compared to full-size examples. It should also be mentioned that I have not personally seen either model, and my interpretations are based on published photographs of the originals, i.e., Mathiassen, 1931: plate 20, no. 7, and Holtved, 1944: plate 45, no.25.

I've chosen very conservative general dimensions for this virtual-modeling: lengths of 15 feet, and breadths of 18 inches for each— fairly ideal dimensions for full-size conjectural replication and sea-trials.

The Punuk-Thule form kayak model Mathiassen excavated is fairly straightforward with regards to its shape, although the bottom could be perfectly flat or slight V. My interpretation is presented in plate 105, and is arbitrarily given a slight V-bottom. The resemblance to historic forms, e.g., types I and V is clear. While the bow looks very high (particularly due to how it is drawn), it should be expected to sit lower in the water, thereby presenting a deep bow-skeg at the stem-keel transition.

The Birnirk-Thule form kayak model from Holtved's excavations at Uummannaq, Polar Greenland, does not even lend a hint as to its cross-sections, although working forward from Arima's descriptions of Birnirk influenced kayak forms and working backwards from historic type II Greenland kayaks I have arrived at the hull shape depicted in plate 106. It is perhaps also worth noticing this kayak's resemblance to the Lc.148 (plate 82), particularly with regards to the sheer line.

My interpretation of this second model is somewhat literal in profile: Note the slightly hogged keel-line, giving a slight bow-skeg effect. Also, my rendering depicts the fore deck as being humped slightly — a possibility discussed in the analysis chapter (page 533). This interpretation's cross-sections draw entirely on type II kayaks, with their somewhat boxy forward sections and twisting gunwales.

The value of this exercise is uncertain, particularly due to the level of conjecture and interpretation required, and the fact that I have not yet built and used either craft at the time of this study's printing. Hopefully these renderings will somehow assist those interested in early comparative/developmental kayak studies.

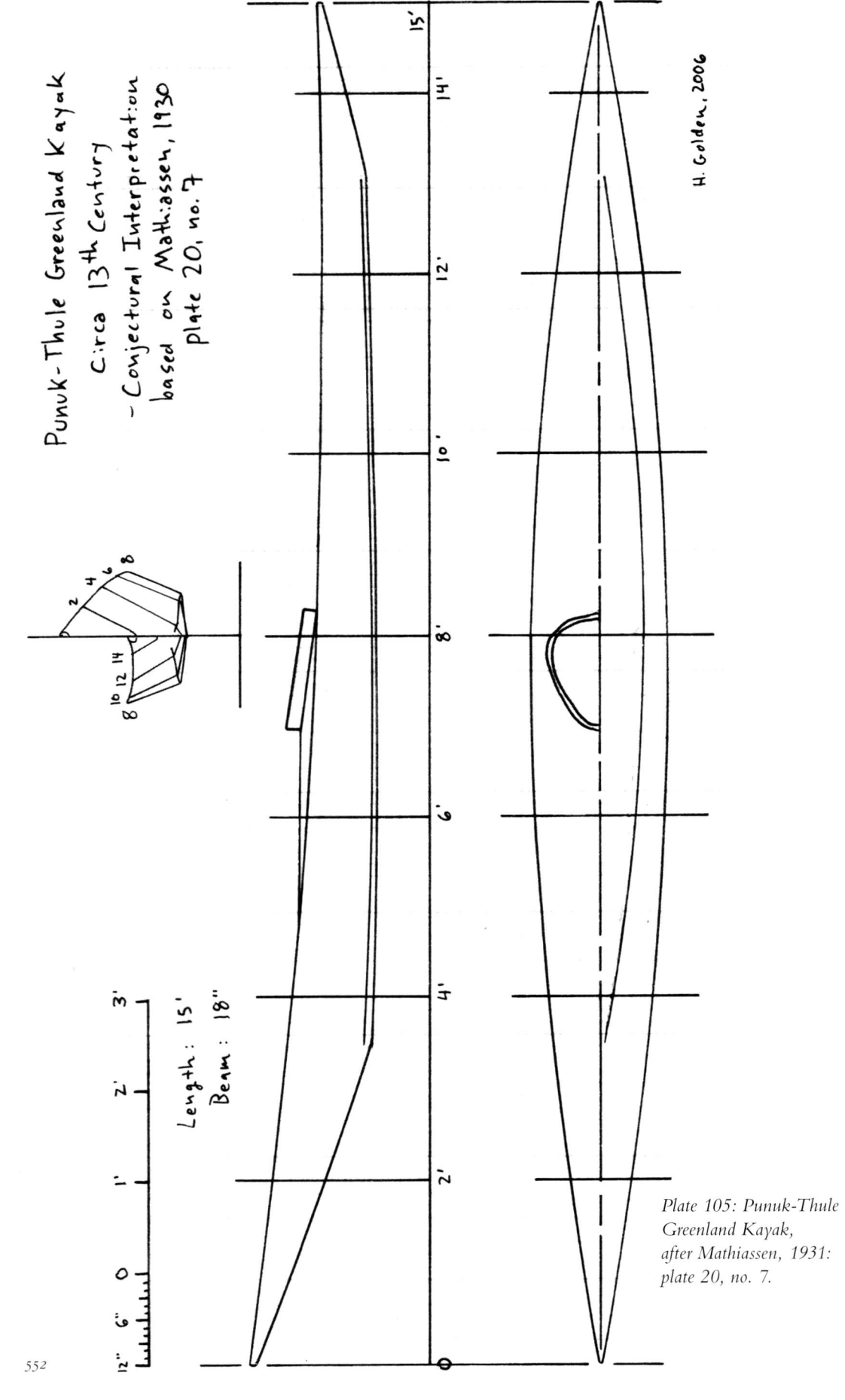

Plate 105: Punuk-Thule Greenland Kayak, after Mathiassen, 1931: plate 20, no. 7.

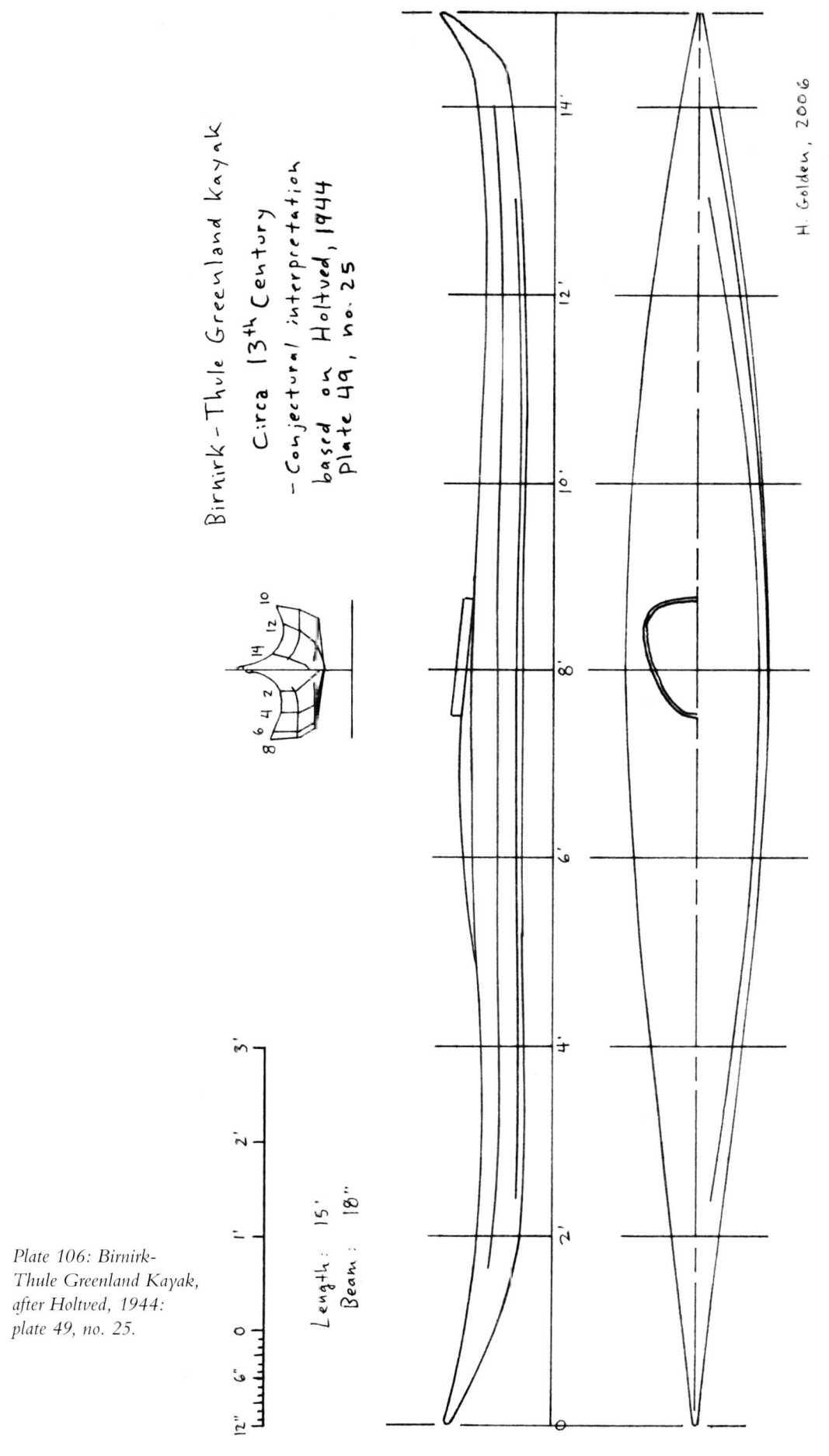

Plate 106: Birnirk-Thule Greenland Kayak, after Holtved, 1944: plate 49, no. 25.

APPENDIX C: THE QUESTION OF GREENLANDERS HAVING PADDLED KAYAKS TO EUROPE

The following is an elaboration on the matter of Greenlanders appearing in their kayaks off the northern coast of Scotland in the 17th and early 18th centuries. As mentioned in the first chapter (page 31), Scots had sighted kayakers at sea off Scotland in the late 1600s – early 1700s. Some of these kayaks were recovered; one is presently in the Marischal College Museum of Anthropology.[70]

Several scholars have dismissed the possibility that Greenlanders could survive a kayak journey from Greenland to Europe. I think such journeys were possible, and have little doubt that they did occur. Dr. Gert Nooter succinctly outlines his reasoning for doubting such journeys were possible:

1. A kayak is not really a suitable vessel for this passage.

2. The distances— even via the way-stations indicated by Whitaker[71]—
are too great, if only in terms of the most obvious problems:
a) the procuring and consuming of food,

b) the procuring of water,

c) the elimination of waste products from the body,

d) the maintenance of a speed of about five miles per hour for two full days, and

e) the lack of knowledge of the shortest route.
      (Nooter, 1971:10)

Nooter's reasons are sound, but inconclusive. "Suitability" of vessels' hasn't prevented ocean crossings in dugout canoes, kayaks, balsa and reed rafts, and even sailboats only four feet long. Each one of Nooter's reasons can be refuted, save for the lack of knowledge of the shortest route, which may in fact not have been such a critical factor.

To suggest that the kayak of the Greenlander is an unsuitable vessel is to underestimate the skill and ability with which Greenlanders used them. There are instances of Greenlanders being swept out to sea in their kayaks during storms and enduring horrendous conditions for long periods. British Arctic Air Route Expedition member F. Spencer Chapman writes that "In 1931 at Cape Farewell, [expedition leader Gino] Watkins met an Eskimo who had recently been blown out to sea for four days in a phenomenal storm: he had had to roll his kayak many times"(1934b: 115). Chapman himself and Kidarsi, an East Greenlander, spent 24 hours in their kayaks without getting out (1934b: 269), though Chapman men

---

[70]John Heath surveyed this kayak, and his drawing appears in *Eastern Arctic Kayaks* (Heath, et.al, 2004:10, fig. 1.5); the paddle associated with this kayak is shown in paddle-plate 8, this volume.

[71]Whitaker's "way-stations" are Iceland, the Faeroe Isles, Shetland Isles, and Orkney Isles (1954:103).

tions napping when the two rafted up, and they undoubtedly rafted up in order to relieve themselves as well. A personal account of a hunter from West Greenland being trapped at sea in a storm over New Year's 1899-1900 is presented in *Eastern Arctic Kayaks* (Rosing, *in* Heath, 2004:103-105).

The 'distances being too great between waypoints' (the greatest being about 280 miles [450km]; Iceland to Faeroe Islands) argument overlooks the likelihood of the occurrence of sea-ice— particularly in a period of rapid cooling: the Little Ice Age which roughly spans 1550-1850 (Fossett, 2001:29). That sea ice likely occurred along the course suggests that procuring drinking water and eliminating bodily waste may not have been such problems. Also, a kayak with a water-saturated skin could be dried out on top of sea-ice.

Nooter suggests that a rate of about five miles an hour for two full days is necessary for a Greenlander to reach Europe: This is based on how long it takes for a kayak's skin-cover to become water saturated and the distances that must be traversed. Again, ice adrift on the sea could provide opportunity for a kayaker to dry out the skins.

With regards to Greenlanders not knowing the shortest way to Scotland, there was of course no chance of knowing this; Even if a Greenlander had gotten to Scotland and back in a kayak, he would undoubtedly be hard-pressed to have recorded sea directions accurately. Despite this point, currents from Greenland to Scotland are favorable. Near Cape Farewell (southernmost Greenland) in September 1998, a European woman in a kayak capsized and died during a storm. Her kayak was not immediately recovered, instead washing up in the Shetland Islands a couple of months later (Cunningham, 1999:7) Any amount of time a kayaker spent sleeping, resting, or eating— either in the kayak or on sea ice— would have been time drifting towards the British Isles.

Historian Renée Fossett speculates that Greenlanders were not only capable of such voyages, but that they deliberately set off on them so as to discover new lands and resources during difficult times (2001:75-83). Whether or not this was the case will never be known.

In any case, the mystery of whether or not Greenlanders traveled from their homes to the shores of Scotland is one that has received pretty much constant scholarly attention since 1883 (Tudor). MacRitchie (1912a and b), Souter (1934), Whittaker (1954 and 1977), Mikkelsen (1954), Nooter (1971), Heath (1987b, and 2004), Iciens (1987), Fossett (2001), and Longyard (2003) present some of the more significant writings on this topic.

APPENDIX D: A PRIMER FOR GATHERING OFFSETS AND LOFTING KAYAKS FOR DESIGN ANALYSIS OR REPLICATION.

For readers wishing to make a table of a kayak's dimensions either for study or reconstruction, the following method may be of some help. The process is more or less the same whether measurements are sought for installing into a computer analysis program, or for drawing the kayak full-size (lofting) on butcher paper for replication.

The only tools needed are a pair of dividers and a straight edge— preferably a triangle. Two basic forms of measurements are needed: breadths and heights of the various lines of a kayak (these lines are the sheer, chine, keelson, gunwale edge, etc.). These breadths and heights are taken at distances (or stations) from 'zero,'— the bow. The scale plates in this book have stations drawn at 2' increments from the bow; of course if an accurate table of offsets is desired, more stations will have to be drawn in so as to catch sharper curves in the kayak, particularly at the bow and stern.

Additional stations can be drawn onto copies of the surveys at any desired increments, such as 12", 6", 3", etc. Likewise metric stations can be added as well. Figure 405 shows how such additional stations can be added to a drawing.

Once all the desired stations are drawn, offsets can then be taken with a pair of dividers. For example, the height of the sheer above

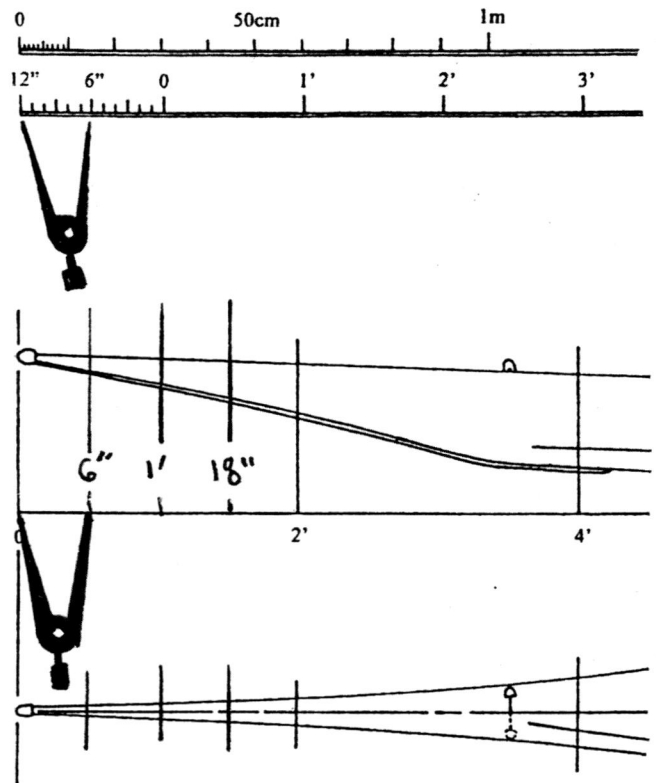

Figure 405: Using dividers to add stations at desired increments, in this case stations spaced every 6".

the baseline (datum) at 2' aft of zero is found by touching the divider's points to the sheer and the baseline at the 2' station, and then transferring this span to the scale— 13" is the height.

The result of this process is a large pile of numbers— the table in figure 407 shows a good method for keeping these numbers organized. Another method is to simply jot the numbers on the survey drawing itself, also shown in figure 407.

Increased accuracy in taking offsets is aided by using larger copies of the survey drawings, though this is usually not necessary for building an accurate replica of a particular kayak. By taking offsets at close stations along the kayak, small dips and bumps in the measurements can be faired-out when re-drawn full-size. Bear in mind the original survey drawings in this book were drawn in the scale of 1"=1-1/2'— a worthy size for small craft, but the line weight used in inking them measures about 3/16 of an inch to scale. If a particular station measurement is considerably 'off the curve' it may have been measured incorrectly.

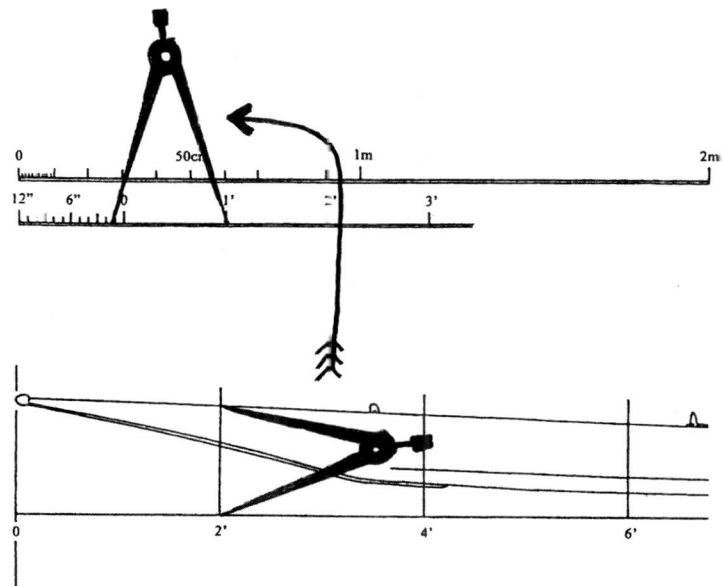

Figure 406: Lifting offsets— for example the height of the sheer above the datum 2' aft of the kayak's bow (0); the calipers are spread this distance and then moved to the scale, for a result of 13".

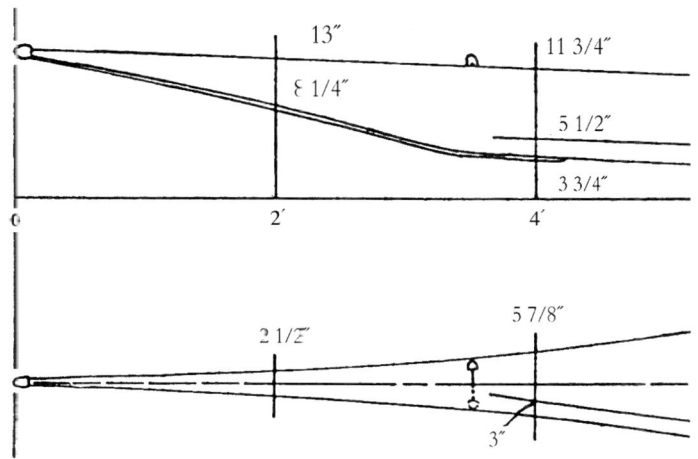

Figure 407: Two methods for recording offsets: Left, directly onto the scale drawing, and right, in a table. Note how the chine is only drawn in 1/2 breadth— simply double the callipered result for its full breadth.

	HEIGHTS			BREADTHS	
	Sheer	Chine	Keel	Sheer	Chine
2'	13"	–	8 1/4"	2 1/2"	–
4'	11 3/4"	5 1/2"	3 3/4"	5 7/8"	3"

557

Glossary

Amidship(s): The middle of a boat or kayak. This is not always the widest part of a kayak, and it is used in the present text to denote a general area, e.g., the cockpit, or in terms of deck lines, the lines the kayaker can reach with his hands.

Beam: The width of a kayak's hull— measured at the maximum breadth except in cases where the masik projects over the gunwales. See figure 18a.

Bilge: Generally, the area of transition between a vessel's bottom and sides— usually a rounded vicinity. On account of Greenland kayaks' usually having hard-chine form and construction, their bilges are abrupt and distinct.

Birds-mouth (scarf): See figure 27.

Blade: The 'power' portion of the paddle— the broad ends of a double bladed paddle. This is a somewhat nebulous vicinity as the loom of many Greenland paddles transitions into the blade very gradually.

Bottom: Generally self-explanatory, but specifically the area of a kayak's hull between the chines and the keelson. Occasionally refers to the keel-line itself, e.g., "a highly-rockered bottom."

Breadth: See also "Beam." Width.

Camber: Curved or crowned edge or surface, such as a paddle's face or the deck of a kayak.

Cant, Canted: See "Dihedral."

Chamfer(red): Tapered, usually abruptly at the end of a structural piece, e.g., ribs are usually tapered at their ends so as to fit into mortises.

Chine: An edge, specifically appearing between the sheer of a kayak and its keelson.

Clipper(ed) (bow): A concave stem-line, as depicted in figure 20; the opposite of a convex stem.

Coaming: Generally referring to the wooden hoop mounted to the kayak's skin covering around the cockpit. Technically, the coaming is not part of the kayak's frame, being made fast to the skin instead. In Greenlandic, the coaming is referred to as *paa*.

Concave/Concavity: A hollow in a line or surface, for example: A concave stem is depicted in figure 20. The opposite of convex.

Convex: A bulge or crown in a line or surface, such as a kayak's stem, keel-line, or sheer-line. See figure 20 for a depiction of a convex stem. The opposite is concave, or hollow.

Cross-section: The shape of a kayak's hull at any given point, cut perpendicular to its longitudinal axis. Cross-sections are presented in the plates, and are generally given at 2´ increments along the kayak's length.

Deadeye: In this study, a deck line's fitting through which a different deck line passes, appearing as if a pulley, or ship's 'deadeyes.'

Deadrise: The angle between the keelson's outer edge and the outer edge of the chines, effectively determining whether a hull-shape is flat-bottomed or more V-bottomed. The deeper the "V" shape in a hull's cross-section, the greater the deadrise. See figure 18f.

Deck: The upper surface or top-sides of a kayak; anything above the sheer line.

Deck fittings: See "Fittings."

Deck-Line: The straps that span a kayak's deck, used to hold hunting tools and/or the paddle.

Depth overall: The height of the kayak measured at the peak of the fore-deck to the bottom of the keelson— measured at the cockpit's front edge, and excluding the height of the coaming. See figure 18b.

Depth to sheer: The height of the kayak's hull, excluding the fore deck and coaming— essentially the depth from the sheer-line down, measured at the forward edge of the cockpit. See figure 18c.

Dihedral: Somewhat analogous to "deadrise" (see), but it comes from a more aeronautical background. It used in the present text to denote the form of certain paddles when viewed from the top or bottom. Dihedral is the amount the blades angle up from their midpoint, much as the deadrise of a kayak's bottom angles up from the keelson to the chines. See figure 387f for an example of a paddle with marked dihedral.

Dowel: Same as a peg, but can also mean any cylindrically shaped piece of wood. See "Peg" and or "Pin."

Draft: The depth of a kayak below the waterline, i.e., how deep the kayak sits in the water. This is an extremely variable factor, as a kayak's load may well vary from between 100 pounds to 250 pounds depending on who is using it, and with what hunting equipment or 'catch' on deck.

Edge scarf: An edge scarf is the joining of two pieces of wood along the woods' edge (narrower surface), such as is illustrated in figure 118, right. Contrast to "Face Scarf," e.g., figure 118, left.

Edging: The ivory or bone strips found along the kayak's keelson or chines, usually just at the ends of the former. Also, the ivory or bone found along the blade-edges of paddles. These pieces protect the kayak or paddle from excessive wear.

Elevation: A side-view of a kayak, depicting the kayak's heights over a level base-line. From this view, rocker, sheer, the rake of the ends and other features are clearly depicted.

Face scarf: A face scarf is the joining of two pieces of wood along the pieces' faces (wider surface) such as is illustrated in figure 118, right. Contrast to 'Edge Scarf,' e.g., figure 118, left.

Fanger: The word "fanger" means 'catcher' in Danish, and refers to seal-catchers, as kayaking seal hunters are known as. "Fangst" is the art of catching sea mammals and other quarry.

Fangst: See "*Fanger.*"

Feathered: This refers to whether or not a double-bladed paddle has its blades in the same plane. A feathered paddle means that one blade is twisted a certain number of degrees from the other. Blades that are not feathered are referred to as 'flat-pitch' or un-feathered.

Fish-form: A boat whose maximum breadth is carried ahead of the mid-point or cockpit; the opposite of 'Swede-form," both depicted in figure 21.

Fittings: The clasps, knobs, buttons, and equipment holders found on the kayak's deck, generally threaded onto the kayak's deck-lines. Fittings are usually made of ivory, antler, or bone.

Flare: The angle made by either the gunwale or the kayak's sides as seen from head-on. See figure 18d.

Freeboard: The surface of a kayak above the waterline, i.e., exposed to wind and weather. Generally (and in this study), this will exclude any surfaces above the kayak's sheer-line (coaming and raised fore-deck). This is a significant element of how a kayak handles, particularly in dynamic conditions (wind/waves).

Gain(s): Additions of wood, in the forms of scarfs or patches to in effect make a piece of wood larger. For example, if a keel board does not reach to the desired height to meet the gunwales, a chunk of wood may be nailed to it in order to close the gap; this piece is a gain. The same term is used when a strip of wood is fastened to another in order to make a kayak paddle blade wider.

Gunwale(s): The large wooden boards that form the sheer and breadth of a kayak; the main structural members of a kayak. (In Greenlandic: *Apummat*). See figure 16g.

Heel, Heeling: From the kayaker's perspective: Leaning the kayak over, as if to roll to the side.

Heel guide(s): See "Leg-Slats."

Hollow, Hollowing: Referring to concavity (see), reflective of volume or 'fullness.'

Hull: The kayak below the sheer-line (see "hull-shape").

Hull shape: Fairly self-explanatory, however, there are several different ways a kayak's hull can be viewed, and thereby its appearance better understood. The hull viewed via cross-sections, elevations, and plan-views. Each method of study presents different information, and each will lack the ability to present an aspect that the other can. Characteristics such as Swede-form/Fish-form are brought to light when a kayak is viewed in plan-view. Rocker and sheer become plain to see when viewed in elevation. Cross-sections do show both, but not well; cross-sections do depict dead-rise, flare, and chine-breadths especially well.

Initial stability: Resistance to heeling. A kayak with high initial stability will be harder to lean. Low initial stability is easier to lean, and to tip over, but generally easier to control in dynamic conditions, e.g., waves and swells, particularly taken broadside.

Inset: This term is used within the context of paddles, and specifically how their ivory or bone edging is positioned on the edges of the wooden paddle. Inset edging has its ends flush with the paddle's edge; the opposite term is "raised." Both are illustrated in figure 387.

Keel: Generally, the centerline of a kayak's bottom; the lowest edge along the kayak's length. It is also shorthand for 'keelson.' See figures 16c and 17b.

Keelson: The longitudinal stringer along the kayak's bottom centerline. See also "Keel."

Lashing(s): A binding of line used to secure structural pieces. The line may be string, baleen, wire, sealskin or any other strong material that can be threaded and knotted.

Leg-slats: Analogous to "Seat-slats" (see), but specifically placed so that the kayaker's legs will be supported by them. These are illustrated in figure 87.

Lock pegged: See "Peg" and/or "Pin."

Longitudinal(s): Along the length of the kayak. Movement along the longitudinal axis of the kayak is known as heeling. The noun longitudinal refers to the stringers running fore and aft, such as chines, keelson, and occasionally gunwales.

Loom: The 'hand-hold' area of a paddle, which is often a nebulous region on Greenland paddles. Generally, the two parts of a (double-bladed) paddle are the loom and the blades. See also "Blade."

Mortise: Hole or pocket into which a tenon is inserted. Mortises are generally found on the gunwales, and receive the tenons of the ribs and the deck beams. Mortises for deck beams may go all the way through the gunwale's face, or just part way. See figures 26 and 34.

Peg: A rod of wood (dowel) used to fasten pieces together, as if a nail. In later kayaks metal nails often replace pegs. Ivory can also be used as a peg.

Pin: A peg used to lock in place another peg or dowel. Pins are usually made of ivory, as they are often of a very small diameter, e.g., 1/16″ (1.5mm). See figure 25.

Pinch(ing): See "Hollow(ing)."

Pitch, Pitching: A kayak's movement along a transverse axis, the bow and stern 'pitching' up and down opposite each other while paddling across waves, for example.

Plan, Plan-view: A top and/or bottom view of the kayak. From this view, one can see whether the kayak is Swede-form or Fish-form, details of the fittings, deck-stringer arrangements and the breadths of the chines and gunwales.

Plumb: Straight up and down; vertical: 90 degrees to horizontal or flat. Usually used to refer to the flare (see) of the gunwales.

Rake: The angle of a stem, 'high-rake' is a steep angle.

Re-curved: See "Sinuous."

Reverse-sheer: See "Sheer."

Ribs: Transverse frames that generally reach from a gunwale's lower edge down to the chines and keelson and then back up the other side. Ribs can be made from bent pieces of wood, or can be pieced together from two or three straight pieces (see figures 16d and 143).

Rocker: The curve of a keel-line between a kayak's raked stems. A kayak with heavy rocker has a strongly curved keel-line, e.g., the DNM Lc.148 (plate 82). An example of a kayak with very little rocker is the KNK 2237 (plate 66).

Rudder: See "Skeg."

Scantlings: The dimensions of the structural members of a boat. For the purposes of this study, these are measured through the cockpit opening, though the dimensions may change along the length of the kayak.

Scarf: A joint that serves to make a piece longer. For example to short boards could be scarfed together in order to make one long piece. Scarfs are fastened via many different means, and take on many different forms.

Shaft: See "Loom."

Sheer: The amount of curve of a kayak's sheer-line (see below). A kayak with 'high-' or 'considerable-sheer' is one significantly curved. 'Sheer' alone suggests a kayak with some curve. 'No sheer' would suggest a flat kayak. Reverse sheer would refer to a kayak whose sheer-line is convex, being higher amidships than at the ends. Sheer is occasionally used as a contraction of 'sheer-line.' See figure 17a.

Sheer-line: The upper-most and outer-most line of a kayak's hull— by 'hull,' it excludes any raised fore deck or coaming. The sheer line is primarily defined by the gunwale's upper/outer corner, though it carries to the kayak's ends whether the gunwales themselves do or not. (Figure 17a) See also "Sheer."

Sinuous: A sheer line or keel line (for example) that curves one direction, and then curves back— essentially "S" formed, though of course much more subtle. Re-curved is also used to describe this. A good example of this is the keel line of the KNK 2050 (plate 49).

Skeg: A fin, either affixed to the exterior of the kayak— along the keel towards the stern, or integral to the kayak's frame resulting in a fin-like protrusion in the same vicinity. (See figure 132.)

Stability: Resistance to leaning or tipping over. Also resistance to turning, i.e., directional stability.

Stanchion: A support post, usually from the keelson to a deck beam or a deck stringer. See figures 57-65.

Stem: The end of a kayak, either front or stern. This often refers to the raked part of the kayak's keelson, at either end. See also "Stem Piece."

Stem piece: A separate piece of wood that forms the kayak's actual tips. These are used in kayaks whose gunwales don't extend to the very ends. See figure 16a.

Step(ped) (scarf): See figure 27 and accompanying text.

Stopped (scarf): See figures 116i–j and accompanying text.

Stringer(s): Longitudinal pieces of the frame. It usually does not include the gunwales, and is most often just referring to the longitudinals on the deck, i.e., the forward and aft deck stringers.

Swede-form: A boat whose maximum breadth is carried aft of the mid-point or cockpit; opposite of fish-form. Both depicted in figure 21.

Tenon: The part of a structural piece that is fitted into a hole or mortise in another piece. See figure 26.

Transverse: Across the deck, or side-to-side, such as the deck lines usually run. Deck beams and ribs run in a transverse direction to the kayak.

Trim: Essentially the 'balance' of a kayak— how it sits on the water, i.e., bow high or low, with regards to the waterline. The hull-volume and its distribution as well as the weight of the kayaker and the equipment on-deck are all factors in a kayak's trim. See also "Waterline."

Waterline: The waterline of a kayak is the line around a kayak's hull to where the water's surface reaches. It is a highly variable reference point dependent on the weight and volume and their respective distribution in the kayak. Many performance calculations can be based on the shape and proportions of a vessel's waterline, but in practicality, as soon as a vessel starts moving, the waterline is inclined to change dramatically.

Weathercock(ing): The tendency for a kayak to point nose towards the eye of the wind while at rest or gliding to a stop— much the same concept as a weather vane always pointing towards the source of the wind.

Yaw(ing): Movement of the kayak along a vertical axis— as in turning the kayak towards a new course. Directional stability and weather-cocking are factors that occur along the vertical axis. 'Resistance to yaw' would suggest a kayak that tracks well, having favorable directional stability.

GREENLANDIC TERMS:

(Cross-reference English Glossary for definitions)

Ajaat: Deck Beams.

Akuillisaq: Spray skirt.

Amiq: Skin Covering; kayak skin.

Ammassalimiut: People of Ammassalik District, East Greenland. See also *Tunumiut.*

Appumaak: Gunwale Strakes.

Asaloq: Harpoon-line stand.

Avasisaartoq: Curved kayak— as related by H. C. Petersen (1986:49). See page 204.

Avataq: Sealskin float, attached to the end of the harpoon head's line.

Inuhuit: Polar Greenlanders; Polar Eskimo.

Isserfik: deck beam defining the aft-end of a kayak's cockpit.

Kujaannalik: A "storm kayak"— described by H. C. Petersen (1986: 50-51). Literally a kayak with only a keel.

Kuujak: Keel of a kayak.

Masik: Aft-most curved deck beam of a kayak, defining the forward end of the cockpit.

Paa: A kayak's coaming; also known as the cockpit hoop.

Pautit: Paddle.

Pequngasoq: 'Curved kayak,' as defined by H. C. Petersen (1986: 48-49). See pages 276-277.

Sianniit: Chines.

Tikpiit: Ribs.

Tuilik: Paddling jacket.

Tuitsoq: Spray skirt.

Tunumiut: East Greenlanders, as termed by West Greenlanders; see "*Ammassalimiut.*"

BIBLIOGRAPHY

Adney, E. T. and Howard Chapelle
1964   The Bark Canoes and Skinboats of North America. Washington, D. C.: Smithsonian.

Andersen, David
1999   Greenland-Style Paddles. *Sea Kayaker* Vol. 16, no. 2: 39-43.

Anderson, Douglas D.
1984   Prehistory of North Alaska. Pp.80-93 in David Damas, ed., *Arctic*, Handbook of North American Indians, vol. 5. Washington, D.C.: Smithsonian Institution.

Anonymous
1838   Transactions of the Natural History Society of Northumberland, Durham, and Newcastle Upon Tyne, Vol. II. London: Emerson Charnley, and Longman and Co.

1860   A Guide to the Museum of the Literary and Philosophical Society of Hull. (Museum pamphlet).

1914   Illustrated Catalogue to the Museum of Fisheries and Shipping, Pickering Park, Hull. (Museum pamphlet).

2001   Westfrisian 'mummy' is not a Greenlander. Arctic Peoples Alert; http://home01.wxs.nl/~innusupp/english/news.html

Arima, Eugene
1963   Notes on the Kayak and Its Equipment at Ivuyivik, P. Q. *Contributions to Anthropology* 1961-62, II. *National Museum of Canada Bulletin* 194:221-261. Ottawa.

1975   A Contextual Study of the Caribou Eskimo Kayak. Canada. *National Museum of Man. Mercury Series. Ethnology Service Paper* 25. Ottawa.

1985   Qainnat Origins. *Inuktitut*, Summer, no.60:19-30.

1987   Inuit Kayaks in Canada: A Review of Historical Records and Construction. Canadian Museum of Civilization Mercury Series, Canadian Ethnology Service Paper110. Ottawa.

1994 Caribou and Iglulik Inuit Kayaks. *Arctic* Vol. 47, no. 2:193-195

2002 Greenland Kayaks: A Luxuriant Fluorescence from an Old Bering Sea Root. *Atlantic Coastal Kayaker* Vol. 11, no. 9:12-13, 26-27.

2004 Kayaks of the East Canadian Arctic. Pp. 111-148 in J. Heath, et al., Eastern Arctic Kayaks. Fairbanks: University of Alaska Press.

_____, ed.

1991 Contributions to Kayak Studies. *Canadian Museum of Civilization Mercury Series, Canadian Ethnology Service Paper* 122. Ottawa.

Arutyunov, S.A. and M.G. Levin and D.A. Sergeyev.

1964 Ancient Burials on the Chukchi Peninsula. Pp.333-346 in Henry N. Michael, ed. The Archaeology and Geomorphology of Northern Asia: Selected Works. Arctic Institute of North America, Anthropology of the North: Translations from Russian Sources/ No. 5. University of Toronto Press.

Birket-Smith, Kaj

1924 Ethnography of the Egedesminde District with Aspects of the General Culture of West Greenland. *Meddelelser om Grønland* Vol. 66. Copenhagen.

1928 The Greenlanders of the Present Day. Pp. 1-207 in Vol. 3 of Greenland, M. Vahl, et al., eds. Copenhagen: C. A. Reitzel; London: H. Milford, Oxford University Press.

1971 Eskimos. New York: Crown Publishers, Inc.

Blæsild, Benno

1988 *V.C. Frederiksens Grønlandssamling Sisimiut-Svendborg tur/retur.* Svendorg: Svendborg and Omegns Museum, Vol. 25.

Boas, Franz

1901-07 *The Eskimo of Baffin Land and Hudson Bay: From Notes Collected by Captain George Comer, Captain James Mutch, and Reverend E. J. Peck.* New York: Bulletin of the American Museum of Natural History, Vol. XV.

Bobé, Louis

1952 Hans Egede: Colonizer and Missionary of Greenland. Copenhagen: Rosenkilde and Bagger.

Brand, John

1984, 1987, 1988 The Little Kayak Book, vols. I-III. Colchester, U.K.: John Brand.

Bray, Maynard

1986 Mystic Seaport Museum Watercraft. Mystic, Connecticut: Mystic Seaport Museum, Inc.

Buel, J. W.
1889   The Story of Man. San Francisco: Pacific Publishing Co

Burch, Ernest S. Jr.
1988   The Eskimos. Norman, Oklahoma: University of Oklahoma Press.

Bure, Kristjan, ed.
n. d.   Greenland. Denmark: The Royal Danish Ministry for Foreign Affairs.

Chapman, F. Spencer
1934a   Northern Lights. Oxford University Press: New York.

1934b   Watkins' Last Expedition. Chatto and Windus: London.

Collinson, Richard
1889   Journal of H.M.S. Enterprise, on the Expedition in Search of Sir John Franklin's Ships By Behring Strait. London: Sampson Low, Marston, Searle, and Rivington, Ltd.

Crantz, David
1767   The History of Greenland: Containing a Description of the Country, and its Inhabitants: ... etc. 2 vols. The (Moravian) Brethren's Society for the Furtherance of the Gospel among the Heathen: London.

Cunningham, Christopher
1999   Editor's Note. *Sea Kayaker*, October, 7.

2003   Building the Greenland Kayak: A Manual for its Construction and Use. Camden, Maine: Ragged Mountain Press.

Cunningham, Richard
1989   California Indian Watercraft. San Luis Obispo, California: EZ Nature Books.

Dam-Mikkelsen, Bente
1980   Ethnographic Objects in the Royal Danish Kunstkamera, 1650-1800. *Nationalmuseets Skrifter, Etnografisk Række* 17. Copenhagen.

Damas, David, ed.
1984   *Arctic*, Handbook of North American Indians, vol. 5. Washington, D.C.: Smithsonian Institution.

Ellis, Richard
1999   Men and Whales. New York: Lyons Press.

Feest, Christian, ed.

1989 Indians and Europe: an Interdisciplinary Collection of Essays. Aachen, Germany: Alano Verlag/edition herodot.

Fitzhugh, William

1984 Paleo-Eskimo Cultures of Greenland. Pp.528-539 in David Damas, ed., *Arctic*, Handbook of North American Indians, vol.5. Washington, D.C.: Smithsonian Institution.

Fossett, Renée

2001 In Order to Live Untroubled: Inuit of the Central Arctic, 1550-1940. Winnipeg: The University of Manitoba Press.

Gad, Finn

1971 The History of Greenland, vol. I: Earliest times to 1700. Montreal: McGill-Queen's University Press.

1973 The History of Greenland, vol. II: 1 700-1782. Montreal: McGill-Queen's University Press.

1982 The History of Greenland, vol. III: 1782-1808. Kingston and Montreal: McGill-Queen's University Press.

1984 History of Colonial Greenland. Pp. 556-576 in David Damas, ed., Arctic, Handbook of North American Indians, vol.5. Washington, D.C.: Smithsonian Institution.

Gilberg, Rolf.

1984 Polar Eskimo. Pp.577-594 in David Damas, ed., *Arctic*, Handbook of North American Indians, vol.5. Washington, D.C.: Smithsonian Institution.

Gosch, C. C. A., ed.

1897 Danish Arctic Expeditions, 1605 to 1620, vol. I. London: Hakluyt Society.

Grønnow, Bjarne

1994 Qeqertasussuk— The Archaeology of a Frozen Saqqaq Site in Disko Bugt, West Greenland. Pp. 197-238 in David Morrison and Jean-Luc Pilon, eds., *Threads of Arctic Prehistory: Papers in Honour of William E. Taylor, jr.* Archaeological Survey of Canada; Mercury Series Paper 149. Ottawa.

Hansen, Johannes

1914 List of the Inhabitants of the East Coast of Greenland Between Cape Farvel and Angmagsalik 1884. In The Ammassalik Eskimo, vol. 1. W. Thalbitzer, ed *Meddelelser om Grønland* 39:188-202. Copenhagen.

Hansen, Keld

1980 Umiaq— En Skindbåd fra Grønland. Denmark: Mallings.

1997   Jigs From Greenland. Pp. 149-156 in R. Gilberg and H.C. Gulløv, eds., *Fifty Years of Arctic Research: Anthropological Studies from Greenland to Siberia*. Department of Ethnography, The National Museum of Denmark; Ethnographical Series, vol. 18. Copenhagen.

Hansen, Keld, and Birthe Clausen, eds.

1991   Kajjakker. Denmark: Vikingeskibshallen I Roskilde.

Heath, John

1978   Some Comparative Notes on Kayak Form and Construction. Pp. 19-26 in David Zimmerly, ed., *Contextual Studies of Material Culture*. Canadian Ethnology Service; Mercury Series Paper no. 43. Ottawa.

1987a   The Greenland Kayak Club: Qajaq Atoqqilerparput. *Sea Kayaker*, Spring, 15-18.

1987b   The Phantom Kayakers: A Scottish Mystery. *Sea Kayaker*, Summer, 15-18.

1987c   The Greenland Kayak and the Canadian Connection. *Sea Kayaker*, Fall, 13-18.

1990   Manasse, 1915-1989 *Sea Kayaker*, Spring, 10-13.

2000a   Maligiaq Makes Waves on his U. S. Visit. *Sea Kayaker*, June, 55-61.

2000b   Paddling with Maligiaq. Video Produced by John Heath, Houston. Distributed by Jessie Heath, 1142 Thornton Rd. Houston, TX 77018-3233 USA.

2004   Kayaks of Greenland. Pp. 5-44 in J. Heath, et al., Eastern Arctic Kayaks. Fairbanks: University of Alaska Press.

Heath, John, et.al.

2004   Eastern Arctic Kayaks. Fairbanks: University of Alaska Press.

Hodgson, George B.

1924   History of South Shields. Newcastle upon Tyne, U.K.: A. Reid.

Holm, Gustav

1888   Ethnologisk Skizze af Angmagsalikerne. *Meddelelser om Grønland* 10(2):43-182. Copenhagen.

1914   Ethnological Sketch of the Angmagsalik Eskimo. In The Ammassalik Eskimo, vol. 1. W. Thalbitzer, ed. *Meddelelser om Grønland* 39:1-147. Copenhagen.

Holtved, Erik

1967   Contributions to Polar Eskimo Ethnography. *Meddelelser om Grønland* 182(2):1-180. Copenhagen.

1944   Archaeological Investigations In the Thule District, Vols. I and II. *Meddelelser om Grønland* 141,1and 2. Copenhagen.

_____, ed.

1962 Otto Fabricius' Ethnographical Works. *Meddelelser om Grønland* 140(2):1-137. Copenhagen.

Hornell, James

1946 Water Transport: Origins and Early Evolution. Cambridge, U.K.: University Press.

Hoyle, Gwyneth

2002 The Collector: Kirk Wipper. Pp. 242-249 in John Jennings, et.al., *The Canoe: A Living Tradition*. Toronto: Firefly Books, Ltd.

Idiens, Dale

1987 Eskimos in Scotland. Pp. 161-174 in Christian Feest, ed. *Indians and Europe: An Interdisciplinary Collection of Essays*. Aachen, Germany: Alano Verlag/ edition herodot.

Jennings, John, et al.

2002 The Canoe: A living Tradition. Toronto: Firefly Books, Ltd.

Jensen, P. Scavenius

1975 Den Grønlandske Kajak og dens Redskaber. Copenhagen: Nyt Nordisk Forlag Anrnold Busck,

1982 The Greenland Kayak and its Implements. (Trans. by G. A. W.). Ottawa: National Museums of Canada.

Jones, A. G. E.

1996 The Greenland and Davis Strait Trade, 1740-1880. Huntingdon, U.K.: Bluntisham Books.

Jordan, Richard H.

1984 Neo-Eskimo Prehistory of Greenland. Pp. 540-548 in David Damas, ed., *Arctic,* Handbook of North American Indians, vol.5. Washington, D.C.: Smithsonian Institution.

Kleivan, Inge

1984a History of Norse Greenland. Pp. 549-555 in David Damas, ed., Arctic, Handbook of North American Indians, vol.5. Washington, D.C.: Smithsonian Institution.

1984b West Greenland before 1950. Pp. 595-621 in David Damas, ed., Arctic, Handbook of North American Indians, vol.5. Washington, D.C.: Smithsonian Institution.

Krabbe, Thomas N.

1930 Greenland, Its Nature, Inhabitants and History. Levin and Munksgaard Publishers, Copenhagen and Humphrey Milford, Oxford University Press, London.

Kroeber, Alfred
1900   The Eskimo of Smith Sound. *Bulletin of the American Museum of Natural History* 12(21): 265-327. New York.

Laughlin, William S., and John D. Heath and Eugene Arima
1991   Two Nikolski Aleut Kayaks: Iqyax and Uluxtax From Umnak Is. Pp. 163-209 in Eugene Arima, ed. *Contributions to Kayak Studies*, Canadian Museum of Civilization Mercury Series, Canadian Ethnology Service Paper 122. Ottawa.

Lembcke-Otto, Carl Ernst
1930   Unpublished letter sent to Dr Thomas Thomsen of the Danish National Museum. Greenland National Museum and Archive, Nuuk.

Leshikar, Margaret E.
1988   The Earliest Watercraft: From Rafts to Viking Ships. Pp.13-32 in George F. Bass, ed., *Ships and Shipwrecks of the Americas*. London and New York: Thames and Hudson.

Lindbergh, Anne Morrow
1974   Locked Rooms and Open Doors. New York and London: Harcourt Brace and Jovanovich, inc.

Longyard, William H.
2003   A Speck On the Sea: Epic Voyages in the most Improbable Vessels. International Marine/ McGraw Hill, Camden, Maine, New York, Chicago, etc.

Low, James G.
1943   Industry in Montrose. Brechin, Scotland: The Tryst, Trinity.

MacMillan,
1925   The MacMillan Arctic Expedition Returns. *The National Geographic Magazine*, XLVIII:477-518.

MacRitchie, David
1912a   The Aberdeen Kayak and its Congeners. *Proceedings of the Society of Antiquaries of Scotland*, XLVI:213-241. Edinburgh.

1912b   Kayak of the North Sea. *The Scottish Geographical Magazine*, XXVIII:126-133. Edinburgh.

Madsen, Jan Skamby, and Keld Hansen
1992   Sivbåde. Denmark: Vikingeskibshallen I Roskilde.

Magnus, Olaus
(1555) 1996 Description of the Northern Peoples, 3 vols. London: The Hakluyt Society. (Originally published 1555, Rome.)

Mary-Rousselière, Guy

1984 Iglulik. Pp. 431-446 in David Damas, ed., *Arctic*, Handbook of North American Indians, vol.5. Washington, D.C.: Smithsonian Institution.

1991 Qitdlarssuaq: The Story of a Polar Migration. Winnipeg: Wuertz Publishing, Ltd.

Mathiassen, Therkel

1928 Material Culture of the Iglulik Eskimos. Report of the Fifth Thule Expedition 1921-24, vol.VI, no.1. Copenhagen.

1930 Inugsuk: A Mediæval Eskimo Settlement in Upernavik District, West Greenland. *Meddelelser om Grønland* 87(4):145-340. Copenhagen.

1931 Ancient Eskimo Settlements in the Kangâmiut Area. *Meddelelser om Grønland* 91(1). Copenhagen.

McCullough, Karen M.

1989 The Ruin Islanders: Early Thule Culture Pioneers in the Eastern High Arctic. *Canadian Museum of Civilization Mercury Series, Archaeological Survey of Canada Paper* 141. Ottawa.

Mikkelsen, Einar

1954 Kajakmanden fra Aberdeen. *Grønland*: 53-58.

Moser, Charles K.

1918 The Isle of Frankincense. *The National Geographic Magazine*, XXXIII: 267-278.

Murdoch, John

(1892) 1988 Ethnological Results of the Point Barrow Expedition. Washington, D. C.: Smithsonian Institution Press.

Nansen, Fridtjof

1893 Eskimo Life. London and New York: Longmans, Green, and Co.

1895 The First Crossing of Greenland. London and New York: Longmans, Green, and Co.

1911 In Northern Mists: Arctic Exploration in Early Times. New York: Frederick A. Stokes.

Neugebauer, Werner, and Arnulf von Ulmann and Ulrich Gabler

1982 'Der Grönlander' – Ein EskimoKajak im Hause der Schiffergesellschaft zu Lübeck. *Mitteilungen der Geographischen Gesellschaft zu Lübeck* 55:199-230.

1993 'The Greenlander' – An Eskimo Kayak at the Lübeck Barge Masters Guild. (Translated by 'M. P.') Hull, Quebec: National Historic Parks and Sites Canada.

Neyret, Jean
1974 Pirogues Océaniennes, vol. II. Paris: Association Des Amis Des Musées De La Marine.

Nooter, Gert
1971 Old kayaks in the Netherlands. *Mededelingen van het Rijksmuseum voor Volkenkunde* 17. Leiden.

1976 Leadership and Headship: Changing Authority Patterns in an East Greenland Hunting Community. *Mededelingen van het Rijksmuseum voor Volkenkunde* 20. Leiden.

1980 Improvisation and Innovation: Social Consequences of Material Culture Changes. Pp. 113-121 in *From Field Case to Showcase: Research, Acquisition, and presentation in the Rijksmuseum Voor Volkenkunde (National Museum of Ethnology), Leiden.* W. R. Van Gulik, H. S. Van der Straaten, and G. D. van Wengen, eds. Amsterdam: J. C. Gieben.

1984 A century of changes in East Greenland. Pp. 121-143 in Gert Nooter, ed., Life and Survival in the Arctic: cultural changes in the polar regions. Ethnological serie Verre naasten naderbij. Leiden.

1991 The East Greenland kayaks. Pp.319-347, in Eugene Arima, ed., *Contributions to Kayak Studies*, Canadian Museum of Civilization Mercury Series, Canadian Ethnology Service Paper 122. Ottawa.

_____ and Emil Rosing
1983 Qajatoqqat Pukkitsormiuniittut (Holland). *Kalaallit Nunaata Katersugaasiviata Naqiterttitai* 1. Nuuk, Greenland.

Ostermann, Hother B. S.
1929 The trade from 1870 to the present time. Pp. 165-214 in Vol. 3 of Greenland. M. Vahl, et al., eds. Copenhagen: C. A. Reitzel; London: H. Milford, Oxford University Press.

Oswalt, Wendell
1979 Eskimos and Explorers. Novato, California: Chandler and Sharp, Inc.

Peary, Josephine
1893 My Arctic Journal: A Year Among Ice-fields and Eskimos. New York: Contemporary Publishing Co.

Peary, Marie and Josephine Peary
1903 Children of the Arctic. New York: Frederick A. Stokes Co.

Peary, Robert
1910 The North Pole: Its Discovery in 1909 Under the Auspices of the Peary Arctic Club. New York: Frederick A. Stokes Co.

Peqatigiiffiat Qaannat Kalaallit Nunaanni Katuffiat

1986   Kajak Klubben, parts 1-3. Video produced by the Greenland National Kayaking Association. Distributed by Jessie Heath, 1142 Thornton Rd. Houston, TX 77018-3233, USA.

Petersen, H.C.

1981   Qaanniornermut Ilitsersuut— Instruktion i kajakbygning— Instruction in Kayak Building. Nuuk: Greenland National Museum and Archives/ Atuakkiorfik.

1986   Skinboats of Greenland. Ships and Boats of the North, Vol. 1. Roskilde: The National Museum of Denmark, The Museum of Greenland and the Viking Ship Museum in Roskilde.

1987   Umiat Qaannallu Kalaallit Nunaanni – Skinbåde I Grønland — Skinboats in Greenland. Charlottenlund, Denmark: Arktisk Institut.

1997   Den Store Kajakbog. Nuuk: Atuakkiorfik.

Petersen, Robert

1984   East Greenland Before 1950. Pp. 622-639 in David Damas, ed., Arctic, Handbook of North American Indians, vol.5. Washington, D.C.: Smithsonian Institution.

Peyrère, Isaac De La

(1647) 1855   Description of Greenland. Pp.132 - 249 in Adam White, ed., A Collection of Documents on Spitzbergen and Greenland. London: Hakluyt Society.

Porsild, Morten

1915   Studies on the Material Culture of the Eskimo in West Greenland. *Meddelelser om Grønland* 51(5):113-239. Copenhagen.

Putnam, David

1926   David Goes to Greenland. New York and London: G. P. Putnam's Sons.

Rasmussen, Knud

1908   The People of the Polar North: A Record. London: Kegan, Paul, Trench, Trübner and Co. Ltd.

(1921) 1976   Greenland by the Polar Sea: The Story of the Thule Expedition from Melville Bay to Cape Morris Jessup. New York: AMS Press, Inc.

Rink, Hinrich

(1875) 1997   Tales and Traditions of the Eskimo. Mineola, N.Y,: Dover Publications, Inc.

(1887) 1914   The East Greenland Dialect According to the Annotations Made by the Danish East Coast Expedition to Kleinschmidt's Greenlandic Dictionary. In The Ammassalik Eskimo, Vol. I, William Thalbitzer, ed. *Meddelelser om Grønland* 39:203-223. Copenhagen.

Rink, Signe, ed.
(1897) 2005 Kayak-Men: Tales of Greenland's Seal Hunters. *Qajaq Journal*, vol.3, nos 1-2:3-21, 24-43. Cambridge, Mass.

Robert-Lamblin, Joëlle
1997 Death in traditional East Greenland: Age, causes, and rituals. A contribution from anthropology to archaeology. Pp. 261-268 in R. Gilberg and H C. Gulløv, eds., *Fifty Years of Arctic Research: Anthropological Studies from Greenland to Siberia*. Department of Ethnography, The National Museum of Denmark; Ethnographical Series, vol. 18. Copenhagen.

Rosing, Johannes (Ataralaa)
1991 En Dramatisk Kajaktur ved Årsskiftet 1899-1900. Pp.29-33 in Hansen and Clausen, eds. Kajjaker. Roskilde: Vikingeskibshallen.

2004 A Dramatic Kayak Trip, 1899-1900: Ataralaa's Narrative. Pp.103-105 in Heath, et al. Eastern Arctic Kayaks. Fairbanks: University of Alaska Press.

Ross, J. Gillies
1985 Arctic Whalers, Icy Seas: Narratives of the Davis Strait Whale Fishery. Toronto: Irwin Publishing.

Smith, Eric Alden
1991 Inujjuamiut Foraging Strategies. Hawthorne, New York: Aldine De Gruyter.

Souter, William Clark
1934 The story of our kayak and some others. Aberdeen: University Press.

Stamer, Greg
2004 Using Greenland Paddles: An Overview. Pp. 45-59 in J. Heath, et al., Eastern Arctic Kayaks. Fairbanks: University of Alaska Press.

Starr, Mark
2002 Building a Greenland Kayak. Mystic, Connecticut: Mystic Seaport Museum.

Steensby, H.P.
1910 Contributions to the Ethnology and Anthropogeography of the Polar Eskimos. *Meddelelser om Grønland*, Vol. 34, no. 7. Copenhagen.

1917 An Anthropogeographical Study of the Origin of the Eskimo Culture. *Meddelelser om Grønland*, Vol. 53, no.2. Copenhagen.

Steffen-Schrade, Jutta
1997 'I Wish No Longer Go To Sea....:' Five Early Kayaks in German Collections. European Review of Native American Studies, 11(2): 11-20.

Storey, Arthur
1967   Trinity House of Kingston upon Hull. Kingston Upon Hull: Trinity House.

Sturtevant, William and David Quinn
1989   This New Prey: Eskimos in Europe in 1567, 1576, and 1577. Pp. 61-140 in C. Feest, ed., Indians and Europe: An Interdisciplinary Collection of Essays. Aachen, Germany: Alano Verlag/edition herodot.

Symons, John
1898   The Hull Museum: A Walk Round. Hull News Supplement, Feb. 12th. 13-14. Hull, U.K.

Taylor, Kenneth I.
1961   The Construction and Use of Kayaks in North-West Greenland: Preliminary Report. The Polar Record, Vol. 10, No. 68:494-500.

Thalbitzer, William
1914   Ethnographical Collections From East Greenland (Angmagsalik and Nualik) Made by G. Holm, G. Amdrup, and J. Petersen and Described by W. Thalbitzer. In The Ammassalik Eskimo, Vol. I, William Thalbitzer, ed. *Meddelelser om Grønland* 39:319-741. Copenhagen.

_____, ed.
1914   The Ammassalik Eskimo: Contributions to the Ethnology of the East Greenland Natives. *Meddelelser om Grønland*, 39. Copenhagen.

Tudor, John R.
1883   The Orkneys and Shetland. London: Edward Stanford.

Vahl, Martin, F. C. Amdrup, L. Bobé, and A. S. Jensen, eds.
1928-1929   Greenland. 3 vols. Copenhagen: C. A. Reitzel; London: H. Milford, Oxford University Press.

Van Gulik, W.R., H. S. Van der Straaten, and G. D. van Wengen, eds
1980   From Field Case to Showcase: Research, Acquisition, and presentation in the Rijksmuseum Voor Volkenkunde (National Museum of Ethnology), Leiden.. Amsterdam: J. C. Gieben.

Ventress, Monica
1998   Admiral Sir Robert Moorsom, 1760-1835. Whitby, U.K.: Whitby Literary and Philosophical Society.

Vernon, Jennifer
1984   The Lincoln Kayak. *The Mariner's Mirror* Vol. 70, No. 4:415-426.

Victor, Paul-Emile and Joelle Robert-Lamblin
1989   La Civilisation du Phoque: Jeux, Gestes et Techniques Des Eskimo D'Ammassalik. France: Armand Colin/ Raymond Chabaud.

Wipper, Kirk
1985   The Kanawa Story: The Beginning (1957-1983). Pp.3-16 in *The Journal of the Kanawa International Museum of Canoes, Kayaks and Rowing Craft* Vol. I, no. 1. Toronto.

Wissler, Clark
1909   Notes on new Collections. *Anthropological Papers*, American Museum of Natural History, Vol. II(3):318-321. New York.

Whitaker, Ian
1954   The Scottish Kayaks and the Finn-men.' *Antiquity* 28:99-104.

1977   The Scottish Kayaks Reconsidered. *Antiquity* 51:41-45.

Zimmerly, David
2000   Qayaq: Kayaks of Alaska and Siberia. Fairbanks: University of Alaska Press.

Index

Aappilattoq: 354-355.

Aasiaat: 23, 34, 88, 107, 487, 543.

Amdrup, Georg: 516.

American Geographical Society: 325

American Museum of Natural History, NY: 40, 238, 323, 374, 412, 468, 508-509, 514, 519, 520.

Ammassalik: 26, 36-37, 41, 51, 95, 109, 111, 390, 394-401, 411-415, 423, 431, 434, 518, 524, 519, 541-542, 545.

Amsterdam: 158.

Appat: 34, 296, 322, 326, 535.

Arctic: 328-329.

Arima, Eugene: xiii, 42, 116, 333, 472, 474, 532-533, 542, 553.

Avagait: 229, 537.

Avasisaartoq: 109, 112, 204, 229, 239, 242.

Balance Stick: 94

Beebe, Jr., Major William M.: 234

Birnirk Culture: 25, 530-533, 540, 551.

Brand, John: 164, 201, 204, 392, 415, 418, 488.

Brøndlund, Peter: 326, 500.

Bryant, Henry G.: 447.

Byrd, Admiral Richard E.: 274, 466.

Canadian Canoe Museum, Peterborough: 40, 242, 325, 343, 451, 459.

Canadian Museum of Civilization: 279, 282, 328, 332-333, 338, 477, 506-507.

Cape York: 242, 447, 449, 451

Chapelle, Howard I.: 317-318, 412, 447, 449-451, 527.

Chateau de Ramezay, Montreal: 332.

Chines: 43-44, 65-66, 97-99.

Clark, Captain William: 164-165.

Coaming: 43, 83-89, 100.

Comer, Captain George: 323.

Construction, of kayaks: 26, 47-100.

Crantz, David: 26, 49-50.

Crockerland Expedition: 323.

Dalrymple, J.: 195, 223.

Danish National Museum, Copenhagen: 39, 138, 229, 335, 354, 377, 380, 382, 387, 392, 397, 415, 455, 465, 486-487, 522.

Davidsen, Kunuunnguaq: xiii, 439.

De Hidde Nijland Stichting, Hindeloopen: 135, 490.

DeRijp: 134.

Dorset culture: 29.

Doucette, Vernon: xiii, 332, 439-440.

Driftwood: 47, 49-50, 452-453.

Dunbar, Max: 279.

Eenoolooapik: 222.

Egede, Hans: 388.

Employment: 37, 542-543.

Enkhuizen: 142.

Fabricius, Otto: 27, 35.

Findlay: 218.

Fortescue, W.I.: xiii, 222.

Fram Museum, Oslo: 265-267, 268-269, 499, 506.

576

Gaimard, Paul: 198.

Gibbon, Captain William: 188.

Green, F.: 282.

Greenland National Museum and Archives, Nuuk: 39, 153, 237, 284, 287, 289-290, 293, 295, 335, 345, 397, 426, 455, 466, 479, 487, 503-505, 508-510, 514-517, 522-524, 527-528.

Gunwales: 53-54, 62-64

Hall, James: 127-128, 164.

Hancock Museum, Newcastle: 166, 498.

Hansen, Keld: 354-355.

Harpooons: 26-28, 35, 49, 76-83 88-89, 168, 351, 535-537.

Heath, John: xiii, 42, 154, 223-224, 280, 326, 333, 349-354, 438, 479, 490, 513.

Hindeloopen: 135, 490.

Hollböll, Carl: 392.

Holm, Gustav: 24, 34-35, 48-50, 392, 397-399, 409, 517, 540.

Holtved, Erik: 530-532, 540, 551

Hoorn: 131, 488.

Hørring, H.C.: 237.

Horton, J. Kenneth: 343.

Hull Maritime Museum: 33, 196, 225, 227, 497.

Hunterian Museum, Glasgow: 195, 218, 223, 497, 500, 505.

Hutchinson, Derek: 201-202.

Ikertoq: 127.

Ikorfat: 322.

Ilorsuit: 24, 34, 74, 296, 349-352, 513.

Iluliarssuk: 27.

Ilulissat: 24, 39, 107, 296, 322, 326, 335, 480, 538-539, 543.

Inugsuk cultural phase (Also see Inussuk): 531, 542.

Inussuk: 531.

Inuhuit: 38, 85, 109, 449, 483-484.

Inuhuit Kayaks: 38-39, 96-100, 441-475, 544.

Jakobsen, Apollus: 387.

Jensen, Peter: 466.

Jonathansen, Billiam: 432-433.

Kanawa International Museum: 242.

Kangaamiut: 101, 107, 244, 272-275, 477.

Kangek: 28, 271.

Kangersuatsiaq: 242, 537.

Keel, Keelson: 43-44, 60-66.

Korneliussen, Emanuele: 349-353, 513.

Kristiansen, Martin: 384.

Kujaannalik: 190.

Kullorsuaq: 343, 346, 356, 538.

Kunstkammer, Royal Danish: 485-487.

Lady Jane: 166-167.

La Gorce, John Oliver: 512.

Laing Gallery, Newcastle: 200.

Latona: 188.

Leask, Captain (?): 166-167.

Lembcke-Otto, C.E.C.: 335, 503, 538.

Lindbergh, Charles: 280.

Lindenov, Godske: 31, 127-128.

Lindow, Harold: 330-331.

Livingstone-Learmonth, Walter: 320.

Lübeck—*see Schiffergesellschaft*.

Magnus, Olaus: 30.

Maniitsoq: 34, 36, 107, 243, 272, 277, 284, 487, 510.

Mariners' Museum, Newport News: 321.

Marischal College Museum, Aberdeen: 189, 490, 495.

Matheussen, Manasse: 33, 479.

Mathiassen, Therkel: 415, 531, 551.

Maud: 320.

McDonald, Eugene F.: 276.

McManus Galleries, Dundee: 193, 240, 598-599, 501.

MacMillan, Donald: 276, 323.

Medico-Chirurgical Society, Aberdeen: 222.

Michigan State University Museum: 276, 502.

Moorsom, Richard: 190.

Montrose City Museum, Scotland: 193.

Morrisey: 242-243.

Musée de la Marine, Paris: 298, 272, 274, 291.

Musei Wormiani: 30.

Museon, The Hague: 142, 281, 341, 421, 429, 432, 489, 511, 520, 523-524.

Nanortalik: 29, 42, 358, 377, 380, 384, 387.

Nansen, Fridtjof: 265-267.

Naskapi: 328.

National Museum of Finland: 330, 503, 518.

National Museum of Natural History (US): 232, 234, 317, 447, 496, 511-512, 522, 527.

National Museum of Scotland: 163, 192, 199, 231, 320, 502, 529.

National Museum of the American Indian (US): 40, 242, 325, 343, 449, 459, 525-526.

Nonas, Richard: xiii, 332, 438, 440.

Nooter, Gert: 94, 131, 134-135, 140, 142, 152-154, 158, 184, 341, 429-430, 432-433, 489, 554-555.

Norcross, Arthur: 412, 508, 519-520.

Norse: 28-29, 31, 531.

Norton, Frederick: 374.

Nualik: 516.

Nuuk (See also Greenland National Museum): 28-29, 32, 34, 48, 107, 153-154, 244, 265, 267-269, 284, 287, 291, 439, 474, 477, 485, 499, 506.

Nuuk Kayak Club: 287.

Nuussuaq: 117, 346.

Nuussuaq Peninsula: 326, 535.

Oqaatsut: 326.

Orchard, W.C.: 459.

Öregaards Gymnasium: 415.

Outriggers: 92-94, 266-267, 282.

Paamiut: 34, 36, 107, 229, 295, 535-537.

Paddles: 23, 481-529.

Padilla, Maligiaq: 33, 438-440, 525.

Peary: 276.

Peary, Robert: 238, 447, 449-453, 525-526.

Peqatigiiffik Qajaq Nuuk: 287.

Pequngasoq: 112, 276-277, 284, 287, 350.

Percy, Charles: 451.

Petersen, H.C.: 39, 106, 108-110, 293.

Petersen, Johan: 409.

Polar Greenland— see Inuhuit, Inuhuit Kayaks, and Thule.

Porsild, A.E.: 338.

Porsild, Morten: xii, 106.

Porsild, R.T.: 333, 507.

Punuk culture: 25, 530, 532, 540, 551.

Putnam, David B.: 448.

Putnam, G.P.: 242.

Qaanaaq: 466.

Qaannat Kattuffiat: 439-440, 479.

Qaqortoq: 34, 107, 229, 358, 370, 374, 482, 513, 536, 543.

Qasigianguit: 25, 34, 48.

Qeqertarsuaq: 34, 77, 242, 296, 322, 328, 543.

Qillaq: 38.

Rasmussen, Knud: 38-39, 281, 377, 380, 415-416, 511.

Recherche: 198.

Repair: 101-105.

Ribs: 59-61, 65-66, 70-71, 97-99.

Rifles: 28, 37, 49, 76-78, 82, 95, 108, 204, 244, 286, 288, 329, 340, 342, 347, 355, 368, 385, 432, 448, 530, 534-537, 539.

Rijksmuseum voor Volkenkunde, Leiden: 39, 152, 154, 184, 370, 424, 491, 494, 513, 521.

Rijper Museum: 134, 489.

Robertson, Captain Thomas: 240.

Roosevelt: 451, 454.

Rosing, Ulrik: 272-274.

Ross, Sir John: 32, 196-197, 225-228.

Royal College of Surgeons: 163.

Royal Ontario Museum: 470, 472.

Ruin Island: 530-531, 533.

Ryberg, Carl J.P.: 370.

Saint Andrews University: 192.

Sakeouse, John: 32.

Sakkit: 24.

Samuelsen, Karl: 295.

Schiffergesellschaft, Lübeck: 31, 127.

Scotia: 240.

Scudder, N.P.: 232.

Seal skin: 47, 71-76, 79.

Singhertek, Henrik: 429.

Sisimiut: 34, 107, 232, 242, 277, 279-280, 374, 481, 485, 503, 506, 511-512, 525, 532, 543.

Skegs: 90-92, 243-244, 270, 278, 283-284, 286, 295, 326-328, 333, 341, 354, 387, 539.

Skins, kayak: 71-76.

Souter, William Clark: 47, 165, 186, 188, 193, 195-196, 199-200, 222, 225, 227-228, 231, 320.

South Shields Museum: 200-202.

Stamer, Greg: 349, 525.

Starr, Mark: 468.

Stein, Robert: 321.

Stems: 43, 45-46, 61-64, 98-100.

Swart, Claudius Clavus: 30.

Tasiusaq: 344.

Taylor, Ken: 349-353.

Thomsen, Thomas: 335.

Thule culture: 25, 29, 530-532, 534, 540, 542, 551.

Thule District: 107-109, 530.

Tinbergen, Nico: 421, 424, 520-521.

Tiniteqilaaq: 37, 39, 48-49, 429.

Trade, domestic: 49-50, 392, 530, 543.

Trade, foreign: 50, 59, 144, 452-453, 530, 542.

Trinity House, Hull: 164, 186, 493, 495.

Trinity House, Newcastle: 200.

Trost: 127.

Types of kayaks; Typology: 106-117.

Umiak: 23-24, 26, 29, 35, 50, 358, 409, 481, 540, 542.

Unicorn: 164.

University Museum of Cultural Heritage, Oslo: 368, 397-498, 409, 515-518.

Upernavik: 29, 34, 39, 75, 106-108, 117, 242, 296, 317, 335, 343, 345, 354, 503-504, 531, 535, 537-539, 541.

Upernavik Kujalleq: 51, 107-109, 296, 317, 343.

Uummannaq, Northwest Greenland: 34, 107-109, 345, 352, 482, 504, 535, 538-539.

Uummannaq, Polar Greenland: 460, 472, 531, 540, 542, 551.

Viking Ship Museum, Roskilde 387.

Watson, Commander ____(?): 218.

Weltmuseum, Frankfurt: 158.

Wereldmuseum, Rotterdam: 161, 493.

Westfries Museum, Hoorn: 131, 488.

Whales, Whalers, Whaling: 25, 31-33, 49, 52, 124, 131, 134-135, 158, 167-169, 188, 190, 194, 218, 222, 225-226, 240, 320, 481, 530, 542-543.

Whitby Museum: 190.

Winning, Duncan: 349, 351.

Worm, Ole: 30.

Zierikzee: 140, 492.